D1557038

BLUE GUIDE

GREECE
THE MAINLAND

Somerset Books • London
WW Norton • New York

Blue Guide Greece
Seventh edition

Published by Blue Guides Limited, a Somerset Books Company
49–51 Causton St, London SW1P 4AT
www.blueguides.com
'Blue Guide' is a registered trademark

© Blue Guides Limited (except as noted on p. 736, which forms part of this copyright page)
Maps by DIMAP Bt and Kartext. We gratefully acknowledge the valuable contribution of
ROAD Editions, the leading Greek mapping company, on whose maps we have drawn in
preparing the cartography in this guide. Their maps are available in the travel sections of good
bookshops worldwide, and are sold throughout Greece in petrol stations, newsagents and
bookshops, as well as at Athens international airport.

All rights reserved. No part of this publication may be reproduced or used in any form or by any
means—photographic, electronic or mechanical, including photocopying, recording, taping or
information storage and retrieval systems—without permission of the publisher.

ISBN 1–905131–10–0

A CIP catalogue record of this book is available from the British Library

Published in the United States of America by
WW Norton and Company, Inc.
500 Fifth Avenue, New York, NY 10110
US ISBN 0–393–32836–8

The author and the publisher have made reasonable efforts to ensure the accuracy of all the
information in *Blue Guide Greece the Mainland*; however, they can accept no responsibility for any
loss, injury or inconvenience sustained by any traveller as a result of information
or advice contained in the guide.

All other acknowledgements, photo credits and copyright information are given
on p. 736, which forms part of this copyright page.

Your views on this book would be much appreciated. We welcome not only specific comments, suggestions or corrections, but any more general views you may have: how this book
enhanced your holiday, how it could have been more helpful. Blue Guides authors and small
editorial and production team work hard to bring you what we hope are the best-researched
and best-presented cultural and historical guide books in the English language. Please write
to us by email (editorial@blueguides.com), via the comments page on our website
(www.blueguides.com) or at the address given above. We will be happy to acknowledge useful contributions in the next edition, and to offer a free copy of one of our titles.

PREFACE

The first Blue Guide to Greece appeared in 1967, compiled—and largely written—by Stuart Rossiter. That famous volume has been a lodestone ever since. Subsequent editions of the guide concentrated on updating and providing supplementary information: the tone and format remained largely unchanged. In fact, much of Rossiter's original text still survives, unaltered and needing no alteration, almost 40 years on. Greece is, however, a very different country from what it was then, and this new Blue Guide represents a significant departure from the older editions. 'Greece,' in Rossiter's words, 'will continue to be visited for its landscape, beauty and a great past contribution to human civilisation; and to all these aspects the Blue Guide provides the best companion.' This is still true; but the companion has adapted. Readers are no longer assumed to have received a Classical education, and more background is given for all references to Classical literature, history and myth. Descriptions of routes to take by car are no longer described: instead each region has its own detailed map so users can plan an independent itinerary.

This book aims above all to be a handbook and reference book to the Classical world, making that world visible and comprehensible to new generations of readers. Byzantine and Ottoman Greece also receive extensive coverage. This edition pays more attention to practical information, on the hypothesis that a good lunch and a comfortable bed are all part of the cultural experience. This remains a tricky area in Greece. There are large parts of the country where there is little to be said. In cases where there are good hotels and restaurants we have tried to include them, though the information is often patchy. All reader input in this area will be gratefully received.

A note on transliteration

Most names and place-names from the Classical world are spelled in the way most familiar from literature, eg: Asclepius, not Asklipios; Olympus, not Olimbos. Famous names from art and history (eg: Socrates, Polyclitus, Michael Palaeologus) are also given traditional spellings. Street names on maps are spelled in the way most likely to correspond to the map the reader will find on site (although it is difficult to predict what this will be). Like any system, this one has flaws. Many anomalies have crept in, and readers will be able to pick holes in it. In general, we have striven for familiarity, and for spellings which do not wound the eye. Accents denoting stressed syllables (local people often simply will not understand you if you get the stress in the wrong place) are given on place names in the index.

CONTENTS

THE GUIDE

MAPS

The authors and contributors

Charles Freeman is a freelance academic historian with a long-standing interest in the history and culture of ancient Greece. Among his books are *The Greek Achievement* (Penguin Books, 1999) and *The Closing of the Western Mind* (Heinemann, London, 2002 and Knopf, New York, 2003), which deals with the end of the Greek philosophical tradition in the 4th century AD. He has travelled widely in Greece and its islands and has dug at the ancient site of Cnidos in southern Turkey.

Sherry Marker took her BA in Classics at Harvard, an MA in Ancient History at the University of California at Berkeley, and studied archaeology at the American School of Classical Studies in Athens. She has worked on the excavations at Morgantina, Sicily and Sardis, Turkey. She has written on Greece for the *New York Times* travel section, *Travel and Leisure*, *Berlitz Travellers* and *Frommer's*. She divides her time between Massachusetts and the Peloponnese. She is co-author of this edition, in which she provided the chapters on Athens, Attica, the Peloponnese, and parts of Boeotia and Phocis.

Nigel McGilchrist has lived in the Mediterranean area—Italy, Greece and Turkey—for over 25 years, working for the Italian Ministry of Arts and then as Director of the Anglo-Italian Institute in Rome. He has taught at the universities of Rome and Massachusetts, and was for seven years Dean of European Studies for a consortium of American universities. He lectures widely in ancient art and archaeology in Europe and in the United States. Since working in Greece in the early 1980s, he has been a dedicated student and explorer of its landscape, customs and history. He is currently writing a new and enlarged Blue Guide to the Greek Islands (pub. 2008). He has provided introductory chapters to this guide, and additional material on Thermon, Dodona, and much of Boeotia.

James Pettifer is a professor at the Defence Academy of the United Kingdom and an author and broadcaster on southeast Europe. He has written extensively from the region for *The Times*, *The World Today*, *The Times Literary Supplement* and other publications. Among his recent books are *The Turkish Labyrinth*, *Blue Guide Bulgaria*, *Blue Guide Albania and Kosovo*, and *Kosova Express*. He is co-author of this edition, in which he provided the chapters on Epirus, Thessaly, Macedonia, Thrace, and parts of Central Greece.

Paola Pugsley is a professional archaeologist with a particular interest in ancient technologies, especially woodwork. She can normally be found working on location in the summer in Greece and Turkey. She has provided updated material on the archaeological sites of Demetrias and Pagasae, Dimini and Sesklo, Dion, Ephyra, Kassope, Oiniadae, Pella, Trikala and Vergina; the town of Kavala; and assisted the editor with the glossary and chronology.

Nikos Stavroulakis has lectured on Byzantine art and architecture at the University of Tel Aviv, and taught Byzantine and Islamic Studies in Athens. He was instrumental in setting up the Jewish Museum of Greece in 1977, and acted as its director until 1993. He has published numerous books and articles, and has been active in raising interest in the preservation of Jewish and Ottoman sites. He is also a painter and illustrator, and has exhibited in the UK, US and France. He has provided introductory chapters and advised the editor on sections relating to Byzantine, Ottoman and Jewish subjects, in particular relating to Hosios Loukas, Arta, Thessaloniki, Veroia and Trikala.

ANCIENT GREECE

by Charles Freeman

The first civilizations

The origins of the peoples who came to live in the country we now know as Greece are mysterious, largely because the Greek peninsula has been so open to migrations. The seascape of the Aegean—notably the pattern of its islands, which are continuations of the mainland mountain ranges—ensures that travel throughout the region is comparatively easy, especially in the summer months. Thousands of inlets and harbours allow access to the sea, and with so much of Greece itself mountainous, it makes sense to move along the shore from one shelter to the next.

The earliest inhabitants of Greece were there by 40,000 BC, but it was not until the end of the Ice Age (c. 12,000 BC) that the climate warmed and the present ecology emerged. At a cave at Franchthi, in southern Greece, there is evidence of a hunter-gatherer group from this period, hunting deer, catching fish and gathering wild cereals (*see p. 255*). By 6000 BC, in the Neolithic period, the first farmers appear, some two thousand years after a similar agricultural revolution in Mesopotamia. It is difficult to say whether the cultivation of crops was introduced by migrants from the east or was the natural result of population increase forcing more intensive methods of production. In the eastern Mediterranean were some of the most ancient and innovative societies in the world: those of Egypt and the ancient Near East. Greece was never isolated from these civilizations, and the relationship between the Greeks and the east was to be crucial in defining the Greeks' own identity.

With agriculture comes settlement, mainly in small villages where the households lived alongside each other in mutual support. Only 20 per cent of Greece is good agricultural land, and these early inhabitants had to find a way to sustain themselves in a climate which allowed for a modest surplus at best. Ingenuity was always called for, and different ecological niches were exploited, so that vines (known from 5000 BC), olives and cereals (barley was the best suited to the low summer rainfalls) could be grown alongside each other, with the higher, less fertile ground being used for sheep and goats. Those communities nearer the sea would also have fished. While the better sites would have been continuously occupied, other plots were often scattered, and social kinship groups could extend across a region so that if one crop or area failed the surplus of others could be called on. Occasionally, as at Dimini on the plain of Thessaly (*see p. 560*), there is a larger central hall, a *megaron*, set in a cluster of walls and houses which suggests the emergence of chieftains or local 'big men'.

The coming of bronze from the east around 3000 BC marks the beginning of the Greek Bronze Age. Bronze is produced by mixing tin (usually about ten per cent of the whole) with copper. It has a much lower melting point than pure copper, allowing it to be worked more easily. It is also harder, which means it can be used for armour, weapons and cutting tools. Societies with access to bronze can distinguish themselves from those without, giving the material a prestige value in itself. Centuries later it was still the preferred metal for the finest statues of the Greek and Roman world. Greece itself lacks the raw materials for bronze; those had to be imported: copper from Cyprus, tin from Spain or eastern Asia. Alongside these came other goods, so bronze-working also stimulated trade. The celebrated Ulu Burun (or Kas) wrecked ship from the coast of southern Turkey, dating to about 1350 BC, contained tin and a host of subsidiary goods: pottery, ebony, and even a writing tablet in addition to its main cargo of six tons of copper.

With increasing trade, new types of settlement emerge. At Lerna, in the Argolid, an impressive fortified settlement survived for some centuries in the third millennium BC (*see p. 254*). Artefacts found on the site come from as far afield as Troy, Crete and the Cyclades, while at its core is the so-called House of Tiles (after the quantity of tiles found in its ruins), which appears to have acted as a centre for food storage. The site may have been a trading outpost of easterners, and there are several others like it in Greece.

Minoans and Mycenaeans (17th–12th centuries BC)

Compared to contemporary civilizations in the Near East and Egypt, Greece had little to show by 2000 BC. However, on the fertile island of Crete, this period sees the emergence of the Minoans, so called from Minos, a legendary king of the island. The civilization begins with the appearance of an elite which had contacts with the east, and who traded with the Aegean and Egypt. Records were kept on clay tablets in a script known as Linear A, which is still undeciphered. The Minoan civilization was centred on 'palaces': sophisticated buildings with courtyards and wide staircases, which acted as centres for storage, craftsmanship and probably ritual as well.

Meanwhile, on the mainland, some time before 1600 BC, newcomers had arrived from the east, bringing the earliest form of Greek, a member of the Indo-European language family. Natives and newcomers intermingled, and Greek became the dominant language. None of this was known until 1952, when a brilliant linguistic scholar, Michael Ventris, deciphered a script, Linear B, which had been preserved on clay tablets both on Crete and the mainland (*see p. 217*). He found words in it which were recognizably Greek, such as 'tripod', 'boy' and 'girl'. It was an exciting moment, as it confirmed Greek as the oldest surviving language in Europe. Even the names of the gods Zeus, Poseidon and Athena were already being recorded. It was clear that the writers of Linear B were adapting the script of the Cretan Linear A to express their own Greek language.

The Linear B tablets had been written by the Mycenaeans, a people who originated in the Peloponnese, where their three most famous sites (Mycenae itself, Tiryns and the palace of Pylos) are to be found. The Mycenaeans appear to have exploited the growing Aegean trading opportunities provided by the Minoans. Their typical settlement was a citadel on a low hill near fertile land and a good water supply. At Mycenae, from 1650 BC, their leaders were buried in shaft graves, the bodies covered by gold face masks (now in the National Archaeological Museum in Athens) and surrounded by trinkets from the east. The Mycenaeans were impressive stone-workers, both in their famous tholos tombs and in their massive fortifications. They were also skilled traders, and their exuberantly painted pottery, notably small perfume jars, is found throughout the Mediterranean. Yet their power was also backed by force. One vase shows a procession of warriors (*pictured on p. 32*), and Mycenaeans may have served as mercenaries in Egypt. Bronze armour and weapons have been found at one site, Dendra, while there are fragmentary records of Mycenaean raids on the coasts of Asia. It is assumed that the Homeric epics draw on campaigns, mythical or real, of Mycenaean expeditions.

In the middle of the 15th century (although the evidence is disputed), all the palaces on Crete were destroyed with the exception of Knossos, which survived a further 75 years. There may well have been some natural disaster, but the same period also sees the arrival of Mycenaean influence from the Greek mainland. Whether the Mycenaeans caused the destruction or exploited it is not clear, but in the 15th and 14th centuries BC they were at the height of their power, and Crete would have been vulnerable. The Mycenaean presence is confirmed by the presence of the Linear B tablets (which may have been developed in Crete itself) and Mycenaean styles of pottery. The famous Throne Room at Knossos may have been modelled on a Mycenaean *megaron*, although newly painted frescoes are still in the bright colour and styles of earlier Minoan work. However, Crete never recovered the prosperity and stability it had known earlier.

The Mycenaeans did not last either. Between 1200 and 1100 there was an abrupt and total collapse of their civilization. The cause remains a mystery, but it may have been the result of overextended trading networks or overexploitation of land. This was a troubled century, as raiders exploiting the breakdown or refugees escaping from it caused further chaos throughout the region. Linear B tablets from the palace at Pylos are more informative than those at Knossos: they tell a story of impending doom as the inhabitants prepare to face the attack which destroys their settlement.

The re-emergence of Greece (12th–8th centuries BC)

The period between 1100 and 800 BC is conventionally known as the Dark Ages. The collapse of the Mycenaeans saw an end to fine craftsmanship, masonry, writing and frescoed halls such as that of Pylos. Populations dropped dramatically, and in only a few settlements is there evidence of contact with the east—although there was a migration of different dialect groups: the Ionians from Attica to Asia Minor; the Dorians from the Peloponnese to the southern Aegean; and others to Cyprus. In some aspects—worship at a number of shrines, for example—there was continuity, and Zeus, Poseidon and Athena survived. With sources of copper and tin cut off by the collapse of secure trading routes, the remaining Greeks turned to using iron for tool making.

Eighth-century Greece saw a remarkable population increase, and with it came more intensive farming methods. An aristocratic landowning class which had the space to graze cattle (see, for instance, the kingdom of the Phaeacians described in Book Seven of Homer's *Odyssey*) could no longer survive as demands on land grew. This had been the class of heroes, so well described in Homer's epics, where success in battle was the proof of manhood. After 700 BC the graves of individual warriors, buried with their weapons, disappear. What is fascinating, however, is the way the aristocratic class transfers its energies from war into competitive games. According to tradition, the first

Olympic Games were held in honour of Zeus in 776 BC. They were held at four-yearly intervals and were open to the whole Greek world. Heralds from the city of Elis, which was responsible for the administration of the games, travelled to every city of Greece calling for all disputes to be put aside so that competitors could travel safely. (*For details of the games, see p. 366.*) In the 6th century BC other important games were founded, at the Isthmus and Nemea, and at Delphi. These truces and the gathering of Greeks from cites throughout the Mediterranean and the Black Sea helped ensure a common sense of 'Greekness' based on a shared language and rituals. Although victory at the games brought only a token prize—an olive wreath at Olympia, a crown of wild celery at Nemea—in their own cities the winners received enormous honours.

The stadium at Delphi still survives on the hillside above the site of the famous oracle. This becomes important for the first time in the 8th century, although the earliest oracle, according to Greek tradition, is at the beautiful and little visited site of Dodona in Epirus (*see p. 518*). Supplicants visited oracles primarily to ask advice, but the sites were also important meeting places. Mercenaries could be recruited there, for example, and advice on emigration would often be based on the experiences of visitors from across the Mediterranean.

The 8th century also sees the emergence of the *polis*, the citizen state. Essentially a *polis* was a community which banded together to preserve its own territory around the core of a settlement, which often had a piece of high ground—the acropolis—for defence. There were many hundreds of *poleis*, although most have vanished without much trace. Each would have its protecting divinity—Athena for Athens and Sparta, Apollo for Corinth—who would be honoured with a cult statue enclosed in a temple. The sacred part of the city would be distinguished from other public spaces, such as market places or places of assembly. Surrounding the city was its territory, which would be farmed by peasant farmers, exploiting the age-old crops of olives, cereals and vines. It was important to define the limits of territory against neighbours, and boundaries would sometimes be marked by temples. The temple of Hera at Perachora, for instance (*see p. 187*), marked the edge of the territory of Corinth.

It was the intensive involvement of its citizens which made the Greek *polis* distinctive, and citizenship itself was marked by an increased use of slaves—as if the freedom of the individual was emphasized by his dominion over others. Hand in hand with the growing consciousness of the citizen class was the emergence of a citizen army, the hoplites, so-called from the *hoplon*, or heavy shield which they carried. They would assemble in phalanxes, the shields interlocking, and battles would be clashes of the two armies with slashing and poking of swords between the shields until one side was broken. The conventions of warfare were that no fighting should begin until the harvest was in and hoplite warfare was, in essence, a ritualistic show of strength. It was impossible for a small hoplite army to hold territory or actually take a rival city. As with any team, morale was vital, and within the city it was cemented by festivals and rituals binding each year group together at adolescence or the coming of manhood. The more successful *poleis*, such as Athens, had a highly sophisticated interlocking set of rituals which reinforced communal identity.

This period also sees a massive expansion of Greeks overseas. The confidence to travel came initially from trading—to western Italy in search of metals, for instance—but the richer soils of Sicily, southern Italy, the northern Aegean and later the Black Sea were too tempting to ignore, and one finds *poleis* springing up wherever the Greeks could get a foothold. The new settlements were founded by bands of young males, and although they would usually intermarry with the native population, they nevertheless retained their Greek identity, and their athletes were sent to compete in the Panhellenic games.

The Archaic period (720–480 BC)

The period between 720 and 480 is termed Archaic, after the Greek *archaios*, 'old'. It was an age of tension within the *poleis* as different social groups, the old aristocratic class, the traders and peasants, battled among themselves to achieve stable forms of government: but these tensions were also creative. The age saw the birth of philosophy—almost certainly as a result of the intense discussions which took place within the city. It was the fluidity of the Greek world which was so important. Although religious rituals both within the city and at the Panhellenic sites were of crucial importance, there was never a powerful priesthood, nor any attempt to impose dogmatic beliefs.

From an economic point of view, the most successful *polis* of the 7th century was Corinth, which was able to exploit its position on the isthmus between the Peloponnese and the rest of Greece for trade. The city valued craftsmanship, above all shipbuilding (it may have invented the trireme); but the most widespread symbol of its success is its pottery (*see p. 33*). Corinth is also associated with the first limestone temples. The transition from wood to stone takes place about 600 BC with the earliest stone temple being built in Corcyra (Corfu), one of Corinth's colonies.

In the 650s the aristocratic clan which ruled Corinth was overthrown by one Cypselus. Cypselus' power was passed on to his son Periander, and then to his great nephew, Psammetichus. Such seizures of power became a common feature of the age, and these rulers are known as *tyrannoi*. These 'tyrants' were strong individual leaders who exploited the political impasses that arose when members of the old aristocracy, trading groups and peasants battled within a city for power. Often a tyrant would at first be the popular choice of one faction. With time tyrants did tend to become genuinely tyrannical, particularly with a second or third generation, but they were also known for great building works and the patronage of the Panhellenic shrines.

Sparta, in the southern Peloponnese, was alone among the Greek city-states in never being ruled by tyrants. It had its own preoccupations, not least the suppression of the Helots, the Greek inhabitants of the neighbouring Messenian plain. They were used as slave labour so the citizens of Sparta could train continuously for war, not only against the Helots themselves, who were regularly brutalised, but against surrounding cities. Such was the preoccupation with internal control that the city itself became increasingly isolated from the prosperous trading cities elsewhere in Greece. Sparta was still using iron bars for exchange, for example, when everyone else had moved on to coins.

Athens was exceptional in the extensive territory—the plains of Attica—which it controlled, but at the beginning of the 6th century its political system was in deadlock as aristocratic landowners retained a stranglehold on the economy. In the 590s a reformer, Solon, had attempted to break down divisions between the classes and had initiated the opening up of Athenian trade. From about 580 Athens eclipsed Corinth as the leading city of Greece. Its success rested on the export of olive oil in exchange for wheat from the Black Sea, but there was also an expanding trade in pottery. In the 560s a tyrant, Peisistratus, took control. He was a shrewd ruler, taking care to appease the different classes of the city. He built the first Parthenon and extended the great Panathenaic Festival (*see p. 78*), which was open to all Greeks and advertised the growing prosperity of the city. However, with time, the tyranny, which passed to Peisistratus' sons, grew less popular. In 510 the Peisistratids were overthrown by a democratic uprising, consolidated by a remarkable politician, Cleisthenes, who reorganised Athenian politics so as to break down the power both of the aristocratic clans and of regional loyalties. The way in which he instituted equality of rights for male citizens set Athens out as a distinctive society where the citizen body, meeting in an Assembly, had prominence.

The Persians and the Classical age (430–348 BC)

Now, once again, the east was to have a major impact on Greece. The Persian empire was the largest the world had ever seen. In the 6th century it had absorbed the Greek peoples of Asia Minor, and when Athens, their Ionian mother-city, gave support to their revolt in the 490s, the Persians decided on retaliatory action. In 490 an invading force reached the plain of Marathon, north of Athens, where it was roundly defeated by a small but well-led Athenian army. Marathon was a stunning victory, and glorified as such in the city; nevertheless, a Persian counter-attack was inevitable. In 480, under the 'king of kings', Xerxes, the Persians reappeared, this time with a massive army and supporting fleet. Not all Greeks opposed him (the oracle at Delphi counselled caution), but a group of 30 Greek cities under the leadership of Sparta agreed to form an alliance. There was the brief but famous resistance of the Spartans at the pass of Thermopylae (*see p. 431*); but it could not prevent the Persian army from sweeping down to Attica. The population of Athens fled and the Acropolis was sacked. The Persian navy, though depleted by losses in storms, arrived to consolidate the victory. And then, when all seemed lost, came the turning point. Themistocles, the most cunning of the Athenian commanders, lured the Persian navy into the straits of Salamis in what appeared to be a pursuit of the fleeing Greek triremes. Just as the Persian rowers were tiring, the Greeks counter-attacked and destroyed much of the Persian fleet. The Persian army remained in Greece over winter, but the next year a combined Greek force, under the leadership of the Spartans, defeated that too (at Plataea) and Greece was saved. (The war inspired the first great history by Herodotus. In a long, rambling account he tells of how the 'free' Greeks triumphed over barbarians who had succumbed to the tyranny of monarchy.)

The year 480 is seen as a major turning-point in Greek history; the start of the so-called Classical age. (The Latin word *classicus* refers to the highest class of the five into which the citizens of Rome were divided, and so denotes status.) The age is often symbolized by a revolution in art, when the Greeks break through convention and see the world—above all the human form—as it really exists. The *Critian Boy*, in the Acropolis

Museum in Athens—'life deliberately observed, understood and copied', as the art historian John Boardman has put it—is often seen as the exemplar of the new era (*pictured on p. 80*). Attempts have been made to relate the birth of Classical art to the new mood of self-confidence in (Greek) human achievement, but the truth may be more prosaic than that: the development of realism may simply be the result of working in bronze, a technique developed in the late 6th century. Even so, a sense of cultural superiority, emphasized by Herodotus and playwrights such as Aeschylus, became crucial to the Greek experience, and centuries later we find peoples of the east trying to pass themselves off as Greek, such was the status that 'Greekness' still gave in the Roman empire.

In 461 a democratic revolution occurred in Athens. Its events are obscure, but it placed total power in the citizen assembly which met on the Pnyx (*see p. 99*). Any major decision—on peace and war, the treatment of subject cities, the running of the city—could now be made by majority vote. Obviously this was not 'democracy' as we know it: the Assembly was confined to citizens, and the whole apparatus of Athens depended on an enormous slave population. Nevertheless, it was an important step. It was not easy to sway an assembly, however, and in the first years after 461, it tended to defer to aristocratic speakers who had the know-how and confidence to dominate it. Famous among these was Pericles, elected year after year as one of the city's ten generals, and whose supremacy was such that he was able to push through important projects such as the building of the Parthenon. (The historian Thucydides records his famous speech about Athens as providing an education to the whole of Greece.)

The Peloponnesian War and the descent to anarchy (431–362 BC)

Throughout this period Athens' major rival remained Sparta. An important result of the Persian Wars had been to boost the position of Athens, who offered herself as the protector of the mass of cities and islands that lay between her and Persia. At first her protection was welcomed; but during the century Athens tightened her grip, imposing taxation and even settlements of Athenian citizens on the smaller cities. By 440 BC one can talk of an Athenian empire, a subject realm paying tribute to its overlord. Sparta viewed Athens' expanding power with anxiety. Things came to a head with an attempt by Athens to subdue her subject city of Potidaia (in the northern Aegean), which led to Potidaia turning for aid to its mother city, Corinth; who in turn called on Sparta. In 431 the two rivals and their allies drifted into war. The Peloponnesian War, as it became known, is the subject of one of the finest histories of the period. Its author was Thucydides, an Athenian aristocrat who had been an unsuccessful general in the northern Aegean and was determined to create a scientific account (in comparison to what he saw as the poetic musings of Herodotus). Few historians have described the realities of war and the cruelty it brings more graphically.

In this war it was hard to see how either side could win. Athens was impregnable behind its walls, which ran down to its harbour, the Piraeus, and its navy could keep it supplied with food. However, its land forces were unlikely to defeat the ruthlessly disciplined Spartan army. Much of the war consisted of sideshows, attacks on each other's allies. In 413, however, a large Athenian expedition sent to conquer Sicily ended in disaster when the Syracusans, aided by a Spartan force, cut off the troops on land. Sparta grasped the advantage, unscrupulously called on Persian money to build a navy, and by 404 had closed off Athens' grain supply from the Black Sea. Athens surrendered, her empire collapsed, and even her democracy was temporarily overthrown

The 4th century BC was a time of inter-city anarchy. The Spartans proved clumsy diplomats and soon threw away the advantages of their victory. In 371, at the Battle of Leuctra, the unthinkable happened. The Spartan army was defeated in open battle by a brilliantly led Theban force. Two centuries of Spartan military pre-eminence vanished never to be restored, after Theban forces entered the Peloponnese and freed the Helots from Spartan control. However, Thebes was no more successful than Sparta in achieving a stable hegemony, and a combined force of Athenians, Spartans and other Peloponnesian cities—unlikely allies brought together by Theban expansionism—defeated her army at Mantineia in the Peloponnese in 362 (*see p. 271*). In the free-for-all that followed, some cities maintained their stability, but others degenerated into civil war as the stresses of the age depleted their economies and led to open class conflict.

The coming of the Hellenistic age (323–31 BC)

Macedonia was a mountainous and unwieldy kingdom in northeastern Greece, whose borders fluctuated with the ability of its successive monarchs to hold off rival rulers. It was here in 359 that Philip II emerged as one of the most brilliant figures of the 4th century. Philip reorganized his kingdom and embarked on a programme of expansion. His aim was land for his followers and the control of natural resources. His success lay in his combination of military prowess with political guile. Through victories, marriage alliances, and the exploitation of the internecine disputes and economic weaknesses of the Greek cities, he had penetrated to the heart of Greece by 352. A few years later he even presided over the Delphic Games. In vain did Athens' greatest orator Demosthenes warn, in a series of Churchillian speeches (his 'Philippics'), of the threat Philip posed. Careful diplomacy might have avoided confrontation, but a muddled Athenian response led to open war, and in 338 Philip's well trained army took on a combined force of Athenians and Thebans at Chaironeia and destroyed it. Philip now dominated Greece.

However, Philip was assassinated at *Aigai*, the ancient capital of his kingdom (the modern Vergina), in 336 and buried there in a tomb which has been, with others alongside it, the most exciting archaeological discovery in Greece of the past 30 years (*see p. 632*). The new capital of Macedonia was Pella, to the north of Vergina, which was the birthplace of the brilliant but impetuous Alexander. Alexander was not popular in Greece: he was more ruthless and less politically astute than his father, and he subdued a revolt at Thebes by killing 6,000 Thebans and enslaving 30,000 others. He then left garrisons to keep control while he set off on his adventures in Persia. His conquests meant little to the cities of the mainland, and news of his death in 323 sparked off a revolt by the Athenians against the Macedonian occupiers. The revolt was suppressed, and Athenian democracy was finally extinguished in the process.

Alexander's conquest of the Persian empire was to transform the nature of the Greek world. In the so-called Hellenistic period (323–31 BC) Alexander's conquests in Asia and Egypt were maintained by three successor dynasties established by his generals: that of the Ptolemies, based in Alexandria (Alexander's foundation on the coast of Egypt); that of the Seleucids in Asia; and that of the Antigonids in Macedonia. Their birth was a bloody one, as the former generals fought each other for power. Figures such as Demetrius Poliorcetes, 'besieger of cities', son of one of these generals, fought across the eastern Mediterranean in a series of campaigns which saw an ebb and flow of power as one temporary victory followed another. Eventually the surviving monarchs, as they termed themselves, defined their borders and the Greek world was to have some stability. In Greece itself two leagues, the Achaean League in the Peloponnese (*see p. 400*) and the Aetolian League in western central Greece (which expanded to control Delphi), provided fora through which disputes could be solved. As peace settled, there were even new foundations. Cassander, the son of Antipater, Alexander's governor of Macedon, founded Thessalonica, named after his wife, as a new port for the kingdom. It was well situated, on what was later to be the Roman Via Egnatia, and was to become one of the most prosperous cities of the Roman empire.

The Hellenistic age was remarkable in many ways. There was relative peace between the cities, even though the days of their independence were over. No city army could ever challenge one of the Hellenistic kings, and it was common for a city to offer cult worship to these kings in the hope of getting patronage. Athens, in particular, benefited from the largesse of outsiders. The stoa (now reconstructed in the agora) was originally the gift of Attalus II of Pergamon, and his beneficence set off a rush of patronage from other rulers. By the end of the 2nd century BC, the agora was crowded with columned buildings and had become a much grander place than it had ever been in the 5th century. With the influx of precious metals from the east, jewellery and ornament become important and homes more comfortable (some with mosaic floors for the first time). Marriage contracts suggest that women gained more status—certainly in comparison to that of their 5th-century predecessors. It was an age of new cults, such as Tyche (fortune), who was honoured as a goddess. Old boundaries broke down as Greeks migrated to the new 'Greek' cities of Egypt and Asia. In Egypt, there were Greek emigrants from no less than 200 cities. Local dialects disappear as a common Greek, *koine*, the language of the New Testament, emerges.

Roman Greece (31 BC—AD 330)

At the end of the 3rd century BC Greece had its first contact with the expanding empire of Rome. Pyrrhus, king of Epirus, a mountainous state in northwestern Greece, agreed to come to the help of the Greek city of Tarentum (in southern Italy) in its struggle with Rome (280). Although Pyrrhus won several victories, the remorseless toll on his men eventually led to his withdrawal from Italy, and the Romans went on to subdue the Greek cities of southern Italy and Sicily, hauling off their treasures as plunder. Roman expansion then led to war with the Carthaginians, whose empire stretched across the western Mediterranean. When the Carthaginian general Hannibal—one of the most effective enemies Rome ever faced—allied with Philip V of Macedonia, Roman intrusion into mainland Greece was inevitable. The first major defeat of a Greek army was that of

Philip's at Cynoscephalae in Thessaly in 197. Philip was confined to Macedon and the Romans announced that they had brought liberation to the cities of Greece. At first the Romans respected Greek independence, warning off rivals rather than incorporating the territory into their empire. Such informal arrangements did not usually last; and after the thrashing of another Macedonian ruler, Perseus, at the Battle of Pydna in 168 (*see p. 585*), the Romans began absorbing Greece. Macedonia became a province of the empire, and after the crushing of the Achaean League, another province, Achaea, was established in southern Greece. The Romans sacked Corinth in 146, and built a new 'Roman' Corinth as the province's capital. Athens retained its independence, but then suffered badly in 86 BC at the hands of the Roman dictator Sulla, after the city unwisely sided with another of Rome's enemies, Mithridates of Pontus. Greece also became caught up in Rome's civil wars from the 50s BC. It was at Pharsalus in Thessaly that Julius Caesar defeated his rival Pompey in 48 BC; it was at Philippi in Macedonia that Mark Antony and Octavian defeated Brutus and Cassius in 42 BC; and it was off Actium on the north-west coast of Greece that Octavian (the future emperor Augustus) defeated Mark Antony and Cleopatra in 31 BC, thus bringing the civil wars to an end.

Though the glory of the Greek city-states was over, for cultured Romans (who by now were used to seeing plundered Greek statues and works of art in their capital), Greece remained a centre of culture. It was the mark of an educated man to be able to speak Greek, and ambitious Romans (Cicero and Julius Caesar among them) came to Greece to study rhetoric. The poet Horace wrote famously of 'Greece, the captive, having taken her savage victor captive'. In the wake of the destruction came new patronage. The emperor Augustus' son-in-law, Agrippa, donated a huge concert hall, the Odeion, to Athens, which was placed prominently in the agora. Yet Rome's attitude to Greece was highly ambivalent, as can best be seen in the reign of Nero. Anxious to show off his culture, the emperor honoured Greece with a visit in AD 66, and somewhat ludicrously competed in games and music contests, knowing that he was sure to be awarded first prize by overawed officials. This was perhaps harmless (Nero also relieved Greece of all taxation for a short period); but when the oracle at Delphi denounced the emperor for his murder of his mother, Nero appropriated at least 500 statues from the shrine. Greece was ultimately at the mercy of her masters. When a temple (the monopteros) was erected in honour of Rome and Augustus alongside the Parthenon, Athens' new subordinate status could hardly have been made more obvious.

In the longer term, however, Greece benefited from the *Pax Romana*. For 300 years there was no invasion of the Greek provinces, and it was now that cities such as Thessalonica grew wealthy. The apostle Paul was able travel freely along the highways of the Greek east, even if he encountered opposition to his attempts to win converts. In fact the survival of Christianity, from the 1st century, is a tribute to the peaceableness of Greek society: the early Christian communities of the east thrived more successfully than those of the Roman west.

In the 2nd century AD there was an important cultural revival in Greece. The emperor Hadrian (reigned 117–138) had a genuine and informed interest in Greek culture, and a real love for Athens. He contributed an aqueduct, library and stoa to the city, as well as finally completing the Temple to Olympian Zeus, which the Peisistratids had begun 600 years before. He also organised a league, the Panhellenion, through which cities sent representatives to Athens to celebrate their common culture. (It lasted until c. AD 250.) There was a renewed sense of confidence and interest in the Classical past. Rhetoric was revived, and the more effective speakers would act as pleaders for their cities before the emperors. Some, such as Herodes Atticus, a friend of the emperor Marcus Aurelius, became important patrons in their own right. A tourist trade began, with Romans flocking to the ancient sites. The guide to the ancient monuments written by Pausanius in c. AD 150 only bothers to mention monuments from before 150 BC. (The guide has therefore proved helpful in showing what Classical and Archaic buildings were still standing at the time.) At Sparta an ancient ritual which involved the beating of adolescents was revived for the delectation of tourists. A few Romans were even initiated into the ancient mysteries of Eleusis (*see p. 146*).

Fall of Rome and the coming of Christianity (267–395)

In 267 the unexpected happened. The Roman empire had been increasingly threatened by outsiders, but Greece had been relatively undisturbed and the threat had been little felt. Then a raid from the sea by a group called the Herulians led to a severe sacking of Athens. Agrippa's odeion and Attalus' stoa were among the buildings destroyed, and the shattered city had to build a defensive wall around its centre. (Parts can still be seen in the agora.) Throughout this period, the most important Greek cities—Ephesus, Antioch, Alexandria—had been outside Greece; with the founding of Constantinople as a second capital of the empire in 330, power shifted firmly to the east. At the end of the 4th century Corinth was sacked by Alaric and the Visigoths, and Athens may also have been attacked again. Even so, some of the ancient festivals survived, and Athens remained a centre for philosophy until its schools were finally closed down by the Byzantine emperor Justinian in 529 AD as part of his policy of Christianisation. Soon afterwards, in the 580s, Slav invasions led to further disintegration of the Roman provinces, and by the 7th century the Roman administration of Greece had collapsed.

Christianity now proved as powerful a force for destruction of the old Greece as the barbarians had been. Constantine had given toleration and patronage to the churches in 312, probably in the hope of using the well established authority of the bishops in support of his regime. A massive church-building programme and tax exemptions for clergy meant that the Church was a visible presence in his cities. The emperor Theodosius I (379–395) went further. He imposed the concept of the Trinity on the Church, and began a persecution, first of all other Christian groups, and then of pagans and Jews. The Eleusinian Mysteries, on a cult site which stretched back to Mycenaean times, were closed down and the Olympic Games, always a festival in honour of Zeus, were held for the last time in 393. A poignant message addressed from Delphi to the last pagan emperor, Julian, reads: 'Go tell the king: Apollo's lovely hall is fallen. No longer has the god his house, his bay leaf oracle, his singing stream. The waters that once spoke are stilled'.

THE ANCIENT GREEK TEMPLE

by Nigel McGilchrist

One of the most lasting gifts of the Greek genius is simplification; and a Doric temple is the physical embodiment of that spirit. Orderly, unpretentious and immediately comprehensible, it is fundamentally a simple idea. It has no complex forms, its interior is plain and dark; but its exterior is a paradigm of unity, clarity and symmetry. Asked to imagine an ancient temple, most people think of the Parthenon in Athens: poised high on its rugged limestone outcrop, rising serenely above city and plain, the Temple of Athena Parthenos has one of the most dramatic settings that a building dedicated to the divine could ever have. Viewed from the hillside opposite, the Pnyx, the perfect clarity and proportion of the building are a vivid contrast to the rough and irregular rock on which it stands: the image suggests in immediate visual terms the triumph of order and intelligence over rude and accidental nature.

Development of the temple form

When we look for the origins of the Greek temple we find that the setting comes first, long before the building. The early Greek mind, which was not monotheistic, found divinity in a myriad aspects of nature. A promontory, a spring of water, a cave, a grove of trees—any unusual or life-giving phenomenon could seem to possess divinity; and to mark such a spot as sacred was an expression of gratitude and respect for an unseen power. The first thing necessary to mark such a spot was a rock or table to act as an altar, so that offerings could be made to the divinity. Since the place became thereby a site of interaction between human and divine, the humans needed to be purified before approaching. Hence a perimeter, or *peribolos*, had to be established: a sacred area around the altar, which humans might enter only once they were physically and symbolically cleansed. This perimeter defined the *temenos* or sacred area. In earliest times the gifts brought to these altars were simple edible offerings: with time, more durable offerings became customary—votive objects, figurines etc—which required a repository in which to be housed. There might also be a physical image of the divinity in order to give the act of cult more focus. Some construction was then needed to protect this often precious image; hence the simple, roofed hut which was later to become known as the *naos*. These then are the primary elements which define most ancient Greek places of cult: the altar, the *temenos* (or sacred area), and the *naos* (or chamber).

Given this evolution, it is important to see an ancient sanctuary in its entirety and to give as much importance to the natural setting, the sacred area and the altar, as to the temple building itself. It is also important to remember that the nature of any temple building or *naos* was not congregational. Human gathering and ceremony took place around the altar or offering table, never inside the *naos*, which remained sacred for the image of the divinity and for any permanent gifts which were offered to it. By the time

Pausanias visited and wrote about the temples of Greece in the 2nd century AD, these chambers were often like store-rooms, stacked with dedications, trophies and gifts.

The first temples

It is difficult to know when the earliest temple sanctuaries emerged. None of the great Bronze Age sites in Greece appears to possess what we can definitely call a 'temple'. Places of cult, mostly centred at the burial places of ancestors, are well attested, but these do not in any real way prefigure the emergence of the later Greek temple and its sanctuary. Foundations do survive, however, from the Geometric period (10th and 9th centuries BC), which appear to be of a simple, single-chamber temple with an entry porch. These early buildings were made of the commonest materials: wooden posts and mud bricks over rubble or stone foundations. So little remains that we cannot be sure of anything more than their floor plan; but that floor plan seems to show the emergence of what was to be the most characteristic feature of later temples: the colonnade on the exterior of the *naos*, which distinguishes the Greek temple from earlier Egyptian and Middle Eastern religious buildings. Several possible reasons, one symbolic, the others more practical, may explain this uniquely Greek evolution.

The scarcity of forest in Greece meant that any beautiful and substantial grove of trees had a special importance or sacred quality, and might be felt to be the abode of a divinity. Particular trees, too, came to be associated with particular gods: the laurel with Apollo, the olive with Athena, the oak with Zeus. The oldest oracle in Greece, in the remote mountain valley at Dodona in Epirus, was famous for its grove of monumental oaks, and the will of Zeus would be read there from the movement and sound of the wind in one particular, sacred tree (*see p. 520*). Early on, a hut had been constructed in the grove near the Sacred Oak as a treasury to contain votive offerings. From that simple hut in a grove of trees, it is a short step to the design of the classic Greek temple, with its peristyle of tree-like columns around a central 'hut' (the *naos*). A row or rows of columns before or all around the *naos* was not only a great embellishment to a plain rectangular building, but a symbolic enceinte which hedged the building about with divinity, just as the sacred grove had done.

The plan of columns around a central chamber also fits with an element of cult believed to have been important since earliest times, namely circumambulation around the dwelling of the divinity. If the chamber that houses the image and the gifts given to the deity is too sacred—or too small—to be entered by a large crowd of people, devotion could be expressed by processing around the walls of the holy place. A peripteral colonnade therefore provides shade, protection and a defined space for a religious circumambulation.

But there are also two practical functions to a peripteral colonnade: it provides an architectural support for greatly extended eaves, taking the weight off mud-brick walls which might otherwise have difficulty bearing the weight of a wide roof alone; and it keeps the damaging effects of rain away from the adobe walls.

Confirmation of this evolution can be seen in a late Geometric temple building at Thermon in Aetolia (*see p. 487*). The structure possesses an apsidal colonnade at the end opposite its entrance, indicative possibly of the practice of cultic circumambulation. At Thermon, in fact, three successive re-buildings of what appears to be a place of worship have been found superimposed, the lowest and earliest level of the 9th century BC, covered partially by subsequent constructions of the 8th and, finally, the late 7th centuries. The first construction was a simple thatched, mud-brick building with a central rectangular *naos*, a porch on the south end, and an apsidal chamber on the north end. But it is the 8th century BC re-building of this which is particularly significant, because the rectangular *naos*, divided just as later temples were to be into three successive areas, is now surrounded by the bases for a wooden colonnade of 36 posts which runs parallel to the long walls of the *naos* and then circles the north end in an apsidal formation. The final version, built over the same site in the late 7th cen-

The Temple of Apollo Epikourios at Bassae, clearly showing its peripteral structure, with the inner naos surrounded by a colonnade.

tury BC is a longer rectangular building, with a peripteral colonnade all around: more like the classic Greek temple with which we are familiar.

Materials and elements of construction

Little survives beyond the foundations of these early buildings because their construction materials were all perishable. That we have any surviving Greek architecture today is due to the fact that around 600 BC the Greeks began building in stone. Greece is a land without good timber, but with plentiful resources of stone, in particular of fine marble. This imbalance forced the Greeks to raise stone buildings in order to conserve supplies of large timber for boat building.

It is perhaps witness of the innate conservatism of architecture in Greece that, as the Greeks began to build their temples in stone, every element of the construction and design of the preceding buildings in wood and mud-brick was punctiliously copied. The earliest marble temples tell the story of this transformation graphically. Stone columns replaced wooden posts, their fluting (shallow at first) perhaps mimicking the shaping of the wood with an adze. The architrave in stone replaced the wooden lintel-beam; above it the triglyphs evoke the incised ends of the roof-timbers resting on the architrave, and stone metopes replace the decorated terracotta squares which formerly filled the regular intercalations of the roof timbers—perhaps originally used to prevent birds from nesting in the spaces. Even the wooden, hammered pegs which secured the roof-supporting timbers to the lintel beams were faithfully—and, from a functional point of view, quite unnecessarily—rendered in marble in the mutules and *guttae*. As if further to underline this transformation, it is interesting to note that the Greek word *architekton* means a 'master carpenter'.

Principles of design

We know that the Egyptians prepared scale drawings for buildings on squared papyrus, but it appears that the Greek builders proceeded more by rule of thumb, laying out the full dimensions of the plan on site and working stage by stage through the construction with each new element conceived and executed in relation to what had already been completed. This gives rise to one of the strangest anomalies of Greek temple construction: namely that the peristyle of columns with its architrave was commonly completed before work on the building of the *naos* was even begun—in spite of the fact that this must have severely restricted access during the construction of the *naos*, and risked damage to the peristyle during the passage of materials through to the inside. Perhaps once the peristyle had been built, the dimensions of every other element could more easily be calculated in the absence of a precise, scaled plan.

The way in which a temple was not so much planned beforehand, but rather evolved on site, can be seen in many unusual aspects of its construction. The stepped platform (crepidoma) of a temple, finishing in a stylobate of dressed stone was, for example, never perfectly flat, but rose evenly towards the centre so that water could drain away. Only a minuscule rise was necessary to facilitate drainage, but it may soon have become clear that an upward curve in the platform gave an energy and vigour to

Village church on Mount Pelion, a descendant of the first wood and mud-brick temples, with colonnaded porch surrounding the inner sanctum.

the whole building which was pleasing to the eye. The rise then became a habitual architectural feature: in the case of the Parthenon, it amounts to a significant 17cm and can be easily observed when the eye is placed at the level of the steps.

This curvature in the base in turn meant that a series of minute adjustments had to be made to each element added on top, in order that the whole building should still appear perfectly regular: columns needed to be cut on a slight bias, and might all have minutely different heights because the architrave now needed to curve slightly too—though not necessarily to the same extent as the stylobate. In short, every element of the temple's construction had to be individually fashioned, with compensations made according to its position. And once there was a common realisation that small variations could enhance the energy of the building—just as though it were a piece of sculpture with its own plasticity—no element was spared the attention of the designers. Columns at the four corners of the building were given a larger diameter, and spaced more closely to their neighbours so as to give a sense of added strength; the columns of the peristyle all leant slightly inwards towards the *naos*, to give a greater tautness and tension to the whole; and every column was given entasis, a subtle and regular swelling and tapering from base towards capital which, once again, imparted a vital sculptural energy. While never distracting the eye, these optical variations enhance the coherence and the vigour of the finished building. And they give rise to the famous adage that a Greek temple has very few straight lines or right angles in its design.

Greek builders were familiar with cement and mortar, but in the construction of temples they chose not to use it, preferring the greater beauty of perfectly dressed and joined stone. In a country as seismically active as Greece, it was clearly essential that every element should be bonded to the next: this was normally done by the use of a butterfly-shaped clamp or dowel, at first made of wood, but later of iron, protected from oxidisation by a surround of molten lead. The earliest temples had columns that were cut from a single block of stone; but these monolithic pieces later gave way to the use of columns assembled from superimposed drums. Each had to be perfectly cut so as to fit the one above and below, and all comprised their own refinements and adjustments for the overall entasis of the column, as well as for its slight inclination. No element, therefore, in the construction of the whole building was straightforward.

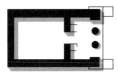

Early temple (distyle in antis), meaning that it has two columns nestling between the projecting piers (antae) of the side walls. The inner chamber (naos) is preceded by an antechamber (pronaos).

More complex temple design, again with two columns in antis, but this time also amphiprostyle, meaning that each end has a colonnaded porch (prostyle). The temple and its porches are built onto a crepidoma, a stepped platform.

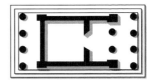

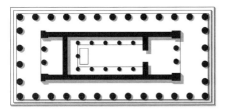

Peripteral temple, with peristyle (colonnade surrounding the naos). The naos is flanked by a pronaos in front, from which there is access to the chamber. The room at the back (with no access to the naos) is the opisthodomos.

Geometric principles of design and orientation

Parallel with a general development in Greek thinking away from the intuitive perceptions of the Archaic world to the more analytical cast of high Classical philosophy, we find that the ideas underpinning the design of a temple also change, favouring a more cerebral geometric plan over earlier organic, *ad hoc* processes. The design of the Parthenon, for example, appears to embody Pythagorean relationships in almost every proportion. It uses the common ratio, found in many temples, in the proportion of its width (8 columns) to its length (17 columns), namely <x : 2x+1>. But this ratio expressed as 4:9, or $2^2:3^2$, is fundamental to many of its other proportions: the height of the front in relation to the width of the front; the distance separating the central axes of two adjacent columns (except at the corners) in proportion to their height; and so forth. And if we examine the floor-plan of the Parthenon, we see that it can be broken down into three equal rectangles, each one of which is composed of two Pythagorean triangles, that most sacred of geometric forms, whose three sides measure 3, 4 and 5. Two of these same Pythagorean rectangles placed end to end give the dimensions of the *naos*.

The question of the orientation of these buildings is perplexing. In Egypt and in Mesopotamia temples had always been positioned in relation to the celestial bodies, in particular the cardinal points, and although the orientation of Greek temples appears to be similarly important, it often seems inconsistent. Most temples are orientated on an east–west axis, with the front facing east and into the sunrise. But this is by no means always the case. We would expect temples dedicated to Apollo, the god most associated with the sun and its light, to be positioned on an east–west axis; but there are several, for example the temple of Apollo Epikourios at Bassae, that are built on a north–south axis. Even within a single sanctuary, as at Delphi or Olympia, or on the acropolis of Athens, temples can jostle together with slight variations of orientation, conspicuously flouting any overall axial scheme. Nevertheless, an eastern orientation was mostly the norm for Greek temples, because sunrise was the commonest time of day for acts of worship, and, with the altar placed before the eastern entrance, this meant that any officiating priest would face the rising sun while the other celebrants saw the first light touch the front of the temple and penetrate, if the doors stood open, into the dark chamber of the *naos* where the deity's presiding image might have gleamed fleetingly.

The architectural orders

The severity of so much of the landscape in mainland Greece means that the austere and simple Doric style is the architectural order which predominates. The more graceful, decorative Ionic style was the natural product of a landscape with softer and fuller vegetation—that of Greek Asia Minor. Both styles appear to emerge simultaneously. The Doric column is massive, possesses the simplest form of capital, and stands directly on the temple platform with no intermediary base. The Ionic column is more refined, with a moulded base and deeper and narrower fluting. In Ionic building, lightness is emphasised over sturdiness and height over horizontality. The enduring characteristic of the Ionic Order, however, is the beautiful form of its scroll capital. In the passage from a vertical column to a horizontal architrave, the gentle curve of the volutes constitutes so perfect and obvious a solution that we scarcely notice its genius. But to look at an Ionic capital close to is to witness the astonishing plasticity and sensuality that could be imparted to what was, after all, a mere architectural element. And when, in Corinth, the idea emerged of further decorating the Ionic scroll with the symmetrical forms of the acanthus leaf, what was lost in tactile sensuality was compensated for by greater decorative quality. The Corinthian Order is not really an architectural order in its own right; it is an aspect of the Ionic. But it contrasts perhaps even more acutely with the simple severity of the Doric.

DORIC

IONIC

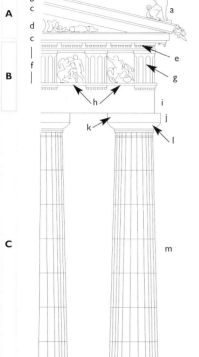

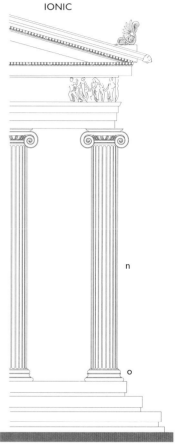

Corinthian capital

A	Pediment	**B**	Entablature	**C**	Column	**D**	Crepidoma

a	Acroterion	e	Mutules & Guttae	j	Capital	p	Stylobate
b	Cyma	f	Frieze	k	Abacus	q	Stereobate
c	Cornice	g	Triglyph	l	Echinus		
d	Tympanum	h	Metopes	m/n	Shaft:		
		i	Architrave		(m) flutes meet in sharp ridges (arrises);		
					(n) flutes lie between flat ridges (fillets)		
				o	Base		

By the mid-5th century BC, the early geographic distribution of the these orders—Doric principally in mainland Greece and Magna Graecia; Ionic in the islands and in Asia Minor—has ceased to be so clear cut. In the shadow of the greatest example of all Doric temples, the Parthenon, there are two exquisite examples of Ionic delicacy: the tiny temple of Athena Nike, and the idiosyncratic Erechtheion.

Colour and appearance

From vestiges of often quite brilliant colour, mostly from the areas of the entablature which have been protected from erosion, we know that the ancient temple was a decorated and colourful building. The colours used are iron oxide pigments (a yellow ochre, a red, and a warm brown), a naturally occurring mercuric sulphide (cinnabar red), a manufactured blue (Egyptian blue) and a blue-black colour based on charred vine wood. Some of these can be seen clearly (particularly the reds) in elements from the Temple of Asclepius in the museum at Epidaurus. What is unclear is whether this red is a remnant of the final appearance, or an undercolour, which would have been modified by the superimposition of other layers, in order perhaps to look like wood itself. Polychromy appears to have been used only above the level of the columns, which were normally left either in the natural colour of their marble, or washed with an ivory white stucco when stone of a lesser quality (poros or sandstone) was used.

The greatest variety of colour was reserved for the pediment, where the facing wall was often painted in a dark colour so as to set off the marble sculptural figures, which were themselves also coloured—the drapery and features being painted, and the uncovered flesh being waxed and polished to a highly-prized ivory tone. The whole was then completed with the addition of spears, helmets, thunderbolts, and other elements in gilded or polished bronze, which glinted in the light of the sun.

Ultimately, however, we can never know exactly what these colours looked like. The same is true of the famous cult statues. In earliest times these were mostly simple: a figure in wood decked out in clothing and jewellery, or even a sort of painted plank of wood, similar to an icon. But with the great humanistic and scientific revolution which occurred in the early 5th century BC, these statues became more humanly descriptive of the divinity. At the same time they became far more extravagant: between one half and two thirds of the total cost of the Parthenon project was incurred in making Pheidias' huge, chryselephantine statue of Athena, which towered 15m high in the dark chamber of the *naos*, with a shallow pool of water in front of her which served to humidify the ivory of her arms and feet and face, and which must also have broken and reflected the low light entering by the door against the gold of her robes. Similar to this was the seated figure of Olympian Zeus at Olympia—one of the 'Seven Wonders' of the ancient world— which was also the work of Pheidias and measured about 12m in height. It, too, was fashioned from solid gold and ivory supported by a complicated wooden armature. The spirit of these creations may seem to us very different from the restrained proportions of the buildings that enshrined them; but both were aspects of the same aesthetic. In fact Greek writers dwell often with greater enthusiasm on the magnificence of the cult statues than on the refinements of the temples' design.

The uses of a temple and sanctuary

When visiting an ancient sanctuary, it is helpful to recreate in our minds what actually happened there. Until we see the pure, impassive symmetry of the temple as the backdrop to a crowded altar, heaped with fire and an often ungainly mass of cooking entrails, with noisy, chanting supplicants and a milling crowd of humanity, we miss much of the purpose of its design. Similarly, if we do not see that it is in functional terms the very opposite of the Byzantine church which was to supersede it in Greek lands, we miss the real extent of the psychological revolution that took place during the Christianisation of the pagan world. The temple was a building whose outside was everything; as opposed to early Christian churches whose exteriors were bare and insignificant, but whose whole purpose was the glorious and decorated interior which enfolded the congregation and hinted at the splendour of paradise.

What took place at the altar before a temple? Ancient Greeks ate little meat: their diet was largely of fish, eggs and vegetables. Their offerings at an altar were of a similar nature. Animal sacrifice would only happen on an important feast. The more inedible parts—femurs and other large bones—were wrapped in fat, as Homer describes in the *Iliad*, and offered on the fire to the divinity. The meat and offal were cooked and distributed amongst the priests and the group who had gathered to pay their respects to the divinity. If the animal were large, some of the meat might also be taken home after the celebration was over. As such, it was not only a timely offering of thanks for the providence of nature and for the food that the gods bestow, but also a method of feeding the needy, who could always be present at the sacrifice. In this way, the central act necessary for human survival—eating—was raised to the sacramental, and made the temple both the visual and the social focus of a community's life.

Temple design in modern times

In the intense light of the Greek sun which projects such deep shadows, the temple functions optically as a cage of light and dark, with its rhythmically broken surfaces, its fluted columns and regular juxtaposition of flat and curved surfaces. Whether in an urban setting, where it rises calmly above the cluttered mass of habitations, or in an isolated site where it tames the power of a rugged landscape, the temple's simple and symmetrical form unfailingly quells human anxiety. This may go some way to explain its disproportionate influence as an architectural model in contexts, climates and ages very different from those in which it was conceived. Whether in Roman Africa or in Confederate Louisiana, as an adornment to an English landscape garden or to Bavarian royal ambitions, as an institutional building in Scotland or Tennessee or the Philippines, the temple has lent a vocabulary to world architecture which has always spoken, in whatever context, of clarity, authority and order. Its success far exceeds its rather limited practicality as a building. But what Greek sport did for human aggression, Greek philosophy for irrationality, and Greek science for superstition, the Greek temple did for the conspicuous waste of pyramids and palaces.

GREEK PAINTED POTTERY

by Charles Freeman

Pottery is essential to community living. Pots are used for storage; for transporting liquids such as perfumes, wines and olive oil, for carrying water from the well, and for celebrating social occasions. They can be used to contain the ashes of the dead, or as grave goods to record a person's status while he was alive.

While pottery vessels break easily, the sherds are virtually indestructible and thus provide important clues for the archaeologist. The pottery of ancient Greece is especially fine due to the sophistication of its making and the superb quality of much of its decoration. A large number of complete pots survive, too, as so much pottery was buried in graves.

The colour of pottery depends on the clay from which it is made. Pottery from Corinth, for example, is a pure clay without impurities which fired to an off-white colour. The clay around Athens contains iron, which makes for a deep red finish when fired. Most pots were shaped on a wheel to the standard shapes illustrated here (*pp. 36–37*), although large storage jars, *pithoi*, would be built up layer by layer. Handles would then be added (and sometimes the neck and foot of a pot would be made separately and joined before firing) and the lips of jugs shaped. Then the decoration would be added. A slip was made of clay mixed with potash and painted on to the clay surface of the pot when the latter was still damp.

The real skill of the potter lay in the firing. To give one example: Athenian pottery of the Classical period is known for the fine contrast between red and black. This was achieved by a three-stage process. The first part of the firing took place with air allowed into the kiln and at a temperature of some 800°C. This turned both the body of the pot and the slip red as the iron oxidised. Then the air vents were closed and the temperature raised to 950° at which point both slip and body turned black. Then air was allowed in again for the final part of the firing, and while the slip remained black the body of the pot turned back to red. An expert potter would be able to refine the process to produce slightly different tones.

The Mycenaeans (1600–1100 BC) first drew heavily on Minoan styles for their early pottery, but they were less inventive in their decoration than the Minoans were and one finds common themes such as marine life (a favourite subject is dolphins or octopuses cavorting with a mass of other sea creatures) or flowers repeated without much variation. At first there are a number of different styles, but by the 14th century recognisable 'Greek' shapes such as the *kylix* (a stemmed cup), the *amphora*, the *krater* (a mixing bowl for wine and water) and *alabastron* (an ointment container) appear and are found on Mycenaean sites throughout the Mediterranean. Another favourite shape is the stirrup jar, so called from the stirrup-like handle next to the spout (*see picture on p. 266*). Any kind of narrative scene is very rare which is why the *Warrior*

Vase from Mycenae, with its parade of helmeted warriors with a woman bidding them farewell (now in the National Museum in Athens), stands out.

Athenian pottery

Skilled pottery-making in Athens began in the second half of the 11th century BC, when the city and surrounding Attic plain began to develop a new cultural identity. The earliest style is known as Protogeometric. Pots, often in similar forms to those of the Mycenaeans, are carefully made (the speed of the wheel was faster than in Mycenaean times) and covered in a much more formal decoration of concentric circles, semi-circles or hatched-in triangles between thick black bands. The stirrup-jar disappears and the *lekythos*, or perfume jar, with a handle now on the side of a longer neck, replaces it. Various shapes of amphora are common, as are *skyphoi*, deep bowls with side handles. Early examples of the *hydria* (water jug), and the *kantharos*, a cup with long 'folded' handles stretching above it, appear for the first time. (A *kantharos* with only one 'folded' handle is known as a *kyathos*.) For pouring there is the jug known as the *oinochoë*. By 900, the Geometric period begins. The same shapes remain common but the decoration now consists of meanders, row upon row with the black rims reduced to thin bands or even just lines. The whole surface of the pot is now covered in patterning. It is assumed that woven baskets or carved wood (which have not survived) provided models for the potters.

The most exciting development of the 8th-century Geometric style is the appearance of humans and animal figures. The animals—deer grazing, ducks, birds feeding, or goats—run around a frieze. Human figures are stereotypes, a triangle for a body, a dab of paint for a head and elongated legs. There are often funeral scenes, with the body surrounded by mourning women or a procession of chariots, presented either in a frieze or in a panel. Some are scenes of shipwrecks or sea battles. Not surprisingly the finest of these pots have been associated with graves, either as markers or containers for libations. (See the exceptional collection of Geometric pots from the Dipylon cemetery, by the so-called Dipylon master, in the National Archaeological Museum in Athens.)

The Mycenaean *Warrior Vase* (c. 1200 BC), one of the earliest narrative scenes in pottery (National Archaeological Museum, Athens).

Athens, with its inexhaustible supply of fine clay from the plain of Attica, led the world of pottery making for 300 years and other cities often imitated its wares.

Corinthian pottery

In the 7th century, Athens' pre-eminence was challenged by Corinth. Corinth was near to the isthmus which joins mainland Greece to the Peloponnese, and so was able to exploit the growth of Mediterranean trade. One of the commonest new shapes was the *aryballos*, the small perfume jar, which probably contained perfume from the east. (In contrast to the elongated *alabastron*, the *aryballos* is a more rounded vessel.) While the *oinochoë* shape continues, there is also the *olpe*, a pouring jug whose belly rounds nearer the foot. Corinth's openness to the east is shown by the painted decoration of its pots. In the so-called Proto-Corinthian period (from 725 BC), a profusion of images from the east—animals, flowers and foliage—run round the surface. One source for the images may have been

'Ripe' Corinthian *olpe* (7th century BC) with a typical design of paired animals against a flowered ground. From the collection of the British Museum.

imported cloth. The most popular animals are panthers, lions, boars, bulls, geese and hares with fillers between them provided by rosettes. One common technique, borrowed from metalworking, was the incision, after firing, of anatomical details on black animals. The combination of the finely defined silhouettes and the meticulous incisions produces work of real quality.

By the 'Ripe' Corinthian period (late 7th century), a more formal setting of animals, often with the animals facing each other in pairs, or grouped in threes, takes over, in contrast to earlier friezes where the animals chase each other around a pot. Black is the predominant colour for figures (and incision continues), but another feature of Corinthian work is the addition of white and purple as colours for detail. Human figures are relatively rare and animals and humans never mix other than when men are shown on horseback or with chariots. The most famous example of a frieze of humans is that of the hoplites marching to a piper on the so-called *Chigi Vase* (in fact an *olpe*, now in the Villa Giulia in Rome). These Corinthian styles are widely copied throughout Greece and can be spotted in most museum collections.

In the 7th century Corinth's domination of the international market was such that the Athenians' production was confined to their own territory. If there is a theme for Athenian pottery of this period, it is a retreat from the Geometric patterning towards the human figure which, for the first time, shows a defined individual. For instance, in the museum at Eleusis there is a large (1.44m) amphora of c. 650 BC with a representation of Odysseus maiming the giant Polyphemus on its neck. Another myth, Perseus and the Gorgons, is shown on the main body of the jug. The figures are still crude—Odysseus and his companions have body shapes which are still Geometric in inspiration—but an important step forward, the showing of a myth in narrative form, has begun. By the end of the century Athens has adopted oriental motifs and black-figure techniques from Corinth.

Black-figure ware

In the 6th century Athens regains the initiative over Corinth, most importantly capturing the Etruscan market. The aristocratic Etruscans would place fine pots in their graves—sometimes using a large amphora as an ossuary—and the Athenians would paint pots specifically for this market. It is, ironically, in Italy rather than in Greece that many of the finest Athenian pots have been found. When the fashion came to England, brought by Robert Adam, the style was initially known as 'Etruscan', not Greek.

Pottery-making was now concentrated within Athens itself (in the Kerameikos district, for instance) rather than out on the plain, and for the first time the names of the

potters and the painters of a vase may be recorded on the vase itself. Two famous painters of the third quarter of the 6th century are Exekias (who was his own potter) and the Amasis painter (so-called because he painted vases made by one Amasis). Other painters are unnamed but recognisable through their styles. By this time the figure and the story dominate the design, and the decoration with rosettes or other patterns become secondary. With the best black figure painters, such as Exekias, the space left around the figures is left bare so that everything is focused on the characters and their actions. The design and relationship of figures to each other

Black-figure *lekythos* showing Dionysus drinking from a *kantharos*, attributed to the Amasis painter (6th century BC), from the Kerameikos in Athens.

are carefully plotted for immediate impact. White is still used for detail and is obligatory for the faces and hands of women, while red is used for beards, hair and some garments. Overwhelmingly, the themes are taken from myths or show heroes in action. Scenes from the Trojan War are a favourite, and reflect the cultural importance of the Homeric poems throughout Greek history.

The most popular shapes of these exceptionally fine black-figure wares reflect their manufacture either for the Etruscan market or the symposium, the aristocratic drinking party. For the latter, the wine for the occasion would come in an *amphora* and water would be brought to the symposium in a *hydria*. It would be mixed in a *krater* and then distributed by the master of the symposium from jugs into drinking cups (the *kylikes*) which would be decorated inside and out.

Red-figure ware

About 530 a revolution takes place in Athens: the birth of red-figure pottery. One can guess that the innovative painters of the Kerameikos were getting bored with their black-figure pots and were on the search for new ideas. Someone started experimenting with painting the outlines of figures on the surface of the pot and then drawing the details within the outlines. It was now possible to get a much more 'real' human body—faces with emotions, for instance— than with the incised technique. When the figures were complete, a 'black' slip was painted around them and the pot then fired, so that the figures came out as red against a black background (*example pictured on p. 630*). Some of these early pots have black figures on one side and red on the other.

As the red-figure painters gained confidence, a group called the Pioneers (c. 510 BC) began exploiting the possibilities of showing the human body in new contortions and angles and even in a foreshortened form. ('The invention of the technique of showing foreshortened figures was,' writes the art historian J.J. Pollitt, 'both from a technical and conceptual point of view one of the most profound changes ever to have taken place in the history of art.') We now have wrestling scenes, drinking orgies and armed combat. Pain and ecstasy can be shown on faces, and everyday life—from athletic contests to erotic encounters at the drunken end of symposia—is more commonly portrayed (especially after 490). Women are found gathered around fountains, craftsmen busy at work and athletes preparing for their events or scraping their bodies down afterwards. There is often a deliberate attempt to set a scene, with the walls of Troy, or a house in the background.

Between 510 and 480 BC, red-figure painting is at its finest. Most experts feel that it then loses its freshness and originality. There is still work of quality, but it is interesting that fewer and fewer potters and painters sign their work. One view is that the pottery painter was losing status in an age when the greatest works of art were in marble and bronze. One of the few innovative shapes is the *rhyton*, a drinking cup set within a pottery animal head, but even this appears to have been copied from metal originals, as if these now set the tone. It has also been argued that the best painters were now working on walls where they could use colour more easily. (These wall paintings have almost all vanished.)

TYPICAL POT SHAPES

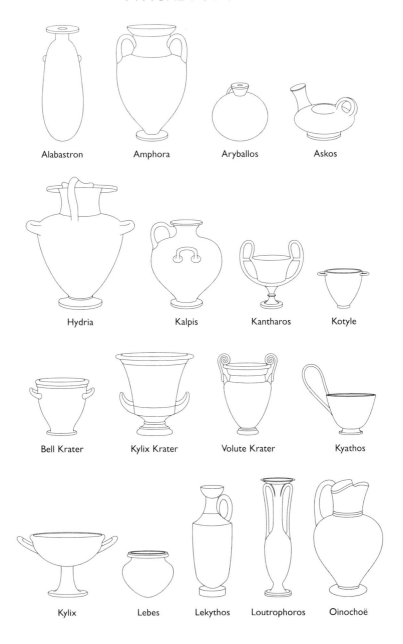

Alabastron   Amphora   Aryballos   Askos

Hydria   Kalpis   Kantharos   Kotyle

Bell Krater   Kylix Krater   Volute Krater   Kyathos

Kylix   Lebes   Lekythos   Loutrophoros   Oinochoë

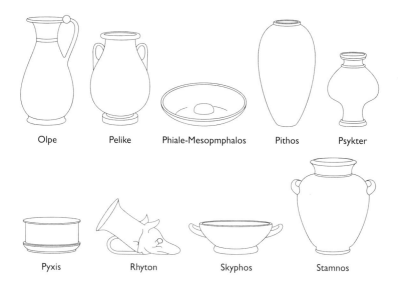

Olpe   Pelike   Phiale-Mesopmphalos   Pithos   Psykter

Pyxis   Rhyton   Skyphos   Stamnos

Fifth-century pottery

Some trends can be spotted as the century continues. One is a decline in the large symposium pots in favour of smaller domestic containers. The *pyxis*, a box shape known from Protogeometric times, is one of these. Then there is the distinctive *lekythos*, an oil container used for funerals. The shape had long been known, but in this period the *lekythoi* are covered with a pure clay slip before firing, which leaves them with a white background. After firing they were then painted with a variety of colours: blue, brown, mauve or red. These were not as hard wearing as colours: fixed by firing and white-ground pottery was largely used on one-off occasions—of which a funeral is an obvious example. Some, for instance, show a figure, perhaps the deceased, sitting at a tomb and being approached by mourners. Others are a specific dedication to a deity. In the museum at Delphi there is a fine white cup of about 480 BC showing Apollo with a raven, which must have been brought by a pilgrim to the oracle for dedication to its presiding god. Some of the larger *lekythoi* appear to be 'cheap' copies of marble originals (which were painted with very similar colours).

For larger pots, the amphorae and kraters, later 5th-century work is characterised by a mass of human figures. There are layers of these, those further away in the landscape being placed higher on the vase than those in the foreground. Clothing is much more elaborately painted, with hair and jewellery detailed. One innovation is the appearance of personifications: figures representing *eunomia* ('good order'), *eros* ('love'), or *eudaimonia* ('happiness'), for instance. The crowded effect is far less aesthetically pleasing than the more simple scenes painted earlier in the century, and it has been argued that the painter is now trying to reproduce wall paintings (which carried more prestige) onto vases. While at the beginning of the 5th century the best painters were working directly onto pots, now we find copyists working from what they have seen on walls.

One form of large pot which kept its shape and function all the way through from c. 560 to the 2nd century BC is the Panathenaic amphora awarded as a prize at the four-yearly Panathenaic festivals. These amphorae were filled with the finest olive oil but were clearly prized in themselves. One which has survived has no less than 58 repair holes, while another was found buried with its proud owner. The typical decoration showed Athena on one side with a representation of one of the contests of the festival on the other; but what is interesting is that these pots were always produced in black-figure, long after red-figure had taken over for all other prestige commissions. Such was the power of tradition, even in a city which was innovative in so many other ways. These pots are of special interest to the historian as most are marked with the name of the *archon*, the presiding magistrate, for the year.

The end of a great tradition

Red-figure ware maintained its vitality certainly until 330 BC but vanishes by 300. With it dies the predominance of one city and its styles throughout the Greek world. By the end of the century Alexander's conquest of the Persian empire has spread that world to the far east. With the influx of gold and silver from the east, metal containers become more popular for prestige objects, and many pots are clearly modelled and even moulded from metal examples. Some new forms appear from the east—breast-shaped vessels from Persia—for instance, but in Athens in 220 BC these are being made from moulds. The painter who constructs his own composition has disappeared: now he is merely a decorator copying from other craftsmen. In Athens, there is the West Slope Ware (so-called because examples have been found on the west slope of the Acropolis) produced between 300 and 50 BC. Painting is crude: figures are rare and most decoration is from a limited repertoire of plants and motifs such as rosettes. The quality seems to degenerate with time, and even the shapes of the pots become more solid and heavy. Although West Slope Ware was exported throughout the Aegean, a long tradition of fine pottery making has come to an end.

BYZANTINE & OTTOMAN GREECE

by Nikos Stavroulakis

The *Pax Romana*, imposed under Augustus in the 1st century AD, brought an end to the internal strife that had characterised the Greek city states for over a thousand years. The city states were transformed into administrative centres within the two Roman provinces of Macedonia and Achaea. Thessaloniki became a productive economic centre; Sparta and Thebes became insignificant; and Athens was transformed into a quiet university town dominated by its architectural magnificence, and by the academies of Plato, Aristotle and Zeno. Several emperors richly endowed the city, and its Agora became filled with statues, cult centres, stoas and libraries. Despite its cultural prestige, however, Greece—and Athens especially—were depositories of an age that had little to offer a world that had changed completely.

Towards the end of the 2nd century the first signs of a break-up of Roman unity were felt following the attacks of an alien tribe from across the Danube. In 175, Greece witnessed a successful penetration of Goths, who sacked Athens. The invasion was an ominous sign of what was to come, as Germanic tribes massed along the Roman frontiers.

Parallel to this external threat was an internal malaise concerning authority in the empire. Theoretically a republic, the Roman state after Augustus was in fact ruled by a single individual. In the course of the 3rd century the Roman armies discovered an effective (and lucrative) means of replacing weak or absentee emperors: namely through revolt, murder and the elevation of someone of their own choice. The sheer size of the empire and its culturally and economically disparate parts exacerbated the problem, and the intrusion of the army led to situations in which two or three militarily appointed 'emperors' went to war with each other. In 284, a Dalmatian named Diocletian was appointed emperor through an army coup. He divided the empire into two parts with two *Augusti*: one ruling from Milan and the other from Nicomedia (Izmit in present-day Turkey). Each Augustus was to have a *Caesar* under him: one administering from York and the other from Thessaloniki.

The Tetrarchy of Diocletian came to a sudden end when shortly after his abdication the new Augustus of the West, Constantius Chlorus, died at York. His son Constantine was appointed by the army as successor to his father. The years that followed saw Constantine systematically destroy his rival emperors, and the experiment of Diocletian came to an end when the Empire was once again re-united into a single entity.

The Emperor Constantine

In 324 Constantine opened up a formal dialogue with the Christian Church by calling a Council at Nicaea (Iznik in modern Turkey). Within a year (and at Imperial expense) bishops from the entire Roman world had assembled, and at the council's first session the emperor was proclaimed 'Thirteenth Apostle'—despite the fact that he was not a formal Christian. His mother, Helen, was, and this may have played some part in determining his sympathies. At Nicaea what was uppermost in his mind was the universal character of Christianity. As a universal 'catholic' empire, Rome had never managed to create a single religious ideology to meet the needs of its complex cultural and ethnic composition.

The interest of the Christian bishops in Constantine was partly opportunistic. Constantine's understanding of the Christ of Christianity was defective. He associated the Messiah with Apollo as Sun God. He incorporated pagan sun symbolism with the Christian Cross, and established December 25th, the date of the feast of *Sol Invictus*—the Unconquerable Sun—as the official date of the birth of Jesus. But this was a matter of indifference to the Fathers of the Council. Ostensibly the Council was called to reach a consensus on the basic dogma of Christianity. This took its form in what was to be called the *Nicene Creed*.

On 11th May 330 Constantine, accompanied by a great procession of pagan augurs and Christian priests, solemnly established the boundaries of 'New Rome', which was to be called Constantinople, on the site of the ancient Greek city of Byzantium. Constantine I chose Byzantium because of its location, dominating the important sea route from the Black Sea to the Aegean. It also straddled the point where Europe and 'Asia' met. Added to this was its highly defensible position, on a promontory naturally protected on two sides by water. A significant problem caused by this moving of the centre of the Roman world from the West to Byzantium was that of the Bishop of Rome. Constantine elevated the hitherto insignificant see of Byzantium to the status of Patriarchate, and henceforth the Bishop of Old Rome and that of New Rome vied for pre-eminence. As western Europe became a backwater through the Germanic invasions, the Popes were left more and more to their own devices. Questions of title, precedence and administration were never resolved. The most definitive schism took place in 1054, leading to the permanent division that marks Latin Catholicism from 'Greek' Orthodoxy.

Constantine left his empire to his three sons. No doubt his aim was to avoid fratricide and civil war, but this was not avoided. Until the end of the 4th century there were essentially two empires: that of the West, ruled either from Ravenna or Milan; and that of the East, with the senior Emperor, ruled from Constantinople. During this time also, and up until the end of the reign of Theodosius II (d. 450), Greece proper underwent dramatic changes that were to affect its link with the past as well as its demography. Despite the attempts of Julian the Apostate, a nephew of Constantine, to reinvigorate paganism between the years 361 and 363, Christianity asserted its influence. In 395 the Olympic Games were abolished. The great Temple of Zeus was dismantled, the oracular shrine at Delphi was sealed, and both the Temple of Demeter at Eleusis and that of Artemis at Ephesus were desecrated and closed. Officially paganism and its rites and ceremonies were no more.

Barbarian invasions and shifting populations

Shortly before 376 the Visigoths appeared at the Danube frontier. The Visigoths had been converted to Christianity, albeit in a heretical form (Arianism, which had been condemned at the Council of Nicaea). Their king, Alaric, requested asylum and re-settlement in the Empire, and the Emperor in Constantinople (Valens) saw this as an opportunity to re-populate Anatolia. The Visigoths, to the horror of witnessing Byzantine officials, crossed over the Danube not as a tribe, but as a nation, their intention being to settle in the Balkans. Like many of the German tribes that had been in close contact with the Huns, the Visigoths had acquired horsemanship, and their military tactics depended on swift cavalry attacks. The Byzantine army, true to its Roman and Greek roots, was infantry orientated and hence slower; for centuries a cavalry had been used for little more than littoral attacks. In 378 after inconclusive negotiations, and when an Imperial army led by the Emperor Valens was making its way toward them through Thrace, Alaric turned his forces on the city of Adrianople (modern Edirne) and there confronted the Byzantines. Routed, Valens was driven for safety into a barn, where he was burnt to death.

The subsequent movement of the Visigoths took them deep into the lands of ancient Greece, ravaging the countryside and its cities. Athens and Sparta were both savagely attacked. After wintering in the Peloponnese the Visigoths made their way to Italy where they descended on Rome. The wanton destruction of the 'Eternal City' prompted great speculation and fears, amongst both pagans and Christians, and it was not long after that St Augustine wrote *The City of God* as a means of comprehending the horrific events.

Athens and Sparta certainly never recovered from the Visigoth attacks, though the importance of both cities was of only limited interest to the Byzantines. Athens remained stubbornly pagan until well into the 6th century, though its highly conservative schools were hardly productive. Sparta, depopulated and restricted in territory, had already ceased to be of interest to anyone other than as a memory of a lost world.

Continually harassed by the Huns, other Germanic tribes began to break through the borders of the Empire. By the end of the 5th century things began to settle. The Visigoths found a permanent home in Spain; the Vandals in North Africa; the Herulians and Ostrogoths in northern Italy, to be followed later by the Lombards; the Burgundians and Franks in Gaul. In 476 the last Roman Emperor in the West, Augustulus Romulus, was put to death at the age of twelve by the Herulian Odoacer. Out of this fragmentation of the Western Roman empire, medieval Europe was to emerge, built on the rubble of conquered imperial patrimony. As far as the Byzantines were concerned, there was henceforth only one emperor, ruling in Constantinople as the successor of the Caesars and the Vicar of Christ on earth. It was this dual capacity that later came to be symbolized by the double-headed eagle.

A much more serious threat struck Greece and the southern Balkans in the course of the 6th century with the arrival of other invaders. Slavs, Bulgarians, Avars and Pechenegs began to settle in the central Balkans, and under the emperor Justinian I (527–65) new defences were erected along the Danube to prohibit their further passage into Greece. These efforts were part of Justinian's larger plan to reconquer the western portion of the empire (Italy, Spain and North Africa) and to wage war against Rome's hereditary enemy, Persia. Justinian reconquered much, but his aspirations carried a heavy price. In the reorganisation of his newly reconquered territories, he made

Ravenna capital of an exarchate which included Old Rome in its administrative domain. A number of fine churches, outstanding among them being San Vitale, were constructed. The building programme was costly, and following on the heels of the expensive and militarily exhausting programme of reconquest, it proved unsustainable. On Justinian's death in 565, the imperial treasury was empty. Justinian was succeeded by three ineffectual emperors. One went mad, and the two others followed a policy of entrenchment that proved ineffectual in the face of ever more aggressive barbarians. The great inundation of Slavs into Greece as far south into the Peloponnese, which took place during the reign of Tiberius, resulted in demographic changes of far-reaching consequences: unlike the Visigoths, the Slavs settled permanently.

The rise of Islam and the Seljuk Turks

The early 7th century saw the rise of the Persians. By 619 they had succeeded in seizing most of the great cities of the Near East including Jerusalem, from where the most sacred relic of Christendom, the Holy Cross, which by tradition had been found by the Empress Helen, the mother of Constantine I, was taken to the Persian capital. Determined to retrieve it, and to recover Jerusalem, the Byzantines launched themselves into an exhausting war, finally brought to an end in 630 with the defeat of Persia and the restoration of the Holy Cross, which was taken to Constantinople. It was a victory, but it came at a price, for it had distracted the Byzantines' attention from another threat. Between the years 621 and 632, the Prophet Muhammad had drawn most of Persia into the fold of Islam. By 643 all of Mesopotamia, Palestine and Egypt had fallen to the new conquerors, who proceeded to conquer all of North Africa (Carthage fell in 697) as far as Spain, which ultimately was taken as well. The Byzantine Empire was reduced to little more than the City of Constantinople itself, and this was annually besieged by Slavs, Bulgars, Avars and Arabs. In the following years several counter-attacks were launched by able emperors, but little was gained. Cyprus was re-taken from the Arabs, though almost at the same time (826) Crete and Sicily fell into Arab hands.

Recovery of Byzantine fortunes began during the reign of the Emperor Basil I (867–86). Of Armenian extraction, he had risen to the throne as the favourite of his predecessor. During his reign and that of his dynastic successors, great gains were made in re-establishing Byzantine power in Anatolia, the Adriatic and Aegean, as well as in ending the Bulgarian threat. In 1014 Basil blinded 14,000 captured Bulgarian troops and had then led back through the passes into Bulgaria by their generals, who were only blinded in one eye. Their king, Samuel, was said to have died of shock on witnessing their misery on arrival. Efforts were also made to Byzantinise the Slavic settlements in Greece. Salonica and Athens are witness to imperial foundations in the form of new churches, whose mosaics and paintings indicate a new approach to the Slavs: their 'Byzantinisation' involved learning Greek, being baptised as Orthodox Christians and accepting the absolute authority of the Emperor.

To the Arab conquests were added those of the Seljuk Turks, who harassed the borders of eastern Anatolia. Just at the point when the empire needed a strong and decisive ruler, government fell into the hands of two sisters who not only hated each other, but whose legitimacy on the throne could only be maintained through male associates of dubious abilities. The choice of husbands by both was unfortunate, especially on the part of Zoe; and when Theodora, certainly the abler and more intelligent (and popular) of the two, finally came to the throne in 1054, she was already well advanced in age. Just at a time when the Empire could have benefited from allies in the West, the hauteur that characterizes these latter years of the dynasty came into its own. The Patriarch Michael Kerularios, undoubtedly with the agreement of Theodora, disputed the claims of Pope Leo IX to ecclesiastical jurisdiction in southern Italy and Sicily, and in 1054 mutual excommunications led to the Great Schism. The immediate consequence of the Schism was the Norman conquest of southern Italy, sealed with papal approval. It also created an inimical atmosphere between Greek and Latin Christians.

The first Crusades

The period of the early Crusades, from 1096 until 1204, was to have ultimately disastrous effects not only on Constantinople but in Greece itself. The First Crusade set a seal on all of those that followed insofar as it was essentially a muddle of irreconcilable interests. The Papacy was seeking a feudal army under its suzerainty; the Byzantines were seeking an army under suzerainty to the Emperor to drive the Seljuks from Anatolia. The Crusaders themselves were, for the most part, members of the minor nobility in a Europe that had little social mobility save what could be found in the Church or through fratricide. Most of the land in Europe had now been settled by hereditary nobles or was in the process of being drawn together by kings. The offspring of both had very limited horizons, and easily ignited the smouldering discontent and misery of an impoverished peasantry. The First Crusade (1096–97) was already a horror before it even entered the Balkans and Byzantine territory. The massacre of the Rhineland Jews by the forerunners of the real combatants, the 'People's Crusade' led by a two fanatic rabble-rousers, Peter the Hermit and Walter the Penniless, set an ominous tone. Penetrating the Balkans ill-armed and with no provisions, they stole from the villages and savagely ravaged the countryside. Their arrival at Constantinople was but an affirmation of news that had filtered down. They numbered over 12,000 and were not permitted to enter the City but were given safe passage across the Bosphorus into Anatolia, where the Seljuks quickly annihilated them. Not long afterwards, the Crusaders proper arrived, numbering 30,000 at a low estimate. Again, after negotiations, they were given passage over the Bosphorus but were accompanied by Byzantine troops, and despite heavy losses they made their way to Antioch (which was when they broke with the Byzantines) and then descended on Jerusalem, which fell in 1099. The zeal of the Crusaders was so intense that they massacred almost the entire population of the city, even those who under a truce had taken refuge at the Dome of the Rock. The word *Franko* in Greek, Arabic and even Turkish to this day has connotations of barbarity and distrust inherited from this initial contact with Latin Christians.

The First Crusade was only ephemerally successful, though Italian merchant states such as Genoa, Venice and Pisa were quick to realize the commercial potential in the new Crusader kingdom. A Second Crusade to assist this kingdom set out in 1147, led by Louis VIII of France and the Holy Roman Emperor, Conrad III. Badly organized and fraught with problems, it came to nothing, though it diverted attention from the movements of the Norman king of Sicily, Roger II, who seized Corfu and then turned on Corinth, Athens and Thebes.

A Third Crusade was called in 1189, shortly after news reached the West that Jerusalem had been taken (with safe passage offered to all inhabitants) by Saladin. At the death by drowning of Frederick Barbarossa, the Crusade was left under the leadership of Richard I of England and Philip II of France, who quickly heightened the atmosphere of distrust that by now accompanied any western Christian. After several decisive defeats by Saladin, the Crusade came to a miserable end. The Byzantines took no part in any of these endeavours; in fact they allied themselves on occasion with Muslims to protect themselves from the Latins.

The Fourth Crusade

The Fourth Crusade in 1204 dealt Byzantium its death blow and caused havoc and ruin in Greece. In 1197 Henry VI of Sicily laid claim to the throne of Constantinople through his marriage to Irene Angelus, the daughter of deposed emperor Isaac Angelus. To the Venetians the new Crusade offered the possibility of undreamed-of commercial expansion by shipping supplies to the Crusaders. Doge Dandolo also saw his chance for revenge. Twenty-two years before he had lost the sight of both eyes in Constantinople, in a pogrom against Latin Christians. The fact that Constantinople was the only antique city that preserved an unbroken line of continuity into the past was of no moment to its assailants. For three days the Crusaders were given the freedom to do as they wished, and the accounts of eye-witnesses are supported by the laments that were written after the City was re-taken in 1261. Churches were sacked for their relics, sacred images ripped from walls and mosaics scraped down in order to retrieve the gold in the tesserae. Manuscripts, books and liturgical objects in gold and silver, bejewelled and enamelled, were carried off as booty. Many are still to be seen in the treasuries of Western cathedrals: especially of note is St Mark's in Venice. The bronze statues in the Hippodrome placed there at the time of the foundation of the City, and many original works by Praxiteles and other Greek sculptors, were melted down, and the marble statues broken to provide building material. Hagia Sophia was converted to the Latin rite after being stripped of the accumulated wealth of almost 1,000 years. It was said by Runciman that when the Ottomans seized the City in 1453 they found only its body, as the soul of Constantinople had been killed by the Latin Crusaders.

Partition of Greece under the Franks

Subsequent to the capture of the City, Venice, through Doge Dandolo, dictated to a degree the division of the Empire. The newly appointed Latin emperor, Baldwin, was to receive five-eighths of the City, and Venice was to have the remainder (the length of its sea walls, docks and harbours). Venice assumed rule over the Ionian Islands, most of those in the Aegean and the most important cities on the coasts such as Euboea and Gallipoli, and in a short time it also acquired Crete. Salonica was seized by the Lombard Boniface of Montferrat. The remainder of Greece was parcelled out among the lesser nobility. In 1205 Attica and Athens (as well as Thebes) were taken by a Burgundian, Otho de la Roche, who established a Duchy that was to last until 1460, when it was finally taken by the Ottomans.

The Peloponnese was more difficult to subdue, and was achieved through the leadership of Geoffrey de Villehardouin, who assumed the title of 'Prince of Achaea'. After its subjection it was feudalised under twelve baronies, with Mistra as its principal city.

The feudalisation of Greece after the pattern of feudal states in Europe was hardly productive or even economically lucrative. On the whole the new nobility exploited the land mercilessly, and many were personally involved in their fiefs only until such time as they could return to Europe, their places taken by sons. The Latin Church, seen as heretical by the Orthodox, was imposed on all territories conquered: a Latin Patriarch in Constantinople and Latin bishops in the remainder of Greece, not to mention considerable numbers of monks, especially the Cistercians, who arrived from Europe. Society was dominated by the Latin clergy and lords, and yet below this mantle, maintaining its own form and episcopal structure, the Greek Church and the Greek urban and rural population survived, nurturing a hatred for the Latin Church and its lords. Greek identity was clearly defined during this period, perhaps even more than by the Byzantinising of the Slavs in the 10th–11th centuries.

The Byzantine Church in exile

Many of the Byzantine nobility not only survived the destruction of Constantinople but managed to recover their fortunes and regroup. In Epirus, in northwestern Greece, Michael Angelus Comnenus entrenched himself and assumed the title of Despot. His capital was at Arta and his influence and authority extended into Larissa and Trikala in central Thessaly, and was to endure against Albanian, Serbian and Crusader attacks until 1336, when it was united again to the restored Byzantine Empire.

Outside Greece two important Byzantine governments in exile were formed. Not long after 1204 the son-in-law of the last emperor, Theodore Lascaris, drew to himself a number of émigrés from the fallen City and established imperial claims from the city of Nicaea. Alexius Comnenus established the Empire of Trebizond, which despite being surrounded not only by the Seljuk Turks, but also feeling the first effects of the Mongol invasions, managed to hold out against the Ottoman Turks until 1461.

It was out of Nicaea that effective moves were taken against the Crusaders. Greater proximity to Constantinople was also an important factor in keeping alive aspirations for re-establishing a Byzantine line on the throne. In 1259 Michael Palaeologus, who for a period was co-emperor with John IV Lascaris, had Lascaris blinded and put in prison and assumed the throne for himself. He was astute, allying himself with the Bulgarians and Seljuks, as well as offering promises to Byzantium's great rivals, the Venetians and Genoese. After securing his allies, Michael concentrated his energies on Constantinople. When in 1261 it became apparent that the Emperor Baldwin II was in Europe (reduced to selling relics of dubious authenticity), the City was taken without out incident, thus ending Latin rule and establishing Michael Palaeologus as Emperor.

The new Byzantium

Michael VIII and his successors were beset by enemies on every side. The City that awaited the Byzantines was a shambles, its churches destroyed or ruined beyond repair. The Sacred Palace of the Daphne, where the emperors had resided since the time of Constantine the Great, was in such a state that it was never inhabited again; the adjoining Hippodrome had been used to quarry stone for Venetian caulking sheds; and Haghia Sophia, the greatest church in Christendom, had been stripped of its gold altars and great silver plated tribune.

Externally Michael had many enemies, the most notable being the Bulgarians, who turned their energies to seizing Thrace and Macedonia, and what remained of the Crusader baronies. Many of these allied themselves with Charles of Anjou, the king of Sicily, who was determined in the name of the former Latin Emperor to seize Epirus and from there launch an attack on Constantinople. He was only defused when Michael set a precedent that was to plague the Empire until its demise in 1453, if not beyond. In 1274 he formally accepted the primacy of the Pope as well as the Latin form of the Creed (both problems that had led to the Schism of 1054). As a shrewd political move it was superficially successful; however, it drove a deep wedge into the Greek Church. The upper clergy supported the imperial decision. The monastic and lower clergy, who had immediate contact with the people, were violently opposed to the 'union', which effectually did nothing except create discord amongst the Greeks. The greatest threats, however, were from Serbia; from the Ottoman Turks; and from internal religious strife in Byzantium and the degenerate character of the Palaeologue dynasty itself.

In 1346 King Stefan Dušan of Serbia pronounced himself Emperor of Constantinople and set out to capture the City. He had considerable support amongst the monks and common people of both nations, as his claims rested on condemning the 'union' with the Pope. Undoubtedly what played a major role in his success, at least initially, was a religious controversy in Thessaloniki between the 'rationalist' theologians and 'Hesychast' (Quietist) monastic party. After a revolt of some violence the city became for a short period almost an independent state. On Dušan's death in 1355 the Serbian claims were retained as an important and dangerous national memory that has been re-awakened, albeit framed in different terms, in our own day.

The Ottoman Turks

The last century of Christian Constantinople witnessed the emergence of the Ottoman Turks. Beginning as a small tribe that had been released from dependency on the collapse of the Seljuks; by the mid-14th century they had seized the important city of Bursa and made it their first capital.

The arrival of the Ottomans into Europe was the result of continuing dynastic problems besetting the Byzantines as well as the menace from Serbia. Both Serbs and Byzantines at odd times called on the Ottomans to assist them against each other, and after Stefan Dušan, claiming the throne for himself, marched on Constantinople, the Emperor John VI Cantacuzene brought the Ottomans in as mercenaries, the alliance being sealed by the marriage of his daughter Theodora to their Khan Orkhan. The

Serbs were defeated, whereupon the Ottomans promptly made it clear that they had not the slightest intention of returning to Anatolia. Thrace was seized and in 1365, under the son of Orkhan, Murad I, *Hadrianopolis* (Edirne) was taken and made the new Ottoman capital. By 1389, Murad had succeeded in reducing Bulgaria to vassalage, was active in dictating terms to the Byzantines, and destroyed all Serbian hopes at the Battle of Kosovo polje, where the Serbs were cut down by the 'red wind' of the Ottoman scimitars. Murad's successor, Bayezid I, began his reign by invading Greece as far as the Corinthian isthmus. Mehmet I added to these gains large victories over the Anatolian khans, and his son Murad II inherited an Empire that comprised most of Anatolia and the Balkans. Constantinople was almost all that remained of the Byzantine Empire save for the Peloponnese: an island in a Turkish sea. It appears that Murad was hesitant about giving it a death blow, probably sensing that it was impossible for it to survive as it was. In 1439 the Emperor John II (1425–48) made a humiliating trip to the West to seek assistance against the Turks. The Council of Florence was convoked for the purpose of uniting the Latin and Greek Churches. The Union was rejected when John returned to Constantinople, and an anathema was put on the church of Haghia Sophia after a Latin Mass was celebrated at its altar. For the last four years of its existence as Constantinople the great City saw internal religious division, and a mass exodus of people who realized that it continued to exist only at the disposal of the Sultan, with hardly any assistance from the West. It was non-payment of the annual tribute to the Sultan which became the pretext for the city's final collapse in 1453.

The fall of Constantinople

In 1451 Murad died, and was succeeded by his 21-year-old son Mehmet. Mehmet had not inherited his father's withdrawn and contemplative nature. Almost immediately he erected an enormous fortress on the Asiatic side of the Bosphorus, at the point where the land masses of Europe and Asia meet. This, to be known as *Anadolu Hissar*, gave the Ottomans complete control of whatever entered or left Constantinople. As the Dardanelles were already in Turkish hands, there was no hope of relief from the Black Sea. The love-hate relationship between Byzantium and the Latin West came to an end on the 29th May 1453, when after breaching a section of the land walls that had protected the Constantinople for a thousand years, the Ottoman forces overcame the defenders, who perhaps numbered no more than 6,000 as opposed to the 150,000 Janissary troops. The last Emperor, Constantine XI, was killed early in the assault, his body identified only by his purple buskins. By early morning the City was completely in Ottoman hands after the seizure of Haghia Sophia, where only hours before the hysterical population had sought refuge. Those who survived the ensuing massacre were collected in its great atrium and sold into slavery.

Within careful limits, set by Mehmet himself, the City was given over to the troops for the accustomed three days of pillaging. Libraries and the accumulated riches of the churches and residences, of the wealthy as well as the poor, were seized and ransacked.

Mehmet had never liked Constantinople, and it was only out of deference that he made it the new capital of the Ottoman state. The City was quickly re-populated through the conscription of Greeks, Armenians and Jews, who were given rights to settle and trade. The finest of the churches were converted into mosques to serve the needs of the still small Muslim population. The Sultan chose a Greek monk, Gennadios, a man who had been been active in the monastic party that had repudiated the Union of the Greek and Latin Churches, and appointed him Patriarch of the Greek Christians in the Ottoman Empire. When the Sultan invested him with the cross and staff of his office, he did so as Caesar, Emperor, Sultan and Khan.

Greece and the Greeks under the Ottomans

The appointment of Gennadios as Patriarch of the Greek *millet* (minority) was to have far-reaching effects on the Greek Orthodox Church and the formation of modern Greek identity. Initially it gave Gennadios enormous authority: his office was such that he could serve on the Imperial Divan with some of the chief viziers, and his jurisdiction over matters of Greek custom, inheritance, marriage, social organisation and religion was effected through the ecclesiastical courts. Especially after the turn of the 15th century, when the Ottomans had seized the Near East, it also established the precedence of the Greek Patriarch of Constantinople over those of Alexandria, Antioch and Jerusalem. Proximity to the source of power also made it easier to further Greek interests. It was inevitable that the Greeks living in Constantinople should evolve as a privileged class. They came to be called the Phanariots, after the name of the area—the Phanar or Fener—that was the centre of the Patriarchate. The vast majority of Greeks, however, were living either in Anatolia, or in Greece itself and the islands of the Ionian and Aegean. Here they were easy prey to unscrupulous local Turkish administrators, the Pashas and Agas. Moreover, these Greeks found themselves at the centre of the great conflict fought from the 16th–18th centuries between the Ottoman Empire and Venice.

In 1503, after Venice had suffered a serious defeat, a treaty was signed forcing it to abandon several key ports. Having seized Coron (Koroni), Modon (Methoni) and Navarino (Pylos) as well as Lepanto (Nafpaktos), the key port of the Gulf of Corinth, the Ottomans were now masters of the Peloponnese.

One of the most interesting aspects of Ottoman imperial structure was the social mobility it allowed. Service of the Sultan could be highly lucrative, and many Europeans converted to Islam, became Ottomanised, and brought highly sought-after skills in ship-building and in contemporary naval warfare. Turkish maritime prowess was to a great degree dependent on Greeks, who provided not only ships but also manpower for the navy. Many Greeks were also absorbed through the institution of the *devşirme*, a system for recruiting boys to the Janissaries (the *Yeniçeri* or 'Young Troops'). These troops, directly subservient to the will of the Sultan, were conscripted through an elaborate system of examinations of 12-year-old Christian boys. These boys were initially sent to Anatolia where they were converted to Islam, given new names, and were exposed for several years to Turkish manners and mores. At the age of around 15 they were re-examined, and those who showed an aptitude for learning were put into the engineering corps. The others were siphoned off into the Janissary army proper, after being initiated into the Sufi order of the Bektashi Dervishes. They were after this sworn to celibacy and absolute obedience to the Sultan. Of this group a very select few, who showed particular promise and intelligence, were sent to the Palace School in the Enderun, the most secret part of the Palace in Istanbul, under the tutelage of the White Eunuchs. This elite, who lived in intimate association with the Sultan, were eventually groomed to become the governors, representatives and viziers of the Ottoman Empire. Many Greeks, Serbians, Croats, Armenians and Dalmatians were absorbed into the ruling class in this way. Ibrahim Pasha, the Chief Vizier under Sultan Suleiman II in the 16th century, was a Greek from Parga. Between the years 1523 and 1536 he practically ruled the Ottoman Empire. The Turkish fleet which defeated the Venetians off of Modon in 1503 was commanded by Kemal Re'is, also a Greek. The corsair Kheir ad-Din (or Barbarossa as he is sometimes known), High Admiral of the Turkish navy and terror of the Venetians, was a Chiot, either of Greek or Genoese extraction.

During the reign of Sultan Suleiman I (1520–66), the Ottoman conquests were extended, beginning with an attack on Christian Central Europe. In 1534 it was the turn of Venice, when after attempting to regain Coron in the Peloponnese they were savagely attacked by Kheir ad-Din. By 1540 Venice was forced to abandon all her holdings in the Peloponnese as well as several important islands in the Aegean.

Decline of the Ottoman Empire

The first indications of Ottoman vulnerability came in 1571, when Pope Pius V created the Holy League, principally an alliance of Venice, Spain and the Papal States. The navies of the League and that of the Ottomans met at Lepanto in the Gulf of Corinth, and after a battle of three hours the greater part of the Ottoman navy was destroyed.

After the death of Selim II in 1574 the Ottoman state began to show the signs of its long descent into decline and fragmentation. Greek influence became especially marked in the court and elsewhere. Their preferred roles as ambassadors of the Porte and as dragomen in European courts put them in easy contact with the West, where already there was a sizeable Greek presence. The late 17th–late 18th century was to see the consequences of a weakening of the Ottoman state and the loss of effective control by sultans who were ill equipped to handle contemporary internal, much less international problems. One of the causes of Ottoman decline were the changes made to the Janissary army. The *Yeniçeri* Corps as a Praetorian Guard fell into inner confusion after ethnic Turks were permitted to swell its numbers, and after its members were permitted to marry, hence dividing their interests. One of the immediate results of this was the abuse of land ownership. Grants of land had been normally allotted to retired military personnel for life tenure. Once these land grants became hereditary, it brought a new evil in the form of almost independent beys who ignored the central government and levied heavy taxes on Greeks as well as other minorities. The problem was at its most acute in Thessaly and the Peloponnese. Exacerbating this situation was the greed that motivated army members who could not, as in the past, depend on acquiring wealth through the great wars that had accompanied the initial growth of the Empire.

Brigandry became rife, and though romanticised in nationalist literature of the 19th century, the *klephts* (Greek mountain bandits) especially were a terror to both Greeks and Turks alike. The Ottoman response to *klepht* attacks was the creation of *armatoli* forces, some of which were Greek and others Albanian, but their activities were never clearly defined, and both *klephts* and *armatoli* changed sides indiscriminately. Piracy was also common, and was a major cause of the breakdown of law and order in coastal areas. The insecure living conditions that prevailed led to a change in Greek demography, many Greeks fleeing their villages to settle in Thrace or cities in Turkey proper such as Izmir, Bursa and Istanbul, thus increasing the Greek presence in these areas. Those Greeks who did remain in Greece were left almost to their own devices, and in many areas of the Peloponnese local administration was carried out under Greek landowners and *klepht* chiefs. It was in these conditions that the seeds were sown that would ripen into the Greek revolt of 1821, and would bear fruit in the next two centuries.

Infancy of the Greek revolution: the role of Russia

In the 18th century Greek influence in the Ottoman Empire became very important in the areas of commerce and seafaring. Many Geeks became enormously wealthy, especially in Constantinople and the coastal islands of the Aegean, where they were in a position to influence the highest official of the Empire. By the century's end many of the most important posts in the Imperial government were held by Phanariot Greeks, especially in the admiralty, which put them directly into contact and influence with Greek shipping magnates operating a merchant marine that had links with Marseilles, Nice, Vienna, London and Paris. Greeks thus became a powerful and favoured bloc in the Ottoman state, and it was inevitable that European monarchs would begin to find ways to influence them in their own favour.

The involvement of Russia in the now quite obviously faltering Ottoman Empire began under Czar Peter I (1689–1725) as part of his double-pronged tactic to secure bases in the Baltic south into the Crimea and hence the Black Sea by way of Azov. This latter move involved him in a successful war against Turkey. Under Catherine II (1762–96) an equally aggressive policy led, in 1770, to her dispatching a naval force under Alexei and Grigori Orlov, two brothers who led the putsch that had put her on the throne in 1762. Catherine's ambition was based on a long and ill-founded fantasy that had obsessed the Russian Czars since the time of Ivan III, who had married Sophia Palaeologus, a cousin of the last Byzantine Emperor, in 1472. Rights to the Byzantine throne did not rest on bloodlines, hence the Russian claim on Constantinople had no dynastic basis. Nonetheless, Catherine hoped to stir up revolt amongst the Greeks in the Peloponnese, and to this end the Orlovs chose to penetrate deep into the peninsula by way of the Bay of Navarino. They were defeated by the Turks at Tripolis, but despite the failure of the expedition, the Russians were eventually (in 1770) to move their fleet into the Aegean where they seized the island of Paros. Hostilities came to an end in 1774 when the Russians were granted protective rights over Orthodox Christians within the Ottoman Empire. Greek hopes of further Russian intervention were high.

A new element of hope was infused into Greeks after the French Revolution, though with little point of reference until Napoleon's rise to power as head of the army that was sent to defeat the Austrians and drive them out of Italy. Italy was invaded and the

Venetian Republic extinguished by Napoleon in 1797. Venetian holdings in the Ionian Islands were transferred to French control. Corfu, Cephalonia and Zante (Zakynthos) became important planning ground for planned intrusion into Ottoman lands, especially by assisting an Albanian-born warlord, Ali Pasha (*see p. 517*), who had managed to create an independent state in Epirus against all attempts of the Sultan to drive him out. For a highly divisive people, these hopes were an important means of cementing an identity that was rapidly assuming primitive nationalistic form.

The Greek 'nation'

The romantic and fanciful interpretations of Greek history by certain Greek intellectuals such as Adamantios Korais, which promoted a form of 'Hellenism' that had no historical authenticity, were to conjure in many Greek hearts the dream of a state that had no precedence either in Classical Antiquity or in the Medieval Byzantine Empire. The ideas of Korais were elaborated by Rigas Feraios as early as 1798. He went a step further in calling for a Greek Republic on the lines established after the French Revolution. With Constantinople as its capital and a constitution and national assembly in which all minorities were to have seats, the cultural milieu was to be purely Greek, but it was to embrace the entire Balkans as well as much of Anatolia. This unblendable cocktail of idealistic aspirations found no common appeal until a more practical approach to Greek freedom was offered by an organization known as the Philike Etaireia. This secret society, founded in Odessa by Greek merchants, rapidly set up sister societies in the Greek diaspora. Whereas Rigas had sought a non-violent transition from Ottoman to Greek dominance, the Philike called for revolution. They even implied that the Russian Czar was its benefactor and hence would endorse an 'Orthodox' revolt. As might be expected the Phanariot Greeks, through self-interest and fear of Turkish repercussions, were not enthusiastic. This was not the case in Greece proper, more especially in the Peloponnese, where a number of *klepht* chieftains, the most active being Theodoros Kolokotronis, espoused the cause of the Etaireia.

Initially the Etaireia was presided over by Ioannis Capodistrias, who had been a delegate at the Congress of Vienna representing the Czar (*see p. 234*). Capodistrias was a genuinely gifted statesman, and it was this that caused his growing hesitation to head the Society, the main interests of which were now turned to the Peloponnese and its more or less brigand (and naïve) leaders, many of whom were of Albanian extraction, as well as the fiery Bishop of Patras, Germanos. In 1820 Capodistrias' position as head of the Etaireia was assumed by Alexandros Ypsilantis, a young Phanariot Greek who had also been in the service of the Czar. His grandiose and unrealistic vision was of a great revolt in Greece and in Serbia (which had just wrested itself from Ottoman control), despite the fact that the Serbs had little if any enthusiasm for assisting the Greeks.

Ypsilantis' hoped-for revolt never happened, partially due to a crisis that arose between Ali Pasha of Ioannina and the Sultan. An Albanian by extraction, Ali Pasha was one of a great number of ethnic Albanians whose careers were to be inextricably intertwined in the complicated web of events that marked the emergence of modern Greece. Ali's capital was the city of Ioannina which, by 1820 had been fitted out with schools, new mosques, libraries and all of the trappings of an oriental court. His apparently pro-Greek façade took the form of promises to create a free Greek state under his aegis.

With extraordinary naivety, Ypsilantis failed to take into account the continued influence of Prince Metternich of Austria. After the fall of Napoleon in 1814, the Congress of Vienna had adopted a conservative stance that defined the 'rights of kings', and by doing so legitimatised the rule of the Sultan. The driving force behind the Congress was Metternich, whose main aim was to put an end to the wave of revolutions that had swept Europe and at the same time to prevent Russia from rousing the Greeks to revolt. The Sultan ruled by Divine Right, therefore, according to the Congress of Vienna as much as in his own estimation, and hence when Ypsilantis took the opportunity to raise revolution in the provinces of Moldavia and Wallachia, his plans were disavowed by Austria and Russia both. Ypsilantis' hopes were completely destroyed at Draganitsa in February 1821 by Ottoman forces though, by mid-March of that year, a violent and ultimately successful revolt broke out in the Peloponnese, where the Turkish presence was actually quite small.

The Greek War of Independence

On 25th March 1821, Bishop Germanos of Patras, an active member of the Philike Etaireia, raised the standard of revolt in the presence of a large following. The news quickly spread north and into the islands of the Aegean. The Ottoman response was to call a meeting of the insurgents at Tripolis, in order to quash the rebellion peacefully. The natural greed that motivated most of the insurgents, however, who were set on gaining land from Turks, plus the firm belief on the part of others that they would be aided by Russian intervention, destroyed any hope of return. By order of the Sultan the Greek Patriarch was hanged from the gates of the Patriarchal Palace in Constantinople (they remain closed to this day). In response, Russia sent an ultimatum to the Sultan claiming a right to protect the Christians in the Ottoman Empire. Had it not been for the intervention of Metternich and the British Prime Minister Castlereagh, this could have resulted in Russia's entry into the hostilities.

By October 1821 Tripolis had been seized by the revolutionaries, and a slaughter of its Muslim and Jewish population, who had sought refuge within its walls, brought down the wrath of the Sultan, Mahmoud II. In retaliation, he turned his attention to Ali Pasha, who was accused of collaboration with the revolutionaries. Ioannina was besieged, and when it capitulated, Ali's head was sent to Constantinople. The focus then became the Peloponnese, where an army numbering over 30,000 was sent in July of 1822. In the Aegean Kara Ali Pasha, treating the defection to the revolutionaries of the Chiot merchant navy as an act of treason, took the island, massacred most of its inhabitants, and sold the remaining women and children into slavery, many ending up on the markets of Kalamata and eventually Cairo.

The hiatus created by the Powers as they debated their role in the revolt had already been taken advantage of by the Greek insurgents, who had met at Epidavros in January, and there had formally declared Greek independence and drawn up a constitution providing for a parliamentary system and a five-member executive council. Personal rival-ries were paramount amongst not only the members of the parliament but more importantly amongst the members of the council, foremost among whom were Kolokotronis and Koundouriotis. Their squabbling led to such dissent that the energy of the new parliament was entirely dissipated in internal feuding. In 1824 Kolokotronis was defeated, and a new government was set up at Nafplion on the Gulf of Corinth.

The governments in Europe were obliged to take action in the face of a new threat when Mehmet Ali of Egypt who had come to the assistance of the Sultan, sent his son Ibrahim Pasha to besiege Missolonghi. It fell after six months, heralding what was tantamount to an end of the Greek revolt.

Greece: a new sovereign state

In Europe a strange Philhellenic romanticism had taken root. Rather than looking back into history, the tendency was to judge the modern Greeks by the historical achievements of Athenians and Spartans and, even less relevantly, of Alexander the Great. It was against this almost theatrical backdrop that men such as Byron set off to take part in the rebellion. It was also due to this popular support of the Greek cause that serious discussions were carried out at St Petersburg by the Powers with a view to creating a Greek state. Semi-autonomous, it was to be made up of three self-governing but tributary states. Russia's highly charged and belligerent stand against Turkey caused both Austria and Great Britain to withdraw their support for the plan, however, and not long after the fall of Missolonghi the Greeks put themselves under the protection of England. At the Treaty of London France joined Russia and Great Britain in issuing an ultimatum to the Sultan threatening to send their combined naval forces into the fray.

The Sultan refused to accept the terms of the Treaty, calling instead for an armistice. The 'allied' naval forces were then instructed to blockade all Turkish transports of men, weapons or provisions, thus catching the main armada of the Turks at Navarino. In response to what some historians have said was an accidental salvo, the British, Russian and French squadrons entered the unnavigable harbour, where the Turks were caught off guard. Almost the entire fleet was sunk, thus stranding Ibrahim's army on shore, to be finally evacuated with the assistance of the French in 1829.

On 22nd March 1829 an ambassadorial conference took place to settle the issue of Greece and Turkey in what was called the London Protocol. Greece was declared a sovereign state with geographically defined borders. All territories south of a diagonal line between Volos and Arta were to constitute a principality that also included the islands of the Aegean but not Crete. The ruler of this new state was to be a European prince, but not a member of any of the ruling families of France, Britain, Russia or Austria. During this complicated process the ruler of the new state was effectively Capodistrias, who had assumed almost personal control after the fall of Koundouriotis. His assassination led to a second Greek civil war between two claimants for his position. Urgency dictated that a choice of monarch for Greece be made quickly, or that all that had been accomplished at the London Protocol would evaporate into chaos. After Leopold of Saxe-Coburg refused the honour, the choice fell on Otho of Bavaria.

BYZANTINE ART
& ARCHITECTURE

by Nikos Stavroulakis

The Byzantine world was born in AD 332. In that year the Emperor Constantine I chose the ancient site of Byzantium as the new capital of the Roman Empire. The 4th century was an era of crisis and change, much of which was to be the dominant factor in the emergence of Byzantine art and architecture, rooted in the challenges posed by the adoption of Christianity in its self-defined form as both Catholic and Apostolic. Lawgivers in Rome needed a justification for the role of a single imperial ruler over what was still termed the 'Roman Republic'; likewise Christianity was engaged in a search for unity as it waited for the Second Coming of its absentee monarch, the Imperial Christ of the Last Judgement. The convergence of these two needs led to the union of catholic (universal) Christianity with the Catholic Empire in the course of the late 4th and early 5th centuries, and it was not long before the Emperor could justifiably be seen as the Vicar of Christ among men, whose duty it was to govern Christian society in the name of a Monarch whose coming would herald the end of the world and the advent of the Millennium.

Art and architecture have important didactic roles to play in society, and in Antiquity both served as the means for promulgating ideas to a largely illiterate population. Paganism was given its official death blow through imperial edicts of the late 4th and early 5th centuries. The Olympic Games were put to an end and the great statue of Zeus disassembled. The shrine at Delphi was also plundered and closed to worship. Unpinning paganism from the hearts and minds of the populace was understandably hard; one way was to create new monuments that made the victory of the Church and the new role of the emperor acceptable and relevant.

As it was through the Church and its teachings that the Emperor had been given his new role, it was only natural that it should be the Church that proclaimed this role to the people. Under Constantine's patronage edicts called for the creation of 'basilicas' on sites that marked important events in the life of Jesus. Some of these were built in conjunction with 'martyria' (*see p. 602*) or 'memoria'. Both play an integral role in the creation of Byzantine architecture in its fully developed form.

Structure of the early Church

Fourth-century Christianity was essentially an urban religion, and in the most important cities of the Empire its bishops and their interaction became—ironically—modelled on Imperial administration. Cities with wealthy and influential Christian communities (Rome, Alexandria and Antioch) were presided over by chief bishops, known as 'Patriarchs'. One sign of the unity within the 'catholic' Church could be found in special tablets (diptychs) found in churches listing the names of the chief bishop of the province and averring their orthodoxy. Another sign was the manner in which the liturgy was performed, following the custom of the particular Patriarch within whose jurisdiction a church lay. Under Constantine the Great bishops were given magisterial authority, which naturally increased their power. With the founding of Constantinople, it also received a bishop, elevated to the rank of Patriarch. To give him an area of jurisdiction, Greece was taken from the Roman Patriarchate and a large portion of Anatolia from the Patriarch of Antioch. This potentially polemical process dictated to a great degree the evolution of the form of the Byzantine church. It was to lead to a deep resentment on the part of the Patriarch of Rome, who continued to claim primacy over the others.

Ravenna, Milan, Salonica, Ephesus, Alexandria and Antioch all shared a common artistic and architectural vocabulary, and were naturally dominated by developments in Constantinople itself. It will be noted that Athens, Corinth and Sparta do not figure in the list. By the late 4th century the Visigothic invasion of Greece had left the country ravaged and vulnerable to attack. For centuries to come it remained provincial. Despite this, however, it is in Greece that some of the most important surviving Byzantine monuments—many of them imperial foundations—can be found.

The Early Byzantine period (332–565)

Unfortunately for the study of Byzantine architecture (and art) in Greece, a great deal of the evidence was destroyed in the course of the 19th and 20th centuries. A cursory look in the courtyard of the Byzantine Museum in Athens reveals a mass of broken pediments, marble revetments, pillars and capitals. Almost all of these are from small, very early Christian churches that stood in many cases over pagan shrines. Zealous eagerness to reach the bedrock of Athenian civilisation led to these structures being thrown down in order to reveal the temple foundations. Only a very few churches of this early period (customarily seen as stretching from the foundation of Constantinople in 332 to the end of the reign of the emperor Justinian in 565) have actually survived in any recognisable form.

Until it was ecclesiastically annexed to Constantinople, Greece lay within the jurisdiction of the Patriarch of Rome. It appears that the liturgy as performed in Greece remained for some time closely allied to that of the Roman Church, and by the 5th century had accommodated itself comfortably to the form of the basilica. The basilica plan was so well suited to liturgical needs and simple to execute that basilica ruins exist all through Greece proper: there are several hundred excavated sites. One of the most striking of all is at Corinth-Lechaion, which was some 120m long by 30m wide. The low platform (*solea*) extending well out into the nave that terminated in the ambo can still be made out.

Structure of the basilica

From the surviving floorplans of a number of basilicas of this early period we can deduce the main components, arranged in three distinct, horizontally defined zones. In front would have been an atrium or colonnaded court giving access to a porch that ran along the western façade of the structure: the narthex. After this would have been the nave of the basilica proper. Depending on its width, and the availability of suitable building materials, this would most likely have taken the form of a longitudinally orientated space divided into three parts: a wide central aisle and two or four side aisles. Lighting for this area was provided for by windows along the flanks as well as a clerestory. Where feasible a balcony could have been constructed above the side aisles. At the east end of the church the focal point was the apse, central to which was a semicircular bench with a throne, before which the altar was located. Peculiar to many early basilicas of this type (in Italy and in Greece) would have been a triumphal arch that spanned the area just before the apse, and acting as the terminal point for the colonnades or architraves of the aisles. This entire area—apse, altar and synthronos—was separated from the nave by means of a rail and columns and constituted the tribune.

In the very centre of the nave or slightly off-centre, would have stood the ambo; an elevated reader's platform or pulpit. Another more or less common feature was an offertory table where bread and wine were placed by the faithful for inclusion in the liturgy proper.

Diagrams showing the evolution of the basilica, from the early Roman model of a simple aisled hall with apsidal end, to more elaborate structures (eg Aghios Dimitrios in Thessaloniki) with transepts creating a Latin cross.

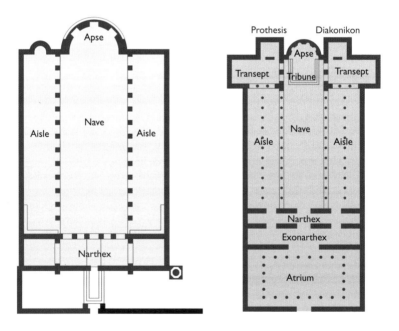

EVOLUTION OF THE BASILICA

The term 'basilica' originally appears to have been used to designate structures that provided the space in which 'Epiphanies', or revelations of semi-divine kings, could be made dramatically manifest to large numbers of people. These buildings were usually quite large, rectangular, and at one end would have had a deep apse pierced with windows to allow in plenty of light and give optical emphasis to the *Theophania*, or revelation of the monarch as divine. The Greek word *basileus* for king or royalty lent itself easily to describe these buildings, though the term was also expanded to apply to any official building that took this simple form. After the Roman conquest of the Hellenistic monarchies in the East, this type of building became the focal point of Roman administration. Roman magistrates, judges, and regional governors—as representatives of the Emperor—would exercise their authority from a throne in the apse. In many cases there was a 'synthronos': a semi-circular bench or series of benches on which important officials or even co-judges and lawyers would assume positions. It is interesting that some of the earliest Christian depictions of Christ show Him standing in such an apse surrounded by the Twelve Apostles. He is portrayed as a Philosopher-teacher, unbearded and in the white garments of a philosopher or as the new Moses revealing the Law.

When exactly the first basilicas were introduced into Rome we do not know. At the very time that Constantine may have been contemplating the creation of a new capital for his Empire he was in the process of constructing an enormous basilica in conjunction with his palace at the Lateran. This building was destined to become the imperial audience hall, though it never functioned as such. It remains today essentially what it was then: a long building divided into three aisles by columns that provided the architraves for supporting a timbered roof, and terminating in an apse though preceded by what is termed a transept—an extension on either side to where the main body of the building meets the apsidal area. It was in the apse that the emperor would have taken his position on the throne, and the court and important officers would have been located in this transept. The rest of the building was for the onlookers.

The Lateran palace and audience hall were ultimately taken over by the Bishops of Rome, and thus the tripartite nave, transept and apse became the model for most of the great cathedrals of Europe. In fact, Western Christian architecture never really evolved much further beyond this point. It was to be in Constantinople and the Byzantine world that we can trace a rich and exciting period of experimentation that created Byzantine architecture in its classic form.

The early liturgy

We know only the bones of the liturgy as it was performed at this time. It had two major divisions: the Liturgy of the Catechumens and the Liturgy of the Faithful. The former was didactic and terminated in readings from the Gospels or Old Testament, as well as perhaps a homily. The catechumens were non-Christians in the process of receiving instruction prior to their baptism. The Liturgy of the Faithful was restricted to baptised Christians and was the formal ceremony of worship during which time the bread and wine were consecrated, offered to God as a commemoration of the Mystery of the death of Christ and the redemption of the Universe, and then consumed by the community.

The action and inter-action of these participants—catechumens, priest, bishop and laity—was well orchestrated. On a given festival all participants would have assembled in the atrium and the presiding priest or bishop would be made ready in either a wing of the colonnade or the narthex. The church proper would have been unlit. At a given moment a procession, preceded by a cross and an elevated book of the Gospels, would precede the celebrant and slowly enter the church. As this was done the interior lamps of the church were lit, thus symbolising the entrance into time of the Incarnate Word of God. This procession would make its way into the apse where the celebrant would take his seat on the throne and his attendant priests or deacons would seat themselves on the bench around it. The apse itself was very early decorated with a scene of either Christ standing amidst the Apostles or seated enthroned. It was only after the bishop had assumed his position that the congregation would enter the church to see him seated in much the same manner as the teaching or authoritative Christ. Many would leave their offerings on the offertory table and then assume their positions. It seems most likely that men would have occupied the right-hand aisle and the women the left, divided between 'Widows' and 'Virgins' (there are interesting accounts of contentious behaviour between both over who had the right to be closer to the tribune). The catechumens would have been toward the back (west end) of the nave. The high point of this part of the liturgy was when the lector processed to the ambo and read the appropriate Gospel for the day. An announcement was then made that the catechumens were to leave the assembly, and they would move either out into the narthex or, in some less formal instances, up into the balconies (which would be hung with heavy curtains). The Liturgy of the Faithful would now begin, with yet another procession as the officiating priest, with the bread and wine from the offertory table, would proceed to the altar, and there, facing the bishop (who was presiding) would have carried out the consecration.

At the end of this part of the liturgy the catechumens were allowed back into the community and final prayers were said, after which the celebrant would leave in procession out of the church.

The most important influence on this initially quite simple liturgy was to be Constantinople. There existed from the time of the Emperor Diocletian (c. 300 AD) an imperial liturgy of sorts, glorifying the emperor as the representative of Helios, the sun-god. It was only a matter of time before the hieratic appearance of the Emperor in ceremonial dress, surrounded by his court and receiving divine honours as the representative of Christ on earth, was adopted by the emperors in Constantinople. It seemed quite natural that the newly established Patriarch of the City should seek to elaborate its liturgy by recourse to the Imperial liturgy.

Early Byzantine architecture

Though never theologically defined in the way that sacred art was, Byzantine architecture adapted itself to changes and refinements in liturgical requirements in the course of centuries to come. What is most noticeable about it are the numerous processions and the displacement and movement of the community in their progress. Unlike the Latin West, where the division of static laity in the nave and active clergy in the apse made the basilica type of church entirely practical, increasingly in the East the elaboration of the liturgy and its processions demanded easy movement and visual access to what was happening.

Four key structures dating from this early period survive in Thessaloniki: the Rotunda of Aghios Georgios (311 and 395), the Acheiropoeitos (c. 430), Aghios Dimitrios, and Hosios David. The Rotunda was originally constructed as a mausoleum for the Emperor Galerius (d. 311), though it was never used as such. Its conversion to Christian usage occurred during the reign of Theodosius I (379–95) and quite feasibly celebrates several edicts that announced Catholic Christianity as the sole religion of the Roman state, hence forbidding any form of pagan worship to continue.

The early 5th-century church of Hosios David was built as a martyrium (*see p. 602*) but functioned as a katholikon: a monastic church. In its original form (it has lost part of its west end) the building was a square, from the centre of which radiated four bays, the eastern one extended so as to provide room for the apse. The four bays form a very distinct cross, and small interconnecting chambers were constructed between the arms. This inscribed-cross plan had precedents in both Syria and Armenia, and was to play an important role in the evolution of high Byzantine architecture.

The evolving liturgy of the Byzantine church appears to have concentrated more and more on the elaborating processions, but also in adapting certain architectural forms to accentuate the form of its action. By this time most of the community had been baptised, and catechumens no longer posed a problem for which accommodation had to be provided in galleries and the narthex. The reading of the scriptures thus became more elaborate, and the ambo the central focus of the first part of the liturgy—though unlike the altar in the semicircular apse, it had no architectural setting befitting its role. A dome was thus placed over it, and the spatial challenge involved in resting a circular or elliptical structure on a rectangular base was solved with the introduction of two important architectural devices. These were the squinch and the pendentive. The area of the basilica that was to be domed was transformed into a square by means of piers, which interrupted the columns on either side of the nave. At the angles of this square, small arches (squinches) were set that transformed it into an octagon, and on this base a dome could easily be set—either directly or resting on a drum. The corners of the squared area were inset with segments (pendentives), which transformed the square into a circle. Unlike the squinches, which created the octagonal shape on which the dome was to rest, the pendentives partially filled the areas beneath.

The finest of all such churches is Haghia Sophia in Istanbul, for centuries the Mother Church of Christendom. In many respects it represents the end of this period of early Byzantine art, a culmination of a period during which Christianity and its

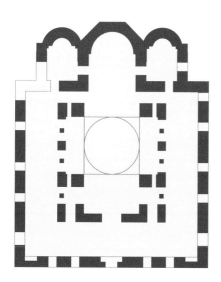

The cross-domed basilica (eg Aghia Sofia in Thessaloniki). A square central bay with four arms of equal length (Greek cross) is surmounted by a dome.

inherited architectural traditions had arrived at a *modus vivendi* out of which emerged a tradition that was entirely Byzantine. Its volume, great dome, filtering light and mysterious casing in dark side aisles was to make it the wonder of the Middle Ages, and it still inspires awe today. Its role in Byzantine history was intimate, and many of the successes and tragedies that the Empire was to endure were enacted within its walls, though it never functioned as a 'normal' church. Special liturgies were enacted there, which saw the Emperor enter the narthex, in the presence of the court, remove his crown and then perform *proskynisis*: lowering himself to the floor in adoration of his prototype Christ enthroned on the altar of the great church. Haghia Sophia in this sense was the audience hall of God, where He and His earthly vicar met. Nowhere else was this rite performed and in the language of the times. Constantinople had become the New Jerusalem, and Haghia Sophia the sole Temple of Christendom. Haghia Sophia and its role were perhaps best summed up in the words of the Emperor Justinian himself when, according to his court historian Procopius, he stood in its vast interior and cried out 'Solomon, I have outdone thee!'

The Middle Byzantine period (565–843)

After Justinian's death in 565, it was not long before all that remained of his great reign and aspirations was Haghia Sophia. Beginning with the Avars in 583, the Danube defences of the Empire were broken through, and within a short period the barbarians were at the gates of Constantinople. By 600 the Slavs, by-passing Salonica, penetrated into Greece and settled permanently as far south as the Peloponnese. No churches of any significance were built during this period. The great wars with Persia, though ending in a success for the Byzantines (see p. 42), ultimately added to the conditions in the Near East that led to the success of the Islamic invasions and the near collapse of the Empire. Heraclius lay dying as the Arabs conquered the heartland of Christianity—Syria, Egypt and North Africa—not to mention Persia.

The proximity of Salonica to Constantinople and its position in Macedonia to a degree protected the city from these invasions. Thus it is that the sole monument in Greece that marks this period of decline is the church of Aghia Sofia in Thessaloniki (*diagram opposite*), which was erected probably in 783 to commemorate a victory over the Slavs in both Macedonia as well as Greece. It is massive, heavy and dependent on the form of the domed basilicas of a century before; and yet the continued use of this form indicates that it best suited the now fully evolved Byzantine liturgy. Two rooms located on either side both had access to the apse. That to the south (the diakonikon) was used for keeping vestments, liturgical books and the like. The room to the north (the prothesis) was where the two processions of the Scriptures and the Holy Sacraments began and then followed a path around the interior of the church, processing down the aisles.

If the great achievements of the pagan antique world reflected Aristotle's dictum that art was to imitate nature, Christianity now questioned what man's true nature was. '*Creatio ex nihilo*' was not considered in Antiquity to be a necessary aspiration for artists and architects. The public assembled in structures that were often designed to express the security of tradition. The idea of creating something entirely 'new' would have met with failure—though this did not affect the search for solutions to the dictates of change in taste and style, not to mention message. Even in this early phase of the creation of a 'sacred' art, the interaction of new ideas, ideals and aspirations are clearly seen in the way the inherited artistic vocabulary of Graeco-Roman art was manipulated to suit the needs of a new ideology.

The Iconoclast Controversy (787–843)

Towards the end of the 8th century, an internal crisis beset the imperial Church: Iconoclasm. In the Christian East especially there had traditionally been a lenient attitude toward the popular reverence given to sites, relics and images of holy persons. This arose out of the cult of martyrs, and took form through the adoption of portrait images associated with funerary customs common throughout the Near East. There was a fine line between 'honour' to these images and 'worship', and there was already serious theological debate over their justification during the time of Justinian I. This debate now transmuted itself into an intense examination of Christian conscience. Given the condemnation of 'graven images' in the First Commandment, a literal war against their use began, supported by a number of Iconoclast emperors. Churches were stripped of their images, and individuals who opposed this mass destruction were in many cases branded or banished from the Empire. The sole permitted image was henceforth to be the Cross. If one looks closely at the image of the Virgin and Child in the apse of Aghia Sofia in Thessaloniki, one can still see the traces of the arms of a cross, delineated by gold tesserae applied later, when the Virgin was replaced after the controversy had ended.

The controversy was ultimately resolved through compromise, achieved only after an exceedingly violent outbreak of iconoclast persecution under Leo V in 815. It was under the Emperor Michael III in 843 that image-worship was firmly incorporated into dogma.

The effects of this controversy determined a number of important regulations. Henceforth no image that was carved in three dimensions would be used for worship. Those that were executed on walls (in churches) or on panels (icons) had to conform in detail to dogma. A clear distinction was made between 'didactic' images, which received 'honour', and those destined for '*douleia*' (worship). The sources for these were clearly established and could only be derived from certain gospels, or from images that were *acheiropoeitoi* (not made by human hands), some of which were attributed to St Luke himself. Within a relatively short time Byzantine art became intellectualised, and the artist himself a theologian. Rules were laid down that dictated in minute detail the appearances of saints and holy figures, down to their hairstyles, the shape of their faces, the colour of their garments, position of hands and even fingers.

There was, according to this doctrinal clarification, an essential relationship between the icon and the prototype, and worship or honour given to an icon was immediately relayed to the person depicted. In practice the artist creating such an image was creating a communication link, and this was only made effective when the image was inscribed with a name, either that of the saint or a descriptive title of the scene depicted. The artist himself was of little account, and not until very late—and certainly under the influence of Western art—do we know any of the painters. Defined and limited in this manner, Byzantine art after the 9th century is distinctively a 'sacred' art as opposed to a religious art as such.

Middle and Late Byzantine architecture (843–1453)

The monumentality of the old cross-domed basilicas appears to have made them redundant after the 8th century. What emerges is a more compact and certainly less expensive structure: the cross-in-square or inscribed cross (*diagram opposite*). In these churches a dome is elevated on squinches springing from four barrel vaults resting on columns that provide the arms of the cross. Over each of the arms (or over the interstices between them) are set smaller domes, hence these churches are termed five-domed or quincunx.

By the 10th century the quincunx had become the normal form of the Byzantine church, and so it remained until the end of the Empire in 1453. It was relatively small; by the use of squinches it had a higher elevation, and the interior articulation of architectural elements lent itself to the new thinking. As a three-dimensional space it provided an at times dramatic means for making dogma clear and accessible. For example, the dome of the church was now the absolute domain of the Imperial Christ as the Judge at the end of time (Pantocrator) and His image is depicted holding either an open or closed book. Around the drum supporting the dome would normally be arranged the twelve Apostles. (If there were pendentives they would lend themselves comfortably for depicting the four Evangelists.) The apse of the church was dedicated to the Virgin as Theotokos (God-bearer). This concave area was also known as the 'womb', and the iconic representation of the Virgin in it was usually as a standing or seated figure with the infant Christ in her lap. On either side normally stood the Archangels Michael and Gabriel, dressed in courtly garments befitting their role as attendants. In the semicircular area just beneath this, a depiction of the Eucharist was typically portrayed, with some of the Doctors of the Church—St John Chrysostom, St Basil, St Cyril—as participants. On occasion a dual representation of Christ is portrayed just behind the altar: one of these images, turning to the left, offers the consecrated bread to six Apostles, and the other image, turning to the right, offers the chalice of wine to the remaining Apostles, as in the apse mosaic of the 11th-century basilica of Aghii Theodoroi in Serres in Macedonia. The intermediate zone of the church was reserved for depictions of the Twelve Great Festivals (the *Dodekaorton*): depictions of the main incidents in the life of Christ that marked the Redemption of man and the Universe. These are the Annunciation, the Nativity, the Baptism of Christ, the Presentation in the Temple, the Transfiguration, the Raising of Lazarus, the Entry into Jerusalem, the Last Supper, The Crucifixion, the Resurrection, the Ascension, Pentecost and the Dormition of the Virgin. The iconography of these images is very ancient, and in many instances is drawn from apocryphal sources as, for example, the image of the Descent of Christ into the Underworld (the Harrowing of Hell) or even the Annunciation, where the Virgin is shown either

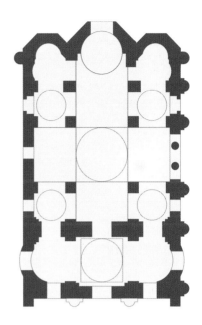

The cross-in-square or quincunx model, where the Greek-cross core, surmounted by its dome, is flanked by side bays all bearing smaller domes.

standing or seated, depending on whether the iconography is drawn from the Gospel of Luke (seated) or the Gospel attributed to Pseudo-Matthew (standing). These images are as a rule set up in the barrel vaults of the interior cross-arms of the church. The inner articulation of the church, with vaults, squinches, pendentives and domes, gave artists ample opportunity to use actual space in order to expound a subject. At Daphni the Annunciation is depicted in a mosaic located in the northeast squinch of the nave. It is a striking example of the art of the Byzantine mosaicist and iconographer. The concave surface of the squinch is filled by a shower of gold mosaic that filters down between the image of the standing Virgin on the right, and the Angel Gabriel opposite. There can be little doubt that this remarkable composition derives from the myth of Zeus descending on Danaë in a shower of golden rain.

The lower zone, that located beneath the depictions of the Twelve Festivals, is usually decorated with single images of saints, and beneath that, in churches that have mosaics, the lower walls are covered with marble revetments.

From the 10th to the beginning of the 13th centuries there was an increased imperial interest in Greece proper. Efforts were concentrated on the conversion and 'Hellenisation' of the great enclaves of Slavs, as well as on defence measures. Prior to this time Greece had sunk into a wretched state through invasions, coastal raids and imperial neglect. Probably the best example of its crude ecclesiastical architecture is the 9th-century church at Skripou in Boeotia (*see p. 427*). Massively constructed of reused segments of stone from other buildings, it bears silent witness to harsh times.

In Thessaloniki the church of the Virgin of the Coppersmiths (Panaghia Chalkeon) was constructed under private patronage in 1028, and is of interest in that it incorporates the now usual cross-in-square floor plan with the dome resting on four columns (though the exterior has only three domes). Built entirely of brick, its exterior reflects a new taste in exterior decoration, though within a tradition that goes back to Ravenna.

The church at Daphni dates from the late 11th century, though the original foundation was of the 5th century and a good amount of marble from an antique pagan temple was used in its building. The present structure is decorated on its exterior with elaborate Kufic designs, and conforms to the type of Hosios Loukas (*see p. 440*). After the Fourth Crusade, the church was given to Cistercian monks, whose austere churches in Europe were a far cry from the rich, Classically imbibed mosaics at Daphni—though they may have taken solace in the stern Pantocrator that dominates the dome. It was under its gaze, according to a tradition, that Franco, the son of the last Acciaioli duke of Athens, throttled his infamous aunt Chiara and then proceeded to behead her.

The evolution of Byzantine painting

The recapture of Constantinople by the Emperor Michael VIII Palaeologus in 1261 ended the Crusader period in the City. The re-unification of the Empire itself, however, shattered beyond recovery by the Crusaders, was never to be achieved. Greece now consisted of small fiefdoms after the Western pattern. Not long after the re-establishment of Byzantine rule in Constantinople, the fortress of Mistra was ceded to the Emperor. Beginning in 1290 a series of churches was erected that were to be the last important Byzantine monuments in Greece.

The paintings in some of the churches are an important clue not only to the developments in Constantinople (as many of its painters were certainly attracted to the new court of Mistra), but also to developments elsewhere. During the period of Latin domination many Byzantine artists had fled to either Serbia or Bulgaria, where they were commissioned to decorate churches in very different circumstances. Many of these churches survive, and artists appear to have been less constrained by Constantinopolitan tastes and reserve. Thus emerges what has been called the 'Macedonian' school, which some scholars have typified as 'humanistic', insofar as the traditional hieratic forms have been replaced, or at least intruded on, by an interest in psychological moment. It has given rise to speculation that Giotto may have been inspired by a time spent with these Byzantine artists-in-exile.

These painters appear to have returned to Constantinople after its recapture in 1261, but the spirit and the techniques of their painting have changed considerably. Many of them may well have been working in Salonica and even further south in Greece. Certainly the newly emerging style and spirit is evident in a number of small churches decorated between the years 1280 and 1320, all well worth visiting, and all related in their polymorphic style and spirit. One of these, Omorfi Ekklisia, is in

Athens (in the suburb of Galatsi). Seldom visited, it is a small, domed, cross-in-square structure in well-cut stone and brick cloisonné. The interior has retained almost all of its wall-paintings, many of which show decided affinities to developments in Macedonia, with animated and emotionally charged figures. This church appears to be one of several that were decorated in Attica at this period, and one of the artists may well be a man who was active in the area: John of Athens.

The mosaics of the Aghii Apostoloi in Salonica can be dated to 1315, and are fine examples of the new spirit. The figures are conceived in terms of volume as opposed to linear values, and the faces are affected by events occurring about them. The deep gravity evinced in the face and eyes of Christ at the moment of seizing the hand of Adam in drawing him out of Hades is quite remarkable, and this inward and power-ful moment is made personal to the viewer through the small head of Abel, also wait-ing to be saved, but who looks directly at us out of the painting.

Two closely related decorated churches are also in this tradition, though much less monumental than Aghii Apostoloi. These are Aghios Nikolaos Orfanos in Salonica (14th century) and the church of the Sotiras Christos in nearby Veroia (1315). Aghios Nikolaos is a small, deceptively plain brick structure with an elevated roof, and a cen-tral cella with a narthex that is extended on either side of it in an embrace. Lacking a dome, there is no dominant *Pantocrator*, though over the apse is a depiction of the Sacred Veil of Edessa (the Veil of Veronica) bearing the face of Christ, an image that becomes more and more common from the 13th century on. The cool, hieratic char-acter of medieval Byzantine painting has here been replaced by intimacy and an inter-pretation of responses, such as in the *Crucifixion*, where the Virgin's head is bent in an anguish reflected above her in the gyrating forms of two angels. In Veroia an equally simple structure was decorated by one of the few artists whose name has survived. So close are the affinities between this church and that of Aghios Nikolaos Orfanos, that it is likely that the artist Kalliergis and his brothers completed commissions in both.

By contrast to these developments in the north of Greece, in Mistra the composi-tions are less rigid, the figures elongated well beyond even conservative practice, and the faces expressive of an anxiety that certainly dominated the Byzantine spirit during this troubled century. Technically there is a strong influence of icon or panel painting on images, with sharp highlighting brushed over figures as if light flowed from above and over them like a ripple. It is under these influences, brought by artists who fled Mistra to Crete when Mistra fell to the Ottoman Turks in 1460, that the genius of Domenicos Theotokopoulos, El Greco, was nurtured.

THE REDISCOVERY OF GREECE

by Charles Freeman

Already by the 4th century AD Greek was lost as a language in the western part of the Empire. (It was in the 380s that Pope Damasus replaced Greek with Latin as the language of the liturgy in Rome and the Western Church.) Some contact was kept, with Latin versions of Greek texts, but the Church was not sympathetic to Greek philosophy and science, and the result was that by 1200 only a couple of works of Plato, and Aristotle's treatises on logic were known in the West. When the bulk of Aristotle's work was rediscovered and brought back into the core of Christian theology in the 13th century (notably by Thomas Aquinas), it was from Arabic translations of the Greek originals. Greece was still difficult to reach, and it took a determined traveller, Cyriac of Ancona, to get to Athens and make the earliest surviving drawing of the Parthenon in the 1440s.

It was the revival of Classical learning in the 14th century that encouraged a new interest in ancient Greece. In 1398 the Chancellor of Florence, Coluccio Salutati, appointed one Manuel Chrysoloras to come to Florence to teach Greek. Chrysoloras agreed, arrived in Florence with manuscripts of important Greek works, such as Plutarch's *Lives* and the *Politics* of Aristotle, and revised the complicated Greek grammars of his native Constantinople so that intelligent and determined Italians could master the language. Soon Florentine scholars were able to make new translations of Greek texts. In the 1420s a Sicilian dealer in manuscripts, Giovanni Aurispa, brought back 238 Greek manuscripts from Constantinople, including works by the great dramatists Aeschylus and Sophocles, and many more works of the philosopher Plato, who was still virtually unread in the West. With the fall of Constantinople to the Ottomans in 1453, refugees brought even more, and in Florence Cosimo de' Medici was able to put in hand, through Marsilio Ficino, the first Latin translation of most of Plato's works. In Venice the great printer Aldus Manutius was able to print the first full edition of Aristotle in the original Greek in the 1490s. Soon most universities had professors in Greek, and in his famous *Courtier* of 1528, Baldassare Castiglione (1478–1529) advocated that his readers learn Greek, 'because of the abundance and variety of things that are so divinely written in it'. By now most of the Greek texts known to us today had been rediscovered.

After this there was a lull in Greek studies. The main problem remained the inaccessibility of Athens, which was still under Ottoman rule. Interest was revived in the 18th century when a mass of Greek pots were found in Etruscan tombs in Italy (an estimated 80 per cent of all Greek pots have been found in Italy). A few intrepid travellers were also reaching Athens again. In 1762, James Stuart and Nicholas Revett's *Antiquities of Athens*, with careful drawings of the surviving monuments, proved a bestseller in Britain. In Italy itself, the *History of Ancient Art* by the German-born librarian at the Vatican, Johann Winckelmann, presented an idealisation of Greek Classical art, which he praised for its 'noble simplicity and calm grandeur'. For Winckelmann, the history of art moved from one peak to another with decline in between, so the art of the Classical age was followed by the decline of the Hellenistic period; this judgement lasted well into the 20th century. Winckelmann never visited Greece, and ironically many of his favourite 'Classical' statues are now known to be much later copies. London was to have its first chance to see the real thing when Lord Elgin shipped many of the finest marbles from the Parthenon frieze from Athens. He sold them to the British government in 1816, and their presence in London has been controversial ever since. But the enthusiasm for Greece spread. A Greek style in furniture and architecture became the rage in Britain in the 1820s. Poets such as Keats and Byron endowed ancient Greece with a romantic glow, and when it achieved independence from the Turks in 1832, the Acropolis was 'tidied up' to recreate the purity of its 5th-century greatness.

By now the study of the language and culture of ancient Greece was central to a university curriculum. The Germans were the most enthusiastic. The Prussians drew on Greece as an inspiration for their national revival after their defeat by Napoleon, and legends were put about that the Dorian Greeks were actually early Germans migrating south. Stories have even circulated that Schliemann forged the Mask of Agamemnon, creating a face with a curling waxed moustache, so that he could demonstrate to his Kaiser that Mycenaeans and Germans shared a common stock. Greece became vulnerable to undisciplined excavation: Schliemann at Mycenae, the Germans at Olympia and the French at Delphi. It was an Englishman, Arthur Evans, who rediscovered a Greek past, Minoan Crete, which had up to then existed only in legend. Amidst this foreign intrusion, it was an important moment when at the revived Olympic games, held for the first time in Athens in 1896, it was a Greek, Spyridon Louis, who won the race which really mattered, the Marathon.

After the First World War there was a reaction against aristocratic and cultural elitism, and Greece and Greek suffered with it. There was a much greater appreciation of the darker sides of Greek culture. Freud discovered his Oedipus and Electra complexes. Others reminded their listeners that Athens had been an empire which had relied heavily on slavery. People began to carp that the study of Greek had simply been a way in which the patrician elite could keep their distance from the commercial classes. Plato had been so popular because his philosophy offered denunciations of democracy and supported the ideal of a governing class who knew what was best for others. In the long term, this rejection allowed a more realistic, detached approach to be made to ancient Greece. Excavations shifted to less important sites and field surveys began to explore the forces which underpinned the survival of the *polis*. Even though the study of Greek in itself has declined dramatically, at both school and university level, new audiences are being attracted by the sheer intellectual power of a period before Christianity had shaped the ways we see the world. There remains a freshness and openness in Greek thought, ethics and literature which is endlessly absorbing and which throws new light on almost every contemporary debate.

ATHENS & PIRAEUS

Athens, the most famous city in ancient Greece and the capital of the country, is set in a bowl of mountains: Hymettus (modern Imittòs) to the south, Parnes (modern Parnitha) to the north, and Pentelicon (modern Pendeli) to the east. The sea and Athens' port, the Piraeus, form its western boundary. Today, as in Antiquity, the countryside around Athens is known as Attica. The modern city was first laid out in the 19th century by the Bavarian architects of Greece's first king, Otho (1835–43). In the 20th century Athens grew rapidly, after the influx of refugees from Turkey in 1922 and thanks to ferocious post-war urban development. Despite the proliferating skyscrapers stretching toward the mountains, Athens' best-known monument, the Acropolis, and the conical peak of Lycabettus (Likavitòs) are still prominent landmarks.

In summer, the mountains often trap Athens' *nefos* (smog), although increasing use of the Metro is cutting down on the city's infamous pollution. Since the August 2004 summer Olympics there are numerous pedestrian walkways linking the principal archaeological sites in the centre. Ten thousand new shrubs and trees are another legacy of the games. In short, the city which has constantly reinvented itself since the days when there was a small Neolithic settlement on the Acropolis, has done so once again.

WHY ATHENS IS CALLED ATHENS

A 19th-century French traveller was once asked why he had bothered to visit Athens, then an undistinguished provincial hamlet. He replied, 'Mais Athènes s'appelle Athènes'. Sigmund Freud reported that when he finally stood on the Acropolis, his first thought was: 'So all this really does exist, just as we learnt at school!' Almost by virtue of its name alone, Athens impresses most visitors—but how did the city get its name? According to legend, both Athena and Poseidon contested for the honour of having the city named after them. Poseidon offered control of the sea, while Athena offered the bounty of the land, as symbolised by an olive tree. The ancient Greeks believed that the trident Poseidon threw down in anger when he lost to Athena scarred the limestone of the Acropolis near the Erechtheion. The olive tree that today grows beside the Erechtheion is a reminder of Athena's victory. In a later contest, Poseidon and Athena vied for control of the countryside around Athens. This time, Poseidon won. Thus Athens and Attica enjoyed the wealth both of the olive and of the sea, and the protection of two important deities.

View of the Agora, including the Temple of Hephaistos and the church of the Holy Apostles.

HISTORY OF ATHENS

Ancient history

The vital presence of a spring on the Acropolis meant that the site was settled early, perhaps around 5000 BC. By Mycenaean times (c. 1600–1200 BC) there was a palace and fortified citadel here. By the 8th century, Athens dominated and unified the surrounding countryside (Attica), and the city's influence is revealed by the presence throughout the Greek world of pottery made in and exported from Athens. A number of social and economic reforms are associated with the figure of Solon, the 'lawgiver' (early 6th century). Under him Peisistratus conquered Salamis, and the popularity that arose from this triumph allowed Peisistratus to seize complete power. The Peisistratid dynasty of tyrants increased Athens' influence. At this time, the 'old' temple of Athens on the Acropolis was built, construction of the Temple of Olympian Zeus was begun, and the Panathenaic festival (*see p. 78*) was extended to last over several days, becoming influential beyond Athens itself. The tyrants were overthrown at the end of the 6th century and a more democratic system of government developed; the leader Cleisthenes is associated with these reforms. In 498 Athens and Eretria responded to an appeal to help the Greek cities of Ionia (Asia Minor) in their revolt against Persian domination. The result was the first Persian invasion of Greece, defeated at the Battle of Marathon (490). Ten years later the Acropolis was sacked in a further Persian attack, but the invaders were repulsed after the battles of Salamis and Plataea.

During the 5th century the Delian League of (chiefly maritime) city-states allied against the Persians was transformed into an Athenian empire, and the Athenians under Pericles used communal funds to beautify their city. The sculptor and architect Pheidias supervised Pericles' ambitious building programme for the Acropolis. Aeschylus, Sophocles and Euripides all wrote at this time, as did the comic playwright Aristophanes (*see p. 117*). Increasing rivalry between Athens and Sparta (not a member of the League) finally resulted in the Peloponnesian War (431–04 BC) which ended in the defeat of Athens. The city's authority revived in the early 4th century but subsequently succumbed to that of the Macedonian kingdom under Philip II. Athens was well treated by Alexander the Great, but had a chequered history under his successors. The city came under Roman control in the 2nd century, but retained a privileged position, though sacked by Sulla in 86 BC. Subsequently the philhellene emperor Hadrian spent long periods in Athens (120–128 AD) and was responsible for many public buildings, as later was Herodes Atticus, whose theatre on the slopes of the Acropolis is still used for performances. Athens remained a leading educational centre until the schools of philosophy were closed in AD 529 by the Christian emperor Justinian, who abhorred the thought of the schools promulgating pagan ideas.

Later history

In the 3rd–6th centuries AD Athens suffered from barbarian raids. If it had little real power during the Byzantine period, its monuments, its port, and the then-fertile Attic countryside gave it some significance in the empire between the 8th and the 12th centuries AD. A number of lovely small churches survive (*see p. 113*). After the fall of Constantinople to the Crusaders in 1204, the city came under Frankish rule for about 100 years. Subsequent control by Sicilians, Florentines and Venetians ended when Athens was annexed to the Ottoman empire in 1456. In 1687 the Parthenon was shattered during a Venetian bombardment of the Turkish position on the Acropolis. Visitors to Athens in the 17th and 18th centuries began to research and publish the city's antiquities. In 1833, thirteen years after the outbreak of the Greek War of Independence, Athens became the capital of a liberated Greece. The Bavarian prince Otho was chosen by England, France and Russia to be King of Greece. During his reign (1832–62), Athens began its transformation from a village backwater to a national capital. A royal palace (now the Parliament building) was built in Syntagma Square, named after the constitution (*syntagma*) which King Otho accepted (not without a struggle) in 1843.

During the First World War the city was occupied by French and British troops. The population was swollen by the exchange of Greek and Turkish nationals in 1923. Athens suffered a harsh occupation by German forces from 1941 to 1944; tens of thousands starved to death. Athens was also the scene of fierce fighting during the Greek Civil War (1944–49). In 1967, the right-wing military cabal known as the 'Colonels' seized power, forced King Constantine into exile, and ruled until the restoration of democracy in 1974. During these decades, Athens' population grew until almost one in three Greeks lived here. In 1981, Greece became a member of the European Community, adopting the Euro in 2001. In August of 2004, Athens hosted the 28th modern Olympic Games, which were the impetus for building the city's new airport and expanded Metro system. There has been much optimistic speculation in Athens that these changes will both make life more pleasant for residents and breathe new vitality into Greece's dwindling tourism industry.

EXPLORING ATHENS

Increasingly, visitors to Greece spend only a day or two in Athens before heading off to visit the Peloponnese, Delphi, Macedonia, or one or more of the 'isles of Greece'. Still, with even a brief visit, it is possible with four excursions to see Athens' most important monuments (the Acropolis and the ancient Agora), to visit Greece's most important museum (the National Archaeological Museum), and to explore the Plaka (Athens' oldest—most touristy—yet still very charming neighbourhood). For those with a bit more time, there are a number of additional itineraries in and around Athens. Some of these may be combined with the four above-mentioned excursions.

NB: In addition to the telephone numbers listed below, information on most public monuments and museums is available at www.culture.gr. A joint ticket is available for the Acropolis site and museum, Ancient Agora, Theatre of Dionysus, Kerameikos, Temple of Olympian Zeus, Roman Agora.

THE ACROPOLIS
Map p. 82, B3
Metro: Acropolis

Site and museum usually open summer daily 8–8; winter daily 8.30–2.30. The museum often closes as much as 30mins earlier than the Acropolis itself. Tickets from the ticket booth below the entrance at the Beulé Gate. T: 210 321 4172. NB: It is no longer possible to enter the individual ancient buildings. In 2004, the north slopes of the Acropolis (closed since the 1990s) were reopened.

HISTORY OF THE ACROPOLIS

The Acropolis rock (156m; 91m above the general level of the city) has been occupied since prehistoric times; the word 'acropolis' means 'upper city'. In the Late Bronze Age (c. 1600–c. 1200) it was the site of a Mycenaean palace with massive fortifications. In the Archaic period it was at times the residence of rulers, as well as a religious centre. In the Classical period its functions were entirely religious. The finest buildings were erected in the later 5th century following the defeat of the Persians, although later Greeks, as well as the Romans, left monuments here. The Byzantines turned the Parthenon into a church, using pieces from various ancient monuments to fashion a rounded apse and the baptistery, narthex and nave. The Acropolis was captured as a stronghold by Franks and Venetians (who reconsecrated the church as Catholic) and Turks, who added a minaret and converted the church into a mosque in the 1460s. For reasons obscure, during a conflict with the Venetians, the Turkish women, children and gunpowder were put in the Parthenon. Some 300 women and children were killed when, in 1687, a Venetian mortar hit the building and ignited the gunpowder. Many columns and much sculpture, as well as much of the roof, were destroyed, leaving the building blown into two separate parts. Serious attempts at excavation and reconstruction began in the 18th century and continue today, devoted in particular to repairing mechanical (earthquakes), biological (invasive plants and lichens) and chemical (acid rain and atmospheric pollution) damage. The Ministry of Culture publication *The Works on the Acropolis of Athens* (Committee for the Preservation of the Acropolis Monuments, 2002) is a handy introduction to past and present work.

The site
The story goes that the great 20th-century Classics scholar Werner Jaeger spent a year in Athens and refused to ascend the Acropolis, fearing that it could not live up to his expectations. Most visitors will not follow his example, but expectations will be best fulfilled if you visit as soon as the site opens, or just before it closes, when most tour groups are not in evidence.

You enter the Acropolis through the **Beulé Gate**, a defensive structure of c. 280 AD whose name honours the 19th-century French archaeologist who unearthed its foundations. Above, a high plinth belongs to the Monument of Agrippa. Originally a Hellenistic monument with a quadriga on top, it later carried statues of Antony and Cleopatra, and finally (after 27 BC) of Marcus Agrippa. You then climb to the **Propylaia**, a monumental gateway designed by the architect Mnesicles, who is known only for this one building. The Propylaia, built almost entirely of local Pentelic marble, was built c. 437–32 to replace an earlier entrance gate. The inner and outer central façades are Doric. The columns in the passage are Ionic. The north wing is still called the Pinakotheke (Picture Gallery), the name Pausanias gave it for its many paintings. In fact, this was probably a ritual dining room with couches. As there was scant room to build a south wing without encroaching on the precinct of the Temple of Athena Nike, only a façade was constructed, to provide a visual balance to the north wing. Two halls at the inner (east) side of the structure were planned but never built. Recent restoration work has concentrated on rectifying problems created by 20th-century restoration work. For example, the iron dowels then used to hold blocks together rusted and harmed the stone. These, here and elsewhere, are being replaced with titanium.

Temple of Athena Nike

The charming 5th-century Temple of Athena Nike, dedicated to Athena the Victor, stands on a projecting bastion, originally a part of the Mycenaean fortifications, to the south of the Propylaia. The original small temple was lost in the Persian sack of Athens in 480. In 449 a new temple, designed by Callicrates, was planned to celebrate the peace with Persia. It was not built until c. 427–424, and then only in modified form. In the meantime Callicrates had erected a similar temple by the Ilissos river. This was still standing in the 18th century, and was included in Stuart and Revett's famous *Antiquities of Athens*. The Temple of Athena Nike was torn down by the Turks in 1686, to free the bastion for use as an artillery position. Today's temple is a reconstruction, built in 1836–42 with the help of Stuart and Revett's drawing. In 1936 it was dismantled again in order to strengthen the bastion, which had become unsafe. At the time of writing, the temple, completely dismantled once again to be reconstructed and restored, was not yet in place; what follows is an attempt to suggest what visitors will see when work is complete.

The temple's bastion conceals its Mycenaean predecessor, part of the defensive system. Tetrastyle amphiprostyle, it has columns in the Ionic order, with double-faced angle capitals. Immediately above the capitals, the architrave is divided into three horizontal bands (*fasciae*): this is the first known example of an Ionic architrave so divided. The frieze showing deities and scenes of Greeks and Persians in combat was removed in 1998 and is in the Acropolis Museum (*see p. 79*); there are plans to replace it here with a copy. The temple platform was surrounded by a sculpted marble parapet with figures of winged Victory (Nike), including the famous *Sandalbinder* (Nike adjusting her sandal), now also in the Acropolis Museum.

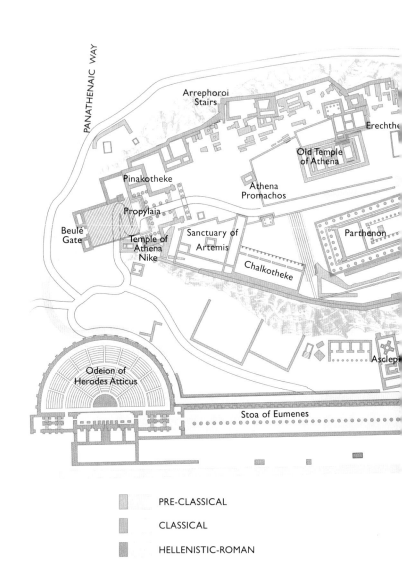

PANATHENAIC WAY

Arrephoroi
Stairs

Erechthe

Old Temple
of Athena

Pinakotheke

Athena
Promachos

Propylaia

Beulé
Gate

Sanctuary of
Artemis

Parthenon

Temple of
Athena
Nike

Chalkotheke

Asclepi

Odeion of
Herodes Atticus

Stoa of Eumenes

PRE-CLASSICAL

CLASSICAL

HELLENISTIC-ROMAN

THE ANCIENT ACROPOLIS

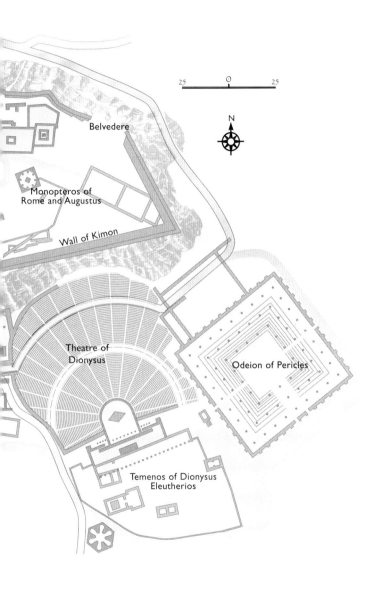

It is from this elevated spot that Theseus' father Aegeus is said to have kept watch for the return of his son from Crete. Theseus had promised to hoist a white sail if his ship was bringing him home alive. He forgot to do so, and seeing the black sail approach and believing his son to have been devoured by the Minotaur, Aegeus hurled himself from the cliff.

Circuit of the Acropolis

Few visitors can resist walking straight from the Propylaia to the Parthenon, but you are strongly recommended to make a circuit of the accessible parts of the Acropolis before approaching it. In Classical times the Parthenon was barely visible from the Propylaia. Some 40 paces in front of the Propylaia are the remains of the base of the famous bronze **statue of Athena Promachos** by Pheidias, erected c. 458 BC as a trophy of the Persian wars. It was 9m high and visible from ships rounding Cape Sounion. The goddess was represented standing, her right arm leaning on her spear, and holding her shield in her left. The shield was decorated with carvings in relief of the battle of the Lapiths and Centaurs, a favourite symbol in Greek art of civilised Greeks prevailing over rude barbarians.

To the left of this, bear towards the Acropolis wall. In an angle of it is a **flight of steps** of Classical date, which may be the secret stairway of the *Arrephoroi*. These were girls of noble birth, between seven and eleven years of age, chosen by the *archon basileus* to perform an obscure annual ritual in the service of Athena. Their duties included the weaving and carrying of the *peplos* for Athena's statue (*see p. 78 below*), and also the carrying down by a secret stair and underground passage to the Sanctuary of Aphrodite in the gardens a burden whose contents are unknown. This they exchanged for another mysterious burden, which they brought back.

At the extreme end of the enclosure is the **Belvedere**, with a superb view over Athens and back over the Acropolis itself. You begin to get a sense of the many layers of building on the Acropolis as you look out on the spot once occupied by a chapel of the Frankish dukes (demolished 1860). Returning toward the Parthenon, you pass the remains of the circular Ionic **Monopteros of Rome and Augustus**, mentioned by the 15th-century traveller Cyriac of Ancona. The monopteros was a kind of gazebo, with a roof supported by columns, but no interior edifice. The path continues west along remains (restored) of the massive retaining **Wall of Kimon**, begun in 460 BC and later completed by Pericles. The west front of the Parthenon, approached by steps partly rock-cut and partly built, was preceded by an entrance court with, on the south side, the **Chalkotheke** or Magazine of Bronzes. To the west was the **Sanctuary of Artemis Brauronia**, a stoa with two projecting wings, ritually connected with the sanctuary of the same name in Attica (*see p. 135*). To the west is a fragment of the Mycenaean wall.

The Parthenon

The Parthenon, or Temple of Athena Polias, represents the culmination of the Doric, indeed of the Classical, style of architecture; as a monument it has no equal. The temple was designed to provide a new sanctuary exclusively for Athena Polias, where her statue might be fittingly housed and the continually increasing treasure stored. It was built in 447–38 BC (the sculpture completed in 432) as the cardinal feature of Pericles' plan. Under the order of Pheidias as 'surveyor general' were the architect Ictinus and the contractor Callicrates. The most celebrated sculptors in Athens, rivals or pupils of Pheidias, such as Agorakritos or Alkamenes, worked on the pediments, the frieze and the metopes. Pheidias supervised the whole of the sculpture programme, reserving entirely to himself the creation of the 12-metre chryselephantine statue of Athena (Thucydides, ever critical of Pericles' building and beautification programme, dismissed it as vulgar). The result was a peerless blend of architecture and sculpture. Indeed, in the veneration of the Athenians the Parthenon was regarded chiefly as an artistic masterpiece and as the state treasury, and it never replaced the Erechtheion, the focus of the Panathenaic procession (*see p. 78*). The name Parthenon, meaning the virgin's apartment, originally applied to only one room in the temple. Its first recorded application to the building as a whole comes in the speeches of Demosthenes (mid-4th century BC).

Except for the roof, which was of wood, the Parthenon is built entirely of Pentelic marble. It is especially remarkable for its entasis. Optical refinements are here executed with great mathematical precision. These include varying the breadth of the intercolumniations throughout the building, thickening the corner columns, and grading the spacing of the triglyphs. Lines that appear horizontal are in fact curved, and lines that appear vertical are slightly inclined.

The Parthenon was larger than most Doric temples (8 by 17 columns), and had more sculpture (all 92 metopes were decorated, as well as both pediments and, most unusually, a continuous Ionic frieze round the outside of the building within the colonnade).

Various additions were made in later Antiquity. In the 6th century it was turned into a church. From 1204 (following the Frankish conquest of Constantinople) until 1258 it followed the Latin rite as cathedral of the Frankish dukes. It was later converted into a mosque. In 1674 Jacques Carrey, a painter in the entourage of the Marquis de Nointel, made drawings of the sculptures (many now lost). In 1687 it was blown up in a Venetian bombardment, when used by the Turks as a powder magazine. The results were disastrous. Pieces of sculpture were removed at various times, most notably by Lord Elgin in 1801. Restoration started in 1834–44; the current programme may be said to have begun in the 1970s and to have accelerated in 2002.

The sculptures

Most of the Parthenon sculptures are in the British Museum (the 'Elgin Marbles'). Substantial sections are in the Acropolis Museum. Some are in the Louvre. The return of all is sought with more and less fervour by each Greek government. The subjects of the sculptures were as follows:

West Pediment: Contest between Athena and Poseidon for possession of Attica;

East Pediment: *Birth of Athena* (springing fully armed from the head of Zeus);

Frieze: *Panathenaic Procession*, whose meaning is still debated. Some see it as simply portraying the procession itself. Others suggest it shows (on the east end) the reception into divine company of the heroes of the Battle of Marathon. Still others see suggestions of a very ancient ceremony involving human sacrifice;

Metopes: (some uncertain) *Battle of Lapiths and Centaurs* (south), *Gigantomachy* (east), *Amazonomachy* (west), *Trojan War*.

Work continues on the extensive restoration of the Parthenon, during the course of which the building is being largely dismantled and reconstituted. At present, the focus is on the pronaos, the room directly in front of the cella, or main temple sanctuary, where the cult statue stood.

Between the Parthenon and the Erechtheion are the foundations of the Archaic (c. 529 BC) **Old Temple of Athena**, destroyed by the Persians, though the opisthodomos survived in use as a treasury.

THE PANATHENAIC FESTIVAL

Housed in one of the *cellae* of the Erechtheion was the highly venerated olive-wood statue of Athena, represented standing and fully armed. The sacred *peplos*, renewed every four years at the Panathenaic Festival, was woven to adorn her shrine. In front of the statue burnt the golden lamp made by the ingenious Callimachus, with an asbestos wick that needed oil only once a year and a brazen palm tree to serve as a chimney. The Panathenaic festival was a ceremonial procession held every four years in high summer to celebrate the 'birthday' of the goddess. Athletic games, animal sacrifice and music contests were all part of the event, and all were permitted to take part, even women and metics (though not slaves). The festival, which under Peisistratus was extended to last several days, culminated in a procession along the Sacred Way to the Erechtheion to do homage to the cult statue.

The Erechtheion

The Erechtheion, designed to succeed the Old Temple of Athena as the joint shrine of Athena and Poseidon-Erechtheus and finally completed c. 395, is one of the most perfect specimens of Greek architecture and an extremely complex building. It is unique not only in plan but also in elevation, since the foundations of the south and east walls stand nearly three metres above those on the north and west. When seen from the east, where the normal entrance is, it has the appearance of an Ionic prostyle temple with a hexastyle portico; behind the facade it is in fact a plain rectangle with a projecting porch on either flank. The surrounding precinct contained altars and other sacred places. Its interior layout remains uncertain because of later alterations: it was converted into a church in the 6th century, and into the harem for the wives of the Ottoman commandant in 1463. The north had an ornamental doorway, refurbished in Roman times; the south is the famous Caryatid Porch, whose roof is supported by six caryatids standing on a parapet. These six caryatids are reproductions; four of the originals are on display in the Acropolis Museum, where a fifth is being restored. The sixth, carried off by Lord Elgin, is in the British Museum in London. The frieze course consists of dark Eleusinian limestone against which the (now fragmentary) relatively small-scale sculptures would stand out. Restoration work (1979–86) on the Erechtheion included replacing a column and part of the entablature removed by Lord Elgin with reproductions. The Erechtheion was the focus of the Panathenaic procession as the repository of the oldest and most revered

The Erechtheion: caryatid porch.

statue of Athena (*see box opposite*). Beyond the Erechtheion, built into the wall, are drums from the unfinished older Parthenon destroyed by the Persians in 480.

The Acropolis Museum

NB: The museum is currently being reinstalled, with an eye to moving displays to the new Acropolis Museum at the foot of the Acropolis (estimated opening in late 2007).

The museum is particularly rich in Attic sculpture. The best holdings are outlined below. The outstanding Archaic pedimental sculpture includes the statue known as the *Calf Bearer* (*Moschophoros*; c. 570 BC). Carved in Hymettian marble, it is one of the earliest examples of native art in marble, still employing techniques suitable to working

The emerging Classical style, as contrasted to the Archaic: *Critian Boy* (c. 480 BC; right) and *Moschophoros* (c. 570 BC; left).

in limestone. An inscription on the base bears the name Rhombos. There are many fine Archaic figures of *korai*, sculptures of maidens dedicated as votive offerings to Athena. All the statues are clothed or painted, and each held an offering in one hand. Under the Peisistratids the Doric dress gradually gave way to the Ionic. We can trace this in the *korai*, as the simple symmetry of the woollen Doric *chiton* are replaced by the Ionic linen *chiton* worn with the *himation*. Parallel to the sartorial changes is a development in the naturalism of the features, including the loosing of the famous 'Attic smile'. A superb example of the emergence of the Classical style from the Archaic is the *Critian Boy* (c. 480 BC). The weight is at last correctly posed and the body liberated from Archaic stiffness. Classical sculpture includes the *Mourning Athena* and the beautiful *Sandalbinder*, with the drapery moulded lovingly onto the contours of the body. Architectural fragments include pediments from the Old Temple of Athena; which preceded the present Parthenon; models and fragments of the originals from the Parthenon pediments and fragments; sections of the Parthenon frieze; also Nike figures from the Nike parapet and pieces of the Erechtheion frieze. The caryatids which originally supported the porch of the Erechtheion are also on display here.

THE AGORA
Map p. 104, C2
Metro: Monastiraki/Thission

The Agora and Temple of Hephaistos are usually open summer daily 8–8; winter daily 8.30–2.30. The site museum in the Stoa of Attalus often closes as much as 30mins earlier than the Agora itself; T: 210 321 0185.

The excellent Athenian Agora Guide *by John Camp (4th edition, 1990); as well as a number of booklets on the agora published by the American School of Classical Studies, are usually on sale at the ticket booth and in the museum. The upper gallery of the Stoa of Attalus (not always open) has useful models showing the Agora at different stages of its development.*

The Agora was the heart of the public centre of the ancient city, where citizens congregated. Before the 6th century BC, some of this area was used as a cemetery; when the Kerameikos (*see p. 100*) became Athens' principal cemetery, farmers from the countryside brought produce here to sell, and this was Athens' principal market area. Over time, this market became a place where most government business took place and law courts met. Here much of the social life of clubs went on and athletes exercised; here Socrates strolled and questioned the everyday assumptions of his fellow-citizens; and here St Paul tried to interest the Athenians in Christianity. The Panathenaic Way, which ran from Eleusis to the Acropolis, ran through the Agora; this was the route taken every four years by the celebrants in the Panathenaic Festival which honoured the goddess Athena (*see p. 78 above*).

Today, the Agora's most conspicuous monuments are the 20th-century reconstruction of the 2nd-century AD Stoa of Attalus, the 11th-century Byzantine Church of the Holy Apostles and the well-preserved 5th-century BC Doric **Temple of Hephaistos**, mistakenly called the 'Theseion' after Athens' great hero Theseus. The temple, which crowns the low knoll of Kolonos Agoraios on the west side of the Agora, was in fact a temple of Athena and Hephaistos (Theseus is depicted in some of the sculptures). It was probably built c. 449 BC. Thanks to its adaptation and use as a Christian church between the 7th and 19th centuries AD, it has survived better than any other antique building in Greece. It is a pleasant vantage point from which to orientate oneself in the Agora and, when that proves difficult, simply to take in the splendid view of the Acropolis.

Monuments of the Agora
Because of the scattered nature of the most of the remains, which come from many different periods, a map or plan of the Agora is invaluable (*a reconstruction is shown overleaf*), as are the plans and the models on view in the Stoa of Attalus. Some of the remains do have stone markers identifying them. The very pleasant landscaping of the Agora helps to define building boundaries; most of the plants are known to have grown in Greece in Antiquity. The flowering trees and rainwater pools brimming with tadpoles and young frogs are charming in spring.

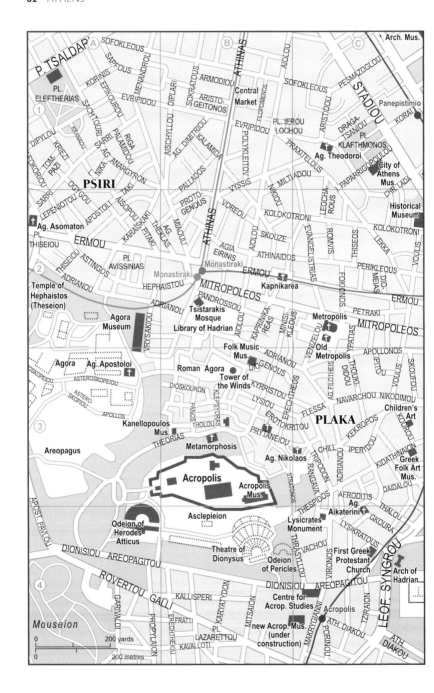

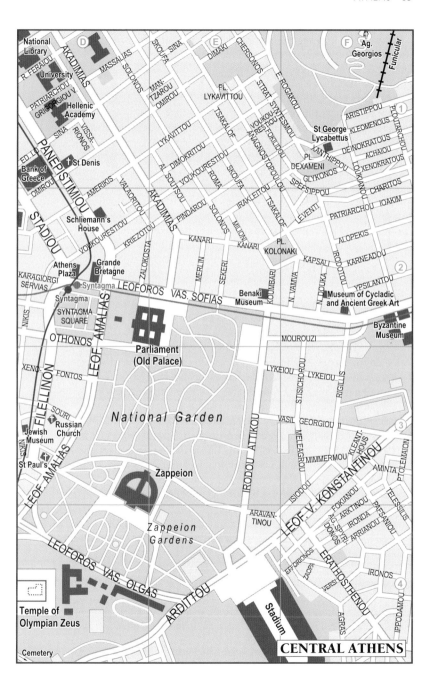

CENTRAL ATHENS

It is reasonable to begin a visit to the Agora near the southwest corner of the excavated area, by the boundary stone of the Agora inscribed in lettering of the 5th century BC 'I am the boundary of the Agora'. The southwest side of the Agora was evidently the first to acquire public buildings. The **tholos**, evident now only from its circular floor, replaced an earlier building c. 465 BC. It was headquarters for the 50 *prytany* or duty officers of the State Council, who had their meals here. The city's official weights and measures were also stored in the tholos. To the northwest are the foundations of the **new bouleuterion** or Chamber of the Council, which prepared legislation for the Assembly. It had semicircular rows of seats, unlike its predecessor to the east (the old bouleuterion), which was subsequently used as a civic archive.

Further north the **Metroön** housed a temple of the Mother of the Gods (Rhea, mother of Zeus) and additional archives. In the Hellenistic period, the Metroön was embellished with a colonnade and a row of statues, some of whose bases remain. Nearby is the long base of the **Monument of the Eponymous Heroes**, which supported ten statues of the heroes after whom the ten tribes of Attica were named. North of the Metroön were the small Archaic temples of Apollo Patroös and one of Zeus and Athena.

THE AGORA EXCAVATIONS: WHAT TO SAVE, WHAT TO DESTROY?

When most of Greece won its independence from the Turks in the 19th century, the hamlet of Athens expanded into the district below the Acropolis now known as the Plaka. By the time that archaeologists began to take an interest in unearthing Athens' ancient Agora, the Plaka was a thriving neighbourhood. The temple known as the 'Theseion' always stood, and parts of other buildings were visible, but most of the ancient Agora had been built over. By the end of the 19th century, there had been several trial excavations in the Agora, but it was not until 1931 that major excavation began, under the supervision of the American School of Classical Studies. Some 400 homes and shops were removed, to the horror not merely of their owners and residents, but of many who saw this as sacrificing Greece's present to its past. As more discoveries have been made outside the periphery of the Agora, along Adrianou, the debate goes on as to how much more of the Plaka should be destroyed so that more of the ancient Agora—which underlies much of the present Plaka—can be excavated.

North end

At the north end of the Agora are the remains of several important stoas. Colonnaded stoas, offering protection from the elements, were popular buildings in Antiquity, used for shops, and civil offices, rather as malls are today. The stoa of Zeus Eleutherios was built c. 430, and is Doric with Ionic interior columns, and had splendid marble Nike acroteria. Beyond, in the railway cutting, are the remains of the **Stoa Basileios** (or Royal

Stoa), only identified in 1970. It was the headquarters of the Royal Archon (*see box on p. 88*) and housed the statutes of Solon and Draco, the two great reformers and lawgivers of the democratic period. In front is the *lithos* (stone) where the archons took their oaths of office. The building probably dates to c. 500 BC. Two porches were added c. 400. Outside the fenced area, in a building plot on the other side of the street, are the excavated remains of the **Stoa Poikile** (or Painted Stoa), the first of the buildings on the north side of the Agora to be investigated (1980). Built c. 460 it is named from the magnificent paintings which originally decorated the walls. It also contained shields captured from the Spartans in 425 BC at the Battle of Sphacteria (example in museum). In the area were many herms. These square stone pillars ornamented with a carved phallus and the bust of a man or god, were commonly used as boundary markers.

Within the archaeological site but largely obscured by the railway cutting is the once impressive **Peribolos of the Twelve Gods**, an enclosed precinct dedicated to the Olympian gods, chief deities in the Greek pantheon: there is a ground altar to the south. The site of the Temple of Ares, a Classical building moved in the Roman period to this site from elsewhere, is marked in gravel. To the south are two huge interrelated structures, the Odeion of Agrippa (c. 15 BC) and a much later (c. 400 AD) gymnasium.

East side

The east side of the Agora is closed by the **Stoa of Attalus**. The original building was erected by Attalus II, King of Pergamon 159–138 BC, and contained shops. The stoa, reconstructed on its original foundations in 1953–56 at the expense of private donors from the USA, pre-eminently John D. Rockefeller, was dedicated as the Agora Museum by King Paul in 1956. Earlier finds below included a Classical lawcourt and Mycenaean and Protogeometric graves. The façade had Doric columns below and Ionic (with a balustrade) above. In front of the centre are a rostrum and a donor's monument. The interior has been somewhat modified to allow the installation of the excellently arranged museum of finds from the Agora (*see below*).

South of the stoa is the so-called 'Valerian' Wall, a Roman fortification using materials from buildings partly destroyed in the Herulian sack of AD 267. The wall follows the line of the façade of the destroyed Library of Pantainos erected before AD 102. Between the Library and the Stoa of Attalus a street led east towards the Roman market (*see p. 90*).

The **Agora Museum** in the Stoa of Attalus has most of its sculpture and many inscriptions on view in the colonnade. Inside, the exhibits are arranged in chronological order. The pottery includes a child's pottery potty seat. In addition, there are are many pottery *ostraka*. Any Athenian citizen (usually a politician) could be voted into exile for ten years if there were enough votes to ostracise him. Prominent 5th-century BC politicians who suffered this fate were Themistocles, credited with saving Athens from the Persians in 480 BC, and Aristides, whose nickname of 'the Just' ultimately got on the nerves of his fellow citizens. Numerous *ostraka* with Aristides' name have been found during the Agora excavations, including one found in 1997 near the

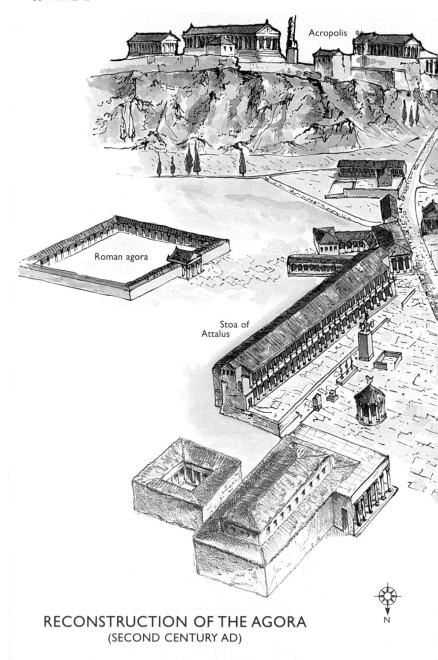

Acropolis

Roman agora

Stoa of
Attalus

N

RECONSTRUCTION OF THE AGORA
(SECOND CENTURY AD)

mphaion

South Stoa

Middle
Stoa

Tholos

Odeion of
Agrippa

Monument of
the Eponymous
Heroes

Temple of Ares

Metroön

New
Bouleuterion

Panathenaic Way

Peribolos
of the
Twelve
Gods

Stoa of Zeus

Stoa
Basileios

Stoa Poikile

Temple of Hephaistos. Bronze voting ballots are also on display. The marble water clock (*klepsydra*) was used to keep long-winded speakers from rambling on in the law court. In addition, there are many fine coins and vases.

THE ADMINISTRATION OF ANCIENT ATHENS

During the Archaic period (700–480 BC) Athens was ruled by a king, who governed with the aid of a council, the Areopagus, named after the hill where it met. This council elected the *archons* or magistrates, to administer the city's affairs, and by degrees the power of the king dwindled, and the government became more oligarchical. In 683 BC the monarchy was abolished altogether. There were three archons: the *archon eponymous*, who was in charge of civil administration; the *polemarch*, who was in charge of military affairs; and the Royal Archon or *archon basileus*, who took over the religious and ceremonial functions of the king. These three, together with the six *thesmothetai*, the judges and lawgivers, formed the governing body. The most famous of the *thesmothetai* is Draco, who in the late 7th century produced the city's first written laws, famously making almost every offence punishable by death (hence 'draconian'): all these laws, except those regarding homicide, were later repealed or moderated by Solon. Before the 7th century BC archons held office for ten years, but after 683 the positions were made annual. Each year took the name of the *archon eponymous*. Years where there was no *archon* were known as an 'anarchy'. In the 6th century BC Solon reorganised the city government, dividing citizens into four groups and allowing the two wealthiest to sit on the Areopagus. From the third group he formed an elected council of 400 (the *Boule*), a sort of lower house, later increased to 500 men, 50 from each of the ten tribes of Attica, of whom 50 were elected to form the *prytany*, leaders of the council. The *prytany* was charged with the routine administration of the state's affairs, and met every day of the year. One of its members, chosen daily by rotation, was on duty every hour of the night and day. Archons who had served a blameless term automatically became members of the Areopagus, which by this time had developed into a court of justice dealing with murder and other major crimes. The lowest class of citizens, the *thetes*, were permitted to vote in assembly on matters presented by the *Boule*.

Southern end

Near the southeast gate is the **Church of the Holy Apostles** (Aghii Apostoloi Solaki) restored to its form of c. 1020. There are 17th-century wall paintings in the narthex. Beneath and to the east are foundations of a nymphaion. Earlier on this site was the mint of Athens. To the north, bordering a roadway, are the remains of a fountain house. The road ran along the back of the first south stoa which formed the south side of the Agora from the 5th century to the 2nd centuries BC. At the west end a large square foundation may be that of the Heliaia lawcourt. The south side of the Agora was remodelled in the 2nd century BC, with the construction of the enormous middle stoa, the second version of the south stoa and other elements forming a south square. The earlier layout of the area has been obscured by the Roman gymnasium.

In the jumble of low remains of houses and other buildings near the south stoa and lawcourt are the putative remains of the Prison of Socrates. The discovery in one substantial stone building of small cell-like rooms and 13 vials, suitable for small doses of hemlock, has made it tempting to identify this as the prison where Plato recorded that Socrates took his fatal dose.

PLAKA
Map p. 82, B2/3–C2/3
Metro: Monastiraki

Plaka, with its sprinkling of antiquities and profusion of souvenir shops, tavernas and restaurants, is both the oldest section of modern Athens and the heart of 'tourist' Athens. It lies between the north-northeast slopes of the Acropolis and Odos Ermou, which runs from Monastiraki Square to Syntagma Square. In high summer, Adrianou and Kidathinaion Streets can have all the relaxed charm of Coney Island or Covent Garden Market: tour groups clog the streets, backpackers stop unexpectedly thumping the unwary with their stout packs, and waiters shout out menu items and thrust menus at all who pause even momentarily. If possible, visit here off-season, when Plaka is reclaimed by the Athenians.

The derivation of the name is uncertain, with some suggesting it refers to the *plaka*, the stone that once marked the district's centre near the Monument of Lysicrates. Most of the buildings date from the mid-19th to the 20th centuries and a number of handsome town houses and Neoclassical buildings have been preserved and restored. The house at no. 96 Adrianou is believed to be the oldest in Athens (17th century). The considerably more modest buildings of Anafiotika, on the slopes of the Acropolis, are charming. This neighbourhood was built in the 19th century by immigrants from the island of Anaphi, many of them stonemasons who worked on the buildings of the capital of the newly independent Greece. To this day, Anafiotika resembles an island village, with its one- and two-storey houses, small churches, and dazzling whitewash.

Monastiraki Square
We begin our visit in Monastiraki Square, whose name honours the monastery that was once here, and from which Ermou and Mitropoleos run east toward Syntagma Square. Pandrossou and Hephaistou run east and west out of Monastiraki Square, each crowded with tourist, junk, and brocante shops. The weekend flea market on and around Hephaistou still offers the chance to find a nice piece of old copper, although many of the 'antiques' on sale in Plateia Avissinias, near the entrance to the Agora, are highly suspicious. The area has a number of small cafés and restaurants, of

which the Avissinias, in Plateia Avissinias, is especially appealing. At the southeast corner of the somewhat inchoate square is the former Mosque of Tzistarakis, built in 1759; its minaret razed after 1821. Used for years as a prison, it now houses the Museum of Greek Popular Art's collection of traditional and modern ceramics (*usually open 9.30–3, closed Tues; T: 210 324 2066; www.culture.gr*). The Thanasis excellent *souvlakia* and *gyro* restaurant is just off the square (*see p. 127*).

Beyond the mosque stand the remains of a façade of the **Library of Hadrian**, which was opened to the public in 2004 (*T: 210 322 0740*). The building consisted of a walled enclosure (122m by 82m) with a cloistered court. The Library was contained in a room on the east side. The interior was probably a garden.

In a square off Odos Mitropoleos is the cathedral (or Metropolis; 1840–55). Beside it is the tiny 12th-century Old Metropolis or Gorgeopikoös, which has all the charm that the new cathedral lacks. Both buildings reuse old material. In the centre of Ermou is a small square with the charming 11th–13th-century Kapnikarea, the university church (*see p. 114*).

The Roman agora and old Turkish Quarter

The Gate of Athena Archegetis, a four-columned Doric portico, forms the main entrance to the Roman agora, the main market of Roman Athens (*usually open 8–7 in summer, 8–3 in winter; T: 210 324 5220*). In the 2nd century AD, a colonnade connected the new Roman agora, with its large central courtyard, colonnades, and shops, with the original Greek agora. A worn inscription on the architrave of the Gate of Athena records contributions of Julius Caesar and Augustus. Nearby stands the **Tower of the Winds** of the 2nd or 1st century BC, one of Athens' most charming monuments. The tower served the triple purpose of sundial, water clock and weather vane. The building (in Pentelic marble), the work of the Macedonian astronomer Andronicos, is octagonal, with each face marking a compass point and adorned with a delightful relief of the appropriate wind: Boreas the north wind blows his icy blast through a conch shell; Kaikias (northeast) scatters hail; Apeliotis (east) bears fruits; Euros (southeast) brings storms; Notos (south) brings rain; Lips (southwest) steers ships; Zephyros (west) brings spring breezes; Skiron (northwest) heralds winter. A semicircular turret attached to the south face was a reservoir for working the water-clock. It was originally surmounted by a revolving bronze triton. In Turkish times it was occupied by dervishes.

At the edge of the Roman agora is the neglected 15th-century Fetiyhe mosque and, on the corner of Odos Aiolou, the gateway of the former *medresse* (seminary), both reminders that this was the heart of Turkish Athens, with an extensive bazaar. On nearby Kyrrestou, a Turkish bath house has recently been restored and is open to the public (as a museum, not a functioning bath; *T: 210 324 4340*).

The enchanting **Museum of Greek Folk Music**, with its collection of more than 1,200 instruments, sheet music and recordings, is a few steps away on Odos Diogenous (*usually open Tues–Sun 10–2; excellent shop; T: 210 325 0198; www.culture.gr*). Just beyond it is the Platanos restaurant, one of Plaka's oldest (*see p. 126*).

Anafiotika

Several streets lead steeply uphill into Anafiotika district on the slopes of the Acropolis, where there are several charming churches (*see p. 115*). From the top of Odos Klepsydrias, it is a short walk along Odos Theorias to the **Kanellopoulos Museum** (*open 8.30–3; closed Mon; T: 210 321 2313*), which houses the Kanellopoulos family's private collection of ancient art and fine icons in their handsome 19th-century house. To the north of the Kanellopoulos Museum, in Odos Tholou, is the Old University (1837–41), recently restored to be a Museum of the University. Further on is Aghii Anargyri, remodelled in the 17th century. Dropping down a street or two brings you to the Byzantine chapel of **Aghios Nikolaos Rangavas**, at the corner of Prytaniou. From here it is easy to explore more of Anafiotika's winding lanes, several with small chapels. It is also almost impossible not to become pleasantly disorientated.

Descending to Adrianou and turning left into Kidathinaion you find, at no. 17, the outstanding **Museum of Greek Folk Art** (*open Tues–Sun 10–2*), with its collection of costumes, embroidery, wood and brass, and frescoes by the eccentric 19th-century artist Theophilos, who wore the foustanella, the pleated white skirt that was traditionally the costume of Greek warriors (and today is still worn by the parliamentary guard).

Several other museums are nearby: the Frissiras Museum of Contemporary Art (*Wed–Sun 11–5; T: 210 323 4678; www.frissirasmuseum.com*) has frequent special exhibitions at 3 Monis Asteriou; the Museum of Greek Children's Art at 9 Kodrou (*Tues–Sat 10–2, Sun 11–2; T 210 331 2621; www.childrensartmuseum.gr*) also has special exhibits

Euros, the southeast wind and bringer of storms, on the Tower of the Winds.

and children's workshops; the Center of Folk Art and Tradition, 6 Hatzimichali Angelou (*Tues–Fri 9–1 & 5–7; Sat–Sun 9–1; T 210 324 3972*), showcases the private collection of Angeliki Hatzimichali in her splendid 19th-century town house.

On the fringes of the Plaka, at Nikis 39, the **Jewish Museum of Greece** (*Mon–Fri 9–2.30; Sun 10–2; T: 210 323 1577; www.jewishmuseum.gr. Poorly marked on the street; ring bell to be admitted*) preserves relics from synagogues and documents Greece's Jewish community, which thrived before its decimation in the Second World War.

THE NATIONAL ARCHAEOLOGICAL MUSEUM
Beyond map p. 82, C1
Metro: Victoria

Odos 28 Oktovriou (also known as Odos Patission) leads from Omonia Square to the National Archaeological Museum; due to heavy traffic the 15-min walk has little to recommend it. The walk from the Victoria metro takes about 10mins, when you include crossing streets busy with heavy traffic.

The museum is usually open summer daily 8–7; winter daily 8.30–2.30. T. 210 821 7717; www.culture.gr. The museum has labels in Greek and English; toilet facilities, café, shop. The shop sells the Ministry of Culture publications The National Archaeological Museum *(2005),* The Prehistoric Collection *and* The Sculpture Collection *(both 2004). The museum is often at its least crowded for an hour or two after it opens and before it closes. NB: It is important to hold onto your ticket, which has to be presented each time you enter or re-enter a series of galleries.*

The National Archaeological Museum still contains Greece's most outstanding collection of ancient art, although almost all new finds now go to the appropriate regional museums. The museum was erected in 1866–89, and a large east wing added in 1925–39. The museum was entirely closed for reinstallation and renovation from 2001–04; by 2005, both the ground floor and much of the first floor galleries were reinstalled and open to the public. Most exhibits are in new cases, with improved lighting, and the rooms are less cluttered than previously. Most of the reopened galleries have helpful wall texts explaining the exhibits' historical context and artistic importance; individual items are usually identified. Room numbers are shown in some, but not all rooms; the order in which the galleries are numbered is not always self-evident (eg, most visitors begin with Gallery 4, the museum's main gallery, with the finds from Mycenae). *National Archaeological Museum,* The brochure handed out with the entrance ticket, has a useful plan of the museum, accurate in most details. This description and plan overleaf follow the numbering in the brochure. As the brochure makes clear, the museum is organised both topically (eg sculpture, bronze, pottery) and chronologically (sculpture, for example, is displayed from the 8th century BC to the 5th century AD). The main periods covered are the Prehistoric, Archaic, Classical, Hellenistic, Roman, and Late Antique (*for a timeline of dates, see p. 713*).

NATIONAL ARCHAEOLOGICAL MUSEUM
(GROUND FLOOR)

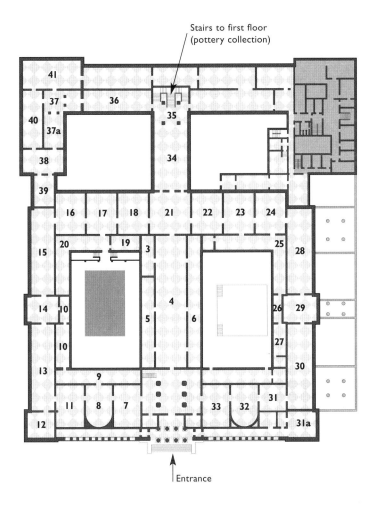

Stairs to first floor
(pottery collection)

Entrance

3–4	Mycenaean objects	
5	Neolithic and Bronze Age	
6	Cycladic objects	
7–35	Sculpture	
36–39	Bronze collection	
40–41	Egyptian collection	

Ground floor, Galleries 3–45 (Prehistoric Collection)

Gallery 3. Mycenaean finds from Central Greece, Thessaly and Skopelos (15th–11th centuries BC): Some superb finds are displayed here, including delicate ivory carvings, gold jewellery and pottery, making the point that this was a rich and widely spread civilisation.

Gallery 4. Finds from Mycenaean centres and cemeteries in the Peloponnese (16th–12th centuries BC): This, the largest gallery in the museum, contains contains the famous gold of Mycenae, including the gold funerary masks, one of which Schliemann identified—wrongly, as it turns out—as the **Mask of Agamemnon** in a jubilant telegram to the King of Greece. Much of what is on display in both rooms comes from graves, including the shaft and tholos graves at Mycenae (*see pp. 212–18*); a wall text gives information on the shaft graves of Grave Circles A and B inside the citadel. Amongst many other spectacular objects are inlaid daggers from Shaft Grave IV, gravestones (*stelae*) with relief decoration, and the elaborately decorated **gold cups from Vapheio** (Laconia; *see p. 309*).

Gallery 5. Objects of the Neolithic period and the Early and Middle Bronze Age, from Central Greece: This gallery has the earliest exhibits in the museum, dating from c. 6800 BC to 3300 BC. Many finds are from two important Neolithic sites in Thessaly, **Dimini and Sesklo** (*see pp. 560–61*) and include stone and pottery vessels, stone and bone tools, and some of the earliest known representational figures found in Greece, including the wide-hipped marble figurine of a woman (c. 6500–5800 BC) from Sparta and the clay figurine of a seated woman holding a child (c. 4800–4500 BC) from Sesklo.

Gallery 6. Objects of the Early and Middle Cycladic periods (3rd and 2nd millennia BC): The Cycladic displays date from the time when the Cycladic islands shared a common culture. A wall text discusses the sequence and chronology of types of vessels and figurines. Most objects—as with the Mycenaean finds—were found in graves. It is uncertain what function other than grave offerings the objects may have had. The best-known exhibits here are the marble Cycladic figurines, from the earliest, 'violin shaped' figurines to the later three-dimensional figures. The figures include the

The golden 'Mask of Agamemnon'.

largest known example of Cycladic sculpture: a 1.5-m figure of a woman with folded arms (c. 2800B–2300 BC) and the charming figure of a musician playing a lyre (c. 2800–2300 BC). The gallery also has displays of tools, both those used in bronze work and obsidian blades, with which stone tools were fashioned. Amongst the pottery, the clay **'frying pan' vessel** (which takes its name from its shape), with an incised scene of a ship at sea, is particularly noteworthy.

Sculpture collection

Most of the ground floor (Galleries 7–35) is devoted to the museum's vast collection of Greek sculpture, from the Archaic period (7th century BC) to Late Antiquity (5th century AD). This is the finest collection of ancient sculpture not merely in Greece, but in the world. Most of the sculpture comes from Athens and Attica, although the numerous works from most of Greece make this truly a national museum. Most tour groups are led through the galleries at a brisk pace and by judicious hovering, it is usually possible to have a moment or two in relative tranquillity with even the best-known works.

Galleries 7–13. Archaic sculpture (8th-6th centuries BC): These galleries have some of the earliest works of Archaic sculpture, such as the **reliefs from the Temple of Athena at Mycenae** (c. 650 BC), and the earliest known life-size statue, possibly of the goddess Artemis, also dating from c. 650 BC. This was a dedication erected by a Naxian, Nikandre, on the island of Delos to the goddess Artemis. These galleries also have examples of the museum's fine collection of statues (usually more than life-size) of *kouroi* and *korai*. Many of the statues were commemorative, and erected on or near graves, such as the statue of the maiden Phrasikleia (c. 550–540 BC), whose youthful rounded body is suggested under the stiff outline of her long gown. As is usual, the *korai* are clad, and the *kouroi*, such as the youth Aristodikos, in Gallery 11 (c. 510–500 BC), are nude. The progression towards more life-like and animated figures is striking: Aristodikos' bent arms and for-

Demeter giving seeds of grain to Triptolemos. 5th-century relief from Eleusis.

ward stride are realistic, and his face seems to be that of an individual, rather than of a stylized type.

Galleries 14–15. Late Archaic and early Classical sculpture (5th century BC): These galleries are dominated by the monumental **bronze *Poseidon* or *Zeus*** (c. 460 BC) found on the seabed off Cape Artemision in Euboea. A wall text explains that it is an example of the Severe style in Classical sculpture. In a few galleries—representing the course of two centuries—Greek sculpture has moved from the stiff, stationary, frontal figures of the first *kouroi* to a monumental statue seemingly on the verge of action. The galleries also contain two of the loveliest of Greek votive relief sculptures: the **youth crowning himself with a victory wreath** found at Sounion (c. 460 BC) and the **Demeter, Persephone and Triptolemos** from Eleusis (c. 440–430 BC; *see p. 146*).

Galleries 16 & 18. Classical sculpture—grave reliefs (5th century BC): These two galleries have a wide range of Athenian funerary stelae. In 460 BC, the Athenian leader Cleisthenes successfully supported a law to outlaw elaborate grave monuments, but when Athens undertook the Peloponnesian War (430–415 BC) the law was largely ignored. These galleries hold some of the results, including the stele in Gallery 16 showing a **youth from Salamis** (c. 430--420 BC), which some think is a work by Pheidias' pupil Agorakritos. Elegant but simple rectangular grave markers of this sort were soon elaborated into monuments that suggested temple façades. The pedimented grave stele of the seated figure of **Hegeso** (c. 410–400 BC), shown choosing a piece of jewellery from the box held by her slave, is an excellent example of this style.

Gallery 17. Classical sculpture—votive reliefs and architectural sculptures: This small gallery has sculpture from the important shrine to Hera, the **Argive Heraion** (*see p. 225*) and 5th–4th-century BC sculpture from other sites in Greece.

Galleries 19–20. Classical sculpture—statues (5th and 4th centuries BC; copies of Classical originals): Tucked away in an inconspicuous spot in Gallery 20 is the small 3rd-century AD statue known as the ***Varvakeion Athena***, from its find spot in the Athenian district of Varvakeion. This very late work is a copy of Pheidias' 5th-century BC chryselephantine statue of *Athena Parthenos* that stood in the Parthenon. The gallery contains several other copies of well-known works of Antiquity, such as the 5th-century BC statue of Nemesis that stood in the sanctuary at Rhamnous (*see p. 140*). In the absence of the originals, these works, along with whatever written descriptions of the originals that have survived, are as close as we can get to some of the best-known monumental works of Classical sculpture.

Gallery 21. Classical and Hellenistic statues and reliefs: This gallery has two well-known works: the 2nd-century BC bronze of a galloping **racehorse and its diminutive jockey**, and a marble copy (c. 100 BC) of the famous 5th-century BC bronze showing an **athlete binding his hair with fillets**. Again, as with the 3rd-century AD miniaturised copy of the *Athena Parthenos*, this is as close as we can get to imagining the famous bronze *Diamoumenos* (fillet-binder) by Polyclitus.

Gallery 22. Classical sculpture: Parts of the sculptural decoration of Asclepius' sanctuary at **Epidaurus**. Perhaps the most impressive of the sculptures on view is the 4th-century BC figure of a Nereid riding side-saddle on a horse, her garments ruffled by the wind.

Galleries 23–24. Grave reliefs (4th century BC): Yet more elaborate grave monuments, in which the relief figures become more three-dimensional and the stelae suggest actual buildings.

Galleries 25–27. Decrees, votive reliefs and statues: A wide number of inscriptions and reliefs from sanctuaries in and out of Athens.

Gallery 28. Grave reliefs (4th century BC): In 371 BC, Athens again passed a law forbidding elaborate grave monuments. Once again, the law was increasingly ignored. The result was monuments like that from the ancient cemetery, the Kerameikos, showing Aristonautes, dressed for battle, shield in hand, his cloak swirling around him, poised for combat in the deep recess of a small temple-like edifice (c. 310 BC). The gallery also contains two famous 4th-century BC bronzes of youths: one, perhaps by the sculptor Euphranor, found in a shipwreck off Antikythera and the boy, perhaps by Praxiteles, found at Marathon.

Galleries 29–30. Hellenistic sculpture (3rd–1st centuries BC): These two galleries have sculpture from the period after the death of Alexander the Great (323 BC), when his successors first ruled—and then lost—the empire Alexander conquered. The figure known as the **Wounded Gaul** (c. 100) is an excellent example of the baroque energy of much of Hellenistic sculpture, while the group of **Aphrodite, Pan, and Eros** (c. 100 BC) captures the charming humour evident in many works. As Eros flutters overhead, attempting to unite Pan and Aphrodite, the goddess, seemingly amused, threatens to swat Pan with her left sandal. The 1st-century BC statue of a child holding a puppy, found at Gerontikon in Asia Minor, became known as **The Little Refugee**, when Greek refugees brought it with them when they fled to Athens from Turkey in 1922.

Galleries 31–33. Sculptures of Greek workshops of the Roman period (1st–5th centuries AD): These galleries contain portrait heads of a number of Roman officials and emperors. There is also a series of portraits of *kosmetai* (officials in the gymnasia), later reused as building stones in a late Roman wall. The bronze statue of the **emperor Augustus**, no longer youthful, is especially fine; there are portraits of both the Emperor Hadrian and his curly-haired, youthful lover Antinous. The bronze portrait statue of the 3rd-century AD empress Julia Aquila Severa, found at Sparta, seems a fitting symbol of the declining fortunes of empire: the statue was crushed when the building in which it stood collapsed, perhaps in a fire.

Galleries 34–35. Grave and votive sculptures (various periods): These two galleries are best seen either as a detour from Gallery 21, or while en route to the first floor galleries. Gallery

34, with a marble altar, attempts to suggest one of the many small sanctuaries of ancient Greece. A helpful wall text gives information on some of these sanctuaries and on the importance of the nymphs and Pan.

Bronze collection (Galleries 36–39)

The museum's collection of ancient bronzes is one of the finest in the world. Many of the displays are small votive offerings from sanctuaries throughout Greece; many others were grave offerings. Some are items of everyday use, such as bronze mirrors and ornamental pins (*fibulae*). Since most of the bronzes are quite small, it is especially helpful to visit the collection when it is not crowded, in order to see the objects clearly. Several things to keep an eye out for: finds from the sanctuary of Zeus at **Dodona** (K. Karapanos Collection; 8th century BC–3rd century AD); the **bronze arrowheads** recovered from the battlefield at Thermopylae, where the Greeks under Leonidas fought the Persians in 480 BC (*see p. 431*); a reconstructed 3rd–4th-century AD **Roman chariot** from Asia Minor; the 2nd-century AD statue known as the ***Lady of Kalymnos***, found by fishermen in 1994. A fascinating wall text explains the process by which the statue was restored to its present condition, complete with the delicate fringe on the woman's flowing robes.

Egyptian collection (Galleries 40–41)

(*Closed at the time of writing*). The Egyptian collection comprises Egyptian antiquities from the Predynastic to the Ptolemaic period (5th millennium BC–1st century BC) and objects up until the 4th century AD. The Fayum portraits (1st–5th centuries AD) are especially noteworthy.

First floor, Galleries 48–56 (Pottery Collection)

This is the best place in Greece to study the evolution of ancient painted pottery (*see also the introduction on p. 31*). The collection spans all periods from the Neolithic to the Classical, with superb examples from each. The finest pieces include the Geometric Dipylon amphora and krater (8th century BC), with scenes of a funeral procession, a body on a bier and mourning women (represented as very simple stick-figures with triangles for bodies, emerging against a background of key patterns in continuous horizontal bands). The Mycenaean *Warrior Vase*, with its procession of armed soldiers, also stands out. The display, which covers both Attic and Corinthian pottery, proceeds chronologically, with black-figure ware (including pieces by the celebrated Exekias), examples of Panathenaic amphorae, and red-figure ware (where we begin to know many more painters' names). There is also a marvellous collection of white-figure funeral *lekythoi*, decorated with likenesses of the deceased; with girls bearing offerings to the dead; with Hermes conducting departed souls to the Underworld; or of Charon the ferryman of Hades.

THE AREOPAGUS, MOUSEION & PNYX
Map p. 104
Metro: Acropolis

The saddle linking the Acropolis to the 115-metre spur of the Areopagus to the west may have been the site of the original agora. The Areopagus gave its name to the council of nobles which became in early times both senate and supreme judicial court. With the rise of democracy the council's importance declined. St Paul spoke here when he visited Athens in 51 AD: the philosophers of the city invited 'the babbler' to the Areopagus to explain himself and his strange god (*Acts 17, 22–34*). Below the summit to the north are the are the ruins of the early Christian church of St Dionysos the Areopagite, one of those who heard St Paul's address to the people of Athens on this hill, and was convinced by it. There are also remains of several Mycenaean chamber tombs. The Cave of the Furies, where the final scene of the *Eumenides* of Aeschylus took place, was traditionally located here.

THE AREOPAGUS COUNCIL

The original and most important function of the council was the conduct of criminal justice, particularly in cases of murder and manslaughter, but in aristocratic times it became the governing body of the state. The Assembly of the people was at this time merely a recording machine for the decisions of the Areopagus, which led to much disaffection and ill-representation of the people's interests. It was Solon who transferred the powers of legislation and administration to the Assembly, when he divided Athenians into four classes (*see p. 88*). Under him the Areopagus was protector of the constitution and guardian of the laws, with control over the magistrates and the censorship of morals. The institution of ostracism (*see p. 85*) c. 488 BC deprived it of its guardianship of the constitution. About 20 years later control over the magistrates was transferred to the people, and the jurisdiction of the Areopagus was once again limited to cases of murder and manslaughter. It was here, according to Euripides, that Orestes was tried for the murder of this mother Clytemnestra. In the 4th century BC the Areopagus dealt also with crimes of treason and corruption, notable cases being the trials of the deserters after Chaironeia (*see p. 434*) in 338; of Demosthenes in 324; and of the courtesan Phryne (*see p. 426*).

The tree-clad slopes of the Mouseion Hill (148m), thought originally to have been the site of a sanctuary of the Muses, is a wooded and pleasant place to stroll and take in the views back to the Acropolis and across Athens. This was always a key point in the fortifications of Athens and the site of a Hellenistic fort. On the summit is the Monument of Philopappus (AD 114–16), built to honour C. Julius Antiochus

Philopappus, a prince of Commagene (northern Syria), who had a distinguished career as a Roman consul and praetor.

A paved path descends through an area that contained many houses in Antiquity. The path reaches the modern drive which also serves the Philopappus Theatre. Here is the 15th-century chapel of Aghios Dimitrios Loumbardiaris, refurbished in the 1950s by the architect Dimitris Pikionis. Pikionis also designed and laid out the elegant marble paths that lead to and link the Acropolis, Areopagus, Mouseion and Hill of the Nymphs.

The adjacent hill of the Pnyx (109m) was the meeting place of the Athenian Assembly under the democracy (a path from the chapel leads to the top). The Assembly deliberately moved here from the Agora so that their sessions would not be overlooked. When a meeting of the Assembly was called, citizens were hustled towards the Pnyx by officials who held ropes daubed with red paint across the Agora and neighbouring streets to encourage people to file quickly past and make it harder for citizens to duck a meeting. There was only one entrance to the Assembly hall, and each entrant was scrutinized to make sure no unofficial persons were attending. Any citizen found to have been touched by the red paint forfeited his allowance.

To the north is the Hill of the Nymphs (104m) crowned by an observatory (founded in 1842). Descending past the observatory to Leoforos Apostolou Pavlou, one passes an overgrown excavated area and can continue past the lively cafés and restaurants to the Agora excavations (*see p. 81*) and to the Kerameikos.

THE KERAMEIKOS & PLATO'S ACADEMY
Map p. 104, B1
Metro: Thission

Open Tues–Sun 8.30–3; T: 210 346 3553.
The Kerameikos, the main cemetery of ancient Athens, includes the remains of the Dipylon and Sacred Gates, where important routes from Piraeus, Eleusis and Boeotia converged and many travellers entered the city. The Kerameikos also included parts of the city walls as well as two cemetery areas. The cemetery for ordinary citizens lay outside the walls and the Demosion Sema, the burial place of Athenian heroes and notables, was inside. The Inner Kerameikos, towards the Agora, was originally the home of smiths and potters (the word 'ceramic' shares its root with 'Kerameikos').

Through the entrance to the site there is a plan of orientation on a prominent mound. A path descends to the city walls with the Sacred Gate spanning both the Sacred Way to Eleusis and the Eridanos stream. The space between the two gates was occupied by the Pompeion, a place of preparation for ceremonial processions. The structure was rebuilt in the Roman period. The Dipylon was a double gateway, as the name implies, on either side of a court. The cemetery area was outside the Dipylon, along the roadsides. The most striking remains are the burial plots to either side of the so-called Street of the Tombs. Sculpted *stelae* are prominent. There is a cast of the stele of Dexileos, killed in the Battle of Corinth in 394 BC.

The Oberländer Museum has funerary sculpture, the contents of graves and a particularly fine and important collection of pottery of the periods Sub-Mycenaean to Proto-Attic. The well-preserved Archaic statue of a *kouros*, found in the Kerameikos by the German excavators in 2000, will eventually be on display either here or at the National Archaeological Museum. Important finds continue to be made here: a severe summer storm in 2002 unearthed the grave stele of the well-known 3rd-century BC comic actor Ariston, with traces of its original paint still in place despite centuries of downpours.

Plato's Academy

Beyond map p. 104, A1. The site of the Academy, which is off Odos Platonos, between Tripoleos and Evklidou, can be reached on foot from the Kerameikos, though the walk (1.5km) is an unpleasant one, through congested streets.

The Academy, made famous by Plato's school of philosophy, was a sacred wood, situated at the end of an avenue than ran into the countryside from the Dipylon Gate. The site was identified by a boundary stone found in 1966. The remains (an Early Helladic house, a Geometric heroön, parts of an (?) Archaic circuit wall, a 4th-century colonnaded court and a Roman gymnasium and baths) and their surroundings remain disappointing, despite recent attempts to create something of a park. The hill of Kolonos, where Oedipus fled in Sophocles' *Oedipus at Colonus*, is at the end of Odos Tripoleos.

NEW MUSEUMS IN THE KERAMEIKOS DISTRICT

There are several other interesting museums in the Kerameikos area: the Museum Alex Mylona (*Plateia Aghion Asomaton 5; open Wed 11–8, Thurs–Sat 11–5.30, Sun 10–5; T: 210 321 5717; www.mam.org.gr*) has examples drawn from more than 50 years of the work of the Athenian painter and sculptor Alex Mylona, exhibited in a remodelled 1920s Neoclassical mansion. The Museum of Traditional Pottery (*Odos Melidoni 4–6 ; open Mon, Tues, Thur, Fri 9–3, Wed 9–8, Sat 10–3, Sun 10–2. T: 210 331 8491*, has a wide-ranging display of traditional and contemporary Greek pottery. In 2004, the Benaki Museum opened the Museum of Islamic Art (*Asomaton 22 and Dipylou; open 9–3, except Weds 9–7; T: 210 322 5550*). The museum is housed in a former Neoclassical mansion (with a section of the Themistoclean city wall in the basement). The exhibit, which covers the entire Islamic world, is arranged chronologically on four floors, spanning the 7th to the 19th centuries. This is a gem of a museum, focusing on a subject seldom covered in Greek museums. As one would expect, the ceramics, including Iznik pottery, are particularly fine, as are the woodwork (elaborately carved doors and windows), metalwork and textiles. The third floor exhibits include a stunning reception room with inlaid marble floor from a 17th-century Cairo mansion.

SOCRATES & PLATO

While the early Greek philosophers came from a variety of cities and set off in a variety of intellectual directions, many were attracted by the wealth and cultural buzz of 5th-century Athens. Here they found the drama festivals, where playwrights such as Aeschylus, Sophocles and Euripides were exposing the underlying ethical conflicts of city life. Alongside these were the comedies of Aristophanes, bawdy, outrageous and totally unrestrained in their mockery of pretension, both intellectual and otherwise.

The visiting philosophers were collectively known as the Sophists. Sophism later became a term of abuse, as the Sophists were accused of taking money for teaching people to think (a practice which the more austere philosophers such as Socrates and Plato frowned on), but between them they spawned a wide range of new ideas. One important functional achievement lay in teaching rhetoric, an essential skill in a democratic state such as Athens. They taught their students how to construct and deliver effective arguments, and thus to think about the nature and purpose of argument itself. Central to Sophism was the belief that, in the words of Protagoras, 'Man is the measure of all things'. The gods were of relatively little importance. 'The subject of the gods is too big and life too short to understand it', said Protagoras. Other Sophists suggested that the gods were the creation of the human mind, or even deliberately evoked by the ruling classes to frighten the masses. If one concentrated on what it meant to be human, then there had to be an analysis of human nature. Were human beings naturally good, or did they have to be forced into goodness by society? Were there moral absolutes or should moral values depend on the situation (moral relativism)?

It was towards the end of the 5th century BC that one native Athenian took philosophy in new directions. His effect was such that all philosophers before him are known as 'pre-Socratic'. Socrates (469–399 BC) was absorbed in himself, uncaring of what others thought about him and ruthless in his challenging of conventional thinking. ('The unexamined life is not worth living', is one of his more famous sayings.) His confrontational approach, known as *elenchus*, involved breaking down a concept, such as virtue, into its component parts by incessant questioning. Then one could begin reconstructing the concepts and achieve a deeper understanding of them. Socrates argued that each human being had a soul, his psyche, and this would be naturally drawn to virtue once that had been discovered. Yet Socrates was teaching in troubled times. Athens had suffered a humiliating defeat at the hands of Sparta in 404, and Socrates had been associated with an unpopular aristocratic government which had temporarily overthrown the democracy. His incessant questioning of convention upset many, and he was eventually put on trial for corrupting the young.

His punishment would probably have been no more than exile if he had not riled the jury with his arrogance: he was eventually sentenced to death (399 BC).

Socrates' death was deeply disturbing to a young aristocratic Athenian, Plato (429–347). Plato reacted strongly against both the Sophists and against democracy. Both, in his view, offered an unstable basis for true knowledge. Plato suggested instead that there was a world on a different plane from this material one, where Forms or Ideas of Beauty, Virtue, Justice, and even objects such as the perfect table, existed eternally and unchanging. Plato presented his arguments in dialogues in which the leading character was often Socrates who, true to his role in real life, would demolish the half-baked views of those around him. So it was shown that rhetoric was little more than a series of tricks which played on emotion (the dialogue *Gorgias*), and democracy a hopelessly muddled way of achieving stable and effective government (*The Republic*). The Forms represented truth, and it was possible to grasp the essence of each through reason—but it required a long intellectual journey to do so. Plato believed in selecting those with the greatest aptitude for this journey when they were young. They would start with mastering mathematical proofs to show how it was possible to use reason (here deductive logic) to reach certainty. They would then progress to greater and greater intellectual challenges, analysing concepts from the examples they saw around them which could, of course, only be echoes of the Form 'above'. So things perceived as beautiful on earth could only be a pale reflection of the Form of Beauty. Plato believed that the soul actually retained the memory of these Forms, so that reasoning was in fact revealing what was already, at some deep, subliminal level, known.

Eventually a few men, perhaps at about the age of fifty, would have reached a true understanding of Virtue, Justice, Beauty and Goodness. They would now be in a position to govern. The 'Guardians', as Plato termed them, would form a dictatorship in which lesser mortals, those consumed with ambition or seduced by the every day temptations of the world (the Guardians were above such things), would be ruled in their own interests according to the Forms.

Plato's Republic, further described in his later work *The Laws*, would have been a pretty joyless state to live in; a place where emotions, love, sexuality, poetry and music were all derided. And yet while the moral absolutism of Plato's Republic is hostile to any kind of personal or emotional freedom, the sparkle of his dialogues and his valid critique of some aspects of moral absolutism confirm his place as one of the world's great philosophers. Even if one despairs of reaching a true understanding of these things called Beauty or Virtue, one can surely benefit from searching for their essence. Plato's belief in a small, disciplined elite who can grasp the reality of what lies beyond our material world, and transmit that understanding to others, was enormously influential in Christian theology, providing a justification for the authority of the Roman Catholic Church.   C.F.

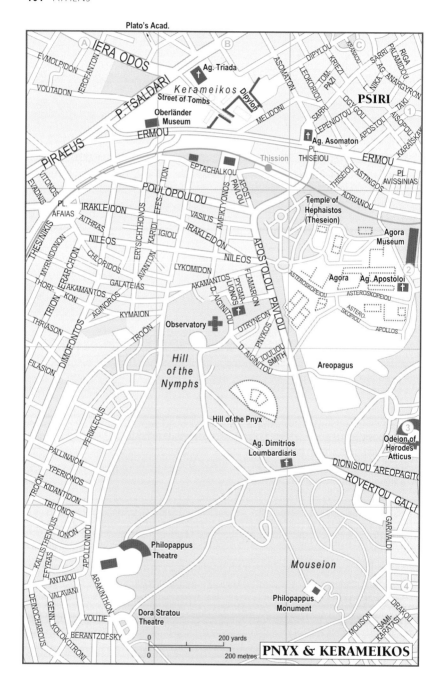

Plato's Acad.

IERA ODOS

EVMOLPIDON
IEROFANTON
VOUTADON

P. TSALDARI

PIRAEUS

ERMOU

Ag. Triada

Kerameikos
Street of Tombs

Oberländer
Museum

Dipylon

MELIDONI
ASOMATON

DIPYLOU
KRIEZI
LEOKORIOU
TOM-PAZI
SARRI
AG. ANARGYRON
NIKA
PALAMIDOU
RIGA
TAKI

PSIRI

SARRI
OGYGOU
LEPENIOTOU
APOSTOLI
AISOPOU
KARAISKAK

Ag. Asomaton

PL.
THISEIOU

Thission

ERMOU

PL.
AVISSINIAS

VITONOS
EVADNIS

PL.
IRAKLEIDON
AFAIAS

AITHRAS
NILEOS
CHLORIDOS

MYRMIDONON
THESPINIKIS

THORI
KON

IERAKAMANTOS
AGINOROS

KYMAION

THRIASON

DIMOFONTOS
FILASION

POULOPOULOU

EPTACHALKOU

APOST.
PAVLOU

AMEIKTYONOS

EFESSION
ERYSICHTHONOS
KARIDI
IGIOU
AVANTON

VASILIS
IRAKLEIDON
LYKOMIDON

NILEOS

AKAMANTOS

FLAMARION
PYGMA-LIONOS
D. AIGINITOU

Observatory

OTRYNEON

PNYKOS
D. AIGINITOU
IOULIOU SMITH

APOSTOLOU PAVLOU

THISEIOU ASTINGOS

ADRIANOU

Temple of
Hephaistos
(Theseion)

ASTEROSKOPEIOU

Agora

ASTERO-
SKOPIOU

Agora
Museum

Ag. Apostoloi

ASTEROSKOPEIOU

APOLLOS

*Hill
of the
Nymphs*

Hill of the Pnyx

Ag. Dimitrios
Loumbardiaris

Areopagus

Odeion of
Herodes
Atticus

DIONISIOU AREOPAGITO

ROVERTOU GALLI

GARIVALDI

PERIKLEOUS

PALLINAION

YPERIONOS
TROON
KIDANTIDON

TRITONOS

IONON
APOLLONIOU

KALLISTHENOUS
EFTRAS
ANTAIOU

ARAKINTHON

VALAVANI

DEINOCHAROUS
GENN. KOLOKOTRONI

VOUTIE

BERANTZOFSKY

Philopappus
Theatre

Mouseion

Dora Stratou
Theatre

Philopappus
Monument

MOUSON

DRAKOU
TSAMI-KARATASI

0   200 yards
0   200 metres

PNYX & KERAMEIKOS

FROM SYNTAGMA SQUARE TO THE ACROPOLIS
Map pp. 82–83
Metro: Syntagma and Acropolis

This route begins in Syntagma Square, through which virtually all visitors pass. It is a pleasant stroll in the evening, something for those those attending performances at the Odeion of Herodes Atticus to consider.

Syntagma (Constitution) Square is the centre of political Athens and is, for most visitors, at the heart of the city they visit. Syntagma is dominated by the old Royal Palace, now the Greek **Parliament building**, from which the Greek Constitution was proclaimed in 1843. A Memorial to the Unknown Soldier, with its honour guard, stands in front of the Parliament building, facing broad Vas. Amalias (Queen Amalia) Boulevard. On Sunday mornings at 11, there is a colourful changing of the guard ceremony, with a brass band and soldiers wearing the pleated white foustanella, the military garb associated with the Greek Revolution.

The square is flanked by offices and luxury hotels, notably the handsome Grande Bretagne (1842). There are several cafés in the square, as well as the inevitable fast-food outlets (known as 'fastfoodtadakia'). Trees and flowerbeds were added to Syntagma on the occasion of the 2004 Olympics; the stray dogs—which were removed for the games—are back, and always welcome snacks.

Southwards along Amalias Boulevard is the attractive **National Garden**, originally belonging to the royal palace; many of the original plants were imported from around Europe by Greece's first queen, Amalia. In Antiquity, Theophrastus' Garden of the Muses was in this area. The garden can be entered from Amalias or from Odos Irodou Attikou, which runs between the east side of the National Garden and the modest former palace, residence of the king after the restoration of the monarchy in 1935, and more recently of the president. There are cafés near both entrances. The **Zappeion Gardens**, adjacent to the National Garden, have the Zappeion exhibition hall (1874–78); both were founded by the Zappas family, wealthy Greeks from Romania. Today the gardens also have a cinema and the distinguished Aegli restaurant and café (*see p. 125*). Both the National and Zappeion Gardens are welcome refuges from summer heat and much used by Athenian families. Across from the National Garden are the Russian Church (originally the Greek Orthodox church of Sotira Lykodemou; c. 1031) and the English Church (St Paul's; 1843). Around the corner at Nikis 39 is the Jewish Museum (*see p. 92*).

Beyond Leoforos Olgas (south of Zappeion) are two monuments built by the philhellene emperor Hadrian: the **Arch of Hadrian** (132 AD), also known as Hadrian's Gate, and the massive Sanctuary of Olympian Zeus, also known as the *Kolonnes* ('the columns'). On one side of the Arch Hadrian is an inscription that reads: 'This is Athens, once the city of Theseus'. On the other side an inscription reminds the Athenians of who is now in charge: 'This is the city of Hadrian, not Theseus'. Behind is an archaeological park with the massive **Temple of Olympian Zeus** (Olympieion; *open Tues–Sun 8.30–3*), most of its 104 columns scattered on the ground. The sanctuary occupies an artificial terrace supported by a peribolos (circuit wall). The temple is the largest is Greece. Begun in the Archaic period, it took 700 years to complete in the course of which Corinthian columns replaced the original Doric order. There are scattered remains of ancient houses overlain by a large Roman bath. Part of the Themistoclean wall can be seen with the Hippades Gate. There is a late 5th-century AD basilica built of Classical fragments.

South of the Olympieion ancient remains have almost all been obliterated by urban development. The river Ilissos has suffered likewise. The Kynosarges gymnasium was hereabouts. To the southeast (via Ath. Diakou) is the main modern cemetery of Athens (Proto Nekrotafeio), with much fine funerary sculpture and the tombs of eminent Greeks and some foreigners. Kolokotronis (*see pp. 51 & 53*) lies here, as do Schliemann, in a magnificent mausoleum, and fellow archaeologist Adolf Furtwängler).

Leaving the Olympieion, one can take Odos Lisikratous into Plaka to the Street of the Tripods (Tripodon), a popular promenade in Antiquity. Bronze tripods, given for success in dramatic contests, were displayed here, often on top of columns or structures. These were known as choregic monuments, from the word *choregos*, the sponsor or financial backer of dramatic productions. There was a legal minimum the *choregoi* were expected to spend, and their sponsorship money was used to pay the actors, to pay for costumes and props, to pay the poet and flute-player, and pay for the monument to Dionysus if their production won the contest. The **Monument of Lysicrates** (334 BC) is a well preserved example: a cylindrical structure on a square base with engaged columns in the Corinthian order (the earliest known external use of the

Corinthian capital). It is surmounted by an elaborate acanthus-leaf finial, which would have borne the tripod. The decoration of the frieze shows Dionysus and the Tyrrhenian pirates, whom the god turned into dolphins. The inscription on the architrave tells us that 'Lysicrates was *choregos*; the tribe of Acamantis won the victory with a chorus of boys; Theon played the flute; Lysiades of Athens trained the chorus; Evainetos was *archon*'.

From the Monument of Lysicrates, Odos Vironos (Byron Street) leads to pedestrianized Dionisiou Areopagitou, which runs along the south side of the Acropolis, past the site of the Odeion of Pericles, a large hall with interior columns used for musical performances at the Panathenaic Festival. There is

The Lysicrates Monument (4th century BC).

The enormous Corinthian columns of the Temple of Olympian Zeus.

an entrance to the south side of the Acropolis near the juncture with Thrasyllou. In 2004, the north slopes of the Acropolis were opened to the public for the first time in several decades. You can make your way from the south slopes around to the north slopes; in time, it is planned to have an entrance directly to the north slopes from Odos Theorias. Opposite the entrance to the south slopes, on the corner of Odos Makriyanni, is the Centre for Acropolis Studies, the intended site of the new Acropolis Museum, where it is hoped that the Elgin Marbles will one day take pride of place.

Past the Odeion of Pericles is the Temenos of Dionysos Eleutherios (*see plan on pp. 74–75*), of which the most important element is the **Theatre of Dionysus** dating from the 6th century but rebuilt in stone in the 4th century and substantially altered (including the shape of the orchestra) in the Hellenistic and Roman periods. The front row of seating consisted of 67 thrones for dignitaries. Other clearly discernible monuments on the higher slopes include, further west, an Asclepieion.

The Theatre of Dionysus was linked to the Roman Odeion of Herodes Atticus, to the west, by the long (163m) Stoa of Eumenes, endowed by King Eumenes II of Pergamon (197–159 BC). This was built against a terrace wall with arches which supported the *peripatos*, a roadway round the acropolis. The Odeion was built in honour of Regilla, wife of Herodes, who died in AD 160. It has the typical shape of a Roman theatre, a well-preserved façade with entrances and niches for statues, and is used annually for performances of the Athens festival.

WHO WAS HERODES ATTICUS?

The sudden rise to wealth of Julius Atticus, father of Herodes, is wittily related by Gibbon. Julius, who had accidentally found a vast treasure buried in an old house, anticipated the officiousness of informers by reporting his find straight to the emperor. On being told by Nerva that he need have no qualms about using—or abusing—fortune's gift, Julius devoted large sums to public works and to educating his son. Herodes (c. 101–177) enjoyed a distinguished public career under Hadrian, becoming *archon* in Athens, where he was famed for his oratory. Under Antoninus Pius he was summoned to Rome as tutor to the young Marcus Aurelius, and was rewarded for his service by a consulship in 143. He retired to Athens and continued the munificence of his father, paying for projects in Thermopylae (baths), Delphi (a stadium) and Corinth (a theatre), as well as for the stadium and this odeion at Athens. He died at his country estate near Marathon.

THE HISTORIC CENTRE & ITS MUSEUMS

Odos Stadiou is one of Athens' busiest shopping streets. Halfway along on the right, at the west corner of Plateia Klafthmonos, is the fine 11th–12th-century Byzantine church of Aghii Theodoroi. At the southeast corner of the square, the Eutaxia-Vourou Mansion (1833) served as King Otho's residence (1836–43) while the Royal Palace (now the Parliament House) was being built. The mansion is now a **Museum of the City of Athens** (*Mon, Weds, Thur 9–4; Sat–Sun 10–3; T: 210 323 1397*), whose rooms recreate the days when King Otho and Queen Amalia held court here; exhibits focus on 19th-century Athens. Farther on on the right is Plateia Kolokotroni with an equestrian statue of Kolokotronis (*see pp. 51 & 53*) and, behind, the Old Parliament Building (Palaia Vouli; 1858–74), now the **National Historical Museum** (*open Tues–Sun 9–2; some labels in English; T: 210 323 7617*), with an extensive and interesting collection of portraits, arms and relics, especially of the War of Independence of 1821–28. Shortly beyond, the street bends to enter the lower side of Syntagma Square.

Neoclassical Athens

Walking down Odos Panepistimiou (University Street; officially Leoforos Eleftheriou Venizelou), you pass a cluster of three important 19th-century Neoclassical buildings: the **National Library**, Athens University, and the Hellenic Academy. The National Library's façade reflects the Agora's Temple of Hephaistos. The main building of **Athens University** was intended to suggest an ancient temple. In front are statues of the British Prime Minister and philhellene Gladstone and four prominent 19th-century Greeks: the political leader Capodistrias (*see p. 234*), the philologist Koraï, the poet Rigas Feraios and the patriarch Gregory. The **Hellenic Academy** faces colossal statues of Athena and Apollo on two Ionic columns and of the seated figures of Plato and Socrates.

Just beyond are the neo-Byzantine-style Eye Hospital, the Italianate Roman Catholic church (1870) of St Denis, the Western version of Dionysios the Areopagite (*see p. 99*). Opposite is the Bank of Greece. Beyond the Archaeological Society (founded 1837), **Schliemann's House** has an inscription on the loggia (ΙΛΙΟΥ ΜΕΛΑΘΡΟΝ: Palace of Troy). The attractively restored house now contains the Numismatic Museum's extensive collection of some 600,000 ancient and modern coins (*open Tues–Sun 8–2.30; T: 210 364 3774*).

At the northeast corner of Syntagma Square you turn left beside the Parliament into Leoforos Vasilissis Sofias, lined on the north with embassies and ministries. Above it, beyond Akadimias, the fashionable district of Kolonaki rises on the south slope of Lycabettus (*see p. 112*).

The museums of Vasilissis Sofias

The **Benaki Museum** (*open Mon, Wed, Fri 9–5; Thur 9–midnight; Sun 9–3; T: 210 922 6330; www.benaki.gr*), the former town house of the wealthy Benaki family, stands at the corner of Koumbari and Vas. Sofias. This irresistible museum houses a stunning collection of antiquities, textiles and costumes, manuscripts, icons and paintings. The wood-carved and painted reception room from two 18th-century Macedonian mansions, the collection of Greek costumes and the extensive collection of watercolours and memorabilia from the Greek War of Independence are particularly fine. The museum shop is excellent (as is the museum guide, on sale there). The café restaurant (which serves a Thursday-evening buffet) is first-rate; it would be easy to spend much of a visit to Athens in the Benaki.

The **Goulandris Museum of Cycladic and Ancient Greek Art** (*open Mon and Wed–Fri 10–4; Sat 10–3; T: 210 722 8321; www.cycladic-m.gr*), at the corner of Vas. Sofias and Odos Neofitou Douka, has Greece's most extensive collection of Cycladic art outside the National Archaeological Museum, including 230 figurines and stone and pottery vessels. The collection also includes objects from Antiquity through to the 6th century AD. Temporary exhibits are staged in the adjacent Neoclassical Stathatos mansion (1895), designed by the architect Ernst Ziller, who was responsible for many handsome 19th-century Athenian buildings. The mansion's conservatory is particularly fine.

Several blocks further along Vas. Sofias (*map p. 111*), on the opposite side of the road, are an improbable trilogy of museums: The Byzantine and Christian Museum,

The War Museum, and the National Picture Gallery. The **Byzantine and Christian Museum** (*open Tues–Sun 8.30–3; T: 210 721 1027*) occupies two large new (2003–04) partly-subterranean galleries, which flank the Villa Ilissia (the former museum, now used for temporary exhibits), which was built (1840–48) in what was then open countryside   for the eccentric, American-born Sophie de Marbois, Duchesse de Plaisance (1785–1854), who held a literary and artistic salon here. This is Greece's main museum of Byzantine antiquities, with a rich permanent collection. The museum's free guide to the exhibits does an excellent job of orientating the visitor and helping, in the guide's own words, to 'interpret and understand the Byzantine world'. Six display areas focus on the period from Antiquity to Byzantium, while another eight illustrate the Byzantine world itself. An exhibit on the post-Byzantine world is planned. Explanatory texts and labels show how ancient iconography (for example, a votive figure carrying a sheep for sacrifice) became Christian iconography (the Good Shepherd). Slides, photographs and drawings show where many objects on display were found and how they were used. 'Aspects of public and private life' illustrates daily life with objects of 'material culture' from pots and pans to portable icons.

A bit further along Vas. Sofias is the squat form of the **War Museum** (*open Sun–Mon 9–3, closed Tues; T: 210 729 0543*), which contains material illustrating Greek military activity from prehistoric times to the present day. The museum was built during the dictatorship of the Colonels (1967–74). The watercolours by Thalia Flora-Karavia (1871–1960) of the Balkan Wars and Asia Minor conflict are highly regarded.

Just off Vas. Sofias on Vas. Konstantinou and opposite the Hilton Hotel is the Ethniki Pinakothiki (**National Picture Gallery**), also known as the Alexandros Soutzos Museum (*open 9–3; closed Tues; T: 210 723 5857*). The collection is devoted mainly to 19th- and 20th-century Greek painting and sculpture. Under the directorship of Marina Lambraki-Plaka since 1992, the gallery has had a series of important special exhibits, including El Greco in 1995 and contemporary Greek artist Alekos Fasianos in 2004. In 2003, the gallery opened a branch, the National Sculpture Gallery, Alos Stratou, (entrance on Katehaki) in Athens' Goudi district (*information at the National Picture Gallery and on T: 210 723 5937*). The National Gallery also has plans to open regional branches, perhaps beginning with Nafplion.

Beyond the Hilton is the imposing **Megaron Mousikis** (Athens Concert Hall; *T: 210 729 0391*), which opened in 1992 and was expanded in 2004. Except in summer, when the Herodes Atticus theatre is used, most concerts take place here, and there are year-round exhibitions, as well as a book and music shop, café and restaurant.

KOLONAKI & LYCABETTUS
Map opposite
Metro: Syntagma/Evangelismos

Mount Lycabettus (Λυκαβηττός, pronounced Likavitòs; 277m) and the chic residential and shopping district of Kolonaki on its slopes, are approached from pedestrianized

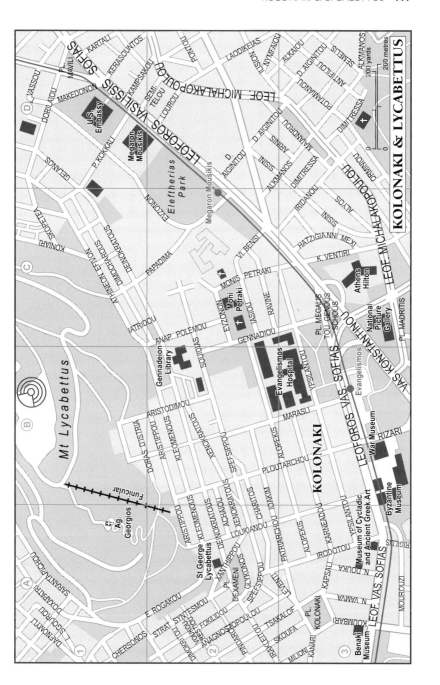

KOLONAKI & LYCABETTUS

Odos Voukourestiou off Panepistimiou, or any of the roads running uphill from Vas. Sofias. The ascent of the mountain (on foot from the southwest) takes c. 45mins from Syntagma Square, via Plateia Kolonaki and a stepped path from the top of Odos Loukianou. The easiest route is by the funicular railway (*usually runs 9am–midnight*), further east, at the top of Odos Ploutarchou. On a clear day, the view over Athens to the sea and mountains is spectacular.

Kolonaki is still Athens' most fashionable district, although stylish suburbs such as Kifissia offer competition. Plateia Kolonaki (officially Plateia Filikis Etaireias) takes its name from its small ancient column (*kolonaki*). Sometimes informally called 'Le Bidet', the square is flanked by cafés where the sound of tinkling ice is drowned out by the varied rings of customers' mobile phones (*kinito*, in Greek). It is not unusual for friends at adjacent tables to conduct lengthy conversations by cellphone. Around the square are Kolonaki's most stylish shops, many on pedestrianized Voukourestiou, and others on Tsakalof, Anagnostopoulou, Kanari, Milioni and Patriarchou Ioakim. Even the smallest side-street will have at least one boutique, with the bored shop assistant draped over her *kinito* and a window display with perhaps one perfect silk scarf snaked around a pair of killer stiletto heels. Kolonaki is also chock-a-block with galleries: The Athens Art Center (*Glykonos 4 and Dexameni; T: 210 721 3938*), Photohoros (*Tsakalof 44; T: 210 321 0448*), and Medussa (*Xenokratous 7; T: 210 724 4552*), are three to look for.

Kolonaki is also home to a number of embassies and foreign schools of archaeology: the British Embassy is on Ploutarchou and Vas. Sofias with the British Council library on Plateia Kolonaki. The American School of Classical Studies and the British School at Athens share a tennis court on Odos Skoufa. Nearby is the imposing Gennadeion Library, founded by the 20th-century diplomat Ioannis Gennadios (*usually open Mon–Sat 9–2: T: 210 721 0536*). The Gennadeion's collection has manuscripts and books focusing on Greek history and literature from the Byzantine to the present era, as well as some memorabilia of Lord Byron. Close by, to the southeast, is the formerly monastic Moni Petraki, now a theological seminary, and below is the large Evangelismos Hospital.

Dexameni and the route to Lycabettus

Several steep blocks above the northeast corner of Plateia Kolonaki is Plateia Dexameni. Here things are less frantic, less ostentatious, less dominated by the *jeunesse dorée*. Here children play, grandmothers sit in the sun, and families come to see films at the open air cinema. This is the site of the Roman *dexameni*, the reservoir of an aqueduct built by Hadrian. The reservoir was recommissioned in 1840 and subsequently restored. Here at Epiphany (6th January) the ceremony of the Blessing of the Waters takes place. Much-sought-after apartments and the stylish St George Lycabettus Hotel overlook the square, with views off toward the Acropolis and up to Mt Lycabettus itself.

Above the Dexameni you can get access (via Odos E. Rogakou) to the series of streets which provides a continuous route (known as the Periferiako Likavittou) round the mountain, and access to or from various points of the city. Near Dexameni

The conical peak of Lycabettus rises above the modern city.

also is the top of Odos Loukianou and the start of the zigzag path up the wooded slopes to the little 19th-century chapel of Aghios Georgios on the summit of Lycabettus, which provides a magnificent panorama of Athens and Attica. Sunsets are memorable. There is an expensive café on the summit and a less expensive café a five-minute stroll down the path that leads down from it.

BYZANTINE CHURCHES IN ATHENS

Little has survived of Byzantine Athens, beyond a number of small churches. Most are of the domed cross-in-square style, the dome usually octagonal and slender. The excellent Ministry of Culture publication *On the Trail of Byzantine Athens* (2001) outlines two walks to see the Byzantine monuments. The route it suggests is followed here, also with metro stops for individual churches.

The most important churches during the early Byzantine period occupied two ancient monuments: in the 5th century, the church of Megali Panaghia was built in the main reading room of Hadrian's Library; of this, virtually nothing remains. Some time around the 6th century the Parthenon became the Church of the Virgin of Athens (Panaghia Athiniotissa). The Temple of Hephaistos honoured St George. Ever fainter traces of the paint from a scene showing the *Annunciation* can be made out with binoculars to the south of the entrance to the Parthenon.

Byzantine Athens encircled the Acropolis, and occupied the areas of the Greek and Roman agoras, and this is where we find most of the surviving churches. The exterior decoration often more than repays a visit even when the churches are locked: many have elaborate cloisonné masonry; many are ornamented with dentil bands; several have handsome spolia built into their walls.

NB: The churches are most often open in the morning and early evening. As always, it is not appropriate to walk about in a church when a service is being conducted.

Kapnikarea (*Plateia Kapnikarea, Metro: Monastiraki. Map p. 82, B2*): This triple-apsed 11th–12th-century church has a charming exonarthex with three roofs. It has elaborate cloisonné masonry and some ancient blocks built into its walls. The paintings are mid-20th century. The name may honour the founder, possibly a tax-collector, or *kapnikarios*, who calculated the taxes on buildings by counting their chimneys.

Panaghia Gorgeopikoös (*Plateia Mitropoleos, Metro: Acropolis or Syntagma. Map p. 82, C2*): This 12th-century church with the lovely name of the 'Swift-Hearing' Virgin (also known as the Old Metropolis), stands in the shadow of Athens' metropolis. The exterior is a jigsaw-puzzle of ancient Greek and Roman spolia, many showing birds and animals, as well as marble taken from earlier Christian churches. Hetherington in his excellent *Byzantine and Medieval Greece* (1991) points out that although this was once the cathedral of Athens, its 'modest scale' was appropriate for the 'large village' that was the Byzantine city.

Russian Church (Sotira tou Lykodemou; *Odos Filellinon, Metro: Syntagma. Map p. 83, D3*): Once part of a monastery, the church was destroyed by the Turks in the 18th century. What

remained was converted into a Russian Orthodox church in the 19th century. As was not uncommon in those days, the Byzantine frescoes were not restored, but covered over by contemporary paintings and a bell-tower was added.

Sotira tou Kottaki (Saviour of Kottakis; *Odos Kidathinaion. Metro: Syntagma. Map p. 82, C3*): This 11th–12th-century church, with its delicate dome, was converted to the Russian Orthodox rite in the 19th century, and later re-established as a Greek Orthodox church.

Aghia Aikaterini (*Plateia Aghias Aikaterinas, Metro: Acropolis. Map p. 82, C4*): This 11th–12th-century church is flanked by the remains of a Roman peristyle. It is a popular church for summer weddings and shows signs of its 20th-century restoration.

Aghii Asomati (The Incorporeal Saints; *Odos Ermou, Metro: Monastiraki. Map p. 82, A2*): Built in the 11th century, and often rebuilt since then, this small church has considerable exterior architectural ornament, including stone crosses set into three walls.

Aghii Anargyri (Cosmas and Damian, the Penniless Saints; *Plateia Aghion Anargyron, Metro: Monastiraki. Map p.*

82, A1): This 11th-century church has a dome divided into two tiers and twin bell-towers. The 20th-century restoration work obliterated earlier frescoes.

Aghii Theodoroi (Saints Theodore; *Plateia Aghion Theodoron, Metro: Monastiraki or Omonia. Map p. 82, C1*): This 11th-century church has foundation inscriptions and ornamental brickwork. It stood on the outskirts of Byzantine Athens, in what was then countryside.

Aghios Ioannis O Theologos (St John the Theologian; *Erechtheos and Erotokritou, Metro: Acropolis. Map p. 82, B3*): The dome of this 11th–14th-century church is supported by columns topped by two Roman capitals. Hetherington suggests that one alone would not have given the desired height.

Interior of the church of Aghia Aikaterini.

Aghios Nikolaos Rangavas (*Prytaneiou and Epicharmou, Metro: Acropolis. Map p. 82, C3*): This 11th-century church with its side chapel was substantially enlarged over the years and heavily restored in the 20th century. It is unusually large, with two storeys and a sizeable gallery.

Metamorphosis tou Sotira (Transfiguration of the Saviour; *Odos Klepsydras, Metro: Acropolis. Map p. 82, B3*): The third church (dated from the 11th to the 14th centuries) on the slopes of the Acropolis), is one of Athens' smallest, sometimes nicknamed '*Sotirakis*' (Little Saviour). There are traces of the original cloisonné masonry, particularly in the drum of the dome.

Aghii Apostoloi Solaki (Holy Apostles of Solakis; *southeast corner of Agora, usually open as Agora. Metro: Thission, Monastiraki. Map p. 82, A3*): This 10th-century church may have been the private chapel of the Solakis family. The façade retains much of its original decoration (restored). Hetherington deems this the most distinguished of the Athenian churches, largely for its unusually spacious and light interior. Some of the 15th-century frescoes remain.

ATHENIAN DRAMA

It was in Athens in the late 6th or early 5th century BC that tragic drama was born. Its origins are obscure. One view is that when the border town of Eleutherai was incorporated into Athenian territory in the late 500s, the rituals accompanying its important festival to Dionysus, the god of wine and wild abandon, were brought to the city and re-enacted for the Athenians. There was a chanting chorus, from which emerged a spokesman who explained the myths involved. (The traditional Greek term for actor is *hypokritis*, which translates as 'interpreter'.) The spectacle involved the spokesman, or actor, and chorus reacting to each other. Then, in a new development, the playwright Aeschylus (525–456 BC) introduced the idea of another actor, so that the relationship between actors and chorus could mature.

After this the drama festivals took on a life of their own, developing interpretations of ancient myths other than the stories of Dionysus. In Athens there were two held each year. The winter festival, the *Lenea*, took place when it was impossible to travel, and so catered only for the city itself. The *Great Dionysia*, held in the summer, attracted enormous crowds from across the Greek world: an audience of some 14,000 with 1,200 actors and singers. It was excellent propaganda for Athens, and as part of the rituals the city's ten generals would be on show. Later in the 5th century, the tribute from the Athenian empire was formally presented to the city during the festival. The plays took place on a circular dancing floor, the *orchestra* (the original Greek word), behind which was the backdrop and changing-booth known as the *skene*, hence our English 'scene'. The space from which a display was watched was the *theatron*. By the 4th century, the whole complex was in stone and the semicircle of the *theatron* gave excellent acoustics. The resonance of the human voice was intensified by the clay masks the actors wore.

Each festival began with a series of dithyrambs, lyric poems sung by dancing choruses of boys and men. After that three poets would have been chosen each to produce a trilogy of tragedies, normally based on ancient myths of gods or heroes but whose storyline could be developed to provide dramatic effect. Aeschylus' trilogy the *Oresteia*, is an example—and happens to be the only one which survives in full. The first play, *Agamemnon*, tells the story of the return of the king of Argos from Troy. The audience knows he bears a terrible guilt: that he sacrificed his daughter Iphigeneia in order to obtain a fair wind for his fleet. His wife Clytemnestra has taken a lover, Aegisthus, and she murders Agamemnon on his return. In the second of the three plays, Agamemnon and Clytemnestra's son Orestes kills his mother and her lover in revenge for his father's death. The guilt passes down the generations until its climax in the final play, *Eumenides*, 'the Furies'. Orestes is pursued by the Furies, who represent his mother's ghost. He is brought before the goddess Athena, sitting as a judge in Athens, and it is she who rules that his retribution was fair. Aeschylus concludes by praising the security and justice of city government. He is known to have been sympathetic to the coming of democracy in Athens.

Aeschylus' pre-eminence as the founder of tragedy was challenged in 468 when first prize at the *Great Dionysia* was won by a playwright 30 years younger, Sophocles (496–406 BC). Although so much younger than his opponent, Sophocles seems more at home in an earlier, Archaic world where loyalties are to kin rather than to the city. Nevertheless, his individuals have greater depth than those of Aeschylus, and their flaws are not so glaring. The chorus plays a less pivotal role in the plots, and it is the unfolding of events over which the leading characters have no control which provides the tragedy. In *Antigone*, Antigone challenges the authority of Creon, king of Thebes, when she insists on burying the body of her brother, Polyneices, who has been killed attacking the city. According to ancient custom and the law of the gods, Creon orders her death: but then finds that she is engaged to his own son, who commits suicide, as does Creon's wife when she learns of this. He desperately tries to call off Antigone's execution, but she too has killed herself. The king is left isolated. Sophocles leaves the moral open. Could either Creon or Antigone have acted differently? Was there an inevitable clash between two systems of authority? Were all the characters simply the victims of circumstance? If one cannot avoid fate, how should one react? The moment of recognition of the inescapability of fate is one of Sophocles' main theatrical devices: he uses it again in his masterpiece, *Oedipus Rex*.

Three days of tragic trilogies must have left the audience gasping for some light relief, and it was fitting that the fourth day of the festival should have been devoted to comedy. Here the genius was Aristophanes (c. 450–385), an Athenian of aristocratic birth who took delight in mocking the pretensions of his fellow citizens. His plays are set in the contemporary world, and Athens' politicians and philosophers are ruthlessly lampooned. In *The Clouds*, the philosopher Socrates appears in a basket among the clouds, making the claim that rain and thunder come from them rather than from the gods. The play's central theme is that philosophers can prove anything and it is to them that one goes in order to make a bad case appear good. Aristophanes is imaginative and colourful. In *Lysistrata*, the women of Greece launch a sex strike to force their men to give up war, while in the wildly escapist *The Birds*, the birds prevent the smoke of sacrifices reaching the gods and so humans are forced to accept the birds' primacy.

Drama fulfilled many functions in ancient Athens. By using myth, the tragedians were able to present contemporary debates over war, the meaning of authority, the degree of respect due to the gods, in a controlled form. The comedies showed no such restraint; and it is a tribute to the maturity of Athenian democracy that it was able to contain such rumbustious attacks on its core values without falling apart at the centre. The legacy of drama, in both tragedy and comedy, is one of ancient Greece's major gifts to civilisation.   C.F.

PIRAEUS

Piraeus, now as in Classical times the port of Athens, occupies a peninsula some 9km from Athens itself. The modern town follows the rectangular plan of its ancient predecessor, whose visible remains are, however, scanty. The Great Harbour (*Megas Limani*) in the west part of the peninsula corresponds very nearly to the ancient *Kantharos* ('goblet'), which was divided between naval and commercial shipping. Today it is still Piraeus' main port. To the east is the smaller, circular Zea (or *Pasalimani*) harbour, where many of the swift island hydrofoils are based. Farther east, below the hill of Kastella (*Munychia*), is a yet smaller harbour, officially the Mikrolimano (Little Harbour), though you will also hear it called the *Tourkolimano* (Turkish harbour). It is home to the Piraeus yacht marina, the Naval College and a string of fish restaurants. The spine of the peninsula divides the modern town into the more fashionable quarter to the south and east, well supplied with restaurants, and a commercial sector surrounding the main harbour.

With its suburbs, Piraeus is the third largest city in Greece; different districts have heavy concentrations of immigrants from individual islands and regions of the mainland. Most visitors come here en route to or from the islands, fewer to take in its antiquities, almost none for its own rough charms, well-depicted in the 1960 movie *Never on Sunday*, which introduced Melina Mercouri to the non-Greek world.

HISTORY OF PIRAEUS

Piraeus gained importance as Athens' main harbour and naval base in the 5th century BC under Themistocles, who began construction of the famous Long Walls, sometimes called the 'Legs' (σκέλη), which linked Athens and the sea. The Themistoclean city wall guarded all three harbours; fortified entrances to each, forming part of the circuit, were probably closed by chains. The first or Northern Long Wall (7km) ran from Athens to Piraeus; the second or Phaleric Long Wall (6.5km) ran from Athens to the east end of Phaleron Bay, where the Athenians stored their triremes before the development of the Piraeus harbours. The walls were completed c. 456 BC. A third or Southern Long Wall, parallel with the first and the same length, was built by Callicrates under the direction of Pericles to guard against an enemy attempting a surprise landing in Phaleron Bay. The northern and southern Long Walls, starting from two points in the outer wall of the Piraeus, converged to within 183m of each other and then ran parallel to the region of the Pnyx Hill in Athens. Piraeus Avenue, the direct modern road from Athens to Piraeus, follows the Northern Long Wall for much of its course, while the Metro line follows the Southern Long Wall.

The rebuilding of the walls in the 4th century BC is usually credited to Konon (*Xenophon, Hellenica, IV, 8*). Though work started before his decisive victory over the Spartans at Cnidos in 394 BC, it was probably finished only after 346 (*Demosthenes XIX, 125*). The defences were shortened on the north side but the circuit was extended round the whole of the peninsula.

Under Pericles, Piraeus was laid out by the town planner Hippodamus of Miletus (*see box overleaf*) on a chess-board plan with a spacious agora at the centre. Boundary stones have been found. Ship-sheds were numerous and prominent and there were dry docks. The 4th-century BC politician Lycurgus constructed a naval arsenal in the harbour of Zea, designed by the architect Philo in 346–329 BC.

In the 5th century Piraeus had a cosmopolitan population consisting largely of metics, or resident aliens, who controlled much of its manufacture and trade. The opening scene of Plato's *Republic* is laid in Piraeus, at the house of the aged Cephalus. Piraeus was a Macedonian and Roman base and commercial centre. After Alaric's raid in 396 AD it declined. In medieval times the city was known as *Porto Leone* from the marble lion (probably purloined from Delos) that stood at the entrance to the Great Harbour; the Turks knew Piraeus as *Aslan-liman* ('lion harbour'). Resettled by islanders after 1834, it grew rapidly through the 19th century. The refugee influx of 1922 from Asia Minor further increased the population. In the Second World War the port was put out of action on the first night of the German air attack (6th April 1941), when ammunition ships blew up. After the war, Piraeus began a period of considerable expansion, as job-seekers poured in from around Greece. The city's politics are usually staunchly leftist.

HIPPODAMUS THE URBANIST

Hippodamus of Miletus in Asia Minor, the 5th-century BC thinker and geometrician, is often considered the father of town planning, and his name is commonly associated with the orthogonal, 'grid-iron' layout of streets and blocks, which was widely used in the ancient world and known as the 'Hippodamian plan'. The grid-plan design in fact long pre-dated Hippodamus, as can be seen in many of the 8th- and 7th-century BC Greek colonies founded in Sicily; Hippodamus' contribution was something different and more sophisticated. Aristotle (*Politics II, 5*), one of our principal sources of information about Hippodamus (describing even his elegant sense of dress), implies that his ideas were as much social and political as purely functional. On a practical level his logical division of a city facilitated movement and ventilation, and produced conveniently equal units of property; but it also gave rise to an important inter-relationship between social classes and land distribution, so that neighbourhoods could be designated to different social groups. Thus there were sacred, public and residential areas which related logically and functionally to one another; residential areas could be further organised with an appropriate social composition, while the artisans' areas could also be planned according to different jobs and tasks. In this way, heavy-duty trades producing effluent (eg tanners or metalworkers) might be placed at the exit of the town's drainage system, while cleaner trades took their place closer to the agora and administrative heart of the community. The design of any settlement was therefore viewed functionally, aesthetically and socially; it was also ascribed an optimum size of 10,000 inhabitants. Hippodamus is sometimes referred to by ancient writers as a *meteorologos*, or astronomer, and his theories of town planning may deliberately have reflected a higher ideal in their imitation of the order of the cosmos.

Four major undertakings are generally ascribed to Hippodamus: the laying out of Miletus; of Piraeus; of the Panhellenic colony of *Thurii* in southern Italy; and of the new city of Rhodes. We can only be certain of his part in two of them: Thurii and Piraeus. At Piraeus he had to contend with a special sort of settlement—a major trading and naval port—as well as with pre-existing temple sanctuaries which, by their nature, could not be moved. Archaeological evidence has not revealed the extent and nature of his plan here; but in its time it was highly influential, and the city's agora was commonly referred to as the *Hippodameia* in deference to its creator. The appeal of his model was so widely felt that it was sometimes applied in incongruous situations. The 4th-century BC town of (New) Priene in Asia Minor was given a rigorously Hippodamian plan in spite of its steep and irregular terrain: this resulted in the need for cumbersome terracing projects and the reduction of many streets to staircases. The value nonetheless of Hippodamus' ideas lay in their characteristically Greek application of logical theory to an area of human endeavour that would otherwise evolve in a chaotic and organic fashion.

N.McG.

Around the Great Harbour

At the heart of maritime Piraeus at the east angle of the Great Harbour stands the Dimarcheion, or Town Hall, in front of which is a clock, a local landmark ('*To Roloï*'). To the southwest is Akti Miaoulis, where cruise ships and international liners berth. It is named after Andreas Miaoulis (1769–1835), commander of naval forces during the War of Independence. Roughly where the old passenger terminal now stands, five ancient stoas lined the quay. From the Town Hall Leoforos Georgiou tou Protou leads shortly to the Tinan Gardens, laid out in 1854 by a French admiral. Opposite stands the 19th-century Aghia Triada Cathedral. Traces of the Emporion are visible in its foundations. On the corner of Odos Filonos in July 1959 was discovered the unique collection of bronze statuary now in the Piraeus Museum, perhaps part of Sulla's loot, after he conquered Greece, awaiting shipment to Rome. Just off Skilitsi, c. 90m east of Plateia Ippodamou, are the remains of the Asty Gate, where the *Hamaxitos*, or 'carriage-road', entered the city. Many neighbouring buildings incorporate Classical masonry from the Long Walls.

The broad Leoforos Iroōn Polytechniou leads southwest along the spine of the peninsula, between pleasant gardens. In the north block between Skouze and Filellinon, an archaeological park has Roman houses and shops of the 2nd–6th centuries AD.

To seaward of the lighthouse is a rock-hewn grave traditionally known as the Tomb of Themistocles, and a poros column (re-erected 1952) that marked the south entrance to the harbour. Here, too, is the Naval School, from where Akti Themistokleous follows the indented south shore of the peninsula. The Wall of Konon is visible in its lower courses, often supporting small tavernas, along Akti Themistokleous, south of the Naval College. A short section of the Wall of Themistocles also survives on Akti Themistokleous, southeast of the signal station (56m) which crowns the highest point of the peninsula.

Around Zea Harbour

In the Zea district is the **Archaeological Museum** (*Harilaou Trikoupi 31; open Tues–Sun 8.30–3; T: 210 452 1598*). Outstanding are the large-scale bronzes (upstairs), including the superb *Piraeus Kouros*, an *Athena* and an *Artemis*; fine Neoclassical reliefs of *Amazonomachia* from Kifissia, c. AD 200; and a massive funerary monument from Kallithea with relief (*Amazonomachia, Zoōmachia*) and free-standing commemorative sculptures, c. 400 BC. Beside the museum are the meagre remains of the Hellenistic Theatre of Zea.

Facing the sea on Akti Themistokleous, the **Hellenic Maritime Museum** (*open Tues–Sat 8.30–2, Sun 9–1; T: 210 451 6264*) is easily spotted by the guns, conning towers and torpedo tubes outside. Opposite the main entrance the building incorporates part of the Themistoclean wall. The museum has a wide range of model ships, from ancient triremes to modern warships. A model of the architect's complete design for the Arsenal of Philo (*see p. 119*), found in 1988, is on display. There are remains of the 196 ship-sheds that spread fan-wise around Zea Harbour in the basement of flats at the east end of the harbour (*sometimes open to public*). Remains of the ancient harbour walls are still present in the two short moles that mark off the present port.

Around Mikrolimano

The picturesque yacht basin of Piraeus' small harbour retains the form it had as the port of *Munychia*, the acropolis of ancient Piraeus. It was protected by two long moles, each ending in a lighthouse tower, and had slips for 82 triremes, of which some foundations can be seen under water to the north and south. The handsome Yacht Club of Greece (perhaps on the site of the Temple of Artemis Munychia) overlooks the harbour. It is a sign of the scantiness of the remains and the paucity of the literary texts that the location of Piraeus' two best-known sanctuaries—Artemis and Bendis—is uncertain. The harbour, which is usually packed with private yachts and sailing boats, is lined with the seafood restaurants that are popular weekend destinations for Athenians.

From the harbour, it is 20mins walk to The **Hill of Munychia** (85m), the ancient acropolis of Piraeus, which commands all three harbours and offers views of Phaleron Bay and the Saronic Gulf. The acropolis hill has been used as a military strongpoint in both ancient and modern times. The modern chapel of Aghios Ilias, near the summit, may occupy the site of a sanctuary to the Thracian god Bendis. About 90m west is the upper entrance to a flight of 165 steps, known as the Cavern of Arethusa, which leads to the stuccoed subterranean galleries that held the water supply of the citadel (65.5m deep). On the west slope of the hill (discovered in 1880, but now covered up) was the ancient Theatre of Dionysus referred to by Thucydides (*VIII, 93*). To the east is the Veakio, a modern open-air theatre.

PRACTICAL INFORMATION

NB: The Athens telephone code is 210.

GETTING AROUND

• **By air:** Eleftherios Venizelos International Airport is 27km southeast of Athens at Spata. The metro links the airport with central Athens in about 1hr; at present, there is a bus and taxi service, but no metro service between 1am and 5am. It is wise to allow a minimum of an hour for the taxi or metro journey from Athens to the airport and 2hrs for the bus journey. Flights on Olympic and Aegean Air depart from here for the Greek islands. For information, T: 210 353 0000; www.aia.gr

NB: Car hire companies levy a steep surcharge (at least 10%) if you collect your car at the airport rather than at their in-town offices.

• **By bus:** There are three stations for KTEL, the Greek national bus company. Buses to and from the Peloponnese and some destinations in Northern Greece use Terminal A, Kifissou 100 (T: 210 512 9233), off the road out of Athens towards Corinth. Terminal B (T: 210 831 7096), on Gousiou, just off Liossion, handles buses to and from Central Greece (including Delphi, Thebes and Meteora) and some destinations to the north and east of Athens. The Mavromation terminal on the corner of Patission and Alexandras, a few hundred metres north of the Archaeological Museum, handles buses for most destinations in Attica.

• **By rail:** Athens has two train stations: Trains from the south and west arrive at the Peloponnese station (Stathmos Peloponnisou; T: 210 513 1601), northwest of Omonia Square on Sidirodromion. Trains from the north arrive at Larissa station (Stathmos Larissis; T: 210 529 8837), just across the tracks from the Peloponnese station on Deligianni. The nearest metro stop for the train stations is Larissa. For train times, T: 145 or 147 or go to www.ose.gr

Train tickets are available at the train stations and at the Omonia Square ticket office, Karolou 1 (T: 210 524 0647) and at Filellinon 17, off Syntagma Square (T: 210 323 6747).

• **By metro:** Athens has an efficient underground network. Maps are available at most metro stops. Tickets are sold at all stations and must be validated in machines in the station before you reach the platforms. Keep the ticket until you end your journey. Metro and bus tickets are not interchangeable (though that may change). Trains currently run from 5am–midnight, but a 24-hour service is being considered. Information on the metro is available at www.ametro.gr

• **By taxi:** Taxis are good value in Athens, but seldom easy to snare on the street. It is not uncommon for a taxi to take a number of passengers going to separate destinations in the same area. The best way to ensure getting a taxi when you really need one is to ask your hotel to call one for you. It's a good idea to check that the meter is turned on and set to 1, unless it is between midnight and 5am, when the meter will be set at 2 (double fare). There are a lot of radio taxi companies in Athens; their phone numbers are prone to change: check the daily listing in the 'Your Guide' section of the *Athens News*. Some established companies include Athina (T: 210 921 7942), Express (T: 210 993 4812), Parthenon (T: 210 532 3300), and Piraeus (T: 210 418 2333).

NB: Because the airport is such a long way from town, taxis can be reluctant to go there. If you have a plane to catch, book your cab in advance.

• **By sea:** Piraeus, Athens' main seaport, is 15–30mins by metro. Piraeus has three harbours: international ships and most island ferries dock at Megas Limani (the main harbour); most hydrofoils use Zea Limani; Mikrolimani (also called Turkolimani) is primarily a yacht marina. For boat times, T: 171 or 1441, or the Piraeus Port Authority T: 210 451 1311 to –1317. The *Athens News* (published on Fri) and the *Kathimerini* insert in the *International Herald Tribune* print major ferry schedules, as do most Greek newspapers. There are ticket agencies on the quay of Piraeus' main harbour.

INFORMATION OFFICE

The main office of the Greek National Tourist Office (EOT or GNTO) is at Tsochas 7, Ambelokipi, (T: 210 870 0000; www.gnto.gr), well out of central Athens. There is a subsidiary office at Amalias 26 (though it may close).

WHERE TO STAY

Most hotels in Athens are clean and acceptably comfortable. Few—with some notable exceptions, such as the Grande Bretagne—are charming. Most visitors will want to be in central Athens, either near Syntagma Square or the Plaka, and this list of suggestions has been compiled with that in mind. Exceptional hotels that are further afield are also included.

€€€ **Andromeda**. Athens' first serious boutique hotel has proved that location isn't everything. Situated well out of the centre of town in an affluent residential neighbourhood, it offers genuine quiet, genuinely helpful staff, and genuine elegance in the decor. Good in-house restaurant. 42 rooms. *Timoleontos Vassou 22 (off Plateia Mavili), T: 210 643 7302, www.andromedahotels.gr. Map p. 111, D1.*

€€€ **Hotel Eridanus**. One of Athens' new boutique hotels, in the newly trendy Gazi district (15mins walk from Omonia or Syntagma Squares). The superb (and expensive) fish restaurant Varoulko is next door. 38 rooms. *Piraeus 78, T: 210 520 5360, www.eridanus.gr. Map p. 104, A1.*

€€€ **Grande Bretagne**. The legendary Grande Bretagne, one of Athens' most distinguished 19th-century buildings, is back after a $70-million renovation. Ask for a room with a balcony overlooking Syntagma Square, the Parliament building, and the Acropolis. You may never leave your balcony—except to go to the hotel pool. 328 rooms. *Syntagma Square, T: 210 333 000, www.grandebretagne.gr. Map p. 83, D2.*

€€€ **St George Lycabettus Hotel**. Popular with Athenians throwing elegant parties and splashy weddings, this is the best hotel in the Kolonaki district, which has Athens' best shops and many fine restaurants. Most rooms have views either of the Acropolis or of Mount

Lycabettus. The in-house restaurants are destinations in themselves for locals. 167 rooms. *Kleomenous 2, T: 210 729 0711, www.sglycabettus.gr. Map p. 111, A2.*

€€ **Acropolis View Hotel**. A moderately priced hotel south of the Acropolis on a residential sidestreet not far from the Herodes Atticus theatre. Small but nicely decorated rooms. 32 rooms. *Rovertou Galli and Webster 10, T: 210 921 7303. Map p. 82, A4.*

€€ **Athens Cypria**. A wonderfully convenient central location just off Syntagma Square. A handful of rooms have Acropolis views. 71 rooms. *Diomeias 5, T: 210 323 8034. Map p. 82, C2.*

€€ **Central**. Central by name and by location, in the busy Plaka district. Small rooms, but minimalist decor and light colours give a sense of space. Rooftop terrace. Good breakfasts. 84 rooms. *Apollonos 2, T: 210 323 4357, www.centralhotel.gr. Map p. 82, C3.*

€€ **Electra Palace**. On a relatively quiet Plaka street, the seven-floor Electra has a very welcome rooftop swimming pool, views of the Acropolis from the top two floors, and an acceptable restaurant. 106 rooms. *Nikodimou 18, T: 210 324 1401 or 210 324 1407. Map p. 82, C3.*

€€ **Fresh Hotel**. A new Athenian boutique hotel, with a popular bar (Orange), and minimalist décor in the bedrooms. Near Omonia Square and the Athens Central Market. 133 rooms. *Sofokleous 6, T: 210 524 8511, www.freshhotel.gr. Map p. 82, B1.*

€€ **Jason Inn Hotel**. On an undistinguished street, but just a few blocks from the Agora, the Plaka, and the trendy Psiri district. This is an excellent value hotel with helpful staff. 57 rooms. *Aghion Asomaton 12, T: 210 325 1106,*

www.douros-hotels.com. Map p. 104, C1.

€€ **Plaka**. An excellent Plaka location on a relatively quiet sidestreet, and Acropolis views from some 5th- and 6th-floor rooms more than compensate for the small rooms and cramped lobby. 67 rooms. *Mitropoleos and Kapnikareas 7, T: 210 322 2096, www.plakahotel.gr. Map p. 82, B2.*

€ **Art Gallery Hotel**. Old-fashioned atmosphere in a former Athenian town house, south of the Acropolis. Popular with academics. 22 rooms. *Erechtheiou 5, Koukaki, T: 210 923 8376, ecotec@otenet.gr. Map p. 82, B4.*

€ **Hotel Carolina**. A popular choice for those on a budget, the Carolina (5mins walk from Syntagma Square) upgraded its rooms recently. 31 rooms. *Kolokotroni 55, T: 210 324 3551, hotelcarolina@galaxynet.gr. Map p. 82, C2.*

€ **Nefeli Hotel**. Flanked by a quiet (except when there are illegal motorcycles) pedestrianized street, the Nefeli has small but characterful rooms and an excellent location. 18 rooms. *Iperidou 16, T: 210 322 8044. Map p. 82, C3.*

WHERE TO EAT

You can get everything from sushi to souvlakia in Athens. Many restaurants are crowded with tourists before 10pm and have a largely Greek crowd later in the evening. Despite the commercialisation of the Plaka district, there are still some excellent traditional restaurants here. NB: many restaurants do not accept credit cards and many are closed on Sundays and in August.

€€€ **Aegli**. Flanked by an open-air cinema, in the Zappeion Gardens, the

Aegli has an elegant French-style menu, often including foie gras, oysters, steak, profiteroles, and yoghurt crème brûlée. A great spot for people-watching and gluttony. *Zappeion Gardens (adjacent to the National Gardens fronting Vas. Amalias), T: 210 336 9363. Reservations recommended. Map p. 83, D3.*

€€€ **Daphne's**. Both the food and the décor are charming and elegant in this 19th-century Neoclassical former town house with a lovely garden in the heart of the Plaka. Evenings only. *Lysikratous 4. T: 210 322 7971. Reservations recommended. Map p. 82, C4.*

€€€ **Spondi**. *Athinorama*, the weekly review of the Athenian scene, has chosen Spondi, in the Pangrati district of Athens, several years running as the best place in town. Excellent fresh fish and a wide range of other dishes featuring innovative modern Greek cooking. *Pyrronos 5, Pangrati (beyond the Stadium), T: 210 752 0658. Reservations recommended. Beyond map p. 83, F4.*

€€€ **Varoulko**. After years in the Piraeus, now in a new location (with a wonderful Acropolis view), Varoulko still serves up the best fish in town, as well as some meat dishes, such as sweetbreads and a tasty goat stew. *Piraeus 80, T: 210 522 8400, www.varoulko.gr. Reservations necessary (several days in advance). Map p. 104, A1.*

€€ **Filippou**. A long time favourite, this traditional taverna continues to serve excellent food at reasonable prices in the heart of fashionable Kolonaki. *Xenokratous 19, T: 210 721 6390. Map p. 111, B2.*

€€ **Ideal**. The oldest restaurant in the heart of Athens, today's Ideal has an Art Deco décor and lots of hearty old

favourites, from egg-lemon soup to lamb with spinach. *Panepistimiou 46, T: 210 330 3000. Reservations recommended. Map p. 83, D2.*

€€ **Ouzeri Kouklis**. Tiny tables, good atmosphere, always full of young people. A wide variety of good *mezedes*, and particularly delicious barrel wine from Santorini. *Odos Tripodon 14, T: 210 324 7605. Map p. 82, C3.*

€€ **Platanos Taverna**. The Platanos has been serving good home cooking since 1932 to locals and visitors alike. There are tables both indoors and outside under the plane tree which gives this Plaka restaurant its name. *Diogenous 4, T: 210 322 0666. Map p. 82, B3.*

€€ **To Kafeneio**. The place in Kolonaki to try artichokes *à la polita*, leeks in crème fraiche and watch the ladies who lunch. A pleasant place to relax after visiting the nearby Benaki and Goulandris museums. *Loukianou 26, T: 210 722 9056. Map p. 111, A3.*

€€ **To Ouzadiko**. A perpetually crowded Kolonaki ouzo bar with more than 40 kinds of ouzo and at least that many *mezedes* (appetisers) from which it's easy to make a light or substantial meal. *Karneadou 25–29 (in the Lemos International Shopping Centre), T: 210 729 5484. Reservations recommended. Map p. 111, B3.*

€€ **To Prytaneion**. One of the finest of Kolonaki's ouzo and *mezedes* places, where you can have a wide range of nibbles, including beef carpaccio, shrimp in fresh cream, as well as traditional staples. *Milioni 7, T: 210 364 3353. Map p. 111, A3.*

€€ **Vlassis**. Amazingly reasonable prices for delicious *paradisiako* (traditional) cooking. In a residential neighbourhood out of central Athens, Vlassis is not easy to find, and you may want to take a taxi. *Paster 8 (off Plateia Mavili), T: 210 646 3060. Reservations recommended. Just beyond map p. 111, D1.*

€ **Damigos** (The Bakaliarakia). This basement taverna on one of Plaka's busiest streets has served delicious deep-fried codfish and eggplant, as well as a variety of roasts and chops, since 1865. The wine comes from Attic vineyards owned by the family. The *skordalia* (garlic sauce) is memorable. Damigos is usually closed July–Sept. Evenings only. *Kidathinaion 41, T: 210 322 5084. Map p. 82, C3.*

€ **Diporto**. A working man's café in the Athens Central Market serves up delicious *revithia* (chickpeas), salads, and stews. *Central Market, Athinas. No phone. Map p. 82, B1.*

€ **Papandreou**. Another famous small café in the Central Market, this one specialising in tripe dishes. *Central Market, Athinas, T: 210 321 4970. Map p. 82, B1.*

€ **Thanasis**. Some of the best *souvlakia* in town, served up at indoor and outdoor tables and available to take away. This Monastiraki restaurant is always crowded, especially at weekends. *Mitropoleos 69, T: 210 324 4705. Map p. 82, B2.*

SHOPPING & MARKETS

There are four main areas of interest for most shoppers in Athens. Monastiraki has a famous flea market, which is especially lively on Sunday. A great deal of what is for sale here is junk, but there are real finds in old postcards and prints of Athens and, occasionally, old copper and wood carvings. Athens'

Central Market on Odos Athinas is the place to get honey, olives, and herbs from all over Greece—and to see the market that supplies much of the meat and cheese that Athenians eat.

There are several distinctively Greek items to keep an eye out for in Athens: first, Korres cosmetics and skin care products. Korres is sold at Liberty and at its own shop on the King's Road in London, but prices are better and the selection is wider in the many pharmacies stocking Korres in Athens. Second, the reproduction ancient and Byzantine jewellery carried at the Zolotas and LALAoUNIS stores is very well crafted. There's a Zolotas at Panepistimiou 10, and a LALAoUNIS nearby at Panepistimiou 6.

BOOKSHOPS & LOCAL GUIDES

The most comprehensive bookshop in Athens is the main branch of Eleftheroudakis, at Panepistimiou 17. This shop covers eight floors and has a wide selection of books on Greece in English, and a wide section of CDs of Greek music. It also has a café. Other bookshops with good selections in English include Compendium, Nikis 28; Reymondos, Voukourestiou 18; Folia tou Bibliou (The Book Nest), Panepistimiou 25–29; Rombos, Kapsali 6, off Plateia Kolonaki.

Good books on Athens include Mary Beard's lively monograph *The Parthenon*; Kevin Andrews's *Athens* and his anthology *Athens Alive*; Nick Papandreou's autobiographical novel, *My Father Dancing*; the anthology *Athens: The Collected Traveler* (ed. Barrie Kerper), and John Freely's superb *Strolling Through Athens*.

The most important festival in Athens—and in Greece—is the Hellenic Festival (also known as the Athens or the Greek Festival), which usually runs from June–Sept. Many performances of music and of ancient and modern theatre are held at the Odeion of Herodes Atticus on the slopes of the Acropolis. Schedules and tickets are usually available at the Hellenic Festival Office, Panepistimiou 39 (in the arcade; *T: 210 928 2900; www.hellenicfestival.gr*). If available, tickets can be purchased at the Herodes Atticus theatre (*T: 210 323 2771 or 210 323 5582*) several hours before the performance.

The Athens International Dance Festival stages contemporary and experimental dance performances during the first two weeks in July at the Technopolis arts complex, Piraeus 100, in the district of Gazi. (*information on T: 210 346 1589 or 210 346 7322*).

Important religious festivals and observations in Athens include Epiphany (6 January), the pre-Lenten Carnival, and Good Friday (movable feasts; also bear in mind that Orthodox Easter falls differently from the Western Easter).

Athens has a lively year-round music and theatre scene. The weekly magazine *Athinorama* has an extensive calendar of events. Some highlights include: the Megaron Mousikis Concert Hall, Leoforos Vas. Sofias 89 (*T: 210 729 0391 or 210 728 2333*). The season runs autumn–spring. Tickets are available either at the Megaron itself or at its kiosk in the Spiromillios Arcade, Stadiou 4. The Greek National Opera performs at Olympia Theatre, Akadimias 59, at Mavromichali (*T: 210 361 2461*). The summer months are usually off-season. The Dora Stratou Folk Dance Theatre gives performances of traditional Greek folk dances on Filopappos Hill from May –Sept. Tickets are available at the box office at Scholiou 8, Plaka (*open 8–2; T: 210 924 4395*) and at the theatre itself before performances.

A 45-minute *son-et-lumière* show on the Pnyx most nights from April–Oct dramatises the story of much of Athens' history. Tickets from the Hellenic Festival Office, Panepistimiou 39 (*T: 210 928 2900*), or at the entrance to the show.

There are a number of spots in Athens where you can hear *rembetika*, often called the music of the urban poor and dispossessed. This music—often songs of thwarted love, with lots of *bouzoukia* sounding in the background—became popular in the 1920s and remains popular to this day. Some places to hear *rembetika* in Athens include the Stoa Athanaton, Sofokleous 18; the Rebetika Istoria, Ippokratous 181; Perivoli Ouranou, Lysikratous 19; Taximi, Isavron 29.

A diminishing number of open-air cinemas remain in Athens. Some of the nicest are Dexameni in Plateia Dexameni, Kolonaki; Cine Paris, on Kidathinaion in the Plaka; Thission on Apostolou Pavlou. Most shows begin after 9pm.

Banks: There are branches of most important Greek banks, including the

National Bank of Greece, on Syntagma Square. Many banks have ATMs which one can use from outside the bank after hours. NB: Many ATMs are not stocked during bank strikes, so it is not a bad idea to travel with some extra cash or travellers cheques.

Emergencies: Tourist Police: The tourist police can be reached on T: 171; the Police are on T: 100; SOS Doctor is on T: 210 331 0310. The KAT emergency hospital in the suburb of Kifissia (T: 210 801 4411) and Asklepion Voulas in Voulas (T: 210 895 3416) have 24-hour emergency services.

Embassies: United Kingdom, Ploutarchou 1 (T: 210 723 6211); United States, Leoforos Vas. Sofias 91 (T: 210 721 2951).

Post Office: The main branch of the Post Office is on Syntagma Square.

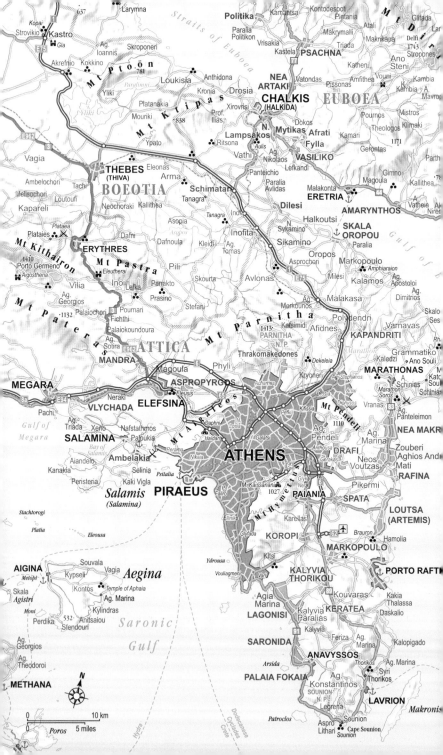

ATTICA

The name Attica ('Ἀττική) derives from the Greek *aktì*, a promontory or peninsula, literally 'the place where the waves break'. Geographically it is a roughly triangular peninsula which ends in Cape Sounion; its base, c. 50km wide, is the almost continuous mountain barrier from the bay of Aigosthena, in the west, to the channel of Euboea, in the east. This consists of the ranges of Pateras, Kithairon, and Parnitha and the coastal hills of Mavrovouni. This barrier formed the ancient boundary between Attica and Boeotia, with disputed areas around the three passes: the Megarid, Eleutherai, and Diakria. Possession of Salamis and the Megarid secured the western approaches, which are effectively cut off from the Peloponnese by the great Geraneia range. Athens itself, protected by the inner ring of Aigaleos, Pentelicon (Pendeli), and Hymettus, but connected by easy roads with the plains beyond, is the natural centre of the region. Many of the Attic mountains, in the time of Pausanias crowned by images of the gods, are now surmounted by ugly radar stations, with restricted access to their summits.

EXPLORING ATTICA

Until recently, it was possible to take day trips from Athens into the pastoral Attic countryside, with its rich vineyards and coastal hamlets such as Vouliagmeni and Glyfada. Today, much of Attica has become a sprawling dormitory suburb for Athens. The efficient and admirable new highway system that links the Eleftherios Venizelos International Airport with Athens, and Athens with north, south, and central Greece, has chopped up much of Attica. Nonetheless, there is much to be seen here.

South to Vouliagmeni

The road south from Piraeus leads first through Palaio Faliro, the old port of ancient Athens, and then through Glyfada, the spot where St Paul is supposed to have landed, on his way to evangelise the Athenians. Vouliagmeni (Βουλιαγμένη), long the most fashionable seaside resort in Attica, sits on a three-tongued promontory, the seaward end of the Hymettus range. In Antiquity it was known as Cape Zoster ('belt'): it was here that Leto unloosed her girdle before the birth of Apollo and Artemis. Vouliagmeni today is famous for its lake of warm, green water enclosed by sheer limestone rocks. The brackish, sulphurous waters help cases of rheumatism, neuritis, arthritis, and skin diseases. The overflow from the lake runs underground to the sea and bubbles up from the sea bottom, raising its temperature for some distance. The fine sandy beaches enclosed by the three headlands are open all year, but the sea here is more often than not polluted.

The Monastery of Kaissariani

Usually open sunrise to sunset, except Mon; T: 210 723 6619.
The visit to the important 11th-century Monastery of Kaissariani (Μονή Καισσαριανῆς)

takes in some of the remaining countryside on the wooded slopes of **Mount Hymettus** (modern Imittòs; Ὑμηττός; 1027m) famous for its sunset glow, its marble, its wild flowers and honey. The violet colour which now, as in Antiquity, suffuses Hymettus at sunset, is peculiar to the mountain and has been much praised by poets, including Ovid, who mentioned its '*purpureos colles*' (violet hills). The monastery sits 341m up Mt Hymettus, at the end of a ravine, surrounded by cypress, pine and plane trees. There have been shrine here since pagan times, commemorating the source of the Ilissos river.

On the brow of the hill just above the monastery is a famous fountain, known in ancient times as *Kyllou Pera*; its waters were supposed to cure sterility. There was a temple of Aphrodite nearby and the spot was made famous by Ovid in his *Ars Amatoria* ('near where his purple head Hymettus shows, and flow'ring hills, a sacred fountain flows'; *Book III*), in the story of Cephalus and Procris, a tragic tale of jealousy and revenge, murder and retribution. The spring supplied Athens with much of its drinking water before the construction of the Marathon Dam. It feeds a fountain on the outside east wall of the monastery where the water gushes from a ram's head (only a cast is there now; the Archaic original is in the Acropolis Museum). Fragments built into the walls belong to an earlier Christian basilica, probably of the 5th century.

The church and convent buildings

The present building is first mentioned in the 12th century. The name is sometimes thought to be derived from Caesarea, perhaps the source of its original icon. In 1458 when the Sultan Mehmet II visited newly conquered Athens, the Abbot of Kaissariani was chosen to deliver up to him the keys of the city, in recognition of which the convent was exempted from taxation by the Turks. During the Second World War the secluded ravine was used by the Germans for the execution of hostages, subject of a popular song. The monastery was restored in 1956–57; the church is still a focus of pilgrimage on Ascension Day, but no longer a working convent.

The conventual buildings (*entered from the far side*), grouped round a pretty court, include a mill and bakery, and a bath-house, now restored after use as an oil-press. The refectory has a finely moulded Roman lintel over the door and a domed kitchen. The church, built of stone with brick courses, is in the form of a Greek cross. The dome is supported on Roman columns. The parecclesion (dedicated to St Anthony) was added in the 16th century, the narthex in the 17th century, and the belfry in the 19th. The frescoes, apart from those by Ioannis Ypatos (Peloponnesian, 1682) in the narthex, are in a 17th–18th-century Cretan style.

SOUNION

Usually open 9am to sunset; T: 22920 39363.

The township of Sounion (Σούνιον), standing at the head of a bay of the same name, where regattas were held in honour of Poseidon, was famously wealthy in Classical times. After defeating the Persians at the battle of Salamis, the Athenians dedicated a captured Phoenician ship here (one of three; *Herodotus VIII, 121*). The famous temple, built above the sea on the remains of an earlier structure, reasonably enough honoured the god of the sea. Because of the promontory's strategic importance, the Athenians fortified it during the Peloponnesian War and, in 413 BC (*Thucydides VIII, 14*), the entire headland was enclosed, the promontory forming the citadel.

The Temple of Poseidon

The Temple of Poseidon at Cape Sounion stands on one of the most visited sites in Greece: a low isthmus separates the sandy and exposed bay of Sounion from the mainland. The temple stands at the end of the isthmus, 60m above the sea. This is a very popular excursion, especially at sunset, when it virtually sags under the weight of tourists, many searching for Lord Byron's name, which the poet carved into a portico column. The visitor wishing to resonate to Byron's experience of 'Sunium's marbled steep, Where nothing save the waves and I may hear our mutual murmurs sweep' should visit the site out of season and in the morning. On Sundays and towards sunset it is overrun by coach parties.

The temple stands near the edge of the cliff, and forms a conspicuous landmark from the sea: this was the last of Attica Athenians saw as they sailed east; the first sight of home on their return voyage. From a distance it presents a dazzlingly white appearance that proves illusory at closer hand: the columns are of grey-veined marble quarried at Agrileza (5km north by an ancient road), where bases of columns of the same dimensions can still be seen. The attribution to Poseidon was confirmed by an inscription.

On stylistic grounds, Professor William Dinsmoor, the dean of Classical architectural experts, ascribed the design of the temple to the architect of the Temple of Hephaistos at Athens, with a date of c. 444 BC. It stands on the foundations of an earlier structure in poros stone, founded shortly before 490 BC and unfinished at the time of the Persian invasion.

The Doric peristyle had 34 columns (6 by 13), resting on a stylobate of 31.1m by 13.4m. Nine columns remain on the south side and six (four re-erected in 1958–59) on the north side, with their architraves. The columns are unusual in having only 16 instead of the normal 20 flutes. The sculptural arrangement also departed from the normal custom, an Ionic frieze lining all four sides of the interior space in front of the pronaos (cf. the Hephaisteion). The external metopes were left blank (perhaps because of the exposed nature of the site); the pediments, which were sculptured, had a raking cornice with a pitch of 12.5° instead of the more usual 15°.

The interior had the usual arrangement of pronaos, cella, and opisthodomos. Both pronaos and opisthodomos were distyle in antis. There survive only the north anta of the pronaos, with its adjacent column, and the south anta, which was reconstructed in 1908.

Thirteen slabs of the frieze, in Parian marble, stand to the east of the approach path. The sculpture, much eroded, is believed to illustrate a contest of Lapiths and Centaurs, the *Gigantomachia*, and exploits of Theseus (cf. the Hephaisteion).

Cape Sounion and the Temple of Poseidon.

The view from the temple over the sea is justly famous. To the east lies Makronisos; about 11km south the rocky island of Aghios Georgios, the ancient *Belbina*. The nearest islands to the southeast are Kea, Kythnos, and Seriphos, to the south of which, on a clear day, even Melos (where the Venus de Milo was found) can be made out. To the west is Aegina, in the centre of the Saronic Gulf.

Lavrion and Thorikos

The lively town of Lavrion (Λαύριον), north of Sounion along the east coast, owes its existence to its mines, which operated from ancient times until the 1970s. The productive measures of silver here were in the possession of Athens, and it is to them that the city owed its commercial greatness: Athenian silver coinage (the 'owls of Athena') had prestige all over the world. By the time of Pericles the mining industry here had reached the peak of its prosperity, and began to decline thereafter. Conditions under which the slaves worked the mines were famously dangerous and harsh, and slaves were constantly trying to escape. It is interesting to note that nearby Sounion was known for its lenient treatment of runaway slaves; the inhabitants were frequently prepared to harbour them, and would often enfranchise them without question.

Today there is a small mineralogy museum in Lavrion, housed in an old 19th-century metal-washing house (*open Tues–Sun 8–3; T: 22920 25295*).

North of Lavrion are the remains of the ancient city of *Thorikos* (*open Mon 12–7, Tues–Sun 8–7 in summer; Tues–Sun 8.30–3 in winter*), home of King Cephalus, who married and then murdered Procris. The ruins include a Mycenaean acropolis with tholos tombs, and the 6th-century BC theatre (unusual because elliptical rather than circular).

THE SANCTUARY OF ARTEMIS AT BRAURON

Brauron (Vravròna; Βραυρώνα), near Porto Rafti, famous for its retsina both in Antiquity and today, is situated in the broad and marshy valley of the subterranean Erasinos c. 1.5km from the sea. This delightful site, shaded by trees, with both pagan and Christian shrines, has an excellent small museum as well as the remains of the Sanctuary of Artemis Brauronia. The site, near the late Byzantine chapel of Aghios Georgios, is reasonably well signposted. Flooding makes it quite damp, something to keep in mind when choosing footwear.

HISTORY OF BRAURON

Brauron is one of the twelve ancient communities known to have existed before Attica was united. Tradition relates that Iphigeneia brought to Brauron the image of Artemis which she and Orestes stole from Tauris (*Euripides, Iphigeneia in Tauris, 1446–67*). In one version she is virtually identified with the goddess and performs the ritual sacrifice of her brother; in another she herself dies at Brauron. A wooden image was taken by the Persians from Brauron to Susa.

In Classical times the savage rites, perhaps involving ritual sacrifice, had been moderated, and Artemis was worshipped in her function as protectress of childbirth. The Brauronia was a ceremony held every four years, in which Attic girls between the ages of five and ten, clad in saffron robes, performed rites which included a dance where they were dressed as bears (*cf. Aristophanes, Lysistrata, 645*). The connection between bears, childbirth and Artemis recalls the legend of Callisto: in one version of the story, the nymph Callisto, a virgin follower of Artemis, is seduced by Zeus and turned into a bear by Artemis for breaking her vow of chastity. The bear later bears Zeus a son. The purpose of the Brauron ritual remains mysterious, however. In the late 4th century BC the site suffered from flooding and by the time of Claudius it was deserted.

The site

Sanctuary usually open 9–3; T: 22990 27020.
Beyond the chapel a small shrine marked the entrance to a cavern, the roof of which fell in the 5th century BC. This seems to have been venerated in Archaic times as the Tomb of Iphigeneia. Other tombs probably belong to priestesses of Artemis.

Excavations, carried out with difficulty in the waterlogged valley by the Greek Archaeological Society under John Papadimitriou in 1946–52 and 1956–63, show occupation since Middle Helladic times (earliest on the hill above). On the lower ground, discovered in 1958, are the remains of a Doric temple of the 5th century BC, measuring c. 20m by 10m, the foundations of which stand on rock-hewn steps (possibly the 'holy stairs' mentioned by Euripides). Here were discovered dedicatory reliefs in coloured terracotta, bronze mirrors, and votive jewellery. Many of these had been deposited in a sacred pool (now dry) below the temple.

Adjoining the temple is a huge Π-shaped stoa, built before 416 BC, in which have been found inscriptions recording it to be the 'parthenon' of the *arktoi*, or bears. It had nine dining-rooms (remains of tables and dining couches). Part of the colonnade (note the tall pillars which would have supported votive reliefs) and entablature was re-erected in 1962. Just to the west is a remarkable stone bridge of the same period. Inscriptions record other buildings (gymnasium, palaestra, stables etc) which have not been found.

THE SANCTUARY OF ARTEMIS BRAURONIA

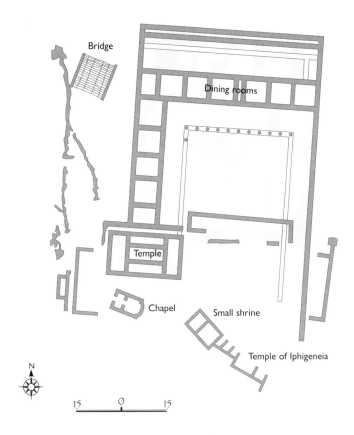

The museum
Labels throughout in Greek and English; site guide and guide to Attica usually on sale.
The large, well-arranged site museum (not in the enclosure with the antiquities, but around the next bend of the road) has marble statues and heads of little girls and of boys, also very fine 4th-century marble reliefs. There are numerous dedicatory offerings from the sanctuary: vases, figurines, mirrors, jewellery, etc. Models reconstruct the appearance of the site. Here also are Geometric finds from the surrounding countryside, including Anavyssos, and important late Helladic pottery from Perati.

THE VORRES MUSEUM

Usually open weekends 10–2; weekdays by appointment; T: 210 664 2520;
www.culture.gr
The town of Paiania (Παιανία), some 25km from Brauron on the other side of
the airport, is the home of the Vorres Museum, founded by Greek magnate Ion
Vorres. The museum specialises in 20th- and 21st-century Greek art, although
it also has some fine 19th-century paintings and sculpture. The collection is
housed in Vorres's villa and its gardens.

MARATHON

The Plain of Marathon extends in a crescent shape around the bay of the same name.
On the landward side it is shut in by stony mountains, which make up for their moderate height by rising abruptly from the plain. The ancient town, one of four administratively linked townships, was the birthplace of Herodes Atticus (*see p. 108*), who
had estates here, and is thought to have been buried in the vicinity. Though many
archaeological discoveries have been made on the plain, Marathon is chiefly famed for
the great battle fought in 490 BC, when a small Greek force halted the massive Persian
advance. As every Greek schoolchild still knows, the victory at Marathon allowed
Greek democracy to flourish and become an example to the rest of the world. This is
a place of pilgrimage for Greeks and many others, a sacred spot on a sacred plain,
where those who fell were honoured with burial on the field. Several helpful site plans
near the burial mound (*see opposite*) help visitors to visualise and understand the battle, battlesite, and nearby sites. As at Gettysburg, there are often battle-aficionados
pacing the plain.

The battle
When the Athenians got word that the invading Persians were approaching Attica by
land and sea, they sent the swift runner Pheidippides to Sparta to ask the Spartans to
stand with them against the Persians. While waiting to learn the Spartans' decision,
the Athenians marched to the Sanctuary of Heracles, which stood in a strong position
commanding the only road into the 10-km long, 5-km wide plain of Marathon. There
the Athenians set camp.

Herodotus does not give the size of the Persian force, which was doubtless grossly
exaggerated by later Athenian tradition. Many scholars think that the Persians had
two divisions of infantry, perhaps 24,000 foot soldiers, and a small force of cavalry.
The Athenians had perhaps 8,000 to 9,000 men, augmented by unexpected aid from
the little city of Plataea, which sent its whole available force, perhaps 1,000 strong, to
stand with the Athenians. The command was vested in the Athenian *polemarch*

Callimachos, whose staff of ten generals included Miltiades (the traditional architect of the victory), and perhaps Themistocles and Aristides.

For four days, the Persian and Athenian forces sat encamped, the Persians being unwilling to attack the strong Athenian position, the Athenians loath to leave it without the expected Spartan reinforcements. The Persian general Datis concluded that he had failed to lure the Athenian army down into the plain to do battle and decided to send his cavalry by sea to Athens, with part of his army heading there on foot.

When Miltiades saw this happening, probably soon after dawn on 12th September 490, he gave the word for action. He had left his centre weak and strongly reinforced his wings; the right wing, the place of honour, was led by Callimachos; on the left wing were the Plataeans. The Greek hoplites advanced rapidly across the mile of No Man's Land before the surprised Persians could get their archers properly into action, possibly helped by tree cover (Professor Burn has pointed out the similarity of tactics used at Bannockburn).

The Athenian wings were successful, while their weak centre was pierced by the Persians. The wings then enveloped the Persian centre, which broke. In the ensuing rout the Persians, weighed down by their armour and weapons, fled to their ships; many were caught and cut down in Marathon's Great Marsh. The Persians lost at least 6,400 men, while the Athenian dead numbered only 192, including Callimachos. The Athenians were buried on the spot where the massive mound (*Soròs*) now stands; the Plataeans possibly at a spot further west, towards the museum: a stone mound containing the skeletons of young men was found here, and we know from Pausanias that the Plataeans had a separate memorial. He also says that the Persian dead were flung unceremoniously into an open trench. A runner (often identified as Pheidippides) is said to have been sent to Athens, where he died of exhaustion after announcing the victory. Since then, the 26-mile race known as the 'marathon' has commemorated his run. (The marathon is re-run each October in Greece; *for information see www.athensmarathon.com.*)

The Persian fleet, having lost only seven ships, put out to sea in an attempt to surprise Athens; but Miltiades, by a rapid march, reached Athens first, and the Persians sailed back to Asia. Marathon proved that the long-dreaded Persians were vulnerable. The Spartan army arrived in time to view the battlefield on the following day—and remained forever embarrassed.

Of the many legends that accrued to Marathon, perhaps the best known are those of the ghostly assistance in the victory of the great Athenian hero Theseus and the goat-footed god Pan. The impressive silence of the plain is said to resound at night to the clash of arms and the neigh of steeds (though it is almost certain that no cavalry took part, the Persian horses having been embarked for Athens).

The battlefield and museum

The site and museum (both between the villages of Nea Makri and Marathonas) are usually open 9–3; T: 22940 55155.

Outside the sprawling agricultural village of Marathonas (Μαραθώνας), a circular road leads towards the coast, to the fenced-in **burial mound of the Athenians** (*Soròs*).

Contrary to usual practice, the fallen at Marathon were buried where they fell, in token of their signal valour. Excavations at the end of the 19th century found ashes and calcined bones, as well as small, black-figure *lekythoi* of the early 5th century. Obsidian arrowheads found on the surface by Schliemann, and which led him to attribute a much earlier date to the mound, may have been used by the Ethiopian archers mentioned by Herodotus. The *Soros* was created from the earth put over the dead and subsequent sacrifices thereon, the ashes being mixed with water and added to the tumulus. It is some 10m high and 180m around; when the winds are strong, it is more than blustery on top. A replica of the tombstone of the *Marathonomaches* (Marathon soldier), now in the National Museum in Athens, stands nearby.

The museum is several kilometres north of the battlefield and the turn-off is signposted on the main road. En route to the museum you pass several obvious burial mounds, including one that might be the resting place of the Plataeans (*see above*). Pottery contemporary with that in the *Soros* was found inside. It is sometimes possible to visit some of these these graves, which have been covered by a protective roof. The small museum is well laid out and has exhibits from the battlefield and from other sites in the area, including the mysterious sanctuary of the Egyptian gods.

RHAMNOUS

Rhamnous (Ράμνους; commonly Ramnoùnda, its name derived from a prickly shrub, the *ramnos*, which still grows in the neighbourhood), is one of the least spoilt sites in Attica, reached by driving through lovely countryside around the villages of Ano and Kato Souli. The site itself lies (poorly signposted) several kilometres north of the little port of Aghia Marina on a rocky promontory that extends into the sea. Rhamnous is worth visiting as much for its romantic isolation and the beauty of its setting as for its archaeological interest. The promontory was famous as early as the 6th century BC for the worship of Nemesis, the fierce goddess who brought mortals low. She took especial care of the presumptuous, punishing *hubris*, the crime of considering oneself master of one's own destiny. Associated with the worship of Nemesis was Themis, the goddess who personified law, equity, and custom.

The promontory's small cove provided shelter on an otherwise inhospitable coast for ships about to pass the dangerous narrows of Aghia Marina. Later a fortress was built to watch over navigation. This gained importance in 412 BC after the Athenian loss of Dekeleia, when Rhamnous became the port of entry for food from Euboea, since it offered the only route wholly on Attic soil that did not involve passing the narrows. Rhamnous was the birthplace of the orator Antiphon (b. 480 BC), whose school of rhetoric was attended by Thucydides.

The site

Usually open Tues–Sun 8.30–3 or 5; the museum and the fenced-off seaside antiquities are open only by pre-arrangement; T: 22940 63477.

A path leads steeply uphill from the ticket booth to the site, which is in a glen above the sea. Along the road are the substantial remains of some of the funerary enclosures with which it was lined. These were topped with sculptured stelae and inscriptions commemorating the dead. The line of the road can be traced back towards the entrance beyond the custodian's hut, where there are the remains of other less well preserved tombs.

At the head of the glen is an impressive artificial platform, 45m wide, constructed in the 5th century BC of large blocks of local marble laid horizontally. Nine courses are exposed at the northeast corner. The sacred precinct thus formed contains the remains of an altar, a stoa, a small fountain house and the temples of Themis and Nemesis. Although none of the visible remains is earlier than the 5th century, both votive offerings and roof tiles of the early 6th century show that there was ritual activity from that time.

The **Temple of Themis** (the smaller temple) was built on a virgin site in the early 5th century. It measures 10.7m by 6.5m and consists merely of a cella in antis with a Doric portico of two columns. The walls which stand to c. 1.8m are built of large polygonal blocks of white marble. Two marble seats (casts *in situ*) dedicated to Themis and Nemesis and three statues from the cella with inscribed pedestals (found in 1890) are in Athens. The building continued in use (as a treasury/storeroom) into the 4th century AD.

The first **Temple of Nemesis**, nearer the sea, was constructed at the end of the 6th century BC in poros limestone as a Doric building, distyle in antis. This temple was probably destroyed by the Persians and replaced by the structure whose remains are still visible. This successor is a Doric peripteral building with six columns by twelve, the last of four sometimes ascribed to the so-called 'Theseum architect'. According to Dinsmoor, it was probably begun on the Festival Day of the *Nemesieia* (Boëdromion 5; ie. 30th September), 436 BC, and is known by an inscription to have been re-dedicated to the Empress Livia, probably by Claudius in AD 45. The interior had the usual arrangement of cella, pronaos and opisthodomos in antis. The unfinished fluting on the remaining drums of six columns (south side) suggests that the building was never completed.

Fragments both of the **cult statue of Nemesis** (including a colossal head, now in the British Museum, London) and of its base have been found. The statue (c. 421 BC) was in Parian marble and the work of Agorakritos, pupil of Pheidias. Pausanias believed it to have been made from the very marble brought by the Persians for use as a victory monument and incorrectly attributed it to Pheidias himself. The base (partly reconstructed, in the museum) has carved decoration on three sides, showing Leda introducing Helen of Troy to her real mother, Nemesis.

Still within the precinct are, to the east of the temple, the foundations of an altar and to the north the scanty remains of a stoa of the 5th century (34m long) which originally had wooden columns in its façade. In front of the stoa was a small fountain house, with a two-columned porch. Opposite the precinct, on the other side of the road, are the foundations of a large Hellenistic structure.

Descending the rocky glen north towards the sea (*access not permitted at present; ask site guard if he will unlock the fence and take you there; gratuity expected*) you reach in 10mins an isolated hill girdled with the well-preserved picturesque enceinte (c. 1km in circuit) of the ancient town. It must have been an exceptionally blustery place to live. The lower part of the south gateway is well preserved, as are short portions (3.7m high in places) of the walls, in ashlar masonry of grey limestone. Nine towers of the fortress can be made out. Recent work has been done on the east gate and four others, smaller, have also been located. There is a shrine of Aphrodite by the road leading in from the east gate to a small open square. Within the town also are some remains of another temple and other shrines, a gymnasium, and an inner citadel. A sanctuary of the healing god Amphiaraus lies outside, to the northwest.

THE AMPHIARAION

This small site, with the remains of a shrine to the healing deity Amphiaraus, some 26km to the north of Marathon, is often uncrowded and offers a pleasant break from the larger, more visited sites. The sanctuary was at once an oracle and a spa. It occupies a sheltered and sunny situation, well suited to a resort of invalids, on the left bank of a wooded glen, watered by a mountain torrent. In spring anemones carpet the site.

The sanctuary commemorated the elevation to divinity of Amphiaraus, the great seer and warrior of Argos, who fought as one of the Seven against Thebes (*see p. 419*). On the defeat of this expedition he fled, but the earth opened and swallowed him up, together with his chariot, near Thebes. His cult was adopted by the Oropians and concentrated here near a spring famed for its healing properties. Whoever wished to consult the god sacrificed a ram and lay down for the night, wrapped in its skin, in the portico allotted for the purpose, and there awaited the revelations to be made in dreams. The cure did not, however, wholly depend on these miraculous communications, for there were medical baths in the precinct. After a cure, the patient had to throw gold or silver coins into the Sacred Spring.

The site
Usually open Tues–Sun 8.30–3; T: 22950 62144.
Descending the path parallel to the stream, you see (right) the little Temple of Amphiaraus, a Doric building of the 4th century, with a pronaos and a cella divided into three by parallel colonnades. The foundations, partly eroded by the stream, have been restored. The base of the cult statue is still in position. The back wall was joined by a porch (door marks in the threshold) to the priests' lodging. Ten metres from the temple is the altar, on which the ram was sacrificed; and below the altar the Sacred Spring, into which the coins were thrown. Its waters were drunk from shells, many of which have been found.

Above the altar is a terrace with a line of over 30 inscribed pedestals of statues, mostly Roman. On a line with these are the remains of a long bench. In front is the museum (*rarely open; enquire at entrance to site*), containing numerous inscriptions, a curious early herm, torsos and, in the back court, reassembled architectural members of the temple and stoa. Beyond are the remains of the *enkoimeterion*, a long stoa, erected c. 387 BC, with 41 Doric columns on the façade and divided internally into two long galleries by 17 Ionic columns. It had a small room at either end, possibly reserved for women patients. Along the walls ran marble benches, resting on claw feet, on which the patients submitted to the process of incubation (*see p. 249*).

Behind the stoa is a small theatre, with a circular orchestra and seating for 300 spectators. Five marble thrones with scroll ornaments are preserved. The *proskenion* (restored) has eight Doric columns surmounted by an epistyle with a dedicatory inscription. Beyond the stoa were the baths. On the opposite bank of the stream are some confused remains of the accommodation provided for patients and part of a *klepsydra*, or water-clock, its bronze plug mechanism visible.

DAPHNI

NB: Daphni was damaged by earthquake in 1999 and has been closed for restoration since then. Tantalising promises are given out from time to time about a reopening date, but at the time of writing, it was still closed. Check with the Greek National Tourist Office (www.gnto.gr; T: 210 870 000) or Ministry of Culture (www.culture.gr) to see whether it has reopened before visiting.

The Monastery of Daphni (Μονή Δαφνίου) has some of the finest Byzantine architecture and mosaics in Greece. The great art historian David Talbot Rice called Daphni the most perfect monument of the 11th century. Both church and walls incorporate ancient materials from a Sanctuary of Apollo, on the same site, mentioned by Pausanias but destroyed c. AD 395. The convent owes its name to the laurels (*daphne*) sacred to Apollo, which once flourished in the neighbourhood.

HISTORY OF DAPHNI

The monastery, founded in the 5th or 6th century, was dedicated to the Virgin Mary. It was rebuilt at the end of the 11th century, but sacked by Crusaders in 1205. In 1211 Otho de la Roche gave it to the Cistercians, who held it until 1458. Two Dukes of Athens, Otho himself and Walter de Brienne, were buried here. The convent was reoccupied in the 16th century by Orthodox monks until its abandonment in the War of Independence. Restorations were made in 1893 after the building had been used in turn as a barracks and a lunatic asylum. The structure was strengthened in 1920, and a more elaborate restoration was undertaken after the Second World War.

THE KATHOLIKON OF DAPHNI

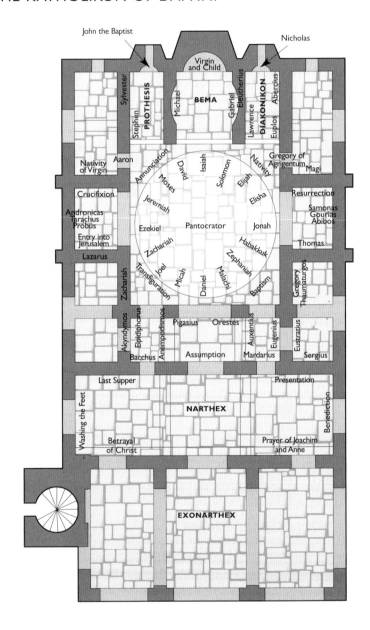

The monastery

The fortified enceinte and a few foundations inside near the northeast corner survive from its earliest Christian period. Of the 11th-century monastic buildings only some foundations of the great refectory can be seen on the north side. The pretty cloister (restored), south of the church, dates from the Cistercian period, with the addition of 16th-century cells. Round it are displayed sculptural fragments, Classical and Byzantine. The two sarcophagi, ornamented with fleurs-de-lys and Latin crosses, are sometimes supposed to be of the Frankish dukes.

The church is a fine example of Byzantine architecture of c. 1080, with an added exonarthex, which was restored in 1961 to the later form given it by the Cistercians. The truncated west tower on the north side bore a Gothic belfry. The three-light windows of the church are separated by mullions and surrounded by three orders of brickwork. The lights are closed by perforated alabaster slabs. The drum of the dome has round engaged buttresses between each of its 16 windows. You enter from the cloister by the south door. The interior is noted for its mosaics (*see plan overleaf*), which, though fragmentary in comparison with their original extent, have no rivals in southern Greece; indeed, apart from those at Hosios Loukas in Phocis, none nearer than Thessaloniki.

Most complete are those on the south side of the narthex, portraying the *Presentation of the Virgin* and the *Prayer of Joachim and Anne*. On the vault of the dome is a celebrated representation, uncompromisingly stern, of *Christ Pantocrator*, on a gold ground. The frieze, round the drum below, depicts saints and prophets. Finely preserved on the pendentives are the *Annunciation*, *Nativity*, *Baptism* and *Transfiguration*. On the west side of the north *choros*, the *Entry into Jerusalem* has interesting perspective effects (note the little boys' foreshortened feet). In the bema, or sanctuary, though the Virgin above the apse is fragmentary and the vault is empty, the flanking Archangels are well preserved. Of the frescoes that once adorned the lower walls of the church, four are still comparatively clear.

ELEUSIS

The ancient city of Eleusis (modern Elefsìna; Ἐλευσίνα), birthplace of Aeschylus (525–456 BC) and home of the famous Sanctuary of Demeter and of the Eleusinian Mysteries, was situated on the east slopes of a low rocky hill (63m) which runs parallel with and close to the shore. The Sacred Way, of which large sections (paved and with kerbs) have been traced, led directly to the sanctuary. Unfortunately, the site is now surrounded by the hideous petrochemical, cement and steel works that make up the industrial sprawl of modern Elefsina. Signs for the ancient site are conspicuous only by their absence, and although it is possible to get here by bus from Athens (*see p. 152*), or to drive, some may prefer to take a taxi.

A plan of the ancient site is given on pp. 148–149.

The legend

According to the Homeric *Hymn to Demeter*, the goddess of crops and fruitfulness herself founded the mysteries here. While gathering flowers, Persephone (Kore, 'the Maiden'), Demeter's daughter, was carried off by Hades to the Underworld. Demeter, searching the world for her daughter, came to Eleusis, where, disguised as an old woman, she found work in the royal palace caring for the sickly son of King Keleos, and vowing that she would neither return to Olympus nor allow crops to grow on earth until Kore was delivered up. Finally Zeus, worried about the famine that would ensue, commanded Hades to return Persephone; but because she had eaten a few pomegranate seeds while in the Underworld she was bound to return there for part of every year. Before leaving Eleusis, Demeter broke the famine and gave to Triptolemos, the son who had been in her care, seeds of wheat and a winged chariot, commanding him to ride over the earth, teaching mankind the use of the plough and the blessings of agriculture. It is this scene that is depicted in the famous relief in the Archaeological Museum in Athens (*see p. 95*). Demeter also commanded that a shrine in her honour be built at Eleusis.

The Mysteries

The legend of Demeter and Persephone is bound up with ideas of death and return from the dead, and therefore with the question of life after death. The cult at the sanctuary of Eleusis aimed to reveal to initiates the mystery of what lay beyond the grave. Candidates for initiation were drawn from all classes, including women, providing that their application was seconded by an Athenian citizen who himself had been initiated. They were first admitted to the *Lesser Eleusinia*, which were held in the month of Anthesterion (February–March) at *Agrai*, in Athens, on the banks of the Ilissos. Being accepted as *mystai* (initiates), they were allowed to attend the *Greater Eleusinia*, which took place in Boëdromion (September), and lasted nine days, with rites and processions beginning and ending in Athens. During the *Eleusinia*, a truce was declared throughout Hellas. In 336 BC the news of the destruction of Thebes by Alexander the Great caused the only recorded instance of the procession's cancellation after it had set out.

The fundamental substance of the Mysteries, the character of the sacred objects displayed, and the nature of the revelation experienced were never divulged. Alcibiades was condemned to death in absentia (though later reprieved) for parodying part of the Mysteries; Aeschylus was almost lynched on suspicion of revealing their substance on the stage. It is thought probable that a pageant (*dromena*) was performed representing the action of the *Hymn of Demeter*. It is known that the *mystai* fasted for a period, and that they broke their fast with a special infusion called *kykeon*, made of barley and herbs. Theories have been advanced about its narcotic effects: if attacked by the parasite ergot, barley releases a substance related to LSD, and it has been suggested that the *mystai* experienced visions induced by this drug. Whatever the nature of the revelation, it seems to have been spiritually uplifting. Under the Roman empire the Mysteries continued to be held, and at least three emperors—Augustus, Hadrian and

Marcus Aurelius—became initiates. Cicero derived great comfort from the experience, saying that Athens had given 'nothing finer to man ... for we learn in [the Mysteries] the principles of life, and from them acquire not only a way of living in happiness, but also a way of dying with greater hope'.

HISTORY OF ELEUSIS

Archaeologists have unearthed remains dating to at least the 15th century BC. Eleusis itself seems to have been a rival of Athens until it came under firm Athenian sway about the time of Solon. Henceforward the cult grew and the sanctuary was constantly enlarged: by Peisistratus; by Pericles; under the Macedonians; and by the Romans. The Imperial transformation of Eleusis probably began under Hadrian. In AD 170 the sanctuary was sacked by the Sarmatians, but was immediately restored at the expense of Marcus Aurelius. At his initiation in 176 he was allowed to enter the *anaktoron* (the chamber at the centre of the site where the ritual objects were stored), the only lay person so honoured in the whole history of Eleusis. The Emperor Julian was initiated, completing his sanctification (according to Gibbon) in Gaul; the last Eleusinian hierophant was invested during his reign. Valerian (253–60) reorganised the defences of the site in the face of threats from barbarian tribes (Goths and Herulians); Valentinian allowed the Mysteries to continue, but Theodosius' decrees of 392 and Alaric's sack a few years later were jointly responsible for their end. The town was abandoned after the Byzantine period and not reoccupied until the 18th century.

The ancient site

Open Tues-Sun 8:30–3; T: 210 554 6019. NB: The site is vast and confusing; a map is essential (plan overleaf). A full exploration of the remains (primarily from the Roman period) takes the best part of a day and requires some scrambling. Care should be taken on the acropolis, where there are unfenced cisterns.

As you pass the entrance gate the Sacred Way changes from a modern to an ancient paved road, which ends on the Great Forecourt before the city walls. This spacious square formed part of the new monumental entrance planned probably in the reign of Antoninus Pius. Here the *mystai* gathered in order to perform the necessary acts of purification before entering the sanctuary. From the square the Greater Propylaia led directly to the sanctuary; to left and right triumphal arches led towards the main gate of the town and to the visitors' quarter of baths, hotels and recreation centres.

Many of the marble blocks to be seen in the **Great Forecourt** came from the buildings that defined its limits. To the left are the remains of a fountain. Beyond it stood a triumphal arch, one of two faithfully copied from the Arch of Hadrian at Athens. The foundations remain; its gable has been reassembled in front; the inscription (replaced nearby) reads 'All the Greeks to the Goddesses and the Emperor'.

ELEUSIS
(SANCTUARY OF DEMETER)

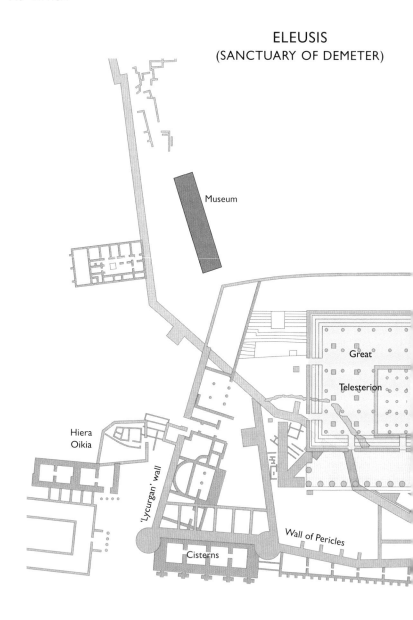

Museum

Great
Telesterion

Hiera
Oikia

'Lycurgan' wall

Wall of Pericles

Cisterns

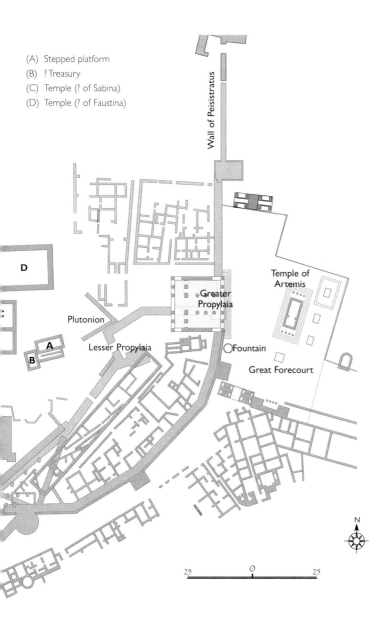

(A) Stepped platform
(B) ? Treasury
(C) Temple (? of Sabina)
(D) Temple (? of Faustina)

Wall of Peisistratus

D

Temple of
Artemis

Greater
Propylaia

Plutonion

B A

Lesser Propylaia

Fountain

Great Forecourt

N

25   0   25

In the centre of the forecourt are the scanty remains of the Temple of Artemis, amphiprostyle in form and built of marble. The **Greater Propylaia**, built in Pentelic marble on a concrete core by Marcus Aurelius or his predecessor, is a close copy of the propylaia on the Acropolis at Athens, both in plan and dimensions. It is approached by six marble steps and faces northeast. Reassembled on the pavement in front are two of the six Doric columns of the façade and the pediment with its central medallion bust of (?) Marcus Aurelius. Crosses scored on the pavement nearby probably derive from Christian fears of pagan spirits.

Close to one corner of the Greater Propylaia is the sacred well that passed throughout Classical times for the *Kallichoron*, or 'Well of the Fair Dances'. The well-head, beautifully fashioned in polygonal masonry with clamps, probably dates from the time of Peisistratus. Mylonas has suggested that this is, in fact, the *Parthenion*, or 'Well of the Maidens', mentioned in the *Hymn* as the place where Demeter sat to rest on her journey to find her daughter, Persephone.

The **Lesser Propylaia**, which form the entrance to the innermost court, were vowed to the goddesses by Cicero's friend Appius Claudius Pulcher in his consulship (54 BC) and completed after his death by two nephews. The structure consisted of two parallel walls, 15m long, with Ionic attached columns, which enclosed a passage 10m wide.

The inner sanctuary

You now enter the inner Precinct of Demeter, for two thousand years an area forbidden to the uninitiated on penalty of death. To the right is the **Plutonion**, a triangular precinct of the 4th century BC, enclosing a cavern sacred to Pluto (Hades). A shrine was built at its mouth in the Peisistratid era; the surviving foundations are of a temple completed in 328 BC (a dated inscription has been found referring to the purchase of its wooden doors). Following the processional road, you come next to a rock-cut stepped platform **(A)** which adjoined a small building, perhaps a treasury **(B)**. The platform may have served as a stand from which the start of a sacred pageant was watched. The levelled terrace beyond the treasury supported a temple **(C)** possibly dedicated to Sabina, the coolly beautiful wife of Hadrian, on whom the Greeks had conferred the title 'New Demeter'. (The temple beyond this **(D)** was probably dedicated to Faustina, wife of Antoninus Pius). You ascend to the large square platform on which stood the Hall of the Mysteries.

The first shrine decreed by Demeter 'beneath the citadel and its sheer wall upon a rising hillock above the Kallichoron' occupied a limited site on ground which sloped steeply away. As each enlargement of the sanctuary was undertaken, it became necessary to extend the artificial terrace on which it stood. Consequently each shrine in turn escaped complete destruction by being buried under the next. The result is an archaeological palimpsest of rare completeness but baffling complexity.

The **Great Telesterion**, the Hall of Initiation and the Mysteries, is an almost square chamber 53m by 52m, partly cut out of the rock of the acropolis and partly built on a terrace. The existing remains appear to be those of the Periclean rebuilding, as finally remodelled by Marcus Aurelius. On each of the four sides were eight tiers of seats, partly cut in the rock and partly built up; these were interrupted at six points only, for two doors on each of the disengaged sides. The hall accommodated 3,000. Six rows of seven columns each supported the (? wooden) roof; they were in two tiers separated by an epistyle (possibly with a frieze). The bases of most remain; one of them has as its top course a reused block of the 1st century AD, showing the extent of the Roman restoration. In the centre, on a site it had occupied from the first, was the *anaktoron*, or holy of holies, a small rectangular room roofed somehow by Xenocles with an *opaion*, or lantern, of which no trace has survived. Excavations have revealed traces of at least six earlier structures on the same site, from Mycenaean to Roman times.

The walls
Sections of the defensive walls of Peisistratus and of Pericles are visible on the site. In addition, looking towards the museum you see the perfectly fitted polygonal masonry (6th century) of the peribolos of the *Hiera Oikia*, a house of the Geometric period, sacred to the memory of a hero. To the right is the 'Lycurgan' wall (? 370–360 BC), one of the best preserved examples of ancient fortification, with both a square and a round tower. On four slightly receding courses in pecked Eleusinian stone are set tooled courses in yellow poros; this is probably a conscious matching of the Periclean style. Beyond the corner the wall is masked by ruined Hadrianic cisterns.

The museum
NB: This important museum has been open only intermittently since suffering earthquake damage in 1998. In theory it is open as the site; T: 201 554 6019.
Outside the entrance are a Roman sarcophagus (c. AD 190) in marble with a well-carved representation of the Calydonian boar-hunt (the lid does not belong); two representations in white marble of torches, c. 2.5m high; a capital from the Lesser Propylaia; and a fine head of a horse. The museum itself contains inscriptions, pottery, coins, architectural elements and statues, as well as copies of some important works found here, including reliefs of Demeter now in the National Archaeological Museum in Athens. As always, at a spot visited by the Emperor Hadrian, there is a dedicatory statue of his beloved who died young, the Bithynian boy Antinous, who was drowned in the Nile in mysterious circumstances, but whose face has remained familiar down the long centuries, with its full, sensuous lips and dreamy eyes.

MEGARA

Megara (Μέγαρα) rises on the slopes of two hills, the twin citadels of the ancient city, whose street plan is reflected in the modern layout. Of the many buildings described by Pausanias, only the Fountain of Theagenes survives, above and to the right of Plateia Iroön, in Odos Krinis. On the slopes of the west hill are fragments of a Temple of Athena built into one of several interesting churches. Numerous traces of Megara's past have been discovered in rescue excavations; many ancient blocks are built into chapels and houses, which are still constructed of the white mussel-stone mentioned by Pausanias.

Megara was prosperous in the Geometric period, and she planted colonies as far west as Megara Hyblaea in Sicily and as far east as Chalcedon and Byzantium. Rivalry with Athens for possession of Salamis led to strife, and the island fell c. 570 to Peisistratus. Possibly about the same time Perachora was finally lost to Corinth. The invasion of Megaris by Mardonius marked the western limit of the Persian advance; 3,000 Megarians fought at Plataea. In 461, menaced by Corinth, Megara formed a short-lived alliance with the Athenians, who built long walls to protect her access to the port, Nisaea. She soon reversed her policy, encroached on sacred Eleusinian land, and murdered an Athenian envoy. Pericles' decree of 432, excluding Megarians from Attic markets and harbours, was one of the causes of the Peloponnesian War. Megara has never been of much importance since then, Pausanias remarking of the Megarians that 'they were the only Greek people whom even the Emperor Hadrian could not make to thrive'.

PRACTICAL INFORMATION

So much of the Attic peninsula can be reached in a day trip from Athens that it often makes sense to use Athens as a base. Hotels tend to be large beach resorts and holiday villages. All towns and smaller villages have their taverna, some good, some less so. The attraction of Attica remains its landscape and its antiquities.

GETTING AROUND

• **By bus:** Faliro and Glyfada are about 30mins from Athens by bus (nos. 155, 103, E2θ) or tram (A1 and A2). Bus 714 goes to the top of Mt Parnitha (c. 2hrs). For Kaissariani bus 224 from Vas. Sofias. Bus 812 (dep. Plateia Eleftherias) for the suburb of Haïdari and Daphni. Buses to Lavrion, Sounion and Marathon depart from Mavromataion.

WHERE TO STAY

Anavyssos
€€ **Alexander Beach**. Hotel catering to the summer tourist market, with Olympic-sized pool and 108 functional, unfussily furnished rooms (white tile floors). T: 22910 80100, www.alexandergroup.gr

Sounion
€€€ **Grecotel Cape Sounion**. A large hotel with bungalows, suites and rooms, set in extensive grounds on the Lavrion side of Cape Sounion. Restaurant and spa centre. T: 22920 69700, www.grecotel.gr
€€ **Aegon**. Unattractive exterior (though it has tried to be low-impact) in a lovely location on a sandy beach on a narrow spur of land. All rooms have balconies, with fabulous sea views. Good size; just 45 rooms. T: 22920 39200.

Vouliagmeni
€€€ **Margi**. Unimpressive from the outside, but nicely decorated within, in a deliberately lifestyle magazine sort of way, with a mix of wood and fabrics, and attention to lighting. 80 rooms. Litous 11, T: 210 892 9000, www.themargi.gr

THE PELOPONNESE

The Peloponnese (Πελοπόννησος) forms the southern extremity of the Balkan peninsula. Joined to the mainland of Greece by a narrow isthmus, it was known to the ancients as the Island of Pelops. Its medieval name, the Morea, was probably derived not from a fanciful likeness to the leaf of the mulberry-tree (μόρον), which it does not resemble in the least, but from the fact that the mulberry flourished in the country. The modern division into the seven *nomes* of Corinthia in the northeast, the Argolid (east), Achaia (north), Elis (northwest), Messenia (southwest), Laconia (southeast), and Arcadia (inland) roughly corresponds to the ancient regional division. The scenery of the Peloponnese combines beauty and grandeur, and its archaeological interest is unsurpassed.

Geography

The north coast, ending in Cape Drepanon, opposite Nafpaktos, is separated from the mainland of Greece proper by the long, narrow Gulf of Corinth, and is comparatively free from indentations. To the south the peninsula sends out the three long tongues of land, separated by the Messenian and Laconian gulfs, which give it a distinctive shape. A fourth but less obtrusive tongue, fringed with islands, stretches southeast between the Gulf of Nafplion and the Saronic Gulf.

An irregular series of mountains, encircling Arcadia, forms the backbone of the region, with articulations almost reaching to the sea in all directions. The highest peaks of this central group are Kyllini (2374m), Aroania or Chelmos (2355m), and Erymanthos or Olonos (2224m). These form a natural barrier across the peninsula from east to west. Two important chains run south from the Arcadian group. The long range of Taygetos, with Aghios Ilias, the highest mountain in the Peloponnese (2408m) separates the Messenian Plain from the Laconian Valley. The parallel chain of Parnon (1940m), continuing the east mountain wall of Arcadia (culminating in Artemision, 1772m), closes the Laconian Valley on the east.

Practically the only low-lying portions are the isthmus and shores of the Bay of Corinth; the coastal district of Achaia and Elis from Patras to Pyrgos, with the vale of Olympia; and the plains or valleys of Messenia, Laconia and Argos. A feature of Arcadia is the bleak Plain of Tripolis, lying 610m above the sea. The vale of Olympia is watered by the Alpheios, the longest and most famous river in the peninsula; the Messenian Plain by the Pirnatsa or Pamisos, the most copious; the Valley of Laconia by the Evrotas; and the Argolic Plain by the seasonal Panitsa or Inachos. The Elean Pineios flows into the Channel of Zakynthos. The whole of the north coast is seared by small torrents, generally dry but occasionally sweeping the road into the sea. A feature of the plateaux of the interior is the number of swallow-holes into which the rivers disappear underground; they are common in Arcadia. The only natural lakes are Pheneos and Stymphalos, both now virtually dry.

History

The Peloponnese was inhabited at least as early as the Mesolithic period (Franchthi Cave, 11th millennium BC). The population increased in Neolithic and Early Helladic times (3rd millennium BC), but neither archaeology nor tradition gives certain indications of the origin or language of its people. From them perhaps come the non-Hellenic place-names ending in -ινθος, -σσος, and -ηνη (e.g. Corinth, Mycenae). They were probably of Asiatic origin. Their implements were of stone, then copper, and later of bronze. Their existence is probably mirrored in the legendary Pelasgians of Herodotus.

Towards the end of the 3rd millennium, a violent upheaval may mark the arrival of new racial groups, of Indo-European stock, possibly the first Greek-speaking people, since their culture develops without a break into the Mycenaean civilisation, which had written records in Greek. The houses of these people were small, with a characteristic horseshoe plan, with a hearth in the centre of the largest room and an open porch; the scheme is the prototype of the later megaron. The dead were buried (originally without or with few offerings) in a contracted position in cist graves. Their traditions survive in the hero legends of Perseus and Heracles. Middle Helladic remains have been excavated at Lerna, Asine and Mycenae. The contents of Grave Circle B (now in Athens) give a good idea of the art of the end of this period of development (c. 1550 BC). Thereafter the mainland becomes influenced by Middle Minoan civilisation, though utilising Cretan ideas in an individual way. Rapid development marks the Late Helladic period—the widespread civilisation known to Homer as Achaean and to us as Mycenaean because both archaeology and tradition confirm that its focus was at Mycenae. The other main centres of the Peloponnese were at Argos and Pylos.

A wave of Greek-speaking people from the north, the so-called Dorian Invasion, brought widespread destruction to the Peloponnese. Classical historians attributed this break to the return of the Heraclidae, descendants of an earlier Mycenaean dynasty (which included Heracles) exiled by the rulers of Mycenae before the Trojan War. This was a political upheaval of a very violent kind, which put back civilisation several centuries, although cultural and racial continuity was evidently not affected: Attica seems not to have been occupied by the Dorians and is neither less nor more Greek than the Peloponnese. Arcadia is said never to have been subordinated to either Achaeans or Dorians. The dispossessed Achaeans supposedly resettled in the north in the area which perpetuates their name to the present day.

The early recorded history of the Peloponnese deals with the rise of Sparta. From 337 BC when the Synedrion of Corinth confirmed Philip of Macedon as leader of the Greek world, the historical centre of the Peloponnese becomes Corinth. After the sack of Corinth in 146 BC, the peninsula formed part of the Roman senatorial province of Achaea; this was temporarily joined in AD 15–44 to Macedonia.

The Peloponnese was ravaged in AD 267 and 395 by the Goths. Placed by the Constantinian reorganisation in the diocese of Macedonia, the province enjoyed (alone of Eastern provinces) proconsular rank. Ecclesiastically it remained subject to Rome (under the Metropolitan of Thessalonica), sending only one bishop (of Corinth) to Ephesus (431). By 457 the Peloponnese had a number of bishops and Corinth had become a metropolitan see. In 540 the Huns penetrated to the gates and Justinian refortified the Isthmus; the western shores were attacked by Totila's Ostrogoths in 549; but in the Peloponnese the ancient era survived into the 6th century. Widespread earthquakes devastated the peninsula in 522 and 551.

Avar and Slav incursions submerged the Peloponnese c. 587, bringing two centuries of barbarism. Plague wrought havoc in 746–47. In 805 the Morea (as it was now called) became a Byzantine *theme*, and under the Orthodox Church slowly refined and assimilated the Slav elements, although predominantly Slav pockets survived in the Taygetos region far into Frankish times and the Mani remained aloof as ever. New menaces soon arose in the Saracen corsairs, beaten off in 881, and the Bulgars, who penetrated the Morea in 924–27 and in 996. In general the 11th century was a period of reconstruction and prosperity, during which Venetian merchants began to acquire the trading privileges that they developed throughout the 12th century.

A year after the fall of Constantinople in 1204 William de Champlitte landed in the western Peloponnese. Assisted by Geoffrey de Villehardouin, he conquered the Morea and divided it up into 12 fiefs among various barons of France, Flanders and Burgundy. Geoffrey de Villehardouin, who became in 1210 Prince of Morea (or Prince of Achaea), governed the country with moderation. The house of Villehardouin lasted till 1301, when Isabella Villehardouin married Philip of Savoy. Philip became Prince of the Morea, sharing his sovereignty with the Marshal of St Omer. In 1318 the principality passed to the Angevin House of Naples, which held it till 1383. The Venetians occupied Methone, Argos, Nafplion, and Navarino; and the Florentine Nerio Acciaioli established himself in Corinth, Argolis and Achaia.

The Byzantine Palaeologi gradually won back the Peloponnese by means of matrimonial and other alliances. In 1453 two rival despots, Demetrius Palaeologus at Mistra, and his brother Thomas at Patras, appealed to Turkey for help against the Albanians, who were devastating the country. The Turkish general Turakhan, after assisting, proceeded to conquer the two brothers, and in 1458 Mehmet II ordered the invasion of the Morea. In 1460 the conquest was completed. The Venetian coastal settlements were abandoned in 1573. Francesco Morosini reconquered the peninsula in 1685–87, and in 1699 it was ceded to Venice by the Treaty of Carlowitz. In 1715 Ali Pasha retook it for Ahmed III, and the Treaty of Passarowitz gave it back to Turkey.

In 1821 the War of Independence was begun in the Peloponnese by the action of Germanos, Archbishop of Patras (*see p. 410*). The same year Peter Mavromichalis, Bey of the Mani, took the field, his example being followed by Kolokotronis, a celebrated *klepht* of the Morea, and by other chieftains. Tripolis fell in October 1821. In 1822 Kolokotronis took Corinth; in 1823 Nafplion fell. The Greeks suffered a setback in 1825, when Ibrahim Pasha invaded the Morea with an Egyptian army; but some months after the battle of Navarino (1827) the French landed in the Gulf of Koroni, under General Maison, and Ibrahim fled. The Turks evacuated the country in October 1828, and the French withdrew soon afterwards. In 1831 an insurrection of the Maniots, who resented sinking their independence even in liberated Greece, was suppressed by Bavarian troops.

CORINTHIA

The Corinthia (Κορίνθια), and the neighbouring Argolid, have the gentlest landscape in the Peloponnese, with seaside plains and low hills and valleys. Bordered to the north by the Gulf of Corinth, to the east by the Argolid, to the south by the Argolid and Arcadia, and to the west by Achaia, Corinthia has an enviable situation, and one which greatly contributed to the importance of the province in Antiquity. The modern *nome* of Corinthia is larger than the ancient district, which did not control Sikyon, with which it shared the western stretches of a fertile plain. Acrocorinth, whose mound is visible throughout much of the Corinthia, rises to 575m; on the western border with Achaia Mt Kyllini rises to 2374m.

Corinthia's history has been dominated by its most important city, Corinth, where stray finds suggest settlement as early as 4500 BC. Mycenaean settlements in Corinthia were probably subordinate to the Argolid. The area's greatest periods of prosperity were during the Archaic and Roman periods.

Throughout much of Antiquity, Corinth's location—and its virtually impregnable citadel, Acrocorinth—allowed it to control sea traffic from east to west and land passage from the mainland into the Peloponnese. This was perhaps particularly significant for Corinth's growth and power because the plain of Corinth, although famously fertile and well watered, was not as extensive as, for example, the plains of Sparta or Argos.

Now, as in Antiquity, the plain of Corinth is well watered, and grain, grapes and olives are cultivated; there is a certain amount of quarrying and a number of gravel and cement works. The coast along the Gulf of Corinth, once dotted with fishing villages, is now a popular Greek summer holiday area: lively, if not restful.

Ancient Corinth and its museum are the greatest draw for visitors to Corinthia. Four sites nearby—Isthmia, Kenchreai, the Diolkos and Lechaion—form an integral part of the city's history, and are recommended detours. On the north shore of the Gulf of Corinth is the energetic spa town of Loutraki and the charming sanctuary of Perachora, long under the sway of Corinth, and still part of the modern province. En route from Corinth to Patras, it is possible to take in more of Corinthia, including the once-noxious, now largely drained Stymphalian Lake and the site of *Sikyon*.

ANCIENT CORINTH

This is one of the largest and grandest ancient sites in Greece; that said, to date, perhaps four percent of the ancient city, which stretched over some two square kilometres, has been uncovered. The most obvious Greek remains are the Temple of Apollo and the early phases of the Fountain of Peirene. The principal excavation area and site museum are close to the village (Ἀρχαία Κόρινθος) crossroads.

HISTORY OF ANCIENT CORINTH

The name *Korinthos* is of pre-Greek origin, a strong suggestion that there was pre-Greek settlement in the countryside around Corinth, perhaps as early as the 5th millennium. The Homeric city of *Ephyra* ('the Lookout'), home of Medea, Sisyphus and Bellerophon, may have been located at Korakou nearer the coast. The Dorians refounded what became the site of Classical Corinth.

According to ancient tradition, and an admixture of traditional scholarship, a picture has emerged of the history of ancient Corinth. Towards the end of the 8th century BC the historical last king of a semi-mythical line gave place to the oligarchy of the Bacchiads, under whom Corinth became a mercantile power, taking advantage of its superb location and two harbours. From that point on, Corinth would be best known for the mercantile and artistic skills that made it prosperous. Corinthian ships carried Corinthian wares, including the city's distinctive black-figure pottery, throughout the Mediterranean world.

Over-population, as well as expansionist aims, may have occasioned the foundation of colonies at *Corcyra* (modern-day Corfu) and Syracuse (c. 734), but Corinthian prowess at sea is attested by the tradition that Ameinocles of Corinth built ships for Samos in 704; by the finding of typical Protocorinthian pottery (*aryballoi, alabastra, skyphoi*) all over the Mediterranean; and by the naval battle of 664 against her disaffected colony Corcyra (at which, according to Thucydides, the trireme was introduced into Greek waters). In the mid-7th century the Bacchiads were overthrown by the tyrant Cypselus, who devoted 30 years to the development of trade and industry.

The prescient Bacchiads had feared the infant Cypselus, whose mother hid him in a chest lest they kill him. In one of his most detailed passages, Pausanias describes an ornate chest, which he believes to be the very one that concealed the infant, which Cypselus dedicated at Olympia. Under Cypselus' son Periander, who reigned for 44 years (629–585), the city reached the level of prosperity and sophistication that Plutarch depicts in his *Seven Sages*, set in the court of Periander. Work began on the Temple of Apollo and the Fountain of Peirene, as well as the Diolkos (the slipway for hauling ships over the isthmus, *see p. 185*). Prosperity continued under the brief reign of Periander's nephew, Psammetichus, and the moderate oligarchy of merchants who deposed and succeeded him.

During the Persian Wars, Corinth's strategic location made it the centre for deliberations amongst the Greek coalition against the Mede. At the end of hostilities, as Athens' rise to power began, that city's increasing expansion robbed Corinth of her foreign markets. She failed to prevent Athens from annexing Megara (457 BC) and for the remainder of the 5th century found herself—not always happily—in the Spartan camp. The war in 434 BC between Corinth and Corcyra was a cause of the Peloponnesian War, in which Corinth supported the

Syracusans against the Athenian-led Sicilian expedition. After the death of the Spartan king Lysander in 395 BC she joined Thebes, Athens and Argos against her former ally, but fared badly in the ensuing Corinthian War (395–87). In 346 Timophanes seized power only to be killed by his brother Timoleon, who became better known for saving Sicily from the Carthaginians than for anything he did at home.

When Philip of Macedon invaded, Corinth shared in the defeat at Chaironeia (338 BC) and received a Macedonian garrison. At the Synedrion of Corinth, the following year, the Greek world ratified the leadership of Philip of Macedon, and after his assassination, that of his son Alexander. The century of Macedonian rule was something of a new golden age for Corinth, with revived peace and prosperity: in exile from Athens and living near Isthmia (c. 369 BC), Xenophon wrote part of the *Hellenica*. The Cynic philosopher Diogenes (412–323), whose tomb Pausanias saw on the road from Lechaion to Corinth, spent some years in Corinth, supporting himself in part as a tutor.

In 224 BC, the Sikyonian statesman and general Aratos expelled Corinth's Macedonian garrison and united Corinth to the resuscitated Achaean League. Corinth's worst moment came in 146 BC, after the Romans under Mummius decisively defeated the League and razed Corinth virtually to the ground. Many citizens were slaughtered, many sold into slavery. Corinth lay desolate until 44 BC, when Julius Caesar planted on its site a colony of veterans, the *Colonia Laus Julia Corinthiensis*, which achieved splendour and importance as the capital of the province of Achaea (the Roman name for most of Greece). Other Greeks regarded (and sometimes envied) the Corinthians their easy living and slack morals. The Greek proverb, latinised by Horace as *Non cuivis homini contingit adire Corinthum*, is usually taken to mean that not everyone could afford to go and partake of the fleshpots of Corinth.

At its zenith under the Romans, Corinth is said to have had a population of 300,000; the number of slaves is put by Athenaeus as high as 460,000. The luxury and dissipation of Corinth did not charm St Paul, who spent 18 months here (c. AD 51–52) plying his trade as a tentmaker (*Acts XVIII, 3*). His *First Epistle to the Corinthians* makes painfully clear his difficulties dealing with the community.

Nero's proclamation of Greek independence at Isthmia in AD 66 was rescinded by his successor Vespasian. Under Hadrian (AD 117–123), Corinth was favoured and embellished with an aqueduct from the Stymphalian Lake; the great 2nd-century philhellene Herodes Atticus also built and restored many monuments here, perhaps including the odeion.

Though it survived the ravages of Alaric in 395, Corinth suffered from disastrous earthquakes in 522 and 551, which contributed to its decline. After a final period of prosperity in the 11th century, it was sacked by the Normans in 1147; thereafter, much of its history is a catalogue of successive captures.

EXPLORING ANCIENT CORINTH

Usually open 8.30–7 in summer; 8.30–3 in winter. T: 27410 31207. Site entrance near the museum. NB: The odeion, theatre and Asclepieion do not lie within the fenced archaeological site and may be visited either before or after. As always, to avoid crowds (Corinth receives over 160,000 visitors a year), it is best to visit as the site opens, during the midday lunch break, or in the hours before the site closes. Parking at site. Plans on pp. 164–65.

This is the oldest American excavation in Greece and the American School of Classical Studies publication *Corinth: The Centenary, 1896–1996*, edited by Nancy Bookides and Charles K. Williams (2002) and the ASCS website (*www.ascsa.edu.gr*) have a wealth of information on Corinth as well as Acrocorinth, Isthmia, Lechaion, and Kenchreai. Guides to aspects of Corinth and its monuments, as well as an excellent monograph on Acrocorinth, are on sale at the entrance and museum; a guide to the entire site is forthcoming.

Most of what remains and has been excavated shows the Roman commercial and administrative centre of the first three centuries AD. The absence of significant finds from late Antiquity in the Roman Forum, combined with the presence there of burials, long led scholars to posit that Corinth was but a shadow of its former self during this period. Recent excavations suggest that in the Late Antique period (6th–7th centuries AD), the Roman Forum was outside the city wall. If so, this would explain the absence of significant Late Antique period finds in the forum, the presence of burials, and indicate a significant redefinition of Corinth's civic space. In short, it is possible that Corinth continued to thrive during what had previously been considered a 'dark age'.

Much of the Byzantine city seems to have been built with virtually the same orientation as Roman Corinth, using the Roman remains as a vast quarry of building material. In turn, the Franks pillaged the Byzantine buildings when they built here, and extended the city south of the site museum, where the important Frankish complex is being excavated. Emerging signs of the vitality of Corinth during Late Antiquity and the Frankish period may provide proof that Corinth was prosperous, if not terribly influential politically, for much longer than previously realised.

Unlike their early predecessors, who destroyed what they encountered until they reached what most interested them, today's archaeologists attempted to document remains from all periods, to record the full history both of sites and their surrounding countryside. To this end, the Eastern Korinthia Archaeological Survey has, since 1999, attempted to document the Isthmia Basin, noting surface finds of pottery and coins as well as signs of buildings. Antiquities in this area, which is under rapid development, are particularly vulnerable. The project should produce an enormous amount of information on life throughout the centuries in the vicinity of one of the greatest cities of Antiquity: in the first three years of the Survey, some 120,000 surface finds were recorded, including remains from the Mycenaean period to a Second World War-era military installation.

The ruins of Corinth, illuminated by electricity and a full moon.

Fountain of Glauke

En route to the museum (left) is a cubic mass of rock, in which are cut the four large reservoirs that formed the Fountain of Glauke, a construction similar to the Peirene fountain (*see p. 174 below*). Pausanias (*II, 3, 6*) attributes its name to Glauke, Jason's second wife, who is supposed to have flung herself into it to obtain relief from the poisoned robe sent her as a wedding-present by the furious, spurned Medea (*see p. 555*). Roman alterations, the decay of the roof in medieval times, and the earthquake of 1928 have all but obliterated its porticoed façade and three drawbasins. The reservoir, which was fed by a small conduit from the base of Acrocorinth, had a storage capacity of c. 64,000 litres (14,000 gallons). Adjoining the fountain to the east is a colonnaded precinct, the entrance to which faced the Sikyon road. Within the court stood a somewhat earlier temple (**Temple C**), perhaps the Temple of Hera Akraia, though not (needless to say) that on whose altar the citizens of Corinth slew the children of Medea.

The museum

The diminutive museum was endowed in 1931 by Ada Small Moore in memory of her father, a philhellene of Chicago, and extended in 1950. In a tale worthy of Pausanias, most of the 284 vases and other objects stolen in a night robbery in 1990 were found packed in plastic boxes hidden in a fish warehouse in Miami, Florida, in 1998. The objects were reinstalled here in 2001. Excavations at Corinth have been under the aegis of the American School of Classical Studies in Athens since 1896 and many of the exhibits are labelled in Greek and English.

Entrance court and Vestibule: Sculptural fragments, including part of a dolphin from the Fountain of Poseidon. The vestibule contains a restored mosaic showing two griffins attacking a horse (c. 400 BC, one of the earliest known Greek pebble mosaics), a marble head of Herodes Atticus and the small shop.

Greek Gallery: This is arranged to show the rise of Corinth from a small settlement to an important manufacturing city-state. The cases contain locally-made vases showing the progression of style from Protogeometric through Geometric to Protocorinthian (725–625 BC), known throughout the Mediterranean; the *aryballos* shape occurs frequently (fine example showing two warriors fighting). Ripe Corinthian pottery (625–550 BC) is at its best in the first 25 years.

At the far end of the gallery are several inscriptions (including an inscribed stone from the sacred spring reading in Archaic Corinthian letters 'Sanctuary boundary; do not come down. Fine 8 drachmai') and several sphinxes, as well as the forepart of a horse (? part of a metope from the Temple of Apollo); small altars, Doric capital, etc, from the Kerameikos (*see p. 177*).

Other cases include black-figure ware (550–450 BC) in imitation of the Attic style which was capturing all the mar-

kets. Compared with vases imported from Attica (kylix signed by Neandros), the black glaze did not adhere firmly to the local Corinthian clay. There are also terracotta figures and plaques, including a fine gorgon. An amphora made in Morocco, and the fish scales found in it, come from the home of a mid-5th-century merchant, and are an indication of Corinth's extensive trading network.

Roman and post-Classical Gallery: The display cases contain some of the museum's finest objects, including protogeometric grave offerings, pottery from Corinthian workshops, black-figure and white-ground *lekythoi*, Roman sculpture and delicate glass perfume bottles.

Along the gallery's walls, a series of statues from the Julian basilica, shows members of the *gens Julia*, including Augustus robed as *Pontifex Maximus* (c. AD 13); head of Nero. Above the statues are mounted three mosaics (2nd century AD) from a villa outside the northwest wall, including one of a shepherd piping to contented cows. The far end of the room is dominated by Colossal figures from the 'Captives' Façade' and a fragmentary sarcophagus of Hadrian's day with reliefs of the departure of the Seven against Thebes and the death of Opheltes. There is also a Roman copy of an athlete (after Myron or Kalamis), and Roman copies of Classical heads from the theatre, probably the *Sappho* of Silanion and the *Doryphoros* of Polyclitus. Other cases contain sgraffito and incised pottery of the 12th century and 'Protomajolica' ware (finds so far paralleled only at Athlit in the Holy Land), Byzantine pottery and glass, and a wooden lute of 10th century.

Cloister: In this pleasantly shaded spot there are frieze reliefs from the theatre (Hadrianic rebuilding) representing the Labours of Heracles and an *Amazonomachia*; the goddess Roma, on a base with other statues from Temple E; Byzantine decorative carvings; inscription reading 'Συναγώγι Εβραίων' (Jewish synagogue; 3rd century AD or later), and a head of Coptic type, perhaps of Egyptian sandstone and imported in the 4th or 5th century AD. In the northwest corner of the courtyard is a base inscribed to Regilla (probably the wife of Herodes Atticus). The Asclepieion Room (*opened on request*) contains finds including typical ex-votos, some anatomically graphic; Early Christian gravestones; and a cache of silver and weapons of the early 19th century.

Roman mosaic of a cowherd piping to his animals (2nd century AD).

ANCIENT CORINTH

Bouleuterion

West shops

South Basilica

South stoa

Bema

Agora / Forum

Captives' façade

Northwest stoa

Propylaia

Temple of Apollo

Starting line

Basilica

Julian Basilica

Peirene Fountain

Peribolos of Apollo

Lechaion Road

Baths of Eurycles

Roman market

Exit

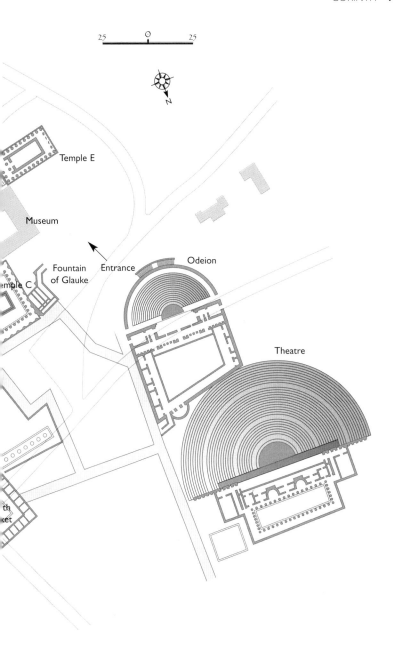

25   O   25

Temple E

Museum

Fountain
of Glauke

Entrance

Odeion

mple C

Theatre

th
et

RECONSTRUCTION OF CORINTH
(ROMAN PERIOD)

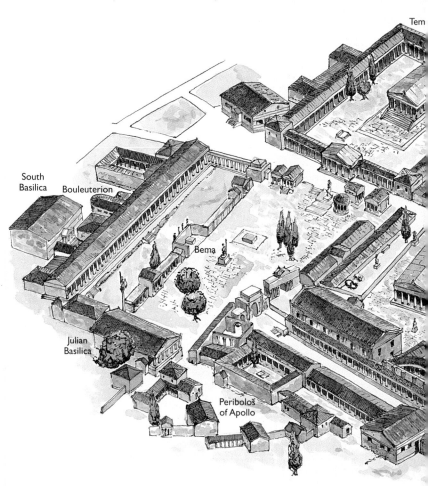

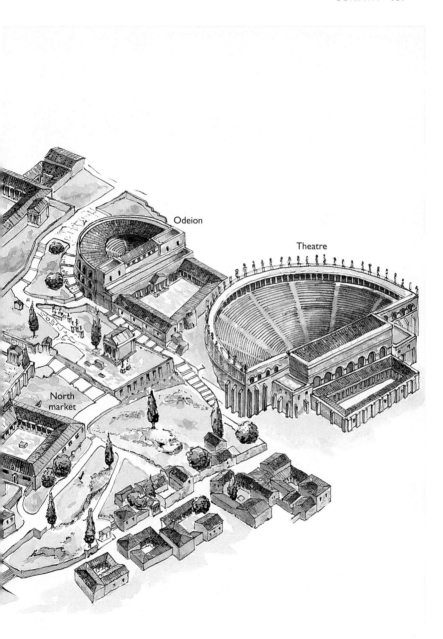

Odeion

Theatre

North market

Temple E

Immediately to the right on leaving the museum and approaching the site is a reminder of Corinth's importance during the Roman period: the foundations of Temple E, an early Imperial building of imposing proportions, probably the temple dedicated either to Jupiter Capitolius or to Octavia, the sister of the emperor Augustus. Pausanias mentions both shrines, but with insufficient precision for certainty of identification. An inscription records that the temple was damaged in the earthquake of AD 77 and rebuilt. Parts of the entablature are displayed on the platform. South of the temple part of the Roman *decumanus* has been exposed.

In the southeast part of the temple temenos, immediately south of the museum, excavations during the last decade have thrown light on the medieval history of Corinth. In particular a Frankish complex (low remains visible; *no access*) contained a church at the north end and partly colonnaded structures on the west and east. The complex, perhaps a monastic establishment frequented by pilgrims en route to and from the Holy Land, was probably destroyed in the 14th century, perhaps by one of the groups of Catalan mercenaries who roamed Greece at this time, but refurbished for use in the 15th–18th centuries. The area has produced coins, jetons, and important and extensive deposits of medieval pottery. The adjacent cemetery has many skeletons showing signs of brucellosis, a malaria-like illness transmitted by goats and goat products.

THE CORINTHIAN CAPITAL

Corinth has given its name to an architectural order, the chief distinguishing feature of which is its capital. The Corinthian capital was invented, according to Vitruvius, by the Athenian sculptor Callimachus in the early 5th century BC. The story told is that Callimachus took his inspiration for the shape of his new capital from a basket twined with acanthus leaves, which he saw left as an offering on a girl's grave. Most Roman building uses the Corinthian order. The earliest external example in mainland Greece is the Lysicrates Monument in Athens (*pictured on p. 106*). Another, very fine, example, also in Athens, is the Temple of Olympian Zeus (*pictured on p. 107*). In modern times, Corinth has lent its name to the currant (*Korinthiaki staphìs*, literally 'Corinthian raisin'), which was first cultivated in the neighbourhood. In world production of currants today, Greece is second only to the United States.

The Temple of Apollo

Opposite Temple E the path leads directly to the site. Before the gate (left) is a display of architectural fragments including column capital types (Doric, Ionic, Corinthian, from left to right along the back wall). The Temple of Apollo, prominent on a knoll to the left, is one of the oldest temples in Greece and the most conspicuous monu-

Architectural fragments at Corinth, including in the foreground, left of centre, an example of a Corinthian capital.

ment on the site (*roped off; entrance no longer possible*). The first temple here was built in the mid-7th century BC and is one of the first known to have had a tile, rather than a thatched, roof; the second temple was built a century later.

The temple, of the Doric order, had a peristyle of 38 columns (6 by 15). Seven adjacent columns remain standing, five on the west front and two more on the south side; the five that form the corner support part of their architrave. Four further columns lie where they fell; foundations remain of four others which Leake tells us were 'demolished by the Turk whose house stands upon the site, because they stood in the way of some new building which he was projecting'. The shafts are monoliths, c. 7m high and 1.8m in diameter at the base, of rough limestone. The lower side of the fallen columns shows the well-preserved Greek stucco and the thicker plaster of a Roman restoration. They have 20 flutes. Their flat Archaic capitals are characteristic of the mid-6th century BC. The naos had two unequal chambers separated by a wall, with a distyle portico in antis at either end. Two rows of interior columns supported the roof. The foundations of a statue base have been found in the west chamber, near the partition wall. In the southwest corner of the pronaos was found a rectangular strong-

The seven surviving monolithic columns of the Temple of Apollo.

box lined with waterproof cement. The precinct of the temple has been cleared, exposing slight but important remnants of the earlier 7th-century temple, which has some similarities with the Archaic temple at Isthmia (*see p. 183*). Before visiting the site, it is helpful to take advantage of the elevated temple knoll to get an overview of the site, most of which is visible, if not immediately intelligible.

North of the temple knoll and partly obscured by a modern road are the remains of the **north market** (? 1st century AD), a rectangular peristyle surrounded by some 40 shops, constructed on the site of an earlier Greek bath. About a third of the market has been excavated and some mosaic pavements survive. The market, which marked the north boundary of the forum, was rebuilt and used in Byzantine times. Beside it, was the long north stoa; some of its coloured terracotta antefixes are in the museum. The gold necklace and hoard of 51 gold staters of Philip and Alexander the Great found here are in the National Archaeological Museum at Athens.

The Agora

The vast (c. 210m by 90m) central agora (more accurately the forum, since what we see is a Roman market-place), cut through by the paved Lechaion road, is girdled by

extensive thickets of stoas and shops, baths and administrative buildings. It is sobering to realize that Pausanias, perhaps rushed for time, mistook the Temple of Apollo
for the Fountain of Glauke. Like many a visitor, Pausanias starts strongly, reminding
his reader that 'What calls for discussion in the city are of course the remnants of
Antiquity, but also and more extensively the product of the later flowering'. Pausanias
(*see p. 175 below*) is famously more interested in Greek remnants than in later flower-
ings, and within a page or two he disposes of Corinth's many baths and numerous
fountains with a cursory reference.

The relentless sprawl of the forum was halted only by the existence of the Greek
south stoa (*see below*). As yet, the location of the Greek and Hellenistic agora is
unknown; it may have been in a totally different location, possibly to the north end
of the Lechaion road. What is known presently is that no earlier buildings of importance have been found below the forum in the area between the temple hill and the
south stoa. In Greek times, this seems to have been occupied by a racecourse and various cult places. Here, as elsewhere, the Greek remains are usually distinguishable by
being at a lower level than the Roman remains.

In a radical Roman replanning the forum area was transformed into two unequal
but more or less level terraces, the upper part being c. 4m higher at the centre. The
division between the two was marked at first by a terrace wall; later, shops were erected in front of this. In Frankish times the forum area was covered with houses. In time,
the village of Old Corinth occupied much of the ancient site.

The north and west sides

On the north side of the forum (south of the temple knoll) are the remains of the
northwest stoa (1st century AD), whose front stylobate is well-preserved, with many
columns still in place, and a colonnade of 15 northwest shops (3rd century AD). The
large central shop, with its stone vault intact, forms the most conspicuous element of
the forum; the concrete vaults of the others have fallen.

The west side of the forum was bounded by a row of shops, fronted by a colonnade
(an inscription on the entablature relates to a repair after an earthquake in AD 375).
Through the middle of these (now seen to the right) one entered the forum. Set forward of the shops were six small Roman temples and a monument, all now so ruined
as to mean little to any but professional archaeologists, were it not for their dedicatory inscriptions, reminders of the fluidity of life under the empire. The monument,
commemorates a former slave of the 1st century AD, Babbius Philinus, who obviously became prosperous enough to dedicate a substantial monument. Of the temples,
one was dedicated to, and one by, the vicious 2nd-century AD Emperor Commodus—
whose name was later erased, presumably when it was safe to do so.

The south stoa

The south side of the forum (the administrative centre of the Roman province of
Achaea) is closed by the **south stoa**, the largest Classical secular building in Greece,
dating originally from the 4th century BC. It had already been reconstructed before

146 BC. Facing the forum was a double colonnade with 71 Doric columns in front and 34 Ionic columns in the middle. Some columns have been collected and restored to position. The rear of the building was transformed in Imperial times. From the stoa's northwest corner, a Roman foundation wall extends at right angles to the building; on it stand Archaic columns, taken possibly from the Temple of Apollo, and across the top a water channel supplied a basin.

In its original form the two-storey south stoa was divided into a row of 33 shops, each with another room behind. All but two of the front compartments had a well, supplied from the Peirene system. From the number of drinking cups recovered from the wells, it is thought that the 'shops' served chiefly as places of refreshment and the wells as refrigerators. A second floor, reached by stairs at either end, probably served as night quarters, and the stoa is believed to have been a huge hostelry built to house delegates to the Panhellenic Union, which Philip of Macedon convened at Corinth. The Greek form is best observed at the west end, where at one point Greek walls stand to a height of 2.75m; a section of the roof has been reconstructed from tiles found in the wells. The building was restored in Julian times, but in the 1st century AD most of the rear half was demolished to make way for administrative buildings: the restaurants and drinking clubs were repressed, bureaucratic offices were created; the colonnades remained.

The Roman administrative buildings begin near the west end of the stoa, where a square hall may be the Duovirs' office; this was later encroached on by a bath-house (well-preserved hypocaust). Towards the centre of the stoa, two shops retained their function in the Roman reconstruction; finds from here included a well-preserved head of Serapis in gilded marble, a base inscribed with the full name of the Roman colony, and the remains of a cash box with coins showing the place to have been destroyed by fire c. AD 267, perhaps in a Herulian raid. Next are the **bouleuterion**, or council chamber. Its curved stone benches have been replaced in position. Through the centre of the stoa a paved road led south towards Kenchreai. To the east (under cover) is a beautiful marble fountain. The next section of the stoa was turned into a forecourt, through which, by a marble stairway and porch, was reached the **South Basilica**. This was similar to the Julian Basilica (*see below*) and, like it, once adorned with Imperial statues. Next is the presumed Office of the Roman Governor, with an antechamber, floors of marble veneer, and (in the antechamber) the base of a statue inscribed to a procurator of the Emperor Trajan. The third hall in from the east end of the stoa was probably the Office of the Agonothetes, who directed the Games at Isthmia.

In front (c. 3m) of the south stoa you cross the line of a low terrace wall below the level of the Roman pavement. Cuttings suggest that this supported over 100 monuments, all probably carried off to Rome during the century following the sack in 146 BC. Pausanias mentions marble or bronze statues (reproductions perhaps) of Zeus, Athena, Aphrodite, Ephesian Artemis, Apollo, and Hermes, as well as gilded wooden statues of Dionysus with faces painted red. During the period of ruin a cart road passed diagonally across the forum (traces at the east end of the wall).

The eastern end and upper forum

The upper forum was the administrative centre of the Roman province of Achaea. The southeast building (right) had a marble Ionic colonnade. It was rebuilt three times and may have been the tabularium, or archive respository, of the Roman colony. In front stands a prominent circular pedestal with a truncated shaft.

The east end of the forum is closed by the **Julian Basilica**, which was probably used for commercial and/or administrative purposes. The well-preserved remains are of a crypto-porticus which formed the base of a Corinthian basilica of the Augustan period. The imperial portrait statues found here are now in the museum.

Parallel to the building and partly underlying its projecting entrance porch is the **starting-line of a Hellenistic racecourse**, preserved for its entire length of 18m and with places for 16 contestants. An earlier 5th-century starting-line with a different orientation lies beneath it. To the south is a curved retaining wall which perhaps supported a judges' grandstand. These remains may be connected with the *Hellotia*, a Corinthian festival mentioned in the 13th *Olympian Ode* of Pindar.

From a circular pedestal, whose function is unknown, a line of buildings extended west, dividing the lower from the upper forum. Its central feature was the **bema**, a monumental rostrum upon which Roman officials appeared before the public. Since later a Christian church was built above its ruins, this may be the place where Gallio, the Roman governor, refused to act upon Jewish accusations against the Apostle Paul (*Acts 18, 12–16*). To right and left of the rostrum extended rows of shops, replaced in Christian times by a flight of steps running the whole length of the forum. In the centre of the lower forum are the foundations of an altar and of an elevated grandstand.

The northern forum

On the north side, almost opposite the bema, towards the centre of the north side, where the Lechaion road enters the agora, stood the **Captives' Façade**, an elaborate two-storey structure of Parian marble, perhaps commemorating a victory over the Parthians. The lower storey consisted of Corinthian columns; the upper storey had at least four atlantes of barbarian captives (portions in the museum); the building reused elements of earlier Roman monuments. The Captives' Façade constituted the final screen of the basilica flanking the Lechaion road (*see p. 176 below*), from which it was separated by an open court.

Adjoining is the **Triglyph Wall**, a low terrace wall decorated with a triglyph frieze, originally painted. It bore tripods and statues, and a surviving base of dark Eleusinian limestone has the signature of the famous 4th-century sculptor Lysippus. Of the two openings for stairways which divide the wall into three sections, one leads down to the **Sacred Spring** (*closed by a grating; key with the custodian*). The spring, which had two bronze lion's head spouts (5th century BC; one now on display in the east room of the museum), was originally in the open air, but was transformed into an underground chamber when the surrounding ground level was raised. It apparently ran dry and was unknown to the Romans, being covered by a later basin fed by a conduit. On the terrace to the north of the Triglyph Wall, and connected with it by an elaborate tunnel, was a small oracular shrine. The tunnel, entered by a secret door disguised as a metope between the triglyphs, probably housed the 'oracle': a priest who pronounced through a small hole below the floor of the shrine. The whole of this area was sacred and public access was forbidden; a minatory inscription forbidding entrance and threatening an eight drachmai fine has been found on its boundary (*see p. 162*).

Returning past the Captives' Façade, you pass through the propylaia, the gateway of the Lechaion road to the agora (now the site exit). Originally a long shallow building, in poros, with a large central arch and two smaller ones on each side, the portal was replaced in the 1st century AD by a typical Roman triumphal arch in marble, surmounted in the time of Pausanias by two gilt bronze chariots bearing Helios and his son Phaethon. Little remains beyond the foundations of the later arch and a portion of the façade of the earlier one. From the road the approach to the propylaia is by a flight of three steps, a landing and a larger staircase.

Fountain of Peirene

The Lechaion road, flanked by the long walls, led into the city from its north port. An impressive monument to Roman town planning, 12m wide, paved and drained in the 1st century AD, it remained in use for centuries. Steps at its steepest part seem to have precluded use by wheeled traffic. To the right, at the foot of the steps which descend from the propylaia, is the **Fountain of Peirene**, the lower one of that name, the upper being on Acrocorinth (*see p. 180*), a natural spring of immemorial antiquity, which has been so much elaborated and remodelled that it looks like an artificial fountain. The water is stored in four long reservoirs fed by a transverse supply tunnel. The reservoirs are hidden by a fountain-house, with a six-arched façade, 'with chambers made like grottoes, from which the water flows into a basin in the open air' (*Pausanias II, 3, 3*). This basin measures 9m by 6m and is sunk below the level of the court of the fountain.

Peirene was turned into a spring by the tears she shed for her son Kenchrias, whom Artemis had killed. Corinth was known in verse and to the Delphic oracle as 'the city of Peirene'. Euripides mentions its 'august waters' (*Medea, 68*). The fountain-house has undergone several modifications. In front of the reservoirs are three deep draw-basins, immediately behind the six chambers of the arcade. Before the arcade was built, the front wall of the basins formed a parapet over which the water was originally drawn in jars. Then the clear space in front of the draw-basins was divided into the existing six chambers. Later (3rd century BC) Ionic columns were erected on the old parapet of the draw-basins, which ceased to be accessible. When Corinth was rebuilt by the Romans the old façade was masked by a new two-storey poros façade—the present series of stone arches. Their engaged Doric columns supported an architrave and a second storey of engaged Ionic columns. This arrangement was continued at right angles to the façade and made to enclose a court 15m square. At the same time the open-air fountain was built in the courtyard. Towards the end of the 1st century AD the walls of the court were lined with marble. At a later time, the court was extensively remodelled to the form which exists today, with massive vaulted apses on three sides. The front walls of the chambers were reinforced and the side walls decorated with paintings of fish swimming in dark blue water (best preserved in Chamber 4). It was long thought that this remodelling took place in the 2nd century AD, but recent work suggests that it occurred much later, in the late 4th or 5th century AD. If so, this would be a startling indication of Corinth's prosperity at a time when it had previously been thought to be dormant at best.

PAUSANIAS

'*On leaving the market-place along the road to Lechaion you come to a gateway, on which are two gilded chariots, one carrying Phaethon the son of Helios, the other Helios himself. A little farther away from the gateway, on the right as you go in, is a bronze Heracles. After this is the entrance to the water of Peirene. The legend about Peirene is that she was a woman who was turned into a spring of water by the tears she shed in bewailing her son...*'. Description of Greece, Book II.

Pausanias was from Lydia, in the west of Asia Minor, and he has left the fullest account of the antiquities of central and southern Greece to have survived. He was writing in c. AD 160–180 when Greece was settled under Roman rule, but his main subject was the monuments of Archaic and Classical Greece and he hardly mentions any buildings dating from after 150 BC unless they are, like the Temple of Olympian Zeus in Athens, benefactions of Hadrian. He provides a mass of material on cults and shrines, and the works of art they held, and these were clearly his major interest. There is very little description of the countryside.

Buildings which survive today correspond so accurately with Pausanias' original descriptions that he is seen as a reliable source for what is now completely missing. In addition to descriptions, he provides historical details and myths such as that above of Peirene. Pausanias muses on the causes of Greek decline and he is sensitive to the outsiders—including, of course, the Romans—who have undermined ancient Greek freedom. It is through Pausanias that one reads of the emperor Nero's looting 500 statues from the oracle at Delphi and other desecrations of Greek shrines by Roman conquerors.

Pausanias is a representative of what is called the Second Sophistic, the revival of interest in the Classical period among educated Greeks. It was emperors such as Trajan, Hadrian and his successor Antoninus Pius who gave wealthier Greeks like Pausanias the chance to explore their heritage, and these rulers earned respect in return. One reason why Pausanias mentions Hadrian's benefactions is because he believed the emperor went some way to restoring the damage inflicted by earlier emperors. And yet however much Pausanias acknowledges the benefits of Roman rule, he remains a Greek writing for other Greeks about the achievements of their forbears, firm in the belief that Greek culture will outlive that of its conquerors. C.F.

Flanking the Lechaion Road

Immediately to the north of the Fountain of Peirene is the **Peribolos of Apollo**, an open court 32m by 23.5m, surrounded by a marble Ionic colonnade, 5m wide, upon a stylobate of Acrocorinthian limestone. Some columns have been re-erected and parts of the epistyle assembled. The heavy foundations in the centre may have supported the bronze statue of Apollo mentioned by Pausanias, who also notes the painting here of Odysseus slaughtering the persistent suitors of his wife Penelope. Below runs the overflow of Peirene, which served the quarter as a main sewer. On the west side, by the Lechaion road, are the foundations of a small Greek temple of the 4th century BC; this was soon replaced by an open shrine in which a covered statue faced its altar across a pebble pavement. Off the south side of the peribolos is an apse, which has been cut into by the east apse of the Peirene court. At an earlier level are scanty remains of a Doric hexastyle stoa and, near the foot of the steps ascending to the Peirene court, some basins from the earliest water system of the Tyrants.

Also on the east side of the road and extending below the modern village are some remains of a great bath of the Imperial era, perhaps the Baths of Eurycles praised by Pausanias as the finest in the city. To the south is a public latrine with some seats *in situ*. The west side of the road is mainly occupied by a terrace on which are the foundations in poros of a **basilica** of the 1st century BC, 64m by 23m, possibly a judgement hall. The basilica terrace was supported at the east by the rear wall of a colonnade which masks 16 small shops. A flight of steps leads through one of the south shops to the extensive though indistinct remains of a Greek market of the 5th century BC, which lies deep underneath the basilica. You return to the road and ascend to the exit from the site, leaving to the left the remains of a square **Roman market**, with colonnades and shops (later replaced by a semicircular court) which is still partly concealed under the modern road.

Around the modern village

To the east of the village are some vestiges of an amphitheatre of the 3rd century AD; of the Isthmian Gate; and of the Early Christian basilica of Kranneion, with a martyrium, that existed in various forms from the 5th century to Frankish times. This lay just within the Kenchreai Gate, where sections of city wall can be traced.

To the south of the village, just below the road to Acrocorinth and on its lower slopes, can be seen the remains of a Sanctuary of Demeter, excavated since 1968 by the American School. The sanctuary dates back to the 7th century BC, and among the finds has been a marble head of the 2nd century from a cult statue of the goddess.

The odeion, theatre, and Asclepieion

Across the road from the site entrance is the **odeion**, (*fenced off, but visible*) cut largely from the rock, resembling in plan that at Pompeii. This roofed theatre held c. 3,000 spectators. Built towards the end of the 1st century AD, it was reconstructed (c. 175) by Herodes Atticus, who, as was his wont, adorned it with marble facing; the interior was totally destroyed by fire and after AD 225 was again restored as an arena or beast-pit by cutting away the lowest rows of seats. Even after a further destruction in 375 by earthquake, the building was patched up to serve until Alaric's holocaust.

Adjacent to the north is the **theatre** (*fenced off, somewhat visible*), with a similar but even longer history. Founded in the 5th century BC, it was here that the multitude acclaimed Aratos of Sikyon after his nocturnal capture of Acrocorinth (243 BC). The cavea of the Greek period is well preserved because the Romans filled it in with earth to produce a steeper rake before rebuilding the seating; the central part has been excavated. Embellished with a three-storey stage-building by Hadrian, the theatre was later modified so that it could stage *naumachiae* and spectacles with wild beasts. In 1925–29 wall-paintings of gladiatorial scenes were found on the late-Roman barrier round the arena; they have since perished. An inscription, scratched in the plaster, was also found recording the story of Androcles and the lion.

About 500m north of the theatre are the remains of the **Asclepieion**, which stood at the edge of the bluff just within the city wall (*cars can get close by taking the road which runs immediately below the former Xenia Hotel*), on the site of an earlier Doric temple of the 4th century BC. Except on the north side the spaces within the colonnades are too narrow to have been an ambulatory, and probably sheltered the dedications of the cured. Many ex-votos are now in the museum; the silver and gold *tamata* dedications placed in Greek churches to this day continue the tradition. Near the entrance to the precinct is a stone offertory box in which copper coins were found. Behind and below the west wall of the sanctuary lies the health centre itself, arranged round a lower court (*for more on Asclepieia, see p. 249*). Off the east side of its peristyle are three rooms, that to the south still with its stone benches; they were probably dining rooms. Over them was a great hall, which closed the west end of the upper court. The south and west walks of the peristyle have access to draw-basins of the Fountain of Lerna, fed by four large reservoirs which extend south into the rock. Another copious supply of water, c. 180m east, is known as the Baths of Aphrodite. Here a Turkish staircase and some fortifications date from the late 17th century. (*NB: These sites are all individually fenced by barbed wire but there is still a reasonable view.*)

The Roman villa and Kerameikos

A road leads west between the odeion and the theatre to the site of a Roman villa (2km), discovered in 1925 and protected by a shelter (*presently closed*). Some of the mosaics from its five rooms have been removed to the museum. More important are the excavations (15mins on foot farther southwest; *also closed*) in the Kerameikos, or Potters' Quarter, on the west edge of the plateau. Remains of workshops and storerooms of the 7th–4th centuries lie inside the Archaic city wall (? 7th century). Through them run the massive foundations of the Classical fortifications. The later wall with remnants of towers and gates may be traced to the gates of Acrocorinth.

Panaghia Field: new discoveries

Since 1995, excavations southeast of the agora in the area known as Panaghia Field, have uncovered an area of 1,300m square with significant signs of habitation, from two 10th-century BC Protogeometric sarcophagi right through to the 20th century AD. A large Roman villa of the late 3rd and early 4th centuries AD had Geometric pattern mosaics, frescoes, and an enviable pool and *euripus* (water folly). The villa is evidence of a greater than expected prosperity here in the early Christian era. In addition, discoveries in Panaghia Field are changing our picture of Corinth from the 17th to the 20th centuries AD. Excavations have revealed, for example, that Christians and Muslims were buried in the same cemetery (17th century). In addition the discovery of imported 19th-century Sèvres and Staffordshire blue decal ware suggests that Corinth was not, as previously thought, an isolated backwater. Pottery (and coins) are one of the most reliable ways of dating the buildings in which they are found. Using the pottery found in Panaghia Field, archaeologists will create a typology and chronology for 19th-century pottery, which can be used to date finds from this poorly documented period elsewhere in Greece.

ACROCORINTH

HISTORY OF THE CITADEL

Acrocorinth (Ἀκροκόρινθος), the Acropolis of Corinth, the limestone mountain (575m) which rises precipitously to the south of the ancient city, is one of the strongest natural fortresses in Europe; in Greece, only Monemvasia can compare. Acrocorinth was the goal of all who aspired to the domination of the Peloponnese and it changed hands many times. Byzantines, Franks, Venetians and Turks have all contributed to its construction; but their walls and towers stand mainly on ancient foundations. In 1208, despairing of victory against the Franks, Acrocorinth's defender, Leon Sgouros, the Archon of Nafplion, who controlled Corinth and Acrocorinth at this time, galloped his horse off one of Acrocorinth's lofty cliffs and perished on the stones below. Thereafter, the defence of the citadel passed to Theodore Ducas, a brother of the Despot of Epirus. In 1210, Ducas sensed the inevitability of defeat and fled to Argos, sensibly taking the church treasure of Corinth with him. Acrocorinth surrendered to Geoffrey de Villehardouin, one of the leaders of the Fourth Crusade, in 1212. Villehardouin then proceeded to turn a large area of central Greece into a powerful Latin state within the Empire of Constantinople. After that came the Acciaioli (1358) and the Palaeologi (1430). In 1458, the citadel withstood Mehmet II for three months, ultimately falling before a concerted artillery barrage. The Knights of Malta conquered it in 1612, and the Venetians in 1687. In 1715 it was retaken by the Turks: the siege of Corinth is described by Byron. Kolokotronis' victory in 1822 over the Turkish general Dramali (*see p. 201*) opened the way to Corinth, which fell into Greek hands after a short siege; Dramali himself died here.

View of Acrocorinth.

The site

Usually open 8.30–5 (summer) and 8.30–3 (winter). A road climbs from ancient Corinth to the citadel summit, where there is a café. It is also possible to follow a track from the ancient site to a cluster of houses below the Fountain of Hadji Mustapha; from there a path winds up to the right round the west face of the mountain to the outer gate (1hr). On foot the visit requires a minimum of 3hrs. Stout shoes and a sunhat are advised. The excellent Ministry of Culture guide The Acrocorinth *is sometimes on sale here; best to get a copy at the site museum.*

The citadel stretches for 24 hectares, with outer walls of 5km; the only approach is defended by a triple line of fortification. You cross a dry moat, once spanned by a drawbridge, to the first of the three gateways which are connected by ramps. The outer gate is largely Turkish, while the middle gate is a Venetian rebuilding of a Frankish structure; traces of ancient walls can be seen. The inner gate is flanked by massive square towers, that to the right little altered since the 4th century BC, the one on the left probably Byzantine. Inside the gates are remains from Acrocorinth's long history, although the basic impression here is of the Frankish inner keep, which encloses the summit. Students of military architecture should not miss the detritus of successive conquerors: the well-preserved Frankish fortifications to the north; the ruins of a Turkish mosque; a 17th-century Venetian cannon.

Visitors pressed for time may prefer to take the path across more gently rising ground amid an overgrown jumble of ruined Turkish houses, Byzantine chapels, and brick-vaulted cisterns, to the south circuit wall of the citadel. Here, near ruined

Turkish barracks at the southeast corner, is the **Upper Peirene Spring**. The subterranean well-house is covered by a vaulted roof of Hellenistic date (protected above by modern concrete). A stairway leads down to a pedimented entrance screen and continues below water level. The water, which is clear and cold (but not safe for drinking), is 3.5m–4.5m deep and has never been known to retreat beyond the screen.

The higher of the two summits of Acrocorinth, due north of Peirene, bore in turn a Temple of Aphrodite, a small basilican church, a watch-tower, a cloistered mosque, and a paved Venetian belvedere. The worship of Aphrodite, the Syrian Astarte, was accompanied by religious prostitution, and the temple is said to have been served by a thousand sacred courtesans. Little remains now but the view, one of the finest in Greece, which Leake, following Strabo, says 'comprehends perhaps a greater number of celebrated objects than any other in Greece'. On a clear day—of which there are sadly fewer and fewer due to industrial pollution—the view extends from Aegina and the Parthenon in the east almost to Nafpaktos in the west, embracing most of the Saronic Gulf and the whole of the Gulf of Corinth.

The north horizon is bounded, from east to west, by Salamis, the hills of Megara, Kithairon, and Geraneia. The Perachora peninsula is prominent in the foreground, then the distant peaks of Helicon and Parnassus. On the south side of the Gulf, the sharp point of Artemision is conspicuous. The tiny Frankish castle of Pendeskoufi (*Mont-Escorée*: bare mountain), built during the 13th-century Frankish siege, boldly crowns the nearest precipitous height of Kastraki.

NEW CORINTH

It must be admitted that Korinthos (New Corinth; Κόρινθος) has fewer charms than its ancient predecessor. It was founded in 1828 when the village of Old Corinth was levelled by an earthquake. The new city was itself largely destroyed first in 1858 and then again in 1928; it has been intermittently damaged by quakes since then, most recently in 1981. It is an undistinguished town of understandably low concrete apartment blocks, on a grid plan, approached by access roads lined by garages and small workshops and factories. The harbourfront is moderately redemptive; the main harbourfront square is Plateia Venizelou. There is a park, along Ermou and Ethnikis Antistasis streets, several blocks inland from the harbour.

EXCURSIONS FROM CORINTH

Four sites near Corinth—Isthmia, Kenchreai, the Diolkos and Lechaion—can all be seen in a vigorous day. On the north shore of the Gulf of Corinth, the sanctuary of Perachora, which was administered by Corinth, can also be visited in a day. On the way from Corinth to Patras, along the coast road, you pass the site of Sikyon. Inland lies the Stymphalian Lake, site of one of the Labours of Heracles.

ISTHMIA & KENCHREAI

Isthmia (in the village of Kyras Vrysi) is some 7km off the main Corinth–Athens road. The modern road follows the ancient one, and passes segments of the Isthmian wall, which extends for c. 9.5km across the narrowest part of the isthmus. The fortification, which follows a natural line of low cliffs, can be traced on foot for practically its whole length. The best preserved section is that immediately east of the Isthmian sanctuary (*see below*), where it is 7m high and 2.5m thick. The remains belong to the original construction of 410–420 AD and to 6th-century repairs of the time of Justinian. Sections of the Classical trans-Isthmian wall mentioned by Herodotus, as well as of a Hellenistic rebuilding of it, have been traced in the countryside northwest of Kenchreai. There are also remains of the wall built c. AD 410–20 in a futile attempt to halt barbarian invasion.

The site

Sanctuary of Poseidon usually open 8.30–3.
Unlike the three other Panhellenic sanctuaries (Olympia, Delphi and Nemea), which were in somewhat out-of-the-way locations, Isthmia was on the main Athens–Corinth road. In fact, Isthmia was one of the most important market towns in Greece. Unfortunately, the road that made it easy for traders and visitors to come here also made it easy for looters. In Late Antiquity most of the town and sanctuary disappeared into the trans-Isthmian wall and fortifications. Consequently, little remains.

Isthmia, like Corinth, has been an American excavation, with the lion's share of the work done by University of Chicago archaeologist Oscar Broneer, who excavated here for several decades beginning in 1952. During the 1990s and into the 2000s, work here by the University of Ohio has concentrated on the Roman bath of the 2nd century AD, the Archaic Temple of Poseidon (where one of the very few blocks *in situ* was discovered), and a geophysical survey of the sanctuary to determine and analyse depositional changes to a depth of six metres.

The museum

Closed for restoration at the time of writing. For information T: 27410 37244.
The first section is devoted to Isthmia itself, with Panathenaic amphorae; athletic equipment including *halteres* (jumping weights); tiles and paintings from the Archaic temple (7 by 18 columns). Beyond are finds from Kenchreai: wooden doors; sculptured ivory plaques with male seated figures; and, most notably, panels in *opus sectile* (in this case glass mosaic) depicting a harbour town and water fowl (these were found packed in crates and may have been imported from Egypt and intended for the home of a wealthy Roman dignitary; they were damaged in an ancient earthquake). There are also finds from the adjacent site of *Rachi*, a 4th–3rd-century settlement where ongoing work suggests the presence of an Archaic/Classical shrine (possibly dedicated to Demeter), of olive oil production and beekeeping, as well as of conflict (slingshots have been discovered). The remains, however, are sparse.

THE ISTHMIAN GAMES

The sanctuary has a history of cult activity and was occupied from the mid-11th century BC until the 3rd century AD. One of the four Panhellenic sanctuaries celebrated in the *Odes* of Pindar, it became famous for its games. The sanctuary's location—just into the Peloponnese from mainland Greece, near Corinth's two harbours—made it a very convenient spot. The date of the main buildings here, as well as the profusion of miniature dedicatory vessels of the 7th and 6th centuries BC, argues that this was the period of the sanctuary's greatest importance. In addition, excavators have noted a substantial increase in the volume of pottery and terracotta figurines around the traditional 582/580 BC date of the first games here.

As is usual, various contradictory legends attempt to explain the foundation of the games. One tradition tells of Melikertes, son of Athamas and Ino. When Ino had been driven mad as punishment by Hera for nursing the son of Zeus and her sister Semele, Ino leapt with her son Melikertes into the sea from the Molurian Rock on the coast of the Saronic Gulf below Megara. Ino was transformed into the sea-goddess Leucothea, and her drowned boy was landed on the Isthmus by a dolphin. Corinth was undergoing a famine at the time, and an oracle declared that this would stop only when the Corinthians gave Melikertes fitting burial and honoured him with funeral games. His name was changed to Palaimon and the Isthmian Games instituted in his honour. The oracle later declared that, to prevent the famine returning, the games must be perpetual.

Other accounts ascribe the games' foundation to Poseidon, to Helios, to Sisyphus, or (in an Attic version) to Athens' hero Theseus. In fact, it would appear that the games were instituted about the time of Periander, the date of the first Isthmiad usually being given as 582 BC. They were held in the 2nd and 4th year of each Olympiad. The Athenians originally had the place of honour while the Eleans were excluded, in a pointed snub to Olympia. In 288 BC the Romans were allowed to compete. The athletic contests were second only to those at Olympia, which they resembled. Musical events were added by the late 5th century BC, on the model of the Pythian Games. The prize for victory in the Isthmian Games was a wreath of pine.

The organisation of the games was in the hands of Corinth until its destruction in 146 BC, when it passed to Sikyon. The venue of the games was probably also transferred at that time, reverting to Corinth after the refounding of the city by Julius Caesar. As is not infrequently the case, politics intruded into the games: at the games of 336 BC Alexander the Great was nominated leader of the Greeks against Persia; at the games of 196 BC Flamininus declared the independence of Greece; and here in AD 66 the second proclamation of independence was made by Nero.

The archaeological remains
Archaeologist Oscar Broneer's comment on Isthmia's Temple of Poseidon that 'the casual visitor will marvel chiefly, perhaps, at the thoroughness of its destruction' applies equally well to the site itself. Inside the site entrance are the scant remains of the foundation of the **Palaimoneion**, by tradition the tomb of Palaimon. The temple had a circular open colonnade of eight columns, which is depicted on local coinage of the Antonine period. Pits found nearby contained the bones of sacrificed animals.

The nearby remains of the **starting gate for the Classical stadium** (constructed 575–550 and removed c. 300 BC) consist of a triangular pavement, scored with radiating grooves, for 16 runners, of the kind alluded to by Aristophanes (*The Knights 1159*). A starter, standing in the pit, operated traps (*balbides*) hinged to wooden posts, by means of cords running in the grooves under bronze staples. The stadium was buttressed by the terraces of the Temple of Poseidon.

On level ground immediately to the north are the sparse remains of the **Temple of Poseidon**, a 5th-century Doric structure, which had a peristyle of 6 columns by 13. The earlier Archaic temple (built 690–650 BC) on the same site is of great importance for the history of Greek monumental architecture because of its early use of dressed stone. An inventory of its surviving blocks in 1990–91 confirmed that it had a peristyle of 7 by 18 columns and wall-paintings. It was completely destroyed by fire. Another mysterious fire in 390 BC damaged the later building (*Xenophon, Hellenica, IV, v, 4*), which was afterwards re-roofed. A colossal statue, unearthed in 1952, formed part of a cult group of Poseidon and Amphitrite of the Antonine period. Excavations have revealed that the temple had some five terraces, built between the Geometric and Hellenistic periods. The sanctuary became derelict after the sack of Corinth and traces of a wagon road can be seen passing across its altar. Reorganisation was undertaken in the middle of the 1st century AD. In the second half of the 2nd century AD the temenos was extended and the temple area surrounded by stoas, the cost of which was defrayed by the high priest, P. Licinius Priscus. To date, the excavations have not turned up any of the boundary markers that customarily marked off the sacred temenos from adjacent land.

The **theatre** is situated in an artificial hollow midway between the precinct and the Isthmian wall. Virtually nothing remains of the building originally constructed in the early 4th century BC and several times modified. Here Nero sang hymns in honour of the Isthmian deities Poseidon and Amphitrite, Melikertes and Leucothea (*see opposite*). Nero sang so long that—so Suetonius tells us—men pretended to have heart attacks and women feigned the pangs of childbirth in order to be carried out of the theatre by their slaves.

At present visible only from the fence are the remains of huge **Roman baths**, in which excavations since 1975 have uncovered the great hall with a superb mosaic floor, an elaborate hypocaust, and traces of an earlier pool.

On the opposite side of the road, in an obvious gully to the southeast of the sanctuary, is the **later stadium**, larger than the first and orientated roughly at right angles to it. This was in use from c. 300 until 146 BC. The starting line at the open end was discovered in 1961. On the slope beyond the stadium are traces of a cyclopean wall of the end of the Mycenaean period. Its function is uncertain. Beyond the stadium are the remains of a Late Antique fortress (? 5th century), constructed of materials pillaged from the sanctuary. In another cautionary tale, this irregular enclosure abutting the Peloponnesian side of the wall was taken by early excavators to be the peribolos of the sanctuary itself.

Kenchreai

Kenchreai (modern Kechries; Κεχριές) was the ancient port of Corinth, which allowed Corinth to dominate trade to the eastern Mediterranean. Its ancient harbour has long since silted up, but remains of the south mole and warehouses are partly visible. The north mole is under water, but the remains of a lighthouse, the foundations of a tomb, and some indeterminate brick buildings are visible. The important Sanctuary of Isis, where the 4th-century AD glass *opus sectile* panels (now in the Isthmia museum) were found is also largely under water. The site was investigated by both land and underwater excavations in 1963 (Indiana University and University of Chicago, under Robert Scranton).

LECHAION

This poorly signposted site can be reached by leaving Old Corinth on the old Patras road and turning right toward Paralia Lechaiou (Παραλία Λεχαίου). If you find yourself in New Corinth, you have overshot Paralia Lechaiou by about 4km.

The harbour of *Lechaion*, the once deep and wide ancient north port of Corinth, is silted up, but the observant will discern its outline. Ships put in here from Italy and the west and this was the home base of the Corinthian fleet. To get a sense of the site, it is helpful to climb one of the sand dunes, created by various ancient attempts to dredge the harbour. The most conspicuous remains today (fenced in) are of a vast basilica, c. 190m by 50m. It was long thought that the basilica was built in the reign of Marcian (450–457) and extended under Justinian I some 70 years later. It was believed that the church was ruined in the earthquake of 551, after which the baptistery, to the north of the narthex, served for worship for two or three centuries. Recent scholarship, however, suggests that the basilica was begun in the early 6th century AD, completed in the mid-6th century, that it survived the earthquake of 551, and was used into the 7th century. If so, this would be important evidence for the continued prosperity of the area.

The basilica may have been dedicated to St Leonidas and the Virgins, who were martyred by drowning off Corinth during persecutions of the Christians at the time of the emperor Decius (3rd century AD). Much of the marble pavement survives and some exquisite capitals; fragments of coloured glass have been recovered. The basilica is a reminder that Lechaion retained its importance well into the early Christian era.

THE DIOLKOS & LOUTRAKI

The easiest way to reach the Diolkos is to forge into New Corinth, take Odos Athinas past the railway station (on the left) and turn left at the road signposted 'Poseidonia/Loutraki'. In about 2km there is a sign for the Diolkos.

The Diolkos ('haulway') was constructed (probably as early as the 7th century BC) so that ships and cargo could be hauled (presumably by oxen) or winched across the Isthmus, thus avoiding the long and dangerous sea journey around the entire Peloponnese. Segments of this 7-km stone slipway remain and are most clearly seen west of the road, emerging from the water. Use of the Diolkos was arduous, and there were numerous attempts in Antiquity to cut a canal through the Isthmus. The tyrant Periander may have financed the first attempt; the emperors Caligula and Nero (the latter using 6,000 Jewish prisoners sent by Vespasian from Judaea) both tried and failed. The present canal took 11 years to build and was completed in 1893. The modern bridge here can be submerged for the passage of ships into the canal.

THE CORINTH CANAL

The history of Corinth is full of tales of men who attempt grand feats and fail: Sisyphus, king of the city, was condemned to roll a huge boulder uphill, only to have it constantly roll down again. Bellerophon, another king, ended his days an outcast, the gods' punishment for his presumption in trying to ride his winged horse Pegasus to heaven. The story of the Isthmus canal is similar. Many people tried to cut it, and many failed miserably in the attempt. Indeed, so miserable were the failures that evil tongues began to wag, saying that the Corinthians encouraged everyone to believe the enterprise cursed, because it was in their interests to keep the Diolkos haulway open (they charged a fee for its use). Periander, tyrant of Corinth, was one of those who tried. In many ways Periander was a ruler on whom the sun shone. His rule saw trade blossom, largely thanks to his wise policies, and Corinth prospered as a result. But there was a darker side to his existence. His detractors assert that he only encouraged his people to produce great pottery so they would not have the leisure to think about politics. He murdered his wife in a jealous fit, and—so Herodotus says—driven madder still by what he had done, slept with her corpse. Though he lived to a ripe old age, he died broken-hearted after the murder of his son at Corcyra. The emperor Nero was another tyrant who had plans to cut the canal. He erected a ceremonial tent near the site, from which he emerged, singing his own compositions and carrying a little golden trowel, with which he proceeded to dig up a small particle of earth, and thus inaugurate the project. Not long after, he was stabbed to death. It wasn't until the late 19th century that a canal was finally cut. The malevolent spirits seem to have departed.

Loutraki

Loutraki (Λουτράκι) is one of the principal spas in Greece, situated at the east end of the Bay of Corinth and sheltered by the towering Geraneia Mountains. Long popular with Greeks coming to take the waters, it now draws a wider and less sedate clientèle due to the presence here since 1995 of Greece's largest casino. In summer, visitors swell the population from about 15,000 to 100,000. Like its ancient predecessor *Therma*, the town gets its name (*loutraki* means baths or hot springs) from the thermal waters that issue from the mountainside only a few metres from the sea. Their saline waters (30–31°C) are used both internally and externally in cases of dyspepsia, arthritis, and liver complaints (*for information on taking the waters and various therapies see www.city-of-loutraki.gr and www.hellas-guide.com/spas*). 'Loutraki' is one of the most popular bottled waters in Greece. The seafront is attractively laid out with eucalyptus and exotic shrubs, and has several parks, but the profusion of new hotels and restaurants, as well as tour buses bringing visitors to take the waters, lends a frazzled air to the town. If possible, visit here in September or October, when it is usually still possible to swim along Loutraki's long pebble beach without having to contend with the summer throngs and the jet skis.

Twelve kilometres northwest of Loutraki, at Schinos, is a rose garden founded in 1995 by the Center for Hellenism-Damianos Foundation (*open Fri–Sun 10–5 in June, July and August, and other times by arrangement; damianou@otenet.gr; www.cfhdf.gr; T: 210 4290 620*).

PERACHORA

There are at least four buses a day from Loutraki to Perachora village, where it is usually possible get a taxi to the site. It is worth noting that it is sometimes possible to visit Perachora from Kiato by boat; inquire at the harbour.

The village of Perachora (Περαχώρα) stands on a small plain about 305m above the sea, dominated to the north by a sheer crag. The road to ancient Perachora skirts the village (bear left, rather than heading into town) and passes Lake Vouliagmeni, the ancient *Eschatiotis*, separated from the sea by a narrow spit through which a channel was cut c. 1880. An Early Helladic settlement (by the lake) and Mycenaean chamber tombs (at Skaloma) have been excavated. Skirting the north shore of the lake, you come to a group of fish tavernas (often closed off-season) to the right of which, fed by a catch-pit, is a well-preserved cistern (? 4th century BC), still in use. Larger cisterns nearby, with staircases descending 30m into the ground, are more difficult to inspect.

Ancient Perachora occupied the greater part of the narrowing peninsula to the west. This was anciently called *Peraion* or Πέρα Χώρα, 'the country beyond the sea' (as seen from Corinth), and commands, as even Acrocorinth does not, the entire gulf. All

The Corinth Canal, cut through the isthmus in 1893.

around jagged rocks tumble towards the sea, except where a valley descends to the sheltered cove which attracted the mariners of the ancient world. Vacation homes are increasingly built here.

The view extends to the heights behind Nafpaktos, 105km away, where a bend in the straits make the gulf seem like a huge lake ringed by mountains. Predominant to the north are Helicon and Parnassus; to the south, Kyllini. Those who have taken in the view from Acrocorinth and from Perachora have seen the best that Corinthia has to offer. As Sounion was the last point in Attica that sailors heading east passed, and the first they saw upon returning home, so was Perachora for Corinthian sailors plying to and from the west.

HISTORY OF PERACHORA

Although signs of occupation from the Middle Helladic and Mycenaean periods have been found here, the important shrine to Hera Akraia ('of the headland') was not founded until the Geometric period. Hera was a goddess much favoured at nearby Argos, but Perachora seems to have been under the sway of Megara until c. 750 BC, when Corinth took over the sanctuary. Thereafter, Corinth held Perachora with brief interruptions: Xenophon, who served on the Spartan side, describes Sparta's capture of Perachora during the Corinthian War of 391–90 BC when refugees from Corinth fled here for sanctuary (*Hellenica* iv, 5). The site was probably destroyed when Corinth fell to Mummius in 146 BC.

The site

Usually open 8.30–3; T: 27440 49423. The museum is no longer open; finds are exhibited at the Archaeological Museum in Athens.

Except for first shepherds and then archaeologists and visitors, the site has been deserted since Roman times, but its remains have suffered from stone robbers from the opposite coast—the Romans ferried much of the building blocks across the gulf to rebuild Corinth. Perachora was excavated in 1930–33 by Humfry Payne and the British School and thereafter by R.A. Tomlinson. Payne, who is buried in the small cemetery between the site and village of Mycenae, died in his 30s. His story and that of the Perachora excavation is poignantly described by his widow, the British film critic Dilys Powell, in *An Affair of the Heart* and *The Traveller's Journey is Done*.

It is possible from the car park, lighthouse or cliffs to gain an excellent overview of the site. The chapel of Aghios Ioannis and the lighthouse (where polygonal walling suggests the evidence of a fortified acropolis) are the two most conspicuous landmarks. The area closest to the harbour has the oldest sanctuary remains: the foundations of an 8th-century apsidal temple and of a 6th-century rectangular Doric temple. Associated with the temple is an altar, which scholars have suggested had triglyphs and metopes and a Doric frieze. The steps nearby may have been for the comfort of spectators.

The temple remains are flanked to the west by two small stoas, and to the east by an L-shaped Doric stoa (4th century BC). By the chapel of Aghios Ioannis there is a large Hellenistic oval water cistern, and immediately to the south of this the remains of ritual dining rooms, such as are regularly associated with Greek sanctuaries. Any number of drinking cups and plates were found here. Another putative dining room is to the east of the chapel.

About 300m east of the temenos a circular structure, 28m in diameter, has been under excavation since 1982. The edifice, belonging to the Classical period, was waterproofed, doorless and has a floor which slopes inward towards the centre—features which suggest that it was a water collection tank. It is almost certainly the monument mentioned by Xenophon (*Hellenica, iv, 5–6*) as the place where King Agesilaus of Sparta sat reviewing his war booty in 392 BC.

Except on summer weekends, when the site is often very crowded, this is a magical spot. Although the remains are scanty, the situation is enchanting. Perachora—small, lovely—is everything Corinth is not. It is not difficult to imagine the first shrine here, which archaeologists suggest was made of simple mud brick and roofed with thatch. It is hard to resist taking a swim in the cove, but bathers should not venture beyond its mouth (danger of currents and sharks).

SIKYON

Approaching Sikyon from Corinth, you cross the Longos near Assos, a village surrounded by cypress groves. Behind, the flat top of Mt Fokas (873m; the ancient *Apesas*) is prominent. Near Zevgolatio are some remains of a late Roman bath explored in 1954. Vrachati, on the Nemea, is a centre for sultanas. Tarsina has an important Byzantine church (of the Metamorfosis). Further inland near Stimanga are remains of a Sanctuary of Demeter and Kore, whose existence is hinted at by Pausanias (*II, 3*). These are at Aghios Ioannis, 1km west of the village. After Vello, where fruit juices are processed, the road crosses the Peloponnesian Asopos, said by Classical tradition to be an extension of the Maeander flowing beneath the sea from near Miletus. Following the defeat of the presumptuous Marsyas in the music contest with Apollo, the satyr's flutes were thrown up on its bank. Pausanias says they were subsequently displayed in the temple of Apollo at Sikyon.

Kiato, with a prominent modern church and some remains of an early Byzantine basilica near the railway station, is a flourishing port exporting raisins. There are several hotels, too, for those who wish to tarry. It is worth noting that it is sometimes possible to visit Perachora (*see p. 187 above*) from Kiato by boat; enquire at the harbour.

The modern village of Vasiliko (c. 5km southwest; served by bus) has readopted the official name of Sikyon, the later site of which it occupies. The museum and site are about 1km from the village; both signposted. Many of the frequent Corinth–Patras buses stop at Kiato, from where there are buses and taxis to Vasiliko. Sikyon has an extensive website: www.sikyon.com

Ancient Sikyon

Sikyon (Σίκυων; 'Cucumber Town' from σικύα, a cucumber), reputedly one of the old-est of Greek cities, was the capital of Sikyonia, a small district, anciently (as now) renowned for its almonds and olive oil. In the Classical period, this relatively small city was a significant centre of Greek art, with a school of sculpture said to have been established by artists from Crete. Famous artists associated with Sikyon include the probably legendary Boutades, said to have fashioned the first portrait relief out of clay. According to the story, Boutades made the relief of his daughter's sweetheart to con-sole her during his absence. Sikyon's school of bronze sculpture was made famous by Aristocles, Canachus, Polyclitus and Lysippus. In addition, Sikyonian dress, and in particular the Sikyonian shoes (most famously a stylish half-boot) manufactured in workshops here, had a wide reputation.

HISTORY OF SIKYON

The traditional list of Sikyon's heroic kings includes the Argive Adrastus, the only survivor of the 'Seven against Thebes' (*see p. 419*). The Homeric 'Catalogue' makes him commander of the Sikyonian contingent to Troy, and Homer gives to Sikyon the epithet εὐρύχορος (wide open). After the Dorian invasions the city became subject to Argos.

About 660 BC Orthagoras, a popular tyrant, established a dynasty lasting a century, during which the city rose to prosperity. Cleisthenes, greatest of the dynasty and grandfather of the great 5th-century BC Athenian legislator, joined the Amphictyonic League in the Sacred War (c. 590 BC). During the war, a num-ber of Greek city states banded together against the city of Krisa, which was destroyed, thus ending Krisa's control of Delphi and its oracle (*see pp. 445–46*). After reorganising the Pythian Games in Delphi, Cleisthenes instituted similar games at Sikyon, abolishing the worship of Adrastus. His successor Aeschines was expelled by the Spartans c. 556, and Sikyon lost its political independence in the Peloponnesian League. The city remained a significant centre of art and industry, and its coinage was in widespread use in the 5th–3rd centuries BC.

The Sikyonians were loyal allies of Sparta during the Persian invasions, in the Peloponnesian War and after, on more than one occasion providing a fleet. The city was conquered in 368 BC by the Theban Epaminondas, but shortly after-wards a Sikyonian citizen called Euphron achieved a brief local notoriety by seiz-ing the government. In 303 BC Demetrius Poliorcetes razed the ancient city in the plain and built a new Sikyon, temporarily called Demetrias in his honour, on the ruins of the old acropolis. In 251 BC Sikyon joined the Achaean League. During the eclipse of Corinth after 146, Sikyon took control of much of Corinth's plain and managed the Isthmian Games but, after the refounding of Corinth, gradual-ly declined. Fulvia, wife of Mark Antony, died in exile here in 40 BC.

The site

The first Sikyon was in the plain; its site and harbour are as yet undiscovered, although road construction in 1966 located a necropolis and mosaics of the old city. Of the 'new' city of Sikyon (303 BC), admirably situated 3km from the sea on an extensive triangular plateau between the gorges of the Asopos and Helisson rivers, there is, alas, little to see, and the excellent small site museum is presently closed. It is to be hoped that future excavations will find what must be considerable remains here. Even taking into account his prejudice for the Greek past, it is striking that Pausanias found much more to describe here than in Corinth. Leake reminds us that Sikyon's location, and fortifications, gave it a military importance in the north Peloponnese second only to that of Corinth. Defended on all sides by precipitous cliffs, Sikyon's expansive plateau is divided by a rocky slope into a lower terrace, the acropolis of the old city, and an upper terrace, forming the apex of the triangle, which became the acropolis of the new. The city walls ran round the edge of the plateau and are least ruined on the west side. Excavations, first by the American School of Classical Studies and then by the Greek Archaeological Society, have uncovered a small part of the city, which seems to have been laid out on a rectangular plan.

What to see

The most impressive remains here are those of the **theatre**, one of the largest in continental Greece, which occupies a natural depression in the slope dividing the city's upper and lower terraces. The building dates from the beginning of the 3rd century BC. The cavea is c. 120m across. The lower diazoma could be reached by two vaulted passages as well as by 16 staircases from the *parodoi*. The fifty-odd tiers of seats, mostly hollowed out of the rock, were divided into 15 wedges, each of which forms one twenty-fifth part of a circle. The front seats have backs, arm-rests, and sculptured feet. The orchestra, of stamped earth, surrounded by a drain, had a diameter of c. 20m. Foundation walls of the stage buildings show that they were twice altered in Roman times. They had as a façade a Doric portico of 13 columns in antis.

In a ravine to the west of the theatre are the remains of the **stadium**, as yet unexcavated. The straight end had a wall of polygonal masonry, still partly standing. East of the temple and stadium, the vigilant may discern the foundations of **two temples**, one Archaic, the other Hellenistic, the two overlain by an Early Christian structure. The temples' patron deities may be Apollo and Artemis. Pausanias mentions a Temple of Apollo as being rebuilt by Pythocles. Remains of Classical and Hellenistic altars and some sculpture have been recovered. The south end of the **agora** was closed by a Hellenistic stoa and the bouleuterion, an almost square hypostyle hall, the ceiling of which was supported by 16 Ionic columns. Later it was adapted to other uses. Near it are extensive remains of the **Gymnasium of Cleinias** on two levels; on either side of the central stairway linking them is a fountain. On the upper terrace are scanty ruins of the **acropolis**. The dividing slope is honeycombed with subterranean aqueducts. The view, especially lovely at sunrise and sunset, embraces Helicon, Kithairon, and Parnassus, with a verdant foreground contrasting with the blue of the gulf.

Western Corinthia

After Sikyon the coast road continues to Melissi where a Mycenaean tomb (500m south; *closed*) was discovered and Xilokastro (*just beyond the map*), a seaside resort, with a number of rent rooms, hotels and apartments, popular with Greek families. The town is agreeably situated amid luxuriant gardens at the mouth of the Sythas valley. It probably occupies the site of ancient *Aristonautai*, a seaport of Pellini, where the Argonauts put in. Along the sandy east shore towards Sykia is a pinewood, called Pefkias, with a campsite. A museum devoted to the memory of the poet Angelos Sikelianos (1884–1951; *see p. 444*) has been established in a villa he once owned. To the southwest on the mountainside stands Zemeno, where a wine festival is held in September.

A road climbs into the Sythas valley, carrying on to Pellini, with the insignificant ruins of ancient *Pellene*, on the top of the mountain separating the valleys of the Sythas and the Forissa. There is an excellent view. Beyond is **Ano Trikala** (1067m), a winter-sporting resort with hotels, standing on the north slope of Mt Kyllini, second highest mountain in the Peloponnese (2377m). In Ano Trikala, several mansions of the Ottoman period have been restored.

An easy path climbs in slightly over 2hrs to Refuge A (1646m; 50 beds; water), and (30mins more) to Refuge B (1737m; 20 beds), from which the west summit may be reached (2hrs further). The Gymnos summit (2134m) to the east overlooks Kefalari on the Kastania road. There is an unsurfaced but driveable road to Refuge B (12km).

THE STYMPHALIAN LAKE & PHENEOS

Southwest of Sikyon and some way inland, on the Arcadian border just beyond the village of Stymfalia to the left of the road, are the conspicuous remains of the 13th-century Frankish-Gothic church of the **Cistercian abbey of Zaraka** and its gate tower, perhaps founded by Cistercians from Hautecombes, near Geneva, who came here at the request of William de Champlitte. Ancient architectural members were extensively used in the construction of the church and these probably came from the nearby Temple of Artemis, mentioned by Pausanias but no longer visible. Some of the medieval architectural carving, especially of the capitals, is very fine. Hetherington, in his *Byzantine and Medieval Greece*, suggests that the carving was done by the western monks, assisted by local masons.

About 500m to the south is the low acropolis of ancient *Stymphalos*, clearly marked by the foundations of the city wall. Crowned by a tower, with a sanctuary consisting of a temple, altars, and auxiliary buildings, it overlooks the dried-up lake below. To the east and north of the acropolis the Canadian Archaeological Institute has discovered (by electrical resistivity and proton magnetometer survey) increasing evidence of the ancient city. The city was carefully laid out to an orthogonal plan in the 4th century BC, abandoned in the 2nd century BC, and resettled in the 1st and 2nd centuries AD. The house blocks are long and narrow and the streets 6m wide. Remains of three Doric structures (probably temples) have been found in various parts of the site. On the north side, by the lake, are the remains of a curious round building and a spring house (cleared by A. Orlandos in the 1920s) which still functions. A small temple and altar to Athena Polias lie on a terrace just to the east of the acropolis. Also by the lakeside are the well-preserved remains of massive polygonal walls supporting a road, whose wheel ruts (1.5m apart) are visible in places. In 2001–02, the Canadian excavators here unearthed the stage building (with *proskene*) of the theatre.

At the east end of the lake are remains of a Roman aqueduct, probably that built by Hadrian to take the abundant local spring waters to Corinth. It can be traced across the valley to the modern irrigation tunnel beneath the pass to Nemea.

THE STYMPAHLIAN BIRDS

Heracles, as his Sixth Labour, was set the task of destroying the monstrous, man-eating birds of Lake Stymphalos. The birds had invaded the lake *en masse*, themselves escaping a pack of ravening wolves. Pausanias was obviously taken with this story: he mentions the birds in vivid detail, describing them as having beaks of bronze, long and tapering as that of an ibis, and strong enough to puncture a suit of armour. At the nearby Temple of Artemis (now lost) he saw effigies of the birds carved in wood on the roof, and marble statues of bird-legged maidens. In some way the birds were sacred to Artemis, whose cults are so often associated with wild creatures. At first Heracles could not prevail against the birds, because he could not persuade them to fly, and was unable to shoot them as they sat on the water. Eventually Athena gave him a pair of bronze rattles. The noise made the birds take fright and fly up into the air in alarm, whereupon the hero shot them down. In some versions, the birds escaped, and flew to the Black Sea, where they harried the Argo and its crew.

Some 10km west of Stymfalia is Kastania, a mountain resort (902m) on the south slope of Kyllini below the saddle that separates Stymphalos from Pheneos. This is a good area for walking and for botanists. From Kastania, it is possible to head east on beautiful, rather rudimentary, roads into the Argolid and to Nemea (*see p. 197*). You can also do a loop through the mountains and regain the sea at Derveni (*map p. 398*). En route you pass the site of *Pheneos*, with remnants of a small Temple of Asclepius and a medieval tower on its acropolis, which locals call *Pyrgos* ('tower'). The church of Aghios Georgios, to the northwest, has frescoes.

PRACTICAL INFORMATION

Ideally, the visitor to Corinthia would have at least four days: the first for Ancient Corinth; another for Isthmia, Kenchreai, the Diolkos and Lechaion (which can be seen in a vigorous day). Loutraki and Perachora can also be fitted into a day trip, as can the Stymphalian Lake and Sikyon.

GETTING AROUND

• **By car:** The roads throughout Corinthia are excellent, and most that all but the most adventurous drivers will encounter are paved. In summer, drivers should keep an eye out for the tour buses that hurtle between Old Corinth and popular nearby destinations such as Argos, Mycenae, Epidaurus and Nafplion. Those travelling on to Tripolis and Patras from Corinth should note that, due to heavy lorry and bus traffic, these are two of the roads with the greatest number of traffic fatalities in Greece.

Corinth is linked by excellent roads to Athens, Patras and Tripolis. The National Highway (tolls) runs from Athens to Corinth and thence to Patras or Tripolis. The 'old' road from Argos and Tripolis to Corinth (no toll) is more pleasant, if one does not mind being trapped behind the occasional tour bus, tractor or lorry.

• **By rail:** Loutraki is served by 4 daily trains from Athens. Trains on the Patras–Tripolis–Athens route stop at the New Corinth station on Athinon, off the waterfront, east of Plateia Venizelos. There are at least 4 trains a day.

• **By bus:** There are about 10 daily buses from Athens to New Corinth (3hrs). There are some 5 buses a day from Tripolis (2hrs) and Patras (3hrs). Athens buses arrive and depart from the station on the corner of Ermou and Koliatsou by the east side of the park. Frequent buses from New to Old Corinth leave from the station at Koliatsou on the west side of the park. Tripolis and Patras buses arrive and depart from the station at the corner of Aratou and Ethnikis Antistasis by the west side of the park. There are frequent buses to Loutraki from New Corinth and from Athens. Loutraki has buses to Perachora.

• **By taxi:** There are usually taxis waiting by the bus and train stations in New Corinth; there is a taxi stand by the site in Old Corinth. There are also taxis at Perachora for the ancient site.

WHERE TO STAY

Corinth
Hotels in New Corinth tend to be noisy. To explore the area it may make sense to stay in nearby Nafplion, which has all the charms Corinth lacks, including excellent hotels and restaurants. For this reason, reservations—especially on summer weekends when Athenians flock to Nafplion—are recommended. For those wishing (or having) to stay in or closer to Corinth, the following are possible choices:

€ **Belle Vue**. (Damaskinou 41; T: 27410 22068), and € **Korinthos** (Damaskinou 26; T: 27410 26701). Both are centrally located between the park and harbour.

€ **Marinos Rooms** (Old Corinth). Advertises—and provides—'traditional greek hospitality' and 'excellent cuisine', and has acceptable rooms, many with a view of Acrocorinth. T: 27410 31209; marinosrooms@acn.gr

Isthmia
€€ **Kalamaki Beach Hotel**. Popular with families. T: 27410 37653; wwwkalamakibeach.gr

Kastania
Xenia Hotel. 17 rooms, on the slopes above town. Open all year. T: 27470 61283.

Loutraki
€€€ **Hotel Poseidon**. Sprawling resort with all the creature comforts. T: 27440 67938; www.poseidonresort.gr
€€ **Angelidis Palace**. Handsome 1920s Art Deco-style hotel on the waterfront, with elegant, chandelier-laden lounge. Open year-round. Lekka 19; T: 27740 26695; www.hotelpalace.gr
€€ **Karelion**. Similar in age and style to the above, with a fine veranda. Open April–Oct. Lekka 23; T: 22740 22347.

Trikala
€€ **Helydorea**. Faux-rustic mountain retreat hotel, popular during the summer and at weekends with escaping Athenians. At other times you are likely to have the place almost to yourself. 14 pretty rooms with lots of wooden furniture. Meals can be bespoke (though dinner is usually served as a matter of course at weekends). T: 27430 91444 or 210 685 4173 (Athens office); www.helidorea.gr
Other options in Trikala include the €€ **Mysaion** (T: 27439 91141), not as architecturally distinguished as the Helydorea, but perfectly comfortable; and the €€ **Pigi Tarlamba** (T: 27430

91267), with 22 rooms and suites, virtually unchanged since the 1930s.

WHERE TO EAT

Corinth
There is a string of interchangeable tavernas along the harbour in New Corinth. Years of catering for groups have led most restaurants in Old Corinth to serve over-priced inferior food; Marinos, the restaurant at Marinos Rooms is a notable and welcome exception.

Isthmia
There are several fish tavernas in town.

Loutraki
€€–€€€ **Oceanos**. Sophisticated international cuisine in seaside setting. Akti Poseidonos 58.
€€–€€€ **Maistrali**. Serves fresh fish, on the waterfront. Akti Poseidonos 83.
€€ **Café Stathmos**. Has coffees, ice creams, and snacks. Lekka, beside the electric train that runs from Loutraki to Athens.

Stymfalia
There are several tavernas (and a simple hotel) in the village.

Trikala
Good local tavernas include Ta Epta Aldephia (The Seven Brothers) and Ta Tria Platania (The Three Plane Trees).

FESTIVALS & EVENTS

The *Pavleia*, a festival honouring St Paul, the patron saint of Corinth, takes place 24–28 June. There is usually a summer music and drama festival; information available at the Dimarcheion at the corner of Koliastou and Ermou and on posters around town.

THE ARGOLID

NB: This chapter is covered by the map on p. 156.

The Argolid (Greek 'Argolidas'; Ἀργολίδας) is the easternmost of the *nomes* of the Peloponnese, bordered on the north by Corinthia and on the west and south by Arcadia. It consists of the Argolic plain and a more mountainous peninsula, the fourth and least conspicuous tongue of the Peloponnese, which separates the Gulf of Nafplion from the Saronic Gulf. Although Homer called the Argive plain 'thirsty', it was praised in Antiquity for grain and horses; today it is green with vineyards and groves of orange and lemon trees. Although Argos was the Argolid's most important city during Classical antiquity, the modern capital is Nafplion, by far the most comfortable and convenient centre for exploration, both here and in neighbouring Corinthia.

As always, geography is destiny. Much of the Argolid's importance in Antiquity stemmed from its position, which controlled the Pass of Dervenaki, the most important route from the Corinthia south into Arcadia and Laconia. And, just as Corinth's isthmian position and two superb ports allowed it to control much sea traffic both to the east and west, the Argolid's long coast and gentle harbours afforded opportunities for trade with Crete and Egypt to the south.

The Argolid is of the greatest historical and archaeological importance. And unlike Corinthia or Laconia, it was not dominated for most of its history by one city: Lerna (first occupied c. 6500 BC) flourished until the end of the Mycenaean period. Mycenae dominated not just the Argolid but much of Greece between the 16th and the mid-13th centuries BC. The importance of Argos is reflected in the fact that in Homer 'Argive', like 'Danaan' and 'Achaean', is a synonym for 'Greek'.

The modern province corresponds roughly to the ancient Argolid; some sites technically in modern Corinthia (eg Nemea) are covered in this chapter. The Argolid is also home to Tiryns, Mycenae's putative port; the massive shrine of the Argive Heraion; the Sanctuary of Asclepius and 4th-century BC theatre of Epidaurus, which is still used for performances.

Into the Argolid

From modern Corinth the old Argos road runs southwest through vineyards. Although the new toll road is faster, the old road follows the path of the ancient road, giving a clearer sense of the landscape, and passing a number of minor sites. To the right rises Acrocorinth. The road climbs the wooded valley between the Oneia hills (563m; left) and Mt Skiona (700m), afterwards passing through a number of undistinguished villages, and skirting the scant remains of several ancient and medieval sites. At Chiliomodi a road branches left to the Pass of Aghionori (8km) with a medieval castle repaired by Morosini (commander in 1687 of the Venetian forces who fired the cannon ball into the Parthenon; *see p. 71*), and continues by Prosymna to the plain of Argos. The Turkish general Dramali succeeded in fighting his way out of the plain along this branch road, at the cost of a further 1,000 men, two days after his defeat at Dervenaki (*see p. 20i*).

The scant remains of *Tenea*, whose precise site has not been determined, lie near this road at Klenia, 1.5km south of Chiliomodi. Tenea is perhaps best known because it was believed that Oedipus, who had been exposed as an infant, was brought up here by the shepherd who found him. Of Tenea itself, little is known: its inhabitants claimed to be Trojans brought captive by the Greeks from Tenedos, where the Greek fleet anchored off Troy. When Corinth founded Syracuse c. 734 BC, most of the colonists came from Tenea. In 146 BC, Tenea sided with the conquering Romans, and so escaped the destruction of Corinth. As the road runs westward, it enters the territory of Kleonai, becoming increasingly shut in by hills as it reaches the summit (392m) near Dervenakia.

NEMEA & KLEONAI

Along with Olympia, Delphi and Isthmia, Nemea (Νεμέα) was one of the four Panhellenic sanctuaries where important athletic festivals took place. The site of ancient Nemea, surrounded by low hills, many covered with vineyards, sits on a small plateau in an upland valley some 4km long and 1km wide in the hamlet of Archaia Nemea. The Nemeios Dias is a very welcome café/restaurant by the site (signposted 'Snak Bar/Souvenir'; *usually open 10am–mid-afternoon*).

The site and museum

Museum usually open Mon 11–3, Tues–Sat 8–3. Site (including stadium) usually open daily 8–3. The site and museum are sometimes open until 5pm in summer; T: 27460 22739. The museum has labels in Greek and English. Several excellent guidebooks are available at the site: S.G. Miller et al: Nemea. A guide to the site and museum *(2004); S.G. Miller:* Nemea: A Brief Guide *(2004); S.G. Miller:* The Ancient Stadium of Nemea *(c. 1994). The museum, site and stadium are best visited in that order. Parking by the site and stadium.*

The museum, immediately inside the site entrance to the right, is one of the finest small museums in Greece. The entrance hall has a display of early travellers' views and accounts and gives a sense of the excavations here. The French School studied the temple in 1884 and 1912; the site was partly excavated by the American School of Classical Studies in Athens (ASCSA) in 1924–27, and again in 1964. Large-scale excavation and restoration work resumed in 1974 under the aegis of the ASCSA and the University of California at Berkeley. The central room has a helpful site model and a video on the starting gate used in the ancient stadium. The well-labelled finds, including pottery, athletic gear, bronzes and coins, have legends explaining their significance and the significance of the site itself. Windows in the central room overlook the site, which makes it possible to see where many of the objects were found. A large display uses coins to make the point that visitors from throughout the Greek world and beyond attended the games.

The museum was reinstalled in 2003–04 and a new gallery has finds from prehistoric sites of the northeastern Peloponnese from the Neolithic to the Late Helladic period, including Tsoungiza and Aïdonia. The displays from some 20 tombs, of which five were unplundered, in the Mycenaean cemetery at Aïdonia are especially impressive. Much of the jewellery found in the Aïdonia shaft graves (c. 1500–1400 BC) was stolen in the 1970s, and recovered and returned here in 1996 when traced to New York City and saved from being auctioned.

HISTORY OF NEMEA & ITS GAMES

Although prehistoric remains have been found on the hill of Tsoungiza, above Nemea, excavation suggests there was no occupation between Mycenaean times and the 8th century, and little activity until the 6th century. In part, this was due to the fact that the valley was subject to severe flooding until the Nemea river was diverted in modern times. The games, which took place in late summer, occurred when the valley would have been dry. For the rest of the year, the sanctuary here sat in a soggy marsh and was probably almost deserted, except for a skeleton staff of guards and priests.

In Roman times, it was believed that the Nemean Games honoured the First Labour of Heracles: the slaying of the Nemean Lion. To this day some of the local red wines commemorate the hero with their name: 'Blood of Heracles'. Earlier accounts of the games' origins say that the Seven Against Thebes (*see p. 419*) held the first games to honour the infant prince Opheltes. Unlike Heracles, who strangled a serpent whilst in his cradle, Opheltes died of a snake bite, when his careless nurse put him down in a bed of wild celery, where the snake lay concealed. Victors at the Nemean Games, which took place every two years, received a crown of wild celery to commemorate the event, and the judges wore the black robes of mourners. It seems that a commemorative 'burial mound' for Opheltes was constructed here as early as the decade before the formal foundation of the games in 573 BC. The games were managed by neighbouring Kleonai from 573 until they moved to Argos in the late 5th century. They returned to Nemea c. 330.

Much of what remains to be seen at Nemea today dates from the burst of building activity when the games returned, and from Nemea's final period of some prosperity in the early Christian era. The 6th-century Slavic invasion put an end to that prosperity, here as throughout much of the Peloponnese.

The xenon, bath and heroön

Leaving the museum, you turn right and follow the path toward the Temple of Nemean Zeus. The path passes to the right a row of 4th-century houses, perhaps used by officials at the games, and a 4th-century BC *xenon*, a hotel or hospice for visitors, including athletes. The building, which had at least five separate entrances from a roadway to the south, is obscured by the remains of the large 4th–5th-century AD basilica built over it, which made use of spolia from the site. Many of the blocks used in the basilica came from the *xenon* and from the Temple of Zeus, including parts of the sanctuary screen and floor. The floor was redone using terracotta in the 12th century. Beside the basilica are the remains of a baptistery and graves of early Christians, buried facing east to greet the Resurrection. To the left of this complex are the substantial remains of a 4th-century bath, a usual feature of athletic sanctuaries; some stretches of the terracotta aqueduct which carried water to the bath house are visible. To the left of the path itself are the remains of the heroön, probably a c. 6th-century BC shrine to Opheltes. It is possible that future excavations in this area will uncover Nemea's hippodrome; the discovery in 2000 of large cistern in this area prompted excavators to speculate that the cistern was a water supply for horses, whose stables and race track might be found nearby.

The path continues toward the Temple of Zeus, passing (right) the remains of nine small buildings (*oikoi*), which excavators suggest may have been combined storehouses, treasuries and meeting houses maintained by cities that participated in the games.

The Temple of Nemean Zeus

This Doric peripteral hexastyle temple (6 columns by 13), was built between 340 and 320 BC of locally quarried stone, on the site of an earlier sanctuary. Preliminary investigations suggest that the pediment of the earlier temple had painted, not sculpted, decoration. When Pausanias visited here he wrote that the 4th-century temple was worth seeing 'except that the roof has collapsed and there was not a statue left'. The lowest course of the cella is sufficiently well preserved to show that it had a pronaos in antis but no opisthodomos. Within the cella 14 columns enclosed the central space, while to the west, between the colonnade and the wall, and below the floor level, is an *adyton*, or secret inner chamber, approached by a flight of crude steps. Parallel to the façade are the foundations of a long narrow altar of unusual type.

The columns are unusually slender; the three columns that remained standing through the centuries (one from the peristyle and two from the pronaos, still supporting their architrave) were much commented on by the early travellers. For centuries, the drums of many other columns lay in order as they fell as the result of deliberate destruction at various times from the 4th to the 13th centuries AD. In 1984 the archaeologists began to inventory and study the fallen columns. Then, between 2000 and 2004, two fallen columns were re-erected in a giant jigsaw puzzle project that involved using both the ancient column drums that survived and new drums created from local limestone. In time, it is hoped to re-erect perhaps four more columns. It is sometimes possible to watch the local masons, who are working on the reconstruction, at work fluting replacement drums.

The stadium

Leave the site by the access road and turn left for the short walk to Nemea's stadium, which was excavated and restored in 1974–81. Though the games were founded here, they were managed by Kleonai until they moved to Argos in the late 5th century, and then again in the 3rd century, probably permanently. As Stephen Miller, director of the Nemea excavations 1974–2004, points out, the games actually took place at Nemea for less than a quarter of their history. Throughout, the games seem to have imitated those at Olympia and not included the musical contests, which Delphi and Isthmia held alongside the athletic heats. In 1996, the revived Nemean games were established here, and have taken place every four years since then (*see www.nemea.gr*). Beside the stadium are the remains of the ancient locker room, the dressing room—or, more precisely, undressing room— where the athletes stripped naked and oiled and dusted themselves before contesting. Of embanked earth, the stadium occupies a partly natural hollow. The starting line is *in situ* and a stone water channel surrounds the course. Foundations of a judges' stand and distance markers are visible. The entrance tunnel (c. 320 BC), approached through a courtyard building of uncertain function, has graffiti (boys' names) written by admirers, including 'Acrotatos is beautiful' in one hand and the qualifying quibble 'to the one who wrote this' in a second hand.

KLEONAI & ENVIRONS

Kleonai, which oversaw the games at Nemea for many years, is signposted 3km east of Nemea, in the village of Archaies Kleones ('Αρχαίες Κλεωνές). The area is dominated by Mt Fokas, where there was an ash altar of burnt offerings to Zeus on the summit in Antiquity. Virtually nothing remains of the city that Homer called 'well-built Kleonai' (*Iliad II, 570*), situated some 80 furlongs from Corinth on the prehistoric road over the hills to Argos. Its site (well fortified, as Strabo remarks) occupies an isolated hill overlooking the valley of the Longos.

Off a by-road to the right a track, initially signposted, leads in the general direction. To the left are the foundations of a Hellenistic Temple to Heracles, which was long almost entirely covered by scrub undergrowth. In 2000–01, the site's German excavators cleaned the area around the foundations and it is now possible to get a sense of the basic layout of the temple. Nearby, ploughed-out blocks and washed-down sherds cover a wide cultivated area.

Phlious and Aïdonia

The road runs from the village of Archaia Nemea through the sprawling, unremarkable village of Nea Nemea, across the plain of Phliasia passing the site of *Phlious* (commonly Phliounda) which is marked by a small chapel (Panaghia Rachiotissa; ? 13th century) on a ridge, round which are scattered the somewhat indeterminate remains (a theatre and a square colonnaded court, between the chapel and the road). It is all wine country round here (*see box*), with Koutsi to the east, and Psari and Asprokambos further north, towards the Stymphalian Lake. To the east is Aïdonia, whose Mycenaean chamber tombs were looted, and which contained much fine jewellery (*see Nemea museum, above*). From Psari it is possible, on equally indifferent roads, to wind one's way north toward the Gulf of Corinth or south into neighbouring Arcadia.

NEMEA WINE

Nemea is an important appellation, chiefly famed for its reds made from the Agiorgitiko grape, whose hallmark hint of ripe cherries has led to it being dubbed the Merlot of Greece. A lot of table wine is made on the valley floors; the finest vintages come from the hillside sites of Koutsi, Asprokambos, Gymno, Psari and Nemea itself. The slight altitude protects the vines from too much heat, allowing good acidity to develop to balance the fruit. The most respected producers are Thanassis Papaioannou in Archaia Nemea, and Georgos Palivos, whose winery is on the road between Archaia and Nea Nemea. Tours and tastings are offered most days in summer; www.palivos.gr.

The Pass of Dervenaki

From Nemea the old Corinth–Argos road leads south, crossing the railway. It is possible to make a brief detour here, and follow the branch road to the left by the old railway station (signposted 'Δερβενάκια'). The road climbs steeply up to a chapel in a grove beside a spring (1.5km). Above stands a colossal statue of Kolokotronis, victor in the battle of 1822 (*see below*). The view is fine.

Rejoining the old Corinth–Argos road, a steep poorly-marked turn to the right takes you to Hani Anesti, a former Turkish *han*, or waystation. This is a pleasant stopping place, with massive plane trees, several tavernas, and springs gushing water. There are the remains of several mills.

The Argos road continues south through the Pass of Dervenaki, between the twin summits of Mt Tretos, the 'perforated' mountain (τρητός), so called because it is honeycombed with caves. Road and railway descend the rocky defile. Nearby, on 6th August 1822, Kolokotronis caught the army of Dramali, which was retreating from the plain of Argolis. The Turks left 4,000 men dead on the field, and though a few cavalry fought their way through to Corinth, Dramali and the remainder retreated to try an alternative route through the Pass of Aghionori.

From the south outlet of the pass you look into the plain of Argos. The view is generally hazy. To the east the bare summits of Aghios Ilias (809m), Zara (660m) and Euboia (535m) overshadow the acropolis of Mycenae. On the right Argos sprawls below its mountain citadel while the east Arcadian mountains rise behind, Artemision reaching 1772m, and Ktenias 1599m. In the centre, the battlemented acropolis of Acronafplion rises for a moment above the blue line of the Argolic Gulf.

The poorly-marked new Mycenae access road is on the left, shortly after the Pass of Dervenaki; it continues past Mycenae and other sites, including the Argive Heraion, Midea and Dendra, before becoming a village road that winds its way to Nafplion.

Near Fichtia are the remains (*signposted*) of two ancient watchtowers. Just beyond (left) are the old turning for the village and site of Mycenae (*see Mycenae, below*). The road runs down the middle of the triangular Argolic Plain; to the east and west it is hedged in by barren mountains. The plain is watered by the capricious Panitsa (the ancient *Inachos*), and other seasonal streams. Their dryness was attributed in Antiquity to the anger of Poseidon because Inachos allotted the country to Hera. Hence Argos is 'very thirsty' in Homer. Close to the sea, however, the land is marshy, and between the marshes and the upper part of the plain is the fertile tract of land which was famed in Antiquity for the horses bred in its pastures. Today, much of the plain is irrigated from deep wells; this makes possible the citrus and olive groves, and vineyards. Some 5km outside Argos, Koutsopodi (*turn off signposted for the new Tripolis road*) exemplifies the land's productivity: there are citrus and olive-groves, vineyards, and cotton and tobacco fields. And, increasingly, there are also proliferating supermarkets, monumental car showrooms, warehouses selling exuberant lighting fixtures, and the emporia that sell all that is needed for two main events in Greek social life: weddings and baptisms.

MYCENAE

Mycenae (Μυκήναι; modern village Mykines), is the city known to archaeology as the centre of the great Helladic civilization and to tradition as the home of Agamemnon, who Homer says led the Greek host to Troy.

From the village of Mykines the road up to the acropolis of Mycenae (2km) runs below an older track which follows some remains of a Turkish aqueduct and over-looks the ravine of the Chavos, or Chaos. The prehistoric road from Mycenae to the Middle- and Late Helladic cemeteries at Prosymna (*see p. 227*) traversed this ravine by a bridge and causeway, the ruins of which may still be seen. The ancient road lies below and to the east of the modern chapel of Aghios Georgios, in whose cemetery Humfry Payne (1902–36), excavator of Perachora (*see p. 188*), is buried (inside the churchyard to the left; simple pedimented headstone).

The site of Mycenae lies 15km from the sea, on a limestone plateau in a mountain glen or recess (μύχος), between Mt Aghios Ilias on the north and Mt Zara on the south. Its position oversees the plain south to the Gulf of Nafplion and controls the natural roads north through the Pass of Dervenaki to Corinth and the Isthmus. All this might not have led to a settlement here had it not been for the Perseia Fountain, a spring which provided a constant supply of water.

The city, which Homer calls 'rich in gold', 'well-built' and 'broad-streeted', was proverbial in Classical times for its wealth. At its zenith Mycenae consisted of a fortified palace and administrative centre with further settlement outside the walls. The acropolis, the residence of its kings (who enclosed within its walls the tombs of some of their predecessors), stands on an almost isolated hill skirted by two deep ravines which fork from the mouth of the Kokoretsa glen running west, and the Chavos southwest. As Leake points out, the acropolis resembles 'many other fortresses in Greece, in its situation on the summit of a steep hill between two torrents'. From the northwest corner of the acropolis a long narrow ridge runs south parallel to the Chavos. In the slopes of this ridge are the tholos or beehive tombs which Pausanias mistook for treasuries.

HOMER

The epics of Homer, the *Iliad* and the *Odyssey*, originated in the Mycenaean world, when warriors from Greece were trading and raiding across the Aegean. They were told by wandering poets who would memorise thousands of lines and continually refine and update them, using real or imagined events as the backdrop. The *Iliad* tells of an episode in the siege of Troy when the Greek hero Achilles seeks revenge on the Trojan hero Hector for killing Patroclus. Hector, the last of the sons of the Trojan king Priam, is killed too, and in one of the most moving moments in Western literature Priam leaves his city to beg for Hector's body from Achilles so that it can be given proper burial. This is the world of the hero, superhuman but mortal, where death and the glory of victory are never far from each other. Behind the blood-chilling accounts of vicious battles, Homer presents a more ordered world of the city, with the civilization of Priam's palace, and domestic affection in the last moments Hector spends with his wife and son before going out to battle.

The *Odyssey* is the famous story of Odysseus' ten-year journey home across the Mediterranean after Troy has been taken. His wife Penelope, besieged by suitors in their court in Ithaca, does not know whether he alive or dead, and the final recognition scene as he returns unannounced is another deeply moving moment. The *Odyssey* has more magic and fantasy than the *Iliad*, and probably drew on new material from the migrations which took the Greeks westwards across the Mediterranean in the 8th century. In the kingdom of the Phaeacians, where Odysseus is cared for by the king's daughter Nausicaa, Homer explores again the rituals and courtesies of a civilised welcome from a well ordered state, the sharing of stories and gifts before Odysseus is helped off on his journey. In contrast, the lawless world of the Cyclops shows how precarious 'civilisation' was in that world.

Scholars have tried to locate the origin of the epics from the dialect in which they were written. The predominant influence is Ionian, which was spoken across the Aegean, but there are traces of Aeolic, the dialect of northern Greece, which suggest a long period of evolution during which new influences entered. Homer is the name given to the poet who brought them to a final form in the 8th century BC, when they were first written down—possibly because the warrior/hero class which is their subject knew that it was under threat and its exploits needed preservation.

For centuries Homer remained the predominant Greek poet, and children would be brought up on his poems. Even as late as the 330s AD we find the future emperor Julian being introduced to the poet at the age of seven. Homer was used to give the young an introduction to the gods, while the manners of his characters—the ways they addressed each other, for instance—were used as models to learn from. Declamations of Homer between rival orators would be part of many festivals.

Robert Fagles' modern translations of the *Iliad* and the *Odyssey* (Penguin Classics) are highly recommended.   C.F.

Mycenaean civilisation

Mycenae was first occupied in the first millennium BC, and some of the most important evidence of its early inhabitants comes from its graves and tombs. During the Late Helladic period, sometime around 1500 BC, a sudden stimulus apparently influences the previously unremarkable mainland culture. Six large shaft graves were dug for a ruling family, the contents of which suggest the existence of a sophisticated and dynamic aristocracy with very considerable wealth. The technique and artistry of the finds is highly accomplished. The dead of the previous generation had been much less lavishly provided. Aware that the Minoan civilisation had flourished before the rise of Mycenae, scholars initially thought that Minoan conquerors or colonists were responsible for the increased sophistication of the mainland culture. This theory has been abandoned, in part because the form of burial, the use of gold, and the warlike accoutrements found on the mainland are largely foreign to Minoan custom. Helladic building types continue unchanged by Cretan influence. Putative sources for the beginnings of the Mycenaean wealth, however, do include Crete, and also Egypt. Some have suggested that the riches of Mycenae's graves were loot from Minoan Crete brought back when Helladic warriors destroyed the Old Palaces. Still others think that there is no evidence of gold on this scale in Crete, whereas contemporary documents in Egypt record that there it was 'like dust beneath the feet'. The Egyptian pharaohs of the 18th dynasty paid their commanders in gold. At the time of the shaft graves (c. 1600 BC onwards) the Egyptians were seeking aid from overseas in their struggle against the Hyksos. It is possible that the heavily-armed Achaean warriors fought as mercenaries on the Nile, when they brought back to Mycenae the Egyptian belief in life after death, the fashion for golden death-masks, and provision of elaborate grave-goods (cf. the representations of cheetah, and the ostrich eggs, among the finds). Legend attributes an Egyptian origin to the hero Danaos (*see p. 222*), suggesting some folk memory of Egyptian contact.

Nevertheless, in Late Helladic I (early 16th century BC), Mycenaean culture does assume in addition many Minoan characteristics in its pottery, jewellery, representation of bulls, and the symbols of the double-axe, the sacred pillar and horns of consecration, associated with a cult of the Mother Goddess. Relations may have led to dynastic marriages; this would account for the presence in female tombs on the mainland of engraved gold seal-rings of a type exactly paralleled in Crete. For whatever reason, Mycenaean craftsmen learned new techniques, some from Minoan masters. One of the most important was the adaptation of the Cretan non-Greek 'Linear A' script for their own purposes, creating the proto-Greek 'Linear B' (*see p. 11*).

The following period (Late Helladic II; 15th century BC) sees the expansion of Mycenaean civilization all over mainland Greece, with considerable trade farther afield. It seems likely that Knossos itself and other Cretan palaces fell to mainland aggression c. 1450. The graves of this period have mostly been plundered and the architecture obscured by later rebuilding so that less of it is known than of the periods before and after. It is characterised by the earliest tholos tombs and represented artistically by the splendid contents of three such tombs (domed burial chambers) found intact at Vapheio, Midea (Dendra) and Pylos. The presence of amethyst and amber beads proves that trading relations already existed with Egypt and the Baltic. The vases are finely made and decorated. The large 'palace-style' vases as well as the beehive tombs typify the insolent exuberance of the age. This type of interment continues to 1300 BC, showing a progressive structural development culminating in fine architecture. Nine such tombs have been discovered at Mycenae.

The full tide of Mycenaean influence (Late Helladic III) is reached in the 14th century. This period is particularly characterised by its fine architecture, of which there are substantial remains. Houses have basements for storage and several rooms. Royal dwellings, with more than one storey and frescoed walls, have become palaces indeed. Accounts are kept in writing, though so far no evidence has come to light of literary composition. The cities are linked by roads and chariots are used.

During the 14th century, the ruler of Mycenae seems to have been the overlord of a loose federation of considerable extent, incorporating the whole of the Peloponnese and extending influence into Attica, Aegina, Boeotia, Euboea, Thessaly, the Ionian Islands (except perhaps Corcyra), Aetolia, Phocis and the islands of the Aegean. Even Crete, which had largely inspired the civilisation of Mycenae, was now subordinated to the younger nation. The principal gates of mainland citadels, which previously faced the hinterland, are rebuilt to face the coast as Mycenaean interests of trade or conquest reach out to the confines of the Mediterranean. There was a vigorous export and import trade with Cyprus and the Levant and on to Egypt. The south Sporades appear to have had settlers. Mycenaean objects have been found in Macedonia, in the Troad, and on the west coast of Anatolia. Ugarit on the Syrian coast had a Mycenaean trading post.

The almost total eclipse of Mycenaean civilisation over the whole area has not yet been adequately explained. A surge of defensive building in the later 13th century, in particular the ensuring of a secret water-supply at Mycenae, Tiryns and Athens, suggests either an external threat or civil war. Many important Mycenaean sites suffered destruction towards the end of the 13th century. The majority of smaller settlements are abandoned at this time, except in Achaea, the Ionian Islands, the eastern Aegean, and Cyprus, where they increase (presumably reflecting an influx of refugees). Before 1100 BC there was a second wave of disasters throughout the region which effectively ended a whole way of life. The 'Dorian Invasions' of Classical historians, internal risings, famine, pestilence, change of climate, seismic disaster, have all been suggested as the reason, none of them by itself accounting for all the conflicting archaeological evidence. What is indisputable is that the continuity of civic life was disrupted and material progress set back for four centuries.

Some small settlement seems to have continued here nevertheless, and in the 5th century the small township still known as Mycenae sent contingents to fight the Persians at Thermopylae and Plataea. Pausanias says that the Mycenaean gesture so irritated powerful Argos that Argos 'utterly devastated' her small neighbour in 468 BC. Later the walls were repaired and a Hellenistic town spread over the west ridge. When Pausanias visited, he remarked on the ruins, which included the walls (which he took to be the work of the Cyclopes who built Tiryns), the Lion Gate, and the tholos tombs, which he took for treasuries. Thereafter, little is known of Mycenae, until the philhellene visitors begin to stop here on their Grand Tours in the 18th century, and the archaeologists began to excavate in the 19th.

Visiting Mycenae

The English philhellene Robert Liddell wrote of Mycenae that 'it should be visited first for the fable, next for the lovely landscape, and thirdly for the excavations'.

THE FABLE OF MYCENAE

According to legend and myth Agamemnon, the leader of the Greeks and lord of Mycenae, led the Greeks to Troy, which they besieged and captured. The result: Agamemnon's sister-in-law, the beautiful Helen, who had eloped to Troy with its handsome prince Paris, returned home to Sparta with her husband Menelaus, Agamemnon's brother. There Helen and Menelaus seem to have lived into peaceful old age. Agamemnon's own homecoming was rather different: he was greeted by his wife Clytemnestra, who promptly slew him, possibly in the bath in which she suggested that Agamemnon wash away the grime and cares of his journey. With the help of her lover Aegisthus, Clytemnestra then murdered Agamemnon's companion Cassandra, the ill-fated daughter of Troy's King Priam. Why had Clytemnestra killed her husband Agamemnon? Perhaps to avenge Agamemnon's sacrifice of their daughter Iphigeneia on the eve of his expedition to Troy, to ensure a smooth voyage across the sea. Agamemnon dead, Aegisthus and Clytemnestra might long have ruled over Mycenae, had not Agamemnon and Clytemnestra had two surviving children: Orestes and Electra. Electra encouraged Orestes to seek revenge for their father's death and their mother's infidelity. Orestes slew his mother and Aegisthus. In many versions of the legend, both matricidal children then went mad. Although Agamemnon and his family were descended from the first hero of the Peloponnese, Pelops himself, the family had always been a troubled one. Pelops, as a child, was served in a stew to the gods by his father Tantalus, but fortunately was recognized by the goddess Demeter as she nibbled on his shoulder. Pelops' two sons, Atreus and Thyestes, continued the family tradition when Atreus invited his brother Thyestes to a banquet at which the main course was a ragout of Thyestes' children. Only one child escaped the stew pot: the very Aegisthus who later took his cousin Agamemnon's wife as a lover and was cut down by Orestes.

The excavations at Mycenae

The earliest systematic excavations, which uncovered the first circle of shaft graves, were initiated in 1874–76 by Schliemann, who was succeeded by Stamatakis. In 1886–1902 digging was continued by the Greek Archaeological Society under Tsountas. Extensive excavations in 1920–23 and 1939 by the British School at Athens under Professor Alan Wace showed that some of the interim conclusions reached by Evans and Myres about the chronology of Mycenae were ill-founded. Wace resumed excavations in 1950–55; in 1951 work of restoration and preservation was begun on behalf of the Greek government. Since 1952, when Grave Circle B was excavated, the Greek Archaeological Society has been actively engaged at Mycenae, with extensive investigations undertaken by Professor George Mylonas. Mylonas, the most prominent excavator of Mycenae in the 20th century, has suggested that in the 17th and 16th centuries BC, the royalty of Mycenae were buried in shaft graves (such as those in Mycenae's grave circles), while the common people were buried in simple graves cut in the rock (cist graves). Later, the royalty was buried in the elaborate tholos tombs, with the common people being buried in underground chamber tombs. Lord William Taylour directed British excavations after Wace's death, first in collaboration with J. Papadimitriou, then with Mylonas. Excavations have continued under the auspices of the Greek Archaeological Service. Since 1991, the Mycenae Survey has worked to record, create a database, and preserve all known remains; in several instances tholos tombs had been used as rubbish pits or used by itinerant fruit pickers as seasonal shelters.

Homer and archaeology

Like Schliemann himself, the visitor to Mycenae may have come here to see the home of '*anax andron Agamemnon*', (Agamemnon, Lord of Men) and to discover how closely Homer's account and the evidence of archaeology coincide. The historical trustworthiness of Homer was first questioned by Herodotus, and the consistency of the texts by Zoilus of Amphipolis. Questions remain as to the authorship of the *Iliad* and *Odyssey*, their dates of composition, and the unity of the texts—although most scholars today think that Homer lived in the 8th century and most credit him with the composition of most, if not all, of both epic poems. Earlier attempts entirely to credit, or discredit, Homer's reliability have given way to a more balanced acceptance that while Homer preserves many legends, and some specific details, of the Trojan War, much of his account is anachronistic, or inaccurate. Still, Mycenaean archaeology has proved the persistence of Mycenaean traditions in Homer in matters of armament, social and burial customs, and religion, of which evidence had wholly vanished by Classical times. The decipherment of Linear B tablets (*see p. 217*) found on Mycenaean sites has given a picture of palace life—down to the very furnishings—that is consonant with much of what Homer suggests. And some scholars suggest that finds at Troy show that the site was destroyed twice during the period of Mycenaean hegemony in the Aegean, while maintaining that there is still no conclusive proof that the Mycenaeans were responsible.

A copy exists of a letter from a Hittite ruler to the king of Ahhiyawa (? Achaea) about events in Lycia; the Homeric letter from the king of Argos to the king of Lycia (*Iliad, VI, 168–69*) may be part of the same correspondence. Myrtilos, the charioteer of Oinomaos, bears a name suggesting that he was a Hittite expert from whom the Greeks learned the art of the chariot. The Attarssyas with a hundred chariots who harried the Hittites in the 13th century was perhaps a member of the house of Atreus.

Hittite documents record Mycenaean activity in Asia Minor amounting to a large-scale expedition. Whether or not this is to be connected with any of the archaeological evidence for destructions at Troy, it implies a fleet and a single leader. The Catalogue of Ships in *Iliad II* reproduces the basic form of Mycenaean lists found in Linear B tablets, and is taken by some scholars to be a quoted document from the Bronze Age. Aulis, where the ships assembled, has a Mycenaean cemetery. It seems, therefore, that a historical 13th-century Mycenaean king, who led a large expedition to Asia Minor, contributed largely to Homer's Agamemnon.

It is probable, however, that the story of the siege of a maritime town ('Troy'), defended by people whose background is known, belonged to Mycenaean tradition as early as the 16th century BC (note the *Siege Rhyton*, Athens Museum). This is confirmed by the discovery on tablets found at Pylos, Knossos and Mycenae of many names that are given in the *Iliad* to Trojan warriors. This traditional story was elaborated for generations in the different Mycenaean kingdoms, gathering later exploits, with changes of locale and dramatis personae, and sometimes of fashion and armament; it could have then been given a new eastern setting when Troy was attacked by an expedition led by a king of Mycenae.

Chronological problems are also raised by the *Odyssey*, the action of which is set after the Trojan War. The correspondence between objects described by Homer (eg Nestor's cup; 'the wrought mixing bowl of solid silver doubled with gold about the rim' given by Menelaus to Telemachus; etc) and those discovered in Mycenaean excavations is sometimes close, though the Homeric object may be more typical of a period before the Trojan War or placed in juxtaposition with an anachronistic object. However, the ascribed provenance of Achaean riches accords with archaeological probability, as when Menelaus mentions his adventures in Egypt and claims to have 'seen Ethiopians in their native haunts'; Polybus of Egyptian Thebes had given him ten talents in gold. It seems that events from several periods of Mycenaean adventure may be telescoped in the *Odyssey* into one ancestral epic; the Egyptian expedition, the Trojan War, and the voyages of colonists to the western Mediterranean. The series of treacheries, improper marriages, and acts of revenge that characterise the Homeric dynasty of Mycenae, and supplied the basis for the embroideries of Classical drama, may actually have happened in the 16th century BC.

THE SITE

A site museum, reached by a path from the main site entrance, opened in 2004. Site and museum open daily 8–7 in summer; shorter hours in winter. T: 27510 76585. NB: The site is slippery and with virtually no shade: a sunhat, stout shoes, and a torch to explore the underground cistern, are advised. There is a telephone that takes phone cards and a post office by the site. At present, museum tickets and guide books are sold only at the ticket booth for the site itself.

Outside the citadel

The area below the citadel contains Grave Circle B; the remains of nine chamber tombs,

Dromos and entrance to the Treasury of Atreus, with the 'relieving triangle' above the lintel. This would originally have been covered by a decorative relief.

of which the best-known are named after Atreus, Clytemnestra and Aegisthus; and the remains of a number of houses. This area, with small habitation centres, was always outside Mycenae; presumably the inhabitants retreated to the citadel in times of danger.

The Treasury of Atreus
The modern road continues to skirt the Atreus Ridge, cutting through a large chamber tomb as it approaches the tholos tomb known as the Treasury of Atreus, or Tomb of Agamemnon. Tholos or beehive tombs are characteristic of the periods Late Helladic II to IIIA at Mycenae but are found over a longer period elsewhere. Over 100 have been located in widely disparate parts of Greece. They are usually composed of two parts, the *dromos*, or approach (an unroofed passage cut horizontally into the hill), and the *tholos*, which formed the actual tomb. This was of masonry, built into a circular excavation in the hill, and rising in a cone like a beehive to about the same height as the diameter of the floor. The top of the cone projected above the slope of the hillside and was covered with earth. Occasionally, as in the 'Treasury of Atreus', an additional chamber, rectangular in shape, opened from the tholos.

Architecturally the tholos tombs at Mycenae fall into three groups, showing a progressive structural development, marked in particular by the increased use of dressed stone and the placing of a relieving triangle above the lintel. They may be dated between c. 1520 and 1300 BC. The tholos tombs of Mycenae had all been plundered before they were excavated.

By the time of Pausanias the original purpose of these structures had been forgotten and they were taken for underground treasuries (hence the tomb's name). The discovery in the late 19th century of six skeletons in the tomb at Menidi (Athens), however, placed the question of their purpose beyond all doubt.

The **Treasury of Atreus** is an architectural masterpiece. As well as being the largest and best-preserved of the tholos tombs, it is also one of the latest, being dated by constructional style and pottery finds to c. 1350 BC. The connection with Atreus (the father of Agamemnon) is speculative. A massive wall of undressed stone supporting a wide paved terrace built of packed boulders fronts onto it. The tomb itself is built into the east slope of the ridge. From the artificial terrace, you pass through traces of the enclosing wall that barred the entrance. The dromos is 35m long and 6m wide; its walls, which naturally rise as it penetrates the hillside, are built of great squared blocks of breccia laid in horizontal courses and water-proofed behind with a lining of clay. At the end of the approach is a doorway nearly 5.5m high tapering slightly towards the top. The lintel is formed of two large slabs of stone, of which the inner one is 8m long, 5m wide, and 1m thick, with an estimated weight of 120,000kg. Above, a triangular space lightens the weight borne by the lintel. On either side of the doorway, on a square stepped base (still in position), stood an engaged half-column of dark green limestone. Parts of the shafts and of the carved capitals have been found; a few of these are in Athens Museum, but most are in the British Museum, London. Above, smaller columns flanked the facing of ornamental coloured bands that masked the 'relieving triangle'; some *rosso antico* fragments of this façade are also in London. They were brought here, presumably in ships owned by the Mycenaeans, probably from quarries at Kypriano near Cape Tainaron. The entrance passage is 5m deep; in the middle a stone threshold has pivot holes on which the double doors were swung. The bronze nails that held the door frame and fixed the wood or bronze covering of the threshold are still in place.

The tholos is a circular domed chamber, 13m high and 14.5m in diameter, formed by well-fitting blocks of breccia in 33 concentric courses, joined without mortar and gradually diminishing in height. The blocks vary from 1.25m to 2.15m in length. Each course overlaps the one immediately below it (corbelling), the topmost course being closed by a single block which, unlike the keystone of an arch, could be removed without endangering the stability of the structure. The overlaps have been cut away, so that the interior presents a smooth unbroken surface curved both horizontally and vertically. The floor is natural rock. From the third course upwards are rows of holes in regular order, some of them with their original bronze nails; these were bored to receive bronze rosettes as at Orchomenos (*see p. 428*). The outside of the dome was wedged with smaller stones. When Leake visited here, his attendants lit a fire inside the tholos; he recorded that 'the strong contrasts of light, the singularity of the edifice, and the recollections connected with the place, all conspired to produce a picture of the highest effect and interest'.

A much smaller doorway, 2.8m high and 1.3m wide, similarly surmounted by a triangular opening, leads from the north side of the beehive chamber into a rock-cut chamber, 8.25m square and 5.8m high. The walls may have been lined and decorated with sculptured slabs as at Orchomenos. In the centre is a circular depression. This may be the actual burial chamber. It was here that Schliemann entertained Pedro II, Emperor of Brazil and himself an amateur archaeologist, to a dinner of roast lamb, coffee and cigars, taking care to point out that a monarch had only once before entered the tholos, several millennia ago.

West and north of the Treasury of Atreus
On the thyme-covered ridge to the west are remains of a settlement of Late Helladic date. The excavations of 1955 showed the walls to be the terraces of outlying villas ('House of Lead', 'Lisa's House', etc), not fortifications; earlier theories of a fortified prehistoric 'lower town' have been abandoned. Just below the conspicuous Panaghia Chapel is the **Panaghia Tomb**, another tholos chamber (of the second group), discovered by Tsountas in 1887; it lacks its upper part. A hundred metres farther north is a tholos of the first group, known as the '**Epano Fournos' Tomb**.

To the north of the Treasury of Atreus are the remains of houses belonging to the Mycenaean settlement outside the citadel. Rounding a corner beyond the Treasury of Atreus you cross an area of confused Hellenistic ruins surrounded by a wall, the course of which can still be traced. Farther on on the right are the excavated foundations of several houses, probably of wealthy merchants of the 13th century BC; all were destroyed by fire. The names given them by the British excavators derive from the objects discovered. Construction is of rubble packed with clay. This supported a timber frame filled in with brick.

In the **House of Sphinxes** were found ivory plaques depicting sphinxes and nine Linear B tablets which had fallen from an upper room. The **House of the Oil Merchant**, adjoining to the north, contained 11 large *pithoi* and an installation for warming them. Thirty-eight written tablets came to light amid the burnt ruins. Across a narrow lane, the **House of Shields** yielded carved ivories, many in the shape of the figure-of-eight shield. The **West House** adjoins the House of the Oil Merchant.

Grave Circle B and Tombs of Clytemnestra and Aegisthus
At the north end of the ridge the road turns east towards the citadel. On the left is the level car park; in the angle of the road (to the right) lies **Grave Circle B**, discovered by accident in 1951 and excavated in 1952–54 by the late John Papadimitriou and others.

Though archaeologically one of the most important of discoveries at Mycenae, there is not a great deal to see. The enclosure, bounded by a wall similar to that of the larger grave circle on the acropolis (*see below*) and containing 25 graves, 15 of them shaft graves, lay partly beneath the road, while the section to the east had been overlapped by the vault of the Tomb of Clytemnestra. The bodies had been buried over a period of years with objects of ivory, gold, bronze and rock crystal, though less sumptuously than the burials of Grave Circle A. The burials are thought to begin to date from c.

1650 BC, slightly earlier those in Grave Circle A. Grave Rho, now roofed, is a built tomb, inserted into the cemetery later, in the 15th century BC.

In the dip below (right; footpath) are two tholos tombs. The **Tomb of Clytemnestra** was partially excavated by Mrs Schliemann in 1876 and more fully explored by the Greek Archaeological Society in 1891–92. It is of the normal type without a side-chamber, and is built on the same principle as the Treasury of Atreus, though a little smaller. From the refined architecture it is thought to be the latest of the tholos tombs (c. 1300 BC). The upper 18 courses of its dome, destroyed probably by Veli Pasha, were restored in 1951. The dromos (65m long) contained a circular depression which seems to have been a woman's grave, as gold trinkets and bronze mirrors were found in it. The doorway is recessed and was flanked by fluted half-columns. Here can be clearly seen how the ornamental façade that covered the relieving triangle was supported. Above the dromos traces of a small theatre of the Hellenistic period show that by then the existence of the tholos had been forgotten. Only one semicircle of seats can be clearly made out.

The so-called **Tomb of Aegisthus**, farther east, was excavated by the British School in 1922. This is on the same plan, but both the style of construction (rubble walls) and the pottery found within align the tomb with the first group (c. 1470 BC), though an earlier (Middle Helladic) date has since been proposed; the collapse of the tholos was due to the weakness of the material. It had been looted before the Hellenistic period.

On the other side of the modern road, in the north slope of the ridge, is the **Lion Tomb**, a tholos of the second group. Its dome has collapsed. Over to the left is **Petsas' House**, where a store of over 600 unused pots, ranged in sizes, was unearthed.

Within the Citadel

The road now reaches the acropolis, built on a triangular hill (278m) of which the north side is c. 320m long and the others c. 180m. In its present form, the enceinte with the Lion Gate, the palace, and most of the houses within, represents the result of architectural developments over a period from c. 1350–c. 1200 BC. The walls are preserved for their whole extent. There is a gap in the middle of the precipitous south slope where there was no need of fortification. They follow the contours of the rocks and in general vary in height between 4.5m and 10.5m, reaching 17m in the middle of the southwest side. The thickness mostly varies from 3m to 7m but in places on the north and southeast sides they are as much as 10–14m wide. There were two gates and a sally-port.

Three different styles of construction may be distinguished. The 'Cyclopean' walls (this masonry takes its name from the tradition that the original walls, like those of Tiryns, were built by the Cyclopes) are of huge blocks of dark limestone, shaped only roughly if at all. The two gateways, with their towers and approach walls, are in squared blocks of breccia, hammer-dressed and in regular courses like the later tholos tombs. This gives extra strength and dignity to the entrances to the city. The so-called Polygonal Towers are built of finely-jointed polygonal blocks of breccia; these and the short sections of wall repaired with similar but curved blocks date from the reoccupation of the 3rd century BC.

The Lion Gate

The famous Lion Gate stands at the northwest angle of the acropolis. It is reached by an approach 14.5m long and 9m wide, formed on the left (northeast) side by a salient of the fortification wall and on the right (southwest) side by a tower or bastion projecting from the wall. This tower commanded the right or unshielded side of anyone that approached. The gateway, unlike the entrances to the tholos tombs, has monolithic gateposts (3.2m high) which slope inwards to provide an opening that narrows from 3.1m at the bottom to 2.9m at the top. Across these, and probably mortised to them, is placed a massive lintel, 4.5m long, 1.9m thick, and 1m high in the centre, diminishing in height towards the sides. In the lintel and threshold are pivot-holes for double doors, and sockets in the side posts show where a wooden bar held them closed. The pavement (no longer visible) was scored to give foothold and rutted on either side for chariot-wheels.

Above the lintel a triangular slab of grey limestone, 3.7m wide at the base, 3.1m high and 0.6m thick, fills the relieving triangle. Carved in relief on it is a pillar supported by two lions (more properly, lionesses), which rest their front paws on the two

The Lion Gate: a carved slab representing two lionesses fills the relieving triangle above a monolithic lintel.

joined altars that constitute its base. Their heads have disappeared. The pillar, which tapers downwards, supports an abacus, and may have had a religious significance. A seal found at Mycenae depicts a similar device, perhaps the badge of the city or of its royal house; in this representation a dove rests on top of the pillar. Leake is not the only visitor here to have wished that Pausanias had mentioned what the lions were thought to represent, even though that almost certainly would have been more interesting for the light it shed on legends about Mycenae than on actual Mycenaean beliefs.

Within the gate (right) is the granary, so-called because *pithoi* of carbonised wheat were found during its excavation. The building, which was of two storeys, was perhaps in fact a guard-house.

Grave Circle A

From the gate the main route climbed by a ramp to the Palace, at first in a southeasterly direction, then north following the line of the wall. Its surface was dug away in Schliemann's excavations, but the massive embanking walls of the ramp remain. The terrace-wall to the north, designed to support the higher ground above, is a modern reconstruction.

To the right is **Grave Circle A**, the Royal Cemetery, a circular enclosure 27m in diameter, consisting of a double ring of dressed slabs 0.9m–1.5m high and 0.9m apart. The space between the two concentric rings appears to have been filled originally with rubble; the top was covered with horizontal slabs, of which one is in place, showing the mortise-and-tenon joints. The entrance, formed by a well made opening in the circle, 3.7m wide and lined with slabs, is opposite the Lion Gate. Ten sepulchral stelae and a small round altar were found over the graves. The stelae, now in the National Museum at Athens, bear crude sculptures in low relief, most of them showing men in chariots fighting or hunting.

Within this enclosure are six shaft graves, cut perpendicularly in the rock at a depth of 7.5m. They vary considerably in size, but all were floored with pebbles and lined with rubble masonry; they appear to have been covered with slabs, which had collapsed beneath the weight of the soil above. In the tombs were found 19 skeletons; the bodies had been interred in a contracted position, not burnt. The burial furnishings, which constitute one of the richest archaeological discoveries ever made, and include the golden 'Mask of Agamemnon', are splendidly displayed in Athens (*see p. 94*).

Archaeologists date these tombs to the end of the Middle Helladic and early Late Helladic periods, and postulate a 16th-century royal house, which they call the 'Shaft Grave dynasty'. The cemetery, of which the graves form part, lay outside the early citadel; when the later 13th-century enceinte was planned the common graves were treated with scant respect and even looted, while this royal group was incorporated within the walls and replanned as a monument. The circle was renewed and the entrance moved from the west to the north. The stelae were lifted and replaced, and an altar installed in the centre.

Grave Circle A, where the Mask of Agamemnon was found.

These were presumably pointed out to Pausanias as the graves of Agamemnon and his companions; the locals adding, following a tradition that goes back to Homer, that the murderers Clytemnestra and Aegisthus were buried outside the walls as they were considered unworthy of burial within. It was Schliemann's unshakeable belief that what he had found was in fact the grave of 'all those who on their return from Ilium were murdered by Aegisthus after a banquet which he gave them'. The belief was fortified by the contents of Grave III, in which were the skeletons of two infants wrapped in sheets of gold together with the remains of three women. Schliemann inferred that these were Cassandra with her two attendants and the twins that she had borne to Agamemnon. For a short time it seemed that Homer might after all be shown to be documentary history.

The grave circle is however undoubtedly centuries earlier than any possible date for the siege of Troy. Just as Homer describes customs (eg cremation) which are unknown at Mycenae at any period, so he seems also to have fused more than one period of Mycenaean events into one saga rife with anachronistic details. The characteristic shape of the inlaid daggers found here and at other Mycenaean sites is curiously echoed in the dagger-shaped marks cut in the trilithons of Stonehenge, the construction of which has elements in common with the final arrangement of the Mycenaean monument; no satisfactory theory yet accounts for what are perhaps coincidences.

The houses

To the south of the royal cemetery several groups of buildings have been uncovered; the remains represent only their basement level, drained and strongly built in stone to support a brick and timber floor above. They were constructed over the Middle Helladic cemetery in the 13th century BC. The first group consists of the Ramp House, the **House of the Warrior Vase**, named after the famous vase found here by Schliemann (*see p. 32*), and the South House.

Further south is Tsountas' House, so-called from its first clearance by the Greek archaeologist in 1886. Further work here in 1950 and in 1970–72 shows the complex to consist of an elaborate shrine, with a separate house on the lower two terraces to the west. Work on the intervening area, the only unexcavated part of the citadel with any depth of deposit, began in 1953 and was completed by a Helleno-British team under Professor Mylonas and Lord William Taylour. The area includes a large handsome hall with a covered passage leading to it and, on the lower terraces, two roughly built shrines which contained unusual clay idols and coiled snakes, a unique fresco and fine ivories (mostly displayed in the Nafplion Museum). This section is now known as the **Cult Centre**.

The palace

From the ramp a modern path follows the contour of the hill to the domestic entrance of the palace. Two guard rooms precede a cobbled court, where the column bases of the propylon are seen. An inner gate gave access to a long corridor and to the state quarters, the official entrance to which was, however, on the south side. These centre round the **Great Court**. In Mycenaean times a grand staircase led the visitor via an anteroom to a room whose use is uncertain. It may have been a throne room, a guest suite or a control post and archive room. From the east side of the Great Court a porch and vestibule lead into the **megaron**, a room 12.7m by 11.8m, in the centre of which was the sacred hearth. Four wooden pillars supported a roof; the bases are still visible. The walls were adorned with gaily coloured frescoes. The rooms to the north are believed to represent the **private apartments**; a small one with a red stuccoed bath is often pointed out as the place of Agamemnon's murder. The topmost point is overlaid by scanty remains of a temple rebuilt in Hellenistic times with material from an earlier structure of the Archaic period. The view takes in the Argolid with the Larissa of Argos prominent.

The eastern end of the citadel

East of the palace on the lower terraces are important buildings, now considered to form an east wing of the Palace. The first is the artisans' quarters, an open corridor with workshops opening off on either side. Below, in the southeast angle of the citadel, lies the so-called **House of Columns** which has close similarities to the palace of Odysseus as described in the *Odyssey*. Beyond are two groups of storerooms. Farther east is the heavily fortified late extension of the acropolis with a sally-port and a **secret cistern**, of the kind now known at both Athens and Tiryns, approached by a passage through the wall and descending (often slippery) stairs. The cistern ensured that Mycenae was not without water, even if an enemy seized control of the spring. A little to the west is a postern gate of the same period as the Lion Gate.

THE LINEAR B TABLETS

In 1900, Sir Arthur Evans' excavations at Knossos unearthed tablets covered with writing in two unknown scripts. For want of a better name, they were called 'Linear A' and 'Linear B'. In 1939—in one of the luckiest moments in excavation history—the American archaeologist Carl Blegen's first trial trench at Nestor's Palace at Pylos intersected what was soon identified as the palace archives. These consisted of stacks of clay tablets written in the same two languages. In both palaces, the tablets—many about the size of a small paperback—had been preserved when they were incinerated in the fires that destroyed the palaces. Many scholars tried, and failed, to decipher the tablets, assuming that they recorded lost Minoan and Mycenaean languages. In 1951, British archaeologist John Chadwick and 23-year-old architect and 'amateur' Classicist Michael Ventris broke the code of Linear B. Astonishingly, it was revealed to be a form of early Greek, recorded on the tablets in logograms and syllabic signs. Greek, it seemed, had been spoken for much longer than scholars had realised. The logograms (or pictograms for items such as cows, oil jars, men and women) and syllabics recorded the accounts and inventories of the ancient palaces. Although it was fascinating to know that the palace of Mycenae had contained an 'ebony chair with ivory braces worked with stags' heads and men and little calves', scholars had, of course, hoped that the tablets would contain records of events which would allow the history of the Mycenaean and Minoan civilisations to be written. While simple inventories, which most scholars have dated to the 13th century BC, do not make writing a historical narrative possible, they have enabled scholars to understand much more about the daily life and economic workings of the Bronze Age. As yet, Linear A remains undeciphered.

The Mycenae Archaeological Museum

Open daily 8–7 in summer; shorter hours in winter. At present, museum tickets and guide books are sold only at the ticket booth for the site itself. The museum is almost invariably crowded, except immediately after the site opens.

The museum displays some 2,500 objects from Mycenae and the surrounding area, displayed as far as possible in groups based on the area in which they were found, to help visitors to relate them to the site. The museum's architecture attempts to suggest the compact, walled citadel itself.

The entrance lobby has a model of the citadel and wall displays on the history of the excavations, depictions of the site by visitors, and ancient myths concerning Mycenae. The first exhibit room (to the right) has finds from buildings inside and outside the citadel and tells the chronology of Mycenae through its pottery, from the end of the Stone Age to the fall of Mycenae (end of the 2nd millennium BC). A reconstruction of the Room with the Fresco and exhibits on the Cult Centre attempt to give a sense of daily life in Mycenae.

A corridor leads down to the lower level where the showcases are said to suggest the shape of Grave Circle B. The first room has exhibits on goods used in life and goods that accompanied Mycenaeans on their last journey. There are copies of the famous objects from Grave Circle A, on view in the National Archaeological Museum in Athens.

The third display room has finds from the post-Mycenaean period (Geometric, Archaic, Hellenistic), a display of coins found on site, and an exhibit focusing on the achievements and legacy of Mycenaean civilization.

ARGOS

Argos ("Αργος) boasts that it is the oldest city not merely in Greece, but in Europe. In Antiquity Argos enjoyed a long period of wealth and power. Today it is a prosperous town of 25,000 inhabitants situated in the centre of the Argolic plain, 8km from the sea. Local industries include cattle breeding and tobacco growing. One of Greece's most distinguished ouzos, Mavrakis, has been made here since 1864 (and can be purchased in the original shop at Vas. Konstantinou 20 on Plateia Aghiou Petrou).

EXPLORING ARGOS

Argos is often ignored by tourists, but the museum and theatre are worth a visit. The city is easy to explore on foot. Much of what you want to see (both ancient and modern) is near Plateia Aghiou Petrou, the main square, dominated by the cathedral of Aghiou Petrou (1859), and flanked by shops, offices, banks and several hotels. A number of fine Neoclassical buildings survive, including the Tsokris, Gordon and Kallergi Houses, the city hall, and the Konsantopoulos House, designed by Ernst Ziller, the Dresden-born Neoclassical architect who built much in the new Kingdom of Greece.

The modern town so thoroughly occupies the site of the ancient city, at the foot of its two citadels ('*duas arces habent Argi*', Livy), that there is relatively little to see of ancient Argos, beyond its fine theatre complex, and a few scattered remains of civic buildings. As in many Greek cities, construction for new buildings almost invariably uncovers ancient remains, whose presence halts, or delays, construction. One example: in 1990–91, extensions to the municipal hospital on the Argos–Corinth road unearthed some of Argos' 'long walls', which Pausanias dated to 417 BC. In order to get on with their work, many builders attempt to conceal—even destroy—unearthed antiquities. Archaeologists are vigilant: 'rescue excavations' in 2003 saved remains from the Protogeometric to the Early Christian and Byzantine periods, including a relief of the healing deity Asclepius that may be the one that Pausanias saw in the Argive Asclepieion (*Pausanias II, 23, 2–5*).

HISTORY OF ARGOS

There are many legends about Argos' foundation (*see p. 222 below*); its first significant semi-historical figure is King Pheidon. Herodotus tells us that Pheidon was
the first to introduce coinage and a new scale of weights and measures into continental Greece—a reform that would transform economic life. Pheidon's dates are
obscure: he is said to have become Argos' first tyrant, and to have led an army to
the banks of the Alpheios and given the neighbouring district of Pisa control of the
Olympic Games. Pausanias dates this to 778 BC. Pheidon is also credited by some
with defeating the Spartans at Hysiae (c. 668 BC), a victory which marked an early
round in the long—unsuccessful—struggle with Sparta for the east seaboard of
Laconia during the 6th and 5th centuries BC. One historian summed up the long
conflict by remarking that Argos fought once a generation with Sparta. In 494 BC,
the Argive poet Telesilla is said to have urged the women of Argos to arm themselves against the enemy after Cleomenes of Sparta routed the Argives.

   Argos did not stand with the rest of Greece in the Persian Wars and resented
the participation of the (by then) insignificant neighbouring hamlets of Mycenae
and Tiryns; in return, the Greeks who did fight in the Persian Wars resented
Argos' inaction. In the mid-5th century BC, Argos allied with Athens, and adopted democratic government. During the Peloponnesian War, in 420, Athens,
Argos, Elis and Mantineia formed a league, defeated by the Spartans at the First
Battle of Mantineia. Argos helped to defeat the Spartans at the Second Battle of
Mantineia (362 BC). Pyrrhus attacked Argos in 272 BC, terrifying the inhabitants
with his siege elephants; he was killed in the abortive street-fighting after being
felled by a tile thrown from a rooftop by an old woman. After Rome conquered
Greece in 146 BC, Argos was included in the Roman province of Achaea. Alaric
sacked the city when he passed through here in 396 AD.

   For much of the middle ages the history of Argos is bound up with that of
Nafplion. During the War of Independence, Ypsilantis' (*see p. 51*) 'National
Convention' of 1821 met at Argos before its move to Epidavros. Argos was left virtually in ruins after three Turkish assaults. Here in 1829 Capodistrias (*see p. 234*)
convened the Fourth National Assembly, which concentrated power in his hands.

   The late 19th and early 20th centuries saw mass emigration from Argos (as
throughout Greece) to the United States. The loss of population was partly offset
by the influx of refugees from Asia Minor. Nea Chios, just outside Argos, was
founded in 1936, but it took decades for the refugees to achieve any degree of
prosperity. Photographs from the late 19th century, and the 20th well into the '60s,
show Argos with one- and two-storey tile-roofed buildings, a large, uncluttered
central plateia, and, beyond, the open countryside. The first three-storey flat-
roofed concrete apartment block was built in 1962; at present, such buildings are
characteristic of Argos' urban architecture, and are infiltrating the countryside.

The Archaeological Museum

The Archaeological Museum (*open daily 8.30–3 except Mon*) is on Vas. Olgas, just off the west side of Plateia Aghiou Petrou. Displays are from Argos and nearby sites in the Argolid. Labels are in Greek throughout, with labels for finds from Lerna also in English, and from Argos sometimes in French. As always, some of the best local finds are to be seen in the National Archaeological Museum in Athens. Although the collection is small, a number of pieces are outstanding. The courtyard, with fine 5th- and 6th-century AD mosaics, is a shady spot to sit.

Foyer: Special exhibit (*text in Greek only*) on the ancient and modern water supply in the Argolid.

Ground Floor Gallery: Middle Helladic, Mycenaean and Geometric pottery and bronze objects from tombs. One of the finest exhibits are the **bronze helmet and cuirass** of the late Geometric period, unique as being an almost complete set of armour. There are also *Krateutai* (fire-dogs) in the shape of triremes (bronze); spits; a red-figured vase by Hermonax showing Theseus and the Minotaur; a terracotta figures playing blind man's buff; beautiful lyre (6th century BC; restored) made of the shell of a tortoise and ibex horns. The superb pottery fragment of a mixing bowl showing **Odysseus and his men blinding Polyphemus** (7th century BC) is said to be one of the earliest known representations of a myth in Greek art. There is a model of ancient Argos and photographs of the ancient agora and theatre.

Pottery fragment from the 7th-century BC showing the blinding of Polyphemus.

First Floor: Roman sculpture, most found in the baths, including copies of Greek works (most of these unlabelled).

Lower Floor: The Lerna Room has important pottery finds from Lerna I–VII, excavated by J.L. Caskey from 1952; they range from Early Neolithic through to Mycenaean. There is an exceptional **terracotta figurine** (c. 3000 BC), the oldest known piece of representational sculpture from the mainland; seal impressions; and a restored Early Helladic ceremonial hearth.

Terrace: Outside are large, well-preserved mosaics of the 5th century AD (Seasons; Bacchus; Hunting scenes).

The square beyond the museum has an animated open market and a covered market building. From here Odos Tsokri, the old bazaar, provides the shortest approach to the Aspis (*see below*).

The agora, baths and theatre

The agora and theatre are all on the Tripolis road, about 1km from the Plateia Aghiou Petrou (open Mon–Sat 9–6; Sun 10–3). The archaeological site is divided by the main road at the point where it turns south towards Tripolis. The theatre is usually open; the agora often is not, but its remains are visible from the road. As noted, modern Argos overlies the ancient city; in consequence, the ancient agora (market and city centre) is largely covered by today's town.

The agora

The large excavated area east of the road, with the scant remains of the agora, requires determination, or imagination, to decipher. Some of what remains is Classical, some is Roman. Nearest the road are the lower courses of a Roman bouleuterion, originally 5th century, whose roof was carried on 16 Ionic columns. To the southeast is a large rectangular complex, with the remains of colonnades to north, west and east. The section of the colonnade immediately east of the bouleuterion was a later addition. In the 5th century BC the interior was an open court: in the 1st century AD baths (their brick construction prominent) were built in the west part and the east section was converted into a palaestra (some column bases from the court, and mosaics of later date, survive). Opposite the northwest corner of the stoa, and east of the bouleuterion, is a square, 1st-century AD nymphaion of brick within a stone surround. This was built over a racecourse (cf. Athens and Corinth), three of whose starting blocks survive beside the nymphaion. The start incorporated a *hysplix* (starting mechanism, as at Isthmia): there were 18 lanes, each c. 1m wide. To the northeast are the poros foundations of a building of the Hellenistic period which was later rebuilt as a Roman temple (base of ? cult statue visible). To the east are the untidy remains of another nymphaion, identified as such by inscriptions on the surviving architrave. The circular superstructure over a cistern is formed out of an earlier building on the same site. South of this is a tomb of the 2nd century AD which had rich finds, and may have been that of the donor of the nymphaion. The east side of the site is bounded by the extensive drainage channels for carrying off the water which flooded down from the hills above. The original open channel of massive limestone blocks was succeeded by watercourses, which were roofed with brick vaults in the Roman period.

Back near the entrance to the site, north of the bouleuterion, is another putative stoa, 4th-century in origin. Attached to it is a circular stepped foundation. A large base within this is composed of reused blocks from a triglyph altar and a Roman honorific base. Originally used for choral performances in honour of Apollo and/or meeting of the old Council of Eighty, it was later converted into an ornamental pool. South of this a trapezoidal enclosure defined by well-preserved limestone posts (of reused Archaic material) enclosed carbonised remains and may be the Fire of Phoroneus; Pausanias mentions that the Argives believed that Phoroneus, not Prometheus, brought fire to humans (*Pausanias II, 19, 5*).

LEGENDS OF ARGOS

According to some accounts, Argos was founded by the river god Inachos. In other versions, Argos was founded by Pelasgians, who came here from another Argos in the north. The mythical Danaos fled here from his brother Aegyptus, who wanted his 50 sons to marry Danaos' 50 daughters. We do not know what fraternal quarrel kept Danaos from wanting his daughters to marry their cousins. Aegyptus and his sons pursued Danaos and his daughters to Argos; the marriages took place, but Danaos had secretly ordered his daughters to kill their new husbands after the mass wedding. All did, except for one, Hypermnestra, whom Danaos condemned to death for her disloyalty. Somehow, the new bride and her husband escaped. Adrastus of Argos, who led the Seven against Thebes (*see p. 419*) to restore his son-in-law Polyneices to his throne, was the sole survivor of that disastrous expedition. Diomedes, successor of Adrastus and next to Achilles the bravest hero in the Greek army, led the Argive contingent in the Trojan War. There are legends as well of a monster named Argos (Argus), who had eyes in the front and back of his head and who terrorised the countryside.

The sanctuary of Apollo Lykeios, from which came the title *Lykeios Agora*), and which Pausanias calls the most 'glorious' object in Argos (*Pausanias II, 19,. 3*), has not been found, but blocks from it may have been incorporated in later alterations to the bouleuterion. Pausanias helpfully explains that Danaos himself founded a shrine to 'Wolf Apollo' when a wolf appeared at a critical moment during a political argument between Danaos and his main rival for power in Argos, Gelanor. Archaic houses (sometimes visible in lower levels) were demolished to make way for the public buildings of the Classical period. Many of these were altered in Roman times and following destructions caused by the Herulians in 267 AD or the Goths in 395. The 18 temples recorded by Pausanias were probably destroyed by the Goths. In the 5th century AD the public buildings fell into disuse.

The baths and theatre

To the west of the main road, the path to the theatre lies above its original approach road. To the south of the ancient road are the remains of a temple of the 1st century AD, perhaps of Asclepius and/or Serapis, remodelled as a bath building in the 2nd century AD. In Antiquity a monumental stepped entrance projected 18m from the façade, joined to the street by a passage. The impressive apse of the west end is preserved to roof height. The layout can best be seen from the hillside to the south of the theatre. The frigidarium was equipped with three plunge-baths and the establishment had three *calidaria* with marble-faced baths. In the crypt below the apsidal reception hall are three sarcophagi. Many architectural fragments and sections of mosaic floor (much now covered over) testify to the original splendour of the building. Sections of the hypocaust heating system can be seen.

Cut into the side of the hill above is the **theatre**, which accommodated c. 20,000 spectators and is thus rivalled in size on the Greek mainland only by those at Dodona, Megalopolis and Sikyon. It dates from the end of the 4th century BC or a little later (construction was probably begun when the Nemean games were transferred here; *see p. 198*), but was twice remodelled in Roman times.

In the south parodos is a small relief of the Dioscuri (Castor and Pollux, sons of Zeus and the twin brothers of Helen of Troy). The orchestra, 25.5m in diameter, was paved in blue and white marble in the 4th century AD when it was turned into a waterproof basin for the staging of naval contests. The late Roman modifications to the stage have been removed to reveal the foundations of the Greek *skene*, largely destroyed in the 2nd century during the Imperial reconstruction. The wings of the cavea, which were built on artificial banks, have disappeared, but 81 rows of seats remain in the rock-cut centre section. Two (later three) *diazomata* and seven flights of steps, not placed regularly, divided the seating. The surviving seats of honour in the front row include an imperial throne, probably of the time of Gratian. The cavea was covered by an awning, supported on wooded poles set in large square holes cut into the back rests of the seats, every 10–14 rows. The national conventions of 1821 and 1829 met in the theatre.

To the south are some remains of the aqueduct that brought water for the *naumachiae*. Fragments of 4th-century walling here probably upheld a road leading to the theatre. Farther on a Roman odeion of the 1st century AD covers vestiges of a second theatre antedating the larger one farther north. Fourteen curved rows remain of the Roman seating. The straight banks of the Greek structure, originally of some 35 rows, probably constituted the meeting-place of the Argive assembly. To the south of the odeion are remnants of an Aphrodision, which survived from the Archaic period to c. AD 405.

From the modern reservoir above the theatres a tiring zigzag path (better used for the descent) leads up in 45mins to the kastro (*see below*), a fortress crowning the ancient Larissa.

Deiras, the Aspis and the Larissa

Argos was protected by its two superb natural citadels, the Larissa and the Aspis, joined by the ridge called the Deiras; at present, they are largely unfenced and often unguarded. They can be reached easily by road from Argos, where they are signposted ('*kastro*'), and also, with determination, on foot, from the ancient theatre. Skirting the base of the Larissa you approach the Deiras; the ancient road from Argos to Mantineia passed through a gate on this ridge. The convent of Panaghia tou Vrachou (Virgin of the Rock; left, above) stands on the site of a Temple of Hera Akraia. The rounded hill of Aghios Ilias, which rises to the northeast of the ridge, is the ancient Aspis ('shield'), the original citadel of Argos, which lost its importance when the Larissa was founded. About 140m northwest the Sanctuary of Apollo and Athena forms a long rectangle divided into four terraces.

At the southwest foot of the Aspis, Wilhelm Vollgraff (a Dutch archaeologist and member of the French School) discovered a Mycenaean necropolis, which was more fully explored in 1955–59. Twenty-six chamber tombs and six shaft graves have come to light as well as a Middle Helladic building of the early 2nd millennium. On the west is a great court with a stone altar, and bases of tripods and statues. A rock-cut staircase of 10 steps, 27.5m wide, leads to the central terrace, which contained the (now destroyed) **Temple of Pythian Apollo** or Apollo Deiradiotes (Apollo of the Ridge) and the *manteion* or oracle, a rectangular building of unbaked bricks on a stone foundation. A large Byzantine church was built on this spot. To the east, on a lower terrace, was a round temple or tholos, and on an upper terrace was the **Temple of Athena Oxyderkes** ('Sharp-eyed Athena'), supposedly dedicated by Diomedes 'because once when he was fighting at Ilium the goddess lifted the darkness from his eyes' (*Iliad, V, 127*). The stadium lay farther north outside the wall.

The summit of the **Aspis** (100m) is crowned by the little chapel of the Profitis Ilias, which today gives its name to the hill. Here the Argives had a small acropolis, built over the remains of a Bronze Age settlement discovered by Vollgraff and now being reinvestigated (along with its pottery) by Greek and French archaeologists.

The polygonal 6th-century walls of the Aspis' Hellenic fortress describe an oval round the chapel. They were built on the remains of the prehistoric enceinte (Middle Helladic), except in the northeast where they formed a triangular salient with two square towers and four posterns. Within the walls, against the east wall and round the chapel, are two groups of pre-Mycenaean houses, in ashlar bonded with clay. To the south and west a group of Macedonian buildings surrounds an Archaic temple. A conspicuous hexagonal tower marks the junction of the acropolis and city walls.

From the Deiras a road runs west before climbing steeply to the summit of the **Larissa** (276m), the principal citadel of Argos. The ancient citadel was formed of two concentric enceintes, an outer wall of Hellenic masonry (5th century) having been added to the polygonal work of the 6th century which protected the Archaic acropolis. Sections of antique masonry can be traced in the medieval kastro, which was built largely on the old foundations by the Byzantines and Franks and enlarged by the Venetians and Turks. The kastro has a double enceinte and a keep. The 5th-century wall survives on the northwest of the outer enceinte, while the polygonal wall is best seen on the northeast side of the keep. This medieval structure, with fine towers, incorporates fragments from a Temple of Zeus Larisaos and a Temple of Athena, the poros foundations of which were excavated in the court by Vollgraff. Traces of Mycenaean wall and a votive deposit of the 8th century BC were also found.

The view embraces the whole Argolid and the Gulf of Nafplion. Far to the east rises Arachnaion. Immediately to the west is Mt Lykoni, crowned by the remains of a small temple of Artemis Orthia; behind rises Artemision.

You can descend by one of two paths, neither distinct and both steep. The more westerly passes close to some traces of the town walls, while that to the east passes a rock-cut relief of a horseman and a snake to reach a rectangular terrace supported by a polygonal wall. At its northeast corner is a relief of seated divinities. Vollgraff identified the place with the *Kriterion*, or Judgement Place, where Hypermnestra was condemned by her father Danaos for refusing to kill her husband (*see p. 222 above*).

THE ARGIVE HERAION

Open 8.30–3 daily except Mon. The Heraion was the most important ancient Argive religious shrine. From Argos it is best reached by leaving town on the Corinth road and taking the right turn to the former Chonikas, now renamed Nea Iraio (7.5km); either name is possible on maps. The Heraion is 1.5 km from the village, which has a 12th-century church (see p. 229 below). There are buses from Nafplion to Nea Iraio. In summer, the view is usually clearest in the evening, when the heat haze dissipates.

The Heraion of Argos, or Sanctuary of Hera (Ἡραίον), dedicated to the tutelary goddess of the Argolid, was the most important religious shrine for both Argos and the surrounding countryside. Here, Agamemnon is fabled to have been chosen leader of the Trojan expedition. The site was discovered in 1831 by the philhellene General Thomas Gordon, who dug here in 1836; its excavation in 1892–95 constituted the first major work of the American School (under Charles Waldstein). Further work was done by Carl Blegen in 1925–28; and a chance discovery led to a short but profitable season in 1949 by P. Amandry and J. Caskey.

The site is little visited; a pity, as it has a fine position on a ridge, affording views over the plain. The terraced remains are extensive, and there is no better place to read Herodotus' account of Cleobis and Biton (*Herodotus I, 31*). The youths' mother was priestess at the shrine here, and when her oxen went missing on the Festival of Hera, her two sons pulled her in the ox-cart from Argos to the Heraion where they were cheered and feasted—and then 'fell asleep in the temple', blessed with death at their moment of greatest accomplishment. Plutarch tells us that Solon used this story to illustrate to King Croesus that indeed there were people on the planet more blessed than he. Some scholars think the tale conceals a darker element of ritual human sacrifice. Astonishingly, the statues of Cleobis and Biton that Herodotus mentions as dedicated at Delphi were found there and are now on view in the Delphi museum.

The site of the Heraion has been occupied at least since Early Helladic times, and tombs dating from the Neolithic to Late Mycenaean periods have been found on slopes west of the sanctuary (*see p. 227 below*). The Archaic and Classical sanctuary is built on three terraces, above which is the Helladic settlement.

Upper terrace

A path to the right leads to the upper terrace, supported by a massive retaining wall in conglomerate, which has all the appearances of Mycenaean workmanship but is believed to date from the Late Geometric period. The surface of the terrace is paved and almost perfectly level. The first temple was probably, like the model found here and now in the National Archaeological Museum in Athens, mud brick with a thatched roof. The next temple, known as the **old temple of Hera**, built in the mid-7th century BC, burnt down in 423 BC when the priestess Chryseis dozed off and left a fire unattended. Traces of the stylobate of the old temple, perhaps the earliest peripteral building of the Peloponnese, survive. Built in the Doric style (6 by 14 columns), its upper structure may have been of wood and unburnt brick.

Middle terrace

In the centre of the middle terrace stands the **new temple**, erected c. 420–410 BC by Eupolemos of Argos. The building was constructed of limestone and poros, with marble adornments. This was a Doric peripteral building (6 by 12 columns) in which was set up a chryselephantine statue of Hera by Polyclitus, said to have deserved comparison with the Olympian Zeus of Pheidias. Pausanias (who says that the statue of Hera was 'very big') claims to have seen here also the ancient *xoanon* in pearwood removed by the Argives from Tiryns in 468 BC; a bejewelled golden peacock (this bird was favoured by Hera) dedicated by Hadrian; and a purple robe offered by Nero.

The buildings bounding this terrace have many unexplained features. Below the wall that supports the upper terrace is the **north stoa**, believed (on the evidence of surviving capitals which do not certainly belong to it) to date from the 6th century BC or even earlier, which makes it one of the earliest known examples of the stoa, later to become such a common feature of all cities and sanctuaries. The foundations are of limestone and the blocks forming the rear wall are well squared. In the centre are statue bases and at the west end a basin, lined with cement, is connected to an elaborate water-supply system. The northeast building, dating from the end of the 7th century, was altered at a later date. The east building is a mid-5th-century rectangular structure in poros with a portico and a triple row of interior columns. The west building, one of the earliest examples known of a peristyle court (late 6th century), has three rooms leading off its north side; it may have been a banqueting place. To the northwest are further foundations, possibly belonging to a late monumental entrance. Farther west are a large Roman bathing establishment and a palaestra.

South stoa

The south stoa, at the third level below the retaining wall of the middle terrace, shows the finest workmanship of any building on the site, and is dated to the mid-5th century. It is now suggested that what were formerly thought to be flights of steps leading up to the south stoa and past it on the east side to the temple, are in fact Archaic retaining walls of stepped construction (*analemmata*). Scholars have noted that these would have provided a perfect vantage point to watch processions coming here across the plain from Argos.

The site guard will show a well-preserved tholos tomb c. 200m below the main site.

PROSYMNA, DENDRA & MIDEA

The following sites are all small, with minimal remains. They are, however, largely unfenced.

Prosymna

The Middle Helladic and Late Helladic cemeteries of Prosymna, explored by Blegen, are in the hillsides to the northwest at approximately the same contour height as the upper terrace. The guard at the Heraion should be able to point them out.

From Nea Iraio/Chonikas a road continues northeast to Berbati (which has read-opted the name Prosymna). Here in 1936–37 the Swedish Institute explored a ceme-tery of Mycenaean chamber-tombs and an Early–Late Helladic settlement. There are scant remains. In the 1980s, the Institute undertook a survey of the surrounding ter-ritory which revealed two Mesolithic sites (9000–7000 BC) in the Kleisoura Gorge, Mycenaean habitation sites, and signs of intensive settlement during the Frankish and Venetian period.

Dendra and Midea

Dendra and Midea are two Mycenaean sites. Midea seems to have been a fortified citadel, with its cemetery (somewhat curiously) 4km away at Dendra. Both sites are clearly signposted on the new Mycenae access road as it continues past the Mycenae turn-off to Nafplion. Both sites can also be reached from Nea Iraio/Chonikas via Aghia Triada (formerly Merbaka), which has an attractive 12th-century church (*see Churches of the Argolid, below*), and is 3km from Dendra.

At Dendra (Δενδρά), the cemetery of Midea, the Swedish Institute dug an unrobbed tholos tomb in 1926–27 (Late Helladic; finds in Athens) and, in 1937–39, richly fur-nished Mycenaean chamber-tombs surrounding it (gold cups, remains of a wooden coffin, etc). Another tomb dug in 1960 yielded the Mycenaean ceremonial armour now in Nafplion museum (*see p. 239*). Horses—an indication of the importance of the deceased—were found in two of three Middle Helladic tombs excavated here. Today, there is little to see.

The site of Midea (Μιδέα) is about 1km from the village of the same name; it has a cyclopean fortress (13th century BC) with impressive walling and gates, and was evidently one of the largest Mycenaean sites. As yet, no palace has been found here, perhaps because Midea was under the control of Mycenae and Tiryns. Linear B (*see p. 217*) inscriptions have been found here, perhaps suggesting that this was an administrative centre. In 1999–2000, Midea's excavators announced that the discov-ery of a clay prismatic nodule with the seal impression of a bull and a Linear B inscription confirmed Midea's position as a 'palatial centre' in the Argolid. The site, founded much earlier in the Bronze Age, was destroyed by what the excavators have described as a devastating earthquake and fire at around the end of the 13th centu-ry BC. Discoveries in 2002–03 of beads of glass and pieces of unworked rock crystal on the acropolis suggest the presence there of workshops. Some occupation contin-ued after the earthquake and, indeed, there is a much later phase of use in the 4th century AD. Excavation on the acropolis and restoration work continues. The view over the plain is fine.

The Pyramid of Kenkreai

Kefalari, 2.5km west of Argos, is a shaded village at the foot of the precipitous Mt Chaon, where the Kefalari river, the ancient *Erasinos*, issues from the rocks. Due to the springs, and a shady park, this is a favourite local excursion, and there are several tavernas, usually very crowded on summer weekends. The ancients thought that the waters came underground from Lake Stymphalos (*see p. 192*). The spring (Kefalovrysi) forms a pool, above which open two caverns, dedicated to Pan and Dionysus. The larger resembles an acute Gothic arch and extends c. 60m into the mountain; the smaller one has been converted into the chapel of the Panaghia Kefalaritissa. The water often attracts numbers of bees. The ancient festival of *tyrbe* (disorder) is recalled by the modern festival on 18th April. Nearby prehistoric remains and a fine large basilican church of the 6th century, probably dedicated to St Paul, were excavated and covered.

The road (signposted Ἑλληνικό, by the church) continues out of Kefalari past a stretch of new houses for several kilometres before reaching (on the left) a hillock, with the remains of the curious **Pyramid of Kenkreai**. The pyramid's first excavators in 1901 concluded that it was not, as Pausanias says, the *polyandrion* (common burial place) of the Argives who fell at Hysiae. In the 1930s, the pyramid was again examined and the English excavators concluded from the workmanship and the pottery remains found that this was a late 4th-century guard house used by patrols; certainly from this vantage point the guards could keep an eye on the approaches from the south into the Argolid. The roof and upper courses of the pyramid are missing, but some ten roughly laid courses of hard local limestone, with both squared and polygonal blocks, still stand. A corbelled arch, at the southeast corner, gives access by a blind corridor to an inner rectangular room. The structure has been used in recent times both as a sheepfold and a latrine. Other 'pyramids' in the Argolid include that at Dalamanara, east of Argos, and the so-called 'tower' at Fichtia. All may be the ground floor of Hellenistic watch-towers; most are now favoured homes of snakes.

SOME CHURCHES OF THE ARGOLID

The churches described here—which can be visited as a half-day excursion—are the Koimisis tis Theotokou at Nea Iraio/Chonikas; Panaghia at Merbaka/Aghia Triada; Aghia Moni at Areia; Aghios Ioannis, Koimisis tis Theotokou and Aghia Marina at Ligourio. All date from the 10th–13th centuries. Although the churches (with the exception of Aghia Moni) are usually locked, it is sometimes possible to get the keys from the custodian; enquire locally.

The churches of the Byzantine Argolid afford a powerful glimpse of the prosperity of the region after Argos became the seat of a bishop in 1189. Several of them have a profusion of spolia, perhaps from Epidaurus or the Argive Heraion. Results of the

ongoing work by the French School and Greek Archaeological Service's photogram-
metric survey of churches and buildings of the Byzantine Argolid in Byzantine times
have appeared since 1996 in the *Archaeological Reports of the British School at Athens*.
The survey is revealing a previously undocumented wealth of material, indicative of
a greater-than-realised local prosperity during the Byzantine era. In addition, the
research will allow for more accurate dating of these monuments.

At Nea Iraio and Aghia Triada

The 12th-century church of the **Koimisis tis Theotokou** (Dormition of the Virgin) at
Nea Iraio/Chonikas is built in an inscribed-cross plan, with four interior columns.
Ancient blocks form a cross on its west front; there are marble windows in the shape
of crosses and circles in the tall, slender drum. The belfry is later than the church.

The 13th-century **church of the Panaghia** in Aghia Triada (by the cemetery southwest of town) is a cross-in-square with three apses; the late Byzantine frescoes were
partially restored in the 1980s. The exterior of this large church is particularly charming: there are 11 ornamental pottery bowls set in the walls, elaborate brickwork ornamentation, and slender windows in the dome. Reused blocks include Classical grave
slabs and reliefs with fish and grapes, and a sundial, presumably from Byzantine
churches. It has long been thought that the church must have been built before 1210,
when the Franks seized Argos and Nafplion. Recent scholarship, however, suggests a
possible late 13th-century date, at the time when Guillaume de Morbecke, a Flemish
Dominican who translated Greek medical texts, was Bishop of Corinth (1278–86).
The village's former name, Merbaka, came from a corruption of de Morbecke's name.

Towards Epidavros

Some 2km out of Nafplion on the Epidavros road, the 12th-century convent of **Aghia
Moni** (also known as the Zoödochos Pigi, the 'lifegiving spring') is signposted and
reached after a steep 2km ascent (*closed from about 2–5*). As often in Greece, if a spot
is sacred, it has been sacred for a long time: the spring that runs through an ancient
conduit into a fountain pond (1836) outside the convent walls is thought to be the
ancient *Kanathos*, or 'Baths of Hera'. Today, its waters are thought to ensure a woman's
fertility, rather than to restore her virginity.

The katholikon (1149) is built on an inscribed-cross plan and has an octagonal
drum supported by four columns. Hetherington points out that the presence of windows in each facet of the drum is characteristic of mid-12th-century church architecture. The architectural ornament inside and out is elegant; the frescoes are modern.
In the 1930s, a fire gutted the convent, which flanks the katholikon. The'nuns say
that a rich Greek-American in Chicago had a vision of the fire, but not of its location.
He was guided here by the Virgin and St Michael (whom the nuns say he recognised
by their heavenly aroma), and underwrote the restoration of the convent.

Ligourio (Asklipieio on some maps), with three handsome churches, is some 27km
out of Nafplion on the Epidavros road. Aghios Ioannis Eleimon is on the east side of
the village. The exterior of this late 11th-century church is thick with reused ancient

blocks, on one of which, a threshold upended in the north wall, a church workman inscribed his name, 'Theophylactos of Chios'. The 13th- or 14th-century inscribed-cross church of the Koimisis tis Theotokou is uphill to the north. Like Aghios Ioannis, it incorporates many ancient marble blocks. It is worth trying to get into the church, as its frescoes are well-preserved. To reach the last church, the little 14th-century Aghia Marina, you must follow a path (*signposted*) on the western outskirts of town. Again, it is worth getting inside, where the four columns that support the cupola have reused Classical column caps and the frescoes are well preserved.

NAFPLION

Nafplion (Ναύπλιο; population 15,000), called by the Venetians *Napoli di Romania*, is the capital of the Argolid. Its situation near the head of the Argolic Gulf made it a strategic fortress for the Byzantines, Franks, Venetians and Turks. It is also one of the most attractive towns in Greece. At the end of the Greek War of Independence, Nafplion was briefly capital of the country (1828–34), a status which has left it with a number of handsome Neoclassical buildings. New development is confined to the outskirts of the old town, and spreads (undistinguished at best, often genuinely hideous) along the coast towards Nea Chios and inland along the roads to Argos and Epidavros.

The picturesque Bourtzi, built by the Venetians in Nafplion harbour.

HISTORY OF NAFPLION

Nafplion's legendary founder was Nauplios, probably a son of Poseidon. His son, Palamedes (after whom the Palamidi fortress is named), is said to have invented lighthouses, the art of navigation, measures and scales, and the games of dice and knucklebones, in addition to introducing the letters Υ, Φ, Χ, and Ψ into the alphabet of Cadmus (historically anachronistic). He was slain by his fellow Greeks in the Trojan War on a false charge of treachery for playing a trick on Odysseus.

Nafplion's long history is attested by the Palaeolithic remains found on Acronafplion, as well as in the Franchthi Cave, south of the town. In Mycenaean times Nafplion may have been the naval station of Argos. Mycenaean chamber tombs have been found on the slopes of the Palamidi. About 625 BC Nafplion sided with Sparta against Argos. When Argos defeated Sparta, Nafplion became Argos' port. By the time of Pausanias, who saw only walls, a sanctuary of Poseidon, the harbour, and the Spring of Kanathos, the town seemed almost deserted.

Nafplion regained its importance during the medieval period, and is mentioned as a trading-post in 11th-century Venetian annals. After the fall of Constantinople (1204), Nafplion remained for a time in Byzantine hands. In 1210 the town was taken by Geoffrey de Villehardouin, who gave it, with Argos, to Otho de la Roche. It remained an appanage of the Dukes of Athens, but on the fall of Athens to the Catalans in 1311 stayed loyal to the Brienne family. In 1388 Nafplion was bought by the Venetians, whose first task was to recover it from the hands of Theodore Palaeologus of Mistra. Turkish sieges were repelled in 1470; in 1500 when Bayezid II attacked in person; and for 14 months in 1538–39. In 1540 the Ottomans captured Nafplion, and it became the Turkish capital of the Morea. Count Königsmark, Morosini's lieutenant, recovered it for Venice in 1687, and until recaptured by the Turks in 1715 it was capital of the kingdom and seat of the Bishop of Corinth. Morosini died within sight of the walls in 1694. After its recapture Ahmed III visited Nafplion in person. As a consequence of a temporary occupation of Nafplion by the Russians in 1770, the capital was removed to Tripolis.

During the War of Independence Nafplion was the most important fortress in the Morea, its two strongholds being regarded as impregnable. The Greeks laid siege for over a year in 1821–22; a few months after the rout of Dramali they seized Palamidi, and the town capitulated. Later the two citadels were for a time in the hands of rival Greek chieftains, who indulged their passion for civil war at the expense of the luckless inhabitants, until Admiral Codrington and Sir Richard Church intervened. The town escaped destruction, and in 1828 Capodistrias, the regent, moved his provisional seat of government here from Aegina. Otho, first king of Greece, disembarked at Nafplion in 1833 after the ratification of his election, remaining till the government was removed to Athens in 1834. The insurrection of the garrison here helped to bring about his abdication in 1862.

Originally walled, the old town huddles along the north slopes of a small rocky peninsula, crowned by the citadel of Acronafplion (85m), towards which narrow streets, lined with old houses attractively balconied and shuttered, many festooned with bougainvillea, rise from the quay. On the southeast the conspicuous fortress of Palamidi (215m) dominates the town, and is a landmark visible from afar. In the harbour, the island fortress called the Bourtzi after its Venetian architect is absurdly picturesque; boats take groups of four or more from the quays to the island. Although construction within the old city is strictly regulated, when construction takes place, antiquities are almost invariably unearthed. Mycenaean remains were discovered on Asklipiou, and in 1999–2000 a burial pithos was unearthed on Mikras Asias, further to the northeast.

Nafplion has lost the importance it once had as the temporary capital of Greece, and is frequented mainly as a popular holiday destination for Greeks and foreigners alike. Facing away from the open sea, it provides the safest harbour on the coast of Argolis, increasingly used by small cruise ships. Tourism is an important source of income, while fishing and agriculture (dairy products, olives, citrus) continue to be important. Agrotourism is being vigorously developed.

Though the seat of a bishop and a military station, Nafplion maintains an air of sophistication befitting the first place in Greece known to have had a piano in a private home—albeit one imported by Count Joseph Ludwig Armensperg, who accompanied King Otho here in 1833. This was also the first town in Greece where European costumes were seen in profusion, first on the members of Otho's court and then on members of the local aristocracy (whilst Otho himself amused his subjects by affecting the foustanella, the short, pleated skirt worn by many Greek men).

In Nafplion, the Museum of the Peloponnesian Folklore Foundation, voted the best new museum in Europe when it opened in 1974, is one of the finest in Greece. Nafplion's restaurants and shops are varied and engaging, the sweet shops (including a branch of Floca's and the marvellous Antica Gelateria di Roma) excellent. The weekly street market along Plateia Kolokotronis sells everything from potatoes to the pots and pans to cook them in. There is a satisfactory bookshop, the Odyssey, with foreign newspapers as well as a wide variety of local guides and translations of ancient and contemporary Greek literature. The town is a stroller's delight, with twisting stepped streets revealing Turkish fountains, small churches, and views over the town and harbour. In short, the opportunities for *dolce far niente* are considerable.

EXPLORING NAFPLION

The 19th-century town

Much of Nafplion's distinction and charm stems from the buildings built here when this was the capital of Greece from 1828–34, before the government was moved to Athens. The Bavarian princelet Otho was accompanied here by a retinue of advisors, including architects, who attempted to turn a provincial hamlet into a national capital. The results may be seen in the Lower Town, where three successive parks at the east end of the old city are punctuated with monuments commemorating revolutionary war

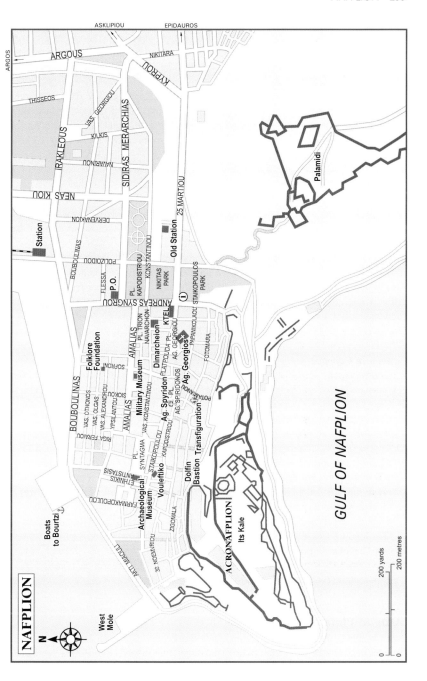

NAFPLION

N

West
Mole

Boats
to Bourtzi

GULF OF NAFPLION

Palamidi

ACRONAFPLION
Its Kale

Station

P.O.

Old Station

Dolfin
Bastion Transfiguration

Archaeological
Museum

Vouleftiko

Military Museum

Folklore
Foundation

Dimarcheion

Ag. Spyridon

Ag. Georgios

KTEL

NIKITAS
PARK

STAIKOPOULOS
PARK

ASKLIPIOU   EPIDAUROS

ARGOUS   NIKITARA

ARGOS

THISSEOS

NEAS KIOU

IRAKLEOUS

SIDIRAS MERARCHIAS

KILKIS

NAVARINOU

VAS. GEORGIOU

KYROU

DERVENAKION

BOUBOULINAS

POLIZOIDOU

FLESSA

25 MARTIOU

PL. KAPODISTRIOU

KONSTANTINOU

ANDREAS SYNGROU

AMALIAS

PL. TRION
NAVARCHON

PLATEIA PL.

PL.
AG. SPIRIDONOS

PAPANIKOLAOU

FOTOMARA

AG. GEORGIOU

POTAMIANOU

SOFRONI

BOUBOULINAS

VAS. OTHONOS

VAS. OLGAS

VAS. ALEXANDROU

YPSILANTOU

SIOKOU

VAS. KONSTANTINOU

AMALIAS

RIGA FERAIOU

PL.
SYNTAGMA

STAIKOPOULOU

PL.
KAPODISTRIOU

ETHNIKIS
ANTISTASIS

FARMAKOPOULOU

ZIGOMALA

30. NOEMVRIOU

AKTI MIAOULI

0   200 yards

0   200 metres

heroes. A bronze equestrian statue shows Theodoros Kolokotronis, the general known as the 'Old Man of the Morea', pointing the way forward to victory. The Turks surrendered the city to Kolokotronis in 1822; in 1833, he found himself a prisoner in the Palamidi, suspected of plotting against the young king, who ultimately freed him 22 months later. A less obtrusive marble statue of Ioannis Capodistrias, Greece's first governor, wearing western garb, stands near the courthouse. Capodistrias is credited with founding Nafplion's eastern extension, Pronia, for those left homeless after the War of Independence. A marble relief commemorates the victory of Nikitas over the Turkish general Dramali at Dervenakia; in the poem inscribed on the relief, Palamas, who wrote the Greek National Anthem, calls Nikitas 'the Turk-eater'.

The adjacent park of Staikopoulos has a statue of the general after whom it is named, in starched foustanella, with his sword sheathed. Staikopoulos captured the fortress of the Palamidi from the Turks in 1822. Slightly to the north is the restored Land Gate of the massive Venetian fortifications and Plateia Trion Navarchon (of the Three Admirals), which commemorates the Battle of Navarino (1827). The square has monuments commemorating the revolutionary war hero Dimitris Ypsilantis, and is flanked by Neoclassical buildings, some with shops, others with offices. The three-storey pedimented building was one of the first high schools in Greece, opened in 1833. Under the Turkish occupation, education was minimal, and there was a rush to build schools after independence.

Ioannis Capodistrias (1776–1831)

Count Ioannis Capodistrias was born on the island of Corfu, at that time a Venetian possession. He was educated (in philosophy and medicine) at Padua, and began a career as a doctor on his native island. In 1801, during the Napoleonic period, the Ionian islands briefly became an independent republic. Capodistrias became a minister of the new state, and in 1809 entered the service of the Russian Czar, acting on diplomatic missions to Geneva and at the Congress of Vienna. The Czar was impressed by his talents, and appointed him Russian foreign minister. Capodistrias sought Russian support for the Greek independence movement, and when this was denied, left Russia for Switzerland, whose unity and independence he had helped secure. In 1827, as the foremost Greek-born international statesman, he was elected Prime Minister of a newly-independent Greece. The measures he introduced in an effort to turn his backward and lawless country into a modern democracy proved his downfall. His imprisonment of the Maniot bey Mavromichalis launched a family vendetta, and Capodistrias was assassinated in Nafplion, on the steps of the church of St Spyridon.

Around Plateia Syntagma

Vas. Amalias and Vas. Konstantinou flank the Plateia of the Three Admirals; Vas. Amalias leads to the waterfront, while Vas. Konstantinou leads into Plateia Syntagma.

Rooftops of Nafplion, with the Vouleftiko, first a mosque and then the parliament house of the Greek republic, prominent on the left.

This was the heart of Venetian Nafplion: the Archaeological Museum occupies the 18th-century Venetian Armoury at the foot of the plateia; the Venetian Lion of St Mark was brought here from the fortifications. This was also the centre of Turkish Nafplion. The mosque on the Plateia is sometimes used for concerts; the mosque just off the plateia was the Vouleftiko, used as Greece's early parliament house. Many of the old buildings now house restaurants, cafés and shops. The façade of the National Bank of Greece is said to attempt a homage to Mycenaean architecture with its top-heavy columns. East of Plateia Syntagma, and several streets above it, on Odos Platpouda, the church of Aghios Georgios is Nafplion's cathedral. It is unclear whether this is a converted mosque, but there seems to have been a church here at least since the 17th-century Venetian occupation. The church's bell-towers and arcaded façade are distinctive; the frescoes (including a reproduction of Leonardo's *Last Supper*), are 19th century. The monument beside the north wall honours the archimandrite Christoforos Kokkinis, executed in 1943 during the German occupation.

The upper town

After following the straight course of Nafplion's parks to Plateia Syntagma, it is pleasant to meander through the streets that climb steeply toward Acronafplion. Some of the houses here date to Turkish times; many have been restored as homes, some as small hotels. Austen Kark's *Attic in Greece* describes the experiences of a British couple who restored one such house. A number of Ottoman fountains survive in this neighbourhood, including a particularly handsome one on Odos Kapodistriou, (which most of the streets that run uphill intersect), across from the church of Aghios Spyridon. Capodistrias was assassinated in front of the church on his way to a service in 1831; a bullet mark is preserved near the door. Odos Potamianou leads on to the secluded church of the Transfiguration, a converted mosque. The wooden commemorative plaque honouring philhellenes who fought in the War of Independence includes a nephew of George Washington. From here the stroll back to the centre of the old town can be accomplished either in minutes or can occupy several pleasant hours.

The waterfront

Nafplion's waterfront is lined with cafés and restaurants, but this is still a working port—witness the cargo and fishing vessels that dock here. The quay commands a fine view across the bay to the mountains of Argolis. The little Plateia of the Philhellenes honours French philhellenes who assisted during the War of Independence. The statue of Bouboulina honours Laskarina Bouboulinas, the wealthy sea captain who was said to fight better than any man. Akti Miaouli, a wide promenade on the site of the old town walls (the walls were demolished 1929–30), leads to the west mole, built on the foundations of the 'porporella', or underwater stone barrier, that once protected the entrance to the harbour. It also ringed the islet of Bourtzi (450m offshore). The Venetians built the Bourtzi in 1471; from it a chain stretched to the harbourfront, to keep out unwanted maritime visitors. Many times modified, under the Turks, the Bourtzi was first a prison, where executions were frequent, then a home for the retired executioners, who feared to live ashore. In the last century, the Bourtzi was briefly a charming hotel; today it is possible to visit it on excursion boats that leave from the dock by the main carpark. A one-hour tram tour of Nafplion also leaves from this dock in season.

Walking on, past the cafés, past the children's playground and popular fishing spots, you come to the 'Five Brothers'. The brothers are Venetian cannons set here to blast anything unwelcome out of the water. Above the Five Brothers is the district of Psaromachalas, a fishermen's quarter of once modest houses, many of which have been restored as holiday homes. From the Five Brothers it is possible to walk the circumference of the Nafplion peninsula, passing the only surviving part of the circuit wall begun in 1502, to the west end of the peninsula. Here, high up, can be seen a postern gate and a few steps of the ascent cut by Morosini's galley-slaves in 1686. En route you pass the municipal beach (*fee*). If you do the entire circuit, it is possible, with some scrambling and climbing, to avoid retracing your steps by getting to Odos Polizoidou, which runs from the beach into town.

The Citadels: Acronafplion and the Palamidi

A fortress has existed on the site of Acronafplion since Antiquity, and traces of Palaeolithic occupation have also been found. In addition, there are the impressive remains of Its Kale (Turkish: *Üç Kalè*), the 'three castles' (Greek, Frankish, Venetian) that constituted Acronafplion.

The original walls of polygonal masonry (still visible from below on the north side) have provided the foundation for each successive rebuilding. The decaying walls were partly restored by the Venetians in 1394–1409 and the lower Castello del Torrione, designed by Gambello, added c. 1477–80. This now supports the former Xenia Hotel. After the erection of the town wall in 1502, the upper castle was allowed to fall into disrepair until 1701–04, when its entrances were strengthened. Within, the former untidy but historic ruins now encircle the former Xenia Hotel and the Acronafplia Palace Hotel, but good views can be had from the panoramic road. From the far end a long flights of steps within the Dolfin Bastion descends to the Porta Sagredo of 1713, above the main square.

The Fortress of Palamidi (215m) stands on the summit of a lofty and almost inaccessible rock commanding the whole of the Argolid and with a view of the surrounding mountains. On foot it is reached by a dizzy climb of some thousand steps requiring stamina even in cool weather; best in the morning. A road now climbs the south side (via Odos 25 Martiou) and passes close to a Mycenaean cemetery of rock-hewn chamber-tombs.

The name preserves the legend of Palamedes, but the difficult terrain seems to have inhibited building here until the fortress was built by the Venetians in 1711–14, in a vain attempt to protect Nafplion from the Turks, who seized the city in 1715. A scimitar carved to the left of the main (eastern) gate marks the spot where the Turks breached the fortress walls. The *caponier*, or covered way, was erected a little earlier to provide a protected retreat from the hill to the city. The complex fortification, entered by a series of gates bearing the Lion of St Mark, consists of outworks and ramparts connecting three independent fortresses, in ascending order named San Girardo (the patron saint of the Sagredo family), San Nicolò, and Sant'Agostino (the *podestà*'s own saint).

Palamidi, inadequately garrisoned, fell after eight days' siege in 1715. The poet Manthos of Ioannina, who was present, slanderously attributed its fall to the betrayal of its plans by Lasalle. More recently the forts were renamed after Greek heroes and Fort Miltiades (S. Nicolò) served as a convict prison. Kolokotronis was incarcerated here, in a small cell that may be visited. Recently, some events in the Musical June festival have been staged here.

The Archaeological Museum

Plateia Syntagma. Closed at the time of writing, with an indefinite reopening time; T: 27520 27502.

The museum, with antiquities from the surrounding area, occupies the upper floors of the Venetian arsenal of 1713. The collection's strength lies in its Mycenaean holdings, from the surrounding Argolid. These include a unique and virtually complete suit of Mycenaean armour, found in a tomb at Dendra in 1960. There is also Neolithic pottery from the Franchthi Cave, and early to Late Helladic pottery from sites in the Argolid (including Grave Circle B at Mycenae), that of Late Helladic I–II showing marked Minoan influences in shape and decoration; a stele from Grave Circle B with the incised figure of a horseman; terracotta idols mainly from the Citadel House shrine at Mycenae (various types of figures, snakes) plus the 'Lord of Asine'; fragments of frescoes from Tiryns and Mycenae; a Mycenaean lamp from Midea, and a sherd inscribed in Linear B. Sub-Mycenaean artefacts include a helmet from Tiryns; finds of the Geometric period and later; votive discs (7th century BC) with painted scenes; grotesque masks (8th century) from Tiryns and Asine, and the 'Tiryns Inscription', the sole inscription found at this site until the surprising discoveries of December 1962. There are also figurines and votive objects; Panathenaic amphorae; a black-glazed krater of the 4th century, and a Hellenistic terracotta bath.

Peloponnesian Folklore Foundation

1 Vas. Alexandros. Open 8.30–3 daily except Tues and all of Feb; T: 27520 28947; www.pli.gr
Despite its name, the museum's superb collection has displays from all Greece. The museum—signposted throughout Nafplion—occupies three full floors in an elegant 18th-century house, with a shady courtyard. The house and much of the collection was the possession of its founder, Ms. I. Papantoniou, who created the foundation and museum when it became clear that the state would never avail itself of her collection. The foundation undertakes research and publications, including the periodical *Ethnografika*. Handsomely displayed exhibits from the collection of more than 25,000 items include coins, ceramics, furniture, and farm implements, as well as a dazzling collection of costumes. A number of dioramas help visitors to imagine town and country life in the last several centuries. There are frequent special exhibits in the entrance foyer. There is an excellent gift shop and café.

EXCURSIONS FROM NAFPLION

Although Nafplion has its own small municipal beach, there are larger beaches 10km away at Tolo and on the Kastraki headland, near the site of ancient *Asine*. Both Tolo and Kastraki are very crowded in season; most of the cheek-by-jowl local hotels are booked by groups, many from Britain.

Tolo (Τολό) is served by a frequent bus service from Nafplion. To get there by car, head out of Nafplion on the road signposted for Epidavros. After 250m a sign points (right) to the 'Bavarian Lion'. This was carved in the rock by order of Ludwig I of Bavaria to commemorate his soldiers who died in an epidemic at Tiryns in 1833–34. It was in this suburb of Pronia, in 1832, that the National Assembly ratified the election of Prince Otho, Ludwig's son, to the throne of Greece.

Beyond the village of Asini, the road continues to Kastraki, the small, rocky headland with the ruins of ancient *Asine*. A path leads past a chapel. Asine was occupied from the Early Helladic period; later by migrants from northern Greece, Dryopians according to Strabo. The inhabitants sided with the Spartans in their invasion of Argos after the First Messenian War, and afterwards fled to Messenia, settling at Koroni. Asine was deserted until the 2nd century BC, when it again became a fortified township. The Swedish excavations of 1922–30 were the idea of Crown Prince (later King) Gustav Adolf, who himself took part. Excavations were resumed in 1970; in 1989, the known-habitation period was pushed back to the Neolithic era with the discovery of a grave from that period with drinking cups and a jug. More recently, in the 1990s and early 2000s, the excavators announced that the acropolis had early been extended by a 'huge' terrace to extend the cultivation and habitation area and that the site was 'densely' populated in the Mycenaean period.

The lower town has imposing sections of Hellenistic ramparts on the north side, with a gate and piece of paved road. Within were found widespread traces of Early Helladic occupation, foundations of many houses of the Middle and Late Helladic periods, and of Roman baths, as well as Venetian additions to the fortifications (Morosini landed at Tolo in 1686). Geometric and Hellenistic remains survive on the acropolis. A Middle Helladic and Mycenaean necropolis and Protogeometric settlement has been explored on Mt Barbouna. Protogeometric and Geometric (including fortifications) finds were also made. Swimming is possible on Kastraki beach, although development has made this considerably less pleasant than formerly. In spring, the wild flowers are varied.

TIRYNS

The Mycenaean fortress-palace of Tiryns, with its massive walls, is at least as impressive as Mycenae, whose port it may have been.

To reach Tiryns (modern Tiryntha; Τίρυνθα), take the road signposted Argos that turns left out of Nafplion (not the road signposted Nea Chios and Argos that runs along the shore); after 1.5km you will see on the right the two limestone hills of Aghios Ilias (111m and 213m), each crowned by a chapel; these hills were used as quarries by the builders of Tiryns. Farther on is the penal Agricultural College founded by Capodistrias. In 1926 in a field belonging to the college was discovered the so-called 'Treasure of Tiryns', 4km from Argos. The site lies just beyond to the east of the road.

The site

Open daily 8.30–5 in summer; Mon–Sat 9.30–3 in winter. Repair work on the site means that it is sometimes closed.

The citadel of Tiryns occupies the summit of a low rocky height known inevitably as Palaiokastro (27m), the lowest and most westerly of a series of isolated knolls rising like islands from the flat plain. It is separated from the sea (now c. 1.5km distant) by reclaimed marshland that stretches towards Nea Chios. The fortress-palace is enclosed by cyclopean walls, the finest specimens of the military architecture of the Mycenaeans. Homer speaks of 'wall-girt Tiryns'; Pindar admires the 'Cyclopean doorways'; and Pausanias compares the walls of Tiryns with the pyramids of Egypt. The palace within is more complex than those at Mycenae and Pylos. The unfortified city lay in the surrounding plain.

HISTORY OF TIRYNS

Tiryns was inhabited before the Bronze Age; the earliest people may have been lake-dwellers in the marsh. In one legend Tiryns is the birthplace of Heracles and the base of operations for his Labours (*Apollodorus II, iv, 12*). The fortifications in their present form belong to the 13th century BC, although there are signs that the upper citadel was fortified a century earlier. Despite its size and wealth, Tiryns seems always to have been secondary to Argos or Mycenae, and many scholars think this was the port of Mycenae, before the subsequent silting up of the coast. Though it continued to be inhabited through Geometric times and sent a contingent to Plataea in 479, Tiryns was never again important. It was destroyed by Argos in 468 BC, so thoroughly that Pausanias says that nothing remained except the Cyclopean wall. Nonetheless, Tiryns became a fortress in the Hellenistic period and the strength of the walls proved an attraction in Byzantine times, when a church was built in the great forecourt. The site was explored by Schliemann and Dörpfeld in 1884–86. There was considerable reconstruction of fallen walls in 1962–64; the long-delayed discovery of the water-supply in 1962 by the late N. Verdelis led to further investigation of the lower enceinte, continued by the German Archaeological Institute. In the last few years, efforts to repair earthquake damage have also confirmed that there were five periods of Mycenaean settlement here, from the early 12th century BC to the Late Helladic era.

The fortress is most impressive from below. The summit on which it stands has the form of a waisted oblong 299m long and from 20m to 34m wide, descending from south to north in three terraces. The whole of the area is enclosed by the walls, nearly 700m in circuit, which are built of two kinds of limestone, red and grey, in irregular blocks of different sizes, laid as far as possible in horizontal courses. They are often called Cyclopean because of Pausanias' remark that the walls were built by Cyclopes, with stones 'so huge that a pair of mules would not even begin to shift the smallest'. The stones, the largest of which are estimated to weigh over 14,000kg, are partially hammer-dressed; smaller stones bonded with clay mortar fill the interstices. Round the lower citadel the walls are 7–8m thick; round the irregular upper citadel, where their line is broken by towers, salients, and re-entrant angles, they vary in thickness from 5–11km, in places containing galleries and chambers. They stand to about half their original estimated height of 20m.

Inside the citadel

The main entrance was in the middle of the east wall. A smaller entrance opened in the great semicircular bastion that projects on the west side, and there were three posterns in the lower citadel. Admission today is by a gate from the by-road (*see plan overleaf*) to the steep and ruinous ramp, c. 5m wide, which formed an approach practicable for chariots. Its disposition exposed the visitor's right or unshielded side to the defenders as at Mycenae, and necessitated at the top a sharp turn. The main entrance opened in the outer wall, here 7.5m thick. The original opening of c. 5m has been reduced to 2.5m by later masonry; there is no trace of a gate. You are now in a long passage running north and south between the inner and outer walls. To the right, passing a square niche below an arch (probably a guard post), it leads down to the lower enceinte.

Approach to the palace

The outer gateway **1** is of similar size to the Lion Gate at Mycenae. In the monolithic threshold are holes for the pivots of folding doors, and in the rebated gateposts are bolt holes, 15cm in diameter, allowing a cross-bar to be shot home into the wall. The right gatepost is intact, the left one is broken, and the lintel has disappeared. Beyond, the passage widens to form a barbican, narrowing again to a point where an inner gate **2** probably guarded the oblong courtyard. Here, to the left, in the thickness of the outer wall, is the first of the two series of galleries and chambers for which the fortress is specially noted. The east gallery, fronted by a colonnade, had a corbelled vault and communicated by six doors with six vaulted chambers, each 3.4m square.

Opposite opens the great propylaia **3**, a double porch divided by a wall, in which was a single doorway. Between antae within and without stood wooden columns, the stone bases of which are still in position. The gateway supersedes an earlier one. From the inner porch a narrow passage leads off direct to the smaller megaron (*see below*).

You enter the forecourt of the palace, from which remains of a Byzantine church have been removed; it is bounded on three sides by the fortress walls and the complex of casemates built into them. You descend by a covered staircase, with a right-angled bend in the middle, to the vaulted south gallery (20m long, 5m high, and 1.5m wide) at a level 7m below that of the court. The sides narrow to a loophole in the east wall by which it was lit. Five doorways open from the gallery into rectangular vaulted chambers. On the southwest side a rectangular tower, with a frontage of 19m, enclosed two cisterns.

The palace

The Royal Palace is reached from the north side of the forecourt by the smaller propylaia **4**. The earliest version of the palace in this form dates to the 14th century BC. There was an important Middle Helladic building here but no architectural remains of Late Helladic I–II have survived. Its present layout belongs to c. 1250 BC. The site was destroyed by fire in c. 1200 BC but continued to be occupied. The walls of the palace stand to a height of only 0.5m–1m; above this limestone base they were of sun-dried brick, the whole being then covered by stucco and decorated with frescoes. The huge stone thresholds of the doors remain *in situ*; the floors are of concrete made of lime and pebbles. In the colonnaded court is a round sacrificial altar. A porch **5**, with two columns and elaborate benches, gives access by triple doors to an antechamber, and then through a door (closed in Antiquity only by a curtain) to the

TIRYNS: THE CITADEL

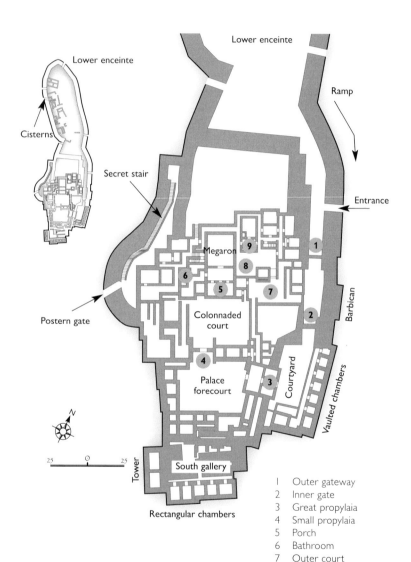

Lower enceinte

Lower enceinte

Ramp

Cisterns

Secret stair

Entrance

Megaron

Postern gate

Barbican

Colonnaded court

Courtyard

Vaulted chambers

Palace forecourt

N

25   0   25

Tower

South gallery

Rectangular chambers

1   Outer gateway
2   Inner gate
3   Great propylaia
4   Small propylaia
5   Porch
6   Bathroom
7   Outer court
8   Inner court
9   Smaller megaron

megaron, or great hall. In the centre is a circular clay hearth, 3.4m in diameter. The roof was supported by four wooden columns, set on stone bases (still present), which had an open lantern to give light and let out the smoke. The base of the throne is well preserved and the painted floor intact in places. The walls were frescoed with scenes of a boar hunt and a life-size frieze of women; the frescoes are now in the National Archaeological Museum in Athens. Reached from the ante-chamber is the bathroom (6), with a floor composed of one huge limestone monolith 4m by 3m.

The apartments described above are duplicated on a smaller scale behind and to the east (outer court, (7); inner court, (8); smaller megaron, (9); and ancillary buildings), sometimes thought to be women's quarters, though a recent study (by K. Kilian) suggests that a double megaron arrangement was typical of advanced Mycenaean palaces. Behind is a large open court separated by the massive inner wall from the lower enceinte. In the Early Helladic period, a massive round building, c. 28m in diameter and with walls 4–5m thick (possibly a granary), occupied the hilltop. It was two-storeyed and roofed with terracotta tiles. This is now concealed beneath the megaron and court. The lower enceinte has been intensively investigated by the German Archaeological Institute (Prof. K. Kilian). The area was occupied as early as Neolithic times and substantial remains of Early Helladic buildings have been discovered. As at Mycenae, there would have been a substantial settlement outside the palace/fortress itself. In times of war, as many people as possible would have taken refuge inside the walls of the palace/fortress. Tiryns' most massive fortifications, however, were only built in the later 13th century. About 1200 BC there was a catastrophic destruction, probably by earthquake, after which the layout of the buildings was completely changed. The most interesting discoveries (not yet accessible) are of a cult room of 12th-century date, with a predecessor on the same site, and associated ritual equipment, including large numbers of terracotta figures of various types. There is also much evidence of industrial activity, including metal working.

Cyclopean masonry at Tiryns.

The site of Tiryns, looking back from the lower enceinte towards Napflion and the Bourtzi.

The western exit

From a square tower to the west of the rear court a well-preserved secret stair winds down within a massive bastion to an inconspicuous corbelled postern gate. You can leave the fortress, turn right, and skirt the outer walls. At the northwest angle of the lower enceinte two secret passages lead steeply downward through the walls from inside to two underground cisterns fed by springs. There are comparable arrangements at Mycenae and on the acropolis at Athens, but the Tiryns passages were discovered by accident only in 1962. Stones covering the cisterns were found (only, unfortunately, after some had been moved) to bear Archaic inscriptions shallowly cut in boustrophedon c. 600 BC.

In the immediate vicinity of the palace, settlement remains of the Early Helladic and Mycenaean periods have been investigated, also a Dark Age and Geometric cemetery.

ANCIENT EPIDAURUS

En route to the site of Epidaurus (Επίδαυρος; Epìdavros in modern Greek) from Nafplion, you enter the valley which separates the slopes of Palamidi, to the south, from the bare, waterless range of Arachnaion to the north. Its highest point rises to 1199m, but the most striking peak is the lower Mt Arna (1079m) above Ligourio. The view is much better on the return journey when the serried ranges of the Peloponnese rise ahead. The road passes a number of ancient remains, including the corbelled arch of a massive cyclopean bridge, perhaps of the 5th century BC but probably of Mycenaean origin, by a modern bridge, 14 km from Nafplion. A little farther on, on the left, rises Kazarma, a small but precipitous hill (280m) with some remains of a citadel of the 5th century, with walls standing to 6m in polygonal masonry (road/track left after cyclopean bridge). Below it, near the road, are the remains of a tholos tomb (fenced). Ligourio has several Byzantine churches (*see p. 229*). The Sanctuary of Asclepius and the Ancient Theatre (called locally *Iero Ligouriou*) are signposted at Ligourio: bear right in the town and 2.5km farther on go left for the Asclepieion.

The Sanctuary of Asclepius

Open daily 8–5 in summer; T: 27530 22090.

The Hieron of Epidaurus, or Sanctuary of Asclepius, combined aspects of a religious shrine, health centre and fashionable spa. The sanctuary is situated in a broad valley between Mt Velanidia, the ancient *Titthion* (858m), on the northeast, and Mt Charani, the ancient *Cynortion*, on the southeast. In addition to the temples and colonnades devoted to the cult of Asclepius (or Asklipios; Æsculapius to the Romans) there were dwellings for the priest-physicians, hospitals for the sick, sanatoria for the convalescent, and hotels and places of amusement—including the nearby theatre—for the healthy. In Roman times baths were added, fed by reservoirs which collected water from the local springs. The sanctuary was also the scene of a number of festivals, including the important athletic and musical festival known as the *Asclepieia*, which was celebrated here nine days after the conclusion of the Isthmian games. Unlike the Isthmian games, where athletes contended for honour and a wreath, the *Asclepieia* carried cash prizes. In 45 AD, one Dionysia of Tralles won the women's sprint; it is not known when the women's games were initiated here.

Excavations

Excavations began in 1881, and became the life's work of P. Kavvadias. The French School also excavated after the Second World War; J. Papadimitriou in 1948–51, and the Greek Archaeology Service more recently. Apart from the theatre, the ruins are not well preserved, although an extensive restoration project is in progress.

EPIDAURUS: THE HISTORY & THE LEGEND

The cult of Apollo at the Epidaurian sanctuary seems to go back into the mists of time, with that of Asclepius being added probably in the Archaic period. There are two sources on which our knowledge of Asclepius depends. For Homer, he was fully mortal, a hero who was also a skilled physician. He and his sons appear in Troy as part of a Greek contingent from *Trikke* in Thessaly—his oldest and most famous sanctuary was indeed at Trikke (modern Trikala; *see page 539*). By the 6th century, Asclepius is presented as a mythical figure, the son of Apollo (who himself had a reputation as a healing god) and Coronis, a maiden probably from Thessaly. While pregnant with Asclepius, Coronis slept with a mortal and Apollo's sister Artemis, in an act of sibling support, killed both the lovers. At the last moment, Apollo (or Hermes) snatched the unborn Asclepius from his mother's womb as she lay on her funeral pyre and gave it to the wise centaur Chiron, who taught the boy the art of medicine. An alternative tradition tells how Coronis survived but exposed her baby at Epidaurus, where it was suckled by a she-goat and protected by a dog. In both versions, Asclepius becomes so skilled in healing that he is even able to raise the dead, but in doing so he enrages the god Zeus into whose domain he has trespassed and is banished to the underworld. Somehow Asclepius transcended his banishment and took root as the supreme healing god. It is said that while Apollo was always remote, Asclepius was more approachable (as is seen in his efforts to raise mortals from the dead, something no god would ever do). This explains his growing popularity. During the 5th century BC the island of Kos and the mainland town of Epidaurus developed as his most important shrines. At Kos, Hippocrates became his most famous follower and is associated with the development of scientific medicine. The sanctuary at Epidaurus developed about 500 BC from an ancient shrine of Apollo. The ancient legend of Asclepius' exposure was commemorated by a ban on the sacrifice of goats and by the keeping of sacred dogs. By the 4th century, the cult of Asclepius had superseded that of Apollo at Epidaurus, which saw itself as the divine physician's birthplace. Asclepius himself fathered several children, including Hygieia (Health).

Epidaurus became as much a social centre, with theatre, athletic contests and philosophical discussions, as a healing centre. Herbs were grown on the hillside and were an important part of some treatments. As with many such sites (and oracles), it remained marginal to city life and therefore there were no restrictions on visitors from throughout the Greek world.

The sanctuary was despoiled by Sulla in 86 BC and the loot distributed among his soldiers. In the late 4th century, a church was built near the sanctuary entrance, effectively ending its long history as Greece's most important shrine to Asclepius.

C.F.

The museum

The pine-clad setting of the site is charming despite the artificial landscaping and paraphernalia of the festival. The museum, on the left as you enter the site, is most conveniently visited before the excavations. To right and left of the entrance are two Corinthian columns from the interior colonnade of the Tholos and two Ionic columns from the Abaton. The collection includes inscriptions recording miraculous cures; Roman statuary; surgical instruments; building stelae with accounts for the Tholos and Temple of Asclepius. There is also sculpture (mostly casts) from pediments; a reconstruction of the entablature of the propylaia, as well as of part of the Temple of Asclepius (380–375). The splendid pavement of the Tholos is also displayed. The Tholos (*see p. 248 below*), a curious building of which two different conjectural versions are illustrated by drawings, was built c. 360 BC, possibly by Polyclitus the Younger. A Corinthian capital, section of circular wall, ornate ceiling, and decorated doorway, all from the same building, are preserved, and finally a reconstruction of its entablature.

The Epidaurus Festival Museum (*usually open daily 1 May–30 Sept when the site is open, and until 9pm on performance nights; some labels in English*), near the site entrance, has displays of props, costumes, programmes and memorabilia from past performances.

The sanctuary

You come first to the remains of a large square building, probably the katagogeion, a hotel comparable with the Leonidaion at Olympia (*see p. 370*). It had four cloistered courts from each of which opened 18 rooms. The polygonal walls stand to a height of 0.6m and most of the threshold blocks are in place. To the west are the ruined Greek baths (3rd century BC). The so-called gymnasium (more probably a ceremonial banqueting hall), a huge colonnaded court with exedrae and other rooms off it, survives only in one course of the outer walls. The two rooms at the southeast and southwest corners have off-centre doorways for the convenient insertion of dining couches, and the large east hall preserves traces of stone couch-supports with dowel holes in their upper surfaces. The Romans built an odeion in the court, of which considerable portions of the brick auditorium and stage buildings survive. The courtyard may have been the location of musical and theatrical ritual in earlier times. The whole base of the great propylaia of the gymnasium, at the northwest corner, is preserved with its pavement and ramp, though the Doric colonnade has vanished. The indeterminate ruins to the northeast may be of the Stoa of Kotys, a building originally of unburnt brick that collapsed and was rebuilt (along with other parts of the sanctuary) by a Roman senator Antoninus, whom some have identified with the 2nd-century AD Emperor Antoninus Pius. Others think him a 3rd-century AD senator of Greek Asia Minor heritage.

The Temple of Asclepius

As you continue into the sanctuary, the most important group of buildings in the Hieron stretches ahead from right to left (east and west); this area would in Antiquity have been crowded with the sick and potentially dying, their families and friends, and visitors here for prophylactic treatments. The remains at the southeast corner, immediately north of the stoa, may be those of the little Greek Temple of Themis **(1)**, with an unidentified Roman building beyond. Turning to the west, you find the foundations of the Temple of Artemis **(2)**, a Doric prostyle building with six columns on the front (4th century BC). Almost adjoining on the north is a large rectangular building which may have included the original Abaton **(3)**, where patients slept expecting the visitation of the god and a cure by miraculous dreams. The Abaton seems to have been expanded several times, probably in the 4th century and perhaps again in Roman times (*see below*). Various inscribed bases may be seen to the north, which probably bordered the sacred grove.

The temple is approached by a paved path and ramp. It was Doric peripteral hexastyle, with 6 columns by 11, about 24m long, and dating from c. 370 BC. Nothing, however, remains but foundations; architectural fragments are on display in the museum.

A stele found in 1885 supplies many details of the method and cost of construction. The work was supervised by the architect Theodotos and the temple took four years and eight and a half months to build. The sculptor Timotheos made the models for the pedimental sculptures and may have been responsible for some of them, though other artists were certainly involved. The doors were of ivory, and the cult statue in gold and ivory was by Thrasymedes of Paros. According to Pausanias, Asclepius was represented seated on a throne, grasping a staff in one hand and holding the other over the head of the serpent; a dog crouched by his side. Two marble reliefs, possibly copies of the statue, were found (now in Athens).

To the east, facing the temple entrance, are the foundations of the Great Altar of Asclepius; farther south, crossed by the line of the Byzantine wall, are the foundations of a small building which may be the Epidoteion, or sanctuary of the bountiful healers.

The Tholos and Abaton

Along with Delphi and Olympia, Epidaurus has a tholos (or rotunda), and, as at those shrines, its function is not entirely understood. Pausanias thought that this tholos (reconstruction project in progress), built c. 360–320 BC was built by the famous sculptor Polyclitus; he was almost certainly wrong. Nothing is left but the foundations, but a very good idea of the appearance of the building may be obtained from the partial reconstructions, drawings, and plans in the museum (*see above*). This tholos seems to have been more elaborate than those at Delphi and Olympia, with foundations consisting of six concentric walls, in conglomerate, with a maximum diameter of 22m.

The rotunda stood on a crepidoma of three steps. The three outer foundation walls supported a peristyle of 26 Doric columns, in poros, stuccoed and painted; the main circular wall of the building with a large portal flanked by windows; and an interior colonnade of 14 marble columns with fine Corinthian capitals. The three inner foundation walls form a miniature labyrinth, the purpose of which—as indeed of the whole building—is obscure. A sacred well or a snake pit are among possibilities; more likely perhaps is that it was the focus of a chthonic cult of Asclepius. Above the labyrinth was a spiralling chequered pavement in black and white marble (now displayed in the museum). The ceiling was coffered, carved and painted. Lion's-head gargoyles were regularly placed at the edge of the roof, on the apex of which was a carved floral acroterion.

GREEK MEDICINE

'And whoever came suffering from the sores of nature, with limbs wounded by grey bronze or far-hurled stones, or with bodies wasted by summer's heat or winter's cold, he [Asclepius] delivered them, different ones from different pains, tending some with kindly incantations, while he set others on their feet again with the knife.'

This description of the healing styles of Asclepius by the poet Pindar shows that the god, or his priests, were able to cure either by mystic spells or elementary surgery. Asclepius' method of healing depended on incubation (confinement to a small cell or chamber). According to one inscription at a healing centre, each patient would deposit a gift of silver and have his name and city recorded before proceeding to a sacred enclosure where men would sleep on one side of the altar and women on the other. In their dreams they might have a vision of the god himself, which might contain instructions on how to treat the ailment or perhaps lead to a miracle cure. Much of the advice made good sense in that it involved diet and exercise. The healed patient would often record any recovery in a votive inscription. These make good reading. A woman emaciated by an internal worm visits the sanctuary. The priests remove her head, pull out the worm, but cannot put the head on again. Luckily Asclepius himself intervenes to do so. A man with a stomach abscess is tied by the priests to a door knocker; the abscess is cut out and the wound sewed up. He leaves a pool of blood behind him but survives.

One important feature of Asclepius' cult was the use of snakes, one of which is habitually shown twined around the god's staff. (Ironically, today's symbol of medicine is not this staff but the two-serpent wing-topped staff of Hermes, the swift-footed messenger god, who also dabbled in astrology and some healing arts.) Some scholars see the serpent as a chthonian symbol of the underworld and death, both of which Asclepius may be said to have triumphed over with his medical skills. An inscription records how a man with a malignant ulcer on his toe was healed when a snake came out from the sanctuary and licked it while he was asleep. All the time he was dreaming of a beautiful youth administering a potion. At Epidaurus a species of yellow snake was kept in a pit in the sanctuary. It was through snakes also that Asclepius' cult spread. In one famous example, after the devastating plague in Athens in 431 BC, a snake was sent by the god from Epidaurus to Athens in a chariot. The cult caught hold in the city and spread further from there. In other cases cult centres were set up on the coast where it was said that snakes had swum ashore. Altogether some 400 such centres have been identified, and some were still in active use until the 6th century AD.

Asclepius is usually depicted standing and with a beard: in the great chryselphantine cult statue at Epidaurus, however, he was seated, his hand stretched over the head of a snake, with a dog in the background.   C.F.

To the north of the Tholos and forming the north side of the area enclosed by the Byzantines, is a line of two adjacent stoas, each 10m deep, but now reduced to their foundations. Their combined length was nearly 71m; the west colonnade was built, owing to the slope of the ground, in two storeys, so that its upper floor continued the level of the single storey of the east colonnade. The two together comprised the expanded Abaton ('place not to be stepped on'), or *enkoimeterion* ('place of incubation'). One or two of the benches which lined the walls and joined the columns still survive. A staircase of 14 steps led up to the second storey. In the east colonnade were found tablets (now in the museum) inscribed with accounts of miraculous cures. In the southeast corner is a well, 17m deep; in the southwest corner an underground passage. The well was sunk in the 6th century BC and incorporated in the 4th-century building.

The stadium
The stadium was laid out in a natural declivity during the 5th century BC, with seats partly cut from the rock and partly built up in masonry. The starting and finishing lines survive, c. 180m apart, and the construction, without sphendone and with an inclined entrance tunnel, somewhat resembles its counterpart at Olympia. A stone water channel with basins at intervals surrounds the track.

The northwest
To north of the site is a small Temple of Aphrodite **(4)**, beyond which is the main propylaia of the sanctuary with part of the sacred way from the town of Epidavros. The limestone pavement and the ramps leading to the great gate are in good condition. To the south of this is a large Roman thermal establishment fed by water from Mt Cynortion, and further south, among the trees, are some indistinct remnants of a large and very early basilican church with double aisles and a large atrium.

The theatre
On nights when there are performances, the theatre is open only to ticket holders. Performances of the ancient tragedies, usually offered in modern Greek, are given June–Sept on Sat and Sun c. 9pm. Many productions are staged by the National Theatre of Greece, some by foreign companies. Information from the Hellenic Festival Box Office in Athens, Panepestimiou 39, T: 210 322 1459; or the Epidaurus Festival Box Office, T: 27530 22006. It's also possible to buy tickets at most of the travel agencies in Nafplion and at the theatre itself, starting at 5pm on the day of a performance.

The theatre is one of the best-preserved Classical buildings in Greece, having escaped significant looting. It dates from the 4th century BC and seems to have escaped alteration until recent years, when judicious restoration has been carried out. The building is on the World Heritage List. It is now the centre of an annual summer festival of drama. Its acoustics are unusually perfect, the slightest whisper or rustle of paper from the orchestra being clearly audible from any of its 14,000 seats—as is more than evident when visitors put the acoustics to the test. The cavea, c. 114m across, faces

EPIDAURUS:
THE SANCTUARY & THEATRE

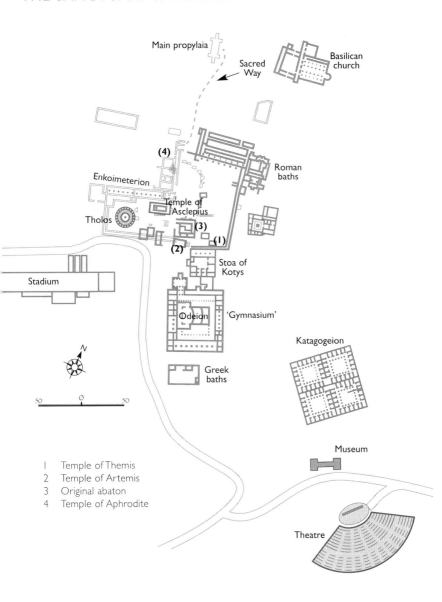

1   Temple of Themis
2   Temple of Artemis
3   Original abaton
4   Temple of Aphrodite

north. It has 55 rows of seats, 34 below the diazoma and 21 above. The lower block is divided into 12 wedges by 13 staircases; the upper block has 23 staircases. The seats of honour were of red, the ordinary seats of white limestone. The two flanks of the theatre were supported by poros retaining walls, now restored. The orchestra is a complete circle 20m in diameter, the circumference of which is marked by a ring of limestone flags. The floor was of beaten earth. In the centre is the round base of the *thymele*, or altar. Between the circle and the front row of seats is a semicircular paved depression, 2.1m wide, placed to collect rainwater. Access to the theatre is by two *parodoi*, passing through double doorways (restored) with pilasters embellished with Corinthian capitals. The foundations of the stage can be seen when they are not covered by temporary wooden scenery. Plays here usually begin as the sun sets, touching the marble and surrounding landscape with red hues.

THE THEATRE OF EPIDAURUS

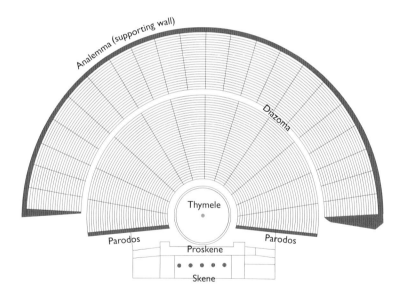

Sanctuary of Apollo Maleatas

The site is intermittently open; inquire at the entrance booth to the main site. Best access is via a good dirt road (1.8km) from behind the tourist pavilion: to reach it leave the car park at the northeast corner, just before the police post and post office hut. Keep right at doubtful junctions on the hillside. The site gates are immediately to the left of the track.

The sanctuary of Apollo Maleatas, which pre-dated the Asclepieion, spanned the centuries from the Mycenaean era to at least the 2nd century AD. The location made expansion difficult, hence the development of the sanctuary of Asclepius on the ground below. The site has been intensively excavated since 1974; work has begun to restore the Altar of Apollo and the Hellenistic terrace of the sanctuary. On entry, you pass some Middle Helladic houses to the left. You leave the cistern to the right, pass by the side of the nymphaion and enter the sanctuary proper. To the left, below the hill with the houses, a Mycenaean terrace was converted into an open air temple-shaped enclosure in the Roman period. Next to it is the Classical Temple of Apollo, overlying an Archaic predecessor. In front, at a lower level, are remains of earlier altars, going back to the Mycenaean period (votives). The north side of the area is bounded by the remains of a Hellenistic stoa, on a buttressed terrace of splendid masonry. In the centre is the 4th-century altar and other structures. On the east side is an entry staircase beside which is a rectangular Temenos of the Muses, with a back wall of rough stones recalling the caves frequented by the Muses. The site may have been damaged in c. 80 BC by pirates. It was refurbished in the 2nd century AD at the expense of one Antoninus (*see p. 247 above*). To this period belong the remarkable and well-preserved vaulted cistern and the nearby nymphaion which it fed. Also of the Roman period, behind the Temenos of the Muses and outside the main sanctuary area, are a complex priests' house and a propylon with stepped approach.

Archaia and Nea Epidavros

The ancient city of Epidavros, which controlled the sanctuary, stood on the headland to the south of the harbour. Cyclopean walls still stand, and a group of Mycenaean chamber tombs was excavated in 1888. There have been sporadic discoveries of remains of Archaic–Roman date. Submerged buildings have been identified and a Theatre of Dionysus excavated in 1972 with 10 *kerkides* and 18 rows of seats (late 4th century BC), many inscribed with names of citizens who endowed the seating. This is now the scene of the 'Musical July at Archaia Epidavros' festival. (*For information on tickets, see p. 250.*)

Nea Epidavros, a little inland to the north, is where the first 'National Assembly' met on 20th December 1821 to declare the independence of Greece ('Constitution of Epidavros'). Above the town are ruins of the Frankish castle of Nicholas de Guise, Constable of the Morea.

MYLI & LERNA

NB: The coast road via Nea Chios is much more pleasant than the inland route via Argos.

Myli (Μύλοι, 'the mills') lies between Mt Pontinos and the sea, 1.5 km from the site of ancient Lerna. Nearby, on 25th June 1825, Dimitrios Ypsilantis, with 227 men, checked the advance on Nafplion of Ibrahim Pasha and a much larger force of Egyptians, after Ibrahim's capture of Tripolis.

The enchanting little site of prehistoric **Lerna** (Λέρνη; *open 8.30–3 except Mon. A useful short guidebook in English is sometimes on sale at the ticket booth*) is less than 1km south of Myli. The site (poorly signposted) is reached by a left turn into a dirt road that ends at the site. The remains are simple—as one might expect of a site that may have been here since 6500 BC. Some remains are marked off by plants and flowers which the excavator J.L. Caskey thought would beautify the site and make the courses of the walls and shapes of the buildings easier for visitors to understand.

Here, in a sacred grove of plane trees, were celebrated the Lernaean mysteries in honour of Demeter, and here Heracles slew the Hydra. On a mound fortified by the Germans in 1943 stands the conspicuous concrete shelter protecting the excavations made by the American School under Caskey in 1952–58. It appears that Lerna was first occupied during the Early and Middle Neolithic period (6500 to 5300 BC) and then again in the Early Helladic period (3000 to 2000 BC). Lerna is one of the most important known sites in Greece for Early Helladic remains. The fortifications are virtually unique for their period. The House of Tiles, so called from the extensive remains of its rectangular terracotta roof tiles, is one of the most elaborate Early Helladic buildings yet found. A palace, or administrative centre of the corridor-house type, it is 25m long and 12m wide and had two storeys—a precursor, perhaps, of later Mycenaean structures. It was destroyed by fire at the end of Early Helladic II, so helping to preserve its mud-brick walls. The Early Helladic III levels had some pottery from Troy, whereas the Middle Helladic settlement, which here seems to follow without any violent upheaval, has pottery imports from near Niš (Balkan) as well as from Crete and the Cyclades. Two Mycenaean royal shaft graves (robbed in Antiquity) cut through the House of Tiles. Geometric graves have been found to the southwest of the site. (Remains found here are in the Argos Archaeological Museum.) Recent work is concentrating on cataloguing pottery from the 9th–4th centuries BC—long after Lerna's most significant period—in the hopes of developing a useful typology for local ceramic ware of those centuries.

Hysiae and Mount Parthenion

West of Myli is Achladokambos, a village of fewer than 1,000 inhabitants on the hillside, with its railway station (273m) in the fertile valley below. The place gets its name from the wild pear (αχλάδι) which once grew on the mountain slopes.

Just before the village, on a ridge to the left, are the inconspicuous ruins of *Hysiae*, whose acropolis is marked by good polygonal walling. Here the Argives defeated the Lacedaemonians in 669–668 BC. The town lay on the frontier between Argos and Tegea, and was destroyed by the Lacedaemonians in 417 BC.

Towards the head of the valley the vegetation becomes scrubby and alpine. On a hill near the summit (780m), just over the border with Arcadia, are the remains of Mouchli, a Byzantine fortress used by the Franks and destroyed in 1460. Mt Parthenion (1215m) lies to the southeast. On its slope a sanctuary once marked the spot where Pan promised the runner Pheidippides that he would aid the Athenians at Marathon (*see p. 138*). The road descends into the Plain of Tripolis, famous in Antiquity for the three Arcadian cities of Mantineia, Tegea and Pallantion (*see pp. 266–72*).

INTO THE ARGOLIC PENINSULA

Those travelling on to Spetses from the Argolid will sail from Kosta or Portocheli, while those visiting Poros will take the ferry from Galatas. Others may simply wish to tour the peninsula, to see the ancient site of Troezen and the very developed coast. It is possible to do the circuit of the peninsula in a day by car (longer by local bus, given the vagaries of scheduling). The relevant roads are well marked.

The western peninsula

Didyma, which with its mountain preserves an ancient name, lies below in the centre of a circular plain. A road leads to Kilada, an active fishing and boat-building village. On the north side of the bay is the 150m long **Franchthi Cave** (Σπήλαιο Φράγχθι), one of the most important sites for the study of the Early and Middle Neolithic in Europe (*sadly not open to visitors*). Here, a stratigraphical sequence going back to the Palaeolithic period (10th millennium BC) was excavated by the University of Indiana from 1968–77 to a depth of 11 metres. The earliest complete skeleton found in Greece was discovered at the bottom of the Mesolithic deposit, as was obsidian from the island of Melos. The remains here cover up to 25,000 years of human habitation from Palaeolithic hunting and gathering to Neolithic plant and animal husbandry. The excavators regard the remains from the transitional Mesolithic era as especially important, believing Franchthi to have been the 'base camp' for a band of hunter-gatherers. Remains found some 100m from the cave near the sea (Paralia) suggest that the cave-dwellers established a beach-head settlement outside the cave during the Neolithic era.

Kranidi (Κρανίδι) is the market centre of the peninsula. The Greek senate removed here in 1823 following their rupture with the executive. The chapel of the Aghia Triada (Holy Trinity) has frescoes by John of Athens (*see p. 65*), dated to 1244. These include the *Ascension* and the *Hospitality of Abraham*.

Ermioni (Ερμιόνη), where boats from Piraeus to the islands of the Argo-Saronic Gulf often make a stop, is, like most of the coastal towns of the Argolic Peninsula, in the throes of over-development. It stands at the base of a spit of land, which separates the two excellent natural anchorages that gave ancient *Hermione* its importance. On the promontory, which has been laid out as a park, are some foundations of a Temple of Poseidon. A mosaic exposed near the school belonged to a complex of Early Christian buildings dependent on a basilica of the 6th century. A chasm in the neighbourhood was supposed in ancient times to be a short cut to Hades, avoiding the Styx. The frugal Hermionians accordingly put no passage money in the mouths of their dead. South of Ermioni is the monastery of the Aghii Anargyri, whose church and fine frescoes may be 16th century. By some obscure coincidence, these 'penniless saints' (Cosmas and Damian, the doctor saints, who took no fee for their ministrations) are venerated here, where the ancients left no coin for the ferryman.

From here the coast road leads west to Portocheli (Πορτοχέλι), on the north side of an inlet. In times gone by this was a pleasant fishing village. Today huge summer hotel complexes, many booked solidly by package holidaymakers, have been built on the adjacent coasts. There is a ferry to Spetses (40mins). The remains on the south side of the harbour have been equated with *Halieis*, settled by refugees from Tiryns in the 5th century BC. Here, from 1962–68 and subsequently, the American School of Classical Studies explored the ancient site which is now partly under water. The fortification system is visible on the acropolis and its continuation has been traced beneath the sea. The lower town was laid out, in the 4th century BC, on a grid plan with typical small courtyard houses; the higher zone is earlier in date and unplanned. The agora and an industrial quarter have been identified. To the southeast of the town were found graves of the 6th–4th centuries BC, one group covered by a tumulus.

Troezen and the eastern peninsula

Trizina (Τροιζήνα), a village lying below the north shope of Mt Aderes (719m), occupies part of the site of *Troezen*, the ancient capital of the small and fertile territory of *Troezenia*. To the south between the deep ravines of Aghios Athanasios (to the east) and the Gefyri (to the west) rises an isolated hill, on which a Frankish tower marks the site of the acropolis. The principal ancient ruins, however, lie to the west of the village.

HISTORY OF TROEZEN

Troezen has an early history rich in myth and legend. It was said to be the birthplace of Theseus, the great hero of Athens. When Theseus' chaste son Hippolytus rebuffed the advances of his stepmother, Phaedra, she killed herself, leaving a message accusing Hippolytus of rape. Theseus called upon Poseidon (his father, in some accounts) to assist him in revenge, and Poseidon sent a sea serpent to make the horses of Hippolytus take fright and drag their master to his death. It was also believed that it was here that Orestes was purified after killing his mother Clytemnestra.

Troezen was a small, independent city state in 480 BC when the Persians occupied Athens and the Troezenians gave hospitality to Athenian refugees. The famous stele detailing Themistocles' plan of evacuation was found here. The Athenians captured the city in 457–446. In the Peloponnesian War the Troezenians sided with Sparta. The city fell under Macedonian control in the 4th century, was visited by the peripatetic emperor Hadrian in the 2nd century, and was the seat of a barony and bishopric under the Franks. The Third Greek National Assembly, at which Capodistrias was elected President of Greece, was held at Troezen, in March 1827. In May of that year, the Constitution of Troezen, usually known as the Charter of the Liberties of Greece, was published, though it was put into immediate abeyance at the time. This was the third of the 'constitutions', the others being those of Epidavros (1821) and of Astros (1823).

The site

The scanty but scattered remains (sign in village), exposed by the French School in 1890 and 1899 and re-examined by the German Institute in 1932, lie near three ruined Byzantine chapels incorporating ancient fragments. You come first to the so-called 'Theseus Stone', then (left fork; 10mins) to the remains of the city walls with a fine tower, 13m square and 10m high, with a postern and a staircase. The lower half is ancient, the upper medieval. From here there is a path along the course of an ancient aqueduct to the gorge of Gefyraion, spanned by the picturesque single-arched Devil's Bridge (*Gefyra tou Diavolou*). The surroundings are cool and pleasant and it is possible to swim.

Of the other remains the most interesting (15mins west of the tower; right fork at the Theseus Stone) is a building c. 30m square, consisting of a colonnaded court surrounded by rooms and, on the west side, a hall with benches and a channelled floor. This has been identified by Welter as an *enkoimeterion* and the building may therefore be an Asclepieion. Beyond this, the deserted Palaia Episkopi, or bishop's palace (or church), is perhaps the site of the Temple of Aphrodite Kataskopia ('Peeping Aphrodite'). Pausanias records such a temple built on the spot where the amorous Phaedra used to watch Hippolytus at his manly exercises; their graves were in its precinct.

Methana

From Troezen, the road leads on to Galatas, where the ferry plies across the straits to Poros. In spring, when the trees are in bloom, it is well worth visiting the lemon grove (λεμονοδάσος) outside town (signposted). Later in the year, when the lemons are ripe, roadside stands sell lemonade.

The road in the other direction leads to Methana (Μέθανα). To get there you go over an isthmus, less than 300m across. The name, properly ἡ Μεθάνα, was corrupted as early as Pausanias to Τὰ Μέθανα.

The peninsula has terraced hills and its interior consists of the bare ridges of Mt Chelona (742m), an extinct volcano. Strabo gives an imaginative or derivative account of the seismic disturbance that gave birth to the mountain, which Pausanias places in the reign of Antigonus Gonatas. The peninsula, which was by confusion called *Methone* even in early texts of Thucydides (as Strabo mentions), was fortified by the Athenians as early as 425 BC in the Peloponnesian War. The fortifications, traces of which are visible, were strengthened during the Ptolemaic occupation (3rd century BC).

The little port of Methana has the usual attractions of a watering-place that has suffered rapid growth. The warm sulphur springs, used in the cure of rheumatic and allied afflictions, give the name Vromolimni ('stinking shore') to the village on the hillside above. Nisaki, a rocky islet connected by a causeway with the waterfront, is charmingly planted with pines and oleanders. Both here and on the Thrioni plateau above Vromolimni are traces of ancient walling.

A walk (40mins) leads via Steno on the isthmus to the west slope of the peninsula where, below the village of Megalochori, are (2.5hrs) the remains of the acropolis of ancient Methana. The view from Kaïmeni Chora ('burnt village'; *45mins farther; the volcano crater is another 30mins*) is delightful: across the Bay of Methana the majestic Mt Ortholithi (1114m) and Mt Arachnaion (887m) rise sheer from the water. Above the village is an ancient tower. The tiny chapel of the Panaghia Krasata, on the west point of the peninsula, was erected by a wine merchant saved from shipwreck; wine is said to have been used to mix the mortar, hence the dedication of the church, from the Greek *krasì*, wine.

PRACTICAL INFORMATION

A week would be no time at all to see the most important sites and enjoy Nafplion. At a minimum, visitors should hope to have a day for Mycenae and Tiryns; a day for Argos itself, with its twin citadels and nearby Lerna; a day for Epidaurus and Nafplion, with the chance to take in some of the area's 12th-century churches.

GETTING AROUND

• **By bus:** Argos and Nafplion are served by frequent buses from Athens via Corinth (where you often have to change). The journey usually takes about 3hrs. Buses for Athens and other destinations in the Argolid leave Nafplion from Kapodistriou 8, just off Plateia Aghiou Petrou. Buses south to Arcadia, Messenia and Laconia leave from the station on Pheidonos. There is a frequent local service between Nafplion and Argos (it is possible to request to be let off at Tiryns); to Kranidi and Galatas. **Epidaurus** is served by frequent buses from Nafplion; make sure that the bus is going to the Sanctuary and Theatre and not to the town of either Nea Epidavros or Palaia/Archaia Epidavros. There are also usually special buses from Athens on the nights of performances. **Mycenae** is served by several buses a day from Argos and Nafplion and Corinth–Argos buses usually stop at Fichtia; after that you need to take a taxi (4km) to the village of Mykines and the Lion Gate.

• **By rail:** Argos is served by train from Athens. Most trains stop at the Mycenae station (some 4km from the site) and at Corinth. The journey usually takes at least 4hrs. Nafplion is served by frequent daily trains from Athens, via Corinth and via Argos. The journey is long and recommended only if you enjoy train journeys. The train station is on the quay, on Bouboulinas.

• **By taxi:** At Argos there is an informal taxi stand on Plateia Aghiou Petrou. At Mycenae, taxis are usually available in Fichtia to go to the site. At Nafplion there are taxis by the bus station on Plateia Nikitara.

INFORMATION OFFICES

Argos At present, there is no tourist information office in Argos. The useful annotated map 'Argos', published by the municipality, is usually on sale at kiosks and the archaeological museum.

Nafplion The tourist office is on 25 Martiou diagonally opposite the bus station. It keeps unpredictable hours. The free handout *Nafplion Day and Night* is useful.

WHERE TO STAY

There is a growing number of 'traditional hotels' in the Argolid, though at present they are all in Nafplion. Elsewhere the choice is more or less confined to basic rooms or large, coastal holiday blocks. The locations may be lovely, but the hotels themselves are lacklustre.

Argos
It is much more pleasant to stay in Nafplion than in Argos. If you need or prefer to stay, two possible options are: **Hotel Mycenae**, Plateia Aghiou Petrou 10 (T: 27510 68754) and **Hotel Telesilla**, Danaou 2 and Plateia Aghiou Petrou (T: 27510 68317). Both are adequately comfortable business hotels.
Epidaurus
€€ **Xenia**. Although somewhat down-at-heel, with a unmemorable restaurant, this has the inestimable advantage of being on the site itself. On nights when there is a theatre performance, reservations are essential (it's a good idea to ask for printed confirmation; T: 27530 22005).
There are hotels in Ligourio and in Palaia Epidavros, about 8km from the site. Even a short drive can be harrowing when theatre performances finish and everyone takes to the road.
Mycenae
€€ **La Belle Helene**. This renovated eight-room hotel in the village of Mykines is where Schliemann and

guests such as Virginia Woolf have stayed. T: 27510 76225.
€€ **Petite Planete**. More modern than the above, and larger (30 rooms), with a usually quiet location (it is the last building in the village before the ancient site). It is a pleasant walk to the site at night, especially impressive at full moon. The hotel also has a swimming pool. T: 27510 76240.
Nafplion
Nafplion is a lovely little town, and you are not alone in noticing. It is always a good idea to book well in advance, especially at weekends, when many Athenians escape the capital, and certainly during summer and the Epidaurus Festival, when hotels tend to get booked up very fast.
€€€ **Ilion**. Boutique hotel in a restored town house on a stepped street above Plateia Syntagma. Good-sized rooms with wall frescoes of Greek mythology and garlands of fruit and flowers. Quiet neighbourhood location, and good breakfasts. 15 rooms, 10 of them suites. Efthimiopoulou and Kapodistriou, T: 27520 251, www.ilionhotel.gr
€€€ **Nafsimedon**. Attractive 19th-century building with large rooms painted in shades of salmon pink and furnished with period items. Overlooks Kolokotronis Park. 13 rooms. Sidiras Merarhias 9, T: 27520 25060, www.nafsimedon.gr
€€€ **Nafplia Palace** (formerly Xenia Palace) Supreme location, with the best view in town, of the harbour and Bourtzi. The rooms are large and comfortable, with balconies. The restaurant is less cheery. 51 rooms, 54 bungalows, T: 27520 28981, helios@helioshotels.gr
€€ **Allotino Pension**. Simple guest-

house above a café, right in the heart of town. Furnishings are well chosen and unfussy. Floors are bare wood, windows and ceilings high. 7 rooms. Vas Konstantinou 19, T: 27520 96150, www.allotino-pension.gr

€€ **Byron**. One of the first and still one of the nicest small, distinctive hotels, with a quiet location (up a steep street) overlooking Aghios Spyridon church, rooms (some on the small side) with bits of Victoriana, a pleasant breakfast terrace, and lots of devoted return customers. 17 rooms. Plateia Aghiou Spiridona, T: 27520 22351, www.byronhotel.gr

€€ **Hotel Leto**. A steep climb up to the hotel, fine views over town from many of the simply furnished, perfectly comfortable rooms. 15 rooms. Zigomala 28, T: 27520 28098.

€€ **Pension Acronafplia**. There are rooms in five restored buildings scattered through town; some are very charming, some are not, so it is a good idea to check your room for cross-ventilation, size and view before you check in. 30 rooms. Papanikolaou 34, Vas. Konstantinou 20, Aghios Spiridon 6, T: 27520 24481, penacrop@otenet.gr

€€–€€€ **King Otho**. At two locations. The Farmakopoulou Otho (12 rooms) has been here for decades, and is now delightfully renovated, with a beautiful hanging staircase and garden. The new Staikopoulou Otho (10 rooms) is more up-to-date—and more expensive, because all rooms have views over the town. Farmakapoulou 4, T: 27520 27585; and Staikopoulou 21, T: 27520 97790.

€€ **Omorfi Poli Pension**. Small pension has nicely restored rooms, several with sleeping lofts suitable for families. High ceilings, simple furnishings, tasteful atmosphere. Staff are helpful, and there is a nice café/restaurant on the ground floor. (7 rooms). Sofroni 5, T: 27520 21565. www.omorfopoli-pension.com

WHERE TO EAT

Argos

None of the small cafés and restaurants in Argos is worth seeking out, but the conveniently located Retro and Aigli, on Plateia Aghiou Petrou are perfectly fine. 'Swet Cookies', the small café directly across from the Archaeological Museum, has snacks and drinks.

Epidaurus

Leonidas. On the main Epidavros road, with a garden and good food. Popular with post-theatre-goers, sometimes including cast members as well as spectators. T: 27530 22115.

Myli

Myli has a string of *souvlakia* places (the best set down from the main road), a bakery with excellent *spanakopites* (spinach pies), and several fish tavernas where the main road turns toward the sea and the town of Nea Chios.

Mycenae

Restaurants in Mycenae tend to cater to large tour groups, with predictable culinary results; the restaurants of the Belle Helene and Petite Planete hotels, and the Mykinaiko Taverna (all on the main road) do better than most.

Nafplion

€€–€€€ **Savouras Psarotaverna**. This fish taverna has been drawing customers for decades for its succulent fresh fish (all priced by the kilo) and simply prepared vegetable side-dishes.

Often crowded in summer. Bouboulinas 79, T: 27520 27704.

€€ **Hellas**. Popular with tourists, but still draws locals too, with a good central location. Eat either inside or out, under shady trees and awnings. The menu offers standard taverna fare. Plateia Syntagma.

€€ **Karamanlis**, **Kanares** and **Hundalos** are three fish and grill tavernas on Bouboulinas, along the harbourfront. Popular with locals.

€€ **Palaio Archontiko**. Usually open for dinner and weekend lunch only in winter; but all day in summer. Tables are either inside or spill out into the narrow, largely pedestrianised street. Excellent traditional Greek cooking. Siokou 7.

€€ **Ta Fanaria**. Popular, bougainvillea-clad place serving all the usual taverna favourites, just steps from Plateia Syntagma. Staikopoulou 13.

OUZERIES, CAFÉS & ZACHAROPLASTEIA

Nafplion

Antica Gelateria di Roma. The best ices and sorbets in the Peloponnese, perhaps in Greece. Freshly-made sandwiches, good coffee, and a variety of pastries. Farmakopoulou and Komninou.

Episkinis. Tiny hole-in-the-wall place for an ouzo and some *mezedes*, especially on a chilly day. Amalias 19.

Stathmos. In the old Nafplion train station, with places to sit outside under the shade trees. Serves snacks.

MARKETS

The lively **Argos** market takes place Wed and Sat, off Tsokri and Pheidonos, just west of Plateia Aghiou Petrou. The street market in **Nafplion** is also Wed and Sat, beside Kolokotronis Park.

FESTIVALS & ENTERTAINMENT

Epidaurus Performances are given in the ancient theatre from June–Sept (*see p. 250*). The *Musical July* Festival takes place at the Little Theatre of Palaia Epidavros, 7km from the ancient site. Information from the Athens Concert Hall (Megaron Mousikis), Kokkali 1 and Vas. Sofias (T: 210 728 2000), the Greek National Tourism Organisation (T: 210 327 1300 or 210 331 0562). The Nafplion Dimarcheion usually has information about the *Musical July* festival.

Nafplion The *Musical June* festival (often held in at least partly in July) stages concerts at various venues. The *Fruits of the Land* festival in July is an agricultural show held both along the quay in Nafplion, Nea Epidavros and Ancient Epidaurus. On 20th November, Nafplion commemorates the capture of the Palamidi in 1822, with a procession up to the fortress.

BOOKS & BACKGROUND READING

Argos Marcel Pierart and Gilles Touchais's *Argos: Une ville grecque de 6000 ans* (Paris Mediterranée CNRS Editions, 1996) is a useful survey of the city and its monuments.

Nafplion Timothy Gregory's *Nauplion* (Lycabettus Press, 1980), remains a very useful guide to the history and monuments.

ARCADIA

Maps of Arcadia are on p. 156 and 296 (south and east Arcadia) and p. 340.

The largest of the *nomes* in the Peloponnese, Arcadia ('Αρκαδία) occupies the centre of the peninsula and shares borders with all six of the other provinces. To the east (*map p. 296*), the coast of Arcadia stretches to the Argolic Gulf and the portion of the Aegean known as the Myrtoön Sea. Arcadia is extremely mountainous; to the north, the Mainalon and Gortynian ranges divide Arcadia from Elis, Achaia, Corinthia and the Argolid. The Parnon range separates much of eastern from western Arcadia. Much of the mountains is covered by wild kern, oak, pines (many planted by reforestation projects, often after the fires that plague Arcadia almost every summer).

Arcadia is blessed with rivers, (including the Alpheios, Ladonas and Lousios) and numerous springs, which nourish chestnut and plane trees. As in Antiquity, the district is known for its flocks of goats and sheep and the remoteness of many of its mountain villages. There are broad, fertile plains in central Arcadia around Tripolis, Megalopolis and Tegea, and smaller plains to the east on the coast between Astros and Leonidion. There are also upland plains where wheat is still harvested by scythe and threshed by mule-drawn sledges on stone threshing floors. Olives and citrus trees flourish throughout Arcadia, wheat is raised on the plains, and the southern Arcadian village of Leonidion is famous throughout Greece for the sweetness of its slender aubergines. Throughout, hills and mountains are terraced with olive trees. Uncultivated land is often covered by the dense maquis that makes rambling a surprisingly difficult activity, although a network of goat tracks, footpaths, and old stone foot and animal roads, connects many pasturages, monasteries and villages.

In Antiquity, Arcadians boasted that, unlike the rest of the Greeks, they had lived here forever, and were, in fact, autochthonous, having sprung from the earth itself. Other Greeks sometimes sneered at the Arcadians as being rough bumpkins and called them 'acorn eaters'—a slur, since pigs are fed on acorns. Arcadia stood with the rest of Greece against the Persians, alternately supported Athens and Sparta during the Peloponnesian War, and formed the Arcadian Federation, centred at the new city of Megalopolis, to withstand Thebes during the 4th century. Along with the rest of Greece, Arcadia was dominated in turn by the Macedonians and the Romans, the Byzantines, Franks and Turks. Large numbers of Slavs settled here and inter-married with the native population during the Middle Ages—a subject best not broached locally, although some villages retain names that suggest the earlier foreign presence.

A centre of resistance during the War of Independence, Arcadia suffered from extensive emigration during the 19th and 20th centuries: there are large communities of Arcadian immigrants in Athens, as well as in Chicago, Toronto and Melbourne. In recent years, increased prosperity has diminished emigration, and in many villages the descendants of those who left to work abroad are returning to ancestral homes for their own retirement years. In addition, Arcadia has recently had a new wave of immigrants (some legal, much not) from Albania, and from parts of the former Soviet Union. Often these new immigrants are day labourers on farms, in construction, and at restaurants.

Increasingly, Arcadia is turning to tourism as a way of supplementing traditional means of livelihood. Mountain villages of north Arcadia (notably Dimitsana and Stemnitsa), only a few years ago virtual ghost towns, now attract increasing numbers of Greek and foreign visitors with their famous monasteries, such as Philosophou and Prodromou; beauty spots, such as the Lousios Gorge; and museums, such as the Open-Air Water Power Museum at Dimitsana and the Folklore Museum at Stemnitsa. The coastal villages of eastern Arcadia, running south from Astros to Leonidion, many with decent sand and pebble beaches, attract summer holidaymakers.

Visitors could easily spend a week in Arcadia, dividing their time between the mountain villages of the north, the coastal villages of the east, and taking in some of the ancient sites around Tripolis (Alea, Tegea, Mantineia, Pallantion), as well as Orchomenos further north, and Megalopolis. Bassae and Phigaleia, although technically over the border in Elis, are also included in this chapter.

TRIPOLIS

NB: Tripolis and the sites of Mantineia, Tegea, Pallantion and Orchomenos are covered on the map on p. 156.

Tripolis (Τρίπολη, pop. 26,000) is the capital—and indeed the only large town—of the *nome* of Arcadia; its central location in the Peloponnese makes it something of a crossroads, with excellent road links. Almost all travellers to the Peloponnese will pass by, or through, Tripolis. Roads radiating out from the town lead to all the major cities of the Peloponnese; to Olympia; the villages and monasteries of northern Arcadia; and virtually every destination in Arcadia and the neighbouring districts.

Tripolis lies at the south foot of Mt Apano Krepa (1559m), a peak of the Mainalon range which dominates the Plain of Tripolis, a monotonous plateau enclosed by an amphitheatre of barren mountains. The site is most attractive in winter, when the mountains are topped with snow. The plain consists of two adjoining level tracts, the Plain of Tegea in the south and the Plain of Mantineia in the north. About 30km long from north to south, and with a maximum width of 16km, it averages 655m above sea-level and suffers extremes of temperature with violent hail and thunderstorms in summer. Vines, wheat and barley are grown, but, apart from the mulberry, the plateau is now almost treeless. There are several marshes, but few rivers or streams; such as exist mostly disappear into the swallow-holes (*katavothrai*) which are common in Arcadia. The plain was famous in Antiquity for the three Arcadian cities of Mantineia, Tegea and Pallantion (*see p. 266 below*).

HISTORY OF TRIPOLIS

In Greece, Tripolis constitutes a young town, although the surrounding countryside was long inhabited: in 1990 six Early Helladic metallurgical kilns—the earliest known in all Greece—were discovered just east of Tripolis in the hamlet of Steno. Tripolis was founded, under the name of *Droboglitza* or *Hydropolitza* about the 14th century to take the place of Mantineia, Tegea and Pallantion, the three derelict ancient cities of the plain, and the eparchy to which it belongs still keeps the name of Mantineia. Later it was called Tripolitza (in Turkish *Tarabolussa*) and became in 1770 the fortified capital of the Pasha of the Morea. This, during the War of Independence, led to its destruction. On 23rd September 1821, Kolokotronis captured the town and massacred the Turkish population. In June of 1825, Ibrahim Pasha recaptured Tripolis, which again fell to the Greek forces in 1828. As the Greeks entered Tripolis, Ibrahim Pasha and his troops withdrew, torching the town, which burned for a week and was almost completely destroyed. The town slowly revived after 1834.

Tripolis today is a modern manufacturing town, as one is all too aware on the approaches to the city. Two buildings are known to have survived the torching of 1828: the present Municipal Library at no. 41 Odos Georgiou I, and the Turkish *medresse* at no. 6 Aghiou Dimitriou. Revival and rebuilding was haphazard, however, and the present confusing town layout testifies to the lack of any guiding principle except growth. The occasional late 19th- and early 20th-century Neoclassical building survives (including the Archaeological Museum, Municipal Theatre and Town Hall), but most of Tripolis consists of resolutely anonymous, flat-roofed, two-to-five-storey, mid-to-late-20th-century concrete structures. The best features for the traveller, in addition to the Archaeological Museum, are the three successive main plateias: Kolokotroni, Vasileos Georgiou (also known as Aghiou Vasileou, from its church), and Anechartisias (also known as Makariou). These three squares, along with Plateia Aghiou Petrou and the expansive Plateia Areos park, lend some spaciousness and greenery to this energetic, but somewhat charmless, city. Some of the shops and cafés in the sidestreets (especially in and around Odos Taxiarchon) have kept their traditional style. There are a theatre and cultural centre in Odos Ethnikis Antistaseos, the latter opposite Plateia Areos, with its pleasant cafés and restaurants.

The Archaeological Museum

Odos Evangelistrias 2, off Plateia Kolokotroni. Open 8.30–3 daily except Mon. Some items are unlabelled. T: 2710 242148.

The museum (which opened in 1986) occupies the former Panarcadian Hospital, designed by the architect Ernst Ziller. The collection of finds from throughout Arcadia includes some 7,000 items, many of fine quality. Unfortunately, visitors are few; the custodians trail behind what few visitors there are, turning the lights on and off in each room. If time is limited, try to begin in the basement, where the splendid finds from the Villa of Herodes Atticus at Eva (*see p. 289*), are on view. Highlights are given below.

Ground Floor: Inscriptions, pottery, worked obsidian, bronze weapons, Mycenaean pottery and several small Neolithic clay idols; bronze weapons and gold jewellery from the Mycenaean chamber tomb cemetery at Palaiokastro Gortynias (*see p. 279*); Classical sculpture, including the 6th-century BC figure of a seated goddess (? Athena); finds, including terracotta vessels and figures and small bronzes, from the sanctuaries of Arcadia, including Tegea, Lykosoura (*see p. 276*), Mantineia; bronze finds, including an unusual Late Hellenistic helmet found at Megalopolis (the only other known to exist in the same style is in the British Museum, London).

Basement: Extensive statuary, pottery, bronze finds from Tegea and Mantineia; important Mycenaean pottery and a bronze sword blade from the Mycenaean cemetery at Palaiokastro Gortynias; sculpture found at the villa of Herodes Atticus at Eva, near the Monastery of Loukou, including a

Mycenaean stirrup jar from Palaiokastro Gortynias, with typical octopus design (12th century BC).

round marble plaque showing Heracles and a young woman (? goddess), a head of Marcus Aurelius, and a head of a beautiful youth, Polydeuces, identified as in the circle of Herodes Atticus.

Garden: Sculptures, mainly Hellenistic, and Roman funerary reliefs.

TEGEA, MANTINEIA, PALLANTION & ORCHOMENOS

NB: All four sites are covered on the map on p. 156.

In Antiquity, Tegea, Mantineia, Pallantion and Orchomenos dominated the plain of Tripolis. The sites can be visited in a very long day, which involves a good deal of doubling back, as they are on different sides of Tripolis. Tegea and Mantineia were the most important cities and constant rivals for land and water rights. From Tripolis, Tegea is 8km to the southeast, Pallantion 19km to the southwest. Mantineia is 12.5km to the northeast and Orchomenos 30km to the north. Pallantion is the least rewarding.

TEGEA

Tegea is best reached by leaving Tripolis on the Sparta road. (Keep an eye out for the combination Jet Oil Garage and Antiques Shop after 4km on the left. There are large ceramic pots in front of the garage/shop, where you will find everything from old dowry chests and olive presses to Victorian lamps and horseshoes.) At 5km take the left turn signposted Astros and/or Leonidion. Alea, Tegea and Episkopi are (poorly) signposted after about 6km. NB: The Folklore Museum of Tegea at Palaia Episkopi, where there is a year-round café/restaurant, is only open weekends 10–4 in July and August.

HISTORY OF TEGEA

In mythology, Tegea (Τεγέα) is best known as the birthplace of Atalanta, the fleetest runner of the age and the heroine of the Calydonian boar-hunt (*see p. 491*). One of the oldest and most important cities in Arcadia, Tegea was the largest city in the plain (an amalgamation of some six local villages) and its known remains are scattered between the modern villages of Alea, Akra, Episkopi and Stadio. Tegea and Mantineia were long enemies, contending for possession of the plain and water rights. Tegea also waged a long war with Sparta until beaten into submission c. 560 BC as a vassal state. The Tegeans sent 500 men to Thermopylae and 1,500 to Plataea, and after the Persian Wars tried unsuccessfully to throw off the yoke of Sparta with Argive aid. In the Peloponnesian War the Tegeans sided with Sparta. In 370 BC, after the Battle of Leuctra, Tegea joined the Arcadian League, and at the Second Battle of Mantineia (362 BC) fought on the side of Thebes against Sparta. In 222 BC Tegea became an unwilling member of the Achaean League. Still a flourishing city in the time of Strabo and in the time of Pausanias, Tegea was destroyed by Alaric in the 5th century AD. The city was refounded by the Byzantines, and under the name of *Nikli* it became one of the most important centres in the Morea. In 1209 Geoffrey de Villehardouin established a barony here.

The site was excavated by the French School in 1889–90, 1902 and 1910, and by the Greek Archaeological Service in 1965 and during the 1990s. Since 1998, the Norwegian Arcadia Survey has studied the landscape of the area in an attempt to document changes in the countryside through the centuries, to comprehend more fully Tegea's role in the area in Antiquity, and to locate its ancient acropolis.

The museum and Temple of Athena

In the village of Alea there is a well-arranged little museum (*open 8.30–3; closed Mon; some objects now moved to the Archaeological Museum in Tripolis*). There are finds from the temple, from ancient Tegea, from Byzantine Nikli, and the surrounding area. The temple sculpture from the workshop of Skopas is particularly noteworthy.

The Temple of Athena Alea is a few minutes' walk from the museum. The guard can point the way. The temple, excavated in 1889 and 1902, was freshly investigated by the Norwegian Institute and the Greek Archaeological Service in the 1990s. Pausanias says the temple was built by Aleos, legendary founder of Tegea. Votive offerings found in the temple have led some scholars to suggest that the epithet 'Alea' may recall an earlier goddess of fertility worshipped here. Of the 4th-century temple, the excellently preserved remains, with pronaos, cella and opisthodomos clearly demarcated, are flanked by scattered fragments of their fallen columns. Excavations have identified traces of the Archaic temple (late 7th century) and traces of two yet earlier structures. Of these, one is almost entirely lost, while six identifiable layers have been documented of the second structure. This earlier cult building has yielded remains (including suggestions of a wood with wattle and daub structure) from the Mycenaean period to the early 7th century BC. Mycenaean votives found here (in addition to numerous Late Geometric and Archaic votives) also suggest prehistoric cult activity. There is evidence for metallurgical activity in the sanctuary.

The scant remains make it difficult to realise that this was one of the most famous sanctuaries in Greece; here two kings of Sparta, Leotychides and Pausanias, took refuge, as well as Chryseis, the careless priestess of the Argive Heraion (*see p. 226*). After the Archaic temple was burnt down in 395 BC, the rebuilding was entrusted to the architect and sculptor Skopas of Paros. This was the temple that Pausanias ranked first in the Peloponnese in size and construction. The new temple had a Doric peristyle of 6 columns by 14, and an internal colonnade of Corinthian half-columns, with Ionic above. There was an open court to the north, and to the northeast a fountain (foundations remain), probably dedicated to Heracles and Auge, the nymph who bore him Telephus, here at Tegea. The temple pediments were decorated with sculpture (? by Skopas), fragments of which survive in the local museum and in the National Museum at Athens. The east pediment represented the *Hunt of the Calydonian Boar*, with figures of Meleager, Theseus, Atalanta and Ancaeus; Pausanias mentions that the hide of the Calydonian Boar (shrivelled, with not one remaining bristle) was preserved in the temple. The west pediment depicted the fight of Telephos and Achilles on the banks of the Kaikos in Mysia. As yet, the ancient stadium mentioned by Pausanias has not been discovered, although a starting block was unearthed in the 1993–94 excavation season.

The marble for the Tegea temple sculptures came from Doliana, c. 10km southeast as the crow flies. The quarries are accessible from Mavriki, 13km by road from Tegea. The very scanty remains of the 6th-century Temple of Artemis Knakeatis, also thought to have been built using marble from the Doliana quarry, are on a shelf just below the summit of Psili Korfi (1520m). The temple is thought to be one of the earliest marble temples in Greece.

Palaia Episkopi and Byzantine Nikli

A ten-minute drive from Alea, there are remains from ancient Tegea and Byzantine Nikli at Palaia Episkopi, whose name ('old church') recalls the Byzantine basilica once here. Palaia Episkopi is a green and pleasant place, with a park with avenues of shade trees, benches, and monuments laid out in the 19th century by local benefactors in the League of Tegeans. There is a shaded café restaurant.

The Folklore Museum of Tegea (*open weekends in July and August 10–4; T: 27105 56021*) is housed in the former Tegean School of Domestic Science, a substantial stone building, where local girls were taught to read and write while studying domestic arts in the 19th and 20th centuries. In spring, the surrounding plain sometimes floods and the marshes here are a haven for migrating waterfowl.

A huge church of 1888 rests on the foundations of the (? 10th-century), Byzantine church (fragments of the earlier church and of antiquities are rebuilt into the walls, and Byzantine mosaic icons are venerated). Both the church of 1888 and the Byzantine structure partly overlie the ancient theatre, rebuilt in marble by Antiochus IV Epiphanes (175–164 BC). The retaining wall of the cavea has been cleared: the stage building was to the west. Opposite the west door of the church an avenue leads through the great park. At the far side are remains of an Early Christian basilica (? 6th century) whose mosaics (*enclosed but visible, best seen by obtaining key from the Alea museum*) of the 12 months of the year are the most substantial surviving feature. Excavations in the 1990s confirmed that this church and its outbuildings overlay much of the ancient agora. Off the same avenue but nearer the church the medieval wall carries an inscription and busts commemorating a meeting of the International Olympic Commission here in 1934. Behind the wall, and north of the church, a recently excavated area is hard to interpret unaided. Medieval houses were found in the upper levels. Below (the curve of its central and northern apses visible, close to remains of the theatre at the east side of the site) was a large Early Christian basilica. The narthex contained mosaics (covered). The basilica was probably destroyed in the Slav incursions of the 7th century AD. Beyond this building (towards the medieval wall) were later built a small Byzantine church and a bath building. At the south side of the area part of the stylobate of the south stoa of the ancient agora (3rd century BC or later) can be made out.

A long avenue leads directly to the main Tripolis–Sparta road at Kerasitsa, where the bus stops.

Wine-lovers may also wish to visit the Tselepos Winery outside Tegea in Rizes (*14km, Tripolis–Kastri road; T: 27105 44440; www.tselepos.gr*). The winery produces some 250,000 bottles a year, and the white Mantineia, red Nemea, and Cabernet-Merlot blend are especially admired.

MANTINEIA

Mantineia (Μαντίνεια) is best reached by heading out of Tripolis on the Pyrgos–Olympia road (also accessible off the ring road). To the left is the long range of Mainalon with the village of Merkovouni on the hillside. The cornfields give place to vineyards producing a celebrated non-resinated red wine. You approach the narrow gap (1.5km wide) between the projecting spurs of Mainalon and Mt Ktenias that marked the ancient frontier between Tegea and Mantineia. Six kilometres out of Tripolis, left of the road, are the ruins of a square watchtower of polygonal masonry, doubtfully identified as the *skopi* ('look-out') from which the dying Epaminondas of Thebes (*see p. 419*) watched the Second Battle of Mantineia. This district, once covered by an oakwood, was called *Pelagos* ('the sea'), thus satisfying the oracle's prediction that Epaminondas should beware of the sea. The plain lies on a major route in Antiquity from Corinthia and the Argolid into Arcadia, and was the scene of several great battles. Today, the marella cherries used in the manufacture of *vissinada*, a popular soft drink, are grown here. The road passes over a low bridge and through Mantineia's southern fortifications. Half a kilometre further, to the left, is an exceptionally eccentric church (1972), a Minoan-Classical-Byzantine folly dedicated to Aghia Photini, with other curious monuments in its grounds. Opposite, approached by a fenced avenue, are the most substantial remains of ancient Mantineia.

The site

NB: The site of Mantineia is marshy and stout shoes or boots are often useful.
There are extensive remains of the circuit of the city walls, which ran for about 4km, with 120 watchtowers, of which a number remain, along with parts of ten of the city gates. Although no longer standing to any height, Mantineia's walls are among the best examples of Greek period fortification. They are contemporary with the walls of Messene (c. 370 BC), and may have been built by the same Theban architects. The walls, encircled by the diverted but now characteristically dry Ophis, are built of large square or polygonal blocks; up to four courses are still standing. The curtain wall was 4m thick.

Within the circuit of the walls, the remains are primarily from the 4th century BC and the 2nd century AD, when Mantineia had an infusion of wealth under Hadrian. Recently, the layout of the site has been plotted with use of ground-penetrating radar. Most of the visible remains are Roman (note concrete construction), but parts of earlier structures are visible. The path comes first to a small theatre (? 4th century BC). Immediately east of the *skene* the foundations of two Roman temples lie between the remains of narrow paved roads. There are three further temples here, one to the north and two to the south. Ancient sources mention temples of Hera, of Zeus Soteros and of a bouleuterion. Two small 'wings' project from it into the agora: between them were statue bases. The building was later divided longitudinally, with a colonnade in the south façade. The east end became a temple for emperor worship. The agora stretches further to the east, crossed by narrow paved roads and bounded by stoas on the north and east. To your left is the stylobate of the north stoa, with some column settings. Walls of an earlier phase of the agora can be made out beneath semicircular Roman foundations (perhaps of an Exedra of Epigone, who is known from inscriptions to have paid for refurbishment of the agora at the time of Augustus). The foundations of the east stoa of the agora and its associated buildings are in the further enclosure. Additional stoas and other buildings were constructed to the southeast, probably in the 2nd century AD.

The remains of several early Christian churches have been found and an inscription testifying to the presence of a synagogue. Tombs (late Classical to Roman) belonging to the site have been excavated at Milia nearby.

HISTORY OF MANTINEIA

Mantineia (629m), one of the most important Arcadian city-states, was the inveterate rival of Tegea, and its whole history is coloured by this mutual antagonism, based probably on disputes over land and water-supply. Like Tegea, Mantineia was made up of a union of nearby villages (probably 6th century). The acropolis, occupied from prehistoric times, was 1km north on the hill of Gortsouli (*see below*), known to the ancients as *Ptolis*. On top of the hill was an Archaic shrine. In the Peloponnesian War the Mantineans were generally allies of Athens, the Tegeans being on the side of Sparta. After the Peace of Nikias in 421 BC Mantineia joined Athens, Argos and Elis in the quadruple alliance against Sparta, in the First Battle of Mantineia (418 BC); described by Thucydides.

After the Kings' Peace of 387 BC, Sparta moved to eradicate Mantineia. In 385 BC King Agesipolis, at the head of the Lacedaemonian army, besieged and took Mantineia after undermining the mud-brick fortification walls with the help of the dammed-up waters of the Ophis. He razed most of the city to the ground and dispersed the population. Some returned to the countryside whence they had come to found Mantineia in the 6th century. After the Battle of Leuctra in 371, the Mantineans, with the help of Thebes, returned to their city, and built the extensive fortifications whose ruins we see today. They rearranged the course of the Ophis so that it became a protection instead of a danger. The foundation in 370 BC of the Arcadian League was due to the efforts of Lycomedes, a native of Mantineia, but six years later the Mantineans themselves seceded from it and joined the Spartans.

At the Second Battle of Mantineia (362 BC) Tegea, the ancient ally of Sparta, fought on the side of Thebes, while Mantineia shared in the defeat of her former enemy, Sparta. Epaminondas of Thebes was mortally wounded in the moment of triumph and the battle marked the end of the fourth and last Theban invasion of the Peloponnese. Joining the Achaean League the following century, the Mantineans fought against Agis IV and helped to defeat Cleomenes III at Sellasia. Revolting against Macedonian dominance of the Achaean League, the city was captured in 222 BC by Antigonus Doson, who changed its name to Antigoneia, a name it kept until Hadrian's time. In 208 BC occurred another 'Battle of Mantineia', in which the Achaeans under Philopoemen defeated the Lacedaemonians, Philopoemen killing the tyrant Machanidas with his own hand (*Polybius, 11.11*).

Continuing along the road from the site entrance, the road again cuts the line of fortifications, visible to the right (track) opposite the first house (left). Half a kilometre further a narrow road (right) climbs in 1.5km to the 'Panaghia Gortsouli'. From the summit there is an excellent view of the site and fortifications (binoculars useful).

PALLANTION

For Pallantion, leave Tripolis on the road for Megalopolis; the modern village of Pallantio (Παλλάντιο) is signposted after 12km. Ask for directions to the site of *Pallantion*, which lies several kilometres out of town, on the cypress-covered slopes in front of Mt Kravari, the ancient *Boreion* (1143m). Pallantion is firmly in the category of ancient site often described as 'probably of interest only to the professional archaeologist'. There are traces of the city wall and the scant remains of three temples (Archaic and later); the chapel of Aghios Ioannis is built on the foundations of one of the three.

As not infrequently, the legends surrounding Pallantion overshadow the site itself. According to legend, 60 years before the Trojan War, King Evander, the son of Hermes by an Arcadian nymph, founded from Pallantion a colony by the river Tiber. The name of the Palatine Hill reflects his native town, and Pallantion was accordingly regarded as the mother-city of Rome itself—although not by Pausanias, who is quite dismissive of the story. When Megalopolis was founded, Pallantion dwindled to a village, but Antoninus Pius, in memory of Evander, restored its civic status and privileges. It was explored by the Italian School in 1940. Just southeast of the ruins are the remains of an embankment, of rammed earth encased with stone, that served both as a dyke against the waters of the Taka Marsh and as a frontier barrier against Tegea.

About 1.5km to the southwest of Pallantion (also accessible from the Kalogerikos pass, via the railway line) a chapel of the Metamorfosis overlies a temple which may be that of Athena and Poseidon mentioned by Pausanias. The site was quarried in the 19th century by the inhabitants of Valtetsi, where, in 1821, Khurshid Pasha's Turks, marching to the relief of Tripolis, were defeated by Kolokotronis.

ORCHOMENOS

Orchomenos (Ορχομενός), about 8km north of Levidi, is not much visited, but well worth the trip, because it gives an excellent sense of an ancient precursor of the villages that today dot the Arcadian hills, and in part also because the panorama from its acropolis (remains of Frankish and Venetian watch-towers) is splendid.

As you turn onto the road that runs steeply uphill to the site, a sign notes the few walls of a 'Prehistoric Water Works' in a gully, partly filled with garbage. The road then proceeds up through the modern village, climbs the mountainside (presently unpaved) and finally becomes a footpath leading to the main site. The site is largely unfenced, although the theatre is fenced off (*fence usually unlocked*). Classical *Orchomenos* was in ruins when Pausanias visited; today, the scanty remains are scattered and overgrown; keep an eye out for site signs on tall poles ('Agora', 'Temple', etc).

Arcadian Orchomenos occupied a strategic position on the midland route between the north and south Peloponnese; today, the situation of the site with wide views over the plain is more impressive than its remains. Homer called Orchomenos 'rich in sheep'. Herodotus tells us that 120 Orchomenian soldiers fought at Thermopylae and 600 at Plataea. Just before the First Battle of Mantineia (418 BC) the Athenians and Argives besieged and took the city. The remains excavated in 1913 by the French School include the foundations of the temple of Artemis Mesopolitis, two stoas, cisterns and a small 4th–3rd-century BC theatre, with ten rows of its seats partly intact. The two throne-like marble chairs were for dignitaries; an inscription on the front row honours a local citizen, Dionysos. The foundations of two stoas, one 70m and the other 40m long, lie above and south of the theatre. Inscriptions found here suggest the presence of the bouleuterion. Further down the slope are the temple foundations. In the 1990s, excavations were resumed which indicated that the stone heaps mentioned by Pausanias may indeed have been funerary monuments.

From the theatre, it is possible to climb to the top of the acropolis (936m), which stands on an almost isolated hill dividing the plain into two halves. On the east a narrow defile connecting the two parts of the plain is guarded on either side by ruined Frankish and Venetian watch-towers. The view is extensive. To the southwest across the plain towers Mainalon, while farther southeast you see into the Plain of Mantineia. To the north loom the high peaks round Mt Pheneos.

Near Orchomenos is the church of Aghios Nikolaos sta Kambia, with a frescoed crypt of Aghia Varvara beneath. Together they reproduce on a small scale the architecture of Hosios Loukas (*see p. 436*), of which this monastery was a dependency. The crypt is of the inscribed-domed cross plan with ten groin-vaulted bays with barrel-vaulted extensions east and west. The frescoes in the crypt are assigned to the 12th century.

Levidi has close ties (it was his parents' natal village) with Alexandros Papanastasiou (1879–1936), republican statesman and prime minister in 1924, and often called the 'father of parliamentary democracy' in Greece. Papanastasiou is remembered in a small museum in the Town Hall and by the former Agricultural School (2km out of Levidi on the Orchomenos road), which he founded in 1930; it was for a time a wood-carving school. Examples of wood-carving, a strong tradition in this part of Arcadia, are usually on sale in the central plateia. A chapel of the Panaghia on a low hill to the east of the school is supposed to mark the site of the sanctuary of Artemis-Hymnia, common to the peoples of Mantineia and Orchomenos. Beyond, the road commands a wide view back across the plain of Orchomenos, magnificently backed by the Chelmos range.

MEGALOPOLIS & ENVIRONS

Megalopolis and western Arcadia are covered on the map on p. 340.

There is little to detain the traveller en route from Tripolis to Megalopolis. Some 17km south of Tripolis, just off the main road, the railway station of the village of Asea is near the springs that form the source of the Alpheios. An isolated hill 150m northeast of the station and to the right of the road inland to Epano Asea is the **acropolis of** ancient *Asea*, shown by Swedish excavations in 1936–38 to have had a continuous existence from Neolithic to Middle Helladic times and to have been reoccupied in the Hellenistic period. During the 1990s, the Swedish Institute Asea Valley Survey examined 10km square around the site and established that Asea had occupied a much larger area than previously thought. The area, occupied from the Neolithic period to the present day, seems to have been most prosperous in the 4th–2nd centuries BC and again in the 13th century AD. Some ancient and medieval remains can be seen. Beyond (3km) Epano Asea, on the slopes of Mt Aghios Ilias (and close to the church of the same name) are remains of a temple which is another candidate for that of Athena and Poseidon (*see p. 272 above*).

HISTORY OF MEGALOPOLIS

After the decisive defeat of Sparta at the Battle of Leuctra in 371 BC (*see p. 433*), the Arcadians banded together to found the Pan-Arcadian League. Mutual jealousies precluded the choice of any existing city as capital. Epaminondas of Thebes chose to construct Megalopolis as the capital. The position was determined in accordance with Epaminondas' concept of a strategic barrier to contain the Spartans, the other bastions of which were to be Messene, Mantineia and Argos. The 'Great City' ('η Μεγάλη Πόλις) as it was called by the Greeks (Megalopolis being a Roman corruption), was built in 371–368 BC, and populated by wholesale transplantation from 40 local villages and smaller migrations from Tegea, Mantineia, etc. The League had a Federal Council of 50 members and an Assembly called the Ten Thousand; the executive power was held by a *Strategos* who had an army of 500 *eparitoi* at his command. The confederation soon broke up; Mantineia withdrew in 364 after the League had tampered with the sacred treasuries at Olympia; and in 362 half the Arcadians fought with the Spartans against Thebes. The inhabitants of Megalopolis had to be prevented from returning to their former homes by Pammenes' Theban soldiers. Spartan attempts to reduce the city were foiled in 353 with Theban aid and again in 331 when Megalopolis sided with Macedon. Having joined the Achaean League in 234, the city again suffered Spartan attack; saved once by a hurricane, it was sacked in 223 BC by Cleomenes III. Two thirds of the population escaped to Messenia under the leadership of Philopoemen (253–183 BC), one of perhaps only two famous sons of Megalopolis, the other being the historian Polybius (204–122 BC)—who, as it happens, was present at Philopoemen's funeral. Although many settlers returned to Megalopolis after Cleomenes' defeat at Sellasia in 220, the city was in decline. Strabo quotes an unknown comic poet to the effect that 'the Great City was a great desert', and Pausanias found it 'mostly in ruins'. In the Christian era, there was a settlement here, and later the seat of a bishop. It finally disappeared in the Slav invasion, but was again a provincial centre by the 18th century.

The modern town

The Plain of Megalopolis, or great west plain of Arcadia, in which Megalopolis (Μεγαλόπολις) stands, is about 30km long from north to south and 16km wide. With an average altitude of 427m, it has a much more temperate climate than the Plain of Tripolis. It is pleasantly wooded and well watered by the Alpheios, while the outlines of the encircling mountains make a fine background. The modern town is small, but confusing to navigate. Megalopolis tempts few visitors to linger after seeing its 4th-century theatre and ancient site.

The site

To reach the site, take the road signposted for Andritsaina from Megalopolis' main plateia. The widespread ruins of the 'Great City' are about 1km out of town (left turn just before the bridge over the river). The view and atmosphere are marred by the large power station which dominates the area, and whose cones and fumes can be seen for miles around.

The city straddles the Hellison (Ellison), one of the seven tributaries of the Alpheios. The federal capital (with the theatre) *Oresteia* occupied the nearer bank while the

The theatre at Megalopolis, the largest in ancient Greece.

municipal city lay across the river to the north. Ploughing has seriously damaged much of the site. Megalopolis was excavated by the British School in 1890–93, and the School has undertaken a survey project in the area in recent years.

The **theatre**, which is built up against the north side of a hillock, 100m from the river, was the largest in Greece. It dates, in its original form, from the 4th century BC, but is later than the Thersileion (or Assembly House; named after its donor), which lies immediately behind the stage. The cavea is divided by ten stairways and two *diazomata*, to make 59 rows of seats for c. 20,000 spectators. The lowest tiers are well preserved; of the upper tiers only the outline in the grassy hillside remains. The orchestra is 30m in diameter. To the west was a large *skenotheke*, or property room (leading off stage right). The stone stage, adorned by 14 marble columns between *antae*, is a Roman addition. The portico of the Thersileion, immediately behind, seems to have served also as a permanent *skene* for the theatre. In 2000, the Greek Archaeological Service resumed examining the theatre with an eye to further restoration work. Initial work suggested that the theatre was one of the first public monuments built here after Megalopolis was founded in the 270s and one of the first theatres in Greece to have a circular plan for the cavea and orchestra.

The **Thersileion** is perhaps the most elaborate example known of the square hall. Measuring 52.5m by 66.5m, it had five concentric rows of columns, set parallel to the outside walls and arranged on radials from a tribune offset from centre. The bases of the columns remaining *in situ* show that the wooden floor sloped down towards the tribune, above which the roof line was probably broken by a lantern. Facing the theatre and originally separated from the hall only by piers (later by a continuous wall with doorways), was a Doric prostyle portico with 14 columns beneath a single pediment. The building, which was built to accommodate the Assembly of the Ten Thousand (*see p. 274 above*), was destroyed in 222 BC and not rebuilt.

On the other side of the river the Sanctuary of Zeus Soter and the Stoa of Philip, demarcating the agora, are now barely identifiable. Sections of the town wall have been found.

Lykosoura and Lykaion

Both Lykosoura and Lykaion are seldom visited, remote, and very rewarding. From Megalopolis the road to Kalamata (60 km) runs southwest, crossing the Alpheios. Just beyond the bridge to the right is the by-road to **Lykosoura** (Λυκόσουρα), via the hamlet of Apiditsa), where you again branch right, and at 11km turn left and steeply uphill to the site (*small sign*). The Sanctuary of Despoina and of Demeter here was one of the most important religious sanctuaries in Arcadia. Pausanias remarks that Lykosoura was the oldest settlement not just in Arcadia, but in the world, and that it was from its example than men learned to build cities. Disappointingly, finds go back only to the 5th century BC.

The museum (*usually open 8.30–3 daily except Mon*) contains inscriptions and many of the colossal cult statues (and casts of heads, which are in Athens) mentioned by Pausanias, the work of the 2nd-century BC sculptor Damophon. Beyond the museum, there are considerable remains of a prostyle temple (? 3rd century BC) with a side door on the south of the cella (cf. Bassae). In front is a stoa, some remains of a megaron, where sacrifices may have taken place and, in the hillside (south), a stepped retaining wall. The site, planted with flowering fruit trees, is particularly evocative in the spring—until one recalls Pausanias' remark that sacrificers did not slit the throats of their victims, but rather chopped off their limbs. Across the road, usually well-hidden in underbrush, are the remains of a fountain house and cistern (*this part of the site is fenced, but often unlocked*).

From Lykosoura a good road leads to **Lykaion** (Λύκαιο; 4km), where it continues unsurfaced to Ano Karyes (7.5km). Turn left just before the village (dangerous in wet weather) and ascend past the stadium, hippodrome and stoas (11km) to the summit of Mt Lykaion (1407m; fine views), in Antiquity the centre of a primitive cult of Zeus involving rainmaking, human sacrifice, werewolves, and athletic games. Within its precinct neither man nor beast cast a shadow. The entire summit and much of the slopes are bare, wind-whipped, and often covered in snow until late into the spring, when sheep pasture here. A number of handsome stone threshing floors are reminders of when the slopes were cultivated.

The summit is a conical mound, the great sacrificial pyre which, with the precinct below, was excavated in 1903. Below are column bases seen by Pausanias which originally supported golden eagles. Six of the starting-line blocks for the stadium were found in the 1990s. On the south side of Mt Lykaion (at 1195m) is a sanctuary of Pan. There are also several modern structures for the Pan-Arcadian games that take place here in summer.

South into Laconia

The road from Megalopolis to Sparta is slow but spectacular, high along the north shoulder of Taygetos. The modern village of **Leondari** (Λεοντάρι) occupies a commanding position on the top of the hill (578m) forming the north end of the Taygetos range and overlooks a narrow pass separating Arcadia from Messenia. It preserves the remains of the Byzantine village founded here in the 13th or 14th century. The Frankish castle is in ruins. Here Thomas Palaeologus was defeated by the Turks in 1460; the inhabitants fled to Gardiki only to be massacred there. The little two-domed church of the Apostoloi (14th century) was converted into a mosque; the minaret is now the bell-tower. The frescoes have been restored. Nearby, the smaller 12th-century church of Aghios Athanasios has 14th-century wall paintings and ceramic decorations in the exterior fabric. (*Both churches are usually locked, though it is sometimes possible for the priest to unlock them.*) About 2.5km northwest of Leondari, on the left bank of the Xerillas, are the scanty vestiges of **Veligosti** (Βελιγοστή), important in Byzantine times. It is reached from the bridle-path that leads in slightly under 2hrs between the Samara Hills and Mt Ellenitsa to Paradeisia.

Beyond Leondari routes lead south to the scattered villages on the west slopes of Taygetos. At 22km, a signposted left turn leads to Skortzinos, with a frescoed 14th-century church of the Taxiarchs. Continuing the road crosses the Arcadian frontier into Laconia. At Longanikos, a narrow mountain village, the church of Profitis Ilias has a restored painting of St George from a Byzantine church dedicated to the saint. Beyond Georgitsi, a left turn leads 4km to **Pellana** (some signs also say Koniditsa). About 800m beyond the plateia (rough road between kafeneions) a small sign points right to 'Mycenaean Tholos Tombs'; a newer sign for 'Archaeological Area' is promised. Five rock-cut chambers of tholos shape have been discovered here, though it is not possible to enter them. The largest is 10m in diameter. The size of this tomb, the cluster of important tombs, and their finds have led some to speculate that this may have been Homeric Sparta; other scholars think that Vapheio, the Menelaion, or an as-yet unknown site nearer Sparta must have been the Homeric Sparta. Finds from the tombs and from Palaikoastro, the acropolis, with finds from Early Helladic to Byzantine times, are in the Sparta Museum; some on display (*see p. 304*).

KARITAINA & ANDRITSAINA

The road north from Megalopolis is one of the most scenic routes in the Peloponnese, taking in the mountain towns of Karitaina and Andritsaina, and the Temple of Bassae (*see below*), as well as a number of lesser sites.

Leaving Megalopolis, the road runs past the ancient remains and crosses the Helisson. (A minor road leads right in 15km, via Trilofos to **Likocheia**, near which a late Archaic and Classical sanctuary of Artemis—perhaps that of Artemis Kalliste, mentioned by Pausanias—was excavated in 1972 and 1975.) The main route follows the Alpheios at varying distances from its right bank. At Katsimbalis, a track diverges (left) across the river to Kyparissia, between which and Mavria, just to the north, are some remains of *Trapezous*. Soon after, Karitaina appears against the sky, spectacularly perched on an isolated hill at the northwest corner of the Plain of Megalopolis above the right bank of the Karitaina (as the Alpheios is called at this point). The town, with its medieval kastro-crowned acropolis and clutch of Byzantine churches, is some 3km up a winding road above the junction with the road from Dimitsana.

Karitaina

Karitaina (Καρίταινα) occupies the site of ancient *Brenthe*, a deserted city which became a refuge for the people of Gortys (*see p. 285 below*) when they were driven out by the Slavs. The name is, in fact, a corruption of *Gortyna*. In 1209 the Franks made Karitaina the capital of a barony of 22 fiefs. The castle was built by Hugh de Bruyères c. 1254. His son Geoffrey I de Bruyères (d. 1272) was the 'Sire de Caritaine' and the pattern of Peloponnesian chivalry. The castle passed by sale in 1320 to Andronicus II Palaeologus. In the War of Independence, Kolokotronis used it as a stronghold from which he defied Ibrahim Pasha. A precipitous path climbs in 10mins to the castle (583m) which occupies the summit of a high rock, extremely steep and in places overhanging the riverside. En route, you pass the (? 11th-century) church of the Panaghia tou Kastrou. The triangular enceinte, adapted for defence by artillery as well as musketry, is a notable example of feudal fortification. In the central court is a large vaulted hall and on the west the remains of a gallery with large windows and of numerous cisterns (care needed). The view is superb.

At the foot of the kastro, the 14th-century church of Aghios Nikolaos has five domes and badly preserved frescoes. The church of the Zoödochos Pigi (? 14th century) on the outskirts of the village is identifiable by its detached bell-tower, with elaborate brickwork, which Hetherington points out 'suggests an interesting use of Western forms by Greek builders'. (*For all these churches, inquire in the plateia or at nearby houses as to who has the keys.*)

From the square below the castle, an asphalt road leads on to Atsicholo and Palaiokastro Gortynias (12km further), with a large cemetery of Mycenaean chamber tombs.

From the main road below Karitaina, a branch leads north to the Lousios Gorge; *see p. 283*. The Andritsaina road crosses the river on a new bridge beside the medieval bridge, renovated (as an inscription once recorded) in 1439 by Manuel Raoul Melikes, a member of a noble Turkish family serving the Palaeologi at Mistra. The road climbs high along the north slopes of the barren Mt Lykaion with views into the Gorge of the Alpheios. The Lavda hill above Theisoa is the site (fortifications etc.) of the ancient settlement of the same name.

Andritsaina

Andritsaina (Ανδρίτσαινα) is an attractive ramshackle village of wooden houses, which was shaken by earthquakes in 1965. It is beautifully situated on elevated ground (765m) facing northwest and watered by a mountain stream. Water is channelled through several plane trees in the small square, with several cafés and tavernas, where the Saturday market takes place. In the main square there is a monument to Panayotis Anagnostopoulos, one of the Philike Etaireia (*see p. 51*), who was educated at the local school. The town has an excellent library of 16th–19th-century manuscripts and books, founded with a bequest in 1860 (*hours irregular; enquire at the library*). There is also a small, engaging Folklore Museum (*irregular hours; enquire at the Taverna Sigouri*).

BASSAE

A well-engineered road (14.5km; taxi; bus daily, not returning) ascends from Andritsaina through spectacular scenery to the remote Temple of Bassae (alas, shrouded under the 'temporary' protective tent erected in 1987). The 2.5-hr walk to or from the temple through the valleys is rewarding.

The celebrated Temple of Apollo Epikourios is situated at 1131m on a narrow rocky terrace of Mt Kotilion (now Palaiavlachitsa), whose summit rises above it to the northeast. The mountain is scored with ravines (βάσσαι) from which the place takes its general name; the temple site is called locally 'the columns' ('*stous stylous*'). The temple,

The lonely temple of Apollo Epikourios, before it was swathed in a protective cover.

which long owed its fine preservation to its inaccessibility, and more recently owes it to girders and an obtrusive protective tent-like covering, is built of a cold grey local limestone that contributes to, rather than lightens, the melancholy bleakness of the landscape. The immediate surroundings are softened a little by a few oak trees and, in spring, the wild flowers.

The present temple (5th century BC) replaced earlier 7th-, 6th-, and 5th-century structures. Its isolated situation vexes scholars, as does the epithet '*epikourios*' ('protector'). Some suggest that this refers to Apollo's help in warding off the plague; others suggest that Apollo was perceived as the protector of Arcadians, especially Arcadian mercenaries.

The temple was rediscovered in 1765 by Joachim Bocher, a French architect employed by the Venetians in Zante. In 1811–12 the party of British and German antiquaries who had previously stripped the Aegina temple, explored the ruins and removed the sculptures. The 23 marble slabs of the cella frieze were bought by the British Government for £19,000 for the British Museum. In 1902–06 the Greek Archaeological Society replaced some fallen column fragments and restored the cella walls. Additional fragments of the frieze were unearthed in 1961. The foundations have been shown to incorporate reused blocks from an Archaic predecessor on the same site. Some of its terracotta decoration has been found (antefixes and disc acroteria).

The temple design

The Classical temple is a Doric peripteral hexastyle, 38.3m long and 14.6m wide, longer, therefore, by about one fifth and fractionally wider than the Temple of Hephaistos in Athens. Attributed by Pausanias to Ictinus, its style makes it almost certainly an earlier work than the Parthenon, and so designed c. 450–440 BC, though the execution may not have been finished before 425 BC. The orientation is unusual, being north and south. The peristyle, 6 columns by 15, on a stylobate of three steps, is complete but for the southeast corner column. Most of the architrave blocks are in position, but nothing of the pediments or the roof. The pediments were prepared for sculptured groups which Dinsmoor concludes were taken off in ancient times to Rome: the roof-tiles have been identified variously as being marble from the island or Paros or from the quarries at Tainaron in Laconia. The colonnade had a coffered ceiling of different patterns.

The interior has the conventional pronaos, cella and opisthodomos, but the arrangement is unusual. The pronaos, 5.5m long, had two columns between *antae*. It was decorated with a metope frieze, now in a very fragmentary state. A metal barrier, with gates, shut it off from the colonnade. A door led into the cella. The opisthodomos, 4.1m long, was similarly distyle in antis, open to the colonnade, and cut off by a wall from the cella.

The cella, 16.8m long and 7m wide, was in two parts. The north section, 12.2m long, had on each side a series of five half-columns engaged in buttresses that projected from the side wall, the first four pairs at right angles and the fifth pair (at the south end) diagonally inward. The half-columns are most unusually located not opposite the peristyle columns but between the intercolumniations. They had bell-shaped bases, resting on a step, 10cm high, and volutes on three faces of the Ionic capitals. The fifth pair had between them a single Corinthian column, in marble, with 20 flutes. Its capital, now lost, is recorded as having acanthus decoration, and thus formed the earliest example of the Corinthian order yet known to us. A theory suggests that the Corinthian column in this curious position was in fact an aniconic representation of the deity and there was no other cult statue (no sign of a base has been found), in spite of the comments of Pausanias (*see below*). The height of the interior colonnade (6.3m) is greater by a foot than that of the peristyle. It supported an Ionic entablature with a frieze, richly carved in island marble and depicting the battles between Greeks and Amazons, and between Lapiths and Centaurs.

The inner adyton, occupying the remaining 4.6m of the cella, is also of unusual design, with a door on the left (east) side. This fact prompted speculation as to whether a cult statue stood against its west wall, and whether the plan follows that of an earlier sanctuary on the site. Pausanias records that the figure of Apollo in bronze was transferred in 369 BC to the agora at Megalopolis and replaced by an acrolithic statue.

As well as the traces of an earlier Archaic temple, votive offerings have been recovered going back to Geometric times. Buildings over a wide area, especially to the north of the Classical temple, indicate that the sanctuary contained a variety of buildings and there was probably an adjacent settlement, although the temple sanctuary was under the supervision of the hamlet of Phigaleia.

Excursion to Ancient Phigaleia

From Bassae a road, sometimes unsurfaced before Kato Figaleia, continues and descends past Dragogi to Perivolia where there are scant remains of a Doric temple. A left turn in the village (sign for Φιγαλεία) leads in 3km to Ano Figaleia, which is situated within the fortifications of **ancient *Phigaleia***, an Arcadian city on the borders of Elis and Messenia, which had a reputation for wizardry, witchcraft and drunkenness. Its walls and towers occupy a high and uneven plateau, with precipitous sides, surrounded by mountains. On the south the Neda flows far below. The antiquities on this attractive site are scattered and difficult to find. A sign on the edge of the village (fork right) indicates a path in the direction of Platania. A short distance along this are the most accessible parts of the fortifications. Near the fork, cut by the road, are the remains of a stoa. Through the village (left fork and downhill), by a plane tree, are the impressive remains of a fountain house (draw-basin and columned façade) of the 4th–3rd centuries BC. The church in the cemetery (above), with ancient columns, is 11th-century and has frescoes. A *kouros* from the site is in the Olympia Museum. In the 1990s, a Middle Helladic settlement was discovered near what is thought to be a 4th-century BC temple.

STEMNITSA & THE LOUSIOS GORGE

Stemnitsa (Στεμνίτσα; on some maps Ipsouda) is one of the most beautiful Arcadian villages, both in location and architecture. Together with Dimitsana. it is a listed site: officially, nothing can be built or altered without government permission. Both villages are popular destinations for Greek school trips and for Greek families visiting the area, which was important during the War of Independence. The area is also popular with hikers and bird-watchers.

Stemnitsa appears as a clutch of 16th- and 17th-century churches and *archontika* tumbling down a slope of Mt Klinitsa (1548m), crowned with the remains of a Byzantine kastro, the 16th-century church of Aghios Nikolaos, the 17th-century chapel of the Panaghia Bafero, and some still-occupied medieval houses. Scattered through the village, five additional churches dating from the 17th–19th centuries have frescoes and the imposing church of Aghios Georgios in the main plateia has a fine limestone relief of St George. Several cafés and restaurants flank the plateia's 19th-century bell-tower, built by stonemasons from Tinos.

Stemnitsa was a centre of metalwork and jewellery in the 19th century; visitors should check to see whether the jewellery school in the former schoolhouse is open. The Folklore Museum (*open 1 June–1 Oct Mon, Weds, Thur, Fri 6pm–8pm, Sat 11–1 & 6–8, Sun 11–1; Oct–June usually open 11–1. Closed Tues and Feb; T: 27950 81252*), which occupies a handsome 19th-century town house, has engaging dioramas recreating local life a hundred and more years ago, including workshops of a local goldsmith, cobbler and bell-maker; the museum also houses the extensive Savvopoulos collection of icons, costumes, weapons and household goods made and used here.

Beyond Stemnitsa the road forks: right for Karitaina and Megalopolis; left for Tripolis via Davia. Off this road, at Limbovisi is the restored birthplace of the revolutionary war hero Theodore Kolokotronis (*see p. 287 below*).

The Lousios Gorge

NB: Despite the shade trees and wading possibilities in the perpetually cool river Gortys, this excursion is best not done on foot on a hot day.

Two rivers dominate northern Arcadia: the Ladonas to the north (now much diverted to the Ladonas dam) and the Lousios (also known as the Gortys) to the south. The Lousios runs for 26km across the entire prefecture of Gortynia, finally merging with the Alpheios near Karitaina. The gorge itself, running between Dimitsana and Karitaina, cut through by the Gortys river, is some 20km long, with red limestone cliffs rising to 100m. Bats live in the caves in the cliffs (and in abandoned chapels and mills), falcons and hawks nest on the cliffs; the vegetation along the river is lush (and home to tree snakes); even the cliffs have an astonishing amount of vegetation in spring. Although it is possible to hike the length of the gorge, mostly on marked paths, the gorge's difficulty of access centuries ago made it a popular place for hermits and monks. Several monasteries survive, most notably Old and New Philosophou and the Prodromou. The river's waterpower has long been harnessed, most notably from the 17th to the 19th centuries, when there were countless mills along the gorge. Tourism is gradually bringing a new prosperity to the area as visitors explore the gorge.

Anyone exploring the gorge should obtain the excellent *Walker's Map of the River Lousios Valley with Cultural Information*, on sale at the Open-Air Water Power Museum in Dimitsana (*see p. 286 below*).

The monasteries

The monks at the monasteries of Our Lady of Aimyalon, the Old and New Philosophou, and the Prodromou welcome visitors who come properly dressed (long sleeves and skirts for women; trousers, not shorts, for men) and who avoid the siesta hours (usually 2pm–4pm). It is traditional to leave a donation in the chapel collection box.

Each of the monasteries has one or more foundation legends, but in the absence of helpful written records before the 17th century, it is difficult to know just when and why the monasteries in the Lousios gorge were founded. Like many monasteries in Greece, the oldest foundations here were caves in the cliffs, the homes of solitary hermits, who kept a few sheep and goats and planted small vegetable gardens on the narrow terraces below the caves. In time—as at the Meteora in Thessaly (*see p. 546*)—other monks appeared and simple wooden dormitories were built, cantilevered out from the caves. The earliest chapels, simple shrines within caves, were preserved but larger churches were built on nearby terraces, some natural and some laboriously created by the monks. If the dormitories of the Monastery of the Prodromou are any indication, the communities may once have contained a hundred or so brethren. Today, there are perhaps a dozen monks in residence year-round at Philosophou (fewer at Prodromou and Aimyalon), although monks from other monasteries often visit. On feast days, pilgrims fill the dormitories. Although there are more grey than black beards among the monks, most of the monks look shocked if asked whether they are worried that there may come a day when the monasteries are not merely just short-staffed, but empty. For now, they pray, maintain their gardens, keep an eye on their small flocks of sheep and goats—and speak to the monks in nearby monasteries on their mobile phones.

The 17th-century **Monastery of Our Lady of Aimyalon** (Μονή της Παναγίας των Αιμυαλών), like many monasteries, is built into a cliff-side, protected by several circuits of walls. There is a well-tended vegetable and flower garden by the courtyard with a fine bronze bell. A monk sometimes offers guests coffee and *loukoumi* (Turkish delight) after showing them the simple chapel, itself in a hollowed-out cave in the cliffside.

At the village of Palaiochori a signpost indicates the turning to the old and new Philosophou monasteries (Φιλοσόφου; right) and to the Monastery of the Prodromou (Προδρόμου; left). The Church of the Dormition at **New Philosophou**, where you park, has an elaborately carved wooden altar screen and well-preserved (restored) frescoes. A cliff-side path leads on in 20mins to the cliff-side remains of **Old Philosophou**, founded in 963 by the chief secretary of the Byzantine emperor Nicephorus Phocas, and now home to innumerable bats. One of the many 'secret schools' that existed under the Turkish Occupation, when studying the Greek language and Orthodox religion were forbidden, met here. Every Greek child still learns the poem *Fengaraki mou Lambro*, which urges the 'little moon' to shine, and which children recited to keep up their courage when they went under cover of darkness to the secret schools.

From the monasteries of Philosophou, take the road back to the turning, and follow the sign for the **Monastery of the Prodromou** (John the Baptist). Those doing this excursion on foot will find the footpaths well-marked. In spring, many stretches of the paths can be very slippery, as rain and melting snow turn them into channels feeding the river below. The road climbs high above the gorge, with fine views of the Philosophou monasteries, which, as intended, are well-camouflaged against the cliffs. Park by the modern chapel, where the paved road ends, and follow the path to the Monastery of the Prodromou, which may have been founded as a hermitage in the 12th century; the most recent foundation here is the 20th-century church. The monastery is very crowded on its feast days (17th May and 29th August), when the devout hope to stay in the guesthouse.

Ancient Gortys

To reach Gortys by car from Dimitsana or Stemnitsa, follow the route above for the Monastery of the Prodromou. Instead of parking by the new white church, continue steeply downhill and park beside the arched stone bridge. Gortys lies across the bridge. Those coming to Gortys from Andritsaina and Karitaina will approach Gortys via Elleniko or Asticholo, following signs for Ancient Gortys and/or Moni Kalamiou. Those coming this way will first pass by Moni Kalamiou and the acropolis of Gortys and then reach the Asclepieion.

This excursion is one of the nicest in all Arcadia, taking in a small, well preserved ancient site near the bottle-green river Gortys; a Byzantine chapel; a monastery; and, in spring, sheep bells and wild flowers. It is a superb spot for picnicking.

Little is known of Gortys (Γόρτυς), a small city which apparently declined after the foundation of Megalopolis; the Asclepieion, however, did not lose its importance. Pausanias mentions that the river was called the 'Wash' (Lousios) because this was where the infant Zeus was washed. Pausanias also mentions that the Lousios was the coldest known river, an opinion which those who wade or swim here may agree with.

To visit the main Asclepieion, cross the arched stone bridge, probably built by the Venetians. The charming small church of St Andrew (? 11th century), with attractive stone and brickwork, and some frescoes, stands on an earlier Roman foundation (*the church is usually locked*). From the bridge, bear left and head uphill, keeping the shepherd's house to your right. You will be aware of ancient defence walls here and there along the river bank. The main elements of the site (foundations of a temple of Asclepius and a bathing establishment)—are compact and easily explored. The temple (no opisthodomos) was built in the 4th century and probably had sculptures by Skopas. The bathing establishment was built in the Hellenistic period and reconstructed in the 4th century AD. Bathers entered through a portico at the east, turned left into a changing room and passed into the main central hall equipped with benches and water fountains. A small circular room off to the northeast was for dry heat. A modest waiting area gave access to the circular bathroom with individual niches. The functions of the two rooms at the northeast are uncertain. The hypocaust system is well preserved. The furnace, with the main water reservoir beside it, is at the far end of the complex from the entrance. Further east, across ravines, are the remains of another temple, a stoa, a watchtower and houses.

From the Asclepieion, it is about 3km by the dirt road to the Acropolis of 'Archaia Gortys'; those on foot with the *Walkers Map to the Lousios Gorge* can follow suggested short-cuts. For much of the year, the Acropolis serves as an unofficial sheepfold. It stands above the Lousios river, and has fine walls and towers (4th-century trapezoidal masonry). There is a smaller walled enclosure (? 3rd century) at the southeast. Fifty metres to the south of this are the remains of a second Asclepieion (inscriptions) with a stoa (abaton), spring or bath and a temple of the 5th or 4th century.

Continuing past the Acropolis, the road leads to **Moni Kalamiou**. The original Byzantine monastery is in ruins, but the new monastery and church (17th century) have been well cared for, with the church recently restored, although there are no monks in residence. A sign points the way between the two monasteries.

DIMITSANA & NORTHERN ARCADIA

Dimitsana (Δημητσάνα) is built amphitheatrically in the deep cleft between two steep hills above the Lousios river. From outside town, it is easy to pick out the bell-towers of churches and pinpoint individual four- and five-storey stone houses, with their narrow windows and slate- and red-tile roofs. Once in town, it is just as easy to lose one's bearings as one loses sight of both church towers and individual houses in the narrow cobbled streets that are layered down the mountainside.

Dimitsana is probably built on the site of the 8th-century BC settlement of *Teuthis*, although some possibly Mycenaean walls (signposted in town on the ancient acropolis) suggest even earlier habitation. Dimitsana's heyday was in the 18th and 19th centuries AD, when it was an important market and mill town, whose school (founded 1764) was a centre of anti-Turkish and revolutionary sentiment. Patriarch Gregory V and Germanos, the Archbishop of Patras who raised the revolutionary standard in 1821 (*see p. 410*) and was born here, both attended the school. Kolokotronis called Dimitsana his 'arsenal', because of the gunpowder its 14 mills supplied to his troops.

In 1998, Greece's first museum of pre-industrial technology, the **Dimitsana Open-Air Water Power Museum**, opened just outside town on the road to Stemnitsa (*open April–Oct daily except Tues 10–3 & 5–7; Oct–April 10–4; T: 27950 31630*). The museum has a restored tannery, raki still, flour and powder mills, and signposted walks to other nearby mills. When the museum's two functioning mills are operating, visitors get an idea of how noisy this now quiet valley once was, before electric power made the mills obsolete. The museum sells a number of books, including the excellent (and misleadingly titled: these are both guide books) *Cultural Map of Arcadia* and *The Walker's Map of the Lousios Valley*.

Dimitsana's churches of the Archangels (16th century); Aghios Georgios, the Dormition (both 17th century); Aghia Kyriaki, Aghios Charalambos, the Transfiguration (all 18th- and 19th century), preserve frescoes, wood-carvings and fine stonework. The small Ecclesiastical Museum (*irregular hours*) and town Library (some incunabulae; *irregular hours*) are both well worth visiting.

Langadia, Vytina and environs

From Dimitsana, the main road winds through rocky gorges in an increasingly barren landscape to a summit of nearly 1220m, clothed in ferns, then crosses the infant Lousios until **Langadia** (Λαγκάδια) appears ahead, tumbling vertically down an outcrop of rock above the valley. The road winds sharply downwards to the centre of the village, where a little plateia forms a superb belvedere.

Langadia is famous throughout the Peloponnese for its stone masons, who travelled from village to village for most of the year from the 17th–20th centuries. Many of the finest stone houses in the Peloponnese bear the mason's marks of Langadian workmen. As one would expect, the village has many handsome stone churches, fountains, and two-, three- and even four-storey stone houses, of which that owned by the

Deligiannis family is perhaps the finest. Theodore Deligiannis (1826–1905) served several terms as prime minister. The 19th-century church of the Archangels has an interesting stone relief.

Magouliana (Μαγουλιανά), the highest village in Arcadia (1367m), has three substantial 19th-century churches, two arched stone bridges, and many fine stone two-storey houses. The village calls itself the 'balcony of Arcadia', and has a splendid plateia, shaded by massive chestnut trees, that is vertiginously cantilevered over a cliff. In the 13th century, this was a summer residence of the powerful Frankish Villehardouin dynasty, whose ruined fortress (known locally as Argirokastro), was the highest fortified spot in the Peloponnese. Continuing through Magouliana from the plateia, a 30-minute walk culminating in a steep uphill climb leads to the fortress, with splendid views across Arcadia.

Valtesiniko (Βαλτεσινίκο) lies just east of the site of ancient *Glanitsa*, where the French School found a late Archaic bronze head in 1939. En route, you pass a former sanatorium, one of many built in the 19th and 20th centuries for those seeking to improve their health by taking the mountain air. The village has several watermills, fine stone houses, an arched stone bridge, and the remains of a Venetian tower and a monastery (? 17th century).

Vytina (Βυτίνα) is a popular summer resort, beloved of Greeks seeking the mountain air. It is on the brink of losing its rustic charms to over-development, as clusters of holiday homes spread across the surrounding hills. Its main plateia is flanked by cafés, restaurants, shops selling wood-carvings, and local agricultural products such as the justly famous local yoghurt, mountain tea, oregano, and cheeses. There are many handsome stone buildings, some undergoing restoration, throughout the village. There is a small Folklore Museum (*usually closed; enquire at the plateia*). Like many villages in this part of Arcadia, Vytina until well into the 20th century had numerous watermills, of which one at the junction of the road to Pyrgaki, to the south, still functions.

The road ascends to Alonistaina (Αλωνίσταινα), a pretty mountain hamlet founded c. 1300 amid wooded crags. En route, in spring, the mountain slopes are covered with bee hives. Alonistaina was the birthplace and family home of Kolokotronis's mother. It has at least one fortified tower-house, and the handsome 19th-century two-storey Dimitrakopoulos house, but is virtually deserted most of the year, though somewhat more lively in winter, as it is a stopping-off point en route to the Ski Centre on Mainalon. At other times, this is not a spot to count on finding a functioning café.

Between Alonistaina and Piana, several signs point (right) to Limbovisi (Λιμποβίσι), the birthplace of the Theodore Kolokotronis (*see p. 51*), hero of the War of Independence. The birthplace has been restored (over-restored, some might say), and is now approached past a small plateia, fountain and chapel. An exhibit in the house, now a museum (*open May–Sept daily 10–7; April and Oct 11–4; labels primarily in Greek*), gives highlights of Kolokotronis's life. From Limbovisi, several good dirt roads (the best one via Chrysovitsi) through dense forests lead to the turn off for Stemnitsa (right) and Karitaina, Andritsaina and Megalopolis (left).

SOUTHERN ARCADIA: THE EAST COAST

A spectacular coast road runs from Argos south along the southeast coast of Arcadia as far as the village of Leonidion (maps pp. 156 and 296). There, a good route runs inland to Kosmas and beyond, to a crossroads whence one can continue to Geraki, Sparta, Megalopolis, and Monemvasia and the Mani.

Southern Arcadia's coast offers many pleasures, of which swimming is not the least. The Monastery of Loukou 5km west of Astros on the Tripolis road is one of the most charming in the Peloponnese. Directly across the road are the extensive remains of the enormous Villa of Herodes Atticus, still under excavation. Although the villa is not yet open to the public, it is easy to get a sense of its dimensions and wealth from outside its fence. Other monasteries in the area (most indicated on good maps) can easily be visited by car, as can a number of villages with handsome tile or slate-roofed traditional stone houses.

Much of this route runs through the sub-prefecture of Kynouria, where, until recently, most people spoke both Greek and Tsakonian, a dialect (some would say a language) which preserves many elements of ancient Doric. The coast was landlocked until after the Second World War, when the first steamrolled dirt road linked the area with the north. In 2004–05, one of the steamrollers was lovingly restored and is now on view by the bridge on the road from Leonidion to Plaka. It will be moved to Leonidion's Museum of Local History, now under construction. The present road is asphalted and excellent (although with many sharp bends), with splendid views across the Myrtoön Gulf to the cliffs of Nafplion, the mountains of the mainland, and the island of Spetses. On a clear day, Hydra is clearly visible beyond Spetses.

Astros and environs

Astros (Ἄστρος), like most of the following villages, has both a coastal and an inland settlement. Astros Paralion is attractively situated on the sea, with a clearly visible medieval fort, with some Classical remains, as well as signs of Turkish fortifications. Much of the low plain between here and the main road was once under water; the lake that remains (Moustou) is a sanctuary for migrating and local birds, often including swans, who feed on the fish and eels that live here. The waters of the lake are thought to be therapeutic, and this is a popular local spot less for swimming than soaking, where the springs that feed the lake bubble up beside the road (small pull-off and parking place; take care when rejoining the road).

Astros itself is a sprawling agricultural centre, growing olives and fruit, and especially noted for peaches. In April 1823 the Second National Assembly called by various *klepht* leaders of the insurrection to revise the constitution of 1821 was held in the courtyard of the handsome stone school building, now the Archaeological Museum (*open 9.30–2, closed Mon; sparse labels; T: 27550 22201*). The Tripolis road passes the museum, which is not visible from the road, as it is obscured by the modern public high school (park by the high school).

The museum is entered through a gate in the high whitewashed wall which conceals the lovely sculpture garden, with rose bushes (and adjacent chained watchdogs). The custodian can point out three items which she says are unique in Greece: a tiny figure of a masturbating satyr; a trick wine jug in the shape of a blowfish, which does not pour wine from its mouth spout; and a bust whose base carries the inscription *aristera mesa*, believed to be the sculptor's indication of where it should be positioned (centre left) amongst a group of busts in an exedra in the Villa of Herodes Atticus. The museum has some fine sculpture (mostly Hellenistic and Roman) and architectural fragments, all from the villa. Amongst the sculptures are two fine grave reliefs, one of a naked warrior resting his arm on a herm. Other reliefs show Hermes and nymphs and feasting heroes. There is a statue of Antinous (*see p. 466*) and portraits of the 2nd century AD emperor Commodus and his son Aelius Verus, as well as the beautiful youth Polydeuces, an intimate of Herodes Atticus. The bust of a little boy is believed by the custodian to depict a mentally handicapped son of Herodes Atticus. The remaining displays come from various sites in ancient *Thyreatis* (Astros and its surrounding plain), which made up much of today's Kynouria. There are grave goods, including bronzes, from Classical/Roman cemeteries at Ellinikon (*see below*). There is some Mycenaean and Geometric material; also some coins, and Byzantine moulds. In the gardens is a Roman sarcophagus lid with a reclining headless figure. Photographs are not allowed.

The remains of **ancient *Ellinikon*** are some 4km southwest of Astros on the road to Aghios Petros. The site tops a hill beside the road and the ancient circuit walls and remains of a system of 12 towers that protected the acropolis are clearly visible in winter. The walls have been dated tentatively to the second half of the 4th century, and were perhaps built at the instigation of Argos to protect the settlement and the plain against Spartan incursions. See Yvonne C. Goester, *The Plain of Astros: A Survey*, Pharos I (1993). The road continues to the Malevi Monastery, which was largely rebuilt after the Second World War.

Moni Loukous and the Villa of Herodes Atticus

The main Tripolis road (good surface; pleasant route) continues beyond the museum through the outskirts of Astros. After 4km, immediately left of the road, is the delightful **Moni Loukous**, whose name comes, so the local guide tells you, from the Latin *lucus*, a grove. The short drive (or climb) up to the monastery passes a segment of a Roman aqueduct, heavily encrusted—draped, really—with mineral deposits. The monastery is a foundation of c. 1100 and its church has a complete cycle of relatively recent (probably 18th- and 19th-century) frescoes. The compound is lovely, beautifully planted, with paintings of saints and religious symbols in niches. Various architectural remains of the ancient town of *Eua*, important in the Roman period, are build into the walls and in the courtyard, although many pieces have been removed to the Astros and Tripolis archaeological museums. The nuns often invite visitors inside for coffee, *loukoumi*, and to inspect the shop, which has religious literature and items and small, handloomed rugs in the local Tsakonian style, made by two sisters who are among the nuns here.

Across the Tripolis road from the monastery, in a fenced enclosure (*no admission*), are the substantial building and other remains, including a nymphaion and mosaic floors, of the **Villa of Herodes Atticus**. Herodes Atticus (110–77), born into a wealthy Greek family that had taken Roman citizenship, increased the fortune he inherited. He seems to have been incapable of making a day trip without funding at least a small fountain as a memento of his visit. Like many a Greek shipping magnate today, he had a string of imposing villas in and out of Greece.

There are plans to cover the villa, which is already known to cover more than 20,000m square, with a protective roof. The villa, which has been compared in size and magnificence to Hadrian's Villa at Tivoli, had a central courtyard flanked on three sides by arcades and courtyards. On the fourth side there was an exedra, or recess. The entire complex included baths, several small temples, a library, pool, extensive gardens, and guard houses. Statuary found to date includes copies of famous works such as the *Aphrodite* of Praxiteles; original works include the dancing maidens known as the *Orchoumenous Lakaines*, done by the 5th century sculptor Callimachus. In short, Herodes Atticus decorated his villa with reproductions and antiques, as well as commissioning mosaics and contemporary works of art by the best craftsmen and artists of his day. Finds here suggest that the villa was occupied long after Herodes' death in 165 AD, perhaps well into the 6th century AD. The Greek Archaeological Service excavations, under Theodoros Spropoulos, continue.

Aghios Andreas to Leonidion

From Astros, the coast road continues south to Aghios Andreas. From here a signposted road leads west to the Monastery of the **Panaghia Orthokosta** (Artokosta). The original foundation was (?) 12th century; the new foundation was built in 1617, burnt by the Albanians in 1770, by the Turks under Ibrahim in 1826, and repeatedly restored. The present monastery is a compact building complex built in a square, with a verdant courtyard around the church, which has 19th-century frescoes. Since 1982 this has been a convent, with a handful of nuns in residence. This is a popular local spot for baptisms, especially on summer weekends.

A few kilometres beyond the monastery is the handsome village of **Prastos**, which spills down a steep hill. This virtually deserted village was the most prosperous town in the area in the 18th century, and has many fine stone houses, including five imposing tower-houses with gunslit windows. There are several ruined mills (and a seasonal waterfall) in the stream bed, off the Prastos–Kastanitsa road, accessible on foot.

From Prastos, it is possible (partly on dirt roads) to visit the 17th-century Monastery of **Aghios Nikolaos Karyas**, 15km to the east. Although the two-storey arcaded slate-roofed monastery was recently renovated with a rather intrusive hand, it remains charming and remote. There are several monks in residence.

From Aghios Andreas, the coast road continues south past Arkadiko Chorio, a bleak retirement development for Arcadians returning from overseas, to Tyros. The signposted remains of Tyros' ancient acropolis are densely overgrown and not easy to locate in summer, although the walls that crown the acropolis summit are usually visible.

The coast road, with spectacular sea and mountain views, winds its way from Tyros to **Leonidion** (Λεωνίδιο), the chief town of Kynouria, the Arcadian eparchy which is separated from the hinterland by the abrupt ranges of Mt Parnon (1936m), with Taygetos, one of the two principal mountain ranges in the area. Two factors led to the rise of Leonidion in the 18th and 19th centuries: the decline of piracy and the decline of Prastos. A woodland tract was designated in the surrounding area on Parnon in 1961; wolves are still found here, as well as the fox, badger, eagle, hawk, tortoise and hedgehog. Leonidion is framed by its imposing cliffs, which change colour from the most austere grey to the most flamboyant violet and rose. The cliffs, and the fertile valley in which Leonidion sits, have been carved by the Daphnios river, which flows through a mountain pass which runs from Leonidion to Kosmas. Leonidion (named after the martyr St Leonidas, not the Spartan hero Leonidas) is a listed village, which in theory necessitates planning permission for any changes to existing homes or the construction of new ones. The town has three plateias, a riverside promenade, a number of handsome *archontika* (mansions), a tower-house, and a bustling agora.

Just outside Leonidion, on the sea, is its port, Plaka, with a small harbour, a pebble beach, a chapel dedicated to Aghios Leonidas and a string of harbourside restaurants. Blocks from the ancient harbour foundations have been recorded in the present harbour. The promontory above the harbour has signposted remains of ancient walls and defence towers (? 4th century) and is topped by the chapel of Aghios Athanasios. The ancient town was probably the *Brasiai/Prasiai*, one of the League of Free Laconian Cities, mentioned by Pausanias.

Moni Elonas and Kosmas

An excellent asphalt road leaves Leonidion (signs to Kosmas, Elonas and Sparti), with views of the cliffside monastery of Tsintzas (Aghios Nikolaos) high on the cliffs south of town. The road turns inland past a memorial to the dead of a battle (1949) in the Civil War, climbs through a deep gorge to pass below Moni Elonas (sideroad), as it crosses Parnon (spectacular scenery). This imposing cliffside monastery is one of the most important pilgrimage spots in the Peloponnese; pilgrims come from throughout the area for the feast of the Assumption of the Virgin on 15th August. The resident nuns say that the small cave-chapel here was founded by refugees from Constantinople in 1454, one year after the city fell to the Turks. Much of the present foundation is 17th century and the church probably 18th. A slippery stone path leads from the massive gate into the monastery, home to a handful of nuns. The views over the gorge and surrounding countryside are spectacular. The ornate wooden iconostasis is very fine; the icon of the Virgin, as is often the case, is almost entirely obscured by votive offerings.

Many monasteries have foundation legends similar to those of the Monastery of Elonas. In the case of Elonas, one story says that villagers repeatedly saw a distant light flickering high in the mountains. In time, a procession (led by the local priest) set out to investigate. High on the cliffs, hanging from an almost inaccessible tree, was an icon of the Virgin Mary. The icon was lowered to safety and the monastery was built where it stands today. According to another version, a decision was made to build a monastery on the more accessible slopes below the present monastery. As the walk here from nearby villages was a long and difficult one, the workers left their tools on the site of the prospective monastery. Over and over again, when the workers returned in the morning, their tools were gone. Each time, the tools were discovered at the present site—and one morning, an icon of the Virgin was discovered beside the pile of tools. At that point, it was clear to one and all where the Virgin wanted her monastery, and it was built where the tools and icon were found. In both versions, the icon is one of a number in Greece which the faithful believe to be the work of St Luke.

From Elonas, the road winds steeply uphill to the village of **Kosmas** (1200m), with sweeping views across to the village of Palaiochori; the sea is sometimes visible. During the Second World War, in 1944, the Germans torched Kosmas, which has since largely been rebuilt in its original style. The stone houses, many with slate roofs, spill over two hills. The central plateia, on the main Leonidion–Geraki road, has seven massive plane trees, and is a pleasant spot to break a journey. A talented local potter, Evangelos Stathakis, has his workshop and showroom on the plateia. The town fountain, on a level lower than the plateia, has fine lion's-head spouts and excellent water. The large modern church is just that.

SOUTH INTO LACONIA

The predominantly mountainous coastal region south of Leonidion is one of the less visited parts of Greece (*map p. 296*). Haste is impossible, accommodation limited and sometimes very simple. Visitors will, however, be rewarded by superb scenery and unexpected traces of the past. The two small ports of Kyparissi and Gerakas can be reached by car, with difficulty, on beautiful, but often unpaved and always narrow roads. For lovers of mountain scenery with no fixed schedule, we offer a route via secondary (at best) roads.

The road from Leonidion runs south past Plaka and continues to the village of Poulithra, a popular seaside retreat for Greek families in the summer. Here, the road turns steeply uphill and runs inland to traverse an upland plain, passing near a series of farming hamlets. The road leaves Arcadia and enters Laconia near Kremasti, from where it is possible to continue via Lambokambos to the tiny port of **Kyparissi**. Until recently one of the last undiscovered seaside hamlets in the Peloponnese, Kyparissi is rapidly being developed, and has several small hotels and a string of tavernas. Just outside Kyparissi, a striking rock cleft has springs and other remains almost certainly of an Asclepieion mentioned by Pausanias (path signed '*Panaghia sto Vracho*'; none beyond to highest spring and sanctuary terrace).

Immediately south of Paralia, just east of Kyparissi, twin peaks linked by a saddle have Archaic/Classical fortifications to the west and medieval ramparts to the east. The latter also has a ruined Byzantine church.

Limeni Gerakas is the small port of **Gerakas**, an attractive mountain village 3.5km inland. The harbour, like that of Kyparissi, shows increasing signs of touristic development. Gerakas is enchantingly situated on a narrow fjord. Dominating the entrance on the north, immediately above the village, is the fine acropolis of *Zarax*, of whose ancient history little is known, with Archaic/Classical walls and towers, an interesting gate to the small inner acropolis, and several later churches and other buildings. The fortifications were probably reused in medieval times. To the south there is a (mainly unsurfaced) road on to Monemvasia (*for Monemvasia, see the following chapter: Laconia*).

PRACTICAL INFORMATION

GETTING AROUND

• **By road:** The National Highway (tolls) runs from Athens–Argos–Tripolis, in part through an impressive tunnel. The 'old' road (no toll) from Corinth via Argos has fine views of the countryside.
• **By rail:** Tripolis is served by train from Athens (about 5hrs). There are trains to Kalamata (about 3hrs) several times a day.
• **By bus:** The main bus station in Tripolis (T: 2710 222560) is in Plateia Kolokotroni; it is possible to get anywhere in the Peloponnese (with changes) from Tripolis. Important direct destinations include Athens (13 daily), Argos (connection to Nafplion) (4), Patras (2), Pyrgos (3), Sparta and Kalamata (10), Megalopolis (9), Andritsaina (2). Buses also go to the site of ancient Tegea.

KTEL 6 Arkadias buses go from the bus station in Tripolis to (8km) Alea, formerly Piali, the site of the Temple of Athena Alea, the most important shrine of ancient Tegea.

There is a daily bus service to many of the coastal villages south of Argos from Athens and from Argos and Tripolis.

INFORMATION OFFICES

Tripolis The tourist information office in the Dimarcheion, on Ethnikis Antistasis, is usually open Mon–Fri 8–2.

WHERE TO STAY

Andritsaina
€€ **Theoxenia**. Old (if not venerable) 1950s hotel still awaiting its oft-promised renovations. 45 rooms. T: 26260 22219.
€€ **Epikourias Apollon**. New small hotel. 5 rooms. T: 26260 22840.
Dimitsana
€€€ **Pyrgos Xeniou**. Old 19th-century tower-house, once the home of a currant merchant, now attractively renovated as a hotel by a writer-and-artist couple. Spacious rooms have an airy feel. In general the place has an air of gracious living. 7 rooms. T: 27950 31750.
€€ **Hotel Dimitsana**. On the Stemnitsa road just outside the village. Completely remodelled in 2000–02, it has quiet rooms with fine views toward the Lousios Gorge. Restaurant desultory. 30 rooms. T: 27950 31518.
Karitaina
This is not a good place to arrive with-

out a reservation (there are one or two 'Rent Rooms' signs). Those wishing to stay here might try **Vrenthi Rooms** (T: 27910 31650).

Kosmas

€€ **Apollo Maleatis**. Simple but pleasant 10-room hotel. T: 27570 31494.

Langadia

€€ **Hotel Langadia** Views over the mountains from the back rooms. 20 rooms. T: 27950 43202). €€ **Kentrikon** (also known as the Maniatis). Front rooms here have balconies but overlook the main road. The hotel has its own restaurant. T: 27950 43221.

Leonidion

Rooms are available on the road into town at **Kostarini** (T: 27570 22273) and the **Ithaki**, which also has a restaurant (T: 27570 22977).

Plaka

Dionysos. Harbourside hotel operated by the same family that runs the Margarita/Michaelis restaurant; moderate. 18 rooms. T: 27570 23445.

Stemnitsa

€€ **Hotel Trikolon**. Family-run, in a restored 19th-century house, with its own excellent restaurant (undergoing renovation at the time of writing). 21 rooms. T: 27950 81297.

Tripolis

Tripolis is not the loveliest place to stay. Its hotels tend to cater to businessmen and families visiting relatives in the large Panarcadian Hospital. All are on noisy central streets. If you do stay here, you might try the €€ **Arcadia**, 1 Plateia Kolokotroni 1 (45 rooms; T: 27102 25511) or the €€ **Anaktorion**, Konstantinou XII (35 rooms; T: 27102 22545), recently renovated.

Vytina

€€ **Aigli**. Family-owned and operated, with its own restaurant. 20 rooms. T: 27950 22216.

€€ **Art Hotel Mainalon**. On the main street. Has sculpture and paintings by contemporary Greek artists and some rooms overlooking a quiet garden. 50 rooms. T: 27950 22217.

WHERE TO EAT

Andritsaina

There are a number of simple tavernas along the main street and Kyria Vasso's excellent **Sigouris** taverna, across from the metal-workers' shop on Sofokleous, just off the plateia with the plane trees. (Kyrias Vasso also usually has the keys to the Folklore Museum.)

Dimitsana

A clutch of restaurants on the main streets (**Archontiko**, **Baroutadiko**, **Tholos**, and **To Limeri tou Trypa**) do grills and stews, as does the **Kali Thea**, across from the Hotel Dimitsana.

Karitaina

There are two cafés and one restaurant in the village: but don't arrive hungry at midday, as they all seem to observe the siesta.

Kosmas

The Apollo Maleatis restaurant does excellent goat stew.

Levidi

Souvlakia places on the main plateia.

Leonidion

1812 Restaurant. In a nicely restored building on the main street. Dinner only.

Megalopolis

Restaurants on the main plateia, though none heartily recommendable.

Plaka

The Plaka waterfront is lined by four restaurants (sometimes closed in winter): the oldest (1830) and most charming is **Margarita/Michaelis**. The best fish (caught by the owners) is to be had at the **Taverna tou Psara**. **Ta Delfinia** has a varied menu and attractive veranda.

Tripolis

Locals speak well of two traditional tavernas, the **Klimataria Piterou**, Kalavrytou 11 (T: 27102 22058) and **To Panarkadiko**, Washington 3 (T: 27102 23328). **Faces**, Ethnikis Antistasis and Deligianni (T: 27102 27750) run by a Greek-American, has a more adventurous menu and slightly higher prices.

Vytina

On and just off the main plateia, there are a number of cafés and 'traditional' restaurants, of which the best-known is the Klimataria.

BOOKS & BACKGROUND READING

The *Cultural Map of Arcadia* (ETBA Cultural Foundation), often on sale at Eleftherodakis Bookshop in Athens and at the Open-Air Water Power Museum in Dimitsana, is excellent. Michael Cullen's *Southern Peloponnese* (Sunflower Books, 2003), has car and hiking itineraries in the area.

FESTIVALS & EVENTS

Leonidion Easter celebrations here, with the release of hundreds of hot-air balloons (*aerostata*), are famous. Leonidion's aubergine festival, held by the harbour in Plaka in late August, attracts visitors from throughout Greece.

Palaia Episkopi In August, the annual Peloponnesian Exhibition takes place here, with displays, athletic contests, dancing, and a fair.

LACONIA

One of the seven *nomes* of the Peloponnese, Laconia occupies the southeast of the peninsula, and is framed by its most imposing mountain ranges: Taygetos to the west and Parnon to the east. The river Evrotas, fed by melting snow from Taygetos, waters the plain around Sparta and is one of the few Peloponnesian rivers that do not usually run dry in summer. As a result, the plain around Sparta is unusually verdant, and the Langada mountain pass from Sparta to Kalamata is densely forested. To the south, Laconia fronts on the Laconian Gulf, and takes in most of the Mani peninsula to the west and all of the Malea peninsula to the east. The Mani peninsula is one of the most barren districts in Greece, and stretches of the Malea peninsula are also quite arid. By contrast, the land around Sparta itself and its ancient port of *Gytheion* (modern Gythion) are well-watered, with fruit and olive trees. There are fine beaches west between Gythion and Areopolis, the capital of the Mani, and east to the medieval fortress town of Monemvasia.

HISTORY & SIGHTS OF LACONIA

The earliest signs of habitation in Laconia date from the Neolithic era and were found in the Alepotripa Cave in the Diros Cave complex south of Areopolis in the Mani. It is frustrating that the site of Homeric Sparta—the home of Agamemnon's brother Menelaus and his wife Helen—has not been identified. It may or may not have been at the site of the Sparta of Classical antiquity, much of which lies under today's town. Sparta's remaining antiquities are few, but hold interest, largely because of Sparta's great past. As the poet Chateaubriand wrote when he visited Sparta in 1806, 'If I hate the manners of the Spartans, I am not blind to the greatness of a free people; neither was it without emotion that I trampled on their noble dust'.

The remains of the Byzantine city of Mistra just outside Sparta are considerably more than 'noble dust': this is one of the best-preserved medieval sites in Greece. To the southeast, the medieval fortress of Monemvasia is equally spectacular. In recent years many of the houses below Monemvasia's citadel have been restored as chic vacation homes and small hotels. Two other sites near Sparta—Chrysafa and Geraki—have clusters of medieval churches, and Geraki has a fine fortress.

Considerable work has been done and is being done on Laconia's long history of habitation. In the 1980s, the Laconia Survey (British School at Athens) examined remains from some 45 ancient sites; in 1993, the British School at Athens began its Laconia Rural Sites Project, examining soil samples as evidence of past human activity in small rural sites throughout Laconia, and in 1999 undertook a Geoarchaeological Survey of the Evrotas valley.

SPARTA

Athens is the only ancient Greek city more famous than Sparta. Sparta today, with some 15,000 inhabitants (more town than city), is the capital of Laconia, seat of the Metropolitan of Sparta and Monemvasia, and the agricultural centre of the Evrotas valley. The site is impressive: to the west, the sheer Taygetos range, rising to 2404m and snow-covered well into summer, seemingly bisects the sky. To the east, the gentler slopes of Parnon (1940m) encircle the fertile Spartan plain. Small wonder that the ancient Spartans boasted that they had no need for defensive walls: the Taygetos and Parnon ranges were the only protection needed. When fortifications were built, between the 4th and 2nd centuries BC, they were a sign of Sparta's fading strength.

Little enough remains of ancient Sparta to make visitors think that Thucydides was particularly prescient when he said that should the city ever fall, and only the ruins of its temples and public buildings remain, posterity would be hard pressed to believe that mighty Sparta had been such a modest place. Sparta was, Thucydides suggested, a collection of villages rather than a notable city such as Athens. Much even of what Thucydides knew as Sparta was destroyed in the horrific earthquake of 364 BC; Plutarch in his *Kimon* says that only five houses remained standing. Enough was rebuilt—largely under the Romans—to entertain Pausanias when he passed through. Alas, virtually all that that tireless traveller saw has been destroyed (or lies, unexcavated, under today's town). Still, the acropolis, the Sanctuary of Artemis, and the Menelaion remain; the small Archaeological Museum, with its pleasant rose garden, has several fine pieces, including a marble bust thought to be that of Leonidas, the 5th-century Spartan hero who fell at Thermopylae in 480 BC in the Spartan attempt to halt the Persian invasion.

After the Greek War of Independence (1821–27), there was an understandable impetus to revive Greek cities that had been glorious in Antiquity, and Sparta was refounded (laid out on a strict grid plan) in 1834. Several handsome Neoclassical buildings (the Town Hall, the Coumantaros Art Gallery, the Menelaion Hotel, and a number of private homes) date from, or commemorate, Sparta's 19th-century revival. The central streets are broad, and lined with orange trees, a reflection that much of Sparta's current wealth comes from its citrus groves. In spring, the scent of orange blossoms overcomes even the automobile exhaust on Sparta's main thoroughfare, Odos Palaiologou. The Saturday street market is lively, and the evening *volta* (promenade) in the main square is famous throughout Greece.

Excavations by the British School in 1906–10 and 1925–29 were resumed in 1988; in addition, numerous salvage excavations under the supervision of the Greek Archaeological Service have uncovered remains of ancient and medieval Sparta.

Homeric Sparta

Fittingly, the city that was best-known for its military exploits entered recorded history in Homer's account of the Trojan War. In the *Iliad*, Menelaus, King of Sparta, was the younger brother of Agamemnon, ruler of Mycenae, and leader of the Greeks. Agamemnon led the Greeks to Troy to reclaim Menelaus' wife, the beautiful Helen, after she eloped with the Trojan prince Paris. Nothing has as yet been found in or near Sparta to suggest a palace complex worthy of Menelaus, although important Mycenaean finds have been made at the Menelaion and at Vapheio (*see pp. 307 and 309*).

Foundation and growth

Sparta's enduring reputation as the ancient Greek military state *par excellence* is deserved, for much of Sparta's history is the history of conquest. By the 10th century, a number of small villages seem to have clustered around the Spartan acropolis. The original Laconians were conquered by the Doric-speaking newcomers known as the Spartans in around the 8th century BC. During the next several centuries, the Spartans gained control of most of Laconia. Spartan expansion began near the end of the 8th century BC with the attack on the fertile territory of Messenia. This conquest was later followed by a long revolt of Messenians (685–668). After the region had been subdued, Sparta began to increase her power in the Peloponnese. A long war with neighbouring Tegea (c. 600–560) showed that expansion was possible only by dominating vassal allies not by annexation. By the end of the 6th century BC, Tegea and Thyreatis (the ancient name for the coastal plain of Argos, which extended as far as today's Astros) were subdued, and c. 500 BC the Peloponnesian League was founded with Sparta at its head. Appropriately for Sparta's expansionist aims, the league was known as a *symmachia*, or 'fellowship in fighting'. Argos, the only neighbouring state that could hope to defy Sparta, was decisively defeated at Sepeia c. 494 BC.

The Persian invasions and the Peloponnesian Wars

Sparta took no part in repelling the first Persian expedition, but in 480–479 added to her prestige by the exploits of Leonidas at Thermopylae and the victory of Plataea under Pausanias (*see pp. 431 and 432*). The later intrigues of Pausanias in Byzantium and the campaign of Leotychides in Thessaly, both opposed by Athens, showed Sparta that better policy lay in maintaining strength in the Peloponnese; control of the Aegean was left to Athens. In 464 BC the Helots revolted, and only outside aid saved the state from destruction. The imperialism of Athens in the second half of the 5th century BC forced the Greeks to turn to Sparta as their champion.

The Peloponnesian War (431–404 BC) ended with the defeat of Athens, leaving Sparta the most powerful state not only of the mainland, but also in the Aegean. This was the apogee of Sparta's military success and political importance, and Sparta's fortunes begin to decline from here. The Greeks found her a worse master than Athens and in 395 BC she was attacked by a coalition led by Athens, Thebes, Corinth and Argos. Although Sparta triumphed on land at Corinth, her fleet was defeated at Cnidos in 394 BC and all hopes of an overseas empire were abandoned. In 386 BC, Sparta was instrumental in forcing the rest of the Greeks to accept the terms of the King's Peace, whereby Persia established its dominion over Asia and Cyprus, and scuppered any further Athenian or Spartan empire-building.

Sparta soon faced a powerful new enemy in Thebes; Theban hoplites, using new tactics devised by their leader Epaminondas, defeated Sparta at the Battle of Leuctra in Boeotia (371 BC). This broke for ever the legend of Spartan invincibility. Epaminondas led his troops south from Leuctra, invaded Laconia—the first known invasion into Spartan territory—and reached the outskirts of Sparta itself. To keep Sparta powerless, Epaminondas revived Messenia as an independent state, founded the Arcadian League, and encircled Sparta's northern frontier with a threatening line of fortresses.

Not surprisingly, others sensed Sparta's vulnerability. The Achaean League (*see p. 400*) and the Macedonians continued the campaign against Sparta. In 295 BC Demetrius Poliorcetes all but captured the city, and in 272 BC Pyrrhus could easily have taken Sparta after defeating its army. Cleomenes III of Sparta abolished the ephorate and ruled as a tyrant in a vain attempt to restore Spartan hegemony, but was utterly defeated at Sellasia. Sparta became a dependency of Macedon, regaining momentary independence only under the tyrants Machanidas (207 BC) and Nabis (195–192). After Nabis' assassination Philopoemen forced Sparta to join the Achaean League, razed the city walls, and repealed the laws of Lycurgus (*see below*).

Later history

In 195 BC (along with much of Greece) Sparta fell to Rome. Under the Romans Laconia had a period of prosperity in the 2nd century AD as a province of Achaea, and under Septimius Severus was even allowed to a degree of self-rule under a revived Lycurgan constitution. Numerous discoveries (including some of the fine mosaics on view in the Archaeological Museum) found in emergency excavations have attested to the prosperity of Roman Sparta.

In AD 396, Sparta was destroyed by Alaric the Goth, and when the Slavs invaded in the 9th century much of the population migrated to the Mani. The Byzantines refounded a town under the name *Lacedaemonia*, but by 1248 it was completely overshadowed by the thriving city of Mistra. For the next 15 centuries until Sparta was refounded in 1834 in its present location, the site of ancient Sparta was but a hamlet clustered on and around the ancient acropolis.

During the Second World War, 118 Spartans of the resistance movement were killed by the Germans on 26th November 1943; a monument at the south end of the Kleisoura Pass, the long defile that provides the best approach into Laconia from the north, commemorates the massacre. Fighting was also fierce around Sparta during the bloody civil war that followed after 1945.

The Spartans have retained their ancient reputation for conservatism: for years after the 1974 referendum that abolished the Greek monarchy, pictures of the deposed King Constantine II were still displayed in many Spartan shops.

SPARTAN INSTITUTIONS & CUSTOMS

Certain Spartan institutions and customs were unique in ancient Greece, notably, the caste system and the dual monarchy. The Spartan Constitution is credited to Lycurgus, an elusive figure whose dates vary between the 9th and 7th centuries BC (with most scholars favouring a 7th-century date). According to the Lycurgan constitution, Spartans were divided into three classes: *Spartiates* (full citizens), *Perioikoi* (free 'dwellers-around' without citizen rights), and *Helots* (serfs, with no rights). Within the three classes, professions were largely hereditary: the first-born son of a flute player was destined to play the flute.

Unusually, Sparta was headed by not one, but two kings. Herodotus mentions that this curious dual monarchy came about when twin sons were born—indistinguishably close together—to a monarch. What to do? The oracle at Delphi was consulted and its advice to accept both babies as king was accepted. Some scholars think that the dual monarchy actually came about as a way of uniting disparate factions when Sparta absorbed the settlements of the Laconian plain in the 10th century BC. The kings' main function was military: they commanded and led the Spartan army .

In addition to the two kings, Sparta's government was made up of five ephors (magistrates), the *gerousia* (council of elders), and the *apella* (assembly of citizens over 30 years old). The *gerousia* consisted of 28 citizens over 60 years old and the two kings. The *gerousia* prepared necessary legislation and put it to the assembly. The ephors were elected annually and while in office were the most powerful men in Sparta, more powerful even than the kings. Nonetheless, final decisions of war and peace were in the hands of the *gerousia* and the *apella*. All citizens could attend the assembly, but its power was limited to accepting or rejecting proposals put to it by the *gerousia*. In short, Sparta was governed by a complex, conservative system of checks and balances.

Our best information on the Spartan 'caste' system comes from the Classical period. The Spartiates, whose numbers may never have exceeded 10,000, were the rulers of Lacedaemonia. Each was given an estate of public land which was cultivated by slaves, leaving the Spartiate to spend virtually his whole life in military and public service. From birth he was subject to stern discipline. Weak or deformed children were left to die—some say cast over cliffs—on Taygetos. Stronger male children remained with their mothers until their seventh birthday. Their education in camps was supervised by young soldiers and discipline enforced by pack leaders; drill exercises and brutal competitive games figured largely. At 20 the Spartiate entered the army proper (perhaps after a period in the *krypteia*, or secret police, which was at intervals let loose upon the Helots). He was expected to marry but continued to live in barracks and to eat in a mess on prescribed rations supplied from his own estate. He became a full soldier-citizen at the age of 30.

Perioikoi, or 'dwellers around', lived in a number of villages in Laconia and neighbouring Messenia. They had no citizen rights but were free-men. Their only duty to the state was to serve, when called upon, as hoplites. The Helots were serfs and completely under the control of the Spartiates, whom they always greatly outnumbered. They consisted of the descendants of former inhabitants of Laconia and of surviving Messenians who were enslaved. They were obliged to cultivate the Spartiate's estates and to deliver the required produce from them.

Though the system itself had all the characteristics least acceptable to the 'democratic' ideal, either ancient or modern, the Spartan regime seems to develop its ruthlessly illiberal and wholly militaristic nature only about the time of the Persian Wars. From the Geometric period to the 6th century, Spartan arts flourished; pottery, sculpture in bronze, and basic architecture—though never opulent—kept pace with those of other cities. The music and dancing of Spartan festivals was famous throughout Greece. In the 7th century poetry flourished with the native Kinaithon, Terpander of Lesbos, Tyrtaios and Alcman—although Pausanias remarked that no people appreciated poetry less than the Spartans. By the 5th century every setback—the numerical inadequacy of the ruling caste, the earthquake of 464 BC, the chronic Messenian discontent—was countered only by greater austerity. This policy was superficially successful while the war machine functioned and the quality of Spartan troops made up for their dwindling numbers, but did nothing in the long run to stave off the inevitable effects of depopulation and an outmoded economy.

Little is known of the lives of Spartan girls, still less of Spartan women. Girls seem to have undergone a fairly rigorous athletic training (designed in large part to produce physically fit future child-bearers) that included racing, wrestling and boxing. They sometimes trained naked, sometimes in the short slit skirts that shocked other Greeks, and were celebrated for their dancing.

The poet Alcman said that compared to all others the Spartan dancing maidens stood out 'as if among a herd of cows someone placed a firmly-built horse with ringing hooves', while the Athenian playwright Aristophanes praised the 'nimble-footed maidens' who leapt not like does but 'like stags'. At the annual festival of the *Hyakinthia* at the Shrine of Apollo and Hyakinthos at Amyklai (*see below*), the girls actually competed in chariot races. Female competition in chariot races was not allowed at Olympia, or any of the other Panhellenic games. (The daughter of the Spartan King Archidamos, Kyniska, won a chariot race at Olympia—but only by entering, not racing, the chariot.) After marriage, these energetic maidens became invisible matrons, whose husbands lived in army barracks and visited them at night for sex. In short, the Spartan woman's main task after marriage was bearing and rearing future Spartiates; a high proportion of female babies, however healthy, seem to have been abandoned at birth. The most famous—and virtually the only—remark attributed to a Spartan matron is a mother's injunction to her soldier son to return from battle with his shield, or on it.

EXPLORING SPARTA

The Archaeological Museum

Open Tues–Sat 8.30–3; Sun 8.30–12.30; T: 27310 28575.

Sparta's handsome central plateia is dominated by the Dimarcheion (Town Hall). To the east, across busy Odos Palaiologou (Sparta's main north–south thoroughfare), on the square between Odos Aghios Nikolaos and Odos Palaiologou, the Archaeological Museum sits in a rose garden with sculptural remains, including a procession of statues of headless Roman dignitaries. The dignitaries were not decapitated; rather they were made to receive changeable, screw-in heads. In the days of the later Roman empire, when emperors came and went, this was an economical way to have an up-to-date representation of those in power.

Much of what is on display in the museum is unlabelled; there are some labels in Greek, some in English. Displays come from throughout Laconia and range from prehistoric finds from the Diros Cave to sculpture from the late Roman period. The bust of Leonidas and terracotta masks used in festivals are particularly fine. Helen's fabled charms do not appear to best advantage in the several Archaic sculptural reliefs on view.

The collection

The famous bust of a Spartan hoplite (5th century BC), thought to represent Leonidas, hero of Thermopylae.

Vestibule: Stelae and inscriptions once bearing inlaid votive sickles of iron, dedicated to Artemis Orthia (*see p. 307*) by boy-victors in ordeal contests. One stele even retains its sickle.

Room 1 (right): Roman mosaics from public and private buildings in 3rd- and 4th-century AD Sparta.

Room 2: Architectural fragments from the sanctuary of Apollo at Amyklai (*see p. 309*); reliefs of the heroised dead; Archaic reliefs, including Helen and Menelaus; terracotta figurines, plaques, also pottery from the Sanctuary of Zeus, Agamemnon and Alexandra–Cassandra (*see p. 309*).

Room 3: Leonidas in marble (5th century), upper part of a superb warrior statue, perhaps the memorial raised to Leonidas on his reburial at Sparta (it inspired the modern memorial at Thermopylae); Stele of Damonon, victor in chariot races, with a long mutilated inscription recording the circumstances of its dedication (5th century BC); colossal heads of

Hera (? Archaic) and Heracles (Hellenistic); other Archaic and Classical free-standing sculpture; votive stelae and inscriptions.

Room 4 (left): Terracotta votive masks, lead votive figurines and limestone reliefs from the Sanctuary of Artemis Orthia; kraters and amphorae showing Spartiate warriors in combat; statuary representing Heracles; Archaic bronze figurines; pottery and other votives from the shrine of Athena Chalkioikos and from the Menelaion (*see p. 307*) and Amyklai; burial *pithoi* and craters with relief decoration.

Room 5: Mainly Hellenistic and Roman sculpture, including Archaising. Head

of Artemis; Hermes; torso of Asclepius; Dioscuri; wild boar in steatite; fragmentary relief from a sarcophagus. Triglyph and two metopes from the acropolis; clay votive model of a Roman galley found in the sea off Cape Malea.

Room 6 (stair): Finds from Diros Cave (*see p. 329*). Pottery, stone, bone and terracotta.

Room 7 (upstairs): Prehistoric finds (pottery, bronzes and figurines) from various sites in Laconia, mostly cemeteries and including Pellana (two large palace-style jars), Epidauros Limera, Palaiokastro Gortynias; photographs of site at Pellana.

SPARTAN OR LACEDAEMONIAN?

According to mythology, Lacedaemon married Sparta, the daughter of Eurotas, and named the territory Lacedaemonia after himself, and its fairest city Sparta after his wife. In the *Iliad*, Homer uses Sparta and Lacedaemon more or less interchangeably. In classical times, Lacedaemon was the preferred term for both the main city and its territory. The inhabitants were called Lacedaemonians. The Roman preference for the term Sparta seems to have fixed it in historical consciousness, overshadowing Lacedaemon. It is possible that the term Sparta derives from *spartos*, the ancient Greek term for the broom plant which still grows and blooms in the spring on the slopes of Taygetos above the town.

The Museum of the Olive and Coumantaros Gallery

Two small new museums, each off Odos Palaiologou, look beyond Antiquity in their collections. The Museum of the Olive and Greek Olive Oil is at Othonos-Amalias 129 (*open 10–4 & 5–7 April 11–Oct 10; Wed–Mon 10–4 Oct 11–April 10; T: 27310 89315*). The museum, which opened in 2002 in a restored olive warehouse, chronicles all aspects of the olive in Greece. Photographs and displays of both household and industrial tools show how how olive oil was made, stored and used in Antiquity, and how that is done today. Some of the earliest exhibits include fossilised olive leaves from the island of Santorini from 50,000–60,000 BC, and reproductions of Linear B tablets mentioning olive trees and olive oil. Exhibits on how to make soap from olive oil include photographs, posters, and machinery from the Linardakis Factory in Kalamata, which produced soap from 1890–1993. The small museum shop sells olive oil, soap, and reproductions of some of the exhibit photos and posters. This is one of several new industrial museums in Greece (the Silk Museum in Serres, Macedonia and the Outdoor Museum of Hydroelectric Power in Dimitsana, Arcadia, are others). The Coumantaros Gallery (*Tues–Sat 9–3; Sun 10–2, closed Mon*), at the corner of Palaiologou and Thermopylon (north of the intersection of Palaiologou and Lykourgou), is a branch of the National Gallery of Athens. The gallery has temporary exhibits from Easter until autumn (*often closed in winter*).

The acropolis

Tues–Sun 8.30–3; T: 27310 28275. No admission charge at present.
At the top of Odos Palaiologou, beyond the Coumantaros Gallery, there is a modern memorial to Leonidas (*see p. 431*), whose body was brought here from Thermopylae and buried near the theatre, where the broken statue believed to represent him (exhibited in the Archaeological Museum) was found. To the left of the sports stadium a partially paved road runs through olive groves to the south gate of the acropolis (20m above the plain), the highest of Sparta's six low hills (the others were known as the Kolona, the Hill of Argive Hera, the Issorion, the Diktynnaion and the Hill of Armed Aphrodite). The acropolis walls were built between AD 267 and 386 and completed on the east side after the Slav invasion in the 8th century.

The course of the city walls has been traced for most of the 10km circuit. The walls of Sparta—which had boasted that it had no need for walls other than the Taygetos and Parnon mountain ranges—were a symptom of her decline. The first defences were made in 307–295 BC and supplemented when Pyrrhus threatened the city in 272 BC. By 218 BC walls and gates existed. These were strengthened by Sparta's last king, Nabis, against Flamininus, pulled down by the Achaeans in 188 BC and rebuilt by Appius Claudius Pulcher four years later.

The contour of the acropolis has been altered by a modern reservoir and the view is obscured by trees. Most of the (scanty) remains are Roman. Immediately inside the gate in the Roman defence wall is a brick-built Roman portico or stoa (2nd century AD), which some scholars have suggested incorporated the Persian Stoa, built from spoils of the Persian War, mentioned by Pausanias. The Roman stoa was some 188m long and 14.5m wide and, at least partly, double fronted, extending as a monumental revetment to the acropolis hill from a round building on the west—and may have continued along the east side. The façades probably had Doric columns, whose archaising characteristics may copy those of its much earlier predecessor. To the east there are barrel vaulted chambers (also visible to the east; some with facilities for the provision of water) at the lower level. Part of the east section was radically transformed in the 10th–12th centuries AD, perhaps into the monastery of Aghios Nikon Metanoeites, which is known from sources to have included a double-fronted stoa.

Late houses were built over the west end of the structure. (After the fall of Mistra, this was the centre of Byzantine Lacedaemonia.)

THE SPARTAN VOLTA

Virtually every Greek town has its evening *volta* (promenade), but Sparta's is famous. When the weather is fine—and sometimes even when it is not—Spartans flock to the main plateia for the evening promenade. In past years, unmarried women (usually chaperoned by their parents) walked one way around the square, while unmarried men the other way; there was a good deal of eye contact, but little conversation. From time to time, parents who had ideas of marrying their children would stop, feign surprise at running into each other, and chat, allowing the prospective matrimonial couple to do the same. Today's *volta* is more relaxed, with virtually no young woman chaperoned, with gaggles of men and women chatting (often on their mobile phones) and strolling together, or lounging in the cafés that line the east side of the square. Still, Sparta's *volta* remains an important clearing house for gossip, political scheming and matchmaking.

The theatre and Temple of Athena

If you follow the left-hand lane from the gate along the crest of the hill past the ruins of two 11th-century churches, and the remnants of one of the mysterious round buildings that turn up often at Greek sites, you reach (below; left) the 1st-century BC theatre. Next to the theatre at Megalopolis it is the largest in Greece, and shows signs of a massive rebuilding under the Romans, but much of its masonry went into late fortifications or was quarried for Mistra. New excavations and site clearance was resumed in the 1990s by the British School at Athens. The diazoma was rediscovered in 1992, along with signs of occupation and abandonment of the site in late Antiquity. The theatre, used for public meetings as well as theatrical performances, shows signs of having passed through three building stages: The earliest theatre had a movable stage building (evidently begun c. 30–20 BC and modified c. 78–79 AD and again in the early 3rd century AD), which was pushed into position on wheels. The grooves of the tracks can be made out and portions of the stage mechanism were discovered by British excavators here in 1997; scenery was also probably moved about on a wooden platform on wheels or rollers. The east parodos wall has more than 30 inscribed blocks, bearing lists of magistrates of the 2nd century AD. Around 400 AD, the stage building was incorporated into the site's fortifications.

Excavations in 1907 to the north unearthed the 6th-century BC **Temple of Athena Chalkioikos**, a building lined with bronze reliefs (*chalkiokos* means bronze) dedicated by Spartan warriors. At the beginning of the first Messenian revolt, the Messenian leader Aristomenes slipped into the sanctuary at night to hang up a shield with an insulting dedication. Today virtually nothing can be seen of the temple, and little remains of the usually overgrown Roman bath and gynmasium complex nearby.

Sanctuary of Artemis Orthia

Tues–Sun 8.30–3. No admission charge at present. NB: It is possible to walk from the Acropolis to the Sanctuary of Artemis Orthia in about 30mins, but the route mainly follows the busy Tripolis road and is best made by car. Leaving Sparta, on the Tripolis road, turn right and head downhill on the signposted path to the sanctuary.

Today often the scene of a gypsy encampment, with exceptionally determined child beggars, this was once the scene of the endurance tests by flogging that featured in the upbringing of Spartan boys. The youths were flogged until they bled; those who endured this torture with appropriate courage were awarded a bronze sickle, which they later dedicated here. There may also have been other contests of a milder sort; singing, oratory, and rougher games for boys of 10 and upward. The sanctuary existed in the 10th century BC, and in Archaic times comprised a walled enclosure with an altar on the east side and a small Doric temple on the west. In the 2nd or 3rd century AD the whole complex was reconstructed and a massive Roman theatre built to accommodate spectators, incorporating the temple almost as a stage set. Farther north along the Evrotas are a heroön and a huge stone altar. All in all—except for the gypsies—a gloomy and forlorn spot.

EXCURSIONS FROM SPARTA

Three sites give a glimpse of Sparta's Mycenaean past; one, the Menelaion, has impressive remains and superb location. The Shrine of Apollo and Hyakinthos has a pleasant situation, but virtually no ancient remains. Vapheio also has a nice location and it is possible to see, but not enter, the Mycenaean tomb where the gold Vapheio cups (now in the National Archaeological Museum in Athens) were found. All three sites can be visited in a half-day.

The Menelaion

Tues–Sun 8.30–3. No admission charge at present. The Menelaion is about 5km out of Sparta. To get there, leave town on the Tripolis road (going north) and turn right on the Geraki road immediately after the bridge across the Evrotas. At 4.5km a road (signed 'Menelaion') leads left to the chapel of Aghios Ilias. From the chapel, a footpath leads to the site (c. 20mins).

On the hill are low remains of the Menelaion, or Shrine of Menelaus and Helen, and a c. 15th-century BC mansion. There are other Mycenaean remains in the vicinity, suggesting that the site covered a large area, perhaps as much as a kilometre in length. The shrine's identification, originally based on the records of Pausanias, has recently been confirmed by the discovery of dedications to the unhappy couple. Although a shrine was surely here in the Mycenaean period, the present remains date from the 8th to the 5th centuries BC. The low walls of the Menelaion, built on several levels, are imposing and the view across the Laconian plain to Taygetos is superb.

Archaeologists C. Mee and A. Spawforth have suggested that the ramp on the west side of the Menelaion was 'thoughtfully provided for the sacrificial victims which might have balked at steps' (*Greece: An Oxford Archaeological Guide*).

Just below the summit to the northeast are Mycenaean remains uncovered in 1910 and since 1973. These consist of a 'mansion' with three distinct building periods (usually called Mansions 1 2, and 3) between the 15th and 13th centuries BC. The consequent profusion of walls, on two levels, is confusing for the non-archaeologist. What is important here is that the arrangement of rooms in all phases closely resembles (albeit on a considerably more modest scale) that of the developed Mycenaean palaces built a century and more later at Mycenae, Tiryns and Pylos. Mansion 1, dated to the 15th century BC, is one of the earliest known 'proto-palaces'. The mansion was destroyed by fire in c. 1200 BC and not rebuilt.

The Shrine of Apollo and Hyakinthos

To reach the Shrine of Apollo and Hyakinthos at Amyklai (modern Amykles), leave Sparta to the south on the Gythion road. Amykles (Ἀμύκλες) is signposted to the right; in the village, head left at the sign for the Temple of Apollo Amyklaios to the chapel of Aghia Kyriaki.

The chapel stands on the site of the *Amyklaion*, the shrine of Apollo and Hyakinthos, which was excavated by the German School in 1925. Ancient *Amyklai* itself, the capital of the Mycenaeans in Laconia, was probably at neighbouring Palaiopyrgi, the largest Late Helladic settlement (unexcavated) yet discovered in Laconia.

There is nothing whatsoever to see of the shrine, where the great festival of the *Hyakinthia* took place every July, except an inscribed base honouring a 3rd-century AD matron who participated in the rites here with appropriate 'modesty and reverence'. The site seems to have had continuous occupation since Mycenaean times (Hyakinthos is a pre-Greek deity). The sanctuary surrounded the Tomb of Hyakinthos, whom Apollo loved and accidentally killed; the hyacinth sprang from the youth's blood as he fell. The shrine included an Archaic statue of Apollo seated on a throne so elaborate that Pausanias said he would only summarise its decoration, lest he weary his readers.

The church of Aghia Paraskevi, to the south, may occupy the site of the Sanctuary of Zeus, Agamemnon and Alexandra–Cassandra, from which a huge Archaic votive deposit with hero-reliefs was unearthed close by in 1956.

Vapheio

Turn left just beyond the turn-off for Amykles on the Gythion road for the village of Vapheio. In 1888, the Greek archaeologist C. Tsountas found the famous gold cups and sealstones (now in the National Archaeological Museum in Athens) in an unplundered Mycenaean tholos tomb here. Some scholars suggest that the tomb may have belonged to the ruler of the Mycenaean settlement at *Amyklai*.

Spring blossom in the countryside near Sparta.

MISTRA

Open daily 8–5 in summer; 8–3 in winter; T: 27310 93377. The local bus stops at the main gate of the site of Mistra, at the foot of the hill. A modern road (often with tour buses hurtling up and down) ascends the hill to a point above Aghia Sofia (car park), providing the easiest approach to the kastro. It is best to enquire at the main gate whether this entrance is open. Stout shoes, binoculars, a hat, sunscreen, and water are recommended.

The road from Sparta runs west to the foot of Mt Taygetos, along the reedy banks of the Evrotas river and through a luxuriant plain, thick with orange, fig and mulberry trees; several restaurants and discos have invaded the countryside. The eroded mountainsides are scored with *langades* (deep gorges), each with its torrent when the snow on Taygetos melts. The gorge of Parori, the gloomiest and most forbidding ravine, has been identified both with the *Apothetai*, where the Spartiates used to expose their weakly children, and with the *Kaiadas*, or criminal pit, from which Aristomenes made a miraculous escape. Tripi, at the entrance to the Langada Gorge, also claims the dubious honour, however. Human remains recovered from a cave nearby seem to support the identification.

For much of the drive, the odd conical hill of Mistra stands out against the flank of Taygetos; gradually, the ramparts of the fortress, then the looming shape of the Palace of the Despots, the domes of churches, and the walls of hundreds of houses in this medieval city are visible. The modern village of Mystras (Μυστράς) stands at the entrance to the Mistra Gorge. The imposing statue is of the last Byzantine Emperor, Constantine XI, who was crowned at Mistra on 6th January 1449. One street was recently renamed in honour of Sir Steven Runciman, the great historian of Byzantium, whose *Mistra* (1980) is a graceful and erudite companion for any visitor.

EXPLORING THE SITE

One of the last outposts of the Byzantine Empire, Mistra was a flourishing city considerably larger than modern Sparta. In fact, the remains of Mistra are so impressive that generations of early travellers misidentified them as ancient Sparta.

Mistra is divided into three districts: the Lower Town (Katochora), with the cathedral and museum and the remains of many modest houses; the Upper Town (Chora), with the Despot's Palace and the homes of those wealthy enough to live in its vicinity; the Kastro (fortress) crowns the summit. Both the lower and upper town have a profusion of churches; many prosperous families had private chapels.

This division into three quarters is characteristic of Byzantine fortified cities and can be clearly appreciated from the Kastro itself, with its splendid view over the city and the Vale of Laconia. Until one reaches that vantage point, map or no map, one may be most taken with what one Byzantinist called Mistra's 'picturesque incoherence'. Quite helpful noticeboards in Greek and English beside the most important buildings explain aspects of the site.

HISTORY OF MISTRA

It was in 1249 that the Frankish prince William de Villehardouin, Prince of Achaea, began to build a palace and a fortress on this rocky spur of Taygetos which the Greeks called *Mezythra* (a kind of cheese, sometimes of a conical shape). William probably had two aims in fortifying Mistra: to have a stronghold against the marauding Slavs and to strengthen the Peloponnesian empire his father Geoffrey had seized from the Greeks after the Fourth Crusade. William had but ten years to enjoy his palace; in 1259 he fought at the Battle of Pelagonia alongside his father-in-law, Michael II, the Greek Despot of Epirus, in an attempt to overthrow the Byzantine emperor, Michael Palaeologus. Things went badly for William, who was defeated and captured by the Greeks. Some accounts say that he almost escaped, but was identified by his well-known buck teeth when plucked from his hiding place in a haystack. He gained his freedom by handing over his strongholds at Mistra, Monemvasia, Great Maina and Geraki. Even holding the fortresses William had surrendered, it took the Greeks another 50 years completely to reconquer the Peloponnese. Initially, Monemvasia was their seat of power, but in 1348, Mistra became the seat of the Despot (*see p. 315*) who ruled over the entire Peloponnese.

In the hundred years before it fell to the Turks in 1460, Mistra was a centre of learning, art and culture, which rivalled Trebizond and even Constantinople. The distinguished philosopher Gemistos Plethon, a student of Aristotle, Plato and Zoroastrianism, lived here (except for a brief sojourn in Italy) from 1407 until his death in 1452. Plethon's presence here attracted scholars from throughout the Greek world. Artists, assured of the patronage of the despots and prosperous citizens, came to paint frescoes in Mistra's multiplicity of chapels and churches.

Mistra was held by the Turks from 1460 until 1687, when much of the Peloponnese was captured by the Venetians. Under Venice (1687–1715) Mistra reached its second peak of prosperity, with a population of 42,000. Outside the city walls to the east, the already flourishing Jewish quarter increased in size. The mulberry trees on the plain below Mistra are reminders of its once-flourishing silkworm cultivation. On the return of the Turks, Mistra continued to prosper until it once more was a casualty of international affairs. In 1770, during the Russo-Turkish War, Albanian troops fighting for the Russians torched Mistra. The Turks themselves, under Ibrahim Pasha, burnt what was left to the ground in 1825, during the Greek War of Independence. After the refounding of Sparta in 1834, Mistra was virtually abandoned; some families settled further down the slopes in what is now the modern village of Mystras, which has a number of handsome homes from this period, one of which is being restored as a folk museum. The French School saved the site from complete ruin in 1896–1910, but it served as a battlefield in 1944 between various partisan forces. The last 30 families were moved by the Greek Archaeological Service in 1952, and wholesale reconstruction was undertaken.

The Lower Town

The Metropolis and museum

Despite being a fortified town, most of the churches that have survived are monastic foundations and are well preserved. The most important of all is the basilica of the Metropolis (1291), reached by a signposted path from the entrance gate. The Metropolis of Aghios Dimitrios; like many churches here (notably the Hodeghitria and Pantanassa; *see below*), combines the standard three-aisled plan of the Roman basilica with the domed Greek cross. The imposing cathedral stands in a spacious court with an antique sarcophagus and a fountain dated 1802, which was probably built on the site of an earlier fountain. Little survives of the Episcopal Palace, part of which gave place to monastic cells in 1754. In the cathedral floor a relief with a two-headed marble eagle is believed to commemorate the coronation here of the Emperor Constantine XI. The 17th-century walnut episcopal throne is richly carved. The basilica, probably begun in the 13th century, was altered in the 15th when a second storey, with a women's gallery, was added, along with five domes after the model of the Hodeghitria church (*see below*). As a result the original paintings in the nave were cut in two. Art historians suggest that the paintings were done by at least ten different artists in three periods. Those in the north aisle (portraits of saints; torture and burial of St Dimitrios; sufferers from dropsy and leprosy) are shown by their symmetry and repose to be the earliest works. In the south aisle are more realistic representations of prophets, the life of the Virgin, and the miracles of Christ (14th century). In the narthex, also 14th-century but by a different hand, is a *Last Judgement*. When Chateaubriand visited, he did not worry about who had painted what, but dismissed all the frescoes as resembling the 'daubings of the school that preceded Perugino'.

Next to the cathedral is the museum, housed in buildings erected by Bishop Ananias Lambardis, whom the Turks executed here in 1770. An iron grille in the courtyard wall covers a stone with dark stains—blood?—and an inscription commemorating his execution. The museum itself was founded by the Byzantinist Gabriel Millet (d. 1954), who did much to save Mistra from further ruin. Displays include a somewhat dusty collection of ecclesiastical garments and church plate, as well as sculptural and fresco fragments, and some distinguished icons.

Churches of the Lower Town

The path continues up to the 14th- or 15th-century **Evangelistria**, a simple mortuary chapel (two ossuaries) with good sculptural detail (notably the iconostasis), and lovely brickwork revetments. Just off the main street to the right is the **Vrontochion**, a great monastic complex, the richest of its time in the Peloponnese, the burial place of the Despots, with two churches. Both were built by the Archimandrite Pachomios, a shrewd politician and fund-raiser. The first **Aghii Theodoroi** (c. 1296), heavily restored in 1932, is Mistra's oldest surviving church.

Farther on, is the monastic church proper, the 'katholikon' of the **Panaghia Hodeghitria** (or Aphentiko), completed in 1322. It was the earliest church at Mistra

The 14th-century church of the Panaghia Hodeghitria.

built to a composite plan, a fusion of the basilica and the cross church with domes, an idea revived from earlier practice. It has a beautiful bell-tower, four small cupolas and a central dome (rebuilt, along with much of the structure, in the 19th century). There are also the remains of cells and a refectory. The interior is remarkable for its proportions, its purity of line, and the carved ornamentation. The marble facings that richly decorated the walls have disappeared. A side chapel on the north side of the narthex contains the tomb of Theodore II, with his frescoed portrait, both in the robes of the Despot (*Aphentis*) and in the monk's habit he wore when he rejected imperial concerns. Here also is the tomb of the founder Pachomios. In the corresponding south chapel the walls have copies of chrysobuls (imperial edicts) detailing the foundation, properties, and privileges of the monastery. The excellent frescoes, in bold colour, include the *Miracles of Christ* (narthex), with delicate angels who appear perfectly capable of flight; group of martyrs (in the northwest chapel); and a panel of *St Gregory the Illuminator of Armenia* (in the apse). Restoration work has made it possible to see individual brush strokes and the delicate shading and contouring of facial expressions. Some scholars have suggested that the sophistication of these frescoes points to artists from Constantinople having worked here; this would make sense, as the Abbot Pachomios clearly intended the Aphentiko to rival imperial churches such as Haghia Irene in Constantinople. Indeed it is possible that some of the inspiration for this structure was derived from Haghia Irene, as it is a solidly defined basilica with a dominating dome resting on piers and side galleries that rest on the columns of the nave.

Beyond the Evangelistria the road passes under a machicolated Gothic archway and higher up divides: by the right branch you enter the Upper Town (*see below*). The left branch leads to the Pantanassa.

The **Pantanassa**, the most beautiful of the churches of Mistra, was the last church built under the Despotate, and shows signs of western influence in some of its architectural details, such as the pointed Gothic arches in the belfry. Begun in 1365 by Manuel Cantacuzene, it was enlarged by John Frangopoulos, *protostrator* (minister) of the Emperor Constantine Palaeologus, in 1428. Today the Pantanassa belongs to a convent, whose nuns sometimes sell embroidery. Inside the convent courtyard, steps lead up to the church itself, with its a shaded portico commanding a fine view over the Evrotas valley. The Pantanassa's richly varied exterior decoration has three distinct zones: the lowest is plain stone; the middle has pointed Gothic arches and garlands; the top has the elaborate brickwork characteristic of so many Byzantine churches. A gallery over the narthex, reached by an external staircase, opens into the Gothic tower (splendid view; *not always open*). The side galleries are continued over the aisles as far as the apses.

The paintings in the lower registers of the church are post-Byzantine (with the exception of the fine portrait of Manuel Chatsikis in the narthex; 1445) and not terribly distinguished. The paintings in the galleries (binoculars are very useful here), on the other hand, are exceptional. Scholars of Byzantine art see in the decoration of Mistra's churches something of an international style, with hints of the colour and modelling of Giotto and Duccio, as well as the best of the Byzantine style. The Byzantinist David Talbot Rice has called these frescoes in the Pantanassa Monastery 'the very flower of late Byzantine art'. The *Raising of Lazarus*, with one bystander holding his nose against the stench from the grave, is particularly fine, as is the scene showing the absolute amazement of the startled figures pointing up to heaven when they found Christ's tomb empty after the Resurrection.

The Perivleptos

From the Pantanassa an unmarked path leads you down the open flank of the hill to the Monastery of the Perivleptos, with splendid lions over its entrance (1714). Only two buildings from the original extensive monastery remain. The church (latter half of the 14th century) in stone and brick, with pentagonal apses and an octagonal dome, has the pure style of three centuries earlier. Below the east end is an unusual little chapel with a tiled pavement. To the south of the church is a square battlemented tower, richly ornamented on its east face. The superb frescoes give a good idea of the iconography of a 14th-century Byzantine church, and some prefer them to those of the Pantanassa. The dome has retained its *Pantocrator*. Above the side entrance is a fine *Dormition of the Virgin*; in the Prothesis Chapel to the left, the *Divine Liturgy*, celebrated by Christ and the angels; in the bema, an *Ascension*; in the vaulting of the south transept, the *Nativity*; in the west nave, the *Transfiguration* (note the silhouette of Christ); in the south aisle, *Childhood of the Virgin*.

Returning towards the main gate you pass (on the right) the 18th-century House of Krevatas, a mass of ruins, like almost all the houses here. The chapel of Aghios Ioannis lies outside the walls near the Marmara Fountain. On the inner path which leads back to the Metropolis are the two small churches of Aghios Georgios (962, restored 1953) and Aghios Christophoros (14th century, restored 1954).

THE DESPOTS OF MISTRA

From 1349 until 1460, Mistra was ruled by a series of despots. While the Despot of Mistra (the term may be taken to mean 'lord' or 'master') was, in theory, subordinate to the emperor in Constantinople, in practice, he held virtually absolute power. Almost always, the Despot was a son or a brother of the emperor (often his heir presumptive, sent here for some training in imperial management). The Despots of Mistra were successively Manuel Cantacuzene (1349–80); Matthew, his brother (1380–83); and Demetrius (1383–84). Here, after his abdication in 1354, the Byzantine emperor John VI Cantacuzene lived with his sons as the monk Ioasaph Christodoulos (d. 1383). The Cantacuzenes were followed by the Palaeologi; Theodore I Palaeologus (1384–1407), his nephew, Theodore II (1407–43), who ended his days as a monk. Constantine Dragatses served as Despot from 1443–48. When Constantine was crowned Emperor Constantine XI in January 1449, his brother Demetrius became Despot and served from 1448–60, assisted for part of that time by another brother, Thomas. The emperor Constantine was killed in the defence of Constantinople as it fell to the Turk in 1453; the Despot Demetrius surrendered Mistra to the same foe in 1460.

The Upper Town

The Palace of the Despots

You enter the upper town by the Monemvasia Gate, through which the road to Monemvasia once passed. After passing below the remains of a tall 15th-century house with arcades and machicolations, and skirting the remains of a small mosque, you reach the square in front of the recently restored Palace of the Despots. This square was the heart of medieval Mistra, where citizens gathered to chat by a fountain, much as today's Spartans enjoy their evening *volta* in the main plateia. In Frankish times there were jousts here, with knights on horseback astonishing Greek locals with their elaborate armour and courtly combat. Throughout Mistra's history, this is where citizens gathered, in part because Mistra's steep terrain made this the only place in the entire city with enough level space for people to throng together.

The massive Palace of the Despots (*Anaktora*), was begun by William de Villehardouin (1249), and added onto by many who followed him; there is a handy plan in front of the Palace. Return visitors will have to decide whether they find the recent restorations admirable, or too much of a good thing. The Palace was always the best-preserved monumental Byzantine civic building in Greece; now it is in the process of becoming the most thoroughly restored. The Palace has two long wings, which meet at a virtual right angle. The wing nearest to the ruins of a mosque has four clearly discernable sections. The first was begun under the Franks (13th century; note the three pointed Gothic windows on the lower level, and five above). The second and third additions (kitchen and storage area) were made in the late 13th century. In the mid-14th century the fourth addition, with the private quarters of the Despot, was built. Beginning in the 14th century, and continuing well into the 15th, a series of despots added the second wing, with basement storage, ground-floor barracks, and a vast ceremonial room, with an Audience Chamber and Throne Room, above. The low stone bench that runs around this room provided seating for petitioners who came to see the despot—or even the Emperor himself, when he visited here in 1408 and 1415. Much of the Palace's façade was painted, and its flamboyant windows are framed in poros mouldings and covered with stucco.

At present, two sections of the Palace are open to the public: the kitchen (with a display suggesting a medieval kitchen) and a portion of the basement storage area, with an engaging display showing how the palace was built. One of the eight enormous fireplaces that piped heat up to the third floor Audience Chamber is clearly visible in the wall above the exhibit on brick- and tile-makers.

Behind the palace are other official buildings which extend to the massive Nauplia Gate, protected by an external redoubt. The road to Nafplion and Central Greece passed through this gate, hence its name.

Aghia Sofia and the Kastro

NB: If the church is locked, the guard on duty at the ticket booth at the upper entrance will sometimes have it unlocked.

Uphill to the west of the palace, beyond a small Turkish bath, is the church of **Aghia Sofia**, built in 1350 by the first Despot, Manuel Cantacuzene, as the katholikon of the Zoödotos monastery. It is possible that the emperor dedicated the church to Aghia Sofia, the Divine Wisdom, in tribute to Constantinople's great church of that name. This was the palace chapel, and the wives of several emperors are buried here. Theodora Tocco (d. 1429), wife of Constantine, is one; and Cleopa Malatesta (d. 1433), wife of Theodore II, another. The polychrome marble floor-paving is ornate, and gives some idea of the original richness of this royal chapel. Little remains of the frescoes except for some fragments (including a fine Nativity scene) preserved under the Turkish whitewash that was meant to obliterate them. There are also remains of the refectory and cells, and of the cistern. Mistra had running water piped up as far as the Despot's Palace; above, water came from cisterns, or was carried up from the fountains below.

From here you begin a steep ascent, passing under a small aqueduct, to the **Kastro**, built in 1249 by William de Villehardouin and repaired and re-fortified along existing lines by all who came after him. The plan, however, remains Frankish even though much of the masonry is later. The keep (564m) and the round look-out towers command a magnificent view, well demonstrating the kastro's strategic importance. It is possible, but quite dangerous, to walk the circuit of the walls.

On the descent, if you pass by Aghia Sofia and several ruined houses, you reach (right) the **Palataki** (Little Palace), a private Byzantine house which won its name from archaeologists impressed by its size and by the architectural distinction of its three floors. Steps lead down to **Aghios Nikolaos** (17th century), Mistra's only post-Byzantine church, whose frescoes include a scene of the *Seven Sleepers of Ephesus*, slumbering side by side.

CHRYSAFA, THE SHRINE OF ZEUS MESAPIOS & GERAKI

This excursion has to recommend it that you may encounter no other travellers and have a true sense of discovery when you find what you set out to see; it has as a drawback, especially in Chrysafa, that you may have trouble finding the guards and custodians who will help you locate what you are after.

Chrysafa (Χρύσαφα), with its clutch of churches with ornamental brickwork and frescoes, makes a good day trip from Sparta. The churches are usually locked, although those in town are usually open for services on Sunday morning. If you present yourself at the house of the priest next to the Church of the **Koimisis tis Theotokou**, in the centre of the village, he may escort you to the churches, if he is free and if you have not appeared at a meal or nap time. If he, or anyone else does this, a gratuity is indicated. If you are not able to get inside, be of good heart: the churches' locations and exterior decoration are well worth seeing. The Koimisis tis Theotokou (14th century), with frescoes, ornamental brick- and tilework, and decorative carved heads, is within the town itself, as is **Aghios Dimitrios** (1641), with its monumental modern bell-tower.

The **Panaghia Chrysafiotissa** (Our Lady of Chrysafa; 13th century) and **Aghios Ioannis Prodromos** (St John the Baptist; 14th century) are in the countryside about 1km south of town; keep a sharp eye out for the two faded blue signs on the main road out of town that point steeply downhill to the left. Plunge downhill onto the (presently) unpaved road that leads to the churches. Bear left almost immediately at the small blue and white sign for the churches (ignoring a modern dome-and-cross church visible on a hill to your right). In about 1km, you see a tower. Park, and walk toward the tower and the two churches. If you do this in the spring, keep an eye out for irate sheepdogs. Both churches were evidently part of a monastic complex; both have wall paintings, ornamental brickwork, and idyllic settings. Other neighbourhood churches include **Aghii Pandes** (1367), as yet unsignposted.

The Shrine of Zeus Mesapios

Beginning in 1989, members of the British School in Athens have conducted excavations at the Shrine of Zeus Mesapios, on a rounded hilltop 50m from east to west and 30m north to south, near the Monastery of Aghios Tesserakonda 5km northeast of Sparta and about 5km outside the village of Afisiou. The remains here are meagre, but the site is interesting and has fine views toward Sparta, Taygetos, and the Menelaion. The site is unfenced at present. Excavations were begun to see what could be learned before future plough damage destroyed the site, sometimes referred to as Tsakona. The discovery of numerous ithyphallic terracotta figurines, along with figurines of women squatting in a childbirth position, has led the excavators to speculate that this was some sort of fertility shrine. The grotesque simian faces of some figurines have been compared to masks in the Sparta Archaeological Museum, which citizens may have worn in ritual obscene dances, and which the dancing Helots mocked at public festivals may also have used. The sanctuary seems to have been in use from the 5th to the 2nd centuries BC and, after a period of little or no use, again in the 3rd and 4th centuries AD.

Geraki

The main Sparta–Geraki road takes you along the left bank of the Evrotas, heading into a large plain. At Skoura the road turns east. Two kilometres north of Skoura, at Melathria, on the hill of Profitis Ilias, a cemetery of Mycenaean chamber tombs was found. Beyond Goritsa you have a distant view towards Geraki across a wide valley.

Geraki (Γεράκι), a large village not much visited, has steep, narrow two-way streets; the plateia, with cafés and a restaurant, is pleasantly shaded. It occupies the site of ancient *Geronthrai*. Its imposing acropolis (591m) has walls in the cyclopean style, best preserved on the north and east. The acropolis is unfenced at present. It was investigated in 1905 by the British School (and by Dutch archaeologists in the 1990s). Initial conclusions that the acropolis walls are Mycenaean were questioned by the Dutch in the 1990s because of the paucity of Mycenaean remains found during excavation. The site seems, however, to have been occupied since the late Neolithic period, with the earliest architectural remains Early Helladic. Geronthrai seems to have been abandoned in the mid-3rd century BC, when quite possibly the inhabitants felt able to move onto the plain below. A small museum contains local finds.

Medieval Geraki

To get there, take the bypass round Geraki village. The site of Geraki is now fenced, and its most important medieval churches are usually locked. The phylax (guard) can be found most days between 9–1, and often in the afternoon, by enquiring at cafés in the main square, or on the road from the village (not the by-pass) to the kastro, or at the entrance to the kastro. Visible on a long detached ridge of Parnon, Geraki was one of the original 12 Frankish baronies. It preserves the remains of 15 small medieval churches and an imposing kastro, probably begun by Guy de Nivelet c. 1254. Along with Mistra and Monemvasia, Geraki passed from the Franks to Michael Palaeologus in 1262 as part of the ransom for William de Villehardouin (*see p. 311*). Thereafter, it was part of the Greek line of defence in the Morea, until Byzantium fell to the Turks in the 15th century.

The kastro, at the north end of the ridge (path in 20mins to the summit) has fine views of Parnon and Taygetos and of a string of windmills and a Turkish fort, some 3km out of the village of Kallithea. In medieval times, a system of bonfires and signal lights allowed the kastros at Mistra, Monemvasia, and Geraki to communicate. Aghios Georgios tou Kastrou, the basilican castle chapel (13th century), has both Frankish and Byzantine elements, including frescoes and a marble shrine, perhaps the tomb of Guy de Nivelet himself. The west door of the Zoödochos Pigi (1431), and the shrine in Aghia Paraskevi, both lower down the slope, have rude incised and sculptured decoration in a local Gothic idiom, as well as Byzantine frescoes. The frescoes in the citadel churches are being restored.

Further down the slope, within the boundaries of Geraki itself, are five more churches, all with frescoes (some restored), all with ancient and medieval blocks used in their fabric. Aghios Athanasios, with a heavily restored exterior, has been dated variously to the 12th and 14th centuries; the frescoes are probably 14th century. The little Evangelistria is 12th century, as are its frescoes. Aghios Ioannis Chrysostomos (13th century) has fine frescoes and, as its door jambs and lintel, marble blocks carrying an inscription which is one of the few surviving copies of Diocletian's *Edict of Prices* (4th century), an early (unsuccessful) attempt at price-fixing. Aghios Sozon's frescoes (12th–13th centuries) are damaged, as are those of Aghios Nikolaos (13th century).

Traces of Ancient Sparta en route to Monemvasia

The village of *Krokeai* (modern Krokeës) was famed in Antiquity for its stone quarries (*Lapis lacedaemonius*). The ancient town lay to the southeast of its modern counterpart and the quarries beyond. Traces of ancient *Helos* lie among rice and cotton fields 3km outside Vlachiotis, a depressing village, which is connected by road with Geraki (17km). By tradition, Helos was the first town to be enslaved by the Spartans, providing an etymology for the word 'Helot'.

MONEMVASIA

Monemvasia (Μονεμβασιά; 300m high; 1.8km long), one of the most important medieval cities in Greece, is often called the Gibraltar of Greece, or simply 'the rock'. Monemvasia's name comes from the single entrance ('*moni embasis*') through which it is reached from the landward side. Once this was a promontory, linked to the mainland by a long-since eroded natural stone causeway. Today, an artificial causeway links Monemvasia's lowering bulk to the mainland. This is one of the most spectacular places in Greece to arrive from the sea.

Unlike Mistra, Monemvasia was never abandoned and never became an absolute ghost town, although as recently as the 1970s most houses were deserted and many were falling down, and only one small restaurant awaited visitors and catered to the 32 permanent inhabitants. Since then, the Byzantine Lower Town has been substantially restored and has a number of excellent small hotels, restaurants, and shops selling handicrafts, local wine, ceramics and guide books. There is also a noticeable scattering of restored old houses, now holiday homes.

HISTORY OF MONEMVASIA

The rock's sheer sides and height gave it enormous strategic importance as a lookout point and potential fortress for southern Laconia and the sea routes past the harbour at *Epidauros Limera* (*see p. 324*). The earliest name known to have been attached to the site was *Minoa*, a name that hints at Cretan influence—of which no traces remain. Successive waves of conquerors had their own names for the rock: it was *Monemvasia* to the Byzantines, *Napoli di Malvasia* to the Venetians, *Malvoisie* to the French, and *Menefsche*, the violet city—a tribute to the colour of the cliffs at sunset—to the Turks. The Venetian and French names pay tribute to the local wine, Malmsey, a famous wine in the middle ages. The younger brother of King Richard III of England is said to have drowned in a butt of it.

There are hints that the Greeks of Laconia took refuge here during the Slav invasions of the 4th and 5th centuries, but the first significant settlement seems to have been established by the Byzantine emperor Maurice in the 580s. By the mid-8th century, imperial documents referred to Monemvasia as the most important city on the east coast of the Peloponnese. The fortress city, whose Lower Town was girded by seaward and landward walls, withstood the Arab pirates who dominated the Mediterranean in the 8th and 9th centuries, and repulsed an attack by the Normans of Sicily in 1147. By the time of the Crusaders' conquest of the Peloponnese in the 13th century, Monemvasia's population was at least 40,000. William de Villehardouin laid siege to it in 1246; the city surrendered three years later when there were no more cats or rats to eat. In 1260, William's expansionist dreams got the better of him; he was soundly defeated by the Byzantine Emperor Michael VIII Palaeologus, and the rock once more became an outpost of the Byzantine empire.

Monemvasia was not merely of strategic importance; it was also the commercial capital of the Byzantine Morea, and enjoyed special trading privileges. Like Mistra, Monemvasia had a profusion of churches and monasteries and was a centre of learning. After the fall of Constantinople in 1453, Monemvasia passed to a succession of foreign overlords: the Pope (1460–64), the Venetians (1464–1540 and 1690–1715), and the Turks (1540–1690 and 1715–1821). When the Venetians were defeated in 1540, many of the local Greeks fled, destroying their famous vineyards as they went—and taking some vines with them to new homes. Some say that the wine of Santorini is a direct descendant of the medieval Malmsey.

Humiliatingly, during the last period of Turkish occupation, the small community of Greeks that still lived here (perhaps 150 families) largely supported themselves by refining and exporting the red dye used to colour Turkish fezes. Monemvasia was the first fortress to be liberated when the Greek War of Independence broke out in 1821; the Turkish garrison first surrendered and then was massacred—a not-uncommon occurrence on both sides during the war.

EXPLORING MONEMVASIA

Like Mistra, Monemvasia is a fortified medieval city, encircled by walls, crowned by a fortress, with an Upper and Lower Town. Unlike Mistra, it is also a thriving holiday destination. Many bus tours have added a stop in Monemvasia to their itinerary. In consequence, Monemvasia is at its best in the early morning and at night, when it is usually quiet. At weekends and in summer, a hotel reservation is essential, although it is sometimes possible to find a room on the mainland. Fewer than 100 locals live here year-round, while another thousand live just across from the rock on the mainland in Gefyra (Γέφυρα). Odos Ritsos, the main thoroughfare, can be clogged with visitors on summer weekends, with travellers videocam-ing each other and the occasional donkey that passes by, often carrying supplies for a house that is being restored. The causeway from the mainland, across which all these visitors and donkeys come, links the mainland and the rock itself. Monemvasia's most famous son, after whom its main—and virtually only—street is named, is the great 20th-century poet Iannis Ritsos. He is buried in the small cemetery on the causeway. At times, Ritsos's poems, set to music by Mikis Theodorakis, can be heard on the radios and CDs playing in the cafés that have sprung up to serve the Greek and foreign tourists who have turned Monemvasia into one of Greece's chic destinations. The causeway (20mins on foot) ends at the narrow town gate in the impressive west wall, with its towers and bastions, which descends precipitously from the Upper Town to the sea. Inside, the two- and three-storey houses in the Lower Town are closely packed and the cobbled streets steep, narrow, slippery and intricate. It is almost impossible not to get lost here at night; unlit narrow passageways twist and turn unexpectedly (torch recommended), and several stepped streets dead-end against garden walls.

The Lower Town

The present 'agora', strung out along Odos Ritsos, with shops, cafés, hotels and restaurants, probably reflects the main Byzantine street and artisans' quarter. Above the main plateia, Odos Ritsos widens slightly, and the handsome stone houses, many with fine gardens, often with bougainvillea, are less narrow. Some of the finest houses in the Lower Town have been restored as hotels; the Stellakis House, with its enviable seaside balcony, and marble door and window frames, is part of the Hotel Malvasia (*see p. 337*).

In its heyday, Monemvasia had more than 40 churches and monasteries, of which a handful remain. The 13th-century **cathedral** (*open much of the day; box for offerings just inside the entrance*), the largest medieval church in Laconia, stands across from a Venetian cannon in the small plateia just off Odos Ritsos. A stone relief of the lion of St Mark over the lintel of the house beside the cathedral is another reminder of the Venetian presence here. The portal was rebuilt in 1687 with Byzantine fragments, including a cornice with two awkwardly dancing peacocks. Inside, the church is somewhat bare and gloomy, in large part because robbers stole the cathedral's valuable icons in 1980. Massive piers with pointed arches support the heavy barrel-vaulted nave and aisles. The cathedral's dedication to *Elkomenos Christos* (Christ in chains), commemorates Christ's sufferings before His crucifixion. The famous icon here that showed the scene was purloined by a Byzantine emperor and taken off to Constantinople, where it disappeared.

Opposite the cathedral, Aghios Pavlos, built in 956 and transformed by the Turks into a mosque, serves as a small but pleasant **Archaeological Museum**, where an admirable attempt has been made to let the exhibits (including clay pipes, drinking vessels and sculpture) tell something of life here through the centuries (useful guide book).

Just above the museum stands the decayed Panaghia Kritiki (or Myrtidiotissa) and farther on, near the sea, the 17th-century **Panaghia Chrysafiotissa**. For some years, this church housed an icon of the virgin which locals said 'flew' here from a church at Chrysafa, outside Sparta (*see p. 317*). The inhabitants of Chrysafa suspected that more than a miracle might be involved, and reclaimed the icon, which later 'flew' back here. In time, the Chrysafians were pacified with a reproduction. The celebration of the *Panaghia Chrysafiotissa* on 2nd May is Monemvasia's greatest festival. Nearby is the large Aghios Nikolaos (1703). Other churches scattered through the lower town include a double building dedicated to Aghii Dimitrios and Antonios, Aghia Paraskevi, Aghii Saranda and the Panaghia Katelchoumena.

The Kastro and Aghia Sofia

The visit to the fortress and church is best done first thing in the morning, as there is little or no shade on the ascent or at the summit. Kastro open most days 8am–7pm. No admission charge at present. Aghia Sofia open all day most days. Likewise no admission charge at present.

Just inside Monemvasia's main gate, a sign points along a narrow path that zigzags uphill, passing under several impressive archways, to the **Kastro**, sometimes called the *Goula*, perhaps from an Albanian or Turkish term for a fortification. The original entrance was via a path and a gate (still visible) on the north side of the promontory: this was blocked by the Turks with what the Venetians came to call the *Muro Rosso*. The ascent along the present path is designedly difficult; any attackers would have found it virtually impossible to storm the Kastro, whose defenders could have rained fire down on them from the parapets above. Bullet holes in the walls and main gates along the ascent attest to past combats here. At the massive iron-reinforced tunnelled gate to the Upper Town, with an inscription stating 'Christ Reigns Here', it is possible to make out the opening through which boiling tar could be poured on attackers. The Upper Town lies in shambles, in part because of an explosion in the munitions storehouse in the fortress in 1689. What remains today is a confusing thistle-infested wasteland of cisterns (into which it is all too easy to tumble) and the ruins of houses, mosques, churches, the fortress, and the defensive walls that ringed the summit. Snakes are not unknown here. Beginning in the early 1990s, the British School at

Athens and the Greek Archaeological Service has conducted a Survey of Upper Monemvasia in the hopes of better understanding the 'growth and functions' of the complex. Monemvasia had no springs, no wells, and its only source of water was rain. The survey has identified numerous small private and three large civic cisterns (? 9th century AD) for gathering rainwater on the citadel; the archaeologists noted that slugs were a 'visible menace' for those who explored the massive Bastada Cistern.

The church of **Aghia Sofia**, built against the sheer edge of the cliffs, dates back to at least the 13th century, as do some of the frescoes. The church was restored in 1958. The plan, a domed cruciform church with octagonal support, is similar to that of the great church at Daphni, outside Athens. A two-storey Venetian loggia stands in front of the church and there are remains of a convent nearby. Inside the church, a *mihrab*, the niche in a mosque wall facing Mecca, is a reminder of the Turkish occupation. As was their custom, the Turks whitewashed the frescoes, some of which nonetheless remain, including four frescoed medallions in the squinches, above which a 16-sided drum of impressive proportions supports the dome. In the sanctuary, frescoes show the *Ancient of Days* in the vault; busts of saints in medallions in the drum of the dome; and *Christ Pantocrator* between worshipping angels in the narthex, above the entrance to the nave.

The views down over the red-tiled house roofs and church domes of the Lower Town are spectacular; on exceptionally clear days in winter, Crete may be seen across the sea.

The coast around Monemvasia

About 5km north of Monemvasia, a left turn at Aghios Ioannis (also signposted 'Epidauros Limera Archaeological Site') leads in about 4km to the seaside hill crowned by the remains (fortifications most prominent) of *Epidauros Limera*, a colony of Epidaurus in the Argolid and one of the free Laconian cities. There are remains of the Classical fortifications, but not of the four sanctuaries Pausanias admired; the beach overlooking the harbour, which was important in Antiquity, is excellent, with the multi-coloured pebbles Pausanias noted.

The port of Neapolis in the south, lined with largely unappealing holiday flats and small hotels, fronts the Voiatic Gulf; this and the peninsula (Vatika on most maps) are named after the free Laconian town of *Boiai*, scant remains of which are on the shore south of town. The Vatika peninsula (4WD often useful) is a hiker's delight, with a number of charming villages (including Faraklo, Kato Kastania and Velanidia), castles, most notably Aghia Paraskevi near the hamlet of Mesochori) and beaches (especially Aghios Pavlos).

SPARTA TO GYTHION

The road from Sparta to Gythion (46km) runs beside orange groves (and past several kilometres of garages, supermarkets, furniture stores and an army base), crossing one tributary of the Evrotas after another. At Trapezanti, a road leads left for Palaiopanaghia, from which a steep but driveable track leads to the climbers' refuge at Aghia Varvara (c. 27km) on Taygetos. From the refuge (1399m), the summit of Taygetos (2404m; Profitis Ilias) can be climbed.

As the orange groves outside Sparta give way to olive groves and mulberry plantations, the road passes the turn for Xirokambi, where the torrent is spanned by a single-arched bridge in Hellenistic polygonal masonry. The turn (23km) for Vasilaki leads to the church of Aghios Ioannis Prodromos, with 13th-century frescoes. The road ascends, climbing through wooded country. From the summit (300m) there are fine views of the Helos plain and the Laconian Gulf. Aghios Nikolaos gives access (*rough track from plateia, and path*) to the castle of Bardounia, guarding a pass over Taygetos. Near the village of Aigies are the ruins of *Aegeiai*, which had a temple to Poseidon by a lake.

Gythion

The port town of Gythion or Gytheion (Γύθειο)—where Helen fled with her lover Paris in the elopement that sparked the Trojan War—has a pleasant waterfront. Gythion is the ancient and modern port of Sparta, and the second largest town in Laconia, the seat of an eparchy, and the eastern entrance to the Mani. With the advent of excellent roads into the Mani, tourism is increasingly an important source of revenue, although olive oil continues to be produced here. Gythion has Neoclassical houses, steeply stepped streets running up to its acropolis, an energetic seaside promenade and a bustling daily market just off the harbour. It is flanked by excellent sand beaches.

In Antiquity, the inhabitants of Gythion claimed Heracles and Apollo as joint founders. Classical tradition speaks of Minyan colonists and Phoenician traders in purple dye. The town became the naval arsenal and port of Sparta, and was sacked by the Athenian admiral Tolmides in 455 BC. Epaminondas of Thebes besieged it in vain. Nabis of Sparta (2 BC) rebuilt and fortified the site. Under the Romans, Gythion was the most important city of the League of Free Laconians.

The ancient city was to the north of the harbour. In 1999–2000, the discovery of three graves on Odos Ermou led archaeologists to think that the ancient town extended further east than previously thought. The late Hellenistic theatre (excavated 1891), near an army post, is c. 250m from the north end of the seafront (signs). Some of the front-row throne-like seats for dignitaries are preserved. Nearby, various Roman buildings, including a bath, have been found. The site museum contains local antiquities.

According to legend, when Paris and Helen eloped from Sparta, they spent their first night together at the islet of Marathonisi, the ancient *Kranaë*, now connected to the mainland by a causeway. Before the lovers continued to Troy, Paris erected a statue here to the Aphrodite of Erotic Love. When Menelaus reclaimed Helen at the end of the Trojan War, he destroyed the statue of Aphrodite and pointedly erected in its place statues to Themis (Justice) and Praxidica (Punishment). Some prehistoric finds have been made here and the chapel sits on ancient foundations. The Tsanetakis tower house has been restored and is used as a local Historical and Ethnological Museum (*open Tues–Sun 8.30–3; no admission charge at present*). A scattering of tables under the pine trees makes this a popular (if mosquito-ridden) picnic spot.

INTO THE MANI

The road from Gythion to Areopolis is good. If you wish to take in Cape Matapan (the ancient Tainaros, in mythology one of the entrances to the Underworld), the coast road is much better than the inland route. NB: The peninsula has been cut through by roads that now make visiting its once-isolated villages, tower-houses and chapels easy enough for tour buses to hurtle through on 'day tours'. Almost all tours stop at the Caves of Diros, south of Areopolis, which means it is best to visit early in the morning. Almost no tours spend the night in the Mani—which makes it a pleasant place to spend a night or more.

The austere Mani (Μάνη), or Maina, is the 77-km spur of Mt Taygetos that stretches to Cape Tainaron (Matapan) at the southernmost tip of the Peloponnese. The Mani has long been famous for its blood-feuds and dirges, tower-houses and chapels. It is the subject of what many consider the finest book written in English on Greece in the 20th century: Patrick Leigh Fermor's *Mani*. No other part of the Peloponnese has led a more isolated and independent life. As recently as 30 years ago, visiting here involved a great deal of waiting for the occasional bus and a good deal of walking. Now, secondary roads link most villages to the main roads across the peninsula.

The Mani has two distinct parts: the relatively green Outer, or Messenian, Mani includes the west coast from the Bay of Itylo (Oitilo), also known as the Bay of Limeni, north to Kalamata. (*It is described below on p. 333; map p. 340.*) Deep Mani is south of the pass from Itylo in the west to Gythion on the east coast, and is itself divided into Inner Mani (along the Messenian Gulf) and Lower Mani (along the Laconian Gulf). Inner Mani is known locally as Kakavoulia ('Evil Council') or Kakavouna ('Evil Mountains'). The terracing and wild wheat on the barren mountains are a reminder of the time before most Maniots fled their harsh life here; olive trees, stunted by the fierce wind resemble miniature bonsai trees. By contrast, prickly pears and thistles grow to considerable heights, and are festooned with sticky webs made by memorably large spiders.

With the notable exception of Areopolis, which has several hotels and restaurants, as well as a number of shops, most Maniot villages are perched on apparently inaccessible mountain ledges. Many do not have a bakery, let alone a grocery. Until recently, in summer the Mani was a place for the very old and the young, as families hard at work in Athens and abroad sent their children to their grandparents. In recent years, Maniots are beginning to return, and the sound of the cement mixer is heard in the land, as abandoned houses are restored with an eye to retirement, or even development for tourism. Still, there are fewer than 5,000 year-round residents here, as opposed to the 30,000 that Leake noted when he visited in 1806.

The Mani offers one of Greece's most distinctive and harmonious combinations of landscape and architecture: grey limestone tower-houses, some four storeys tall, cluster in villages that, from a distance, seem to be outcroppings of the mountains themselves. Almost all of the Mani's churches, many dating from the 9th–11th centuries, are built in spots that must have been chosen for their spectacular view.

HISTORY OF THE MANI

Seemingly inconsequential in Antiquity, the Mani flourished in the Middle Ages—which some say lasted here into the 19th century. The area was extensively settled in the Neolithic period, and there is some archaeological evidence of activity in Mycenaean times, through to the 9th century BC. Urban settlements are known to have existed since Homeric times when *Messe*, *Las* and *Oitilo* contributed ships to the expedition against Troy. The Dorians established small city-states which later became satellites of Sparta. As Sparta declined, many towns formed the Confederation of Free Laconians, whose independence was recognised by Augustus, while the rest of the Peloponnese was subject to Rome. Their descendants acquired the name of Maniots and continued in the same independent spirit. They clung to paganism until the reign of Basil I (867–86), but when the Mani converted to Christianity, it embarked on a frenzy of church-building, in the 10th–12th centuries. The Frankish invaders of the mid-13th century, as was their wont, built or restored fortresses. Although Byzantine rule was re-established in the Peloponnese after 1259, the Mani led something of a separate existence. Most Maniots lived in clans commanded by chieftains and did not welcome strangers. Indeed, the strongest Maniot chieftans cunningly exploited the endemic confusion caused by the attempts of the various foreign powers—notably the Turks and Venetians—to control the area. Until well into the 19th century, blood feuds were common in the Mani, and tower-houses served both as homes and fortresses. As Colonel Leake recorded, 'To pull down the adversary's house is generally the object and end of the war'. During conflicts, women (whose principal role was to bear sons, colloquially known as 'guns') were allowed out to tend the crops and the wounded and to bury the dead. One legacy remains of these feuds: the *mirologia* (dirges), which Maniot women still sing at funerals.

The Maniots boast that even when the rest of the Peloponnese fell to the Turk in 1460, the Turks never truly subdued the Mani. A series of sultans appointed a series of powerful Maniot leaders as Bey of the Mani, and the region largely benefited from the benign neglect of the Ottoman overlords. Nonetheless, it was the Maniot leader Petrobey Mavromichalis who led the Maniot uprising against the Turks in 1821 in the conflict that became the Greek War of Independence. Once independence was won, however, the Maniots strongly resented merging their own freedom in the new Greek kingdom, and were with difficulty incorporated into Greece. Indeed, it was two members of the Mavromichalis clan who assassinated the first President of Greece, Ioannis Capodistrias in 1831 (*see p. 234*). Today the Mani remains profoundly conservative, despite the growth of tourism. Travellers of either sex wearing shorts are more likely to be looked on askance here than in almost any other part of Greece—and are guaranteed to lacerate their legs on the undergrowth, a dense mixture of thorns, prickly pears, and thistles.

Across the Mani to Areopolis

Just out of Gythion, the medieval castle of Gythion, known locally as *To kastro tou Goula*, overlooks the village of Mavrovouni. About 3km after Mavrovouni, on a prominent sandy hill (Skina, right), Mycenaean chamber tombs were found. The road crosses the fertile and marshy plain of Pasavas and then turns inland through woodland. The first of the Mani's many towers (many medieval) stand on the hills. The ruined Frankish **castle of Pasavas**, built in 1254, and incorporating fragments of ancient Greek masonry, stands on a sheer cliff left of the road (8km). This was probably the site of Classical *Las*, but no Mycenaean remains have so far come to light to justify identification with the Laas of the *Iliad*. There are fine views. The fine enceinte is best reached by a steep path starting from just before the sign to the village of Chosiari. If in doubt, get directions at the family-run roadside Kali Kardia restaurant (*T: 27330 93250*), which, incidentally, serves good *spitiko* (homestyle) food.

Beyond Karyoupolis, probably founded as a stronghold in the 6th or 7th century AD, with a castle and a fortified settlement of c. 1800, a picturesque defile emerges high above Limeni, the harbour of Areopolis. The road from Itylo is joined on the bare grey slopes of Profitis Ilias (813m). The equally grey bulk of **Kelefa**, the long-walled frontier post erected by the Ottomans in the 17th century to control the Maniots, dominates the landscape. **Areopolis** ('Αρεόπολη), with many of its houses, buildings and cobbled streets made from the same limestone that was used at the fortress of Kelefa, can itself seem very grey. The tower-houses, lowering over the narrow streets are handsome, with their narrow windows and slate roofs. The main plateia on the outskirts of town is charmless, despite several restaurants and an imposing statue of Petrobey Mavromichalis, the Maniot hero of the War of Independence (*see p. 327 above*). The main street into the old section of Areopolis runs west from the plateia to the church of Aghii Taxiarchi (1798) with its tall campanile and primitive reliefs of martial saints and astrological symbols. A 20-min walk downhill past either the Tsimova or Kapetanakou hotels leads to Aghios Ioannis, with fine frescoes.

South into the Mani for caves and churches

Good roads make it possible to see a considerable amount of Deep (Inner) Mani, with its tower villages, chapels, seaside villages, and the Pyrgos Dirou caves. The stunted vegetation of Inner Mani (where cacti are often taller than olive trees) is vividly memorable. The excursion described below involves leaving the main road and taking lesser (not always paved) roads to see churches and villages.

NB: It is always a good idea to stop at the Dimarcheion (Town Hall) in Areopolis to see if the elusive guard with the church keys is available. If not, some of the churches are open early in the morning or at twilight, or on Sundays. It never hurts to ask anyone you see near one of the churches where you might find the keys. As a certain amount of exploration and back-tracking is involved in seeing the churches, it is possible to see many, but by no means all the most important chapels in a day. Roadsigns pointing to the chapels are elusive and impermanent.

Two books are invaluable: Peter Greenhalgh and Edward Eliopoulos's Deep into Mani *and Bob Barrow's* The Mani *(the latter often available in Areopolis).*

Typical rural Maniot church, diminutive in size, built of grey limestone, with a small belfry.

The landscape south of Areopolis, dotted by tower-houses, is dominated by the Kakavoulia and the Sangias range (1218m), which rises between Pyrgos Dirou and Kotronas on the east coast. A turning off the main road south from Areopolis leads from the nondescript hamlet of Pyrgos Dirou to the **Bay of Diros**. Here two spectacular caverns, Vlikada (or Glyfada; *open daily 9–7 in summer; 9–3 in winter incl. boat on underground lake. T: 27330 52222*) and Alepotripa ('fox-hole'; *closed for some years*), were opened to the public in 1963. This is a very popular destination with Greeks; and on summer weekends there is often a long wait for a tour boat.

The caves were discovered when a local dog disappeared into a sinkhole and returned home three days later, covered in red clay, arousing the curiosity of a local spelunking archaeologist, Anna Petrocheilou. Both caves have stalactites and stalagmites, produce sonorous echoes when visitors call out, are rumoured to contain giant eels, and are lit by electricity. Alepotripa has yielded extensive Neolithic finds. There is a museum of Neolithic material found in the caves, which usually keeps the same hours as the caves. Recent excavations in a third cave (Kalamakia; *not presently open to the public*), near Areopolis, have produced signs of habitation by the Neanderthals of the Mani between 100,000 and 40,000 BC.

Some two dozen of the Mani's distinctive primitive barrel-vaulted chapels (probably 9th century) and small domed Byzantine churches (mainly from the 11th and

12th centuries) are clustered between Pyrgos Dirou and the little port of Gerolimenas. Often these churches are hidden in the folds of the hills, their presence sometimes revealed by stands of cypress trees. Two **chapels of Aghios Michaïlis Taxiarchis** (signposted on the main road just south of Pyrgos Dirou) are at Glezou and at Charounda. Both have the elaborate brickwork set in decorative fan-shaped bands around windows and in herringbone patterns in the exterior walls that distinguishes so many Maniot churches. A left turn toward Briki (ruins of small monastic community) leads on to Vamvaka, where the church of **Aghios Theodoros** is dated by an inscription to 1075. There are fine marble carvings around the door and set in the walls. A right turn leads to Erimos, with the (heavily restored) domed cruciform church of **Aghia Varvara** (1150), distinguished by its fine proportions and masonry. Mezapos, possibly the site of Homeric *Messe*, lies on the coast.

On this road a right turn past the hamlet of Aghios Georgios and a walk 10mins downhill between two tower houses leads to the 12th-century **church of the Episkopi**, once the seat of the Bishopric of Maina. The fine frescoes are mainly 12th century, with a *Last Judgement* in the narthex. Church and frescoes have been restored. Episkopi's perfect proportions, ornamental brickwork, and idyllic situation on a hillside overlooking the Bay of Mezapos are enchanting. On the shores of the bay, modern homes threaten the solitude of several farms and the elegant little 12th-century chapel of Vlacherna. On a sharp-edged slope to the west of Episkopi, what appears to be a ruined sheep-shed, is all that remains of the **chapel of Aghios Procopios**. The absence of figures in the frescoes and the presence of simple painted crosses, has led scholars to date Aghios Procopios to the 9th-century Iconoclastic period.

Jutting into the sea, on the promontory of Tigani ('frying pan'), stands the **Castle of Maina**, the Frankish fortress erected by William de Villehardouin in 1248. An earlier wall with three towers on this promontory may be Mycenaean. A considerable portion of the ramparts remain. There are the ruins of one of the largest (22m by 15m) and earliest Christian basilicas (5th–6th centuries). To reach it turn right to the hamlet of Stavri (Tsitsiris Castle Hotel) and the conical hill of Aghia Kyriaki (45mins walk; no shade).

Kita (Koita), now almost depopulated, was reported by Leake to have 22 towers and almost 100 usually feuding families. Above Kita the decayed church of Aghii Asomati has a carved marble iconostasis. The village of Kato Boularioi has the **Anemodoura tower**, one of the earliest towers (possibly 1600), built of huge dry stones tapering to the top. There is also the well-preserved late 18th-century tower of the Mantouvalos family. Just above Ano Boularioi is the cruciform 11th-century church of **Aghios Stratigos**, its dome supported by Roman Ionic columns. It contains an almost complete cycle of frescoes (mainly 12th century). An offshoot of the main road leads down to Gerolimenas, a small fishing village (and increasingly popular Greek summer day-trip and holiday destination), where boats no longer call. Beyond, on the main road, in Alika, there are two inscribed stelae in the square. One is the dedication to Gaius Julius Laco by the League of Free Laconians, the other to an 'excellent citizen' named Tanagros from his own 'City of the Tainarians'.

Vatheia, one of the Mani's celebrated tower villages.

The southern tip

The coastal hamlet of Kyparissos, ancient *Kaenipolis*, was one of the most important cities in the Messenian Gulf in the 1st century AD and later. There are extensive remains round the two bays of Almiros and Psarolimeni and up to the village of Alika. On a headland, the hill of the Metamorfosis, stands a ruined 19th-century tower surrounded by fragments of marble, possibly the site of Pausanias' Megaron of Demeter; there are remains of a monumental building to the west. By the beach the church of **Aghia Paraskevi** incorporates ancient marble and pieces of columns possibly from the Temple of Aphrodite mentioned by Pausanias. Behind the church is a massive inscribed stele in honour of the emperor Gordian. In the olive groves southeast are the ruins of the basilica of **Aghios Petros** (early 6th century), incorporating ancient material. The jambs of the west door are two inscribed stelae, to the Empress Julia Domna (wife of Septimius Severus) and to a generous citizen Lysicrates.

The winding main road follows the coast before climbing steeply inland to **Vatheia**, which is one of the most spectacular of the tower villages. The road continues to climb with superb views north up the coast to Cavo Grosso, before rounding a headland to a dramatic section cut into the cliff with a precipitous drop to a long narrow plateau high above the sea (view south to Cape Matapan, ancient *Tainaron*). A turning to the left leads steeply down to **Porto Kagio**, with the 16th-century Turkish castle of Porto Kagio, perched high on a cliff edge overlooking the almost circular Bay of Porto Kagio, the name of which is a corruption of the Venetian '*quaglio*' (quails). The Venetians prized the quails that passed through here each spring on their migration, slaughtered them in their millions, and sent them off, pickled, by the barrelful to Venice. Below (right) between two sandy inlets, is Porto Marmari, ancient *Achilleion*, with restored tower houses and the remains of a medieval castle. On the highest point of the isthmus (left) is the prominent tower of Charakes. The small sandy (often dirty) beach of Porto Kagio, ancient *Psamathous*, has several small tavernas.

From the highest point of the road before it descends to Porto Kagio, an hour's hike leads on to the tip of **Cape Tainaron** (Matapan), the southernmost point in Europe. Alternatively, keeping Vathi Bay on the left, one can walk on a descending path along a scarp; the right fork leads south to the shoulder of the promontory of Livadi, which forms the bottom end of Vathi Bay. Over the low saddle is the hamlet of Kokkinogia and, below, the Bay of Asomatos. The Asomaton chapel on the headland occupies the site of the famous Temple of Poseidon (5th century BC), part of the extended shrine of Poseidon Tainarios where the Free Laconians had their religious headquarters. The large blocks on the north wall formed part of the ancient temple. On a pebbly beach (left) is the cave of the Oracle of Poseidon mentioned by Pausanias. There are remains of a religious complex attached to the oracle which was still in use during the late Roman period. In the bay (right) are numerous cisterns which inspired the name of Porto Chisternes. In the next small bay to the south is a pebble mosaic. The track continues (30mins) to the lighthouse at the tip of the cape. The Greeks thought that one of the entrances to Hades was in this remote spot. It was here that Heracles, as one of his Twelve Labours, dispatched the three-headed watchdog Cerberus.

Up the eastern coast

The main road leads on though a valley skirting the southern tip of the Kakavoulia and crosses the watershed (view of the Laconian Gulf) to Lagia (bus to Sparta daily), 400m above sea level. Now depopulated, it was once the main town of southeast Mani. There are some fine towers.

About 500m before the village of Dimaristika the main road cuts across an ancient road from the harbour of Aghios Kyprianos to the marble quarries of *rosso antico* (Tainaron marble), highly prized in Antiquity and used (*inter alia*) in the decoration of the Treasury of Atreus at Mycenae. The road loops down through scattered towered settlements (view north to the great promontory of Stavri) to the small harbour of Kokkala (beach, rooms). At Nymfi, a steep path up the Kournos ravine leads to the monastery of the Panaghia and the ancient shrine of *Kionia* (500m beyond; 1.5hrs from Nymfi). Below the monastery is a circular cistern incorporating ancient material. The cistern has a constant water supply from a spring above the monastery. Water was supplied to the sanctuary and settlement of Kionia. Situated on a high plateau 480m above sea level are the scant remains of the foundations of two Doric temples built in local grey limestone. The larger (peripteral) temple dates from the second half of the 2nd century BC; the smaller (in antis) from the Augustan period. There are extensive remains of a settlement with cisterns, a cemetery with rock-cut reliefs and a fortified acropolis. Magnificent views look east to Cape Malea and southeast to Kythera.

The road continues with the grey, barren Kakavoulia rising steeply to the west, punctuated by sombre ravines and towered villages. Across a small coastal plain with olives and cypress the high towers of Flomochori are visible. A right turn leads to the delightful small fishing village of (3km) Kotronas, ancient *Teuthrone*, with a sandy beach and rooms to rent. On the small peninsula of Skopa to the southwest are the remains of a Byzantine fortress. To the east, on the high point of the Stavri peninsula, are remnants of fortifications associated with Spartan defences during the Corinthian War. The road climbs to Loukadika, with its once-fortified citadel, and turns west through a pass with oaks and cypress opening onto the cultivated plain of Pyrrhichos, which still bears its ancient name. According to Pausanias the city derived its name either from Pyrrhus, the son of Achilles, or from the god Pyrrichos, who was one of the Kouretes, a band of minor gods who served as attendants to the infant Zeus. Beyond, the road descends through a valley, with a view of the Bay of Diros, to join the Areopolis–Gerolimenas road.

Itylo (Oitilo; Οἴτυλο), once the capital of the Mani before Areopolis, is now better known for its potent retsina. Its name survives unchanged from Homeric times. Here Napoleon I put in on his way to Egypt. The village is divided by the Ravine of Milolangado, which divides Inner and Messenian Mani. A narrow road signposted Dekoulou leads to the cliff-side deserted 18th-century monastery church, with splendid views over the bay and toward Pendedaktilos (five fingers), the mountain range whose knuckle-like folds separate Messenia and Laconia.

MESSENIAN MANI

The coast road into Messenian Mani, north to Kalamata, takes in some of the most beautiful countryside in Greece, with sweeping views out over the sea. The excursion described below involves leaving the main road and taking lesser (not always paved) roads to see churches and villages. The latter part of the excursion is covered by the map on p. 340.

The main road from Itylo continues to **Langada**, with terraced tower-houses (and a tumbledown house on the left of the road just outside town with a charming relief dated 1859, portraying the builder, wearing a top hat and his wife, with kerchief). The church of Aghios Sotiris by the road is 9th century with exterior decoration and fine frescoes, long covered in plaster and concrete. The seaside village of Trachila has a cave.

The road widens at Thalames (or Koutifari), which has been suggested as the site of ancient *Thalamai*. The small, privately-run Museum of the Mani (*open daily in summer from about 9–5*) has local curiosities; the owner is usually more than willing to expound (usually in German) on his collection. The countryside between Thalames and Platsa is dotted with Byzantine churches and arcaded foundations incorporating ancient masonry fragments. Some of the most appealing churches are Aghios Nikolaos Kambinari, south of Platsa (11th–12th centuries); Aghios Ioannis Prodromos at Platsa (12th century) with frescoes of several periods; Aghii Anargyri at Nomitsis (12th–13th centuries) with 14th-century frescoes; the Metamorfosis at Thalames (12th–13th centuries), with 14th–15th-century frescoes. The isolated church of Aghios Dimitrios, on a spur above Platsa, commands a superb view to the north. Selinitsa, or Aghios Nikolaos, off the main road by the sea, has a prominent war memorial. Aghios Dimitrios, to the south, has a stalactite cave.

Stoupa, with its good beaches, is rapidly becoming a popular Greek and German seaside resort. Nikos Kazantzakis lived here and Stoupa is one of many Greek villages to claim that the 'real' Zorba was a local character. Beyond Stoupa, the road, cut from the rock, clings to the coast. It passes below Proasteio, near which (turn right at the end of the village) is the ruined 11th-century monastic church of Aghios Nikolaos and its 13th-century successor dedicated to the Aghii Theodoroi, with 13th-century paintings.

The seaside village of **Kardamyli** (Καρδαμύλη), perpetuates the name of *Kardamyle*, one of the seven cities that Agamemnon offered to Achilles to appease his wrath. It was transferred by Augustus from Messenia to Laconia. More recently, it has been the home of the British philhellene, war hero and writer Patrick Leigh Fermor. Of late, Kardamyli's good beaches have begun to attract both Greek and foreign tourists, and the main street is lined with shops (including a bookshop), restaurants (Lela's, off the main street, by the sea, is excellent), and cafés. There is good hiking through the countryside around Kardamyli and into the Vykos Gorge (local maps available in bookshop). The medieval castle (300m inland, visible from road to the north; signs in main street to 'Old Kardamyli') incorporates ancient masonry. It houses a tower complex of the Mourtzinos family and an 18th-century Venetian church with some interesting exterior carving. Here Kolokotronis set up his headquarters in 1821 prior to the seizure of Kalamata. The acropolis (path from church starting through a fine gateway) has rock-cuttings of probably Mycenaean date. Offshore is a fortified islet.

North of Kardamyli, views back to the south have a tremendous view right down the Mani: Kardamyli in its little plain of olives is seen below as from the air. Venetiko Island, off Cape Akritas, is evident across the Gulf.

Kambos, with a conspicuous church, a tholos tomb (dug in 1888), and vestiges of an ancient temple, is dominated by the **Castle of Zarnata**. Best reached from the next village, Stavropigi (keep left in village), this is a huge Frankish enceinte (before 1427) with a Turkish keep built by Ahmed Kiuprili in 1670. It was captured by stratagem in 1685 by Morosini. The kastro rests on polygonal foundations, perhaps of *Gereneia*. The south wall was torn down during the disturbances of 1943–49 and further damage done by earthquake in 1947. The Byzantine church of Zoödhochos Pigi has a carved wooden templon. Farther on, the square battlemented Tower of Koumoundouraki crowns a second height.

After Kambos, the Mani begins to slip away, as Kalamata makes itself known. There is a fine castle at Sotirianika, and there are splendid views out over the sea. At Verga, the road slips through a narrow gorge, which was blocked by a wall—the 'Mandra tis Vergas'—in 1826, when the Mani successfully turned back Ibrahim Pasha's ravaging army; Kalamata (*see p. 342*) is at hand.

PRACTICAL INFORMATION

Ideally, the visitor to Laconia would have at least six days: one for Sparta and Mistra; one for Geraki and Chrysafa; one for Monemvasia; one for the drive from Sparta to Kalamata through the Langada pass; two for the Mani peninsula.

GETTING AROUND

• **By air:** Kalamata, 60km southwest of Sparta, has daily flights from Athens into Asprochoma airport, 8km north-west of Kalamata (T: 27210 69442).
• **By car:** Sparta is most easily approached from the north, on the Tripolis–Sparta highway (63km), which continues south (45km) to Gythion. From the east, a road runs through a rugged mountain pass from Leonidion to Sparta (90km). From the west, routes to Sparta pass through the Langada Pass, spectacularly beautiful for those who do not suffer from vertigo.

While good new roads make it possible to visit Gythion and the Mani in a brisk day's drive, it is better to allow a day or two, to take in the rugged landscape and isolated tower villages and chapels. The Mani is still primarily the haunt of independent travellers, but a few bus tours do now spend a night here.
• **By bus:** About nine daily buses connect Sparta to Athens via Tripolis in about 4hrs (225km). Buses connect via Tripolis, Megalopolis, Kalamata and Gythion to most destinations in the Peloponnese. Sparta's main bus station (T: 27310 26441) is at the corner of Lykourgou and Thivronos, several blocks east of the Archaeological Museum. There is frequent bus service to Mistra. Buses regularly link Mistra and Sparta, though with a long midday interval. There is a daily bus service (8hrs) to Monemvasia from Athens and daily services from Sparta. There is a bus service from Gythion to Areopolis and many points in the Mani.
• **By sea:** Monemvasia is presently served by Hellas Flying Dolphin hydro-foils from Athens (T: 210 419 9200; www.dolphins.gr) and by Minoan Flying Dolphin hydrofoils from Piraeus (T: 27320 61266). It is possible to visit here on a day trip. Neapolis is linked to Athens (Piraeus) and the island of Kythera by Flying Dolphin Service and by ferry. Gythion is connected by ferry and hydrofoil service with Piraeus, ports in the western Peloponnese, several of the Argo-Saronic islands, Kythera and western Crete; information and

336 THE PELOPONNESE: LACONIA

tickets available at Rozakis Ship Brokers and Travel Agency, Vas. Pavlou 5 (the harbourfront).
• **By taxi:** In Sparta there is a taxi stand in front of the Hotel Menelaion on Palaiologou.

Sparta Information is usually available at the Dimarcheion, T: 27310 26517, on the main square open Mon–Fri 8–3. An English-language brochure *Laconia Traveller* is sometimes available. The Hellenic Alpine Club of Sparta, at Gortsologou (near the central square; T: 27310 22574) has information on climbing Mount Taygetos and local hikes as does the Sparta Alpine Club (T: 27310 24135). *Taygetos*, published by the Municipality of Sparta, is an invaluable guide.

Gythion
Gythion's harbourfront hotels include the venerable (but recently restored) €€ **Aktaion** (T: 27330 23500) with its seaside balconies; the €€ **Gythion** (T: 27330 23452), in a restored 19th-century businessmen's club; the €€ **Pantheon** (T: 27330 22289); and €€ **Leonidas** (T: 27330 22389).
The Mani
Since hotel rooms are limited, even in Areopolis, it is advisable to pre-book a room. The desultory hotels on the main plateia on the outskirts of Areopolis are to be avoided. Fortunately, a number of tower-houses have been converted into small hotels and one large hotel has been built to replicate clusters of tower-

houses. There are several other small hotels in Maniot villages.
Areopolis The €€ Kapetanakou Tower Hotel (T: 27330 51233), originally operated by the Greek National Tourist Office, is now in private hands and has its own garden. The charming €€ Londas Tower Guesthouse (T: 27330 51360; londas@otenet.gr) overlooks the town and is TV-free. The €€ Tsimova Guesthouse (T: 27330 51301) is at once a private home, a small museum of local history, and a guest house. The €€€ Limeni Village Hotel (T: 27330 51111), a reconstituted tower village just outside Areopolis, overlooks the Bay of Itylo, has a swimming pool, and serves martinis.
Gerolimenas For decades a modest harbourfront hotel with 12 rooms over a seafood taverna, the €€ Akroyiali Hotel (T: 27330 54204) now has 20 more rooms in a handsomely restored adjacent building and 23 apartments in a new building up the hill.
€€–€€€ **Kyrimai**. Beautiful, family-operated seaside hotel in rambling, stone-built house. Designer-planned decor (you can tell; it's sometimes a bit too contrived), offering elegance and comfort. Swim either in the sea, off a rocky cove, or in the hotel pool. 21 rooms and suites. T: 27330 54288, www.kyrimai.gr
Neo Itylo The nicest rooms at the €€ Hotel Itilo (T: 27330 59222) are in the original seaside hotel; there's also an annexe across the road. The children's playground and sand beach bring many families here. The restaurant is good and full-board and demi-pension are available.
Stavri The €€ Tsitiris Castle Hotel (T:

27330 56297) in this hilltop hamlet has a restaurant in a restored 200-year old tower. Rooms flanking a rose garden, and helpful owners with tips on what to see in the area.

Mistra

€€€ **Pyrgos Mystra**. Converted mid-19th-century *archontiko*, built of mellow stone, now beautifully renovated as the finest hotel for miles around. Cool shades of palest blue, cowslip and white within, with well-appointed rooms and bathrooms. Citrus trees crowd the garden. (NB: No smoking throughout the building.) 7 rooms, T: 27310 20870, www.pyrgosmystra.gr

€€ **Byzantion**. Pleasant, family-operated hotel, in Mistra itself, on the Sparta–Mistra road. Back rooms quietest; several nearby tavernas;usually open all year. T: 27310 83309.

Monemvasia-Gefyra

Monemvasia has become a popular Greek holiday destination and rooms are often at a premium. At weekends and throughout August, reservations are recommended.

€€€ **Lazaretto**. On the causeway. Very pleasant indeed. T: 27320 61991.

€€–€€€ **Byzantion**. Right on the main street, in a restored old house, built against the rock. Some rooms a bit poky. T: 27320 61351.

€€–€€€ **Malvasia**. Rooms and suites in a number of handsomely restored houses; the nicest place to stay on the rock. T: 27320 61323, malvazia@otenet.gr

€€ **Kellia**. Former monastery beside the chapel built on the spot where the icon of the Panaghia Chrysafiotissa was found (*see p. 322*). A terrace at the front faces the water. Rooms are simply fur-

nished, with a combination of wood, wrought iron and bright white plaster. T: 27320 61520, www.kellia.gr

€€ **Pramataris**. Almost directly on the beach, in Gefyra. T: 27329 61833; hotelpr@hol.gr

Sparta

There are a number of acceptable, if undistinguished, hotels in Sparta. The front rooms, especially on lower floors, in the hotels on busy Palaiologou are usually very noisy.

€€ **Maniatis**. Centrally located. Flash lobby, austere rooms, acceptable restaurant; open all year. Palaiologou 72, T: 27310 22665.

€€ **Menelaion**. Centrally located, in a handsome 1935 Neoclassical building. Decent-sized bedrooms, thoroughly renovated in the 1990s, when the courtyard swimming pool was added. Open all year. Paleologou 91, T: 27310 22161.

€€ **Hotel Sparta Inn**. Centrally located on relatively quiet side street, with decent rooms and bathrooms and two small swimming pools. Open all year. Thermopilion 109, T: 27310 21021.

WHERE TO EAT

Gythion

Seaside fish tavernas line the harbourfront; fish is priced by the kilo and expensive. Off the waterfront, the €€ **General Store and Wine Bar**, Vas. Georgiou 67, concentrates on meat dishes.

The Mani

Those who remember travelling to the Mani with their own provisions will be pleased at the availability of restaurants. **Areopolis** The fish taverna €€€ To

Limeni (T: 27330 51327) on the harbour, is superb. Much of the fish is so fresh that you may see it scaled before it is prepared for you. Reservations recommended at weekends. In Areopolis itself, € Barba Petros (T: 27330 51205), on the main street by the cathedral, has tables indoors and out and excellent home cooking.

Kardamyli The village has a number of restaurants, including €€ Lela's (T: 27210 73541) by the sea, reached by the twisting road from the main plateia. When Lela's is closed, there's usually a sign with directions to another family-run place.

Gerolimenas The €€ Akroyiali Hotel has an excellent seafood taverna.

Monemvasia-Gefyra

Matoula's has been serving Greek favourites since the '50s. **To Kanoni** has fresh fish and pasta dishes, and **Marianthi** has a pleasantly old-fashioned interior and usually has fresh fish.

Sparta

As better roads have lured more visitors into Laconia, decent hotels and restaurants have appeared, making travel here markedly less 'Spartan' than in earlier years, when it was often difficult not to think that the ancient tradition of subsisting on gruel had been preserved through the centuries. Today's visitors are not likely to make a journal entry like that made by the 17th-century botanist Francis Vernon when he visited Sparta: 'Lodging bad. Sup. bread wine'. (Quoted in R. Stoneman's *Literary Companion to Travel in Greece*.) Most of the restaurants in Sparta are on Palaiologou, the main north–south street, with a number of cafés occupying the block between Palaiologou and the main square, Plateia Kentriki. Most have tables outside facing the main square in fine weather.

€€ **Diethnes**. Has tables outside in a pleasant walled garden in fine weather, usually thronged on Saturday market days, consistently serving the best food (and good local wine) in town. Palaiologou 105, T: 27310 28636.

€€ **Elysse**. Some attempt at continental dishes. Palaiologou 113, T: 27310 29896.

MARKETS

Sparta The weekly Saturday outdoor market is on on the streets north of Lykourgou, from about 8–3. Fruits, vegetables, plants available in season, as well as a wide variety of other goods.

FESTIVALS & EVENTS

Monemvasia Festival of the Panaghia Chrysafiotissa, 2 May.

Sparta There is usually a summer music and drama festival; information available at the Dimarcheion, or on posters around town.

HIKING & CLIMBING

Alpine Club of Sparta, Gortsologou 97, T: 23710 22574 (for Taygetos). It is important to check weather conditions and availability at the refuge before setting off.

BOOKS & NEWSPAPERS

The Mani Bob Barrow: *The Mani* (often available in Areopolis); Patrick Leigh Fermor: *Mani*; Peter Greenhalgh and

Edward Eliopoulos: *Deep into Mani*. Michael Cullen's *Southern Peloponnese* (Sunflower Books) is a very useful guide to trekking and car excursions in the Mani and Vatika peninsula.

Mistra Sir Stephen Runciman's *Mistra* and Nicolas Cheetham's *Medieval Greece* are recommended background reading.

Monemvasia A.G. and H.A. Kaligas' *Monemvasia* (1986), in the Greek Traditional Architecture series, and Rainer W. Klaus and Ulrich Steinmuller's *Monemvasia* (English translation) are usually available at the bookshop just inside the main gate; W.R. Elliott's *Monemvasia* is excellent. Shops in the lower town sell guide books. In Gefyra there is a shop selling foreign newspapers.

Sparta Lampropoulou and Liakos, both on Odos Palaiologou, stock English-language books and newspapers.

MESSENIA

Messenia (Messinìa; Μεσσηνία), one of the six ancient divisions of the Peloponnese, is bounded on the north by Elis and Arcadia, on the south by the Mediterranean, to the west by the Ionian Sea, and to the east by Laconia. Its capital and principal trading port is the sprawling city of Kalamata, which overlooks the Messenian Gulf.

If any part of the Peloponnese could be called lush, it is central Messenia, with its fertile, well-watered plains of grain, fruit trees and olives (Messenian figs and olive oil are highly esteemed). In recent years, cultivation using hothouses has increased, and Messenian produce, along with that from Crete, is often the first on the market. The border between Laconia and Messenia runs across Mt Taygetos' highest point, Profitis Ilias (2404m), from where the sea off the Messenian coast is visible on a clear day. Messenia includes the southwest peninsula of the Peloponnese, containing the triangular mass of high ground that culminates in Mt Aigaleos (1225m). To the east of this range lies the fertile Messenian Plain watered by the Pamisos, which runs 43km from its source on the western slopes of Mt Taygetos down to the Gulf of Kalamata. It is while discussing the Pamisos that Pausanias remarks reassuringly that 'Greek rivers are quite unterrifying as to monsters'. The eastern coast of the Messenian Gulf, which takes in Messenian Mani (part of the middle 'finger' of the southern Peloponnese), has a splendid corniche and some sand beaches. The western coast of the Messenian Gulf is more gentle; its most significant site is the Venetian fortress of Koroni. The west coast of Messenia fronts the Ionian sea, and has the splendid Bay of Navarino (Pylos), flanked by Venetian kastros.

It seems that Messenia has been inhabited since the Neolithic period (c. 7000–3000 BC). In Homer much of Messenia belonged to the Neleid princes of Pylos, of whom the most famous was Nestor, while the eastern part was included in the joint kingdoms of Agamemnon and Menelaus. According to legend, in the Dorian Invasion Messenia was assigned to Cresphontes, a descendant of Heracles. The original inhabitants absorbed their conquerors, and their prosperity excited the envy of Sparta and sparked a series of wars. In the First Messenian War (? 743–724 BC) the Spartans conquered Messenia and, notwithstanding the courage of the Messenian king Aristodemos, captured the fortress of Ithome, reducing the inhabitants to the condition of helots. A rebellion known as the Second Messenian War (? 685–668 BC) was with great difficulty suppressed, when the fort of Eira was captured. The hero of this was Aristomenes, 'the first and greatest glory of the Messenian name', who held out against the Spartans for 11 years. After defeat, Aristomenes lived in comfortable exile in Rhodes, whilst many of the Messenians emigrated to Sicily, where, in 493 BC, their descendant Anaxilas of Rhegium captured Zancle and renamed it Messana (now Messina). The Third Messenian War (464–455 BC) had far-reaching consequences. The Athenians, who had sent an expeditionary force to help the Lacedaemonians, were rudely dismissed. After the fall of Ithome they therefore befriended the exiled Messenians, settling them in Nafpaktos. It was these Messenians who in 425 BC aided the Athenians at the siege of Sphacteria. After the Battle of Leuctra in 371 BC, Epaminondas repatriated the Messenians and founded for them the city of Messene. They remained independent till the Roman conquest in 146 BC.

The ancient topography of the area has been the subject of intensive study since 1958 by the University of Minnesota Messenia Expedition, which has published much of its findings. Work continues also under the auspices of the Minnesota Pylos Project and the Pylos Regional Archaeological Project.

KALAMATA

Kalamata (Καλαμάτα), a manufacturing town and port (pop. 50,000) with avenues of citrus trees, is the capital of Messenia. On the main roads into town, in addition to the usual sprawl of garages, furniture shops and supermarkets, there are a number of potteries, using the clay found in the marshes created by the Pamisos.

Kalamata's centre lies on the level land below its kastro and runs for several kilometres down to the harbour, once the principal outlet for exports from the Peloponnese, including Messenian olive oil and figs. The main avenues linking the town and harbour (Aristodemous, Aristomenous, Faron, Psaron and Akrita) are wide, and a pleasant park runs from the foot of Aristomenous (between Psaron and Aristodemous) to the sea. The narrow streets at the foot of the kastro, many with nicely restored Neoclassical houses, are charming.

Many of the houses, and much of the entire town, was rebuilt after the severe earthquake of 14th September 1986, which caused extensive loss of life and serious damage to Kalamata and nearby villages. Many demolished buildings were initially replaced by prefabricated structures, virtually all of which have now been replaced. Today, Kalamata is a prosperous town, with more banks per square metre than almost any other city in Greece. The annual International Dance and International Documentary Film Festivals make the city unusually lively for a provincial centre, whose chief claim to importance long resided in its boast to be the first Greek city to have revolted against the Turks in 1821.

Kalamata's most appealing aspects are its harbour and seaside (with cafés and restaurants), its tree-lined boulevards, and the old town around the convent of Aghios Konstantinos and Aghia Eleni at the foot of the kastro. It is about 3kms walk from the harbourfront to the kastro. En route, one passes the open-air Railway Museum (on Aristomenous by the railway station; *free*) and, in the market area, the church of Aghii Apostoloi, which has a Byzantine core of 1317 and badly damaged frescoes in the apse. Ypapandis, lined with trees, leads north to the cathedral church of Tis Ypapandis (1859), in the oldest surviving part of Kalamata. The nuns of the convent of Aghios Konstantinos and Aghia Eleni (signposted from the plateia in front of the cathedral) sell weavings and embroidery, including silk shawls that reflect Kalamata's once-thriving silk industry. Nearby, the Chandrinou Wineshop at no. 8 Aghiou Ioannou, has been selling wine from massive barrels since 1888.

Museums of Kalamata

The excellent Benakeion Archaeological Museum of Kalamata (*signposted in the plateia in front of the cathedral; open Tues–Sun 8–3; T: 27210 26209; protocol@zepha.culture.gr*) is housed in the 18th-century Venetian-style mansion at the corner of Benaki and Papazoglou, that was the home of members of the Benaki family, benefactors also of Athens' Benaki Museum. Well-displayed and labelled exhibits include objects from throughout Messenia from the Early Helladic to the late Roman period. The ground floor has sculpture from Petalidi (ancient *Korone*); grave monuments; architectural fragments; Roman mosaics, including a scene of a chariot pulled by lions. Upstairs there are finds from the Mycenaean tholos tomb of Nichoria; Middle Helladic and Mycenaean finds from Malthi, including a superb thumb-sized marble figure of a naked female (? goddess); finds from the Mycenaean necropolis at Antheia-Ellenika, including gold jewellery from the temple of the river god Pamisos near Aghios Floros. An exhibit documenting stray finds from throughout Messenia makes clear how much remains to be found.

Nearby, there are two other small museums. The Municipal Art Gallery, at Papazoglou 5 (*open Mon–Fri 8.30–2.30; T: 27210 88991; labels in Greek; no toilet facilities*), has displays of contemporary Greek artists. The Historical and Folklore Museum, at Ag. Ioannou 12 and Kyriakou, in a carefully restored 19th-century town house, focuses on life in Kalamata, and has a fine collection of agricultural implements, domestic furnishings (including the recreation of an upper class *saloni* (sitting room), costumes, prints, and mementos of local industry. Although the labels are in Greek only, there is usually someone on duty who speaks English.

The kastro

Several streets run from the old town up to the kastro (*often closed*), erected by Geoffrey I Villehardouin in 1208 on the acropolis of ancient *Pharai*. There are traces of walls as far back as Mycenaean times. The castle consists of an outer enceinte, an inner redoubt, and a keep. A Byzantine double enceinte had already fallen into disuse before 1204, and in 1208 its church was encased within the walls of the new keep. The castle was held by the Villehardouins for nearly a century and here William (1218–78, *see p. 311*) was born and died. It was captured by the Slavs in 1293 but won back, and passed by marriage to Guy II, Duke of Athens, in 1300. Florentines and Angevins held the site in turn until it passed to the Palaeologi in 1425. Held by the Venetians during the first Turko-Venetian war (1463–79), it was sacked by them in a raid in 1659. The Turks blew up a part in 1685 and the Venetians continued its demolition. It is now sometimes used as a venue for performances.

In the eastern suburbs of town is the interesting (originally 12th century, with later building periods through to the 18th century) cemetery church of Aghios Charalambos, two-storeyed and partly underground. Recent work on the structure indicates it is typical of churches of the middle Byzantine period in Messenia (*ask for directions at the Benakeion, or the municipal information centre*).

EXCURSIONS FROM KALAMATA

The main road north from Kalamata leads through **Thouria**. Ancient *Thouria*, further to the north, was destroyed in 464 BC by the Spartans and rebuilt by Epaminondas. It was given by Augustus to Laconia to punish the Messenians for siding with Antony. The Classical remains are at the north end of a long ridge in which many Mycenaean tombs have been found: this may be the place known to Homer as *Antheia*. To the west a road leads to **Androusa** (Ἀνδρούσα), the medieval *Druges*, once a bishopric of Frankish Messenia and one of the most important centres of medieval Greece. John Palaeologus seized it from the Navarrese, whose capital it was, for the Byzantines. It is well situated on an elevated terrace overlooking the plain and blends into the modern village, where some of its walls have been reused. To the north of the imposing Frankish castle (stretches of wall 50m long survive) on the other side of a ravine, is the small 12th-century church of Aghios Georgios (*usually locked*), with attractive exterior brickwork and, within, a simple unadorned nave and apse.

In a peaceful valley 7km northwest of Androusa by road, beyond the village of Kalogerorachi (*key*), is the hamlet of **Ellinokklisia**, with an elegant church beside the road outside the village. The church was probably built in the 12th century, and little altered since then, except for a discreet restoration in the 1990s. The church is locked, but its exterior repays a visit. The dedication of Zoödochos Pigi (Fount of Life) comes from a spring beneath the church. Built in horizontal layers of brick and stone (including massive marble blocks), it has three apses and a dome supported by ancient marble columns. The narthex supports a square belfry. Within, the mosaic borders, the marble icon frames, the iconostasis, and frescoes are of interest. Some column drums nearby show that an earlier building occupied the site.

After Hania Labaina, a by-road (signposted 'Ithomi', with other signs mentioning Mavromati and Messene) ascends (left) in 10km to Mavromati (Μαυρομάτι), the pretty, well-watered village (419m) that occupies part of the site of ancient Messene. The spring in the centre of the village (ancient construction) is that of Klepsydra, mentioned by Pausanias. The village's name of Mavro Mati refers to the 'black eye' or hole from which the spring emerges.

ANCIENT MESSENE

Visitors may wish to check in Mavromati and at the site to see whether the excellent site guide is in print and on sale. At the far end of the village is the small Archaeological Museum (open Tues–Sun 8.30–2.30; T: 27240 51201) with an impressive collection of sculpture, including a head possibly by 2nd-century BC Messenian sculptor Damophon. From there a paved road descends to the site. There is also a footpath from the centre of the village.

Messene is one of the most impressive and least visited sites in the Peloponnese. The almost 10km of surviving walls, with massive gates and well-preserved defence towers, are a spectacular example of 4th-century Greek military architecture. The Asclepieion is so large that the excavators originally thought that this one shrine might be the entire ancient agora. The city dates from 370–369 BC, when Epaminondas restored the Messenians to their country and encouraged them to build a capital. The city was built, probably on the Hippodamian system (*see p. 120*), in a hollow between three steep hills: Eva to the southeast, Psoriari to the west, and Ithome to the north. The situation is charming. The acropolis was on Ithome (802m).

HISTORY OF MESSENE

Messene, with Megalopolis, Mantineia and Argos, completed the strategic barrier against Sparta organised by Epaminondas after the Battle of Leuctra in 371 BC (*see p. 433*). Diodorus says that the city was built in 85 days—astonishing, if true. In 214 BC Messene was besieged by a Macedonian general, Demetrios of Pharos, who was killed under its walls; in 202 an attack by the Spartan tyrant Nabis was frustrated by Philopoemen. After the demagogue Dinocrates had incited the Messenians to revolt against the Achaean League (*see p. 400*), Philopoemen attacked the rebels, but was taken prisoner by them, thrown into a dungeon in Messene, and forced to take poison. He was avenged and succeeded by Lycortas, the father of the historian Polybius. The 2nd-century BC sculptor Damophon, who repaired Pheidias' statue of Zeus at Olympia (*see p. 377*), was a native. The discovery of a 4th-century AD Roman villa with a fine mosaic indicates that the site continued to flourish in late Antiquity. By the 7th century AD, much of the agora was covered with a settlement, which, along with many of the remaining monuments from Antiquity, was dismantled by the Byzantines to build their own structures here and in the neighbourhood. Later, the village of Mavromati, now partially relocated, grew up here.

The site

Open daily 8.30–3; no entrance fee at present; T: 27240 51201.
Entering the site past the theatre, with fine archways in the parodos retaining walls, one continues toward the foundations of the large Roman north stoa (c. 80m long), recently investigated. The stoa enclosed the north side of the agora, whose layout is now partially obscured by the trees that make this site so pleasant. This stoa incorporated (west) a fountain, which the excavators have identified as that of Arsinoë, mentioned by Pausanias. The fountain was built in the late 3rd century BC and expanded during the Augustan era with flanking buildings to house dedications.

The Sanctuary of Asclepius
The south side of the agora was likewise bounded by a Roman stoa (*shown on the plan*). Entrance to the sanctuary was provided through the north propylon. A monu-

mental stairway led from the propylon up to the *sebastieion*, a Roman-era temple for emperor-worship and for the cult of the goddess Roma, the deified city of Rome. To the south of this is the thoroughly cleared Hellenistic (2nd-century) Sanctuary of Asclepius, c. 69m square surrounded by a colonnade whose Corinthian columns had winged Nike figures rising from their acanthus-leaf capitals. Finds unearthed here in the 1990s suggest that deities worshipped were healers, heroes, heroines, and a mythical Messenian king, as well as Asclepius himself.

In the centre of the court is the Temple of Asclepius and Hygieia (or ? the heroine Messene), peripteral with 6 columns by 12. The building in the centre of the east side of the agora seems to have been a propylon, flanked by a small odeion to the north and a bouleuterion and archive hall to the south. Recent work has shown that there was a bathing establishment on the agora's south side in the Hellenistic period (part of heating system visible) and that the complex previously identified as a priests' house or prytaneion (square with inner court) formed part of the bath. To the west are various rooms of which the most important is a tripartite 4th–3rd-century Second Temple of Artemis Orthia (northwest corner) with bases for the cult statue and other dedications; seats with lions' feet may point to a mystery cult. The first sanctuary of Artemis was to the north of here. A temenos of Athena Kyparissia has been discovered recently and identified by inscriptions, also a Sanctuary of Demeter (votive plaques) southwest of the agora. In a building to the southeast, with inlaid marble and mosaic floors, a fine intact statue of Artemis was discovered in 1989.

The stadium and heroön

A few minutes walk to the southwest is the stadium, which abutted onto the city wall; work continues here, and there are signs that the stadium was used for wild animal battles in late Antiquity. Some of the seating was inscribed and stoas enclosed the curved (north) end. Beyond the west stoa are remains of a temenos of Heracles and, to the northwest, a palaestra (40m square). Roman copies of the *Doryphoros* of Polyclitus and the *Heracles* of Lysippus were found nearby in the 1990s.

At the south end and occupying a monumental podium projecting beyond the city wall was a heröon (the details now difficult to make out). Here, in an enormous stone-pile tumulus, were probably the graves of distinguished (heroised) Messenian citizens. You can follow traces of the walls west and then north beyond the stadium, or return to the road and continue past the museum to the Arcadian Gate, which forms, with the adjoining section of the city wall and the tower to the east, the best-preserved part of the fortifications.

The Arcadian Gate and fortifications

The gateway, through which a road still runs, consists of an outer and an inner entrance, separated by a circular court. The outer entrance was flanked by square towers, 10m apart, the foundations alone of which survive. The gateway is nearly 5m wide. The open court, 19m in diameter, is remarkable for the perfection of its masonry, laid without mortar on a base of two or more massive courses. On either side, near

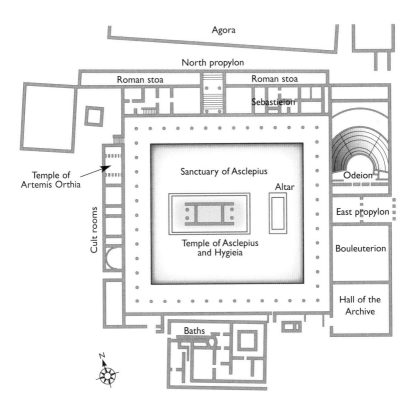

ANCIENT MESSENE:
SANCTUARY OF ASCLEPIUS

the outer gate, is a niche for statues of the protecting gods, one doubtless the *Hermes* noted by Pausanias. Under the right niche a worn inscription describes the restorations of Q. Plotius Euphemion. The Inner Gate has an enormous monolithic doorpost, now half fallen. A short section of paved road with chariot ruts is visible. Outside the gate is the stepped base of a large monument. The main road continues west within the walls towards a line of towers standing to their original height. Recent work on funeral monuments outside the north wall by tower 17, northeast of the Arcadian Gate, unearthed sarcophagi bases and a coin horde with 1,400 coins of the 5th century AD.

The circuit of the walls, c. 9km long, follows the line of the ridge descending from the acropolis on Ithome and was continuous except at various inaccessible points.

This vast enceinte, planned to enclose cornfields, doubtless served also as a refuge for the surrounding population in time of danger. The battlemented curtain consists of an outer and inner facing of unmortared squared blocks, with a rubble core; it is 2–2.5m thick and averaged 4.5m high. The steepness of the escarpment prevented the approach of siege engines. The curtain was flanked at irregular intervals (30–90m) by projecting battlemented towers, of which there were at least 30. These were square or, at the salient angles, semicircular. Seven are still partly extant. They had two storeys, the lower with four loopholes, the upper with six small windows. Four of the gates have been distinguished.

Mount Ithome

To the northeast of the village, the path to Mt Ithome (Ιθώμη) passes the aqueduct which fed Klepsydra and reaches the recently reinvestigated shrine of Artemis Limnatis or Laphria (circuit wall, Ionic naïskos, cult statue base, altar, ancillary buildings). Another shrine has also been located 500m further northwest. The ascent of Ithome (90mins from the village) can be made by taking the track from Mavromati to the Laconian Gate and following the path from there. Recent paving of the summit road makes it possible to drive to the top. The view embraces most of Messenia and extends to Laconia.

The summit (802m) is really a ridge running southeast to northwest. Mentioned by Homer, Ithome figured as a refuge in the First and Third Messenian Wars. On the summit stands the small monastery of Voulkano, dating from the 16th century, and the mother-convent of the later monastery below. It was finally abandoned in 1950 and its icon removed from the ruined katholikon. A paved threshing floor may have been the scene of the festival of the *Ithomaea*, which survives to this day in an annual festival of the Panaghia. The convent occupies the site of an altar-sanctuary of Zeus Ithomatas, where human sacrifice was occasionally offered. To the south are two large cisterns. The thistles that grow on the windswept summit are home to sizeable spiders and beetles. From the summit, one can descend to the Laconian Gate, and from there to the saddle between Mts Eva and Ithome and reach the functioning **Monastery of Voulkano**, which is visible from afar half-way up (383m) the north slope of Mt Eva. The convent is an offshoot of the older foundation of the same name on the summit of Ithome and offers hospitality (try not to arrive at midday, when it is usually closed). On the 15th-century entrance gate is the escutcheon of the Knights of St John. The conventual buildings, which date only from 1712, are set round a cloistered court, with an earlier church in the centre. The beautiful situation commands a view of southern Messenia and of the Arcadian mountains.

From Messene to the coast

The route to the Ionian coast traverses the Lower Messenian Plain, known to the ancients as *Makaria* ('Happy Land'), and described by Euripides in a lost play, quoted by Strabo, as a 'land of fair fruitage and watered by innumerable streams, abounding in pasturage for cattle and sheep, being neither very wintry in the blasts of winter, nor yet made too hot by the chariot of Helios'. Curtius (the excavator of Olympia) observes: 'High hedges of cactus divide the well-tilled fields; the great aloe stands in thick clumps, lemons and oranges flourish plentifully, the date itself ripens under the Messenian sun, and the superabundance of oil and wine is exported from Kalamata'. Today, in addition, bananas are grown.

From Messene's Arcadian Gate an upper road leads to Meligalas, crossing the triple Mavrozoumenos Bridge, built over the confluence of two rivers. The west arm spans the Upper Mavrozoumenos, the east arm the Amphitos. The north arm forms a causeway over the apex of land between them, which is liable to be flooded. The bridge has seven arches (span 5.2m, height above water 4m) and one rectangular opening 2.2m high by 1.2m wide. The piers are ancient, probably contemporary with Messene; the arches mainly Turkish. The river is the Pamisos.

Meligalas (pop. 1,405) is the largest town in the Upper Messenian Plain, or Plain of Steniklaros, the home of the Dorian dynasty of Cresphontes. The site of the royal city is unknown. This beautiful and fertile valley, watered by many streams, enjoys a temperate climate. Its vegetation includes figs, olives, oranges, mulberries, cactus and date palms. Meligalas itself has a prominent clock tower.

Vasiliko has a small museum containing objects from Malthi, and a Roman mosaic found near Koroni. Above Vasiliko (turn left at sign 'Malthi 6' in village; after c. 2km small sign points right and left to 'Tholos Tombs' and 'Acropolis'. The acropolis can be reached by a very rough track to the left a little further on) is the **site of Malthi**, doubtfully identified with the Homeric *Dorion* where Thamyris lost his eyesight. Excavations in 1927–36 revealed chiefly Middle Helladic material. Two small tholos tombs (to the other side of the road below; *closed*) and a sanctuary containing a bronze double-axe were discovered.

Continuing on, one passes Psari, with recently excavated Mycenaean tholos tombs at Metsiki. Kato Kopanaki, on the watershed between the Archadeïka (Aëtos) and the western tributaries of the Pamisos, lies 5km north of **Aëtos**, a village on the north slope of Mt Sechi (1391m) where there are cyclopean ruins and remains of a 14th-century Venetian fort. At Kalo Nero you join the coastal road to continue south to Kyparissia.

Kyparissia (Κυπαρισσία) is the chief centre of the eparchy of Messenian Triphyllia and the seat of the Bishop of Triphyllia and Christianoupolis. The ancient city of *Kyparissiai* was founded by Epaminondas as the port of Messene. During the Slav invasions it became a refuge of the Arcadians, whence its medieval name: *Arcadia*. It was taken after a seven-day siege by William de Champlitte in 1205. The town was destroyed by Ibrahim Pasha in 1825 and, when rebuilt, resumed the ancient name. Today's town, with pleasant broad streets, and a number of restaurants and cafés, has expanded from the foot of the acropolis down to its small harbour and beaches, which are backed by groves of trees. The acropolis is a craggy rock 152m high connected with Mt Psychro (1116m), the northeastern end of the Aigaleos range. Pieces of Hellenic masonry survive in the impressive Byzantine and Frankish castle (*open sunrise to sunset; no admission charge at present*) from where the view takes in Zakynthos, Cephalonia and the Strophades. The castle reintroduced the round tower to Greece. There is a modern amphitheatre in a fine position below.

PYLOS & ENVIRONS

Pylos (Πύλος), known locally as Neokastro, is the historic Navarino. The clean and attractive little town, built with arcaded streets by the French in 1829, rises from the south shore of Navarino Bay at the foot of a promontory, on which a castle guards the south entrance to the bay. With its shaded harbourside plateia, stepped sidestreets and sprawling kastro with landscaped grounds, Pylos is the most pleasant base from which to explore southern Messenia. In addition to the important Mycenaean Palace of Nestor at Epano Englianos, the immediate environs include the island of Sfaktiria (scene of the famous battle between the Athenians and Spartans in 425 BC) Palaiokoastro; Nestor's Cave; and the sand beaches and nature preserves of Voidokilia.

HISTORY OF PYLOS

It seems that modern Pylos was not occupied in Antiquity, and that the ancient settlement lay to the north, close to the remains of Palaiokastro. In 1572 the Turks built a fortress here, called Neokastro to distinguish it from the Palaiokastro to the north of the bay. The name of Navarino, locally obsolete, is probably a Venetian corruption of *Ton Avarinon* (Castle 'of the Avars'), originally given by the Byzantines to the old castle and carried over to the new castle during the Venetian occupation of 1686–1718. In 1825 Ibrahim Pasha made it the centre of his operations in Messenia, which he utterly devastated. The intervention of the powers in 1827, the consequent Battle of Navarino (*see box*), and the arrival of French troops under General Maison, brought about Ibrahim's evacuation of the Morea in September 1828. The present town dates from the French occupation and has attracted to itself the Classical name of Pylos.

The town centre and Neokastro

Despite Pylos' recent growth and sprawl, the harbourside Plateia Trion Navarchon remains the town's centre. The plateia is planted with planes and limes, flanked by cafés, restaurants and arcaded shops, and has a memorial, erected in 1927, to Admirals Codrington, de Rigny and von Heyden, who commanded respectively the British, French and Russians at Navarino. The (signposted) Antonopouleion Archaeological Museum (*open Tues–Sun 8.30–3; T: 27230 22448*), a block off the plateia, includes exhibits on the Battle of Navarino, objects found in Hellenistic tombs at Gialova and Mycenaean finds from Koukounara (9.5km northeast).

The attractively restored Turko-Venetian fortress of Neokastro above the town (*open daily in summer 8.30–7; 8.30–3 in winter*) is reached in 10mins by the shore (ascend steps beyond school and follow path beside walls) or from the Methoni road, along which are remains of the Venetian-Turkish aqueduct. The fortress consists of a large crenellated enceinte, enclosing a citadel with six bastions, and with an attractive domed mosque converted into a church. The outer bastion, to the southwest, with a platform above the sea, gives a good view of the enceinte as a whole and commands the entire bay; the best view is from the keep. The citadel was rebuilt in 1829 by the French and was in use as a prison until recent years. The former barracks now houses a museum (*open daily 8–3; sometimes 7pm in summer*). The view from the walls at sunset is splendid.

Navarino Bay

Navarino Bay forms a magnificent natural harbour, 5.5km long and 3km wide, with a depth of 12–30 fathoms (22–55m). Its west side is formed by the island of Sfaktiria (*see below*). The only practicable entrance, on the south, is 1190m wide and divided into unequal channels by the islet of Pylos and the Tsikhli-Baba Rocks. On the islet are a lighthouse and the French Monument, erected in 1890 when the remains were transferred here from the mainland cemetery of the fallen from Navarino and from the Morea Expedition of 1828–30. In the centre of the harbour a low rock called Chelonaki ('little tortoise') is crowned by the Memorial to the British Sailors.

THE BATTLE OF NAVARINO

The Treaty of London (6th July 1827) provided that Great Britain, France and Russia should guarantee the autonomy of Greece, under the suzerainty of Turkey, without breaking off friendly relations with the Porte. Their fleets were, without open hostilities or bloodshed, to intimidate Ibrahim Pasha into withdrawing the Turkish and Egyptian fleets from the Morea. A wide discretion was left to the senior admiral (Codrington). The allies called for an armistice; the Greeks accepted but the Turks rejected the demand. On 20th October the allied fleet of 26 sail (11 British, 7 French, 8 Russian), mounting 1,270 guns, entered the Bay of Navarino, which sheltered the Turko-Egyptian fleet, numbering 82 warships, 2,438 guns, and 16,000 men. After an ultimatum to Ibrahim Pasha demanding his withdrawal from the Morea, a few shots fired by the Turks brought about a general action. At nightfall the Ottoman fleet, reduced to 29 ships, had lost 6,000 men. The wrecks of many of the ships can be seen underwater in the harbour when the sea is calm. The allies had 174 killed and sustained 475 wounded, but lost not a single ship. The news of this unexpected victory was received in England with mixed feelings (being referred to in the King's speech of 1828 as 'an untoward event'). In Russia it was received with ill-concealed satisfaction, and in France with frank delight. Prince Metternich denounced the action as 'an unparalleled outrage'.

The Island of Sfaktiria

It is possible to visit several of the offshore islands, including Sfaktiria, by one of the caiques that leave from Pylos harbour.

The uninhabited island of Sfaktiria, or Sfagia, which all but closes the bay on the west, is 4.5km long and 450–900m wide. Sfaktiria was long famous as a nest of pirates and it is said to be the scene of Byron's *Corsair*. The uneven interior of the island is covered with thickets. On the harbour side the cliffs, 30–90m high, are precipitous. The highest point, Aghios Ilias (168m), near the north end, is partly surrounded by a ruined cyclopean wall—the 'ancient wall made of rough stones' (*Thucydides IV, 31*), where the Spartans made their last stand in the Battle of Sphacteria. At the south end of the island is the tomb of Captain Mallet, a French officer killed in the War of Independence. Below the clear waters farther north, the wrecks of Turkish ships sunk at Navarino can sometimes be seen and in 1990, the remains of a ship sunk at the Battle of Sphacteria was also discovered.

Most excursion caiques cross from Pylos to the south end of Sfaktiria and cruise up its east coast before landing in the Bay of Panagoula. Here, near a chapel, is the monument to the Russian Sailors who fought in the Battle of Navarino. A path ascends in 10mins to a plateau with two brackish wells. Here for 72 days in the summer of 425 BC, 420 occupying Spartans held out against an Athenian force under Demosthenes and Cleon. When the 292 survivors eventually surrendered, the myth that Spartans always fought to the death was exploded. Thucydides describes the affair in great topographical detail, which can still easily be related to the terrain.

Palaiokastro and Voidokilia

The area around Palaiokastro can be visited by boat from Pylos harbour. Alternatively, it is possible to walk or drive here from Pylos.

A rough and largely overgrown path runs from the Pylos–Kyparissia road to the north side of Koryphasion. Since paths here are usually very difficult to find, local help is advisable and the directions given in Cullen's *Southern Peloponnese* are invaluable. A path leads up in 30mins to the acropolis of 'Old Pylos', surmounted by a Venetian castle, the **Palaiokastro**. It seems probable that here also was the harbour town of the prehistoric Palace of Nestor (*see below*). Strabo records that some of the inhabitants of Messenian Pylos 'at the foot of Mt Aigaleos' moved to this site, which the Spartans called *Koryphasia* (*Thucydides IV, 3*) from κορυφή, 'summit'. Its occupation by the Athenians in 425 BC was the first act in the drama of Sphacteria.

From the 6th to the 9th centuries AD this side of the bay was the home of a colony of Slavs and Avars: hence its name *Avarinos* or *Navarinon*. In 1278 Nicholas II of St-Omer built a castle here. In 1353 the Genoese captured a fleet under its walls. In 1381 it was occupied by Gascon and Navarrese adventurers; to the latter is sometimes attributed the origin of the name of Navarino. The castle was purchased by the Venetians in 1423 and fell to the Turks in 1501. After it had been bombarded by Don John of Austria in 1572 it was superseded by the Neokastro and known as Palaiokastro. Its capture in 1686 by Morosini and Königsmark ended its utility.

The spacious castle (*some of the interior inaccessible because of undergrowth; circuit of walls possible, with care*) is fairly well preserved. Its crenellated walls and square towers rest partly on 4th-century foundations. The area enclosed is about 180m by 90m. There are outer and inner courts. Fragments of ancient walls, both polygonal and cyclopean, can be traced near the middle of the south wall, on the northeast side, and on the west side of the castle. There are also ancient cisterns and staircases cut in the rock.

Below, to the north, is **Voidokilia** (good beach) probable site of the Mycenaean harbour. The marshes of the protected Voidokilia Wetland extending toward Gialova offer havens to migrating birds, including egrets and herons. The steep path (red spots) leads down from the castle in 10mins to the mouth of the so-called **Grotto of Nestor**, on the north slope of Koryphasion (easy ascent from Voidokilia). The arched entrance is c. 9m wide and 3.5m high. The cave itself is 18m long, 12m wide and 12m high. Clinging to the walls are stalactites with the shapes of animals and of hanging hides, whence the legend that Neleus and Nestor stabled their cattle here. The grotto is identified with the cavern of the Homeric *Hymn to Hermes* in which Hermes hid the cattle stolen by him from Apollo and hung up the hides of the two beasts that he had killed. Sherds attest its intensive use in the Mycenaean period; Neolithic material has also been found.

On the promontory opposite to the north, reached by walking round Voidokilia Bay, is one of the earliest tholos tombs (not easy to locate) in mainland Greece. Recent researches have shown that it was inserted into a Middle Helladic tumulus. An Early Helladic settlement preceded the tumulus, and Neolithic finds have also been made. Votive offerings of the Classical and Hellenistic periods show that a later cult grew up centred on the tholos.

NESTOR'S PALACE & CHORA

Palace open Tues–Sun 8.30–3, sometimes to 7pm in summer; T: 27630 31358. Sometimes there is a stand with light refreshments. Excellent site guide usually on sale at the ticket booth.
Below the village of Chora is the low but abrupt hill of Epano Englianos, on which stand the remains of the Palace of Nestor (site roof prominent). The remains here were first explored in 1939 and excavated after the Second World War, beginning in 1952, initially by Carl Blegen (University of Cincinnati), who identified the remains as the Palace of Nestor. On the first day of his excavations, Blegen had the incredible good luck to discover the palace archives, with the first of the more than 600 Linear B (*see p. 217*) tablets calcified in the fire that destroyed the last palace. Although some scholars still have reservations as to the identification of the site with Nestor, most accept that this was indeed the home of the garrulous elderly warrior whose rambling reminiscences punctuate the *Iliad*. The *Iliad* preserves a tradition of a Messenian Pylos ruled by a Neleid dynasty, led by Nestor for three generations. In the 'Catalogue of Ships' Nestor is credited with the second largest fleet (90 ships against Agamemnon's 100); the palace of Englianos compares in size and richness with that of Mycenae and has associated tholos tombs. In contrast to Mycenae, Pylos seems to have had minimal fortifications for most of its existence (c. 14th–late 13th centuries BC). Recent electromagnetic investigations of the site area suggest the presence of fortification walls for the as-yet unexcavated lower city, and suggest that the settlement stretched over the countryside for at least a kilometre.

In recent years, the Minnesota Pylos Project (1990–), along with the the Pylos Regional Archaeological Project (1998–) have embarked on an ambitious plan to reanalyse Blegen's findings and bring advanced technology to bear on the site. Thus far, the projects have sought to create a state plan of the excavated architectural remains of the Palace of Nestor at Pylos; to re-excavate much of Blegen's work and to sift through his dump (leading to the discovery of more fragments of Linear B tablets); to do a topographical survey of palace plateau and surrounding area; and, with the use of phyto-archaeology, to understand the local 'relationships between vegetation and archaeology'. In addition, a study has been undertaken of what has been described as one of 'best preserved collections of human remains from any Mycenaean palace' with an eye to studying the health of the population. Intriguingly, the study of animal bones found here reveals many defleshed burnt bones, suggestive of Homer's mention of burnt offerings to the Gods of thigh bones wrapped in fat.

The site

Although many of the palace rooms are labelled, and there is a site plan, the site guide is very useful both for identifying individual rooms and visualizing the palace complex. Also useful for imagining the palace is Homer's account of the visit here of Odysseus' son Telemachus, who came seeking news of his father. Homer shows us Telemachus' arrival, his bath, assisted by handmaidens, and the elaborate banquet Nestor hosted to honour his old friend's young son (*Odyssey Book III*).

The final palace consisted of three main blocks of two-storeyed buildings, whose construction somewhat resembled that of Tudor half-timbered buildings, with wooden columns, roofs and ceilings; at present, one visits the main palace building, with the megaron. The palace's exterior walls were faced in squared blocks of limestone; the inner walls were of rubble, with a plaster surface, and decorated with brightly-coloured frescoes, some of which are on view at the Chora Museum (*see p. 356 below*). The upper storey had brick walls between the wooden beams. The presence of so much wood meant that the superstructure was devoured by the fire, leaving only the few non-inflammable objects from the upper floor to fall to the ground floor. Most of the surviving walls stand to c. 1m above floor level giving a clear ground plan.

As one enters the palace, one passes on the left the room where the Linear B tablets (the first to be found on the mainland) were unearthed, within two hours of the first day's digging in 1939, on the day Italy invaded Albania. They were stored in a bank vault in Athens throughout the war.

The main building

The main building was approached across an open court paved in stucco. Jutting out (right) beyond the entrance stood a guard tower. The simple propylon had one column in each façade with a single door in the cross-wall between. The stone bases of the columns survive and show that the wooden pillars had 64 flutes. A sentry-box (left) guarded the palace door and also two small rooms beside the gateway, where nearly 100 clay tablets inscribed in Linear B script were found. Here perhaps was the tax collector's office. A large interior court, open to the sky, gives access to other parts of the palace. To the left are a pantry, its wine jars and cups lying in ruin, and a waiting-room with a stuccoed bench and several thoughtfully-provided large wine jars.

A wide portico, distyle in antis, opened into a vestibule and then by another door into the megaron proper, 12.8m long by 11.3m wide. In the centre a great ceremonial hearth of stuccoed clay forms a circle 4m across and raised 20cm above the floor. Round this four great columns, each with 32 flutes, supported a galleried upper storey, probably with a lantern above to let light in and smoke out. The floor was divided into patterned squares, all abstract in design except for one with an octopus. This is directly in front of a depression in the floor against the right-hand wall where a throne almost certainly stood. Beside it in the floor is a hollow from which a channel leads to another hollow, 1.8m away. These may have been used in some libation ceremony performed from the throne. The chamber was decorated with paintings, the wall behind the throne with reclining griffins and lions.

Corridors either side of the megaron served suites of service rooms and gave access to staircases leading to the upper floor. Five small rooms filled with thousands of cups and pots of more than 20 types must have formed as much a central depot for issue or sale as the palace pantry. There are, in fact, so many cups that archaeologists have suggested that each was used but once. Behind the megaron are store rooms with larger *pithoi* (some identified by the Linear B tablets as containing olive oil) fixed in stucco. The bathroom is evocative, its fixed terracotta tub (*larnax*) still *in situ*, together with *pithoi* for water and its pouring vessels (*kylikes*). Blegen, who himself lived to a great age, suggested that the small step beside the tub was added when the aged Nestor had difficulty climbing in and out of his bath.

On the southeast side of the court a colonnade (which supported a balcony) gives access to a duplicate but smaller set of apartments surrounding what appears to be the queen's megaron. The suite includes a small room with a drain hole, either another bathroom or a lavatory.

The adjacent buildings

The Southwestern Building (much of which is covered over) is thought to be an earlier and less sophisticated palace, perhaps turned into a dower house when the new palace was completed. Despite differences in plan (the arrangement is not axial and the storerooms open one from another instead of from corridors), it is a self-contained unit with most of the features of the later construction (megaron, etc). Much of its stonework has been robbed, though parts of the supporting ashlar wall survive.

The Northeast Building may have housed the palace workshops, and seems to have had an altar in the court. The functions of various workrooms have been identified from fragments found in them and tablet lists; they included a chariot repair-shop and an armoury. Traces of an elaborate water-supply system are visible. Farther to the north is the wine magazine, a separate building, in which a large room contains 35 or more large jars. Clay sealings were found marked in Linear B with the character interpreted as 'wine', and indications of its source (or vintage?).

As at Mycenae, there are tholos tombs near the palace. Outside the northeast gate of the citadel (100m) is the tomb excavated by Lord William Taylour in 1953 and restored in 1957 by the Greek Archaeological Service. It is crude in construction compared with those at Mycenae. Three other *tholoi*, south of the palace, excavated in 1912, 1926 and 1939, have been filled in.

Chora and beyond
The Archaeological Museum in Chora (*open Tues–Sun 8.30–3; T: 27630 31358*) contains Mycenaean antiquities from Messenia, including the Palace of Nestor, although many of the best finds are in the National Archaeological Museum in Athens. The three rooms contain objects from tholos and chamber tombs, including swords, and gold cups from one of the Peristeria *tholoi*; frescoes from the palace; reproductions of frescoes from the palace; Linear B tablets; reproductions of Linear B tablets; pottery from the palace 'pantries'.

Filiatra is a well-planned and prosperous town set amid amid currant fields and orchards of citrus fruit. All the towns in this area have been consideraby rebuilt since the earthquake of 1986. At the coast, one passes by Aghia Kyriaki, whose little port (4km southwest), had more important days as *Erane*, as is shown by remains of basilica and baths (5th century AD) and coins from its Frankish mint.

There is one important Byzantine church in the area: 10km southeast of Filiatra is **Christiani**, the *Christianoupolis* of the Byzantines and seat of an archbishop in the 11th century. It lost importance in the 14th century and the bishopric was transferred in 1837 to Kyparissia. The large and impressive 12th-century cathedral (*locked*) of Aghia Sotira, wrecked by earthquake in 1886, has been restored, and there are remains of ancillary buildings, including the bishop's palace

METHONI & KORONI

Koroni (Κορώνη), on the Messenian Gulf, and Methoni (Μεθώνη), on the Ionian Sea, stand 35km apart and were fortified ports for the Venetians by the 12th century. The two fortress towns, overlooking the east–west shipping routes, were so important that they were known as the 'twin eyes of Venice' (*oculi capitales communis*), and so wealthy that in 1201 Venice ordered them to pay an annual tribute of 1,000 pounds of gold. Both were thriving commercial centres, shipping goods throughout the Mediterranean and across Greece. Both were ports of call for pilgrims en route to and from the Holy Land. Each had extensive shipyards to repair the vessels that put in here. Both fell to the Turk in 1500 and both were liberated by the French army after the Battle of Navarino (*see p. 351 above*). When Leake visited, the principal trade of Methoni was the sale of slaves from Africa to the Turks, while the export of olive oil was an important source of revenue at Koroni. Now, Koroni's fortress and considerable present-day charms merit a visit, while Methoni offers an indifferent town (albeit with one excellent restaurant) but the best-preserved Venetian fortress in the

Peloponnese. The two towns can easily be visited in a day trip from Pylos, by a road engineered in 1828–29 by the French army after the Battle of Navarino. There are glimpses of an aqueduct, built by the Venetians and repaired by the Turks.

HISTORY OF METHONI

Methone or *Mothone* was said to be one of the seven cities which Agamemnon promised to Achilles, perhaps ancient *Pedasos*. Homer calls it 'rich in vines'. Its location overlooking the east–west shipping routes guaranteed its strategic importance. It received a colony of *perioikoi* from Nauplia (modern Nafplion) about the time of the Second Messenian War. In 431 BC an Athenian attack was foiled by the bravery of Brasidas the Spartan. The descendants of the Argive immigrants remained here even after the restoration of the Messenians by Epaminondas. Marcus Agrippa's capture of the site in 31 BC cut off Mark Antony's supplies from Egypt. Trajan granted independence to the city.

Having become a haunt of pirates, Methoni was razed in 1125 by the Venetians, and after a period of desolation firmly assigned to Venice in 1204. Until 1206, however, Geoffrey de Villehardouin and William de Champlitte used it as a base, establishing a bishopric. The Venetians fortified it as their main port of call on the way to the Holy Land, to which were sent an annual convoy of pilgrims. The town, known as *Modon*, was noted for its wine and bacon. Early travellers often comment on the pervasive stench of pigs: a German pilgrim who visited here in 1483 reported that more than 6,000 pigskins filled with lard were shipped to Venice during his short stay. Methoni also had a flourishing silk industry, but although it was a naval station, its public buildings were never lavish. The Venetian navy, totally defeated at the Battle of Sapienza in 1354 by the Genoese under Andrea Doria, took their revenge here in 1403, defeating a Genoese fleet commanded by the French marshal Boucicault. In 1500, after resisting a month's bombardment, Methoni fell to Sultan Bayezid II when the defenders prematurely deserted the walls to welcome a relieving force sent from Corfu. An attack by the Knights of Malta in 1551 was unsuccessful, and save for a second brief Venetian period in 1686–1715, following Morosini's conquest, the town remained in Turkish hands until 1828. Chateaubriand landed here in 1806 and admired the views from the ramparts; here, too, Ibrahim Pasha disembarked his army in 1825. The story of the captive told in *Don Quixote* may reflect Cervantes' own experience here as a Turkish prisoner. During the Second World War, three pillboxes were constructed here and the fortifications again saw action.

The fortress

Today Methoni's imposing medieval fortress (*open daily 8.30–7 in summer, 8.30–3 in winter; no admission charge; T: 27230 31255*) still stands, on a promontory opposite the island of Sapienza. The fortress walls enclosed a city of several thousand during the Middle Ages, and while today's modern town swells to that size in summer, it is a quiet place off-season. Methoni's once-important harbour is almost sanded up, and one can wade quite far out in shallow water. There is a good beach to the east.

The strongest fortifications on the landward side are separated from the mainland by a great ditch, or moat. This is crossed on an attractive bridge, rebuilt by the French in 1828, to a Venetian monumental gateway of c. 1700. Within, a covered way leads through a second gate to a third, opening into the area occupied by the medieval town (pulled down by the French when they built the modern area on the mainland). A granite column with a weathered inscription probably commemorates Rector Fr. Bembo (1494). Little remains except a Turkish bath, the ruin of the Latin cathedral, and cisterns. The curtain wall shows masonry of all periods from Classical (exposed when a section was dynamited in 1943) to the 19th century. The citadel contains many subtleties of Venetian defence, including casemates and underground passages for counter-mining. Numerous lions of St Mark (which Leake mentions that the Turks of his day referred to as the 'holy dog'), escutcheons and dated inscriptions survive. At the south end of the enceinte an imposing sea gate (restored) and causeway lead to the little islet (some fortifications Turkish), with the octagonal Venetian Bourtzi tower, where the Turks massacred the 7,000 strong remnant of the Venetian force in 1500.

Offshore lie the Oinoussai Islands, a group consisting of Sapienza and Schiza (caves; prehistoric occupation) or Cabrera, with the tiny islet of Aghia Mariani between them. The islands are home to wild deer and sea birds. The storms here are very dangerous.

KORONI

NB: The road from Methoni via Finikounda is often heavy with traffic in summer. Koroni's kastro grounds are open all day and there is no admission fee. Driving up to the kastro is not recommended, as there is almost never parking available, and one has to back down the narrow street as the next hapless visitor drives up.

Koroni, a picturesque medieval town, stands on a promontory at the foot of a Venetian castle, whose grounds are now occupied by a convent and its rose gardens. The antique remains along the harbour (breakwater, cisterns, walls, etc.) are of *Asine*, a colony planted by *perioikoi* from Argive Asine. The derelict site was reoccupied in the Middle Ages by the inhabitants of *Korone* (now Petalidi, to the north), hence its modern name. This was corrupted by Frankish conquerors into *Coron*. In 1206 after a year's tenure the Franks had to cede it to the Venetians. Coron was attacked from the sea in 1428 by the Turks. In 1500, the inhabitants, demoralised by the news from Methone (*see above*), mutinied and gave in to the Turks only to be banished to Cephalonia. The Genoese Andrea Doria captured Coron in 1532 for the Holy Roman Empire but, being besieged in turn by Kheir-ad-Din Barbarossa, was taken off with the inhabitants in a squadron of Sicilian ships, leaving the empty town to the Turks. It fell in 1685 to Morosini who massacred its 1,500 defenders. Its final period (1718–1828) under Turkish rule was ended by General Maison.

The castle and town

The principal points of architectural interest in the castle, which occupies a triangular headland, are Venetian, although there is reused Classical masonry in the outer curtain and the Gothic entrance gate. In addition, a Byzantine wall of reused fragments divides the inner from the outer court and the southeast and southwest artillery bastions may be Turkish. Here and there are cannons and piles of cannon balls, reminders of Koroni's bloody past, especially the massacre of 1685. Today, this is a pleasant place to stroll at twilight, with the inhabitants of the small dwellings tucked into the walls tending their gardens. The convent of Aghios Ioannis Prodromos is partially built over a 12th–13th-century Byzantine church, which was for a time a mosque (remains of the base of the minaret). There are several small graveyards in the convent grounds.

Koroni has a string of seaside tavernas, one or two small hotels, and narrow streets lined with narrow houses with the characteristic arched ground-floor doors and windows and the wrought iron balconies that may reflect the long Venetian occupation. The four and five layers of tile on the eaves are also characteristic of the local architecture. If at all possible, see Koroni from the sea, from where its cliffs and walls are most impressive; alternatively, it is possible to get a sense of the cliff and walls by peering over the escarpment, especially on the east side.

PRACTICAL INFORMATION

Ideally, the visitor to Messenia would have four days, to visit Nestor's Palace and the modern town of Pylos, the Venetian fortresses of Methoni and Koroni, ancient Messene, and Kalamata.

GETTING AROUND

• **By air:** Kalamata has daily flights from Athens into Asprochoma airport (8km northwest of Kalamata). There is a bus service from the airport into Kalamata.
• **By car:** Kalamata is linked by good roads to Patras, to the west; Sparta, to the east; and Megalopolis, Tripolis and Corinth to the north. The route from Sparta to Kalamata through the Langada Pass is one of the most scenic in Greece. Pylos is joined by excellent roads to Kalamata, Patras, and thence beyond. Although the roads are excellent, most travellers will be surprised at the amount of time they can spend on the 51km from Kalamata to Pylos, especially if they get behind a bus.
• **By bus:** About 10 daily buses connect Kalamata to Athens (8hrs), via Tripolis. There is also a frequent bus service to Patras, Sparta, and to Messenian Mani and beyond to Areopolis. The main bus station is on the outskirts of town where the road from Sparta enters Kalamata. Information on T: 27210 23145. Frequent buses link Athens, Patras and Kalamata with Pylos, whose bus station is on the main plateia (T: 27210 23145).

There are also buses for Methoni, Koroni, and the Palace of Nestor (Chora bus) several times a day.

• **By rail:** There are 4 daily trains linking Athens and Kalamata. Kalamata is connected by train to most parts of Greece (frequent changes involved). The train station is on Franzi, a right turn off Aristomenous.

• **By taxi:** There is an informal taxi stand on the main plateia in Pylos; as always, be sure that you have agreed on a price before undertaking an excursion.

• **By boat:** Caiques from Pylos offer excursions to see the Turkish shipwrecks and the island of Sfaktiria.

INFORMATION OFFICE

Kalamata The municipal tourist office is signposted on Makedonias. Information is also available from the police at Aristomenous 46. Several bookshops, including Euporia and Hobby on Faron sell foreign language newspapers, maps, and guide books. Information on hotels is also available at www.kal.gr/tourismos (available in English). The website for Messenia is www.messenia.gr

Pylos At present, there is no information office, but the book and newspaper store on the main plateia sells local guides and often functions as a surrogate information office.

WHERE TO STAY

Kalamata
€€ **Hibiscus**. Renovated Neoclassical town house offering excellent central location and relative quiet (ask for a room facing the courtyard). In an area where it can be hard to find a hotel with character, this has it. 7 rooms. Faron 196, T: 27210 62511; www.traditionalhomes.gr

€€ **Messenian Bay Hotel**. Large, charmless 77-room hotel with charming situation on sea 4km south of Kalamata at Almyros Vergas. Open all year. T: 27210 41001; www.messenianbay.gr

€€ **Rex**. With a convenient central location, some rooms with (distant) views of the harbour, and unusually large and comfortable for a Greek provincial hotel. A good choice if you want to stay in town. Aristomenous 26, T: 27210 94440; rex@galaxynet.gr

€ **Ostria**. Convenient location, some rooms with sea views. Navarinou 95.

Koroni
The 42-room €€ **Auberge de la Plage** (T: 27250 22401) is 60m from the beach and popular with families in summer (closed Nov–March).

Mavromati (Messene)
The family-run € **Pension Zeus** (T: 27240 51025) has five simple rooms, some with balconies. The only drawback is that the hotel is on the only through road in town.

Methoni
Methoni offers a wide variety of rent rooms and holiday flats, popular with Greeks, as well as with German and Italian tourists. The 36-room €€ **Hotel Amalia** (T: 27230 12931) has a quiet location on a hill a 5-min drive outside Methoni; disadvantages are that it is not on the sea and does a brisk tour group business (closed Nov–March). The 14-room €€ **Achilles** (T: 27230 31819; achilles@conxion.gr) is on the main street in Methoni (not the quietest location), but it does have a garden. Open all year.

Pylos

€€ **Eleonas Villas**. Self-catering studios and apartments, at Gialova, opposite Pylos across the bay, and close to the beaches of Voidokilia. Clean and attractive in a functional way; a good base for exploring the area. T: 27230 22696, www.eleonas.com

The 15-room €€€ **Karalis Beach** hotel has a marvellous location beside a park of pine trees overlooking the water, although overpriced for the service it offers. T: 27230 23021. The 26-room €€ **Karalis** is in town and in a somewhat noisy location, but is well run. T: 27230 22980.

€€ **Miramare**. Conveniently located 26-room hotel just off the plateia, across the street from the public bathing beach; some rooms with balconies; restaurant. Paralia. T: 27230 22751.

WHERE TO EAT

Kalamata

€€ **Akrogiali**. A very popular, year-round fish restaurant, by the shore. Navarinou 12.

€€ **Toscana**. The oldest Italian trattoria in Kalamata, with decent food and prices. Navarinou 79.

€€ **Ximeroma**. Popular restaurant at Aghia Sion, serving lunch and dinner year-round. Excellent fresh seafood at good prices.

Koroni

The waterfront restaurants and ouzeries all serve seafood, but The Kagkelarios seems to attract more locals with its grilled octopus, fish and snails.

Mavromati (Messene)

The Ithome Restaurant on the square serves stews and *souvlaki* and has fine views over the ancient site.

Methoni

€€ **Klimataria**. This restaurant is famous in Methoni, and for good reason: it serves the best food in town, and indeed for miles around, with inventive Greek cooking served under the vine shade, including a wide variety of delicious *mezedes*. The Klimataria is understandably popular, and reservations are recommended, certainly for the garden in summer. Closed mid-Oct–March. T: 27230 31544.

Pylos

€€–€€€ **Diethnes**. A long-time favourite, at Paralia, serving fresh fish right next to the government fish-inspection station. Prices depend on the catch.

Restaurant 1930, on the Pylos–Kalamata road by the Karalis, takes its name from the décor, which recreates the mood of the 1930s. The food is good.

FESTIVALS & EVENTS

The *Kalamata International Dance Festival* takes place for about 10 days in mid-July. Information from the Kalamata International Dance Center, T: 27210 83086; www.elia-artschools.org and www.culture.gr

The *Kalamata International Documentary Film Festival* takes place for a week in mid-October.

BEACHES

There is excellent swimming at Pylos' own small municipal bathing beach, and at the sand beaches of Gialova, Voidokilia, and nearby Methoni.

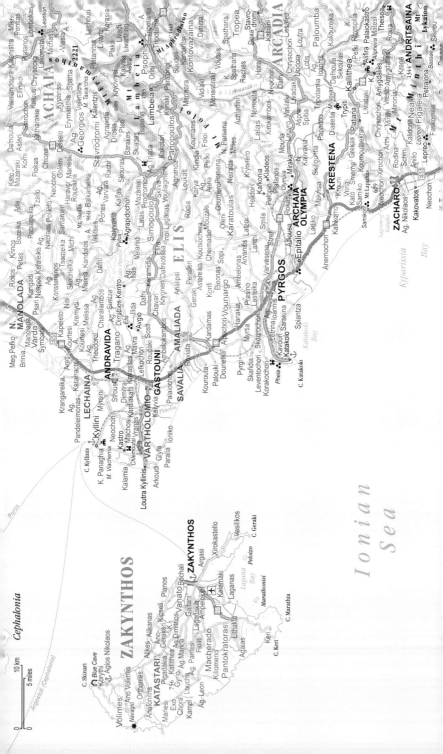

ELIS

Elis is the smallest of the seven *nomes* of the Peloponnese. It is bounded to the west by the Ionian Sea, is remote from the Aegean, and cut off from the rest of the Peloponnese by a mountain barrier intersected by the easily guarded ravines that have worked to its advantage in time of war.

In Antiquity the region was divided into three parts: Hollow Elis, or Elis proper, in the north, watered by the Elean Pineios; Pisatis, the country of Pisa, on the Alpheios, in the centre (including Olympia); and Triphyllia, between the Alpheios and the Neda, in the south. The district was noted for its horses and especially suited to the growth of fine flax. Pisa and Elis were often in contention, especially for stewardship of the Olympic Games; the eponymous towns in both Pisa and Elis were virtually eradicated in Antiquity. Famous for the grove of Altis and the Temple of Zeus at Olympia and for the Olympic Games, Elis was regarded as a holy land and its neutrality was largely respected until the Peloponnesian War.

As in Antiquity, Elis today has a fertile plain, cultivated with olives and fruit trees, well-watered by the Alpheios (Ἀλφειός), one of the most important rivers in the Peloponnese. It rises in southeast Arcadia, close to the source of the Evrotas, and flows through Arcadia and Elis, past Olympia, into the Ionian Sea. Pausanias describes it as 'a broad and noble stream, fed by seven important rivers', one of which was the Ladonas, today regarded as the main stream. According to legend the river-god Alpheios fell in love with the nymph Arethusa. Spurning his advances she fled to Ortygia, an island off Syracuse in Sicily, and was there changed into a fountain, whereupon Alpheios flowed under the sea to join her. The Alpheios was the river that Heracles diverted to clean the fetid stables of King Augeas (*see p. 389*). It was said to be the favourite river of Zeus, and on its banks first grew the wild olive, which supplied the garlands which were the reward of victors in the Olympic Games.

Most signs of early habitation in Elis are concentrated in the region around Olympia, where there are signs of prehistoric settlements and Mycenaean cemeteries. The Mycenaean tombs discovered at Miraka, for example, are near the site of Olympia's sometime rival, Pisa. The discovery in the late 1990s at Kafkonia, north of Olympia, of a 17th-century BC sanctuary with a Linear B (*see p. 217*) inscription on an egg-shaped stone with a double headed axe on its other side was hailed by Greek archaeologists as the 'oldest written survival of Greek language'.

During Antiquity, Elis was dominated by Olympia. More recently, the coastal plain became an important centre of the Frankish occupation. Many of today's place-names attest relatively recent occupation from the north and west by Avars, Slavs and Albanians. Elis has a number of well-preserved medieval monuments, such as Issova, Katakolo, Gastouni, Andravida, Kyllini and Chlemoutsi; these sites reflect the area's close historical connections with western Europe. In recent years, the excellent sand beaches of the Ionian coast have sparked touristic development.

OLYMPIA

Olympia is situated in the territory of Pisatis, the quietly beautiful valley of the Alpheios, at its confluence with the Kladeos. Confusingly, the modern village is called Ancient Olympia (Ἀρχαία Ὀλυμπία). The setting, in great contrast with most Greek sites, is pastoral, green and lush; the ancient remains shaded by evergreen oaks, Aleppo pines, planes and poplars, as well as olive trees. The Kladeos bounds the site on the west and the Alpheios on the south, while to the north rises the conical Mt Kronos (123m).

Olympia was not a city, but a sacred precinct, occupied exclusively by temples, dwellings for the priests and officials, and public buildings connected with the games, which took place every four years from 776 BC to at least 393 AD. Gradually, Olympia became a sanctuary in which were concentrated many of the choicest treasures of Greek art. In the centre was the sacred enclosure known as the Altis, from the Greek word for a sacred grove. This precinct was dedicated to Zeus, in whose honour were held the quadrennial festival and the games. At those times, spectators camped out on every available inch of ground—and probably saw no events at all if they had not staked out a seat in the stadium before the games began. Between festivals, Olympia was a sleepy place, watched over by its priests and a skeleton crew of administrators. It is difficult to realise that after the official cessation of the Olympic Games in 393 AD, repeated earthquake damage and the gradual silting up of the site led to Olympia's precise location being unknown for centuries. In 1766, the English antiquarian Richard Chandler rediscovered Olympia, and in 1874, the Germans began to excavate here.

Rediscovery and excavation

The first known western traveller to visit Olympia in modern times was Dr Chandler, in 1766. In 1768 the German scholar Winckelmann planned a restoration of Olympia. In 1811 Stanhope had a plan made of the site. A French expedition of 1829 partially excavated the Temple of Zeus. In 1852 Professor Curtius revived the plan of Winckelmann for the excavation of Olympia and interested the German royal family in the project. In 1874, a convention with Greece was reached, whereby the German government was permitted to carry out excavations. Their work covers three periods: 1875–81, 1936–41, and since 1952. Everything of importance has been housed in the museum, except for some bronzes (now in the National Museum in Athens). The temples of Zeus and Hera, along with several other monuments, have suffered from exposure since they were uncovered. In 2000, restoration work began on several columns of the Temple of Zeus, on the Echo Colonnade and the Treasury of Gela.

Since the 1980s, the excavations have concentrated on Roman Olympia, especially in the southern area of the site. Neither the main entrance nor the route of the ceremonial way during Roman times is yet known. Still, enormous progress has been made since Leake visited here, before excavations began, and could identify with certainty only the Temple of Zeus. He mused that 'at Olympia, as in many other celebrated places in Greece, the scenery and topography are at present much more interesting than the ancient remains'.

HISTORY OF OLYMPIA

The history of Olympia and of the Olympic Games are virtually synonymous. Excavations since 1959 have shown that Olympia was already flourishing in Mycenaean times. According to some accounts, Heracles founded the games to celebrate his successful cleansing of the Augean Stables. In other accounts, Pelops founded the games to celebrate his victory in the chariot race that won him the daughter of the King of Pisa.

The official era of the Olympiads started in 776 BC. Control over the games seems at first to have been disputed between Pisa and Elis, and ancient authorities differ widely as to the date when the Eleans finally prevailed (between 572 and 471 BC). Despite the vicissitudes of fortune and of war, the Olympic Games were held with the utmost regularity, the wealth of the various sanctuaries steadily accumulated, and the prestige of Olympia increased, reaching its zenith in the 5th century BC. A sacred truce (*ekecheiria*), fortified by severe sanctions, universally suspended hostilities during the week of the festival, forbade armed forces to enter the confines of Elis, and proclaimed the inviolability of visitors. This truce was strictly observed, with one or two exceptions. In 420 BC the Lacedaemonians were excluded from the festival on the grounds of truce-breaking (*Thucydides V, 49*). In 364 BC, during the invasion of the Pisans and Arcadians, a battle was fought in the Altis in the presence of the crowd that had come to watch the games.

After the age of Hadrian, Olympia ceased to have much religious or political significance, but was visited for sentimental reasons or out of curiosity. The games were, however, kept up until AD 393, when the edict of Theodosius I, prohibiting all pagan festivals, brought them to an end. In 426 Theodosius II ordered the destruction of the temples and the Altis was burnt. Soon afterwards the ruins were quarried to transform the Workshop of Pheidias into a Christian church and to build a fortification against the Vandals. In 522 and 551 the ruins were devastated anew by earthquakes, the Temple of Zeus being partially buried, while a landslip from Mt Kronos destroyed the buildings at its foot. A new settlement was swept away when the Kladeos overflowed and buried all the buildings on the western side of the precinct deep in sand and mud. Further landslips on Mt Kronos occurred and the Alpheios, changing its bed, carried away the hippodrome and part of the stadium, thus completing the ruin of Olympia, which for centuries remained an uninhabited waste covered with a layer of debris 3–3.75m deep.

THE ANCIENT GAMES

The most important of all the festivals at Olympia was the Quadrennial Festival of Zeus, accompanied by the Olympic Games. Lasting five days, it took place at the time of the second (or possibly first) full moon following the summer solstice, ie in August or September. Participants came from as far away as Asia Minor and Italy, and the entire Greek world observed a truce to allow athletes and spectators to make their way to Olympia safely. During all the years that the games took place, the truce was broken only a handful of times.

Ten months before the date of the games the Elean magistrates chose a body of ten *hellanodikai*, or umpires, who supervised training and discipline as well as the actual contests. The competitors had to train for the whole ten months, the last month being spent at Elis (*see p. 396 below*). A ceremonial procession to Olympia took place just before the festival began. The competitors took the oath at the bouleuterion on the Altar of Zeus Horkeios, swearing that they would loyally observe all the regulations of the games, and involving not only their family but their native town in the penalties consequent on any infraction.

By the time the games opened, thousands of people—almost all men—had flocked to Olympia, turning the surrounding countryside into an enormous campsite. Only men and boys who spoke Greek as their mother-tongue were originally allowed to compete; barbarians were admitted as spectators, but slaves were entirely excluded. No married woman might be present, or even cross the Alpheios while the games were going on, under penalty of being hurled from the Typaeon Rock. No woman was permitted to compete in the games, although women could participate in the festival as patrons; women are known to have owned and entered teams of horses in chariot-races. Unmarried women (usually described in the sources as 'virgins') did have their own games, also held every four years, in honour of Hera. The only event in the women's games was a 160-metre foot race in the stadium. The women runners were organised into three groups, by their age. The Museum of the History of the Olympic Games in Antiquity has a charming 6th-century bronze of a girl contestant, lifting the hem of her *chiton* to increase her stride. For the duration of the games, the special representatives of the various cities and states were publicly entertained, being housed in buildings adjoining the Altis and fed at the prytaneion. The *theoroi* or special ambassadors from foreign states, were sent at their national expense. The crowd of humbler pilgrims was accommodated in tents, or like the competitors slept in blankets on the ground. The scene was described by the 2nd-century AD philosopher Epictetus: 'There are enough irksome and troublesome things in life; aren't things just as bad at the Olympic festival? Aren't you scorched there by the fierce heat? Aren't you crushed in the crowd? Isn't it difficult to freshen yourself up? Doesn't the rain soak you to the skin? Aren't you bothered by the noise, the din, and other nuisances? But it seems to me that you are well able to bear and indeed gladly endure all this when you think of the gripping spectacles you will see'.

The events

It is not known precisely what the order of events at the games was. The most prestigious event was the *stade*, or short foot-race, the oldest of the events, which gives its name to the 'stadium'. To this, over the years, were added other competitive events: a longer foot-race, long-distance running, and, most notably, the pentathlon (discus, javelin, long-jump, running and wrestling). Boxing came at the end of the 7th century, as did chariot-racing and horse racing (the 'hippic'—as opposed to gymnastic—contests, at which tyrants and nobles competed, employing professional charioteers and jockeys). The vicious *pancration*, a kind of no-holds-barred boxing, was introduced in 650. Events for boys were inaugurated in 632.

The athletic programme was varied by the presence of historians, orators, and sophists, who read their works aloud to the assembled spectators. Herodotus here read extracts from his history. Themistocles attended the 76th Olympiad in celebration of the Persian defeat. The 211th Olympiad was postponed two years to AD 69 to allow Nero to compete and win special musical contests and a chariot-race. The records were later expunged.

The victors

The Eleans kept registers of the winners of the *stade*, after whom the next Olympiad would be named. An athlete such as the 2nd-century BC Leonidas of Rhodes, who won at four consecutive Olympics, would have become a Panhellenic hero. While the competitors never forgot that they were Athenians or Spartans, Milesians or Syracusans, they knew that an Olympic victory was regarded as the highest possible honour for any Greek. After each event a herald announced the victor's name and handed him a palm. On the last day the successful competitors (*Olympionikai*) were each given a garland of wild olive and entertained in the prytaneion. There was only one winner in each contest. The simple reward of the Olympic crown not only immortalised the victor and his family, but redounded to the glory of his native city.

A victor who had won a total of three events gained the right to erect a statue in the Altis, which might represent his own features. By the time of the older Pliny the statues numbered 3,000, a real hall of fame. On returning home, the victor was publicly entertained and a lyric composition was recited in his honour. The best known such poems are Pindar's fourteen *Olympian Odes*.

An Athenian took the prize for the first time in 696, and in 688 the inaugural boxing contest was won by a man from Smyrna, the first overseas city to gain an Olympic victor. Southern Italy records its first victory in 672. The Spartans were frequent winners.

Revival: the modern Olympics

The Greeks used the Olympiads as the basis of their chronology. The games were held regularly in peace and in war for over 1,000 years from 776 BC until their suppression in AD 393. From the first Olympiad to the time of Hadrian, the embellishment of Olympia never ceased. The vitality of the festivals is reflected in the architecture and works of art that have survived.

In 1896 a quadrennial international athletic festival, taking the name of the Olympic Games, had its inception at the stadium in Athens, where a Greek—the Athenian water-seller Spyridon Louis, running in a pair of shoes bought for him by friends—won the 'marathon'. The games have since been held successively in different countries, and there was rejoicing throughout Greece when the 2004 games were awarded to Athens—followed by considerable grumbling at the enormous disruption of daily life caused by getting the city ready for them. There is no modern Olympic truce: the First World War prevented the games' celebration in 1916, as did the Second in 1940 and 1944.

EXPLORING OLYMPIA

Archaia Olympia

The modern village, which grew up largely in response to visitors drawn by the German excavations, is undistinguished architecturally. It consists of one long central street, Kondili, flanked by a few sidestreets, most lined with small hotels, restaurants, fast-food outlets, and shops. The village has one museum worth a visit: the small **Museum of the Olympic Games** (*signposted on Kosmopoulou, which runs parallel to and above Kondili; open daily 8–3, Sun and holidays 9–2; T: 26240 22544*). Displays include medals and photographs of victorious athletes (including the former King Constantine of Greece).

The site and museums: planning a visit

This sprawling site and its three fine museums (Archaeological Museum, Museum of the History of the Olympic Games in Antiquity, Museum of the History of Excavations in Olympia) are often crowded. Crowds are usually much less early in the day, at lunch time, and an hour before the site closes. The Archaeological Museum reopened in 2004 after extensive renovations, and most visitors will want to visit this and the site before taking in the two other, new museums. It is perfectly possible to walk to the site from the village, but be wary of the tour buses that hurtle back and forth. To the site you take the Tripolis road, pass the old museum (now the Museum of the History of the Olympic Games in Antiquity), prominent on a hill (right) and cross the Kladeos river, which now, as in Antiquity, is channelled away from the site. The site is to the right and the museum to the left. Visitors may wish to check to see if the new museum guide is available at the museum shop; guides such as A. and N. Yalouris's *Olympia. The museum and the sanctuary* (1987) are now out of date; S. Photinos's *Olympia, Plan and Reconstruction of the Sanctuary* (1994) is still useful, but does not show recent excavations. The model of the Altis sanctuary is helpful in envisioning the site, and the museum's superb collection brings home the wealth of ancient Olympia. That said, bear in mind that on Mondays the museum usually opens 3hrs later than the site. It is useful to know that the site sometimes opens informally half an hour or so in advance of its official hours. This is as close as visitors ever get to seeing this usually crowded place in solitude.

THE SITE

As one makes one's way into this vast—often confusing—site, it is pleasant to remember Pausanias' remark that although there are many wonderful things to see in Greece, there is a 'unique divinity' about the mysteries at Eleusis and the games at Olympia.

The site has two parts: the sports and administrative complex; and the sacred Altis, where the temples and shrines were. The difficulty in comprehending the site stems in fact from the fact that remains of buildings from virtually every period of Olympia's long history stand side-by-side: remains of a prehistoric house or shrine are only metres from much later Greek and Roman remains. In recent years, the German excavators here concentrated their efforts on Roman Olympia and on restoration work.

The sports complex

As one enters the site, the first buildings that one passes are part of Olympia's extensive sports complex, lying outside the precincts of the sacred Altis. To the left, past the entrance, are the remains of a Roman bath. A section of the mosaic floor was restored in 2003–4 and there were plans for it to remain on view, with a protective roof. On the right, immediately beyond the entrance, some remains parallel to the path mark the ***xystos***, or covered running track, the length of the Olympic stadium (roughly 200m). The *xystos* formed a wing of the gymnasium, a large quadrangle extending to the Kladeos. Its propylon (? 1st century BC) consisted of a Corinthian portico raised on three steps.

Adjacent on the south is the **palaestra**, often called a 'wrestling school', but in fact a place for meetings and social intercourse, as well as for athletic practice of various kinds. It corresponds closely with Vitruvius' description of such a building. An open court, 41m square, is surrounded by a Doric colonnade with 19 columns on each side. Behind the colonnade, on three sides, were rooms of various sizes, entered through Ionic porches or through plain doorways. Some of them retain ancient stone benches set against the wall. On the south side the colonnade was divided into two long corridors by an inner row of 15 Ionic columns. The main entrances were at the east and west ends of the south side, through porches of two Corinthian columns in antis. The capitals are of unusual design, with parallels in Pompeii and Asia Minor rather than in Greece. The style generally suggests a date in the 3rd century BC.

A water channel, entering the palaestra at its northeast corner, ran round its four sides. In the north part of the court is a pavement of grooved and plain tiles, 25m by 5.5m; its object is unknown. From the central room in the north colonnade a plain doorway gave access to the gymnasium.

The theokoleion and Workshop of Pheidias

The **theokoleion**, lying immediately south of the palaestra, was the official residence of the priests. The ruins belong to three periods. The original Greek structure (c. 350 BC) consisted of eight rooms round a central court and covered an area 18m square. The foundations and pavement are well preserved. In the court is an ancient well lined with blocks of sandstone. Later three rooms were added on the east side and a large garden court, with cloisters and rooms, was constructed. The Romans took down the east half of the extended Greek building and enlarged the garden court. A colonnade was built round it, with eight columns on each side.

To the west is a small round **heroön**, c. 8m in diameter, enclosed within a square. The lower blocks of the circular wall are well preserved; the upper courses were probably of mud brick. Within was found an altar of earth and ashes, coated with stucco. To the southwest are the **remains of baths**, a critical feature of any sports complex, dating perhaps from c. 100 BC.

Adjacent on the south side is a Classical building, the sandstone walls of which are still standing to a height of 1.8m with later brickwork above. In its later form it was a Byzantine church divided by columns into nave and aisles with an apse on the east and a narthex on the west. Near the east end is a ruined ambo (left) with two flights of three steps, and, beyond it, a perforated marble screen of Byzantine workmanship. The original building was none other than the **Workshop of Pheidias**, mentioned by Pausanias as the place where the great sculptor worked 'detail by detail' on the statue of Zeus. The identification of Pheidias' workshop was confirmed first by the discovery of tools and terracotta moulds used in the manufacture of the great 12-metre high chryselephantine statue of Zeus (*see p. 377*), and finally in 1958 by the cup bearing Pheidias' name (now in the Archaeological Museum). The workshop had the same measurements as the cella of the temple for which the statue was destined and a similar orientation; it probably also had a similar internal structure, being divided into two compartments with galleries supported on columns. A long narrow building, to the south, divided by cross-walls into small rooms, is believed to have sheltered Pheidias' working technicians.

To the west (*not accessible*) remains of **Roman baths** overlie baths of the Archaic period, near the bank of the Kladeos, together with part of a swimming pool of the 5th century BC. This was 23m long and 1.5m deep. In the same area (south) was a Roman guesthouse.

The Leonidaion

The enormous **Leonidaion** was erected in the 4th century BC by a certain Leonidas, the son of Leontas of Naxos, who is known only by the inscription that identifies him as the donor of the building that perpetuates his name—possibly a hostel for distinguished visitors. The Leonidaion stands at the crossing of the roads from Arcadia and Elis outside the processional entrance to the Altis. This was the largest building in Olympia, possibly 6,000m square. As originally built it had an open court, 30m square, surrounded by Doric colonnades of 12 columns per side, off which rooms opened on all four sides. The main entrance was on the south side, principal rooms on the west. Outside ran a continuous colonnade of 138 Ionic columns, the bases of which are almost all *in situ*, together with many of the capitals. Their bases and capitals were of sandstone, the shafts of shell limestone; the whole was covered with stucco. In Roman times the rooms were remodelled and an ornamental garden with elaborate ponds was laid out in the middle of the court. The Roman governor of Achaea—in an act of conspicuous consumption, if not pure hubris—took over the entire complex as his residence. Many fragments of the colonnades were found built into the Byzantine wall (*see below*) and these, especially those from the terracotta cornice, show great richness of decoration. Recent research suggests that the main (south) entrance to the Leonidaion may have opened on to the processional approach to the sanctuary which presumably crossed the Kladeos by a bridge. The outer boundary of the whole sanctuary complex (including the secondary area) would have been defined at the west by the retaining wall by the river.

On the other side of this route, opposite the Leonidaion, is an imposing **Roman building**, formerly thought to be baths (the 'southwest baths'), with the main entrance facing the roadway. Across the court behind the north façade, a doorway is surrounded by three statue niches and fronted by a swimming pool. The courtyard has an ambulatory. Excavations here throughout the 1990s suggest that this was a club house of an athletic guild, begun under Nero and finished later in the 1st century, with the baths perhaps added in the 3rd century AD. A bronze plaque was found here in 1994, inscribed with the names of victorious athletes from throughout the Greek mainland and Asia Minor from the 1st century BC to the 4th century AD. This discovery pushed the date that the sanctuary was known to be thriving forward in the 4th century to the 291th Olympiad (381AD) from the 267th Olympiad (369 AD).

Immediately west of the southwest corner of the Leonidaion the so-called 'Spolienhaus' is probably an Early Christian structure and incorporated architectural elements from several earlier buildings in the sanctuary.

The Altis

The Altis, or sacred precinct of Zeus, was bounded on the north by Mt Kronos and on the other three sides by walls, the lines of which can still be traced. On the west side are remains of two parallel walls, the inner one Greek and the outer one Roman. The south wall is Roman. The original south wall, now called the South Terrace Wall, was more to the north, the Altis having been enlarged about the time of Nero. The Greek walls seem to have been merely low stone parapets and the inner precinct was probably not fully enclosed by high boundary walls until the Roman period. Within were the Temple of Zeus, the Heraion and the small Metroön; as well as the Pelopion, or shrine of Pelops, and innumerable altars to Zeus and other divinities. Much of the remaining space was taken up by statues of Olympic victors and other dedications and inscriptions. In short, the Altis was, depending on your point of view, a treasure-trove of sculptural elegance, or a confusing thicket of statues and shrines. Those who have visited the Church of the Evangelistria on the island of Tinos will have some idea of the concentration of offerings here.

The Altis proper was reserved for the gods; the dwellings of the priests and officials were in the secondary area outside. Entering the precinct by the processional entrance, a small triple opening with an external porch of four columns, we see on the right a row of large oblong pedestals, mostly belonging to equestrian statues. On the left are two pedestals bearing respectively the names of Philonides, courier of Alexander the Great, and of Sophocles, the sculptor. Turning to the right you pass on the right a wilderness of scattered remains recovered from the Byzantine wall, but originally forming part of the Leonidaion, bouleuterion, and many other buildings. Passing between the remains of two unidentified Greek buildings with several small partitions, you reach the bouleuterion.

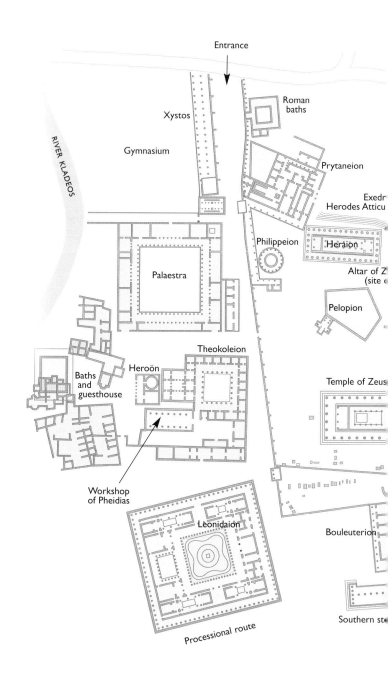

ANCIENT OLYMPIA
(PRINCIPAL EXCAVATIONS)

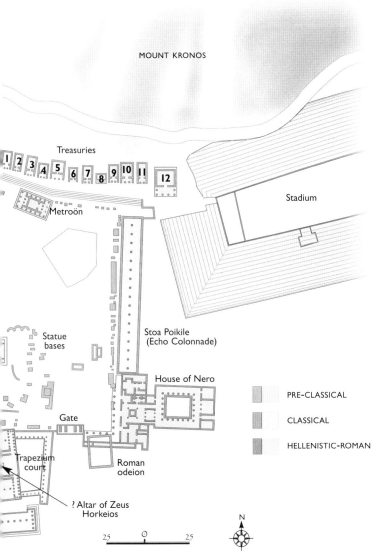

MOUNT KRONOS

Treasuries

1 2 3 4 5 6 7 8 9 10 11 12

Stadium

Metroön

Statue
bases

Stoa Poikile
(Echo Colonnade)

House of Nero

PRE-CLASSICAL

CLASSICAL

HELLENISTIC-ROMAN

Gate

Trapezium
court

Roman
odeion

? Altar of Zeus
Horkeios

25   0   25

N

THE GOVERNMENT OF OLYMPIA

Olympia's supreme governing body was the Council, or Senate, elected from the Elean aristocracy, which met in the bouleuterion. The senate had control of the revenue and the Olympian officials were responsible to it. The magistrates and priests, Eleans of good family, were elected for the period of each Olympiad. They lived in the prytaneion. Though each individual sanctuary had its own staff, a superior hierarchy looked after the administration as a whole and regulated the service of the temples. At its head were three *theokoloi*, or high priests, who lived in the theokoleion and dined at the prytaneion. Next were three *spondophoroi* (heralds), whose duty it was to travel abroad and proclaim the date of the festival and of the Olympic truce. Finally the two (later four) hereditary soothsayers interpreted the oracle. In addition there was a host of minor officials such as the *kathimerothytes*, or priest of the day; the *exegetes* (who doubled the role of master of ceremonies with that of cicerone to visitors), the *epimeletes*, or keeper of the Sanctuary; three *epispondorchestai*, or dancers; as well as a flute-player, an architect, a doctor, a chef for the prytaneion, a wood-cutter (who provided the wood for the altars), and still other lesser functionaries.

The bouleuterion

The **bouleuterion**, or Council House, seat of the Olympic Senate, consists of a square hall flanked north and south by larger apsidal wings of practically equal size and plan. The building may have been begun in the Archaic period and substantially added to and modified until at least the 4th century. Each wing consisted of an oblong hall with a central row of seven Doric (?) columns on separate foundations and a cross-wall cutting off its apse. Each apse was divided into two by a central wall. There has been speculation that the bipartite form of the building reflected the long-standing rivalry between Elis and Pisa. A triglyph frieze appears to have decorated the exteriors of the wings. On the east side, each wing ended in a screen of three Doric columns in antis. A spacious Ionic portico with 27 columns on its front ran along the whole length of the east façade, providing the only means of communication between the three parts of the building. The central hall, which is much later than the wings and may be contemporary with the Ionic colonnade (3rd century BC), may have contained the Altar of Zeus Horkeios, beside which competitors, their relatives, and their trainers swore that they would be guilty of no foul play in the games. Of the north wing, the oldest part of the building (6th century BC), very little except foundations, is left. The south wing (5th century) is the best preserved and differs from the north wing in that its long walls are not straight but form with the apse an elliptical shape recalling ancient structures at Sparta and Thermon (*see p. 487*): it may have been rebuilt on old foundations. In front of the connecting portico is an irregular colonnaded court of Roman date, usually called the Trapezium Court.

To the east of the bouleuterion, a system of ditches has been uncovered, probably representing temporary defences erected by the Arcadians in the course of the battle fought in the sanctuary during the 104th Olympiad. Nearby are the foundations of a Roman odeion and of a gate, which may have been a minor entrance to the hippodrome (*see below*). To the south of the bouleuterion is the ? c.350 BC **southern stoa**, over 78m long, built of tufa and raised on three limestone steps. It was closed on the north by a wall, with a narrow passageway at either end. The other sides were open and had Doric columns. Within it was divided longitudinally (probably in Roman times) by a central row of sandstone Corinthian columns. The Byzantines used the stoa as the south wall of their fort.

To the south of the Leonidaion is assumed to have lain an agora, where temporary booths would have been erected at festival times. Pausanias mentions statues of deities with the epithet *agoraios*. There were no permanent buildings or statues here, at least in Hellenistic and Roman times.

The Temple of Zeus

The Temple of Zeus, dedicated to the sovereign god of Olympia, is the most important temple in the Altis and one of the largest in mainland Greece. It was built from the spoils of Pisa, after its sack by the Eleans c. 470 BC, and completed before 456, when an inscribed block (quoted by Pausanias and since found) was let into the east gable to support a gold shield dedicated by the Spartans in commemoration of their victory at Tanagra. The architect was Libon of Elis. After an earthquake c. 175 BC both façades were dismantled and rebuilt and three of the west pedimental statues replaced. In the early 6th century AD the building was completely shattered by earthquakes. In 2003, one of the columns was re-erected in honour of the 2004 Athens Olympic Games.

The building, which is a Doric peripteral hexastyle, stands on a crepidoma of three unequal steps, itself borne on a massive platform. The foundations, which are of shell limestone with inter-spaces filled with earth, are complete. They were sunk 90cm deep in the soil and rose 3.1m above its natural level. Unlike many temples, which stood on rises, here an embankment was raised all round, giving the appearance of an artificial hillock. Access was by a ramp at the east end. There is no evidence of optical curvature such as distinguishes the Parthenon, though it has now been established that the columns had *entasis*.

The peristyle had six columns at either end and 13 at the sides; these also were made of shell limestone, but covered with fine white stucco to give the appearance of marble. Their height was twice the axial spacing. Each of them had the usual 20 flutes and three incised rings round the neck. The echinus of the capitals was similar in outline to those of the Temple of Aphaia on Aegina. Apart from one or two drums in their original positions, only the column restored in 2003 stands. On the south side they lie as thrown down by the earthquake of the 6th century.

Fragments of the entablature lie around. Above the architrave a frieze of triglyphs and plain metopes ran all around the peristyle; 21 Roman gilded shields, dedicated by Mummius to commemorate his destruction of Corinth in 146 BC, were placed on the ten metopes of the east front and on the adjacent metopes on the south side. The marks of their attachment can still be seen.

The two pediments were filled with sculptured groups in Parian marble: on the east pediment the preparations for the chariot-race between Pelops and Oinomaos; on the west pediment the battle of the Lapiths and Centaurs at the wedding of Pirithous. Pausanias attributed these to Alkamenes and Paionios (Paeonius). The surviving sculptures are in the museum (*see pp. 384–90*). At the apex of the east pediment was the gold shield dedicated by the Spartans (*see above*), crowned sometime later by a gilt bronze Victory, by Paionios. The corner-acroteria were in the form of gilded bronze tripods.

The roof was of marble tiles, many of which are preserved in the shrine to Pelops, the Pelopion. The earliest tiles are of Parian marble, the later ones (replacements of the Augustan period) of Pentelic. There was a continuous marble cyma interrupted by 102 lion's head water-spouts, of which 39 survive (some are crude later replacements). Traces of colour found on the architectural members show that parts of the temple were painted.

The wide ambulatory surrounding the *sekos* was occupied by bronze statues and votive offerings. The ceiling was of wood. The pavement was of large blocks of conglomerate covered with river pebbles embedded in mortar. This was replaced in Roman times by a mosaic pavement, traces of which remain. The *sekos* had the usual arrangement of pronaos, cella, and opisthodomos. It was raised one step above the stylobate. The pronaos and opisthodomos each ended in a portico of two Doric columns between *antae*, surmounted (unusually) by a Doric entablature consisting of an architrave and triglyph frieze. The 12 Parian marble metopes were decorated with sculptures depicting the Labours of Heracles, six at each end. Some were removed by the French expedition of 1829 and are now in the Louvre; the rest are in the museum.

The pronaos was closed by three folding bronze doors. On the floor are the remains of the earliest known Greek mosaic (now covered), representing a triton with a boy seated on his tail. Pausanias noticed here the statue of Iphitos being crowned by Ekecheiria (personification of the Olympic Truce). According to legend, before the official Olympics began in 776 BC, there was a time when the original games were suspended, for unknown reasons. The games were believed to have been restored by Iphitos, who is also credited with devising the Olympic truce. Different versions of the truce were inscribed on a number of discs (some on display in the Olympia museums. Traces of various bases here indicate the former presence of other statues he mentions. A great door, about 4.9m wide, led into the cella. The cella was 28.7m long and 13.3m wide. It was divided down the middle by two-tiered colonnades of seven Doric columns to form a nave c. 6.7m wide. This colonnade supported the wooden ceiling and galleries above the aisles from which the public were allowed to view the image of Zeus. The only light came from the doorway.

The nave was divided laterally into four sections. The first formed a kind of vestibule (open to the public) extended to the second column. On either side, by the first column, was a wooden staircase leading to the galleries. The next two sections were forbidden to the public. The second, closed by a barrier, extended to the base of the statue, and had side screens made of slabs of conglomerate to divide it from the aisles. A square, the full width of the nave, was paved with black Eleusinian limestone, bordered with a kerb of Pentelic marble, to form a receptacle for the sacred oil used for anointing the statue (*see below*). This probably served two purposes, both practical: mirroring light from the doorway, and providing oil for the wooden core in order to prevent swelling in the damp climate, which might have split the ivory. (As Pausanias mentions, the statue of Athena in the Parthenon needed not oil, but water, to protect it from the dry air of the acropolis.) The nave's third section, from the fifth to beyond the seventh column, is entirely occupied by the base of the statue of Zeus. The fourth section is merely a passage 1.7m wide connecting the two aisles behind the statue. The similarity in both proportion and decoration with that of the Parthenon makes it certain that the interior arrangement was designed by Pheidias himself.

The **chryselephantine statue of Zeus**, the masterpiece of Pheidias, was accounted one of the Seven Wonders of the ancient world. If Pausanias is correct that Pheidias took as model for one of the throne figures the youth Pantarkes, who was victor in the boys' wrestling in 436 BC, the work at Olympia would seem to have been done in 436–432, after the Athena Polias was finished. Apart from one or two Hadrianic coins of Elis, no authenticated copies of the statue of Zeus exist. Pausanias alone of ancient writers describes it in detail, and even he devotes more attention to the throne than to the figure. It is believed to have been about seven times life-size or c. 12m high. Pausanias, noting that the measurements had been recorded, says that they did not do justice to the impression made by the image on the spectator. Strabo, on the other hand, tells us that the artist is thought to have missed true proportion, as the head of the seated god almost touched the ceiling, giving the impression that if he rose he would knock the roof off. The ancients on the whole, however, concur in praising the extraordinary majesty and beauty of the statue. Cicero, in his *Orationes*, says that Pheidias made the image not after any living model, but after that ideal beauty seen with the inward eye alone.

The pedestal, 90cm high, and decorated with gold reliefs of various divinities, was of blue-black Eleusinian stone, fragments of which have been discovered. Zeus was represented seated on a throne made of ebony and ivory overlaid with gold and precious stones. The four legs of the throne were adorned with carvings and strutted with stretchers which bore golden reliefs of combatants. Some of the great weight was taken by four pillars underneath, hidden by screens on which were paintings by Panainos; and by the footstool which had golden lions and a relief of Theseus fighting the Amazons. The figure of Zeus held in his right hand a chryselephantine Victory and in his left a sceptre with an eagle. The undraped parts of the statue—head, feet, hands and torso—were of ivory. The statue's robe was decorated with figures of animals and lilies. In 167 BC Antiochus IV Epiphanes, King of Syria, dedicated (?) behind the statue, 'a woollen curtain, a product of the gay Assyrian looms and dyed with Phoenician purple' (*Pausanias V, 12, 4*). There are grounds for believing this to have been the veil of the temple at Jerusalem which Antiochus carried off (*II Maccabees I, 22*).

The care of the statue devolved upon the descendants of Pheidias, who were called the 'Burnishers'. By the 2nd century BC, however, the ivory had cracked and had to be repaired by Damophon of Messene. In the time of Julius Caesar it was struck by lightning. The Emperor Caligula wanted to remove it to Rome and to replace the head of Zeus with his own, but every time his agents came near the statue it is said to have burst into a loud peal of laughter. It is believed that after the reign of Theodosius II the statue was carried off to Constantinople, where it perished in a fire in AD 475. No trace of it has ever been recovered.

The opisthodomos had no direct communication with the cella. It was reached from the west peristyle and does not appear to have been enclosed by gratings. It had a long stone bench where people used to meet and talk.

Votive statuary
In front of the entrance ramp to the temple are some pedestals of statues detailed by Pausanias. It was the custom to erect in front of the east façade of the temple the statues of the *Olympionikai* and the chariots dedicated by them. The latter included the *Chariot of Gelo*, by Glaukias of Aegina, and the *Chariot of Hiero*, by Kalamis and Onatas of Aegina. Near the large rectangular bases of these is the semicircular base of a group of *Nine Heroes of the Trojan War*, dedicated by the Achaean cities and made by Onatas of Aegina; they are represented as drawing lots for the honour of the duel with Hector. Opposite, on a round base, stood Nestor shaking the lots in his helmet. Close by is the restored triangular base of the *Nike* of Paionios, dedicated by the Dorian Messenians (*and now in the museum; see p. 389*). Adjacent were statues of famous *Olympionikai*. Rather more to the west are the base of Diagoras of Rhodes, his son Praxiteles, a Mantinean athlete (484–461 BC), and the cylindrical plinth of a statue of Zeus, dedicated by the Lacedaemonians in the 6th century after the Third Messenian War. Near the northeast corner of the ramp are three semicircular moulded plinths which bore statues of the *Elean Women* (1st century BC). Adjacent are the pedestals of the *Eretrian Bull*, by Philesios (5th century BC) with an inscription on its east margin (*fragments in the museum*); and of the historian Polybius (146 BC). These bases and others transferred to the new museum were within the trapezoidal area enclosed by the 6th-century Byzantine wall, which had as its north and south limits the Temple of Zeus and the south stoa. The wall, made of ancient blocks from many buildings in the Altis, was demolished by the excavators and the fragments recovered.

House of Nero
Moving southeast you reach a heap of grey limestone blocks belonging to a pedestal that supported an equestrian group of *Mummius and the Ten Legates*. Close by to the east are remains of a **Roman triumphal arch**, erected for Nero's visit. It was largely built of older materials, including the pedestals of statues, destroyed lest the memory of their prowess should overshadow that of the megalomaniac emperor.

In the southeast corner of the Altis are foundations of the southeast building, perhaps the shrine of Hestia, mentioned by Xenophon. It was demolished to make way for the **House of Nero**, the peristyle of which lies farther east, hurriedly built for the emperor's visit. This house has been identified by the discovery of a lead water-pipe inscribed 'NER. AVG'. The Doric columns of the Greek building were broken up into small pieces to form the *opus incertum* of the walls. Later a large Roman structure was constructed immediately east of Nero's house, which was partially sacrificed to the new building. This contained over 30 rooms, one octagonal, and explorations in 1963–64 showed it to have been baths.

Farther east lay the hippodrome, long since washed away by the Alpheios. Here was installed the *hippaphesis*, an ingenious starting gate invented by Cleoitas in the 6th century BC and described by Pausanias. To the south of the House of Nero, in 1963, was uncovered the Altar of Artemis.

Stoa Poikile and stadium

The greater part of the east side of the Altis is occupied by the foundations of the late 4th-century Echo Colonnade or **Stoa Poikile**. The former name is due to its seven-fold echo, the latter to the paintings with which it was decorated. In front of the Stoa Poikile are numerous statue bases including a long plinth bearing two Ionic columns, which supported statues of Ptolemy II Philadelphus and Arsinoë, his queen.

The vaulted entrance (Hellenistic) to the **stadium** is clearly apparent. Immediately outside the entrance is a row of 12 pedestals which supported the *Zanes*, bronze images of Zeus erected out of the fines for cheating imposed on athletes in the 98th and 112th Olympiads. In 2004, the finals of the shot put in the Athens 2004 Summer Olympics was held in the stadium; ironically, the results were later questioned due to allegations of drug use by contestants.

The stadium was completely explored in 1958–62 by the German Institute and restored to the form it took in the 4th century BC. The artificial banks never had permanent seats, but could accommodate c. 40,000 people. The track originally extended northeast from near the Pelopion and was not separated from the Altis until the 5th century when the Stoa Poikile was constructed. The embankments were several times enlarged and the German excavators found many older weather-worn votive offerings (helmets, shields, etc), which had been buried during the alterations as sacred objects not to be profaned by re-use. The starting and finishing lines are *in situ*, 600 Olympic feet apart, and turning marks for athletes were discovered in the 1990s. The stone kerb round the track and the water-supply opening at intervals into basins are visible; the paved area for judges on the south side has been uncovered.

Throughout most of Antiquity, the only woman spectator officially in attendance would have been the Eleian priestess of Demeter Chamyne, whose stone altar is visible on the north embankment; there are rumours of the mothers of athletes disguising themselves and risking death to attend. Of these, the most famous is Pherenike (5th century BC), who disguised herself as her son's trainer. When she was discovered, she was spared death out of respect to her father, husband, brother and son—all Olympic victors. Thereafter, trainers entered the precincts naked.

The treasuries and Metroön

Outside the stadium entrance, a flight of ancient steps ascends to the treasuries, which are arranged roughly in line on a terrace overlooking the Altis at the foot of Mt Kronos, the soil of which is kept back by a substantial retaining wall. Each treasury takes the form of a small temple, consisting of a single chamber and a distyle portico in antis facing south. All but two of the treasuries were built by cities outside Greece proper, for the storage of various items, including sacrificial vessels used by the *theoroi*, weapons and gear used in the games, and 'treasures' and antiquities. Little remains but the foundations. The description of Pausanias is problematic and the identification of several of them is uncertain. They seem to have been added roughly chronologically from east to west from c. 600–450 BC.

The oldest and largest, built c. 600 BC and modernised about a century later, belonged to **Gela (12)**. Though constructed of shell limestone, those parts of the masonry which were most exposed to the weather, eg the pediment cornices, were encased in painted terracotta plaques and tiles—a survival from the days when buildings were made of wood. The terracottas were made in Gela and the building was presumably designed by Sicilian architects.

Though little more than the foundations of the **Treasury of Megara (11)** remain *in situ*, many fragments were recovered from the south Byzantine wall. It was erected c. 570 BC between those of Gela and Metapontum, as is shown by the fact that all ornamentation (fluting, mutules, etc) was omitted where it could not be seen. The pediment may not have received its sculpture until c. 510. Adjacent are foundations of the **Metapontum Treasury (10)**, slightly earlier in date. That of **Selinus (9)** is next, squashed in later between existing buildings, then **(8)** a structure which was probably not a treasury but the **Altar of Gaia**. The next three treasuries, which are very ruinous, are assigned to **Cyrene (7)**, to which two sculptured fragments of African limestone probably belong; **Sybaris (6)**, which must date before 510 BC when that city was destroyed; and **Byzantium (5)**.

The architectural remains of the next building **(4)** belong to the 6th century BC, suggesting that it is more likely that of **Epidamnos** than (as usually proposed) of Syracuse. The **Syracusan Treasury**, which contained the spoils of the victory at Himera (480 BC), may have been farther along **(2)**, but both this building and that tentatively assigned to **Samos (3)** seem to have been obliterated in Roman times. The **Treasury of Sikyon (1)**, by contrast, has well preserved foundations. Many blocks of the superstructure in Sikyonian stone with identifying inscription have been recovered, and the building has been partially reconstructed. They date from c. 480 BC. A Sikyonian treasury was dedicated by Myron to celebrate his chariot victory in the 33rd Olympiad, when the two huge bronze shrines also dedicated necessitated a special strengthening of the floor. This must have concerned an earlier building, but the existing floor is also strengthened. Immediately beyond is an **Altar to Heracles** and, north of it, an ancient shrine with a pronaos facing south.

Descending the terrace steps you immediately reach a small peripteral hexastyle Doric temple of the 4th century BC. This was the **Metroön** (dedicated to Rhea, the

Mother of the Gods). It measured only 20.5m by 10.5m. The remains include most of the foundations and a portion of stylobate with the drum of one column and a fragment of another. In Roman times the temple was re-dedicated to Augustus; excavators discovered in the foundations a statue of Claudius and another of Titus.

To the west of the Metroön, six prehistoric houses were uncovered by Dörpfeld. Traces of two of them may be seen in front of the **Exedra of Herodes Atticus**. This was a reservoir, the termination of a much-needed supply of pure drinking water brought to Olympia between 157 and 160 by an aqueduct c. 3km long. The water was stored in a large semicircular tank from which it flowed through lion's-head spouts into an oblong basin in front. The upper tank was paved with marble and backed by an apse supported by eight buttresses which rose to a half-cupola. The inner side had 15 niches which held statues, primarily of the relentless benefactor Herodes Atticus (*see p. 108*), his family, and their imperial patrons. At each end of the lower tank a small circular Corinthian temple enclosed a statue. A large marble bull bore an inscription recording that Herodes dedicated the reservoir to Zeus in the name of his wife Regilla, who was a priestess of Demeter.

The Heraion

The Heraion, the oldest but the best preserved building at Olympia, is situated near the northwest corner of the Altis. It was originally probably a temple of Zeus, then of Zeus and Hera. After the grander temple of Zeus was built, it was reserved to the goddess alone. The worship of Hera, which played little part in the history of Olympia, may have been introduced by Pheidon of Argos, who supposedly usurped control of the festival. By the 2nd century AD, Hera was patron of the women's games that took place every four years. The temple is not earlier than the beginning of the 6th century, and was originally built of wood, which was gradually replaced by stone. Even in the time of Pausanias columns of wood survived.

The temple, raised on a single step, was a Doric peripteral hexastyle with 16 columns at the sides. Thirty-four of the columns survive in part; two of them were re-erected in 1905 and another in 1970. They vary in diameter, in the height of the drums (while three are monolithic), and in the number and depth of the flutings, while the 18 surviving capitals show by the outlines of their echinus that they belong to every period from the foundation to Roman times. As no trace has been found of the entablature, it is believed to have been of wood. The roof tiles and acroteria (museum) were of terracotta.

The division of the interior into three chambers was conventional, though the details are unusual. Both pronaos and opisthodomos were distyle in antis. The walls of the *sekos* were nearly 1.2m thick; the four courses forming the inner face are well preserved to a height of 90cm. The upper part was of mud brick with wooden doorposts. The cella, long in proportion to its breadth, was lighted only by the door. Four internal cross-walls, recalling the structure of the much later temple at Bassae, served to buttress the outside walls and to support the cross-beams of the roof. At a later date the cella was divided longitudinally by two rows of Doric columns, every sec-

Fallen remains of the Temple of Hera at Olympia.

ond one being engaged with the corresponding buttress. There was a flat wooden ceiling.

Pausanias tells how, during the repair of the roof, the body of a hoplite was found between the ceiling and the roof. The soldier had apparently fought in the war of 401–399 BC between Elis and Sparta, during which a battle had swept over the Altis. Wounded, he had crawled to shelter only to die, remaining undiscovered for 500 years.

At the west end of the cella stands the pedestal of the Archaic group of Zeus and Hera. The head of Hera has been recovered. Of all the other treasures and statues known to have been in the Heraion, only the *Hermes* of Praxiteles has been found. It was lying in front of its pedestal between the second and third columns from the east on the north side. Six bases in the pronaos bore statues of noble Elean women. The opisthodomos is known to have held what was believed to be the cedar-wood Chest of Cypselus, in which the future tyrant of Corinth was hidden as an infant; the Disc of Iphitos, on which was inscribed the Olympic Truce; and the gold and ivory Table of Kolotes, on which the victors' crowns were displayed.

The Pelopion and Altar of Zeus

To the south of the Heraion, on the site of a prehistoric (Early Helladic) tumulus, is the Pelopion, a grove containing a small eminence and an **altar to Pelops**, the principal Olympian hero, enclosed by a pentagonal wall. A Doric propylon at its southwest end, of which foundations remain, appears to date from the 5th century BC and to have replaced an older entrance. Immense quantities of Archaic bronzes and terracottas were recovered in the enclosure as well as roof-tiles from the Temple of Zeus. Apsidal houses nearby are Early Helladic.

Somewhere to the east must have stood the **Altar of Olympian Zeus**, the most sacred spot in the Altis, where a daily blood sacrifice was made. The altar, Pausanias notes, had a circumference of 42m and the mound of ashes from burnt sacrifices rose some seven metres. Animals were evidently sacrificed at the foot of the altar; their thigh bones were burnt near the summit. An easy-to-miss heap of stone marks the altar's supposed location; in Antiquity, the stench of the animals' blood and the smell of their burning flesh would have made the altar impossible to miss. Pausanias mentions that while some say that Idean Heracles built the altar, others claim that it was constructed by 'local divine heroes'.

The Philippeion and prytaneion

Turning towards the exit you pass, in the northwest corner of the Altis, the foundations of the **Philippeion**, a circular monument begun by Philip of Macedon after the battle of Chaironeia (338 BC) and probably finished by Alexander the Great. In 2003–04, the Germans restored part of the stylobate and three columns. Two concentric colonnades stood on a crepidoma of three steps, the outer peristyle had 18 Ionic columns, the cella 12 engaged columns with Corinthian capitals. The roof had marble tiles and a bronze poppy on the top which held the rafters together. Within was a group of five chryselephantine statues, by Leochares, representing Philip, his mother and father, his wife Olympias, and their son Alexander. Finely carved fragments of their bases have been recovered.

Beyond stood the **prytaneion**, the official residence of the magistrates, in which Olympic victors were ceremonially feasted. The remains are scanty. The building, which dates in some form from the Archaic period (?), was later remodelled more than once in Roman times. The later Greek prytaneion was a square of 33m with an entrance on the south side and a vestibule leading into a central chamber, 6.7m square. On both sides of the central chamber were open courts. In Roman times a banqueting hall was added to the west.

Beneath the prytaneion is what seems to be a foundation for the piers of a Geometric bridge over the Kladeos, which originally took this course. Discoveries in this area (wells, hearths, food remains) have demonstrated that it was used as a campsite by visitors to the festival from the 6th century or earlier.

On leaving the enclosure there are (right) remains of a Roman dining pavilion, to which yet another bath was later added.

THE ARCHAEOLOGICAL MUSEUM

Usually open Mon 12–7, Tues–Sun 8–7 in summer; in winter it usually closes by 5pm; T: 26240 22742 and 22529.

The museum, built in the 1970s, has a monumentally dull exterior but contains one of the finest collections in Greece. The reinstalled museum, which reopened in time for the 2004 Summer Olympics, is better lit than formerly and displays are much more clearly and fully identified. Immediately inside, the entrance a plan of the museum's twelve galleries describes their contents. Most material is arranged chronologically, although some displays are also themed. Throughout, photos and drawings suggest the sanctuary itself and remind visitors of where objects were displayed.

Museum layout

Hall 1: Prehistoric;

Hall 2: the Protogeometric-Geometric and Early Archaic;

Hall 3: the Archaic Period;

Hall 4: the Classical Period;

Hall 5: Pediments of the Temple of Zeus;

Hall 6: the *Nike* of Paionios;

Hall 7: Pheidias' Workshop;

Hall 8: the *Hermes* of Praxiteles;

Hall 9: the Late Classical–Hellenistic Period;

Hall 10: the Nymphaion and Roman Period;

Hall 11: Roman Statues;

Hall 12: Roman and Post-Roman

The exhibits

This is a museum in which virtually every object is of superb quality, and often of both artistic and historic interest (note particularly the Mycenaean boars'-tusk helmet in Hall 1; the Geometric and early Archaic bronzes, including orientalising bronze plaques, griffins, cauldrons, armour and weapons in Hall 2; the Helmet of Miltiades and terracotta of Zeus bearing off the youth Ganymede in Hall 4; objects from the Workshop of Pheidias, including terracotta moulds for forming sections of drapery for the cult statue and a cup inscribed with the name of Pheidias in Hall 7. In Hall 4, the exhibit case with ringlets that are all that remain from some of the countless bronze statues that once stood here is a poignant reminder of how much was lost, destroyed and stolen over the centuries.

Highlights of the museum

The pedimental sculpture from the Temple of Zeus

These, together with the metopes and some fragments of the cornice, with lion's-head water spouts, are in the huge central hall (Hall 5). Explanatory panels on the sculptures are in place in the gallery, although scholars continue to dispute the identity of some of the individual figures.

The pedimental sculptures depict two myths important in the history of Olympia and the Peloponnese: the chariot-race between Oinomaos and Pelops and the wedding feast of the Thessalian prince Pirithous, badly disrupted by drunken Centaurs. The metopes depict the Twelve Labours of Heracles, ancestral hero of the Dorian Peloponnesians.

The sculptures are all of Parian marble with the exception of the two old women in the west pediment, the young woman in its left hand corner, and the arm of the other young woman, which are of Pentelic marble and are thought to be Antique restorations. From traces of colour discovered it is clear that all the figures were painted. *NB: the terms 'right' and 'left' used below are in relation to the central figure in each pediment, as the viewer views it.*

East pediment sculptures: Attributed by Pausanias to Paionios, the scenes represent the start of the chariot-race between Oinomaos and Pelops, from whom the Peloponnese derived its name, the 'island of Pelops'. All the figures are sculpted in the round except the three inner horses of each team, which are in moderate relief. Not a trace of either chariot has been found, but the marks of attachment can be seen on the horses. The figures, none of which is complete, are 1.5 times lifesize and in the Severe style, consistent with a date in the early to mid-5th century.

Oinomaos, King of Pisa, warned by an oracle that he would be killed by a son-in-law, was unwilling to give his daughter Hippodameia in marriage. Aspirants to her hand were challenged to a chariot-race from Olympia to Isthmia, and given a start with Hippodameia while Oinomaos sacrificed a ram. By the fleet-footedness of his horses Oinomaos overtook his potential sons-in-law, spearing them in the back. He had thus disposed of 13 suitors when Pelops appeared as claimant. He bribed the charioteer Myrtilos to tamper with the axle-pins of his master's chariot so that Oinomaos was killed when his

chariot crashed. Pelops thus won both his bride and her father's kingdom. This unedifying story of cheating and treachery—generally accepted as the root cause of the curse of the Atridae (Agamemnon and Menelaus, sons of Atreus, who was in turn the son of Hippodameia and Pelops)—seems to have provided one legendary version of the founding of the Olympic Games. Alternative versions have omitted Myrtilos' part and attributed Pelops' victory to his magical steeds (a present from Poseidon) and Oinomaos' death to *hubris* punished by Zeus. The pediment seems to omit Myrtilos, and this may have been the Elean version of the story.

At the centre of the composition is the colossal figure of Zeus, whose preserved height is 2.91m. Zeus is flanked by the principal figures in the chariot-race. To his right (according to the most generally accepted of a long series of suggested reconstructions) stand Oinomaos and his wife, Sterope; beside Sterope are the figure of a kneeling youth, which some have identified as the charioteer Myrtilos, and Oinomaos' four-horse chariot. Then come the fragmentary figures of a second charioteer, or servant, and the figure identified as a

The Centaur Eurytion grasping Deidameia at her wedding feast. Fragments from the west pediment of the Temple of Zeus.

Seer. In the extreme corner of the pediment is the personified figure of the Alpheios river. To Zeus' left stand the figures of Pelops and his bride Hippodameia. Zeus, who is invisible to the contestants, is slightly turned toward Pelops, perhaps to indicate his goodwill. The rest of the composition mirrors that which flanks Zeus on his right side. Beside Hippodameia are the four-horse chariot of Pelops, the kneeling figure of a servant, another figure of a Seer—recoiling in horror at what he foresees—flanked by a servant, and the personified figure of the Kladeos river.

West pediment sculptures: Executed according to Pausanias by Alkamenes, these illustrate the fight between the Lapiths and Centaurs at the marriage-feast of Pirithous. Again, none of the figures is complete, though the Apollo is almost perfect. Scholars have suggested that most of the figures of Lapiths and Centaurs are 4th- and late 1st-century BC replacements for the originals, which were perhaps destroyed by a series of Olympia's frequent earthquakes.

Pirithous, King of the Lapiths in Thessaly, and a reputed son of Zeus, invited his friend the Athenian hero Theseus and the Centaurs (whose usual home was Thessaly) to his wedding. The Centaurs had too much to drink and assaulted the women and boys present. One of the Centaurs, Eurytion, attempted to carry off the bride, Deidameia. Pirithous, assisted by Theseus, defended the attacked, slew many of the Centaurs, and routed the rest. Contests of Lapiths and Centaurs are not uncommon in Greek art, and usually carry the subtext of the triumph of civilisation (as represented by the Lapiths, as stand-ins for the Greeks) over barbarism (as represented by the bestial Centaurs.)

The central figure is Apollo, who has come to the assistance of the Lapiths, and is shown calmly towering above the tumult. To the right of Apollo, the fragmentary figure of Pirithous stands ready to strike the centaur Eurytion with his sword to free Deidameia, whom Eurytion clutches. Deidameia is attempting to push the centaur's hand from her breast. Beyond, a Lapith is being picked up by a Centaur. Next comes a Lapith woman, her garment torn, trying to tear herself free from a Centaur who has already been transfixed by the sword of a kneeling Lapith. They are watched from the corner by crouching and recumbent Lapith women. As with the east pediment, the composition of to the left of the central figure of the deity mirrors that to the god's right. To the left of Apollo, the figure of Theseus attacks a Centaur, who is abducting a Lapith woman. The series of fragmentary figures that follow represent more struggling Lapiths and Centaurs. The well-preserved figure of a boy being savagely bitten in the arm by a Centaur encapsulates the fury of the battle. Again, in the corner of the pediment are the figures of two reclining Lapith women, watching the fray.

The metopes

The twelve sculptured metopes from the cella illustrate the Twelve Labours of Heracles. The metopes decorated the west and east sides of the cella, six on each side. The metopes are displayed in the museum in a way that suggests their original location in the temple. Each slab measured 1.6m by 1.5m, the figures being slightly under lifesize. The metopes were originally painted, the brush completing the details of hair, clothes, etc, which the chisel has merely indicated.

Western metopes

(1) The Nemean Lion: It is generally agreed that Heracles slew the Nemean Lion, which had ravaged the countryside around Nemea. Heracles then skinned the lion and used its impregnable hide as his cloak. In ancient representations, Heracles is almost invariably shown wearing his lion's-skin cloak, but here, the young, beardless hero is shown standing with one foot astride the slain—but not yet skinned—beast.

(2) The Hydra of Lerna: On the second metope, Heracles is shown in battle against the Lernaean Hydra, a nine-headed monster (which grew multiple new heads for each head cut off) which exhaled poisonous vapours from each of its mouths. On this badly damaged metope, Heracles is shown cauterizing the stump of one of the Hydra's decapitated heads to prevent its growing back.

(3) The Stymphalian Birds: On the third metope, Heracles is shown offering the Stymphalian Birds to Athena. Heracles overcame the birds, which could shoot their feathers as arrows, by the Stymphalian Lake (*see p. 193*).

(4) The Cretan Bull: The fourth metope depicts Heracles capturing the animal. According to some accounts, Heracles delivered the bull to King Eurystheus, who released it. The bull wandered off and lived in the neighbourhood of Marathon, in Attica.

(5) The Cerynean Hind: The fifth (very fragmentary) metope depicts Heracles' capture of the Cerynean Hind. This deer was beloved of Artemis, who allowed Heracles to take it to King Eurystheus, but insisted on its safe return. Although King Eurystheus had hoped to keep the hind as a pet, Heracles successfully released it, and it made its way back to Artemis.

(6) Slaying the Amazon: The sixth (very fragmentary) metope shows Heracles slaying the Amazon Hippolyte and capturing her magic girdle, which King Eurystheus' daughter Admete had coveted.

THE LABOURS OF HERACLES & THEIR REPRESENTATION AT OLYMPIA

Heracles, one of the most popular of the Greek heroes, was the son of Zeus and the nymph Alcmene. Some say that his name was chosen in a (vain) attempt to placate Zeus' wife Hera about the arrival of yet another love child (the name means 'Glory of Hera'). Hera was not placated, and when the infant Heracles strangled the serpents she sent to kill him in his cradle, she bided her time. When, as a young man, Heracles married Megara and had three children by her, Hera took her revenge: she inflicted a fit of madness on Heracles, who killed his wife and children. The Delphic Oracle told Heracles that to atone for his crime, he must seek out his enemy Eurystheus, King of Mycenae and Tiryns, and serve him. Eurystheus set ten Labours for Heracles; in each instance, Heracles had to deliver proof that he had succeeded. When Heracles had performed all ten Labours, the king claimed that he had had assistance in performing two of them and insisted on two more. There are variants on what the Twelve Labours were and how—and in what order—they were accomplished. In one way and another, each of the Labours represents a triumph of life over death and of civilisation over raw nature. The description here gives the Labours in the order in which they appear on the twelve metopes on view in the museum.

Eastern metopes

(1) The Erymanthian Boar: The first of the eastern metopes depicts Heracles' capture of the Erymanthian boar, which lived on Mt Erymanthos in Arcadia. Heracles is shown delivering the boar's body to King Eurystheus. Eurystheus, terrified, had leapt into a large, bronze crater, from which he gesticulates in alarm.

(2) The Horses of Diomedes: The second (very fragmentary) metope shows the capture of the flesh-eating horses that belonged to Diomedes, King of Thrace. The horses evidently lost their taste for flesh and lived peacefully in the kingdom of King Eurystheus. It was generally thought that Alexander the Great's famous steed Bucephalus descended from these horses.

(3) The Cattle of Geryon: The third metope shows Heracles' capture of the Cattle of of the monster Geryon, whose upper body was composed of three complete torsos, three heads, and six arms. The (very fragmentary) metope seems to show Heracles subduing Geryon.

(4) The Apples of the Hesperides: The fourth metope shows Heracles receiving the Apples of the Hesperides from Atlas. The Hesperides were nymphs who lived is the blessed isles located somewhere on the edge of the world (or, according to other versions, hidden in a mountain glen). Heracles is shown struggling to support the weight of the heavens, as Athena assists him with one graceful hand.

(5) The Capture of Cerberus: The fifth metope shows Heracles' capture of Cerberus, the terrifying three-headed dog who guarded the entrance to Hades. Heracles' ploy was to treat the serpent-tailed beast kindly, which no one else had ever done. As soon as Cerberus relaxed, Heracles put him on a leash and dragged him off to King Eurystheus.

(6) The Augean Stables: In the sixth metope, Heracles is shown at Olympia itself. In this labour, Heracles cleared in a single day the accumulated filth of years from the stables of King Augeas. The goddess Athena is shown looking on with approval.

Votive statues

The *Nike* of Paionios: The important late 5th-century *Nike* of Paionios, of island marble (Hall 6), originally stood on a tall triangular pedestal in front of the southeast corner of the Temple of Zeus. The base is inscribed with the name of the sculptor, a native of Mende in Thrace, and a dedication to Zeus from the Messenians of Nafpaktos 'as a tithe from their enemies'. It was probably dedicated at the Peace of Nikias in 421 BC after the exiled Messenians had aided the Athenians in the Spartan defeat at Sphacteria (*see p. 352*). The winged Nike is shown swooping down to land on the pedestal, the drapery pressed against the body, almost transparent in places, but billowing out

The famous *Hermes* of Praxiteles. Greek original of the 4th century BC, or 2nd-century BC Roman copy?

worth no more than the briefest remark. One of the best preserved Classical statues to have survived to modern times, it was protected by the fallen clay of which the upper walls of the temple had been built. The statue is of Parian marble, its original polish scarcely marked by the passage of time.

Hermes, the messenger of the gods, was charged by Zeus to take his infant son Dionysus (Bacchus) out of the reach of the jealous Hera. Hermes took the infant to the nymphs of Mount Nysa for safekeeping. Hermes is represented as resting on his journey. He stands in an attitude of easy grace, the left knee slightly bent, leaning his left arm on the trunk of a tree. In his left hand must have been his herald's staff, the *caduceus* (missing). Hermes' cloak is carelessly thrown across his arm and falls in simple, graceful folds over the tree trunk. On his left arm sits the infant Dionysus, reaching up towards an object (a bunch of grapes?) which Hermes holds in his right hand. The form of Hermes, which is entirely nude, presents an ideal combination of grace and strength. The head is slightly turned towards the child. The hair is in short crisp locks, indicated rather than sculptured in detail. Both behind and before can be traced the groove of a metal wreath. Traces of paint have been detected on the hair, lips, and sandal. The date of this masterpiece is usually put between 363 and 343 BC, though some authorities consider it a 2nd-century BC Roman copy.

behind in thick curling swathes—a fine example of the dramatic use of drapery in the sculpture of this period.

The Hermes of Praxiteles: This sculpture (Hall 8) was found in the Temple of Hera in 1877, in the place where it was noted by Pausanias. Its attribution to the 4th-century BC sculptor Praxiteles rests on Pausanias' summary description; he seems to have considered the work

THE MUSEUM OF THE HISTORY OF THE
OLYMPIC GAMES IN ANTIQUITY

Open Mon 12–7, Tues–Sun 8–7 in summer; 8–5 in winter; T: 26240 22529.

The museum (opened 2004) occupies a well-proportioned Neoclassical building, the original archaeological museum. Both collection and its labelling are excellent. Busts of Olympia's first excavators, Ernst Curtius and William Dörpfeld, stand in the entrance hall. The 12 galleries have themed displays, as follows:

Gallery 1: the Beginning of the Games at Olympia;

Gallery 2: Zeus and his Cult;

Gallery 3: the Organisation of the Games;

Gallery 4: Preparation of the Athletes;

Gallery 5: Women and Physical Exercise;

Gallery 6: the Champions;

Gallery 7: the Events;

Gallery 8: the Prizes;

Gallery 9: the Spectators;

Gallery 10: the Hellenistic and Roman Periods;

Gallery 11: Delphi and the Pythian Games;

Gallery 12: the Isthmian Games and Nemea and the Nemean Games.

The museum's exhibits detail all aspects of the games' history. The early beginnings are documented with some of the more than 6,000 dedications (many bronze) from the 10th–8th centuries BC. From the 7th century on, dedications from city-states begin to appear. The exhibits chart the expansion of the events from the first sprint in the stadium (776 BC) to chariot-races and boxing in the 7th century, races in armour in the 6th, a competition for heralds and trumpets in the 4th, and a *pancration* for young boys c. 200 BC. The games, which lasted only one day when they began in the 8th century BC, lasted some five days by the 5th century BC. In wrestling, breaking fingers was forbidden; eye gouging was permitted. Victorious athletes were awarded free meals for life by their home towns, paid no taxes, had front-row seats at theatre performances—and often became trainers for the next generation of Olympic athletes. The central gallery (7) suggests the Temple of Zeus in its dimensions and has a dazzling display of chariot wheels, javelin heads, and musical instruments used in contests, as well as prizes won and commemorative statues of victorious athletes that were erected at the sanctuary.

MUSEUM OF THE HISTORY OF THE EXCAVATIONS

Open Mon 12–7, Tues–Sun 8–7 in summer; 8–5 in winter; T: 26240 20128.

This characterful little museum is housed one of the houses used by the original German excavators. Exhibits document the history of the excavations from 1766 (when Dr Chandler identified the site) to the present. A wonderful photograph shows the Temple of Zeus just beginning to emerge from under five metres of earth. Some of the shovels and whisk brooms used by the archaeologists are on display.

SOUTH OF OLYMPIA

Issova and Alipheira

Just south of Olympia, near Krestena, is Skillountia (or Mazi), the site of ancient *Skillous*. The stylobate of a Doric temple was proposed by Yalouris (1954) to be that of Athena Skillountia mentioned by Strabo, rather than that known to have been erected at the cost of the exiled Xenophon on his estate here c. 444–434 BC. Recent work by I. Triandi has clarified the character of the temple (peripteral, internal colonnade) and revealed another substantial building, as well as a fortification wall and tower; also fragments of pedimental sculptures.

From Krestena the road leads east to Kallithea, a village standing just south of the confluence of the Ladonas with the Alpheios. Its situation suits the name ('Beautiful View'). Before you reach the village, a left turn leads in 4km to Trypiti (or Bitzibardi) with a Classical acropolis at Kastro. A kilometre through the village are the impressive remains (called locally *To Palati*) of the Gothic monastery of **Notre Dame d'Issova**. Built by the Franks and burnt in 1263 (either by the Byzantines or by Turks, possibly hired by them), the monastery ruins are unfenced at present. The remains abut a farm, and care must be exercised to avoid damaging crops or irritating any dogs. One comes first not to the monastery, but to the ruined east end of the three-aisled basilica of St Nicholas, with decorative brickwork, built after the monastery was burned in 1263.

The monastery, presumably built by western craftsmen, had Gothic pointed windows, a single nave, and was some 43m long. Little remains but the church, whose walls survive to an impressive height. Hetherington notes that on the north side of the nave there are indications of where the wooden roof of the adjoining cloister and dormitory were attached. It is not known whether the monastery was Cistercian or Benedictine, although Hetherington suggests that it may be the Cistercian foundation mentioned in a 1210 letter of Pope Innocent III.

Beyond Kallithea is the little visited and very scenic **site of ancient *Alipheira***. The route from Kato Amygdalies passes by Moni Sepetou (a convent of nuns), whose arcaded façade is visible against the rockface. Although the structure is modern, the original foundation is attributed by some to the 12th century. On the edge of the village of Alifira, a sign ('Archaia Alipheira') indicates the steep uphill turn to the site, aptly described by Mee and Spawforth as one for 'lovers of impressive ruins set in remote countryside'. After about 5mins on the dirt road, another sign (right) points up a steep footpath set off by stones which leads past shaded benches (c. 20mins to the site).

The buildings are laid out on a series of surprisingly large terraces. You reach first a Sanctuary of Asclepius (late 4th century), whose small temple has an altar and statue base; above, on a terrace, are the remains of the peristyle court of an associated building, perhaps the hospice for ailing pilgrims. From the terrace immediately above are broad views north and south. Beyond a further terrace to the east are a section of the wall defending the acropolis, and a tower. On the furthest terrace, at a slightly lower level, are the foundations of a Doric Temple of Athena (6 by 15 columns; built mid-6th century), also an altar and monumental base. From the top of the track where you approached the site, another path (left) partly follows the line of the northern fortifications; a good tower on this side is most clearly seen from above.

Typaneai and the Kaïafas Lagoon

West of Kallithea is Platiana. Below Kallithea you cross the Temberoula; from the climb on the other side can be seen an Ottoman bridge across the river. Platiana is just off the main road to the left. The hill behind the village (climbed by a dirt road leading eventually to Zacharo (Ζαχάρω) on the coast), is crowned by the walls of **ancient Typaneai**, in fine regular isodomic masonry (? 3rd century BC). Their perimeter encloses a narrow ridge, 594m long, rising at its west end to 599m. Within are remains of a theatre (with stone throne), cisterns and two Christian churches. Cars can be taken nearly 4km up the Zacharo road (keep left above the village) and parked near two wayside shrines. From here the site (the interior reasonably accessible) is 20mins walk further up the track and 5mins up a steep footpath. About 1km farther east (on an extension of the Typaneai ridge) are the scant ruins of Cumba, a Frankish castle held in 1364 by Marie de Bourbon, widow of Robert of Taranto.

Beyond Zacharo, the road passes between the sea and the **Lagoon of Kaïafas**, which is 5km long and contains valuable fisheries. On the lake-island of Aghia Aikaterini (*cross by causeway right at 32km*) are the sulphur Baths of Kaïafas, a somewhat desultory spa, with hotels and rent rooms open May–Oct. Migrating birds stop on the lake and adjacent marshes. The lake's waters come from springs in two large sulphurous caverns, the Cave of the Anigrian Nymphs and the Cave of Geranion, to which the ancients resorted for the cure of skin diseases. The first feeds the baths, the second is used for drinking. Local tradition ascribes the name of the lagoon to Caiaphas, High Priest of Judah, who bathed here after having been shipwrecked. To him is attributed the offensive pungency of the sulphur-laden waters.

Two small ancient sites are in the vicinity of the springs. Turn (right) signed again for Kaïafas Thermal Springs. A little further on, to the left across the railway line in the area called Kleidi, a low hill has some prehistoric remains. At the east foot are excavations of part of an important cemetery of tumuli (Middle–Late Helladic), one covering a tholos tomb. The first tumulus to be excavated, now in a sad state, is in a lemon grove to the north of the hill. On the other side of the main road from Kleidi, on a western spur of Mt Kaïafas (744m) is **ancient *Samikon*** (path from opposite Kleidi or track by road sign for Kato Samiko). The walls are impressive (best view from main road to the north) but close access is difficult. The imposing enceinte in developed polygonal masonry of c. 450 BC stands in places to 12 courses. Within is a less well preserved and earlier defensive wall dated before the 6th century BC. The place was taken by Philip V of Macedon in 219 BC.

Triphyllian Pylos and Lepreon

South of Zacharo is Kakovatos (Κακόβατος), well known to archaeologists for the site (15mins to the east) identified by Professor Dörpfeld, following Strabo, as **Triphyllian Pylos**, a place confused until the discoveries at Englianos with the Pylos of Nestor (*see p. 353*). Three tholos tombs and traces of a palace or sanctuary (Late Helladic) were excavated in 1909–10, and the position of the lower town was identified in 1961 (*unfenced at present, scant remains*).

Further south and further inland is Lepreo (Λέπρεο). On the heights above the village is the site of **ancient *Lepreon*** (*signposted*); there is a short, steep drive uphill followed by a short (uphill) walk to the site (*unfenced at present*). One comes first to a modern storage shed, which is partly built from blocks of the ancient walls which encircled the site; it is possible to follow the course of the walls for much of their circumference. The most important remains are the foundations of the 4th-century BC Doric Temple of Demeter and its altar. The temple, built of local limestone, had an external colonnade of 6 by 11 columns. The views over the surrounding countryside to the sea are splendid, as are the wild crocus and orchids in spring and autumn. One would be unlucky to encounter other visitors.

WESTERN ELIS

Just north of Pyrgos, at the end of a small peninsula, lies **Katakolo** (Κατάκολο) a small port founded for the currant trade in 1857, and often used by cruise ships as a base for the visit to Olympia. Close by are the **remains of *Pheia***, which with *Kyllene* (*see below*), was an important harbour for ancient Elis. Pheia was partially engulfed by the earthquake that overthrew the Temple of Zeus at Olympia in the 6th century AD. Remains of Pheia's walls can be traced under water, where they were explored by N. Yalouris and John Hall in 1957–60. Pheia's low acropolis (Pondikokastro or 'mouse castle') had a Byzantine kastro, which became the *Beauvoir* of the Villehardouins. The steep site is considerably overgrown, with low remains, one or two towers, and a plethora of potentially dangerous cisterns. The main thing here is the view, still beautiful.

To the northwest of here is **Gastouni** (Γαστούνι) a town that takes its name from the Frankish fief of *Gastogne*. Under the Turkish occupation it was the chief town of Elis. The 12th-century single-apsed church of the Panaghia (*usually locked*) has an elegant façade with decorative brickwork. The frescoes are badly sooted-over. The 13th-century Frankish castle which was once here has been entirely obliterated, as have signs of the minaret which once adorned the church, during its period as a mosque.

Andravida (Ἀνδραβίδα) further north, is an uninteresting market town, the successor to *Andreville*, once the flourishing capital of William de Villehardouin's Frankish principate of the Morea and seat of a Catholic bishop. Of the cathedral church of Aghia Sofia (c. 1250), two Gothic bays of the east end with the apse and east aisle chapels survive in a ruinous state. Hetherington remarks that the Gothic vaulting seen here is also seen in the Peloponnese only at Chalandritsa, in Achaia. There are traces of reused Byzantine ornament, as well as of Frankish trefoil decoration. Aghia Sofia was probably later used as a mosque. Of the Templars' church of St James, where the Villehardouin princes were buried, and of the Franciscan Church of St Stephen, nothing remains.

Kyllini (Κυλλήνη) west of Andravida, off the Patras–Pyrgos road, is reached by a heavily trafficked road to its harbour, which has ferry service for Zakynthos. Ancient *Kyllene* was an important port for ancient Elis, a trading point with Magna Graecia, and in the Peloponnesian War served as a Spartan naval station. Kyllene was captured by Sulpicius in 208 BC. In the Middle Ages *Clarence*, as it was then called, became the residence of the Villehardouin princes of Achaea, and their Angevin successors here developed the court life described in the *Chronicles of the Morea*. As *Chiarenza* it became the port of transit for Venetian and Genoese galleys from Brindisi or Taranto. In 1428 it passed to Constantine Palaeologus, who systematically destroyed it as soon as he held the last Frankish outpost (Patras).

Scattered foundations of the medieval city remain on the low plateau northwest of the modern village with a large ruined church similar to that at Andravida. A medieval castle was dynamited during the German occupation. Earlier remains may be traced near the 12th-century Byzantine Moni Vlachernai (30mins to the east; *closed at present*), completed by the Franks. The 13th-century church of Vlachernai may be a Frankish edifice built over an earlier Byzantine church. This would explain the mixed elements of the structure, including Byzantine cloisonné, reused Byzantine spolia, and the western porch and keystone of the narthex. The three-aisled barrel-vaulted church is some 40m long. More of the church, and possibly of its monastic complex, may lie under the nearby modern buildings.

The Castle of Clairmont at **Chlemoutsi**, impressive from afar on its hilltop, sits south of Kyllini, from which it is reached via the coast road, with a turn inland (6km) to Kastro (*site usually open 9–3*). The lone height on which the castle conspicuously stands was known to the ancients as *Cape Chelonatas* (from its resemblance when seen from seaward to a tortoise-shell). Above the village towers the crenellated enceinte of the best-preserved Frankish monument in the Morea. The castle keep is unique in Greece. The site has long been occupied: Some traces of Middle Helladic occupation of the hill have been recognised in the castle foundations. On the lower east slopes of this hill Palaeolithic implements were found in 1960.

Chlemoutsi was built in 1220–23 with revenues confiscated from the Latin clergy by Geoffrey I Villehardouin, who called it *Clairmont*. The castle was held by Ferdinand of Majorca in 1314–16. It fell in 1427 to Constantine Palaeologus, who based here his campaign against Patras. The Turks refortified the site after 1460.

The original recessed entrance gate has been obscured by the Turkish addition built flush with the curtain into the outer passage. Within to the left is a well-preserved 13th-century construction, but most of the buildings that backed the curtain wall have disappeared; only fireplaces remain. The breach made by Ibrahim Pasha's guns in 1825 can be seen near the southwest angle. The keep, a huge irregular hexagon, consists of a series of vast vaulted galleries arranged round a court. These were divided into two storeys either by an intermediate vault (as in the north and northwest) or by wooden floors (south and southwest). The massive barrel-vaults, in fine ashlar masonry, were strengthened by reinforcing arches; though these have mostly fallen, much of the vault has held, or been repaired. The view (exercise care when walking on the walls) commands the Zakynthos channel and the whole plain of Elis.

It is possible from Chlemoutsi to visit the rather disappointing spa town of Loutra Kyllinis, with a long sand beach and a number of hotels.

ANCIENT ELIS

Site and museum (labels in Greek and German) open Tues–Sun 8.30–3; T: 26220 41415.

Ancient Elis was excavated by the Austrian School in 1910–14 and jointly with the Greek Archaeological Service from 1960–81 and more recently. The small museum has a plan of the excavated remains and finds from the site, including Hellenistic and Roman mosaics. At the site, the remains are scattered and, with the exception of the theatre, considerably overgrown. Signs of habitation from the 12th century BC have been found here, but Elis became important only from the 5th century, both as the main city of Elis, and because of its dominant role in the organisation of the Olympic Games. Elis had another burst of prosperity under the Romans, when it was honoured for its connection with Olympia. In the 4th and 5th centuries AD, a cemetery spread across much of the former agora and a large basilica was built (cf. Nemea, in Corinthia).

Athletes trained at Elis under supervision for one month before the start of the games, and facilities for them (palaestrae, gymnasia) and the officials (*Hellanodikaion*; Stoa of the Hellanodikai) were provided. Remains of these buildings have been identified in the vicinity of the agora, where there is also the south or 'Corcyraean' stoa, mentioned by Pausanias, although his explanation of its name—which requires a foundation date in the 5th century—cannot be reconciled with the archaeological evidence for one in the 2nd or 1st century BC. A Late Roman building has fine mosaics of the Muses and the Labours of Heracles. A path leads to the theatre, a Hellenistic reconstruction of a Classical structure, again altered in Roman times. The cavea was banked, probably with radials in stone, but did not have stone seats. Stone 'tickets' were found. An Early Helladic tomb came to light and nine slab-covered graves attributed to the transitional period between sub-Mycenaean and Protogeometric. The boundaries of the city have been fixed and two cemeteries explored. The acropolis was on the hill locally called *Kaloskopi*, a name which led to the erroneous location here of *Beauregard*, a lost Frankish castle.

About 5km farther up the river, near Kentro, is the huge Pineios irrigation dam, built in 1961–62 by American engineers, forming a large lake. In a series of international 'salvage digs' in the area, the flat-topped hill of Armatova, near Agrapidochori just on the other side of the swollen river, upheld its claim to be the site of Elean *Pylos*.

PRACTICAL INFORMATION

At a minimum, the visitor to Elis should have a full day at Olympia. Those interested in Elis' medieval monuments will want another day or two.

GETTING AROUND

- **By car:** Olympia is a 4–6-hr drive from Athens; heavy traffic in Patras means that the drive from Patras to Olympia can easily take 2hrs.
- **By bus:** There are three buses a day to Olympia from Athens (Kifissou 100; T: 210 513 4110 or 210 512 9233). Also frequent buses from Patras to Pyrgos, with connecting service to Olympia.
- **By rail:** There are several trains a day from Athens to Pyrgos (change here for Olympia). Information from the Stathmos Peloponnisou in Athens (T: 210 513 1601).
- **By taxi:** In Olympia there are usually taxis waiting by the museum and on the small plateia on the main street.

INFORMATION OFFICES

Olympia The tourist office (T: 26240 23100 or 26240 23125), on the way to the ancient site near the south end of Kondili, is usually open daily 9–9 in summer; in winter, hours are erratic.

WHERE TO STAY

Olympia

There are plenty of hotels in Olympia, but it is still a good idea to book in summer.

€€€ **Europa**. Excellent 80-room hotel, with its own restaurant, a few mins' drive out of town on a hill overlooking the village and site. Garden and pool. Archaia Olympia, T: 800 528 1234 in the US; 26240 22650, or 26240 22700.

€€€ **Grecotel Lakopetra Beach**. 200-room resort, 30mins by car from Olympia (*map p. 398*), set in extensive gardens a short walk from the beach. Two restaurants and two pools. Kato Achaia, T: 26930 51713.

€€ **Olympia Palace**. 58-room hotel on the main street. Good-sized rooms, most with balconies. Restaurant. Praxiteleous Kondili 2, Archaia Olympia, T: 26240 23101.

€€ **Hotel Pelops**. Pleasant, centrally located 25-room hotel (sometimes closed in winter) completely renovated after being occupied for most of 2003 by the Olympics Committee. Varela 2, Archaia Olympia, T: 26240 22543, www.hotelpelops.gr

Loutra Kyllinis (for Chlemoutsi) €€€ **Robinson Club Hotel-Kyllini Beach**. 330 rooms, open May–October. T: 26230 95205; €€ **Xenia**. 80 rooms, open April–October. T: 26230 92270.

WHERE TO EAT

Olympia

As with any establishment where the staff does not expect to see you again, the service and food at most Olympia restaurants is poor. The €€ **Taverna Ambrosia** behind the train station (often closed in winter) is better than average, and is probably the locals' choice. There is a nice outside terrace.

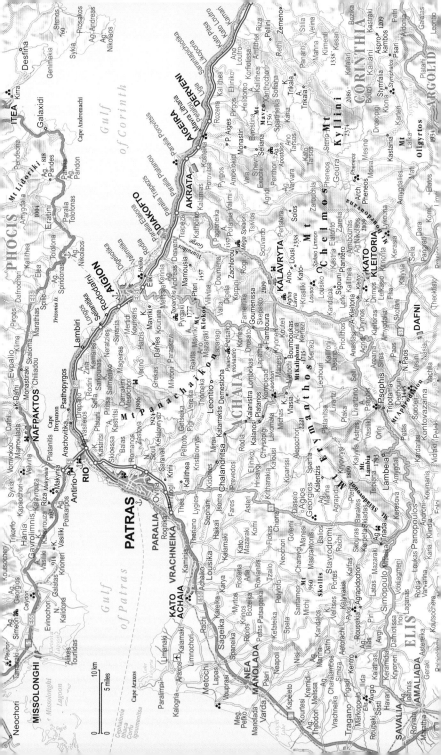

ACHAIA

Achaia (Ἀχαΐα, also Achaea), the mountainous, earthquake-prone northwestern division of the Peloponnese, borders on the south with inland Arcadia and maritime Elis, and faces to the north and west the gulfs of Corinth and Patras and the Ionian Sea. Achaia—as is more than evident from afar—is very mountainous; its major ranges are Panachaïkon (1924m) to the north, Erymanthos to the west (2221m) and Chelmos (Aroania; 2338m) to the east. The capital is Patras, the largest city in the Peloponnese, the third largest in Greece, and one of the country's most important ports. Most visitors from Europe who arrive in Greece by ship, arrive in Patras, which is served by high-speed ferries from Ancona and Brindisi. In 1809, Byron first set foot on Greek soil here. The vineyards around Patras, especially those of the Achaia Clauss winery, are among the most productive in Greece.

Achaia has no major ancient sites, and its medieval remains do not equal those of neighbouring Elis. Its pleasures come rather from its landscape, which affords chances to hike Chelmos and the Selinous Gorge, and its villages, especially those in the mountains around Kalavryta, and on the coast, near Aigion, Achaia's second largest city.

In the Mycenaean period the name of the province seems to have connoted almost the whole of the Peloponnese. According to legend, Agamemnon convened the Greek host at ancient *Aigion* before setting off for Troy. Although no substantial site has been found, remains from cemeteries testify to settlement during the Mycenaean period. In Classical times Achaia was the name given chiefly to the north coastal area. When the Romans conquered the Achaean League (*see overleaf*) they gave the name Achaea to the whole peninsula.

During the Frankish occupation of the Peloponnese, Achaia was occupied (1204–1422) and Aigion was the capital of a barony. Under the Turks, Achaia's mountain villages enjoyed a fair amount of independence, while the coast was firmly under Turkish control. The War of Independence began here on 25th March 1821, when the banner of Revolution was raised at the monastery of Aghia Lavra near Kalavryta by Archbishop Germanos of Patras. Aigion (then called Vostitsa) was the first town liberated from the Turks, and it resumed its ancient name. During the Second World War, Kalavryta suffered one of the worst massacres in Greece under the German occupation (*see p. 408*). Today the district's prosperity depends on wine, currants, light industry, the port towns of Patras and Aigion, and tourism, including ecotourism and skiing.

PATRAS

Patras (Πάτρα), the largest town (pop. 160,000) in the Peloponnese and the third largest in Greece, is a furiously energetic port town with a diabolical system of one-way streets. It has the usual virtues and vices of a port town: lively squares and streets, some of which, near the waterfront, it is best not to explore alone at night. The University of Patras is one of the best in Greece; there is a winter music and theatre season, and the Patras International Festival of the Arts in the summer. Carnival in Patras is the most lavishly celebrated in all Greece. Although Patras' ancient remains are sparse, the area below the Kastro has a Roman odeion, as well as pleasant side-streets. Further down toward the centre, on Boukaouri, is the only Turkish bath in Greece still in operation. A great deal of sprucing up took place, and new museums— including a new archaeological museum—were projected, for Patras' role as 'European City of Culture' in 2006.

THE ACHAEAN LEAGUE

The Achaean League was a confederation for mutual defence and protection of the 12 coastal cities of Achaea (*Aigai*, *Aigeira*, *Aigion*, *Boura*, *Dyme*, *Kerynea*, *Olenos*, *Patrai*, *Pellene*, *Pharai*, *Rhypes* and *Tritaia*). Founded at an unknown date, the league met until 373 BC at Helike (*see p. 407*). It was refounded in 280 BC as an anti-Macedonian organisation and admitted non-Achaeans. Aratos of Sikyon united Sikyon, Corinth and other cities to the League, became its general in 245 BC, and made it the chief political power in Greece. The admission of Megalopolis antagonised Sparta, whose king Cleomenes III attacked Corinth, Argos and Megalopolis before being defeated by the combined forces of Aratos and his powerful ally Antigonus Doson. The League went over to Rome in 198 BC under the leadership of Philopoemen of Megalopolis (252–183 BC), sometimes styled the last great man of free Greece. After the Roman conquest of Greece in 146 BC, the Achaean League lost all power.

EXPLORING PATRAS

Patras' rapid growth in the last several decades means that it is now approached by the usual disheartening, anonymous urban sprawl. The focus of the city continues to be on the harbour, and the most pleasant spots for visitors are the squares, such as Psila Alonia and Aghiou Georgiou; the old quarter around the kastro; and the harbourside promenade. Residents speak highly of the new suburbs in the hills above town.

The waterfront

The quay, with the railway station, is generally animated to a point of considerable frenzy; parking here is virtually impossible, although it is often possible to hover by one of the ticket agents. A number of kiosks sell foreign language newspapers and periodicals. Plateia Olgas stands several blocks inland, beyond the busy commercial arcades of Aghiou Andreou. Here is the Archaeological Museum (*closed at the time of writing because of earthquake damage*). The collection has material from Patras and

Achaia itself, including grave finds from the Mycenaean through to the early Christian periods (some Classical and Hellenistic gold jewellery); Greek and Roman sculpture and pottery; Roman mosaics; and inscriptions.

HISTORY OF PATRAS

Patrai was a substantial though not conspicuous member of the Achaean League. The ancient city lay some distance inland from its port, to which it was connected by long walls, the idea for building which came from Alcibiades (*Thucydides V, 52*). During an invasion of the Gauls, the Patraians were the only Achaeans to cross into Phocis to help the Aetolians and they suffered accordingly. After the Battle of Actium, Augustus settled many of his veterans in the depopulated city, which he refounded as the *Colonia Augusta Achaica Patrensis* (16–15 BC). Under the Romans, Patras had holdings on both sides of the Gulf of Corinth, was a vital port, and was linked by an excellent coast road (whose course the modern road largely follows) to Corinth. Although Patras was favoured by the Romans, relatively little remains of the Roman town because of recent urban development. There are important traces of the Early Christian and Byzantine city, and of a significant Jewish community, during the Roman period and again during Byzantine times, when Benjamin of Tudela recorded a community with two rabbis. In the 17th century, a third of the 5,000 inhabitants were Jews, but the community disappeared during the War of Independence, when many left, lest they be forced to convert or killed.

St Andrew, the first disciple, preached at Patrai and is said to have been martyred here. Invading Slavs, assisted by a Saracen fleet, besieged Patras in 805 when the supposed intervention of St Andrew confirmed his veneration as the city's patron saint. In the 9th–10th centuries the city's prosperity grew, especially with the development of a silk trade and the growth of its port. In 1205 Patras became a Frankish barony with a Latin archbishop.

In 1408 Patras was sold by its archbishop to Venice. After a series of skirmishes, Constantine Palaeologus seized the city in 1429. Patras was held by Constantine's brother Thomas until 1460, when it passed to Mehmet II. It remained the commercial capital of Greece despite the political changes. During the 17th century, Patras, along with Kalamata, was involved in the slave trade. Both in the abortive rising of 1770 and in 1821 Patras claims to be the first town to have taken up arms against the Ottomans.

Patras is celebrated throughout Greece as the see of Archbishop Germanos, who raised the standard of the Cross at Kalavryta in 1821, in the opening sally of the War of Independence (*see p. 410*). The Turks, however, aware of the archbishop's intention to march on Patras, occupied the citadel, from where they bombarded the town. It remained under Turkish control until 1828. The modern city was rebuilt, on a grid plan with broad arcaded streets, by Capodistrias (*see p. 234*).

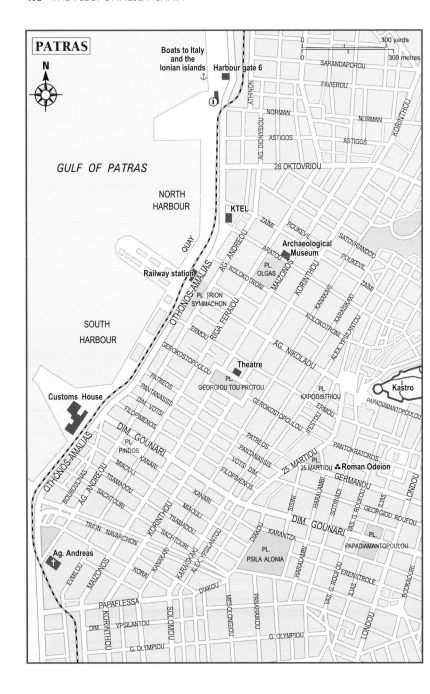

The kastro

Open 8–3; closed Mon.

At the top of Aghiou Nikolaou, a broad flight of steps (view) leads to the kastro, with its pleasant park, built on the site of the ancient acropolis. The upper town on the slopes of the acropolis has a distinctive neighbourhood atmosphere which is lacking nearer the quay; nonetheless, driving here on the steep, sometimes one-way, sometimes dead-end streets, is not for the faint-hearted.

The lower ward of the kastro has round and polygonal towers and is planted with flowering shrubs. The north curtain wall, of early Byzantine date, incorporates Classical drums and blocks; similar elements occur in a flanking tower of the south curtain. All periods of Byzantine–Turkish–Venetian rebuilding up to the 17th century are represented, with the Byzantine remains especially notable. The well-preserved keep (*no admission*) has square towers but is equally indeterminate in date. The view embraces Zakynthos and Cepahlonia, the mountains of the Roumeli coast above Nafpaktos, and, to the south, the peaks of Erymanthos. In Papadiamantopoulou nearby, the remains of a Temple of Augustus have been identified.

From opposite the east gate of the kastro a narrow paved road, skirting below the radio station in the park, passes (15mins walk) through two sections of a Roman aqueduct, the first well-preserved, the second ruinous.

The odeion and Roman Patras

Much of what remains of Roman Patras has been saved by numerous aptly-termed 'rescue operations'. In 1999 alone, there were 29 rescue operations, uncovering signs of the Roman agora on Londou, a number of Roman roads, a late Roman bath complex, parts of the north and south Roman cemeteries, as well as public buildings and private houses, often with mosaic floors and fine objects. In other years, streets have been traced and evidence of agricultural activity (wine presses, etc) discovered, as well as remains of the numerous graves and funerary monuments that lined the roads outside the city. To the southwest of the kastro, on Plateia 25 Martiou, is a characteristic imperial Roman odeion (*open Tues–Sun 8–2.30; free entry*), made of brick and faced with marble, which, when rediscovered in 1889, had 25 rows of seats (in 4 wedges). Much of the odeion's marble was later removed by enterprising local builders. Pausanias said that this, and the odeion of Herodes Atticus in Athens, were the two most distinguished in Greece. The theatre was extensively restored in 1960 and is now used for dramatic productions. The cavea faces south; the orchestra is 9.6m in diameter. In Germanou, just beyond, are the remains of a 3rd-century AD nymphaeum. In this area of Patras the ancient buildings seem to have been laid out on a series of terraces c. 4m high. On the lower side of Plateia 25 Martiou are the remains of a substantial Roman building, which excavations (visible) in the streets below (Ifestou, Gerokostopoulou) have suggested may be the amphitheatre. You can then take Odos Sisini, passing other Roman remains, to the Plateia Psila Alonia. From this irregular space, planted with palms, a vigorous bronze of Archbishop Germanos raising the standard dominates the city. A substantial Roman terrace wall, typical of those needed to support buildings in this sloping area of Patras, can be seen in Odos Diakou, immediately below the Plateia. In Kanari (Vlachou) to the west, a probable bath complex with nymphaeum has been partly excavated.

Aghios Andreas

Odos Trion Navarchon descends to the west towards the huge ungainly neo-Byzantine church of Aghios Andreas, in reinforced concrete by G. Nomikos. A venerated gold reliquary contains the head of St Andrew, returned by Pope Paul VI from Rome in 1964, where, according to one tradition, Thomas Palaeologus fled from the Turks with it in 1460. According to a much older tradition, the relics of St Andrew had already been removed in the 4th century by St Regulus, or Rule, Bishop of Patras, who, guided by an angel, travelled to Scotland, where he was shipwrecked off Muckcross, in Fife, but survived to found St Andrews.

Patras' Aghios Andreas is widely believed to be on the site of the Apostle's crucifixion, but is more likely over a Temple of Demeter. An earlier Byzantine church, restored in 1426, was essentially destroyed in the fire of 1821. The park beside the church, with a children's playground, is a pleasant place to pass some time.

You can return to the quay via Odos Korinthou or Odos Maizonos, passing solemn public buildings to Plateia Georgiou tou Protou, the imposing central square of the city, with numerous cafés and the municipal theatre, the Apollo, one of Patras' proudest buildings. Built by Ernst Ziller, it is said to be modelled on Milan's La Scala.

On the west side of the town in the Scagliopoulou Park (Odos Koritsas and Odos Mavrokordatou; *beyond the map*) is the Folk Museum, which keeps irregular hours (*check at the tourist office for current opening times*).

EXCURSIONS FROM PATRAS

Achaia Clauss

Usually open 8–1 & 4–7 in summer; 10–4 in winter. T: 2610 325051; www.greekwinemakers.com

The Achaia-Clauss winery, a popular tour-group stop, is 8km southeast of Patras. The no. 7 bus leaves from the corner of Kolokotroni and Kanakari and follows a pleasant route through the hilly suburbs of Patras to the vineyard; by car, take Odos Gounari (signposted) out of town.

The Bavarian Baron von Clauss founded the winery in 1854; its most famous wine, the very sweet Mavrodaphne ('Black Laurel'), is said to commemorate the beautiful black eyes of the baron's wife, who died young. Visitors are given conducted tours and a sip of Mavrodaphne. The buildings, with huge wooden barrels, occupy the site of a partly excavated Mycenaean chamber-tomb cemetery.

Rio and the coast

At Rio the new Rio–Antirio bridge linking the Peloponnese and Central Greece threatens to put the old car ferry (*frequent crossings in 20mins*) out of business. This, the world's largest cable-stayed bridge, opened in time for the August 2004 Athens Olympics. It has a 2,252-metre fully suspended continuous deck, 40km of cables, and was built to withstand both earthquakes and acts of terrorism. With the bridge in operation, cars and lorries no longer have to take the ferry, though that will continue to operate for an indeterminate period. The bridge is an important component of Greece's radically revamped road system from the Peloponnese north to Thessaloniki and into Central Europe, and east to Turkey. The bridge's website is www.gefyra.gr

At Rio, the **Castle of the Morea** or *Kastelli*, on the shore, formerly a prison, is usually open to the public and well worth a visit. It was built by Bayezid II in 1499 before his campaign in the Morea. Parts of its aqueduct still exist by the roadside. Here took place the last stand of the Turks in October 1828, when Ibrahim Pasha's troops held out for three weeks against a combined Anglo-French force under General Maison. The moated fortress is also impressive from the sea.

The coastal plain is well watered by torrents descending from Panachaïkon, and bamboo is grown. The villages of Rododafni, Selianitika and Lambiri are popular with Greek holidaymakers. Psathopyrgos ('thatched tower') lies in the midst of very fine scenery resembling the Italian Riviera, with a lovely coastline across the Gulf. The mountains, thickly clothed with firs, plane-trees, arbutus, oleander, and a variety of flowering shrubs, run down to the coast, while the road and railway pass immediately above the sea, crossing a number of torrents. **Cape Drepanon**, northeast of Arachovitika, is the northernmost point of the Peloponnese.

AIGION

The small commercial port of Aigion (Αἴγιο) is the second largest town (after Patras) in Achaia, the chief town (pop. 24,000) of the eparchy of Aigialeia and the seat of a bishop. Called *Vostitsa* after it was conquered by the Slavs in the 8th century, it gave its name to the finest currants grown in Greece. In the 19th century, this was one of the most important ports for the export of currants throughout the Mediterranean and beyond. Currants and olive-oil are still exported and there are large paper-mills. There is also a ferry across to the Gulf of Corinth to Aghios Nikolaos (*usually morning and afternoon*). A lively provincial centre, Aigion has made few efforts to attract foreign tourists, but has pleasant squares, an archaeological museum, decent restaurants and pastry shops, and good beaches near town. At Oikonomou 43, the Demeter shop sells local produce, mostly organic.

According to legend, *Aigion* (which is mentioned in the Homeric 'Catalogue') took its name from a goat (αἴξ) which suckled the infant Zeus. The Achaean League met here in the Homarion and after the destruction of *Helike*, this was the chief city of Achaia. Along with the rest of Greece, it was conquered by the Romans in 146 BC. The name *Vostitsa* is of Slav origin. After the division of the Morea in 1209 it was given by Geoffrey de Villehardouin to Hugh de Lille de Charpigny as the barony of *La Vostice*. After a period under the Acciaioli, it surrendered to the Turks in 1458, and except for a Venetian interlude in 1463–70 remained Turkish until 1821. It was partly destroyed by earthquakes in 1819 and 1888.

The town

The town is built on a cliff 30m high above a narrow strip of shore, and has several fountains. The suburbs are nondescript, but the old core has considerable charm. The harbourside church of the Panaghia Tripiti houses a revered icon. A plane tree of great antiquity is said to be one mentioned by Pausanias. From the main square, Plateia Aghia Lavra, Odos Mitropoleos, with the cathedral, ascends to the attractive Plateia Psila Alonia (cafés with a fine view of the Gulf of Corinth). Near the cathedral a mosaic floor depicting the *Good Shepherd*, probably from the narthex of an Early Christian basilica of c. AD 500, was found in 1973–74. Above Psila Alonia, at the junction of Odos Solomou (left at lights) and Odos Rouvali are substantial remains of a Hellenistic naïskos.

In Odos Aghiou Andreou, north of Plateia Aghias Lavras, the handsome old market, designed by Ziller (1890), was refurbished to house a cultural centre and the Archaeological Museum (*open 8.30–3; T: 26910 21517*). The centrepiece of the museum is a fine Roman marble figure, beautifully displayed at the far end of a series of galleries which contain material from the Neolithic to Late Roman periods from Aigion and the eparchy of Aigialeia. The main hall in the centre of the building has finds (mostly architectural fragments) laid out round the sides. These include terracotta antefixes and cornices from the Temple of Artemis (?) at *Aigeira*, c. 500 BC; capitals and other fragments in various styles, chiefly from Aigion and Mamousia; also inscriptions. A tile fragment from Mamousia is inscribed ΚΑΡΥΝ[ΕΙΟΝ] confirming the identification of the ancient site. Displays in the other galleries include Neolithic-Mycenaean material, with pottery and jewellery from the Kallithea Mycenaean cemetery (Aigion); Protogeometric and Geometric pottery from various sites and two bronze bowls from Kato Mavriki; Archaic, Classical, Hellenistic and Roman finds from Aigion, Mamousia (ancient *Keryneia*) etc, including a gold Hellenistic necklace and diadem and a silver cup, also terracotta figurines and moulds, as well as Roman bronzes, and tile fragments stamped ΑΙΓΙΟ.

EXCURSIONS FROM AIGION

The Selinous Valley

Immediately before the crossing of the rapid Selinous, or Vostitsa, amid vineyards of currants, a road diverges (left) for Pteri or Fteri (20km) a summer hill-resort with fine views which have earned it the sobriquet of the 'Balcony of God'.

A pleasant excursion up the Selinous Valley can take in two monasteries, the Taxiarchis (small ecclesiastical museum) beyond the river on the right bank, to which site it was transferred in the 17th century from (1hr farther on) Palaiomonastiro. Another road, further west, mounts the foothills of Panachaïkon (1925m), where at Dafnes (12km) are two refuges of the Greek Alpine Club.

Ancient Helike

Eliki recalls the name of the Classical city of *Helike*, already a prominent settlement in the Bronze Age. The important sanctuary of Helikonian Poseidon was the early meeting-place of the Achaean League, until Helike was drowned by a tidal wave in the earthquake of 373 BC; Pausanias states that Poseidon sent the earthquake as punishment when Achaians dragged supplicants from the temple and murdered them. Following a similar seismic disturbance in 1963, underwater investigation was undertaken in 1966, without conspicuous success. Later geophysical examination of the area by the American School of Classical Studies in Athens and the University of Patras suggested that ancient Helike no longer lay under the sea, but under the coastal plain, due to the shift in the coastline, and extensive silting caused by severe earthquakes. Excavations beginning in the late 1990s confirmed this hypothesis. In 2000, part of the Roman coast road from Corinth to Patras, which Pausanias would have taken when he passed this way, was discovered. Then, in 2001, the Helike Project, uncovered evidence of Classical Helike and the startling remains of a previously unsuspected Early Bronze Age town dating from perhaps 2400 BC, the period when Troy flourished. As Steven Soter of the American Museum of Natural History put it, 'We were looking for a Classical Pompeii and we found a Bronze Age Pompeii'. (*New York Times*, December 2, 2003; see also *Archaeology*, January 2004). Work in the 5m-deep excavation pit has been slow, and complicated by repeated flooding.

The coast towards Corinth

The small town of Diakofto is the railway junction for Kalavryta, and the excursion by train, up the Vouraikos Gorge as far as Zachlorou is a 'must' (*see p. 409 below*).

Between here and Akrata the mountains reach to the sea and the road runs higher with views ahead and across the Gulf of Corinth. From Akrata station, below the village, tracks climb to Solos (6hrs) providing a possible approach to the Styx; its waters feed the Krathis, crossed by the road just before Akrata.

Further along the coast, a detour between Aigeira and Mavra Litharia leads to the **site of Classical *Aigeira***, with a Hellenistic theatre and fine views. Turn under the railway just before Mavra Litharia and take the steeply rising inland road towards Palaies Aiges. After c. 5.5km there is a sign for the theatre. The antiquities lie to the left (theatre etc, though not immediately visible) and right (acropolis) of the road. The site seems to have been occupied in Antiquity, deserted in the Middle Ages, resettled in the 19th century, and then once more abandoned. The city was called *Hyperesia* by Homer (*Iliad II, 573*); there are signs of prehistoric settlement (pottery) on the acropolis. There has been speculation that the 12th-century pottery found here was made by invaders, not locals. In the 7th century, the inhabitants are said to have frustrated a Sikyonian invasion by collecting goats after dark and tying torches to their horns, thus misleading the enemy into believing reinforcements had arrived: hence the later name of the city.

Aigeira has been excavated by the Austrian Archaeological Institute (1915, 1926, and from 1972). The Hellenistic theatre, remodelled in the Roman period, is the most impressive monument. Beyond it are a group of *naïskoi* arranged in a semicircle, in one of which was found a head by the sculptor Eucleides. Naïskoi D and E (to the west, with some painted plaster) were dedicated to Zeus and Artemis-Iphigeneia respectively. A large complex (Hellenistic/Roman) lies to the north. It seems to include the bath building of a gymnasium, as troughs and channels for water control have been found.

Remains on the two main terraces of the acropolis (sharp climb; view) are less tangible. Mycenaean buildings and pottery have been discovered, and a Hellenistic/Roman square with shops. Architectural fragments and foundations of the 7th century BC at the highest point may be from a Temple of Artemis-Iphigeneia mentioned by Pausanias. Terracottas from the buildings are in the Aigion Museum. There are some traces of the wall on the side of the hill above the road, beyond the theatre.

About 12km further inland, beyond the villages of Aiges and Monastiri, at Seliana (or Felloï), the Monastery of Aghii Apostoloi has a 17th-century church, with frescoes, and a carved wooden templon of 1730.

KALAVRYTA & ENVIRONS

A magnificently scenic road (165km) runs from Tripolis, through the Mainalon mountains of Arcadia into the Erymanthos mountains of Achaia. NB: The mountain roads of southern Achaia, best taken slowly at any time, can be impassable (snow and ice) for most cars in winter.

Kalavryta (Καλάβρυτα), the successor to ancient *Kynaithes*, whose inhabitants were distinguished for their independence, wildness, and irreverence, is situated on the Vouraïkos river at the foot of Mt Velia. The town is known throughout Greece because of two events. First, it was at the nearby Aghia Lavra Monastery (*see overleaf*) that Archbishop Germanos of Patras raised the banner of Revolution on 25th March 1821. Second, this was the site of an infamous massacre during the Second World War. On 13th December 1943, German occupying troops, in reprisal for the shooting of 81 of their men taken prisoner by ELAS guerrillas, massacred 1,436 males over the age of 15 at the Kapi Hill outside Kalavryta and then torched the town. The hill is topped by a memorial to the massacre (signposted from town 'Sacrifice of 1943'). Kalavryta is a member of the Association of Martyred Towns, whose members include Coventry, Guernica and Lidice. Since 1962 the German Federal government has re-endowed Kalavrytan schools. The clock on the metropolitan church stands at 2.34, the exact hour of the massacre. Well into the 1960s, this was a village of old women in black.

Kalavryta today is a thriving town, with its rack-and-pinion railway popular in summer, and the Kalavryta ski centre (15km outside town) drawing visitors in winter with slopes of 1800m and 2499m. Cool mountain springs and the freshness of the air make Kalavryta especially attractive in summer, when tables are set up outside the cafés and restaurants along the main plateia. The local rosehip sweet is on sale at most shops.

The kastro of Kalavryta

The kastro stands on a rocky height reached by a steep path. There are sparse remains (walls; cisterns; portions of the 6m by 10m keep) of '*Tremolo*', or the '*Kastro tis Oraias*'. The first name derives from Humbert de la Trémouille; the second from the beautiful Katherine Palaeologus, daughter of a baron from Chalandritsa, who is said to have committed suicide rather than fall into Turkish hands in 1463. The views (gained after a steep climb) over the surrounding countryside are splendid.

EXCURSIONS FROM KALAVRYTA

Taxis are usually available in Kalavryta for these excursions, and there is sometimes a local bus service to the Mega Spilaion and Aghia Lavra monasteries. It is also possible to arrange for a taxi to meet the rack-and-pinion railway at its stop at Zachlorou for the excursion to Mega Spilaion.

The rack-and-pinion railway and Mega Spilaion

The schedule for the train, which usually runs year-round, is posted both in the Kalavryta and Diakofto stations. The train can be crowded on summer weekends, when it is sometimes necessary to purchase a ticket a day in advance. Allow 3hrs for the 45-km round trip, more if you visit Mega Spilaion.

The Kalavryta railway, reopened in 2005 after extensive repairs, was engineered in 1885–95 by an Italian company in the fantastic, sombre gorge down which the Vouraïkos, or Kerynites, tumbles its boulder-strewn course. The replacement of the original steam rolling-stock by diesel railcars from 1960–62 has ended the former discomfort—and for period enthusiasts much of the romance—but nothing detracts from the awe-inspiring scenery or from the achievement of the engineers. Sometimes pushing, sometimes pulling, the little locomotives (75cm gauge) proceed partly by adhesion (max. gradient 1:28), partly by rack-and-pinion (Abt system; gradient 1:7), rising 700m in 22.5km. The line crosses the water several times on bridges and runs in tunnels or on overhung ledges. The sites of ancient *Bura* and *Keryneia* occupy hilltops to east and west of the entrance to the gorge. Just below Zachlorou, where the gorge is only a few feet wide, an original tunnel on the east side suffered a partial collapse and after the Second World War was replaced by another, cut in the solid cliff on the west, and a new bridge constructed.

The ride begins gently, running through the valley that extends to Zachlorou. Gradually, the track becomes more precipitous, at points seemingly perpendicular. From Zachlorou, a steep zigzag ascent (with a superb view towards Kalavryta up the cypress- and fir-clad valley) leads east in 45mins to the **Moni Mega Spilaion** (Μονή Μέγα Σπήλαιο), or monastery of the great cavern, built against a vertical and almost smooth cliff. If you decide not to visit the monastery, the train will rush you on through dense vegetation into the plain (noted for its cherries) of Diakofto, the railway junction for Kalavryta, with frequent bus connection with Patras.

Visiting the monastery

Taxis often meet the train, but it is not a bad idea to arrange this in advance in Kalavryta.
It is best to visit the monastery in the morning (usually open daily 9–2 & 6–7 in summer;
admission fee. It has a hostel of 50 beds.

After a disastrous fire in 1934, when a powder magazine (said to date from the War of
Independence) exploded, the monastery was rebuilt in an uncompromising 20th-cen-
tury style. Visitors are shown around by a monk. There is a miraculous icon of the
Mother of God, supposedly found in the great cavern by the shepherdess Euphrosyne
in AD 362, and attributed to St Luke. The image is in relief, of wax and gum mastic. An
interesting museum of sacred relics, including seraphim, carved in wood (c. 1700),
illustrates the history of the convent; note two *epitaphioi* from Asia Minor, one of Russian
workmanship; gospels on vellum (9th–11th centuries), with Byzantine enamel-work
covers; reliquaries containing the left hand of the martyr Charalambos in the attitude of
blessing; the heads of the monks Simeon and Theodore, founders of the monastery;
hands of the Sts Theodore; crosses, etc. There is a 17th-century wooden iconostasis.

Aghia Lavra

Usually open 9.30–1.30 & 6–7.30.

Seven kilometres out of Kalavryta is Aghia Lavra, the celebrated monastery where
Germanos, Archbishop of Patras, raised the standard of revolt on 25th March 1821.
Kalavryta, along with coastal Vostitsa (the present Aigion) was a centre of anti-Turkish
revolutionary sentiment, and local leaders planned the moment when Archbishop
Germanos would raise his standard in a series of meetings. A hermitage, started in 961,
developed into a monastery, many times destroyed and rebuilt. The present building,
begun in 1839, has suffered by earthquake and fire, most recently at the hands of the
Nazis in 1943, but retains the church of the Koimisis tis Theotokou from before the sack
by Ibrahim Pasha in 1826. A little museum contains historical relics and medieval manuscripts. On a hill 2.5km to the west stands the imposing monument to the national
uprising of 1821, erected on the 150th anniversary. On the back is a relief of the banner of the *Dormition* on which Archbishop Germanos administered the oath of revolt.

Ancient Lousoi

One bus daily links Kalavryta and Kato Lousi.

The remains of *Lousoi* (near the road between Kato Lousi and Sigouni) are not spectacular, but the scenery is. A few hundred metres from the main road are the excavations
(Austrian Archaeological Institute), which have uncovered a Hellenistic house with peristyle, bathroom and farming equipment. Another building includes a dining room with
space for 11 couches, also two phases of a bathroom. The area was reconstructed in the
Roman period and there are also signs of pre-Hellenistic occupation. In the 1990s, part
of the network of ancient roads from Lousi to Kalavryta, Kleitoria, and in the direction
of Aghia Lavra, was traced, and some ancient wheel-tracks were noted south of Lefki.

Higher up the track (left), on a bluff above the valley, lies a Hellenistic Sanctuary of
Artemis (Austrian Institute 1898–99 and renewed excavation since the 1990s). The

Theodoros Vryzakis: *The Oath at Aghia Lavra* (1851).

temple (3rd century but with a ? 7th-century predecessor, and votives back to the Geometric period), by the roadside, is of an unusual design, which has been compared to that of the Temple of Apollo at Bassae: the cella (with a base for the cult statue) had five semi-engaged columns on each side and external supporting pilasters. Below are remains of a semicircular building, with propylaia, and of a fountain house whose water was said to banish any desire for wine. The fountain-house was supplied by an aqueduct whose line has been partly traced higher up the valley. The acropolis of the ancient town (walls, remains of towers) is on the hill of Profitis Ilias, above the temple. In 2000, excavators announced the possible discovery of a temple/stoa complex.

After visiting the ruins, it is pleasant to continue 4km to the village of Planitero, outside which, by the springs of the River Aroania, both trout and salmon are raised. A number of restaurants, shaded by massive plane trees, flank the springs, and local honey and herbs are sold.

Between Kato Lousi and Planitero are the spectacular Kastria Caves, perhaps better known as the *Spilaio ton Limnon* (Cave of the Lakes; *usually open daily 9.30–4, but check the hours in Kalavryta or on T: 2692 31633*).

Kleitoria and the Arcadian border

Kleitoria, locally known as *Mazeïka*, a market village at the junction of two valleys, lies at the southwest foot of the Chelmos mountains. At the west exit of the village, a track (left; signed) leads in 500m to ancient *Kleitor*, a rival of nearby *Lousoi*. Kleitor stood on the flat ground between two rivers; its most impressive remains are remnants of its imposing walls and towers and theatre. Further west, past Ano Kleitoria, the mountain view opens, becoming immense as the road climbs in increasingly rough country to *Avchena tou Chelmou* (the 'Aroania neck'; 1049m), a saddle where a road diverges to Tripotama. The road descends in loops to Priolithos (799m) at the head of the long and pretty valley of the Vouraïkos.

THE SLOPES OF ERYMANTHOS

Dafni, in a delightful situation, right on the border with Arcadia, has a monastery (Evangelistrias) of the late 17th century and some small medieval churches. To the northwest lies Paos. At the far end of Paos, a dirt road (to the left; signed Kontovazaina) passes after 8km the chapel of Aghios Petros (views), which stands in the **Sanctuary of Aphrodite Erykine**, just over the Arcadian border. It was the seat of an oracle. The church is on the site of the temple and a *telesterion*. Nearer the road are the base of a monumental altar and a section of paved ancient road, also a tripartite building. A fountain was fed via terracotta pipes from a spring on the mountain above (Mt Aphrodision). The stadium was in the hollow immediately to the north (sections of the judges' seats survive). Hephaistos, Aphrodite's husband, was also worshipped here and the sanctuary included metalworking installations. Pausanias had this to say about the site: 'In Psophis there is a sanctuary of Aphrodite surnamed

Erykine (of Eryx); I found only ruins of it remaining, but the people said that it was established by the sons of Psophis. Their account is probable, for in Sikelia (Sicily) too, in the territory of Eryx, is a sanctuary of Erykine, which from the remotest times has been very holy, and quite as rich as the sanctuary in Paphos'. (*Pausanias 8, 24, 6*). A sacred road in fact connects the site with Psophis (modern Tripotama). Sanctuary finds are of the 7th century and later, but the area has yielded material from prehistoric to Frankish in date.

North of here is Tripotama (550m), a small village and bus junction, which stands at the confluence of three rivers ('*tria potamia*'), the Seiraios, Aroanios and the Erymanthos, as well as of three frontiers: those of Achaia, Arcadia and Elis. Here are scanty remains of **ancient *Psophis***, destroyed by Philip V of Macedon in 219 BC. The situation, hemmed in by mountains, is subject to extremes of heat and violent winds. In ancient times it was the scene of Heracles' Fourth Labour, in which he was set the task of capturing alive the Erymanthian Boar, which was ravaging the town of Psophis.

From here the main road skirts the Erymanthos range, while mountain roads traverse it. Kalentzis is a pleasant mountain village (975m), from which the Ionian islands can be seen and the second summit of Erymanthos (2221m) climbed. It is the birthplace of George Papandreou (1888–1968), prime minister in 1961–65, father of the prime minister Andreas Papandreou, and grandfather of foreign secretary George Papandreou. There is a small museum honouring him. At weekends, residents of Patras sometimes escape the summer heat and stay at the the 22-room Xenia Hotel (*T: 26940 31240*).

West of Kalavryta

From Kalavryta the Patras road heads west across the valley to enter the winding gap between Panachaïkon to the north and Erymanthos to the south. The signposted hamlet of Vrisari (or Goumenissa, to the right of the main road) has a Mycenaean cemetery near the church of Aghia Paraskevi. The jagged peaks of Erymanthos are well seen from the village of Flamboura. A few kilometres further along, Boumbouka retains a Turkish appearance. The road climbs to nearly 1067m before descending to Kato Vlasia under the north face of Erymanthos. At Kastritsi, about 3km southwest of the road, is the site of **ancient *Leontion*** with the remains of a theatre (4th century BC) excavated by N. Yialouris in 1958. New engineering has removed many loops of the road, which climbs steadily up the north side of a wild gorge. The dizzy ledge runs along the south outliers of Panachaïkon. The villages of Platanos and Kalanos are superbly sited, facing vistas of epic grandeur extending west to the sea.

Beyond Kalanistra the road reaches a further summit (721m) with a magnificent retrospective panorama. A by-road diverges (right) to **Demesticha** (8km) with vineyards producing well-known wines bottled by Achaia-Clauss (*see p. 404*). Mycenaean remains have been found near Leontio and Katarraktis, which lies in an enclosed valley above which Mycenaean settlements (and traces of Middle Helladic occupation) were located in 1957 in the region of ancient *Pharai*.

The hamlet of **Chalandritsa** was once a small Frankish barony held by Robert de la Trémouille. There are fine views over the coastal plain towards Zakynthos, a fine church, and virtually no other remains. The 11th–12th-century Byzantine domed inscribed-cross church (Aghios Athanasios) has a groin vault, a Frankish addition. Hetherington notes that the base of a tower 50m to the north, once thought to be part of the Frankish castle, is more likely simply a medieval storage tower.

At Kallithea, remains have been found of a Late Helladic cemetery (at Laganidia). The road descends through olive groves, past Krini, where remains of a Mycenaean cemetery were discovered, into the sprawl of Patras.

PRACTICAL INFORMATION

GETTING AROUND

• **By air:** The Patras/Araxos airport (T: 26930 23598) is used presently only by charter flights.
• **By bus:** There are some 15 buses to Patras daily from Athens. The main Patras bus station (T: 2610 623 886) is on Amalias. From Patras one can reach destinations in the Peloponnese and throughout Greece (change usually necessary). There are frequent bus links between Patras and Diakofto, for the train to Zachlorou. Daily buses also link Patras and Kalavryta.
• **By rail:** Frequent trains to Patras from Athens. The Patras train station at Othonos-Amalias 14 (T: 2610 273694). If you're catching a ferry, bear in mind that Greek trains usually run late and allow plenty of time.
• **By taxi:** Taxis in Patras can be found in Plateia Aghiou Georgiou. Getting a taxi when boats dock is a scramble.
• **By boat:** Daily service to Cephalonia (Sami), Ithaca and Corfu; also to Brindisi (car ferry), Ancona (car ferry), and Venice. International departures are presently from Gate 6 (but these change, so check beforehand).

INFORMATION OFFICES

Patras The main tourist office is by the main ferry terminal for Italy. Patras' website is www.infocenterpatras.gr

WHERE TO STAY

Aigion
€€ **Archontiko tou Gero Foti**. 6 rooms in a pretty stone-built house, at Lakka, 9km from Aigion. T: 26910 25126.
Kalavryta
€€–€€€ **Archontiko Zafeiropoulou**. 10 studios decorated in traditional style. On the hills outside town. T: 26920 24500.
€€ **Aphrodite's Inn**. On the wooded slopes outside town. 10 rooms, some with balcony. Popular with skiers. T: 26920 23600.
€€ **Filoxenia**. 26 small rooms looking over the town or hills. Perfectly acceptable. T: 26920 22290.
€€ **Xenonas Fanaras** 12 newly-restored rooms and fine views over the town. T: 26920 23665.
Patras
€€€ **Primarolia Art Hotel**. Boutique hotel with its own art gallery in an elegantly restored former brewery.

Certainly the most stylish hotel in town. Good restaurant. Othonos-Amalias 33, T: 2610 624900, www.arthotel.gr
€€ **Astir**. Convenient 120-room hotel with roof garden and pool. The bedrooms are nothing special, but the hotel is relatively quiet. Aghiou Andreas 16, T: 2610 277502.
€€ **Vyzantino**. New boutique hotel (17 rooms and 8 suites), in a nicely-restored 19th-century building several streets back from the waterfront. Repro furniture throughout. Riga Feraiou 106 and Asklipiou, T: 2610 243000; www.byzantino-hotel.gr

Zachlorou
The small **Romantzo** taverna and rent-rooms hotel (T: 26920 24097) is virtually on the station platform. Those making the trip by car, not train, can consider staying at the 5-room **Pandocheion o Stathmos** (T: 26920 22360), decorated with a railway theme, on the Kalavrita–Diakofto road (6km mark).

WHERE TO EAT

Kalavryta
In town, **To Spitiko** and **O Afstraios** both serve grills and stews. On the Mega Spilaio–Kalavryta road, **Katafygio** is open year round, serves good grills and goat or rabbit stews, and has spectacular mountain and sea views.

Patras
€€€ **Mesogeios**. Best to take a taxi to this hard-to-find place, with what many think is the best food in town. There's an open kitchen, a courtyard by the sea, and lots of well-dressed locals eating risottos and inventive seafood dishes; open Tues–Sun year round. Leof. Petmeza, Kastellokampos.

€€ **Beau Rivage**. One of Patras' finest restaurants, with a classic menu of favourites, as well as some innovations, such as curry. Open evenings May–Oct. Germanou 6.
€€ **Faos**. A relatively new innovative restaurant with chic modernistic décor, excellent sea food, and a menu with lots of choices for seafood. Pantanassis 83.
€€ **Lavyrinthos**. Long-time (since 1928) family-run favourite with excellent goat or rabbit stews, vegetable dishes, and excellent wine, some from the barrels lining the walls. Open Mon–Sat Sept–June lunch and dinner. Poukevil 44, T: 26102 26436.
€ **Trikogia**. Tiny taverna with a mainly fish menu. The **Pharos** next door is equally good. Amalias 46 and 48.

FESTIVALS & EVENTS

Patras The Patras International Festival usually runs from early June–late Sept, with music by international and Greek artists. T: 2610 223342, 2610 278206, and www.infocenterpatras.gr. Carnival celebrations (the three weeks before *Kathara Deftera*, the Mon before Shrove Tuesday) are elaborate. Information on T: 2610 226063. The feast day of Patras' patron saint, Aghios Andreas (St Andrew), on 30 November, is usually celebrated with special church services and a procession.

HIKING & CLIMBING

Aigion Alpine Club Sotiriou Pontou and Aratou, T: 26910 22308.
Patras Alpine Club (for Chelmos). Pantanassis 29, T: 26102 26225.

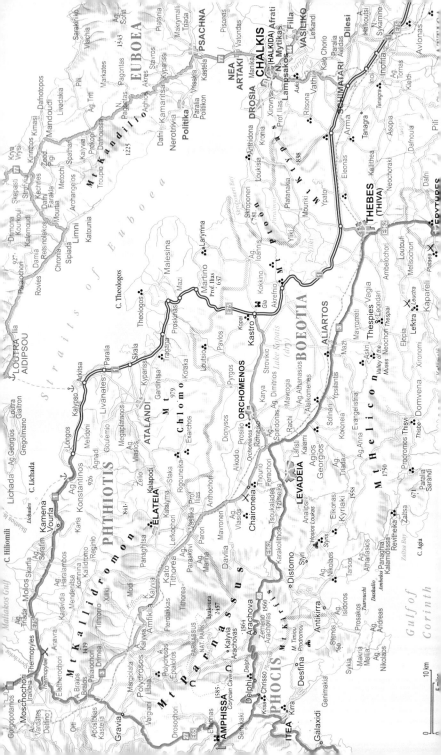

CENTRAL GREECE

The official administrative territory of Sterea Ellada (Στερεά Ἑλλάδα; Central Greece) extends from Attica to Acarnania, and includes Boeotia, Phocis, part of Phthiotis, and Euboea. The low-lying interior is nearly surrounded by mountains. To the south is the barrier of Parnes (Parnitha) and Kithairon. In the west are Helicon and Parnassus, and in the north the Opuntian mountains. The highest summit in Boeotia is Helicon, which rises to 1750m. On the east coast the Asopos plain reaches to the sea. This plain is adjoined on the north by the plain of Thebes, beyond which extend the Boeotian Lakes. The Kopaïs, once the largest lake in Greece, is now a fertile plain growing cereals and cotton and grazing pedigree cattle. The Boeotian Kephissos, the other notable river, finds its outlets in swallow-holes.

Boeotia flourished in prehistoric times with Mycenaean centres at 'Minyan' Orchomenos, at Gla, and at 'Cadmeian' Thebes. With two sea coasts and good harbours, Boeotia was well placed for maritime trade. All land routes between northern and southern Greece pass through it. The soil was fertile. Despite these natural advantages the Boeotians never (save for nine short years under Epaminondas) took the leadership in Greek affairs, because, in the opinion of Strabo, 'they belittled the value of learning and of sociability, and cared alone for the military virtues'. In Antiquity they had a reputation for slow-wittedness, illiteracy and boorish manners.

Among the many battles fought in Boeotia, three were of vital importance: Plataea, in 479 BC, which secured the independence of Greece at the end of the Persian Wars; Leuctra, in 371, which ended the long-suffered hegemony of Sparta and gave Thebes her nine-years' leadership over the rest of Greece; and Chaironeia, in 338, at which city-state democracy was virtually extinguished by the victory of Philip of Macedon.

On account of its Classical interest and sparse modern habitation, Boeotia was one of the earliest regions to attract the interest of archaeologists. Some of the sites, especially those of battles, are only rewarding to dedicated antiquaries, though many of them still enjoy that romantic isolation fast being lost elsewhere. Places of natural beauty include the Valley of the Muses on Mt Helicon and the north coast of the Gulf of Corinth, the latter offering a number of impressive fortified sites.

THEBES

Thebes (Thìva; Θήβα) is as undistinguished today as it was glorious in Antiquity. As the birthplace or home of the god Dionysus and the hero Heracles, as well as of the poet Pindar and the statesmen and military leaders Epaminondas and Pelopidas, the 'seven-gated city' of Thebes is inextricably bound up with Greek myth, literature, and history. The city founded by the legendary Phoenician immigrant Cadmus (or Kadmos), brother of Europa, claimed the invention of the Greek alphabet. The historical city consistently strove to dominate Boeotia and, for a very short period in the 4th century BC under Epamindondas, led the whole of Greece.

Still, only the most pious will linger in Thebes; the hotels are desultory and the restaurants, although lively, basic. The museum has a fine collection, but the remains of the ancient city—famous already in the Mycenaean period—largely lie under the modern town. Rescue excavations in recent years have turned up finds ranging from a Mycenaean chamber tomb to a Byzantine bath house, as well as a horde of Hellenistic gold plaques and coins found in works on the railway line and national road. The outline of Thebes' ancient acropolis or Cadmeia, a plateau 800m long and 400m wide, some 30m above the surrounding plain, is difficult to discern. Modern Thebes has nibbled away at the slopes of the acropolis, and visitors who have trouble locating the ancient summit may be comforted to know that some locals are equally unsure of the acropolis' location. The Mycenaean palaces are thought to have been on the acropolis, while the Classical city around the acropolis had a circuit of 8km.

Foundation of Thebes

The traditional foundation of Thebes by Cadmus (trad. date 1313 BC) and the sowing of the dragon's teeth begin a saga of tragedy and bloodshed paralleled in the troubles of the House of Atreus at Mycenae. According to the myth, Cadmus slew a dragon and then sowed the creature's teeth. These teeth grew into a crop of fully-armed soldiers, who proceeded to slaughter each other. Five alone survived, the ancestors of the better class of Thebans, known as the *spartoi* (sown). Among Cadmus' own descendants was the Laius who married Jocasta, the mother of Oedipus. Thus Thebes was the cradle of the tragic destiny of Oedipus. Rivalry between Eteocles and Polyneices brought about the intervention of the Argives under Adrastus (father-in-law of Polyneices) and the disastrous war of the Seven against Thebes (trad. date 1213 BC; *see box*). In the reign of Laodamus, son of Eteocles, the Epigonoi (sons of the Seven) took Thebes and razed it to the ground (trad. date 1198 BC).

Classical and Hellenistic Thebes

From the earliest times Thebes is represented as a flourishing city, large enough to have had seven gates. Sixty years after the fall of Troy, Thebes is said to have defeated Orchomenos and to have become the capital of a loose federation, later known as the Boeotian League, which dominated smaller cities such as Thespiai and Thisbe. This federation of the greater cities of Boeotia was governed (in the 4th century BC, at any rate) by eleven magistrates called *Boeotarchs*, Thebes supplying two, whereas the other members were allowed only one each. Thebes was a member of the Amphictyonic League (*see p. 445*).

An inveterate rival and opponent of Athens, Thebes favoured Athenian enemies and Medised in the Persian Wars. The Spartans are said to have forced some Thebans to help them at Thermopylae, but they deserted at the first opportunity. The fortified city of Thebes was the base of Mardonius before the Battle of Plataea (479 BC) and his Theban allies shared in his defeat. Shortly before the Battle of Tanagra in 457 the

Lacedaemonians marched into Boeotia and re-established Thebes at the head of the Boeotian League. At the beginning of the Peloponnesian War Thebes attacked Plataea (431); as an ally of Sparta she helped to bring about the downfall of Athens. In 394, however, she joined a confederacy against Sparta. The seizure of the Cadmeia (the acropolis of Thebes) by the Lacedaemonian Phoebidas in 382 in defiance of the Peace of Antalcidas and its recovery in 379 by the Theban exiles under Pelopidas precipitated war. The Battle of Leuctra (371), won by the genius of Epaminondas, gave Thebes for a brief period of nine years the hegemony in Greece. By restoring Messenia, helping to found Megalopolis, and organising the Arcadian League, Epaminondas completed the humiliation of Sparta. After his untimely death at Mantineia in 362 the Theban supremacy, which depended entirely on himself, disappeared, and the subsequent history of Thebes is a record of disasters.

OEDIPUS & THE SEVEN AGAINST THEBES

Oedipus never knew his father, King Laius of Thebes. Having been warned by an oracle that his own son would kill him, Laius had exposed the baby boy to die on Mt Kithairon. There the infant was found by a kindly shepherd, who presented him to the ruler of Corinth, Polybus, who took the baby in. The adult Oedipus came to Thebes to deliver the city from the Sphinx, a monstrous hybrid creature who devoured anyone unable to answer her riddle: what goes on four legs in the morning, two at noon, and three in the evening? Oedipus answered that it was man: crawling as a baby, walking as an adult, and hobbling on a stick in his dotage. In fury the Sphinx dashed herself to pieces. Oedipus was acclaimed leader of the city. He slew King Laius, married his wife (his own mother Jocasta), and fathered four children: Eteocles, Polyneices, Antigone and Ismene. When Oedipus and Jocasta discovered that they were mother and son, Jocasta hanged herself and Oedipus went into wandering exile. The two brothers Eteocles and Polyneices agreed to rule Thebes in alternate years. When after the first year Eteocles refused to yield the sceptre to his brother, Polyneices gathered an army under six leaders: Adrastus, Amphiaraus, Capaneus, Hippomedon, Parthenopaeus and Tydeus. All but Adrastus were killed, and Eteocles and Polyneices slew one another.

Joining her traditional enemy Athens against Philip at the instigation of Demosthenes, Thebes shared in the defeat of Chaironeia in 338, and a revolt shortly after Philip's death was ruthlessly suppressed by Alexander the Great in 336. The city was completely destroyed, with the exception of the temples and—because of Alexander's admiration of the poet—Pindar's house; 6,000 inhabitants were killed and 30,000 enslaved. In 316 Cassander rebuilt Thebes, but in 290 it was taken by Demetrius Poliorcetes. The Thebans sided with Mithridates in his war with Rome, but eventually went over to Sulla. In spite of this the city was finally dismembered in 86 by Sulla, who gave half its territory to the Delphians, by way of compensation for his plundering of the oracle. Strabo found Thebes hardly the size of a respectable village. In the time of Pausanias only the Cadmeia was inhabited. In AD 248 and again in 396 it was taken by the Goths, being spared (by Alaric) on the second occasion.

Later history of Thebes

Thebes enjoyed a second period of renown in the Middle Ages. From the 9th century it was the seat of the *Strategos* (Military Commander) of Byzantine Hellas. In 1040 it surrendered to the Bulgarians after fierce resistance. In 1146 it was sacked by the Normans of Sicily led by their great admiral, George of Antioch. The city was now famous for its silk manufactures, and it was from Thebes that King Roger introduced the cultivation of silk into Sicily, from where it reached Lucca a century later, and eventually spread to the rest of Europe. The silks of Thebes, which were worn by the Byzantine emperors, were ultimately supplanted by those of Sicily, and with the decline of the silk trade the prosperity of Thebes faded. In 1205 it was taken by Boniface III of Montferrat, who granted it to Otho de la Roche. Under his house Thebes was the capital of the Duchy of Athens. Half the city subsequently passed by marriage to the family of St-Omer. Under the Turks Thebes degenerated into a wretched village, overshadowed by Levadeia, which was made the seat of the pasha. Today, it is a lively provincial centre, which most travellers catch a glimpse of en route from Athens to Delphi.

EXPLORING ANCIENT THEBES

The plateau which was ancient Thebes' acropolis is covered today by a grid of parallel streets. Beneath them—under the heart of the modern town—lie two superimposed Mycenaean palaces, the extent and positions of which have been tentatively plotted.

Excavations, led by the Greek Archaeological Service, have taken place in Thebes since 1906, with spectacular finds (including hundreds of Linear B tablets) discovered in the 1960s and again in the 1990s. Many of the excavations have been rescue operations when antiquities were discovered during construction of modern buildings. A Mycenaean megaron complex excavated by Keramopoulos in 1906 on Od. Pindarou, behind the present market place, was identified by him as the 'House of Cadmus', mentioned by Pausanias. Annexes of both palaces, including comparable jewellers' workshops, have been explored. The palace known as the 'Cadmeion' seems to have been built in the 14th century, destroyed in the early 13th, and rebuilt on a different alignment in the late 13th. Archaeologists speculate that Thebes and Orchomenos, which also had an extensive Mycenaean settlement (*see p. 427*), may have been rivals. Classical masonry, which overlies parts of the two Mycenaean palaces at the junction of Pindarou and Antigonis, and continues under those streets, has been identified with the peribolos wall of the Sanctuary of Demeter Thesmophoros (which Pausanias placed within the House of Cadmus).

Other remains of ancient Thebes (not easy to locate; directions sometimes available at the museum) include a large frescoed Mycenaean chamber-tomb (*closed*) on Kastelli hill; the remains of the ancient agora and theatre; the 'Fountain of Oedipus' (spring of Aghios Theodoros); the 4th-century Ismenion temple (some foundations remain); and the scant remains of the defences and gates of Thebes (the best-preserved remains are the two towers of the Electra Gate at Odos Amphionos. Near the gate was the extensive Sanctuary of Heracles, now probably occupied by the church of Aghios Nikolaos (Byzantine lintel in the interior).

The museum

Usually open Tues–Sun 9–3. NB: At press time the new museum was reported open, though no details were available. The reinstalling of the collection may affect the displays.

The museum, at the north end of Pindarou, stands below the surviving 13th-century tower of the Frankish castle of Nicholas II de St-Omer, largely destroyed in 1311 by the Catalans. The pleasant garden and courtyard, which occupy the enceinte of the castle, are strewn with inscriptions of varying dates, sculptural remains including fine Byzantine reliefs, Turkish tombstones, architectural fragments and Early Christian mosaics (the Seasons). Below are some of the highlights.

The entrance has a display of important inscriptions from different parts of Boeotia, including Nero's proclamation at the Isthmian games in AD 67 that he was freeing Greece from Roman rule. The first room has 7th- and 6th-century statues of *kouroi* and a display of Classical grave monuments. The second room has the museum's most impressive finds: 30 cylinder seals of lapis lazuli, 14 with cuneiform inscriptions, nearly all from the Near East (a few are Cypriot, 15th–13th centuries BC), the greater number being of the Kassite-Babylonian period of the 14th century BC, seemingly confirm-

Mycenaean painted larnax (13th century BC).

ing the traditional connection of Thebes with Phoenicia; bronze plates and shoulder pieces from a Mycenaean corselet; the largest pieces of worked ivory so far found in Greece; Linear B tablets; fragments of a fresco from the old palace, showing a procession of women bearing gifts. These displays bring home the wealth of Mycenaean palace life in Thebes. The third room has unusual black stone grave monuments, which were first incised and then painted. The fourth room has rather rare Mycenaean painted *larnakes* (terracotta coffins) with scenes of funeral processions and other finds (pottery, terracottas, bronzes etc) from a large cemetery near Tanagra (*see below*).

TANAGRA FIGURINES

Delicate, poised, brilliantly coloured and with naturalistic features and poses, the majority of the Tanagra figurines depict fashionable and finely dressed women, wrapped in a coloured *himation* or cloak, often wearing hats or elaborate hairstyles, and sometimes carrying fans. Some figures in the repertoire may deliberately recall characters from the urbane world of 'New Comedy', made popular by Menander. The pieces were generally mass produced: by varying the position of the head and arms, a single figure could be made to serve several poses. An original model would be created in wax or terracotta, from which a concave mould would be formed in clay. The mould was generally split in two between the front and the back; but on occasions, the head or limbs might be separately moulded and joined before firing. A thin, white slip of dilute clay, which served as a preparation for the colour decoration, was added to the surface before the final firing. Water soluble pigments were generally used to colour the skin and garments, and define the features of the face. Although this final polychrome layer is fragile and has sometimes not survived in more than faint traces, the tones are always brilliant and afford us a unique vision of the colourfulness of Hellenistic taste and fashion.

The figurines represent a new departure in Greek fictile art in the Hellenistic age. Small, votive figures and masks were common throughout the 5th and 4th centuries BC. But the 'tanagras' show a primary interest in narrative and decorative qualities, and their charm and elegance is more suited to the secular environment. It would seem that the style evolved here, but rapidly spread throughout the Greek cultural area, with new and prolific centres of production in Asia Minor and southern Italy. The fact that the figures so predominantly represent women is a reflection of the new economic and social status of women in this period, which began in the cities of Attica and Boeotia, and spread out from there. Though the figurines were found in graves, this does not exclude their being primarily intended as gifts and adornments for the living environment of the house, only later to be included with the burial paraphernalia of their owner, according to time-honoured tradition. In the stillness of the tomb, they may simply have survived better than in the houses for which they were originally created.   N.McG.

ENVIRONS OF THEBES

Tanagra

About 25km east of Thebes is the town of Tanagra (Τανάγρα), famed for the small moulded terracotta figurines of the 3rd century BC found in its cemeteries during excavations in the last three decades of the 19th century (*see opposite*). The figurines have given the town a fame which goes beyond the interest of the place today. So numerous and popular were these figurines when they were first uncovered, that they were known simply as 'tanagras'; and they corresponded so closely to the taste of the Victorian world, that they were forged extensively in centres such as Athens and Paris, and passed—often unobserved—onto the international antiquities market.

Eleutherai

The fortress of Eleutherai (Ἐλεύθεραι), which is visible from the old Thebes–Athens road, crowns a steep and rocky knoll. Originally Boeotian, Pausanias says that it went over to Athens in the 6th century BC, out of hatred for Thebes. The fortress guards the main route between Athens and Thebes, and is some 300m long and 125m wide. It may have been one of a number of border forts built by Athens. The defences, in excellent masonry of the 4th century BC, are nearly complete on the north side. Eight rectangular towers, 35m–45m apart, are connected by walls about 3.5m high. Several of the towers stood three storeys high and had slits for archers in the second-floor walls and catapults on the top storey. Each tower had a door to the central court. The massive blocks in the walls are limestone.

In the fields opposite the Aigosthena fork (and well seen from the east wall of Eleutherai) is the substructure of a temple dating from c. 300 BC, perhaps that of Dionysus mentioned by Pausanias.

Aigosthena and Mount Kithairon

The turn for Aigosthena (Αἰγόσθενα) is at Eleutherai; it is about 20km from the turn-off to the fortress, which overlooks a good beach by the village of Porto Germeno. The beach and village (which has hotels and tavernas) can be very crowded with Athenian day-trippers on summer weekends.

The city, which overlooks the eastern end of the Gulf of Corinth, belonged not to Thebes, but to the city of Megara. The fortress overlooked both sea traffic through the Gulf of Corinth and land traffic between Boeotia and the Peloponnese. Although its fortifications are among the finest in Greece, written sources that mention Aigosthena are few, and its history is obscure. It is known that the Spartans retreated to Aigosthena after their defeat at Leuctra in 371 BC (*see p. 433*). The fortress sits on a slope of Mt Kithairon, with its walls running some 450m down to the sea. The walls enclosed a rectangle c. 550m by 180m. The east wall, partly of polygonal masonry, with four square towers in regular ashlar courses, is the best preserved, despite earthquake damage from 1981. The tower at the southeast angle, one of the best examples of Greek defensive architecture of the 4th century BC, rises over 10m above the top of the wall. Joist-holes for wooden floors can be seen in the middle towers. Within the enceinte two small churches locate the remains of late-Byzantine monastic cells; lower down is a larger basilica with floor mosaics. The north wall runs 450m and had eight towers, of which a good deal remains.

Mount Kithairon rises to 1410m. This is the mountain where Oedipus was exposed and where Pentheus, grandson of Cadmus and himself king of Thebes, was torn to pieces by the Bacchantes, the frenzied followers of Dionysus. It became the frontier between Attica and Boeotia when the Eleutherians cast in their lot with Athens.

HELICON & THE VALLEY OF THE MUSES

'Music', 'amusement', 'museums', or the simple act of 'musing'—so many of the profounder pleasures of our earthly life were first acknowledged by the Greeks in the person of the Muses. Their emergence as tutelary divinities of the acts of creation and performance marks a significant moment in the development of human thought: a growing awareness that things other than martial prowess and the exercise of power could be important and divinely inspired qualities. We first hear of the Muses in both Homer and Hesiod, in the 8th century BC. But it is primarily Hesiod, in the long, enchanted opening of his poem *Theogeny* (*ll. 1–115*), who first gives their names, their story and their authority, and tells us that, although imperious by nature as all the Olympian deities were, they aimed with their arts above all 'to soothe men's troubles and make them forget their sorrows'. It is Hesiod, too—a native of this area of Boeotia—who is largely responsible for the establishment of their cult on Mount Helicon.

The Muses

Always present at important festivities on Olympus, and sometimes invoked at the Castalian spring on Mount Parnassus, the Muses' preferred abode soon became the 'Valley of the Muses' on the south slopes of Helicon. Here their cult was well-established by the Hellenistic period, and superseded an older one at Pieria, north of Mount Olympus, where, according to Hesiod, the Muses had been born. Taken together with the important cult of Eros at nearby Thespiai (*see below*), this meant that Mount Helicon became sacred to the many aspects of earthly delight, in contrast to the loftier resonances of Parnassus and Olympus.

Born appropriately of the marriage of Zeus with Mnemosyne ('recollection'), the number of the Muses, following Hesiod's version, was generally considered to be nine: Calliope (epic poetry), Melpomene (tragedy), Thalia (comedy), Erato (lyric and love poetry), Terpsichore (choral song and dance), Polyhymnia (sacred hymns and mime), Euterpe (harmony and instrumental music), Clio (history and narrative), Urania (astronomy and speculative thought). The fields of creative endeavour ascribed to each Muse are an addition of later literature, and belong to the world of post-Aristotelian thought, with its passion for taxonomy and its innate opposition to the creative ambiguity of earlier poetry, which left such matters undefined.

Hesiod (8th century BC)

The poet Hesiod, writing shortly after Homer, probably about 700 BC, has an attractive story of himself tending sheep on the slopes of Mount Helicon in Boeotia, from where the Muses call on him to be a poet. The task they set him is to leave aside the heroics of epic poetry and concentrate instead on poetry which reflects everyday life. In fact, the first of his surviving works, the *Theogeny*, is an account of the evolution of the world through a series of conflicts between the gods. Uranus (Ouranos), the god of the heavens, is overthrown by his son Cronus (Kronos), whose family of Titans is in turn overthrown by Zeus and the Olympians. Under Zeus a more stable world emerges in which justice and moderation are possible. Hesiod appears to have absorbed this story from the ancient Near East, either directly or through Greek intermediaries.

In his *Works and Days*, Hesiod produces an alternative story, of the three ages of man in which silver succeeds gold and iron silver as life becomes more decadent. The poem appears to have been inspired by the misdeeds of Hesiod's grasping brother Perses, who—he claims—has cheated him of land. While again talking of the power of Zeus to bring justice (through the personification of his daughter Dike), Hesiod also stresses the importance of unremitting hard work as an antidote to the wickedness of mankind. *Works and Days* includes advice on farming, on how to survive winter, and how to undertake a sea journey. It is full of myth, including the famous story of Pandora, sent to earth with her box of evils by Zeus in revenge after Prometheus steals fire from heaven (thus bringing the possibility of culture to humanity). These complex but important myths became deeply embedded in the Greek mind. The historian Herodotus tells how it was Hesiod and Homer who taught the Greeks of 'the descent of the Gods, their names, honours and arts and their outward forms'.   C.F.

Thespiai

Virtually nothing remains of *Thespiai* (modern Thespiès; Θεσπιὲς), whose inhabitants were said to honour the god of love above all others. The famous courtesan Phryne, famed for the beauty of her breasts, lived at Thespiai, and the sculptor Praxiteles honoured her with a statue of Eros, which was still on view when Cicero came here. The sanctuary of the Muses lay on the summit behind the town. Here the Thespians instituted both a festival of the Muses, and a 'Museion' which, according to Athenaeus, contained manuscripts of Hesiod and statues of those who were distinguished in the arts. It is from this original institution that we take our modern notion of the museum. Higher up towards the summit of Helicon were the sacred springs and the sources of the streams mentioned in the *Theogeny* (ll. 5–6): Permessos, Olmeios, Aganippe and Hippocrene. The name 'Hippo-crene', which literally means 'horse fountain', may derive from its once being a source of water for the high, summer pasturing of horses; but poetic tradition related how the winged horse Pegasus struck the ground here with his hooves at the bidding of an angry Poseidon, and released the sacred water. In later literature, Pegasus himself came to represent the soaring of the poet's mind when inspired by the Muses. Hippocrene has remained a talisman of poetic inspiration throughout the history of literature, even up to the time of Keats's *Ode to a Nightingale*. Keats, however, runs counter to the spirit of Antiquity in conflating in his poem the spring's sacred water with the effects of fresh, red wine: the Muses desired libations of water, milk and honey, but never of wine.

At Thisbe (Thìsvi; Θίσβη), a stretch of Classical defence walls alone remains to remind visitors of the city which Homer called 'the haunt of doves'.

PHRYNE & PRAXITELES

Thespiai was renowned in Antiquity for its Sanctuary of Eros, and for the beauty of its most famous daughter, Phryne: Strabo commented that 'there was little else worth seeing there'. Phryne appears to have been an exceptionally gifted courtesan, of rare physical allure. When she was brought before the Areopagus on a charge of sacrilege against the Eleusinian Mysteries, it is said that she stripped before the judges. Overcome by her loveliess, and believing it next to godliness, they acquitted her instantly. Phryne also directly inspired two great works, both now lost, but considered by ancient writers to be amongst the very finest productions of all Greek art: the *Aphrodite Anadyomene*, a painting by Apelles in which the goddess rises from the sea; and the *Aphrodite of Cnidos*, Praxiteles' most celebrated sculpture, which portrays the deity bathing in a pool of still water—both masterpieces of an artistic golden age in Greece during the 4th century BC. Phryne appears to have been the mistress of Praxiteles and the model for a large number of his works, amongst them a golden portrait-statue, which was set on a column at Delphi, and another portrait in marble, which was placed within the sanctuary of Eros at Thespiai. It seems, in addition, that she was accorded the honour of dedicating the main image of Eros there, a work also by Praxiteles. Pausanias relates how she obtained this statue from the sculptor: although Praxiteles had promised to give her his most prized work, he continually prevaricated as to which one it was that he treasured most. Contriving to let the artist know that his studio was on fire, she tricked him into exclaiming that all his life's work was for nothing if the fire should claim either his *Eros* or his *Satyr*. Other writers—Pliny and Athenaeus of Naucratis—tell how it was the artist's unquenchable love for Phryne that imparted the magic that is found in his greatest works. This is borne out by an inscription, spoken as if by the god, which he had placed below his statue of Eros: *[In me] Praxiteles shows exactly the love he suffered, conceiving this image from his own heart. Phryne received me as a gift. I no longer shoot the darts of love with my bow: love blazes just by looking on me.*   N.McG.

ORCHOMENOS & LAKE KOPAÏS

Orchomenos (Ὀρχομενὸς), combining the former hamlets of Petromagoula and Skripou, lies at the foot of a desolate rocky ridge, known in Antiquity as *Akontion* ('Javelin') and today as Dourdouvana. The church of the former convent of the Dormition (also known as Panaghia Skripou) was built in 874, and admirably restored since its fabric was split by an earthquake in 1895, and torched by vandals exactly a century later, in 1995. Designed in a Bulgar tradition of Byzantine building, and similar in plan to Aghia Sophia at Ohrid, it is the unique example of its type in Greece. The single cupola on a high drum rests on solid walls, but the proportions are good. The exterior of the apse is decorated with an elaborately carved frieze of stylized animals and flowers. There is also the famous (and beautiful) vertical sundial, contemporary with the building. The whole fabric of the church consists of column-drums from a temple (of the Graces, or *Charites*, the local cult) and blocks from the theatre where songs and games were performed in their honour (*see below*). The interior is architecturally unadorned but contains some lovely 9th-century frescoes, notably of St Helen, St Constantine and the True Cross at Golgotha on the north wall of the nave.

HISTORY OF ORCHOMENOS

The Minyans were supposed to have come from the Thessalian seaboard (or, more fancifully, directly from Egypt) to Orchomenos and made it their capital. They drained Lake Kopaïs and built a series of fortresses of which the most remarkable is Gla (*see p. 429*). Their dominion extended across Boeotia, and Thebes itself came, for a time, under their sway. According to myth, Dionysus punished the daughters of King Minyas for refusing to participate in his rites by sending horrific visions of orgiastic scenes to drive them mad. Minyan ware, so-called because Schliemann first discovered it at Orchomenos, is a 'fine wheel-made ware of well refined, grey clay with a very smooth polished surface which is curiously soapy to the touch'. Its origin is a mystery, its period Middle Helladic, and it comes also in yellow and other colours.

About 600 BC Orchomenos joined the Boeotian League, but did not put its emblem on her coinage until 387 BC. She took the side of the invader in the Persian Wars. Orchomenos joined Sparta against Thebes in 395 and 394 BC, and was saved after Leuctra (371; *see p. 433*) only by the good offices of Epaminondas. In 364 Thebes seized the pretext of a conspiracy to destroy her venerable rival during Epaminondas' absence. Eleven years later the Phocians rebuilt Orchomenos, but it was again destroyed by the Thebans in 349. Under Philip of Macedon and Alexander the Great it was again rebuilt. In 87 Sulla defeated Archelaus, the general of Mithridates, under its walls.

Ancient Orchomenos

Ancient *Orchomenos* (*open daily 8.30–3; later in summer*), occupying a strong position at the east end of Akontion, was one of the richest and most important centres of Mycenaean times. Traditionally it was the capital of the Minyans. Homer compared its treasures with those of Egyptian Thebes. It appears to have been inhabited almost continuously from the Neolithic period to the time of Alexander the Great.

Immediately west of the church, excavations have revealed a probable **Mycenaean palace** built c. 1350 and destroyed in 1200 BC, with extensive remains of fresco decoration. Across the road are impressive remains of the **theatre** of the 4th century BC, where the *Charitesia*, poetical and musical games in honour of the Graces (or *Charites*, first worshipped here), were held. About 150m southwest of the church, in a walled enclosure, is the so-called **Treasury of Minyas**, a Mycenaean tholos tomb recalling the Treasury of Atreus at Mycenae. It was excavated by Schliemann in 1880–86. The stone revetments of the dromos were robbed in 1862 and the roof of the tholos has fallen in, but the gateway still has its threshold and enormous lintel of dark grey Levadeia marble, and eight courses stand of the tholos itself. The most remarkable features were the bronze rosettes, which decorated the walls, and the *thalamos*, or inner sepulchral chamber cut out of the rock. In its ceiling are slabs of green schist, carved with spirals interwoven with fan-shaped leaves, and surrounded by a border of rosettes. In the middle of the tholos are remains of a marble pedestal belonging to a funerary monument of the Macedonian period, once erroneously taken for the tomb of Hesiod, which was in the agora. Restoration work was carried out by the Hellenic Ministry of Culture from 1994.

The **Archaic city walls** ran along the north and south sides of the ridge forming a long triangle, whose apex was the acropolis. Within these walls excavations in the early 20th century revealed a series of superimposed settlements.

To the west and east of the Treasury of Minyas are the remains of a Neolithic settlement (? 6000–3400 BC), consisting of beehive huts built of unfired brick on stone socles. Above this was a town of Early Helladic date (3000–2000), characterised by deep circular ashpits, 6–8m in diameter. Above this again appear the apsidal house and rectangular megaron common in Thessaly and Elis (2000–1750) and yielding the so-called Minyan ware (*see previous page*) of Middle Helladic date.

Near the cemetery is the substructure (21m by 85m) of a Geometric/Archaic temple, of the 9th or 8th century BC, resting, as at Tiryns and at Mycenae, on much older remains. This was a part of the Middle Helladic town of 1700–1450 BC. About 350m west of the cemetery, on an intermediate terrace, are the remains of a Temple of Asclepius, measuring 22m by 11.5m. From there are reached the upper terraces, the location of the Macedonian town.

An ancient stairway mounts to the acropolis (308m), in size hardly more than a square keep. The cliffs on the east and north formed a natural defence; on the south and west the site was protected by massive walls, dating from the 4th century BC and among the finest extant examples of ancient Greek fortification. The view is extensive including the entire Kopaic plain.

Gla

The main road from Orchomenos crosses the channelled effluents of Lake Kopaïs, which spreads out to the right. On a hill to the left, once an island in the lake, rises Kastro; here vestiges of polygonal walling and inscribed stones in the church mark the site of *Kopai*, the city mentioned in Homer's 'Catalogue of Ships' which gave its name to the 'Kopaic' lake. To the right, on a low eminence, also an island in Antiquity, is the magnificently atmospheric ruined Mycenaean stronghold of Gla, a remarkable fortress about seven times larger than Mycenae itself. The fortifications, 2.8km in length, run along the edge of a precipitous low cliff, and were pierced by four gates. The south or Royal Gate had double bronze-faced doors. From here a road led directly to the vast walled 'agora', a space enclosed by long parallel buildings. These were apparently store- and work-rooms, with limited access and provision for the manipulation of heavy loads (? sacks of grain); also some living quarters. Fragments of large storage jars encourage this identification. The best-preserved ruins are of a complex at the highest point of the site (72m above the plain) right up against the north wall. Usually described as a 'palace', the building consists of two symmetrically arranged wings forming an L-shape. This arrangement is unlike any other known Mycenaean 'palace'; the two megarons also lack the distinctive features (eg hearths) of other such palaces. The two wings allow for some intercommunication, and it has been suggested that they housed two high officials of equal status.

Lake Kopaïs

Lake Kopaïs (or Copais) is named after the ancient city of *Kopai*. It was the largest lake in Greece, measuring 24km by 13km; Strabo says that it had a circuit of 380 *stadia* (68km). For most of the year it was a reedy swamp, while large tracts dried up completely in summer. In the rainy season the surrounding basin used to be frequently inundated and it is doubtless to some exceptionally severe flood that the tradition of the Ogygian deluge is due. The eels of Kopaïs were very large and succulent, and the reeds which fringed its shores were the raw materials of the Greek flute.

The natural outlets of the lake (all on the east and northeast) were swallow-holes (*katavothrai*). These were not, however, sufficient to cope with a sudden inrush of water, and from early times attempts were made to increase the natural outflow. The massive, prehistoric project to drain and control the waters of Lake Kopaïs gives a vivid sense of the scale on which the earliest Greeks were accustomed to think and the ingenuity that they could bring to bear on technological matters. It is the earliest major hydraulic work in European history, and it would have revolutionised life for the settlers of this strategic corridor of the Greek mainland. The lake is an enclosed, limestone-bound basin, fed by several streams descending from the Helicon massif, and by the larger Kephissos river to the west. At the northeastern extremity, a number of natural swallow-holes provided an uneven drainage of the water from the basin into the Straits of Euboea. In the winter the streams in spate caused the lake to flood; in summer the area dried out and became an insalubrious marsh. A high-water mark can still be seen on the cliffs around the lake at approximately two metres above ground level. The first and boldest project to circumvent this cycle so as to guarantee an area of arable land and to give a more constant form to the remaining water, was undertaken in the middle of the 2nd millennium BC, by the Minyans, a proto-Greek people with a major centre at Orchomenos (*see p. 427 above*). They channelled the waters to various *katavothrai* with such success that the whole basin was reclaimed. Strabo repeats the tradition that it was dry cultivated ground in the days when it belonged to Orchomenos. Heracles is said, out of enmity to the Orchomenians, to have blocked up the *katavothrai*; Strabo explains that the chasms were affected by earthquakes. After the destruction of the Minyan drainage works and throughout the historic period, the Copaic basin remained a lake. Aristophanes, writing in the 5th century BC, could once again comment on the quantity and quality of the large eels in the marshy waters of the lake, and the suitability of its reed-beds for the making of flutes. Theophrastus also mentions that the ancients would read and predict the qualities of the seasons from the variations in performance of the lake's waters.

Attempts were made, however, in historical times to supplement the *katavothrai* by means of tunnels. Two artificial emissaries have been discovered. The more extensive is the tunnel towards Larymna. This may have been the work of Krates, engineer to Alexander the Great. We know that Krates was forced to abandon work because of local political problems. Roman engineers under Hadrian also did much to repair and reinforce the existing dykes. But it seems that none had the boldness and tenacity to think on the same scale as the Minyans, more than a thousand years earlier. The definitive drainage of the area was only accomplished by French and Scottish engineers in the mid-19th century. Since then the reclaimed land has been intensively cultivated, and ploughing has begun to obliterate the traces that remain of the ancient Minyan constructions.

At the Battle of Lake Kopaïs, in 1311, the Catalan Grand Company practically annihilated the chivalry of Frankish Greece. The battle was fought near Orchomenos.

FOUR IMPORTANT BATTLEGROUNDS

Four very important battles took place in Central Greece: at Thermopylae, in 480, the Spartans under Leonidas attempted to delay—or if possible, halt—the Persian invasion of Greece. At Plataea, in 479, the Greek forces defeated the Persians and sent them in retreat from the Greek mainland. At Leuctra, in 371, the brilliant Theban military tactician Epaminondas defeated Greece's most fabled soldiers, the Spartans, and gave Thebes a nine-year period of leadership over Greece. And at Chaironeia, in 338, Philip of Macedon defeated the combined Greek forces, and took control of most of Greece, effectively ending Greek city-state democracy. Leuctra and Plataea can be visited en route to or from Thebes, while Chaironeia and Thermopylae are best visited en route north from central into northern Greece. The battles are described here in chronological order.

THERMOPYLAE

Thermopylae is on the Athens–Thessaloniki National Road, between Kamena Vourla and Lamia. It is signposted and easy to identify because of the modern monument on the battlefield. The hot springs here are said to be good for various complaints.

In the most famous battle of the first Persian invasion, the Greeks defeated the Persians at Marathon in 490 BC (*see p. 138*). In 480 BC, Xerxes at the head of the Persian army and navy, led a second Persian force against Greece. The Greek Confederacy (those Greek city-states that chose to resist the Persians) wanted to stop the invasion as far north as possible and decided to make their stand at the pass of Thermopylae, which links Thessaly and southern Greece. There, the Spartan general Leonidas sent the rest of the Greek army to safety and attempted to hold the pass and delay the advance of the much larger Persian army. Estimates of the size of the Persian force range from ten to several hundred thousand men to Herodotus' inflated count of five million. When the fighting was finished, only two of the Spartans survived. One atoned for his survival by his valour at the Battle of Plataea; the other hanged himself on his return to Sparta. The dead were buried on the battlefield; the burial mound is visible today. The dead are today commemorated with a monument, dedicated in 1955, showing Leonidas and scenes from the battle that bears the famous lines 'Stranger, tell the Spartans that here, obedient to their laws, we lie'. In Antiquity, a stone lion honouring Leonidas, which survived to the time of Tiberius, stood on the battlefield. Forty years after the battle, Leonidas' body was taken to Sparta. A fine bust thought to be of Leonidas is on view in the Archaeological Museum at Sparta (*see p. 303*). Leonidas' desperate stand at Thermopylae cannot be explained solely as high-principled and impractical self-sacrifice, because it served three tactical purposes. First, the considerable delay which it inflicted on Xerxes' forces kept the Persians inconveniently separated from their supply ships; second, it gave the Greeks important time to re-group, or (as in the case of the Athenians) to evacuate their cities; and lastly, because by August, the time of the confrontation at Thermopylae, any further delay could only favour the Greeks over the invaders. The later in the season the moment of final encounter between the two sides could be pushed, the greater the chance that the autumnal weather and winds would limit the Persians' room for manoeuvre. It was this, in fact, which forced Xerxes' hand in engaging with the Greeks at Salamis, almost a month later.

In Antiquity, the pass of Thermopylae, which runs between precipitous mountains and the sea, was the main route from north to south and was the only practical route for any large force to take. The defile, which was just under 6.5km long, was extremely narrow at both ends, but widened in the middle, where there were the hot springs. To understand the ancient topography, you must imagine the sea much closer on the right than it is today. Over the years, the silt brought down by the River Spercheios has advanced the coastline by nearly 5km, though the plain is still marshy. The modern road coincides with the ancient road for most of the way, except at the critical narrows where it runs north of the old course; here you must visualise the ancient road nearer the cliffs with the sea extending to within a few metres of their foot.

The battle

While the small Greek army of perhaps 6,000–7,000 men under Leonidas occupied Thermopylae, the Greek fleet lay off Artemision (Euboea) to prevent the Persian fleet sailing down the Euboean Gulf in support of their army. The superior size of the Persian land force did not help it to seize the pass, where the Greeks were securely protected by the pass itself and by their fortifications. Xerxes had almost given up hope of forcing a passage when a Greek, named Ephialtes, showed the Persians a route that would take them through the pass and allow them to outflank the Greeks. His motive might have been perfidy, or he may simply have wanted to get the huge, food-consuming Persian army off his territory. A detail of perhaps 2,000 Persian soldiers made a night march through the pass, and by morning they held both ends. Once Leonidas was aware of this, he ordered the withdrawal of the main force, retaining only his 300 Spartans, the 700 Thespians, and 400 Thebans, to block the pass for as long as he could. Before the final engagement of battle, the Persians—ignorant that this was a ritual sacred to the Spartans in the face of having to make the supreme sacrifice—were astonished to see their adversary calmly combing and preparing their hair in the early morning light. The pro-Persian Thebans were held as hostages and they deserted in a body to the Persians as soon as opportunity offered. The course of the desperate battle, the death of Leonidas, and the famous 'last stand' of the Spartans on the hillock of Kolonos is told in detail by Herodotus (*Bk. VII*), and visitors wishing to traverse the ground in detail cannot do better than follow his vivid and dramatic account.

Later battles

In later years, the tactics of Xerxes were copied by all who wished to force the Pass of Thermopylae. In 279 Brennus, at the head of his Gauls, finding himself checked by the troops of Kallipos, used the Anopaia path to turn the Greek position; but this time the Greeks were able to escape to their ships. In 191 Antiochus III, King of Syria, with 10,000 men, tried to deny the pass to the 40,000 legionaries of the Roman consul Manlius Acilius Glabrio and his legate M. Porcius Cato. Antiochus raised a double wall, with trenches, across the defile, and built forts on the slopes of Mt Kallidromon. Cato succeeded in carrying the forts and in taking the position in the rear, while Glabrio made a frontal attack. Antiochus escaped with only 500 men.

In AD 395 Alaric entered the pass without opposition. In the 6th century, according to Gibbon, 'the straits of Thermopylae, which seemed to protect, but which had so often betrayed, the safety of Greece, were diligently strengthened by the labours of Justinian'. In 1204 Boniface of Montferrat came through unopposed. Retreating British troops began to take up position here in 1941, but evacuation was ordered before the Germans reached the area.

PLATAEA

The turning for Plataea, some 15km from Thebes, is signposted on the Athens road and then in the villages of Erythres (Ἐρυθρές) and Plataies (Πλαταιές). There are considerable remains of ancient *Plataea*, including some stretches of excellent 4th-century ashlar masonry and other less well-preserved pieces of polygonal work.

Plataea, a small Boeotian town near the border with Attica, early turned to Athens in an attempt to avoid Theban domination. In 490 BC the Plataeans achieved fame by sending their entire army of 1,000 men to stand with the Athenians against the Persians at Marathon. The Battle of Plataea in 479, during the second Persian invasion, is described in detail by Herodotus (*IX, 19*). The Greek victory here clinched the defeat of the Persian campaign.

The battle

In 479, after sacking Athens, the Persian commander Mardonius retired by way of Tanagra to Boeotia, where the terrain was better suited to his cavalry. He encamped before the Asopos river near Plataea, facing the foothills of Kithairon, over whose passes armies from Attica or the Peloponnese would of necessity come. The forces of the Greek league, commanded by the Spartan Pausanias, with Aristides' Athenians on the left wing, took up their first position along the foothills. They were outnumbered three to one and lacked a cavalry arm. For three weeks the opposing generals manoeuvred for favourable positions. The Greeks suffered constant harrying by the Persian cavalry, though a picked force of 300 Athenians succeeded in killing Masistius, the Persian cavalry commander. A Greek attempt to outflank the enemy and cut them off from Thebes miscarried; in the subsequent retreat the Greek forces became split into three. Mardonius attacked the Spartans, whose fighting qualities proved superior, and the Persian general was slain. The Athenians fought a pitched battle with the Boeotians, annihilating the Theban Sacred Band, which was made up of pairs of warriors who had taken an oath never to surrender, but to fight to victory or death. When the Persian camp was stormed, no quarter was given and though its outcome was decided more by the quality of the men than the tactics of their generals, the three weeks' campaign was a notable achievement of Greek unity (despite the defection of the Thebans). In honour of the dead, the member states instituted a Panhellenic festival to Zeus Eleutherios (the Liberator), which survived many centuries.

During the invasion of Xerxes the Plataeans remained staunchly loyal to the Athenian cause and their city was destroyed by the Persians and Thebans. For much of its history, Plataea was a pawn—and prey—of Thebes, Athens, and of Sparta. Plataea was destroyed by Sparta in 427 and yet again by Thebes in 373. After the Battle of Chaironeia, Philip, in fulfilment of his policy of humiliating Thebes, refounded the town, which lasted into Byzantine times, though without particular importance.

LEUCTRA

Leuctra (Λεύκτρα) is signposted at the village known both as Lefktra and Parapoungia about a mile out of Thebes on the Athens road. Here, in 371 BC, the Boeotians defeated a much larger force of Spartans and dealt a lasting blow to the legend of Spartan invincibility. Leuctra is intimately associated with the Theban commander

Epaminondas, who was credited with routing the Spartan forces with an ingenious attack with his unexpectedly strong left wing. Epaminondas went on to lead Thebes, and Boeotia, and to free Messenia and Arcadia from Spartan control. After a string of successes, which made Thebes a leading power in Greece, Epaminondas attempted to defeat Sparta utterly, but was killed during the Spartan victory at the Second Battle of Mantineia in 362 BC. Plutarch highly praised Epaminondas, for his military prowess, political skills, and the strength of his character.

Visible up a valley to the right on the approach to Leuctra (also signposted) is the **Tropaion** (locally 'Màrmara'), a monumental trophy erected by the Thebans after the victory and now restored. A circular plinth of triglyphs has a dome-shaped roof of nine stone shields sculptured in relief; it probably supported a warrior figure in bronze.

CHAIRONEIA

Chaironeia (Χαιρώνεια) is on the old Thebes–Lamia road, by the village of the same name. The lion monument on the battlefield makes Chaironeia easy to spot. There is a small site museum (*often closed*).

Philip of Macedon came to the throne in 358 BC and almost immediately began to alarm Greeks with his territorial ambitions. Demosthenes of Athens was particularly hostile to Philip and engineered an alliance between Athens and Boeotia to stand, if necessary, against Philip. Philip did, indeed, invade southern Greece, and at the Battle of Chaironeia in 348 defeated the Greek forces and took control of Greece.

The campaign began when Philip intervened in Greece during the Fourth Sacred War (*see p. 446*). After capturing Delphi's neighbour Amphissa, Philip entered Boeotian territory at the head of 30,000 foot and 20,000 horse. He found the allied army, perhaps slightly inferior in numbers, barring his way in the plain to the east of Chaironeia. The Athenians, attacking on the left wing, gained an initial advantage. The Macedonian cavalry, led by the 18-year old Alexander, overwhelmed the Theban Sacred Band, who fought on to the death. The Athenians (among them Demosthenes himself), taken in the rear, fled. Philip buried the Macedonian dead in a great tumulus (still visible); he burned the Athenian corpses and sent the ashes to Athens. The Thebans were permitted to bury their dead in a common tomb. After the battle Philip treated Thebes with the utmost severity, but was unexpectedly lenient towards Athens.

The most notable feature of the battlefield is the lion monument, which stands by the *polyandrion*, or common tomb, in which the Thebans buried the fallen members of their Sacred Band. Pausanias suggests that the lion represented the fighting spirits of those who stood here against Philip. Many scholars assume that the monument was erected after Philip's death, when Thebes was rebuilt in 316. This remarkable—but not very realistic—sculpture, which was discovered by a party of English visitors in 1818 almost buried in the ground, was smashed during the War of Independence by the brigand patriot Odysseus Androutsos under the impression that it contained treasure. In 1902–04 the Greek Archaeological Society restored the lion and replaced it on its ancient plinth. It is constructed of three hollow sections of bluish-grey

Boeotian marble, and is represented seated on its haunches; its height is 5.5m (8.5m with the plinth). The ossuary which it adorned was a rectangular enclosure surrounded by a peribolos wall; inside were found 254 skeletons and various objects, now in Athens.

A second battle was fought here in 86 BC when the Roman general Sulla defeated the Greek general Archelaus, who had led the troops of King Mithridates of Pontus on a war of conquest into Greece.

The ancient city, whose chief industry was the distillation of unguents from the lily, rose, narcissus and iris, was the birthplace of Plutarch (AD 46–?127), who kept a school here, holding a priesthood for life at Delphi from AD 95. One of Plutarch's many biographies in his *Parallel Lives* was that of Demosthenes, Philip's great opponent. The acropolis (270m) occupies two summits separated by a saddle. There are remains of Hellenic walls and fragments of earlier walls in polygonal and Cyclopean work. At the north foot of the hill is a little theatre.

THE EURIPOS

NB: A new bridge crosses the strait well to the south of the Euripos. The older entry is described here.

Chalkis (commonly Halkìda; Χαλκίδα), attractively situated on the Euripos at its narrowest, is the capital of the *nome* of Euboea. Ancient *Chalcis*, was famous for its manufactures in bronze, exporting arms, vases, and votive tripods; it was the mother-city of many early colonies: so many, in fact (32 in the Macedonian peninsula between the Thermaic and Strymonic gulfs), that the whole peninsula was called *Chalcidice* (modern Chalkidiki).

The mainland approach to the Euripos is guarded by Karababa, an Ottoman fortress of 1686; scanty rock-cuttings suggest an ancient fortress on this site, supposedly a Macedonian fort built c. 334 BC. The walls afford a wonderful view of the strait and whole town. In the mainland suburb below are (left) the town beach and (right) the railway station and an information office. The unusual bridge that carries the old road over the Euripos opens by a double action; the carriageway descends just sufficiently to allow each half-span to roll on rails under its own approaches.

The Euripos is notorious for its alternating currents, which change direction six or seven times a day and on occasion as often as 14 times in 24hrs. The current flows from north to south for about three hours at a rate which may exceed six knots. It then suddenly subsides; and, after a few minutes of quiescence, it begins to flow in the opposite direction. The passage of the channel with the current is dangerous and the bridge is opened only when the direction is favourable. A red ball indicates a north–south current; a white ball a south–north current. The phenomenon is alluded to by Aeschylus (*Agamemnon 190*), as well as by Livy, Cicero, Pliny and Strabo. The cause is complex and still not fully understood. According to a popular tradition, Aristotle, in despair at his failure to solve the problem, flung himself into the water.

The Euripos was first spanned in 411 BC. In 334 the Chalcidians included the Boeotian fort of Kanethos within the city boundaries. Under Justinian the fixed wooden bridge was replaced by a movable structure. The Turks replaced this with another fixed wooden bridge. In 1856 a wooden swing bridge was erected; in 1896 a Belgian company enlarged the channel, demolished the Venetian fort that had guarded the approach, and built an iron swing bridge. This gave place in 1962 to the existing structure. A new road bridge, considerably further south, was opened in 1993.

Ancient Aulis

South of Chalkis across the inlet is the site of *Aulis* (*open Nov–March daily except Wed, Sun 8:30 –3; Wed, Sun 11–3*), famed in the heroic epic as the place where Agamemnon sacrificed his daughter Iphigeneia to Artemis, to secure a strong wind to blow his fleet to Troy. The pathetic story of the young woman's death, and the bloody family imbroglio that followed, inspired the famous plays of Euripides and in modern times captivated the imagination of Goethe. The long, narrow Temple of Artemis (who indeed granted the longed-for wind) was discovered in 1941, during the building of the road. Its identification is certain from the inscription on the statue base found here. The cella dates from the 5th century but was restored in the Roman period; it originally had a porch, with two columns in antis, rebuilt with four columns in Hellenistic times, from which time the coroplasts' workshops, remains of which lie to the south of the temple, also date. East of the temple are the remains of a sacred well. The whole complex was destroyed during the sack by Alaric in the 4th century AD.

HOSIOS LOUKAS

Usually open daily 8–2 & 4–7 in summer; in winter usually 8–5. Hosios Loukas is popular with tour groups. Though there are still monks here, and Greek Orthodox pilgrims, the mood is often more touristic than monastic. Nevertheless, it is appropriate to observe the usual formalities of dress and decorum when visiting. There is a little café inside the precincts. A torch is useful for examining the mosaics and frescoes, especially in the crypt.

Hosios Loukas, the 10th-century Monastery of the Holy Luke, stands outside the village of Styri on the brow of a peaked hill that faces south and commands wonderful views of Mt Helicon and the surrounding country. It is one of the largest, best-preserved, and most impressive Byzantine monuments in Greece; on the mainland only the Monastery of the Koimisis tis Theotokou at Daphni (*see p. 143*) can compare in richness of architecture and decoration. In fact, the art historian Richard Krautheimer cites Daphni and Hosios Loukas together as 'probably the most beautiful representatives of the Greek-cross-octagon plan'.

Hosios Loukas is actually two churches co-joined. The northern church of the Theotokos is the earlier (late 10th century) and is a cross-in-square with four interior supporting columns. The adjoining katholikon, which was used primarily by the monks of the monastery, was erected in the early 11th century.

The monastic complex of Hosios Loukas, looking towards Mount Helicon.

HISTORY OF HOSIOS LOUKAS

The monastery, with its two churches and monastic buildings, is dedicated not to St Luke the Evangelist, but to a local 10th-century beatified hermit, the Blessed Luke. According to a 10th-century *Life of Luke*, as well as to popular legend, Luke's family fled from the island of Aegina when it was invaded by the Saracens, and Luke was born in '*Kastorion*' (probably Kastri, ie Delphi). After a peripatetic life, Luke came to Styri, the hamlet outside which the monastery now stands, where he died in 953. It seems that there was already a church dedicated to St Barbara here, and the establishment of the present complex took place after Luke's death. According to some accounts, the Emperor Romanus II financed the larger church in 961 after recapturing Crete from the Saracens, perhaps to honour the fulfilment of Luke's prophecy that Crete would be liberated by an emperor named Romanus. In other accounts, the monastery was founded in the 11th century. Over the years, the monastery has suffered from repeated earthquakes and undergone various renovations and alterations which complicate dating its foundation.

The monastery

The monastery's rebuilt *tràpeza* or **refectory** (now a museum of Byzantine sculpture) flanks a flagged terrace, above which rises the south side of the katholikon set off by the flowing line of its dome. The foundation walls are of stone with stone and brick above—the same frugal brick and stone mixture which one sees throughout Greece in countless Byzantine churches, both modest and grand. Columns of various stones, including Hymettian marble, divide the windows, each of which is surmounted by a large impost bearing a Greek cross. The lower parts of the windows are filled with sculptured marble. An inscription in the outer wall records the dedication by Xenocrates and Eumaridas of a fountain; the slab probably came from ancient *Styris*.

The **katholikon** may once have had an exonarthex, perhaps added in the 12th century, and demolished in the late 19th. Now, the west door opens into a narthex, which has a vaulted ceiling and mosaics on a gold ground. On the arches are depicted the Apostles; in the lunettes, *Christ Washing of Feet of His Disciples*, the *Crucifixion*, and the *Resurrection*. On the ceiling

St Peter the Apostle.

are medallions of the Baptist, the Virgin with angels, and Saints. On the pavement are slabs of *verde antico* marble.

One enters the central domed nave through a vestibule which, with the two transepts and the bema, form the arms of the cross enclosed within the external rectangle of the walls. The angles are filled in by twelve groin-vaulted or domed bays, surmounted by a second storey of equal height; this is frescoed (interesting graffiti of medieval ships) and carried over the transepts by open galleries. The piers have fine, ancient polychrome marble revetments. The bema and its flanking chapels are each closed off by a *templon*; that in the centre forming the iconostasis, those to left and right open colonnades.

The interplay of light and shade produced by the multiplicity of arches gives an air of solemn mystery, enhanced by reflected light from gold mosaics, which are the finest feature of the church (*see box*). Those in the dome were damaged in 1659 by earthquake and replaced by paintings. The mosaics are most complete in the vestibule and its aisles, and in the north transept. The monk on duty is sometimes willing to point out the portrait of Hosios Loukas himself, among some 130 saints represented. On the squinches supporting the dome are mosaics of the *Nativity*, *Presentation* and *Baptism*. In the apse are mosaics of the *Virgin and Child*; above, in the vault, the *Descent of the Holy Ghost*. The katholikon also has early 11th-century frescoes in the northeast, northwest and southwest chapels, and in the gallery above the narthex.

THE MOSAICS OF HOSIOS LOUKAS

The mosaics of Hosios Loukas are of prime importance. We know nothing of the workshop that made them, and their appearance in a relatively isolated area is today surprising. At the time, however, this church, as the focal point of a monastic community and honouring the tomb of its founder—a miracle-worker and man of great holiness—would have attracted a great number of pilgrims.

Unfortunately we very seldom see mosaics of this genre in the conditions in which they are most effectively brought to life. Byzantine liturgies often began well before dawn or as the sun was setting. The vast gold backgrounds would only have been visible as sparkling magic lit by flickering oil lamps. As the sun rose in the morning they would slowly reveal their depth and come to scintillating life, and in the evening they would sink again into the lamplit darkness. Light and optics and the angled application of tesserae were all part of the total art form.   N.S.

The **crypt**, which has three tombs, including that of the Blessed Luke, is supported by square bevelled columns with imposts. It is lavishly decorated with 11th-century frescoes of the *Passion of Christ*. The groin-vaults are divided into panels containing busts of saints and monks in medallions. Beneath is a rock-cut refuge with its own water supply. Opinions differ as to whether the crypt originally belonged to the earlier church here of St Barbara.

The church of the Theotokos

The smaller church of the Theotokos is attached to the north transept of the katholikon. As you leave the katholikon by the door off the north bay, to enter the Theotokos, you pass a wall with a fresco of *Joshua as Warrior*. This fresco, which was uncovered in 1965, has led some art historians to conclude that the church of the Theotokos must have been built before the katholikon, the result of an extension (997–1011) of part of an earlier building, presumably the church of St Barbara, traces of whose construction have been recognised. Questions not only about the Hosios Loukas monastery, but about the style of 10th- and 11th-century painting and church architecture, hinge on understanding the sequence of these two churches.

The exterior of the Theotokos is noteworthy as the earliest example of decorative devices that are apparently a completely Greek innovation. Most of the major building material was 'quarried' from the nearby ruins of the ancient city of *Styris*. In between courses of stone, triple and quadruple layers of brick laid horizontally, and at the edges vertical single bricks, create cloisonné effects. Houndstooth brick patterns are also used on the upper courses and above these are relatively wide bands of brick inlays that reflect strong Islamic influences in that they reproduce fanciful—though often surprisingly accurate—simulations of Kufic Arabic script. The church is fronted by a exonarthex (16th century) with triple portico. Beyond, the narthex proper has two columns with Corinthian capitals. The church itself is a plain cross-in-square, the dome borne on four large granite columns with Byzantine capitals and imposts. The floor mosaics are fine, but the church's principal glory is in the sculptural decoration of its columns and other architectural elements.

Distomo

A few kilometres from Hosios Loukas is the village of **Distomo** (Δίστομο), with several small hotels and restaurants. Distomo is today the scene of an annual autumn wine festival. Here, on 10th June 1944, 218 villagers (including many children) were killed in one of the most infamous Nazi reprisal massacres of the Second World War.

PRACTICAL INFORMATION

GETTING AROUND

• **By car:** Boeotia has a wealth of sites, all scattered over a relatively wide area. Public transport can be erratic, and a car is much the best way to get around and see everything you want to see.

• **By train:** Trains link Athens with Livadeia, the regional capital.

• **By bus:** Daily buses run (roughly hourly) from Athens to Livadeia (2hrs), Thebes (1.5hrs), Distomo and Chalkis.

WHERE TO STAY

Boeotia lacks hotels of charm, though Thebes and Livadeia are well stocked with basic accommodation.

Kamena Vourla (for Thermopylae) The speciality here is large spa hotels, for example the **Levendi** (Best Western chain; T: 22350 32251) or the **Sissi** (T: 22350 22277). All have restaurants. Perhaps the nicest is the €€ **Galini**, built round a courtyard, sanatorium style. The rooms have extraordinary Barbie-doll décor, and the bar looks like a ski chalet. The swimming pool, with mountains high above, is beautiful.

Livadeia

€€ **Erato**. Basic hotel, with functionally decorated rooms, in the lively regional capital. Restaurant. T: 22610 20351, www.hotelerato.com

€€€ **Levadia**. Peculiar combination: a modern exterior (of no architectural merit), and rooms with wooden ceilings to give a rustic feel. Restaurant. Papaspyrou 4, T: 22610 23611, www.levadia-hotel.gr

Thebes

€€ **Niovi**. Central location. Functional, sparsely-furnished rooms. Epaminonda 63, T: 22620 29888.

FESTIVALS & EVENTS

Easter celebrations are very colourful in Livadeia. An enormous public barbecue is held, with folk music and dancing.

HIKING & CLIMBING

Livadeia Alpine Club, Karagiannopoulou 27, T: 22610 20711

PHOCIS, PHTHIOTIS & EVRYTANIA

Phocis (modern Fokìda; Φωκίδα) is a small region famous for containing the city and oracle of Delphi. At one time its territory extended across Greece to the port of Daphnous, on the Atalante Channel. The interior is unproductive and mountainous, culminating in Parnassus (2457m). None of the 22 Phocian cities was very large.

DELPHI

NB: Delphi and its immediate environs are covered by the previous map on p. 416.

Delphi (Δελφοί) is by common consent the most spectacularly beautiful ancient site in Greece. In Antiquity Delphi was regarded as the centre of the world, the spot determined when two eagles loosed from the ends of the earth by Zeus met overhead here. Delphi was also the site of the most famous oracle in the ancient world. Delphi seems to have been regarded as a sacred spot at least from Mycenaean times, and early in its history it became closely associated with Apollo. From the early 6th century, important games honouring Apollo were held here every four years, although they were always second in importance to those held at the shrine of Zeus at Olympia.

The sacred precinct is superbly situated below the south slopes of Mount Parnassus, within the angle formed by the twin Phaedriades ('Shining Rocks', so called because they reflect the light), which form a tremendous precipice 250–300m high. The western rock is called Rhodini ('Roseate'), anciently *Nauplia*. From the eastern rock, Phleboukos ('Flamboyant', anciently *Hyampeia*) the Delphians used to hurl those found guilty of sacrilege. The cleft between the two, hollowed out by seismic activity and cascades from the upper plateau, is continued on the south by a line of ravines, through which spring and rain water flows into the river Pleistos. To the west the rocky spur of Mt Aghios Ilias (700m) completes the theatre-like setting. To the south, Delphi is bounded by the ravine of the Pleistos, in which the pipeline that channels water to a reservoir at Marathon, near Athens, is conspicuous; beyond rises the barrier of Mt Kirfis. The site is in a seismic area. On several occasions earthquakes and storms have caused the fall of great fragments of rock from Parnassus, and serious landslips endangering the safety of the monuments. When the mountains and plain are not enveloped in the mists that are frequent here, the view down the sacred plain to Itea, with its myriad olive-trees, and out across the Gulf of Corinth, is spectacular.

Approaches

Most visitors will approach Delphi either from the south, via the road from Itea, or from the east, via the road from Arachova. Either route is impressive. From Itea, after passing through the magnificent plain of olives—said to be the largest concentration of olive trees in Greece (*see p. 472*)—the road climbs steeply, with many sharp bends, upwards to Delphi. There are several stopping points where one can take in the views out to sea, and up into the Parnassus range to Amphissa, which has an impressive 13th-century Frankish castle. Delphi itself is hidden until almost the last moment. Bear in mind that one will almost certainly encounter a number of coaches barrelling down the road from Delphi as one proceeds uphill. The road enters Delphi on its main street and passes through the village to the site and museum.

Approaching from Arachova, the road descends gradually, skirting the cliffs of Parnassus on the right and keeping high above the Pleistos river, whose ravine is hidden by vineyards. Egyptian vultures (often wrongly identified as eagles) are not uncommon overhead, riding the currents above the cliffs. The road passes through the site of one of the ancient cemeteries of Delphi. To the left of the road (1200m before the Castalian Spring) are the sparse remains of a square tower, probably of the 4th–3rd centuries BC and one of a chain that guarded the Levadeia–Delphi road. The tower was subsequently used as a burial place in the Roman period. On the right are the Phaedriades, the stark precipices that shut in Delphi on the west. The road continues through what was the centre of ancient Delphi. On the left, below the road, is the part of the site known as the Marmaria, with the Sanctuary of Athena. The road then makes a sharp bend to the left at the Castalian Spring, which is on the right, shaded by trees. The Sanctuary of Apollo is also on the right, beyond which the road sweeps round to the right to enter the modern village.

The modern village

In the modern village of Delphi is the House of Angelos and Eva Sikelianos Museum (*hours irregular, but officially open Wed–Mon 10–3; T: 22650 82173*), which commemorates the work of the 20th-century poet Sikelianos and his American wife, Eva Palmer. Palmer was a set and costume designer, and together the couple staged revivals of Greek tragedies in the theatre at Delphi in the 1920s and '30s. Theirs was one of the first attempts to use the ancient theatres to stage performances; today, virtually every ancient theatre in Greece has its drama festival. Exhibits include manuscripts by Sikelianos and costumes designed by Eva. The house itself, built by local workmen in 1927, is elegant and attractive, with spectacular views from the windows.

HISTORY OF DELPHI

The early sanctuary

Originally, Delphi seems to have been sacred to Mother Earth (and probably Poseidon and Athena), and was called *Pytho*, the name by which it is known in Homer (*Iliad IX, 405; Odyssey VII, 80*). There was a Mycenaean settlement here and from the 15th century this was the seat of an oracle with a priestess (Pythia) who officiated near the cave of the serpent Python, a son of Mother Earth (Ge), who was worshipped here. Delphi was in the territory of *Krisa* (the modern hamlet of Chrisso, some 10km to the south) and was partially subject to that city. When the cult of Apollo Delphinios, an island deity worshipped in the form of a dolphin, was imported to Krisa from Crete (? 8th century), the cult was soon introduced at Pytho, which was renamed Delphi. According to the Homeric *Hymn to Apollo*, Apollo slew Python; the name 'Pytho' comes from the Greek *pythein*, 'to rot', and evidently refers to the decaying corpse of the dead serpent. After dispatching Python, Apollo travelled north to Tempe, where he gathered laurel boughs to build his temple at Delphi. Some say that the laurel (*daphne* in Greek) commemorates the nymph who turned herself into a laurel to escape Apollo's advances. Although Apollo was the most important deity honoured at Delphi, Dionysus and Athena Pronoia (Foresighted Athena) were associated with the sanctuary; indeed, Dionysus is shown on the west pediment of the Temple of Apollo (*see p. 463*). The Pythian Games, one of the four great national Greek festivals, were instituted in honour of Apollo, Artemis and Leto, and at first were held every eight years. The fame of the oracle spread all over the ancient world, and the festival attracted competitors and visitors from far and wide.

The Amphictyonic League

After the Dorian Invasion (c. 1100 BC) the sanctuary became a centre of an association called the Amphictyonic League. This was by false etymology supposed to have been founded by the hero Amphictyon, but really only means the league of the dwellers round a particular locality. Peter Levi, in his commentary on Pausanias, nicely renders the Amphictyonic League as the 'League of Neighbours'. The league was composed of twelve tribes, each of which dominated various city-states, large and small, all of which (in theory) had equal status within the group. This rudimentary United Nations included Thessalians, Dorians, Ionians and Achaeans. In addition, the more distant and more powerful city states of Athens and Sparta belonged to the league. In spite of the theoretical equality of members, votes could be transferred and political power was reflected in the decisions made. The administration of the sanctuary was conducted by the council of the League together with the community of Delphi.

The First Sacred War

Unlike Olympia, which was virtually deserted when not hosting its four-yearly games, the presence of the oracle ensured year-round traffic to Delphi and a year-round community to serve pilgrims. From the 8th century on, Delphi received rich gifts not merely from Greek cities, but from foreign powers: Gyges, King of Lydia sent gifts of gold in the 7th century, as did his descendant Croesus in the 6th century. The massive silver bull on view in the museum was made by artists from Ionia in Asia Minor.

The city of Krisa capitalized on the traffic to the sanctuary by imposing transit fees on all pilgrims to Delphi, many of whom had to disembark at Krisa's port of *Kirrha* (today's Itea). At least by the early 6th century, pilgrims were complaining of extortionate charges, and the Delphians appealed to the Amphictyonic League to rid the sanctuary of Krisa's influence. The league, urged on, it is said, by Athens, declared war against the Krisaeans. The ensuing conflict was known as the First Sacred War (c. 595–586 BC), the first of four wars fought for control of Delphi and its oracle. The tyrant Cleisthenes of Sikyon seems to have led the attack, and Krisa, with its port, was destroyed and its territory confiscated. The Amphictyonic League took over management of the Temple of Apollo and the state of Delphi was made autonomous. The Krisaean Plain was dedicated to the god and no one was allowed to till it or use it for grazing.

About this time the Pythian Games were reorganised and, from 582 BC, like the Olympic Games, were held every four years. Cleisthenes of Sikyon is said to have won the first chariot race. He later instituted Pythian Games at Sikyon. Now followed a period of great prosperity for Delphi, with gifts not just from throughout Greece, but throughout the known world. The Treasuries of Corinth, Sikyon and Clazomenae were built in the sanctuary (*see p. 450*). Croesus, last king of Lydia (560–546 BC), was a great benefactor of the sanctuary; it was Croesus who asked the oracle whether he should invade the territory of his enemy, Cyrus. 'Invade', said the oracle, 'and you will destroy a great empire'. What Croesus did not realise was that the empire he would destroy would be his own. In 548 BC, the Temple of Apollo burnt, but was soon rebuilt, with the powerful Athenian Alcmaeonidae clan financing much of the work.

Later Sacred Wars

During the Persian Wars, the oracle was inclined to Medise. Nevertheless, in 480 BC, Xerxes sent a detachment to plunder the temple. The Persian soldiers had reached the Sanctuary of Athena Pronoia when, according to Herodotus, thunder was heard and two huge crags rolled down and crushed many of them to death. After the Persian defeats, trophies, statues, and new treasuries were set up in celebration, with the Athenian treasury and stoa especially splendid.

After the Persian Wars, the territory of Phocis (with help from Athens) again exerted considerable influence on Delphi, which appealed to the Amphictyonic League for help. In the Second Sacred War (448–446 BC), Sparta attempted to assist Delphi to throw off Athenian and Phocian influence. No sooner did the Spartans return home than the Athenians returned to Delphi, seized the temple, and handed it back to the Phocians. The Delphians soon got it back, and their possession was confirmed in the Peace of Nikias (421 BC).

In 373 the temple was again destroyed, this time by an earthquake, and it was again rebuilt, by international cooperation. In 356 the Phocians, who had, on the accusation of Thebes, been fined by the Amphictyonic League for having cultivated a portion of the Krisaean Plain, retaliated by seizing Delphi with all its treasures. This precipitated the Third Sacred War (356–346 BC), during which Phocis seized the sanctuary and much of its wealth, giving Philip of Macedon a welcome pretext to intervene to 'protect' Delphi. Phocis was expelled from the Amphictyonic League and Macedon took Phocis' place in the League, with Philip elected president of the Pythian Games. The Fourth Sacred War (340–338 BC) broke out when the league accused the Amphissans of cultivating the Krisaean Plain. The Amphictyons appealed to Philip, who was delighted to invade Greece. Philip captured Amphissa and then, at the battle of Chaironeia (338 BC; *see p. 434*), defeated the Greeks led by Athens who had rallied against this northern invader. Philip now controlled not merely Delphi, but much of Greece. Although Delphi continued as a pilgrimage destination, its greater influence began to decline once it was perceived to be a mouthpiece for Macedon.

Roman Delphi

In the 3rd century, the Aetolians, who had united in a confederacy along the lines of the Amphictyonic League, succeeded the Macedonians as masters of Delphi. In 279 BC Brennus and his Gauls advanced to the attack of Delphi by the same route as the Persians in 480. They were repulsed in the same supernatural manner, by landslides and rockfalls. Their retreat was disastrous and celebrated in years to come by the festival of the *Soteria* (Salvation).

In the early 2nd century BC, the Aetolians lost Delphi to the Romans. Under Roman sway the oracle lost further prestige, as the Romans did not take its utterances seriously. In fact, the precinct was plundered by Sulla in 86 BC; by way of compensation, he gave the Delphians half the territory of dismembered Thebes.

In the imperial era the fortunes of the oracle depended on the whim of the emperor. Augustus reorganised the Amphictyonic League. Nero seized over 500 bronze statues in a fit of rage at the oracle's condemnation of his matricide. Domitian restored parts of the Temple of Apollo. When Pliny visited here, he counted more than 3,000 statues and Pausanias described a Delphi still rich in works of art. Under Hadrian and the Antonines, Delphi was restored to much of its former splendour and adorned with new buildings and monuments. Constantine carried off several of its treasures (notably the serpent column; *see pp. 453–54*) to adorn his new capital at Constantinople. The oracle was consulted by the pagan emperor Julian the Apostate, but was finally abolished by Theodosius when he closed down pagan shrines and institutions c. AD 385. Towards the end the oracle's utterances were almost entirely concerned with private and domestic matters such as marriages, loans, voyages and sales.

Rediscovery and excavation

During the Byzantine period, Cyriac of Ancona copied inscriptions here in March 1436, after which the site appears to have been ignored—indeed, virtually lost: several early travellers thought that nearby Amphissa was the site of ancient Delphi. In 1676, the English travellers Wheler and Spon realised that the contemporary village concealed much of the ancient site of Delphi. Byron and Hobhouse were disappointed at how little there was to see, and considered the names of two fellow countrymen, which they found scratched on a pillar, infinitely more inspiring than the Castalian Spring. In 1851 Flaubert records finding Byron's own name on a column of the now-destroyed Panaghia church in the Marmaria. Beginning in 1892, the village was moved from the ancient site to its present location, to allow for excavation by the French School of Archaeology. Excavation has continued under the French (excavation reports published in *Fouilles de Delphes*) and, more recently, the Greek Archaeological Service. In recent years, the archaeologists have concentrated less on excavation than on consolidating what is known: re-examining and cataloguing inscriptions, architectural blocks and fragments, and sculptural and ceramic finds. New publications on Delphi's topography and architecture are planned for the near future.

THE ANCIENT SITE

Planning a visit

Usually open 7.30–7 in summer; 8–5 in winter; check for current hours upon arrival. NB: The main sanctuary is constructed on a steeply terraced hillside, has virtually no shade, is packed with often elusive ancient remains, and demands concerted energy. Stout shoes, a sunhat, and water are useful. There is a small (over-priced) café, and a museum shop between the museum and the main sanctuary. The site is a short walk from the village. The views en route of the surrounding mountains are spectacular.

A visit to Delphi and its museum is, for better or worse, an excellent way to experience the sort of crowding that took place here in Antiquity, especially on those days when the priestess was prophesying. No matter when you go, it is virtually impossible to avoid tour groups. The site and museum are less crowded immediately after opening or late in the day.

There are three distinct components of the ancient site: The Sanctuary of Athena (known as the Marmaria, or marbles), below the Delphi–Arachova road; the Castalian Spring; and the Sanctuary of Apollo, where the Pythian priestess prophesied in the temple. Pausanias begins his visit to the Sanctuary of Apollo with the words, 'The city of Delphi is a steep slope from top to bottom, and the sacred precinct of Apollo is no different from the rest of it'. These are words most visitors will find all too apt as they explore the slopes of both the sanctuary of Apollo and that of Athena. Pausanias also mentions that he intends to 'record those dedications that seemed to me most memorable'; we will follow him in this, attempting to help visitors make sense of this most beautiful—but vast, fragmentary, and poorly labelled—site. Like Pausanias, we will not worry unduly about the dedications of 'athletes or obscure musicians'. The best guide to the site remains Pausanias, supplemented by a detailed site map (*plan on p. 451*). It is sobering to realise that the exact location of much of what Pausanias identified remains uncertain. In addition, since Pausanias did not mention monuments that he considered less than significant, many remains, in the absence of his identification, an identifying inscription, or other literary evidence, are as yet unidentified.

The Sanctuary of Apollo

NB: The entrance to the sanctuary is above the Arachova–Delphi road, between the Castalian Spring and the Archaeological Museum. The drinking fountains by the ticket booth are often out of order and it is an excellent idea to arrive with one's own supply.

Unlike the Sanctuary of Zeus at Olympia, which sprawls across a valley, the Sanctuary of Apollo is a triumph of engineering, where as many monuments and statues as possible were wedged onto a series of narrow mountain terraces. Because of the demands of its location, the sanctuary is an irregular quadrangle or trapezium, measuring about 183m by 128m. The south wall is built of squared blocks and dates from the 5th century BC; the west and north walls, which are polygonal, from the 6th century; while the splendid east wall was rebuilt on the old foundations by the architect Agathon in the 4th century. The sanctuary (including the theatre, but not the stadium) was delineated by a peribolos, or enclosure wall, with several gates.

From the main entrance, modern steps lead to a paved rectangular square, which was enclosed by Roman porticoes and doubtless used as a market place for the sale of religious objects, such as the bronze and pottery votive dedications on view in the museum, and souvenirs. In short, this was an area that probably had something of the ambience of the streets and souvenir shops of modern Delphi. One ancient block, with an inscribed cross, is a reminder of the early Christian community here; much of ancient Delphi was reused in the building of later settlements on the site.

Dedications on the Sacred Way

Four steps lead up to the main gate, 3.7m wide, through which you enter the Sacred Way, which winds up to the Temple of Apollo. This is 3.7 by 4.9m wide, and was paved in the Roman period with slabs taken from nearby buildings. Some of this makeshift pavement is intact. The Sacred Way was lined on either side with the votive monuments given by cities, citizens, kings—and the athletes and obscure musicians whom Pausanias chose to ignore. Walking along the Sacred Way in Antiquity must have been, if anything, even more claustrophobic than it is today, with hundreds of pilgrims toiling along this relatively narrow route, which ascended to the Temple of Apollo through a multitude of dedications, some humble, some spectacular.

Ⓐ Base of the Bull of Corcyra: The base, which survives, supported a bronze bull by Theopompos of Aegina, dedicated c. 480 BC from the proceeds of a catch of tuna. According to the story, which Pausanias gives, a bull went down to the sea and bellowed at an enormous school of tuna fish for a long enough time that the people of Corcyra (Corfu) sent to the oracle to ask what to do. Precise for once, the oracle suggested sacrificing the bull. The bull was sacrificed, the fish were caught, and with a tithe of the takings, the commemorative bronze bull was dedicated in thanks.

Ⓑ Offerings of the Arcadians: The line of bases supported nine bronze statues of Apollo, Victory, and Arcadian heroes. They were erected to commem-orate a successful invasion of Laconia in 369 BC and placed, out of bravado, facing the nearby Spartan Monument of the Admirals, insult being added to injury by employing the ageing sculptor Antiphanes, who had previously made the Spartan dedication.

Ⓒ Monument of the Admirals: This monument, dedicated by the Spartan Lysander in 403 BC after he had crushed the Athenians at Aegospotami, was one of the most impressive at Delphi, with 37 bronze statues of gods and Spartan admirals. Nine Peloponnesian sculptors, including Antiphanes of Argos, worked on the monument. The poet Ios of Samos was then commissioned to write verse inscriptions (some of which have been found) for the statues.

D **Offering of Marathon**: This was dedicated by the Athenians 30 years after the victory at Marathon, in honour of their leader Miltiades. The long base supported 16 statues attributed to Pheidias. One theory assigns the Riace Bronzes (two Classical Greek bronze masterpieces, recovered from the sea off southern Italy and now in the museum in Reggio Calabria) to this monument.

E **Argive Exedrae**: The Sacred Way passes between the site and remains of two semicircular exedrae, both dedicated by the Argives. The exedra on the left was erected c. 450 BC in honour of the Epigonoi, the successors of the Seven Against Thebes (*see p. 419*). To the right, stood the 4th-century exedra known as the 'Kings of Argos', which had only ten statues of a planned 20 statues of Argive kings and heroes; some of the bases remain in place along with four plinths, which once supported yet other commemorative statues.

The Treasuries

At this point, one leaves this dense concentration of commemorative statues and monuments and enters the section of the Sacred Way that is primarily devoted to treasuries, similar to those at Olympia that flank the Temple of Zeus. The treasuries contained cult equipment, smaller votive offerings, and important documents—but not, Pausanias says, money. Cities tried to outdo one another in the splendour of their treasuries, which were frequently redecorated, rebuilt, and generally enhanced.

F **Treasury of the Sikyonians**: A Doric edifice in antis, built about the beginning of the 5th century. The foundations of the treasury contain remains of two earlier buildings, probably given by Cleisthenes of Sikyon: a tholos of 13 columns (c. 580 BC) and a rectangular monopteros of 14 columns surmounted by a roof, perhaps designed to shelter the chariot of Cleisthenes; to this belong the metopes showing scenes from mythology now on view in the museum (Room III; *p. 461*). According to some accounts, the treasury was topped by the actual chariot which Cleisthenes drove when he won the chariot race in the Pythian Games of 582.

G **Treasury of the Siphnians**: After the remains of several unidentified treasuries come the massive foundations of the Siphnian treasury, built in 526–525 BC with a tithe of the profits from the famously productive gold-mines of Siphnos. This treasury was intended to surpass in opulence all other existing treasuries at Delphi. It was an Ionic temple in antis, with two Caryatid columns between the *antae*. Fragments of the Caryatids were found on the site. Along with the surviving sculptured frieze of Parian marble showing battling Greeks and Trojans and Gods and Giants, are in the museum (Room V; *p. 462*).

At this point, one has reached the so-called 'Crossroads of the Treasuries'. A branch-road, 27m long, runs to a west gate. Little remains of the Treasuries of the Thebans **(1)** or the Boeotians **(2)** and still less of what have tentatively been identified as those of the Megarians **(3)**, Potidaians **(4)** and Etruscans **(5)**.

DELPHI
SANCTUARY OF APOLLO

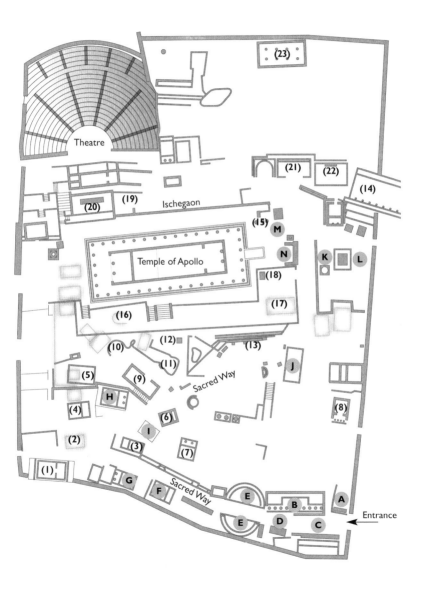

H **Treasury of the Athenians**: This is easily identifiable, since it is the only one of the treasuries which has been restored. The French School, aided by a large grant from the municipality of Athens, re-erected the building in 1904–06. The structure was reassembled from scattered stones (more than four-fifths of them recovered) to its original state, though the foundations had to be readjusted and new columns supplied. According to Pausanias, the treasury was built just after 490 BC with a tithe of the spoils of Marathon, but some scholars think it was built earlier (? c. 500 BC). A Doric building, distyle in antis, it measures 10m by 6m. It stands on a terrace ending in a triangular buttress and reached by a staircase from the Sacred Way. The triglyph frieze depicted the exploits of Heracles and of Theseus; the originals are in the Museum (Rooms VII and VIII; *p. 463*; the sculptures on the restored treasury are arbitrarily-placed casts). The treasury walls are covered with more than 150 inscriptions. Many of them, decorated with crowns, refer to the Athenian *pythiad*, special embassies sent here; others include honorific decrees in favour of the Athenians. The two *Hymns to Apollo*, with the musical notation in Greek letters above the text that were here are now in the museum (Room VIII; *p. 463*). On the south the terrace ended in a triangular space on which were displayed the Persian

weapons captured at Marathon with the dedication 'The Athenians dedicate to Apollo the spoils of the Medes after the battle of Marathon'. The inscription is a 3rd-century copy replacing the damaged original.

I **Treasury of the Syracusans**: This is a conjectural identification, but it is probable that here stood the Syracusan treasury, which (true to form) was erected here after Syracuse had routed the Athenian expedition to Sicily in 413 BC, in one of the decisive battles of the Peloponnesian War. This part of the sanctuary was dug into by a Christian cemetery, but some surviving foundation blocks mark the treasury's location. Adjacent are the foundations of the **Treasury of the Cnidians (6)**, built in Parian marble before the capture of Cnidos in 544 BC by the Persians, and the **Treasury of Clazomenae (7)**. A lateral road leads east to the remains of the **Treasury of Cyrene (8)**, probably of mid-4th-century date.

J **Treasury of the Corinthians**: A little apart from the rest of the treasuries is the site of the once-splendid Treasury of Corinth, ascribed by Herodotus to Cypselus, tyrant of that city. It was not only the oldest but the richest of the buildings of this kind, thanks to the generosity of the kings of Lydia.

Beneath the Temple of Apollo
Next to the Treasury of the Athenians are the remains of the rectangular **bouleuterion (9)**, the seat of the Delphic senate. Some attempt has been made to restore the foundations of this building. Little at all remains of the **Sanctuary of Ge-Themis (10)**, part of which was destroyed to make way for the great retaining wall. This shrine was guarded by the serpent Python, and was the site (or one of them) of the primi-

tive oracle of Ge-Themis, the earth goddess. One of the nearby rocks, supported by modern masonry, and with an identifying sign, was the **Rock of the Sibyl (11)** on which, according to ancient local tradition, recorded by Pausanias, the sibyl Herophile prophesied and foretold the fate of Helen long before the Trojan War. Another rock supported a statue of Apollo's mother Leto. Nearby stood the spectacular **Monument of the Naxians (12)**, dedicated c. 570 BC. This was an Ionic column with 44 flutings, surmounted by a sphinx (now in the museum, Room V; *p. 462*). The lower part of the column is *in situ*. An inscription of 322 BC on the base renews to the Naxians the right of *promanteia* (the privilege of consulting the oracle before other petitioners).

A little higher up, the Sacred Way crosses the threshing floor (*halos*), a circular place 15m in diameter, surrounded by seats, where the *Septerion*, a morality play celebrating the death of Python, was staged. To the north was the **Stoa of the Athenians (13)**, dedicated after the end of the Persian Wars. The stoa was long (30m) and thin (4m) so that it could nestle in the prominent position close to the Temple of Apollo. A three-stepped limestone basement supported a colonnade, 30m long and 4m deep, consisting of eight Ionic columns in Parian marble, set four metres apart. The architrave was of wood, as well as the roof, which leaned against the wall of the temple terrace. The building is gone, but on the top step of the basement is an Archaic inscription recording the Athenian dedication of cables (from the pontoon bridge thrown by Xerxes across the Hellespont) and figureheads (from captured Persian ships).

Beneath the Byzantine paving in front of the portico was found a deposit of ivory, gold, and bronze objects (museum, Room IV; *pp. 461–62*), which had been damaged in a fire in the mid-5th century and deliberately buried in a sacred pit.

Approach to the temple

The Sacred Way now describes another curve (to the north; 561m), below and to the right of the remarkable polygonal wall, which supports the platform on which stands the Temple of Apollo, the reason that most travellers, whether ancient or modern, have come here. The beautiful and elegant wall is worth a long glance before one continues to the temple. The wall, site of the first excavations at Delphi, is built in irregular interlocking blocks with curved joints, in a style unique to Delphi. This has both practical and aesthetic advantages, giving strength in seismic shocks without appearing to be a rigid barrier across the sanctuary. The dressed face was covered in the 2nd century BC–1st century AD with more than 800 inscriptions: in short, an ancient notice board. Towards the southeast end the inscriptions are particularly numerous. Records, public and private, important and trivial, are all mixed together; they relate above all to the emancipation of slaves, and constitute an invaluable record of Delphic life.

K **Tripod of Plataea**: The circular pedestal is all that remains here of this once tall and impressive monument. It was dedicated by the Greeks from the spoils of victory over the Persians at the Battle of Plataea in 479 BC (*see p. 433*). On the stone base was a gilt bronze pedestal about 5.5m high, consisting of three intertwined serpents, on which were engraved the names of the 31 city-states contributing to the victory. The three serpent heads supported a golden tripod, which was seized by the Phocians after 356 BC. This remaining serpent column was carried off by Constantine the Great and still reposes in a mutilated state, in the site of the ancient Hippodrome, at Istanbul.

Ⓛ Chariot of Helios: To the right and adjacent to the site of the Plataean Tripod, is the rectangular plinth that once supported a chariot of the sun-god, dedicated by the Rhodians. Examination of the cuttings into which the hooves of the horses fitted has suggested that the missing steeds may be none other than those now adorning St Mark's basilica in Venice—though these have been derived by other authorities from a similar group made for Alexander the Great and set up at Corinth in 336 BC. On the left are a ruined treasury (Acanthians ?), and two enormous bases, which bore statues of Eumenes and Attalus, kings of Pergamon. Above, extending across the temenos wall, are the ruins of the 2nd-century **Stoa of Attalus (14)**; Attalus was also the donor of the stoa in the Athenian agora.

Ⓜ Crossroads of the Tripods: At the top of the slope on which the temple rests, you come to a place where stand the bases of long-vanished votive offerings. The most remarkable were the Tripods of Gelon and Hiero, tyrants of Syracuse, and of their brothers. The offering which commemorated Gelon's victory at Himera over the Carthaginians in 481 BC, comprised four monuments supporting golden tripods and Victories, weighing 50 talents in all. They were some of the earliest objects to be looted when in 353 BC the Phocians needed funds for the Sacred War. The stele in front, adorned with a bull, bears an honorific decree in favour of a citizen of Kleitor in Arcadia. The base adjoining that of the tripods on the left is that of the **Acanthus Column (15)** with the dancing girls, now in the museum (Room XI; *p. 464*).

Ⓝ Altar of Apollo: This great rectangular structure with steps in black and white marble, stands in front of the temple. The altar, dedicated by the Chians in gratitude for their deliverance from the Persians, was piously re-erected in 1920 at the expense of the inhabitants of Chios and restored more accurately in 1960. Between the altar and its temple is an esplanade with some of the bases that remain of the dedications that were crowded around the temple. Of these one of the most spectacular was the bronze palm tree, supporting a gilt statue of the goddess Athena, which the Athenians dedicated after defeating the Persians at the Battle of the Eurymedon (468 BC).

The Temple of Apollo

Even in ruins, the Temple of Apollo still dominates the sanctuary and it is not difficult to imagine the effect it had in Antiquity on those who had toiled up past so many elegant, but small treasuries, to this massive building. The temple rests on its north side on the living rock, and on the south is supported by a huge substructure of irregular courses nearly 61m long and 3–4.6m high. The foundations consist of two concentric rectangles, the outer supporting the peristyle and the inner the *sekos*. The stylobate, on three steps of fine bluish local limestone, has been partially restored and many of the pavement blocks returned to place. One complete column of the 4th-century façade and portions of the others have been re-erected; in Antiquity the columns were covered with stucco, which probably contained marble dust, and which was polished until it shone. A stone ramp leads up to the entrance of the temple on the east; entering the temple is no longer allowed. The walls of the pronaos had inscriptions of well-known quotations from the Seven Sages of Ancient Greece, such as 'Know Thyself' and 'Nothing in Excess'.

Pausanias recounts and scholars discount the legends that a series of three early temples here were made first of laurel boughs, then of beeswax, and finally of bronze. In fact, it seems that the existing building had two predecessors. A structure of the 7th century was burnt in 548 BC, and replaced by a larger temple, started perhaps in 536, but completed in 513–505 by the Alcmaeonids, who were in exile from Athens. Of this Archaic temple, which was admired by Aeschylus, Pindar and Euripides, fragments, including some of the pedimental sculptures by Antenor, have been found (now in the museum; *p. 463*). This temple seems to have been destroyed by an earthquake in 373 BC. The present temple was built in 366–329 under the supervision of the Amphictyonic League and financed by contributions from across Greece. This temple was burned in 88 BC by Thracian invaders, sacked by the Roman general Sulla in 86 BC and restored by the 1st-century AD Roman emperor Domitian. In the Middle Ages the temple, like so many ancient buildings in Greece, was dismembered for the valuable metal clamps that had held column drums and building blocks in place.

The temple was the usual Doric peripteral hexastyle, 60m by 22m, with six originally stuccoed poros columns at the ends and 15 on the sides. Both pronaos and opisthodomos had two columns between *antae*. The architrave was decorated with shields captured from the Persians at Plataea (east side) and from the Gauls (west and south sides). Some of the spouts and marble tiles have been discovered, but not a fragment of the pediments described by Pausanias. Earthquakes and systematic spoliation have left practically nothing of the *sekos*, so that there is no clear indication of the arrangement of the adyton, or inner shrine. This was an underground chamber, in which were the *omphalos* (*see p. 464*) and, according to later authorities, the oracular chasm.

The south walk

To the west of the temple are the foundations of a Roman building, in which was found the statue of Antinous, now in the museum (Room XII; *p. 466*). From the southwest angle of the temple you can descend past the **House of the Pythia (16)** to the south walk. This may or may not have been where the Pythia lived. In the southeast corner was probably the **Offering of the Messenians of Naupaktos (17)**, erected to commemorate their victory at Sphacteria (*see p. 352*). Below the temple ramp was the **Monument of Aemilius Paullus (18)**, also in the museum (Room XII; *p. 466*).

THE DELPHIC ORACLE

The enormous importance of the oracle at Delphi stemmed from the fact that it was believed that Apollo himself spoke through the the Pythia, or priestess, who delivered the oracles. The priestess' utterances—famously obscure, often seemingly incoherent —were interpreted and put into scanning if recondite hexameters by one of the temple priests. Usually the priestess was a local woman, often a middle-aged matron, who led a celibate life during her time as priestess, when she seems to have worn the robes of an unmarried girl (ie of a virgin, to emphasise her chastity). When the oracle was at its most popular, there may have been as many as three priestesses, working in shifts.

There are varying accounts of what happened when supplicants arrived at the Temple of Apollo. It seems that the oracle functioned nine times a year: after the new moon in the spring, summer and autumn months, but not during the winter. In principle, petitioners drew lots to determine when they would be seen. The crowds waiting with requests must have been enormous, and it is not surprising that exceptions were made. Some cities had the right to jump the queue and others could seek advice from the oracle at any time, if the sacrificial signs were favourable. The emperor Nero characteristically demanded to be heard when the signs were not favourable, and when the oracle failed to tell him what he wished to hear, stormed off in a rage, taking hundreds of the sanctuary treasures with him.

Customarily, the petitioner would sacrifice a goat to Apollo and hand his written question to a priest, who would give the question to the Pythia. The priestess, according to most accounts, purified herself at the Castalian Spring before her sessions and then proceeded to the Temple of Apollo. There, she took her seat on a tripod (examples of these are in the museum) in the adyton, an underground chamber beneath the temple itself. It is what happened next that is the real mystery. According to many accounts, the priestess chewed laurel leaves, entered a trance, and delivered the garbled message that the priest then interpreted. Some have suggested that the laurel may have had hallucinogenic effects, but these have been hard to duplicate. Many ancient accounts mention that the priestess seemed somewhat intoxicated during her sessions, and others suggest that her tripod sat above a chasm in the earth through which vapours rose.

Scholars recently discovered that two seismic faults, riddled with fissures through which gases can escape, do indeed run under the Temple of Apollo. Earlier scholars, looking for a large chasm, overlooked the importance of these small fissures, in which signs of methane, ethane and ethylene were discovered. Ethylene was long used as an anaesthetic. In different concentrations, it can produce the states of altered consciousness—which ranged from mildly hallucinogenic trances to incoherent frenzies—attributed to the priestess.

The Temple of Apollo at Delphi.

Above the temple

The Sacred Way was protected above the Temple of Apollo by a retaining wall, called the ischegaon, constructed c. 355 BC of reused material from the Alcmaeonid temple. At the northwest angle of the terrace was the **Offering of Polyzalos (19)**, which was buried in some catastrophe (? 373 BC) and from which the celebrated *Charioteer* was recovered (museum, Room XIII; *p. 466*). Adjoining on the west is the **Lion Hunt of Alexander the Great (20)**, a large rectangular exedra of dressed stones. An epigram on the back wall has established the identity of this exedra with the monument described by Pliny and Plutarch. It was dedicated in 320 BC by Krateros, who had saved the life of Alexander the Great during a lion-hunt near Susa. A bronze group by Lysippus and Leochares represented the incident (cf. also the mosaic at Pella; *see p. 621*).

The theatre

From the temple of Apollo you can climb (via a Roman staircase) to the theatre. This is one of the best-preserved theatres in Greece, built in the 4th century BC, and restored by Eumenes II in 159 and by the Romans. The 35 tiers of seats were divided into two uneven sections by a paved diazoma (23 rows in the lower section and seven in the upper). The seats were of white marble from Parnassus. The orchestra was paved with polygonal slabs and measured 18m across. It was surrounded by an enclosed conduit. In the 1st century AD, the front of the stage was adorned with a frieze in relief depicting the Labours of Heracles, now in the museum (Room XII). There is speculation that the frieze was a rushed job, erected to flatter the Emperor Nero before he visited here in 67 AD. There is a fine view of the sanctuary from the top of the theatre (596m), which is sometimes used for special events.

Between the stage buildings and the Alexander exedra a pathway runs east above the ischegaon, passing the remains of a semicircular exedra. Beyond is the **Monument of the Thessalians (21)**, a rectangular exedra, dedicated by Daochos II of Pharsalus, who as *hieromnemon* represented Thessaly in 336–332 at the Amphictyonic League, over which he presided. On a plinth 12m long (now in the museum, Room XI; *p. 464*) stood statues of his house, also in the museum. Beyond is the ruined **Temenos of Neoptolemos (22)**, the son of Achilles, beneath which have been excavated remains of a settlement of the Mycenaean period. In front is a long base attributed to the Corcyraeans.

Somewhere northeast of the theatre was the **Fountain of Kassotis**, the water of which descended into the adyton. This was an artificial reservoir fed by the Delphousa (now Kerna), a spring which rises from a rock 70m north. The Pythia drank the waters of this spring before prophesying. Two stages of the Kerna Fountain, one Classical, the other Archaic, have been uncovered between the theatre and the stadium. Farther east of the theatre was the **Lesche of the Cnidians (23)**. This was a clubhouse (used also for ritual dining) dedicated by the Cnidians c. 450 BC. The clubhouse must have been among Delphi's most splendid buildings, as it was adorned by Polygnotus with paintings described in detail by Pausanias. The paintings showed the

Greeks departing from Troy and included scenes of people gazing at the beautiful Helen, the Trojan women lamenting the fall of Troy, and Greek soldiers taking down Menelaus' tent as they prepared to sail back to Greece.

The stadium

A path winds steeply uphill from the diazoma of the theatre to the stadium, situated in the highest part of the ancient city (645m). The north side is cut into the rock. The south side was artificially supported, and excavations now afford a fine view of the massive supporting blocks of Classical masonry (5th century BC). Four pillars remain of the Roman triumphal arch which decorated the southeast entrance of the final form given it by Herodes Atticus. The track was then established at 600 Roman feet (177m).

THE PYTHIAN GAMES

The Pythian Games, founded in 586 BC, were the second-oldest Panhellenic festival in Greece, preceded only by the more famous contests at Olympia (776 BC). In fact, the original Pythian Games may have been little more than a religious ceremony taking the form of a hymn honouring Apollo and commemorating his slaying of the Python. After the First Sacred War (*see p. 445*), when the Amphictyonic League managed Delphi, the festival was expanded. While athletic events dominated the festivals at Olympia, the Pythian Games emphasised theatre and music—as was appropriate for a festival honouring the god of music. The festival, which lasted a week, began with sacrifices and a sacred play about the fight of Apollo and the serpent. There followed, in the theatre, musical contests of cithara, flute and song, and hymns of praise in honour of Apollo; later tragedies and comedies were added. Then came athletic competitions in the stadium, and finally chariot races in the Krisaean Plain. As at Olympia, Nemea, and Isthmia, victors won a wreath of laurel—although many victors became wealthy from the honours heaped upon them by their native cities. For most of their history, the games were held every four years, although the earliest and the last festivals seem to have been every eight years. As with the Olympics, a sacred truce was in effect to allow contestants to travel to and participate in the festivals. The Greek states sent *theoroi*, or sacred embassies, loaded with gifts to the god, to the games. The Athenians also sent on occasions not connected with the games a special embassy or *pythiad* for the purpose of holding a separate festival, which included athletic games and plays. Exhibits in the museum that recall the athletic contests include the famous *Charioteer* and the statue of the athlete Agias of Pharsalus, who won contests at Olympia, Delphi, Isthmia and Nemea. The musical contests are recalled by a 2nd-century BC inscription, the earliest known written notation of a melody, with both the instrumental and choral parts of a hymn to Apollo, and a 5th-century BC bronze statuette of a flautist, his cheeks puffed out as he plays his tune.

Structure of the stadium

Both starting point (*aphesis*) and finishing post (*terma*) had stone sills with posts separating the 17 or 18 runners. The north long side had 12 tiers of seats; 13 staircases divided it into 12 rectangular blocks. A rectangular tribune, on which are benches with backs, was the stand of the *proedria*, or presidents of the games. At the west end was a conventional semicircular sphendone (unlike the stadia at Olympia and at Epidaurus). Here were six tiers of seats divided by three staircases into four *kerkides*. The south long side had only six tiers of seats. There was accommodation for 7,000 spectators.

West of the stadium

Above the stadium, to the west, on the slopes of Mt Aghios Ilias (700m), the Fortress of Philomelos, the sole fortification of Delphi, was built in 355 BC as a defence against the Locrians of Amphissa. The hill again saw fighting in the civil war that followed the Second World War. To the south of the fortress are threshing-floors and tombs. Here was the west necropolis. Sepulchral relics of every period, from the Mycenaean to Byzantine, have been found in this area. The chapel of Aghios Ilias, on the road between the sanctuary and the village, stands on a rectangular platform partly built of ancient masonry. This was the site of the *synedrion* or place of assembly built by Hadrian for the Amphictyonic League. The spot was called *Pylaea*. The name was afterwards given to a suburb which came into existence here in Roman times.

THE ARCHAEOLOGICAL MUSEUM

Usually open Mon 11–7; Tues–Sun 7:30–7 in summer; in winter, it usually closes by 5; T: 22650 82312. To avoid disappointment, it is a good idea to check the hours upon arrival in Delphi. Flash photography is not allowed in the museum, and it is forbidden to photograph people beside the displays.

The museum reopened in 2004 after extensive renovation and expansion. Much that was previously in storage is now on view. At the time of writing, the labels for individual objects and the explanatory room-by-room wall texts were still sparse and the anticipated museum guidebook had not yet been published. Until it is, the 2004 edition of Photios Petsas's Delphi, Monuments and Museum *is the best available guide.*

This museum has some of the finest works of art in Greece, and is especially rich in Archaic sculpture from the site. Most material is arranged chronologically, although some displays are themed. The rooms do not have their numbers displayed, and a certain amount of doubling-back is required to proceed through in sequence. The few texts posted are virtually the same colour as the walls, and disconcertingly hard to spot.

Terrace: The most prominent pieces here are a handsome sarcophagus, known as the *Sarcophagus of Meleager*, discovered by Capodistrias; and a large panelled mosaic (5th century AD) depicting animals and birds.

DELPHI MUSEUM

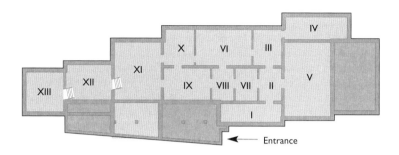

I & II	Beginnings of the Sanctuary	IX	Votive offerings (5th century BC
III	Early Archaic period	X	Tholos of the Sanctuary of Athena
IV	Sacred pits (chryselephantine	XI	Late Classical and Hellenistic ages
	objects)	XII	Late Hellenistic and Roman periods
V	Treasury of the Siphnians	XIII	The Charioteer
VI	Temple of Apollo	XIV	The end of the Sanctuary
VII & VIII	Treasury of the Athenians		

Rooms I and II: These rooms display some of the earliest offerings found, including clay votive figurines of women with upstretched arms (c. 1400–1500 BC) from the Sanctuary of Athena; a large bronze cauldron and tripod, bronze shields, and decorative bronze griffin heads (all 7th century). Also bronze votive offerings of animals (10th–7th centuries); a bronze statuette of Apollo, perhaps of Cretan workmanship (7th century); a heavily restored marble stand for a fountain in the shape of three maidens (6th century). A wall text stresses the importance of Delphi's early relations with Crete and Asia Minor.

Room III: Here are the two famous Archaic statues (6th century), 2.16 m tall identified variously as the Argive twins

Cleobis and Biton (*see p. 225*), or possibly the Dioscuri; painted terracotta architectural fragments (6th century), including lion's-head spouts; five metopes from the Sikyonian monopteros, a circular building open to the sky (6th century). The surviving (badly damaged) metopes, on which signs of paint are still visible, show mythological scenes thought to be the expedition of the Argonauts; the abduction of Europa by Zeus; Castor and Polydeuces stealing the Arcadian Cattle; the hunting of the Calydonian Boar; a scene from the quest for the Golden Fleece.

Room IV: The displays in this room, found in 1939, are thought to have been buried as a sign of respect in pits after a fire in the 5th century. In short, they were found in a sacred dump. Most seem to have been made in western Asia Minor, in Ionia, and are reminders that offerings were sent to Delphi from afar. Wall cases contain (restored) chryselephantine heads, with gold head-dresses, probably of Apollo, his sister Artemis, and their mother Leto (6th century); and an ivory statuette of a god, perhaps Apollo, with his hand resting on a lion (7th century), of the type known as the 'master of the beasts'. The room is dominated by the silver statue of a life-sized bull (6th century), whose original length was 2.30m. The bull, whose horns and hooves are gilded, was made of three sheets of silver placed over a wooden core, hammered into shape, and fastened by bronze bands and silver nails (some still evident). Most scholars think the bull to be the work of a Greek artist living in Ionia.

Room V: The room contains the the **Naxian Sphinx** (6th century), which stood on a column near the temple of Apollo. The total height of the column was 14.40m; the sphinx loomed over the sanctuary and would have been visible from afar to all who came here. It was intended to demonstrate both the wealth of the Cycladic island of Naxos and to imply that Naxos' gift was watching over the sanctuary. The sphinx has the head of a woman (with a quintessential Archaic smile), the torso of an eagle, and the body of a lion.

Also here are the massive **entrance door of the Treasury of the Siphnians**; and **temple sculpture** from the treasury (6th century). The sculptures are well-preserved and bear out Herodotus' remark that the Siphnian treasury was

one of the richest in Delphi. Most scholars think that the south and west friezes were done by one or more 'conservative' artists (still adhering to Archaic styles) and the north and east friezes by one or more less conservative artists, perhaps influenced by Athenian sculptors. The east pediment represents the dispute between Heracles and Apollo over the Delphic tripod. The two sons of Zeus, less than dignified, each tug at the tripod. Between them stands a figure variously identified as Athena, Zeus or Hermes, who seems to be attempting to restrain the brawling deities. The four sculptural friezes that adorned the treasury are displayed almost at eye level, which allows visitors to see the clearly remaining traces of the colours used on the figures. The east frieze shows a group of Olympian gods watching the fighting at Troy. Ares, god of war, holding his massive shield, sits behind a figure variously identified as Aphrodite or Leto, who leans forward, resting her hands on the shoulders of Artemis, who herself leans toward her brother Apollo. Ahead of Apollo, and larger than the other figures, is the seated figure of Zeus. On his knee, one can just make out part of a female hand, which some have suggested is the hand of Achilles' mother Thetis, who may have been shown pleading with Zeus to spare her son. Next come scenes of the fighting at Troy, with several dead warriors stretched on the ground. The north frieze shows a *gigantomachy*, a battle of gods and giants, always a popular theme for the Greeks, and usually taken to represent the triumph of Olympian reason over less civilised powers. Heracles is noticeable with his lion's-skin cloak and

Hera is the figure bending forward over a giant whom she has struck down. Originally, many of the names of the contestants were painted at the bottom of the composition, as on vases. The west frieze shows the judgment of Paris, when the apple of discord, inscribed 'For the fairest' was contended for by Hera, Athena and Aphrodite. The unfortunate Paris had to resolve the dispute; Aphrodite, easily the most beautiful female shown in the frieze, is depicted alighting from her chariot, toying with her necklace. The south frieze is so fragmentary that scholars either say that it is not possible to interpret it at all—or interpret it, in any one of a great many ways.

Room VI: The displays here, with several helpful texts, are devoted to the **Temple of Apollo**, covering several periods in the temple's history and stressing the importance of the Alcmaeonids of Athens in its rebuilding after destruction by fire in 548 BC. It is also suggested that scenes on the 4th-century temple of Apollo and Dionysus are meant to show that the two gods of music were coexisting in harmony at Delphi. Some of the sculpture on display here had been in museum storerooms for so long that it had been lost track of and was thought to have been looted by the Romans. The sculpture includes figures from the west pediment of the temple during both its 6th-century Archaic period (depiction of a *gigantomachy*) and its 5th-century Classical period (Dionysus and Maenads). From the east pediment, there is the scene from the Archaic temple—stark in its simplicity—of Apollo's arrival at Delphi

from Athens, and from the Classical temple scenes of gods and muses flanking Apollo seated on a tripod. One of the most splendid figures on display is the **Nike acroterion**—one knee bent as she hurtles along—which topped the 6th-century temple.

Rooms VII and VIII: The **Treasury of the Athenians** had 30 metopes, of which 24 have been preserved and are on display. There is a helpful text posted on the metopes, which are variously dated to the years just before, or just after, the Battle of Marathon (480 BC). As with the Siphnian Treasury, scholars discern several hands at work on the metopes, one more conservative (Archaic) than the other, which represents a transition to the Classical style. The contrast in the two styles may be seen most easily by comparing the metope showing Heracles and the Cerynean Hind with that showing Heracles and Kyknos, son of the bandit Ares, who preyed on visitors to Delphi. The figure of Heracles with the hind is noticeably less fluid, less anatomically detailed, than that of the Heracles with Kyknos. The metopes show scenes from three popular subjects: an *Amazonomachy*; the exploits of Heracles; the exploits of the Athenian hero Theseus. The subject of the sculpture on the treasury's east pediment is uncertain (Theseus and Pirithous, King of the Lapiths?), while the west pediment focuses on Heracles. Easy to miss, flush against a side wall in Room VII, is the 2nd-century BC inscription with the **oldest known notation of melody**; an explanatory text is on the wall beside the room entrance.

Room IX: This room, with votive offerings of the 5th century BC, has a text on the **Sanctuary of Athena** and its treasuries, focusing on the 6th-century Treasury of Massalia (Marseilles). The votive offerings include statuettes of athletes and flautists who would have contended in the Pythian festival. The elaborate figure of a woman supporting an incense burner with an intricate crown-like lid is particularly notable. There are also a number of statues of *korai*, which stood at unknown places in the sanctuary, as well as architectural fragments from buildings of the sanctuary. The room is something of a mixed bag, but gives a glimpse of the enormous profusion of votive offerings left at the sanctuary.

Room X: *Tholoi*, round buildings of uncertain origin and use, are always mysterious. Although today the **tholos at the Sanctuary of Athena** is its most visible building (thanks to restoration), Pausanias did not even mention it when he visited here. The displays focus on the architecture of the 4th-century tholos, which combined the architectural orders. The tholos had interior and exterior friezes, of which fragments showing *Amazonomachia* and *Centauromachia* survive. Some have suggested that both this tholos and the tholos at the Asclepieion at Epidaurus were designed by the same architect, Theodoros of Phocaia.

Room XI: Several exhibits vie for attention in this room: first, are the figures from the impressive 4th-century **Monument of the Thessalians**, dedicated by Daochos II of Thessaly, head of the Amphictyonic Assembly of Delphi from 338–334 BC. Daochos' monument showed nine of his family members, including three famous athletes. The group, identified from the surviving inscription of the plinth, forms a genealogical succession of seven generations from the 6th century BC. The best-preserved figures are those representing Agias, great-grandfather of the dedicator (depicted as an athlete), who had not only won an Olympic wreath, but had five victories at the Nemean, three at the Pythian, and five at the Isthmian Games; and Agelaos, his young brother, who won a track event at Delphi. Some think that the composition copies one in bronze by the famous sculptor Lysippus. Even in its present form—missing a figure of Apollo—this monument clearly conveys the sheer bulk of many of the dedications at Delphi. Nearby stands the **Acanthus Column**, which originally stood 13m high, one of many dedications whose donor is unknown. It takes its name from its large, fleshy acanthus-leaf base and is topped by three figures of women dancers in scanty chitons. This would be a flamboyant monument as is, but some scholars think that the whole composition was topped by a bronze cauldron (lost) holding a massive marble *omphalos* (navel). An *omphalos* stone was found in the south wall of the Temple of Apollo, marking the spot where the two eagles loosed by Zeus met, at the very centre of the world.

Detail of the celebrated *Charioteer*, a bronze original of c. 475 BC.

Room XII: This room contains the earliest known monument with a relief depicting an actual event in Graeco-Roman history: the **Monument of Aemilius Paullus**, commemorating the Roman general's victory in 168 BC over King Perseus of Macedon at Pydna. Erecting the monument must have been particularly sweet for Paulus: Perseus had commissioned a monument to celebrate his victory before the battle. When Paullus triumphed, he used the marble set aside for Perseus' monument to commemorate his own victory. Also here is one of the best and best-known marble statues of the youth **Antinous**, the beloved of the emperor Hadrian. When Antinous drowned in the Nile in 130 BC, Hadrian was inconsolable. He deified the youth, and dedicated statues of him wherever he went on his journeys. This statue captures the enormous appeal of Antinous' brooding, sensual looks.

Room XIII: The 5th-century bronze figure of a winning **charioteer** is not only the best-known piece in the museum; it is one of the most famous pieces of Greek sculpture to have survived from Antiquity. Originally, the charioteer was one of a group, which included the winning four-horse chariot. The scant remains of the horses (three hooves) and their chariot (the reins are well preserved) are on display in a separate case. A good deal has been written

pointing out that the charioteer was designed to be seen from a distance and from below; its proportions seem odd when viewed up close and virtually at eye-level. The eyes, for example, of magnesium and onyx, wonderfully preserved, are not symmetrical. The figure was discovered in 1896 where it had fallen during the earthquake of 373 BC. The charioteer, dressed in a long tunic (*xystis*), is represented life-size. On his head is a victor's fillet. He holds the reins in his right hand. Some have suggested that the charioteer's calm and formal pose suggests that he is depicted performing his lap of honour. The work, one of the few great surviving bronzes of the 5th century, dates from c. 475 and was dedicated by a Sicilian prince to commemorate a chariot victory in the Pythian Games in 478 or 474 BC. The sculptor may have been Pythagoras of Samos, who was in exile at this time at *Rhegion*, in southern Italy.

Room XIV: The final room has an assortment of busts and statues from the 1st–4th centuries AD, one of which has been tentatively identified as the historian Plutarch, who served as a priest at Delphi. Several inscriptions bear testimony to the interests various Roman emperors took in Delphi. There is a model of the sanctuary on a low table near the exit; oddly, the period that the model shows is not indicated.

THE MARMARIA

The Marmaria is about 1.5 km east of the main sanctuary on the road to Arachova. From the road, the columns of the tholos and the outline of the gymnasium are clearly visible. A path leads down from the road, passing a small café, which proclaims fast service.

The Marmaria was the Sanctuary of Athena; it is a reminder of how much is not known about Delphi that scholars disagree as to whether Athena was worshipped here as Athena Pronoia (Athena of Foresight) or as Athena Pronaia (Athena before the Temple). If the latter, the epithet may refer to the fact that Athena's temple was lower in the sanctuary than Apollo's, and one reached it before coming to the Temple of Apollo.

The earliest remains found here are Mycenaean, including the clay figurines of women on view in the museum (Room I; *p. 461*). Some of the finest sculptures found here are also in the museum (Room X; *p. 464*). The precinct is roughly rectangular, with the entrance on the east. With the exception of the 4th-century tholos (partly reconstructed, with three standing columns) the remains here are primarily of foundations and fallen architectural members. The most important part of the sanctuary lay between the two temples of Athena, whose foundations are still visible.

An upper terrace north of the gate supported the small Precinct of Phylakos; one of its two buildings was the Heroōn of Phylakos, who, with Autonoös, routed the Persians in 480 BC. The other may have been dedicated to the saviours of Delphi at the time of the onset of the Gauls in 279 BC. An inscription on the retaining wall locates the Altars of Athena Hygieia and of Eileithyia (childbirth).

The oldest part of the sanctuary, dedicated to Athena Hygieia, was entered through a gateway, whose huge lintel lies on the ground. Here the excavations of 1922 revealed the existence of a Mycenaean settlement. The Old Temple of Athena was a Doric peripteral hexastyle structure in tufa, built at the beginning of the 5th century BC on the site of a still older building (7th century) from which capitals survive. The temple was damaged in 480 BC by the fall of rocks that routed the Persians and its ruin was completed by the earthquake of 373. Fifteen columns and the stylobate had been found when in 1905 another landslip demolished all but three of the columns.

The centre of the precinct is occupied by three buildings. A **Doric treasury** (490–460 BC) of marble stood on a limestone foundation. The **Aeolian Treasury of Massalia**, in antis, built c. 530 BC in Parian marble, was of remarkably fine workmanship, recalling the Treasury of the Siphnians in the Sanctuary of Apollo (*see p. 450*). The third building, a Pentelic marble **tholos**, or rotunda, of the early 4th century, was one of the finest in Delphi. Its dedication and purpose are unknown. It has a circular peristyle of 20 slender Doric columns on a platform of three steps. Three columns with their entablature were re-erected in 1938; the cornice and metopes have been restored in replica from the best surviving fragments. The entrance to the circular cella was on the south. The paved interior was decorated with Corinthian half-columns. To the west of the tholos c. 360 BC rose the New Temple of Athena, a severe prostyle edifice with a portico of six columns of the Doric order. Beyond this temple, and partly beneath it, is an earlier rectangular building (5th century), probably a priest's dwelling.

The gymnasium

To the northwest of Marmaria are the remains of the gymnasium, originally dating from the 4th century BC, but rebuilt by the Romans. The slope of the ground necessitated its arrangement on different levels. On the upper level was the *xystos*, or covered track,

Delphi: the Marmaria, with the famous tholos. The function of this building is still unknown.

where the athletes practised in bad weather, with a parallel track in the open air. The lower terrace was occupied by the palaestra, also used for exercise. This is divided into the palaestra proper, a court 12m square surrounded by a colonnade on all four sides, and the baths, comprising a circular (cold) bath 9m in diameter and 1.8m deep, and, in the retaining wall at the back, a series of douche baths. The hot baths, north of the court, are a Roman addition. A column, which was reused in the building of the church of the Panaghia (now in ruins), bears the names of Byron and Hobhouse.

THE CASTALIAN SPRING

The spring lies between the Sanctuary of Athena and the Sanctuary of Apollo, in a sharp bend of the Arachova–Delphi road, where a deep ravine separates the two cliffs of the Phaedriades. According to legend, Apollo planted a cutting of the laurel he

brought from Tempe to Delphi by the spring. The base of a statue of Ge, the goddess of Earth, found here shows that the spring was an early place of cult worship. All those who came to Delphi for any religious purpose had to purify themselves in the Castalian spring. Murderers bathed their entire body, but others simply washed their hair—as legend says that Apollo himself did here. In Roman times, it was believed that the waters of the Castalian fountain inspired the muse of poetry. This belief—or homage to it—has driven many of today's visitors to slide precariously along the slippery rocks to drink the waters here, despite signs forbidding the practice. Some prize the medicinal qualities of the spring which, as often as not of late, is but a trickle.

Originally the spring simply flowed through a cleft in the rocks, but it was soon embellished. Remains of 7th- and 5th-century fountains have been found, but what one sees today dates primarily from the Hellenistic and Roman periods. The spring had a façade of seven marble pilasters. The four niches within (clearly visible in the cliffside) were presumably for votive offerings; in the largest is a column drum once used as the altar of a Christian chapel. The water was collected in a long narrow reservoir (9m by 1m) which fed seven jets (holes still visible). These jets fell into a rectangular court, 9m by 3m, reached by rock-hewn steps. The overflow from the fountain joins the water of the gorge dividing the Phaedriades, which plunges into a deep rocky glen, to join the Pleistos flowing in the valley far below. An Archaic square fountain house, discovered in 1957, lies nearer the road.

PARNASSUS

Parnassus (Παρνασσός) is a complex mountain mass, with two main peaks: hence Ovid's *biceps Parnassus*. The higher summit is called Lyakoura or Lykeri ('Wolf Mountain', anciently *Lykorea*; 2457m) and the lower Gerontovrachos ('Old Man's Rock'; 2435m). To the Greeks Parnassus was sacred to Dionysus and the Maenads; it was the Latin poets who made it, with the Castalian Spring, the home of Apollo and the Muses. Deucalion's ship was believed to have rested on the top of Parnassus during the Flood. Climbers (in summer months) and skiers (winter and early spring) come to Parnassus. Those who wish to drive up may do so easily on the wide new road that leads to the ski centres. The ski centre at Fterolakkas (c. 1500m) is reached by road (c. 26km) from Arachova via Kalyvia (*centre closed in summer*).

ARACHOVA

Arachova ('Αράχοβα), 11km east of Delphi, once noted for its thick hand-loomed *flokati* rugs, wines and embroideries, and as the best starting-point for the climb of Mount Parnassus, is now more famous for its *après-ski* winter pleasures. The proliferation of highways and the development of skiing on Mount Parnassus have made this a popular weekend destination for Athenians. The surrounding hills are sprouting villas and small apartment blocks with vacation flats. Where once copious streams of water ran down Arachova's narrow street, now cars race through the town en route to the ski slopes. Nonetheless, off the main street—usually clogged with traffic—Arachova retains much of its charm. The houses rise in terraces on the mountain spur; near the top is the church of Aghios Georgios. The views down over the lower town from vantage points in the upper town and even from along the main street are splendid. Once off the main street, it is easy to get lost in the narrow, twisting lanes that run up and down the steep slope that Arachova clings to. This is a pleasant spot to come in the evening for a meal by one of the springs along the main street—although on winter weekends, Arachova is usually very crowded. The shops sell local honey, wine, some folk art (carved wooden utensils, etc), and local cheeses and sausages.

Arachova may occupy the site of a small Classical place called *Petrites*, which succeeded the two prehistoric towns of *Anemoreia* and *Kyparissos*. There are traces of these below and above the Katoptirio rock (*enquire locally for directions*).

CLIMBING PARNASSUS

Arachova Climbers' Association, T: 22670 31118. Due to changes in road and accom-modation facilities, it is desirable to seek up-to-date information as to the best approach.

The lower ski centre functions as an excursion resort in summer. July and August are the only practicable months for climbing to the summit, when the paths are free of snow. With a car and guide (or precise directions) it is possible to drive to within 45mins' walk of the summit via the access roads to the skiing installations. The traditional method of making the proper climb is to spend a night at the Hellenic Alpine Club refuge (Katafygion Sarandari; 1890m, 28 beds, only food need be taken). A robust vehicle can get to within 15mins' walk of the refuge. The climb is usually made before dawn and takes about 5hrs there and back, though fell-walkers would do it in less. It is practicable for a fit climber, who does not mind the heat, to do the whole expedition in the day from Kalyvia, ignoring the refuge.

The view from high on Parnassus at sunrise, before the mists gather, exceeds in grandeur and interest almost every other prospect in the world. Little by lit-tle the map of Greece unfolds. To the northwest are Tymfristos and Pindus; to the north, beyond Kallidromon, are Oiti, Othrys, Pelion, Ossa and Olympus. To the northeast lies the Atalante Channel and the island of Euboea, with the Gulfs of Lamia and Volos, and the northern Sporades beyond. In the far distance the grey mass of Mount Athos rises from the sea. To the southeast are Helicon, Attica and the Cyclades; to the south the Gulf of Corinth, with its isthmus; beyond, the Peloponnesian mountains; Kyllini, Maenalon, Aroania, Erymanthos, and Panachaïkon, with Taygetos in the background. To the west, beyond the vale of Amphissa, the view is masked by the mountains of Locris and Doris, two of which, Kiona (2500m) and Vardousi (2495m), are higher than Parnassus.

THE CORYCIAN CAVE

Allow at least six hours for this excursion. NB: Recent development of skiing (and consequent ski lodges and holiday homes) means that this is no longer an excursion into untouched coun-tryside and some may wish to visit the Corycian Cave only in their imaginations or with Pausanias (see below). It is very easy to lose the path once one leaves the Phaedriades; a guide is advised for the full climb. With a car the cave is more easily reached from Kalyvia, above Arachova, by a signed road.

From Delphi the site fence now blocks the ancient rock-cut path that starts above the stadium. The modern path (marked) begins above the Sikelianos Museum. The path zigzags upwards; there are a number of black and yellow diamond markers indicating the way. There is a good view down over the ancient stadium. About an hour out of Delphi (at a brisk pace) you reach the top of the Phaedriades cliffs. In Antiquity murderers were thrown off the peaks here; today, they are known as the *Kaki Skala* (Evil Stairs). From here, there are fine views over Delphi and the surrounding countryside.

The path continues on the Plateau of Livadi, used as a pasturage by ancient and modern shepherds alike, as far as the conspicuous watering troughs. Here we turn right (east) and cross the low ridge. On the east slope a broad path will be found at the entrance to the forest, leading down the valley (marked with red arrows and signs). These are not easy to follow near two small tarns, where you make for the gap between two hills. From this gap a rough path climbs in zigzags. After a ruined chapel, a sign in Greek and English points ahead to the cave. In another half hour or so, you reach (1299m) the low arched entrance to the Corycian Cave, now called *Sarantavlì* ('Forty Rooms'). This cave, which Pausanias thought the finest he had seen, was sacred to Pan and the Nymphs (inscriptions). Above it Dionysiac orgies were celebrated by the Thyiades (*Aeschylus, Eumenides 22*). According to Herodotus, when the Persians were marching on Delphi, the inhabitants took refuge in the Corycian Cave; it was again used as a refuge during the War of Independence. Within a faint light reveals pink and green walls and the stalactites and stalagmites. Excavations of the French School in 1970 showed the periods of use to be Neolithic, late-Mycenaean, and 6th–4th centuries.

AMPHISSA & THE COAST

Amphissa ('Άμφυσσα; 20km from Delphi) perches on a steep slope of the Locrian mountains at the northwest end of the Krisaean Plain; it is visible from afar by day, and its distant lights are tantalizing by night from Delphi. The drive from Delphi is winding with fine views. Amphissa's chief glory are its olives. The olive groves of Amphissa, especially when viewed from the summit of the steep descent from Delphi, have the appearance of a riverbed of dense aquatic vegetation. They are amongst the most ancient olive groves in Greece, established by the ancient Greeks, exploited by the Romans and maintained in production almost continuously since that time. They yield a variety of *koroneiki* olive, producing a fruit similar to the purple Kalamata, but a little smaller. A combination of an exceptionally sheltered habitat, well watered and drained soil, with a customarily light pruning regime, has allowed the trees to grow older, larger and fuller than almost anywhere else in Greece. The sound and sight of this dense and ordered olive jungle when lightly moved by the wind is unforgettable.

The town of Amphissa

In Antiquity Amphissa was the capital of Ozolian Locris. Its ancient remains are inconsequential (although mosaic floors from Roman buildings have been found in various parts of the town), but the ancient acropolis is crowned by a ruined but impressive Frankish castle (1205), accessible by road (follow Odos tou Frouriou uphill). In the 13th century, Amphissa was held by counts from Picardy who owed their allegiance to the Kings of Thessaloniki. Some think that this is the origin of its medieval name *Salona* (from Salonika). The castle (known locally as the kastro or frourio) has three well-preserved gates, three enceintes and a circular keep, partly built on the walls of the ancient acropolis. Antique survivals include the remains of Classical and Hellenistic walls, and of two towers. There is a reasonably well-preserved cistern, but the remains of several medieval churches are more than elusive.

At the south foot of the castle are the remains of a Turkish fountain and the 12th-century church of the Sotiros, which has several reused Corinthian columns and architectural decoration on its exterior walls including two sundials and two crosses. In the centre of Amphissa, on a site to the north of the cathedral, are the remains of a baptistery of the late 4th century AD, with marble facings and fine mosaics. The small Archaeological Museum has finds from the area.

Itea and Kirra

From Amphissa, one can continue to Lamia (*see p. 477*) on a magnificent road with a sharp winding ascent and descent through the Pass of Gravia (870m), between Mt Gkiona and Parnassus. The earth hereabouts is rich in the colours of manganese and bauxite, which are extensively quarried near the mouth of the valley at Itea.

The main road from Amphissa winds south to the coast at Itea, a dull little place full of eucalyptus trees: but it is possible to stay here if Galaxidi (*see below*) is full and/or your budget is limited. The modern harbour, built round a promontory at the head of the gulf, is a fresh and pleasant small resort, busy at intervals with cruise ships disembarking their excursions to Delphi.

Immediately east of here is Kirra. French (and more recently Greek) excavations show that ancient *Kirrha* flourished in Early and Middle Helladic times, though it is best known for its part in the First Sacred War. Recent work has revealed part of a Classical harbourfront building, and some remains of the harbour itself can be made out beneath the sea. There is a Frankish tower on the seafront, mainly constructed of reused Classical blocks. This (rather than Galaxidi, as usually supposed) may have been the port of medieval *Salona* (Amphissa). There are Early Christian and Byzantine remains at Aghios Nikolaos (2km north of the tower) where there was an important settlement.

Beyond Kirra a spectacular road climbs 610m up the face of Koutsouras and across its saddle to (155km) Desfina, continuing in an enclosed valley. At (159km) the large Moni Timiou Prodromou, it divides. The right branch makes a steep descent to Andikira, while the left branch crosses another ridge to (168km) Distomo (*see p. 440*) and Hosios Loukas.

The coast road from Itea to Galaxidi is scarred with quarries and mines: bauxite is loaded by cableway and tipped direct into ships. The little Bay of Salona was the site of Salona's medieval port, now Ormos Iteas.

GALAXIDI

Galaxidi (Γαλαξίδι), on the west side of the Gulf of Itea, is a well-built old seafaring town that boomed at the end of the 19th century, leaving many pretty buildings from that period. With many absentee householders, it is picturesquely situated on a wooded bay with a fine view of Parnassus. The church of the Metamorfosis was reputedly rebuilt by Michael II Angelus in gratitude for his recovery from an illness; it has an exceptionally good altar screen. There is an interesting Maritime Museum, with paintings, equipment and relics; also some antiquities and material relating to the Wars of Independence. There is an ecological forest area, and the yachting marina is being expanded.

HISTORY OF GALAXIDI

The town has sections of ancient wall dating from the 4th century, which may have belonged to ancient *Chaleion*. Mycenaean objects have been found on the site. The first city was built on the hill above the modern town, and coastal settlement followed later. In the Peleponnesian War Galaxidi was connected with Sparta. In 216 it was conquered by the Macedonians, and remained a very small maritime and trading port for several hundred years. In medieval times it was held by the Angevins, the Duke of Patras, and the Knights of St John. It was fortified in 1448, but taken soon afterwards by the Turks. In 1703, the *Chronicle of Galaxidi* was compiled, giving a great deal of information about the town in Byzantine times. After the Ottoman conquest it became the seat of a Bey. In 1580 an earthquake caused serious damage. A traveller in 1673 noted that the town had been reduced to a small, semi-ruined village, but in the 18th century conditions improved with the growth of maritime trade in the Gulf of Corinth and elsewhere. The English traveller Edward Dodwell, visiting in 1805, noted the size of the houses and the quality of their construction. The town that you see today was built as a showpiece port for the new Greek state by King Otho I, in appreciation for the help the local shipowners had given in the War of Independence, but fell into decline with the end of sailing ships in the early 20th century.

NAFPAKTOS & ENVIRONS

Nafpaktos (Ναύπακτος), officially in Aetolia, is a charming town though rather congested. A new bypass is being built that will improve conditions considerably. Ancient *Naupaktos*, a town of the Ozolian Locrians, was taken in 455 by the Athenians. Here they established a colony of Messenians, who had been dispossessed by their Spartan conquerors. The place played an important part in the Peloponnesian War; it was successfully defended in 429 by Phormion and in 426 by Demosthenes against the Spartans, and became a base for the Sicilian expedition.

Nafpaktos was an early Christian centre, and sent a bishop to the Synod of Sardiki in 343. After 899 it was part of the Theme of Nicopolis. After 1204 it was taken by the Venetians when the name Lepanto appears. In 1320 it fell under Angevin control, and was taken by Albanians in 1361. In the last decades of the 14th century Albanians, Venetians and Ottomans all held it for periods, but it reverted to the Venetians in 1407, then fell to the Turks in 1499. It became part of the Greek state after 1829. In 1909 Baedeker observed that it was 'picturesquely situated but poor'.

Nafpaktos today is worth a detour on any through journey to visit the wonderful castle, one of the finest examples of Venetian and Ottoman military architecture in northern Greece, and once one of the most important fortresses in the country. Attractively floodlit at night, its ramparts and interlocking walls loop down the steep hill to enclose the little harbour, a formidable obstacle to attackers. There are magnificent views from the castle across the Gulf of Corinth and towards the new road bridge, and there are some fine old houses below the walls. There are four gates in these perimeter walls, which were strengthened by towers in the Ottoman period. On the way down from the castle, the Café Tapia is very pleasant. The plateia, shaded by jacaranda trees, looks across the Gulf to Mt Panachaïkon. The Eviva sweet and wine shop is very good.

THE BATTLE OF LEPANTO

It was here at Nafpaktos, in 1571, that the Turkish admiral fitted out before the decisive Battle of Lepanto, fought in fact off the Echinades Islands. The allied fleet, under Don John of Austria, natural son of the Holy Roman Emperor Charles V, included contingents from Venice, Genoa, the Papal States, Spain, Sicily and Naples. The Turks were assisted by the Bey of Alexandria and the Bey of Algiers. The result was an overwhelming victory for Christendom, with Muslim sea-power suffering a blow from which it never recovered. The young Cervantes, author of *Don Quixote*, who was fighting with the Spanish force, here lost the use of his left hand. There is an attractive new bronze statue of Cervantes by the harbour wall.

UP THE MORNOS RIVER

Just east of Nafpaktos the ways part beside the Mornos river. The new road (right), crosses nearer the mouth of the river, and then follows the coast. There are few villages hereabouts, and place-names are often derived from beaches or isolated churches. The pretty village of Monastiraki is where Herodotus located *Erythrae*.

Leaving Nafpaktos on the inland route takes you up the west side of the Mornos valley. At Kato Dafni the road turns right onto a five-span bridge which carries the road across the Mornos near its mouth. The broad river valley is now completely empty of water. The way continues through rolling hills interspersed with orchards and little streams, climbing gradually. Prominent on a bluff to the right is a radar station commanding the Rio strait. The mountains behind Patras become very prominent across the Gulf and there are splendid retrospective views southwards before the descent past Filothei. A turning to the left leads to the **Varnakova Monastery**, a Byzantine foundation rebuilt by Capodistrias (*see p. 234*) in 1831. The road turns north, crosses a ridge, then follows a ledge high up the mountainside above a side valley of the Mornos. During the gradual descent to the main river, the horizon becomes increasingly filled with peaks; those to the north barren, those to the east clothed with forests. Beyond a sign to Teichio (right) the road drops to cross the Mornos, now virtually dry, at its confluence with the Loufoloreko. Minor roads lead into the mountains to Chrisovo and Katafygio, once refuges from the Turks.

The road climbs high above the north bank of the Mornos and a series of wooded valleys opens out to the east. There are dark pine forests on the higher slopes. Descending again, the valley becomes broader with views ahead towards Mt Gkiona (2507m). **Krokileio** was the native village of Yiannis Makriyiannis, a hero of the 1821 revolt. A succession of bridges cross gullies and minor streams. The 850-metre Mornos Dam creates the artificial Lake Mornos.

To the north of the lake rises Mt Vardousia (2495m). Beyond Diakopi, rising immediately above the road to the right, is a conical hill with the remains of **Kallion** (ancient *Kallipolis*). The lower part of the site was excavated from 1976 in advance of flooding for creation of the Mornos barrage. Further work is in progress. Classical remains are of the Hellenistic to Late Roman periods and include parts of the city wall, houses, public buildings and the Roman cemetery. The site suffered destruction by the Gauls in 279 BC. More prominent on the higher slopes of the acropolis are substantial walls and buildings of a fortified medieval settlement (*Loidorix*), perhaps built by the Catalans who certainly occupied the site in the 14th century. It was one of the three Catalan strong-points of the county of Salona. Below on the shore are some sad remains of the drowned old village of Kallion, now again above water level. A short distance further along the road is the newer hamlet of Kallio, and there are good retrospective views of the ancient site.

Lidoriki, on the east side of the lake, is a pleasant mountain village with an archaeological collection. With just under a thousand inhabitants, it is the chief market centre of Doris, one of the two eparchies of Phocis. Just beyond **Aigitio** on the south side of the lake there is a fortified acropolis that may be ancient *Aegition*, with other forts in its territory (on Mts Vounichora and Zerza). The road winds down towards the coast through scrubby and uninteresting countryside. Beyond the village of Vounichora, however, the view opens out to the right giving a glimpse of the Bay of Galaxidi with Chrisso and Delphi lying on the slopes of Parnassus. The site of ancient *Tolophon*, with a well-preserved enceinte, lies near Aghii Pandes.

LAMIA & ENVIRONS

Lamia (Λαμία), the chief town of the *nome* of Phthiotis (Fthiotida) and the seat of an archbishop, is a lively and pleasant town of 44,084 inhabitants, lying below two wooded hills. It is a market centre for cotton, cereals and garden produce. A characteristic sight are the storks' nests on the roofs.

Lamia is remembered for the Lamian War (323–322 BC), in which the Athenians attempted to free themselves from Macedonian domination. Leosthenes seized Thermopylae and shut up Antipater, the Macedonian viceroy, in Lamia. After Leosthenes had been killed in a sortie, the command passed to Antiphilos. A Macedonian relief force freed Antipater, and Antiphilos was defeated at Krannon. A stronghold in the Middle Ages, Lamia was known to the Franks as *Gipton* and to the Catalans as *El Cito*, whence perhaps the Turkish name *Zitouni*. Rescue excavations have revealed many traces of the ancient city, its walls and cemeteries.

The town

Round the central Plateia Eleftherias are grouped the Nomarchia, the cathedral and several hotels. Odos Diakou leads to Plateia Diakou, adorned with a characteristic statue of Athanasios Diakos, a local patriot. From here a stepped street ascends the hill of Aghios Loukas. Just to the east of Plateia Eleftherias is the shaded Plateia Laou, where the waters of the Gorgopotamos gush from a fountain. Dominating the town on the northeast is the kastro, a castle of the Catalan Duchy of Neo-Patras (1319–93). Traces of Middle and Late Bronze Age occupation and a Protogeometric tomb have been found. The walls stand on Classical foundations and show masonry of many later epochs (including Roman, Catalan and Turkish battlements). They command a fine view to east and west.

On the summit of the kastro, a military barracks of the time of King Otho has been attractively restored to provide offices for the Archaeological Service, a lecture theatre and an excellent museum. The latter contains a wide range of prehistoric finds from Neolithic to Mycenaean, including material from Lianokladi (*see below*) and Elateia (*map p. 416*), interesting sub-Mycenaean and Geometric objects, with models of tomb types, outstanding finds and architectural elements from the Temple of Apollo and Artemis at Kalapodi (*map p. 416*); pottery, sculpture and small finds of the Classical, Hellenistic and Roman periods.

WEST FROM LAMIA

Leaving Lianokladi station behind you, you cross the railway and gradually ascend the lush broad valley of the Spercheios. The huge mass of Mt Oiti (Ὄρος Οἴτι; pronounced Iti) looms to the left as you continue through the village of Lianokladi. Excavation of a mound by the Ypati turn revealed a Middle Helladic apsidal house.

Diverging left across the river take you to Loutra Ypatis, a thermal establishment whose waters (25.5°C) are good for skin diseases and bronchial infections. The same road continues to **Ypati** (Ὑπάτη), the ancient *Hypata* (some finds) and the Neo-Patras of the Franks and Catalans, finely situated on the north slope of Mt Oiti. In Antiquity it was the capital of the Aenianes, a tribe which migrated south from Mt Ossa. During the Lamian War it was the centre of the military operations of the confederate Greeks. The remains of the Catalan castle (some ancient masonry) are slight but the situation and views are fine. It is reached via the lush area of Perivolia either by following a rough but driveable track (*to the left; small sign includes 'Kastro'; 3km*) just before the entrance to the village, or from the church of Aghios Nikolaos (*35min walk*). In the 13th century it was the capital of the dominions of John Ducas, who with help from Athens here defeated the forces of Michael VIII Palaeologus in 1275. In 1318 it became the second capital of Alfonso's Catalan duchy of Athens and Neo-Patras. The town was taken by the Turks in 1393 and made the seat of a pasha. Here were born Leo the Mathematician (c. 800) and St Athanasius the Meteorite (1305–83). The inhabitants cultivate tobacco and weave linen. At Sarandari (3km northwest) is a Macedonian tomb and at Mexiates (9km northeast) three others. Ypati is the starting-point for the ascent of **Mt Oiti**, legendary scene of the death of Heracles, whose summit (2153m) may be climbed from the Trapeza refuge of the Greek Alpine Club (3.5hrs from Ypati).

Kastri, further along the main road towards Karpenisi, takes its name from a ruined fortress with square towers. Varibobi has readopted the name of Makrakomi, a town known to Livy, the ruins of which stand on the hill to the northeast of today's little market town. Beyond the Spercheios, Spercheiada is visible. To its east, on the left bank of the tributary Inachos, is Aghios Sostis, site of ancient *Sosthenis*, mentioned by Ptolemy. About 5km to the north of Makrakomi are the baths of Platystomo (Loutra Platystomou), the waters of which are recommended in cases of dyspepsia, anaemia, disorders of the stomach, and spinal complaints.

Beyond Makrakomi a road crosses the river to Palaiovracha on the north slope of Mt Goulinas (1466m). Between this village and its neighbour Fteri are some remains of ancient *Spercheiai*. The vegetation becomes increasingly temperate as the valley narrows to a gorge. Above Aghios Georgios the slopes become more wooded and the climb gradually steeper. The valley divides. Aghia Triada is a beautiful mountain village which upheld a tradition of learning in Turkish times. You climb out of the valley by continuous turns to Tymfristos, known for its cherries. The road now zigzags across the spruce-clad saddle between Pikrovouni to the north (1503m) and Kokkalia to the south (1721m). As you reach the road-summit (c. 1430m), on the watershed of the Southern Pindus and the boundary between Phthiotis and Evrytania, there is a fine view of the peak of Mt Tymfristos. Along the summit ridge a road runs south to Krikello.

EVRYTANIA

Karpenisi (Καρπενήσι) is the chief and only sizeable place (pop. 5,868) of Evrytania, which by population is the smallest nomarchy of mainland Greece. Most of it is covered with vast impenetrable pine forests, and tourism is focused on skiing. Karpenisi's houses occupy both slopes of a torrent that descends to a small plain, wholly enclosed by mountains and dominated on the north by the peaks of Tymfristos. The older parts are attractive but some of the modern buildings are quite out of scale with their surroundings.

Agrafa and the Prousos Gorge

Lake Kremaston, west of Karpenisi, is the largest artificial lake in Greece. Several villages were drowned during its construction, and rebuilt on the slopes above. Beyond a small plane-shaded opening with springs, grass and a café, the road continues to Frangista, after which it climbs to Agrafa and the remote northern villages of the **Agrafa mountains**. Good walking country today, this and adjacent regions were some of the wildest and most backward places in Greece in Ottoman times. Agrafa, meaning literally the 'unwritten' or uncharted places, was a region where the tax collectors' writ did not run.

There is one outstanding excursion from Karpenisi, which is the mountain route to the magnificent **Prousos Gorge and monastery**, across the Kalliakouda mountains. Most of the journey (about 40km, depending on the exact route taken) is on dirt roads, but a 4WD vehicle is not essential in dry summer weather. The most obvious route is to take the road that follows the Karpenisiotis river valley through deciduous forest, running south between Mega Chorio on the north slope of Mt Kalliakouda, and its companion village, Mikro Chorio, which was overwhelmed on 13th January 1963 by a landslide, mercifully while most of the 336 inhabitants were at a church festival in another village. After Dermati, climbing all the while, the road crosses another river, the Krikeliotis, and enters the Prousos Gorge, with the monastery set into the cliff at a dizzy height above you. Prousos village is 2km to the north on top of the cliff.

The monastery (800m) is a medieval foundation with some modern buildings that were constructed to replace those lost in a fire in the Civil War. According to tradition it was founded by two monks, Dionysios and Timotheos, in 829. Its most treasured icon was the *Panaghia Prousiotissa*, brought from Asia Minor and claimed to be the work of St Luke. This is now housed in a cave chapel at the site. Framed in silver, it boasts an inscription by Georgios Karaïskakis, the celebrated *klepht*, and later general in the War of Independence. Today's church dates from the mid- to late 18th century. The monastery complex also includes a museum with some personal effects of Karaïskakis (clothes and a sword).

INTO THESSALY

The road between Lamia and Domokos is part of the traditional north–south route through Greece. Soon after Lamia it begins its gradual ascent of the Furka Pass (850m), the main route through the brown western foothills of Mt Othrys (*see map p. 552*). There are fine views to the left over the Spercheios to Mt Oiti. On the curving descent is the Khani Dragoman Aga, an old caravanserai, now a taverna. You cross the level cultivated plain formed by the draining of Lake Xynias. Some walls of ancient *Xyniai* survive near its southern limit (south of the modern village, 3km west of the road). On the banks, near the village of Omvriaki, two Neolithic settlements have been identified. The road passes chromium mine workings and surmounts another ridge. Due west of here is **Loutra Smokovou**, with alkaline sulphur springs (38.9–40°C), particularly good for nervous, rheumatic, catarrhal and skin complaints. The spa is beautifully situated at an altitude of 450m in a shady ravine and is an excursion centre. Secondary roads (mostly asphalt to Rendina) continue a serpentine course through or past **Rendina**, 6km from which (on a rough road) is a fine and beautifully situated old monastery, said to be an 8th-century foundation, with good and extensive frescoes of 1662, some recently cleaned. The roads south of the monastery are rough.

Domokos (Δομοκός), chief town of an eparchy and seat of a bishop, is picturesquely situated 1km above the road on a rocky hill (520m). Good Classical walls can be seen on the hill near the bus station and built into various houses; parts of the 4th-century fortifications have been traced. The railway station, a distance away in the plain to the north, keeps the ancient name, Thavmakoi. The town, which commanded the defile of *Koile*, was so called because of the astonishment (*thauma*) of the traveller from the south who had climbed over rugged hills and had suddenly been confronted with the vast plain of Thessaly. Thavmakoi (*Thaumakoi*) was vainly besieged by Philip V in 198 BC and was taken by Acilius Glabrio in 191. During the Graeco-Turkish war of 1897, Domokos was the last stage in the retreat of the Greek army under Constantine I (17th May). The advance of the Turks, who reached the Furka Pass two days later, was halted only by the intervention of the Powers.

The abrupt descent affords a fine view of the Thessalian Plain. Near Neo Monastiri (on a hill to the right of Gynaikokastro) some well-preserved walls remain to locate ancient *Proerna*; its Temple of Demeter has been recognised in the village and prehistoric material (Early Helladic and Mycenaean) has also been found.

Farsala

After Neo Monastiri the road forks. The right fork leads through Vrysia to Farsala (Φάρσαλα), four-fifths destroyed in the earthquake of 1954, and now mainly noted for its halva. Its bishopric was suppressed in 1900 and incorporated in the see of Larissa, but with 7,094 inhabitants, it is still the largest place in its eparchy.

The Battle of Pharsalus (9th August 48 BC), which took place in the plain to the west, probably on the left bank of the Epineas, decided the issue between Pompey and Caesar and the fate of the Roman world. Pompey, trusting to his overwhelming superiority in cavalry, led by Labienus, planned to turn Caesar's right wing and fall upon his rear. Labienus' cavalry charge was put to flight, panic spread through Pompey's army, and Pompey himself fled with an escort of only four men. His army lost 15,000 and the remainder surrendered next day.

Archaeological discoveries are mostly more interesting to the specialist. Traces of the walls can be made out on a tree-clad ridge southwest of the town, which has been occupied since Neolithic times.

There are other remains on the ancient acropolis, and notably also on the acropolis slopes, beneath and beside the church of Aghios Nikolaos. The bus station has desecrated the ancient centre, where there are the sad remains of a spring, associated with Thetis. Further out, to the left of the Lamia road, is an interesting tholos tomb in polygonal masonry, perhaps of Archaic date; other rectangular-built tombs are beside and to the south. Prehistoric material was excavated on the hill of Aghia Paraskevi.

NB: Thessaly, the Pelion region and the towns of Larissa and Volos are covered on pp. 552 and 574.

PRACTICAL INFORMATION

GETTING AROUND

• **By car:** In the mountain regions around Karpenisi driving should not be attempted in very wet or winter weather. Carry food, drink, compass and full spares kit.
• **By bus:** Buses link Athens and Galaxidi about 3 times a week. Buses link Lamia with Ypati, Farsala, Athens, Thessaloniki, Patras, Karpenisi, Chalkis, Grevena, Trikala and Volos. Buses run daily from Nafpaktos to modern Thermo. Daily bus to Distomo, and to Amphissa (3.5hrs). Buses link Athens to Delphi (3hrs) and Galaxidi (4hrs).
• **By rail:** Lamia is on the main Athens–Thessaloniki line.

INFORMATION OFFICES

Lamia Kalivion 14, T: 22310 666050.

WHERE TO STAY

Agrafa
The small village of Agrafa itself has hotels, the € **Hotel Niki** (T: 22370 93209), and the € **Hotel Agrafa**. There is a booking number for rooms in tradi-

tional houses (T: 22370 25102).
Arachova
Maria. Prettily furnished, with carved wooden bedsteads and cosy rugs. 7 rooms, T: 22670-31803.
Santa Maria Arachova. Small boutique hotel attractively furnished, open year-round. Restaurant. T: 22670 312304. Other options are the **Nostos** (Plateia Xenia, T: 22670 31385); **Sfalaki** (T: 22670 31068). There are also agencies who have rooms in traditionally decorated buildings in Arachova village: **Alexandros Rooms** (T: 22670 32884) and **Katafygio Rooms** (T: 22670 32232).
Delphi
The village has two hotels in the 'old-fashioned' category, meaning that they are in older buildings and have traditional décor: **Apollo** (20 rooms; T: 22650 82580); **Hermes** (23 rooms; T: 22650 82710). The **Acropole** is a pleasant enough place with views of the mountains. An easy walk from the site. 42 rooms. No restaurant. T: 22650 82675.
Galaxidi
€ **Argo**. Pleasant and good value. T: 22650 41996.
€€ **Galaxa**. Pretty old house in its own

garden, with blue painted shutters and brightly whitewashed walls. Café and bar serving snacks. 10 rooms. Eleftherias 8, T: 22650 41620.

Karpenisi

Hotels here cater mainly for a winter sports clientèle. The Anessis is in a traditional old building with wooden balconies. T: 22370 80700. A locally available leaflet gives information about village rooms. Koryschades (to the southwest) is one of a group of 'listed' villages, and has an old-style hotel called Archontiko Lappa (4 rooms), T: 22370 25102.

Lamia

There are several hotels in the central plateia, eg Samaras, T: 22310 28971.

Mega Chorio

€€–€€€ **Anerada**. Homely comfort from Athens-based artist. Everything has been carefully thought out, and the result is an unexpected surprise in the wilds of Evrytania. 6 rooms. T: 22370 41479.

Dryas. Small, low-slung building in fine mountain setting. Convenient for a trip to the Prousos monastery. 20 rooms. T: 22370 41131.

Nafpaktos

Nafpaktos is very popular in the summer, and hotel reservations are essential.

Akti. Modern, four-floor exterior, eclectically decorated within, offering views of the sea and of the castle. T: 26340 28464, www.akti.gr

Diethnes. Tiny pension (4 rooms) near the central square. Messolongiou 3, T: 26340 27342.

Ilion. The best hotel in Nafpaktos, in attractively restored old stone-built houses, in a panoramic location in the kastro district, with views of the Gulf of Corinth. Carved wood, wrought iron and rosewood hues predominate in the décor. Daliani 7, T: 26340 21222.

WHERE TO EAT

Nafpaktos

Tsaras has fine historic 19th-century ceilings. **Taverna Papoulis** near the harbour wall has very good traditional Greek food in a lovely old building. In summer hotel reservations are necessary.

HIKING & CLIMBING

Arachova Climbers' Association (for Parnassus) T: 22670 31118.
Karpenisi Alpine Club (for Tymfristos). T: 22370 23051.
Lamia Alpine Club (for Mt Oiti). Palaiologou 5, T: 22310 31644.
Nafpaktos Alpine Club For the very interesting old fashioned hill villages in the hills north of Galaxidi. T: 26340 25153.

FESTIVALS & EVENTS

Amphissa At carnival time the story of the famous ghost, a sort of mascot of the tanners' guild, who walks the town rattling chains, is re-enacted.
Arachova The *Feast of St George*, patron of shepherds, is celebrated here with enthusiasm (23rd April, unless it falls in Lent, in which case on Easter Tuesday).
Galaxidi People celebrate carnival by sprinkling one another with flour.

BOOKS & BACKGROUND READING

Agrafa A very interesting book on this area is *The Unwritten Places* by Tim Salmon.

Battle of Lepanto A useful book is *Crescent and Cross: The Battle of Lepanto 1571* by Hugh Bicheno.

Galaxidi *Galaxidi*, by Christina Paschou and George Manousskis, sold in local shops, is very useful, particularly on the 19th-century maritime history.

Parnassus Tim Salmon's *The Mountains of Greece, A Walker's Guide* (Cicerone Press) is very useful.

BEACHES

There are decent beaches within a mile or so of Nafpaktos in both directions. The best swimming at Galaxidi is off the small beaches beyond the pine eco-forest on the far side of the town.

AETOLIA–ACARNANIA

NB: *The first part of this chapter is covered on the previous map on p. 442.*

Aetolia and Acarnania together ('Αιτωλοακαρνανία) form the most westerly nomarchy of Central Greece, lying between Epirus and the Gulf of Patras. Aetolia, on the east, is divided from Acarnania by the river Acheloös. The interior of Aetolia is roadless, wild and mountainous, with numerous peaks exceeding 1800m, and is accessible only to determined travellers.

Aetolia derives its name from Aetolus, son of Endymion, who fled here after killing Apis. The five cities of Old Aetolia (the western half) all took part in the Trojan War. The three tribes living in New Aetolia to the east were barbarous, ate raw flesh, and spoke an unintelligible dialect (*Thucydides III, 94*). Loosely connected by a religious tie, they had a common temple at the sanctuary of Thermon. After the battle of Chaironeia (338 BC), they formed the Aetolian League which, at the beginning of the 3rd century BC, was strong enough to frustrate the invading armies of the Gaul Brennus. Before the expansion of the rival Achaean League under Aratos, the Aetolians reached the zenith of their power. They acquired or dominated Locris, Phocis, central Acarnania, and Boeotia, as well as numerous cities in the Peloponnese. In the ruinous War of the Leagues (219–217 BC), Philip V of Macedon, with the Achaeans as allies, invaded Aetolia. In 211 the Aetolians allied themselves with Rome, and in 197 helped the Romans to win the battle of Cynoscephalae (*see p. 562*). In 31, after the Battle of Actium, Octavian (Augustus) depopulated the region by transferring most of the inhabitants to his new city of Nicopolis, on the Epirus side of the Ambracian Gulf. In the War of Independence the Aetolians defeated the Turks at Karpenisi, and Missolonghi endured three sieges.

Acarnania has the sea on three sides. It is bounded on the north by the Ambracian Gulf. The Acarnanians emerged from obscurity at the beginning of the Peloponnesian War (431 BC). Like the Aetolians, they were uncivilised, living by piracy and robbery, and like them formed their towns into a league, which first met at Stratos. South and central Aetolia are entirely agricultural. Currants are grown near Missolonghi, olives round Aitoliko, and tobacco near Agrinion. The mountain eparchies depend upon the produce of the forests; Xeromeros, in Acarnania, exports *valonia*, the acorn of the *Quercus aegilops*, used for tanning.

THERMON

Modern Thermo (Θέρμο) is an attractive hillside town grouped around a shaded plateia with plentiful springs. From the town centre follow signs to 'Museum' at 'Palaio Bazari', for the remains of ancient *Thermon*. This is one of the most important ancient sites in this area of Greece, not just for the regional significance of Thermon in ancient times, but because of the interesting archaeological evidence it has provided for the genesis of the classic temple design, and for the quantity and beauty of the decorative elements surviving from its Archaic temples, which can be seen in the small museum. Thermon—which takes its name from the hero Thermos, accidentally killed by a discus thrown by his brother Oxylos, later king of Elis—was the spiritual centre of the Aetolians, who held their elections of magistrates here at an annual festival. The festival was the occasion also for a great fair and for athletic games. Thermon became a Panaetolian sanctuary centred on the temple of Apollo Thermios. Some 2,000 of the statues erected here were destroyed by Philip V of Macedon when he sacked the place in 218 BC. The Greek Archaeological Service excavated the site in 1898–1916 and new work is in progress.

The site

Site and museum usually open Tues–Sun 8.30–3.

The site lies on a wide plateau to the right of the road: from the entrance, the excavations of the temple of Apollo Thermios are visible below the path immediately to your right, while straight ahead, in the centre of the area, is the well-preserved pool of the sacred spring which probably determined the site of the sanctuary in the first place. Beyond extend the remains of the stoas and public buildings. All of these date from the Archaic to Hellenistic periods; though at the northern end of the site the buildings stood on top of earlier prehistoric constructions. The two building periods can be clearly distinguished by the masonry used: small, irregular stone elements in the prehistoric foundations; larger and more carefully cut rectangular elements in the later buildings.

With its east side against Mt Mega Lakkos, the ancient sanctuary was surrounded by a roughly rectangular peribolos protected by over a dozen towers dating from the 3rd century BC. There were three temples—two dedicated to Apollo and one to Artemis— all clustered at the northern extremity. Of these only one claims attention with significant, visible remains. This was the **Temple of Apollo Thermios** (630 BC), the largest and most important of the three: it was a narrow peripteral building with five columns at the ends and 15 at the sides (unusually aligned north–south, in similar fashion to the Temple of Apollo Epikourios at Bassae). A row of columns down the centre which supported the hipped roof, divided the building lengthwise. The walls may have been made of sun-dried brick. The entablature was of wood; the metopes, acroteria, antefixes and cornice facings of painted terracotta. Directly below this Archaic temple base (now largely covered over again by the archaeologists) are the foundations of the previous temple of the Geometric period (8th century BC) built with an apsidal peristyle. It is one of the earliest examples we have of the emerging feature of a colonnade of posts or columns around the exterior of a temple. Visible a little to the north, and at a still lower level, are the bases of the buildings of a prehistoric settlement of the 9th century BC. One particularly large and well-built construction with a clearly visible apsidal end has excited much curiosity: some scholars see this as an early place of cult, and, in its tripartite division and apsidal form, observe

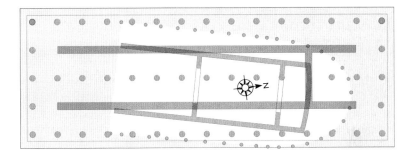

Plan of the Temple of Apollo Thermios, showing its peripteral structure, and the central row of columns which supported the roof. The earlier Geometric temple (which now lies largely buried), with its apsidal exterior colonnade, is also clearly marked.

the genesis of the later temple form. Immediately northwest of this are remains of a Hellenistic **Temple of Artemis** while to the east are the scant remains of the prehistoric **Temple of Apollo Lyseios** (or Lykeios).

To the south are the remains of a beautiful and well-preserved **fountain-house** with three spouts: the spring is still flowing, and its paved floor and surround are in good condition. Beyond this to the south are two parallel stoas, defining an unusually long and narrow area. These are being reinvestigated. The west was 165m long and had wooden columns; the east has interior benches. Both had predecessors. At their southern extremity and against the wall of the sanctuary is a building which may have been a bouleuterion. A third stoa, so far only partly investigated, runs west at right angles to the other two across the south side of the enclosed area.

The museum

The museum contains decorative elements from the Archaic temples of extraordinary beauty and importance, although displayed somewhat like a stack-room. Most striking are the painted terracotta antefixes and metopes. The modelled heads, lively faces, and harmonious, muted earth colours contribute significantly to our sense of the appearance of a decorated early Greek temple. Both colour and design show marked Corinthian influence. Also exhibited are some Middle Bronze Age pottery; part of a Mycenaean helmet; and a fine pair of bronze horses mounted on a single base (Geometric).

Environs of Thermon

Aghia Sofia is a long pretty village with gushing streams; its Byzantine church incorporating blocks from a Temple of Aphrodite. Myrtia, further on, has a monastery of 1491, and a charming rural square with a modest hotel and restaurants, reminiscent of Mt Pelion. The road runs above orange groves along the shore of Lake Trichonida, to Paravola (*map p. 484*), where there are substantial remains of ancient *Boukation* (Classical and 4th-century with Byzantine towers).

THE ACHELOÖS RIVER

The Acheloös, or Aspropotamos, is the longest river (217km) in Greece. Rising in the Pindus, it forms the boundary between Aetolia and Acarnania, and falls into the sea opposite the Echinades Islands. Since 1960 the river has been harnessed to provide power and irrigation. A new construction project, high in the Pindus to the east, to divert part of its waters to irrigate the Thessalian plain will alter the nature of the river here, with potentially disastrous consequences for the Aetolian wetlands. In myth the Acheloös plays an important role in the story of Heracles, who is said to have wrestled the river for the hand of Deianeira, daughter of Oeneus of Calydon.

AGRINION & STRATOS

Agrinion ('Αγρίνιο) is the capital of the eparchy of Trichonidos and the largest place in the nomarchy. It is a tobacco-growing centre, which grew to prominence as the terminus of the new railway in the 1890s. It was originally called *Vrachohori*, 'settlement of the Vlachs', and most of the population is indeed of Vlach or Albanian descent. In Ottoman times the most important building nearby was the Han of Dogri, used by travellers and caravans on the road north to Arta and Ioannina.

The town was almost completely rebuilt after an earthquake in 1887, and there is nothing of historic interest to see. There is a small archaeological museum. The site of ancient *Agrinion* has been located above the village of Megali Chora, 4km northwest.

Stratos (Στράτος), a melancholy village, stands in the centre of the ruins of *Stratos*, the ancient capital and largest city of Acarnania. Vlachs were forcibly resettled in lower Stratos in the aftermath of the Greek Civil War. There are some fine surviving farmhouses. The walls, dating from before 429 BC and particularly well preserved, stand on a low bluff commanding the broad Acheloös. A new survey of the site is in progress.

The site

The site was occupied in early times but first became important in the 5th century BC. In 429 BC, during the Peloponnesian War, Stratos was vainly besieged by Sparta. In 314 it passed to the ruthless Macedonian leader Cassander (*see p. 681*). In 263, when Acarnania was partitioned, Stratos fell to the Aetolians. After the dissolution of the Aetolian League (188), the Romans held it against Philip V and Perseus of Macedon, but by the late 1st century it had lost all importance. The site was explored by the French School in 1892, 1910–11, and 1924. Some minor work is currently in progress.

The walls embrace four parallel north–south ridges with their three intervening depressions. A transverse north–south wall divides the city into two parts. With the exception of the theatre, most of the public buildings seem to have been in the western sector. In the centre of the south wall, to the right of the track to the village, is the Main Gate, with a defensive interior court. The remains of the agora are scanty. The central wall leads up past the ancient quarries to the acropolis, seemingly a fortified refuge rather than a religious place. Curiously placed athwart a projecting section of the west wall is the Doric Temple of Zeus, built on a platform c. 70m from east to west. Peripteral (6 by 11 columns) and somewhat larger than the Athenian Hephaisteion, it dates from the 4th century, probably after 338 BC. An Ionic colonnade surrounded the cella on three sides. The stylobate and parts of the cella walls survive. The temple is built of a stern grey stone. It appears never to have been finished: column drums were found here with their protective bosses unremoved.

AITOLIKO & PLEURON

Aitoliko ('Αιτωλικό), a medieval refuge-town, originally *Anatoliko*, stands on an island between its lagoon and the larger seaward Lagoon of Missolonghi, and is joined to the mainland (to which the town has spread) at either end by fine stone bridges. The local sailing boats have affinities with the Egyptian felucca and the nets are unusual. The 15th-century church of the Panaghia has wall paintings. The island was originally connected by stone bridges to the mainland. West of the town there was, until after the Second World War, the vast Swamp of Leziri, from which ancient Oiniadae (*see p. 492*) stood on a small hill. The area was notorious until recent times as a breeding ground for malaria. Many of the villages between Aitoliko and Agrinion were Vlach, although the language is not spoken nowadays.

Beyond Aitoliko the new road continues through rice fields. To the right are salt flats. **Ancient *Pleuron*** (Plevron), high above the main road, is reached from the restaurant (Plevron) opposite a turning to Missolonghi. Just north of the restaurant a rough track (c. 5km, passable with care; poor in the final stages) leads indirectly towards the site. In the early stages you pass below the two lower hills (Petrovouni and Gyftokastro) which have some Archaic remains of an enceinte that probably represents Old Pleuron, the city of the Kouretes (attendants of the infant Zeus), destroyed by Demetrius II, son of Antigonus Gonatas, in 234 BC. The track climbs to the enceinte of ashlar masonry (Kastro Irinio), the New Pleuron built soon afterwards. The splendid walls, have 36 towers and seven gates; the circuit is almost complete and stands in places to 15 courses of Hellenistic masonry.

Within are the ruins of a theatre, perhaps the smallest in Greece. The stage, with the proscenium, backed on to the city wall; a small doorway led through the orchestra to a square tower. In a hollow to the southeast is a cistern, 31m by 20m by 4m deep, divided into five rectangular basins by four partition walls pierced by triangular openings. Near the east wall is the agora, a flat rectangular terrace 145m long. It is crowded with the debris of buildings; among them a portico 60.5m by 10m, with enclosing walls still standing to a height of c. 0.6m. There are also exedrae and pedestals. To the north (half an hour's steep climb; best to follow the east wall) is the acropolis, which had square towers. Below the terrace the hill sinks rapidly east towards the city walls. At the foot of the depression is a fine gateway 1.7m wide, 2.7m high and 2m thick. The lintel is formed of two large horizontal blocks; in it and in the stone of the threshold are the holes for the gatepost.

MISSOLONGHI

Missolonghi or Mesolongi (Μεσολόγγι), with 10,916 inhabitants, is the capital of the nomarchy of Aetolia and Acarnania, and the seat of a bishop. The town is more familiar to the English-speaking world than many others in Greece of greater importance, for here Lord Byron died of fever on 19th April 1824, after ten months of incessant activity in the cause of Greek independence. Missolonghi, now by-passed by the main highway, is situated on the east shore of a vast lagoon (Limnothalassa), partly given over to fish hatcheries and the haunt of many water-birds. It has always been too shallow to allow access to vessels of any size, and a long causeway extends south to deep water at Tourlida. Tribal people lived in the lagoon area from the earliest times, but urban settlement was limited by the marshy land and encroaching sea, which in Antiquity and early medieval times flooded inland much further than it does now. The modern town grew as a minor Venetian settlement and fishing centre. Drainage and reclamation work is hastening the disappearance of the fishing community and their characteristic reed huts built on piles. It is well worth driving out towards the sea along one of the narrow tracks across the marshes, for the outstanding birdlife, and unique if often bleak and lonely atmosphere. In winter mist and fog is common.

The town
The town is entered through the Venetian walls by the 'Gate of the Sortie', rebuilt by King Otho to protect the hastily repaired earthen rampart through which the *Exodos* (*see opposite*) was made. Within the gate (right) is a pleasant garden with the heroön (*admission free*) commemorating the heroes of the town's three sieges. A large central tumulus contains the bodies of unnamed defenders; to the right is the tomb of Botsaris, and, between the two, a statue of Byron erected in 1881, beneath which is the poet's heart. The centre of the town is the Plateia Botsari, where the Dimarcheion houses the Museum of the Revolution, with Byron relics and several dramatic pictures of the war. Odos Trikoupis leads west and, at the end, Odos Levidou brings you to a small square where a memorial garden occupies the site of the house in which Byron died: the house was destroyed in the Second World War. Round a school is the causeway, with a bust of the poet Kostas Palamas and the reconstructed base of the historic windmill blown up by Christos Kapsalis on 11th April 1826.

MISSOLONGHI IN THE WAR OF INDEPENDENCE

Missolonghi was the western centre of resistance against the Turks in the War of Independence, and it endured three sieges. In 1822 it was defended by Mavrogordato against a force of 10,000 led by Omer Vrioni and Reshid Pasha. In 1823 its commander was a Souliot, Markos Botsaris. In January 1824 Lord Byron came to Missolonghi and inspired the defenders with his enthusiasm; he died the following April before the beginning of the final siege. In April 1825 Reshid Pasha appeared before the town with 15,000 troops. The defenders numbered only 5,000. Hampered by furious sorties and by a lack of supplies, Reshid Pasha could make no headway for six months. Then Ibrahim Pasha, with 10,000 Egyptians, advanced to his aid from the Peloponnese. After fluctuating struggles for the islands in the lagoon, the enemy closed round the town. At the end of their resources after 12 months of siege, almost the whole population determined to break out. Their attempt (the '*Exodos*') was made on the night of 22nd–23rd April 1826. Though they managed to get clear of the town, they were frustrated by the treachery of a Bulgarian deserter, who had forewarned the besiegers. The fugitives, imagining themselves safe, were ambushed by 1,000 Albanians on the slopes of Mt Zygos. Of the 9,000 who left Missolonghi—soldiers and civilians—only 1,800 made good their escape to Amphissa. Meanwhile those who had stayed behind fired their magazines, overwhelming themselves and their enemies in a common destruction. In 1828 the Turks surrendered Missolonghi without firing a shot.

CALYDON

From Missolonghi the road runs east towards the dark mass of Varasova. To the right are seen the mountains that rise behind Patras. After 5km you come to a turning (on the left) to **Aghios Simeon**, the monastery where the people of Missolonghi made their last stand after the *Exodos* in 1826 (*see above*). At 8.5km a track (on the left; signpost-ed) leads in a few minutes to **ancient *Calydon***, celebrated in the heroic age as the home of Oeneus, the first man to plant the vine, newly brought to Greece by Dionysus (hence the Greek word for wine, *oinos*, and our word oenology and its derivatives). Oeneus had two sons, Tydeus, one of the Seven Against Thebes (*see p. 419*) and father of Diomedes, who fought at Troy and, with his brutal masculine allure, won Cressida from Troilus. The second son was Meleager, slayer of the Calydonian Boar. The mountain slopes here, culminating at Mt Zygos (950m), were the scene of the hunt. The boar had been sent to ravage Oeneus' lands by an angry Artemis, who felt the king had failed in his duty to her. Atalanta, who assisted Meleager in the chase, was given the boar hide as a gift. It is said to have been kept in the temple at Tegea (*see p. 268*). Though Strabo couples Calydon with Pleuron as an ornament to Greece, it was historically insignificant. The city received a death blow when Augustus transferred its inhabitants to Nicopolis and most of the public treasures to Patrai. There is substantial new excavation going on about 200m from the main road at the bottom of the site track, with what appear to be extensive remains of (?) Roman buildings coming to light.

After a few minutes, signs point to a heroön (right) and the temple (left). The heroön consists of rooms grouped round a peristyle court with a well and cistern. Under the main room is an impressive sepulchral chamber with stone furniture. The path continues to a ruined church (left) standing on ancient foundations, near the south fortifications of the ancient town. The Sanctuary of Artemis Laphria is impressively situated on a spur immediately to the southwest, commanding the plain and gulf. A massive foundation platform locates the 4th-century temple, erected on a terrace supported by 6th-century retaining walls. Remains of painted terracotta metopes were recovered from earlier temples of c. 570 and c. 620 BC. Major finds are in the National Archaeological Museum in Athens.

ANCIENT OINIADAE & ENVIRONS

Oiniadae (modern Iniades) is a beautiful and evocative site in the Acheloös river delta. The easiest way to approach it is probably from Katochi, a village that was the main town of the region in medieval and Ottoman times. Leake records that 100 families lived there in 1807, and there are picturesque fragments of very old buildings mixed up with modern market town development. The large old church of Aghios Panteleimonos is impressive, and there is a medieval (?) tower on a large rock in the centre of town. Hellenistic inscriptions have been found on rocks elsewhere in the town.

HISTORY OF OINIADAE

Oiniadae was visited by Leake in 1807, when it was known as *Trikardo*. Leake saw an isolated hill site, covered in oak forest and surrounded by vast marshlands. It was explored by the American School in 1901 and new work is in progress. In summer dancing and singing contests take place in the theatre.

Though unhealthily situated and until recently totally inaccessible in winter, Oiniadae was strategically important in Antiquity as the key to southern Acarnania. It was taken after a siege in 455 BC by exiled Messenians established at Naupaktos, and attacked in vain by Pericles in 453. Demosthenes in 424 forced the town to join the Athenian alliance. It fell to the Aetolians in 336 and, without bloodshed, to Philip V in 219. Captured by the Romans eight years later, it was handed over to the Aetolian League. The town was restored to the Acarnanians in 189. With changes in sea level and the Slav invasions, most of the vicinity sunk into saline marshland, with widespread flooding in the winter and spring.

The site

NB: The site is in a very poor and deserted area, and it is easy to get lost. The area is prone to flooding in very wet weather, when a 4WD is recommended. There are numerous unfenced and deep drainage channels across the marshes, some of which are dangerously near the edge of the asphalt road. Drive with care; unaccompanied travel is perhaps unwise.

Taking the first turn into the site, over a drainage ditch, and through fine fortifications in Archaic polygonal masonry (6th century), you climb to near the theatre, cleared and used occasionally for performances. It has 27 rows of seats; inscriptions on the lowest three rows record the freeing of slaves and date the building (late 3rd century BC). The site, though generally wooded, is easily accessible at this point (and pleasantly filled with oak trees) but it is thickly overgrown at the periphery and some is fenced off. On all sides, except the south, it is surrounded by the marshes of Lesini, the ancient Lake Melita. To the south a plain slopes down to the Acheloös.

The main gate (to the south), is one of many with arched openings, a feature unusual in Greek architecture. From the theatre a road on the outside of the city walls leads to the north harbour where the ship-sheds are. These consist of five slipways hewn in the rock on a slope from the back wall down to the water's edge. The slides would originally have been lined with wooden planks to facilitate the hauling up of ships. Five rows of rough, functional limestone columns standing on ridges supported a tiled gabled roof about seven metres high. The sheds, which also included a storage area, were improved and fortified by Philip V (*Polybius 4.65.11*); they are comparable in size and scope to those of the Piraeus, the port of Athens. The site is enclosed and if the gate is locked you can get a good look by walking around the fence.

Environs of Oiniadae

Pendalofos, with its prominent church, skirts the north end of the lagoon of Aitoliko and joins the main road just south of the Stena Kleisouras, 16km from Lesini. This route also gives access to the 5th-century (?) fortifications of Palaiomanina, perhaps ancient *Sauria*, reached via Pendalofos and the village of the same name (11km further north).

Astakos (᾿Αστακός), formerly *Dragomestre*, was the coastal base of Sir Richard Church's operations in Western Greece in 1828. Church, the son of a Quaker, born in southern Ireland, occupied the Ionian Islands for Britain during the Napoleonic wars, and gained a great reputation as a commander. Appointed head of the disorganised Greek army, he attempted to turn the anarchic, rag-bag troops into an efficient fighting force. The Turks routed his army at Athens, whereupon Church devoted his attention to western Greece.

Today Astakos is a quiet and old-fashioned former resort, with one or two fine houses on the front dating from the 1930s. The bay is used by visiting yachtsmen and cigarette smugglers in the summer. There is a summer ferry service to Ithaca and Cephalonia, and connecting buses to Athens (twice daily). It makes a good place to stay a night en route.

THE AMBRACIAN GULF

Amfilochia (Ἀμφιλοχία) stands at the head of the Gulf of Karvasara, the farthest inland reach of the Ambracian Gulf, on a volcanic outcrop. The town was founded by Ali Pasha as a military station; its former name, *Karvasaras*, is a corruption of 'caravanserai', and a small *han* was used here until the early 20th century. On the hill (189m) above are some remains of an ancient town with long castle walls, perhaps to be identified with *Heracleia Limnaia*. In Ottoman times it was an important garrison castle on the road north to Arta and played an important part in Sir Richard Church's campaign in the Greek War of Independence in March 1829. The capture of this castle and that at Vonitsa (*see below*) prevented the Ottoman army from moving forces from Arta and Ioannina to threatened southwest Greece. The Greek forces were able to secure the Makrynoros passes into the interior, and as a result to set what was to become the border of northern Greece after 1881.

In the late 19th century Amfilochia became quite prosperous as the terminus of daily steamers to Patras and a weekly boat to Piraeus. It suffered extensive damage in the Second World War and in the Greek Civil War, and most of what you see today is dull modern concrete. Busy, down-to-earth and cheerful, it is a useful place for an overnight stop on the main road north–south.

The main road north from here follows the coast, below the oak-clad slopes of Makrynoros, a long mountain ridge parallel to the shore. The pass *en corniche* thus formed, sometimes called the 'Thermopylae of Western Greece', was guarded in Antiquity by a string of forts. Anoixiatiko marks the south end of the pass; Menidi the north. Just before Krikellos is (right) the little church of Aghios Ioannis, behind which (road signposted) rise the insignificant remains of *Amphilochian Argos*, a town of some importance in the Peloponnesian War.

Vonitsa

The road west from here follows the south line of the Ambracian Gulf, often away from the shore amid marsh, cotton fields, or low hills. To the left Mt Bergandi rises to 1428m. At **Thirio**, on its north slope, is a museum with Classical and Roman material, including inscriptions, from ancient *Thyreion*, where Cicero, sailing along the Acarnanian coast, spent two hours at the house of his friend Xenomanes.

Vonitsa (Βόνιτσα) is a little port on the Gulf with a magnificent Byzantine, Venetian and Ottoman citadel, one of the chain of fortresses protecting Arta. It formed part of the dowry of Thamar, the daughter of the Despot Nicephorus I, when she married Philip of Taranto in 1294. It was refortified by the Ottomans after 1460. The houndstooth brick ornamentation indicates the parts of the buildings constructed by the Epirots. The magnificent polygonal keep is Ottoman work.

The entrance to the citadel (*open Tues–Sun during daylight hours*), through an imposing Ottoman gatehouse, leads into a rocky, grass-covered knoll, with a curtain of inner walls following the contour. These walls are mostly Venetian, but built on foundations dating from the time of the Despotate of Epirus. When the citadel was built, and for several hundred years afterwards, there was a small port below it on the Gulf which silted up in the late Ottoman period, but some remains of low harbour walls can be seen in the surrounding marshes. On the upper slopes of the knoll within the walls there are remains of churches, domestic buildings and a garrison mosque. The top of the hill is dominated by a massive Ottoman keep, indicating the importance of Vonitsa for Imperial sea defences. There are outstanding views over the Ambracian Gulf. The incursions of the sea and marshes meant that by the time of the Greek War of Independence and the conflicts of the late 19th and 20th centuries, the citadel had little or no military importance; thus it now stands largely as it stood in the 18th century, an unrivalled example of Venetian and Ottoman military architecture.

The west coast

Further south, below Peratia, there is a right turn (no sign) for the impressive Venetian **Fort St George**, which lies beyond the village of Plagia. There are remains of (?) an Early Christian basilica in the centre of the fort and of ancient buildings in the vicinity.

Above Peratia the road crosses a long causeway to the Frankish **Kastro Santa Maura**, guarding a gap between the mainland and the island of Levkas. While taking this castle in 1809, Sir Richard Church's arm was shattered by a bullet. The strait is crossed by a moveable bridge, whence another causeway carries the road into Lefkas.

The countryside just south of Vonitsa is rich and undulating, with cornfields and pasture. At Palairos you join the coast road, a lonely but pleasant route, with wonderful scenery. The road passes close to the southeast limit of Lake Voulkari where, near the village of Kechropoula, are the impressive fortifications and other remains of **ancient *Palaerus*** (now called Kastro; an unsigned track allows access in c. 8km, roundabout, but seek directions; also possible by bad track from Pogonia). Near Mytikas there are some remains of ancient *Alyzia*, by-passed by the main road. The modern village is pleasant but very busy in season. Opposite are three islets, of which the largest is Kalamos. A few people live on them, mostly in summer. About 2km east of Mytikas, not far from the sea, are the substantial remains of the Early Christian basilica of Aghia Sofia.

PRACTICAL INFORMATION

This is a region with few tourists, and facilities for visitors are correspondingly sparse. Most towns and larger villages—among them Thermon and Mytikas—have basic hotels and rooms, as well as tavernas.

GETTING AROUND

• **By car:** There are many empty and unfrequented places off the main roads and garages can be few and far between.
• **By bus:** Agrinion KTEL has regular Athens and regional buses. Athens and Missolonghi are also linked by bus (4hrs). Twice daily buses link Athens and Astakos (5hrs). Buses run daily from Nafpaktos to Thermo.

WHERE TO STAY

Agrinion
€ **Esperia**. Well run, cleanly furnished. T: 26410 23033, www.esperiahotel.gr
Amfilochia
€ **Amvrakia**. Clean and helpful. T: 26420 23162.
€ **Oscar**. A little more upmarket, with good views of the Gulf. T: 26420 22155.
Astakos
€ **Stratos**. Pleasant and helpful. T: 26460 41096.
Missolonghi
€€ **Liberty**. There is a dearth of reliable hotels in Missolonghi, and this is the best of a dismal bunch, housed in a grim concrete block, built in 1984 but looking like a junta-period construction. Prices slightly higher than you

would expect. Popular with overnight coaches. T: 26310 24831.
Vonitsa
€ **Vonitsa**. On the beach road. A dull-looking concrete block, but very friendly and helpful, all rooms with shower. There is a pebble beach in front of it. T: 26430 22594.

WHERE TO EAT

There are numerous cafés and small tavernas near the sea in Amfilochia, and small fish tavernas in Astakos. Local fresh fish is worth finding, but not cheap. There are a few fish tavernas on the lagoon side of Missolonghi which are worth visiting. If you are lucky they serve eel and lagoon fish specialities.

BEACHES

These are very good except where they adjoin marshy inland areas and lagoons. The sea is warmer than off northern Epirus but still cooler than is usual in southern and island Greece. Mosquitoes can be a problem in some places.

FESTIVALS & EVENTS

Stratos A folk-dancing festival is held annually in September.

EPIRUS

Maps of Epirus are on p. 484 (Preveza and Arta) and p. 508.

The province of Epirus lies south of the modern Albanian border, and is separated from Thessaly by the Pindus range. For many British or American visitors to Greece it is familiar as the mainland backdrop to holidays in Corfu or Paxos. On the south it is washed by the Gulf of Arta and on the west by the Ionian Sea, with the island of Corfu lying opposite the frontier between Greece and Albania. The mountainous character of the interior and difficulties of communication have always isolated Epirus, whose inhabitants were and are only partly Hellenic. In Antiquity the few Greek colonies were confined to the coast and to the low-lying regions.

Epirus is the wettest region in Greece, and its hills and mountains are densely forested. It has long been famous for its flocks and pasturage, and for its breed of dog, the Molossian mastiff. Today depopulation is affecting many agricultural and mountain areas. In Ottoman times Epirus was very ethnically mixed, and large ethnic Albanian communities remained in the region, which was known as Çameria (pronounced 'Chameria'), after the Çams, the ethnic Albanians who lived here until the Second World War. Albanian settlement has resurged in recent years with population movement after the end of Communism in Albania in 1990.

The principal rivers are the Arta (Arachthos), the Kalamas (Thyamis), and the Acherondas (Acheron), the 'woeful', principal river of the Underworld. Epirus is divided into four nomarchies: Ioannina, Preveza, Arta and Thesprotia. The main roads are now good. The most important archaeological site is the oracle of Dodona, renowned as the oldest in Greece. The history of Epirus in the 20th century was not always very happy, and the legacy of its multiple conflicts—the Balkan Wars, the First and Second World Wars, and the Greek Civil War—has been the destruction of some communities, depopulation, ethnic tension and emigration.

Tourism in Epirus suffered for many years from the Cold War and the aftermath of the Greek Civil War (1944–49), which left more or less closed military zones near the border and northwest coast. These have now been abolished and visitors are free to travel wherever they wish (with one or two minor exceptions such as the coast north of Sagiada; *see p. 509*). As a result of this improved access, in this edition of the Guide it has been possible to incorporate wonderful archaeological sites such as the medieval fortress of Pyrgos Raghiou, which were absent from previous editions.

Southern Epirus and the associated fringes of old Çameria (*covered by the map on p. 484*) is a little-known region for tourists. That said, it contains some of the most rewarding and neglected landscapes and antiquities in the region: the southern Souli mountains, the Preveza fortresses, ancient Nicopolis, the Classical, Byzantine and Ottoman monuments of Arta, and the site of the Battle of Actium.

HISTORY OF EPIRUS

Epirus was inhabited by Illyrian tribes in late prehistoric times. Of these, the chief were the Chaones, the Thesproti and the Molossi, who gave their names to the three main divisions of the country. Each tribe was governed by its own prince. The Molossians, who claimed descent from Neoptolemos, son of Achilles, later took over the whole country as kings of Epirus. The most famous of these kings was Pyrrhus (318–272 BC). In 286 he invaded Macedonia, of which he became king for a brief period. In 280 he accepted the invitation of the Tarentines to join them in their war against Rome. After his victory at *Heraclea*, he came within 24 miles of Rome. A second victory, at *Asculum* (Apulia), in 279, was gained with such heavy losses on his own side that the term Pyrrhic victory came to mean a victory gained at too high a price. Later he turned against Sparta and Argos, where he was ignominiously killed, it is said by a tile thrown from a rooftop by a woman. (In the local collection of antiquities at Polydroso is the first complete Etruscan 'jockey-cap' helmet to be found in Greece, perhaps brought to the area by a veteran of Pyrrhus' campaigns.) After his death the kingship of Epirus was abolished, and the country divided between three generals. In the Macedonian wars, Epirus joined the Macedonians, went over to the Romans (198), and then turned against them (170). After the defeat of Perseus, last king of Macedon, at Pydna in 168, 70 towns in Epirus were destroyed, 150,000 of the inhabitants enslaved, and the country became a Roman province.

In the Middle Ages Epirus was constantly invaded. After the division of the Byzantine empire the country was divided into New Epirus, with *Dyrrachium* (Durazzo), and Old Epirus (*Epirus Vetus*), with Acarnania. After the capture of Constantinople by the Franks in 1204, a Despotate of Epirus was set up. The first despot, Michael I, made Ioannina his capital. A later despot, Theodore Angelus, seized the Latin kingdom of Salonica in 1223. The dynasty expired at the end of the 13th century. In 1318–35 Epirus with Cephalonia came under the domination of the Orsini, returned briefly to Byzantium, fell to the Serbs (1348–86), and then returned to Cephalonia. The Turks captured Ioannina in 1431. In the 15th and 16th centuries the Venetians occupied several strong-points in the country.

Epirus took no part in the War of Independence but was a focus for European attention in the Romantic era, exemplified by Lord Byron's visit in 1809 to the court of Ali Pasha. In 1881 the District of Arta was freed from Ottoman rule. During the Second Balkan War the Greek army took Ioannina, and occupied all the north of Epirus, brutally driving out the Albanian majority population. In the First World War much of central Epirus was the focus of further ethnic conflict, and many Muslim Albanians found themselves forced to migrate to Turkey after 1920. During the Second World War there were attempts to eradicate the coastal Albanian Çam population (*see p. 509*).

PREVEZA & ENVIRONS

Preveza (Πρέβεζα), the main town of a small nomarchy, stands on the north shore of the shallow strait, here only 1km wide, through which the waters of the Ambracian Gulf reach the sea. In 1809 Byron and his friend Hobhouse went from here to view the scene of the Battle of Actium (*see below*).

The name Preveza is of Albanian origin and is derived from the word for a crossing or ferrypoint. Preveza occupies the site of ancient *Berenikia*, founded c. 290 BC by Pyrrhus in honour of his mother-in-law Berenice, queen of Ptolemy Soter. For centuries the town was the naval gateway to western Greece. It was occupied by the Venetians in 1499. Ceded to the Turks by the Treaty of Carlowitz (1699), it was retaken in 1717. In 1797 Preveza passed, with the Ionian Islands, to the French, but the next year was retaken by Ali Pasha in the name of the Sultan of Turkey. Ali Pasha marched on the town and the defenders were outnumbered among the ruins of Nicopolis and massacred. Ali Pasha forced 147 Preveza prisoners to march to Constantinople with a pyramid of skulls to present to the Sultan. Leake observed in 1809 that Preveza, as a town, 'was the principal sufferer' from the Napoleonic Wars in the region; the population fell by half between 1798 and 1807. Preveza remained in Turkish hands until it fell to the Greek army in 1912. From 1881 to 1912 the Graeco-Turkish frontier ran through the strait. Malaria was a major health problem in the region until after the Second World War.

In Byron's time Preveza was little more than an enormous Ottoman fortress with accompanying support installations. Nowadays, the waterside esplanade is a favourite evening promenade. Preveza is a much more interesting and pleasant town than the grim streets by the main through road would suggest, and is a good centre for regional exploration. The harbour is developing rapidly as a fashionable yachting centre, and there are some well restored 19th-century buildings, and a pleasant pedestrianised shopping area. The main attraction are the great Venetian and Ottoman fortresses, no fewer than four of them, although two are occupied by the Greek army and are not accessible. There is a fine Ottoman clock tower in the town centre, wrongly described in local guides as Venetian.

The Battle of Actium

On the south side of the strait the sandy promontory of Aktio (Latin, *Actium*) is sharper in outline than that of Preveza and almost closes the entrance to the gulf. At the naval Battle of Actium, on 2nd September 31 BC, Agrippa, Octavian's commander, with a smaller but more manoeuvrable fleet, routed the combined navies of Antony and Cleopatra. The royal leaders deserted the army they had massed for an invasion in Italy, and it surrendered a week later. This decisive naval battle was of great importance in the Roman period of ascendancy in the ancient world. Ships sunk in the conflict have been located beneath the sea and archaeological investigation is planned.

On the promontory, 1km north, are scanty remains of the Temple of Apollo Aktios. A temple, under the protection of neighbouring *Anaktorion*, existed here in the 5th century BC. From it came two *kouroi* now in the Louvre. Gymnastic games and horse races were held. After his victory at Actium, Augustus rebuilt the temple and, in special boathouses, consecrated examples of the vessels captured in the battle. The festival he transferred to his new city of Nicopolis (*see below*), adding naval and musical events. The *Actia*, held every five years and declared sacred, thus took rank with the four great Panhellenic games.

ANCIENT NICOPOLIS

Nicopolis, slightly to the south of the modern village of Nikopolis (Νικόπολη), is a large and once very neglected site, now being tended and with some archaeological work in progress. This was the city founded by Augustus after his victory over Antony and Cleopatra at Actium in 31 BC. To the west is the Bay of Gomares, where Augustus concentrated his forces before the battle.

In commemoration of his victory, Octavian (Augustus) made Patrai a Roman colony and founded the new *colonia* of Nicopolis ('victory city') on his camp site. To populate the new city, he resettled the inhabitants of most of the towns of Aetolia and Acarnania, including Calydon, Ambracia and Amphilochian Argos, and Nicopolis was made a member of the Amphictyonic League. St Paul spent a winter (? 64) at 'Nicopolis of Macedonia', where he wrote his *Epistle to Titus*. By AD 67 the city was the capital of an Epirot province. The philosopher Epictetus (c. 60–140) had a school here, and the city was the reputed birthplace of Pope St Eleutherius (175–189). Thriving in the time of Strabo, it was plundered by Alaric, Genseric and Totila. Justinian rebuilt its defences, reducing their compass. At the coming of the Slavs, the Byzantines removed the seat of the *theme* to Nafpaktos, and Nicopolis decayed. The Greek Archaeological Service has excavated at intervals since 1913 and a new survey is in progress. The main current work is the restoration of the South Gate area, which will make a dramatic and impressive approach to the site if driving north towards it from Preveza.

The site

Open daily 8.30–3; T: 26820 41336. Parts of the widely scattered site are very overgrown and a visit can be arduous in summer. Other parts have sunk into the marsh after changes in sea level and are not accessible.

Though now classified as a dangerous structure and fenced off, the **theatre** is prominent to the right of the road. The walls of the proscenium still stand, and the auditorium rises to the upper portico, its niches and arcades the haunt of storks. In several places the holes in which the poles for the *velarium*, or awning, were fixed may be seen. The line of the *cunei* can be distinguished though the stone seats have mostly vanished.

A dirt road (signed 'Temple of Apollo', though this was not the temple dedication; *see below*) to the left skirts the **stadium** which, unusually in Greece, was rounded at both ends like those of Asia Minor. A new entrance bridge of wood has recently been built, and undergrowth tidied up inside it. The road leads in 450m to the village of

Smirtoula, above which are the remains of the **commemorative monument** erected by Augustus after the Battle of Actium, on the site where his tent had been pitched (*at the time of writing this part of the site was closed*). A massive podium of masonry fronted by a stepped terrace is preserved. In its face are cuttings where the bronze prow rams (*rostra*) of captured ships were attached. The positions of 23 have been identified. There were probably originally 33–35, a tenth of the c. 350 captured in the battle. The largest was two tons in weight. Above these was a long inscription (parts preserved) recording the dedication to Mars and Neptune (not Apollo as mistakenly reported by Cassius Dio). On top of the podium was a structure with Corinthian columns.

The Byzantine city

The road runs south, meeting the inland road from Parga near some ruined baths, then enters the Byzantine enceinte. To the left, just inside the circuit, is Basilica G (Γ). Further on are the excavated remains of the **Basilica of Alkyson** (= Basilica B), a double-aisled church with tripartite transept, founded by Bishop Alkyson (d. 516). Two heads in mosaic survive from its Christian decoration. Beyond the basilica a track leads (right) through a fine gate in Justinian's walls, here well preserved for c. 500m. The path may be followed past the Augustan odeion, restored for use in the annual festival of ancient drama (August), to the Great Gate in the city walls of the Augustan period. Some remains of the aqueduct that supplied the city with water from the Louros survive to the north, as well as part of the nymphaeum in which it terminated.

Further along the main road is the **museum**. On the walls of the lobby are inscribed stelae bases and gravestones. Two rooms display statues, sarcophagi, Roman portraits (notably Agrippa, Augustus' general at Actium, and Faustina the Younger, wife of Marcus Aurelius) and capitals; in the centre of the first room is a grave lion (3rd century BC); in the second, a huge cylindrical base with *Amazonomachia* reliefs (reused as the ambo of the Alkyson basilica); a large glass cinerary urn and rings and lamps.

In the field nearby is the **Basilica of Doumetios** (Basilica A), dated from its fine floor mosaics to the second quarter of the 6th century. Adjacent to the west is the palace of the archbishops of *Epirus Vetus* who had their seat here. North of that are remains of baths and a cistern. To the northeast, on the other side of the road, are slight remains of the 6th basilica of the area (ΣΤ in Greek letters). **Basilica D** (Δ; the 'Asomatos'; 5th–6th centuries) with a peacock mosaic floor is off the road to the left, 400m beyond the main walls. To the west of that is a church of the Ascension (Analipsis). The amphitheatre lay outside the city walls, to the south.

INLAND FROM NICOPOLIS

Just north of Michalitsi (where 4th-century tombs were found), the Louros river meets the sea. The area to the east is a marshy lagoon, the haunt of herons and other wildfowl. Following the river's course inland, the narrow isthmus widens into a peninsula, turning into a lush plain around the large village of Louros.

The impressive ruins of **Roghi Castle** (ancient *Bouchetion*) stand on a low hill near Nea Kerasounda, protected by a marshy loop of the river. The modern name is derived from the Albanian word for a guard-house. Though very overgrown and in need of restoration, it is an atmospheric and major edifice. In 1807 it was visited by Leake, when it was surrounded on three sides by a lake, with a narrow seasonal passage through marsh to the sea. The castle was one of the main defending strongholds of the boundaries of the Despotate of Epirus (*see p. 505*), but stands on the site of much earlier fortifications: Illyrian tribes constructed a hilltop fort here as early as the 5th century BC. Various outer walls were built in the time of the Despotate, with large guarded gatehouses connecting them, and secured by outer towers. An excellent outer polygonal enceinte encloses a medieval citadel, built on ashlar foundations (late 5th century BC, then three subsequent phases of alteration and reconstruction before it was abandoned after 31 BC), with a church (defaced frescoes). The walk up through sheepfolds and following the path in the undergrowth is very worthwhile, with the romantic ruined walls high above the river valley and fine views in all directions.

ARTA

Arta ('Άρτα), from the Albanian word *Narta*, meaning lagoon, is pleasantly situated in a loop of the Arachthos. It is a friendly town, a pleasant place to stroll, with numerous leafy squares, good shops, and a profusion of orange and lemon trees.

HISTORY OF ARTA

The lagoon and rivers were inhabited by tribal people from the earliest times, and Illyrian hilltop fortresses were built in many places. Ancient Arta, *Ambracia*, was colonised by Corinth c. 625 BC and had a grid plan at least by the 5th century BC. Pausanias found only ruins. Arta's rise to importance began after AD 259, when Pyrrhus transferred his capital to Ambracia. After the fall of Constantinople and of the Morea to the Franks in 1204, Michael I Angelus, with the approval of the exiled Emperor Alexius III, set up the autonomous Despotate of Epirus (*see p. 505*). In the 12th and 13th centuries Arta prospered as a producer of ceramics and agricultural goods used in trade with Ragusa and Venice. After 1259 a period of anarchy in the region meant that the town changed hands many times. It was controlled by the Toco Albanian feudal lords after 1416. The town fell to the Turks in 1449, but soon passed to the Venetians. The French held it for two years after the Treaty of Campoformio (1797) but, after a period of subjection to Ali Pasha of Ioannina, it fell again under direct Turkish rule. Hodja Ishak Efendi (1774–1834), the accomplished linguist who first introduced western science into Turkish education, was born at Arta. The town became part of Greece in 1881.

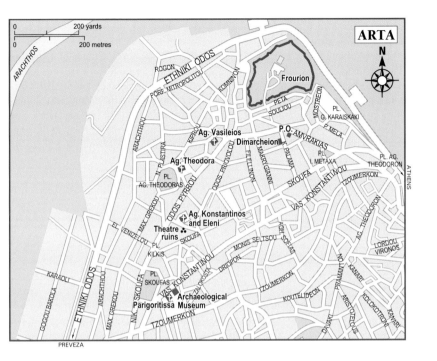

The frourion and churches

The frourion (*open 9am–11pm*), a 13th-century fortress on earlier foundations and with Ottoman additions, commands the bend of the river. The restored outer walls (virtually complete), with reused Classical blocks, can be followed and give pleasant views northward to Xerovouni. Within the walls there is a grassy knoll and pleasant paved walks and citrus groves. The derelict hotel building in the centre is an eyesore. There are very good views over the entire river valley. The fortress was extended by Ali Pasha, who used it as the citadel on the southernmost boundary of his domains. Some scanty remains of a Classical temple survive near the river bank.

To the southwest, off Odos Pyrrou is **Aghios Vasileios**, a small, single-aisle 14th-century church with the elaborate brick-and-tile decoration characteristic of the area. Farther to the west is the 13th-century **Aghia Theodora**, properly the church of St George the Martyr, a conventual church where Theodora, consort of Michael II and now patron saint of Arta, took the veil and ended her days. The domed narthex, perhaps added in her lifetime, has outstanding brick-and-tile decoration; within stands a reconstruction of Theodora's tomb (excavated in 1873), originally erected by Nicephorus I, her son. Theodora (c. 1225–after 1270) was the only woman sanctified by the Byzantine church in the 13th century. Miracles are said to have been performed at her tomb, which is still an object of veneration. Her festival, 11th March, is observed with great devotion.

Plateia Skoufas is dominated by the former metropolitan church of **Panaghia Parigoritissa**, a huge square building crowned by six domes. It was erected in 1282–89 by Nicephorus and John, sons of Michael II. The gloomy interior has a certain majesty; the curious sub-structure of the central dome, borne on antique columns on a primitive cantilever principle, appears unsound, but is in fact ingenious. The mosaics of the Pantocrator and the prophets in the dome (cleaned) belong to the original decoration. There is an archaeological museum (*open Tues–Sun 8.30–3; T: 26180 28692*) in the refectory of the former convent.

CHURCHES OF ARTA

NB: The churches are often locked: it is safest to visit on a Sunday.

Arta was for some time after the Crusader period the centre of a Byzantine principality, its Despots even claiming a right to the Imperial crown that had been appropriated by the Latin occupiers of Constantinople in 1204. The churches built under the dynasty fit uneasily into the categories of architecture that one finds elsewhere, even in Greece. If one can sense the distant influence of Constantinople in churches such as Nea Moni on Chios, or even Daphni, in Arta there is a more provincial application of general rules and tastes. They have heavy external decorations of brick and stone. Some of them are cross-vaulted, which is common enough in Greece. The most noteworthy of the churches erected under the Epirot Despotate is the church of the Parigoritissa, built between 1283 and 1296. It shares in the idiosyncratic (though derivative) nature of many of the churches erected during the period, notably in that its exterior reflects almost nothing of the complicated system of overhangs, inaccessible galleries and the use of double columns to support a precariously balanced interior: nonetheless it has a certain (almost Italianate) grandeur about it. The mosaics are of some interest, especially the somewhat troubled-looking figure of the Pantocrator in the central dome. N.S.

Ancient Arta

Remains are coming to light of Arta's ancient past as *Ambracia*, capital of Pyrrhus, Illyrian king of Epirus. Parallel to Odos Pyrrou is Odos Priovolou, in which the ancient bouleuterion was found in 1976. Remains of a substantial Hellenistic public building can be seen further south in a plot on the same side of the street. Towards Odos Skoufa, by the church of Aghii Konstantinos and Eleni, are the remains of the tiny 4th–3rd-century theatre. There are pretty 19th-century cafés in this street, too.

Towards the bottom of Odos Priovolou (on the right) are the foundations of a large Doric **Temple of Apollo** of the early 5th century BC, uncovered in 1964–69. Its tiles were stamped AMBP. This is much the most impressive antiquity in the town, with great stone blocks lying in scattered confusion on the grassy pavement.

Sections of the ancient town wall (c. 500 BC) have been located in the north of town, on Porfiriou Mitropolitou and Rogon; also, prominently, to the northwest in the vicinity of Arachthou 15, where there are towers and a gate.

On the south side of the town by the Athens main road (*beyond the map*) is the **House of Zorbas**, a fine *konak* with an overhanging roof (*open 9–2*), housing the ephorate of Byzantine antiquities.

THE DESPOTATE OF EPIRUS

When in 1204 the army of the Fourth Crusade set up the Latin (Frankish) Empire of Constantinople on the ruins of Byzantium, the Eastern Empire split into three states in exile: at Trebizond, Nicaea and Epirus. The Greek state stretched from Durazzo in the north to the Gulf of Patras in the south, and was governed from Epirus by rulers known as *despotes*. The first of these was Michael Angelus Comnenus Ducas, first of the Ducas dynasty. He became known as the 'Byzantine Noah' saving his people from the Frankish flood. The despots' primary ambition was to win territory back from the Franks: in 1222 Epirus took Salonica from them; in 1259 the Greeks won Mistra. For a time the Despotate of Epirus was a rival of the empire of Nicaea in the struggle for the restoration of the Byzantine Empire. The ensuing civil war was unproductive, and ultimately Epirus accepted vassal status. When the Byzantine Empire was restored at Consantinople in 1261, the territory of Epirus fell under the control of the Serbs and Albanians, and after that to the Ottomans. The Despotate of Epirus, though short-lived, was the channel through which Hellenic culture survived in this part of Greece.

ENVIRONS OF ARTA

The **Bridge of Arta**, an Ottoman packhorse bridge, is on the western outskirts, about 200m away from where the modern road to Ioannina crosses the river. It is a wonderful monument to the artistic, architectural and civil engineering genius of the Ottoman civilisation, with a vast central arch that seems to defy the laws of gravity and architecture, and three smaller side arches. It is best seen in winter or early spring, with the torrent rushing far beneath it over the bright pebbles. The legend that the mason built his wife into the foundations to strengthen the bridge is enshrined in a song that is known among several Balkan peoples. There is a small gatehouse on the south side that also served as a customs post when this river was the border between the Ottoman Empire and the Greek state, between 1881 and 1913. It is an ethnographic museum, though currently closed, and the building has been vandalised. The bridge is in use as a footbridge, and as long as you have a reasonable head for heights it is well worth walking across to see the views into the surrounding hills and to give a moment's thought to the greatness of Ottoman culture in Greece.

Another remnant of Arta's Muslim past is the **Imaret**, the Mosque of Faik Pasha, one of the numerous Albanian pashas who ruled the city in the Ottoman era. This lovely little mosque, dating from the early conquest period, is hidden in an orange grove about 3km outside the town. (*Follow the signs from the main road; it is about 5mins drive from the bridge. Turn right about 200m from the bridge, taking the sign to Gramenitsa village, then turn right down Odos Aghios Ioannis, and follow a track for about 2km.*) Construction is dated to about 1444. Though there has been some vandalism to the interior by Orthodox extremists, the structure, with its single high dome, is standing. Ruined Islamic buildings covered in undergrowth nearby would merit excavation and identification. One appears to be a (?) hammam, another a small (?) *medresse*, or a Bektashi shrine.

Four kilometres away is a Byzantine church in the village of Vlacherna. The monastery of **Moni Vlachernai** (Panaghia Vlachernitissa) was built in the early 10th century, and transformed into a convent of nuns by Theodore Angelus c. 1225, not many years after its foundation. It was reconstructed, and embellished with cupolas, by Michael Comnenus in the middle of the 12th century, as the burial chapel for the Epirot ruling dynasty. Fragments of the original marble *templon* are built into the narthex doorway. Within are two marble tombs, believed from their fragmentary inscriptions to belong to Michael II and to two of his sons. The builder's assistant went on to build the church of Parigoritissa in Arta (*see p. 504 above*).

By the river 3.5km south of Arta, on a road which follows the east bank of the river, is the **Kato Panaghia**, a nunnery founded by Michael II, whose monogram can be traced on the south wall of the church. It shelters 20 orphaned girls who weave blankets and carpets (for sale). The church incorporates prophyry columns, perhaps from a Syrian Temple of Aphrodite (Classical foundation blocks visible in the terrace). The exterior walls are adorned with bands of cable and meander patterns with decorative motifs worked in red tile. The frescoes within are mainly of the 18th century; fragments in the apse date from the 13th century.

Near Plisioi is the 8th–9th-century church of **Aghios Dimitrios Katsouri**, the chapel of a Patriarchal monastery. The frescoes are assigned to the late 12th–early 13th centuries. The nearby church of **Aghios Nikolaos tis Rodias** (12th–13th centuries) also has frescoes of the early 13th century. Two unusual scenes are preserved in the west corner bays: the three *Hebrews in the Fiery Furnace* and the *Seven Sleepers of Ephesus*.

Leaving Arta and turning southeast, the road runs through orange groves to Komboti, the native town of Nikolaos Skoufas, one of the founders of the Philike Etaireia, the secret society formed in 1814 with the aim of establishing a free Greek state and overthrowing Ottoman rule (*see p. 51*).

IGOUMENITSA & THE COAST

The remainder of this chapter is covered by the map overleaf.

Igoumenitsa (Ηγουμενίτσα) is the first port of call on the Greek mainland for car ferries from Brindisi and other Italian ports, and the terminus of a frequent local ferry
from Corfu. The modern town was an insignificant village until, in 1936, it became
the seat of the nomarch of Thesprotia. Rebuilt on the ruins left after the Second World
War, it is now a flourishing transit town (pop. 6,807) with a pleasant seafront. A
major expansion scheme for the port is in progress, and a controversial new motorway through Çameria/Thesprotia runs from the new lorry port to the south of the
town. Although it speeds lorry travel, it has destroyed unique countryside and many
fine Greek and Çam traditional buildings.

In Ottoman times and until the Second World War Goumenitsa (to give it its old
name) was an insignificant little place, with most Ottoman trade between Ioannina
and the coast going through Sarande, in Albania, or Muros/Vola (modern Syvota), or
the now abandoned port of Sagiada, a short distance to the north. Development began
after the Second World War, and has accelerated ever since, so the port is now the
most important point of departure for many Greek agricultural exports.

Igoumenitsa is a scruffy, lively, workaday sort of place. There is a small kastro hill
behind the main square, covered in pine forest, with the remains of a castle that may
have Byzantine origins. The low walls that are visible today date from Ottoman times.

THE KALAMAS RIVER VALLEY
& NORTHERN COAST

Through the formerly marshy plain to the north of Igoumenitsa, the Kalamas, the
ancient *Thyamis*, winds its way to the channel separating Corfu from the mainland. A
barrage (1962) at the exit of the last defile now controls irrigation, and experiments are
being made in rice growing. In Antiquity the sea level was different along the coast, and
most of the modern lowlands were flooded marshland. The small hills which rise above
the marsh are considered by some authorities to represent the ancient Sybota Islands,
near which a naval battle was fought in 433 BC between the Corinthians and
Corcyraeans (*Thucydides I, 45*). Their name is now held by modern Syvota and its
islands between Igoumenitsa and Parga to the south. The Kalamas delta is an important
wildlife site, and offers good birdwatching, particularly in the migration period.

The fortress of Pyrgos Raghiou

The magnificent fortress of Pyrgos Raghiou should be a priority on any visit to the
region. On the way there, you pass the long, sandy beach at Drepano, with very
attractive views of the bay. The road winds through sand dunes and marshes covered
with forest and scrub towards the modern village of Raghio. The castle is a massive
fortress dating from the 5th century BC on a hillock sticking out of the marshlands that

dominated this part of the coast for two millennia before changes in sea levels and in the course of the Kalamas river led to its current inland isolation.

Evidence of Neolithic habitation has been found at the site. A large fortress was built by Illyrian tribes which, according to Thucydides, was colonised by Greek settlers from Corfu in the 5th century BC, when it was known as *Peraia*. In the Classical and Hellenistic period, the fort protected this and other local settlements from mainland invaders. The hill was refortified in Byzantine times, and became an important Venetian and then Ottoman coastal stronghold in the 17th century. In later Ottoman times it fell into disrepair until the late 19th century when a small garrison post was built

The hillock is about 250m high with rocky limestone extrusions, and in its centre is a large depression about 15m deep, near a huge isolated rock that was probably used as a cult centre from the earliest times. You enter, after a stiff climb, through the south gate. There is a pleasant walk around the summit of the hill, with massive polygonal masonry walls on the seaward side, and an ancient carved throne that probably dates from Archaic times. On the north side is a well restored Albanian *kulla* tower house and Ottoman garrison post, which the local guides incorrectly describe as Venetian. Inside is a small museum representing events of the recent past from an unapologetically Greek standpoint. The top floor has an interesting exhibition of photographs by the Swiss photographer Frédéric Boissonas (1858–1946), who made many photographs of interwar Epirus. There are magnificent views over the coastal marshes and towards Corfu.

Lisi

The melancholy but evocative ruins of Lisi are reached via the pretty village of Smertos. The land hereabouts is used for mandarin orange and fruit growing. The modern village of Asprokklisi lies on the main road: from here you walk up the hill to the east through the modern houses to the upper village of Lisi. (*NB: Though it is possible—but difficult—to get to the top of the hill with a 4WD vehicle, it is safer and easier to walk. Remember your route through the scrub: it is easy to get lost on the way down, and a compass is useful.*) The village was probably originally established on this high site in Byzantine times as a protection from pirates. Lisi today has a remarkably well preserved complex of ruined and semi-ruined Albanian *kulla* tower-houses, and a ruined church. It is possible to see the pattern of settlement of a traditional Çam village, with most properties dating from the times of prosperity here in the 18th and 19th centuries. The tower-house *kullas* are similar in design to those found in northern Albania today. The houses are all abandoned now, since the pogroms of 1943–45, when over 40,000 people were driven from their homes, leaving many villages depopulated. Most went to Turkey or the United States as refugees. The survival of the houses in Lisi is due to the fact that for many years the village was in a closed military zone.

Sagiada and the road inland

Sagiada (Σαγιάδα), on the coast, is nowadays a jumble of nondescript houses by a lovely sandy beach with a deserted acropolis hill, but in Ottoman times it was a thriving port, trading in fish and Epirot agricultural products. There are some very good small fish tavernas popular with smugglers on the southern harbour pier. The ancient settlement was centred around the acropolis that dominates a small spit of land protruding into the sea, with bare windswept hillsides to the north giving the place a slight end-of-the-world atmosphere.

Inland the main road takes you to the little town of Filiates. This is a dull and nondescript garrison town today, but prior to the Second World War it was a thriving centre of Albanian culture. As late as the early 1960s the British authority on Epirus, Arthur Foss, found Albanian speakers in the villages nearby. There is a beautiful drive inland north of Filiates through Giromeri, which has a monastery founded in 1285. To the west of here is Plaisio, a decayed old town with a 17th-century church, which in the 19th century had flourishing tanneries. It was the birthplace of Kyra Vasiliki, consort of Ali Pasha. At the end of the road (about 3hrs drive, round trip), on the Albanian border, the dramatic, isolated village of Tsamandas nestles below the grim and remote Mount Tsamanda (1819m). Three kilometres before Tsamandas is the Monastery of Aghios Georgios, an early Byzantine foundation with fine wood carvings. Tsamandas has a museum of ethnography (*currently closed*).

THE SOUTHERN COAST ROAD

The forested coastline south from Igoumenitsa is beautiful and generally unspoilt. At Ladochori, near the sea, a Late Roman mausoleum of brick and stone was found in 1975, with four fine sculptured marble sarcophagi (now in the Ioannina Museum). A courtyard house was associated with the mausoleum. The road runs near the sea to the attractive little fishing village of Plataria, with good fish tavernas and a lovely beach, and then along the coast past Cape Chironisi and south to Syvota, with very good swimming at several beach coves en route.

Syvota (Σύβοτα), once Venetian *Muros*, later Ottoman *Vola*, is an attractive place, its ancient Byzantine harbour popular with yachtsmen. According to Leake, a castle was built on the small wooded island in the bay by an Albanian feudal lord called Murtza. Muros became the main harbour on this part of the coast in Venetian and Ottoman times, and a powerful Çam merchant class developed, their prosperity based on trade with Corfu. In the 19th century trade was dominated by timber and food exports to the island. In the early 20th century the town declined as a result of ethnic conflict in Epirus. The modern town dates from rebuilding in the late 1950s, although some older buildings have been restored.

The Castle of Karvostasi

Karvostasi Castle is a magnificently situated coastal fortress, set in a dramatic position opposite the southern coast of Corfu. It is signed up a track 2km along the main road as you leave Syvota. Drive into dense woods near the sea, and climb towards the summit of a low hill. In very wet weather a 4WD vehicle is best. The castle is a rough climb through scrub and oak forest—long trousers needed. The site is a superb natural fortress that has been inhabited since the earliest times, with breathtaking views across the Corfu Straits, and remains of many low walls and scattered masonry from different historical periods. The main walls of massive cyclopean blocks were constructed in the Illyrian period, and the castle continued as a military stronghold until the Roman pacification of Epirus. It fell into disrepair after the Ottoman conquest, but was used as a watch-tower over the coast until the 20th century.

A rough track, probably on the site of an ancient or medieval road, does follow the coast all the way down to Parga, but it is better to return to the main road.

The Castle of Valtos

Eighteen kilometres north of Parga is a fine beach at Sarakiniko, and the Christos taverna (recommended). Six kilometres south of here, reached up a good track right from the main road 1km before the village of Anthousa, is the Castle of Valtos, an austere late 18th-century building standing in a lonely windswept position on top of the often windy coastal cliff. It was constructed by Ali Pasha, to the same architectural specification as the fortress of Porto Palermo in Albania, although it is appreciably smaller than the Albanian edifice. This castle, also like Porto Palermo, was designed by the Italian military architect Monteleone, and completed in 1814, with Romanesque entrance arches and a dark, sinister internal chamber. A severe mathematical structure, it occupies an operatic situation, with magnificent views of Paxos and Antipaxos. Nearby (about 800m down the hill) there is a ruined small garrison mosque, in a sad, roofless state. A new village called Aghia was established here after the departure of the Çams in the Second World War.

PARGA

Parga (Πάργα) is a clean and picturesque little seaside town backed by slopes of orange and olive groves, opposite the island of Paxos. The town spreads across the neck of a rocky headland, crowned by a castle of Norman origin (its keep is adorned with the lion of St Mark). The tiny bay has rocks and islets and many cafés along the waterfront.

There was a small port and trading centre on the site in Antiquity, and in the early medieval period a port was developed by the Angevins. Activity was dominated by local trade along the Adriatic coast and to Corfu. Parga was already important in the 14th century. In 1401 it came under the protection of the Venetians, who dominated it until the fall of their republic in 1797, except for brief intervals in 1452–54 and after 1701 when it fell into Turkish hands. It was taken by the French in 1797, who left a small fort on the densely wooded islet of the Panaghia. In 1800–07 it enjoyed a brief existence as an independent state under the aegis of Russia, before passing again to the French at the Treaty of Tilsit. Ali Pasha bought it from the British, who had replaced the French in 1814. He drove out its people, who sought refuge in the Ionian Islands. Some of them later returned, but Parga remained subject to Turkey until 1913, when it became Greek.

Although Parga is picturesque and interesting to visit for a day or two, it has been considerably affected by package tourism. Bad drains and some tatty buildings spoil the overall aspect. There are pleasant day trips in boats from the harbour to the River Acheron and other locations. There is an interesting small castle above the harbour, and ruins of Venetian naval fortifications. The clifftop walk to Valtos Castle (*see above*) takes about 2hrs.

IOANNINA

The university town of Ioannina (Ιωάννινα) is the capital of the nomarchy of the same name. It occupies a rocky promontory jutting into Lake Pambotis opposite the foot of the precipitous Mt Mitsikeli. A busy and friendly town, it lies in the midst of a plain divided between pasture and the cultivation of cereals and tobacco. A large proportion of the population is of either Vlach or Albanian descent. Local industries include the manufacture of filigree silver jewellery. To the east and southeast rise the highest peaks of the Pindus. In summer the temperature is oppressive; winters are long and cold.

HISTORY OF IOANNINA

In very early times the lake vicinity—at that date probably a large marsh, rich in wildlife—was inhabited by Illyrian tribes. In the 6th century Justinian fortified the castle site. Nothing remains of this fort. The lake in its modern form is believed to have developed in the early Byzantine period. Ioannina is first documented in 1020 and may have taken its name and site from a monastery of St John the Baptist. Taken by Bohemond, eldest son of Robert Guiscard, in the 11th century, it was visited in 1160 by Benjamin of Tudela. Ioannina dates its importance, however, from the influx of refugees in 1205 from Constantinople and the Morea and its consequent fortification by Michael I Angelus Ducas. An archbishopric was established here between 1284 and 1307. In 1345 Ioannina was captured by Stefan Dušan, proclaimed Emperor of Serbia and Greece in the following year. In 1431 it surrendered to the army of Sultan Murad II. In 1611, after an abortive rising led by Dionysos 'Skylosophos', the fanatical Bishop of Trikala, the Christians were expelled from the citadel and their churches destroyed. Nevertheless in 1666 Jacob Spon found the town rich and populous. It reached a zenith under Ali Pasha (*see p. 517*). Ioannina was long famous for its Schools, founded by Michael Philanthropinos (1682–1758), Leondati Giouma (1675–1725), and Meletios (1690), later Bishop of Athens and a noted historian and geographer. They were all destroyed in the fire.

The Congress of Berlin (1878) assigned Epirus to Greece, but it remained in Turkish hands for over 35 more years, until 1913.

The town

Life in Ioannina centres on Odos Dodonis, which connects Plateia Dimokratias, a beautiful belvedere laid out in front of the Nomarchia (Municipal Offices), and Plateia 25 Martiou with its clock tower (*To Roloï*) farther down the hill. The square is home to Ioannina's Archaeological Museum (*see below*).

Immediately below the Nomarchia, Odos Mikhaïl Angelou (running west) has, in a restored Ottoman building, a good **Folk Art Museum** (*open Mon 5–8, Wed 11–1*) with an extensive collection of Epirot costume, and also ceramics and domestic and agricultural implements.

Archaeological Museum

Plateia 25 Martiou. Open 8.30–2.30, closed Mon; T: 26510 33357.

Hall A: Cases are arranged chronologically from right to left. The exhibit includes stone and bone objects from Cambridge University excavations in Palaeolithic caves at Asprochaliko and Kastritsa; Neolithic and Bronze Age finds, chiefly from cist graves (swords, daggers, axes); Protogeometric vases from the region of Agrinion; finds from the cemeteries of Vitsa, ranging from 9th-century Geometric to late-Classical—notable are the small stylized Geometric horse and a fine bronze kylix; two superb bronze beaked pitchers; vases and terracotta figurines of Persephone from the Necromanteion of Ephyra (*see p. 528*), also the windlass mechanism. Note the finger ring of crystal with a sculptured bull in case 11, and also the elaborate gold earrings, from Ambracia; small gilded bronze plaque depicting Clytemnestra and Orestes. There are also heads of various goddesses, Epirot coins, and some of the large bronze vessels from the Votonosi hoard, discovered in 1939. From Dodona there are votive bronzes (eagle, warriors, boy with dove, lion), oracular tablets of lead, and a reconstruction of the door of the bouleuterion, using original fittings.

Corridor: Grave stelae from various sites; inscriptions from Dodona; Ionic capitals from Kassope, and grave goods from Michalitsi (model cart from a child burial).

Hall B: Marble sculptures from Michalitsi include female heads and an elaborate sarcophagus.

Hall C: Finds from recent excavations at Panepistemioupolis (site of the university), including iron tools and weapons and two 'Illyrian' helmets; three impressive Roman sarcophagi with mythological scenes, from Ladochori. There are also prehistoric finds from tumuli at Kato Meropi, near the Albanian border; bronzes from *Stephane* (Preveza); a fine Thracian or Phrygian helmet; tools and weapons from Dodona and material from the Vitsa cemetery.

Halls D and E: 19th–20th-century paintings and sculpture.

Hall F: Fine Frankish-Byzantine capitals from a church at Glyki; hoards of Venetian coins; an ecclesiastical collection of icons, Church plate and jewellery.

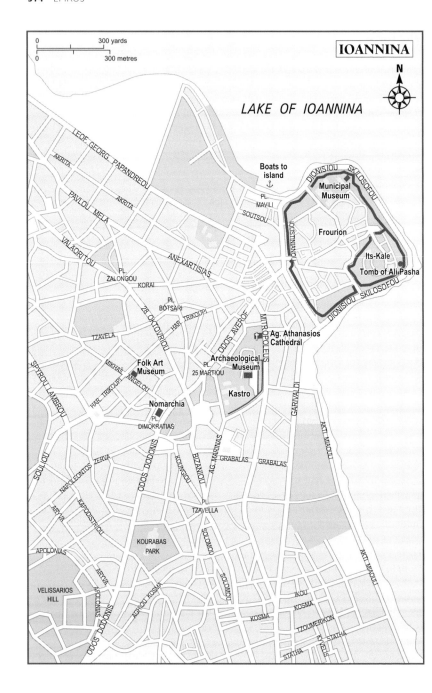

IOANNINA

0 ——— 300 yards
0 ——— 300 metres

N

LAKE OF IOANNINA

LEOF. GEORG. PAPANDREOU

AKRITA

PAVLOU MELA

AKRITA

VALAORITOU

ANEXARTISIAS

PL. ZALONGOU

KORAI

28. OKTOVRIOU

PL. BOTSARI

HAR. TRIKOUPI

TZAVELA

MIKHAIL ANGELOU

HAR. TRIKOUPI

SPYROU LAMBROU

Folk Art Museum

Nomarchia

PL. DIMOKRATIAS

IOULIOU

NAPOLEONTOS

ZERVA

KAPODISTRIOU

ARIVA

ODOS DODONIS

KOUNGGIOU

BIZANIOU

AG. MARINAS

PL. TZAVELLA

GRABALAS

GRABALAS

Boats to island

PL. MAVILI

SOUTSOU

DIONISIOU SKILOSOFOU

Municipal Museum

IOUSTINIANOU

Frourion

Its-Kale

Tomb of Ali Pasha

DIONISIOU SKILOSOFOU

ODOS AVEROF

MITROPOLEUS

Ag. Athanasios Cathedral

Archaeological Museum

PL. 25 MARTIOU

Kastro

GARIVALDI

AKTI MIAOULI

APOLONIAS

VELISSARIOS HILL

ARIVA

APOLONIAS

ODOS DODONIS

AGRIOU KOSMA

KOURABAS PARK

SOLOMOU

SOLOMOU

IKOU

KOSMA

KOSMA

TZOUMERIKON

STATHA

STATHA

RIVELIS

AKTI MIAOULI

Behind the archaeological museum and its gardens is the levelled upper esplanade of the **kastro**, which once sheltered the Christian quarter of Litharitsa: its walls were demolished by Ali Pasha and the material used to build his palace and outer fortifications of the town.

The frourion

Odos Averof, lined with silversmiths, descends directly to the market. Lower down, off to the left, the narrow streets have small traditional shops and kafeneions crowded together. The frourion, the fortress of the Despots, was restored in 1815 by Ali Pasha as his headquarters. The walls, though impressive, preserve very little Byzantine work. The landward side was protected by the *khandaki*, a moat (now filled in) joining the two little landing places (*see below*) and crossed by three wooden bridges.

At no. 16 Ioustinianou, in the former Jewish quarter, is a **synagogue** of Romaniot type, still in use. The (Romaniot) Jewish community is thought to date from the reign of Alexander the Great. In 1904 it numbered 4,000 but was practically obliterated in the Second World War, when nearly half of all Ioannina's Jews were deported to their deaths. Towards the northwest is the former Turkish library, restored in 1973. Enclosed by a wall in the northwest corner, overlooking the lake, is the picturesque Djami of Aslan Pasha, a conventual foundation of 1618. Tradition places here the rape and murder in 1801 of Kyra Phrosyne and her 17 companions (*see p. 517 below*).

The so-called Asian mosque, which continued in use until 1928, now houses the crowded **Municipal Museum** (*open in summer Mon–Fri 8–8, Sat–Sun 9–8; in winter Mon–Fri 8–3, Sat–Sun 9–3*). Note the recesses for shoes in the vestibule. The mosque has a well-proportioned dome, still retaining traces of the original painting. It was built in 1618 on the rubble of a demolished church, destroyed in revenge for the Skylosophos revolt. Striking among the exhibits are the Epirot costumes and adornments of the 18th–19th centuries; also a Roman sarcophagus, and an interesting collection of the Jewish and Islamic communities.

The minaret (*closed at present*) has a superb view of the lake and the surrounding mountains. To the southeast you look down on the inner citadel of Its-Kale (military) with the Fetihe Djami (or Victory Mosque), a circular tower, the **Tomb of Ali Pasha**, and the restored palace or *serai* where the 'Lion of Ioannina' entertained Byron and Hobhouse in October 1809. Nearby was the residence of the Byzantine archon. North of the palace are some remains of a Byzantine bath complex.

The shady Leoforos Dionisiou Skilosofou runs by the lakeside beneath the walls. In the cliff is the cave where the hermit-rebel Skylosophos was caught and flayed alive in 1611. From the south corner of the frourion, roads wind westwards to the cathedral (Aghios Athanasios), rebuilt in 1820, with ornate carved woodwork and the tomb of a local patriot of 1828.

The lake

The Lake of Ioannina, or Lake Pambotis, is fed by torrents from the precipices of Mitsikeli and discharges its waters into swallow-holes. In 1849 the artist Edward Lear noted the 'placid solemnity of the dark waters reflecting the great mosque and battlements of the citadel as if in a mirror'. It is first mentioned in 12th-century documents. It is 10–11km long, averages 3km across, and ranges in depth from 9–20m, with shallow reedy shores. After very wet weather it may join up with the Lapsista marsh to the north. This marsh was once Lake Lapsista, which dried up in the last century. The general condition of the lake is poor, and is a matter of concern to ecologists. There is a 2000m international rowing course. The local boats are similar in design to those on Lake Kastoria. Boats (*half-hourly in summer, from Plateia Mavili, by the castle*) cross to the island in the lake, on which are numerous monasteries very prettily situated amid trees and flowers. There is also a choice of tavernas. East of the little island village is the **Monastery of the Prodromos** (St John the Baptist). The oldest (13th-century) parts are the katholikon and the east aisle. It was restored in the 16th century; the 18th-century frescoes in the 19th century. In the 16th-century **Monastery of Panteleimon** nearby Ali Pasha was killed on 17th January 1822; the bullet marks on the floor bear witness to his execution.

The dark waters of Lake Pambotis (Ioannina Lake), where Ali Pasha is said to have drowned Kyra Phrosyne and her seventeen handmaidens.

Ali Pasha (1741–1822)

Born in 1741 at Homovo, near the Albanian town of Tepelena, this brilliant, resourceful and vindictive adventurer alternately fought and served the Ottoman Sultan. Having assisted the Turks in their war of 1787 against Austria, he was made Pasha of Trikala in 1788, in which year he seized Ioannina, then a town of 35,000 inhabitants, and made it his headquarters. In 1797 he allied himself with Napoleon, but the next year took Preveza from the French. In 1803 he subdued the Souliots. After 1807 his dependence on the Porte was merely nominal. Byron visited Ioannina in 1809, while Colonel W.M. Leake (*see p. 544*) was British resident, and Henry Holland was Ali Pasha's doctor. In 1813 Ali Pasha made the entire population work as forced labourers to build the fortifications. In 1817 he entered into an alliance with the British, who gave him Parga. At length the Sultan decided to eliminate this daring rebel. He was captured at Ioannina after a siege, and executed there in 1822. The Ioannina lake island was the scene of some of the most notorious episodes of Ali Pasha's tyranny. His daughter-in-law Kyra Phrosyne was drowned in a sack here to disguise the fact that the despot had drugged and raped her in a frenzy of rage after the discovery of his son Veli's failure to subdue the Morea. Other versions of the story say she was drowned for refusing her father-in-law's libidinous advances. Tradition has it that she was bound hand and foot, had rocks fastened to her body, and was tossed into the lake to drown, along with her 17 waiting women. The gypsies who carried out the drownings were then beheaded by a dumb black slave to ensure secrecy. Ali Pasha's own murder took place after negotiations with Kurshid Pasha, who he believed had secured a pardon for his crimes from the Sultan in Constantinople.

The **Philanthropinon Monastery** (Aghios Nikolaos Spanos), on a rocky height to the north of the village, was founded in 1392 and rebuilt in the 16th century. It has a katholikon with decorated doors and outstanding 16th-century frescoes. The 15th-century *Chronicle of Epirus* was written here. In the apse is the *Communion of Saints*. In the nave vault, the *Almighty* and the *Evangelists*; on the walls the *Life of Jesus*. In the narthex vault is the *Annunciation*, with the five founders of the monastery kneeling before St Nicholas on the north side, and above the *Head of Christ*. In the northwest corner are portraits of Greek philosophers.

The **Monastery of Aghios Nikolaos Dilios**, or Stratigopoulou, is the oldest (11th century). It lies to the east of the Philanthropinon. The eminent Stratigopoulou family arrived in Ioannina after the Fourth Crusade. In the katholikon there is a fresco (restored in the 16th century) of Judas returning his pieces of silver. In the narthex are the *Life of the Virgin*, *Life of St Nicholas* and *Last Judgement*. To the south the **Monastery of Eleouses** takes its name from a 15th-century icon of the Panaghia Eleousa, brought here from the kastro. The katholikon (before 1584) has 18th-century frescoes.

ENVIRONS OF IOANNINA

At the north end of the lake, towards **Perama** (Πέραμα) are a spectacular series of caverns, discovered by accident when places of refuge were being sought in the Second World War. Their stalagmites and stalactites are carefully lit and well worth a visit; parties are taken through the half-mile of galleries by guides (*open 8–sunset*).

Beyond Perama a road diverges right (signed Amphithea) to follow the lakeside (pleasant tavernas) reaching in 4km the monastery of **Panaghia Dourahan** (Koimisis tis Theotokou), which is reputed to have been founded in 1434 by Dourahan Pasha as a thank-offering to the Virgin for protecting his night ride across the frozen lake.

At the south end of the lake, on the hill of Kastritsa, near an old monastery, is the site of ancient *Tekmona*. Below this, Palaeolithic remains were dug in 1966 by the British School. At Bizani is the **Pavlos Vrellis Museum** of wax effigies of figures from Greek history. Three main themes are illustrated in the tableaux: the pre-revolutionary period after the execution of Skylosophos (1611–1821); the 1821 revolution and assassination of Ali Pasha; the Second World War. At Konstaniani the 12th-century church of the Archangel Michael has frescoes.

Near Rodotopi, northwest of Ioannina, are slight remains of **ancient *Passaron***, a Molossian town which survived into Roman times. The site of its Sanctuary of Zeus Areios was identified by inscriptions in 1954. **Zitsa**, to the north again, is a picturesque little town locally renowned for its sweetish semi-sparkling wine (there is a wine festival at the monastery). Prosperity in Turkish times is attested by its stone houses and paved streets. The 14th-century monastery of the Pateron, fired with nationalist zeal by Kosmas Aitolou in 1778, fostered Greek schools. Byron sings the charms of the view in *Childe Harold*:

> Monastic Zitza! From thy shady brow
> Thou small, but favour'd spot of holy ground!
> Where'er we gaze around, above, below,
> What rainbow tints, what magic charms are found!

> *Canto II, xlvii*

ANCIENT DODONA

The theatre and oracle at Dodona is the most notable ancient site in northwest Greece and and is of great beauty, interest and importance. Leaving Ioannina on the Arta road, and passing the modern buildings of the university on the hillside (site of a large Archaic and Classical cemetery) on your right, the road at first runs level through tobacco fields with distant views of the Pindus. After turning off to the right you wind over a ridge (fine retrospective views of the lake) into the enclosed valley of Tsarkovitsa at the foot of Mt Tomaros, whose long ridge rises from the north end (1332m) to two higher peaks at the south. A tourist pavilion (5 rooms) lies at the entrance to the ruins of Dodona. The modern village of Dodoni (Δωδώνι) stands a little farther west.

HISTORY OF DODONA

Strabo says that Dodona was moved from Skotoussa, in Thessaly, in obedience to the command of Apollo. Herodotus tells of the arrival of a black dove from Egyptian Thebes, which settled in an oak tree at Dodona. Archaeological evidence, however, suggests that Dodona became a place of chthonian cult first in early Mycenaean times, and was consecrated to a Mother Goddess of the earth, whose abode was in the roots of an oak tree: this cult was superseded in early historic times by that of celestial Zeus, who as a 'new dweller' in the oaks, came to Dodona with the epithet '*Naīos*' or 'inhabitant', while the earlier goddess now took the name Dione. The two divinities shared the abode: three preistesses called '*Peleiai*' (doves) were assigned to Dione; and a varying number of soothsaying priests called '*Selloi*', to Zeus. Homer, who refers to 'Wintry Dodona' in both the *Iliad* and the *Odyssey*, says that these *Selloi*, or prophets of Zeus, slept upon the ground and did not wash their feet. The mention of such curiosities of personal hygiene in epic poetry should be taken as an indication of the deep spiritual significance of the priests' remaining in close symbolic contact with the earth from which they were believed to draw their oracular power. According to Herodotus the divine oracle spoke in the rustling of leaves of the sacred oaks, and in the sound of acorns dropping into a ring of large, resonating bronze cauldrons, placed in a contiguous circle around the principal sacred tree. Divination was made by the interpretation of the accidental sounds and harmonies. The site was identified in 1873 by Constantine Karapanos, who discovered a number of bronze artefacts and small lead tablets inscribed with questions to be put to the oracle (now in the Archaeological Museum at Ioannina). More scientific excavations have been undertaken by the Greek Archaeological Service since 1952, and the theatre considerably restored.

The ancient oracles

Widely scattered throughout the Greek world and frequently consulted at both trivial and momentous moments, the ancient oracles are a defining aspect of Greek private and public life. Although the oracles of Apollo at Delphi and of Zeus at Dodona are perhaps the best known and attested, there may have been more than 20 recognised centres of such divination in Greek lands. They functioned at different moments in the year, operated in different ways and offered different types of response from one another: but all had in common that they were the focus of a larger centre of cult, where the suppliant would generally need to spend perhaps several days. Both Delphi and Dodona have—in common with most oracular centres—theatres, stadia, sports facilities and numerous temples: both are in remote places (a fact which helped at times to preserve their independence) and would have involved the suppliants in long and arduous journeys. Visiting an oracle, therefore, was not undertaken lightly, and the experience may have been similar to our going away to a retreat: it involved a journey away from home, obligatory rituals of spiritual cleansing, and a protracted period of meditation on a problem or dilemma. Furthermore, there was always much that was dramatic or poetic in the nature of the great oracles: the response of Zeus at Dodona came through the rustling of leaves or the sound of acorns breaking the silence by dropping from the sacred oak into the bronze cauldrons that stood beneath its boughs; at Olympia his will was consulted by 'empyromancy': reading the movement and appearance of flames on his altar. At Delphi, 'far-seeing' Apollo spoke though the entranced utterances of a priestess, who was heard only and remained hidden from view; whilst at Didyma, in Asia Minor, Apollo's oracle was at a spring deep in the floor of his vast temple there, the centre of which was dramatically and quite unexpectedly open to the skies and flooded with light. All of this imagery, combined with a sometimes veiled response from the divinity and with abstraction from the familiar environment, may in the end have prompted the suppliant to arrive at his or her own solution: this may indeed be the implication of the famous epigram 'Know Thyself', which was written beside the oracle at Delphi. Whatever their process and efficacy, oracles as a phenomenon remained popular throughout Antiquity, right up until the time of their suppression in the 4th century AD.

As the small, leaden tablets, inscribed with questions to be put to the oracle, found at Dodona show, there was often a much more ordinary side to the divination. Suppliants sought advice on whether to undertake a sea-voyage, whether to adopt a son, to marry, divorce, or how to discover the patrimony of their children. One anxious suppliant asks, 'Is my wandering boy still alive?'; another 'Did Pistos steal the wool from the mattress?'. For such questions a simple 'yes' or 'no' answer was sought. From another invaluable source, the Oxyrhynchus Papyri (no. 1477), which lists over 100 types of question that were considered 'appropriate to be asked of an oracle', it seems clear that even slaves could consult (at least some) oracles with questions such as, 'Am I to be sold as a slave?', or 'Shall I receive my pay?'. In the absence of orthodoxy and of a clergy, the oracle was also the ultimate authority on matters of cult practice, on purifications, and on questions of what might be done to please or placate a particular divinity who had apparently turned away. Most notably, however, an oracle—particularly the Delphic—was consulted by whole communities and cities at times of great moment, such as for the founding of colonies, or in the emergency of war. Byzas, founder of Byzantium, asking for guidance as to where to plant a new colony, was told to '...settle opposite the land of the blind': the people of Chalcedon on the Sea of Marmara had indeed been blind not to see the far superior strategic advantage of the site which Byzas chose on the entrance to the Bosphorus. And when pressed, after at first recommending submission to Persia during the Persian Wars, the Delphic oracle then told the delegation from Athens that 'only a wooden wall will assist you and your children', these words gave much-needed support to Themistocles, the architect of the Greeks' ultimate victory, in his efforts to convince the Athenians that their only salvation was to trust to their navy of (wooden-walled) ships at Salamis. Crucially helpful at times; discouraging or irrelevant at others; occa-

Ancient theatre at Dodona, with the snow-capped Pindus mountains in the background.

sionally political, often aloof; sometimes wrong; sometimes even apparently flippant; the greatest oracles were always poetic and metaphorical in their expression. They were a divine gift and therefore not frequently available for consultation: the Delphic oracle spoke only on a small number of auspicious days—perhaps only once a month, and then only in spring and summer, because in the winter Apollo was away in the remote lands of the Hyperboreans and would therefore give no pronouncements.

The site

Open 8.30–5 every day.

You enter along the axis of the stadium, of which part of the sphendone has been uncovered. The seating rises on the north side on a bank thrown up against the west retaining wall of the theatre at the end of the 3rd century BC. The superb **theatre** was judiciously restored in 1960–63 for use at the annual festival of drama. Constructed originally in the time of Pyrrhus (297–272 BC), it was destroyed by the Aetolians in 219 BC and rebuilt shortly afterwards by Philip V out of the spoils taken from Thermon. It suffered at the hands of the Romans in 168–167 BC and was converted into an arena about the time of Augustus, when the lowest seating was replaced by a high protective wall.

The *skene* is built in good isodomic masonry. The outer façade consisted of a stoa of 13 octagonal columns. An arch gave admittance to the centre of the stage. Double gateways, with Ionic half-columns, open into either parodos, leading to the orchestra. The fine horseshoe-shaped drainage channel is well-preserved: this may also have been used for illuminating the edge of the stage, by filling it with water and floating oil flares in terracotta cups on the surface.

The cavea is partly recessed in the side of the acropolis hill and partly supported by massive retaining walls (up to 21m high) of excellent rusticated ashlar masonry, buttressed by towers. It is divided by two *diazomata*, the three resulting banks of seats having 21 (reduced later to 15), 16, and 21 rows (the lower two banks restored to position). Ten stairways divided the lower banks into nine *kerkides*, while the topmost bank has 18. Two broad staircases added later against the façade lead up to the upper diazoma, while a ceremonial entrance from the direction of the acropolis opens into the topmost gallery; here cuttings show where a gate fitted. The back retaining wall is almost complete, though some wall slabs of the gallery have fallen forward. The base of the *thymele* (the symbolic altar to Dionysus, god of drama) is still visible in the centre of the *orchestra*, or stage: standing here and declaiming clearly gives a better sense than almost any other theatre in Greece of the ability of the acoustic design of the building's shape to magnify the human voice. It is a strange and instructive experience to have the voice pulled out of you apparently by nothing more than the carefully calculated shape of the auditorium. The view from the theatre down the wide valley towards the south forms a characteristically impressive backdrop.

Behind the theatre a well-preserved gate leads into the acropolis. The surrounding wall, 3–4.5m wide, is now less than 3m high. The enclosure is roughly quadrilateral with towers on three sides. The fabric is of various periods with Hellenistic predominating.

The sanctuary

A path descends to the terrace, east of the theatre, site of the sanctuary. Only foundations remain. The large hypostyle hall immediately on the left is shown by inscribed decrees and an inscribed altar to be the bouleuterion of the Epirot confederacy, built by Pyrrhus. Opposite this and to the south is a rectangular building which has been the focus of recent work (Prof. S. Dakaris). Built in the early 3rd century and destroyed in 169, it was probably the prytaneion. It has a large room with benches for delegates, and a Doric colonnaded court to the east. The west wall of the peristyle was part of the original boundary of the sanctuary. Late 3rd-century additions included dining and service rooms and an Ionic stoa to the east. Further to the east is the base of a small, rectangular Temple of Aphrodite. Beyond this is the Temenos of Zeus Naïos, or *Hiera Oikia*—a complex ruin in which four phases can be distinguished. At first worship centred upon the sacred oak; fragments of votive tripods of the 8th century BC have been recovered, and it was probably these which supported the bronze cauldrons which surrounded the tree. A stone temple was not built until the 4th century, and then consisted merely of cella and pronaos. This and the oak were then surrounded by a peribolos wall. The wall was replaced in the time of Pyrrhus by an enclosure of Ionic colonnades facing inwards on three sides with a blind wall on the east next to the tree. It was at this time that the ring of contiguous cauldrons was replaced by a votive offering presented by the Corcyraeans: this was a bronze statue of a boy holding a whip with three chains of *astragali*, or knuckle-bones, which, when agitated by the frequent winds in the valley, chimed against a bronze bowl placed nearby. After the burning of the sacred groves in 219 BC the temple was enlarged with an Ionic portico and an adyton, and the peribolos rebuilt with an Ionic propylon. A solitary large oak has been planted by the archaeologists beside the site of the original sacred tree.

Beyond are two successive versions of a Temple of Dione, and a Sanctuary of Heracles. These are overlain by an Early Christian basilica, which incorporates an honorific decree of 180 BC. A depression in the ground towards the east end marks the original baptismal pool. Dodona sent a bishop to the Council of Ephesus in AD 431, but the basilica is probably of Justinianic date.

THE VIKOS GORGE

The Vikos Gorge (Farangi Vikou; Φαράγγι Βίκου) lies at the northeast end of the Pindus mountains north of Ioannina and is one of the most magnificent natural landscapes in Greece. According to the Guinness Book of Records it has the steepest walls of any gorge in the world, and has a scale and grandeur comparable to the Grand Canyon in the United States. The Zagoria region was inhabited by pastoralists in Antiquity. Little is known of the history after the Slav invasions, when the area was settled by the invaders. The name Zagori is of Slav origin. After 1431, and the occupation of Epirus by the Ottomans, the 14 villages of the central Zagoria were granted a degree of autonomy providing they supplied horses and stablemen for the Ottoman army. This arrangement continued until 1868, and benefiting from contact with the Ottoman civilisation, Zagori citizens travelled all over the Empire and often traded as merchants, bringing capital and a degree of investment to their home villages. Zagoriots also served the Empire as diplomats, soldiers and doctors. After about 1870, the Zagoria went into decline, and continual wars and inter-ethnic violence has reduced the population from the 30,000 or so people who lived here in the late 19th century to about 6,000 today. The region was a stronghold of the resistance to the Nazi occupation, and many villages were burnt by the Germans and Italians. Today's cultural and economic revival began after about 1980.

EXPLORING THE VIKOS GORGE

Vitsa (Βίτσα) is an old stone-built village with extensive views of forest-clad mountains. Excavations here have revealed a settlement and cemetery of the 9th–4th centuries BC (finds in Ioannina; *see p. 513*). Some of the graves were covered with stone tumuli and have produced rich material. Monodendri (Μονοδένδρι) at 1090m is a traditional village, with a church dating from 1620. There are plenty of small hotels heareabouts. There is a staggering view down into the gorge from the upper village, a sight 'beyond words', in the view of one 19th-century traveller. A path beyond Monodendri's square leads in 600m to the monastery of Aghia Paraskevi (1612), perched high on a sheer cliff above the Vikos Gorge itself. The cells and frescoed chapel have been restored and vertiginous paths with perilous bridges lead on to caves and hermits' cells. In the lush gorge (long stepped descent) the river Voïdomatis runs northwest to Vikos village.

Monodendri is also a good place for walking. The there is a marked path that is reasonably clear, which follows a walk (7–8hrs) that can be terminated by ascending to Vikos. The road from Monodendri continues to the Oxya viewpoint (car park). The village of Kipi (Κήποι) has a wonderful little Byzantine church, Aghia Paraskevi, on dizzy heights above the gorge.

Papingo (Πάπιγκο) or Megalo Papingo is a delightful stone-built village (perhaps a little self-consciously 'Epirot') with good tavernas and shops, overshadowed by the surrounding mountains. The road climbs through lush country and then, after spectacular views north over the plain of Konitsa, descends through the pleasant village of Aristi, where there is a turn to Vikos (4km), above the gorge. At Kleidonia, on the north bank of the Voïdomatis (path, left, in 30mins), near the small deserted monastery of Aghii Anargyri, excavation of a Palaeolithic rock shelter began in 1981. A steep zigzag ascent leads back to Papingo. A mountain stream

Typical Epirot cobbled street in the village of Monodendri.

between Papingo and Mikro Papingo has been dammed to provide a swimming pool. Mikro Papingo is a good place to begin walks on Mt Gamila (3hrs to the refuge at 1950m; 4hrs to Lake Drakolimni; almost 6hrs to the summit at 2480m).

THE VIKOS-AOÖS NATIONAL PARK

Vikos Alpine Club: Megalo Papingo, T: 26530 41138.

The National Park covers about 13,000 hectares,and extends from about 500m above sea level to 2480m at the summit of Mount Gamila. To the north it is dominated by the massive range of Tymfi, with many peaks above 2000m, and the deep ravine of the river gorge. The Zagoria region, with its fine traditional villages, is developing as an ecotourism and walking centre.

There are some outstanding Ottoman monuments, mostly bridges, some within the Aoös river ravine. The region has a unique natural flora which for hundreds of years was used as the basis for traditional medicinal practice in Greece: the so-called 'Vikos doctor' herbalists.

The fauna of the park includes the brown bear, otters, wild goats, wild boar, deer, eagles and other rare birds. Illegal hunting and taxidermy, however, have led to a threat to the survival of many species.

Kipi and Koukouli make good bases for exploration. The Anavasi map of the Zagori National Park is highly recommended for walkers and all those who wish to explore the region fully. The routes centre on the Tymfi mountains to the north. There is a mountain refuge hut at Astraka, at an altitude of 1900m on the brow of the peaks between Astraka and Lapakos (*open May–Oct*). There is also cross-country skiing in the winter. NB: Mountain rescue facilities are limited, and it is better to travel accompanied, and to take a mobile telephone.

KONITSA & ENVIRONS

Konitsa (Κόνιτσα) is a pleasant and friendly mountain market centre, which commands the road from the hillside above the gorge. The birthplace of the mother of Ali Pasha, it was conquered by the Turks of Murad II in 1440. In the winter of 1947–48 its army garrison withstood attacks from the Democratic Army led by General Markos Vafiades, who intended to make it his capital.

Just before the town you pass (right) the narrow entrance to the colossal gorge through which the Aoös river emerges from the Pindus. To the right of the modern road, the river is spanned by a fine one-arched bridge (1871), with a Bailey bridge carrying the old road in between. About two hours' delightful walk up the gorge is the Monastery of the Genisis tis Theotokou, founded in 1774 and restored after its destruction (apart from the church) by the Germans in 1944 (*key must normally be obtained from the office of the Metropolitan in Konitsa but this will not admit you to the church unless a church official is present).* The scenery is especially dramatic from the more arduous upper level path which has to be used when the river is high. To the northeast towers Smolikas (2637m), highest peak of the Pindus; to the south Gamila. Mount Smolikas has numerous summer Vlach settlements.

Above Konitsa's central square can be seen the house of Hussein Bey, a fine mansion made by local builders and, higher, the more ruinous family house of Hamkos, the mother of Ali Pasha. Above is the kastro. In the lower part of the town survives the minaret of the mosque of Sultan Suleiman the Magnificent (1536). There is also a small folk museum. The Ottoman monuments are in a very neglected condition.

The Albanian border

About half an hour to the west of Konitsa is the Kokkini Panaghia (Koimisis tis Theotokou; 1412), with frescoes. As it flows towards the Albanian frontier, the Aoös is crossed by two ancient bridges at Bourazani and Mertzani. The road runs through beautifully lush and fertile country to the delightful and beautifully kept **Monastery of the Koimisis tis Theotokou** below Molybdoskepastos. This dates to the reign of Constantine IV Pogonatus (668–685), founder of the archbishopric of Pogoniani. It was restored by Andronicus Comnenus in c. 1183. The frescoes were restored in 1521 and there is 14th-century woodwork. In **Molybdoskepastos** itself there are several interesting churches. Aghii Apostoloi, with frescoes, has a belvedere overlooking the river Sarandaporos and Albania. Kalpaki, a road junction of great strategic importance, commands the chief route into Greece from Albania.

The main road makes a steep ascent with views of Mt Gamila, whose rugged peaks rise to 2480m. After the junction below Geroplatanos, the road descends in loops to the Voïdomatis, crosses it below the Vikos Gorge, and runs through an upland plain growing melons. To the north and west of Geroplatanos, Vasiliko has a 17th-century church of Aghios Georgios with frescoes; Palaiopyrgos and Kato Meropi have several excavated tumuli with cist tombs and finds from the 11th–4th centuries BC, also some later, as well as a partly investigated prehistoric settlement (see Ioannina Museum; *p. 513*).

SOULI & ITS MOUNTAINS

Paramythia (Παραμυθιά), a large village picturesquely scattered on the slopes below the west scarp of Mt Korillas, is the chief place of the eparchy of Souli. Its name, which means 'consolation', is variously derived. It was called by the Turks *Aij Donat Kalessi* and by the Venetians *Castel San Donato*, names again variously explained as a corruption of the ancient *Aidonati* or after the 4th-century Donatus, Bishop of Euroia.

In the 18th century Paramythia was the capital of one of the three sanjaks of Epirus, and was one of the most important urban centres of the Ottoman administration. The Pashas of Paramythia reported directly to the military governor of Roumelia, based at Monastir, now Bitola in modern FYROM. There is a magnificent Ottoman fortress above the town, but this and other Ottoman monuments and antiquities are obscure and difficult to find: the only building the inhabitants will be able to direct you to with certainty is the late Byzantine church of the Panaghia Paramythias in the lower town. Its original structure dates from the 13th century, with 19th-century additions. Also in the lower town are one or two bey's houses. At the top of the town there is a very fine Albanian *kulla* tower house of a large clan, incorrectly described as Venetian in much local literature.

Above the town is the ruined kastro, built on Hellenic foundations. It is difficult to find, in the forest roads (you go north for c. 5km along the main road, then turn towards Petousi). At Veliani, southeast of Paramythia, remains of a 7th-century basilica may mark the see of the Bishop of Photiki.

Ancient Elea and the Acherondas Valley

The hilltop Illyrian **fortress of *Elea*** is an outstanding Archaic site 2km from Paramythia in the little village of Chrisavgi, where a winding track leads to up to the ruins. Walls of huge cyclopean blocks dating from the 4th century BC enclose a natural rock platform. The walls are best preserved on the east side, and run about 800m around the site perimeter, 6m high and up to 4m wide. The central area is divided into two zones, with remains of a large tower on the perimeter. Huge limestone boulders litter the hillside by the gatehouse in the east wall. There are magnificent views in all directions. Elea was destroyed by the Goths in the 6th century. In the middle of the site the remains of a small Hellenistic theatre, market and temples can be seen.

The road south follows the enclosed valley of the Cocytus (Kokytos; one of the rivers of the Underworld) below the steep scarps of Mt Paramythias. At Prodromi a rich Macedonian warrior cist burial beneath a mound was found in 1979. Finds included a fine bronze hydria used as the ash urn, gilded wreaths and iron weapons and armour.

Further south the road diverges from the Cocytus to meet the **Acherondas**, just above Glyki, possibly the site of *Euroia*. There are the remains of a church of the Despotate, supposed to be the burial place of Bishop Donatus. The Acherondas is the mystic Acheron of mythology, the 'river of woe' across which Charon ferried the dead to the Underworld. It comes down from the mountains of Souli and flows through a deep and gloomy ravine with precipitous sides, suggesting the terrors of Hades. At Glyki the gloom lifts and the river enters the wide plain of Fanari, where it traverses meres and swamps, never wholly dry even in summer, and which were known to the ancients as the Acherousian Lake. This is a lovely place with a poetic atmosphere. There is canoeing and white water sports on the rushing turbulent river. The river (boat trips from Parga) flows past Ephyra, site of a mystic cult of the dead (*see overleaf*) and enters the sea at the pleasant village of Ammoudia on the Bay of Fanari, south of Parga.

Souli

A track from near Glyki (signed 'Σκάλα Τσαβελαίνας') leads through the gorge, and after 1hr turns north and enters by a narrow pass into the region of Souli, with its grand and impressive scenery. The **Castle of Souli** stands on an isolated hill near the village of the same name (memorials), 366m above the Acheron. It was one of the strongholds of the Souliots, a tribe of Christian Albanians who played a seminal role in the Greek War of Independence, mustering about 4,000 fighting men and women. Their territory, like Montenegro, was a centre of stubborn resistance to Ottoman rule. From 1790 they were at war with Ali Pasha until 1803, when at great cost he captured their principal fastnesses, and they retired to the Ionian Islands. At the outbreak of the War of Independence most of the Souliots returned to the mainland, where they again engaged the Turks. Among them was Markos Botsaris, defender of Missolonghi.

Margariti, the Çam *Margelleci*, is now a tiny place, with a few hundred inhabitants, but despite its size controls an eparchy of a few neighbouring villages. In medieval and Ottoman times it was an important centre. In 1850 there were about 40 main families, of which the vast majority were Muslim Çam. They had close relationships with Albanian landowners in Souli. Remains of two fortresses crown neighbouring heights: that to the south is substantial; that to the north has a Albanian bey's mansion.

The Souli road winds up through Tsangari, and across desolate, treeless mountains with an occasional flock and isolated farmhouse to **Koukouli**, where there is a short dirt track section near the dramatic and isolated summit, with magnificent views in all directions. Descending eastwards back towards Ioannina, you cross wooded hills and prosperous small farms, meeting the Ioannina–Arta main road near Aghia Paraskevi.

EPHYRA & KASSOPE

Southeast of Morphi, in a part of the Acheron valley planted with cotton bushes, Kastri occupies the site of *Pandosia*, with imposing Classical walls. Immediately before the Acheron crossing, a right turning leads in 5km by a dyke-road to Mesopotamos. Here, on a rocky hill above the confluence of the Cocytus and the Acheron (Periphlegethon), are the remains of the Necromanteion of Ephyra, oracle of the dead and sanctuary of Persephone and Hades. From the site the extent of the ancient Acherousian Lake is obvious; the river flows on to the sea through willows and poplars. The acropolis of Ephyra (under excavation) rises at the north end of the ridge on which the Necromanteion stands and c. 600m distant: it has a prehistoric cyclopean wall and tumuli with Late Helladic burials.

THE NECROMANTEION OF EPHYRA

Open daily summer 8–8; winter 8–3. Entrance charge.
The Necromanteion is the most remarkable example of an ancient oracle that has survived. The buildings are unique in Europe, and should be a top priority on any visit to the region. It is an astonishing construction set on top of a small hill near the Acheron river valley, sinister in atmosphere with labyrinthine corridors and windowless rooms, both above and below ground. The structure, excavated between the late 1950s to the mid-1970s by Sotirios Dakaris, extends over three levels. At the top the small church of

Aghios Ioannis Prodromos, a modern development, dates from the 18th century. Immediately below are the Hellenistic levels destroyed by fire in 168 BC. These consists of a rectangular structure in polygonal masonry with outer walls 3.3m thick and inner partitions in fired and unfired brick c. 1m in width. They define a central area and three long north–south rooms on either side. Below the central area is a chamber measuring 4.50m by 4.50m with a stone roof supported by 15 arches. Finds include bronze rings, ratchet wheels (now in the museum in Ioannina), jars full of broad beans, wheat, barley and lupins, agricultural and woodworking tools, 22 iron blocks, several libation vessels and a number of figurines of Persephone, the goddess of the Underworld.

Ephyra as the House of Hades: the romantic interpretation

Influenced the proximity of the Acheron and the Cocytus, two of the rivers of the Underworld, Dakaris interpreted the site as the House of Hades, the Necromanteion of Thesprotia, one of the entries to the Underworld where the pilgrims came in Antiquity to communicate with the dead. The location first mentioned in Herodotus (*V, 92*) in connection with Periander, tyrant of Corinth, who sent emissaries to contact his murdered wife Melissa in the 6th century BC, is described in detail in the *Odyssey* (*X, 505–32*), though Homer mentions no buildings. His is a purely geographical description complete with instructions for the correct libation procedures to raise the dead.

According to Dakaris, the ancient visitors entered from the north end of the building and progressed towards the inner sanctuary, moving in a labyrinth through stages of preparation and purification to confront the dead—a stressful undertaking, since the dead were apparently always angry. Pilgrims were helped in the process by the priests, who fed them on a diet of lupins and broad beans, which can have hallucinogenic effects. Eventually the deceased was made to 'appear' by the priests operating a machinery of weights and counterweights (the 22 iron blocks, the bronze rings and the ratchet wheels). Although Dakaris's interpretation was not unanimously accepted, the tourist industry was quick to cash in: it is possible take a boat ride from Ammoudia up the Acheron to Ephyra, with a local dressed as Charon, the ferryman of the Underworld.

Ephyra as stronghold: the prosaic interpretation

James Wiseman who co-directed the Nicopolis Project, a Greek-American survey of southern Epirus in the 1990s, focused on the evolution of the landscape of the area. In Antiquity the Acheron flowed more to the south of the ridge where Ephyra stands. It emptied directly into the *Glykis Limen*, the 'sweet harbour' (modern Fanari Bay). Over time the river became impounded and formed the Acherousian Lake first mentioned by Thucydides (5th century BC); this gradually filled by natural alluvial processes and by Turkish times was a swamp. It was eventually drained after the First World War. According to Wiseman, the Acheron only carved out its present course close to the Necromanteion in the 18th–19th centuries. At the same time the coastline underwent alterations. The modern Fanari Bay, now a modest 700m by 350m, and ten metres deep, was much larger in Antiquity. The ridge where Ephyra stands would have been a promontory jutting into it. The Glykis Limen could accommodate 150 ships (according to Thucydides, talking of the Corinthians in 433 BC) and as many as 250 in 31 BC (according to Cassius Dio describing Octavian's preparations before the Battle of Actium). Over 1,000 years later, Anna Comnena was able to anchor a large fleet there (1089 AD). Wiseman therefore sees Ephyra as a site of strategic importance and the building itself as a fortified farmhouse for a large household, an arrangement of which there are other instances in the area, all with the same fine polygonal masonry. He interpreted the underground room as a possible water reservoir and pointed out that lupins and broad beans were staples in Antiquity, and that if properly processed presented no hallucinogenic danger. This interpretation has received support from Dietwulf Baatz, an expert on ancient military equipment, who re-examined the metal remains identifying the bronze rings as part of a catapult and other remains as missile points.

KASSOPE

The road reaches the coast at Loutsa and follows it south. About 3km beyond Lygia, as the road begins to ascend again, a right turn (unsurfaced; signed 'Restaurant Artolithia') leads in c. 1.5km to the concealed site of an impressive 3rd-century Roman nymphaeum. Keep left at houses until the road bends sharply over a stream. The remains, surrounded by thick undergrowth and hard to see from a distance, are c. 100m above the road before the turn. The main chamber (of three) has four entrances and six semicircular niches and belongs to the 3rd AD. It may have been in the grounds of a private estate. Returning to the main road you turn right and rejoin the new highway near Riza, where a site at Panaghia may be ancient *Kassope* (signposted from Kamarina). The ruins were discovered in 1951–55; excavations were resumed in 1977–83.

The site
Open daily 8.30–3. Free entry.
The attractive site sits on a broad plateau facing south, with a high acropolis behind. The city was laid out on the Hippodamian system and protected by polygonal walls. It was founded before the middle of the 4th century BC in order to protect the fertile valley to the south from the exploitation of Elean colonists. The city flourished in the 3rd century, when large public buildings and private houses were built. In the same period it even had its own mint. Its prosperity came to and end in 168–167 BC, when it was torched by the Romans, and later it was abandoned in favour of Nicopolis.

The excavations have concentrated around the agora. This was bound on the north by a stoa, its north side supported by buttresses, the interior divided into two by a row of 13 square pillars. The anterior colonnade was of 27 Ionic columns, in front of which are 21 bases with inscriptions dated to the 3rd and 2nd centuries. The prytaneion, on the west side of the agora, had a central peristyle court with Doric columns and six rooms arranged around it. On the east side was a stoa with 13 Doric columns, in front of which extended an open precinct with bases and altars. The katagogeion (probably a hostel) had a central peristyle court surrounded by four stoas. At the back of these were 17 rooms with table and hearth, all with independent access. A number of houses have been excavated north of the katagogeion. One of them, House 5, had a central court, an open courtyard, the men's quarters (*andron*), kitchen, baths and subsidiary rooms. It was damaged by the Romans in 167 BC and temporarily repaired afterwards.

Kassope's two theatres, though of similar date and style, are different in size and located at opposite ends of the town. The smaller odeion (with capacity for c. 2,500 spectators) in the agora is probably the earlier, and doubled as a bouleuterion. The larger theatre, seating 6,000, affords superb views to the distant sea.

Continuing up the road you see (100m, left) the remains of a Temple of Aphrodite (Ionic, prostyle) and, beyond that, part of a defence wall blocking the pass. The road climbs a further 400m to the **Monastery of Zalongo**, where the Souliot mountaineers took refuge when attacked by Ali Pasha. Sixty women escaped with their children to the summit, where, after performing their traditional dance, and singing the famous song, 'As the flower cannot grow on sand, so the women of Souli cannot live without freedom', they threw themselves over the precipice. This act is commemorated by a huge sculpture above the monastery (footpath).

PRACTICAL INFORMATION

GETTING AROUND

• **By air:** Preveza is the main regional airport, though there are few flights, except a daily Olympic airways shuttle to Athens, and some summer charters. Even in summer, it is closed on some days of the week. Ioannina airport has services once or twice daily to Athens; three times weekly to Thessaloniki.
• **By car:** The Souli Pass is often closed by snow in winter, and travel should not be attempted unaccompanied, or if thunderstorms or snow are forecast. **Car hire:** There are car hire offices from Avis, Hertz and the main companies at Preveza airport, but they seem to have few vehicles and prior reservation is essential.
• **By bus:** Daily buses link Igoumenitsa to Athens, and more frequent services to Ioannina, Parga and Preveza. Buses link Patras to Arta (regularly); to Preveza (more scanty service). Preveza KTEL has good bus connections to Igoumenitsa, Athens, Arta, Parga, Ioannina and Patras. There are good, fast services between Ioannina and Thessaloniki. Other buses go regularly from Ioannina to Arta; also Preveza, Perama, Igoumenitsa, Konitsa, Metsovo. There are daily bus links between Ioannina and Dodona. Local buses also run to the Vikos Gorge, mainly to Megalo Papingo.
• **By sea:** In winter stormy seas can sometimes cause problems with services. A foot ferry crosses the strait from Preveza to Aktio.

INFORMATION OFFICES

Arta Plateia Kristalli, T: 26810 78551
Igoumenitsa Port of Igoumenitsa, Hellenic Tourist Association (T: 26650 22227). See also www.epirus.com
Ioannina Dodonis 39, T: 26510 41868.

Good basic accommodation can be
found everywhere, although coastal
resorts only function fully between
Easter and Oct. There is often nowhere
much to stay in small towns in the interior or in the mountains.

Arta
€ **Hotel Ambracia**. Small and cheap,
in a small street below the castle. T:
26810 28311.
€ **Kronos**. In Kilkis square. Convenient.
T: 26810 22211.

Igoumenitsa
Hotels are very good value indeed, and
the town makes an adequate base for a
no-frills trip to see the major Epirus
sites. The main disadvantage is the
noise from traffic connected with the
port and harbour. Options include:
Hotel Egnatia. Friendly and helpful, on
the main square. T: 26650 23648.
Hotel Oscar. Odos Ag. Apostolon 149,
T: 26650 22675.

Ioannina
For a city of its size and importance,
Ioannina does not have a particularly
extensive choice of hotels, and some of
the cheaper places are really very poor
indeed: grubby concrete barracks with
little attention to the guests, and not
particularly cheap. The best choices are:
€€€ **Epirus Palace**. Massive new
place on the main road south of the
town. Restaurant. T: 26510 93555,
www.epiruspalace.gr
Hotel Galaxy. In Pyrrhus square
(Dimokratias). T: 26510 25432.
€€ **Hotel Kastro**. Highly recommended if you like a traditional place to stay,
in a town house inside the frourion
walls. Beautifully renovated and aston-

ishing value. T: 26510 22886 and
22780; www.epirus.com/hotel-kastro
Hotel Xenia. Very helpful staff, and
good modern facilities. T: 26510 47301.
Konitsa
Filoxenia. Very traditional and friendly.
T: 26550 23330.
Perama
€ **Hotel Ziakas**. Small and traditional
and prettily situated near the lake. T:
26510 81013.
Preveza
€€ **Preveza Beach**. Large seafront
hotel, probably the best in town. T:
26820 51481.
Preveza City. T: 26820 89500;
info@prevezacity.gr
Syvota
There are several small hotels and
apartment buildings near the harbour.
For a list, see www.syvota.info
€ **Criana Studios**. T: 26650 93521.
€ **Hotel Filakas**. Perhaps the best-situ-
ated. T: 26650 93345.

Vikos Gorge
Ano Pedina: € Hotel Ameliko, T:
26530 71501; €€€ Primoula, T:
26530 71133, www.primoula.gr
Koukouli: € Dimon Hotel, T: 26530
71760; € Guest House Koukouli, T:
0653 71070.
Megalo Papingo: € Lakis Inn, T:
26530 41087; €€ Papaevangelou, T:
26530 41135, www.epirus.com/
hotelpapaevangelou
Kipi: €€ Artemis' House, T: 26530
71644, www.epirus.com/spitiouartemi; €
Robinson Expeditions, T: 26530 51217.

Arta
Taverna Spiros Tomas. Very good

meat and game. Kilkis square.
Ioannina
By far the best restaurants are on the
lake island where lake fish like eel, pike
and carp is cooked, along with organic
local trout from Pindus mountain
streams. The latter can be expensive.
Sputino. Under the kastro walls.
Elegant, with good Italianate cuisine. T:
26510 73984.
Igoumenitsa
Restaurants and tavernas are cheap and
traditional. It is worth bearing in mind
that, like any other major port, there
are some places best avoided if alone,
especially at night.
Syvota
There are good tavernas along the harbourside.

FESTIVALS & MUSIC

Threspotia Festival, held each year,
usually in early August.
Ioannina CDs of local musicians playing the famous Epirus clarinet are well
worth buying, and live concerts in the
summer can be outstanding.

LOCAL SPECIALITIES

The old Ottoman market in Ioannina is
still more or less intact and still has
some local craft goods; you can also
watch them being made. Silverwork is a
Ioannina speciality, with some very fine
work for sale at reasonable prices.

BEACHES

There are very good Blue Flag beaches
near **Syvota**, mostly to the south of the
town. Try Mega Ammos or Zavia, with

lovely views and a café, or Aghia
Paraskevi. There are also good beaches
near **Igoumenitsa**. As elsewhere in
Epirus, however, the sea only really
warms up in the July–Sept period. The
bay of Chrysogiali, 1.5km to the west of
Parga, has a superb sweep of beach.
Lichnos beach, 2km to the south, has a
good campsite and a Blue Flag.

VISITOR SERVICES

Preveza
Airport Information T: 026820 22355;
Police T: 026820 22225;
Tourist Police T: 026820 25489;
Port Authority T: 026820 28854.

BOOKS & BACKGROUND READING

Arta
A useful tourist booklet (1993) is avail-
able in various languages and, for those
with some knowledge of Greek, there is
K.T. Yiannelos' Τα Βυζαντινά Μνημεία τής
Ἄρτας, 1990, published by the Town
Council, and Ὁδοιπορικό στην Ἄρτα by
B.N. Papadopoulos (2002).
Ephyra
A useful book in English is *The Ancient
Underworld and the Oracle for
Necromancy at Ephyra* by Spyros
Mouselimis, Ioannina, 1989.
Ioannina
A fine book depicting the Second World
War period, in English, is Nigel Clive's
A Greek Experience 1943–1948. A useful
local guidebook is *A Tourist Guide to
Epirus* by Lambros Malamas.
Parga
A useful local volume is *Parga* by
Periklis Karaminas.

THESSALY

Thessaly (Θεσσαλία), one of the most fertile areas of Greece, and in summer one of the hottest, consists of a vast plain surrounded on three sides by mountains, with the Aegean sea to the east. It has a reputation as a dull and flat agricultural area, inhabited by politically curmudgeonly small farmers—but there is much to see and do. Meteora is a famous monastic centre, and Pelion is a lovely region for ecotourism.

The province has three large towns: Larissa, its political centre; Volos, its chief port; and Trikala. They are all recommended centres for exploration. Thessaly's most important archaeological remains are from the prehistoric era. In the Tertiary epoch the whole plain was under water. It is nowadays drained by the Pineios (Peneios), which rises in the Pindus and, joined by substantial tributaries, flows through the Vale of Tempe into the Gulf of Thessaloniki. The surrounding mountains are covered with forests of pine, oak and beech; the plain yields corn, tobacco, cotton and fruit. The horses of Thessaly have always been famous; Thessalian cavalry helped the Athenians in the Peloponnesian War. Cattle and sheep thrive on its pastures. In the mountains bears, wolves, and wild boar used to be common, but uncontrolled hunting has led to badly depleted numbers.

The population includes Albanians and Vlachs. Few are still nomadic shepherds, but there are large communities in the towns.

The convent of Rousanou in the Meteora.

HISTORY OF THESSALY

In Antiquity Thessaly also included the long narrow valley of the Spercheios between Othrys and Mt Oiti, in which is the city of Lamia (*see p. 477*). Thessaly was divided into four tetrarchies, an organisation which subsisted up to the Peloponnesian War. The divisions were *Hestaeotis* (region of Trikala) in the northwest; *Thessaliotis* (including Pharsalus, now Farsala) in the southwest; *Pelasgiotis* (Larissa) in the east and northeast, in which was Skotoussa, the original home of the Dodona oracle; and *Phthiotis* (Othrys) in the southeast, which included the Homeric city of *Phthia* and was the country of Deucalion and of Achilles and his Myrmidons. There were also four secondary divisions: *Magnesia*, covering the peninsula of that name; *Dolopia*, south of Thessaliotis, inhabited by the ancient race of the Dolopians who fought before Troy; *Oetaea*, in the upper valley of the Spercheios (now part of Phthiotis and Phocis); and *Malis*, a district on the shores of the Maliac Gulf (Gulf of Lamia), which extended as far as Thermopylae.

For some time after the conquest, Thessaly was governed by kings who claimed descent from Heracles. Later the kingship was abolished and the government in the separate cities became concentrated in the hands of a few great families descended from the kings. The most powerful of these were the Aleuadai, who ruled at Larissa, and their kinsmen the Skopadai, whose seat was at Krannon. Pausanias tells us that the Aleuadai betrayed Thessaly to the Persians in 480 BC. The attitude of these northern oligarchs was never cordial to the rest of Greece, although, according to Thucydides, the common people of Thessaly liked the Athenians. As time went on, the rulers formed themselves into a kind of confederation. Each of the four main divisions remained politically independent but, to guard against the contingency of war, a chief magistrate (*Tagos*) was elected, who had supreme command. He was generally one of the Aleuadai.

Other cities of importance in Antiquity were Pharsalus and Pherai (modern Velestino). About 374 BC Jason, tyrant of Pherai, was elected Tagos. His rule and that of his successor Alexander (d. 357) was so harsh that the Thessalians solicited aid from the Thebans and threw off their yoke. Twenty years later, Philip of Macedon, similarly invited, annexed the whole country to his own dominions. In 275 Pyrrhus, king of Epirus (*see p. 498*), made himself master of Thessaly and Macedonia. In 197, the Romans took Thessaly under their protection, as part of a Roman province. Larissa soon became the political and religious capital.

In the 12th century, after a succession of invaders, Thessaly became the centre of a Bulgar-Vlach kingdom known as Great Wallachia. The Turks conquered the country in 1389 and held it for five centuries. The Congress of Berlin (1878) assigned to Greece Thessaly and the district of Arta; three years later Turkey ceded to Greece the whole of Thessaly south of the Pineios. Greece obtained the remainder of Thessaly after the war of 1912–13.

TRIKALA & ENVIRONS

Trikala (Τρίκαλα; also Trikkala; pop. 50,000), the third largest town in Thessaly, is attractively situated on both banks of the Lithaios (locally *Trikkalinos*), some distance from its confluence with the Pineios, at the end of a low ridge. Modern Trikala is a busy regional centre, clean and well organised. It was the birthplace of the great *rembetika* musician Vassilis Tsitsanis (1915–84). It is also the watermelon capital of the country.

HISTORY OF TRIKALA

Trikala is the *Trikke* of Homer, the domain of Podaleirios and Machaon, the two sons of Asclepius, 'cunning leeches' who led the Trikkeans to the Trojan War (*Iliad II, 729*). The earliest of all the temples to Asclepius stood here, and in later times the town had a medical school of repute. The plain of Trikke produced the finest of the renowned Thessalian horses, the features of which are reproduced in the frieze of the Parthenon. The name Trikala first appears in the 12th century. Under the Turks Trikala was the chief town of Thessaly despite periodical uprisings such as that of Dionysios 'the Skylosophos', its bishop (*see p. 512*). Reuters correspondent W. Kinnaird Rose gives an interesting picture of the revolutionary atmosphere in the liberation period in his book *With the Greeks in Thessaly* (1897). In the 20th century the town was firmly Venizelist and anti-royalist. After the battle for Athens in 1945, Trikala became one of the ELAS (Communist guerrilla) strongholds, and has always had a strong radical streak in its political identity.

The town centre

The river Lithaios divides the town. On its banks are numerous cafés, under attractive avenues of plane trees. The Plateia Riga Feraiou on the south bank (with a bronze group commemorating five local resistance heroes hanged by the Germans in 1944) is connected by bridges with Plateia Ethnikis Antistaseos and the large central Plateia Iroön Polytechniou. There are a number of important bronze statues in and around the plateia, the most important of which is a statue of General Serafis (1890–1957), the military leader of the ELAS anti-Fascist resistance. The central bridge across the river was built in 1886, and the conflux of water and fountains is very attractive.

The archaeological potential of Trikala received confirmation in 2005 with the identification during building work in the centre of town of the first sanctuary dedicated to Hermes discovered in western Thessaly. So far the perimeter sandstone walls have been uncovered together with clay votive figurines dedicated to the god of commerce.

On the north bank of the river, Odos Sarafis leads west to the impressive kastro, a Byzantine fortress on Hellenistic foundations, where the lower ward has a tourist pavilion with very attractive fountains and a good view. There is a very fine and richly decorated late Ottoman castellated clock tower.

The mosque

The Kursum or Osman Shah Djami is a mosque built by local craftsmen in 1557 to the designs of the great Ottoman architect Sinan Pasha. It has a fine soaring dome and (originally) an external arcade. The building has been superbly restored as an exhibition centre, and is a glorious tribute to Sinan's architectural genius. Immediately to the south of the mosque is the Mausoleum of Osman Shah (d. 1567/8), a probable nephew of Suleiman the Magnificent, who commissioned the mosque.

Mimar Sinan (1490–1588)

The architect Mimar Sinan, said to have designed the mosque in Trikala, was a genius the first order and a wonderful example of the social mobility that was possible in the Ottoman Empire. He was the son of either an Armenian or a Greek priest, and as a boy was taken in a *devşirme*, the Ottoman system of taking children from Christian families and training them as Janissaries. Sinan entered the Janissary engineering corps, where he was involved in designing barracks and bridges and other civil projects. Later he was commissioned by the Porte (actually by wife of the Sultan, Roxana) to design a public bath (near Haghia Sophia) and afterwards was set to designing the new kitchens in the Topkapi. It was the beginning of a great career. The combination of enthusiastic patronage (he worked under three Sultans) and his own genius resulted in some 90 buildings. What is most interesting is the way in which Sinan adapted Christian prototypes to Muslim use. Haghia Sophia (after some 1,000 years of standing inert, un-copied, un-developed and with a good number of structural problems that were never solved) became the main influence on his creation of a distinctly Ottoman architectural idiom. In a Christian basilica attention is focused through the apparently diminishing columns, on the apsidal area, or else divided between the dome and the apse. In either case the focus is within the building. For a Muslim the focus is many miles away, in Mecca, hence what is important is the *kibla* wall (the wall against which the faithful queue up to pray), which faces Mecca. What Sinan did was to take the Byzantine-Roman-Hellenistic tradition that had evolved in Christianity and invert it in such a manner that it became Islamic.   N.S.

The Varousa district

On the east slopes of the kastro is Varousa, a picturesque quarter of Ottoman houses. The principal Byzantine churches are here. While several lay claim to an early foundation, many surviving remains were rebuilt and redecorated in the 19th and 20th centuries. Aghios Dimitrios, which incorporates ancient blocks in its construction, has a gilded wooden *templon* and 17th-century frescos. Aghia Marina (18th-century) also has frescoes. Aghii Anargyri was refurbished in 1575 and painted soon after: the figures include the two bishops Bessarion, both later canonised. Aghios Ioannis

Prodromos is 17th-century with frescoes. Aghios Stefanos, the cathedral church in Trikala in the 14th century, was probably founded by Symeon Uroš, Emperor of Serbia, who had his capital in Trikala until 1355. The church was destroyed and rebuilt in the late 19th century and many of its contents transferred to Panaghia Faneromeni (damaged by fire in 1991), and to Aghios Nikolaos, cathedral church of Trikala since 1967. The earliest cathedral may have been the church of the Archangelos, the remains of which are on the Byzantine kastro. There is an archaeological collection (*not often open*) at Odos 25 Martiou 31.

The Asclepieion

Close to the church of Aghios Nikolaos (north of Odos Sarafis) are some remains of what may be the Asclepieion, excavated by the Greek Archaeological Service intermittently since 1902. In view of the legends concerning the origins of the Asclepius cult in ancient *Trikke*, this site is of great potential interest (*for more on the cult, see Epidaurus, pp. 246 & 249*). Visible buildings (badly kept, and partly overlain by the foundations of a Byzantine church, probably that of the 10th-century monastery of Aghios Nikolaos) include a Hellenistic stoa and a Roman bath, perhaps representing different phases of a therapeutic complex laid out round a court.

ENVIRONS OF TRIKALA

Gomphoi and Dousiko

Passing the railway station the road leads southwest across the plain, which is often flooded by the Portaïkos torrent, above which stands the village of Lygaria. At 12km there is a left turn to **Gomfoi** (Γόμφοι; 3km), a village on a hill overlooking the Pamisos. Lazarina, to the east, has a stud farm.

Ancient *Gomphoi*, on a wooded ridge between the modern village and Mouzaki (sign to 'Archaeological Site' on the road between them), was of considerable importance by reason of its domination of the chief pass from Thessaly into Epirus. It was fortified by Philip II. In the civil war it supported, to its cost, Pompey against Caesar. On its site the Byzantines founded the city of *Episkope*. The situation is pleasant and some sections of the walls can be traced, but there is not a great deal to see. Many ancient blocks are incorporated in the houses of the village.

Returning to the main road, you see the great cleft of the **Stena tis Portas**, a beautiful defile through which the Portaïkos emerges from the Pindus. On the right, halfway up the mountain, is the monastery of Dousiko (*see below*). Pyli stands at the entrance to the defile, with an attractive single-arched bridge built in 1514 by St Bessarion as one of his civic projects to help the people of his native region; a pebble mosaic decorates the rock face on the far side. A kilometre and a half upstream is the delightful **church of Porta Panaghia** (founded 1283; the narthex probably later). Within, the figures of Christ and of the Virgin are amongst the finest Byzantine mosaics in Greece and, as icons, unique. On the splendid marble iconostasis the figure of Christ is on the left, a reversal of customary Orthodox iconography.

On the same side of the river, but further east (signs from bridge) is the **Monastery of Dousiko** (5.5km; *women not admitted*), known locally as *Ai Vessaris*, which stands at 762m above its village amid chestnuts and limes. It was founded in 1515 by St Bessarion (later Archbishop of Larissa), and completed in 1556 by his son. The monastery is on a grand scale with 336 cells, a library of importance and an imposing church with a full cycle of frescoes and a carved wooden iconostasis (1767).

The heights of Kerketion

The road climbs from here, at first through a broad valley. The scenery is spectacular, a combination of tree-clad slopes (firs dominating as the altitude increases) and bare towering peaks. Elati, with rooms and hotels, lies on the west side of Mt Kerketion. The village is delightful in the summer and a centre of winter sports. Local produce is sold by the roadside. Higher up to the right is the Hatzipetros refuge (1250m) from which the summit of Kerketion (1900m) may be climbed.

Seven kilometres beyond Elati is a Thessaloniki University Forestry plantation (the research station is further on, at Pertouli). The road drops into an attractive plateau where, every May, the Sarakatsanoi (*see box*) hold a gathering. Pertouli, cold even in August at nearly 1220m, lies beyond the watershed. Neraïdhochori, with some unappealing new building, stands above the infant Acheloös. The 18th-century church of Aghia Paraskevi, with a separate upper-storey chapel, lies 4km further on to the left. Major construction works at Mesochora mark the site of the controversial Acheloös project, which will divert part of the westward-flowing river to help with the irrigation of Thessaly, east of the Pindus. The consequences for the environment of western Greece are far from clear.

Argithea and the Panaghia Spilias

A green and gentle landscape spreads between Trikala and Mouzaki. Passing through Mouzaki, you leave to the left a turn for Pevkofito and Moni Spilias (*see below*). The road runs through a delightful valley, rich in vegetation. Beyond a turn for Drakotripa the road climbs and there are retrospective views over the valley and Thessalian plain. At Oxya bare peaks rise above high fir-covered slopes to a height of 1758m. On reaching the summit you descent to **Argithea**, nestling deep in its mountain valley.

The antiquities of this region, ancient *Athamania*, are not well known. Athamania sided with first Sparta and then Athens in the alliances of the 5th and 4th centuries. In the 3rd century it was dominated by Pyrrhus, later becoming an independent kingdom, which reached its greatest extent in the 2nd century when it stretched into the Thessalian plain. In 191 it became a Macedonian province and in 168 gave allegiance to Rome. Ancient townships have been identified with varying degrees of certainty. One settlement may be the ancient capital of *Argithea*: numerous tombs (4th–1st centuries BC) belonging to the site have been examined. Near Petroto (at Palaiokastro) a fortified Hellenistic site and associated cemetery have been investigated.

Intrepid explorers with tough vehicles can assay visits to two interesting churches in the Argithea area. Ten kilometres further beyond the village there is a turn right for

Anthiro, which is 3km away. Four kilometres further is the small monastery of the **Genisis tis Theotokou**, with 17th- and 18th-century paintings (*at present being attractively restored*). The katholikon has two storeys, the upper (19th-century frescoes) being a double church dedicated to to Zoödhochos Pigi and Aghii Anargyri (*keys must be sought from the priest in Anthiro*).

In the mountains to the south is the spectacularly situated 17th-century monastery of the **Panaghia Spilias** with 17th–18th-century paintings (*accommodation and food available in summer*). The smaller church (Koimisis tis Theotokou) is 17th century, the larger (Zoödhochos Pigi) is 19th century. (*NB: if Moni Spilias is the sole objective, it is faster to get there via Vlasi and Pevkofito to the turn outside Mouzaki, 42.5km from the monastery: this route also involves about 25km of bad roads, stretches of which are being improved.*

THE SARAKATSANOI

The Sarakatsanoi are the nomadic shepherds of mainland Greece. Their traditional pasturelands were among the Pindus mountains, and the pattern of their transhumance was to spend the summer in the Rhodope region of Thrace and Bulgaria, migrating south on 26th October, St Dimitrios' Day. Today the nomadic lifestyle is no more, and the people have settled in Thrace, Epirus and Attica. Greek-speaking, their origins are unknown, but they are believed to be a pre-Neolithic race; indeed scholars have traced a line between their folk art and the Protogeometric styles of Antiquity. Patrick Leigh Fermor writes of them in *Roumeli*; A.Wace and M.Thompson's *The Nomads of the Balkans* is another classic work.

Lake Megdovo and Karditsa

NB: The entire lake area is covered by the map on p. 442.

Lake Megdovo (Lake Plastiras) can be approached from several different points. The lake is formed by the Tavropos Barrage (conceived in 1925 by Plastiras; *see opposite*, and opened in 1959) on a tributary of the Acheloös. After serving electrical generators, the water provides irrigation in the plain and finally discharges into the Pineios. Above the lake's eastern shore stands the monastery of Koroni, with a 16th-century church. The circuit of the lake is an attractive drive, especially through the wooded landscape at the northwest. There is a belvedere at Neochori to the southwest about 15km above the dam, which is crossed by the road (cars only).

Mitropoli, east of the lake, stands on the site of ancient *Metropolis*, which was a civic centre made up of several towns, including Ithome (*see below*). With *Trikke* (Trikala), *Pelinnaion*, and *Gomphoi*, it was part of a fortified rectangle protecting the approach to the Thessalian plain. Excavation has revealed fragments of the town, including sections of the walls. The circuit was apparently 16-sided, a small acropolis within. Metropolis was captured in 191 BC by Flamininus and occupied by Caesar before the Battle of Pharsalus (*see p. 480*). A Mycenaean tholos tomb was discovered to the south in 1958.

Further east, at **Kallithiro**, excavated sections of 4th–3rd-century ancient *Kallithera* have been excellently displayed (visible from street) at basement level below the modern buildings.

Lake Megdovo.

Outside Katafygi is the interesting **Moni Petras**, dedicated to the Panaghia. The church (*under restoration; guard on site in summer, otherwise key from Katafygi*) dates from c. 1600, with extensive frescoes (including a fine donor scene) and a carved wooden *templon* and other furniture. A side chapel is dedicated to Aghios Sotiros (the Holy Saviour). At the village of **Philia**, an important pan-Thessalian sanctuary of Itonian Athena was located in 1963. Excavations yielded fine Geometric and Archaic bronzes and other material from Mycenaean to Early Christian. There is now nothing to see at the site though Roman inscriptions from the sanctuary are built into the church of the Taxiarchs at Melissochori to the west. On a prominent hill to the north, near the hamlet of **Pyrgos**, are some remains (also partly beneath the village) identified by an inscription found at Mataranga (*map p. 442*) as ancient *Kierion*, a place Stephanus of Byzantium equated with Thessalian *Arne*. At Mascholouri, a fine bridge over the Sofaditikos may be as early as the 13th century.

Karditsa (Καρδίτσα), the capital of its nomarchy, is an uninteresting town, laid out on a rectilinear plan in Turkish times. It has no ancient associations. An important market centre attracting custom from the Thessalian plain and from the mountainous Agrafa region, it trades in tobacco, cereals, cotton, silk and cattle, and is served by the Thessalian railway. Its buildings are liberally adorned with storks' nests. There is a pleasant park. Methane gas has been discovered in the vicinity. Karditsa was the birthplace of Colonel Nikolaos Plastiras (1883–1953), leader of the revolution of 1922, and republican prime minister for just three months in 1945.

Fanari is situated on the west side of a rocky hill called 'the Beacon' (φανάρι). The fine Byzantine fortress which marks the summit is conspicuous for miles around. The wall is preserved to c. 14m and there are six towers, a cistern and (?) church within. Its foundation date is uncertain but it was important in the 13th–14th centuries. The structure incorporates ancient masonry. This was the site of 'rugged Ithome' of the *Iliad*; it was 'a heap of stones' in Strabo's day.

FROM IOANNINA TO METSOVO

This road across the northern Pindus, the main arterial route across northern Greece, is one of Europe's great mountain journeys, and has views of unsurpassed grandeur and scale. Though major improvements to the road are in progress—including the construction of a controversial tunnel through a section of the mountains near Metsovo—it remains a tough drive, but in spring, summer and autumn is well worth undertaking. In winter the road can be closed by blizzards; in bad weather conditions at other times, a 4WD vehicle is helpful.

In 1807 Colonel Leake (*see box overleaf*) observed that the Ioannina–Metsovo road, 'although the high road to Constantinople and the only frequented communication between Epirus and Thessaly, is in the most neglected condition. The late autumnal rains have left it only just passable'. Ali Pasha established *hans* along the entire route, from Ioannina to Trikala, but only a handful had individual rooms; in most, conditions were squalid, with travellers often accommodated with their animals. The road in those days and up until the 20th century followed a more southerly route than it does now, using the river valleys, so the hard-pressed traveller left Ioannina by tracks above the lake and then ascended the hills to stay the first night at one of the better *hans*, that of Drysko, modern Driskos village, 3km south of the modern main road near Aghia Paraskevi monastery, and then followed the bed of the Arachthos river up to Metsovo. The paths by the river are suitable for summer hiking trips, and there are some fine surviving Ottoman bridges along the way. A particularly fine single-span bridge is the so-called 'Papastathis Bridge', near Driskos, in a ravine on the old river course. The final arduous day would have been spent ascending the valley, reaching the Three Hans, near modern Votonosi village, arriving in the northern Ottoman *mahalas* of Metsovo, then called Prosilio. The main task of the people of Metsovo in those days was to run a band of *armatoli* for the Sultan, whose job was to protect travellers from bandits. Ali Pasha instituted a system whereby each village where a *han* was situated was obliged to nominate a *han*-keeper and supply food for sale to travellers, often an onerous obligation. There are many fine accounts of the colourful difficulties of *han* life in the works of British and American travellers in the late Ottoman Empire.

The downward route from Metsovo to Thessaly left the modern road at Malakasi village, and proceeded through the forests south of the modern road by the gravel river bed to the *han* of Kotovazdi, and then a further six hours' ride down to the *han* of Kalarytes, to Kalambaka and Meteora.

William Martin Leake (1777–1860)
Lieutenant Colonel Leake has been called the greatest of modern topographers. He is chiefly remembered for his work on the topography of ancient Greece, and for three great tomes: *The Topography of Athens* (1821), *Travels in the Morea* (1830) and *Travels in Northern Greece* (1835). All three are still used as source material today, especially for the identification of ancient sites, where Leake's conclusions—made through a combination of science and instinct—have often proved spot on.

Leake was educated as a soldier, meaning to take up a career in the Royal Artillery. It was thus that he acquired the skills of surveying and reconnoitring terrain. During the Napoleonic Wars, in 1789 and again in 1804, Leake set off on military missions to Turkey and Greece. His task was to consult the Ottoman governors on how best to defend their territory against the French. The mission stretched over several years, during which time he travelled all over the country on reconnaissance trips, for some of the time staying in Ioannina at the court of Ali Pasha (*see p. 517*). After the fall of Napoleon and the repartition of Europe, Leake never visited Greece again. He used his journal and notebooks as the source of his published works, settled down and married the widow of an old friend, and was a founding fellow of the Royal Geographical Society.

Modern Metsovo

NB: If you are travelling mainly to visit Metsovo, there is a lot to be said for making the jour-ney by KTEL coach, to enjoy the views and avoid the trouble both of driving and of finding somewhere to park. An overnight stay in Metsovo is highly recommended. In spring, autumn and winter, take plenty of warm clothing. Hiking boots are useful in wet weather, even in the town—and essential outside it.

Metsovo is a charming little mountain town lost in the remote heights of the north-ern Pindus. Set below the main road in a vast mountain chasm, below the alpine Aoös Lake, at an altitude of about 3000m, this characterful place, with its picturesque tra-ditional houses, its predominantly Vlach population—and some Sarakatsan settled pastoralists—is well worth a visit.

There are about 6,000 permanent inhabitants in Metsovo and its immediate envi-rons, although the population rises considerably in the summer, when diaspora Vlachs return home. Metsovo was originally a Vlach village which grew to prosperity as an essential stopping point on the route across the Pindus for ancient and medieval traders, and for Ottoman mule caravans. The name appears in chronicles in 1380. In the 18th century, with the improvements in economic conditions in the Ottoman Balkans, it became a trading centre based on the products derived from the large flocks of the Vlach herdsmen, and was a boom town in the time of Ali Pasha. It trad-ed mainly with Ioannina and the Epirus coast. The French traveller Pouqueville observed in the early 19th century that 'the Metzovites are all concerned with mer-chandise: and the most active *kiradgis* or muleteers of Turkey in Europe belong either to Metsovo, or its neighbour Zagori beyond the mountains'. Metsovo was liberated from Ottoman rule in October 1912. In the 20th century it was best known as the home town of the political and philanthropic Averof family. To the south of the main square in a house constructed in 1988 in traditional style, there is an interesting art museum holding parts of the Averof collection of modern Greek art (*open 9–1.30 & 4–7.30; T: 26560 41210*).

KALAMBAKA & THE METEORA

NB: A visit to the Meteora needs at least half a day, even if confined to the three principal monasteries, and with the use of a car.

The attractive little town of **Kalambaka** (Καλαμπάκα) spreads fanwise on the green slopes at the foot of the Meteora near the point where the Pineios emerges from the Pindus gorges. Kalambaka is the *Aiginion* of Antiquity, a town of the Tymphaei, stated by Livy to have been impregnable. Here Caesar joined Cnaeus Domitius before marching on Pharsalus. The Byzantines called the town *Stagoi*, perhaps a corruption of ἐις τοὺς ἁγίους, and established a bishopric here in the 10th century; the see is now at Trikala.

The cathedral, dedicated to the Dormition of the Virgin (Koimisis tis Theotokou), bears an inscription ascribing its foundation to Manuel I Comnenus (mid-12th centu-ry). The chrysobul of Andronicus III painted on the north wall of the narthex concerns the privileges of the diocese, not the building of the church. The present building, an aisled basilica, stands on even earlier foundations; some mosaics survive below the sanctuary floor. The *synthronon* in the apse as well as the ciborium and centrally-placed ambo probably belonged to the earlier building. There are several layers of paintings. From the 12th-century decoration have survived some frescoes on the north wall of the diakonikon. The remaining scenes were painted by Cretan artists after a reconstruction in 1573, when the narthex and cloisters were added. The church of Aghios Ioannis Prodromos (11th–14th centuries) is constructed of Roman materials.

The Meteora

The Meteora (Τα Μετέωρα) are a series of monastic buildings perched on a cluster of detached precipitous rocks. These are composed of a stratified conglomerate of iron-grey colour scarred by erosion of wind and streaked by centuries of rainwater. 'They rise' (in the words of Dr Henry Holland, who visited them in 1812) 'from the comparatively flat surface of the valley; a group of isolated masses, cones, and pillars of rock, of great height, and for the most part so perpendicular in their ascent, that each one of their numerous fronts seems to the eye as a vast wall, formed rather by the art of man, than by the more varied and irregular workings of nature. In the deep and winding recesses which form the intervals between these lofty pinnacles, the thick foliage of trees gives a shade and colouring, which, while they enhance the contrast, do not diminish the effect of the great masses of naked rock impending above'. Awe-inspiring in the most favourable conditions, the landscape in lowering weather or by the light of the full moon is daunting in the extreme.

Visiting the monasteries

The monasteries can mostly be visited daily 9–1 & 3.30–6; Aghios Stefanos is closed on Mon, the Metamorphosis on Tues, the Great Meteoron on Thur and Barlaam on Fri. There is now no guest-house. Rules of dress must be observed (no trousers for women or shorts for men). The best place for a quiet visit to the site, to escape the crowds and to sense the grandeur of the rock formations, is from Kastraki. Beyond the Kastraki turn the road bends right. On the left stands the Doupiani Chapel, rebuilt in 1861. To the left is the 'Broad Rock' (*Platys Lithos*; 534m), on which stands the Great Meteoron, rising above several lesser pillars. These are the cleft rock of the Prodromos, whose scanty ruins—already deserted in 1745—are now inaccessible; Aghios Nikolaos tou Anapavsa (c. 1388), on a higher point near the road, partly repaired in 1960 when its frescoes, by Theophanes the Cretan (1527), were restored; and the inaccessible Aghia Moni, dangerously perched on its slender pinnacle in 1614 and ruined in an earthquake in 1858. Leaving Rousanou to the right, you take the left fork, passing Barlaam on the left, and arrive at the largest and loftiest of the monasteries, the Great Meteoron, or coenobite Monastery of the Transfiguration.

The monastery of Aghia Triada.

HISTORY OF THE METEROA

The earliest monastic community here, the 'Thebaid of Stagoi' at Doupiani, developed before 1336 among the hermits who sought in these caves religious isolation and a secure retreat from the turbulent times. Their *protaton*, or communal church, is located by a small chapel on old foundations. Before the end of the century this had been eclipsed by the Meteoron, which, with other communities, was encouraged and endowed by the Orthodox Serbian conquerors of Thessaly. During the Turkish conquest the monasteries became an asylum for refugees. At its largest the community numbered 13 monasteries, all coenobite—in other words with all property held in common—and around 20 smaller settlements. They flourished under Abbot Bessarion in the time of Suleiman the Magnificent, deriving revenues from estates on the Danube granted by the *voivodes* of Wallachia. The Patriarch Jeremias I (1522–45) raised several of them to the rank of imperial *stavropegion*. They declined in the 18th century, and were already a decaying curiosity to early 19th-century travellers. They lost their independence to the Bishop of Trikala in 1899. The road that now makes the visit a commonplace of tourism has shattered the solitude and isolation. There are now only a handful monks and nuns, largely occupied in receiving visitors. However, continuing religious occupation seems assured by the Church's policy of a period of monastic service for its priests.

Access to the Meteora was intentionally difficult, either by a series of vertical wooden ladders of vertiginous length (20–40m), which could be retracted at night or in emergency, or in a net drawn up by rope and windlass to specially built towers, overhanging the abyss. The old methods, uncomfortable at best and often perilous, gave way in the 1920s to steps cut on the orders of Polycarpos, Bishop of Trikala, though the rope and windlass remained in occasional use for taking in provisions.

The Great Meteoron and Ypapandi

The **Great Meteoron** (Μεγάλο Μετέωρο) was founded by St Athanasius as the poor community of the Theotokos Meteoritissa, the Virgin of Meteora. Its privileges were guaranteed in 1362 by the Serbian Emperor Symeon Uroš and under the guidance of John Uroš, his son, who retired here c. 1373 as the monk Ioasaph, it became a rich monastic house. Euthymius, Patriarch of Constantinople (1410–16), made it independent of local jurisdiction, but its head was not officially granted the title of Abbot (*hegoumenos*) until c. 1482.

The katholikon was reconstructed by Ioasaph in 1387–88, at his own expense. His apse and sanctuary, painted in 1497–98, form the east extension of the existing church, which was enlarged after an earthquake in 1544. It is a Greek cross-in-square with a dome set on a drum. The paintings are well preserved. The refectory (1557), on the north side of the church, has a vaulted roof set on five pillars.

From the southeast corner of the monastery (or from the path in the ravine towards Barlaam) there is a striking view of the neighbouring rock. Here among the vultures' nests can be made out two painted icons and broken lengths of the ladders that once gave access to **Ypselotera** (Ὑψηλοτέρα), highest of the monasteries and dedicated to the 'Highest in the Heavens'. This convent was founded c. 1390 and disappeared in the 17th century, possibly owing to the danger of the ascent.

About 30mins north of the Broad Rock is the seldom-visited **Ypapandi** (Ὑπαπάντη), derelict but still accessible, in a huge cavern. It deserves a visit for its brightly painted frescoes and gilded iconostasis. The inaccessible Aghios Dimitrios stands on top of a nearby rock. It was destroyed by Turkish gunfire in 1809 after having served as headquarters of a local klephtic band.

Barlaam and Rousanou

The monastery of **Barlaam** (Βαρλαάμ) is approached by bridge from the road. The windlass and rope in the tower (erected in 1536) were much used for materials in 1961–63 when the refectory was reconstructed as a museum for the monastic treasures. The founders in 1517, Nectarios and Theophanes Asparas of Ioannina, reoccupied a site where a 14th-century anchorite named Barlaam had built a church dedicated to the Three Hierarchs. This they restored and it survives (repaired and frescoed in 1627–37) as a side chapel of the present katholikon erected in 1542–44. This is a good example of the late-Byzantine style, with a carved and gilded iconostasis and frescoes by Frangos Kastellanos and George of Thebes (in the narthex; 1566).

Rousanou (Ρουσάνου) is a small monastery compactly set on a lower hill. The approach is by bridges, built in 1868. It was founded before 1545 by Maximos and Ioasaph of Ioannina, but by 1614 had decayed to such an extent that it was made subject to Barlaam. It is now occupied by a convent of nuns. The church, with an octagonal dome, is a smaller version of that of Barlaam, with frescoes of 1560.

Aghia Triada and Aghios Stefanos

Aghia Triada ('Αγ. Τριάδα), the monastery of the Holy Trinity, situated on an isolated pillar between two ravines, is entered by 130 steps partly in a tunnel through the rock. Off the passage leading into the courtyard a round chapel carved out of the rock was dedicated to St John the Baptist in 1682. The little church of 1476, ornamented in brick and tile, was not improved by the addition in 1684 of a large and ugly narthex. The conventual buildings are in an attractive half-timbered style with a pretty garden.

The **Moni Aghiou Stefanou** ('Αγ. Στεφάνου), or nunnery of St Stephen, is the only monastery visible from Kalambaka. It is easily reached since its solitary pinnacle is joined directly to the Kyklioli hill by a bridge. The convent was founded c. 1400 by Antonius Cantacuzene (probably a son of Nicephorus II of Epirus), whose portrait in the parecclesion (the original katholikon) was defaced by Communist rebels in 1949. The new katholikon, rebuilt in 1798, is dedicated to the martyr Charalambos, whose head is the monastery's chief relic.

PRACTICAL INFORMATION

GETTING AROUND

• **By car:** Do not attempt to travel across the Pindus if heavy snowfall is forecast. If the weather is doubtful, carry a mobile phone, snowchains and supplies.

• **By rail:** Thessaly is traversed south–north by main-line trains, with branches to Volos, Karditsa and Trikala. Trikala is on the main Volos–Kalambaka line, with slowish trains about three times a day, T: 24310 73130. To Kalambaka from Trikala (40mins) trains go six times daily.

• **By bus:** Trikala is linked to Larissa (frequently), Karditsa (frequently), Athens (regularly), Volos, Thessaloniki and Ioannina (2–6 times daily); also to Grevena (once daily). Local buses to Pyli and Mouzaki (regularly), to some Pindus villages: Desi, Mesochora (2 or 3 times a week). Buses from Karditsa also serve many of the villages, though infrequently. There is a weekly bus from Trikala to Argithea, continuing to Arta. There are frequent and fast services from Trikala to Kalambaka and Metsovo (c. 45mins).

INFORMATION OFFICES

Kalambaka Kondyli and Hatzipetrou 38, T: 24320 75306, www.kalampaka.com
Trikala Tzitzani 31, T: 24310 76817

WHERE TO STAY

It is not difficult to find a room in this part of Thessaly: there are plenty of small hotels dotted around everywhere and rooms are very cheap.

Karditsa
Arni. Small hotel (31 rooms) in an early 20th-century stuccoed building, occupying a corner site in the centre of town. Completely modernised within. Karaïskaki 4, T: 24410 22161.
Meteora (Kalambaka)
The town has some of the classic attributes of a tourist trap. That said, there is no shortage of accommodation, though none of it is outstanding, and there is a bit of a rip-off mentality. It is worth paying for one of the more expensive places.
€€ **Amalia**. Attractive modern hotel on the southern side of town, about 2km south (car needed).
€€ **Divani Meteora**. This is probably the best option, on the southern outskirts by the National Road. T: 24320 23330, www.divanis.gr
€ **Antoniadis**. Basic modern decor. Trikalon 148, T: 24320 24387. €
Kaikis. Next door to the Antoniadis. Trikalon 146, T: 24320 75280.
€ **Rex**. Modern, clean, good facilities. Slightly unsympathetic decor, but an acceptable choice. Patriarchou Dimitriou 7, T: 24320 22042, www.hotelrex.gr
Meteora (Kastraki)
Odysseon. Situated on the road between Kalambaka and Kastraki village. 22 rooms. T: 24320 22320.
Trikala
Trikala has some very good value middle range hotels. Air conditioning essential in summer. For some reason most Trikala hotels do not serve breakfast.
€ **Divani**. Pleasant, near the river. Dionisiou 11, T: 24310 027286.
€ **Lithaion**. Convenient for a quick stopover, by the KTEL bus station. T:

24310 20690, www.litheon-hotel.gr
€ **Ntina**. Perhaps the best situated in
town, in the pedestrian area, in
Asklipiou. Helpful staff. T: 24310
74777.
Penellenion. A finely restored late
19th-century building opposite the
river bridge. Many famous politicians
have perorated on its balcony. The hotel
was opened in 1914 and is a rare survivor from that era in northern Greek
hotels. Plateia Riga Feraiou, T: 24310
73545, panellin@compulink.gr

Metsovo

There are plenty of nice rooms in traditional buildings, most near the main
square. In mid-summer reservation is
necessary. It can also be busy in winter,
particularly around Christmas and New
Year. Options, all good value, include:
Bitouni. T: 26560 41217; **Egnatia**. T:
26560 41263; **Kassaros**. T: 26560
41800; **Godevenos**.T: 26560 41166;
Profitis Ilias. T: 26560 41095.
Neochori (Lake Megdovo)
Katsaros. Stone-built chalet-style guest
house with five suites, some with self-
catering. A good base for exploring the
region. T: 24410 93195.

WHERE TO EAT

Metsovo
The Café Krini is a good taverna, as is
the Galaxias hotel/restaurant. Lamb and
kid is the main speciality.

Trikala
Trikala is rather short of good restaurants. Two suggestions are given below.
Aigli. A fine historic restaurant, within
the Neoclassical Panellenion Hotel, with
some—mainly winter—local specialities. Plateia Riga Feraiou, T: 24310

73545, panellin@compulink.gr
Taverna Ethlos. Around the corner
from the Aigli; cheap and cheerful.

LOCAL SPECIALITIES

Metsovo has outstanding traditional
craft shops, particularly for carved
wood products, wool sweaters and
rugs, and for local sheeps' cheese and
other food products. Smoked cheese is
a Metsovo speciality. There is a drink-
able local light red wine, from Katogi.

VISITOR SERVICES

Metsovo has the only reasonably efficient banking and money changing
facilities for miles around. Many places
do not accept credit or debit cards.

HIKING & CLIMBING

The plain can be very hot and tiring in
mid-summer, and serious archaeological
exploration or hiking are best undertak-
en in milder weather. Both mountains
and plains can be subject to sudden
changes of temperature, particularly in
spring and autumn. In winter the
Pindus mountains have a very cold climate and in some years there are major
blizzards. Metsovo is a lovely place to
walk and the National Park to the north
preserves many elements of traditional
pastoral life. Take care with sheepdogs.
Wolves and bears live in the forests but
are not often seen.
Kalambaka Alpine Club. Vlahava 13,
T: 24320 22386.
Metsovo Alpine Club. N. Gotsou 2, T:
26560 41689.

MAGNESIA &
MOUNT PELION

VOLOS

Volos (Βόλος; pop. 90,000), a characterful and historic town, is the chief port of Thessaly. The town is the gateway to the popular and famous Mount Pelion tourist area, with its wonderful rugged beaches and winter skiing. The modern harbour dates from 1912, but some form of maritime town has existed in the area from prehistoric times. It is the main channel of Thessalian exports: cereals, cotton and olives. With its mills, tanneries and refineries, now of industrial archaeological interest, Volos was a potential rival of Piraeus until stricken by two disastrous earthquakes in 1954 and 1955. The town's attractive site between Mt Pelion and the Gulf, its excellent museum and the quality of its hotels and restaurants, make it a pleasant base.

EXPLORING VOLOS

Entering the town from the junction with the Larissa road, you pass, on your left, the rising ground where lay ancient *Iolkos* (Iolcus), also with medieval buildings. The road then enters Plateia Riga Feraiou, a huge triangle bordering the picturesque fishing harbour. The Dimarcheion (Town Hall), in traditional Pelion style with interesting doors, is by Dimitris Pikionis (1887–1968), an architect who was much influenced by Greek vernacular styles, as well as by the art of Giorgio de Chirico. De Chirico was born in Volos, where his father was working as a railway engineer, and studied Fine Art in Athens. Inside the building is a series of woodcuts illustrating episodes in the history of Volos and upstairs, a fascinating series of late 19th- and early 20th-century photographs of the town and its environs. On the corner of Odos Metamorfosios, at the east end of the square, is the Volos Odeion (Music College), in a lovely Neoclassical building with a fine interior.

Beyond the fishing harbour, the busy quayside leads to an open space, the social centre of the town, which fronts the landing stage. Here a model of the Argo forms a graceful monument to the past. The quay is continued east for nearly a mile as the Argonafton, a splendid esplanade, venue of the *volta*.

Old Volos

West of Riga Feraiou, between the railway station and the football stadium, is the older part of Volos, known as Palaia. The red-light district is opposite the port entrance, a maze of tiny Ambleresque streets and alleyways. The area used to be known as the 'Russian Market', and had a resident Russian population. The railway station building is a remarkable Art Deco fantasy designed by Evaristico de Chirico, Giorgio de Chirico's father.

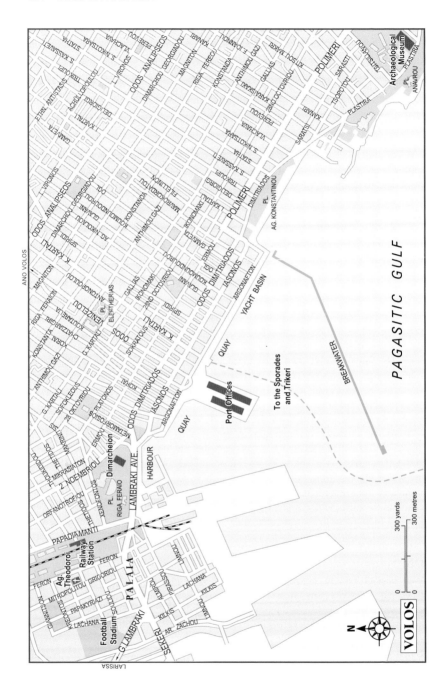

Archaeologically, the most important part of this area of Old Volos is the mound (412m by 320m by 9m high) of Aghii Theodoroi. Excavations close by the church (in Mitropolitou Grigoriou) have revealed the remains of a Classical temple (columns reused in the balustrade of the terrace) and later remains. Pieces of ancient masonry can be seen round about. Opposite the church are the remains of an Early Christian basilica. Extensive finds have been identified (D. Theocharis, 1956) as those of **ancient Iolcus**. In the modern suburb of Nea Ionia, to the north, parts of the ancient cemetery have been excavated.

Iolcus (Iolkos), famous in legend as the place from which the Argonauts set out in quest of the Golden Fleece, had a flourishing existence. The site at Aghii Theodoroi was important in Early, Middle and Late Helladic times and probably had continuity of occupation down the ages. Greek mythological personages (King Pelias, the uncle of Jason, Eumeios and Alcestis), have inevitably been associated with the site. With other towns, it was depopulated by Demetrius Poliorcetes and its inhabitants moved to Demetrias (*see p. 558*). Other locations (*see Dimini, p. 560*) have also been proposed for Iolcus in Mycenaean times.

The main prehistoric excavations (overgrown and little to see, but thought to include Mycenaean palatial structures) are in Souliou and, at the northwest foot of the mound in Lachana, at which points the impressive remains of the Ottoman fortifications can best be seen. Prehistoric structures are preserved for the visitor in the basement of 68–70 Odos Papakyriazi. At the junction of Kreontos and Mitropolitou Grigoriou is a fine mediaeval cistern. At the south edge of this area (junction of M. Grigoriou and G. Lambraki) excavations on the site of the old vegetable market in advance of rebuilding have revealed basements with *pithoi*. To the west a dried-up river bed may be the remains of the ancient *Anauros*.

JASON & THE ARGO

Jason was the son of Aeson, and heir to the throne of Iolcus in Thessaly. When the throne was usurped by Aeson's half-brother Pelias, Jason retired to the mountain fastnesses of Pelion. There he was brought up by Chiron, the wise centaur. As a grown man he returned to Iolcus to claim his birthright, whereupon his uncle set him a challenge: to fetch the Golden Fleece from Colchis. The Argo, the first longship ever built, with its crew of Argonauts, set sail from Volos harbour for Colchis in the Crimea. The sorceress Medea, daughter of the ruler of Colchis, helped Jason secure the Fleece. With her Jason sailed to Corinth, and the couple lived together there until Jason abandoned Medea for Glauke. Medea murdered the girl in revenge, together with her two children by Jason. After this, Jason lived a life of aimless, wandering solitude beside the Saronic Gulf. He was killed as he lay on the seashore, of a blow on the head, caused by a falling beam from the rotting Argo's prow.

The Archaeological Museum

Athanasakis 1. Open Tues–Sun 8.30–5 (3 in winter); T: 24210 25285. Bus no. 3 from oppo-site the Dimarcheion to its terminus; useful leaflet in English, free.
The attractive, lemon-yellow museum, at the southeast extremity of the town, was founded in 1909 by Alexis Athanasakis. Rebuilt after the earthquakes, it was reopened in 1961. Its collection of c. 300 painted stelae is unique.

Vestibule (Theocharis Room): A changing exhibition of finds from recent rescue excavations in the area con-trolled by the museum, together with a map of sites investigated. A 4th-century sarcophagus from Velestino has a recon-structed burial.

Room A: Painted Hellenistic grave stelae from Demetrias (*see overleaf*); Mycenaean vases and bead jewellery from various sites; Mycenaean and Protogeometric finds from the palace of Iolkos. Geometric pottery from Thessalian sites. In doorway, head of a youth from Meliboias, (modern Melivia), reminiscent of the Critias Boy (*see p. 80*).

Room B: Relief grave stelae and votive reliefs from a variety of sites; Geometric bronzes from Thessalian sites; Palaeolithic flints and bone implements from Larissa, Sesklo (*see p. 561*) and sites in the Pineios valley; Pre-pottery Neolithic tools (7th millennium BC), including a bone and flint saw.

Room G: Excellent displays illustrating various aspects of life in the Neolithic period: architecture, agriculture, stock rearing, implement technology, manu-facture of pottery, jewellery and fig-urines; spinning and weaving.

Room D: More painted grave stelae; good model of site of Demetrias and Pagasae. In the centre, a good male torso in marble (? Roman copy of origi-nal of the 5th century BC). Vases and figurines of Archaic to Hellenistic date; Hellenistic glass vases and gold jew-ellery.

Room E: Offerings from various graves; drawings of tombs and graves; fine case of gold jewellery.

Room Z: An excellent display of recon-structed burials of all periods from Mycenaean to Classical with the skele-tons and grave offerings in place (in some cases, also stelae). Here also are the later stelae from Demetrias.

Ano Volos and Anakasia

Odos Venizelou (popularly known as Iolkou) heads northeast through the centre of town, crosses Odos Analipseos, and ascends towards Ano Volos and the villages of Pelion. A stiff climb (possible also by bus) may be made through the pretty suburb of Ano Volos. The church of the Koimisis tis Theotokou, built in the 17th century, has carved spolia and fragments of bas-relief—some of them very beautiful—incorporat-ed into its exterior walls. The doorway preserves a 13th-century plaque commemo-rating Anna Angelina, a lady of the Comnenus dynasty, who ended her life here as a nun under the name of Anthousa.

Beyond Ano Volos is Anakasia, a medieval village, with houses built on the sides of steep hills rising to 793m. One of the houses has frescoes (1912) by the folk painter Theophilos Hatzimichaïl (1873–1934), famous among other eccentricities for his penchant for dressing up as Ares, god of war, at carnival time. A native of Lesbos, he came to Pelion to work as a shepherd, painting frescoes and murals in his spare time. The murals here were painted as a way of paying for his board and lodging. Though never acknowledged as a genius in his lifetime, his naive style gained many plaudits after his death, and his work now commands fantastic prices. The Kitsos Makris Folklore Centre, at no. 38 Kitsou Makri, also preserves a number of his works.

Goritsa

On the eastern outskirts the road passes a prominent hill (access by road behind the stadium) on which is the site of *Goritsa*. The settlement, above the sea and probably of the 4th century BC, is laid out on a strict grid plan and surrounded by a fortification wall with towers. There was a cemetery outside the west gate. The quarries from which the building stone was cut have been located in the vicinity. Excavation is currently in progress, and a massive tower base on the north side is visible. The outlines of a large ancient urban settlement are being delineated: Goritsa may develop into a major archaeological site. There is a remarkable—if Dickensian and very polluted— view down into the huge open-cast mine beyond the Goritsa hill.

Byzantine fragments built into the wall of the Church of the Dormition at Ano Volos.

DEMETRIAS & PAGASAE

NB: It is a good idea to study the topographical model of the area in the Volos Museum before you visit these sites. In general, access is poor and visiting conditions less than ideal. The remains of the two cities lie c. 3km south of Volos and can be reached by car or bus (take no. 6 opposite the Dimarcheion) along the Almyros road heading southwest.

Pefkakia

A left turn is signposted to Pefkakia, an important a late Neolithic (4500–3200 BC) and Bronze Age settlement with remains of rectangular building with stone foundations, clay floors and hearths. Finds suggest that this was an important commercial harbour and trading post between Thessaly and Thrace, Asia Minor, the islands of the Aegean Sea and southern Greece. Further on is the ancient city of Demetrias.

Demetrias

Demetrias (Δημητριάς) was founded by Demetrius Poliorcetes, the son of Antigonus Monophthalmos (the One-eyed), who assumed control of Asia after the death of Alexander the Great. Demetrius made the town his base and launched from there a number of expeditions against Alexander's successors. One of them earned him his nickname 'the Besieger', from his extensive use of siege machines in an unsuccessful attempt to take the island of Rhodes in 305 BC. His career as warlord was not a great success and came to an end when he attempted the invasion of Asia Minor. Imprisoned by Seleucus, he died in captivity in 283 BC.

Demetrias blossomed as a commercial and political centre between 217 and 168 BC when, after the Battle of Pydna, its fortifications were razed. From the 1st century BC it went into decline. The greater part of its territory was abandoned and the residential nucleus shrunk considerably. It experienced a revival in the early Christian period when important public buildings and two churches with mosaic floors and rich architectural decoration were built. The first one is by the north harbour (Basilica of Damocratia), and a second church at the south end of the town outside the city walls (Cemetery Basilica). In 902 invading Saracens sacked the town which went into terminal decline from c. 1000 when it was supplanted by Almyros as a trading port used by the Venetians, the Genoese and the Pisans.

The site

Excavations in Demetrias began at the end of the 19th century. The ancient town was protected by a strong wall which can be traced for a large part of its length (c. 11 km) except for a large stretch by the harbour. The towers of the east side were repaired and enlarged in a hurry, probably at the beginning of the 1st century BC, during the Mithridatic war. Fortunately for posterity, painted gravestones carried off from the town cemeteries were used in the foundations. Protected from humidity and light, the stelae (349 of them) have maintained their original polychromy. The themes of the paintings include the farewell of the dead, the funeral feast, the servant preparing the corpse, as well as, more rarely, scenes of war and hunting. A particular poignant example is the stele of Hedisti, who died in childbirth. The stelae are now in Volos museum.

The other main feature of Demetrias is the Anaktoron, the Macedonian palace built on a hillock in the eastern section of the town. Situated on the highest spot of the hill, it has a peristyle courtyard with Doric columns, apartments on the three sides, and metal workshops at the north end. A two-storey building, the Anaktoron had four towers at its corners. Walls were painted in grey, red, white and yellow in imitation of marble. The palace was abandoned in the middle of the 2nd century BC at the end of the Macedonian domination in Greece. Part of it was used during the Roman times as a cemetery.

The theatre is some 300m to the west. Built during the 1st half of the 3rd century BC, it was repaired at least four times and permanently abandoned in the second half of the 4th century. Above the theatre is the Heroön, a temple or a mausoleum, while a temple to Artemis Iolkia has been identified on the agora situated south of the Anaktoron.

Painted grave stele from Demetrias (3rd century BC). This and many others found at the site are on display in Volos museum.

Pagasae

Pagasae (Πάγασαι), after which the Pagasitic Gulf is named, predated Demetrias. It has not been identified with any certainty. The port of Iolcus and afterwards of Pherai, Pagasae played a central role in the legend of the Argonauts: it is here that, according to the poet Callimachus, the ship destined to sail to the Colchis was built by order of Athena using the timber from nearby mount Pelion. The town also boasted a famous oracle mentioned by Hesiod and a temple to Apollo built by Trophonius, a mythical architect of Antiquity who, with his brother Agamedes, first used stone in the making of monuments (wood and brick having been used until then).

Pagasae flourished in the 5th century becoming eventually a dependency of the newly-founded Demetrias. The site seems likely to have been partly incorporated in that of Demetrias, and it is often thought that the more southerly loop of the walls belonged originally to Pagasae. The centre may, however, have been further south (2.5km at Soros, otherwise identified as ancient *Amphanai*) or in the area north and east of the theatre where early material has been found.

DIMINI & SESKLO

Open Tues–Sun 8.30–5 (summer); 8.30–3 (winter). Tickets from the Ephorate; T: 24210 85690. Leaving Volos on the Larissa road, take a left turn signposted to Dimini while still in the outskirts of Volos. Dimini is c. 6.5km to the west. Finds from the sites are in the Volos Museum. A descriptive leaflet in English is available. To reach Sesklo, follow the road to Larissa a further 10.5km and turn left over a railway crossing. A tarmac road continues towards the village; after a further 3km follow a sign to the left.

Dimini

The site of Dimini (Διμήνι) stretches over a low hill, today located c. 3km from the shoreline of the Pagasitic Gulf. Excavations and geological investigations found evidence that the settlement was situated very close to the sea in the Late Neolithic era. The excavations have so far extended over 4,000m square, making Dimini one of the better-known Neolithic sites in Greece.

The hill of Dimini was inhabited almost from the beginning of the 5th millennium BC. Curvilinear enclosures (five) built in local slate arranged around a central enclosure suggest times of trouble. About 40 to 50 houses with mud brick walls on stone foundations were built against the enclosure walls. Spaces for communal activities and slated-paved passages between enclosures have been identified.

The largest building of the settlement and probably one of the most important was House N (10m by 5m). The structure showed all the architectural features of a Neolithic house: floor in beaten clay, clay and stone hearths, and rectangular storage areas edged by stones. In the southwestern part of the settlement, a ceramic kiln belonging to a workshop specialising in the production of vessels with incised decoration, typical of Late Neolithic II (also known as Dimini culture) was found between the second and the third enclosure. The kiln consisted of a circular stone foundation where the leather-dry decorated pots were piled. These were completely covered with branches and a layer of fresh clay, a procedure assisting in the control of the firing temperature (c. 850°C).

The economic and social changes observed at the end of the Late Neolithic age are reflected in the use of the hill of Dimini during the Final Neolithic and the Early Bronze Age. House 13 in the central enclosure was enlarged, the passages to the central court blocked, and the hill used exclusively by one family.

After a period of abandonment the site became again an important centre in Mycenaean times. Mycenaean Dimini, which developed east of the Neolithic settlement, has been extensively plotted by remote sensing and has revealed two large *megara* as well as cult and residential areas. Finds show connections with the Levant and Asia Minor, prompting an identification with ancient Iolcus, the city of Jason (*see p. 555*). Two impressive Mycenaean tholos tombs complete the picture.

Sesklo

Sesklo (Σἐσκλο) has given its name to a culture of the Neolithic period extending from Serbia to western Macedonia and covering 100 square miles. The site was discovered at the end of the 19th century. The first excavations, led by Christos Tsountas, took place in 1901–02; they were followed by investigations by Dimitris Theocharis in 1956–77 (both archaeologists are commemorated in memorials on the approach to the site). The site covering Kastraki hill and the surrounding area has a very long occupation dating from the Pre-pottery Neolithic period to the Late Bronze Age. This is due to the fertile arable soil, the abundance of water and the direct access to both the Pelion mountains and the sea of the Pagasitic Gulf. The first inhabitants farmed and raised stock, founding a small settlement on the acropolis in 6500 BC. It consisted of rectangular, one-room buildings with or without stone foundations and with mud-brick walls, built, as in Achilleio (a Neolithic site near Farsala), at a distance from each other. The intervening spaces were used for various activities, including cooking. The earliest settlement may have had a fortification wall, but the evidence is not conclusive (some traces of an unusually thick wall are to be found at the east end of the site).

In the second period, the main phase of the Thessalian Middle Neolithic, the same construction methods were used, and evidence for fortification of the settlement is stronger. Evidence of occupation is found both on the acropolis and in the lower town for an estimated total population of about 3,000 people. There are possible indications of houses with a second storey, and in general the dwellings are more crowded together. One large building of megaron type was found on the acropolis. It was partly overlain by a similar but larger structure belonging to the later phase of occupation. The Middle Neolithic is the major period of the site and is characterised by the distinctive Sesklo pottery (painted red on a light background). This was found in the acropolis, but not in the lower town, prompting suggestions of emerging social stratification. About 4400 BC this settlement was destroyed by an earthquake followed by fire. A half-century hiatus in occupation followed before the site was reoccupied—but only on the acropolis—from the Late Neolithic to the middle of the 2nd millennium BC.

EXCURSIONS FROM VOLOS

Velestino and Skotoussa

The small town of Velestino (Βελεστίνο) is pleasantly situated amid gardens and fountains in a ravine of the Chalkodoni mountains. It was the birthplace of the revolutionary poet Rigas Feraios (1757–98), who was executed by the Turks in Belgrade for working towards a Balkan confederacy.

Velestino occupies the site of **ancient *Pherai***, at one time one of the great cities of Thessaly; its port was Pagasae (*see p. 559*). Pherai was the legendary home of Admetus, whose wife Alcestis sacrificed her life for him, a story that inspired a celebrated tragedy of Euripides and an opera by Gluck. In the 4th century BC the rulers of Pherai tried to dominate the whole of Thessaly and to interfere in the Greek world generally. The most notorious were Jason (not the Argonaut), elected *Tagos* of Thessaly in 374 and assassinated in 370; his successor Alexander; and Lycophron II, driven out in 352 by Philip of Macedon. Rich prehistoric remains (Middle and Late Bronze Age) have been found beneath the modern village. The ancient acropolis is on a trapezoidal plateau to the north of the Vlach quarter; here are the remains of the Larissan Gate and of a temple of Heracles. The city proper extended to the southwest; by the church of the Panaghia (prominent amongst trees above the outskirts of the town) are remains of the walls. Walls and towers uncovered on the hill of Aghios Athanasios show that this too was within the enceinte. Pherai was noted for two fountains, Hypereia and Messeïs. The former is in the centre of Velestino; the basin and conduit are covered with tiles. On the Larissa road, to the right on the edge of the town, a Hellenistic stoa (remains fenced), at least 49m long, was found in 1983. Further on (left) are the remains of a Temple of Zeus Thaulios, rebuilt in the ? 4th century. Archaic bronzes were removed to Athens and Geometric pottery to Volos.

South and west of Velestino rise the mountains of Chalkodoni or Kara Dagh, anciently called *Cynos Cephalai* or **Cynoscephalae** ('dogs' heads') and famous for two battles. The first (364 BC) was between Alexander of Pherai and the combined forces of Thessalians and Thebans. Alexander was defeated but the Theban general Pelopidas was killed. At the second, more famous Battle of Cynoscephalae, in 197, the power of Macedonia was irreparably weakened when the Romans, under Flamininus, totally defeated Philip V of Macedon, the issue being decided by an elephant charge. An uneasy period followed, ending in the Battle of Pydna and complete Macedonian dependence upon Rome.

Further west is the village of **Skotoussa**, near which (to the east) are some remains of the ancient *Skotoussa*, the supposed original home of the Dodona oracle.

Nea Anchialos and Mikrothives

South of Volos, the road leads to **Nea Anchialos** (Νέα Ἀγχίαλος), a village by the sea, founded by refugees in 1906, and occupying the site of ancient *Pyrasos*. This is one of the most important Early Christian/Early Byzantine sites in Greece. Nine basilicas (mid-4th to mid-6th century AD), remains of the city wall, graves and parts of the settlement (including two bathing establishments, sections of a roadway and other houses and public buildings) have been excavated. The city was abandoned about 620. In five large areas of excavation (three of them along the main road) are the five most important basilicas: A, B, G (the basilica of Archbishop Peter), D, and 'Martyrios'. G had two predecessors, the first of them earlier 4th century AD. Beneath this are two even earlier building complexes, one of which might be a shrine of Demeter mentioned in literary sources. Immediately southwest, close to the city wall, a rich monumental baptistery of early Constantinian type, with octagonal font and elaborate facilities for the sacrament of baptism, was found in 1983. It must belong to the original phase of the basilica. Several of these buildings have produced fine mosaics, paintings and architectural fragments, some of which may be seen in the small museum which lies within the site enclosure to the left of the road.

To the west of here is **Mikrothives** (Μικροθήβες), which stands below the flat hill of *Phthiotic Thebes*, ringed by ruined Classical walls with 40 towers, and with remains of a Temple of Athena, a theatre, and a stoa; the walls can be seen from the road (two fields' length away) about 1.5km outside Mikrothives. Finds are in the Volos Museum.

West of here, near the village of Asprogeia, is a **Dervish monastery** of the Bektashi sect (*Tekkes tou Bekasi*) perhaps on the site of a Byzantine foundation. The cemetery includes two domed mausoleia (the earlier ? 16th century). On a hill above Eretria are the remains of *Eretreia* of Phthiotis, a prehistoric site with a fortified acropolis. According to Strabo, it was one of the cities under the sway of Achilles.

Glyfa and the south

Almyros ('Αλμυρός) is the capital of an eparchy, with a small museum. Benjamin of Tudela remarks on the presence of numerous Italian and Jewish merchants at Almyros, and the Emperor Alexius III in 1199 granted trading concessions here to the Venetians. Hellenistic *Halos* lies beside the motorway to the south, its acropolis on a hill to the right. The site, which has been surveyed but not excavated and partially destroyed by quarrying, was probably founded in the Hellenistic period. The town was laid out on a grid plan and surrounded by a wall with numerous towers. The small acropolis (subsequently crowned by a Byzantine fortress) was connected to the town by similar walls which ran down the hillside in a V-shape. The fortifications and the absence of public buildings (though there was an agora) suggest that Halos was a military foundation. At the time of its construction, the site was closer to the sea and effectively dominated the passage between Mt Othrys and the Pagasitic Gulf.

Continuing south on the old road you come to a turn to the left, which leads under the motorway to the Moni Xenias, dating from the 17th century, when it moved down from a higher site, where there are ruins of the 5th–13th centuries. Sourpi, further south, is a nesting-place of storks. Magoula Platanhiotiki, on the Bay of Sourpi is probably the site of Old Halos, destroyed by the Macedonians in 346 BC. Just beyond Sourpi is Mt Chlomon (893m) which guards the Trikeri Strait, the landlocked entrance to the Gulf of Volos, scene in 480 BC of the first encounter between the Greek and Persian fleets. On the mountain's southern foot, by modern Pteleos, lies the site of Homeric *Pteleon*, marked perhaps by a medieval tower on a height nearer the sea (Mycenaean tombs to the northwest). Achilleio, on a deep bay to the south, is a popular bathing-place. Due south again is Glyfa, with boats to Euboea.

About 1.5 hours north on foot from Pelasgia are the remains of *Larissa Kremaste*. Paralia Pelasgias has an Early Christian basilica.

MOUNT PELION

Mount Pelion or Pilio (Πήλιο; 1624m), the long mountain range that occupies the greater part of the peninsula enclosing the Pagasitic Gulf, is one of the most attractive regions of Greece. There are three distinct climatic regions, the very wet and heavily wooded north, which is more or less uninhabited, the central region, centred on Tsangarada, and the dry and arid south. Most visitors head for the Tsangarada villages, but tourism is developing in some small coastal resorts in the south, and road improvements have made most of the region accessible. There are some very interesting Byzantine and Ottoman buildings in the south, and remarkable unspoilt coastal scenery. A car is required here; there is virtually no public transport.

The north and central region, cool in summer but often subject to heavy snowfall in winter, with abundant streams from the upper slopes, encourages a lush vegetation scarcely found elsewhere on the Greek mainland, but winter winds make agriculture more or less impossible on north slopes.

From Pelion's slopes the sea—often hundreds of feet below—is rarely hidden from view, so Pelion life has an Olympian quality. The delightful villages, well-watered and shady, have timber-framed houses with balconies; stone-paved mule paths wind between the gardens. The Pelion churches are low and wide and have an exonarthex supported on wooden pillars, which often extends from the north and south sides of the nave in the form of a covered walkway.

MOUNT PELION IN MYTHOLOGY

The Centaurs were a tribe of wild creatures, half man-half horse, who lived in the mountains of Thessaly. In myth they symbolise unbridled brutish desires, are described as drunk, debauched and brawling, and are frequently depicted battling the serene and noble Lapiths, the forces of civilisation and restraint. One of the centaurs' number transcended his bestial nature and allowed his human, perfectible side to triumph. This was Chiron, who lived in a cave on Mount Pelion, possessed great skill as a healer, and was the tutor of Jason.

Pelion was also where the gods celebrated the nuptials of the mortal Peleus and his bride, the sea-goddess Thetis. Their son Achilles was brought up a mortal (though Thetis dipped him in the Styx to wash his mortality away), and was taught the art of music by Chiron. The trees of the mountain supplied timber for the Argo. Peleus was one of the Argonauts, and it was Thetis who saved the vessel from foundering on the Symplegades.

View of the Monastery of the Taxiarches, near Zagora.

Makrynitsa and the heights of Pelion

The road above Volos winds steeply to **Portaria** (Πορταριά), a beautiful summer resort with a magnificent plane-tree and spring in its square. It has excellent cheese and unresinated red wine. The small church (1273) has frescoes of 1581. From here a by-road diverges round the Megarevma ravine to **Makrynitsa** (Μακρυνίτσα), capital of the the old Ottoman *vakoufia*, a religious endowment of land, of which Pelion was one. Today it is a delightful village, tumbling down its hillside. It contains a number of fine old mansions, many of which now operate as guest houses. The picturesque little plateia has a huge hollow plane-tree, a sculptured marble fountain, a small church with sculptural decoration in the apse, and a fine view. Higher up is the formerly monastic church of the Panaghia (18th century) with Greek inscriptions and Roman and Byzantine carvings built into the walls. A small chapel, with a school below, has frescoes. A street name commemorates Charles Ogle (1851–78), special correspondent of *The Times*, who was killed here (it is said in cold blood by order of the Turkish commander) while reporting on a fight between local insurgents and the Turks. The Votsareas café is famous as much for its ouzo and coffee as for its mural by Theophilos (*see p. 557*) of the freedom-fighting *klepht* Katsantonis, betrayed to the Turks by a shepherd, tied to a plane tree, and battered to death in 1808.

Portaria is the starting-point for the 3.5-hr climb to Pliasidi (1548m), one of the main heights of Pelion. The road climbs in zigzags, then runs along a high ledge with enormous views over the Gulf. Hania (Χάνια; 1158m), the main winter sports centre, is named after the Ottoman *han* that was once an important resting place for imperial travellers crossing the mountain ridge. The village is a pretty, if overdeveloped place, amid beech woods, and stands at the head of the pass with a wide panorama in either direction.

AGRIOLEFKES WINTER SPORTS CENTRE

Information: Volos Alpine Club, Dimitriados 186, T: 24210 25696.
Agriolefkes ('Αγριολεύκες) was one of the first ski centres built in Greece, and is still one of the best. At an altitude of about 1500m, there are five ski lifts of different types, and a total length of piste of about 5,000 metres. There is snow-boarding and cross-country skiing, and a shelter with 80 beds. It is well worth a visit at any time of year if it is a clear day for the extraordinary views, with the Aegean sea to the east, and the Pagasitic Gulf to the west. In the summer mountain biking is popular. It is possible to drive up from Hania and there are good car-parking facilities.

Under the radar-capped crests of Pelion, you descend a tremendous valley through chestnuts, oaks and planes, joining the road from Tsangarada just over a mile short of Zagora.

View down on the rooftops of Makrynitsa.

Zagora and Kissos

Zagora (Ζαγορά), on the mountain's east slope facing the Aegean, is a large community of four hamlets. In the plateia is the church of Aghios Georgios, a typical Pelionic construction, with an 18th-century iconostasis. The countryside around is famed for the variety of its fruit (plums, damsons, pears, peaches, wild strawberries) and its aromatic red wine. The inhabitants of Zagora traditionally earned their living not from agriculture, but as merchants and silk weavers. Zagora was also famous for its school, the first in the region, whose alumni included Rigas Feraios (*see p. 561*) and Anthimos Gazi (*see p. 568 below*).

Below Zagora, on the coast, is **Chorefto**, with a fine sandy beach, from which excursions to the Sporades can be made by boat. The poet Georgios Drossinis found inspiration here, writing his *Ode to Peace*.

Frescoes by the 19th-century artist Pagonis in the church of Aghia Triada at Anilio.

The road from Zagora to Tsangarada is one of the most beautiful in Greece, a splen-did day's walk (29km) in spring or autumn; not so in summer, when visitor traffic is heavier. The road runs fairly level at c. 488m on the slopes, which are clad with oak forests and plane-trees. It passes through the village of Makryrrachi and then **Anilio** ('Ανήλιο), a pretty place, wealthy in the Ottoman period, when it had a flourishing silk industry. It is thought to have been built by immigrants from Epirus, who named it after a village of the same name near Metsovo. Certainly many Epirots came to Pelion to find work. Among them was the painter Ioannis Pagonis, whose early 19th-centu-ry post-Byzantine frescoes decorate many a Pelion church, including that of Aghia Triada at Anilio. The crowning glory of his achievement is at **Kissos** (Κισσός), in the church of Aghia Marina (*open every day; T: 24260 31619*), where the interior is cov-ered floor-to-ceiling with his work. In the four shallow domes the images show Aghia Marina, the Virgin, Christ Pantocrator, and the Eternal Father. The church also boasts a gold-plated limewood iconostasis of exquisite craftsmanship, carved between 1720 and 1760. Below Kissos lies Aghios Ioannis, one of the best beaches on Pelion.

Tsangarada and Milies

Tsangarada (Τσαγκαράδα), verdantly situated amid oak and plane forests at 472m, enjoys superb views down to the sea. A road descends to the fine beach at Milopotamos. Milies (Μηλιές), known for its apple trees, is the birthplace of Anthimos Gazi (1764–1828), who raised the Thessalian revolt against the Ottomans in 1821. During the Second World War it was a stronghold of the anti-Axis resistance and suffered serious reprisals from the German occupiers. Today it is a charming village, and a good base for walks in the Magnesian peninsula. It also has an excellent small museum.

From Milies the road runs east to join the main road above Neochori. After Lambinou the road winds vertiginously in and out of the deep clefts that fissure the east face of Pelion; the view extends to the island of Skiathos.

SOUTHERN PELION

Southern Pelion has had a long history. Under the Ottomans, the south of the peninsula was the centre of Peliot economic and political life. The chief town during Ottoman rule was Promyri, now no more than a small village. When the railway came to Volos, the remote south fell into rapid decline; quarrying remained the only real economic activity, and there was extensive depopulation. In the Second World War the area came under the control of ELAS, the Communist guerrilla resistance, and vil-

Milopotamos beach.

lages were subject to Axis reprisals. After the defeat of the Communists in the Greek Civil War in 1949, Trikeri was used as a place of internal exile.

Tour of the region

A drive through the region can usefully begin from Argalasti, the largest of the villages, from there running down to the coast at Paou, and to **Milina** (Μηλίνα), a developing little fishing village, with nice beaches and rooms for rent (recommended if you wish or need to stay here). The ruins of ancient *Olizon* are on a hill above the village.

From Milina you follow the coast road south into increasingly remote and arid country, with the Monastery of Aghia Tesserakonda on a little island in Milina bay. The new coast road leads to Mavri Petra, and round the bay to Koulouleika, with some Byzantine remains, before veering inland to Marathias, a tiny place in a beautiful deserted bay. Further down the landscape becomes bare and largely treeless, with the isolated little miniature port of Kottes, below Trikeri. There are three very good fish tavernas here (particularly the Tseta). A farmhouse by the sea appears to have ancient or Byzantine masonry in the farmyard wall. Trikeri is 5km away up a hill overlooking both the Pagasitic Gulf and the Euboea channel.

The hilltop town of **Trikeri** commands an important strategic position over the Pagasitic Gulf, with fine views across to northern Euboea. Until comparatively recently, it was accessible only by sea. Although there has been settlement on the site since ancient times, most of the historic town visible nowadays dates from the late 19th century. The minuscule port of Aghia Kyriaki, below the town cliff on the north side of the gulf, is nowadays only used for fishing boats and yachting, although in the past there was a ferry over the gulf to Euboea. The little shipyard using traditional construction methods is interesting, and there are very good fish tavernas. North of Trikeri is Cape Trachili, with the little island of Palaio Trikeri, referring to the Byzantine castle that once stood here, now the monastery of the Evangelistria.

NORTH TO MOUNT OSSA

Roads north from Volos wind up past the marsh of Lake Karla, the ancient *Boïbeis*, once 15m long and 5m wide, with a depth of about 3–4m. Numerous ruins exist of cities that once clustered on its shores. At modern Glafyres are the remains of ancient *Glaphyrai*, where there are the foundations of a temple. Armenio, to the west of the old lake, is named from Homeric *Armenion*, said to lie a little farther west, at Kokkines. The entire plain is dotted with mounds showing prehistoric occupation.

The range of Olympus lies ahead, the highest and mightiest of this coastal chain of peaks. The giants, in their war with the gods, are said to have piled Pelion, the southernmost and lowest of the range, on top of Ossa, in order to reach the summit of Olympus. Mount Ossa, a bold isolated mountain, rises to 1978m between the plain of Larissa and the sea. Its western slopes provided *verde antico* and Atrax marble (serpentine) for the buildings of ancient Rome.

Aghia ('Αγιά) is situated on the southern slopes of Ossa above the gorge dividing Ossa from Pelion, and c. 11km from the sea. It has several post-Byzantine churches with interesting decoration. The town is a base for expeditions on Mt Ossa. The summit commands a magnificent view, taking in Mt Athos and, in clear weather, the Turkish coast.

To the northeast of Aghia is the attractive 16th-century convent (restored) of Aghios Panteleimon. There are frescoes of 1721 in the narthex and of the early 17th century in the refectory; also an abbot's tower, with chapel. The same road continues to Melivia (Μελιβοία), sometimes thought to be the site of ancient *Meliboias*, native place of Philoctetes. A recent theory however locates this at the kastro of Kato Polydendri (18km southeast). Near there, on the hill of Mavrovouni, two small churches both have frescoes: that of the Panaghia (16th century) originally monastic, and the Koimisis tis Theotokou (16th century with 17th-century decoration). The royal estate of Polydendri was donated by King Paul to the State in 1962 as a training school for farmers.

Kokkino Nero ('Red Water') is a busy resort with mineral springs producing the eponymous reddish water. Stomio is a peaceful seaside town with a sandy beach, trees and thermal springs, below the steepest face of Ossa.

PRACTICAL INFORMATION

Pelion is a beautiful and evocative place, but it is worth bearing in mind that it has high rainfall by Greek standards and even in mid-summer it can be very wet on occasion. If you wish to have a standard Greek summer beach holiday, with guaranteed weather, Pelion is not the right place. In winter, even up to late March, blizzards come along and motorists often need snowchains on their tyres.

The east coast beaches are wonderful, but the sea can run a heavy swell and sometimes swimming is not allowed. Some beaches are unsuitable for small children and/or weak swimmers. West coast beaches on the Pagasitic Gulf do not have these problems but are polluted near Volos. A car is necessary to reach the east beaches from the high Pelion villages where most people stay. In the south and in the northern mountain forests there are large areas which are more or less deserted most of the time; carry a mobile phone and supplies in case of emergency. A 4WD vehicle is useful.

GETTING AROUND

• **By air:** Volos airport has the usual Olympic and Aegean internal flights but is also developing as a May–Sept charter flight destination from Britain, mainly with Sunville Holidays. Some of these flights can be very good value, and very cheap indeed at either end of the summer season.

• **By car:** A car is needed for touring Pelion; there is very little public transport. If you are staying in the Tsangarada region, the south can be covered in a day's drive, although more time is need for detailed exploration.

• **By bus:** The local Volos KTEL (T: 24210 35555) in Zakhou is excellent, truly a great Greek bus station, with brilliant lighting, and a dramatic sweep as the vehicles enter and leave the building, full of the excitement of bus travel in Greece. Regular services to Athens, Thessaloniki, Patras, Trikala, Pelion and Thessaly towns. Cross-Pindus services to western Greece are limited. Almyros has an hourly bus connection (45mins).

Two buses a day link Volos with Zagora; to Portaria and Makrynitsa 10–11 times daily. Daily bus to Milies and Tsangarada, continuing to Makryrrachi.

• **By rail:** The railway has regular if slow services to Larissa, where you can change for fast trains to Athens and Thessaloniki. Also trains to Trikala and Kalambaka.

• **By boat:** Volos is the main port for Skiathos and the northern Sporades. If you need to move a car to Skopelos or Alonissos, prior reservation is a good idea in the summer season. Limited services to Euboea; it is necessary to use other ferries further down the gulf (Glyfa). For hydrofoil information, Hellas Flying Dolphins bookings, T: 210 419 9000 or 210 419 9950, in Piraeus.

INFORMATION OFFICES

Volos Plateia Riga Feraiou, T: 24210 23500.

WHERE TO STAY

Volos
Most Volos hotels are on or near the port and seafront, and are fairly straightforward commercial establishments. The €€ **Aegli** (T: 24210 25691), the €€ **Alexandros** (T: 24210 31221) and €€ **Nefeli** (T: 24210 30211) are all Greek category B. There are numerous category C and D hotels too.

Argalasti
The **Hotel Argalasti** is nice, in a traditional house, with a pool 24230 54557.

Makrynitsa
The village boasts a number of three-storey traditional *archontika*, restored as guesthouses. A selection is given below: **Karamarli** (T: 24280 99570); **Pandora** (T: 24280 99404); **Repana** (T: 24280 99548); **Sissilianou** (T: 24280 99556); **Xiradaki** (T: 24280 99250).

Milies
Two ancient (17th-century) village houses have been restored as guesthouses. The **Evangelinaki** (T: 24230 86714); and the **Dereli** (T: 24280 93163).

Milina
For accommodation, contact the helpful, British-run Milina Holidays (T: 24230 65020, milina@vol.forthnet.gr, www.milinahols.gr).

Mouresi
There is good accommodation here at **Villa Olga** (T: 24260 49651) and **The Old Silk Store**, British-run (T: 24260 49086, www.pelion.org/oldsilkstore, jill@pelionet.gr).

Portaria
Archontiko Kandartzi. 150-year-old house. 14 rooms. Restaurant. T: 24280 99388.

Archontiko Kleitsa. Tiny (4 rooms) stone-built village house with traditional decor. T: 24280 99418.
Marios. Old village house, nicely restored with period furnishings. 7 rooms. T: 24280 99535.
Tsangarada
Kastanies. T: 24260 49135.
Konaki. Hotel in a well-preserved Ottoman building. T: 24260 49481.
Lost Unicorn. Run by a Greek-English couple, and decorated a little like an English country house inside. T: 24260 49930, www.lostunicorn.com
Theophilos. 19th-century exterior, modern within. T: 24280 99435.

WHERE TO EAT

Volos
Many restaurants are on or near the quay, and are full of traditional atmosphere. Some are in very attractive interwar buildings which have been well restored; others have fascinating collections of old photographs on the walls. *Tsipouradika* serve the local aperitif *tsìpouro*, a variety of raki, each order being accompanied by a different *meze*. Especially recommended for devotees of traditional Greek entertainment is the modest restaurant I Skala tou Milanou on the corner of Iolkou (officially El. Venizelou) and Analipseos, whose proprietors play traditional Greek music (especially *rembetika*) after serving the food. The best cafes stretch along the seafront north of the harbour, opposite the Civil War monument.

Pelion
There are plenty of cafés and tavernas in the coastal resorts and in the inland villages, though sparser in the south. Milina is the most developed place in southern Pelion, with good fish tavernas.

VISITOR SERVICES

As elsewhere outside cities in northern Greece, many places do not accept credit cards, and cash in Euros is needed. On Mount Pelion this is more or less universal. Some cash machines are badly maintained and unreliable. Travellers cheques are often not accepted in smaller places.

HIKING & CLIMBING

Larissa Alpine Club (for Mt Ossa), Skarlatou Soutsou 11, T: 24105 35097.
Nea Anchialos Alpine Club, T: 24210 25696.
Volos Alpine Club (for Mt Pelion), Dimitriados 186, T: 24210 25696.

BEACHES

There are very small, deserted beaches on the east side of the southern peninsula, accessible by dirt roads. Some are popular with nudists; all have fine views of Skiathos. Further north, the coast is indented with fine, sandy coves, the prettiest being Aghios Ioannis, Milopotamos and Chorefto.

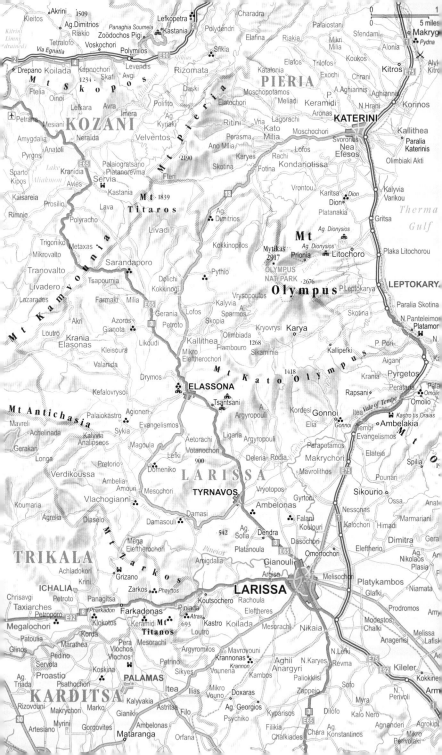

LARISSA & MOUNT OLYMPUS

Larissa (Λάρισα; pop. 133,000), the capital of the province of Thessaly, is an important transport hub situated in the middle of the Thessalian plain. With its spacious squares and busy streets, it has more the air of a city than anywhere else in central Greece. Evidence of Larissa's long history is not prominent, though traces of the Turkish enceinte still survive to the south of the town. There is good local ouzo, halva and ice cream. Unusually for Greece, bicycles are much used. The presence of storks on the roofs adds a pleasant touch to the townscape.

HISTORY OF LARISSA

The name Larissa, meaning 'citadel', is pre-Hellenic, and a settlement seems to have existed on the site from earliest times. An early ruler, Aleuas, who claimed descent from Heracles, founded the powerful family of the Aleuadai. The dynasty attracted to their court the poet Pindar, the sophist Gorgias, and the physician Hippocrates, the last two of whom died at Larissa. At the end of the 5th century BC their power was weakened by a democratic revolt and by the rise of the tyrants of *Pherai*, the most formidable of whom was Jason. The last Aleuadai injudiciously invited the aid of Philip of Macedon, who annexed Larissa and the whole of Thessaly. After the second battle of Cynoscephalae (197), the Romans made Larissa the capital of the reorganised Thessalian confederation. In 171 Perseus, king of Macedon, defeated the Romans near Larissa. Pompey passed through the city on his flight after the Battle of Pharsalus.

Achilleios, bishop and patron saint of Larissa, was present at the Council of Nicaea (325), and by the 5th century the city had metropolitan rank. Larissa fell to the Bulgars in 985. Byzantine rule was restored and survived until after the Fourth Crusade, when Thessaly fell to the Franks. Theodore Angelus drove them out and Michael II, his nephew, ruled Thessaly from Arta. When the last Epirot despot, John II, died without an heir in 1318, Thessaly was invaded from all sides, until Andronicus III restored uneasy Byzantine rule. During the latter half of the 14th century Larissa was ruled by the Serbs. By 1393 the Turks were encamped on the Spercheios; they took the town soon afterwards. Their garrison inhibited Thessaly's participation in the War of Independence. Larissa succeeded Trikala as the Turkish capital of Thessaly in 1870. Thessaly remained Turkish until 1881.

The town

The centre of Larissa is the huge Plateia Sapka, shaded by limes and orange trees and lively with cafés, patisseries, and cinemas. Above its northwest corner, in Odos

Papanastasiou, the 3rd-century theatre (capacity c. 10,000) was found in 1968 and has been intensively investigated and restored. Further west, at Odos Velissariou and Odos Ergatikis Protomagias, is a Roman theatre of the 2nd century AD, though with an earlier history. Odos Papanastasiou leads to the low hill, once the acropolis of the ancient city, now crowned by a clock tower (*To Roloï*). Northeast is the impressive Byzantine frourion (traces of an Early Christian basilica). To the west are the new cathedral and some vestiges of a Classical temple, overlooking the new bridge which replaced a medieval span of 12 arches across the Pineios. Beyond, along the river, extends the Alkazar, a fine shady park (cafés), a favourite promenade in summer.

Returning by Odos Venizelou, you pass between the Philharmonic Hall and the covered market. Opposite a small public garden is a mosque with a conspicuous minaret. Here is the Archaeological Museum, containing Thessalian antiquities from the *nome* of Larissa. In the single hall are displayed a menhir from Soufli tumulus (Middle Bronze Age); Archaic temple fragments; 5th-century Roman funerary stelae from Larissa and other sites; Classical bronzes from Tyrnavos and Argiroupolis; later sculpture, typically Thessalian in character; late-Imperial stelae depicting mounted warriors (the Graeco-Roman antecedents of the Byzantine portrayal of St George). Important are the Palaeolithic and Neolithic finds from the valley of the Pineios.

AROUND LARISSA

Ancient Krannon

Southwest of Larissa (3km south of the main road to Karditsa) are the ruins of *Krannon*, once one of the foremost cities of Thessaly and the seat of the Skopadai, kinsmen of the Aleuadai, whose wealth was proverbial. The poet Simonides (556–467 BC), who beat Aeschylus in a competition for the best elegy on the fallen at Marathon, lived for a time at Krannon under the patronage of the Skopadai. At Krannon in 322 BC, Antipater, the Macedonian regent, defeated the confederate Greeks and so put a stop to the Lamian War. South of the village, the low hill of Kastro, with a pleasant church of the Panaghia at its northern foot, was the ancient acropolis (excavations but little to see). Passing behind the kastro, passable dirt tracks lead (4.5km from village) to three tholos tombs of the 5th century BC, showing a remarkable survival in Thessaly of a Mycenaean form. Five kilometres southeast of Krannon, excavations at two cemetery sites in the vicinity of the village of Aghios Georgios produced rich finds including weapons and huge Thessalian fibulae of c. 650–550 BC. There are several tumuli in the area, as at Doxaras. The finds are in the Larissa Museum.

The road running west through the plain is interrupted ahead by isolated moderate hills culminating in Mt Titanos. At Koutsochero the village fountain has been cut from a large Doric column drum. To your right, one behind the other, are the twin heights above Gounitsa between which, through the impressive defile of Kalamaki, the Pineios emerges into the plain. About an hour southwest of Koutsochero, on a spur of Mt Titanos, is the Palaiokastro of Alefaka, the wreck of a Byzantine fortress built on ancient foundations. The ancient remains belong to *Atrax*, once inhabited by the warlike Perrhaeboi. One of the city gates, flanked by a fine piece of polygonal wall, partly survives. A number of gravestones and inscriptions from the site are in Larissa Museum and the Trikala archaeological collection.

West and north of Larissa

Further west both road and river pass between Titanos and the abrupt spur of Zarkos, the vertical western scarp of which looms over the village of the same name, 3km north of the road, with a Neolithic and Early Bronze Age mound. Here was an ancient city, possibly *Phayttos*, which in the Middle Ages became the seat of a bishop. Six kilometres north of modern Farkadonas is Grizano, with a Byzantine fort.

Northeast of Larissa a road runs through Omorfochori to Sikouri, continuing to Spilia, 8km farther on, the departure point for the mountain refuge (3hrs) on Mt Ossa. A group of Mycenaean tholos tombs was identified in 1969 near the village.

The mound (*Magoula*) of Gremmou, near Dendra, 10.5km northwest of Larissa off the Kozani road, represents the site of Homeric *Argyssa*, though the principal antiquities excavated are Neolithic. The road then continues northwards through Tyrnavos, a centre of ouzo production, and where a Dionysiac carnival is celebrated before Lent, to **Elassona** (Ἐλασσόνα), a base for hiking on Kato Olympus. It occupies the site of the 'white Oloösson' of Homer; the epithet apparently derived from the limestone rocks in the neighbourhood. Chief town of the warlike Perrhaeboi, it had a Bronze Age origin, but declined after the 5th century BC. A fine Byzantine bridge spans the river. On a steep rock overlooking the road is the attractive 13th-century Panaghia Olimpiotissa, a monastery with a Byzantine church whose plan resembles that of the Dodeca Apostoloi at Thessaloniki. It has cushion capitals and a carved wooden door of 1296. A torch is needed to inspect the fresoces. Two Classical tombstones are built into the gate.

About 4km east of Elassona is **Tsaritsani** (Τσαριτσάνι), a village said to have been founded by a colony of Bulgarians in the 10th century. Later they were replaced by Greeks, who preserved a kind of independence under the Ottomans. Thriving on agriculture and the manufacture of silk and cotton, their prosperity declined with the plague of 1813. About 1.5hrs east of the village, on a western outlier of Kato Olympus, is the monastery of Valtetsiko ('the Child'), founded by the Bulgarians, with a legend of a royal child miraculously healed.

TEMPE

The Vale of Tempe (Κοιλάδα Τεμπῶν) is a beautiful glen between Olympus and Ossa. In the early 20th century it was a famous attraction; though somewhat spoiled by traffic today, it is still well worth a visit, for its natural beauty and romantic associations. The praises of this vale have been sung by innumerable Roman and other poets. The glen, called *Lykostoma* ('Wolf's Mouth') in the Middle Ages, is 10km long and only 27–50m wide; it is the most practicable way out of the Thessalian plain to the northeast. It was formed in the Quaternary Epoch by a convulsion that rent the mountains and, by providing the Larissan Lake with an outlet to the sea, allowed the Thessalian plain to emerge. The Thessalians, according to Herodotus (*VII, 129*), attributed the convulsion to Poseidon, the god of storms and earthquakes. This violent topographical distortion finds an echo in the legends of the War of the Gods and Giants (*Gigantomachia*).

The attraction of the valley is one of dramatic contrasts. The stern, almost vertical cliffs, scarred by winter torrents and only partly clothed with ivy and other climbing plants, are offset by the peaceful river scenery below. The swift and turbid Pineios river is overshadowed on either side by plane trees and willows. Beyond the Spring of Venus, from which the goddess is reputed to have drunk, you reach the Wolf's Mouth. On a rocky hillock (right) stand the ruins of the medieval Kastro tis Oraias (Castle of the Beautiful Maiden), the redoubt which used to guard the gulf; at the foot of the rock are the remains of an ancient fortress.

In Classical times Tempe was a centre of the worship of Apollo. The god, having killed the serpent Python, purified himself in the waters of the Pineios, and cut a branch of laurel which he replanted by the Castalian Fountain at Delphi. In memory of this event, every eight years a mission of well-born youths was sent from Delphi to Tempe, to bring back cuttings of the sacred laurel to weave into wreaths for the victors of the Pythian Games.

In 480 BC a force of 10,000 Greeks occupied Tempe, to deny passage to the Persians. However, hearing that Xerxes was already turning their position by the inland roads, they withdrew to Thermopylae, abandoning Thessaly to the invader. Herodotus tells us that the Persians came over the shoulder of Olympus and down (via *Kallipeuke*, modern Kallipefki) on Gonnoi (as did the Germans in 1941). Before Pydan, in 168 BC, the Romans entered Thessaly by way of Gonnoi, and established a military post in the Vale of Tempe. Grave stelae from Gonnoi are in the museum at Volos.

Omolio in ancient times had a Temple of Poseidon Petraios; a tomb near the river produced an exquisite hoard of Classical jewellery in 1961 (now in Larissa Museum). Protogeometric tombs have yielded iron, bronze and gold objects.

THE WINE OF OLYMPUS

Edward Clarke, an early 19th-century English visitor to the Vale of Tempe, was much struck by the wines he tasted there, claiming that they were the best he had drunk in Greece. Wine is still made here today, and it is still some of the finest in the country. The Rapsani vineyards cluster around the villages of Rapsani, Ambelakia, Krania and Pyrgetos. A stony soil, rich in iron but poor in humus, forces the vines to put their roots down deep to find sustenance. This, coupled with the fresh sea air, creates red wines that are both distinctive and distinguished, all made from the indigenous grape varieties Xynomavro, Krasato and Petroto.

MOUNT OLYMPUS

Mount Olympus ('Ὄλυμπος), the highest mountain range in Greece, rises at the north-east limit of Thessaly and falls away into Macedonia. The massif soars to 2917m and wears a crown of snow from early autumn to the end of April. On the seaward eastern side is a line of vast precipices cleft by tree-filled ravines. Although it is an imposing peak, and should be treated with respect, even by experienced hikers, it is possible to drive quite a significant part of the way up the mountain, and enjoy the fine views.

To the south the main range is separated by a depression from Kato Olympus ('Low Olympus'), a region of wooded hills rising to 1587m. It is easily accessible from Karya. To the north rises High Olympus, with the loftiest peaks grouped round the centre of the massif in the form of an amphitheatre enclosing the deep Mavrolongos valley. Oak, chestnut, beech and plane trees flourish at the lower levels; higher up pine forests reach almost to the snow line. The principal summits are in three groups. To the south are Serai (2704m), Kalogeros (2701m) and Palaiomanastri (2815m). The central group comprises Skolion (2911m), from which fine precipices fall into the Tigania glen; Skala (2865m); Mytikas ('the needle'; 2917m), highest of all the pantheon, more broken; and Stafani, the 'Throne of Zeus' (2909m), a majestic curve of limestone arête. Then, separated from the central group by the Col of Porta (2682m) come Toumba (2784m) and Profitis Ilias (2787m), an easy shale-covered peak on the top of which is a tiny chapel, which used to be visited once a year by monks. From here an arête called Petrostrounga descends towards the valley of the Varkos.

In Greek mythology Olympus was the abode of the gods, whose life of pleasure there was imagined in human terms unencumbered by moral philosophy. Hesiod incorrectly reports Olympus as 'never struck by the wind or touched by snow'. Lions seem to have survived here down to Classical times. Evidence of a Sanctuary of Zeus of the Hellenistic period with animal sacrifices was found in 1965.

Sultan Mehmet IV is said to have attempted the highest peak without success in 1669, and in 1780 a French naval officer, G.S. Sonnini, reached Aghios Dionysios. Leake toured the lower area in 1806. After 1821 it became a famous haunt of nationalist bands and bandits. The difficulty of the approach and the insecurity of the region deterred all but the keenest climbers and geologists. As late as 1910 Edward Richter, on his third attempt at the climb, was captured and held to ransom by bandits after the escorting gendarmes had been killed. In 1912 the territory passed from Turkey to Greece and the following year two philhellene Swiss artists, Daniel Baud-Bovy and Frédéric Boissonas, with Christos Kakalos, a local guide, climbed the Throne of Zeus and Mytikas. In 1921 an official mission of two Swiss topographers, Marcel Kurz and Hans Bickel, completed the exploration of the range and mapped it. Since the Greek Alpine Club established a shelter in 1931, the mountain has been explored by increasing numbers.

Litochoro

Litochoro (Λιτόχωρο) is a pleasant well-watered town standing nearly 305m up on the east flank of Olympus. The inhabitants have long had a reputation as mariners and were prominent in the abortive uprising of 1878. It developed in the 1920s as a health resort for the tubercular, and is now the principal centre for climbing in the Olympus massif. It is home to the Olympus office of the Greek Mountaineering Club (EOS).

South of Litochoro, on the coast, is Platamonas. The Castle of Platamonas is a massive Byzantine and Ottoman fortress in an imposing coastal position.

CLIMBING OLYMPUS

Information from the EOS office in Litochoro: T: 23520 81944; eos@olympus.gr
The mountain-climbing website www.summitpost.org is also useful.

The ascent (arduous rather than difficult for mountaineers) is made in two days, the night being spent at a refuge. July and August are the best months. The road (asphalt to Prionia) ascends northwest passing the lower monastery of Aghios Dionysios (the *Metochì*) and climbs steadily up the slopes of Stavros (950m), where there is abundant water. You wind along the north side of the Mavrolongos valley, shaded with pines, in which flows the Enipeas. Below is the ruined monastery of Aghios Dionysios, a building of c. 1500, blown up by the Turks in 1828, but rebuilt before 1856. It was destroyed in 1943 by the Germans, who believed it to be used by guerrillas. The ruins can be reached in 20mins by a path across a hollow, but you continue almost level on the main path (following the red marks). At Prionia (c. 1600m; car park, restaurant), the springs of the Enipeas afford the last running water.

From this point the route rises fairly steeply amid thick beech woods in a region rich in botanic interest. You climb almost to the head of the Mavrolongos to reach (3hrs) Refuge A, the Spilios Agapitos at 2100m (*100 beds; T: 23520 81800*), on a spur facing east towards the sea. From the refuge the climb to one or other summit takes c. 3.5hrs; the vegetation gives out after c. 1hr. The mountain is usually shrouded in cloud at the midday hours in hot weather. Waymarks continue to the summit of Mytikas.

PIERIA

The summit of Mount Olympus forms the border between Thessaly and the region of Pieria in Macedonia. Pieria takes its name from another mountain, where there was a spring, sacred to the Muses, and made famous in later times by Alexander Pope:

A little learning is a dang'rous thing;
Drink deep, or taste not the Pierian spring:

Essay on Criticism, Part II.

The Mavrolongos valley and the Enipeas river, on the lower slopes of Olympus.

DION

Dion (Δίον) is a beautiful and poetic site of outstanding natural beauty and historical importance situated on the northern foothills of mount Olympus, some 5km from the Pierian shore. A visit in spring with the rampant wild flowers is particularly recommended. The ancient site was first identified by Leake in 1806, in the ruins adjoining the village of Malathria. Léon Heuzey visited in 1855 and again in 1861 and identified the perimeter of the city walls. Systematic archaeological exploration did not begin until 1928 (the area was under Ottoman rule until 1912). From then until 1931, G. Sotiriadis carried out a series of surveys, identifying part of the street plan, the west and east city gates, a 4th-century BC Macedonian tomb and an early Christian basilica. Excavations were resumed in 1960 under the direction of Georgios Bakalakis in the area of the theatre and the wall. Since 1973, Dimitrios Pandermalis of Thessaloniki University has conducted archaeological research.

HISTORY OF DION

According to tradition, Dion stood where king Deucalion of Thessaly erected the first altar to Zeus after the mythical flood. It was used from the earliest times as a cult centre and rose to prominence under Archelaus (413–399), who according to Diodorus Siculus built a temple to Zeus, a stadium for festival games dedicated to Zeus and the nine Muses, and a theatre. The ancient dramatist Euripides was active at Dion during the last years of his life when he lived in exile from Athens at the Macedonian court, and it is likely that his plays *The Bacchae* and *Archelaus* received their first performances at Dion.

In Macedonian times the place was a troop concentration centre rather than a city. Both Alexander the Great and his father Philip used to celebrate their military victories at Dion, with impressive sacrifices to Zeus. Here Philip II celebrated his triumph after the capture of Olynthos, and Alexander sacrificed before invading Persia. With Dodona, the city was laid waste by the Aetolians in 220 BC, Philip V taking revenge in 218 by destroying Thermon. Dion was quickly rebuilt, for Philip made it his base before Cynoscephalae as did Perseus his before the Third Macedonian War and Pydna.

Macedonia's independence ended with the Battle of Pydna in 168 BC; the *Colonia Julia Diensis* was established at Dion by the Romans in 31 BC, though the town itself remained Greek in character. Dion had a bishop in AD 346. It was sacked by Alaric in the 4th century; hit by floods and earthquakes, it was deserted by its inhabitants, who fled to higher ground.

The archeological park

Open Mon 10.30–5, Tues–Fri 8–5, Sat–Sun 8.30–3. T: 23510 53206. Shop at the kiosk with material for the general visitor and archaeological specialists. Local guide Dion: The Archeological Site and Museum *by Dimitrios Pandermalis is excellent. The park is fitted with paved walkways, bridges and panoramic towers. NB: The site is in a low lying area subject to waterlogging and flooding. Mud and mosquitoes in the summer can be a problem.*

The Roman town measures some 500m by 460m, is square in shape and enclosed in well-preserved walls. At the entrance to the town you cross the line of the city wall and step onto the main south–north street, part of the original 4th-century BC layout but paved with large blocks in the Roman period. To the left is a row of buildings, storerooms and workshops of the 3rd and 4th centuries AD, though the large squared blocks of earlier Hellenistic structures can be seen beneath the floors. Farther on (left) an impressive Roman façade has relief sculptures consisting of alternating shields and cuirasses, which may originally have been the base of a victory monument taken apart and moved here. To the right, a road leads to a residential area with splendid Roman mosaics. The vast 2nd-century AD **Villa of Dionysus**, with its mosaic showing the god emerging from the waves on a chariot pulled by amphibious panthers, is the principal attraction.

Southeast of the villa, a viewing tower marks an oddly shaped extension of the wall at the corner of the site, which may have served as a jetty over the River Baphyras (modern Helopotamos), which was navigable in Antiquity. In the same area is located the **Praetorium** a building recently uncovered by Pandermalis. According to a Latin inscription found in the vicinity, the Mestri family of Dion had ordered the construction of accommodation for officials (*praetorium*) and for ordinary travellers. The structure with five bedrooms, triclinia, two taverns, kitchen and stable has been shown by Pandermalis to correspond to the instructions set out in the inscription.

On the other side of the main street, a side lane has remains of private houses of the 2nd and 3rd centuries AD and of an Early Christian basilica, whose predecessor on the same site had a mosaic floor. Climbing the bank (right) you can look down into the east apse and the aisle of the building. The narthex lay beyond. Architectural fragments from the buildings are visible. Turning west, you reach the town wall, of which a substantial section can be observed. The original Hellenistic structure was mainly of large squared blocks; the later (Roman and Early Christian) repairs can be easily distinguished. There are projecting square towers.

Back towards the entrance note the well-preserved latrine and beyond it, the **Severan bath**, whose hypocaust system is the most immediately obvious feature. Statues of the god Asclepius and his family (now in the museum) were found here. The building may have been part of a larger therapeutic complex, a view supported by the presence, close by to the east, of an odeion, which can be reached by a path along the south side of the baths.

The sanctuaries of the gods, two theatres, one Greek and one Roman, and the stadium were located outside the city walls. Among the gods worshipped at Dion, the most important was Olympian Zeus, after whom the city was named (from the Latin). The **sanctuary of Zeus** has recently been identified by Pandermalis through his finding of dedicatory inscriptions, marble eagles, the base of the cult statue and the seated statue of Zeus himself. Pandermalis also excavated the altar, a 22m long limestone structure filled with half-baked bricks, and, in the area immediately to the west, the location where the sacrificial animals were tethered to large blocks fitted with a bronze ring, before being dispatched.

Nearby are shrines to other gods including Demeter (the most ancient, 6th century BC) and Asclepius. Recently Pandermalis excavated the **Temple of Artemis Baphyras**, identified by the presence *in situ* of an inscribed statue of the goddess. The epithet added to her name shows that she was the protectress of the local river flowing through Dion to the sea.

Beyond the bridge crossing the river, lies the **Temple of Isis**. The structure was found intact in 1978, just as it fell after an earthquake in Antiquity and was covered by the mud of floods.

The archaeological museum

The new archaeological museum has mainly Roman and Hellenistic finds from the ancient town and the surrounding area. Not to be missed are the remains (fragments of the copper pipes, 24 large and 16 small; keyboard and water pump have not survived) of the 1st-century BC *hydraulis* from the Villa of Dionysus. This musical instrument, invented in the 3rd century BC by Ctesibious, an engineer from Alexandria specializing in water and air powered mechanisms, produced a wailing, melancholic sound punctuated by the clacks of the keys, according to the reconstruction by the European Cultural Centre in Delphi. Known in the Classical west, it was later forgotten until AD 757 when a specimen was sent as a gift by the Byzantine emperor to Rome. It is the ancestor of the modern church organ.

This is not the only connection of Dion with music. A stele representing a *nabla*, a six string instrument of the harp family described by Ovid in his *Ars Amatoria*, has also been found here—and Dion is in the area where Orpheus met his cruel death, torn to pieces by the women he had shunned, on the slopes of Mount Olympus.

KATERINI & PYDNA

Katerini (Κατερίνι) is a brisk, busy, modern town, with almost no buildings dating earlier than 1912, when it developed as a railway town after the integration of Macedonia into modern Greece after the First Balkan War. There is good, cheap shopping along the main pedestrianised central area. Seven kilometres east, on the coast, Paralia has literally hundreds of fur shops, mostly branches of Kastoria businesses, which open Easter–Sept to cater for the numerous Russian and East European tourists. The beach is excellent clean sand, but Paralia town is downmarket, and not particularly recommended for non-Russophiles except as an overnight stop—unless you are planning some really serious drinking. It is an ideal place for a real 'Lost Weekend', with some of the strongest Russian vodka on sale in Greece, 100% proof spirit in some bars. Men enjoy 12- or 15-hour sessions while their wives and girlfriends buy fur coats. Russian beer and dried fish are provided for breakfast to attack the hangovers. Less robust spirits (pun intended) may prefer to stay in Katerini itself and use the bus for the beach.

Pydna (Πύδνα) is a site of some interest most easily reached by car. Pydna gave its name to the famous battle of 168 BC. When Lucius Aemilius Paullus took command of the Roman forces in 168, Perseus, the last king of Macedon, held an impregnable position southeast of Dion. By a feigned attempt to turn the Macedonian position, the Roman general induced Perseus to retire to a point 11km south of Pydna, near the Aison, where the decisive Battle of Pydna took place between 38,000 Romans and the Macedonian forces. At the acropolis of ancient Pydna (Byzantine *Kitros*) there are substantial remains. A Byzantine basilica of the 10th century succeeded Early Christian churches. The original fortifications were of the time of Justinian. The site was taken by the Franks in 1204 and turned into a military camp (a tower and cistern were constructed within the church). It was captured by the Turks at the end of the 14th century. Other remains of the ancient settlement (houses, a fragment of the mud-brick fortification wall) and its cemeteries have been discovered here and beneath the modern village to the north.

PRACTICAL INFORMATION

GETTING AROUND

• **By car:** A car is unnecessary to explore Dion and Olympus unless you wish to drive up the mountain road onto the Olympus range, or explore the inner Pierian mountains west of Katerini.
• **By bus:** Frequent KTEL buses run between Thessaloniki and Katerini, c. 1hr. Local buses run every 30mins between Katerini and the Paralia. Buses run between Volos and Larissa, and also link Larissa with major towns in Epirus, Thessaly and Macedonia, including Karditsa, Trikala, Kozani, Farsala, Grevena, Ioannina, Veroia, Tyrnavos and Elassona.
• **By rail:** Trains link Thessaloniki and Katerini (frequent service; c.1hr).

Larissa is a rail hub on the main Athens–Thessaloniki line.
• **By taxi:** A taxi from Katerini to Dion costs about €15 return. The journey is 14km, and takes about 20mins.

INFORMATION OFFICES

Larissa Epirou 58, T: 24106 18189.

WHERE TO STAY

Katerini
If you plan to stay the night to explore the Pieria region, in winter, spring and autumn Katerini is a useful little town with surprisingly good cheap hotels. In summer Paralia Katerinis (7km east on the shore) is popular, with plenty of rooms and small hotels, and a wide,

sandy open beach with the first clean sea south of the murky Thermaic Gulf.
€ **Lido**. Friendly and helpful middle-range place off the main square. Tsaldari 16, T: 23510 25300.
€ **Orfeas Classic**. Nice-looking place, good value. Ethnikis Antistasis 3, T: 23510 77800.

Larissa
€€€ **Larissa Imperial**. Luxury hotel in a grand, royal villa-style mansion, sumptuously decorated with rich fabrics. Pool and poolside bar. Spa centre. Attractive skylit restaurant. Farsalon 182, T: 24106 87600, www.grecotel.gr

WHERE TO EAT

Katerini
There are numerous good tavernas, try Tsanakas, in Filippon for excellent pork and lamb.

Larissa
The Konstantinidis Zacharoplasteion at Panagouli 4 is particularly recomended.

HIKING & CLIMBING

Olympus is a mountain to climb in summer. Only experienced mountaineers should attempt the ascent in winter, when snow and ice make climbing treacherous. Arrangements to stay in mountain refuges should be made beforehand with the Alpine Club in Litochoro (*see below*). Proper hiking equipment is essential. Study of the weather forecast is important prior to departure. Problems with mist and thick cloud can occur at very short notice, at any time of year. Every year there are accidents and sometimes fatalities caused by visitors neglecting basic precautions, or having inadequate equipment. Unaccompanied exploration is not recommended. Keep to signed paths. The EOS (Greek mountaineering association) has a map of the mountain. Road Editions also has a detailed 1:50,000 map showing marked trails and refuges.
Elassona Alpine Club Kentriki Plateia, T: 24930 22261.
Litochoro EOS T: 23520 81944.

MACEDONIA

The province of Macedonia (Μακεδονία), one of the two northernmost of modern Greece, has been under Greek sovereignty only since 1912. The region has great natural beauty and interest, and is increasingly fostering tourism, though remoter parts can still be primitive. The province is only part of the large but ill-defined area to which the name of Macedonia has been given since Classical times; much of it is now within the territory of bordering states. The Greek province is shaped like a gigantic capital L, with the short arm extending north from the Thessalian border and the long arm bounding the Aegean Sea as far as its junction with Thrace, with FYROM, and Bulgaria beyond the frontier to the north. On the west Macedonia marches with Albania. In the south Mount Olympus rises on the Thessalian border and extends into both provinces.

The climate is Balkan rather than Mediterranean, with extreme temperatures in summer and winter and considerable rainfall. The topography has few affinities with that of southern Greece. The coastline is little indented and safe anchorages are scarce. The larger rivers are perennial. The mountains are for the most part covered with dense forest or scrub. The interior is mountainous, the western regions being traversed north–south by part of the mountain backbone of Greece. A noteworthy geographical feature of Macedonia is the Chalkidiki peninsula, with its three prongs projecting boldly into the Aegean.

HISTORY OF MACEDONIA

During the long Middle Ages the population of Macedonia became very mixed. Slavs—chiefly Bulgarian, with a strong admixture of Bosnian and Serbian elements—and Turks were predominant inland, while the coast from the Aliakmon to the Strymon, including Chalkidiki, was mainly Greek. A profound change was caused by the provisions of the Treaty of Lausanne (1923), whereby 348,000 Muslims living in Macedonia were exchanged for 538,600 Greeks from Asia Minor. As a result of the Second World War and the civil wars, the greater part of the Slav population retired or was exiled across the neighbouring frontiers. The northern provinces suffered great depopulation by emigration in the mid-20th century, largely to Western Germany, Australia and Canada.

The problem of whether Macedonians were Greeks has been endlessly debated, from the time of Herodotus to the present day (usually to the accompaniment of political polemic). Some Greek tribes probably settled in the southern part of Macedonia. According to one tradition their leaders were the three sons of the Heraclid Temenos, who had fled from Argos. The youngest of the three, Perdiccas, is said to have founded the Macedonian monarchy and to have made his capital at *Aigai* (modern Vergina). Another tradition makes an earlier Heraclid, Karanos, the founder of the dynasty and Perdiccas only the fourth of the line. It seems reasonably certain that by the 7th century BC a kingdom was established at Aigai, from which the whole region was subdued and unified. The Greek settlers intermarried with the indigenous population and spoke a dialect akin to Doric, but with many barbarous words and forms—so much so that while seldom actually called Barbarians, the Macedonians were never regarded as genuine Hellenes. After the 6th century BC Greek influence increasingly filtered north from Thasos.

From written record little is known of Macedonia until the reign of Amyntas I (c. 540–505), under whom it was virtually a satrapy of Persia. His son Alexander I was a secret philhellene, despite the fact that he accompanied Xerxes on his invasion to Greece. He later extended his kingdom to the Strymon. The reign of Perdiccas II (454–414), coinciding with the period of Athenian expansion, is characterised by vacillation between Athens and her enemies. Archelaus (413–399) was a patron of Greek art and literature and established cordial relations with Greece, which remained friendly until the advent of Philip II (359–336). That king, intent on universal conquest, began by seizing various Greek cities on the Macedonian coast, such as Amphipolis, Pydna, Potidaia, Methone and Olynthos. The well-meaning but misdirected efforts of Demosthenes to rouse the Athenians against the danger met with little response. The Athenians were not really roused until Philip, invited by the Amphictyonic League (*see p. 445*), marched through the pass of Thermopylae on the pretext of punishing the Locrians of Amphissa. The Athenians and their Theban allies were defeated at Chaironeia in 338 and the independence of the Greek city-states was lost. A congress held at Corinth after the victory decided on war against Persia; but in the midst of his preparations, Philip was murdered. He was succeeded by his son Alexander (the Great; 336–323), who was destined to fulfil the ambition of world conquest that Philip had cherished.

On Alexander's death there was general upheaval. His regent in Macedonia, Antipater, won the Lamian War against the Greeks with the victory of Krannon. Antipater's son Cassander, who had been deprived by his father of the succession to the regency, proclaimed himself king of Macedonia in 306 and in 301 secured the possession of Macedonia and Greece. On his death in 297, his son Philip IV held the throne for a few months. In 294 Demetrius Poliorcetes, son of Antigonus the One-Eyed, one of Alexander's generals who had become king of Asia, was acknowledged king of Macedonia; but in 286 he was deserted by his own troops, who offered the throne to Pyrrhus, king of Epirus. Two years later Pyrrhus had to hand over Macedonia to Lysimachus, another of Alexander's generals, who had made himself king of Thrace in 306. In 277 Antigonus Gonatas, son of Demetrius Poliorcetes, obtained the throne of Macedonia, though Pyrrhus contested it again in 273. Demetrius II (239–229), son of Antigonus Gonatas, and Antigonus Doson (229–220) tried to win the mastery over Greece. Now came the period of the three Macedonian Wars (214–205, 200–194 and 171–168), and of the last Macedonian kings. Philip V (220–179) was defeated by the Romans at Cynoscephalae in 197, and his son Perseus (178–168) at Pydna in 168. After Pydna Macedonia was divided into four republics with capitals at Thessalonica, Pella, Pelagonia (*Heracleia Lyncestis*), and Amphipolis.

The arrangement did not last long, for in 148 Macedonia became a Roman province. In 27 BC, as a senatorial province, Macedonia was separated from Achaea, and extended north to the Danube, east to the *Hebros* (Evros), and south and southwest to include Thessaly and Epirus. After the Roman subjugation of Thrace in AD 46, Macedonia, no longer a frontier province, recovered some of its prosperity, attracting the missionary zeal of St Paul.

The Goths invaded Macedonia in AD 252. In 289 Diocletian altered the province's boundaries by taking away Thessaly and Epirus. Constantine created the diocese of Macedonia, which took in Thessaly, Epirus and Crete. The Byzantine centuries saw repeated incursions by Goths, Huns, Ostrogoths and Slavs. In the 7th century the Serbs reached the gates of Thessalonica. The 9th century was marked by the invasions of Bulgars and Saracens who, at the beginning of the 10th century, seized Thessalonica. In 1014 Macedonia came under the rule of Byzantium. In 1185 William of Sicily sacked Thessalonica. After the capture of Constantinople by the Franks in 1204, the Latin kingdom of Thessalonica was given to Boniface of Montferrat; but his successor was expelled in 1223 by Theodore Angelus, Despot of Epirus, who styled himself Emperor of Thessalonica. He was defeated in 1230 by the Bulgarian ruler Ivan Asen II, who incorporated northern and central Macedonia into the second Bulgarian or Bulgar-Vlach Empire, the remainder being absorbed in the Nicaean (Byzantine) Empire in 1246. On the extinction of the direct line of the house of Asen, the power of Bulgaria declined, and northwest Macedonia again came under the Despotate of Epirus. In the 14th century Macedonia fell under the domination of the Serbs. Stefan Dušan (1331–55) conquered all Macedonia except Thessalonica, as well as Thessaly, Epirus, and part of Bulgaria. In 1364 Murad I, Sultan of Turkey, routed the united Serbs, Hungarians and Vlachs on the banks of the Maritsa and by 1375 the whole of the Balkan peninsula, with Macedonia, came under Turkish domination. The invasion of Timur (Tamerlane) reversed the trend of expansion. After the battle of Ankara in 1402, in which the Turks under Bayezid I were totally defeated, Timur reinstated the various principalities that had been suppressed, including the Christian ones in eastern Europe. Under Murad II the Turks defeated the Christians at Varna in 1444 and established Ottoman rule in east Europe. This survived until the Balkan Wars of 1912–13.

In 1900–08 the so-called 'Macedonian Struggle' took place, when armed bands (Greek *andartes*, Bulgarian *comitajis* and Serb *chetniks*) contended for supremacy in the mountain regions. Greek Macedonia became a reality in 1912. The Treaty of Bucharest (1913) fixed the Mesta as the frontier with Bulgaria, which retained its seaboard on the Aegean until the end of the First World War. The treaties of St-Germain (1919), of Neuilly (1919), and of Sèvres (1920) attempted to solve the problem of Macedonia. For some years until the war with Turkey in 1922 the whole of Thrace passed to Greece. The Treaty of Lausanne (1923) restored eastern Thrace to Turkey. In the Second World War Macedonia served in 1940 as the base for the successful Greek campaign against the Italians, but fell within a week to the German onslaught in 1941.

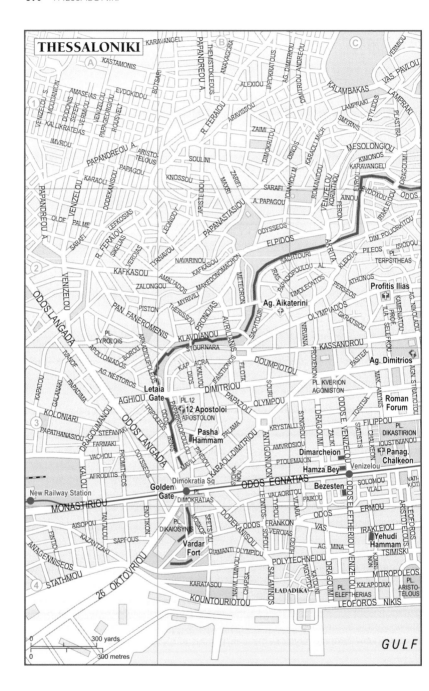

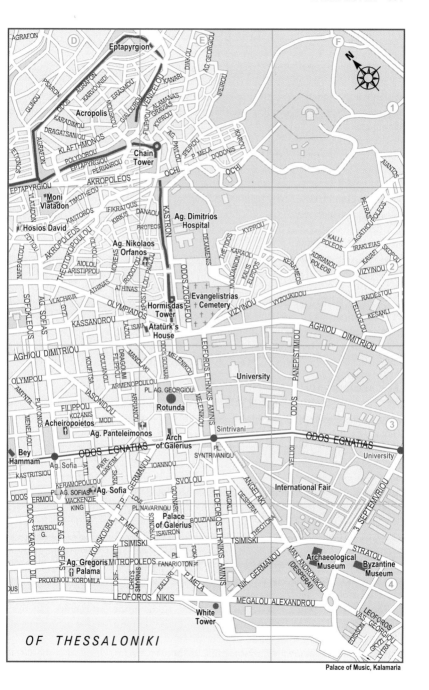

Palace of Music, Kalamaria

THESSALONIKI

Thessaloniki (Θεσσαλονίκη), biblical Thessalonica, often known in English as Salonica, is the second city of Greece and the natural centre of communication with her Balkan neighbours. It is the pre-eminent Byzantine city in Greece, and most visitors come to see the outstanding late Classical and medieval remains, and the famous churches.

The city rises from the Bay of Thessaloniki in the form of a theatre on the slopes of Mt Chortiatis. Its citadel, the battlemented walls, and the huddled hillside houses of the upper town create a character which remains unique despite the devastating fire of 1917, and more recent earthquakes. Its monuments—though sometimes over-restored—are surpassed only by those of Istanbul as an illustration of ten centuries of Byzantine architecture.

Outside the walls the huge grounds of the International Fair and the university divide the old town from the new. Modern Thessaloniki is a bustling, dynamic city, residence of the Minister for Northern Greece, and home to a university. Athenians often call the tough, resourceful inhabitants the 'Bulgarians', which is also the nickname throughout Greece of the city's famous and controversial football team, PAOK, founded in 1926. Thessaloniki is the main centre of large-scale manufacturing and other business, and in some respects is the commercial capital of the nation, though the port has suffered decline with the growth of Igoumenitsa and Volos.

HISTORY OF THESSALONIKI

The ancient city

Tribal people lived in the earliest times on the hills above the coast, which then was probably impenetrable marshland (*see p. 619*). Urban development began in Hellenistic times. The unimportant ancient town of *Therme* was incorporated with 25 others in 316 BC by Cassander (*see p. 681*), son of Alexander the Great's former general Antipater, and given the name of *Thessalonikeia* (in Strabo's spelling) after his wife, who was Alexander the Great's half-sister. In AD 146, when Macedonia became a Roman province, Thessalonica was made the capital. Its geographical position at the head of the gulf favoured development, which was accelerated by the building of the Via Egnatia. Cicero spent part of his exile here in 58; Pompey took refuge from Caesar here in 49. The city's support of Antony and Octavian before the Battle of Philippi promoted its fortunes. In AD 49–50 St Paul preached at Thessalonica, where he antagonised some of the Jews, who attacked the house in which he had been staying. His two letters to the church he founded here have come down to us as the 'Epistles to the Thessalonians'; he revisited the city in 56.

Thessalonica repelled repeated attacks by the Goths in the 3rd century. Galerius, who succeeded to the eastern half of the Roman Empire on the retirement of Diocletian (*see p. 39*), lived in the city. The persecution he instigated claimed as a victim St Dimitrios, afterwards patron saint of the city. Under Theodosius the Great

(379–95) Thessalonica became the seat of the prefecture of Illyricum, a metropolitan see, and the base of the Emperor's operations against the Goths. Here Theodosius himself, severely ill, was converted to Christianity and afterwards issued the Edict of Thessalonica (380), reversing Julian the Apostate's toleration of pagan gods. In 390, after Botheric the Goth, military commander of the city, had been lynched for failing to control his soldiers' outrages, Theodosius invited the populace to a special performance in the circus and there had around 7,000 of those soldiers massacred. For this crime he was made to do penance by St Ambrose, Bishop of Milan.

The medieval city

Favoured by Justinian, Thessalonica rose to become the second city of the Byzantine Empire. Having endured further invasions of the Goths, and resisted five sieges by Avars and Slavs, it remained an enclave in Slav dominions until Justinian II's expedition of 689, and seems only to have returned to direct Byzantine administration c. 783. St Cyril (d. 869) and St Methodius (d. 885), the brothers who converted the Slavs to Christianity, were natives of Thessalonica.

Thessalonica was stormed by the Saracens (led by the Greek renegade Leo of Tripoli) in 904, and 20,000 of its inhabitants were sold into slavery. It served Basil II as a base against the Bulgars, who besieged it without success in 1041. When the city was captured in 1185 by the army and fleet of William II of Sicily, under the command of Tancred, the celebrated Homeric scholar Eustathios, then Archbishop of Thessalonica, left a detailed account of its barbarous sack. At the end of the Fourth Crusade, the city became the capital of the Latin kingdom of Thessalonica under Boniface of Montferrat (1204). The Byzantine Despot of Epirus retook the city in 1222, while the rest of Macedonia came under the sway of Ivan Asen II of Bulgaria; but in 1246 John Vatatzes reappropriated both to the Byzantine empire of Nicaea.

In the 14th century possession of Thessalonica was the first goal of every usurper aiming for the Imperial throne. The same century witnessed the religious struggles of the Hesychasts, or Quietists (*see p. 611*), and the insurrection of the Zealots, a 'people's party' who murdered the nobles in 1342 (*see p. 611*). The short period of reform before they were crushed coincided with the artistic Golden Age of the city. During a long period of anarchy Thessalonica fell to the Ottoman Turks in 1387 and again in 1394, but in 1403, after the Mongol Tamerlane had crushed Bayezid I at Ankara, it was restored to the Byzantines. In 1423 Andronicus Palaeologus, son of the Emperor Manuel II, despairing of keeping back the Turks, placed Thessalonica under Venetian protection. However in 1430 Murad II stormed, sacked, and occupied the already depopulated city. Some churches were transformed into mosques.

The population was suddenly increased by the influx of 20,000 Jews banished from Spain by the Edict of the Alhambra (1492). They absorbed the Bavarian Jews who had arrived 20 years earlier. By the middle of the 16th century they constituted the major part of the population, and had formed a small autonomous community speaking Ladino, a form of Castilian, which they wrote in Hebrew characters.

THE JEWS OF SALONICA

Contemporary Thessaloniki bears little evidence of the Jewish presence that was so much a part of the city until 1943 when some 56,000 Jews were deported by the Nazis to their deaths in Auschwitz. Even this number is deceptive: in 1900 the Jewish community numbered some 90,000, and its depletion was the consequence of several Balkan wars, the absorption of the city into the modern Greek State in 1912, a great fire that destroyed most of the Jewish quarter in 1917, and the arrival of great numbers of Greek Christians from Asia Minor in the mid-1920s.

Jews first settled in Thessaloniki not long after its foundation in the 4th century BC. Most probably they came from Alexandria, where Jews had already begun to assimilate—culturally, linguistically and institutionally—into the great world of Alexander the Great. St Paul's visit to the synagogue in Salonica was unproductive: it appears that the city's Jews presented a somewhat conservative front. When Christianity became the state religion of Rome under the emperor Theodosius I, life for pagans and Jews became more difficult. The uneven growth of the Jewish community probably reflects the crises that the city faced during late Antiquity and well into medieval times. Benjamin of Tudela visited Salonica in 1169 and mentions a community numbering possibly 2,000 (he mentions 300 'householders'). As Byzantine Jews, they referred to themselves as Romaniots, a name which eventually came to denote distinct peculiarities in language, ritual and interpretation of the Mosaic Law.

By the 14th century Thessaloniki became a refuge for Jews fleeing persecution in Hungary, Provence and Sicily. Language and cultural influences kept these Jews distinct from the Romaniots, and this is reflected in the creation of separate synagogues and communities. To add to this growing Babel was the arrival, in 1494, of over 20,000 Spanish- and Portuguese-speaking Jews fleeing the Inquisition in Iberia. Very quickly these Sephardim set to work rebuilding their lives. Equally rapid was the Hispanisation of the other Jews of the city: though they retained their own synagogues, they eventually adopted Spanish as the common language. By the mid-16th century Thessaloniki had over 30 synagogues bearing names such as Castile, Aragon, Provenzia, Apuleia and Magreb, not to mention Etz Hayyim, the ancient synagogue of the Romaniots.

The fortunes of the Jews of Salonica were closely linked to those of the Ottomans and are reflected in an intense creativity on the part of leaders, rabbis, mystics and entrepreneurs, who quickly formed contacts with other Jewish—especially Sephardic—communities within the Empire and in Europe. The severe economic consequences that followed the discovery of the New World by Spain and then the opening of a trade route to the Far East via the southern tip of Africa by the Portuguese brought the economic importance of

Chief *Hanadji* addressing mourners in Salonica Jewish cemetery, 1918.

the Near East to an end, and Jewish fortunes began to dwindle. Attempts to find a meaning in the expulsion from Spain led to musings on the Messianic Age, and in 1669 a rabbi from Izmir, R. Shabbatai Zvi, was proclaimed the Messiah in Salonica. His career is of great importance, and appears to have met with disastrous consequences when he converted to Islam. Not long after his death many of his followers followed suit, forming a schismatic sect of their own in Salonica, the Dönmeh.

With the troubles that affected the Ottoman Empire through the assertion of a national identity by Greeks, Bulgarians and Serbs in the early 19th century, the Jews of Salonica found themselves increasingly marginalised. By the turn of the 20th century the community was struggling to find a *modus vivendi* under new economic and social conditions, and this process was exacerbated when Salonica was absorbed by Greece in 1912. Not long after this the First World War and then the fire of 1917 resulted in emigration of Jews to various parts of Europe, the United States and South America. Those who remained were still trying to come to grips with life in the Greek State when the Nazis invaded Greece in 1941.

Almost immediately severe measures were taken to restrict Jewish movements. The vast Jewish cemetery, with over 300,000 graves, was expropriated and destroyed (the site is now incorporated into the grounds of the University of Thessaloniki) and the remaining community of 56,000 was segregated into ghettos and then, between March and August of 1943, systematically deported to Auschwitz. Only a handful returned.

The present Jewish community in Thessaloniki numbers some 1,200, and is active and well led. There is a new Jewish Museum, a Home for the Aged, a primary school and three synagogues. **N.S.**

The modern city

The rise of modern Salonica began in the 18th century with the improvement in trading conditions in the Ottoman world and the beginnings of the industrial revolution. Greek bourgeois society grew as a result of commercial relationships with French and British traders, who were opening up the hitherto closed Ottoman economic system. The citizens of Salonica established Greek as the language of commerce over a wide area. After the Treaty of Passarowitz in 1718 between the Habsburgs and the Ottomans, trade expanded rapidly, and Salonica was a hub of the caravan routes. Trade with Czarist Russia expanded after 1775. The city soon became the financial centre for the entire region and the French, Dutch, Venetians and others established consulates. In 1821, at the outbreak of the Greek War of Independence, a sympathetic movement at Thessaloniki was savagely suppressed. During the 19th century the Turks made a show of reforms; the Greeks improved their schools; the Jews increased their influence. In 1888 the railway link with the rest of Europe was built, and in 1897–1903 a new harbour constructed.

Thessaloniki (known to the Turks as *Selaïnik*) became a centre of intrigue against the misrule of the last Ottoman sultan, Abdul Hamid (reigned 1876–1909), and both Greek and Bulgarian nationalist movements flourished in the city. The International Macedonian Revolutionary Organisation (IMRO), the first modern terrorist organisation, was founded in Salonica in 1903, followed in 1906 by the Turkish Committee of Union and Progress (*Ittihat ve Terakki Cemiyeti*), which secretly organised the Young Turks Macedonian revolt of 1908. In 1909 Abdul Hamid was deposed and exiled here. In the First Balkan War the Greek Army made a triumphal entry into Thessaloniki on 8th November (26th October O.S.) 1912, and the city was ceded to Greece by the Treaty of Bucharest (1913). During the First World War Venizelos set up his provisional government of National Defence. Fire devastated the city in 1917, making 70,000 homeless, and the shanty town of refugees was swollen in 1923 by the exchange of population with Turkey (*see p. 587*). Replanning of the centre was put in hand in 1925–35.

German tanks entered the city in April 1941, and the city became the centre of Axis occupation of the southern Balkans. Thessaloniki was the focus of the Greek Holocaust, with the mass deportation of the Jewish community (around 50,000 people) from the train station. After the end of the Occupation, the pro-communist ELAS resistance took control, but were soon displaced, and the city was run by the National Army. The post-1949 period was characterised by economic growth. Since then Thessaloniki has become a modern city, though the upper town still retains some of its old atmosphere.

EXPLORING THESSALONIKI

Despite many changes since the fire of 1917, the ancient chess-board plan remains a feature of the town. The principal thoroughfares—Aghiou Dimitriou, Egnatias, and Tsimiski—run roughly parallel to the sea, effectively dividing the old city into four belts. The main sights and monuments are described below.

THE SEAFRONT & EASTERN QUARTER

The original port, constructed by Constantine the Great, was silted up in the Middle Ages. A new harbour was fashioned by a French company in the late 19th century and in 1911, when Thessaloniki was the third port of the Ottoman Empire. Leoforos Nikis, a quayside esplanade, replaces the 10th-century seaward rampart demolished in 1866–74. To the right it leads to Plateia Eleftherias, centre of banking, and to the harbour. Turning left along the promenade, you pass an unbroken string of cafés, some of the most chic and expensive in Salonica, with the gilded youth of the city revelling during warm summer nights with their designer clothes and huge, glittering motorcycles.

On the shore at the far end (1km), among trees, is the famous 32-metre **White Tower** or Lefkos Pyrgos (Λευκός Πύργος; *open Tues–Sun 8.30–3*) which marked the southern angle of the ramparts, and which today, for many residents, embodies the spirit of Macedonia. Built c. 1430 either by the Venetians or the Turks, it served in the 18th–19th centuries as a prison for the Janissaries. Their massacre in 1826 at the order of Mahmoud II gained for it the name of Bloody Tower. Today the tower functions as an exhibition space administered by the Museum of Byzantine Culture. A stepped ramp leads all the way to the top, from where there are excellent views of the mountains behind Thessaloniki, and across the Thermaic Gulf to Mount Olympus.

Beyond the tower, a park (with a friendly café) divides the old town from its huge eastern extension. To the right, a massive equestrian statue of Alexander the Great stands near the sea. Along the foreshore a promenade, flanked by gardens, extends south to the enormous, brick built 'Palace of Music', and eventually (after 4km) to the suburb of Kalamaria and the yacht club (*Naftikos Omilos*) and small marina.

The avenue from the White Tower to the left of the park leads to the entrance of the Fair. The entrance to the Archaeological Museum is across the road.

The Archaeological Museum

M. Andronikou 6. Open Mon 12.30–7, Tue–Fri 8–7, Sat 8.30–3, Sun 8–7, T: 2310 830 538. Map p. 591, F4. Small shop. NB: At the time of writing the museum was undergoing major reconstruction and reorganisation. It is already overdue for reopening (though this is now scheduled for late 2006). The description below covers what is so far on display, and what is projected.

In front of the building are two fine sarcophagi, one showing a battle with Amazons, and another with a scene of Orpheus and his lyre.

The Gold of Macedon

This beautifully curated display shows the astonishing wealth of Macedonia during the Hellenistic age. A wall text explains how the value of gold actually fell during the reigns of Philip II and his son Alexander the Great, because they flooded the market with it. Exhibits are chiefly of gold jewellery, ornaments, wreaths and other artefacts, including great quantities of *alabastra* and other perfume jars, largely recovered from burials. Highlights include a set of dice from a boardgame (the patterns of the dots have not changed since then); an exquisite early 3rd-century BC torque-style bracelet from Europos, with a delicate reticulated body and ibex-head finials; and a coin struck to commemorate the games held at Veroia (3rd century), with a graceful likeness of Alexander the Great's mother Olympias on one side.

Some of the items recovered from Philip II's tomb at Vergina are also here (though most are now at Vergina itself; *see p. 632*), including a pretty silver *askos*. The finds from Derveni are prominently shown, particularly the famous **Derveni krater**. This monumental cremation urn takes the form of a bronze volute krater, dating from the 4th century BC, showing the marriage of Dionysus and Ariadne on one side. Dionysus, naked, places one leg across his bride's lap. His panther sits behind him. Maenads in orgiastic ecstasy (one swinging a kid, another a baby) dance around the rest of the krater, with Silenus, phallus erect, accompanying them. Others, exhausted, sit resting on the krater rim. The krater is made of two metal sheets hammered together, composed of a bronze and tin alloy. It is not gilded, although its colour resembles gold. The figures around the main body of the vase were made using the repoussé technique; that is, they were hammered out from behind.

Also from Derveni is the **Derveni papyrus** (4th century BC), an extraordinary document relating to cults and belief systems which clearly show how paganism, in its development towards monotheism, prefigured Christianity.

The remaining rooms of the museum are planned to be organised as follows:

Room 2: Prehistory
Room 3: The birth of cities
Room 4: The Kingdom of Macedonia up
to late Antiquity
Room 5: Thessaloniki: the early centuries.

The Byzantine Museum

Stratou 2. Open Mon 10.30–5; Tues–Sun 8.30–3; T: 2310 868 570. Map p. 591, F4.
The low-slung modern building of the Museum of Byzantine Culture was completed in 1993. In 2000 the Greek Ministry of Culture made it a listed building; the Council of Europe voted it 'Museum of Europe' in 2005. It is built of attractive mellow brick, surrounding a plain concrete peristyle. The exhibits are arranged over 12 rooms, all with a theme. The sense of how much was destroyed is overpowering.

Room 1 (The early Christian Church): Fragments—architectural elements, mosaic floors, frescoes—from churches in Thessaloniki and elsewhere, including a fine archway from Aghios Dimitrios, an example of a Theodosian capital, and a 4th-century statue of the 'Good Shepherd', a youth in a tunic with a lamb on his shoulders: the same type as the *Moschophoros* (*see p. 80*).

Room 2 (The early Christian city): Artefacts to illustrate public utilities (eg water pipes, made of slender *loutrophoroi* fitted snugly together) and domestic life (eg cooking utensils).

Room 3 (Burials and Cemeteries): Quantities of grave goods from Thessaloniki cemeteries, including sarcophagi, inscribed funeral stelae, and a reconstructed barrel-vaulted tomb with the original fresco remains, showing parents and two children.

Room 4 (middle Byzantine period): Highlights include two exquisite bracelets (9th–10th century) with enamel panels of flowers and birds and carved slabs with floral motifs, crosses and vines from the Iconoclastic period (*see p. 61*). There is a single icon, from the 12th century, of the Virgin and Child, with the Virgin holding the Child on her right arm.

Room 5: Genealogies of the Byzantine emperors from Heraclius (610–641) to the Palaeologues (1261–1453).

Room 6 (Byzantine castles): Mainly wall texts, with some finds (clay pots, axe heads, horseshoes) on defensive castles, chiefly from the 6th, 9th, 10th and 14th centuries.

Room 7 (Twilight of Byzantium, 1204–1453): Glassware, architectural elements, icons, pottery. There is an exquisite small icon of Sts Athanasius of Alexandria and Anthony of Veroia (14th century), and an *epitaphios* sewn in gold thread on a red ground (c. 1300).

Rooms 8–9 (Donated collections): A collection of prints of Byzantine subjects, mainly made in 18th- and 19th-century Venice is followed by the Dimitris Ekonomopoulous collection of icons. There is another superb St Athanasius, and an appealing *Adoration of the Magi* (15th century).

Room 10 (the Byzantine legacy): The survival of the Byzantine church after the fall of Constantinople.

THE ARCH OF GALERIUS & ROTUNDA

Odos Gounari, a busy street filled with junk jewellery and CD shops, leads to Plateia Navarinou (*map p. 591, E4*), a large square formed by the excavations in the **Palace of Galerius**. A deep cutting is surrounded by a low wall so that the remains can be seen from various vantage points. Most impressive is an octagonal building, richly decorated within, perhaps the throne room.

Further on Gounari meets the Odos Egnatias, which once passed through the triumphal **Arch of Galerius** (*map p. 591, E3*; known locally as the *Kamàra*). Now realigned, the road passes to the right of the arch, with a wide section of pavement allowing the arch to be viewed at leisure. The arch was erected to commemorate Galerius' victories over the Persians in AD 297, and is known to have formed part of a larger design, which included a palace, hippodrome and mausoleum. Only part of the western section of the arch survives. Originally two further piers to the southeast carried a similar span, forming a double gate crowned by a central dome. The springers of the transverse arches can be seen above the cornice of the reliefs. Beneath them ran a roadway to the northeast, in the form of a porticoed avenue leading to the Rotunda (*see below*). The structure is of brick. The piers are faced with stone reliefs. These are in four zones, separated by bands of sculptured garlands and crowned by a cyma and cornice.

On east side of the south pier is a scene of sacrifice (on the second zone from the bottom) showing Diocletian, Augustus of the East, in the imperial purple (left), and Galerius Caesar his son-in-law in military uniform (right), celebrating the latter's victories. The altar is decorated with reliefs of Jupiter and Heracles, of whom Augustus and Galerius claimed to be the reincarnations. The scene below represents the surrender of an Eastern town; those above, prisoners begging for clemency, and (top) Galerius addressing his troops. In the adjacent reliefs beneath the main arch, above a row of victories, Galerius is seen (top to bottom) riding in his chariot between two towns which receive him and bid him farewell; fighting on horse-back (crowned by an eagle on the sculptured band); receiving the surrender of Mesopotamia and Armenia. On the north pier the various scenes of combat, some with elephants, are less well preserved.

Just to the north is **Aghios Panteleimonos**, a pretty church with a central dome and a domed narthex, first mentioned in 1169 as a dependency of the Rossikon monastery on Mt Athos. The cloister which surrounded it on three sides disappeared during Turkish use as the Issakié Mescid Djami. This change (c. 1500) was carried out by Kadi Ishak Çelebi, whose magnificent mosque is still the central feature of Bitola. Damage in the 1978 earthquake was severe.

The Rotunda

The church of Aghios Georgios (*map p. 591, E3*) is the oldest as well as the most conspicuous intact monument in Thessaloniki, with the only surviving minaret. Built on the same axis as the Arch of Galerius, it was probably erected in the emperor's lifetime to serve as his mausoleum, though it was never used as such. The building is austere, entirely constructed in brick, including the dome and vaults, with the dome protected by a low-pitched timber roof borne on the outer walls, one of the first known examples of this practice in Europe.

Galerius died in *Serdica* (modern Sofia) and was buried in nearby *Romulianum*, his birthplace. It is said that he died of a mysterious suppurating canker, which caused his flesh to smell so bad that few doctors could come near. Fearful that the sickness might be divine retribution for his persecution of Christians, the dying emperor is said to have revoked his edict of suppression on his deathbed. The Rotunda was transformed into a church before 400, when the southeast recess was converted into an arch and the sanctuary constructed; the main entrance was moved from the southwest to the northwest, and a narthex added. At the same time an ambulatory (now destroyed) was built round the outside and the recesses in the original wall opened into it, giving visual access to the interior. The conversion of this impressive centralised building was without doubt a political statement of some import.

Some time after the 10th century the upper part of the sanctuary fell and the dome was repaired. The buttresses date from this time. This is possibly the church known

Apse of the Rotunda.

in the Middle Ages as the Asomaton, or Archangels, which gave its name to the quarter and its gate. For some time in the 15th century the Asomaton served as the Metropolitan church of the Greeks. In 1591, the year of the *Hegira* 999 (when the end of the world was expected), the Rotunda was turned into a mosque, later renamed after Hortaci Suleïman Effendi, whose tomb (19th century) stands in the courtyard. The elegant stelae surrounding the church date from the time of Mahmoud II (1807–39).

The interior

The circular wall, 6m thick, has eight barrel-vaulted recesses. Over each recess is an arched window; above and between these are small lunettes; the dome is c. 24m across. The interior was lavishly decorated with mosaics. Fragments survive, Hellenistic in feeling and dating from the end of the 4th century. They are some of the finest that remain from this period. The central mosaic in the dome no longer exists but it has been possible to piece together what it represented: a good illustration of the conflation of Roman Imperial and Christian symbolism. Christ here appeared as Emperor, dressed in the purple and seated on a *clipeus* or shield: witness to the manner in which the army often proclaimed an emperor by elevating him on a shield. Here the shield is borne aloft by four Nike or Victories, figures from the Classical lexicon that were to become the iconographic types adopted for angels. This and the surviving representations of martyr saints are superb examples of the new art that was emerging experimentally at this time: a balance between the classic norms of realism and a tendency that will develop further in abstraction. Eight scenes in the drum of the dome (*concealed by scaffolding at the time of writing*) show elaborate architectural constructions with saints in prayer. Their vestments are varied and their features individual; all were martyred in the East, the majority under Diocletian. The stance of the figures is hieratic and in somewhat harsh frontality, but the faces, with bright shining eyes, fully fleshed cheeks and vibrantly virile mien, are among the finest examples of this transitional period in Christian art.

Of the middle zone, which probably represented the Apostles, only some sandalled feet survive. In the southeast recess (restored in 1885) are medallions with birds and fruit on a gold ground. In the apse which, like the bema and the ambulatory, was added to the original building on its conversion into a church, four truncated columns (of a ciborium?) show the original floor level. There are some badly preserved frescoes of the Ascension (second half of the 9th century).

MARTYRIA

During the last years of the reign of Constantine basilicas began to be complemented by another type of building, 'martyria': places that mark or bear witness to something specific, such as an event or a tomb. Unlike the rectangular basilica, which focuses the interior energy of the structure towards the apse, the martyrium is centralised, and it is generally accepted—both by the use of a Greek word to designate them, and by archaeological evidence—that they were of Hellenistic origin. The earliest extant martyrium in Rome is what remains of the mausoleum of Augustus. Originally it would have had a dome and under it would have been the tomb of the Emperor. The Emperor Galerius constructed just such a martyrium to serve as his tomb in Thessaloniki: ironically, it was to become dedicated to St George in the name of the new religion which Galerius had persecuted. The edicts of Constantine indicate that he also ordered martyria to be built: many of these would have resembled the tomb of his daughter Constantia in Rome (Santa Costanza), which remains much as it was. Like the basilica, the martyrium provided space for both worship or visual access. The tomb would be located in the central area under the dome, and around this was constructed an ambulatory around which people who were not permitted access to the tomb itself could pass. In certain instances a martyrium was built in direct conjunction with a basilica, as is the case in Jerusalem and Bethlehem. In Jerusalem the basilica on the site of the Crucifixion is joined to a martyrium built over the Tomb of the Resurrection. In Bethlehem the large basilica is merged with a martyrium marking the entrance to the cave where Jesus was supposedly born. This merging of basilica and martyrium also took place in Rome, when the martyrium associated with the site of the execution of St Peter and his burial was incorporated into a large basilica built over the graveyard. Aghios Dimitrios in Thessaloniki (*see p. 605 below*) is a good Greek example of this model. N.S.

THE ACHEIROPOIETOS & AGHIA SOFIA

In Odos Aghias Sofias (*map p. 591, D3*), is the **Panaghia Acheiropoietos** (pronounced 'achiropíitos'), one of the earliest Christian buildings still in use. It was probably dedicated to the Virgin soon after Her recognition as Theotokos (Mother of God) by the Third Ecumenical Council, at Ephesus in 431 AD, and completed c. 470. The church was most likely was erected, like Santa Maria Maggiore in Rome, to celebrate the decision of the Council of Ephesus which condemned the teachings of the deposed Patriarch Nestorius and solemnly proclaimed the Virgin Mary as the 'Theotokos' or God-bearer. It was named ('Αχειροποίητος: 'Made without hands') at some time after the 12th century, after a celebrated icon supposed to have been miraculously painted. A later popular name, Aghia Paraskevi (Good Friday), is said to come from a mistranslation of the Turkish name *Eski Djuma*, meaning 'old place of worship' (*djuma* also meaning Friday, the Muslim day of worship). The church was converted into a mosque in 1430, not without detriment to its fabric. After restoration in 1910 it suffered further damage in 1923, from the billeting of refugees. Reconsecrated, it has again been restored.

The church is a basilica of Syrian type, with nave and two aisles. The atrium and exonarthex have disappeared. The narthex opens into the nave by a *trivilon*, a triple opening formed by two columns and closed by curtains. The arcades have monolithic columns with Theodosian capitals (capitals decorated with leaf fronds pierced with holes). The interior has lost most of its mosaics but a few survive in the soffits of the arches of Nilotic plants—papyrus and water-lilies—showing influence from Alexandria. Frescoes of c. 1225 have survived in the south aisle, above the arcade between it and the nave. Eighteen of the Forty Martyrs remain, depicted either in bust in medallions or as full-length figures. Near the south chapel (the former baptistery) are some brick walls of a Roman house, and below the south aisle two layers of Roman mosaic flooring are exposed.

Aghia Sofia and its district

Aghia Sofia, the Church of the Holy Wisdom (*map p. 591, D3*), is set in a garden planted with palms and Mediterranean pine, which occupies the site of the basilica's former atrium. The heavy exterior was not improved by the loss of the elegant Turkish portico, ruined by an Italian air raid in 1941, and the building suffered severely in 1978.

The date of Aghia Sofia is disputed. Imperfect pendentives and the masonry style led some scholars to think it older than its Justinianean namesake in Constantinople. More likely the building represents a transitional form between the domed basilica and the domed cruciform church and should be dated to the early 8th century, perhaps to the reign of Leo III the Isaurian (717–40). Beneath are remains of a five-aisled Early Christian basilica and, below again, of a Roman building. In 1585 it was transformed into a mosque by Raktoub Ibrahim Pasha. Damaged by fire in 1890, it was reconstructed in 1907–10 and restored to Christian worship in 1912. The Greeks used its minaret (since demolished) for a machine gun post in 1913 while subduing the Bulgarian garrison barricaded in a school nearby.

The spacious interior is impressive. The drum, borne on pendentives, on which the dome rests, is a square with rounded corners rather than a circle. The dome, 10m in diameter, is decorated with fine mosaics of the *Ascension*. In the centre, in a circular medallion supported by two angels, the Almighty is seated on a rainbow throne; below are the Virgin with an angel on either side, and figures of the Apostles divided by trees. Below the angels is a Greek inscription (from *Acts I, 11*; 'Ye men of Galilee, why stand ye gazing up into heaven?'). The mosaics are now attributed to the 9th or 10th centuries. In the apse are monograms of Constantine VI and of the Empress Irene, and the *Virgin Enthroned*. There are traces of an earlier mosaic of the Cross which, during the Iconoclastic period (*see p. 61*), accompanied the liturgical inscription now interrupted by the Virgin's feet; the existing mosaics, therefore, are dated to 785–97. In the arches of the west wall of the narthex, part of the original fresco decoration of the 11th century remains. Fragments of full-length male and female saints can be distinguished, with busts of saints below.

Odos Aghias Sofias leads south to the principal shopping street of the city, still known by its Byzantine name of Tsimiski. Crossing Tsimiski and continuing towards the sea, you come to **Aghios Gregoris Palama**, built in 1912–13 to serve as the cathedral. Here is re-interred the body of Archbishop Gregory Palamas (c. 1295–1359), champion of the Hesychasts (*see p. 611*).

THE ROMAN FORUM

The Odos Egnatias (Οδός Εγνατίας) runs from the site of the Axios Gate in the northwest to that of the Kassandreia Gate in the southeast (though the actual gates are no more). The street follows an ancient line and, since it was spanned by two triumphal arches, was long assumed to represent the famous Via Egnatia. The evidence of milestones, however, seems to show that the Egnatian Way entered from Pella by the Axios Gate but left again by the Letaia Gate, also to the northwest, without passing through the city, rather as its successor does today.

Halfway along the street, on its upper side, opens the **Plateia Dikastirion**, a vast square cleared by the fire of 1917. Today it serves as a local bus terminal, but once it was the Imperial Roman forum. Preparatory building work for new lawcourts immediately produced ancient finds, and systematic excavations by the Greek Archaeological Service revealed the odeion and two stoas bounding the forum, and a long double cryptoporticus. The projected courts were abandoned and the lower part of the square attractively planted with gardens. On the southeast corner of the square is the picturesque **Bey Hammam** (*Map p. 591, D3; open Mon–Fri 8.30–3*), an old Ottoman bath-house erected by Sultan Murad II in 1444, with separate men's and women's sections, and in use as a bath-house until 1968. The original dedicatory inscription survives. Beneath are remains of late Roman buildings.

On the opposite corner of the garden-square stands the pretty little **Panaghia Chalkeon** (*map p. 590, C3*), set below the road in a garden with two fine date palms.

Founded in 1028 by Christophoros of Lombardy, it was restored in 1934. The name, 'Our Lady of the Coppersmiths', recalls the time from 1430 to 1912 when it served the Ottoman smiths as a mosque (the *Kazançilar-Djami*). The brick church has the form of a Greek cross-in-square, extended to the east by three apses and to the west by a narthex. The central dome, with a straight cornice, is mounted on a lofty octagonal drum, and the arms of the cross have triangular pediments, which give a markedly angular appearance to the whole. Within, the church contains an almost complete cycle of frescoes belonging to the original decoration, which must have been painted very soon after the church's construction. Those in the dome (*Ascension*), round the drum and in the apse, seem to derive from the mosaics of Aghia Sofia (*see p. 603 above*). The narthex fresco shows the *Last Judgement*. The church is often empty: the peace inside, while the traffic roars in the background, is broken only by the gentle tick of an old grandfather clock. It strikes the hours, too.

Beyond Panaghia Chalkeon, where Odos Egnatias crosses Eleftheriou Venizelou, is the **Hamza Bey Djami**, founded in 1468, enlarged before 1592 and partly rebuilt after a fire in 1620. It is the largest mosque on Greek soil.

AGHIOS DIMITRIOS

The most revered church in Salonica (*map p. 590, C3*), and the largest in Greece, is the 5th-century basilica of Aghios Dimitrios. The martyr saint to whom it is dedicated was executed while under arrest in some rooms adjacent to baths connected to the hippodrome of the city. Almost immediately the blood-soaked site became a place of veneration for Christians, and miracles were recorded. By the late 4th century the original rooms of the bath had been modified and a small church erected over the site. Under the city prefect Leontius between 412–13, the site was cleared and an enormous five aisled basilica erected that terminated, as in the case the of church of the Nativity in Bethlehem or old St Peter's in Rome, in the martyrium proper, built as in the case of the latter as a transept constructed over the site of the saint's martyrdom located in a crypt beneath the apsidal area. This dual aspect of the building is especially evident by the fact that the galleries above the side aisles terminate at the transept. As in Bethlehem, access to the underground crypt was by stairs which allowed the pilgrim to descend, pay homage to the martyr and then ascend to the church proper by stairs at the other end of the crypt.

The building was reduced to a shell by the fire of 1917, though the main arcades stood and the sanctuary survived to roof level. It was reconstructed in 1926–48, where possible with surviving materials, more or less as it had been before the fire. The open timber roof however was replaced by one of reinforced concrete.

History of the church

Local tradition makes St Dimitrios a native of Thessalonica, though Sirmium, near Mitrovica in Serbia, also claims him. He was martyred at the command of Galerius.

The saint, as the city's guardian, defended it against enemy attacks. His tomb exuded a sacred oil with miraculous healing powers. A fair, of considerable importance in the Middle Ages, accompanied his feast days (20th–26th October). Immediately after the edict of toleration (311/313) the Christians built a small church on the site of the martyrdom. In AD 412–13 Leontius, prefect of Illyricum, miraculously healed of paralysis, founded 'between the ruins of the Roman bath and the Stadium', a large church which was damaged by fire in the reign of Heraclius (c. 629–34) and shortly afterwards rebuilt by Archbishop John with the addition of the east transepts. The plan seems to have remained unaltered despite later repairs. Here in 688 the Emperor Justinian II celebrated his success against the Slavs. The church was pillaged in 1430 but left to the Christians until 1491 when, in the reign of Bayezid II (as shown by an inscription formerly above the west door), it became the *Kasimiye Djami*. Between 1907 and 1912, when it was returned to Christian use, the wonderful mosaics were rediscovered, only to be largely destroyed in the fire of 1917.

The exterior

The outside of the church appears cruciform because of the transept roofs, which break the line of the aisles although they do not form a true crossing with the nave. Outside the west front, which is flanked by two low towers, stands the great *phiale*, a canopied immersion font. The usual entrance is by the south door.

The interior

The spacious interior, 43m long, has been impressively restored, though the upper surfaces have only whitewashed plaster in place of the destroyed revetment of polychrome marble (traces above the arcade). The nave, 12m wide and ending in an apse, is flanked by double aisles, with round arches supported by columns of green, red, and white marble. The ancient shafts (some renewed) must have been replacements from elsewhere after the first fire since they have pedestals of uneven height. The carved capitals with their imposts repay detailed attention; many are Theodosian. The ancient marble revetment has been renewed on the piers, and the floor repaved in Thessalian marble. The iconostasis and the furnishings are replicas of Byzantine work in fretted marble (fragments of the originals are preserved in the Byzantine Museum (*see p. 598*).

A On the north side is the marble tomb (1481) of Osios Loukas Spantounis, of Florentine workmanship most unusual in Greece.

B A domed chamber survives from a Roman building and probably held the tomb of St Dimitrios; it is poorly frescoed. At the entrance is a damaged mosaic of the saint.

C Housed under a modern polygonal canopy are the revered relics of the saint, in particular part of his skull, in an elaborate silver reliquary.

D On the first pier of the south arcade is a fresco of Archbishop Palamas (*see p. 611*) either with the Hesychast saint Ioasaph, or, as scholars now think more likely, with St Dimitrios himself.

AGHIOS DIMITRIOS

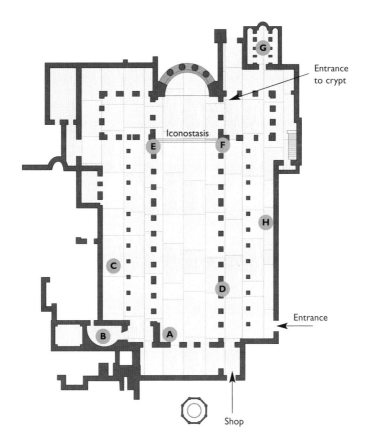

Entrance
to crypt

Iconostasis

Entrance

Shop

E To the left of the iconostasis survive two mosaics, one contemporary with Leontius' rebuilding. This church was essentially the focus of specific veneration of St Dimitrios as the protector and patron of Salonica and not primarily a locus for the liturgy as such, hence the mosaics are mostly in the form of ex-votos showing the saint standing with donors. The left pier shows St Dimitrios with two children, and the Virgin and (?) St Theodore (the date still disputed).

F On the pier to the right of the iconostasis are three more mosaics, two from the time of Leontius: St Dimitrios and the builders of the church (presumably Leontius himself and Archbishop John, defender of the city in 617–19); St Sergius sumptuously attired as captain of the Imperial guard (a later work); St Dimitrios with a deacon (discovered when a Turkish wall was removed).

G At the southeast corner, beyond the treasury, stands the lovely little Chapel of Aghios Euthymios, with frescoes of 1303 and a flagged floor.

H In the outer south aisle are frescoes of St Dimitrios and of the miraculous defeat of a Barbarian invasion.

The crypt

The crypt (now set out as a museum) was discovered in the 1917 fire, and is entered from the south transept. Here is located the martyrium of the saint (early 4th century), perhaps an adaptation of part of the Roman bath in which St Dimitrios was traditionally imprisoned. Beneath its apse was found a small cruciform reliquary-crypt containing a phial of blood-soaked earth. Parts of a fountain from a fish pond described by Archbishop Eustathios (d. 1193) were also discovered. A stretch of paved Roman street shows that the martyrium was originally above the ground level.

Profitis Ilias

The trifoliate church of Profitis Ilias (*map p. 590, C2*), which served the 14th-century convent of Nea Moni, occupies the site of a Byzantine palace. Converted to the Muslim rite of Fethi Murad, it was disfigured by massive external buttresses, the removal of which has revealed its fine brick decoration. The square narthex, with an upper storey supported on pillars, is characteristic of the monastic katholikon (badly damaged mosaics and medieval graffiti). Internally the church needed such thorough restoration that its only original features are the four columns supporting the dome and fragmentary mosaics in the small window embrasures of the drum.

THE ACROPOLIS & RAMPARTS

The acropolis (*map p. 591, D1*) is one of the most evocative and impressive monuments of its age in the southern Balkans, and the massive floodlit Theodosian walls are one of the great sights of the city. The present course of the Byzantine ramparts seems to have been adopted in the 4th century. Whether this perpetuates an enceinte of Cassander is uncertain, but here and there well-laid courses of Hellenistic masonry remain. The length of the circuit in the 4th century AD was c. 8km, about half of which survives, with upwards of 40 towers, almost all square, spaced irregularly. The construction is largely of rubble with courses of brick, though in places it is entirely of brick, sometimes with rows of brick arches to give added strength. This device (which enables the wall to remain standing even if the base is sapped) was not again revived in Europe until the 12th–13th centuries. Inscriptions survive from a number of rebuildings. The walls stand

to a height of 7.6–15.2m, though the upper courses are mostly 14th- or 15th-century work with restorations. All the major gates have now disappeared.

The best way to appreciate the architecture and site is to walk up from the lower town (up Leoforos Ethnikis Aminis from the White Tower; *map p. 591, E4*). On a hot day it is an arduous walk, and it is easier to take a taxi straight to the top.

Odos Apostolou Pavlou

Just below Olympiados, a red house in Odos Apostolou Pavlou (no. 17; *map p. 591, E4*) is the **birthplace of Atatürk** (Mustafa Kemal; 1881–1938), first President of Turkey. A plaque was placed here in 1933. It is an attractive building with interesting exhibitions. Mustafa Kemal, the son of a government clerk, with both Slav and Alabanian family antecedents, was born in Thessaloniki in 1881 and spent his childhood in the city, attending the Military Cadet School. In 1907–11 he was posted to the Turkish Third Army (then in Thessaloniki), and took part in the march to Constantinople that over-threw the last sultan, Abdul Hamid. The house that you see today was purchased by Staff Captain Mustafa Kemal in 1908 for 50 gold coins, though the family had been liv-ing here as tenants since 1877. Atatürk was born on the second floor. In 1937 the house was bought by the Thessaloniki municipality and given to the Turkish government. It was restored to its original condition in 1950, and opened to the public in 1953.

To the west is the **Hormisdas Tower**, high up on which part of a Greek inscription, 9m long in brick, reads 'by indestructible walls Hormisdas completely fortified this town'. Hormisdas the Younger held various offices in Thessaloniki and Constantinople under Theodosius.

The upper section of Apostolou Pavlou is narrow, cobbled and picturesque. Near the top is the lovely little 14th-century church of **Aghios Nikolaos Orfanos** (*entrance in Irodotou, to the west, if the metal postern in the walls is closed*). The interior is very simple: a sanctuary surrounded on three sides by space for the laity under the sloping roof. The frescoes (possibly by Kalliergis; *see p. 65*) are exceptionally fine. Apart from the Twelve Festival depictions are several cycles, one of the life of St Nicholas and another interpret-ing strophes from the *Akathistos Hymn*. This is a very ancient Byzantine liturgical poem dedicated to the Theotokos (Mother of God), and composed during one of the great Arab sieges of Constantinople. During a critical moment in the siege, a procession of the peo-ple from the City, headed by a miracle-working icon of the Virgin, circuited around the walls as the hymn was sung; the eventual departure of the besiegers was attributed to miraculous intervention. This church was decorated shortly after the Catalans attempted to seize the city in 1308, and the *Akathistos Hymn*, may well refer to the event.

The Chain Tower and acropolis

The Chain Tower (*Gingirli Koule*), so called from the heavy stringcourse half way up, is a circular keep of the 16th century. Following the road round to the right of it brings you into the acropolis precinct. The acropolis still has most of its wall; walking along-side it from the Chain Tower gives you an excellent view of its masonry. A series of gateways pierces it at the end of Polydorou: to the right of the gate with the long lintel is the Gate of Anna Palaeologus, first opened in 1355 by the widow of Andronicus III. It has a Byzantine inscription. The triangle here, where the acropolis wall meets the city wall, is probably to be identified with the *Trigonion*, where the storming Turks gained entry in 1430. Within the Acropolis unremarkable suburban villas climb haphazardly to the Eptapyrgion (*Yedi Koule*), a fortress with seven towers until recently used as a prison (also accessible via the cobbled Odos Agrafon). The massive central tower bears an Arabic inscription recording its construction in 1431.

Odos Eptapyrgiou follows the excellently preserved south wall of the acropolis, which is also part of the main circuit of the city. From the top, during the 'People's Uprising' in 1345, the enraged mob hurled the nobles onto stakes below.

The original towers face towards the acropolis which, more vulnerable to an expected assault from the landward, might be invested first. In the 14th century when the likelier danger had proven to be from the sea, four shallow towers were added on the seaward side. The second one bears the device of Andronicus II Palaeologus. A small secret postern survives between the second and third. A modern gate has been opened towards the west end, nearly opposite which stands the Moni Vlatadon.

Moni Vlatadon and Hosios David

The Moni Vlatadon (*map p. 591, D2*), surrounded by tall cypresses and noisy peacocks, was founded in the 14th century by the Cretan Vlatades brothers, probably Hesychasts (*see below*), hence its dedication to the Transfiguration, the Divine Light. Largely rebuilt in 1801, the church has original frescoes in the bema and in the parecclesion to the right. Some recently uncovered paintings are dated to the 11th century. The monastic buildings house a Patriarchal Academy of Patristic Studies.

HESYCHASM

The Hesychasts or 'Quietists' are members of a movement in the Byzantine Church that stems from the monastic traditions of Mount Athos, and sets great store by mystic prayer and contemplation: Hesychasts believe that by complete passivity man can abandon himself to God. Any definite act of will or outward gesture is suppressed: man initiates nothing, does not try to alter his circumstances or those of others, and thereby attains perfection. The similarities with Buddhism are no coincidence: Hesychasm was brought to Greece from India by the prince-saint Ioasaph (his name derives from the Indian *Bodhisattva*). Hesychasts enter a kind of suspended animation, by unceasing repetition of a short prayer, adopting a particular physical posture as they chant, with their eyes fixed on the area of the heart. The aim is to achieve a union of heart and mind; the ultimate goal a vision of the Divine Light, as revealed by Christ at His Transfiguration, and which even the bodily eyes may apprehend if rendered receptive. The greatest exponent of Hesychasm was St Gregory Palamas.

The little visited church of **Hosios David** (*map p. 591, D2; open daily 9–12 & 4–6; small gratuity for expected*) is located in the upper city and is worth whatever inconvenience it may take to find it. This site is also associated with the Emperor Galerius through his daughter Theodora, who had been secretly baptised and, according to the hagiographical account, had built a small chapel on the site under the pretence that it was a bath. When her perfidy was revealed to her father (through the agency of her mother) she (as had been St Dimitrios) was incarcerated on the site and ultimately murdered. The tiny church probably dates from the late 5th century. In medieval times it served the Moni Latomou. Its plan, an inscribed cross of Syrian type and unusually early date, was mutilated and the west door closed up when it became a mosque. A mosaic, discovered in 1921 beneath plaster in the apse and contemporary with the church, shows a youthful, beardless Christ in imperial majesty, elevated on a light-radiating shield, not by Victories but by winged symbols of the Evangelists. On either side stand Ezekiel (left) and Habakkuk (right). The scene seems to interpret the visions of Ezekiel I and II in the spirit of the New Testament, for the two prophets can also represent Sts Peter and Paul. The supple and complicated composition of this mosaic make it one of the finest of its period. The entire upper portions of the structures were originally filled with mosaics that have been lost, though that which survives in the apse is so dramatic and lifelike that it inspired a number of legends—one that it was miraculously revealed at the time of Theodora and another that it was made divinely manifest (hence '*acheiropoeitos*'; made without hands) to an Egyptian monk, Senoufias, who had made three pilgrimages to the site seeking to see Christ as revealed at the Second Coming. Late 12th-century frescoes of exceptional quality cover the south vault. They show the *Baptism of Christ* (west side), *Nativity* and *Presentation*.

THE WESTERN QUARTER

Aghia Aikaterini (*map p. 590, B2*) is a pretty church of similar plan to the Dodeca Apostoloi (*see below*). The outer walk has arcades, closed with glass, and surmounted by a wavy cornice. The church dates from the late 13th century; the contemporary paintings were much damaged during its time as the *Yakob Pasha Djami* after 1510.

The extreme northwestern limit of the city ramparts has more frequent towers and was protected by an outwork. The Letaia Gate, with a hexagonal barbican, was reduced to ruin in th 20th century; there remains some pseudo-isodomic masonry incorporating reused Classical blocks. A few metres inside the gate is the **Dodeca Apostoloi** (*map p. 590, B3*), the least restored and perhaps the most charming of Thessaloniki's churches. Founded by the Patriarch Niphou (1312–15), it was a monastic church until its conversion to the Mohammedan rite as the *Soouk Sou Djami*. The east end has richly patterned brickwork. Round three sides of the central cross-in-square runs an outer aisle with four corner domes. The narthex has an arcaded façade. The inner dome is borne on four columns with capitals from an earlier structure. The wall paintings, extensive but damaged, include a *Tree of Jesse* in the south aisle. The four barrel vaults that support the drum have lively mosaics. In the south vault is the *Nativity*, with a bucolic shepherd and soulful animals; the handmaiden Salome prepares a bath; the midwife tests the temperature of the water, while the Child apprehensively turns away. The *Transfiguration* is a powerful composition.

Just below is the **Pasha Hammam** (16th century) with an attractive dome, in use as baths until 1981. You now descend Odos Irinis, where an animated fruit market largely masks the wall, to Plateia Dimokratias, or Vardari, the busy west entrance to the city. A statue of Constantine, liberator of Thessalonica, occupies the site of the sculptured Golden Gate of the Flavian epoch, described and drawn by 19th-century travellers, but since totally demolished.

Here the two principal routes into the city converge. To the north in Odos Langada stands a fine memorial (1962) to the 50,000 Jews of Thessaloniki who perished in the gas chambers of Auschwitz. The monument, a monolithic block of Pentelic marble, was designed by the Italian architect Manfredo Portino.

From the square, Odos Frangon follows the line of the early Byzantine walls to the **Vardar Stronghold** (*Top Hane*, the Turkish fort and arsenal; *map p. 590, B4*), now restored and laid out as a park. Between here and the modern harbour lay the Classical port, silted up in the Middle Ages. Here is now an interesting quarter of Turkish warehouses, the streets paved with lava.

PRACTICAL INFORMATION

NB: The Thessaloniki telephone code, for all calls, is 2310.

If you wish to see the main sights, two days are sufficient if you are staying in the city centre. More time is needed for a full exploration. Streets at right angles to the sea are numbered from the seaward end; those parallel to the sea from the northwest. The climate of Thessaloniki runs to extremes: the winters are often severe, when the city is swept by the *Vardarats*, or Vardar wind from the northwest; summers can be oppressive.

GETTING AROUND

• **By air:** Thessaloniki Airport is at Mikra, 11.25km to the southeast (T: 473 212). Refurbished in 1998–2000, it is one of the best run and most user-friendly airports in Greece. From London Swiss offer a good and surprisingly cheap service via Zurich. Between Easter and October UK charter flights can be very cheap. There are good flight connections to German cities, and another cheap way to get there involves taking a budget flight from the UK to Munich, or Frankfurt, and then by Lufthansa to Thessaloniki. There are also frequent domestic services to Athens; 1–3 times weekly to Chania, Chios, Corfu, Heraklion, Ioannina, Rhodes; 4–6 times weekly to Limnos, Lesbos.

The bus service between the airport and city is intermittent, and can be non-existent in the evenings and in winter. A taxi is often needed, allow at least an hour during busy periods.

Air Intersalonika (office in airport; T: 2310 492 100) offers helicopter and light plane hire for tourism, business and hunting trips. A flight to Vergina costs about €700.

• **By car:** Thessaloniki is a busy city, and parking is very difficult. For ordinary visitor purposes it is much the best to see the sights on foot. It is possible and not unpleasant to walk to the upper town. Otherwise take a taxi. Cycling is possible, but only for the very brave.

• **By rail:** Thessaloniki station (on Monastiriou, an extension of Egnatia; (T: 2310 517 517) is a characterful centre of town life, though a fair way from the centre on the western outskirts. Trains go to most towns, cheaply but slowly. For routes and timetables, T: 145, or see Greek Railways information office in the station, or www.ose.gr. The OSE (Greek Railways) office is at Aristotelous 18. The main lines go to Turkey, via Serres, Drama and Alexandroupolis; to Skopje via Gevgelia; to Edessa and Florina (highly recommended scenic route); and south to Athens via Larissa. The Express trains to Athens are recommended, even first class is not expensive and it is a magnificent journey with the crossing of the famous Gorgopotamos Bridge. Non-express trains are very cheap indeed, but stop at every tiny station and are extremely slow. For information, T: 2310 517 517. Security on trains is reasonable, but a companion is recommended.

• **By bus:** The new regional KTEL, an ugly, unimaginative pile at Iannitsou 194, has displaced the wonderful old traditional bus stations dotted around the train station. It is no doubt more efficient, but also soulless, and in a grim surrounding area. International coaches run mostly from the front of the train station forecourt and there is an office inside the station for tickets and information. All national buses now leave from here, except for Chalkidiki, which has its own KTEL in the east of the city.

City buses: Thessaloniki has the best local services of any Greek city, as citizens are not slow to remind you. Local Services: 1 (from the railway station) and 2–7 traverse Tsimiski or Nikis and Vasilissis Olgas; 4 terminates at Mikro Karavournou. 22, 23 run from Venizelou to the acropolis. No. 72 to the Agricultural School, Aghia Triada, etc, from 23 Karolou Dil; to Asvestochori from 22 Syngrou.

• **By taxi:** Taxis are plentiful and cheap in Thessaloniki, and easy to hail on the street. Taxi-sharing is absolutely normal: don't be surprised if the driver admits someone else into your cab, if they are going in the same general direction. It is also acceptable to flag down occupied taxis and ask the driver if he is going to the same place you are.

• **By sea:** Ferry services to the port are surprisingly poor for a city of the size of Thessaloniki, and services to Rhodes and Crete are often the only regular boats that run all the year round. A Flying Dolphin service down the coast has been closed down. In summer services improve considerably, with boats to Skiathos, Tinos, Naxos, Samos and elsewhere. A useful agency in the port is Karacharisis, T: 2310 513 005.

INFORMATION OFFICE

Odos Aristotelous 8, T: 2310 271 888.

WHERE TO STAY

The town has hotels to suit all budgets, from glitzy and expensive to small basic places in the streets near the station. Rooms vary from over €200 a night for the best suites in expensive hotels down to about €30 in the cheapest outlying places. Prices vary at different times of the year. It is often difficult to get a room at all during the International Trade Fair period in September and before Christmas, without prior reservation. There are not many tourists in the city, and prices for middle-market hotels are set with the expense-account business visitor in mind, and can be pricey.

Cheap hotels can be very basic, and those along Egnatias are noisy. Some recommendations are given below:

€€€ **Electra Palace**. Step inside the Electra Palace, and you could be almost anywhere in the world. If you are looking for comfort and a well-appointed, international four-star standard place to stay, this is for you. *Plateia Aristotelous 9, T: 2310 294 000, www.electrahotels.gr. Map p. 590, C4.*

€€ **Capsis Bristol**. Small boutique hotel in the old Frankish quarter on the edge of Ladadika, in a building that escaped the 1917 fire. Elegantly restored, this makes an extremely comfortable base for exploring the city. *Oplopiou and Katouni 2, T: 2310 506 500, www.capsisbristol.gr. Map p. 590, C4.*

€€ **Le Palace**. Easy, relaxed, no-problem hotel right in the heart of town, offering basic comfort and good-sized rooms. Pretty dining area and very good breakfasts. *Tsimiski 12, T: 2310 257 400, www.lepalace.gr. Map p. 590, C4.*

€€ **Luxembourg**. In a well refurbished, very attractive 1920s building, just up from the waterfront. *Komninon 6. T: 2310 252 600, www.hotelluxembourg.gr. Map p. 590, C4.*

€€ **Plaza Art**. Modern hotel, comfortable if bland in design, in the Ladadika district. *Paggaiou 5, T: 2310 520 120, info@hotelplaza.gr. Map p. 590, C4.*

€ **ABC**. Functional, clean modern hotel near the Archaeological Museum. *Angelaki 41, T: 2310 265 421, www.hotelabc.gr. Map p. 591, E3.*

€ **Hotel Augustos**. Clean, comfy and central. *Svoronou 4, T: 2310 522 550, augustos@hellasnet.gr. Map p. 590, B3.*

€ **Vergina**. Small, middle-market hotel, conveniently located, though rather noisy. *Monastiriou 19, T: 2310 516 021. Map p. 590, A3.*

WHERE TO EAT

Thessaloniki has some of the best restaurants in Greece, and the local cuisine benefits from a mixture of Turkish, Slavonic and Jewish influences not found elsewhere. The best fish restaurants are in the Kalamaria suburb, on the coast beyond the Palace of Music (*beyond map p. 591, F4*). Tavernas are everywhere, and easily found, with plenty on the acropolis, along Polydorou. The Ladadika area (*map p. 590, C4*) around the old olive market and tram station has good restaurants and some excellent bars. There are also plenty of lively bars and tavernas behind the *Bezesten* (the old Ottoman cloth hall), and between there and Ermou (*map p. 590, C3*). For snacks, there are always the *koulouri* vendors, who sell the traditional round sesame-seed rolls from handcarts.

Louloudakia. Good basic restaurant opposite the old Yehudi Hammam. *Odos Komninon. Map p. 590, C4.*

To Peran. Possibly the finest restaurant in town, if not in northern Greece. Excellent *mezedes*, delicious white *tarama*, superb salads, served in congenial, discreetly elegant surroundings. *Iktinou 22, T: 2310 252 977. Map p. 591, D4.*

Soutsoukakia. No design, no Michelin stars, just a good old-fashioned restaurant, in business since 1928. Blanket windows on two sides give a 1930s diner feel. Excellent appetizers, homemade fried potatoes, and the fattest olives you ever saw. *Corner of Venizelou and Kalapodaki. Map p. 590, C4.*

To Spiti tou Pasa. Rustic-looking taverna in a pretty building on a cobbled street in the upper town. Traditional menu. Ivy-covered terrace in summer. *Apostolou Pavlou 35. Map p. 591, E2.*

Zythos. *Zythos* means 'ale', but this is not only a beer hall. A pretty tile-floor and bentwood-chair café throws white cloths over its tables at lunchtime (1pm) and serves an eclectic menu from across Greece, with influences from beyond. Popular with families on Sunday. A variety of good beers is always available, as well as wine. At two addresses, one in Ladadika, the other overlooking the White Tower. *Katouni 2, T: 2310 540 284, map p. 590, C4; and Tsirogianni 7, T: 2310 279 010, map p. 591, E4.*

VISITING CHURCHES

Churches are open to visitors 8–1.30 & 3.30–8 (but not always regularly). In recent years many are only open on Sundays if they contain valuable icons. If you are planning a short visit to the city, and Byzantine monuments are a priority, it is a good idea to include a Sunday in your plans. As with everywhere else in Greece, you are expected to dress decorously (no bare legs or shoulders).

SHOPPING & MARKETS

Thessaloniki has arguably the best shopping in Greece if judged by the lower prices of all goods in northern Greece compared to Athens and the islands, and the astonishing number of top international-name designer and specialist shops. The main concentration of fashionable shops is on and around Tsimiski. Fur, leather goods and shoes are well represented, but also worth considering are Thessaloniki specialities such as handmade notepaper, tobacco goods, metalwork, icons and religious artefacts, CDs and musical instruments.

There are shops selling icons and Orthodox metalwork artefacts everywhere but some of the most expensive and remarkable are sold in shops near the Arch of Galerius.

The covered markets in the narrow lanes on either side of Aristotelous (Vlali, Vatikioti, and the Kentriki Stoa between Ermou and Irakleiou) are the only sensible place to shop for all foods, spices and herbs. Even those with perfect demotic Greek will find many words used in the vigorous exchanges between market traders that are unknown to them. Some Salonica slang expressions and numerous abusive swear words are said to embody words from the medieval Jewish dialect of Ladino spoken by Sephardic immigrants. Tavernas in the market area sometimes have live (often Roma) musicians on summer evenings.

The Harley Davidson motorcycle showroom, the largest in the world outside the USA, is near the White Tower.

NB: Cash in Euros is normal for all shopping. Credit cards are not widely accepted, and if they are can result in a price surcharge.

BOOKSHOPS & LOCAL GUIDES

There are numerous small guides and street maps available to the city and to individual monuments, but perhaps the best is the *Thessaloniki Tourist Guide* published by Malliaris and available from their bookshop at Aristotelous 9. Molho is an excellent bookshop at Tsimiski 10; highly recommended. Numerous books are available on the long and complex history of the city. Some of the most accessible for the foreign visitor include *Monuments of Thessalonika* by Apostolos Papagiannopoulos. For a general overview of the Byzantine city, see *Byzantine and Medieval Greece* by Paul Hetherington; for the late Ottoman period, Tozer's *Researches in the Highlands of Turkey* and Abbott's *Tour in Macedonia*. For the late-Jewish city there is Leon Sciaky's brilliant *Farewell to Salonika*. For the British military campaign in the First World War, *The Gardeners of Salonica*, by Alan Palmer. On the Second World War period, *Inside Hitler's Greece* by Mark Mazower. Mazower has also written a history of the city, *Salonica, City of Ghosts* (2004). Lord Kinross's monumental

work *Ataturk* gives a good picture of the important role Salonica played in the Ghazi's upbringing and later life.

FESTIVALS

The International Trade Fair is held in early September. The *Dimitriada* is a three-day holiday from St Dimitrios (26 October; religious processions) to Ochi Day (28 October; military parade).

BEACHES & SWIMMING

The harbour and bay seawater is foul and grossly polluted. Avoid swimming anywhere near Thessaloniki (see p. 685 for recommended beaches within easy reach).

VISITOR SERVICES

Banks: National Bank of Greece, Tsimiski 12; Ionian, Mitropoleos 3 and 7; Commercial, Ionos Dragoumi 21. There are numerous small Exchange Bureaux and money changers who often offer better rates, but with a minor risk of forged Euros.
Post Office: Tsimiski 28, open Mon–Fri 7–7; branch offices near the White Tower, and in Plateia Mitropoleos.
Consulates: The American Consulate is at Tsimiski 43, T: 2310 242 908; the British is at Venizelou 8, T: 2310 204 606.
Tourist Police: At airport and railway station.
Aliens Office: Plateia Polytechneiou 42.
Useful numbers: Police T: 100; First Aid Centre T: 166; All-night pharmacies T: 107; On-duty hospital information T: 160.

CENTRAL MACEDONIA

PELLA

Pella (Πέλλα) is the nearest important site to Thessaloniki, and one of the most interesting towns in central Macedonia. The small modern town on a hillock, with one or two tavernas and some cafés, is a nondescript place apart from a fine modern bronze equestrian statue of Alexander the Great, who was born here. Ancient Pella was capital of Macedonia at the height of its greatness.

HISTORY OF PELLA

Writing in the 6th century AD Stephanus of Byzantium, the author of the *Ethnica*, mentioned that Pella developed from an earlier site called *Bounomos* or *Bounomeia*, which may be the prehistoric settlement identified on Phakos hill (the location was later used for a fortified treasury by the Macedonian kings). First mentioned by Herodotus in the description of Xerxes' journey to the Axios river, Pella came to prominence at the end of the 5th century BC when King Archelaus made it his capital, moving from *Aigai* (Vergina). A protector of the arts and later mocked for his ambitions by Aelian (*Varia Historia 14,17*), Archelaus had an interesting entourage which included the poets Agathon and Timotheus, the dramatist Euripides (*see overleaf*) and the painter Zeuxis, who decorated his palace. Pella flourished under the reign of the philosopher king Antigonus Gonatas (274–239 BC). Captured by the Romans under Aemilius Paullus at the Battle of Pydna, it lost in importance to Thessaloniki. In the 1st century BC it was hit by an earthquake and replaced by a Roman colony which did not prosper. In AD 180 the poet Lucian, talking about the tradition of tame snakes from the region, described Pella as 'insignificant, with very few inhabitants'.

The ancient city

In the only known description of ancient Pella, Livy describes it as 'rising like an island on its immense earthwork'. When Pella was the capital of Philip II it was surrounded by a vast marshy fen that through most of the winter was flooded with seawater, forming a shallow, navigable lagoon connecting the city to the Thermaic Gulf. This is somewhat hard to imagine nowadays, with all the surrounding land drained for agriculture, but it is an essential backdrop to understanding the ancient site.

Ancient Pella was discovered in 1957, and is estimated to have occupied 3.8km square. Excavations by Professors Makaronas and Petsas in 1957–68 uncovered outstanding pebble mosaics of c. 300 BC. Pella was the first of the modern archaeological discoveries in Macedonia which have had such a signal effect on the consciousness of the Greek public and the understanding of regional history.

The museum

Open Tues–Sun 8.30–7 in summer, 8.30–3 in winter; T: 23820 31160.

The museum contains collections of finds from the excavations of private houses, the agora, the sanctuaries, the cemeteries and various sites in the district, including the Neolithic and Bronze Age *tell* site of *Mandalon*, northeast of Pella. Note the terracotta moulds for relief bowls and figurines locally made and sold in the agora; a late 5th-century red-figure hydria found in the cemetery near the agora bearing a representation of the fight between Athena and Poseidon for the name of the city of Athens; and a couple of statues of Alexander, one with the horns of Pan. Instances of architectural frescoes imitating marble (the style known as Early Pompeian), and six mosaics from local houses, show the lavish lifestyle of some of Pella's inhabitants. The mosaic floors—which can be compared to those of Olynthos (*see p. 678*)—were made of river pebbles of various sizes with a limited colour range. Special features were outlined with lead strips and baked clay; glass tesserae were used for added effect, and it is

Pebble mosaic (3rd century BC) showing Dionysus, wreathed in gold and riding on a panther.

thought that the eyes were made of semi-precious stones, though they are all now missing. Themes include a lion hunt, thought to represent Alexander the Great's rescue from a lion by Krateros near Susa in 332 BC, commemorated in Delphi (look at the details of the hair and faces for lead strips); a rare female centaur; a griffin attacking a deer, and Dionysus on the back of a panther (*pictured opposite*).

Euripides (c. 460–406 BC)

In his last set of plays, performed in 406 BC, Sophocles dressed his chorus and actors in mourning, as the news had just come through of the death of the great playwright Euripides, at Pella in Macedonia, where he was a protégé of King Archelaus. Euripides is astonishingly contemporary in his approach to his subject matter. He is ready, for instance, to challenge traditional views of the gods, asking why they should allow evil; even wondering whether the gods exist at all. And with divine intervention less prominent, Euripides can allow the psychological make-up of his characters to emerge more clearly. Thus we are presented with the behaviour of powerful women, such as Medea, who kills her own children in revenge for her humiliation at the hands of her husband, Jason; or Phaedra, whose amorous advances are rejected by her stepson Hippolytus. Phaedra commits suicide, but just before she dies she claims that it is Hippolytus who had shown incestuous desire towards her. He too kills himself, when his father lays a curse on him for his supposed transgression. This is recognisably modern drama. Euripides also takes current themes, such as war, and shows how miscalculation and accident can lead to violence. What if Helen of Troy, over whom the Trojan war was fought, never went to Troy, so that the war was based on a false claim? The relevance of Euripides was highlighted by the long Peloponnesian War, which ended in defeat for Athens shortly after the playwright died. In his final play, *The Bacchae*, possibly first performed at Pella (*though see also Dion; p. 582*), Euripides deals with the consequences of religious frenzy. A mother becomes so caught up in the ecstasy of the Dionysiac revels that she even kills her own son when he intrudes.

Euripides died in 407 or 406, either at Pella, or at Arethousa, torn to pieces by dogs. It is not known whether his death was an accident or whether the dogs were set on him by enemies. C.F.

The site

The town was laid out on an orthogonal grid with broad streets and an excellent water and drainage system. It covers a very large area (3.5km square), only part of which has been explored. By the museum are three house blocks cut across by the main road. The richest of the houses to the right is the **House of the Lion Hunt**, a palatial villa of the late 4th century BC, 50m wide and 90m long, with three open courts. The rooms were decorated with mosaic floors now in the museum. Remains of painted plaster, bronze bosses from the doors and terracotta antefixes show it was a splendid building, possibly   with an official function. Roof tiles stamped with the name of the town in the genitive case (*Pelles*) provided confirmation in 1957 that this was indeed the site of Pella. Left of the museum, a building houses a mosaic with a variant of the myth of Helen of Troy: here it is not Paris, but Theseus who carries her away. In the same house look out for an *Amazonomachy* and the *Stag Hunt* (signed 'Gnosis made this'), with a beautiful floral border contrasting with the violence of the scene.

It is the massive square **agora**, occupying 7 hectares at the centre of the city, that gives an idea of the true scale of the size of Pella. On the east side the remains of a kiln show that this was not just a market. Pottery and terracotta figurines were made and traded here. On the north side sanctuaries to Aphrodite and Cybele incorporated ritual areas, banqueting halls and metal workshops. Finds of clay papyrus seals suggest that the archives of the city were located in the southwest corner.

On an acropolis west of the modern village, some distance to the north of the museum and site, are the remains of a very large building complex: over 60,000m square of peristyle courts, public and private rooms and a swimming pool are set on the brow of the hill with an unique view over the Thermaic Gulf. They are though to belong to the **Palace of Archelaus**, in which Alexander the Great and perhaps Philip II were born. It had a monumental façade, an entrance with a ramp and Doric columns. It was famous in Antiquity, and as Socrates put it: 'Nobody would go to Macedonia to see the king, but many would come far to see his palace'.

Two **Macedonian tombs** with monumental façades (*visit by arrangement with the museum*) were excavated in the mid-1990s. Tomb C (c. 300 BC) has remains of painted stucco decorations and the stone base of the funerary couch. In tomb D, the marble door leading to the funerary chamber has a painted relief of a Medusa head and relief shields. Dated to the 4th century BC, it has several later graffiti and votive inscriptions.

NEW DISCOVERIES AT PELLA

In February 2006 an enormous eight-chamber Hellenistic tomb was discovered, quite by chance, when a farmer happened upon it while ploughing. The field where it was found is adjacent to the ancient cemetery of Pella. With a total surface area of over 60m square, it is the largest such tomb discovered in Greece, with more chambers than any other so far unearthed (previous chamber tombs have had up to three). The walls of the burial chambers in the Pella tomb were painted in red, blue and gold, traces of which remain. Votive tomb artefacts, coins and jewellery were found scattered by the entrance, leading archaeologists to conclude that the tomb was plundered in Antiquity. Interestingly, it is of a similar type to chamber tombs in Egypt dating from the time of the Ptolemies, Alexander the Great's successors. Incised slabs bearing the names of the deceased were found *in situ*. Maria Akmati, head of the team excavating the tomb, believes that this was the burial crypt of a wealthy patrician family.

ENVIRONS OF PELLA

At nearby **Agrosikia** (10km from Pella) there is an ancient settlement occupied from Neolithic to Early Christian times and centred on a recently excavated mound at Peliti. Off this road, **Rachona** has a 4th-century cemetery with monumental tombs covered by a mound, and funerary sculpture. At the necropolis in **Archontiko**, in 2005, rectangular trench graves were excavated containing sumptuously apparelled warriors from the 5th and 6th centuries BC. They were buried fully armed, their faces covered in gold masks, clad in gold breastplates and in armour embroidered with gold.

Giannitsa (Γιαννιτσά), the largest town (pop. 40,000) in the nomarchy of Pella, is a dull place today, dominated by intensive agriculture. In Ottoman times it stood by a permanent lake in the marshes, Lake Giannitsa, which was finally drained in the 1930s. As *Yeniceyi Vardar* it was a holy place of the Turks. In a dilapidated mosque are the tombs of the Evrenos family (14th–15th centuries), descendants of the conqueror of Macedonia. A bronze monument by the road commemorates the Battle of Giannitsa (1912), which paved the way for the liberation of Thessaloniki. The battle actually took place at Melissi, further to the west, where the Turks fiercely contested the crossing of the river.

THE AXIOS RIVER

The Axios (Αξιός) or Vardar, the largest river in Macedonia, rises deep in former Yugoslavia and flows through Greece for just 80km from the Iron Gates to the sea. Before the flood and reclamation works, instituted by Venizelos in 1925, gave the river its present bed, the area was largely malarial marshes. Those marshes were flooded in winter and made travel very difficult, as the epic accounts of British travellers' difficulties in the Ottoman period attest. Further irrigation works, jointly controlling the Axios and Aliakmon, undertaken in 1953–63 by Karamanlis, have brought the greater part of the floodplain under cultivation. And though malaria may not plague the region today, over-extraction of ground water for farming and uncontrolled use of chemical fertilisers and pesticides have led to other environmental problems.

The Axios Valley

Tomb hummocks on either side of the road are common as you leave Pella to the east. **Chalkidona** grew up after 1923 round the old timber-framed *han* at the junction where the Via Egnatia and the Veroia road, of Roman origin or earlier, divided to pass Lake Loudias (later Lake Giannitsa). The original Ottoman town was an important garrison centre. To the south is a fertile plain, drained by the Loudias, an artificial river that perpetuates the name of the Classical lake. A series of funerary mounds marks its former perimeter.

Irrigation canals carry water from the Axios river barrage (1954–58) 3km north of the road (approach-road on top of the dyke). At the crossing of the Axios is a girder bridge of 14 spans, built by British sappers in 1945. **Gefyra**, at the junction of the old road to the border, lies where the Axios was bridged before being diverted to its modern bed—hence its name (*gefyra* means bridge). A prehistoric table-mound and Classical finds prove the antiquity of the site. The agreement surrendering Thessaloniki to Greece was signed here in 1912.

At **Sindos** (Σίνδος) important Archaic and Classical cemeteries have been discovered since 1980. The burials, which were in stone cists, stone or clay sarcophagi or simple pits, probably belong to the nearby settlement mound of Anchialos, which is perhaps to be identified with the ancient town of *Chalastra*. Potters' kilns were constructed over the cemetery area in the 4th century. (*The spectacular finds are in Thessaloniki, but not on display at the time of writing; see p. 597*). Pyrgos, another candidate for Chalastra, was on the coast in Classical times. Between Sindos and Pyrgos, Xerxes' fleet waited for the army to catch up. Nea Malgara, a huge refugee settlement amid rice-fields on the right bank of the Axios, is built on land reclaimed since ancient times. Kleidi may represent ancient *Haloros* where, following Preclassical boundaries, the *nome* of Imathia pushes a narrow tongue to the sea.

The approach to Edessa

On approaching Edessa, the visitor first encounters some of the majestic landscape that makes a visit to Macedonia so rewarding at any time of year. Many devotees consider September and October the best time to appreciate the forest hues, although distant views are often clearest and most magnificent on a sunny day after winter snowfall. Ten kilometres away to the north, Meterizi (1598m), the third highest peak of the Paiko Mountains, rises abruptly from the plain. Mt Paiko itself is 1650m.

You cross two of the large flood canals that channel to the Aliakmon the waters of the countless mountain streams from Mt Vermion that once inundated the plain. Edessa and its waterfalls come into view ahead, with the town perched on the edge of a precipitous limestone cliff. To the northeast are Kali and Anydro, which may be the site of ancient *Meneida*. Mandalo has a Neolithic and Early Bronze Age settlement under excavation. Continuing to Edessa you cross the railway and pass among orchards of peaches and pears. Beyond Rizari the valley becomes lush as you again cross the copious streams of the Vodas below Edessa's falls. Turns to the right lead to the archaeological site. The town itself is reached after a short, steep ascent.

EDESSA

Edessa (Έδεσσα), in Macedonian *Vodena*, is beautifully situated on top of a steep cliff rising above the Axios plain.The waters of the Edessos cascade down the cliff in one of the most famous and dramatic waterfalls in Greece. The town itself occupies a semi-circular plateau (350m), backed by the foothills of Mt Vermion. Below the

Edessa cliff is the interesting small site of ancient Edessa. Through it flow numerous cascades, which inspired the Slav name of Vodena ('the waters'). Capital of the nomarchy of Pella, this small town, with a population of 17,128, is a favourite summer resort. A commanding situation on the Via Egnatia has always made it strategically important, and many regional travellers feel that it marks an invisible psychological boundary: here the calmly predictable agricultural landscape ends, giving way to the drama of the Balkans. Local industries include the manufacture of carpets, and Edessa is a prominent trading and agricultural centre. The outstanding views in all directions take in the Pindus to the west, Olympus to the southeast, and the heights beyond Thessaloniki to the east.

The numerous streams that cross the town unite to the east to fall in cascades. The area at the top of the falls has been turned into an attractive park at the cliff's edge. The drop is 24m, after which the water flows steeply to the plain. The cliffs are covered with luxuriant vegetation, including vines, pomegranates, figs and nut trees. There are said to be crayfish in the waters. The volume of water is best seen in spring, when melting snow on the mountains to the north and west produces a raging torrent. Under the falls is a cave with stalactites.

HISTORY OF EDESSA

Until the discoveries in 1977 at Vergina, Edessa was thought to be the site of Archelaus' capital city of *Aigai*, a belief the local inhabitants are disinclined to relinquish. Edessa was a flourishing place in Antiquity, and always a vital transport nexus on the Via Egnatia and the Ottoman road which followed it. Until 1939 it had always had a large Slav population, and was a centre of pro-Bulgarian activism under the late Ottoman Empire. In October 1912 the Greek army entered the town, though it was reoccupied for a time by the Bulgarians in the Second World War.

Edessa was an early centre of the industrial revolution in Macedonia, when merchants from Naousa invested in water-powered textile mills after 1874. The heyday of industrial Vodena was the inter-war period, and as late as 1940 Edessa had 2,500 industrial workers out of 15,000 inhabitants. After the Second World War there was rapid decline, and the last water-powered factory closed in 1962.

The modern town

Edessa has a number of surviving industrial buildings and Ottoman houses, mostly on the east side of town, including a hemp factory (some of the disused machinery is still in place) below the top of the falls. To the west of the park is the old quarter of Varosi, which has been well restored. Odos Makedonomachon, for example, has attractive old houses, as well as a cultural centre—in a startling modern building— where you can buy a useful English-language guide: *Edessa, City of Waters*. Below, in

Odos Megalou Alexandrou, from the terrace near the Archbishop's Palace, there is a splendid view, with the monastery of Aghia Triada in the foreground. The church of the Koimisis tis Theotokou, now the archiepiscopal chapel, has a fine iconostasis, and incorporates antique columns (as does the smaller Aghii Petrou kai Pavlou nearby), probably from a temple on the site. Wall paintings have been revealed in recent investigations. Next to the church is the old Parthenagogeion (girls' school; 1877), now housing a folk museum. Sections of the town's medieval walls can be seen in a lane descending to the right. Nearer the centre, off Odos Egnatias, an attractive mosque, the Yeni Djami (1904), houses an archaeological collection (*sadly not normally open*). There is a fine late Ottoman clock tower in Aris Dimitris. At the north end of the town in the area of Kioupri, reached by various pedestrianised streets (including Odos Konstantinoupoleos) from the park by the falls, is a fine single-span bridge, of Roman or Byzantine date. The acropolis of the ancient city was on the site of the modern town: sections of the walls have been traced and other finds made.

Ancient Edessa

Signs mark a left turn for the site or for Aghia Triada monastery (1865, but incorporating antique material). The site has well preserved walls, Classical in origin but with extensive Roman and Byzantine repairs and alterations. Much of the visible remains are Byzantine, reusing earlier material. A gate leads to a paved main street with a re-erected Ionic colonnade with inscriptions. Further out of town are the hydro-electric works (*no admission*), but you can continue past the gate to the reservoir at the foot of the falls. By the huge pipe are the overgrown remains of an Early Christian basilica.

EXCURSIONS FROM EDESSA

Lake Vergoritis

Lake Vergoritis (or Vergoritida) is one of the largest and deepest lakes in Greece. It makes a pleasant drive from Edessa and is a very good place for birdwatching, particularly in cold winters, when birds of prey from the nearby mountains and forests come to hunt on the lake shores. The ecology of the lake was the first Balkan study project of the prominent British Albanologist and author Edith Durham.

West of the lake is the town of Amintaio or Amindeo ('Αμύνταιο; named after Amyntas, ancestor of Philip II). In 1941 the railway here was blown up before the advancing Germans by British irregular troops led by the author Peter Fleming. The local wines are good. A prehistoric cemetery (222 tombs) yielded valuable finds in 1900. A road leads north along the shore of the little Lake Petron to the archaeological site at Petres. Palaios Aghios Athanasios is well worth visiting to see local architecture at its best. It is a lovely place for summer walking.

The border country

From Edessa a road leads directly north into mountainous country (there is a bus six times daily in summer) via Apsalos to **Aridaia**, a friendly but uninteresting town in a low, well-watered plain hemmed in by the magnificent crests of the Voras range, which forms the frontier with FYROM. There is very good walking up here, and cross-country skiing in winter. Tobacco, and silk and—as ever in Macedonia—peppers are grown. To the southeast, just outside Chrisi (c. 1km on a dirt road) can be seen a substantial section (wall and towers) of the fortifications of what was probably **Byzantine Moglena** overlooking the river Moglenitsa. In the centre of the site is a Middle Byzantine basilica in a bad state; to the north a cemetery basilica and some graves have been investigated.

A road goes on west of Aridaia via Loutraki (rooms) to **Loutra Loutrakiou**, known locally just as Loutra, a large if somewhat down-at-heel spa in a pretty glen with plane trees shading the tumbling waters. Nearby caves have been discovered with ritual carvings.

NAOUSA & ENVIRONS

Naousa (Νάουσα) is a flourishing town standing on a travertine terrace between two tributaries of the Arapitsa, one of which falls near by in a cascade. The town is known for its full red wine, its peaches and its silk. The name is a corruption of *Nea Augousta*, and it was known to the Turks as *Agustos*. It occupies an ancient site, perhaps that of *Mieza* (*but see below*). The town was destroyed in 1821 and again suffered in 1944–48, but its narrow streets remain on an old plan. In its carnival, masked dancers with scimitars symbolise the oppression of the Janissaries. Near the modern church of Aghia Paraskevi a fine park looks out over the plain and there is a small military museum. The wooden Aghios Dimitrios is built over an ancient structure.

Ancient Mieza

Kefalovrysi (Κεφαλόβρυση), off the road from Naousa to Kopanos, where a dressed rockface (with beam holes) backs a terrace (cave shrines etc) overlooking the Isvoria springs, may be the site of the nymphaion of *Mieza*, where Philip II established the school in which Aristotle taught Alexander. The setting is fine and the site has been recently tidied. The site is flanked by the villages of Lefkadia and Kopanos. **Lefkadia** (ancient *Leucadia*), a hamlet west of the road, has given its name to three Macedonian tombs, lying near the main road before you reach the village turn. The discovery of a building with mosaics south of the village and another on a hill near the Arapitsa suggest that Lefkadia was a place of some importance, and is another candidate for ancient *Mieza*.

Signposted to the right, on a by-road crossing the railway, is the **Great Tomb** (or Tomb of Judgement), protected by a concrete hangar. On the façade two outer pilasters and four Doric fluted columns support an entablature with painted metopes and triglyphs, and a frieze in bas-relief depicting a battle between Macedonians and Persians. A second (Ionic) storey, rising above the vault, has seven false doors surmounted by a pediment (of which only fragments survive). Two life-size frescoes in vivid colours represent (left) the deceased with Hermes Psychopompos and (right) Aeacus and Rhadamanthys, the judges of the Underworld. An ante-chamber leads to a square, barrel-vaulted chamber with painted panels between engaged pilasters. Rows of nails remain *in situ* where presumably garlands were hung. The tomb is dated to the beginning of the 3rd century BC.

Two hundred metres further on is the **Tomb of the Flowers** (3rd–2nd centuries BC) with fine floral and figural paintings. Behind an Ionic façade are two chambers. Although the tomb was robbed, a marble sarcophagus was found and ivory fragments apparently of mythological figures decorating a casket.

Returning to the main road 200m farther north (sign), is the accessible 'Kinch' Tomb, and 300m beyond this (left) the much smaller vaulted Lyson Callicles Tomb of the early 2nd century BC, with a plain exterior. It contained the urn burials of three related families. Their names are inscribed on the niches inside, and the walls are painted with garlands and decorative panels.

MOUNT VERMION & SELI

Information from ski resort offices in Veroia, T: 23310 26237 and in Seli itself, T: 23310 49226; www.seli-ski.gr

Mount Vermion (Βέρμιο; 2052m) is one of the most densely forested mountains in Greece, with beech, oak, chestnut, pine, hazel, whitethorn, cornel-cherry and evergreen maquis. It is home to roe deer, red deer, and wild boar. It was a centre of resistance in the Second World War (see N.G.L. Hammond, *Venture into Greece*, 1983). From Naousa a steep road mounts to Ano Seli (1420m, with an 18-bed refuge) on the northeast slope. Here winter sports are held from mid-January to mid-March (Greek ski championship in late February). In late spring and summer delightful walks can be taken on the mountain. The southeastern foothills are given over to the vineyards of the Naousa appellation, which produces noted wines from the Xynomavro grape (the same variety as is cultivated on Mount Olympus). The best internationally-known wineries are Tsantali and Boutari.

Kopanos and Nea Nikomedia

Kopanos has an important cemetery (4th century to Hellenistic, including a Macedonian tomb) which was discovered in 1977. The settlement with which it is to be associated may lie beneath the modern village. South of here, at Nea Nikomedia, is a Neolithic settlement (now little to see) excavated in 1961–64 by the British and American Schools. Radio-carbon tests have given a date of c. 6200 BC, making it by far the earliest Neolithic settlement known on the Greek mainland. Houses of two periods were found, arranged round a central structure, which yielded female idols and serpentine axes. The settlement was fortified.

VEROIA

Veroia (Βέροια; pronounced Vérria) is an old town with some good historic buildings and a very long history. It lies west of Thessaloniki, beyond an exposed and very flat plain that was once a lagoon into which both the Axios and Aliakmon drained, and as late as Classical times was navigable nearly to Pella. Veroia is the *Berea* of the New Testament, and is the capital of the nomarchy of Imathia. It is attractively situated on a travertine terrace (188m) near the east foot of Mt Vermion, commanding the plain below. The Tripotamos, a tributary of the Aliakmon, runs through a ravine just north of the town centre. The local cloth industry, using hemp and flax spun locally, has declined but there is a market (Tuesday) for peaches and apples from the district. Though there has been much undistinguished modern building, the town well repays a visit as numerous churches, traditional houses and Ottoman buildings survive, and the bazaar area (lower part of Vasileos Konstantinou and side streets) gives a good feeling of its original character. On the debit side are a rash of modern cafés and poor food. A useful guidebook (*Veria*, in Greek and English) published by the Town Council, is available from some bookshops. In difficulty, enquire at the Dimarcheion.

HISTORY OF VEROIA

Berea emerges at the end of the 5th century BC as the second city of Imathia, known from an inscription to have been dedicated to Heracles Cynagidas. It was the first Macedonian city to surrender after the Roman victory of Pydna in 168 BC. Pompey spent the winter of 49–48 BC here. St Paul and Silas, having experienced trouble at Thessaloniki, withdrew to Berea, where the Jews, 'more noble' than those of Salonica, 'searched the scriptures daily' (*Acts XVII, 10–12*). At an early date Berea became a bishopric. When Diocletian reorganised the Roman colonial empire, he made Berea one of the two capitals of Macedonia. About the end of the 10th century it endured the Bulgar invasions, and in the 14th century was occupied by the Serbs. The Turks, who called the town *Karaferiye*, established a military colony here. Many ancient Greek and Roman finds have come from rescue excavations in the town. Elements of the fortification system have been traced on the north, south and east. Fragments of the stadium have been recovered outside the walls to the east and temples are mentioned in Hellenistic inscriptions. Many finds have come from graves, including a cemetery of vaulted rock-cut chamber tombs of the Hellenistic period just outside the ancient walls to the north, and the large Classical northeast cemetery near the railway station.

The eastern approach and museum

Near the top of the hill at the entrance to the town, remnants of the ramparts survive. A tower, of pseudo-isodomic construction resembling the Letaia Gate at Thessaloniki, has been dated to the 3rd century AD; among reused blocks are grave reliefs and shield metopes.

The pleasantest approach to the town centre can be made via Leof. Anixeos (left after the top of the hill), which curves round to follow the edge of the plateau—the line of the ancient fortifications—overlooking the plain. The **museum** (*Anixeos 47, open 8–3, closed Mon*) stands in a garden lined with grave stelae of various periods (especially Roman), altars and other architectural fragments. Inside there is a plan of Veroia with the locations of ancient sites, and a model of a typical rock-cut tomb. Grave groups of the 4th–2nd centuries BC include fine bronze vessels and terracottas. Room 2 has sculpture,

Red-figure krater (mid-4th century BC) showing Dionysus and Aphrodite.

mostly Hellenistic grave stelae, one of which, from the Great Tumulus at Vergina, is painted. Inscriptions include the 2nd-century BC gymnasium rules. Roman sculpture (in Room 3) consists of grave stelae, portraits and mythological figures. Marble table supports have figures of Ganymede and the eagle, and a winged demon.

Central Veroia

At the centre of town, where Venizelou and Mitropoleos meet, is the delightful 14th-century **church of Christ the Saviour** (Sotiras Christos; *open 8.30–1 except Mon*) with an external arcade added in the 18th century. The interior has 14th-century frescoes by Georgios Kallierges (*Annunciation*; *Raising of Lazarus*; *Entry into Jerusalem*; *Crucifixion*). According to his own estimation, Kallierges was the 'finest painter in all Thessaly'. The realism of the figures is striking, and scholars have attributed this characteristic of Macedonian art of the period to the region's close links with Constantinople, links which were severed after 1430, when the Ottomans took Thessaloniki.

Parallel with Mitropoleos is Odos Kentrikis, which gives more of a flavour of old Veroia, with its narrow side streets and old houses sloping down to the Tripotamos. At the junction with Perikleous is the 11th-century **Old Cathedral** (*Palaias Mitropolis*), impressive in spite of its poor state (one side-aisle has been demolished), with Early Christian columns and remains of 13th- and early 14th-century wall painting. Attached to the north aisle is a truncated minaret. Opposite stands the plane tree from which the Turks hanged Archbishop Kallimachos in 1436.

Mitropoleos, a busy shopping street with most of the major facilities, rises gently past the modern Cathedral of Sts Peter and Paul, with re-used capitals in the narthex. The street brings you out into Plateia Orologiou. To the right, behind the lawcourts, is the **site of the ancient acropolis**. The major visible structure is a tower, said to be Byzantine, incorporating Classical masonry. On the opposite side of the square, a few yards up the first turn off Odos Kolokotroni, is the so-called 'bema' (a fanciful reconstruction of 1961) from which St Paul is said to have preached.

Nearby is the **synagogue**, in the Jewish quarter of Barbouta. To get there, turn from Mitropoleos up Kentrikis and into 10th Merarchias. Barbouta is on your left, a ramshackle district of mainly 18th-century buildings, some with Hebrew inscriptions.

The lower town

On the other side of Mitropoleos, Odos Loutrou leads to a delightful **Ottoman bath complex** (*Tuzci Hammam*), mentioned by Evliya Çelebi when he visited Veroia. It has been well restored externally, though the interior not accessible. Here Odos Kyriotissis has old houses and at the very end, where it narrows and descends, a remarkable section of the Roman/Byzantine defences supporting a 'modern' house.

The numerous churches (about 40 survive) of wattle and timber construction were the most unusual feature of the lower town. Built under the Ottoman Empire, they were sited inconspicuously behind houses and their appearance disguised. Formerly they were hard to find. Most of the ramshackle old houses have now been replaced by modern blocks and the churches revealed. They are usually locked, though guided walks can be arranged (*enquire at the Byzantine Museum, Odos Mylos Markou; T: 23310 21718 or 23310 25827*).

The road to Vergina

Some of the finest and most accessible Macedonian tombs are near Veroia, and belong mainly to the late Classical and Hellenistic periods. Although subterranean, they were splendid structures, built of local poros stone, with vaulted roofs. The façades of smaller tombs have a pediment or a simply sculptured cornice. Later and grander examples resemble the Classical temple, with columns, entablature and pediment. The doors were generally of marble and hung on metal hinges. The main chamber may be preceded by an ante-room. Furniture consisted of marble couches or thrones. The walls were usually plastered and painted. The façade may also be frescoed.

With the Pieria mountains ahead of you, you descend to the Aliakmon Dam, a graceful concrete structure, 320m long, whose 19 piers carry the road across the river. The approach on the north curves to avoid the 3rd-century BC Temple Tomb, visible to the left (*no admission*), discovered during construction work. The outer doorway has triglyphs, the inner is white with a yellow moulding. The interior is plastered and painted in bands, white below, black and red above.

VERGINA

Vergina (Βεργίνα), a UNESCO World Heritage site in the foothills of the Pierian mountains, is a village created in 1923 by refugees amalgamating the two small agricultural villages of Koutles and Barbes. It replaces a city that was already an important centre in the Iron Age and reached the peak of prosperity in the 5th–4th centuries BC when it was the most important centre of the area. It has now been identified with ancient *Aigai*, which Perdiccas, the founder of the Macedonian monarchy, made his capital. The residence of the kings until the seat of government was transferred to Pella at the end of the 5th century, Aigai (apparently named after the profusion of goats in the area) remained a national sanctuary and a royal burial place. According to tradition, the Macedonian dynasty would perish as soon as one of its kings was buried elsewhere: and so it did, after Alexander the Great was buried in Egypt.

The royal burial grounds were plundered in 274 BC by Celtic mercenaries, 'people with an insatiable appetite for treasure' (*Plutarch, Life of Pyrrhus 25.6*). The Roman conquest of 168 spelled the end of the Antigonid dynasty: Aigai was destroyed. Rebuilt in the 1st century AD, it was later abandoned.

The site was first excavated in 1860 by Léon Heuzey, then in the 1930s by K. A. Rhomaios and from 1959–92 by Manolis Andronikos. The identification with Aigai first mooted in 1968 has been confirmed by later finds.

The site and museum

Open Tues–Sun 8–7; Mon 12.30–7; winter Tues–Sun 8.30–3. An excellent, well-illustrated survey of the site has been provided by Andronikos in his Vergina: the Royal Tombs.

The Great Tumulus is a good starting point. Twelve metres high and 110m across, it is signposted from the village. It covers a smaller mound which overlay the royal tombs and was probably constructed by order of Antigonus Gonatas to protect his own burial and cover the damage caused by the plundering Celts. Excavated by Andronikos in 1977–78, it has now been reconstructed and turned into a spectacular museum. There is an explanatory video left of the entrance. In the hall, the limestone cist tomb dated to 350 BC, looted in Antiquity, is notable for its frieze with a depiction the *Rape of Persephone*, attributed to the painter Nicomachus. The tomb stood next to the destroyed Heroön, a place for the cult of dead kings.

The highlight of the visit is downstairs, where the dimmed lighting allows the gold to shine. The **tomb of Philip II**, a vaulted construction with two chambers separated by a marble door, can only be viewed from the outside. You can admire the façade with a frieze of Alexander hunting lions. The finds, shown nearby, include two marble sarcophagi containing solid gold burial caskets (one weighing almost 8kg; note the 16-point Macedonian star), gold wreaths (one with acorns and oak leaves weighing over 700g), a sceptre, a diadem, chryselephantine ceremonial couches, and weapons. The tomb is thought to have contained, in the far chamber, the remains of Philip II, murdered here in 336 BC. The cremated bones shrouded in purple cloth were examined by forensic experts, who concluded that they belonged to a male aged 35–55, who had sustained a severe eye wound. Philip died aged 46, and had been blinded in one eye by an arrow 18 years before. The remains in the front rooms are believed to belong to his last wife, Cleopatra, who died shortly after him, either by suicide or murder.

The **Tomb of the Prince**, with the cremated remains of a youth and a woman, was also unlooted. The tomb is generally believed to have belonged to Alexander the Great's ill-fated posthumous son Alexander IV, murdered by Cassander c. 311 with his mother Roxane. The façade has moulded shields and the interior a frieze of riders and chariots. Nearby are displayed the finds, including a silver hydria that contained the ashes and the gold oak wreath that was placed around its neck. There is also a funerary couch decorated with gold and ivory (a representation of Dionysus with a flute player and a satyr) and weapons.

Philip II's golden quiver.

The Palace of Palatitsia

The Palace of Palatitsia was named after the old village to the northeast by Heuzey, who first excavated it in 1861—though the name strongly suggests that the local people had an inkling of a palatial structure somewhere in the area. It is situated on a low hill to the southeast of the tumulus next to the acropolis. The site is marked by a very large oak tree. Measuring 105m by 89m, this is one of the largest buildings of ancient Greece. It was built by Antigonus Gonatas, or according to others by Cassander, and destroyed by fire. Constructed in mud brick on stone foundations with marble thresholds, it had been conceived on a grand scale, with a monumental two-storey porch leading to a central courtyard with a Doric colonnade. Several banqueting rooms with drains and off-centre doors to accommodate the couches have been identified. A number of superb pebble mosaic floors, both in the private and public areas of the building, have been uncovered (*not all open to the public*).

On the east side a circular room with a dedicatory inscription to Heracles Patroös, the mythical ancestor of the Macedonian kings, may have been either a throne room, a dining room for people to sit rather than recline to eat, or a place of worship. On the north range, a terrace connected the palace to a small **theatre** discovered in 1982. Here, in 336 BC, Philip II was murdered in full view of the audience, by one of his bodyguard during the wedding celebrations of his daughter. Diodorus Siculus' steamy account of the circumstance leading to the event (*16.91.5*), suggest that all was not well in the Kingdom of Macedon. The **city of Aigai** lies north of the theatre: so far a couple of sanctuaries, one to Cybele and one to Eucleia, have been investigated.

The rest of the site is occupied by tombs: Aigai was already famous in Antiquity for its necropoleis. To the east of the Great Tumulus extends the prehistoric cemetery (10th–7th centuries BC), partly excavated by Andronikos in 1952–61. It had some 300 small mounds over clusters of burials. Though already disturbed in Hellenistic times, it yielded a number of intact burials with iron swords, bronze ornaments (including a curious axe with three sets of double heads), Lausitz ware and Protogeometric pottery showing the area had strong connections with central Europe.

The typical Macedonian tomb, partly underground (probably for security) and covered by a small mound, with a monumental façade, a barrel vault—unique in Greece at the time—marble doors and occasionally stone couches, appeared in the 4th century. About 50 are known in Greece. Aigai has a few more than those mentioned above. Among these, two may have belonged to royalty: both the **Rhomaios tomb**, named after its excavator, and the **Eurydice tomb**, situated northeast of the palace, contained painted marble thrones. It is suggested that the latter—a very early instance dating to 340 BC—may have belonged to Philip II's mother.

The Tripotamos Valley

Orchards clothe the rolling hills and stalls of produce line the road as it climbs into the Tripotamos valley (*map p. 574*), which divides the outlying spur of Mati Pouliou (1238m) from the main Vermion range. A turning (left) crosses a ridge to Lefkopetra, with scanty remains of an ancient temple. There is much evidence of marble quarrying. The road clings to a shelf on the north side of the narrowing valley, beautifully clothed with oak and beech woods. Kastania has a magnificent position on the hillside (902m) amid orchards of apples and nuts. Above the village stands the Monastery of Panaghia Soumela, built by refugees who brought with them (c. 1930) from the Soumela monastery in Pontus an icon of the Virgin attributed to St Luke. It is a focus of pilgrimage on 15th August (the Assumption). As you cross the shoulder of Mati Pouliou there is a tremendous view into the Aliakmon Valley; the river, just over 3km away, is more than 914m below. Beyond it the jagged heights of Pieria tower to 2190m. The road continues to climb, with retrospective views from the steep turns towards Kastania, before turning away from the Aliakmon to reach its summit (1359m) on a south ridge of Vermion. At the summit is Zoödochos Pigi (with restaurants), which is named after a small church built above a spring. Mt Olympus is seen to the east behind Pieria. The road descends by a spectacular ladder and vertiginous curves. At Polymilos, with water mills, it enters a gentle upland valley with the Skopos hills to the south; the villages lie off the road on their slopes. On the edge of the plain at Voskochori a small Christian basilica (? early 6th century) came to light in 1935. At Akrini (11km to the right) another, with delightful animal mosaics, was uncovered in 1959. Aghios Dimitrios has a power station. The road descends gently with long straight stretches, running along the south edge of the drained Kitrini Limni to Drepano and Kozani.

Kozani

Kozani (Κοζάνη) is a prosperous agricultural town with an interesting historic centre despite dull outskirts. There has been much use of European Union subsides to develop fruit tree plantations. It was an important garrison and market town in the Ottoman period, and some parts of the centre, with pretty alleyways and winding streets, recall that era. There is a small archaeological museum and also an ethnographic museum. There is not much reason to stay the night other than in transit, but Kozani is a good transport centre—particularly for those travelling bus—for mountain towns such as Kastoria (*see p. 639*) and Florina (*see p. 644*).

KILKIS & LAKE DOÏRANIS

Kilkis (Κίλκις) is a welcoming town set in rolling green countryside. It has a good museum and an important Neolithic cave, and one or two good new hotels that make it a possible centre for exploration. A substantial number of local people have some Turkish blood in their pattern of descent, particularly town dwellers, as many Turkish-speaking Christians were settled here after 1922.

The rocky hill on which the first settlement has been located was inhabited from early times. A small fortress was built here in the Byzantine era. After the Ottoman conquest, the town became an important garrison centre, and market town for the rich surrounding region. As the Ottoman Empire collapsed, control of the area became a vital objective for both the Greeks and the Bulgarians, and there was extensive fighting for Kilkis in the Second Balkan War in 1913.

The town

Most of the town as it exists today was built in the 20th century after destruction in wars, but it is well worth walking to the top of the hill to see the **Cave of Saint George**, with Neolithic remains and an interesting short underground tour. The cave was discovered by accident in 1925 by a local man during quarrying work. More than 300 important fossils have been found here, including examples of the Giant Deer and hyenas (*for information on opening hours T: 23410 20054*). On the opposite side of the hill is the Church of St George, built in 1917 on the ruins of a Byzantine building that in turn stood within the Ottoman fortress. The **Archaeological Museum** in Odos Outskouni (*open 8.30–3; closed Mon*) is a very good small museum. The main exhibits are the statues found at Europos (*see below*), but there is an excellent picture of the development of the civilisation of the region from Stone Age to Byzantine times. There is an exhibit of the findings of the British School at Tsaouitsa and Axiochori.

AROUND KILKIS

On a rocky extrusion from the plain, about 10km west of Kilkis at **Nea Gynaikokastro**, stands a ruined Byzantine fortress, highly spectacular at sunset. It was built in the 14th century by the Emperor Andronicus Palaeologus to protect the road north from Thessaloniki, but the outcrop was inhabited from early times, with an Iron Age graveyard recently discovered containing 370 urns of human remains. An Iron Age village was also discovered nearby. **Pikrolimni**, south from Gynaikokastro near the village of Gallikos, is the main spa in Greece where heated local clay is used for treatments. The spa is open all the year round and specialises in diseases of the joints and musculoskeletal system, of the skin, internal female genitals, and post-fracture problems (*T: 23410 29971, email pikrol@otenet.gr*).

Across the Axios, about 6km from the modern town of Goumenissa, on the slopes of Mount Païko outside Evropos, is **ancient *Europos*** (Ευρωπός), which was the principal settlement from the Classical period near modern Kilkis. When excavations began in 1989, some magnificent statues were discovered, particularly a 6th-century BC Cycladic *kouros*. It is now in Kilkis museum. Goumenissa itself has some fine old houses and 19th-century streets and tavernas.

Lake Doïranis straddles the border with FYROM and is a pleasant, evocative reed-fringed lake with pleasant villages and rooms to rent. Though there have been recent problems with water levels, the lake fish are very good, eels particularly.

PRACTICAL INFORMATION

The Macedonian summer is hot, but without the extremes of heat of more southern parts of Greece, and the spring and autumn are generally very pleasant. Winter weather in January and February is often severe; indeed the town of Florina is reputed to have the most rigorous climate of any town in Greece.

GETTING AROUND

• **By bus:** Hourly buses link Thessaloniki and Pella. There are also fast, regular buses between Thessaloniki and Edessa, and hourly (approx.) buses to Veroia, and from Veroia to Vergina and Naousa. Kilkis is served by local buses and a roughly hourly service to/from Thessaloniki. Buses run from Kilkis to the villages around Lake Doïranis about twice daily.
• **By rail:** Some Thessaloniki–Veroia trains continue to Naousa and Edessa (journey time c. 2hrs; 70mins to Veroia). The train to Edessa is slower than the bus, but a lovely journey. There is a cheap through service about three times a day from Thessaloniki via Edessa to Florina and the north, with magnificent views. Highly recommended. Trains run from Kilkis (station c. 4km outside town at Kristoni) to Serres in c. 90mins.

INFORMATION OFFICES

Edessa T: 23810 20300; www.edessacity.gr
Veroia Imathia Tourist Office T: 23310 28201.

Edessa

€€ **Xenia**. Modern bunker of a building, but the rooms have spectacular views. Swimming pool. Filippou 35, T: 23810 21898, www.xeniaedessa.gr

€ **Alfa**. Modern hotel with bright, clean rooms. Egnatia 28, T: 23819 22221, hotel-a@otenet.gr

€ **Varosi**. Nicely restored historic building. Arch. Meletiou 45–47, T: 23810 21865.

Giannitsa

€ **Alexandros**. Small hotel with restaurant offering basic but comfortable accommodation. T: 23820 24700.

Kilkis

€ **Evridiki**. Old fashioned but cheap and friendly, in the town centre, T: 23410, reserve@evridiki.lar.forthnet.gr

€ **Kristonia**. A new hotel on the outskirts of town, targeted mainly at business travellers, but with a good atmosphere and facilities. T: 23410 77290, info@kristonia.gr

Kozani

€–€€ **Kyriakidis**. Modern with a nice garden and a good view of the small Polyfitos lake. Restaurant. T: 24640 22975.

€€ **Elimia 3**. Modern and clean, mainly aimed at business travellers, but a useful base. T: 24610 39990.

Lake Vergoritis

€ **Alexander**. 5km south of Panaghitsa village above the main road, 1 km from the east end of the lake, in very attractive country. T: 23810 32025/6.

Naousa

€ **Xatiati**. In a small historic building with outstanding wooden interiors. T: 23320 52120, email hayati@otenet.gr

Vergina

€€ **Arxontiko Dimitra**. Cleanly if slightly sparsely decorated, but comfortable and convenient for the site. T: 23310 92900.

Veroia

Aiges Melathron. Greek category A hotel in a dull place by the ringroad. T: 23310 77777.

Edessa

There are good tavernas, sweet shops and restaurants all over the place, concentrated around Filippou.

Kilkis

Xani is a good restaurant, on Odos Solomos, as is **Kyrils Taverna** on Aristediou. **Leski Kynigon** (21 Iouniou) is good for fish.

Vergina

Fillipon. T: 23310 92892. They can also help with rooms.

Edessa

There are some good small shops selling local craft products such as rugs.

Kilkis

Food shopping is very good in Kilkis, in both the food market and in specialist shops like the Alantika delicatessen on 21 Iouniou, with one of the finest and most extensive selections of Greek cheeses in the entire country.

Naousa

The Imathia region produces excellent wine. To visit vineyards and wineries contact the Macedonian Wine Association, T: 23310 281617, www.wineroads.gr

WESTERN MACEDONIA

KASTORIA & ITS LAKE

Kastoria (Καστοριά; in Macedonian *Kostur*, is one of the finest historic towns in northern Greece, delightfully situated on the isthmus of a peninsula. Many of its inhabitants used to be occupied in the fur trade, and are especially skilled in matching and joining rejected pieces of mink imported from abroad. In recent years the industry has gone into relative decline. Some of the magnificent large houses (*archontikà*) of the 17th–18th centuries, with workshops on the ground floor, survive scattered amid trees and approached by narrow cobbled ways of the Turkish period when the town was known as *Kesriye*. Storks nest on the roofs.

HISTORY OF KASTORIA

The ancient *Keletron*, mentioned by Livy, probably occupied the hill of Vigla above the shoreward suburb. It was captured by the Romans in 200 BC. Removed to the present site, the town was renamed Justinianopolis, after its refounder, but soon called Kastoria after the beavers that haunted the lake (a *kastòri* is a beaver in Greek). The town was occupied by the Bulgars of Tsar Samuel in 990–1018 until freed by Basil II. It was surprised and captured in 1083 by Robert Guiscard from an English garrison of 300 men. Disputed in the 12th century between the despots of Epirus and emperors of Nicaea, Kastoria enjoyed a period of prosperity under Michael Palaeologus. The town continued to thrive under the Serbs, who held it in 1331–80. After five years of Albanian rule, it fell to the Turks in 1385, who remained its masters until 1912. A colony of Jews continued trade with Vienna and Constantinople, and the fur industry flourished for 500 years.

The town

The neck of the isthmus marks the entrance to the town. At the little quay, with a fish market, can be seen the curious wooden boats peculiar to the lake, designed in an ancient tradition. Some remains of the Byzantine ramparts (known as the 'Justinian Wall') can be seen from Plateia Davaki. Odos Mitropoleos, the main street of the town, runs southeast to Plateia Omonias. The pretty Odos Mandakasi descends to the unspoilt Kariaki quarter near the south shore of the lake. Here, to the southeast of Aghii Anargyri (an over-restored church with an unusual west gallery; its screen, carved and gilded, has panels of topographical scenes), are three excellent examples of *archontikà*: the Emanouli, the Basara, and the Natzes, which has fine painted ceilings.

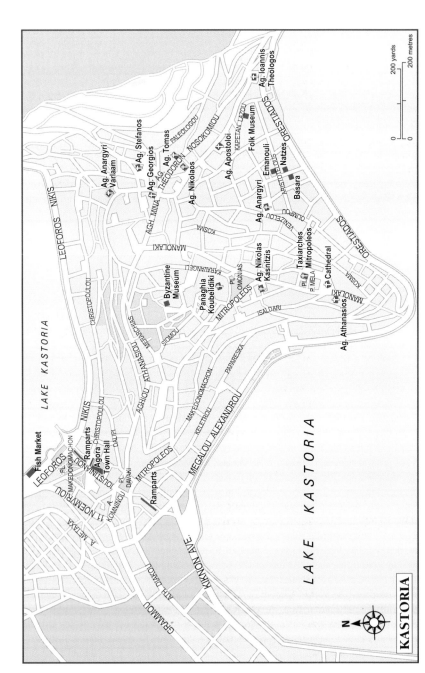

KASTORIA

LAKE KASTORIA

LAKE KASTORIA

LAKE KASTORIA

Fish Market

Ramparts
Agora
Town Hall
Ramparts

Byzantine Museum

Panaghia Koubelidiki

Ag. Anargyri Varlaam
Ag. Stefanos
Ag. Georgios
Ag. Nikolaos
Ag. Tomas
Ag. Apostoloi
Folk Museum
Ag. Ioannis Theologos
Natzes
Emanouli
Basara
Ag. Anargyri
Taxiarches
Mitropoleos
Ag. Nikolas Kasnitzis
Cathedral
Ag. Athanasios

NOSOKOMIOU
PALEOLOGOU
KAPETAN TAZOU
ORESTIADOS
ARISTOTELOUS
OLIMPOU
VENIZELOU
ORESTIADOS
KOSMA
MANOLAKI
ISALDARI
MITROPOLEOS
KARAVANGELI
SIOMOU
MEFRACHIAS
MITROPOLEOS
MANOLAKI
KOSMA
AGH. MINA
AG. THEODORON
NIKIS
LEOFOROS
CHRISTOPOULOU
AGHIOU ATHANASIOU
NIKIS
CHRISTOPOULOU
IOUSTINIANOU
MAKEDONOMACHON
DALIPI
DAVAKI
KOMNINOU
A. METAXA
11 NOEMVRIOU
LEOFOROS
MITROPOLEOS
MAKEDONOMACHON
KELETROU
PAPARESKA
MEGALOU ALEXANDROU
GRAMMOU
ATH. DIAKOU
KIKNON AVE.

200 yards
200 metres
0
0

N

The churches of Kastoria

Of the town's 72 churches, 54 survive. Seven of the Byzantine period and about 30 others of medieval date are listed monuments. With one exception the Kastorian churches are basilican, the earliest with two low aisles while the later ones are without. The naves are barrel-vaulted. Exteriors are either decorated with crude patternwork (including *chi-rho* symbols) in tile, or plastered and frescoed. Most churches are kept locked. Keys are either at nearby houses or with the *phylax* (custodian) and enquiry must be made.

Panaghia Koubelidiki is an 11th-century triconchial church with a high central drum. The frescoes date from the 13th–16th centuries. **Aghios Nikolaos Kasnitzis** is a single-chamber wood-roofed chapel with a semicircular apse. The late 12th-century frescoes are in a bad state of preservation, but include a large number of images from the Orthodox Festival cycle. North of the door leading to the nave is depicted the donor of the church, Nikephoros Kasnitzi the Magistros. South of the door is his wife, Anne.

The **Taxiarches Mitropoleos** is a small three-aisled basilica with fragments of 10th-century frescoes in the diakonikon and prothesis. The remainder of the interior frescoes (1359) were executed by the monk Daniel and include the *Dormition of the Virgin* at the west end of the nave. The external frescoes represent people buried in the church in the 15th century with, over the door, a 13th-century Virgin and Child. In the narthex is the tomb of Pavlos Melas (1870–1904), the hero of the Greek struggle for Macedonia, killed in a skirmish against the Turks near Siatista. **Aghios Athanasios** was built in 1384–85 by Stoias and Theodore Musaki, members of the ruling Albanian family. In the contemporary frescoes the saints are depicted in Byzantine princely or military costume; above are scenes of the life and Passion of Christ.

Aghii Apostoloi was frescoed by Onouphrios in 1545. Of the group of churches just to the north, **Aghios Nikolaos** (by Aghios Tomas) has been restored since it was hit by an Italian bomb in the Second World War; the frescoes date from 1663. **Aghios Stefanos**, with a semi-hexagonal apse, contains some poorly preserved frescoes from the 10th century in the narthex and in the west part of the nave. The remainder have been assigned to the late 12th century. In the adjacent **Aghios Georgios** (rebuilt under the Turks) the Normans assembled to give themselves up to the Emperor Alexius in 1085. **Aghii Anargyri Varlaam**, a small but very high three-aisled, barrel-vaulted and wood-roofed basilica with a semicircular apse, is the oldest church in Kastoria. It contains fragments of early 11th-century frescoes in the narthex (Constantine, a donor; Sts Constantine and Helen; Sts Basil and Nicholas). The remainder of the frescoes were executed by two different painters and are assigned to the late 12th century. The scene of Jesus and Nathaniel is one rarely depicted in Byzantine art. Its screen is also decorated.

The Byzantine Museum

Plateia Dexiamenis. Open Tues–Sun 8.30–5 (summer) or 8.30–3 (winter); T: 24670 26781. The museum has a superb collection of icons from Kastoria churches. Highlights include a beautiful 12th-century *Elijah*, of the so-called Comnene school; various products of the local Kastoria school, noted for its heavily stylized angularity of line; and a *Pantocrator* of the Cretan school, with its more familiar, soft, restrained contours.

LAKE KASTORIA

Kastoria Lake (Limni Kastorias; Λίμνη Καστοριάς), 620m above sea level, and c. 6.5km long by 5km wide, is almost divided into two by a peninsula projecting from the west shore. On the neck of this the town is built. The lake, which varies in depth from 7.5m to 15m, is fished for carp, tench and eels. In summer the waters are hot, turbid and often covered with a green film, and frogs keep up an incessant chorus; in winter it is often frozen. Birds abound, and adders are not uncommon. There are traces of a Prehistoric dwelling on the south shore. The circuit (32km, almost at lake level) can be made by car comfortably in an hour. The surrounding mountains are attractive, as are the apple orchards at the north end.

The lakeside road (or walk) provides fine views of the surrounding mountains. Leaving the town to the northeast by Leoforos Nikis, it is about an hour's walk to the Moni Panaghia Mavriotissa, a one-aisled wood-roofed church with a semicircular apse. The frescoes from the original decoration of the building (on the east and south walls of the nave and on the east wall of the narthex, as well as part of its exterior wall) are assigned to the early 13th century. They have an interesting miniature quality. The two headless figures in the upper register to the left of the *Tree of Jesse* on the exterior of the south wall are variously identified as the Emperor Alexius (1081–1118) and his son John II, or as Michael VIII (1259–82) with his brother John Palaeologus. On its southeast side is attached the chapel of Aghios Ioannis Theologos, with 16th-century frescoes.

SOUTH ALONG THE ALIAKMON

Omorfoklissia and the road south

At Omorfoklissia, 19km southwest of Kastoria, is the outstanding Byzantine church of Aghios Georgios, restored in 1955. A small rectangular structure, built at the end of the 11th century, it was extended under Andronicus II (inscription). In the exonarthex survive vigorous frescoes of seven saints from the beginning of the 14th century. It also has one of the finest wooden statues in Greece, of St George, nearly 3m high. A local tradition claims that it was brought to the village by two nuns from Ioannina.

The main road south from Kastoria bypasses Argos Orestikon, an important garrison town with the airport of Kastoria and a military airfield on the late Roman site (some walls) of *Diocletianoupolis*. Today it is noted for the manufacture of *flokkates* and *kilimia*, varieties of woollen carpet. Just before Kostarazi, a concrete bridge crosses the emissary from Lake Kastoria that feeds the Aliakmon. The road continues to follow the Aliakmon downstream. Vogatsiko, a pretty small town on seven low wooded hills, below the bluish-grey mountain (1361m) of the same name, sits above a gorge. From here the road runs along the hillside above the beautiful valley and winds amid slopes clad with oak. Far to the west is Smolikas, usually snow capped. A series of Bailey bridges carries the road across the Aliakmon and its tributaries. Neapolis makes cheese. Kaloneri, as its name suggests ('good water'), is situated among green and fertile countryside.

Siatista and Grevena

Siatista (Σιάτιστα) is a pretty little hilltop town set below dry, arid overgrazed hills. Its many historic buildings make it well worth a detour or short stay. It was of considerable importance in the Ottoman period, with a large Albanian and Muslim population, and retains some of the atmosphere of that time. Siatista has an economic base similar to Kastoria, with many fur-trade establishments, and has suffered the same problems of industrial decline. It was a tiny village before the Ottoman conquest, and was settled in the 16th century, becoming a caravan centre of merchants trading with Vienna. In the 18th century, as *Sisechte*, it was noted for its wines, tanneries and for industry, but after 1821 these gradually declined. When the vineyards were destroyed by phylloxera in 1928–35, it became more dependent on the fur trade. The town is made up of the two districts of Chora and Geraneia, and (also like Kastoria) is noted for its fine 18th-century houses, timber-framed with jutting balconies and gabled roofs. The Poulikos Mansion, with an elaborately panelled and frescoed interior, was restored in 1962, and others may also be visited. The church of Aghia Paraskevi dates from 1677. The Manousakis Library, left to the town by the 19th-century scholar of the same name, contains local archaeological finds.

Grevena (Γρεβενά) is the chief town (pop. 16,000) of a mainly agricultural *nome* that corresponds roughly to the ancient district of *Elimeiotis*. Situated at the confluence of two branches of the Greveniotikos, it is the focal point of numerous mountain tracks. It was a centre of Greek learning in the Middle Ages and the headquarters of the *Armatoli*, an irregular militia of Byzantine times, kept up by the Turks, from whose ranks arose the patriotic brigand, or *klepht*. Today Grevena has a school of forestry, but from a visitor's point of view it is a dull place, with little to detain the traveller.

FLORINA & ENVIRONS

Florina (Φλώρινα) is a traditional northern Greek town with a conservative popular culture. Local music, dance and hunting traditions are very strong, in both Greek and Macedonian. It makes a good centre to stay to explore the region, or a place from which to visit the Prespa National Park (*see opposite*).

HISTORY OF FLORINA

Florina was a small place in early Antiquity, settled by the Macedonian kings to help secure the military corridor to the south. It grew to prominence as a satellite settlement to ancient *Heraclea* (*see p. below*) on the Via Egnatia. The strategic military situation of the town in the so-called 'Monastir Gap' between the northern Greek border mountain ranges has meant that it has been a central military objective in all invasions of Greece from the north, from ancient times to the Second World War, and as a result has few historic buildings. Christianity developed early, and in Byzantine times it was the seat of a bishop. Under the Ottomans it was a garrison centre. During the Balkan Wars the town was controlled by the Internal Macedonian Revolutionary Organisation, IMRO, and was pro-Bulgarian. It was Hellenised by an influx of refugees from Asia Minor after 1922. In the Greek Civil War the Ottoman town was largely destroyed by Allied bombing. It was rebuilt after 1949 on a grid pattern.

The town

In the last four years the small surviving historic area of the town has been well restored. The main square is rather dismal and militaristic, but go past the market to the little river Crina that rushes through the town, and you will pass historic houses on either side of the river as you walk upstream. Most date from the inter-war period but there are also some fine Ottoman buildings. In the late Empire Florina was very ethnically mixed with Turks, Albanians, Slav Macedonians, Vlachs and a few Jews, and families were often not on particularly good terms with each other—something the architecture and walls reflect. The Archaeological Museum, with some interesting natural history exhibits, is near the main station square.

An excursion to ancient Heraclea

The important Roman site of *Heraclea Lyncestis* lies north of Florina, on the Niki road across the border in the Former Yugoslav Republic of Macedonia (FYROM; *just beyond*

the map). It can easily be visited as a day trip from Florina. There are no visa requirements for EU or US passport holders at the border, and formalities are few. A good
way to approach the trip is to hire a taxi from Florina to Niki, the border village on
the Greek side. The drive (about 15mins) takes you across wide fields below the magnificent Pelister Mountains to the west. In winter there are often wonderful views of
eagles and other birds of prey hunting over the fields.

A few taxi drivers have permits allowing them to take you all the way. If not, after
Greek passport control, tell the driver to go to the '*granitsa*' (the Slav word for 'border') on the FYROM side. He will drive about 400m and leave you at the border post.
Walk through after passport control and take a taxi to Bitola. Ancient *Heraclea* is on
the Niki side of the town, a left turn. The city occupied an important strategic position on the Via Egnatia, and was used by Julius Caesar to store supplies for his campaigns. It was a bishopric from the 4th century, and was overrun by the Slavs in the
6th. Fine 5th- and 6th-century mosaics with animal and flower motifs were found in
the narthex of the basilica. In the summer they are generally uncovered, and there is
an impressive ancient theatre and other buildings.

PRESPA NATIONAL PARK

Information centres: Aghios Germanos (T: 23850 51452); Psarades (T: 23850 51332).
The Prespa National Park straddles the borders of Greece, Albania and FYROM,
and is a vast, wild wooded region of outstanding natural beauty, although a visit
takes a certain amount of commitment. Unless you like really cold weather, it is
better to go between April and November. Three days should be allowed for a visit
if possible, as it takes half a day to get there from Florina and half a day to get back.

This vast and sparsely inhabited wilderness of forest, mountains and remote
lakes, was for many years largely closed to the outside world thanks to its proximity to Cold War borders and its central role in the Greek Civil War. It is now
a flourishing ecotourism centre, the habitat of many rare birds and animals.

All local people speak Greek but most near the lakes are ethnic Macedonians
and often speak the language at home. There are some Vlach villages in the park,
such as Pyli, and others where Albanian is spoken as well, like Vronteron.
Relations between the lake fisherman of all three nations are not always cordial.

The Prespa lakes

Great Prespa Lake (*Prespës* in Albanian, *Prespansko* in Macedonian) is one of the
largest lakes in the Balkans, with a small part in Greece, a larger part in Albania and
the largest section in FYROM. All three borders run through the centre of the lake.
Psarades is a main tourist centre on the Greek side, and it is possible to take a boat
trip to see the remarkable Byzantine and later rock icons and cliff churches on the
limestone crags above the lake. The village itself has some fine traditional wooden

houses. It was built in 1893 with funds from a Russian diplomat who enjoyed wild-fowling in the region. There are very good fish tavernas for the lake trout, carp and other fish. There is an ecology centre in the old schoolhouse in Psarades.

Little Prespa Lake is mostly in Greece but partly in Albania. The view from the Greek side towards Wolf Pass in Albania is of Wagnerian scale and grandeur, especially on a winter evening as the clouds gather. The region was a very important centre of Byzantine civilisation, but since the purging of the Slav Macedonian inhabitants after 1947 has been more or less uninhabited, with ruined and deserted villages common. The church of Aghios Achilleios on the little island in the lake is well worth seeing. On the Albanian side there are important Neolithic cave paintings at Tren, on Spile Rock.

PRACTICAL INFORMATION

The ethnic mix in the borderlands of northern and western Macedonia is rich. Florina is the centre for the large Macedonian-speaking Slav minority in northern Greece, with many villages speaking *Slavika*, as it is known in Florina, every day, although everybody can speak Greek as well. There are also one or two *Arvanites* villages in the region where Albanian is spoken.Visitors will also meet many local people who can speak excellent English as a result of the close links people have with the emigrant communities in Australia and Canada.

Late spring, summer and early autumn are very pleasant but Florina and region enjoy the full force of the Balkan winter, and between mid-November and March it can often be very cold—and in January–March sometimes positively Arctic, with deep snow, howling east winds and outlying villages cut off by drifts. Kastoria is subject to sudden winds and changes of temperature, and the winter climate is often tough.

GETTING AROUND

• **By air:** Kastoria airport has domestic flights to and from Athens.
• **By car:** If driving in the Florina region in winter, snowchains are useful, often essential. A 4WD vehicle is required in winter outside the main towns. Maps are not always a reliable guide to the border areas.
• **By bus:** Fast services link Kastoria with Thessaloniki and Kozani. Buses also run between Edessa and Florina. Florina has regular services to local villages and the Prespa area, although an overnight stop is often necessary. It is magnificent scenic journey lasting about 3hrs, depending on the weather.
• **By rail:** There is a train link between Edessa and Florina.
• **By taxi:** Taxis from Florina are usually good value.

INFORMATION OFFICES

Kastoria T: 24670 26777;
www.kastoriacity.gr

WHERE TO STAY

NB: Hotels in some of the remoter regions are often closed in winter.

Kastoria

Aiolis. Small hotel (14 rooms) in attractive early 20th-century building. Café. Aghiou Athanasiou 30, T: 24670 21070.
Archontiko Alexiou Vergoula. Beautiful old stone-built house, with well-proportioned airy rooms and period wooden furniture. Restaurant. Aiditras 14, T: 24670 23415, sfinas@otenet.gr
Archontiko tis Venetoulas. Built as a family home in the 1920s, and still a family home today. All rooms fully refurbished with modern furnishings, garden and large terrace (lake views). Aghion Theodoron 6, T: 24670 22446, www.venetula.gr
Europa. Modern hotel in modern block. A useful, good-value choice. Aghiou Athanasiou 12, T: 24670 23826.
Kastoria. Modern hotel with friendly service. Rooms small but well looked-after. Lake views. Nikis 122, T: 24670 29453, www.hotel-kastoria.gr
Tsamis. Built in the late 70s in imitation of traditional styles, right on the lakeshore. Restaurant. 4km out to the west on the National Road. T: 24670 85334.

Florina

€ **Antigone**. Opposite the bus station. Friendly service, excellent value. Arianou 1, T: 23850 23180.
€€€ **Lingos**. International business traveller-style four-star hotel, with standard room décor and large restaurant. A comfortable base for touring the region. Naoum 1, T: 23850 28322.

Prespa National Park

The Costas Hotel is on the right as you enter Psarades. The much larger Women's Cooperative Hotel is on the opposite bank of the lake to Psarades village. There is another Women's Cooperative Hotel in Aghios Germanos village. Rooms in surrounding villages are easy to find except in mid-August, when many exiles return home for their holidays.

WHERE TO EAT

Florina

Florina has some good tavernas and local cookshops, and a fine covered food market, by the Metropolitan's house.
Prespa National Park
The Germanos fish taverna at the lake end of Psarades village is very good.

LOCAL SPECIALITIES

Florina and region

Local goat and sheep's cheese is very good, and retsina.
Prespa Lakes
The Prespa region is known for its red peppers.

FESTIVALS & EVENTS

Grevena The fair of Aghios Achilleios, starts first Mon in June.
Kastoria The *Ragoutsaria*, celebrated around Epiphany, is a good time to hear traditional music.
Prespa Lakes Festival of the *Prespoia*, last weekend in August.

BOOKS

For more on the background to Macedonia's ethnic mix, see Hugh Poulton, *Who are the Macedonians*? (London, 1998) and James Pettifer (ed.) *The New Macedonian Question* (London and New York, 1999).

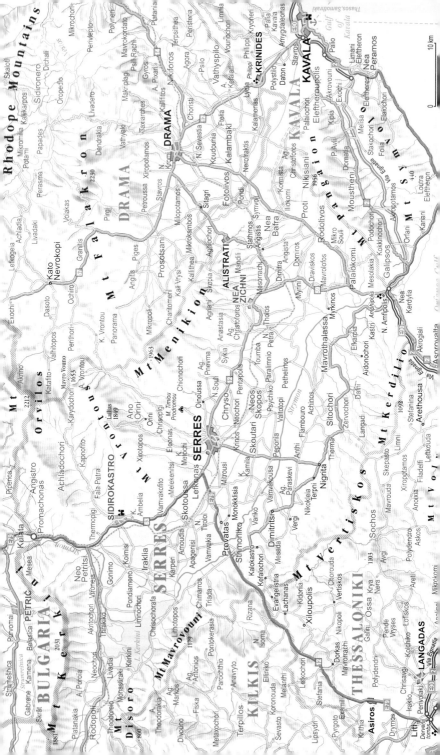

EASTERN MACEDONIA

Eastern Macedonia is a region of cultivated plains and empty, thinly inhabited uplands. Its principal sites are the historic town of Kavala, and the site of Philippi, on a battlefield near which the forces of Brutus and Cassius were famously defeated by Octavian (the future Augustus) and Mark Antony.

LANGADAS & ENVIRONS

The busy highway emerging from Thessaloniki's northern suburbs carries traffic for Lachanas, Nigrita, and Kavala through a gap (290m) in the Chortiatis range that shuts in the town to north and east. After 11km or so you come to **Derveni** (with signs to 'Macedonian Tomb' and 'Ancient Cemetery'). Burial mounds of the 4th century BC covering cist graves were explored here in 1962; they yielded iron weapons, a pair of gilt bronze greaves, vases of silver and alabaster, the burnt remains of a papyrus roll, and the astonishing *Derveni Krater*. All the finds are now in Thessaloniki Museum (*see p. 598*).

Further east, in a cultivated plain is **Langadas** (Λαγκαδάς), with alkaline warm springs. Here the *Anastenaria*, a ritual fire-walking ceremony, takes place on the feast of Sts Constantine and Helen (21st May). Tradition asserts that c. 1250 in the Thracian village of Kosti, the church of St Constantine caught fire. The sacred icons were heard groaning in the flames, whereupon certain villagers dashed into the fire and rescued them without suffering harm. The icons have been handed down by the families concerned from one generation to the next and the descendants honour their saints each year by walking barefoot on fire in a state of ecstasy carrying the icons. The walkers are called *Anastenarides* from their imitative groaning (*anastenàzo* means to groan). In 1914, when their territory was transferred from Turkish to Bulgarian rule, they fled with their icons to Aghia Eleni (Serres), Mavrolefki (Drama), Meliki and Langadas, where, until 1948, their rituals were held in secret owing to opposition from the Greek Orthodox Church. Clerical objections in 1960 caused the ceremonies to be held that year only in Aghia Eleni. The orgiastic dance to drum and lyre with attendant chorus, together with the sacrifice of a bull decked with garlands, suggests an origin far earlier than the 13th century, and the ceremony probably survives, shorn of attendant excesses, from the pre-Christian worship of Dionysus. The dance patterns and primitive music are considered by scholars to have evolved from Thracian Orphism.

The road to Serres

Approaching Asiros, by the side of the road, you will see Toumba Asiros, a prominent mound, excavated by the British School from 1975 and occupied from c. 2000 BC to c. 800 BC. Now begins the long climb into the foothills of the mountains which separate the Axios basin from the Strymon. From the ridges fine views of the plain take in Lakes Koroneia and Volvi and the heights of Chalkidiki. Beyond Dorkas (which has a taverna) the road crosses a declivity with pine-clad slopes. At the top of the next rise, there is a by-road to Vertiskos, which gives its name to the mountains to the southeast. The road undulates to Xiloupolis at the head of another wooded valley.

Lachanas was the farthest point reached by the Bulgarians in 1913, and the road crosses empty, thinly inhabited uplands. You pass a memorial of the bayonet charge that checked their advance, with a small museum. A kilometre west of the village is a British Military Cemetery, in which are buried 270 soldiers who died on this front in 1916–17. The panorama extends to the Kerkini or Beles Mountains (2031m) on the Bulgarian frontier. Evangelistria stands on an irregular spur projecting into the Strymon plain. Kefalochori has wayside tavernas.

THE STRYMON BASIN

The Strymon (or Struma or Strymonas; Στρυμώνας), 250km long, called by the Turks *Kara-Su* (the Black Waters), rises in the Bulgarian mountains, enters Greece through the Rupel Pass, and flows generally southeast through a broad and fertile plain enclosed by parallel chains of mountains. Its upper reaches have been dammed to form a new lake. Its lower course has been controlled and the former Lake Achinos, anciently called *Prasias*, drained. At the southeast end of the lake lay the city of *Myrkinos*, founded c. 510. The modern village of Myrkinos marks the site. The river empties into the Strymonic Gulf. At one time it formed the boundary between Macedonia and Thrace.

At Kalokastro, above the river to the west, Byzantine walls and the remains of a Roman town were found in 1917. To the left of the road is the Struma Military Cemetery, which contains the graves of 932 officers and men of the British, Indian and Maltese forces who died on the Strymon front. Two other places of note lie along the way: Provatas, which produces ouzo, and Monokklisia, which is notorious for its practices of 8th January, when the women confine the men to domestic chores while they revel in the streets and tavernas. The inhabitants brought the custom from eastern Thrace in 1922; it may derive from ancient Dionysiac rites.

SERRES

Serres (Σέρρες; pop. 80,000) is one of the most important commercial cities in Macedonia. Situated at a low elevation (50m) at the foot of mountainous country, it overlooks the fertile plain to the southwest through which the Strymon flows some 24km away. Busy and with a lot of new building, Serres is nonetheless a pleasant town, with wide streets and good general shopping, surrounded by abundant woods and luxuriant gardens. It has always been of military importance to the defence of northern Greece and retains a strong garrison presence.

HISTORY OF SERRES

Siris or *Serrhai* was already chief town of its district in the time of Herodotus; the ancient settlement was built below the rocky outcrop on the edge of the plain. In those days much of the river valley would have been marshy and flooded for several months of the year.

In its plain Xerxes, on his march into Greece, left the sacred mares of the Chariot of the Sun. On his return he found that they had been stolen as they grazed by the Strymonians. Serres played a strategic role throughout the Middle Ages. In 1195–96 it was ravaged by the Bulgarians who defeated a Byzantine army and took prisoner Isaac Comnenus, the *sebastocrator* (second-in-command in the Byzantine Empire). In 1205 the marauding Vlach Johannica besieged Serres; the Frankish garrison was slaughtered when it surrendered. Boniface of Montferrat, hastening from the Morea, recaptured and refortified the town. In 1345 it fell to Stefan Dušan, who here promulgated his legal code (1354). Helen, his widow, retired here under the religious name of Elizabeth. Serres was recaptured for the Byzantines in 1371, but attracted the attention of the Ottoman Turks the following year and in 1383 fell decisively into the hands of Lala Shahin. It remained Turkish (as *Siruz*) until 1913, when it was seized by the Bulgarians who set it on fire in their retreat. On 29th June the town celebrates its freedom from the Bulgarians. In the First World War many buildings were destroyed. Numerous refugees from Asia Minor settled in Serres after 1922. Many inhabitants have close links with the Pontus region on the Black Sea, and Pontic influences are strong in local music.

The town

The town, almost entirely rebuilt since the Bulgarian fire of 1913, is best seen from the ruined 14th-century kastro that crowns the wooded acropolis to the north (take the road from the east of town in the direction of Orini; about 10mins). There are remains of various walls, some over 4m thick, and two impressive Byzantine towers.

To the northeast is a pretty cypress-planted cemetery; to the northwest an ancient aqueduct spans a gully. On the slopes below, in the northeast part of the town, lay the Christian quarter (Varoch). Just below the café on the summit of the kastro is the restored Aghios Nikolaos, an attractive cross-in-square, with an exonarthex wider than the building. Its octagonal drum and small domes are ornamented with brick decoration. In the same general area, but accessible from the town itself, is the Old Metropolis, also restored, dedicated to St Theodore. It is a large aisled basilica of the 11th century, rather too high for its length, with a pretty domed chapel at one corner. In the apse was a huge 11th–12th-century wall mosaic of the *Last Supper*, now in the museum. Close by, at no. 62 Odos Ionos Dragoumi, is a Folk Museum of the Sarakatsanoi (*see p. 541*), whose preserve lay between Drama and the Bulgarian fron-

St Andrew (11th–12th century), from the *Last Supper* mosaic from Serres Old Metropolis.

tier (*museum open Tues–Sun 8–2; closed 15 July–20 Aug*). The west gate of the Byzantine town has been found on Ionos Dragoumi, and other parts of the Byzantine fortifications located elsewhere.

Between here and the busy Plateia Emboriou, to the south, can be seen houses of the old town. Two interesting mosques lie on streets leading out of Plateia Emboriou: the Tsitsirli on the Drama road, and another on the corner of Anatolikis Thrakis and Andrianopoleos.

In the attractive central Plateia Eleftherias, a short distance northwest of Emboriou, a huge Turkish market with six domes, which has seen Muslim and Christian worship in turn, is now an Archaeological Museum (*open Tues–Sun 8.30–3*). In the attractive interior are a 12th-century mosaic of St Andrew from the Old Metropolis, ancient sculpture and other finds: also the marble doors and part of a couch from the Macedonian tombs at Argilos. Accompanying the finds are excellent descriptions, with photographs, of ancient sites in the area, especially Amphipolis and Argilos.

Serres also has a museum of mainly post-Byzantine ecclesiastical art from the area, largely from Moni Timiou Prodromou (*see below*), housed in the modern metropolitan headquarters at Odos Kyprou 10 (*open Tues and Thur 10–12*).

North of Serres

From Serres a steep but beautiful mountain road crosses the pass between the Vrontous Mountains and Mount Menikion. The little village at the ski resort of Laïlias has some very pretty buildings. To the east is Oinoussa, an attractive village with an old church, standing at the mouth of the Kazil Tsai valley, in which there are asbestos mines. Higher up the valley, in a cool wooded site, is the Moni Timiou Prodromou (1275), with wall paintings and the tombs of the founders, as well as that of Gennadios II Scholarios (d. 1472), first Patriarch of Byzantium under the Turks (*see p. 48*).

South of Serres

At the eastern foot of Mt Vertiskos extends the area once occupied by Lake Prasias (now drained), the extent of which is betrayed by the prehistoric mounds that lined its shores. Nigrita, a pleasant and friendly town, overlooks the Strymon valley. It is a centre for tobacco. At Terpni, 2km to the northwest, is an ancient acropolis at Aghios Mandeios (*finds in Serres museum*). At Dimitritsi, continuing northwest on the same road, the Greek general Branas defeated the retreating Normans in 1185, putting an end to their expedition. Vergi, between the two, has a site at Palaiokastro to the north (*finds also in Serres museum*). The road from Dimitritsi continues south to Amphipolis, past a right turn for Aïdonochori, outside which probably stood ancient *Tragilos*. The road meets the Strymon river on the shores of the Strymonic Gulf (here called the Gulf of Orfanos).

ANCIENT AMPHIPOLIS

The *Lion of Amphipolis* guards the old bridge over the Strymon. This colossal animal, reassembled from fragments in 1936–37, has been mounted on a pedestal built on the ancient foundation with blocks of the 2nd century BC dredged from the Strymon, where they may have been reused in a medieval dam. Originally the lion perhaps honoured Laomedon, the sailor of Mytilene who later became governor of Syria. Beyond the bridge, amid low hills to the left, are the scattered remains of ancient *Amphipolis*; the outline of the acropolis walls can be seen above. The site is well worth the short diversion up the Drama road (1km farther on). The city was built on a commanding eminence (154m) above the east bank of the river, c. 5km from the sea. A loop of the river flowed round the west half of the city walls.

The site, which belonged to the Edonians of Thrace, was originally called *Ennea Hodoi* ('Nine Ways'; the original site c. 1km north of Amphipolis), for which reason, according to Herodotus, Xerxes on crossing its bridges buried alive nine local boys and nine girls. It was colonised as Amphipolis by the Athenians in 437 BC after an abortive attempt 28 years earlier (*see p. 656*). Deriving its wealth from the gold mines of Mt Pangaion, Amphipolis was one of their most important northern possessions: hence the consternation when it surrendered to the Spartan Brasidas in 424. The historian (and general) Thucydides (*see box overleaf*) saved its port of Eion, at the mouth of the Strymon, but, for failing to save Amphipolis as well, he was exiled for 20 years by his countrymen. In 421 the Athenians made an unsuccessful attempt to retake the city; in the cavalry battle both Cleon, the Athenian demagogue and general, and his Spartan opponent Brasidas were killed. Amphipolis was seized by Philip II of Macedon in 358. After the Battle of Pydna (168) it became the capital of one of the four republics provisionally set up by the Romans. St Paul passed through Amphipolis on his way to Thessalonica (*Acts XVII, 1*). The city was a station on the Via Egnatia and the seat of a bishop in the Early Christian period. Excavations have been made since 1956 by the Greek Archaeological Service.

Thucydides (c. 455–400 or 399 BC)

By the time of Herodotus' death in the 420s, Athens was at war again, this time not against the Persians, but in the far less glorious struggle against Sparta. The historian of the Peloponnesian War (431–404 BC) is Thucydides. Thucydides was a wealthy Athenian who was appointed one of the city's generals for 424. A naval expedition which he led to the northern Aegean failed to prevent the Spartan capture of Amphipolis, and Thucydides was condemned in absentia by the Athenian assembly. For the next 20 years he travelled widely collecting material for his history of the war, returning to Athens only at the end of the war in 404.

Thucydides self-consciously sets himself out to be a more scientific historian than Herodotus, and his narrative is more tightly focused on a narrative of events. He does not have the fascination with other cultures that Herodotus displays, and he shows little interest in a religious perspective. His subjects are alone in this world and they are subject to the vagaries of natural events. In his description of the plague which sweeps through Athens as the beginning of the war, for example, he drily notes that those who prayed were as likely to die as those who did not. However, he also provides a scientific description of the symptoms. Thucydides has no illusions about the nature of man. He describes the brutal reality of a civil war in Corcyra (Corfu), where moderation is seen as weakness and killing becomes the mark of a man. Some years later, the people of the island of Melos are bullied into support of Athens, their profession of neutrality being met with the rejoinder that the might of the Athenians makes their actions 'right'. There is no sentimentality here. On the other hand, in some of his set speeches—his version of Pericles' famous oration on the superiority of Athens, for instance—he does show an appreciation of nobler virtues, while his description of the ill-fated Athenian expedition to Sicily in 415 must rank as one of the most gripping historical narratives of all time.

There has been much discussion of Thucydides' accuracy. Donald Kagan, the finest contemporary historian of the Peloponnesian War, compares Thucydides' work to Winston Churchill's *History of the Second World War*: finely written but with a bias towards its writer's point of view. There is no doubt that despite his profession for accuracy Thucydides placed his own order on his account.   C.F.

The site

Open Tues–Sun 8.30–3 (to 5pm in summer); T: 23220 32474. NB: For those with limited time the gymnasium and the walls and bridge are the most exciting of the remains.

For the ancient site (signed) you turn left onto the Drama road which climbs, and soon there is a small sign in Greek (Macedonian tomb). Two tombs lie on the hill right of the road (the nearer only a few yards away): one had been plundered, but the other yielded precious articles now in Kavala museum. Further up the road, another sign (on the left) points to ancient walls, and parts of the defences can be seen.

The gymnasium

Opposite the roadsign indicating 200m to the Amphipolis turn, a track leads round the acropolis (c. 400m) to the gymnasium. This interesting complex was built in the 3rd century BC and continued in use, with various alterations, until the 1st century AD, when it was violently destroyed. At the southwest is a palaestra with rooms round a colonnaded court. There was a monumental stepped entrance on the east, later replaced by an Ionic propylon to the north. In the northwest and northeast corners were washrooms, of which the basin stands and water conduits and drains survive. Some exercise areas were tiled. There are several statue bases. In a room to the south of an entrance on the west side was a statue of Apellas, a *gymnasiarch* of the 1st century AD. Outside the north entrance was found an inscription containing an ephebic law of 21 BC, perhaps incorporating an earlier system of regulations, and referring to parts of the ancient city (agora, theatre) as yet undiscovered. Here too are an altar and late structure of reused blocks (triglyphs and metopes). North and east stretch the *xystos* and *paradromis* (covered and fair-weather running tracks; similar to those at Delphi). The *xystos* was fronted by a Doric colonnade. In both the starting blocks have been found and arrangements for supporting string lines dividing the tracks identified.

The modern village and museum

Returning to the main road you continue to the turn (left) for the modern village. The church contains a relief of Totoes, the Thracian equivalent of Hypnos. The museum contains finds from the excavations, from the Archaic to the Byzantine periods. Exhibits are arranged chronologically, and include Neolithic figurines, gold staters with the head of Alexander the Great, a beautiful wreath of gold oak leaves (4th century BC), a stele from the gymnasium with an oil jar and strigils carved in relief, and coins from the reign of Justinian. Signs direct you up the hill to the main archaeological area, on the acropolis of the ancient city.

The Roman and Christian city

NB: This section of Amphipolis is often closed in winter.

The principal remains so far excavated are not of the Classical period but of five churches of the 5th and 6th centuries AD, four basilican and one with a hexagonal internal layout. Some of the mosaics (including fine and varied representations of birds) can be seen, protected by wooden shelters; others remain semi-permanently covered. East of Basilica A a huge Early Christian cistern was later subdivided and finally filled with houses and workshops. South of the basilicas is a section of the wall. A short distance further up the track are the remains of a Roman house, again under a shelter to protect its mosaics. It has a paved courtyard with a well in addition to mosaic floors and an apsidal room which originally had painted plaster decoration. Beside the house and not yet fully investigated is a building with statue dedications in front. A hundred metres below these structures, down a track, is a remarkable Hellenistic house (covered) with fine painted decoration employing architectural motifs of the kind which formed the basis for the First Pompeian style. A Shrine of Clio borders a deep ravine to the southeast.

The city walls and bridge

Returning again to the Drama road, the next turning left leads in 400m to a derelict railway station below a ruined Byzantine tower, which once bore an inscription stating that it was built in 1367 for the monastery of the Pantocrator on Mt Athos. Here and farther on three long sections of the city walls stand in places to a height of 7m. By soundings at 64 places these have now been proved to form a circuit of nearly 7km, with the inner acropolis wall of 2km. Built in fine coursed masonry, with towers, gates, sluices for flood waters resembling archery embrasures, and walkways, the walls extend to guard a crossing of the Strymon. Farther on (500m), within a fenced enclosure are further sections of the wall and the interesting fossilised wooden piles of the ancient bridge. If the site is closed, these can be adequately viewed from the track which runs alongside the river.

DRAMA & PHILIPPI

Drama (Δράμα) is a thriving town, and the capital of the *nome* of Drama, the seat of a bishop, and the headquarters of an army corps. It is ringed but not overshadowed to the north by the heights of Falakron, and commands the 'golden plain', the tobacco which provides its livelihood. The town has a Tobacco Research Station and some timber production. Though it holds no particular interest for the tourist, the large shaded squares and restaurants make it a pleasant place to pause, and there are attractive old houses and shops. An archaeological museum, in Patriarchou Dionisiou to the south of the park, is built but unoccupied. There is a small folk collection in the Nomarchia (municipality).

Drama is thought to occupy the site of an Edonian town called *Drabeskos* by Thucydides, where in 465 BC the Athenians were cut to pieces in their first and unsuccessful attempt to colonise Amphipolis. The Edonians, a Thracian people who dwelt between the Strymon and the Nestos, were notorious for their orgiastic worship of Dionysus. Drama was of some importance in the Byzantine era and its original walls may be as early as the 9th century. Boniface of Montferrat fortified the town in 1205; the Turks occupied it c. 1371.

PHILIPPI

Site open 8.30–5. Museum closed at the time of writing.

Philippi is a site of major importance. It guarded a narrow gap between the hills and the marshy plain through which the ancient Via Egnatia (connecting Rome to Byzantium, via Brindisi and Dyrrachium) had to pass. The highway formed the decumanus, the main east–west thoroughfare of the city. The modern road follows the same course and bisects the excavations. On the plain lies the larger archaeological area with the forum; opposite, on the hills (take care crossing the road) are the theatre and museum. Dominating the plain, the Greek acropolis with its prominent medieval towers, occupies the last outcrop of the Lekanis range, which extends east to the river Nestos. Visible remains are mainly Roman or early Christian.

HISTORY OF PHILIPPI

In 361 BC the Thasians, who were already occupying Kavala (ancient *Neapolis*), founded the colony of *Krinides* ('Little Fountains') to exploit the nearby gold and silver mines and the timber resources of mount Pangaion. Four years later the colony was taken over, probably for the same reasons, by Philip II of Macedon, who renamed it Philippi after himself and settled it with Macedonian colonists. The town received a boost with the Roman occupation and the establishment of the Via Egnatia, a main military artery. After the battle of 42 BC (*see p. 660 below*) Octavian settled the land with his own veterans. From 27 BC it bore the name of *Colonia Julia Augusta Philippensis*, gradually losing its Greek character and becoming a Roman town, as testified by the large body of Latin inscriptions.

In AD 49 St Paul spent some time in Philippi, where he baptised his first convert, St Lydia, a purple dye merchant. Though he was arrested and thrown into prison on this first visit for conducting an exorcism (*Acts 16, 9–40*), he was back in Philippi six years later (*Acts 20, 6*); clearly he had a special affection for the place and its people, to whom he also addressed one of his epistles. Christianity flourished in Philippi, which had a large basilica as early as the 5th century. Occupied by the Goths in 473, it suffered greatly in an earthquake c. 619. An important military centre for the Byzantine empire mainly against the marauding Bulgarians, it prospered again and when the Arab geographer Idrisi visited it c. 1150, he was able to comment on the local wine production. Conquered by the Franks on their way back from the sack of Constantinople, then taken by the Serbs, Philippi was abandoned at an unknown date.

The site

Briefly described by the 16th-century French naturalist Pierre Belon, who reported that the Turks were using it as a quarry, Philippi received its first archaeological overview in 1856 by Perrot, then in 1861 by Léon Heuzey and H. Daumet. Excavations by the French School in Athens, started and then interrupted in the summer of 1914, were resumed in 1920 and continued to 1937. During this time the theatre, the forum, Basilicas A and B, the baths and the walls were excavated. Further work after the Second World War by the Greeks and the French uncovered the bishop's quarter and the octagonal church, large private residences, a new basilica near the museum and two others in the necropolis to the east of the city.

A good place to start a visit is the theatre. Situated on the slope of the acropolis just before the modern town of Krinides; it cannot be missed. There is an open-air café/restaurant set in a green spot nearby, and also space to park.

The theatre

Built by Philip II, the structure retains traces of original building in the outer structural wall (*analemma*) and in the side entrances (*parodoi*). In the Roman era the theatre was remodelled; the orchestra paved, the *parodoi* vaulted. Remains of the Roman *scena* show it resembled the type in Asia Minor, with its rubble wall pierced by five doors. The Roman stage disappeared in the last alteration (3rd century). To this period belong three bas-reliefs of Nemesis, Mars and Victory found on the west parodos. Excavations have shown that the cavea had an upper tier, probably Roman. The lateral passageways dividing the lower tier from the upper, as well as the front wall of the upper tier with draining vents, the rubble foundations for the seating, and the vaulted structure are visible. The building remained virtually intact until the 16th century. According to inscriptions, the theatre hosted drama performances as well as gladiatorial shows, and was eventually turned into an arena with fences for wild animals. It was restored in the 1950s for a summer Greek Drama Festival.

Basilicas A and C and the acropolis

From the theatre, a path leads to **Basilica A**, erected on a man-made terrace in the late 6th century. It was probably ruined in an earthquake a century later, then used as a quarry. It was a large, three-aisled building (130m by 50m) with a transept aisle on the east side, a square atrium, a gallery over the aisles and the narthex. Fragments of the luxurious pavement and part of the pulpit and of the screen are preserved in the middle aisle. It had a separate baptistery at the north end with a well-preserved mosaic floor. (It is comparable to Aghios Dimitrios in Thessaloniki; *see p. 605*). The atrium incorporates part of a Hellenistic heroön later transformed into a cistern taken, in the 5th century, to be St Paul's prison. It became a place of worship and a chapel was built on top of it. To the right of the basilica are several recesses cut in the rock and belonging to a number of 3rd-century sanctuaries dedicated to Sylvanus, Hermes, Dionysus, Heracles and Bendis, the Thracian version of Artemis.

Further west is **Basilica C**, an impressive three-aisled structure with narthex and transept and a double pulpit. Dated to the 6th century, it had a luxurious floor with marble inlays. Finds suggests the presence of stained glass windows. From the nearby museum (*closed at the time of writing*) a path leads to the **acropolis** (331m) with its three medieval towers built on the ruins of the Macedonian walls. The climb is recommended more for the view of the lower town (*see below*) than for the remains of a sanctuary of Egyptian deities (Isis, Serapis and Harpocrates).

The forum and Basilica B

Make your way down and cross the road to the forum, a paved rectangle 99m by 50m with uniform porticoes on three sides approached by steps. The plan is quite clear though the remains do not stand much above the foundations. On the north side are public fountains (you can still make out the name of a donor, Decimius Bassus, and the price of a fountain: 30,000 *sestertii*), flanked by a tribune and monuments to citizens and emperors. The decumanus passing along and above its rear wall, remained parallel and below the modern road leaving a view towards the acropolis. The rear walls of all four sides make an enclosing rectangle. This re-planning of the general ensemble can be dated through inscriptions to Marcus Aurelius (late 2nd century). Two temples stood in the corners at the north end; behind the colonnade to the east, four rooms housed a library.

To the south of the forum rise the conspicuous remains of the *Direkler* (meaning 'Pillars' in Turkish), also known as **Basilica B**. These belong to an unfinished building marking the transition from the true Roman basilica (an aisled building with a gabled roof) to the cruciform church with a dome. The 6th-century architect attempted to cover the east end of the basilica with a brick cupola. The east wall collapsed under the weight and the church was never dedicated. The west end, still standing in 837 when the invading Bulgarians carved a monumental inscription on the stylobate (removed in 1943), fell in turn leaving only the narthex to be converted into a small church in the 10th century by the addition of an apse made of earlier material. The pillars, formed of reused antique blocks, have interesting capitals with acanthus leaf decoration. The central arch of the west wall shows the spring of the narthex vault. Pieces of of the fallen dome survive. Two contemporary annexes to the north form the baptistery; two to the south, designed perhaps as the diakonikon, probably constituted the sanctuary itself after the collapse.

To make way for Basilica B, a covered market and the greater part of a palaestra were levelled; much of the material was incorporated in the church. The most interesting part surviving below the southeast corner is a monumental **public latrine**, almost perfectly preserved; it was approached by a flight of steps and a double portal. The 42 seats are still in place. Farther over are the Roman baths built c. AD 250 and destroyed by fire soon afterwards. The Bulgarians destroyed the mosaics in 1941–45.

The Octagon

Excavations by Stylianos Pelekanides in the 1960s east of the forum uncovered the remains of an octagonal church comparable in size and plan to San Vitale in Ravenna. The building had an inner colonnade of 20 columns on seven sides with a marble screen closing the bema on the eighth. The church was approached from the Via Egnatia by a great gate (perhaps that described by Eusebius of Caesarea). On the north side it had a baptistery communicating with the baths, and to the east was the bishop's palace. The complex can be compared with the site of Nea Anchialos, ancient *Pyrasos* in Thessaly (*see p. 562*).

Excavations have shown a continuity of use of the area for ritual purposes. First there was a 2nd-century BC Macedonian tomb which yielded gold finds. It had a superstructure suggesting a form of hero cult which lasted into Roman times. An early church was built on top of it c. 350, the earliest church in Philippi, dedicated to St Paul. It respected the tomb, which is why its massive stone entrance is still in place. Later, c. AD 400, the Octagon was built in two phases, a hundred years apart.

THE BATTLE OF PHILIPPI

Following Caesar's assassination in 44 BC, the republicans Brutus and Cassius made for the east. By the time Antony and Octavian, Caesar's adopted son, had temporarily assuaged their rivalry by the device of a triumvirate with Lepidus, Brutus (who had seized Macedonia) and Cassius (who had secured Syria) were in control of the eastern provinces and of a huge army of 19 legions. Leaving Lepidus behind to rule Italy, Antony and Octavian marched against them with an equivalent force. The armies met in the plain of Philippi in October 42 BC. The republican camp was west of the town across the main road (traces of their fieldworks have been noted). In the ensuing two battles fought south and west of the city, Brutus and Cassius made the same mistake as Pompey at Pharsalus. With the command of the sea and shorter supply lines, their obvious policy was to exhaust the enemy by avoiding action. A hazardous frontal attack by Antony forced a pitched battle, and muddled generalship contributed to the defeat of Cassius, who committed suicide. Brutus, who had been victorious over Octavian and had actually conquered his camp, was three weeks later forced—against his better judgement—to fight again where the triumvirate's legions were executing a dangerous infiltration between his troops and the marsh. The outcome was disastrous, and Brutus too killed himself. The poet Horace fought on the republican side and joined in the 'headlong rout, his poor shield ingloriously left behind' (*Odes II, 7*).

South to Kavala

On the way from Philippi to modern Krinides look out for the **mud baths** (*open in summer*), signposted right. The establishment is not far and is very basic. The baths consist of two open-air single-sex pools full of a gritty, dense black substance. You are not expected to wear very much, though swimming costumes are tolerated. The beginning and end of the sessions are marked by a siren announcing the opening of the communal showers. You do need the high-pressure water to get the mud off—though expect to find remains of it in unexpected places for a few days after a visit. A total immersion, a good massage and the advice of the locals may not cure you of all your ills, but it is certainly very reviving, and a different way to enjoy a view of the Pangaion. The mud is heated only by the sunlight: it is therefore advisable to go in the late afternoon on a hot day, when the top layers will be reasonably warm. It is also better to lie flat (the mud is very buoyant) rather than stay upright: the deeper levels are really cold.

Krinides has important remains of ancient Philippi. In Odos Merarchias, left of the main road, is a large *extra-muros* cemetery basilica. Part of a second, with a mosaic floor, has been uncovered close by. Right of the main road (before the Jetoil petrol station) is an enclosure with tombs, and a mortuary complex including a church and stoa—part of Philippi's east cemetery. Ancient stone fragments strewn about the tobacco fields show that a large suburb extended to the east.

Continuing towards Kavala on the ancient Via Egnatia, look out immediately after leaving Krinides for a huge Roman funerary monument on the left of the road. It marks the **site of Dikili Tash** ('Big Stone' in Turkish). Opposite, an unmade lane leads to the Neolithic site of that name (signed), where since the 1960s Greek and French archaeologists have been investigating a Neolithic *tell* with an occupation stretching back eight millennia. A part of the excavation, with remains of Neolithic houses and ovens, has been conserved and is on display. To visit you will have to take pot luck and hope that either the Greek or the French team is in residence—normally in late spring–summer. It is the only time when the site is open. Finds are in the museums in Kavala and Philippi.

Late Neolithic pottery vessel from Dikili Tash (4000–3000 BC). It forms part of the display of finds at the Philippi museum.

KAVALA

Beautifully situated at the head of its bay and best seen from the sea, Kavala (Καβάλα) rises like a shallow theatre on the outlying slopes of Mandra Kari, one of the chain of hills linking Mount Symvolo with the Lekanis massif. The old citadel occupies a rocky promontory jutting into the sea.

HISTORY OF KAVALA

Inhabited since Neolithic times, Kavala is ancient *Neapolis*, the port of Philippi and originally a colony of Thasos. At the time of the Battle of Philippi Brutus' fleet was stationed here. It was the usual port of disembarkation for travellers to Europe from the Levant, and is where St Paul landed on his way to Philippi (*Acts 16, 11*). In Byzantine times the town adopted the name of *Christoupolis*. It was burnt by the Normans on their way to Constantinople in 1185 (an event recorded in an inscription from the Byzantine kastro wall). The Catalan Grand Company landed in Kavala from Gallipoli in 1306 at the start of its conquering march to Athens. The town was under Ottoman rule until 1912, prospering as a tobacco processing centre. It suffered Bulgarian occupations in both world wars.

The town

Kavala has a citadel to the east and a lower area clustered around the harbour. It is surrounded by well-preserved Byzantine walls, restored after an earthquake in 926 (inscription) and again in the 16th century, and incorporating ancient blocks. On Odos Theodorou Poulidou on the citadel, just up from the harbour, is the **Imaret**, a former seminary locally known as *Tembel Hane*, the 'lazy man's home', since membership brought free *pilaf* and exemption from military service. It housed some 600 boarders. It was founded by Mehmet Ali (1769–1849), Kavala's most famous son. He was born in Kavala, the son an Albanian tobacco merchant, and went on to become pasha of Egypt, to massacre the Mamluks, modernise the state, conquer the Sudan and found a dynasty that ended in 1953 with King Farouk. Recently restored as a luxury hotel (*see opposite*), the multi-domed construction is certainly the most interesting monument of the town.

   Continuing on the same street is a lively equestrian statue of same Mehmet Ali, a present from the Greek community in Egypt. Below is a belvedere with a view towards Thasos. The monument stands next to Mehmet Ali's birthplace, a house in the Turkish style built in 1720 with stable and kitchen below, and harem (he had six wives) and private quarters above. It is now fully restored, and functions as the restaurant of the Imaret hotel.

   Excavations in 1959–61, north of the Imaret, uncovered the peribolos of a Sanctuary of the Parthenos (6th century BC); finds of imported pottery showed wide-ranging contacts all over the Aegean.

   The citadel's aqueduct, the three-tiered *Kamares*, may look Roman in construction, but it is of a much later date, having been built by Suleiman the Magnificent in 1550.

   Dotted around the town are Ottoman and Neoclassical buildings as well as remains of the 200 or so warehouses where tobacco was graded and stored. In Odos Venizelou these tall buildings originally backed onto the shore, but now the port has been enlarged and in-filled and the warehouses have been converted into nightclubs, cafés and shops. At the west end of the harbour stands the museum.

The Archaeological Museum

Open Tues–Sun 8.30–3; late closing Wed. Exhibits are labelled in English.

Exhibits include finds from Kavala itself as well as from further afield. There are some Late Neolithic and Early Bronze Age objects, mainly from Dikili Tash (though the best finds from this site are at Philippi). The collection of sculpture includes a metope (5th century BC) from Tragilos showing a fight between two hoplites. A Macedonian tomb from Amphipolis with painted funerary couches has been reconstructed. Precious metal finds from the tomb, including a polished silver mirror in a folding case and a man's ring bearing the picture of a youth are displayed nearby. Other finds from Amphipolis include polychrome glass; jewellery with gold wreaths and diadems, coloured busts of goddesses and grave stelae (one painted). Material from Abdera (*see p. 688*) includes the Dolphin Mosaic from a Hellenistic house, a painted Clazomenian sarcophagus from the earliest period of settlement. A lamp and chain in the form of a slave (2nd century AD) come from Drama.

PRACTICAL INFORMATION

GETTING AROUND

• **By air:** Kavala has daily connections to Athens. Airport 30km east of town.
• **By bus:** Hourly buses between Thessaloniki and Serres (journey time 75mins), and between Thessaloniki and Pella. Frequent buses link Kavala with Philippi (c. 20mins) and Drama.
• **By boat:** Boats to Thasos and Samothrace leave from Kavala.

INFORMATION OFFICES

Kavala Ethnikis Antistasis 2, T: 25102 31653.

WHERE TO STAY

Alistrati
€€ **Archontiko Voziki**. Small hotel (9 rooms) in traditional building, renovated inside to Greek Class A standard. G. Stimenidi 11, T: 23240 20400.
Kato Nevrokopi
€€ **Granitis**. Mountain hotel in attractive village, pretty shaded terrace with stunning views. Modern and comfortable. T: 25230 21049, www.granitishotel.gr
Kavala
€€ **Egnatia**. Try-hard hotel with a standard business-hotel feel, but good value for its four stars. Restaurant. 7th Merarchias 139, T: 25102 44891, www.egnatiahotel.gr
€€€€ **Imaret**. Stunningly atmospheric small luxury hotel (26 rooms) in a converted Ottoman complex stretched out above the water. Beautiful stone arcades, central pool. A world of flowers and silks. Theodorou Poulidou 6, T: 25106 20151, www.imaret.gr
Serres
€ **Hotel Metropolis**. An atmospheric inter-war building, fully renovated inside to acceptable two-star standard. Plateia Emporiou, T: 23210 54433.
€ **Xenia**. Medium-sized, near the central park. Aghias Sofias 1, T: 23210 29561.

WHERE TO EAT

Kavala
€€€ Hotel Imaret restaurant, in the house where Mehmet Ali was born (*see opposite*). The town also has a variety of good fish tavernas down by the port.
Serres
The town has some very good tavernas with strong Asia Minor and Pontic culinary influences. There is a row of restaurants near the public park on the road up to the acropolis.

FESTIVALS & EVENTS

Kavala The *Eleftheria*, in June, celebrates Kavala's liberation by Greek troops in 1913.
Langadas The *Anastenaria* is a ritual fire-walking ceremony, performed on the feast of Sts Constantine and Helen (21 May).
Monokklisia On 8 Jan the women exchange roles with their menfolk, making men perform domestic chores while they while away the day at the taverna.
Philippi Drama festival in the ancient theatre, July–Sept.

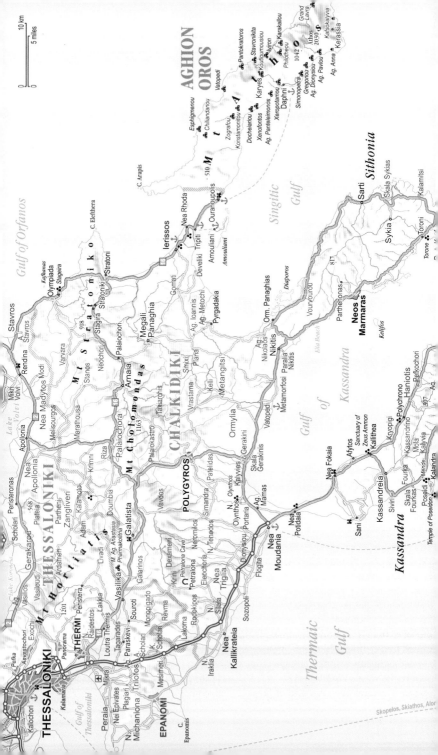

CHALKIDIKI

The peninsula of Chalkidiki (Chalcidice; Χαλκιδική) is often seen—apart from the monastic republic of Mount Athos—as the poor relation of Greek tourism. This lacklustre image is unjustified: investment in better roads and hotels is bringing new life to many resorts, and the region's rich archaeological and historic heritage is becoming more prominent. The Kassandra 'finger' of the peninsula is popular with day trippers from Thessaloniki and elsewhere, while Sithonia, the central 'finger', has more sophisticated resorts (and the best archaeological sites). The east coast, north of the Athos peninsula, is very little visited, but has beautiful coastal scenery, large forests and good fish tavernas, as well as many historic sites, including Stagira, the birthplace of Aristotle.

Chalkidiki received its name from the number of colonies planted here by the city of Chalkis in Euboea. Geographically it is the most prominent feature of Macedonia, projecting into the Aegean between the Gulf of Thessaloniki on the west and the Gulf of Orfanos on the east. It branches into three smaller peninsulas: Kassandra (anciently *Pallene*), Sithonia, and Athos. Other than in the west, along the southern coastal plain, and in Kassandra, the interior is wooded and mountainous, the highest point (Mt Athos), rising to 2030m. On the landward side the limit of Chalkidiki is marked by the lakes east of Thessaloniki, though the official boundary runs a few miles south of them.

Administratively the region is divided into the nomarchy of Chalkidiki, which comprises the greater part of the peninsula, and Aghion Oros, coterminous with the territory of Athos, which has an autonomous constitution. The inhabitants are mainly engaged in agriculture, though the mines are important and tourism is playing a rapidly increasing role. The coasts in the remote past supported flourishing cities, some of them—notably Olynthos—of more than local importance. Finds from the many archaeological sites are in the Thessaloniki and Polygyros museums.

WESTWARDS ACROSS THE PENINSULA

This route takes the old road between Thessaloniki and Mount Athos. It passes through rich agricultural country, with an emphasis on wine and cereal production. If you are on a first visit to northern Greece, it is a good introduction to the region.

Thermi and environs

Just outside Thessaloniki is Thermi (Θέρμη), a small place bearing the name of the predecessor of Thessaloniki. It was an Ottoman centre, and ruins of a small hammam can be seen near the roadside in a wood. Loutra Thermis is a small spa with some interesting Ottoman bath buildings that require restoration. To the south Aghia Paraskevi has a Macedonian tomb (at Mikri Toumba); and a huge Archaic cemetery, largely intact, with splendid finds (in Thessaloniki). To the north, at Peristera, the church of Aghios Andreas has 9th-century frescoes. Vasilika has tavernas. There is a left turn here for the Monastery of Aghios Anastasios, and an imposing bronze and marble roadside monument to Kapetan Hapsa, a local leader who led his *ceta* against the Ottomans in 1821.

The plain changes to a wide valley as you cross the *nome* boundary, then climb along the north side. At a crossroads there is a left turn to the Moni Aghia Anastasia Pharmakolitria, founded c. 888. Galatista, a mining centre, occupies the site of ancient *Anthemous*. There is a Byzantine tower in the village, part of the defence system of the medieval road. The road now climbs round the slopes of Mt Cholomondas (1163m) amid chestnut woods, rising to 1006m on a ridge just below the summit before descending to Arnaia, a characterful old Macedonian town with some fine traditional stone houses, and centre of a fruit and wine-growing region. At Palaiochori, a road runs south to the delightful Megali Panaghia, a focus of pilgrimage on 15th August (Feast of the Assumption).

Ierissos and Tripiti

Ierissos is a straggling fishing village on the shore of the bay of the same name, with nice old-fashioned tavernas. It is a departure point for Mt Athos and there are sightseeing cruises. The ruined medieval watch-tower outside the village to the northwest has Hellenic foundations and reused marbles. Ancient too are the remains of a mole, still in use. The town occupies part of the site of the huge Archaic, Classical and Hellenistic cemetery of *Akanthos*, which extends to the shore, with tombs in the sand. Some of them (4th century) were cremations carried out in a clay-lined grave, the clay being fired in the process to create a kind of terracotta coffin. Finds are in Polygyros museum. Remains (Classical to Byzantine) of the ancient town lie on low hills immediately to the southeast. Fortifications are visible on the east side of the acropolis. The road continues to Nea Rhoda, on the north shore, and to the landing stage of Tripiti, on the south shore of the vale of Provlaka (the narrowest part of the isthmus).

THE PROVLAKA CANAL

In 480 BC, aware of the disaster that had befallen Mardonius eleven years before, when he lost 300 ships and 20,000 men trying to round the promontory of Athos, Xerxes ordered a canal across the isthmus for the passage of his invasion fleet. The citizens of Akanthos awarded heroic honours to Artachaies, who died while in charge of its cutting and was given a state funeral by Xerxes. The canal was apparently dug in a hollow between low banks past the town of *Sane* (long since vanished). Several artificial mounds and substructions of walls can be traced along its course. Its width seems to have been 12–15m. The isthmus is estimated to have risen 14m since the canal was cut. An alternative theory suggests that only part of the line was true canal, the central part of the crossing being in the form of a trackway.

Beyond Tripiti, with views towards the attractive islet of Amouliani (car ferry from Tripiti) is Ouranopolis, with a 14th-century tower. The fishing village, built by refugees in 1922, has adopted the name of a lost town founded by Alexarchos, son of Antipater, in 316 BC. The inhabitants make knotted rugs to Byzantine patterns, a 'tradition' started by an Australian woman in 1928. Beyond lies the territory of the Holy Mountain.

MOUNT ATHOS

The wild, often roadless, and picturesque peninsula of Athos or Aghion Oros ('Holy Mountain'), easternmost of the three prongs of Chalkidiki, is connected to the mainland by a low isthmus only 2.5km across. The peninsula is c. 50km long and 5–10km wide. The population, exclusively male, is around 1,400. The ground rises abruptly from the isthmus, and for the most part is beautifully wooded. Immediately south of Karyes, the administrative capital, the land rises to 610m; from here a rugged broken country, covered with dark forests, extends to the foot of Mt Athos itself (2030m), a cone of white limestone which rises in solitary magnificence from the sea.

The Holy Community
The Holy Community, a kind of monastic republic, is composed of 20 monasteries, of which 17 are Greek, one Russian (Roussiko), one Bulgarian (Zografou), and one Serb (Chiliandariou). There is also a Romanian retreat. Throughout the 20th century the number of hermitages and cells has dwindled, along with the number of monks, though the last few years have seen a revival of interest in the monastic life, and several novices have entered the orders. Divorced from distracting modernity, unaffected by hurry (the Julian Calendar, 13 days behind the rest of Europe, is still in use, and the day divided into Byzantine hours of variable length, with sunset as 12 o'clock), the Holy Mountain affords to the devout a glimpse of life wholly dedicated to God; to the weary a welcome retreat from the world; and to the lover of nature and medieval art a treasury of beauty.

Formalities
Visitors must be male and (unless a theological student) over 18 years of age. All visitors require a permit (for which a fee is payable) obtained in advance. Offices issuing permits are as follows:

For non-Orthodox Christians and all other: Ministry of Foreign Affairs, Churches Directorate, Athens, T: 210 362 6894; or Ministry of Macedonia and Thrace, Political Office, Thessaloniki, T: 2310 270 092.

For Orthodox Christians: Visitors' Office in Thessaloniki, T: 2310 252 575 (Greek nationals); T: 2310 252 578 (non-Greeks); branch office in Ouranopolis, T: 23770 71423.

The maximum length of stay is four consecutive days (three nights). Extensions are sometimes granted. Do not expect to get your permit immediately. Only 120 Orthodox and 14 non-Orthodox visitors are allowed on the Holy Mountain at any one time, and monasteries tend to favour their own denomination.

HISTORY OF MOUNT ATHOS

The fame of Athos rests entirely on its medieval monasteries. Legends of foundation by the Virgin herself, by St Helen, or by one or other Roman emperor of the 4th or 5th century, often supported by documents forged in the 18th century, seem to have been tacitly abandoned with the official celebration in 1963 of the 1,000th anniversary of the founding of the monastic community. It is likely that anchorites lived on the mountain at an earlier time, fugitives, perhaps, from iconoclastic persecution in 726–842; Peter the Athonite, the most famous of the early monks, is supposed to have lived for 50 years in a cave. Existing *lavres* (λαύρα, cloister or monk's cell) were organised by Athanasius the Athonite, friend and counsellor of the Emperor Nicephorus Phocas, the first historical benefactor of the Holy Mountain. He founded the monastery of the Great Lavra (963 or 961) and instituted the strict rule of the Abbot Theodore. Thereafter foundations multiplied under the protection of the emperors (especially Alexius I Comnenus, who placed them under Imperial jurisdiction), until they reached the number of 40, with, it is said, 1,000 monks in each. Andronicus II relinquished his authority to the Patriarch in 1312. The incursions of the Latins, Catalans (1307), Serbs (1346) and Turks caused the abandonment of a few outlying sites, but the importance of Mt Athos was not impaired. It reached its zenith in the 15th century, after which a period of decadence set in, followed by reinvigorating reforms. After the fall of Constantinople in 1453 the monks kept on good terms with the sultans, one of whom, Selim I, paid a state visit to the peninsula. Thanks to this political dexterity, the Holy Mountain remained the spiritual centre of orthodoxy. It built its own schools, one of which, that of Vatopedi, had a famous headmaster, Eugene Bulgaris (1753–59). At the beginning of the War of Independence the community joined the insurgents, but sank defeated under the Turkish yoke.

Despite its seclusion, Mt Athos has always attracted the attention, not necessarily disinterested, of the outside world. The Vatican has frequently, but without success, tried to exercise some influence. The European Union has tried to outlaw its prohibition of women.

Rules of the mountain

The gates of the monasteries are open only during the daytime. Meals are simple: fish, vegetables, rice, cheese, fruits, and wine made on the mountain. Meat, which few of the monks ever taste, is not to be expected. On 159 days in the year the monks have only one meal and then eggs, cheese, wine, fish, milk and oil are forbidden; on the other days they are allowed only two meals. The visitor's contribution to monastic funds on leaving should be at least commensurate with the hospitality he has received. Supplementary rations, purchased before arrival on Athos, are a great advantage. NB: Take plenty of cash when you travel to Athos. At the time of writing there were no ATM machines on the mountain.

Appropriate clothing (long trousers, no headgear indoors) should be worn at all times, and the rules of the mountain observed: no smoking, no filming or video-recording, no swimming, even in secluded coves.

Organisation of the community

By a decree of 16th September 1926, the peninsula forms part of Greece but enjoys administrative autonomy, while in Church matters it depends on the Ecumenical Patriarch. All monks, of whatever race, become Greek subjects on retiring to Mt Athos; no heterodox or schismatics are admitted. Women are excluded. The Hellenic Republic is represented by a governor having the rank of nomarch, answerable to the Ministry of Foreign Affairs, and by a police force. The administrative autonomy is centred in the Synod, or Holy Council (*Hiera Synaxis*), with its seat at Karyes, comprising 20 deputies (*Antipròsopoi*), one from each convent. The deputies are elected annually in January; and four of them, appointed in rotation, form the *Epistasia*, with executive powers. One of the four takes precedence as the First of Athos ('Ο Πρότος του 'Αθωνος).

The 20 convents are divided into two categories; coenobite; 'living in common') and idiorrhythmic ('going their own way'). In the eleven coenobite convents all members are clothed alike, pool their resources, and live on the same meagre fare in the common hall or refectory. The monks of the nine idiorrhythmic convents enjoy a milder rule. They live apart from their fellows, though their convents may have refectories, and they have no property in common. Each monk provides his own clothes and obtains his food from his own resources. All of them attend services for at least eight out of the 24 hours. These include Mass (*Leitourgìa*), Vespers (*Hesperinòn*), Compline (*Apòdeipnon*), and Nocturnal Office (*Nykterinòn*), which may on occasion last throughout the night and even exceptionally for 24 hours.

As well as the convents, there are anchorites, who live apart in cells, some of them well-nigh inaccessible; *sarabaites*, groups of two or three hermits living in hermitages or small houses; and *gyrovakes*, mendicant and vagabond monks. The small retreats and cells have various names, such as *skeìtai, kellià, kathìsmata*, etc.

Each convent is administered by an abbot (*hegoùmenos*), elected for life or for a definite period assisted by two or three coadjutors (*epìtropoi*) and by a Council (*Synaxis*) of Elders (*Proïstàmenoi*). There is also a class of inferior monks (*paramikroì*), who do manual labour. The monk begins as a novice (*dòkimos*, or *rasofòros*, from the name of his black gown). In the next three years he becomes crusader (*stavrofòros*) or *mikròschima* (wearer of short coat); then *megalòschima* (wearer of long coat; with elaborate symbolic embroidery). All the monks are bearded and wear their hair long, either hanging down or tucked into a bonnet; their normal dress is a black gown with a leather girdle.

Among the oldest and most strictly observed of the rules is that of Constantine Monomachos (1060), which forbids access to 'every woman, every female animal, every child, eunuch, and smooth-faced person'. This rule is still officially in force, except that it is no longer incumbent upon a visitor to be bearded. Female cats and hens are openly tolerated.

The coenobitic monastery resembles a cross between an inn and a walled city. It is usually in the form of a rectangle and guarded by towers. The entrance is through a door at one of the four corners. The principal building in the middle of the enclosure is the katholikon, or communal church, cruciform with double narthex and several cupolas. Between the church and one of the short walls is the *phiale*, a canopied stoup containing holy water. Built into the short wall beyond is the apsidal *tràpeza* (refectory), with an ambo from which a monk reads during meals, and, near the seat of the *hegoùmenos*, a platter for the consecrated bread. Against the opposite short wall is the *archontarìa*, or guest-chamber. The monks' cells, adorned with porticoes and balconies, line the long walls.

The art of Mount Athos

Although many treasures, particularly classical manuscripts, have been pillaged, burnt, neglected, or sold in the past, Athos is still rich in minor works of art. Little except charters and chrysobuls survive from the earliest times, but the archives (now jealously guarded) of Grand Lavra, Vatopedi and Iviron, and the library of Vatopedi, are of the first importance. Reliquaries, chalices and illuminated MSS survive in quantity. In the major arts of architecture and painting, if there is not much of the first rank, there is sufficient of interest and merit to give a comprehensive picture of the late Byzantine scene. The principal features in which Athonite churches diverge from general Byzantine practice are the apsidal ends to the transepts and the double narthex, divided into *liti* and *mesonyktikòn*, often flanked by side chapels. Two schools of painting are represented. The Macedonian School skilfully adapts painting to architectural media. Its protagonists are Manuel Panselinos (early 14th century), and his contemporaries. The Cretan School, affected by the art of Italy and south Germany, was founded c. 1535 by Theophanes and continued by Frangos Kastellanos of Thebes. In the refectories (eg at Lavra) the subject of the frescoes is food. There may be local variations of the traditional style. There are few icons of importance.

Approaches

Either by boat from Ierissos to Iviron or Grand Lavra (daily) or from Ouranopolis (at least once daily; calling also at Nea Rhoda) down the south coast to Daphni. In summer there are two daily buses from Thessaloniki to the ports. The morning bus connects three times weekly with the late-morning boat from Ouranopolis.

On Athos, there are buses from the port of Daphni to Karyes (1hr), and from Iviron monastery to Karyes, the latter connecting with the boat from Ierissos. Minibuses go direct from Karyes to most monasteries, and there are also taxis driven by lay brothers. Many of the monasteries can be approached by boat (and a walk inland) through intermediate stops on the routes from Ouranopolis and Ierissos, and there is a service from Daphni to Aghia Anna. Ports at the east end of the peninsula are less frequently served. Otherwise travel is on foot. The best map of the mountain is the Road Edition 1:50,000 Mount Athos map.

AN ATHOS ITINERARY

Xeropotamou and Koutloumousiou

The idiorrhythmic convent of **Xeropotamou** (Ξηροποτάμου) is pleasantly situated c. 140m above the sea. It derives its name ('dry river') from a seasonal torrent. By forged documents the convent acquired in the 18th century a 'traditional' foundation by Pulcheria, empress in 450–457. Its first genuine mention is in the 10th century; it received privileges from Michael VIII in 1275 after an earthquake the previous year, and Sultan Selim I (or, more probably, Selim II) rescued it from a period of decay. The earliest of the present buildings dates from 1763, when the paintings in the katholikon were also executed. Two ancient reliefs are built into the west wall of the court; the 'Roman' inscriptions are 18th-century forgeries and the two busts on the clock-tower (said to be St Paul of Athos and Pulcheria) are of the 15th century. The chief treasures are a piece of the Cross (30cm long) and the so-called 'Paten of St Pulcheria', depicting the Virgin at prayer standing adored by two angels with censers; in the first band is a procession of angels; in the second, the Apostles prostrate in worship. The paten was made in the 15th century; the mounting showing the inscription, with the name, is an 18th-century addition. From the guest-chamber there is a fine view.

Farther on is the coenobite convent of **Koutloumousiou** (Κουτλουμουσίου), situated in the most fertile part of the peninsula, amid gardens, vineyards, olive plantations, and cornfields. This convent is first documented in 1169. It is named after the princely Seljuk family of Kutlumush, of which its convert founder was a member. Bad fires in 1857 and 1870 (and again more recently) wrought havoc with all but the katholikon, rebuilt before 1540, and the arcaded east range, which dates from 1767. The frescoes of the katholikon have been repainted. There is a fine view of Karyes from the monastery.

Karyes

Karyes (Καρυές) is a little town surrounded by vineyards and gardens, with a few shops kept by monks and lay brothers. Its monastery was reputedly founded by Constantine and destroyed by Julian the Apostate. The restored basilican **Church of the Protaton**, the oldest on Mt Athos, dates from the 10th century. In the Chapel of St John the Baptist are frescoes of the *Nativity* and of the *Presentation in the Temple* attributed to Manuel Panselinos (early 14th century) and considered the finest in the peninsula; others, of a later date, are beautifully fresh and delicate. There are also silver filigree crosses and a wonder-working icon. The Council House has a chamber in which the 20 deputies deliberate sitting on divans. Each of the deputies has a lodge at Karyes to accommodate himself and younger monks of his convent attending the school here.

Vatopedi

Vatopedi (Βατοπέδιον), one of the largest and most modern on Mt Athos, is an idior-rhythmic convent. The monastery, rather like a country mansion, is built round a huge triangular court in a charming pastoral setting overlooking a little bay, with a highly picturesque harbour. The southeast wing was destroyed by fire in February 1966.

Foundation traditions tell of Constantine as well as of Theodosius, the miraculous rescue of whose son Arcadius from the sea by the Virgin is supposedly commemorated by the name *Vatopaidion* (βάτος, bramble, and παιδή, child). The story tells of the boy being placed under a bramble for the hermits to find. The name is more likely *Vatopedion* (bramble-ground). The historical founders are Athanasius, Nicholas, and Antony from Adrianople (late 10th century). The Emperor John VI Cantacuzene retired here in 1355 under the name Ioasaph.

Most of the attractive buildings are of the 17th century or later. The katholikon (dedicated to the Annunciation), is an 11th-century basilica adapted to the plan of a Greek cross. It has a massive detached belfry and a double narthex. The 15th-century bronze doors, from Aghia Sofia, Thessaloniki, have panels in relief depicting the *Annunciation*. Over the second door is an 11th-century mosaic of *Intercession* (δέησις): centre, Christ in glory; at the sides, the Virgin and John the Baptist. The inner doors, inlaid with ivory, are dated 1567. The impressive interior, which has a polygonal apse, is decorated with frescoes of the Macedonian School (1312), restored in 1789 and 1819. Porphyry columns support the dome. In the **Chapel of St Dimitrios** (north) are icons of St Peter and St Paul (16th century), in a beautiful frame; of the *Panaghia Hodeghitria*, with reliefs of Christian festivals; of St Anne; and of the *Crucifixion* (13th century) in a 14th-century metal frame. The iconostasis is a fine work of art. The **Chapel of the Holy Girdle** contains a good *Nativity*. The cup of Manuel Palaeologus (early 15th century) is made of a block of jasper 25.5cm across, on a silver base decorated with enamel; the engraved handles are in the shape of dragons. There are some fine crosses with silver-gilt ornamentation. The most notable relic, the 'Girdle of the Virgin', was given to the monastery by Lazar I of Serbia (1372–89).

The **library** contains 8,000 volumes. Especially noteworthy are an Octateuch (first eight books of the Bible); a psalter autographed by Constantine IX Monomachos (1042–54); and a MS of Ptolemy's *Geographia*, with which are 17 chapters of Strabo's *Geography*, the *Periplus* of Hadrian, and 42 maps in colour. Two fragments of frescoes were discovered in the library, the first representing only the heads of the Apostles Peter and Paul. They are attributed to the painters commissioned by Stefan Nemanja and his son (c. 1197–98) to decorate the Refectory.

Esphigmenou and Chiliandariou

The coenobite convent of **Esphigmenou** (Ἐσφιγμένου) stands on the edge of the sea, at the mouth of a torrent in a little narrow valley (whence probably its name, from the Greek for 'compressed' or 'hemmed in'). First mentioned in a document of 1034, it was restored in the 14th century, but plundered by pirates in 1533. Except for short periods of revival, it lay abandoned until the end of the 18th century. Possession of the cave of the hermit Antony of Kiev (983–1073) assured it Russian support, but, though it was restored in the 19th century, it has never been of the first importance. The church (1808–11), overpoweringly ornate, has an iconostasis carved with figures of Adam and Eve. It has a portable mosaic icon of Christ (12th century) and (in the library) an 11th-century Menologion (calendar).

Chiliandariou (Χιλιανδαρίου) is an idiorrhythmic Serbian convent (the monks are all Slavs). It is situated nearly a mile from the sea, in a well-watered valley surrounded by thickly wooded hills. The name is said to be derived from its construction for 1,000 monks (*chilioi andres*). Founded in 1197 by the Serbian prince Stefan Nemanja and his son Sava, it was rebuilt in 1299 by Stefan Milutin, who eventually retired, after his abdication, to Vatopedi. (*NB: There was a serious fire at Chiliandariou in 2004, and it is currently closed. Until damage is assessed and it reopens, it is impossible to give an account of the convent's treasures.*)

Pantokratoros, Stavronikita and Iviron

Pantokratoros (Παντοκράτορος) is an idiorrhythmic convent founded c. 1357–63 by Alexius the Stratopedarch and John the Primicerius, whose inscribed tombs have been found in the narthex. The walls, repaired in 1536, have a massive tower. It is built on a sea-washed rock above a small cove and has a fine view of Stavronikita. The old katholikon has been often renovated (fragmentary 14th-century frescoes). The library has interesting 11th-century MSS.

Stavronikita (Σταυρονικήτα), also idiorrhythmic, was perhaps founded in 1153 (or even earlier) but refounded in 1542 by the Patriarch Jeremiah of Constantinople. The monastery, with its massive tower, crowns a precipitous rock at the edge of the sea. The katholikon has frescoes of 1546 executed by monks. It has a mosaic icon of St Nicholas and a psalter of the 12th century.

Iviron (᾽Ιβήρων; Monastery of the Iberians) is also idiorrhythmic, with Greek, Russian, Romanian and Georgian monks. It was founded in 979 or 986 by three Iberians or Georgians under charter from Basil II the Bulgar-Slayer. Badly damaged by fire in 1865, it is a welter of buildings in an enclosed valley near the sea. The entrance opens into a vast court surrounded by heterogeneous buildings. In the middle is the katholikon, with a pavement that dates from the foundation. In a little chapel (1680–83) adjoining is the miraculous 10th-century icon of the *Panaghia Portaïtissa* which, found by one of the Georgians in the sea, enabled him to walk upon it. The library is rich in MSS, particularly of the gospels including one the gift of Peter the Great. The treasury (*seldom shown*) has a carved cross of 1607, another of carved wood (*Raising of Lazarus*), and remarkable vestments, including an embroidered tunic said to have belonged to the Emperor John Tsimiskis.

Philotheou and Karakallou

The idiorrhythmic convent of **Philotheou** (Φιλοθέου) was supposedly founded in the 9th century by three monks of Olympus (Arsenius, Denys, and Philotheos), but it is first mentioned in the 12th century. It numbered Stefan Dušan among its benefactors.

St Peter and St Paul embracing: an icon from the Karakallou monastery.

The convent was rebuilt after a fire in 1781. Round its church are workshops where the monks employ themselves in wood carving. There is a fine view from here of the convents of Stavronikita and Pantokratoros.

About 30mins farther on through rich and fertile country is the coenobite convent of **Karakallou** (Καρακάλλου), situated in hazel woods (460m). It was founded in the 15th century by Peter Raresch IV of Moldavia and dedicated to Sts Peter and Paul by one John Karakallos. The convent was restored in 1548. There was a fire in 1988. The mountainside falls abruptly to the sea and the view over the Aegean embraces Samothrace, Imbros and Tenedos.

Grand Lavra

The **Grand Lavra** (Μονή Μεγίστης Λαύρας) is an idiorrhythmic convent whose monks include Russians, Romanians and Bulgarians. The largest and perhaps the finest of all, partly because (alone of the 20) it has never suffered from fire, it is comparatively simple in plan, without the multiplicity of buildings characterising some of the others. It was founded in the time of Nicephorus Phocas (963–64) by Athanasius of Trebizond (the Athonite). Resembling a fortified village, with a fine 10th-century tower, it stands on a gently sloping spur (152m) overlooking a little harbour guarded by a fort. The entrance is by a long, winding and vaulted passage, with several massive iron gates. In the court are two ancient cypresses, said to have been planted at the foundation.

The *phiale*, erected in 1635, incorporates Byzantine relief panels between eight Turkish stalactite capitals. Paintings within the dome represent the Baptism of Christ. Below is an antique porphyry basin with a sculptured bronze fountain. The **katholikon**, completed in 1004, which externally resembles a domed basilica, consists of a triconchial Greek cross extended to the west and flanked by pareeclesia in the form of two smaller cross-in-square churches. A hideous exonarthex of 1814 now abuts the three west fronts, occupying the site of St Athanasius's cell. Painted Baroque doors of the Turkish period lead into the church, which was frescoed all over by Theophanes the Cretan in 1535–60. Representations of Nicephorus Phocas and his nephew, John I Tsimiskis, benefactors of the church, dominate the nave. In the right pareeclesion is the Tomb of St Athanasius. To the left the **Chapel of St Nicholas** has frescoes by Kastellanos. The cruciform **Refectory**, built by Gennadios, Archbishop of Serres, in 1512, has frescoes by Theophanes the Cretan. Within the apse is the *Last Supper*. On the side walls, in three bands, are Sts Athanasius, Euthymios, and Gregory Palamas (below); scenes of martyrdom (centre); and an illustration of the hymn *Axion esti* (above). To the south are the *Life of Aghios Solitarios*, *Council of Nicaea*, scenes from the life of the Virgin. To the north, *Death of a Just Man*, scenes from the life of St John. To the east, *Last Judgement* (centre, *Second Coming*; left, *Paradise*; right, *Hell*). The Chapel of the Trinity (Aghia Trias) has an iconostasis of the 15th–16th centuries.

The **treasures** include the icon of *Koukouzelissa* (12th century), reliquary of Nicephorus Phocas (11th century or earlier), and an enamelled icon said to be that of John Tzinitzas (12th century). The **library** has 5,000 volumes and 2,250 MSS, including a Bible belonging to Nicephorus Phocas, set with precious stones; two leaves (from *Galatians* and *II Corinthians*) of the 6th-century *Codex Euthalianus* are preserved.

The summit of Athos and the coast

Directly above the Grand Lavra rises the **peak of Mount Athos** (2030m), with its white cone and its precipices, in striking contrast to the dark foliage of the ridges below. The ascent can be made in a day from the convent via Kerassia. On the summit is the little Chapel of the Transfiguration, in which a service is held annually (on 6th August). The peak was one of the stations of the fire-beacons that carried Agamemnon's signal to Clytemnestra (*Aeschylus, Agamemnon, 284*). The view all round is unsurpassed, embracing the whole northern Aegean.

Around the contour of the peninsula and up the west coast there are numerous hermits' cells (*sketai*), many of them almost inaccessible. A short distance from Kerassia, on the coast, is Kafsokalyvia, a colony of painters and woodcarvers who live in small groups. The *skete* of Aghia Anna, round the cape, is a retreat where monks live in separate houses, which cling in terraces to a steep mountainside. Here is a shrine with a relic of St Anne.

Convents of the west coast

The coenobite convent of **Aghiou Pavlou** (’Αγίου Παύλου) is beautifully situated in an angle of stupendous cliff above a boulder-strewn torrent. Founded in the 11th century by Serbs and Bulgars, it gets its name not from the Apostle, but from a son of the Emperor Maurice, one of its chief benefactors. After a period of desertion, the buildings were renewed wing by wing in the 19th–20th centuries; the katholikon of 1447 was replaced in 1844–50. The library was lost in a fire in 1905. The Chapel of St George has good frescoes in the Cretan style, dated 1423 but probably of the 16th century: figures of saints and Apostles and, in the narthex, the Virgin as the source of life (Zoödochos Pigi).

The coenobite convent of **Dionysiou** (Διονυσίου) was founded in 1375 by Alexius III, Emperor of Trebizond. It stands on a precipitous rock where a bleak gorge reaches the sea, and is approached from its little landing-stage by 420 steps. The huge

676 MACEDONIA: CHALKIDIKI

tower was built in 1520 and Peter IV Raresch of Moldavia restored the buildings (1547) after a fire in 1535. The katholikon has frescoes of 1547 by Zorzis (Cretan School). In the refectory is a *Last Judgement* (1603). There is the silver reliquary of St Niphon and (in the library) a superb chrysobul and c. 600 MSS. Farther up the coast, just above the sea and shut in by rocky cliffs, is the compact and attractive **Gregoriou** (Γρηγόριου), a coenobite convent founded c. 1395 and rebuilt after a fire in 1762–83. Its katholikon has paintings of 1779.

The coenobite convent of **Simonopetra** (Σιμωνόπετρα; or Simonos Petras, or Simópetra) is picturesquely situated over 305m up on a rock isolated on all sides save the northeast, where a bridge of three superimposed arches joins it to the cliff. Its buildings, reconstructed on the old foundations in 1893–1902, with funds from Czar Nicholas II, are supported by heavy beams overhanging the precipice, recalling architecturally the Potala at Lhasa in Tibet. The view is magnificent. The convent was founded in 1257 by St Simon and favoured by the Serbian Emperor John Ugleš. Fires took their usual toll in 1580 and 1625, and Turkish occupation in 1821–30, while the library and much else was destroyed in 1891. From Simonopetra Daphni is 2hrs walk.

The west coast beyond Dafni

Aghios Panteleimonos (Ἅγίος Παντελεήμονος) or **Roussiko** is a huge coenobite convent of Russian monks. It was founded in 1169 in an earlier abandoned building, burnt down by the Catalan Company in 1309, but re-endowed by Andronicus II two years later. It was occupied for about 80 years after 1735 by Greek monks, but rebuilt in 1812–14 in an exotic Russian style. It was swept by fire in 1968 when the assembly hall was destroyed. Above its scattered barrack-like blocks on the waterfront rise many towers and domes surmounted by golden crosses. It has a soapstone paten with a representation of the Virgin and Child, and an illuminated MS of St Gregory of Nazianzen. The singing of its Russian choirs was famous. At the monastery are some architectural and sculptural fragments from the Temple of Zeus Ammon at Kallithea on the Kassandra peninsula (*see p. 680*).

The coenobite convent of **Xenofontos** (Ξενοφώντος), founded at the end of the 10th century by the monk Xenophon, stands at the edge of the sea. The old katholikon has frescoes of the school of Theophanes, while the new katholikon (1837) has two fine 14th-century mosaic panels of saints. In the refectory is a good *Last Judgement*. Farther on, standing 46m above the sea, is the idiorrhythmic convent of **Docheiariou** (Δοχειαρείου), architecturally one of the most charming. It was founded at the beginning of the 10th century by Euthymios, who had been Receiver (δοχειάρης) of the Grand Lavra. The katholikon is one of the finest on Mt Athos; its frescoes, by an unknown artist of the Cretan school (1568) embody the traditional style of decoration in all its completeness. Count Alexander IV of Moldavia and his countess Roxandra are depicted as founders. The convent has an *epitaphios* of 1605, and 11th–12th-century MSS.

The little coenobite convent of **Konstamonitou** (Κωνσταμονίτου) is hidden in a deep defile. It was founded, according to the most probable account, in the 11th cen-

The pleasing proportions of the monastery of Gregoriou, on the west coast of the Athos peninsula. Though a 14th-century foundation, its buildings are mainly mid-18th century.

tury by someone from Kastamon, but tradition has altered the medieval spelling from Kastamonitou to accord with a legendary foundation by Constans, son of Constantine the Great. Its buildings are all of the 19th century.

Zografou (Ζωγράφου) is a coenobite convent of Bulgarian monks founded by Slav nobles from Ohrid at the end of the 10th century. The two churches date from 1764 and 1801 but the rest was largely rebuilt in 1860–96 in an ugly style. Its miraculous icon of St George (Italian style, 15th century) is said to have come from Palestine without human aid, in the same way as the House of the Virgin at Loreto. The monks declare that it was painted by divine will and not by man; hence the dedication to the *Zografos* or Painter. There is a small hole near the eyes of the painting made by an unbelieving bishop from Constantinople, who (it is said) inserted his finger in derision and could not withdraw it, so that it had to be cut off.

The route from Zografou across the peninsula to Chiliandariou is one of the finest on the Holy Mountain.

POLYGYROS & OLYNTHOS

Polygyros (Πολύγυρος) is the chief town of Chalkidiki. Ugly outskirts give way to an attractive small pedestrianised centre with some good late 19th-century buildings. There is a fine 1909 Town Hall in grey stone, and some good craft shops. The Archaeological Museum (*open Tues–Sun 8.30–3*) is to the right at the entrance to the town. It houses finds from all over Chalkidiki. Of particular interest are those from the sanctuary of Zeus Ammon at Aphytis and a head of Dionysus from the associated sanctuary. There is also early black-figure pottery from Olynthos, and a Late Archaic Clazomenian larnax. Three silver coins displayed were found in the hand of a skeleton at Akanthos.

West of Polygyros, near Petralona, is a cave (conducted tours; museum; *open 9am–sundown; T: 23730 71671*), where a Neanderthal skull came to light in 1960 and a full skeleton in 1976. The hominid creature takes its name from its find-site: *Archanthropus europeus petralonsiensis*. The cave may have been occupied c. 500,000 BC.

Beyond Polygyros the road winds south down through rounded hills, passing large quarries, and reaches the coast at a T-junction. The road to the right leads to Olynthos.

ANCIENT OLYNTHOS

To get to the site, take a signed track at the beginning of the modern village, and follow it for 1km, fording the River Retsinika. The site (open Tues–Sun 8.30–3; later in summer) occupies twin flat-topped mounds running north and south, overlooking the river.

HISTORY OF OLYNTHOS

Neolithic dwellings occupied the south spur of the hill in the early 3rd millennium BC. The Bronze Age settlement was at Aghios Mamas, but c. 800 BC the south hill was reoccupied by a Macedonian tribe. Xerxes here requisitioned troops and ships in 480 BC; meditating rebellion in the following year, the city was burnt by the Persian Artabazus and the site given to the Chalcidians. The city paid tribute to Athens until, in 432, Perdiccas II of Macedon moved many inhabitants of neighbouring Chalcidian towns into Olynthos and it became the head of the Chalcidian League. The population grew to c. 30,000 inhabitants, and the town spread to the north hill. It maintained its independence except for a short period of submission to Sparta (379 BC). After first siding with Macedon, Olynthos was reconciled to Athens by Demosthenes, who in his *Olynthiac Orations* urged his countrymen to support the Olynthians against Philip II. In 348, however, Philip took and destroyed Olynthos so thoroughly as to prompt Demosthenes' comment that a visitor to the place would never realise that there had been a city there (*Philippics 3, 117*).

The site

Demosthenes is right that there is little to see at Olynthos. To the archaeologist its remains (best appreciated from the air) have proved fascinating for what they reveal of Greek urban layout. The Classical city was built on the Hippodamian system with *insulae* of uniform area, measuring 300 by 120 Greek feet. Its excavation by the American School in 1928–34 provided a knowledge of Greek town-planning and domestic building comparable with that gained by Roman scholars from Pompeii. Sculptural and architectural fragments, exactly dated by the historic destruction, clarified the relationship between Classical and Hellenistic styles. Its pebble mosaics, forerunners of those at Pella, have been covered over; some mosaics have been uncovered for display but these are not easy to find without help from the *phylax*, and the site otherwise offers little to the layman. There are numerous open cisterns.

The typical Olynthian dwelling

In the 5th and 4th centuries BC Olynthos was the most important of the Greek cities in this part of the Macedonian coast. Nevertheless, the majority of its buildings were undistinguished: carefully planned, compact housing, making maximum use of minimum space, much as any urban housing project in our own day. Dwelling houses had access from one side only, from the street-facing elevation. Houses were built close together, uniform in size, though with some variation in interior layout. They backed onto a narrow passageway between rows. The diagram below shows the typical inside layout of an Olynthian home.

Opening off the entrance was a courtyard with a colonnade on one side. Sleeping quarters and the women's apartments were placed above this. The two principal ground-floor rooms were the communal *oikos* (living room) with its hearth, placed near the kitchen, bathroom and domestic quarters; and the *andron*, reserved for the men of the family, with couches placed around the walls, where visitors and friends could be entertained. This would have been the most lavishly decorated of all the rooms in the house. While most rooms had floors of beaten earth, the *andron* might have been paved in pebble mosaic.

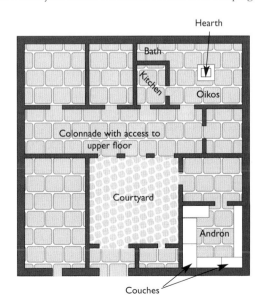

Hearth

Bath

Kitchen

Oikos

Colonnade with access to upper floor

Courtyard

Andron

Couches

THE KASSANDRA PENINSULA

The peninsula of Kassandra (Κασάνδρα), the ancient *Pallene*, is the most fertile of the three prongs of Chalkidiki. It is popular with weekend trippers from Thessaloniki, and has good market gardening. There are some nice sandy beaches in the southern parts. Before the War of Independence it contained a population of cattle- and sheep-farmers. When news arrived in 1821 of the revolt of the Greeks in the south, the people of Kassandra decided at first to join in, but finding themselves unprepared, tried to back out. It was too late. The Pasha of Thessaloniki, entering the peninsula, put all the inhabitants to the sword and razed their houses. Kassandra was left untenanted for two years and only relatively recently has anything been done to restore its former prosperity.

Nea Potidaia and the east coast

Nea Potidaia stands on the site of *Potidaia*, a Dorian colony founded c. 600 BC from Corinth, but which soon minted its own coins. After Salamis the strongly fortified port led the Chalcidian revolt against the Persian lines of communication, resisting a siege by Artabazus. Its revolt from Athens in 432 BC was one of the immediate causes of the Peloponnesian War (*see p. 16*). The city was subdued in 429 after a siege of two years; in the campaign Socrates saved the life of Alcibiades while serving as a hoplite. After destruction in the Olynthian War, Potidaia was refounded by Cassander as *Cassandreia*, and became the most prosperous city in Macedonia. It was destroyed by the Huns in AD 540 but revived by Justinian, who was probably responsible for the fortification of the isthmus. The castle was destroyed by the Turks in 1430.

From Nea Potidaia the road follows the east side of the peninsula. Nea Fokaia has a prominent tower. Diagonally opposite, on the west coast at Sani, there is a 16th-century tower on the promontory, which protected a dependency of the Athonite monastery of Stavronikita. Ancient remains in the vicinity indicate the site of the Euboean colonial settlement of *Sane*. Afytos marks the site of ancient *Aphytis*. A sanctuary of Zeus Ammon (4th century BC) with an associated sanctuary of the Nymphs and Dionysus were found and excavated in 1969–71 (finds in Polygyros museum and at the Roussiko monastery on Mt Athos). At Kallithea, the road divides to form a circuit of 76km round the peninsula.

The pleasant east coast road continues through wooded hamlets. Close to Polychrono are remains of an ancient settlement and cemetery, possibly *Neapolis*, a colony of *Mende* (*see below*). The peninsula ends in Cape Kalogria, the ancient *Kanastraion*.

The west coast

From Paliouri the road turns inland through Aghia Paraskevi, with a large Archaic cemetery, to the west coast at Loutra, which has hot springs. At Nea Skioni, chance finds in 1956 included coins and walls, relics presumably of *Skione*, once the chief town of the peninsula. Two kilometres to the east the church of Panaghia Faneromeni has early 17th-century frescoes. Farther on is Kalandra, the site of ancient *Mende*, noted for its wine and as the birthplace of the sculptor Paionios, whose famous *Nike* is in the museum at Olympia (*see p. 389*). The ancient town lies on a hill called Xefoto, with a walled acropolis (Mycenaean to Geometric periods) on the summit of Vigla to the southeast and, near the Hotel Mende, the ancient cemetery and the *proasteion* (suburb) mentioned by Thucydides (*IV, 130*). An excavated area of the latter has yielded material of the 9th–4th centuries. On Cape Kassandras a Temple of Poseidon, with inscribed votives from the Archaic period, has recently been located.

Cassander (c. 355–297 BC)

The Kassandra peninsula takes its name from Cassander, one of the *diodochoi*, the former generals of Alexander the Great, who disputed the governance of his empire after his death. Cassander emerged as ruler of Macedonia in c. 316. To stabilise his position, he ordered the murder of the boy Alexander, 13-year-old son of Alexander the Great, together with his mother Roxane. He then married Alexander the Great's half-sister Thessalonike. He founded two cities: one, which he named after himself, stood between modern Kassandreia and Nea Potidaia (the site remains unexcavated). The other he named after his wife.

Cassander's life was one of ceaseless struggle to still the strife between Alexander's squabbling successors and to redistribute the conqueror's territories. He had no desire to rebuild the empire, and allied himself with Ptolemy and Seleucus to prevent Antigonus from doing so. He died of dropsy.

SITHONIA

With its trees, sharp hills and rocks, Sithonia (Σιθωνία) is wilder and less domesticated than Kassandra, and still largely unspoilt. There are many small, bright beaches overhung with pinewoods; on the west coast you will find the occasional deserted cove.

Nikitis, at the base of the Sithonia peninsula, is a town rebuilt after destruction by the Turks in the early 19th century. It has some very attractive 19th-century houses, in a traditional Macedonian style. On top of the hill is a fine old mosque, now a church of the Profitis Ilias, by a ravine with sheep-pens. At Aghios Georgios on the coast (2km southwest) are substantial remains of an Early Christian settlement. The early 5th-century **Basilica of Bishop Sophronios** (the name recorded in a mosaic floor) has good mosaics, *opus sectile* and paintings. It is two-aisled with a colonnade to the west and a baptistery nearby. A hundred metres to the north is a bath building, while 60m south is a 5th-century cemetery basilica with a modern church of St George in its ruins (difficult to find, follow signs carefully).

At Elia are the remains of a basilica of the 5th century. Neos Marmaras is a pleasant village with good seaside restaurants. Inland, near Parthenonas, there is a sanctuary (perhaps of Zeus Koryphaios) on the summit of Mt Kostas. Beyond extend the estates of John C. Carras, run as a model farm to produce olives, citrus fruits, almonds and excellent wines for Porto Carras, a village expressly built in a modern but unappealing Mediterranean idiom as a resort for 3,000 guests (two vast hotels) and 1,800 permanent residents. It is popular with wealthy visitors from ex-Yugoslavia and Eastern Europe.

Toroni and the 'lekythos' promontory

Toroni is a pretty little fishing port in a charming tiny bay with good fish tavernas. At the south end of the bay, on the 'lekythos' promontory and the hills behind, are the extensive remains of **ancient *Torone***, where excavations since 1975 have produced important finds from the prehistoric to Ottoman periods.

The name Torone supposedly derives from a daughter of Proteus (or Poseidon) and Phoenix (Phoenike). It was founded as a colony by the Chalcidians in Hellenic times but recent excavations have revealed an important and long-lived Bronze Age settlement. In the Classical period the city gave assistance to Xerxes in his invasion of Greece. After the Persian wars it became subject to Athens. In 424 the gates were opened to the Spartans, but the Athenian Cleon retook it two years later. Later the site was dominated by Olynthos until again recovered for Athens by Timotheus. It became part of Philip's Macedonian Empire. In 169 BC it was unsuccessfully attacked by the Romans in the war against Perseus. In the 14th century it is mentioned in records of Mt Athos and remains of a synthronon in Basilica A suggests that it was the seat of a bishop.

Most striking on the promontory (called the 'lekythos' after Thucydides; *no entry*) are the walls of the **Byzantine and post-Byzantine fortifications**, largely built of blocks from earlier structures. The 'lekythos' has produced evidence for settlement, more or less continuous, from the Early Bronze Age until the Ottoman period. Especially interesting was a Late Geometric (c. 700 BC) structure with storage *pithoi*, found beneath a Byzantine tower. Archaic architectural fragments probably belong to the Temple of Athena, mentioned by Thucydides. Excavated remains outside the 'lekythos' include Classical houses and a large cemetery (sub-Mycenaean to Early Geometric), whose pottery shows connections with Euboea. The well-kept remains of the three-aisled basilica of Aghios Athanasios (5th century) preserve parts of a mosaic floor and a synthronon.

NORTHERN CHALKIDIKI

North of Pyrgadikia lies a large and empty domain dominated by vast forests. To see the recently revealed **Neposi Castle**, a fine Byzantine fortress lost in remote woodland, take the road north from Pyrgadikia towards Palaeochori and Arnaia. After about 4km, take the sign to Neposi Castle, and drive about 7km on good new dirt tracks. These follows the line of the old Byzantine road across the peninsula to the coast. The road is safe and passable in an ordinary car in summer but needs a 4WD in very wet weather. The castle is a romantic ruin bridging a ravine (undergrowth is still being cleared and the interior is inaccessible). It is a gently poetic and sad excursion into deep forest.

Return to the main road to Palaiochori and then to Arnaia (7km), a characterful little town with very good traditional crafts, dependent on sheep farming and forestry.

Returning in the direction east towards the coast, after 12km near modern **Stagira**, amid the remains of a Byzantine fortress, is the fine Monument to Aristotle, a large marble statue of the philosopher who was born here. The road continues to Stratoni on the coast, a mining town with a large 1922 refugee population. Iron pyrite outcrops can be seen on the sandy beach. **Ancient *Stageira*** is a few kilometres north up the coast, with well preserved walls of the ancient town on the hillside above the sea. Olympiada nearby (the ancient *Kapros Limen*) is a nice, friendly old town with some very picturesque 19th-century houses and fish tavernas.

Aristotle (384–322 BC)

Aristotle left his native Stagira to study at the Academy of Plato in Athens. Though he may have shared Plato's views to start with, his ideas developed in very different directions. The cast of Aristotle's mind was more sympathetic to democratic or oligarchic government than Plato's. And while Plato sought for eternal truths, Aristotle wanted to understand the world as it existed around him; he had little time for things which could not be seen. His achievement was extraordinary. He collected an immense amount of knowledge about the natural world, and thus became the founding father of zoology. He tried to understand how organisms grew and developed, seeing each one as having an ultimate purpose to which it naturally tended. The 'purpose' of man, for instance, was the state of *eudaemonia*, a sort of flourishing, centred on the active use of reasoning. His *Nicomachian Ethics* suggest that one must start out with wanting to achieve good, but be prepared to weigh up each situation on its merits and act accordingly. This allowed some flexibility, and the *Ethics* still provides a workable guide to everyday ethical living.

Another major achievement of Aristotle's was to sort out the mechanics of logical thinking. 'All men are mortal, Socrates is a man, therefore Socrates is mortal' is a piece of valid reasoning. 'All dogs have four legs, all cats have four legs, all cats are therefore dogs' is not, and Aristotle draws up the rules to show us why.

Aristotle and Plato represent two major schools of philosophy which have co-existed and conflicted throughout Western history. Plato's belief in a reality beyond the tangible world, which can be apprehended by a favoured few and interpreted for the majority, was clearly sympathetic to Christianity. Aristotle's empiricism and scientific enquiry, on the other hand, was derided by the Church as placing too great an emphasis on mortal man and his limited powers of perception. In the 13th century, however, Thomas Aquinas reconciled empiricism with Christianity, and Aristotle became the dominant philosopher of the Middle Ages.

Aristotle's end was a sad one. His father had been physician to Philip of Macedon, and he himself may have been tutor to Philip's son, Alexander (the Great). Alexander made the Macedonians deeply unpopular in Athens, and when news of his death reached the city in 323, an outburst of anti-Macedonian feeling saw Aristotle driven into exile. He died in Euboea in 322.   C.F.

THE ROAD OF SAINT PAUL

This route follows the so-called 'Road of St Paul', the section of the ancient Via Egnatia that wound eastwards across Macedonia before arriving at Philippi, the other main centre on the route with Pauline associations. Leaving Stagira you drive north for a few kilometres until you meet the busy main road under the hills of Psili Rychi, and turn left. After 6km, the massive overgrown walls of **Rendina Castle** can be seen on the left, a large Byzantine citadel set in a wooded ravine. The castle was later extended and refortified by the Ottomans to guard this important road junction. It is possible to park near the main road and clamber up the hillock to see the castle, a partly overgrown romantic ruin in need of restoration. North of the modern village is **Arethousa**, where the dramatist Euripides (*see p. 621*), in exile from Athens, was supposed in legend to have died after being attacked by wild dogs.

The road continues west to **Apollonia**, a small Ottoman town on the site of a Classical settlement. At the edge of the modern town, on grassland to the north of the main road, there is a small ruined mosque and nearby hammam, and a massive standing rock, where St Paul is said to have preached. It is a quiet, small, but in its way impressive place, well worth a detour.

PRACTICAL INFORMATION

Roads and communications are generally good, and many of the sites can be visited in a day trip from Thessaloniki, although it is more enjoyable to stay a night or two and enjoy the good local food and wine. The east coast of Chalkidiki can be cold in winter, and windy at any time of year. The west-facing coasts of Sithonia and Kassandra can be very mild, even in mid-winter, and are recommended then, although it can be wet on occasion. The sea does not warm up in many places until late June.

GETTING AROUND

• **By air:** There are frequent internal flights to Thessaloniki, and some international scheduled and charter flights.
• **By car:** From Thessaloniki, it takes about 2hrs to drive across the peninsula. Public transport is patchy.
• **By bus:** There is a separate KTEL for Chalkidiki in Thessaloniki, but it offers a sparse service. Although there are local buses, a car or some other form of personal transport is needed in many places. Kassandra has reasonable local buses, Sithonia less so. Some Thessaloniki hotels and travel agents can book day trips by coach.
Buses run at least twice daily from Thessaloniki to Ouranopolis and Mt Athos. There are quite good bus services to Polygyros and Kassandra, and a car is unnecessary for the coastal areas.
• **By boat:** Nea Moudania has a small harbour from which boats leave to the

northern Sporades. Information on getting to Athos is given separately (*see p.
670*).

WHERE TO STAY

The Kassandra and Sithonia branches of
the peninsula are generally well supplied with small hotels and there are
plenty of cheap rooms. Some of the
small towns in the northern central part
of Chalkidiki like Polygyros have basic
local hotels which are some of the
cheapest in Greece.
Sithonia
Elia beach has a very good hotel, the
Hotel Athena Pallas (T: 23750 81410,
www.athena-pallas.gr). Nearby, and very
attractive, also cheaper, is the Villa
Antigoni (T: 23750 81294). Both are
open all the year round.
   Near **Nikitis** is the €€€ Danai
Beach Hotel, one of the best hotels in
northern Greece (T: 23750 22310,
danai-bh@otenet.gr).
   At **Olympiada** the Hotel Liotopi on
the beach is cheap and pleasant (T:
23760 51262).

WHERE TO EAT

There are good restaurants at Neos
Marmaras on Sithonia. Information is
available on www.halkidiki.com/

marmaras. Good fish tavernas are to be
found all along the coasts; particularly
recommended are those at Ierissos,
Toroni and Olympiada.

FESTIVALS & EVENTS

Polygyros There is a local pre-Lent carnival at the end of February each year.

BEACHES

Beaches near Thessaloniki and north of
Nea Moudania on Kassandra should be
avoided, as there is pollution from the
Thessaloniki harbour area, and pesti-
cide residues from agribusiness collect
near the river estuaries. South of Nea
Kallikrateia are decent clean sandy
beaches and the first place south of
Thessaloniki where swimming can really be sensibly recommended.
There are some nice sandy beaches in
the southern parts of the Kassandra
peninsula.

BOOKS

Two excellent books about Mount
Athos, both by British lay visitors, are
The Station, by Robert Byron (1928;
reissued by Phoenix Press, 2000), and
From the Holy Mountain, by William
Dalrymple (1997).

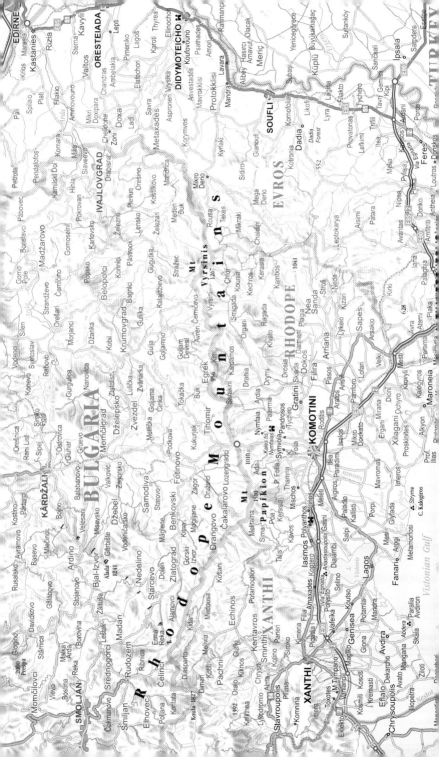

THRACE

Thrace (Θράκη) is the largest and least known region of northern Greece. It lies on a crossroads between Turkey, Greece and Bulgaria, on the border of the old Asia Minor, and only became part of Greece in 1920. The population is diverse, with a large Turkish Muslim minority, and smaller groups of Roma gypsies, Pomaks, Macedonians, Vlachs and Armenians, as well as more recent immigrants from places such as Kurdistan and Romania. The original Thracians were Indo-European but not Hellenic; they came from the Carpathian region, and had fair or red hair and grey eyes. They spoke a language so far undeciphered. The whole area beyond the Strymon seems hardly to have been reached by the Bronze Age, and the ethnic and historical affinities of Thrace are with Bulgaria and Turkey rather than with Greece. In 1923 the Treaty of Lausanne set the parameters for modern boundaries and political and cultural relationships in the north-eastern Mediterranean, and the population of Thrace underwent many changes. Whereas in Macedonia the Turkish population was exchanged, in Thrace it was allowed to remain (as Greeks were allowed to remain in Constantinople). This gives the province a special flavour, with Turkish villages alternating with Greek. The population in many places is dominated by people who left Turkey and Bulgaria as refugees in the early 20th century, and who see themselves as embodying the heart of Hellenism in the region.

The landscape is dominated by the dramatic and heavily wooded Rhodope mountain range running along the northern border with Bulgaria, and the Plain of Thrace down to the coast. For most of the post-Second World War period, there was little tourist activity in Thrace, except for a short summer season along the coast. Travel inland was constrained by the closure of many border zones. It is now possible to travel everywhere without hindrance. The forests and rich wildlife have become a focus for the development of ecotourism, and work has begun on restoring hitherto neglected historic buildings in the older towns—which have the richest surviving heritage of Ottoman buildings in the country.

XANTHI & ENVIRONS

Xanthi (Ξάνθη), the prosperous capital of a nomarchy, is the most attractive and cultured town in Thrace, with a flourishing university, a well looked-after historic centre, many interesting old buildings and good shops. The town was built on tobacco in Ottoman times, and this is still an important crop, though Xanthi has also diversified into light manufacturing, with agribusiness and some local tourism. It is a good centre for the exploration of the rich traditional villages in the Rhodope hills to the north, the Nestos river valley, and for the important archaeological site of Abdera.

In the town itself, there is still some sense of the old Ottoman *mahalas* system, with Muslims living mostly in the northern sector, Armenians in the city centre, and the

Greek majority elsewhere. Traditional culture is very strong, with outstanding music and dance, and it is well worth trying to visit in early September, when there are local festivals; or during the spring carnival.

HISTORY OF XANTHI

In early Byzantine times a small settlement grew up here and during the civil wars between Emperor John Cantacuzene and the Palaeologus rivals it became a metropolis, although it was only of village size. In 1264 Emperor Michael VIII wintered in Xanthi with his army. In 1361 the town fell to the Turks, but was taken from them by the Serbs in 1369. Throughout the Ottoman period it was an important garrison and trading centre on the road west from Constantinople. With the coming of the railway, it superseded Genisea as the centre of tobacco-growing. During the Balkan Wars (1912–13) it was captured by the Bulgarians, and under the Treaty of Bucharest was assigned to Bulgaria. Xanthi became part of the expanded Greek state in 1920. In the Second World War it was under German and Bulgarian occupation, and was held by nationalist forces against the Democratic Army in the latter stages of the Greek Civil War (1944–49).

The town

The Byzantine kastro (sections of fortifications visible) was built to defend the Xanthi defile from Bulgar incursions. Below it, on a hillside to the north of the modern town, clusters Old Xanthi. Its main attraction are its beautiful traditional houses. About 50 remain from the 19th century; monuments to the wealth and prosperity of the tobacco clans who built them, at a time when Xanthi, in common with the rest of Thrace and much of Macedonia, was enjoying a boom period with the development of the international tobacco industry. Xanthi was important enough then for Austria-Hungary, Italy and France to have consulates in the town, and Xanthi merchants travelled over the world. Their houses show them to have been men of taste and distinction. The tobacco is still prized today: the composer Mikis Theodorakis writes in a poem of 'aromatic cigarettes from Xanthi'.

The lower town has been considerably rebuilt in recent years, but as well as sections of Byzantine structures, there are some delightful streets of old low buildings with small shops and cafés.

ENVIRONS OF XANTHI

Abdera

The museum, in the modern village, is open daily 10–1; T: 25410 51003.

Abdera (near modern Avdira; ᾿Αβδηρα) is a pretty site with fine views across the sea to Thasos, and is a pleasant place for a seaside walk or a picnic. Legend says that the city was founded by Heracles on the spot where Abderos was killed by Diomedes' horses: Diomedes was a king of Thrace; the capture of his man-eating mares formed the Eighth Labour of Heracles. The mares were caught, but not before Heracles' companion Abderos had been dragged to his death by them. History tells us that Abdera was in fact colonised c. 656 BC from Clazomenae, in modern Turkey. Refounded c. 500 BC by refugees from a Persian occupation of Teos (southwest of Smyrna), it became a prominent member of the Delian League (*see p. 70*) and famous for the beauty of its coinage. Democritus, the 5th-century philosopher who expounded atomic theory; Protagoras (c. 481–411), the first of the Sophists; and Anaxarchos, the counsellor of Alexander the Great, were all born here. Despite the celebrity of its school of philosophy, however, the inhabitants were generally proverbial for their dullness. Hippocrates and Juvenal inveigh against its sickly air. Abdera shared the fortunes of Macedonia and remained nominally free of Rome down to Imperial times. Abdera was important in the Early Christian and Byzantine periods when a fortress (*Polystylon*) was built on the Classical acropolis.

The Classical acropolis

The nature of the site is probably best appreciated by climbing first the track immediately opposite the gate to the fenced site, which leads in a few metres to **Polystylon**, site of the acropolis of the city from the Classical period. The first conspicuous monument is a small single-aisled church of the 12th century, with the remains of a contemporary cemetery beside it. Below are good sections of the defences, the Byzantine built over the Classical, with the masonry of the two periods clearly distinguishable. A square tower of the Classical system is preserved. Within the wall some parts of a bath building with hypocaust can be made out. In the sea beyond, within the lines of the modern breakwater, can be seen the scattered remnants of the ancient harbour mole.

On the highest point of the promontory, its position indicated from below by a triangulation block, is a fine three-aisled **Middle Byzantine church** on the site of an Early Christian basilica of c. 600, with an octagonal baptistery (from the earlier period) at the northwest. Beyond are the remains of the bishop's palace. From this point, the broader extent of the Greek and Roman city can be best surveyed. It lay in a depression north and east of the acropolis. In Antiquity the sea reached much further inland, approaching the western arm of the walls. The fortified circuit, almost 5.5km in total, has been fully traced. The Archaic acropolis, focus of the earliest part of the fortifications (7th–6th centuries) and predecessor to *Polystylon*, was on the high ground to the northwest. The whole of the valley seems to have been settled and the eastern limit, as defined by the wall, extended to a second (smaller) harbour out of sight beyond the furthest visible promontory. (It can be reached by following the road beyond the archaeological site to Porto Molos, where there is a good beach.)

The main site

Descending from the acropolis you enter the gate to the main site. To the right is a Roman bath building and, beyond, the city wall. Beyond the path are Late Roman houses. A large square structure was a forward tower, into which Roman burials (fragments of sarcophagi visible) were later inserted. North of this is the gateway to the city, protected by two square towers. The wall (and towers) in fine masonry belong, in origin, to the Classical period, but the wall itself underwent many later repairs, and differences in constructional style are evident here and there. Within the gate, the remains are less impressive. They belong almost exclusively to blocks of houses of the Hellenistic and Roman periods, sometimes with Classical buildings shown to underlie them, as in the first units visible, where a paved Roman floor is at the top and Classical house remains at the bottom of the excavated sequence. In general the house remains are disappointing to the visitor, though it is possible to make out paved courts with wells and drainage channels, column bases, threshold blocks, the outlines of rooms, etc. The town was laid out on a grid system from the 4th century, with several houses in blocks of uniform size.

The northwest enclosure

At the northwest extremity of the site, reached by returning for c. 1.3km towards modern Avdira and striking east by tracks, is a fenced enclosure where, in the 4th–3rd centuries, ground altars, probably to Demeter and Kore (Persephone), were approached by steps. Two thousand miniature votive vases were found. Remains of ship-sheds against the wall here are associated with an early harbour when the shoreline was different. Remains of a public building of the Archaic period have been located c. 100m from the northwest corner of the fortifications. Graves of various periods have been excavated outside the walls.

The Nestos river

The Nestos, or Mesta, rises in the Rhodope Mountains in Bulgaria. Geographically it divides Macedonia from Thrace, though the modern *nome* boundaries rather reflect local convenience. Under the Treaty of Bucharest (1913), the river formed the frontier with Bulgaria, which for two or three years enjoyed an Aegean seaboard extending from the Mesta to Alexandroupolis and beyond. To the east, towards Drama, the river is enclosed in inaccessible gorges, and the whole of its basin north to the Bulgarian frontier is hemmed in by the Rhodope chain, the rolling heights of which are swathed in beech forests. The area, which has a good climate and fertile soil, has not found favour with Anatolian Greeks, and since 1923 has remained practically uninhabited. The lower course of the Nestos lies through the alluvial plain of Chrysoupolis, a town of some importance in Byzantine times, and known to the Turks as *Sari Saban*: 'Yellow Plain'.

At Stavroupolis, in the loveliest part of the valley, a *kafeneion* in the attractive little plateia has an interesting collection of bygones. To the southeast of Stavroupolis, reached from the station by minor road (after 3km towards Komnina, take signposted track left for 1.5km), is a remarkable vaulted tomb, excavated in 1953. The chamber is 3m square and the vaulted dromos 4.9m long. The tomb was constructed in local marble with paintings done directly onto the marble surface (a technique unusual in Macedonia). Within are two handsome marble funerary couches.

Toxotes with its minaret, and Megalo Tympano with its wooden balconies, are typical villages of the region, where growers still produce a much-prized tobacco. The picturesque irregularity of the villages, with their gardens, is emphasised by the neighbouring Greek villages, built in rigid, functional lines, as refugee settlements in the 1920s.

THE VIA EGNATIA

The Via Egnatia, the great military road between the Adriatic and Byzantium, was built by the Romans in the 2nd century BC to form, together with the Via Appia, a direct link between Rome and the East. It takes its name from the proconsul who ordered its construction: Gaius Egnatius. It had two branches starting from *Apollonia* (Avlona) and *Dyrrachium* (Durazzo), passing *Lychidnus* (near Lake Ohrid), *Heracleia Lyncestis* (Bitola), Edessa, Pella, Thessalonica, *Amphipolis*, and Philippi. *Neapolis* (Kavala) was the east terminus until the conquest of Thrace in AD 46, when the road was extended through Akontisma and *Trajanopolis*, to end at Byzantium (Istanbul). Augustus founded colonies along its route; Nero installed inns; Trajan repaired it in AD 107–112. Milestones found on its route as far apart as Ohrid, Amphipolis and Akontisma bear witness to repairs by Caracalla in 216–217. An epitaph discovered near the site of *Ad Duodecimum*, a staging post 12 Roman miles west of Philippi, commemorates C. Lavus Faustus, '*institor tabernae*'. From the 4th century AD the Via Egnatia lost importance to the northern route via Belgrade, *Naissus* (Niš), *Serdica* (Sofia), *Philippopolis* (Plovdiv) and *Hadrianopolis* (Edirne), as Milan replaced Rome as the starting-point.

East of Xanthi: along the Via Egnatia

About 1.5km beyond Amaxades, a track to the right leads in 5km to the best-preserved part of **Anastasioupolis** (Byzantine *Peritheorion*). The town was a station on the Via Egnatia, probably taking its name from Anastasius I (491–518): it lies on the north shore of Lake Vistonis. After destruction in the early 13th century, it was rebuilt and renamed under Andronicus III (1328–41). At the edge of the lake, among trees, is a fenced archaeological area. The site is very overgrown but the spectacular remains make the effort involved worthwhile. Preserved nearly to its original height is the south gate of the city, which gave onto the harbour (marble plaques to each side have monograms of the Palaeologi). Also to be seen here are a tower and sections of the fortification wall. Most of the wall circuit can be traced and different periods of construction distinguished.

Beyond Iasmos, you cross the River Kompsatos. Just beyond the bridge (signs) a rough path leads in 5mins to a delightful **medieval bridge** with two arches, a central pier and the original surface partly preserved. Returning to the main road you soon pass (left) the fenced remains of a Byzantine church and shortly (33km) enter Polyanthos, which has a Byzantine castle and, to the north, at Kedik Kazin, the remains of a Hellenistic fort. A Hellenistic cemetery has also been excavated in the vicinity. To the north of Linos, on Mt Papikion, is a Byzantine cemetery and a recently excavated 10th–11th-century Byzantine church with an *opus sectile* marble floor. This was part of a more extensive and impressive monastic complex (refectory, baths, cistern etc.) At Sostis a sign (right) to 'Prehistoric Settlement' can be safely ignored: there is nothing to see.

KOMOTINI

Komotini (Κομοτηνή) a town only 22.5km from the Bulgarian frontier, is the capital of the nomarchy of Rhodope. For many years it was a poor, run-down place, but its fortunes have improved in the last few years, and it is now a town of pleasant broad streets and squares and a delightful old quarter centred round Plateias Ifaistou (metal-workers; the name derived from Hephaistos) and Irinis. It is a flourishing market centre for tobacco, cattle, hides and agricultural goods, with an annual livestock fair in Holy Week. About half of the inhabitants are ethnic Turks, who know the town as *Gümülcüne*, and

many are Bulgarian-speaking (Pomaks). The town is effectively the 'capital' of the Turkish Muslim minority in Thrace.

The seasonal Boukloutza river, on which Komotini stands, has been diverted since the town was flooded in 1960. The walls of the Byzantine fortress are to the left on entering the town. The excellent **Archaeological Museum** (*open Tues–Sun 8.30–3; T: 25310 22411*) on the south side of the inner ring road (Odos Zoïdou) houses attractively displayed finds from the whole of Thrace. Outside is a fine Roman sarcophagus with garlands and bucrania. Within, the outstanding exhibit is the unique gold imperial bust of Septimius Severus, found at *Plotinoupolis* (modern Didymoteicho; *see p.*

Gold bust, identified as the emperor Septimius Severus.

701). Also displayed are a remarkable phallic altar; a Clazomenian sarcophagus from Abdera and fine objects from graves at the same site; Archaic pottery and a grave stele from Dikaia; interesting votive plaques from the Sanctuary of Demeter at Mesembria; finds from the prehistoric tomb at Paradimi, southeast of Komotini, as well as from tombs at Ardani and Oresteiada; honorific decrees from Doriskos and Maroneia (4th century BC); also from Maroneia, an inscribed marble block (3rd century) with impressions of feet and a fine relief of a Thracian rider (4th century).

Komotini has an **Ecclesiastical Museum** (*open daily; T: 25310 34177*) in Odos Xenofontos, which occupies a pretty, domed building, the restored 14th-century *imaret* (an Ottoman boarding house and soup kitchen). It contains a large collection of icons and liturgical objects from Komotini and the diocese, many of them (especially the portable icons) brought by Pontic and Asia Minor refugees in 1922.

ENVIRONS OF KOMOTINI

Porto Lagos

Porto Lagos, the port of Komotini, stands on a tongue of land separating the Vistonian Gulf from Lake Vistonis. The remains of a Byzantine basilica of the 10th century lie right of the road (sign) just beyond the town of Lagos. The church is an early example of the inscribed-cross type and was built over the remains of an Early Christian structure. It stands within a fortified Byzantine settlement. Remains of the defences are particularly evident towards the sea, where they include towers. They can be seen also on the other side of the road. The place still has a bishop. Worth a glance are the old Genoese fort and an attractive church. Beyond the channel through which the lake drains into the sea, the road is carried on a causeway with a marshy lagoon on the right. Fish and eels are caught in great numbers and the area is celebrated for the variety of its water-birds. The eels are almost exclusively exported live in tanks to Germany and Central Europe. The fish traps can be visited.

A low hill rising to the southeast (off the by-road to Fanari) may be the site of ancient *Dikaia*. Graves have been excavated here. Some ruins, identified with *Stryme*, once famed for its wine, have been explored at Mitriko on the remote coast c. 16km farther east. A city wall was traced with houses, which yielded a hoard of Maroneian tetradrachms of the 4th century BC.

Kales tis Nymfaias and Mischos

North of Komotini, a road leads towards Nymfaia, after 5km entering an attractively wooded area, with unobtrusive amenities for picnicking. An unsurfaced road diverges right to Pandrosos. The main road continues to climb and, 3km beyond the Pandrosos turn, reaches the impressive Byzantine fort of Kales tis Nymfaias with splendid views over the plain of Komotini. Nine kilometres further west (on a different road) is Symvola, with a good Macedonian tomb of the 3rd century or earlier.

Gratini (the Byzantine *Gratianos*) is a pleasant village, lying at the foot of the steep hill. At the top (c. 30mins climb) are the ruinous remains of a Byzantine fortress of the Palaeologue period. A fine Byzantine cistern (with some modern repair) is still in use and accessible, by the little chapel on the summit.

West of Komotini is Mischos, with an attractive, silver-capped minaret. Just before the village, a track (left) leads to the site of medieval *Mosynopolis*, the limit of Norman penetration in 1185. Originally *Porsula*, the town was granted city rank by Diocletian with the name *Maximianopolis*, and sent a metropolitan to the Council of Ephesus. Geoffrey de Villehardouin, a chronicler of the Fourth Crusade, accepted it as his fief. The best-preserved section of the walls, with square and round towers, is by the track after 2.5km, but other remains can be seen over a wide area. Inscriptions and architectural fragments from the site are in the Komotini museum.

MARONEIA, MESEMBRIA & MAKRI

The principal archaeological sites of this region, the ancient *Kikones*, lie to the southeast of Komotini on the coast. They are cut off from the hinterland by barren limestone hills scored by ravines and torrents. A road (bus from Komotini) crosses the railway and the Filiouri to Maroneia, with a pleasant square and cafés, and descends from there, past occasional signs to 'antiquities', through the middle of the ancient site, to the coast.

Ancient Maroneia

Maroneia (Μαρώνεια) is a very beautiful coastal site. The general vicinity, with excellent beaches, is perhaps the most attractive and unspoilt part of the mainland Thrace coast. Maroneia was a city of importance from Homeric times to the Genoese period. Extensive archaeological works are currently in progress, and the archaeological staff are most helpful to visitors.

The Classical site of the 4th–3rd centuries BC occupied an enormous area, the wall circuit being 10.5km in extent, running from the sheer-faced acropolis of Aghios Athanasios above the village down to the coast at Aghios Charalambos. The area is thickly wooded and, although several interesting features can be easily approached by roads and tracks, a full exploration of the remains requires time and determination.

The site
Officially open Mon 12–7; Tues–Sun 8–7 (closes earlier in winter); T: 25330 41294.
You follow the road from the village towards the coast. A dirt track (left) leads to the theatre and sanctuary, in 1.3km and 1.6km respectively. The **theatre** (to the right of the track) was a Hellenistic construction, altered in Roman times. Some of the seating survives, part of the stage building (re-using material from earlier buildings) and the foundation for the proscenium columns, with a number of architectural elements. The seating was provided with a protective barrier (*thorakion*) in the Roman period for contests involving wild animals. The theatre was built across the ravine and was protected from damage by storm water by an enormous built drainage channel which can be seen to have passed beneath. Two hundred metres northeast of the theatre is a sub-

stantial section of walling with towers. Farther on, the foundations of the **sanctuary complex** (probably dedicated to Dionysus) can be made out. The main temple had a pronaos and cella (with hearth or base for the cult statue) and ancillary structures but the surviving remains are hardly worth more than a glance.

Returning to the main road, a short distance further down (left) is the most accessible part of the **city wall**, with two square towers. The wall in general is 2.3–3m thick and has square or round towers at irregular intervals; more frequent on flat ground. A sign to 'Mosaic' (left) takes you to a recently restored Hellenistic mosaic. Three hundred metres farther down the road, a second sign ('Mosaic', left) leads to the **Byzantine fortifications**, which have been partly cleared and are impressive. They were constructed on an earlier (Classical) system which protected the harbour. You reach a parking space above the harbour. In an enclosure immediately to the right are the well-preserved remains of a double monumental gateway with three openings in each face, possibly Hadrianic, and the entrance to the agora. Farther right (200m) excavations are in progress. Left from the car park, beside a restaurant, are the fenced remains of the Byzantine **church of Aghios Charalambos**. A 9th-century structure, 8m below modern ground level, was succeeded by an inscribed-cross building, the cathedral of a Middle Byzantine bishopric. There is a synthronon in the apse.

At **Synaxi**, 7km east of Maroneia, an important Middle Byzantine monastery complex (furnished refectory, tombs etc.) was constructed partly over an Early Christian basilica of the time of Justinian.

Mesembria-Zone

Mesembria (Μεσημβρία) is perhaps the most beautifully situated of all the coastal sites of Aegean Thrace. It is sometimes called Aegean Mesembria to distinguish it from another site of the same name on the Black Sea coast of Bulgaria. Recent research indicates that it was actually a twin city in Antiquity, with nearby Zone, and a rich and complex heritage has been revealed. The scrub-covered hills of the hinterland are noted for quail, woodcock and snipe.

The site
Officially open Tues–Sun 8.30–3; T: 25510 96214.
The towns were probably established in 7th century BC as part of Greek coastal colonisation of Thracian tribal lands. It was a Samothracian colony in the late 7th century and is mentioned by Herodotus. He noted that in 480 it was passed by the invading Persian army and he called it 'the last city in the west'. It grew and prospered with the rapid expansion of Greek trade with modern Turkey and the cities of the Black Sea coast. Coins from all over the ancient Greek world have been found here, and impressive goldwork and ceramics indicating a high level of civilisation. The cities remained important until Hellenistic times, but the site was vulnerable to barbarian invaders and pirates and fell into rapid decline with the end of the Classical world.

Parts of the walls always remained visible, but the first excavations were made in the First World War by Bulgarian soldiers, who were digging coastal fortification trenches.

Modern archaeology began in 1966. The most interesting recent discoveries include a store of hundreds of large amphorae, a sign of the trading importance of the cities.

To the left, beyond the site entrance, the south section of the central arm of the wall crosses the road and can be traced to a tower above the sea. A three-roomed structure of fine large blocks which abuts the wall c. 20m inland from the tower belongs to the 4th-century **Sanctuary of Demeter**, from which came an inscribed base and fine votive plaques, in the Komotini Museum. To the right of the main path, inside the east arm of the main fortifications, an Archaic **Sanctuary of Apollo** consists of buildings grouped round a paved open court. There are remains of a prostyle temple and a stoa. The torso of a *kouros* and many vases inscribed to Apollo were found.

The most conspicuous part of the site is an unusual **fortified settlement** which occupies only the southwest corner of the whole walled area, which included an acropolis to the north. The defensive circuit can be traced at many points on the ground but is most easily appreciated in the area of the fortified settlement, against which it is built. The eastern part of the fortifications (which have three north–south arms) may belong to the first period of settlement, with an acropolis at that time on the east hill.

The thickness of the walls of the fortified settlement can be clearly discerned, as can the fact that the earlier buildings excavated outside the limits of the fort (north) and partly underlying its walls are on a different alignment from those within. The fort therefore belongs to a secondary phase of the life of the settlement. Within the complex small one-and two-room units (workshops?) lie against the west and part of the north walls. The buildings are laid out on the Hippodamian system, with streets on an orthogonal grid—three running east–west and two north–south. At the southeast the houses are, unusually, separated from the wall by a road, probably because there was no room for this outside between the wall and the sea. In the centre are house blocks and against the west wall two houses. The rooms of that at the northeast corner (below the tower) can be easily distinguished, with court, threshold block, etc. Three different phases of construction have been noted between the 5th and 2nd centuries BC. Most of the visible remains belong to the second of these, though evidence for the different periods can be seen here and there, with underlying walls on different alignments and layered surfaces to the streets. A large building in the centre of the site may be a public building of some kind. A substantial block of houses outside the fortified settlement has been excavated c. 80m to the north. The city fortifications are best seen at the west side, where there are three towers. The second (from the south) bears inscriptions, the third (beyond the fortified settlement) guards a gate with two marble steps and an unusual circular passage in its north side. The masonry of the walls is in a variety of styles, often of fine quality.

There is a good beach and a fine view west to the mountain spur that hides Maroneia. The road descends to the coast amongst the dense vineyards to Makri.

Makri

Makri (Μάκρη), the ancient *Makre*, was built on the site of a Byzantine settlement. There are important Byzantine and Ottoman monuments near the modern village. In Byzantine times it was an important place, and would repay proper excavation. The Turkish traveller Evliya Çelebi noted its prosperity as a small town in the 17th century, with the fortress in good condition, and a mixed Muslim and Christian population. Then it had a mosque, a *medresse*, five *hans*, a hammam, and commercial buildings. To the east, the Monastery of St George dates from the 13th century. Sections of Byzantine fortifications can be seen, and remains of a medieval basilica that later became a mosque.

The prosperity of the town then and under the Ottomans was built on production from water power in the nearby ravine, and remains of ten water mills dating from different historical periods have been found. The most interesting Ottoman monument is the **Tekke of Sançaktar Baba** and the hammam near it, which is overgrown with vegetation and needs restoration. The *tekke* building complex and dervish monastery were destroyed in 1826, in one of the Sultan's periodic clampdowns on Shi'ite Islamic sects. The name would indicate that the dervish buried here and who founded the *tekke* was from the Sandjak region, but of ethnic Albanian stock; the 'tar' ending is Albanian.

The modern village and archaeological site are about 12km west of Alexandrouplois. Follow signs from the road to the 'Cave of Cyclops'.

The site

Officially open Mon 12–7; Tues–Sun 8–7 (closes earlier in winter); T: 25510 71219.

Makri is the most important Neolithic settlement in Thrace. It is believed to date from about 5000 BC, when primitive Thracian tribes abandoned the hunter-gathering life for settlements where they developed agriculture and animal husbandry. The remains are not spectacular, but are of considerable interest, on a little hillock, about 400m from the sea. The 'Cave of Cyclops' in on the south side of the hill. Sections of the fortification walls can be seen and various churches have been investigated in or near the village. The site itself is of most interest on the east side of the hill, where intact Neolithic layers have been revealed near the earth's surface. They include storage jars, places for cult objects, ovens, hearths, vessels and refuse pits. Archaeologists have also found evidence of basket weaving, stone tool manufacture, jewellery and ceramics. The dead were buried inside their houses, in a hunched position. In the Bronze and Iron Ages, new settlement was built partly on top of the old, but more on the west side of the hill. In the Classical period a small trading post grew up. The visible retaining wall is Roman, and in Byzantine times the hill became a cemetery, and the cave a church.

ALEXANDROUPOLIS & ENVIRONS

Alexandroupolis ('Αλεξανδρούπολις; often written abbreviated to Αλεξ/πολις) is the chief town of the nomarchy of Evros, and a growing and prosperous trading port. It was renamed after King Alexander in 1919. It is noted for its fish; mussels are specialities. It makes a good centre from which to explore Thrace.

The town stands on what is probably the site of ancient *Salis*, parts of whose Roman cemeteries have been excavated under the modern town. The Turkish name ('Tree of the holy man') derives from a colony of dervishes established in the 15th century. The place remained a fishing village until reached in 1872 by the railway from Edirne, after which it rapidly usurped the importance of Ainos (modern Turkish Enez; *map p. 5*).

The main road, parallel with the sea, forms the principal boulevard of the town, Odos Dimokratias. The street is the venue of the *volta*, which necessitates the evening diversion of traffic. On the shore facing the large artificial harbour is a conspicuous lighthouse, to the west of which a broad promenade has been laid out above the beach. The huge modern cathedral of St Nicholas farther inland is prominent. It has an important 13th-century carved wooden icon of the Virgin from Ainos (Turkish Enez). There is an archaeological collection in the Old Dimarcheion in Plateia Polytechniou (also called Eleftherias), the entrance unsigned and well-concealed in an arcade, with sculpture from the area and finds from the Sanctuary of Demeter at Mesembria, also plans of the Sanctuary of the Great Gods on Samothrace.

ALONG THE EVROS

Beyond Alexandroupolis road and railway continue east together, passing the airport. On the far bank of the Tsaï was the Roman and Byzantine staging-post of **Trajanopolis**, which succeeded Doriskos (*see below*). It was the scene in 161 under Marcus Aurelius of the spectacular miracles of St Glyceria, a Roman maiden later martyred in the Propontis. After a long period as a Metropolitan see, the town seems to have been ruined in the wars of 1205 and lost importance to *Demotika* (modern Didymoteicho). To the left of the road is a magnificently preserved *han* built in the 14th–15th centuries when the town itself had gone into decline. The adjacent thermal springs help treat kidney ailments. A turning leads right, in the opposite direction to modern Doriskos village, to **ancient Doriskos**, a Persian fortress town established in 512 BC by Darius I, where Xerxes numbered his armies in 480 (modern scholarship suggests the troops numbered some 200,000).

The Evros river (᾽Εβρος; ancient *Hebros*; Turkish *Meriçi*; Bulgarian *Maritza*), of which there are periodic glimpses, rises in Bulgaria south of Sofia and, after a course of c. 500km, enters the Aegean opposite the island of Samothrace through a delta 11km wide. It is inextricably linked with the Orphic legend. Since 1923 its lower course through the flat Thracian plain has formed the boundary between Greece and Turkey, save where the suburbs of Edirne, ancient *Hadrianopolis*, make a Turkish enclave west of the river. It is navigable for small boats as far as Edirne, below which it is crossed by bridges only at Pythio and Ipsala (in modern Turkey). Its waters abound in fish and water fowl; rare geese and eagles may be seen. The delta region is one of the glories of Thrace, and is a paradise for the birdwatcher and ecological tourist. Round its twin mouths, noted by Strabo, are several swamps and lakes, of which the largest is Gala (*Gölu*), on the Turkish side, the ancient *Stentoris* of

Herodotus. Some way southwest of this lake is the town of Ainos (Enez), familiar to historians as one end of the Enos–Midia line, created at the Treaty of London in 1913: all territory west of the line was to be ceded by Turkey to Greece. Enos is also the ancient *Ainos*, the foundation of which Virgil ascribes to Aeneas.

In the centre of **Feres**, at the highest point, is the church (signed 'Byzantine Temple') of Aghia Sofia, katholikon of the monastery of the Theotokos Kosmosotira, built by Isaac Comnenus in 1152. It is of the domed inscribed-cross plan. The interesting frescoes (in need of cleaning), much defaced by the Turks, are of the same date. There are fine carved capitals. The monastery was provided with defences, parts of which are visible: in the 14th century it became a fortified civilian settlement.

Ipsala, ancient *Kypsela*, the greatest city of the Thracians, lost importance by the 4th century BC and in Livy's time was only a fort. Returning towards Salonica from his meeting here with Henry of Flanders in 1207, Boniface of Montferrat was intercepted and decapitated by a Bulgarian ambush. It now lies on the Turkish side of the river.

THE DADIA FOREST

Visitor Centres: Dadia Centre, http://ecoclub.com/dadia and www.dadia.gr
Hotel Dadia Biotope Agricultural. 20 rooms. Bird-watching hides. T: 25540 32263.
Reservation essential.
The Dadia-Soufli Forest Ecotourist Reserve was designated in 1980. It is the main ecotourist centre in Thrace, with informative exhibits about the vast deciduous Dadia Forest (Δάσος της Δαδιάς) that stretches hundreds of miles west into the Rhodope Mountains. The best times to visit are late spring or late autumn, when water levels rise. There are exhibits of vulture conservation and feeding during the day. Within the reserved area, which covers millions of hectares, there are projects for the preservation of threatened species, such as the black vulture; for the provision of sustainable development for the surviving Sarakatsan nomad pastoral communities; for sustainable forestry and many other projects. There are hiking and birdwatching trails.

Soufli (Σουφλί) is a pleasant town, engaged in the cultivation of vines and silk worms. Most of the native silk production has been replaced by Chinese imports and as a result the place has a slightly melancholy air, but is still very interesting. It has old timber-framed houses, the best of which are up the hill to the left of the main road. One of these, the Archontiko Kourtidi, contains the Silk Museum. The house itself is a fine example of a traditional well-to-do family dwelling (*archontikò*) with rooms opening off a large *salòni* upstairs, workrooms on the ground floor and a summer kitchen and other utility rooms off the courtyard. The ground floor has a display of equipment and illustrative material to demonstrate the process of silk production (the original function of this part of the house). Upstairs are examples of local costumes and silk items. The side rooms contain memorabilia of the original owner and a restored kitchen. In the church of Aghios Georgios is a fine 18th-century carved iconostasis.

At Mandra you meet a by-road that descends a wooded valley from Mikro Derio. Beyond Mandra is the little roadside town of **Lavara**, the so called 'storkopolis', with the marvellous sight of numerous storks' nests on top of lamp posts, houses and telegraph poles. The best time to visit to see these beautiful and characterful birds is late spring and early summer. There is a very good view across the river valley east into Turkey.

DIDYMOTEICHO

Didymoteicho (Διδυμότειχο; often written Didimotiho) is interesting with an out-standing mosque. There are nice cafés in the plateia. It is essentially a market town of Turkish timber-framed houses, clustering round an abrupt hill over-looking the Erythropotamos or *Kizil Remma*. The fortified hill has been important in all historical periods up to the Balkan Wars (1912–13) and the First World War, as it guards one of the easier crossings over the Evros river.

HISTORY OF DIDYMOTEICHO

The town hill has been inhabited since the earliest times. Thracian tribes estab-lished a small town around the castle rock. Little is known about the first Greek town, but a much larger settlement developed in Hellenistic times, which was then conquered by the Romans. An inscription, found in 1937, identifies the site with *Plotinoupolis*, refounded by Trajan in honour of his wife, Plotina. The bar-barian raids forced the Romans to fortify the twin hills, Kales and Aghia Petra, so giving the town the origin of its modern name, 'twin walls'. Plotinoupolis seems to have survived until the 7th century, when it was abandoned. At the same time Byzantine *Didymoticheon* was developing on the Kales hill.

The fortress-town played an important part in Byzantine history. In 1189 dur-ing the Third Crusade, Frederick Barbarossa held the town hostage while nego-tiating with the Emperor Isaac II Angelus. In 1205 it was described by Geoffrey Villehardouin as 'the most powerful and richest town of Romania'. Here, in 1341, John VI Cantacuzene had himself proclaimed emperor. The town fell to the Turks in 1361 and Murad I made it his capital for four years before trans-ferring to Adrianople (Edirne); his son Bayezid was born here. The area was popular with the later sultans as a hunting range. In the later Empire, the town was contested by the Bulgarians, and was the scene of bitter fighting in the Second Balkan War, in 1913, with the retreat of the defeated remnants of the Ottoman army, in appalling misery. There were large Jewish and Armenian com-munities in the town in that period. The town became part of Greece in 1920.

The town

To the right, on crossing the bridge, is the sheer-sided hill of Aghia Petra, crowned by an aerial mast. This was the core of Roman *Plotinoupoulis*. Recent excavations, mainly on the northeast flank and including some of the fortification wall, have revealed little of interest for the casual visitor, though one must recall the fine gold bust from here in the Komotini Museum (*see p. 693*).

The road climbs into the town. In the plateia (off the main road to the left) is a magnificent large square mosque, the **Mosque of Sultan Bayezid the Thunderer**, with a pyramidal roof. It was begun by Murad I in the early 15th century and completed by his son, Bayezid, and has the sweeping confidence and grace of large mosques of the early post-conquest period, when the Ottoman civilisation was being established throughout the southern Balkans. It had a fine interior (wooden ceiling, calligraphic inscriptions) and the minaret has two fretted balconies. The interior has been vandalised and is in a sorry state. The external structure is sound. There are good cafés and tavernas nearby.

Didymoteicho has other interesting Ottoman buildings (including hammams, and the 15th-century Tomb of Orout Pasha), which have recently been studied. They are all in need of restoration. The '**Baths of the Whisperers**' is the oldest Ottoman baths complex in mainland Europe. A short distance above the plateia, in a fine old house, is the outstanding **Folk Museum** (*open regularly in the evenings and at most other times by request*), begun by a co-operative of local schoolmasters in the 1970s. Particularly interesting are items in the basement connected with agricultural, domestic and industrial activities (threshing sledges, liquor still, dyeing equipment, ironworker's furnace).

Above the Folk Museum are the walls of the **kastro**, much of the interior of which is occupied by post-Byzantine buildings, including the cathedral of Aghios Athanasios. The most impressive section of Byzantine walling is to the left, on the ascent. Within the settlement, with its delightful old houses, is the cathedral, a 19th-century structure on Byzantine foundations. Beside it are the conspicuous—though partial—remains of an arched Byzantine building, probably a hostel. Another close approach to the fortifications may be made by ascending Odos Ermou, a narrow street c. 100m north of the original point of entry into the kastro. At first concrete, it soon reverts to its ancient surface and climbs the north face of the fortifications. The walls give a good view of the Evros.

The Turkish border

On the far side of Didymoteicho, a fork (right; asphalt, deteriorated in places) off the main road leads to Petrades and Pythio (*just beyond the map*). At Pythio (Byzantine *Empythion*) are the outstanding remains of a massive and dramatic Byzantine fort of the 13th century, used by John Cantacuzene as a headquarters. The central tower is preserved to a height of two storeys and probably had a third. The interior architecture (arches, brick vaults, stairways) is impressive, and it was probably a partly domestic establishment. Linked to this by a section of wall with a fine gateway is a smaller tower, probably exclusively military in character.

The highway continues north. Beyond Oresteiada, the minarets of Edirne can be seen in the distance (right) from the road into Kastanies (Custom House). The small triangle of Greek soil lying between the Arda and the Evros is served by a road from Kastanies and by railway to Ormeni, its principal village.

Edirne, formerly Adrianople, both names being successive corruptions of *Hadrianopolis*, stands beyond the frontier. Refounded by Hadrian in AD 125 from *Uscudama*, chief town of the Bessi, it remained a strategic stronghold until the decline of the Ottoman Empire. The period of its zenith in 1367–1458 as the Ottoman capital left many fine buildings, though the later Selimiye Çami by Sinan (*see p. 538*) is its masterpiece. It remains the market town of the area and is much visited by local Greeks and Bulgarians.

PRACTICAL INFORMATION

While the mid-summer climate in Thrace is as warm as elsewhere in Greece, spring and autumn are longer, cooler and wetter, and winter can be severe in the hills and mountains. Greek is universally understood, although minority languages are widely used.

GETTING AROUND

• **By air:** Kavala airport (3km south-west of Chrysoupolis) has cheap flights in the summer from international destinations, and numerous Athens flights. It is on a convenient road to Xanthi. Local transport from the airport is often thin. Alexandroupolis airport is 6.5km east of town, with daily services to Athens. An Olympic Airways bus connects Komotini with one flight a day from Alexandroupolis.

• **By car:** The road from Kavala runs up from the coast, and is good quality dual carriageway in parts, but often heavy with lorries, as is the road through to Alexandroupolis. The route from Drama is very attractive in parts, running through the Rhodope foothills, via Stavroupolis. Effective exploration of the Evros region really needs a car. It does not cost much to hire one for a day or two in Alexandroupolis, to get to the more remote places, or to agree a price for a day's work with a local taxi driver.

The border crossing at Ipsala is well run and efficient, but posts can become very busy in summer and sometimes at other times of year. Be prepared for long delays. Generally commercial vehicles are queued separately, and cars get priority, but it is somewhere to expect the worst, and hope for the best. Carry plenty of food and drink. Some of the kiosk shops near the border are very good value for rugs, honey, metalwork and ceramics. Expect courteous but serious searches at customs.

Roads round the Bulgarian border are no longer subject to military control but are popular with smugglers. Do not try to cross the border except at official

crossing posts; some parts are still mined, and extremely dangerous.
• **By bus:** There are regular daily services from Athens (about 14hrs), and from Thessaloniki, Kavala and all regional towns. Buses link Xanthi and Abdera. Other services from Xanthi to the localities do exist but are infrequent to some outlying villages (particularly those inhabited by the Turkish minority).

There is a daily service between Alexandroupolis and Athens (c. 11hrs), with six buses a day. Frequent services link Alexandroupolis with all Thrace towns, including Didymoteicho (2hrs).
• **By rail:** Xanthi is on the main Athens–Thessaloniki–Istanbul line and the journey is picturesque, if slow. Tickets are very cheap. Trains also link Thessaloniki and Alexandroupolis.
• **By taxi:** Taxis are adequate in central Xanthi, but thin on the ground outside.
• **By sea:** Ferries run from Alexandroupolis to Samothrace daily in summer.

WHERE TO STAY

Abdera
There are rooms in modern Avdira.
Alexandroupolis
The massive new €€€ **Thraki Palace** is the best hotel, though not long on charm. There are fine sea views (T: 25510 89100, www.thrakipalace.gr). The **Alexander Beach** is similar, but cheaper (T: 25510 39290, www.alexbh.gr). The € **Hera**, on Leoforos Dimokratous, is very friendly and helpful (T: 25510 25995). The **Hotel Park**, on the outskirts (Dimokratous 458, T: 25510 28647), has a nice swimming pool.

Didymoteicho
The 67-room **Plotini** is in a modern building on the outskirts of town. Comfortable enough, with a pool. T: 25530 23400.
Komotini
Astoria. Fronting a pleasant town square, this 1900 building has been a hotel since 1937. Completely modernised inside to basic guesthouse standard. Friendly staff. 14 rooms. Plateia Irinis 28, T: 25310 35054, www.astoriakomotini.gr
Maroneia and Mesembria
There is not much accommodation or settlement along the coast, but visitors can easily find rooms in inland towns and villages.
Xanthi
The €€ **Z Palace** near the river is recommended, with very helpful staff (T: 25410 64414). Other possibilities are the **Elena** (T: 25410 63901), and, for somewhere cheap and cheerful in the centre of town, the **Orfeas** (T: 25410 20121).

WHERE TO EAT

Abdera
There are cafés and small tavernas in modern Avdira.
Alexandroupolis
The best restaurants are concentrated near the Dimarcheion and the lighthouse, and in the restored Old Town area, by the harbour. **Stathis** in Botsari is very atmospheric and has good seafood. Also **Taverna Kalenterimi**, Emporiou 40, and **To Nisitiko** fish taverna, G. Zarifi 1 (T: 25510 20202). **To Kalamaki**, in N. Chili, is a fine old establishment. **Agora** is a good music

café, at Emporiou 68, and **Café Aigli**, in Nikiforos Foka, is also recommended.

Komotini
There are good tavernas with Turkish food.

Makri
There are very good fish tavernas, like Planatos and To Filarakia, in the central square and near the harbour. Sardines baked in vine leaves are a local speciality.

Xanthi
There are some good tavernas in the lower Old Town below the castle hill, and the restaurants dotted around in the town square have good traditional food. The Archontissa is very popular with young people, the Mikrovolos often has good music. Local red wine can be good.

LOCAL SPECIALITIES

Xanthi produces the Kiretsiler cigarette, which many connoisseurs consider the best Greek cigarette. It is possible to buy exquisite quality handcut loose tobaccos from market traders, often old Ottoman varieties, to roll your own cigarettes, or to mix with a proprietory Virginia mixture for your pipe.
Alexandroupolis is famed for its mussels.

FESTIVALS & EVENTS

Didymoteicho
This part of Thrace has a rich traditional culture and some pagan festivals have become integrated into Orthodox tradition, particularly on St Dimitrios's Day,

with sacrifices of live chickens, and St Athanasios's Day, with sheep sacrifices. The *Eleftheria* festival every May celebrates the end of the Ottoman Empire in the town in 1920. In the first week in August every year there is a castle festival with themes from Thracian and regional history.

Xanthi
The Carnival, dating back uninterrupted to the Roman period, is outstanding. It is held over a ten day period, at varying dates in early spring. Live bands are often superb, particularly from the town's large Roma and Turkish communities. The festival finishes with the 'burning of Tsaros', a large human effigy, in a ritual inherited from ancient Thracian models.

The 'Old Town' festival is held in early September, which also has excellent music but is primarily a food and drink event. See the town website www.xanthi.com for annual details.

SECURITY

Avoid street moneychangers near border areas, as forged currency (particularly US dollars) is not uncommon.

BEACHES

The coast around Maroneia is beautiful and unspoilt, and popular with visitors from northern Europe, often with camper vans. The beaches are usually suitable for small children and non-swimmers. Stray dogs can sometimes be a minor problem.

GLOSSARY OF TERMS

N.B: Typical pot shapes are illustrated on p. 36; temple design on p. 26; the Orders of architecture on p. 28, types of masonry on p. 712 and elements of an ancient theatre on p. 252.

Abacus, upper element of a capital on which the architrave rests

Abaton, literally the 'place of no stepping'; an inner sanctuary for the use only of initiates or priests

Acrolithic, describes a statue where the head and undraped (visible) extremities are of stone, while the remainder is of wood

Acroterion (*pl. acroteria*), plinth surmounting the apex of a pediment and its two corners, often topped by a statue

Adyton, inner sanctum of a temple with no natural light, from where oracular pronouncements were made

Aedicule, small opening framed by two columns and a pediment, originally used in classical architecture

Aghii Anargyri, the 'penniless saints'; a church dedicated to Sts Cosmas and Damian, doctors who refused to accept payment for their ministrations

Aghii Asomati, the 'incorporeal saints'; a church dedicated to the angels, whom Orthodoxy believes to have no bodily substance

Amazonomachia, a contest between Amazons

Ambo (pl. *ambones*), pulpit in a Christian basilica; the two pulpits on opposite sides of the nave from which the Gospel and Epistle were read

Amphora, vase of large dimensions the transport and storage of wine, oil and other liquids

Amphiprostyle, of a temple, meaning that it has a colonnade at front and back

Analemma, outer supporting wall of the cavea of an ancient Greek theatre

Aniconic, material symbol of a deity (pillar or block) not shaped into an image of human form (icon); the worship connected with this

Anta (pl. *antae*), pier or piers at the front of a temple formed when the side walls project beyond the front wall. Columns placed between these piers are said to be *in antis*

Antefix, an ornament at the eaves of the roof to hide the join between tiles

Apse, vaulted semicircular end wall of the chancel of a church or of a chapel

Archaic, period in Greek civilisation preceding the Classical era: from about 750–480 BC

Architrave, the lowest part of an entablature

Archontikon (pl. *archontika*), old (usually 16th–18th-century), traditionally well-to-do dwelling house

Argive, of or pertaining to the city and territory of Argos

Aryballos, (pl. *aryballoi*) a small spherical or globular pottery flask with a narrow neck used for oils and perfumes. It is often depicted as being used by athletes bathing, either attached by a strap to the wrist or hanging from a peg on the wall

Asclepieion, cult centre dedicated to Asclepius, god of healing, where patients would come to seek cures

Atlantes, male figures used as supporting columns (*cf Caryatids*)

Attic, topmost storey of a Classical building, hiding the spring of the roof

Basilica, originally a Roman hall used for public administration; in Christian architecture an aisled church with a clerestory and apse and no transepts

Bas-relief, sculpture in low relief

Bema, a rostrum or raised platform for public speaking. Also the sanctuary of a Byzantine church

Black-figure ware, originally developed in Corinth, black-figure technique first appeared in Athenian pottery c. 630 BC and was used until about 470 BC; after that date it is used almost solely for the ornamental vessels awarded to victors at the Athenian games. Black-figure vases portray their motifs with a black glaze, using the reddish fabric of the vase as a background. Other colours (especially red and white) may be added

Bouleuterion, meeting chamber where the *boule*, or ruling council, held sessions

Boustrophedon, a system of writing that involves alternating lines of left-to-right and right-to-left, so that the eye moves in curves, like an ox ploughing a field (the derivation of the term)

Bucranium, (pl. *bucrania*) originally an ox skull, sometimes covered with plaster and used for ritual purposes. Later a sculptured ornament representing an ox skull

Cardo, the main north–south street in a Roman town; it crosses the *decumanus*

Caryatids, female figures used as supporting columns

Cavea, the part of a theatre that is dug into the hillside, and occupied by the rows of seats

Cella, enclosed interior part of a temple; the naos

Ceta, Serbian word for a military band or company, used in Macedonia during the struggle against the Ottomans

Chiton, Sleeveless linen tunic falling in vertical folds, secured at the waist or bustline with a girdle

Chrysobul, a document bearing the Byzantine emperor's gold *bulla*, ie his seal impressed in molten gold. The term later indicated an important document (with or without the *bulla*)

Ciborium, casket or tabernacle containing the Host

Classical, of the period from 480 BC (second Persian invasion) to 323 BC (death of Alexander the Great)

Clazomenian, coming from the ancient city of *Clazomenae* in Asia Minor, west of the Izmir peninsula. One of the 12 Ionian cities of Asia minor, Clazomenae was the birthplace of the philosopher Anaxagoras

Clerestory, upper part of the nave of a church above the side aisles, with windows

Cleruch, in ancient Greece an Athenian citizen who received an allotment of land in a foreign country but retained his rights as a citizen at home. A cleruchy is an allotment of land so given

Cloisonné, masonry style where the stone blocks are set off by thin red brick courses

Coenobite, a monastery where the monks hold everything in common, having no personal property

Corbel, a projecting block, usually of stone, to support an arch or beam

Corbelling, building system which gives support by superimpositions of projecting courses, each bearing the load of the next. It is used in tholos tomb vaulting

Corinthian, an order of architecture developed—according to the Roman architect Vitruvius—by the Athenian Callimachus in the late 5th century BC. It is characterised by a capital with the shape of a basket or an inverted bell, decorated with two or more rows of acanthus leaves and topped by a four-faced abacus. Columns (which may be plain or fluted), stand on an elaborate base and support an entablature with a continuous frieze and a richly ornamented projecting cornice

Cornice, topmost part of a temple entablature; any projecting ornamental moulding at the top of a building beneath the roof

Coroplast, a worker in terracotta

Crepidoma, stepped platform on which a temple stands

Cross-in-square, type of Byzantine church plan consisting of two intersecting barrel-vaulted naves of equal length. The middle space is covered by a dome supported with pillars

Cuneus (pl. *cunei*), the Roman word for *kerkides*, the wedge-shaped sections of a theatre, filled by seats, with access steps on either side

Cyclopean, masonry (typically Mycenaean) which uses enormous blocks, so large that they appear to have been built by the Cyclopes

Cyma, curved moulding at the top of a cornice

Decumanus, the principal street of a Roman town, typically running east–west

Dentil bands, bands of bricks set diagonally on edge

Diakonikon, auxiliary chamber used as a sacristy where the sacred vessels were stored in a Byzantine church. Originally a separate building it is later normally found next to the apse

Diazoma (pl. *diazomata*) semicircular aisle between the tiers of a theatre

Dipteral, temple surrounded by a double peristyle

Distyle, of a temple or porch, having two columns

Doric, an order of architecture developed in Greece before the 6th century BC. It is characterised by fluted columns standing close together directly on the stylobate (with no base). Capitals have a convex moulding topped by a square abacus. (*Illustration on p. 28*)

Dressed stone, stone worked to a finish on its surface

Echinus, convex stone cushioning between the abacus (the topmost section of a capital) and the top of the column shaft

Engaged column, a column partly embedded in a wall, but with half or more visible, so different from a pilaster

Enkoimeterion, a stoa-type building in the sanctuaries of Asclepius, in which the sick slept. The god appeared to them in their dreams, either curing them miraculously or recommending the appropriate therapy

Entablature, upper section of an order supported by a colonnade, divided (horizontally, from the bottom) into architrave, frieze and cornice

Entasis, a design technique used to counteract the optical illusion of inner sagging created by the parallel sides of a column. Entasis (meaning 'stretching') involved giving the column a slightly convex curvature with the result that the diameter at the bottom was marginally larger than at the top

Ephebus, Greek youth under training (military or academic)

Epistyle, the lower part in a horizontal beam supported by columns; it is topped by the frieze and the cornice

Epitaphios, Liturgical cloth consisting of a large piece of silk, representing that given by Joseph of Arimathea to wrap the body of Christ, used in Holy Saturday processions

Exedra, semicircular recess or any outdoor passage or portico, usually with seats

Exonarthex, vestibule or narthex on the exterior of the main façade of a church

Ex-voto, tablet or small painting expressing gratitude to a saint

Foustanella, the full, pleated white skirt worn by the ceremonial guards in Athens, and until the last century as part of traditional attire by many Greek males

Frieze, strip of decoration usually along the upper part of a wall; in a temple this refers to the horizontal feature above the columns between the architrave and the cornice

Frons scenae, a wall as high as the top of the cavea at the back of the stage, decorated with columns and niches; the ancestor of the modern backdrop

Gigantomachia, In art or sculpture, a contest between giants

Genisis tis Theotokou, a church dedicated to the birth of the Virgin

Geometric, refers to a pottery style with complex abstract decoration (900 –700 BC)

Graffiti, design on a wall made with an iron tool on a prepared surface, the design showing in white. Also used loosely to describe scratched designs or words on walls

Greek cross, a cross with all four arms of equal length

Gutta (*pl. guttae*), small, peg-like projections carved under the mutules of a Doric cornice

Han, in the Ottoman world, a caravanserai

Helladic Period, the Bronze Age in the Greek mainland and islands (3000–1100 BC)

Hellenistic Period, the period from 323 BC (death of Alexander the Great) to 30 BC (defeat of Antony and Cleopatra)

708 GLOSSARY OF TERMS

Hemicycle, a semicircular structure

Herm (pl. *hermae*), quadrangular pillar decreasing in girth towards the ground, surmounted by a head

Heroön, shrine to a deified hero

Hexastyle, having six columns

Himation, cloak, part of a woman's costume in ancient Greece

Hippodamian system, regular grid plan for city streets, named after the 5th-century BC town planner Hippodamus of Miletus

Hodeghitria, icon type showing the Virgin with the Child seated on her lap. The icon painted by St Luke is said to have been the prototype for the Hodeghitria, an icon which functions as a 'guide', presenting the infant Christ as 'the way'

Hydria, a vessel for water

Hypocaust, ancient Roman heating system in which hot air circulated under the floor and between double walls

Hypostyle, a roofed colonnade

Hypostyle hall, a large room with the ceiling borne by rows of columns. The central row could be taller to accommodate a clerestory to provide light

Iconostasis, screen holding icons, separating the sanctuary from the laity

Idiorrhythmic, a monastery where the monks are not subject to a common rule, are allowed to own their own belongings, and do not necessarily eat together

Inscribed cross (*see Cross-in-square*)

Intarsia, a decorative inlay made from wood, marble or metal

Intrados, underside or soffit of an arch

Ionic, an order of architecture developed in Ionia, a region of Asia Minor, in the late 6th century BC, and identified by its capital with two opposed volutes supporting a moulded abacus. Columns are fluted, stand on a base, and have a shaft more slender than in the Doric order. (*Illustration on p. 28*)

Isodomic, masonry made up of blocks of identical size, with the vertical joins coming in the centre of the block below. The variant known as pseudo-isodomic has alternating taller and lower courses

Ithyphallic, representations of the human male figure with an oversize erect phallus

Katagogeion, a feature of sanctuaries, particularly Asclepieia. The term designates the dormitory and reception areas for patients and pilgrims

Katholikon, a monastery church

Kerkides wedge-shaped sections of a theatre, filled by seats, with access steps on either side

Klepht, (from the Greek root meaning 'thief') one of the groups of Greeks who refused to submit to Ottoman power after the conquest in the 15th century; they took to the mountains where they remained after independence, gaining a reputation as bandits

Koimisis tis Theotokou, the Dormition of the Virgin

Konak, in the Ottoman world, a well-to-do dwelling house

Kore (pl. *korai*), from the Greek word for young girl, used to describe standing female figures in the Archaic style

Kouros (pl. *kouroi*) from the Greek word for young man, used to describe a standing, nude male statue in the Archaic style

Krater, a large, open bowl used for mixing wine with water

Kylix, wide shallow drinking vessel with two handles and short stem

Larnax (pl. *larnakes*), chest, urn or coffin normally in terracotta, containing the remains of the dead

Latin cross, cross where the vertical arm is longer than the horizontal

Lausitz ware, a subgroup of the Urnfield culture, the Lausitz culture (1300–500 BC) is best represented in eastern Saxony and in western Silesia; from there it spread east to Poland, south to Macedonia and westwards. The pottery is characterised by biconical ossuaries and vessels with applied relief decoration and incised geometrical patterns which may have influenced the emergence of Greek Protogeometric pottery

Lekythos, tall, narrow-necked Greek vase with one handle, used for oil

Lunette, semicircular space in a vault or ceiling, or above a door or window, often decorated with a painting or relief

Machicolated, of a parapet: having holes in the floor through which stones, boiling oil etc, could be dropped onto attackers

Mahalas (Turkish *mahal*), neighbourhood, quarter, or ghetto: used in the Ottoman world to designate parts of town where particular ethnic groups or craftsmen reside

Mandorla, tapered, almond-shaped aura around a holy figure (usually Christ or the Virgin)

Medise, a term used at the time of the Persian wars meaning to favour the Mede or Persian side

Medresse, (also *madrasa*), an Islamic theological school

Megaron, large rectangular hall, typically the chief building of a Mycenaean city, with a roofed entrance lobby at one end. The form is thought to have been the forerunner of the temple

Metamorphosis (or Metamorfosis), the Transfiguration

Metic, in ancient Athens, a non-citizen resident, either an immigrant or often an ex-slave

Metope, square ornamental relief occurring between triglyphs on a Doric frieze

Metroön, shrine or temple to the mother of the gods, Rhea

Metropolis, the Greek word for a cathedral; the bishop is the Metropolitan

Monolith, single stone; a monolithic sculpture is therefore one carved from a single block

Monopteros (also *monopteron*) a temple, usually circular, without a cella consisting of a colonnade supporting a roof

Mutules, flattish, regularly spaced blocks on the underside of a Doric cornice, decorated with downward-projecting pegs (*guttae*)

Naos, enclosed interior part of a temple; the cella

Naïskos, small temple with pillars and columns with the statue or relief of the deceased. It is part of funerary architecture

Narthex, vestibule of a church or basilica, before the west door

Naumachia (pl. *naumachiae*), mock sea battle as staged in amphitheatres

Nymphaion (pl. *nymphaia,* Latin *nymphaeum*), in the Greek and Roman world originally a natural grotto with springs and streams, traditionally considered the habitat of nymphs. It came later to designate buildings filled with fountains, plants, flowers and works of art. Frequently built on a circular plan, *nymphaia* were used as sanctuaries, reservoirs, assembly-rooms and for the celebration of marriages

Octastyle, a portico with eight columns

Oikos (*pl. oikoi*), dwelling house or domestic quarters

Oinochoë, wine-jug, usually of elongated shape, for dipping wine out of a krater

Opisthodomos, the back section of an ancient Greek temple, entered from the outside of the building and arranged with two columns in antis on the long walls

Opus incertum, building technique where irregular pieces of stone facing are inserted into a rubble-and-cement core

Opus sectile, geometrically patterned floor or wall covering made of coloured pieces (larger than mosaic tesserae) of marble or glass

Opus tessellatum, mosaic formed entirely of square tesserae (pieces of marble, stone or glass)

Orthostat, large vertical stone block in the lower part of a wall

Palaestra, a public place devoted to training athletes in ancient Greece or Rome

Pancration, from 'pan-kration', literally 'all holds': a boxing contest in which no holds were barred

Pantocrator, literally 'he who controls all'; a representation of Christ in majesty, traditionally featured in the central dome of Orthodox churches

Pareeclesion, a subsidiary chapel in a Byzantine church with a variety of functions, often funerary

Parodos (pl. *parodoi*), entrance corridors or

passages at the sides of a theatre, between the stage and the cavea

Patera, small circular ornamental disc, usually carved; Greek or Roman dish for libations to the gods

Pelasgic, pertaining to a pre-Hellenic people (the Pelasgians) variously regarded to have been settled in Thrace, Thessaly, at Dodona and in the Ionian region

Pendentive, concave spandrel beneath a dome

Peplos, Sleeveless woollen tunic made of a square piece of cloth wrapped around the body and fastened at the sides and shoulders

Peribolos, in ancient Greece, the enclosure or court of a temple, the actual wall or the space enclosed; in early Christian times a church enclosure

Peripteral, temple surrounded by a colonnade

Peristyle, colonnade surrounding a court or a building

Phiale, a fountain or stoup in the atrium of a Byzantine church originally intended for the ablution of the faithful; it normally consisted of a shallow bowl covered sometimes by a canopy. In the context of ancient pottery, a *phiale* is a shallow saucer or bowl

Phylax, in ancient Greece a guard or an observer; today used to denote the custodian at an ancient site

Pilaster, a shallow pier or rectangular column projecting only slightly from the wall

Polemarch, Athenian magistrate responsible for military affairs

Polygonal, a style of masonry in which blocks of irregular shape are roughly hewn to fit

Poros, a soft, coarse, conchiferous limestone (tufa)

Pronaos, vestibule at the entrance of a temple

Proskenion, a row of columns in front of the *skene* supporting a high platform used as a raised stage for comedy

Propylon (pl. *propylaia*), entrance gate to a sacred enclosure. Used in the plural form when there is more than one door

Prostyle, temple with columns on the front only

Prothesis, area connected with the preparation by the deacons of the bread and wine for the Eucharist in a Byzantine church; it can be a recess at the north side of the church, a table or a dedicated chapel

Protogeometric, pottery style with simple, non-figurative decoration (1050–900 BC)

Prytaneion, a public building in which the governors of the city in ancient Greece (the *prytany*) conducted their business and had their meals

Quadriga, a two-wheeled chariot drawn by four horses

Quadriporticus, rectangular court or atrium arcaded on all four sides, derived from the atria in front of palaeochristian basilicas

Red-figure ware, pottery style developed in Athens and flourishing in the period 530–330 BC. In this technique the decoration was first painted as a black outline, then the surface outside the outline was filled with black pigment, leaving the figures showing in red; further details were then added in black. The style quickly overtook the earlier black-figure pottery, as it allowed more flexibility and freedom of expression by adding details with a paintbrush rather than with incisions

Revetment thin facing or cladding on a wall, sometimes of marble, to hide a rough construction surface

Rhyton, drinking-horn usually ending in an animal's head

Rosso antico, red marble from the Peloponnese

Rostrum (*pl. rostra*), prow of a warship. Rostra from captured ships were used to decorate speaking platforms, known as *rostra*, and columns, *colonnae rostratae*

Salient, an outward-projecting angle in a fortified wall

Sekos, the naos of a temple; the interior space

Sgraffito, a term derived from the Italian word *graffiare* meaning 'to scratch', and referring to a technique used on walls and ceramics. It consists in applying two layers of contrasting colours in plaster or slip and then scratching an outline drawing thereby revealing the colour of the surface beneath

Skene, originally a simple hut where actors could dress and store props, behind the *orchestra* or stage, also used as a background for performances; it evolved as a purpose-built structure with projecting wings from the 5th century BC

Skyphos, drinking cup with two handles

Spandrel, surface between two arches in an arcade or the triangular space on either side of an arch

Sphendone, the curving end of a hippodrome or racetrack

Spolia, items of masonry taken from an earlier (ruined or demolished) building and reused

Squinch, Supporting block placed across the angles of a square area, to allow a dome to be rested on top

Stamnos, big-bellied vase with two small handles at the sides, closed by a lid

Stater, originally a weight, it designated a coin in silver and in gold

Stele (pl. *stelae*), upright stone bearing a monumental inscription

Stereobate, basement of a temple or other building

Stoa, a covered, colonnaded, free-standing market hall in an ancient Greek town

Stoup, vessel for Holy Water, usually near the west or entrance door of a church

Strigil, bronze scraper used when bathing to remove the oil with which bathers anointed themselves

Stylobate, topmost level of the stepped platform on which a temple stood; literally, the solid base on which the columns stand

Synedrion, council chamber

Synthronon, semicircular structure in the apse of an early church providing seating for the bishop and clergy

Taxiarchs (*Taxiarches*), in the Greek Orthodox Church, the name given to the Archangels

Tekke, the counterpart to the more orthodox *medresse*, it was a lodge for dervishes, and normally part of a complex including mosque and a memorial tomb; a tekke may have contained individual cells

Telesterion, a room in the sanctuary of Demeter at Eleusis where the sacred initiation rites were performed

Tell, mound or hummock occurring from the accumulation of debris over a period of occupation

Temenos, holy sanctuary or enclosure within which a temple and other cult buildings stand

Templon, a partition separating the faithful from the officiating clergy in an Orthodox church

Tepidarium, room for warm baths in a Roman bath

Tessera (pl. *tesserae*), a small cube of marble, glass etc, used in mosaic work

Tetrastyle, having four columns at the end

Thalamos, inner chamber of a tomb

Theme, administrative unit of territory within the Byzantine empire, ruled by a *strategos*, a military and civil governor

Theodosian, describes a stone capital from the early Christian period, decorated with foliage pierced with lines of holes

Theoroi, ambassadors to the Panhellenic games from foreign states

Thermae, originally simply Roman baths, later elaborate buildings fitted with libraries, assembly rooms, gymnasia and circuses

Thesmophorion, temple of Demeter Thesmophoros, goddess of fertility and of the fields; normally situated outside the city and connected to the ancient Greek fertility festival celebrated by women

Tholos, circular building with a roof constructed by corbelling

Transenna, open grille or screen, usually of marble, in an early Christian church

Trapezoidal, a style of stone masonry in which the blocks have two parallel sides, the other two slanting

Tribune, the apse of a Christian basilica that contains the bishop's throne or the throne itself

Triconchial, also known as trefoil, it refers

to a structure with three apses set at right angles

Triglyph, small panel of a Doric frieze raised slightly and carved with three vertical channels

Triptych, painting or tablet in three sections

Triton, a river-god

Trompe l'œil, literally, a deception of the eye; used to describe illusionist decoration and painted architectural perspective

Tympanum, the area between the top of a doorway and the arch above it; also the triangular space enclosed by the mouldings of a pediment

Verde antico, green Thessalian marble

Volute, a form of ornament also called a spiral scroll or helix, possibly derived from a rolled up cushion, and characteristic of the Ionic order

White-ground ware, a type of pottery in which a white slip was first applied as a background and figures were painted on top of it. The style, contemporary with red-figure ware, was employed almost exclusively in the production of funerary vessels

Xenon, guest house for visitors and athletes at a games

Xystos, a covered running track

Zoödochos Pigi, church dedication to the Virgin as 'fount of life'

Zoömachia, in art or sculpture, a contest between wild animals

Zoöphoros, frieze of a Doric temple, so-called because the metopes were often decorated with figures of animals

TYPES OF MASONRY

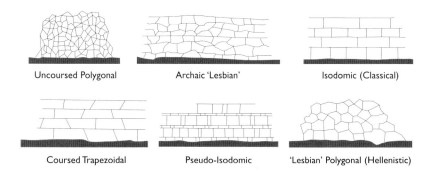

Uncoursed Polygonal   Archaic 'Lesbian'   Isodomic (Classical)

Coursed Trapezoidal   Pseudo-Isodomic   'Lesbian' Polygonal (Hellenistic)

CHRONOLOGY

Palaeolithic and Mesolithic
(240,000–7000 BC)

240,000–160,000: Early man. Petralona cave
10,000–7000: Early burials. Franchthi cave

Pre-pottery Neolithic and Neolithic
(7000–3000 BC)

First farmers, villages, defended settlements:
Nea Nikomedia, Sesklo, Dimini

Early Helladic (3000–2000 BC)

Indo-European populations introduce
bronze-working and new agricultural
techniques
Special-purpose buildings (palaces?): Lerna,
House of Tiles (clay seal impressions)

Middle Helladic (2000–1600 BC)

Minoan civilisation; Linear A

Late Helladic (1600–1050 BC)

Mycenean palaces and shaft graves; Linear B
c. 1230: Tribes of Attica unite under Athens
1200: Dorian Invasion
c. 1180: fall of Troy
c.1100: Athens founds Ionian colonies

Geometric period (1050–700 BC)

Iron working; ancient Greek script; Homer
and Hesiod active; emergence of the city-state
(*polis*)
776: first Olympic games

Archaic period (700–480 BC)

Age of tyrants; development of a citizens'
army of hoplites
700: Black-figure ware invented in Corinth
530: Red-figure ware invented in Athens

492: Persians conquer Thrace and Macedonia
490: First Persian War; Battle of Marathon
c. 480: *Critian Boy*: birth of Classical sculpture

Classical period (480–323 BC)

Delian League and Athenian Empire; Golden
Age of tragedy (Aeschylus, Sophocles and
Euripides), of comedy (Aristophanes) and
history (Herodotus, Thucydides)
480: Second Persian War: victory for
Persians at Thermopylae; victory for
Greeks at Salamis
479: Greek victory over Persians at Plataea
447: Pericles begins the Parthenon
431–404: Peloponnesian War
405: Athens surrenders to Sparta, ending
the Peloponnesian War
386: Plato's Academy founded
371: Battle of Leuctra. Sparta surrenders to
Thebes. End of Spartan hegemony
359–336: Philip II king of Macedon
338: Battle of Chaironeia: Greeks defeated by
Philip II
340s: First Macedonian tombs
336–323: Alexander the Great conquers the
east and dies in Babylon

Hellenistic period (323–31 BC)

Rome 'discovers' the art and culture of
conquered Greece. Greece becomes
fashionable for cultured Romans. Via Egnatia
built, connecting Rome to the east via northern Greece
322–275: Alexander's successors carve up
the empire
279: Celts invade Macedonia and reach
Delphi
215–205: First Macedonian War. Philip V
sides with the Carthaginian Hannibal
against the Romans
197: Romans defeat Philip V at
Cynoscephalae
168: Battle of Pydna. Romans defeat Philip

V's son Perseus of Macedon

146: Romans sack Corinth. Macedonia becomes a Roman province and southern Greece (Achaea) a Roman dependency

86: Sack of Athens by Sulla

31: Victory for Octavian (Augustus) at the Battle of Actium ends Rome's civil wars

Roman period (31 BC–AD 330)

49: St Paul baptises Lydia, his first Greek convert, in Philippi

66–67: Nero visits Greece and wins the Olympic chariot-race

124–125: Hadrian visits Greece and institutes a building programme in Athens

c. 150–170: Pausanias writes the first guide book to Greece

252: Goths invade Macedonia and raid Athens and the Peloponnese (267)

293–330: Thessaloniki capital of the reorganised Roman Empire

Byzantine period (330–1460)

393: Olympic Games outlawed by Emperor Theodosius I

435: All pagan worship outlawed by Theodosius II

529: Athens school of philosophy closed by Justinian

726–843: Iconoclasm; figurative art banned

867–1054: Macedonian dynasty; Bulgars defeated

904: Saracen corsair Leo of Tripoli storms Thessalonica and enslaves 20,000 of its inhabitants

1020: Hosios Loukas monastery church built in Boeotia

1204: Sack of Constantinople by the Crusaders; Eastern Latin Empire established. Greece fragmented; Venice obtains control of Crete, Euboea, the Cyclades, Sporades, part of the Peloponnese and of Thessaly

1261: Michael VIII Palaeologus reconquers Constantinople with the help of the Genoese. Byzantine despotate at Mistra, where Byzantine culture and art flourish

Ottoman period (1460–1830)

1361–93: Ottomans conquer large parts of Thrace, Macedonia and Thessaly

1453: Ottomans conquer Constantinople

1456: Ottomans capture Athens

1460: Ottomans conquer the Morea

1492: Jews expelled from Spain settle in Thessalonica

1687: Turks accidentally blow up the Parthenon

1774: Catherine of Russia's 'Greek project' to free Greece of the Ottoman occupation

1801–05: The Elgin Marbles arrive in Britain

1814: Secret revolutionary society Philike Etaireia founded in Odessa

1821–30: Greek War of Independence. The London Protocol sanctions an independent Greek state but of a reduced size, not large enough to tempt the chosen king Leopold of Saxe-Coburg. Ioannis Capodistrias takes over in his place (assassinated 1831)

Independence to present times

1832: Otho of Bavaria crowned King of Greece

1861: Napoleon III sends Léon Heuzey to investigate antiquities in northern Greece

1864: Constitutional monarchy

1874: Schliemann starts work in Mycenae

1881: Thessaly becomes part of Greece

1912–13: Balkan Wars. Annexation of Crete, Macedonia, southern Epirus and some islands

1914: First World War; initial Greek neutrality

1919: Treaty of Sèvres; Greece gains Izmir, Dodecanese and eastern Thrace

1919–22: Greek army lands at Izmir and invades Anatolia and is repulsed by Atatürk. Population exchange: Greece expels the Turks and absorbs over a million Anatolian and Pontic Greek refugees

1941–44: Nazi occupation

1946–49: Greek Civil War

1967–73: Military dictatorship of the Colonels

1974: Greece becomes a republic

INDEX

Sights and monuments in larger cities (Athens and Thessaloniki) are listed as sub-indices of that city. For the Parthenon, for example, look under 'Athens: Parthenon'. In general, explanatory or more detailed references (where there are many) are given in bold. Numbers in italics are picture references. Dates are given for all artists, architects and sculptors. Ancient place names and works of art are listed in italics. The stressed syllables of modern place names are indicated.

720 INDEX

contd. from p. 6

Editor-in-chief, and editor of this volume: Annabel Barber
Consulting editors: Charles Freeman, Nigel McGilchrist

Design: Anikó Kuzmich
Floor plans and watercolours: Imre Bába
Watercolours of pottery vessels: Edit Nagy
Line drawings: Michael Mansell RIBA & Gabriella Juhász
With special thanks to Kostas Christodoulou, HE Dimitris Costoumas,
Katalin Partics, Niki Sidiropoulou

Photo editor: Róbert Szabó Benke
Photographs by Arion: pp. 107, 113, 134–35, 161, 169, 170, 179, 186, 209, 382, 468–69;
Roger Barber: pp. 23, 25, 213, 243, 244, 262, 275, 280, 308, 521, 535, 541, 557, 565, 567, 569;
Matt Barrett: pp. 329, 331 (www.greecetravel.com); Josephine Bulbulian: pp. 313, 323, 547;
Vangelis Massias: pp. 215, 230, 437, 456, 642; Szilvia Mucsy: pp. 68, 91, 106, 115, 118;
Yiannis Papadimitriou: pp. 601, 609, 677; Zoltán Serfőző: pp. 516, 524, 581; Arkos Arkoulis: p.
235; Annabel Barber: p. 568; Lucretious: p. 79; Efthymios Spais: p. 542; Szilvia Tóth: p. 122
Ministry of Culture of the Hellenic Republic: pp. 95, 163, 303, 559, 620, 652, 692;
Alinari Archives, Florence: pp: 80, 94, 386, 390, 465, 633; © Benaki Museum, 2005: p. 411;
© 2005. Carnegie Mellon/University of Pittsburgh: p. 674; Jewish Museum of Greece: p. 595;
© 2005. Photo Scala Florence/HIP: p. 438.

Cover photographs
Top: The site of ancient Olympia. Photo: Arion
Bottom: Mosaic of the Medusa from a Roman villa at Corinth. Alinari Archives, Florence
Title page: Detail from a 19th-century fresco by Ioannis Pagonis
Spine: The Mycenaean *Warrior Vase* (c. 1200 BC). Watercolour by Edit Nagy

Sherry Marker would like to thank the following for help during preparation of the guide:
Vivian Anagnostaki, Adrian Bartlett, Victoria Bartlett, John Bowman, George and Effie
Constantinides, Gemma Davies, Linda Drury, Michael Drury, Pat Gentle, Evelyn and George
Hatziyannaki, Caroline Houser, Paul Hetherington, Lisa Kallett, Jack Kroll, Stephen Miller,
Thalia Pandiri, Meredith Pillon, Vincent Rosivach, Guy Sanders, Peter Smith, Rebekah Smith,
Sharon Turner, Allen Ward. James Pettifer would like to thank Julia Pettifer for the use of her
research work on the history of northern Greek towns and cities; Alexander Pettifer for
material on Thessaloniki and region; Susan Comely for endless generous assistance while
researching and travelling in the region; Miranda Vickers for historical material on Threspotia
and Epirus; Auron Tare for information on Epirus castles. He would also like to thank the
many local people who offered practical help and advice.

Statement of editorial independence: Blue Guides, their authors and editors, are prohibited from
accepting payment from any restaurant, hotel, gallery or other establishment for its inclusion in this
guide, or for a more favourable mention than would otherwise have been made.

Every effort has been made to contact the copyright owners of material reproduced in this guide.
We would be pleased to hear from any copyright owners we have been unable to reach.

Printed in Hungary by Dürer Nyomda Kft, Gyula.

ISBN 1–905131–10–0